KEYNES, CHICAGO AND FRIEDMAN

VOLUME 1

KEYNES, CHICAGO AND FRIEDMAN

Volume 1

General Editor
ROBERT LEESON

Preface by
MILTON FRIEDMAN

LONDON
PICKERING & CHATTO
2003

Published by Pickering & Chatto (Publishers) Limited
21 Bloomsbury Way, London, WC1A 2TH

2252 Ridge Road, Brookfield, Vermont 05036, USA

www.pickeringchatto.com

BRITISH LIBRARY CATALOGUING IN PUBLICATION DATA

Keynes, Chicago and Friedman
1. Keynes, John Maynard, 1883–1946 2. Friedman, Milton
3. Chicago School of Economics 4. Keynesian economics
I. Leeson, Robert
330.1'5

ISBN 1851967672

LIBRARY OF CONGRESS CATALOGING-IN-PUBLICATION DATA

Keynes, Chicago and Friedman / general editor, Robert Leeson: preface by Milton Friedman
p. cm
Includes bibliographical references and index.
ISBN 1–85196–767–2 (alk. paper)
1. Friedman, Milton, 1912– 2. Chicago School of Economics 3. Keynes, John Maynard, 1883–1946. I. Leeson, Robert II. Friedman, Milton, 1912–

HB119 .F84 K49 2003
330.15--dc21 2002030351

This publication is printed on acid-free paper that conforms to
the American National Standard for Permanence of Paper in Printed Library Materials.

Typeset by
P&C

Printed and bound in Great Britain

CONTENTS OF THE EDITION

Volume 1

Part One: The Initial Controversy

Part Two: The Debate Widens

Volume 2

Part Three: How Unique was the Chicago Tradition?

CONTENTS

Preface

In 1956, I wrote an essay, 'The Quantity Theory of Money – A Restatement' (pp. 33–51 [1956]), as an introduction to a collection of doctoral essays by students in my Workshop in Money and Banking, published under the title, *Studies in the Quantity Theory of Money* (Friedman, 1956). The book was one of the first major steps in the rehabilitation of the quantity theory of money, which the Keynesian Revolution had relegated to the dustbin of history. It was one of the opening shots in the intellectual battle between what came to be known as monetarism and Keynesianism.

In the introductory paragraphs of that essay, I referred to Chicago as

> one of the few academic centers at which the quantity theory continued to be a central and vigorous part of the oral tradition throughout the 1930's and 1940's... The quantity theory that retained this role differed sharply from the atrophied and rigid caricature that is so frequently described by the proponents of the new income-expenditure approach—and with some justice, to judge by much of the literature on policy that was spawned by quantity theorists. At Chicago, Henry Simons and Lloyd Mints directly, Frank Knight and Jacob Viner at one remove, taught and developed a more subtle and relevant version...
>
> The purpose of this introduction is not to enshrine – or should I say, inter – a definitive version of the Chicago tradition... The purpose is rather to set down a particular 'model' of a quantity theory in an attempt to convey the flavor of the oral tradition which nurtured the remaining essays in this volume...

Thirteen years later, in 1969, as if a long-delay time fuse had gone off, Don Patinkin attacked me for claiming the mantle of an oral monetary tradition at Chicago for my interpretation of the quantity theory (pp. 87–120 [1969/1981]). My work, he claimed, was Keynesian, not based on any pre-Keynesian monetary tradition. Two years later, Harry Johnson devoted his Ely lecture at the annual meeting of the American Economic Association to an, if anything, even more vicious attack, coming close to accusing me of having made up a Chicago oral tradition out of whole cloth (pp. 169–82 [1971]).

I was baffled at the time, and have been ever since, at what all the fuss was about. So far as I could see, very little was at stake. What seemed to me important was the validity and usefulness of the theory that I sketched in my essay. Suppose I was wrong in asserting that that theory conveyed 'the flavor of the oral tradition that nurtured the remaining essays in this volume.' That would simply mean that I was confused about the origin of the ideas I was presenting but it would not affect by an iota the validity or usefulness of those ideas. And so far as being Keynesian, in the one reply I wrote to Patinkin and Johnson, I pointed out that 'Keynes was a quantity theorist long before he was a Keynesian, and he continued to be one after he became a Keynesian'. I went on to say that my 'restatement *is* a restatement of the quantity theory and is not Keynesian in any meaningful sense of that term' (pp. 147–66 [1972/1974]).

In that reply, I also defended my view about the Chicago tradition. I have written nothing further about the subject. But surrogates came forth to defend my position, and others to confute them. The many resulting articles and notes have been collected by Robert Leeson in these volumes. They explore the arcana of monetary thought at Chicago, Harvard, and elsewhere in the 1930s.

I am impressed – or perhaps, depressed might be better – by the amount of subtle scholarship and hard research the articles embody. I confess that I come out very much where I came in, but with my knowledge of who was saying what, where, very much enlarged. I remain persuaded that I was the beneficiary of a Chicago oral tradition, but this evidence convinces me that I gave Chicago more credit for uniqueness than was justified. Were I writing the paper now, I would undoubtedly word those first four paragraphs differently, but no change would be called for in the rest of the essay. The issue is entirely about the origin of ideas, not about the validity of content.

Milton Friedman
Hoover Institution
December 28, 2001

Part One

The Initial Controversy

The Initial Controversy[1]

Introduction

During the middle third of the twentieth century, the ideas of John Maynard Keynes and those who described themselves as 'Keynesians' acquired a profound influence over both the economics profession and the macroeconomic policy process. After the publication of Milton Friedman's (1956) *Studies in the Quantity Theory of Money*, Keynesians were obliged to compete with 'monetarists' for policy and intellectual influence.[2] These two volumes examine aspects of this counter-revolution by focusing on Friedman's claim that he was merely formalising the macroeconomic ideas of the first generation Chicago School, at whose 'feet' he 'sat' in 1932–3 and 1934–5 (Friedman pp. 147–66 [1972/1974], 152).

In his introductory chapter 'The Quantity Theory of Money – A Restatement' Friedman (pp. 33–51 [1956], 33–4) launched the monetarist counter-revolution accompanied by the assertion that 'Chicago was one of the few academic centres at which the quantity theory continued to be a central and vigorous part of the oral tradition throughout the 1930's and 1940's'. Friedman sought to 'nurture' the revival of the quantity theory by linking it to this Chicago 'oral tradition'. According to Friedman the 'flavor' of this oral tradition was captured in a model in which the quantity theory was 'in the first instance a theory of the demand for money'. Friedman did not intend to offer 'a full justification' for his 'assertion' adding that to 'the best of my knowledge no systematic statement of this theory as developed at Chicago exists, though much of it can be read between the lines of [Henry] Simons' and [Lloyd] Mints's writings'. Friedman also enlisted the names of two co-editors of the *Journal of Political Economy* (*JPE*), Frank Knight and Jacob Viner (1929–45), in support of his assertion.

Don Patinkin studied at Chicago between 1941–47, a few years after Friedman; both had been taught monetary economics at Chicago by Mints.[3] Patinkin analysed his 1944 notes from Mints' Economics 330 and found no evidence to sustain Friedman's account of the nature of the Chicago monetary tradition. There had previously been other attempts to construct oral traditions and lineages; but none generated as much heat – and light – as this. This introductory chapter sets the Patinkin–Friedman dispute in its political and ideological context and also describes some of these other lineage assertions and disputes.

Patinkin (pp. 87–120 [1969/1981], 87, 99, 102) began his assault with 'an apology for being over a decade late'. The 'nominal' justification was the recent publication of Friedman's encyclopaedia essay on the quantity theory (pp. 71–84 [1968]) in which the Chicago School, its individual members, and *Studies in the Quantity Theory of Money* are not mentioned.[4] Indeed, in the offending sentence of that encyclopaedia entry, Friedman (pp. 71–84 [1968], 77) did not even refer to his own work. Instead, he referred to an essay by Harry Johnson: 'The postwar period has also seen a return to analysis in terms of the quantity equation accompanied by a reformulation of the quantity theory that has been strongly affected by the Keynesian analysis of liquidity preference (Johnson 1962)'.[5] Since Patinkin acknowledged that in 1968 Friedman had already 'admitted' his 'intellectual indebtedness' to 'modern Keynesian monetary theory' this suggests that Patinkin's assault may have a 'real' cause: the increased potency of Friedman's macroeconomic advocacy and ideology, relative to the mid-1950s. In a posthumously published essay, Patinkin (1995, 361–2) stated that in his judgement, Friedman returned to Chicago in 1946 'to continue the school's fundamental ideological advocacy of free-market economic liberalism'.

Studies in the Quantity Theory of Money was published mid-way between Herbert Hoover's defeat in 1932 and Ronald Reagan's victory in 1980.[6] Hoover's defeat by Franklin Delano Roosevelt in 1932 produced a 'political watershed' equivalent to that later created by Reagan's victory in 1980: the 1860–1932 era of Republican ascendancy gave way to the 1932–80 era of Democrat ascendancy (Friedman and Friedman, 1980, 331–2; 1984, 4).[7] Reagan's election was regarded as the death of the New Deal (Graham, 1989, 75); it initiated a period of increased policy influence for Friedman and other Hoover Institution economists.

Political watersheds often occur in conjunction with changes in the intellectual climate. The President and Chairman of Citibank recalled that as a result of the research undertaken by Friedman and his students 'every Friday afternoon, a kind of eerie silence settled over the normally boisterous trading rooms on Wall Street. The computer screens started going blank at about 4.20 as traders waited for the 4.30 announcement of the M1 and M2 figures. The quantity theory of money had come to Wall Street' (Wriston, 1998, 2). Almost half a century earlier, the *Chicago*

Tribune reported that after Roosevelt's victory the quantity theory had come to Washington with the 'brains trust': 'All Washington is going to school to the professors ... Debutantes hang on their exposition of the quantitative theory of money' (cited by Leuchtenburg, 1968 [1933], 50).[8]

Three students of the first generation largely created the second-generation Chicago School: Friedman, W. Allen Wallis and George Stigler. According to Stigler (1969, 229), an incumbent was 'A person of the liveliest interest to the outcumbents'. In 1952, Adolf Berle, a prominent New Dealer, attempted to persuade Senator Paul Douglas, an important inter-war University of Chicago economist, to seek the Democratic Party Presidential nomination (Schwartz 1987, 295; see also Douglas 1972, 193–4). Twelve years later Berle (1973 [1964], 795) confided to his diary: 'Goldwater has picked up Milton Friedman, the economist of the University of Chicago, straight out of the old laissez faire group. He will make the campaign a referendum on everything that has happened since Roosevelt was elected in 1932, and his crowd mean to go for broke ... The worst elements in American reaction have their day.'

The Importance of Lineage and Tradition

Friedman sought to explain the 'transition from the overwhelming defeat of Barry Goldwater in 1964 to the overwhelming victory of Ronald Reagan in 1980 – two men with essentially the same programme and the same message' (Friedman and Friedman, 1982, viii). One partial explanation was lineage. Goldwater was pilloried for using the phrase 'Extremism in defence of liberty is no vice'; Friedman reflected that the reaction would have been so different 'if Goldwater had introduced the statement by "as Cicero said more than two thousand years ago"' (Friedman and Friedman, 1998, 368–9).[9]

Friedman (1953, 3–5) found a lineage for his methodology of positive economics in John Neville Keynes' (1891) *Scope and Method of Political Economy*. Friedman suggested that the 'progress' of such a method of research could allow differences of opinion among 'disinterested citizens' to be 'eliminated', unlike value judgement disputes, about which 'men can ultimately only fight'.[10] Friedman (1977) also found a lineage with which to conclude his Nobel Prize Lecture – a quotation from Pierre du Pont to the French National Assembly of 1790: 'Gentlemen, it is a disagreeable custom to which one is too easily led by the harshness of the discussion to assume evil intentions. It is necessary to be gracious as to intentions; one should believe them good and apparently they are; but we do not have to be gracious at all to inconsistent logic or to absurd reasoning. Bad logicians have committed more involuntary crimes than bad men have done intentionally'. But Friedman was suspected of attempting to perpetrate an ideological coup as du Pont and his fellow Physiocrats had done.[11] Thus some of Friedman's opponents exhibited 'a bitterness beyond reason' – attributed by Donald McCloskey (1986) to the widespread professional acceptance of Friedman's methodology of positive economics.

According to a University of Chicago Public Policy Pamphlet discussion of monetary policy, 'tradition ... is stronger than logic' and could thus be a crucial factor in the 'tactical' process by which policy is formulated and propagated (Whittlesey 1935, 24–5). Tradition and lineage were important not only to Friedman but also to his fellow Mt Pelerin Society libertarians. In his Opening Address to the Society, Friedrich von Hayek (1967 [1947], 158) highlighted the importance of lineage by proposing the name 'Acton-Tocqueville Society'.[12] In a University of Chicago Public Policy Pamphlet, Hayek (1939, 24, n. 15) stated that 'There can be little doubt that the existence of firm tradition has materially helped to preserve free institutions in the Western world, just as its absence has contributed to their downfall in central Europe'.[13] According to Stigler (1988) 'There was no Chicago School of Economics when the Mt. Pelerin Society first met'.

While Friedman's (1953; 1957) methodology and permanent income hypothesis entered the economics mainstream, his monetary research was initially regarded as the work of an eccentric. Meghnad Desai (1981, 2) went as far as to suggest that prior to the publication of *A Monetary History of the United States* (Friedman and Schwartz, 1963), Friedman's use of the quantity theory was regarded as 'a peculiar Chicago madness, indulgently mocked'. According to Robert Barro (1998, 5), Friedman had been treated as a 'right-wing midwestern crank. Most of the derision applied to his views on money'.

Neither Desai nor Barro were dispassionate observers; but according to an unpublished Massachusetts Institute of Technology doctoral dissertation on the 'Demand and Supply Functions for Money in the United States', the implications of Friedman's results were 'limited because the definitions and formulations used are somewhat idiosyncratic, thus insulating his work from the main stream of research effort in the monetary area ... we here neglect our conceptual misgivings about the Friedman approach, allow him his definitions for the sake of argument, and attempt to show that his approach appears to be empirically inferior' (Teigen, 1962, 31, 170).[14]

Eccentrics or 'cranks' can help define the boundaries of professional respectability. Prior to 1936, acceptance of the quantity theory was, for some, the touchstone of professional reliability. For example, Edwin Kemmerer (1935, 66), of Princeton University, concluded that 'it can be said, without fear of successful contradiction, that a large majority of scientific economists, both in the United States and abroad, who have worked intensively in the field monetary theory, accept some form of the quantity theory of money'.[15] Kemmerer (1934a, 174, 51, 56, 77, viii, 151) was alarmed by his belief that the US money supply had increased by 59% between June 1926 and March 1934, resulting in a '59-cent dollar'. The Federal Reserve banks could, he argued, control the money supply but not their velocities: 'You can lead a horse to water but you can't make him drink'.[16] These velocities were 'questions of business confidence and prospects, of hopes and fears, of emotions and prejudices'. According to Kemmerer (1933, 134; 1934b) there was a direct relationship between velocity and business confidence and therefore the 'vigorous reflation program of the Federal Reserve banks' had been counter-productive because it had weakened the confidence of the business community'.[17]

Kemmerer (1934a) opposed 'the money cranks ... a mass of barnacles so bright in appearance and with such clinging properties'. After attending the 1932 American Economic Association (AEA) proceedings, Richard Kahn (30 January 1933) wrote to Keynes from Chicago complaining that American economists were 'still living in the Dark Ages. It was all about the helplessness of trying to expand the economy ... the dead hand of Kemmerer hung heavy on most of the proceedings ... I am thinking that the only way to save humanity is to lead a campaign against the Quantity Theory. I tried it on the [University of Chicago] Graduate Club here and they didn't very much like it, but didn't quite know what to say. These people can see nothing absurd in the president elect being "opposed to currency inflation but in favour of credit inflation". I am enjoying the spectacle'.[18]

Keynes (JMK, XIII [1935], 546, 552; 1936, 351) realised that cranks could also be resurrected as neglected heretics 'which the classics have treated as imbecile for the last hundred years ... I am not really being so great an innovator, except as against the classical school, but have important predecessors and am returning to an age-long tradition of common sense ... which deserves rehabilitation and honour'.[19] As a result of the post-1936 Keynesian revolution, adherents of the quantity theory were relegated to 'crank' status. Until the late 1960s, that is, when Friedman was transformed from 'pariah to priest' (Barro, 1998, 6). Entering the temple, he turned the tables on those who had changed 'money' into Keynesian 'macroeconomics'. For this rebellion against the Keynesian Neoclassical Synthesis, Patinkin sought to have him, if not crucified, then permanently separated from his claimed parentage.[20]

Patinkin explained to his students at the University of Western Ontario (19 November 1973) that with respect to 'Friedman vs. everyone else – after having said everything they could think about one another, they started on their respective intellectual forefathers – and in this context, the worst thing that you can say about your opponent that he's a bastard – or at best an intellectual bastard. That he really isn't the son of the intellectual father he is claiming for himself. That he really doesn't understand the teachings of his alleged fathers – and that his opponent is really the legitimate descendent' (see Backhouse, 2002).[21]

Monetarists and Keynesians

Those who opposed the New Deal were tainted by the 'mark of Cain' (Conkin, 1968, 51); until shortly before Patinkin's assault, the 'mark of Chicago' was perceived to have inspired Friedman's monetarism. For example, Walter Heller (1969, 40–1), chairman of the Council of Economic Advisers (CEA) under both President Kennedy and President Johnson, stated that 'the Chicago School just goes rolling along' with 'great consistency over the years'. Heller's remarks were made in a widely reported debate on monetary policy with Friedman on 14 November 1968, a few days after Richard Nixon's election victory. In response, Friedman (1969, 45) – obviously aware that his remarks would be scrutinised for hints about Nixon's economic policy – declared that he would 'speak not for any mythical Chicago School, nor for any administration or candidate, but for myself'.

Friedman (1968) had just completed the theoretical structure of the monetarist counter-revolution with his 'natural rate of unemployment' AEA Presidential Address. After Nixon's victory it was widely expected that Friedman would exert a considerable influence on American economic policy. Paul McCracken, Nixon's CEA chairman, declared himself to be 'Friedmanesque' (cited by Blumenthal 1986, 109, 111). When Arthur Burns became Chairman of the Federal Reserve Board this was regarded (somewhat inaccurately) by James Tobin (pp. 215–28 [1981], 216) as the '1970 conversion' to monetarism. Between 1973–5, there were two monetary revolutions (domestic and international) which were closely connected to Friedman's advocacy: the destruction of the post-war system of fixed exchange rates and the widespread adoption of the rule of targeting monetary aggregates based on the expectation that the demand for money was a stable relationship.[22]

Since Simons' (1962 [1936]) classic essay on 'Rules Versus Authorities in Monetary Policy' the Chicago School had been regarded as the 'rules party' (Selden, 1962, 323).[23] According to Simons (1948 [1945], 308) the New Deal had delegated arbitrary power to a series of agencies. This 'high-road to dictatorship' was 'terrifying' for 'an old-fashioned liberal'. Elevating the 'government of men' over the 'government of rules' was tantamount to 'accepting or inviting fascism'. Simons was interpreted as undertaking a process of 'public indoctrination with the new rules of the game so that a new "religion of money" can be built up "around which might be regimented strong sentiments against tinkering with the currency"' (Gideonse, 1938, 13).[24]

An early version of Friedman's case for flexible exchange rates can be found in Simons' (1934, 53–4) 'Money and the New Deal'. Mints (1950, 115) also stated that 'the essential problem of monetary policy can be stated as that of "rules versus discretion"'. According to Friedman (pp. 147–66 [1972/1974], 152) this Chicago tradition provided immunity from the Keynesian virus: 'the small minority of economists who did not succumb to the Keynesian revolution consisted disproportionately of Chicago-trained economists ... so far as policy was concerned, Keynes had nothing to offer those of us who sat at the feet of Simons, Mints, Knight and Viner'.

Studies in the Quantity Theory of Money and Friedman's 'Restatement' of the quantity theory were published in the same year as *Money, Interest, and Prices* – Patinkin's (1956) attempt to codify the Keynesian Neoclassical Synthesis. In the ensuing controversy, Patinkin sought to provide 'A Restatement of Keynesian Economics'. Patinkin (19 August 1957; 27 January 1958) informed John Hicks that he was unambiguously an adherent of the Keynesian revolution but that he thought 'we strengthen the revolution by dropping the false issue of "unemployment *equilibrium*" of which so much has been made in the past ... Keynesian economics can and should be restated in a way that it remains valid even after we do take account of' the real balance effect [emphasis in original].[25]

Shortly afterwards, Friedman (1965 [1958], 106) argued before the Joint Economic Committee of the United States Congress that the money supply should grow at a 'predesignated rate'. Further supporting evidence was presented in 'The Demand for Money: Some Theoretical and Empirical

Results' (Friedman 1959). Patinkin (16 November 1959) then wrote to Friedman to complain that 'As an aside, I might add that my only other objection to your [1956] essay is its refusal to recognise the strongly Keynesian flavour of the analysis it presents ... to me it seems that with perhaps one exception (Karl Schlesinger) an exposition with the contents and spirit of yours could not have been written (and was not written) before Keynes. I find it particularly difficult to accept your implication that your essay represents the kind of thing that was taught at Chicago by Knight, Viner, Simons and Mints. My own recollections are different'.[26]

Shortly after he returned to Chicago, Friedman attempted to read 'between the lines' in connection with Wesley Claire Mitchell. Friedman sought to defend the Burns–Mitchell National Bureau of Economic Research methodology, which had been derided by the structural econometricians as 'measurement without theory' (Koopmans 1947).[27] Mitchell induced in Friedman (1950, 465, 489, 478–9) a feeling of 'exasperation, because numerous significant theoretical insights are so carefully hidden'.[28] He attempted to rescue Mitchell's work and to elevate it as 'a contribution to economic theory of the first magnitude'. Friedman believed that 'the theoretical insights are there after one pierces their protective coloring'. He explained the process by which he intended to enable 'economists ... to rediscover [the] essential elements' of Mitchell's work: 'The aim of the free rendering that follows is to show that an integrated business-cycle theory can be constructed from – or read into – Mitchell's work and to express it in terms that bring out its similarities and dissimilarities to other existing theories'.

His Chicago colleague, Lloyd Metzler (25 September 1950), complained in correspondence to Friedman that 'I do not share your views concerning the relative merits of Mitchell's theory and later theories of the business cycle. I doubt very much whether you would be able to interpret Mitchell as you have done in the absence of later developments by Keynes and others'.[29] Friedman later admitted that 'I tried ... in the article I wrote on [Mitchell] to sort of play fast and loose and try to construct an analytical theory'.[30] But the disagreement with Metzler – like the disagreement with Patinkin prior to 1968 – remained in the private domain.

Likewise, Nicholas Kaldor (1970, 54, n. 1) referred to an anti-Monetarist tradition, which remained quasi-oral (including in his 'written and oral evidence' to the 1958 Radcliffe Committee). But Friedman could no longer be dismissed so casually: 'It is a tribute to Friedman's growing influence (in the UK, as well as the US) that I thought it worth-while to publish a paper solely devoted to a criticism of his views in 1970 which I did not think worth-while twelve years before'.

Twelve years after the publication of *Studies in the Quantity Theory of Money* Patinkin became determined to bring the issue to a head in the public domain. On 27 November 1968, he wrote to Friedman enclosing a draft of an essay that was to be published in the first issue of the *Journal of Money, Credit and Banking* (*JMCB*) in which he documented what he believed to be the falsity of Friedman's account of the Chicago tradition (pp. 87–120 [1969/1981]). Harry Johnson (pp. 169–82 [1971]), Friedman's Chicago colleague (1959–77) and former editor of the *JPE*, expanded upon Patinkin's essay to provide a wider critique of Friedman's scholarship and integrity.

Friedman (1962) dedicated *Capitalism and Freedom* to his two children 'and their contemporaries who must carry the torch of liberty on its next lap'. Johnson (pp. 169–82 [1971], 179) concluded that Patinkin had shown 'specifically that the Chicago quantity theorists – Simons and Mints – were no different from their quantity theory colleagues elsewhere in these respects. There was no lonely light constantly burning in a secret shrine on the Midway, encouraging the faithful to assemble in waiting for the day when the truth could safely be revealed to the masses; that candle was made, and not merely lit, only when its light had a chance of penetrating far and wide and attracting new converts to the old time religion'.

The Patinkin–Johnson assaults provided anti-monetarist ammunition to many of Friedman's opponents including Tobin and Paul Samuelson (both associated with the Keynesian Neoclassical Synthesis and the policy process in President Kennedy's White House). In his *JPE* obituary of Viner, Samuelson (1972, 11) asserted that it was 'a perversion of history to believe that there was an oral tradition at the University of Chicago which had already anticipated the valid nucleus of Keynesian analysis'. Tobin (pp. 215–28 [1981], 216) regretted that 'the flaws Johnson detected [in monetarism] have not yet proved fatal'.

Early Disputes over the Quantity Theory

From its formation, the Chicago Economics department and its journal, the *JPE*, had been involved in heated controversy over the quantity theory. J. Laurence Laughlin the founding chairman of the department and the founding editor of the *JPE* (1892–5) was a relentless critic of the quantity theory (Dorfman, 1959, 419; Bornemann, 1940, 4). Laughlin's (1903) work stimulated Kemmerer (1907) and Irving Fisher (1911) to restate and defend the quantity theory (Mehrling 1997, 32). Throughout his career

Laughlin engaged Fisher on the quantity theory: Chicago versus Yale 'with the sides reversed' (Friedman, 1974, 14–15).[31]

Laughlin took his campaign to the public, taking two years leave (1911–13) from Chicago to act as full-time chairman of the National Citizens League to press for banking reform. Friedman (1987) noted that Laughlin's economics was 'marred by dogmatic and rigid opposition to the quantity theory'. Paul Douglas (1972, 42, 334) arrived at the University of Chicago in 1920: 'over the years I developed a greater faith in [Laughlin's] ideas and even less reliance on the rigid quantity theory as the sole factor in the general price level'.

Presumably referring to Keynes (JMK, 1983, 11 [1911], 375–76), Laughlin complained about 'the recrudescence of the archaic quantity theory of money in Great Britain' (Laughlin, 1918, 117). In *The Federal Reserve Act its Origin and Problems*, Laughlin (1933, 222, 229, 231–2) continued to abuse the quantity theory, and Fisher and his 'unquestionable error'. Moreover, Laughlin asserted that 'the American inflationist school of Irving Fisher has called in for reinforcement ... John Maynard Keynes'. Keynes' 'remarks on the abandonment of the British gold standard and the sacerdotal nature assigned to the influence of the quantity of money on prices are scarcely credible'.

H. Parker Willis acquired his aversion to the quantity theory from Laughlin, his Chicago colleague and former teacher (Dorfman, 1959, 314–5).[32] Laughlin and Willis were two of the architects of the Federal Reserve Act (White, 1983, 115). Willis became Secretary of the Federal Reserve Board (1918–22) and was the founding President of the Stable Money Association (Fisher, 1934, 106, 360; Sandilands, 1990, 64).[33] Laughlin, however, had to exert his influence on the Federal Reserve Board via Willis because a Democrat was in the White House and to the Democrats 'Laughlin was *persona non grata*' (Mitchell, 1941, 878; Friedman, 1987).[34]

W. Allen Wallis (1976 [1964], 102) noted that Friedman was '*persona non grata* in the Federal Reserve Board'. Citing Mints (1945), Friedman (1960, 26, 43) argued that the Federal Reserve Board had been 'set up by men mostly wedded to that ubiquitous fallacy, the real bills doctrine'. According to Friedman, this fallacy had contributed to the confusion 'between what might be called the "monetary" effects of monetary policy – the effect on the stock of money – and the "credit" effects – the effects on recorded rates of interest and other conditions in the credit market ... An ancient example of the confusion is the "real bills" fallacy already referred to. More recently, the change in economic ideas associated with the name of John Maynard Keynes led to an almost complete neglect of the "monetary" effects of monetary policy and concentration on the "credit" effects'.

According to Friedman and Anna Schwartz (1963, 193), one of the consequences of this acceptance of the real bills doctrine was that the Federal Reserve began operations 'with no effective legislative criteria for determining the total stock of money. The discretionary judgement of a group of men was inevitably substituted for the quasi-automatic discipline of the gold standard ... Little wonder, perhaps, that the subsequent years saw so much backing and filling, so much confusion about purpose and power, and so erratic an exercise of power'.

Laughlin was an advocate of 'an extreme form of the real bills doctrine' (Mehrling, 1997, 35–6; see also Friedman and Schwartz, 1963, 192, n. 7). Mints (1950, 6–7; 1945, 5) regarded the real bills doctrine as 'almost wholly fallacious'; it was 'utterly subversive of any rational attack on the problems of monetary policy'. This aversion to the real bills doctrine (and the incompetent discretion associated with it) linked the dominant monetary economists of the first and second generation Chicago School 'rules party' (Mints and Friedman) to members of the third generation.

Friedman was not the first Chicago economist to offer a restatement of the quantity theory by reading between the lines. In the *JPE*, Willis (1896, 448, 441) noted that the quantity theory was 'gradually losing ground amongst economists' but 'had lost none of its hold on upon the public mind'. Willis sought to provide 'a clear restatement of the quantity theory'. He noted the difficulties involved in such a project but concluded that 'by comparison of the various bits of exposition on the subject a theory fairly consistent with itself may, if too great nicety in the use of terms is not demanded, be culled from the recent writings of believers in the doctrine'. Friedman (1972, 12) later repeated Fisher's rebuttal to Laughlin that 'the quantity theory is in essence correct. What it needs is to be restated not rejected'. It was this 'Restatement' that Friedman (pp. 33–51 [1956], 33, 51) provided, by 'reading between the lines' as Willis had done six decades before.

Nor was Friedman the first economist to make an assertion about the existence of a quantity theory oral tradition. On two occasions, Keynes made similar assertions: in his review of Fisher's *Purchasing Power of Money* (1911) and in his obituary of Alfred Marshall (JMK, 1983, XI [1911], 375–76; X [1924], 189; see also Whitaker, 1975, 164–78). According to Johnson, Friedman self-consciously imitated the tactics of the Keynesian revolution so as to further his counter-revolution.[35] Johnson (1970, 85–6, 107 n. 48) speculated that during his year 'as a visitor at Cambridge [1954], Friedman became enamoured of the "Cambridge oral tradition" as a concept permitting the attribution to an institution of a wisdom exceeding that displayed in its published work, and unconsciously stole a leaf from Cambridge's book for the benefit of his own institution'.[36]

Edward Cannan (1927 [1922], 311), of the London School of Economics (LSE), noted that to 'outsiders' the 'Cambridge School of Economics' appeared 'as somewhat of a "sect"'.[37] Cannan also attempted to expropriate the analysis of money demand as an LSE oral tradition after having earlier disagreed with Keynes. In a review of Keynes' *Tract on Monetary Reform*, Cannan (1927 [1924], 371–2) took up the 'gauntlet' which Keynes had thrown down. Cannan argued that it was important for the stability of the financial system that the quantity theory was seen to be part of the body of economic theory which is perceived to be 'generally true'. Distracting attention away from the money supply towards money demand would 'constantly tend to make people disbelieve in the workings of the quantity theory'.[38]

In his rejoinder, Keynes (JMK, XI [1924], 415, 419) argued that there could be 'both very large and very rapid' changes in 'the volume of real balances'. Keynes complained that Cannan was 'unsympathetic with nearly everything worth reading ... which has been written on monetary theory in the last ten years'. The 'almost revolutionary improvement in our understanding of the mechanism of money and credit and of the analysis of the trade cycle ... may prove to be one of the most important advances in economic thought ever made'. Cannan was guilty of writing 'as though the last word had been said years ago in elementary textbooks'. In contrast to Cannan's work, Keynes commended the 'impressive' collection of opinions on the topic provided by J. R. Bellerby (1923) 'from many sources'. Cannan (1927 [1924], 384, 386–7) responded by purporting to analyse 'what these textbooks really did say'. Referring to Keynes' 1923 'restatement of the quantity theory' and heightened perceptions about the importance of hoarding and 'the demand for currency' Cannan reported that 'rummaging through old lecture notes, I find I was teaching it orally ten years before I put it in a book in 1918'.[39]

Other Oral Traditions

Richard Kahn's English translation of Knut Wicksell's *Interest and Prices* was published in 1936. It is possible that Keynes learnt of Wicksell's economics through an oral tradition (Skidelsky, 1992, 168).[40] Alternatively, Keynes may have read Wicksell (1907) in the *Economic Journal*, or an earlier German edition of *Interest and Prices*, or may have been exposed to Wicksell's ideas through Kahn (Laidler, 1991, 149, 152, n. 30). Kahn (1933, 1, 14, 6), who visited Chicago in 1932–3, also made an assertion about the existence of an oral tradition. He noted that the marginal revenue curve had been developed by 'a number of independent workers': Edward Chamberlin in Harvard and Austin Robinson in Cambridge. Kahn also 'realised that by a curious coincidence precisely the same term was in use at Chicago' by Viner and Theodore Yntema. Kahn also referred to 'a general theory' and a Cambridge oral tradition: 'Mr Shove has, by way of oral teaching, long been engaged in following up the same lines of thought'.

Patinkin (pp. 87–120 [1969/1981], 98) and his research assistant, Stanley Fischer, located a Chicago oral tradition in George Bach's Chicago dissertation on 'Price Level Stabilisation Some Theoretical and Practical Considerations'. Acknowledging his 'deep obligation' to Mints, Simon and Viner, Bach (1940, iii, 36, n. 1) explained that he was especially grateful to Mints for the 'reductions to essentials' of his theory, 'although it has been in the nature of an "oral tradition" at Chicago for some time and can be found in many writers, but only more or less obscured. (Note, e.g. Vol. 1 of Keynes' *Treatise*)'. This Chicago oral tradition related to psychological factors which changed the 'propensity to hoard consume and invest', 'perverse fluctuations in the volume of money in the system' and 'the existence of "sticky" prices throughout large sections of the economy, of which many are cost-prices, so that costs have a tendency to move more slowly than do the more flexible selling prices'.

This sticky price tradition played a pivotal role separating Keynes' analysis of liquidity preference from his contemporaries in Viner's review of the *General Theory* (Vol. 2, pp. 399–430 [1936/1964], 404): 'In modern monetary theory [hoarding] is generally dealt with, with results which in kind are substantially identical with Keynes', as a factor operating to reduce the "velocity" of money. There has been, I believe, common agreement among economists that when price rigidities are important hoarding could present a serious and continuing problem, and that it is always a significant factor in the downward phase of a short business cycle. Keynes, however, attaches great importance to it as a barrier to "full" employment at almost all times, and apparently irrespective of the degree of flexibility of prices'.[41] Friedman (1968, 3) noted that Pigou's analysis of the behaviour of real money balances exploded 'Keynes' key theoretical proposition, namely, that even in a world of flexible prices, a position of equilibrium at full employment might not exist. Henceforth, unemployment had again to be explained by rigidities or imperfections, not as the natural outcome of a fully operative market process'.

Simons (1948 [1944], 131–2) used sticky prices to build an expectations-augmented-insider-outsider model of the labour market. Where trade unions had power and labour turnover was costly to firms, insiders could 'insulate themselves from the competition of new workers merely by making their costs excessive, that is, by establishing labor costs and *wage expectations* [emphasis added] which preclude expansion of production or employment in their field'. Thus outsiders ('new and displaced workers') would not 'typically migrate' to such firms because 'jobs cannot be had'. The privately optimal strategy for trade unions was to exclude 'lower-wage competitors'. Douglas (1935, 54–5, 61), citing Gardiner Means, also emphasised the causal importance of 'stickiness in prices' in his *Controlling Depressions*. Thus 'an examination of the actual facts of industry' revealed that 'rigid prices in the face of falling costs' were 'probably the chief initiating causes of the present depression.[42]

According to Martin Bronfenbrenner, in the late 1930s 'Simons agreed with Means that administered prices were delaying recovery and should come down. (But Simons was more down on trade union wages than on industrial prices)' (cited by Samuels and Medema, 1990, 169, n. 55). Means used this analysis to implicitly demonstrate the invalidity of the quantity theory: 'In the modern economy, the widespread presence of inflexible prices makes any changes in the relation between the supply of money and the demand for money under given price conditions a seriously disorganising force'. In the 'old flexible-price economy' changes in money demand or supply would lead to price changes which would leave production relations 'essentially undisturbed'. In the modern economy, a monetary contraction would dislocate the price relationships and produce a decline in output in the inflexible price sector (Ware and Means, 1936, 79–81). A 'serious and continuing depression' could follow such a policy. Alternatively, the same outcome could result from the monetary authorities failing to allow the money supply to keep pace with money demand, a scenario that Means (1935, 409–10) advanced as a partial explanation of the Great Depression. Thus a stabilising monetary policy would require the authorities to adjust the money supply so as to eliminate any pressure towards 'a *general revision* of prices either upwards or downwards' [emphasis in original].

Chicago and the Keynesian Revolution

In his AEA Presidential Address (1951, 2–3), Knight hinted at the existence of a Chicago oral monetary tradition: 'It has long been my habit to mention to classes the sinister import of such intellectual phenomena as … the perpetual popular demand for making capital cheap by manufacturing money'. Knight noted that during his career several 'movements' had denigrated the term 'orthodox' as 'a "cuss-word", an epithet of reproach … the latest "new economics" and in my opinion rather the worst, for fallacious doctrine and pernicious consequences, is that launched by the late John Maynard (Lord) Keynes, who for a decade succeeded in carrying economic thinking way back to the dark age'.

Keynes read between the lines to construct his 'classical' straw man caricature.[43] Keynes (1936, 3, n. 1, 175, 177–8) opened the *General Theory* with the admission that much of what followed was possibly a 'solecism' with respect to his characterisation of the 'classical' economists in general and the 'Classical Theory of the Rate of Interest' in particular. But the absence of compelling textual evidence did not prevent Keynes from establishing a potent rhetorical device. Thus Alfred Marshall must have believed that the interest rate was determined by equilibrating investment and savings although this explanation 'is not to be found in Marshall's *Principles* in so many words. Yet his theory seems to be this, and it is what I myself was brought up on … [Marshall] surely believed, although he did not expressly say so, that aggregate savings and aggregate investment are necessarily equal'.[44]

In his review of the *General Theory*, Knight (Vol. 2, pp. 437–60 [1937], 438, 451, 459, n. 22) complained that Keynes' references to 'classical economists' were 'the sort of caricatures which are typically set up as straw men for purposes of attack in controversial writing'. He sought to defend his own Chicago teaching from Keynes' influence: 'In the great majority of cases the doctrines so labelled [as classical] seem to me to be quite at variance with, and often contradictory to anything I was ever taught as academic doctrine in any modern sense … and they are certainly alien to anything I have ever taught as such, and I have been rated, and have supposed myself, an adherent of the general type of position referred to by the term. On the other hand, many of Mr Keynes's own doctrines are, as he would proudly admit, among the notorious fallacies to combat which have been considered a main function of the teaching of economics'. Knight noted that 'where once it was necessary in writing to pose as merely restating and interpreting doctrine handed down from the Fathers, the surest way to public interest and acclaim now lies through pulling down and overturning everything established or accepted'.

Patinkin (like Friedman) offered a 'Restatement' of the doctrines of the Chicago Fathers. In 'Price Flexibility and Full Employment' Patinkin (1952 [1948], 278), then an assistant professor at Chicago, concluded that 'in a static world with a constant stock of money, price flexibility assures full employment ... But in the real dynamic world in which we live, price flexibility with a constant stock of money might generate full employment only after a long period; or might even lead to a deflationary spiral of continuous unemployment. On either of these grounds, a full employment policy based on a constant stock of money and price flexibility does not seem to be very promising. All that this means is that a full employment policy cannot be the fairly simple one of maintaining a constant stock of money and waiting for the economic system to generate full employment automatically through price declines. Other policies will be required. One possible alternative policy can be inferred from the Haberler–Pigou analysis itself: there are two ways to increase real balances. One is to keep the money stock constant and permit prices to fall. An equally effective way is to maintain the price level constant, and increase the stock of money by creating a government deficit'. Patinkin then added a footnote: 'Considered from this perspective, the Pigou analysis presents in a rigorous fashion part of the theoretical framework implicit in the fiscal-monetary policy of the Simons–Mints position'.

Patinkin's Restatement of the doctrines of the Chicago Fathers made an important contribution to the Keynesian Neoclassical Synthesis. With respect to 'the Keynesian–classical polemic' Patinkin (1952 [1948], 253, 257–8, 260) believed that he had demonstrated that 'these two camps have really come closer and closer together'. Patinkin also asserted that 'a successful restatement of the classical position must demonstrate the existence of some automatic mechanism which will always bring about full employment ... To the Keynesian negative interest rate argument replies had been made by both Haberler and Pigou ... by changing the real value of cash balances, desired full employment savings and investment can always be equated at a positive rate of interest'.

In 1947, Friedman provided Patinkin with detailed ('early and often') comments on at least two drafts of his paper. When the essay was reprinted in an AEA volume edited by Friedrich Lutz and Mints (1952), Patinkin (1952, 252, n. 261) added four sentences 'as a result of discussions with Milton Friedman' which followed from this discussion of cash balances: 'It should also be emphasised, as Haberler does, that although this argument has been presented above as an answer to Keynes, it is of much older origin. In particular, it is implicit in classical theorising on the quantity theory of money. The crucial step in this analysis, it will be recalled, comes at the point where it is argued that as a result of increasing the amount of money in the economy, individuals' cash balances are larger than desired at the existing price level, so that they will attempt to reduce these real balances by increasing their money expenditure. The main contribution of Haberler and Pigou is to show how this set of forces must, and can, be introduced into the Keynesian analytical apparatus'.

The year before the *General Theory* was published, Knight (1935, 236) described the economic doctrines of 'the classical school' as 'a mixture of a more or less scientific analysis of a price economy with what is really political propaganda for *laissez-faire*'. But as Kenneth Boulding (1956, 136, 138), one of Friedman's fellow Chicago graduate students noted, the Keynesian 'bulldozer' had left 'the orthodox laissez faire man' stranded. Alvin Hansen played the role of the 'American Keynes'. Simons wrote to Keynes describing himself as 'a vigorous but inconspicuous participant in recent monetary-fiscal controversies' adding that he was 'bitterly anti-Hansen and, if not wholly anti-Keynesian, utterly opposed to your more extreme American disciples' (cited by Patinkin (Vol. 2, pp. 373–92 [1979/1981], 388–9). Hansen favoured a 'dynamic approach' – which stood in contrast to the passive acceptance of 'the play of "natural" forces ... many economists are coming to think that action along these traditional lines would by itself be wholly inadequate. It is increasingly understood that the essential foundation upon which the international security of the future must be built is an economic order so managed and controlled that it will be capable of sustaining full employment' (Hansen and Kindleberger, 1942, 467). In response, Simons (1948 [1942], 199) referred disparagingly to 'Hansen and his school'.

Hansen (Vol. 2, pp. 472–7 [1946], 476) also saw the post-war cleavage widening: 'It may now be useful to contrast the Mints–Simons program with that urged by [Abba P.] Lerner'. Howard Ellis (Vol. 2, pp. 477–80 [1946], 477) saw the dispute as a confrontation between 'a political wing favoring a very large amount of government activity, and another wing which, mistrustful of the concentrated power which the bureaucracy would possess under these circumstances, would reduce it to a minimum'.[45]

In contrast, Patinkin (1952 [1948], 282) thought that 'although these positions are quite distinct theoretically, their policy implications are very similar ... Thus the policies may advocate tax reductions to stimulate consumption and investment (the Simons–Mints school); or may insist on direct government investment to supplement private investment (Hansen, *et al.*)'. But Friedman (pp. 33–51 [1956]) found the Simons–Mints school to be the inspiration for a policy proposal (the x% money growth rule) which contrasted markedly with the consensual policy implication derived by Patinkin.

Thus four paragraphs of Friedman's introductory essay launched an intense and wide-ranging debate that spawned important contributions to theory, methodology and the history of thought, and that also profoundly influenced popular ideology and political action. These two volumes are devoted to all these implications. Part one of this volume reconstructs the initial controversy: Friedman's initial essay (pp. 33–51 [1956]) plus an essay on 'The Monetary Theory and Policy of Henry Simons' (pp. 55–67 [1967]) and the offending encyclopaedia entry on 'The Quantity Theory of Money' (pp. 71–84 [1968]). Pages 87–120 ([1969/1981]) and 147–66 ([1972/1974]) constitute the basis of Patinkin's case; pages 147–66 ([1972/1974]) Friedman's only published response. In pages 169–82, on 'The Keynesian Revolution and the Monetarist Counter-Revolution', Johnson ([1971]) expands on Patinkin's essay original essay. The following pages by David Laidler (pp. 185–212 [1981]) and Tobin (pp. 215–28 [1981]) provide some additional background about the nature of the monetarist assault on orthodoxy. Interestingly, Laidler – a monetarist, and a distinguished monetary historian – takes Patinkin's side of the debate. Pages 231–46 and 249–79 set the dispute in the wider context of the Patinkin–Friedman friendship and the political and ideological disputes of the time.

Notes

[1] I am grateful to seminar participants at Duke University, the 2002 History of Economics Society Conference, the Hoover Institution and the 2001 Patinkin conference plus Tom Cate, Roger Backhouse, Jeff Biddel, William Coleman, Graeme Dorrance, Mathew Forbes, Robert J. Gordon, Geoffrey Harcourt, Rolf Henriksson, Tom Humphrey, David Laidler, Cristina Marcuzza, Perry Mehrling, Don Moggridge, Michael Parkin, Ron Phillips, Dominick Regan, Melvin Reder, Hugh Rockoff, Annalissa Rosselli, Roger Sandilands, Michael Schneider, Anna Schwartz, Frank Steindl, George Tavlas, Warren Young and Richard Watson. Gloria Valentine and the librarians at Special Collections, Duke University, the Modern Archives Collection, Kings College, Cambridge and the Hoover Institution were, as always, most helpful. I am grateful to the Modern Archives Collection, King's College Cambridge for permission to cite from the Richard Kahn Papers, to the Special Collections, Duke University, for permission to cite from the Don Patinkin and Lauchlin Currie Papers, and to the Hoover Institution for permission to cite from the Friedman Papers. I also thank Roger Sandilands for providing me with

copies of Currie's letters. I am especially grateful to Milton Friedman for answering my detailed questions, for being so generous with his time and for allowing me to inspect his 1932 lecture notes which had been gathering dust for almost seven decades. These chapters demonstrate that economists cooperate even when they compete.

[2] The term 'monetarism' was not apparently coined for another decade, by which time it had become a real threat to the Keynesian intellectual hegemony.

[3] Both Patinkin (1981, 261) and Rose Friedman (Friedman and Friedman, 1998, 38) took Mints' Economics 331, 'Banking Theory and Monetary Policy'. According to Milton Friedman's academic transcript he did not attend that course for credit, but he recalls sitting in on the lectures (no reading lists for 331 have apparently survived in the Friedman Papers).

[4] One of the few changes that Friedman made between the first and the final draft of his December 1967 American Economic Association Presidential Address was to delete the reference to Knight in the opening sentence: 'My revered teacher, Frank Knight, was fond of quoting Josh Billing's wry comment "The trouble with most people ain't ignorance; it's what they know that ain't so". That describes my aim to night: to persuade you that something you know simply isn't so'.

[5] Patinkin (pp. 87–120 [1969/1981], 102; pp. 361–6 [1986], 365) misquotes this sentence twice. In the first instance Patinkin misquotes 'affected' as 'influenced'; in the second he misquotes 'analysis' as 'theory'.

[6] Both Friedman and Reagan arrived in Chicago in autumn 1932; Reagan (1990, 20) 'hitchhiked to Chicago ... with visions of getting a job as a radio announcer'. Starting in 1933, President Roosevelt helped re-establish confidence in the monetary system through 'the warm and supportive simplicity of his Fireside Chat lessons' administered through the radio (Karl, 1983, 103). It is interesting to note that the Chicago oral tradition was supposed to exist just as the radio was transforming mass communication in the United States. Ten million households in the US had a radio in 1929; twenty-seven million in 1939 (Hobsbawm, 1994, 195–6). During this period, an amateur monetary reformer, Father Charles Coughlin, emerged as a 'radio priest' (Laidler, 1999, 229, n. 20). Coughlin's biggest breakthrough came when he acquired radio access to the Chicago and Cincinnati areas in 1929–30. By early 1934, *Fortune* estimated that he had ten million regular listeners, probably the largest in the world (Reeve 1943, 132–3, 136).

[7] When Keynes (JMK, XX, 587) arrived in Chicago in June 1931 he found President Hoover's 'stock stood incredibly low. There was not a soul who would say good word for him'.

[8] According to surviving lecture notes, at Harvard in 1903–4, Franklin Roosevelt had been taught that 'The quantity theory holds' (cited by Fusfeld, 1956, 31). In 1932, Roosevelt was re-introduced to the quantity theory in person by Irving Fisher (Tugwell, 1968, 98).

[9] In contrast, Reagan (1990, 230–1, 311) had both faith and a lineage. He was aware that in 1981 he was facing 'what many economists called the greatest economic emergency since the Great Depression' but he had 'faith – faith in those tax cuts and faith in the American people'. His supply side policies were based on his own oral tradition ('you say "I'm not gonna work for six cents on the dollar"') with a lineage

descending from 'that philosopher, Khaldoon' a fourteenth-century Muslim writer on taxes.

[10] Friedman (1987) noted that J. Laurence Laughlin, the founding chairman of the University of Chicago Economics Department, exerted 'no lasting influence on economic thought'. He might have made an indirect impact: in 1894–5, John Neville Keynes considered but rejected an offer made by Laughlin to accept a chair at Chicago (Skidelsky, 1983, 65; Moggridge, 1992, 16). It is interesting to speculate what the consequences for the modern configuration of economics would have been had the Keynes family relocated permanently to Chicago, and had Friedman's parents not migrated (separately) to the United States (also in 1894–5).

[11] According to Schumpeter (1954, 223–4), the Physiocrats 'formed a group united by what amounted to a creed; they were indeed what they were called so often, a sect ... [with] vows to One Master and One Doctrine ... [they were] disciples who absorbed and accepted the Master's teaching with a fidelity for which there are but two analogues in the whole history of economics: the fidelity of the orthodox Marxist to the message of Marx, and the fidelity of the orthodox Keynesians to the message of Keynes ... they founded discussion groups, worked upon individuals and agencies in key positions (the parliaments especially) and produced a large quantity of popular and controversial literature [and] economic journalism'. du Pont and his fellow disciples were 'thoroughly alive to the importance of propaganda'.

[12] Karl Popper favoured the title 'Periclean Society'; Aaron Director preferred 'Adam Smith-Tocqueville' (Hartwell, 1995, 43).

[13] Ludwig von Mises (1974 [1952], 170) recalled that at a meeting of the Mt Pelerin Society, T. S. Ashton, a prominent historian, presented a paper which suggested that much contemporary history was mere ideology, consisting of 'tortured facts' and 'concocted legends'. Hayek also berated the 'appalling effects of the use of history as propaganda' and there was a discussion about history being able to 'demonstrate the importance of freedom in the past' (Hartwell, 1995, 40–1, 38). These concerns led to a 1954 University of Chicago volume on *Capitalism and the Historians*. One essay focused on Charles Beard's responsibility for cultivating the 'Anticapitalist Bias of American Historians' (Hacker, 1954). In his introductory essay Hayek (1954, 7, 9, 4) referred to the 'socialist interpretation of history which has governed political thinking for the last two or three generations ... Most people would be surprised to learn that most of what they believe about these subjects are not safely established facts but myths, launched from political motives'. Historical beliefs were sometimes 'the effects rather than the cause of political beliefs. Historical myths have perhaps played nearly as great a role in shaping opinion as historical facts'. Hayek (1967 [1944], 1) prefaced *The Road to Serfdom* with Acton's dictum: 'few discoveries are more irritating than those which expose the pedigree of ideas'. In his review of Simons' *Economic Policy for a Free Society*, Michael Oakeshott (1977 [1949], 49–50) argued that it was vital to combat the 'deplorable ignorance of the nature of libertarian tradition itself' because this lack of understanding 'threatens liberty'.

[14] Ronald Teigen's thesis was supervised by Albert Ando and accepted by Robert Solow as chair of the graduate studies committee (both Ando and Solow opposed monetarism). In Solow's (1964, 710–11) judgement 'Although only a small minority

of the profession is persuaded by his opinions, around any academic lunch table on any given day, the talk is more likely to be about Milton Friedman than about any other economist'. Teigen (1971, 244) subsequently admitted that it was 'not obvious why monetarism had suddenly become so popular'. Johnson's (pp. 000–000 [1971]) critique was approvingly cited and Teigen asserted (without any supporting evidence) that Patinkin (pp. 87–120 [1969/1981]) had 'shown' that Friedman's 'alleged Chicago oral tradition' was false.

[15] Arthur F. Burns (1929, 562) noted that it was 'true' that economists 'cling to one or another version of [the Quantity Theory] doctrine'.

[16] Friedman (1968, 1) later used this analysis to denigrate earlier analyses: 'Monetary policy was [perceived as] a string ... You could lead a horse to water but you could not make him drink. Theory by aphorism was soon replaced by Keynes' rigourous and sophisticated analysis'. Friedman and Schwartz (1963, 410–11, 171) reinterpreted the Great Depression as a 'Great Contraction' with the money supply falling, rather than rising as Kemmerer suggested. They found Kemmerer's work 'depressing' and unperceptive. They concluded that his involvement in the establishment of the Federal Reserve System led him to believe that the system he had helped create had 'once and for all solved problems of liquidity'. They also noted that during the agitation to establish the Federal Reserve System, Kemmerer's contribution to the National Monetary Commission was a monograph on *Seasonal Variations in the Demand for Money and Capital in the United States*. Friedman's other major ideological-intellectual opponents were also associated with 'systems': the Bretton Woods system and the Keynesian system.

[17] Kemmerer (1934a, 174) was obviously proud of having been a financial adviser to eleven countries. Roger Sandilands (correspondence, 26 March 2002) recalls Lauchlin Currie complaining that Kemmerer's advice had left a 'wretched legacy' to Latin America.

[18] Keynes Papers, L/K/35–8.

[19] Roy Harrod (1951, 460) criticised Keynes for seizing on 'isolated passages [from the mercantilists] to find wisdom that was not really there'. In response to Harrod's attempt to persuade him to treat these heretics with less respect, Keynes (JMK, XIII [1935], 650–1) wrote to Joan Robinson explaining that Harrod 'strongly objected to Chapter 26 [ultimately Chapter 23 of the *General Theory*] as a tendentious attempt to glorify imbeciles. I should like to know how it strikes you'. Robinson replied that 'I hope you won't let Roy intimidate you about 26. I think it is important to have it, and it is very enjoyable to read. I don't think you have overstated matters at all'.

[20] Economists (including Patinkin) often use biblical analogies: Knight (1940), for example, published an essay on '"what is Truth" in Economics?' Patinkin (1995, 388–9) highlighted his studies at the Hebrew Theological College at Chicago (1933–43) as an influence on his historical studies. Patinkin (1990, 224, n. 20) detected religious overtones in post-Keynesian writings. With respect to the Keynesian revolution, Patinkin (1993, 647) referred to the struggle 'for the privilege of having been vicariously present at that Moment of Truth ...'. Perry Mehrling (2002) recounted that Jacob Marshak declined an approached to migrate to Palestine, suggesting Patinkin ('an ardent Zionist') as his replacement. Patinkin's first thesis topic was 'The

International Economic Position of Palestine'. Patinkin's widow informed me that the Federal Bureau of Investigation prevented her and her husband from migrating to Israel in spring 1948, because they had been procuring military hardware for the shortly-to-be-established State of Israel. For a discussion of both 'Patinkin and Talmudic Readings in the History of Economics' and the role of the 'Oral Torah' in the Jewish tradition, see Saunders, 2001.

[21] Don Patinkin Papers, Box 20.

[22] Patinkin (1979, 154) noted that Friedman had previously effected an intellectual revolution by having 'monetary policy' redefined as relating to variations in the money supply rather than changes in interest rates.

[23] Irving Fisher was an earlier advocate of monetary rules.

[24] Simons (1950, 155, n. 23) referred to himself as 'not enough of a scholar' to describe the sources of his ideas and having 'no fear that bibliophiles will point out an army of unacknowledged precursors'. The only source for his ideas on income taxation that he wished to acknowledge was his undergraduate teacher in accounting. Joan Robinson (1962, 77) noted that 'Keynes himself lacked the scruple of a scholar'.

[25] Don Patinkin Papers: http://scriptorium.lib.duke.edu/economists/patinkin.

[26] Don Patinkin Papers, Box 32.

[27] In 1933–4, Friedman attended Mitchell's Columbia University course on 'Types of Economic Theory', lecture notes for which have survived for the year 1934–5. In his final two sentences of the course Mitchell stated that 'the people who are gradually accumulating this factual knowledge are ... laying the basis and actively contributing to our economic theory at large. I hope that every member of the class in the future will have some part in this work of developing economic theory' (Gould and Kelley, 1949, 300).

[28] In the early 1930s, Mitchell told Erik Lundberg (1994, 497) that 'we need another hundred years of empirical research and knowledge before we can generalise about causal relations on your level'.

[29] Metzler continued: 'I was quite strongly impressed, as I read your paper, by the similarity between the theory which you have attributed to Mitchell and Kalecki's theory of the business cycle ... the similarity between your version of Mitchell and chapter 6 of Kalecki's book *Essays in the Theory of Economic Fluctuations*, is so striking that seems to me that it might be advisable to make a footnote to his work somewhere in your paper'. Friedman (30 October 1950) replied that he was 'almost ready to wager that there is no copy in Paris' where he was currently based and was therefore unable to refer to Kalecki's book. Milton Friedman Papers, Correspondence, Meltzler file.

[30] In an interview with Jeff Biddle (6 October, 1993). I am grateful to Biddle for providing me with a transcript of this interview.

[31] In 1879, as an instructor in political economy at Harvard, Laughlin (1924, 307) listened to a paper on 'Taxation' presented by two undergraduates, Theodore Roosevelt and Robert Bacon, a future president of United States and his Secretary of State. Around the same time, Laughlin (1850–1934) heard Simon Newcomb deliver some invited lectures at Harvard. It was Newcomb to whom Fisher (1911) dedicated

The Purchasing Power of Money. When an Iowa Senator declared that the University of Chicago 'smelled of [Rockefeller] oil', Laughlin (1906, 41) defended academic freedom using a monetary analogy: an elastic currency was required to reflect the state of the business cycle, just as tolerance was required to accommodate unpopular views. His last academic appointment to Chicago was Jacob Viner (Friedman 1987).

[32] Wesley Claire Mitchell told Eli Ginzberg (1997, 3) that Willis had never deviated from the 'hard money' views which he had acquired as a Chicago graduate student under Laughlin.

[33] Willis (1874–1937) was one of the first to visit Roosevelt after the 1932 election (Tugwell, 1972, 205). From the outset of the Depression, Willis blamed Federal Reserve officials for the panic (Davis, 1971, 35). He denounced the 1935 Eccles banking bill as 'the most dangerous, the most unwarranted, the most insidious measure' of the New Deal (cited by Schlesinger, 1960, 297). During Friedman's time at Columbia, Willis' Banking Seminar produced a collaborative analysis of *The Banking Situation* (Willis and Chapman, 1934). Friedman's (1956) *Studies in the Quantity Theory of Money* was the collaborative product of his Chicago Workshop in Money and Banking, founded in 1953. Friedman attributed the 'success' of his Workshop to the rule 'no representation without taxation' (Friedman and Friedman, 1998, 208).

[34] Laughlin was a 'staunch conservative and Republican' (Neff, 1934, 4, 1).

[35] Johnson (1975, 124) concluded that in the 1950s, Cambridge people were 'perverting economics in order to defend intellectual and emotional positions taken in the 1930s'. He was implicitly accusing Friedman of perverting economics by pretending to be merely defending an intellectual position (or framework) that had not been (uniquely) taken in Chicago in the 1930s.

[36] In the year before Friedman's visit to Cambridge a *JPE* essay on the 'checkered career' of the concept of the demand for money also referred to 'the oral tradition at Cambridge' with respect to Marshall's use of the 'demand-to-hold' approach in the decades before the publication of his 1923 *Money, Credit and Commerce* (Gilbert, 1953, 145). In a 1871 manuscript on the theory of money, Marshall criticised the approach to the quantity theory which sought to explain the value of money by reference to its supply and its velocity. Marshall objected on the grounds that '"the rapidity of circulation" is not the most convenient thing to be made the basis of our investigations'. Specifically, John Stuart Mill had not adequately delineated the 'balancing of advantages' which underpinned the demand for money (cited in Whitaker, 1975, 166–7).

[37] The Keynes-Cannan dispute had been preceded by an earlier 'institutional' dispute between Cannan and Alfred Marshall (Dahrendorf, 1995, 211–3; Coats, 1967). Lionel Robbins (1971, 105, 85, 83) recalled that the 'slogan' at Cambridge in the 1920s was that it was 'all in Marshall' whereas Cannan emphasised 'this or that weakness of "old Marshall"'.

[38] Cannan (1932, 369; 1927, xiii, 253, 305, 330, 417) explained that 'General unemployment appears when asking too much is a general phenomenon'. He devoted his professional life to the cause of removing the 'scales ... from the eyes of the people of Europe' until they forced disinflation upon their reluctant governments by crying: 'Burn your paper money, and go on burning it till it will buy as much gold as it used to do'. The 'thorough deflationist' cure for the 'diarrhoea of paper' would be disagreeable

'but so is giving up the practice of over-indulgence in intoxicating liquor'. With respect to the unemployed 'byproduct' of this deflation 'Expectation of Government assistance only hinders the mobility of existing workers'.

[39] However, Cannan's attempt to establish an LSE oral tradition is not supported by an examination of the 1918 edition of *Money.* Cannan (1918, 63) explained that economists had 'long been familiar' with the idea that the value of money depended 'upon the various influences which affect demand and supply' and that to restrain prices rises the public should 'insist on adequate limitation of the supply of money'. In the eighth edition of *Money* (after the publication of Keynes' *Treatise*), Cannan (1935, 76, 92) explained that 'the Quantity Theory of the value of money singles out quantity as the thing on which the value of money may be said to depend, other things (including Demand) remaining the same. It would be very astonishing if this were not true'. Cannan believed that the demand for money was fairly stable: 'in the absence of anticipation of future changes the elasticity of demand for money is "equal to unity"'. Prior to his death on 8 April 1935 Cannan's book on *Money* went through eight editions (the Preface to the last edition was dated April 1935). During his time at the LSE (1922–5), Lauchlin Currie (1978, 541) found inspiration in Cannan's insistence of getting 'behind the Money Veil' (see the introductory chapter, part two, below).

[40] Erik Lundberg (1994 [1934], 48) recalled that during his time at Chicago (1931–2) there was 'a real boom of interest in Swedish economics ... especially Wicksell's thoughts'. Wicksell dominated the Stockholm Political Economy Club both through his writings and through 'the Wicksellian oral tradition. This oral tradition was probably most important in monetary theory. It is well known that Wicksell in his last years expressed quite severe criticism of his own earlier work in the quantity theory tradition. At that time Wicksell actually turned against the quantity theory and attempted to explain the development of the price level without any reference to the monetary factors focused on in the equation of exchange' (Henriksson, 1989, 63, 67).

[41] This sticky price tradition can be found in Simons' 'Positive Proposal for Laissez Faire' (1948 [1934], 64–5) in which he explains that it was important to consider 'how different possible [monetary] policy rules would operate given the basic inflexibilities in the price structure ... no monetary system, however perfectly conceived and administered, can make a free-enterprise system function effectively in the absence of reasonable flexibility in the price structure'. It can also be found in Simons' (1933, 550–1) review of Charles Beard's *America Faces the Future*. It was, Simons stated, 'perhaps an incontrovertible position that the excess of booms and depressions are attributable, on the one hand, to the system of commercial banking and, on the other, to an exceeding and increasing "stickiness" in many parts of the price structure ... many prices have become quite inflexible and especially resistant to downward pressure ... Mr Beard beseeches us to adopt measures which will make the 'sticky' prices as much stickier as possible. To adopt such measures, while neglecting the problem of money and credit, is to assure the next depression will make the present one seem altogether trivial'. It was a tradition that Chicago's Greg Lewis (1946, 668–9) referred to in his Memorial to Simons. Some policy implications of this sticky price tradition were outlined by Neil Jacoby, a Chicago Assistant Professor of Finance: 'I think that

government policy should be bent towards trying to get rid of these sticky, rigid elements rather than trying to increase them' (Gideonse, Hansen, and Jacoby, 1938, 10).

[42] In Knight's 'The Business Cycle, Interest and Money: A Methodological Approach' (1941, 59) there is a discussion of sticky intermediate prices and wages: 'Wages are notoriously sticky, especially with respect to any downward change in the hourly wage-rates, which is the important fact in the unit cost or marginal cost of products'.

[43] There is also another oral or more precisely an ethereal tradition in the *General Theory*: 'Madmen in authority, who hear voices in the air, are distilling their frenzy from some academic scribbler from a few years back' (Keynes, 1936, 383).

[44] In 1956, Keynes' caricature was defended by John Dunlop on the same grounds chosen by Friedman: 'Keynes' General Theory ... was soon hailed as the manifesto of a revolution ... With respect to public policy, Keynes and his followers scored a signal victory over the "price flexibility school" but contrary to popular impression (carefully nurtured by Keynes' disciples), this latter was a rather small and relatively powerless group ... Keynes attacked the Pigovian theory – the "classical" thought which had by then reigned supreme for but three years. In dealing with the pre-Pigovian theoretical treatment of wage reductions which was so meagre, Keynes could only pummel that convenient but difficult to define strawman, Say's Law. It is questionable whether Keynes' caricature could be considered a fair presentation of the views of his postclassical predecessors'. James Schlesinger (1956, 582, n. 7), the author of this commentary, then added the following footnote: 'Dunlop has intimated to me that this statement is unfair to Keynes. He points to a strong "body of oral tradition" in favor of wage reductions and suggests that the noted article of Edwin Cannan, "The Demand for Labour" (EJ, Sept. 1932, 357–70) is illustrative of this general attitude'. 'The Demand for Labour' was Cannan Royal Economic Society Presidential Address delivered on 26 May 1931 (four days before Keynes left for a visit to the University of Chicago).

[45] But as Ellis noted, Mints and Hansen 'agree completely' about the need for federal deficits to combat depressions, though Hansen stressed increasing expenditures while Mints stressed reducing taxes.

Bibliography

Bach, G. L., 'Price Level Stabilisation: Some Theoretical and Practical Considerations' (unpublished dissertation, University of Chicago, 1940).

Backhouse, R., 'Don Patinkin – Interpreter of the Keynesian Revolution', *European Journal of the History of Economic Thought*, 9:2 Summer (2002), pp. 186–202.

Barro, R., 'Tribute on the quad', *Hoover Digest*, 4 (1998), pp. 1–9.

Berle, A. A., *Navigating the Rapids, 1918–71*, ed. B. Berle and T. Jacobs (New York, Harcourt Brace, 1973).

Beschloss, M. R. and Cronin, T. E. (eds), *Essays in Honor of James MacGregor Burns* (Englewood Cliffs, New Jersey, Prentice Hall, 1989).

Bellerby, J. R., *Control of Credit as a Remedy for Unemployment* (London, P. S. King and Son, 1923).

Blumenthal, S., *The Rise of the Counter-Establishment from Conservative Ideology to Political Power* (New York, Times, 1986).

Bornemann, A., *J. Laurence Laughlin: Chapters in the Career of an Economist* (Washington American Council on Public Affairs, 1940).

Boulding, K., 'Economics – the Taming of Mammon', in White (ed.), *Frontiers of Knowledge in the Study of Man* (New York, Harper and Brothers, 1956).

Burns, A. F., 'Quantity theory and price stabilisation', *American Economic Review*, XIX:4 (December 1929), pp. 561–79.

Cannan, E., *Money: Its Connection with Rising and Falling Prices*, 1st edn (London, P. S. King and Son, 1918).

——, 'The Demand for Labour', *Economic Journal*, 167.XLII (September 1923), pp. 357–370.

——, *An Economist's Protest* (London, P. S. King and Son, 1927).

——, *Money: Its Connection with Rising and Falling Prices*, 8th edn (London, P. S. King and Son, 1935).

Coats, A. W., 'Alfred Marshall and the Early Development of the London School of Economics', *Economica*, (November 1967), pp. 408–17.

Conkin, P., *The New Deal* (London, Routledge and Kegan Paul, 1968).

Croome, D. R. and Johnson, H. G. (eds), *Money in Britain 1959–1969* (London, Oxford UP, 1970).

Currie, L., 'Comments and Observations', *History of Political Economy*, 10:4 (1978), pp. 541–8.

Dahrendorf, R., *LSE: A History of the London School of Economics and Political Science, 1895–1995* (Oxford, Oxford UP, 1995).

Davis, J. R., *The New Economics and the Old Economists* (Ames, Iowa, Iowa UP, 1971).

Dean, E. (ed.), *The Controversy over the Quantity Theory of Money* (London, D. C. Heath, 1965).

Desai, M., *Testing Monetarism* (London, Francis Pinter, 1981).

Dorfman, J., *The Economic Mind in American Civilisation* (New York, Viking, 1959), Vol. 4.

Douglas, P., *Controlling Depressions* (London, George Allen and Unwin, 1935).

——, *In the Fullness of Time* (New York, Harcourt Brace Jovanovich, 1972).

Eatwell, J., Milgate, M. and Newman, P. (eds), *The New Palgrave: A Dictionary of Economics* (London, Macmillan, 1987).

Fisher, I., *The Purchasing Power of Money* (New York, Macmillan, 1911).

——, *Stable Money: A History of the Movement* (New York, Adelphi, 1934).

Friedman, M., 'Wesley C. Mitchell as an Economic Theorist', *Journal of Political Economy*, LVIII:6 (December 1950), pp. 465–93.

——, *Essays in Positive Economics* (Chicago, Chicago UP, 1953).

—— (ed.), *Studies in The Quantity Theory of Money* (Chicago, Chicago UP, 1956).

——, *Theory of the Consumption Function* (Princeton, Princeton UP, 1957).

——, 'The Demand for Money: Some Theoretical and Empirical Results', *Journal of Political Economy*, 67 (June 1959), pp. 327–51.

——, *A Program for Monetary Stability* (New York, Fordham UP, 1960).

——, *Capitalism and Freedom*, 1st edn (Chicago, Chicago UP, 1962).

——, 'The Supply of Money and Changes in Prices and Output', in Dean (ed.), *The Controversy over the Quantity Theory of Money* (London, D. C. Heath, 1965), pp. 88–107.

——, 'The Role of Monetary Policy', *American Economic Review*, LVIII:1 (March 1968), pp. 1–17.

——, 'Has Fiscal Policy Been Oversold?', in Friedman and Heller (eds), *Monetary versus Fiscal Policy: A Dialogue* (New York, W. W. Norton, 1969).

——, 'Have Monetary Policies Failed?', *American Economic Review*, (May1972), pp. 11–18.

——, 'Schools at Chicago', *University of Chicago Magazine* (1974), pp. 11–16.

——, 'Nobel Lecture Inflation and Unemployment', *Journal of Political Economy*, 85 (June 1977), pp. 451–72.

——, 'J. Laurence Laughlin', in Eatwell *et al.* (eds), *The New Palgrave: A Dictionary of Economics* (London, Macmillan, 1987), pp. 139–40.

Friedman, M. and Friedman, R., *Capitalism and Freedom*, 1st edn (Chicago, Chicago UP, 1962).

——, *Free to Choose: A Personal Statement* (New York, Harcourt Brace Jovanovich, 1980).

——, *Capitalism and Freedom*, 2nd edn (Chicago, Chicago UP, 1982).

——, *Tyranny of the Status Quo* (London, Secker and Warburg, 1984).

——, *Two Lucky People: Memoirs* (Chicago, Chicago UP, 1998).

Friedman, M. and Heller, W. W. (eds), *Monetary versus fiscal policy: a dialogue* (New York, W. W. Norton, 1969).

Friedman, M. and Schwartz, A., *A Monetary History of the United States* (Princeton, Princeton UP, 1963).

Fusfeld, D., *The Economic Thought of Franklin D. Roosevelt and the Origins of the New Deal* (New York, Columbia UP, 1956).

Gideonse, H. D., *The Commodity Dollar*, Public Policy Pamphlet No. 26 (Chicago, Chicago UP, 1938).

Gideonse, H. D., Hansen, A. H. and Jacoby, N. H., *Purchasing Power and Prosperity*, University of Chicago Round Table transcript (31 July 1938).

Gilbert, J. C., 'The Demand for Money: The Development of an Economic Concept', *Journal of Political Economy* (April 1953), pp. 144–59.

Ginzberg, E., *New Deal Days, 1933–1934* (New Brunswick, N. J., Transaction, 1997).

Gould, J. M. and Kelley, A. M. (eds), *Lecture Notes on Types of Economic Theory As Delivered by Professor Wesley C. Mitchell* (New York, Augustus Kelley, 1949), Vol. II.

Graham, O. T., 'Franklin Roosevelt and the Intended New Deal' in Beschloss and Cronin (eds), *Essays in Honor of James MacGregor Burns* (Englewood Cliffs, New Jersey, Prentice Hall, 1989).

Greenfield, H. I., Levenson, A. M. Hamovitch, W. and Rotwein, E. (eds), *Theory for Economic Efficiency: Essays in Honour of Abba P. Lerner* (London, MIT Press, 1979).

Hacker, L. M., 'The Anticapitalist Bias of American Historians' in Hayek (ed.), *Capitalism and the Historians* (Chicago, Chicago UP, 1954).

Hamilton, E. J., Rees, A. and Johnson, H. G. (eds), *Landmarks in Political Economy* (Chicago, Chicago UP, 1962).

Hansen, A. H. and Kindleberger, C. P., 'The economic tasks of the post-war world', *Foreign Affairs* (1942), pp. 466–76.

Harrod, R., *The Life of John Maynard Keynes* (London, Macmillan, 1951).

Hartwell, R. M., *A History of the Mont Pelerin Society* (Indianapolis, Liberty Fund, 1995).

Hayek, F. A., *Freedom and the Economic System*, Public Policy Pamphlet No. 29, (Chicago, Chicago UP, 1939).

——, *The Road to Serfdom* (Chicago, Chicago UP, 1944).

—— (ed.), *Capitalism and the Historians* (Chicago, Chicago UP, 1954).

——, *Studies in Philosophy, Politics and Economics* (London, Routledge, 1967).

Heller, W., 'Is monetary policy being oversold?' in Friedman and Heller (eds), *Monetary versus Fiscal Policy: A Dialogue* (New York, W. W. Norton, 1969).

Henriksson, R. G. H., 'The Institutional Base of the Stockholm School: The Political Economy Club (1917–1951)', *History of Economics Society Bulletin*, 11:1 (Spring 1989), pp. 59–77.

Hobsbawm, E., *The Age of Extremes: The Short History of the Twentieth Century 1914–1991* (London, Michael Joseph, 1994).

Johnson, H. G., 'Monetary Theory and Policy', *American Economic Review,* 52 (1962), pp. 335–84.

——, 'Recent Developments in Monetary Theory – A Commentary' in Croome and Johnson (eds), *Money in Britain 1959–1969* (London, Oxford UP, 1970).

——, *On Economics and Society* (Chicago, Chicago UP, 1975).

Kahn, R. F., 'Imperfect Competition and the Marginal Principle' unpublished mimeo. In the Kahn Papers, Modern Archives Collection, King's College Cambridge, 1933.

Kaldor, N., 'Reply', *Lloyds Bank Review* (October 1970), pp. 54–5.

Karl, B. D., *The Uneasy State: The United States from 1915 to 1945* (Chicago, Chicago UP, 1983).

Kemmerer, E. W., *Money and Credit in Relation to General Prices* (New York, Holt, 1907).

——, 'Discussion. Federal Reserve Policy Since 1926', *American Economic Review,* (March 1933), pp. 130–4.

——, *Kemmerer on Money* (London, George Routledge and Sons, 1934a).

——, 'Controlled Inflation', *American Economic Review,* Supplement, (March 1934b), pp. 90–100.

——, *Money: The Principles of Money and their Exemplification in Outstanding Chapters of Monetary History* (New York, Macmillan, 1935).

Keynes, J. M., *A Tract on Monetary Reform* (London, Macmillan, 1923).

——, *A Treatise on Money: The Applied Theory of Money* (London, Macmillan, 1930).

——, *The General Theory of Employment Interest and Money* (London, Macmillan, 1936).

——, *Collected Writings of John Maynard Keynes* (London, Macmillan, 1972–89).

Keynes, J. N., *The Scope and Method of Political Economy* (London, Macmillan, 1891).

Knight, F., *The Ethics of Competition and Other Essays* (New York, Book for Libraries Press, 1935).

——, '"What is Truth" in Economics?', *Journal of Political Economy,* XLVIII:1 (February 1940), pp. 1–32.

——, 'The Business Cycle, Interest and Money: A Methodological Approach', *Review of Economic Statistics,* XXIII:2 (May 1941), pp. 53–67.

——, 'The Role of Principles in Economics and Politics', *American Economic Review,* XLI:1 (March 1951), pp. 1–29.

Koopmans, T. C., 'Measurement without Theory', *Review of Economics and Statistics,* (August 1947), pp. 161–72.

Laidler, D., *The Golden Age of the Quantity Theory* (Princeton, New Jersey, Princeton UP, 1991).

——, *Fabricating the Keynesian Revolution: Studies of the Inter-War Literature on Money, the Cycle, and Unemployment* (Cambridge, Cambridge UP, 1999).

Laughlin, J. L., *Principles of Money* (New York, Scribner's Sons, 1903).

——, 'Academic liberty', *Journal of Political Economy,* XIV (January 1906), pp. 41–3.

——, *Credit of the Nations* (New York, Scribner's Sons, 1918).

——, 'Roosevelt at Harvard', *The American Review of Reviews,* (October 1924), pp. 391–8.

——, *The Federal Reserve Act: its Origin and Problems* (New York, Macmillan, 1933).

Lewis, H. G., 'Henry Calvert Simons', *American Economic Review,* (September 1946), pp. 668–9.

Leuchtenburg, W. E. (ed.), *The New Deal: A Documentary History* (New York, Harper and Row, 1968).

Lundberg, E., *Studies in Economic Instability and Change,* ed. R. Henriksson (Stockholm, SNS Forlag, 1994).

Lutz, F. and Mints, L. (eds), *Readings in Monetary Theory* (American Economic Association; London, George Allen and Unwin, 1952).

Means, G., 'Price Inflexibility and the Requirements of a Stabilising Monetary Policy', *Journal of the American Statistical Society*, (June 1935), pp. 401–13.
McCloskey, D, *The Rhetoric of Economics* (Great Britain, Wheatsheaf, 1986).
Mehrling, P., *The Money Interest and the Public Interest American Monetary Thought 1920–1970* (Cambridge, Massachusetts, Harvard UP, 1997).
——, 'Economists and the Fed: Beginnings', mimeo (2001).
——, 'Don Patinkin and the Origins of Post War Monetary Orthodoxy', *European Journal of the History of Economic Thought*, 9:2 (Summer 2002), pp. 161–85.
Mints, L. W., *A History of Banking Theory* (Chicago, Chicago UP, 1946).
——, *Monetary Policy for a Competitive Society* (New York, McGraw Hill, 1950).
Mises, L. von, *Planning for Freedom and Twelve Other Essays* (Illinois, Libertarian Press, 1974).
Mitchell, W. C., 'J. Laurence Laughlin', *Journal of Political Economy*, (December 1941), pp. 875–81.
Moggridge, D., *Maynard Keynes: An Economist's Biography* (London, Routledge, 1992).
Nef, J. U., 'James Laurence Laughlin', *Journal of Political Economy*, 42:1 (February 1934), pp. 1–5.
Newman, P., Milgate, M. and Eatwell, J. (eds), *The New Palgrave Dictionary of Money and Finance* (London, Macmillan, 1992).
Oakeshott, M., *Rationalism in Politics and Other Essays* (London, Methuen and Co. Ltd, 1977).
Patinkin, D., 'Price Flexibility and Full Employment' in Lutz and Mints (eds), *Readings in Monetary Theory* (American Economic Association; London, George Allen and Unwin, 1952).
——, *Money Interest and Prices* (Evanston, Illinois, Row, Peterson, 1956).
——, 'The Development of Keynes's Policy Thinking' in Greenfield *et al.* (eds), *Theory for Economic Efficiency: Essays in Honor of Abba P. Lerner* (London, MIT Press, 1979).
——, *Essays on and in the Chicago Tradition* (Durham, North Carolina, Duke UP, 1981).
——, 'On Different Interpretations of *The General Theory*', *Journal of Monetary Economics*, 26 (1990), pp. 205–43.
——, 'On the Chronology of the General Theory', *Economic Journal*, 103:418 (May 1993), pp. 647–63.
——, 'The Training of an Economist', *Banca Nazionale del Lavoro Quarterly Review*, 195 (December 1995), pp. 359–95.
Reagan, R., *An American Life* (London, Random, 1990).
Reeve, J. E., *Monetary Reform Movements: A Survey of Recent Plans and Panaceas* (Washington, American Council on Public Affairs, 1943).
Robbins, L., *Autobiography of an Economist* (London: Macmillan, 1971).
Robinson, J., *Economic Philosophy* (England, Penguin, 1962).
Samuels, W. and Medema, S. G., *Gardiner C. Means: Institutionalist and Post-Keynesian* (New York, M. E. Sharp, 1990).
Samuelson, P., 'Jacob Viner, 1892–1970', *Journal of Political Economy*, 80 (1972), pp. 5–11.
Sandilands, R., *The Life and Political Economy of Lauchlin Currie: New Dealer, Presidential Adviser and Development Economist* (Durham, Duke UP, 1990).
Saunders, S., 'Patinkin and Talmudic Readings in the History of Economics', paper presented to the Patinkin Conference, Lausanne, September 2001.
Schlesinger, A. M., *The Politics of Upheaval* (Boston, Houghton Mifflin, 1960).
Schlesinger, J. R., 'After Twenty Years: The General Theory', *Quarterly Journal of Economics*, 71 (1956), pp. 581–602.
Schumpeter, J., *A History of Economic Analysis* (Oxford, Oxford UP, 1954).
Schwartz, J. A., *Liberal: Adolf A. Berle and the Vision of an American Era* (London, Macmillan, 1987).

Selden, R. T., 'Stable Monetary Growth' in Yeager (ed.), *In Search of a Monetary Constitution* (Cambridge, Mass., Harvard UP, 1962).

Simons, H. C., 'Mercantilism as Liberalism', *Journal of Political Economy*, (August 1933) pp. 548–51.

——, 'Money and the New Deal: Review of Pasvolsky's *Current Monetary Issues*', *New Republic*, 21 (February 1934), pp. 53–4.

——, 'Postwar Economic Policy: Some Traditional Liberal Principles', *American Economic Review*, XXXIII:1 (March 1943), pp. 432–45.

——, *Economic Policy for a Free Society* (Chicago, Chicago UP, 1948).

——, *Federal Tax Reform* (Chicago, Chicago UP, 1950).

——, 'Rules Versus Authorities in Monetary Policy' reprinted in Hamilton *et al.* (eds), *Landmarks in Political Economy* (Chicago, Chicago UP, 1962)

Skidelsky, R., *John Maynard Keynes: Hopes Betrayed 1883–1920* (London, Macmillan, 1983).

——, *John Maynard Keynes: The Economist as Saviour 1920–1937* (London, Macmillan, 1992).

Smith, B. D., 'Real Bills Doctrine' in Newman *et al.* (eds), *The New Palgrave Dictionary of Money and Finance* (London, Macmillan, 1992), vol. 3, pp. 298–300.

Solow, R., 'Friedman on America's Money', *Banker*, (November 1964), pp. 710–17.

Stigler, G., 'Does Economics Have a Useful Past?', *History of Political Economy*, 1:2 (Fall 1969), pp. 217–230.

——, *Memoirs of an Unregulated Economist* (New York, Basic Books, 1988).

Teigen, R. L., 'Demand and Supply Functions for Money in the United States: Some Structural Estimates' (unpublished doctoral dissertation, Massachusetts Institute of Technology, 1962).

——, 'Some Observations on Monetarist Analysis', *Kredit and Kapital*, 4 (1971), pp. 234–63.

Tugwell, R., *The Brains Trust* (New York, Viking, 1968).

——, *In Search of Roosevelt* (Cambridge, Mass, Harvard UP, 1972).

Wallis, W.A., *An Overgoverned Society* (London, Free Press, 1976).

Ware, C. and Means, G. C., *The Modern Economy in Action* (New York, Harcourt Brace, 1936).

Whitaker, J. L. (ed.), *The Early Economic Writings of Alfred Marshall, 1867–1890* (London, Macmillan, for the Royal Economic Society, 1975), vol. 1.

White, E. N., *The Regulation and Reform of the American Banking System, 1900–1929* (Princeton, Princeton UP, 1983).

White, L. T. (ed.), *Frontiers of Knowledge in the Study of Man* (New York, Harper and Brothers, 1956).

Whittlesey, C. R., *Banking and the New Deal*, Public Policy Pamphlet No. 16 (Chicago, Chicago UP, 1935).

Wicksell, K., 'The influence of the rate of interest on prices', *Economic Journal*, 17 (June 1907), pp. 213–20.

Willis, H. P., 'The History and Present Application of the Quantity Theory', *Journal of Political Economy*, (September 1896), pp. 417–48.

Willis, H. P. and Chapman, J., *The Banking Situation: American Post War Problems and Developments* (New York, Columbia UP, 1934).

Wriston, W., 'Tribute on the Quad', *Hoover Digest*, 4 (1998), pp. 1–9.

Yeager, L. B. (ed.), *In Search of a Monetary Constitution* (Cambridge, Mass., Harvard UP, 1962).

'The Quantity Theory of Money – A Restatement'

M. Friedman, 'The quantity theory of money – a restatement', in Friedman (ed.), *Studies in the Quantity Theory of Money* (Chicago, Chicago UP, 1956), pp. 3–19.

The Quantity Theory of Money—A Restatement

THE quantity theory of money is a term evocative of a general approach rather than a label for a well-defined theory. The exact content of the approach varies from a truism defining the term "velocity" to an allegedly rigid and unchanging ratio between the quantity of money—defined in one way or another—and the price level—also defined in one way or another. Whatever its precise meaning, it is clear that the general approach fell into disrepute after the crash of 1929 and the subsequent Great Depression and only recently has been slowly re-emerging into professional respectability.

The present volume is partly a symptom of this re-emergence and partly a continuance of an aberrant tradition. Chicago was one of the few academic centers at which the quantity theory continued to be a central and vigorous part of the oral tradition throughout the 1930's and 1940's, where students continued to study monetary theory and to write theses on monetary problems. The quantity theory that retained this role differed sharply from the atrophied and rigid caricature that is so frequently described by the proponents of the new income-expenditure approach—and with some justice, to judge by much of the literature on policy that was spawned by quantity theorists. At Chicago, Henry Simons and Lloyd Mints directly, Frank Knight and Jacob Viner at one remove, taught and developed a more subtle and relevant version, one in which the quantity theory was connected and integrated with general price theory and became a flexible and sensitive tool for interpreting movements in aggregate economic activity and for developing relevant policy prescriptions.

To the best of my knowledge, no systematic statement of this theory as developed at Chicago exists, though much can be read between the lines of Simons' and Mints's writings. And this is as it should be, for the Chicago tradition was not a rigid system, an unchangeable orthodoxy, but a way of looking at things. It was a theoretical approach that insisted that money does matter—that any interpretation of short-term movements in economic activity is likely to be seriously at fault if it neglects monetary changes and repercussions and if it leaves unexplained why people are willing to hold the particular nominal quantity of money in existence.

The purpose of this introduction is not to enshrine—or, should I say, inter—a definitive version of the Chicago tradition. To suppose that one could do so would be inconsistent with that tradition itself. The purpose is rather to set down a particular "model" of a quantity theory in an attempt to convey the flavor of the oral tradition which nurtured the remaining essays in this volume. In consonance with this purpose, I shall not attempt to be exhaustive or to give a full justification for every assertion.

1. The quantity theory is in the first instance a theory of the *demand* for money. It is not a theory of output, or of money income, or of the price level. Any statement about these variables requires combining the quantity theory with some specifications about the conditions of supply of money and perhaps about other variables as well.

2. To the ultimate wealth-owning units in the economy, money is one kind of asset, one way of holding wealth. To the productive enterprise, money is a capital good, a source of productive services that are combined with other productive services to yield the products that the enterprise sells. Thus the theory of the demand for money is a special topic in the theory of capital; as such, it has the rather unusual feature of combining a piece from each side of the capital market, the supply of capital (points 3 through 8 that follow), and the demand for capital (points 9 through 12).

3. The analysis of the demand for money on the part of the ultimate wealth-owning units in the society can be made formally identical with that of the demand for a consumption service. As in the usual theory of consumer choice, the demand for money (or any other particular asset) depends on three major sets of factors: (*a*) the total wealth to be held in various forms—the analogue of the budget restraint; (*b*) the price of and return on this form of wealth and alternative forms; and (*c*) the tastes and preferences of the wealth-owning units. The substantive differences from the analysis of the demand for a consumption service are the necessity of taking account of intertemporal rates of substitution in (*b*) and (*c*) and of casting the budget restraint in terms of wealth.

4. From the broadest and most general point of view, total wealth includes all sources of "income" or consumable services. One such source is the productive capacity of human beings, and accordingly this is one form in which wealth can be held. From this point of view, "the" rate of interest expresses the relation between the stock which is wealth and the flow which is income, so if Y be the total flow of income, and r, "the" interest rate, total wealth is

$$W = \frac{Y}{r}. \tag{1}$$

Income in this broadest sense should not be identified with income as it is ordinarily measured. The latter is generally a "gross" stream with respect to human beings, since no deduction is made for the expense of maintaining human productive capacity intact; in addition, it is affected by transitory elements that make it depart more or less widely from the theoretical concept of the stable level of consumption of services that could be maintained indefinitely.

5. Wealth can be held in numerous forms, and the ultimate wealth-owning unit is to be regarded as dividing his wealth among them (point [*a*] of 3), so as to maximize "utility" (point [*c*] of 3), subject to whatever restrictions affect the possibility of converting one form of wealth into another (point [*b*] of 3). As usual, this implies that he will seek an apportionment of his wealth such that the rate at which he *can* substitute one form of wealth for another is equal to the rate at which he is just willing to do so. But this general proposition has some special features in the present instance because of the necessity of considering flows as well as stocks. We can suppose all wealth (except wealth in the form of the productive capacity of human beings) to be expressed in terms of monetary units at the prices of the point of time in question. The rate at which one form can be substituted for another is then simply $1.00 worth for $1.00 worth, regardless of the forms involved. But this is clearly not a complete description, because the holding of one form of wealth instead of another involves a difference in the composition of the income stream, and it is essentially these differences that are fundamental to the "utility" of a particular structure of wealth. In consequence, to describe fully the alternative combinations of forms of wealth that are available to an individual, we must take account not only of their market prices—which except for human wealth can be done simply by expressing them in units worth $1.00—but also of the form and size of the income streams they yield.

It will suffice to bring out the major issues that these considerations raise to consider five different forms in which wealth can be held: (i) money (M), interpreted as claims or commodity units that are generally accepted in payment of debts at a fixed nominal value; (ii) bonds (B), interpreted as claims to time streams of payments that are fixed in nominal units; (iii) equities (E), interpreted as claims to stated pro-rata shares of the returns of enterprises; (iv) physical non-human goods (G); and (v) human capital (H). Consider now the yield of each.

(i) Money may yield a return in the form of money, for example, interest on demand deposits. It will simplify matters, however, and entail no essential loss of generality, to suppose that money yields its return solely in kind, in the usual form of convenience, security, etc. The magnitude of this return in "real" terms per nominal unit of money clearly depends on the volume of goods that unit corresponds to, or on the general price level, which we may designate by P. Since we have decided to take \$1.00 worth as the unit for each form of wealth, this will be equally true for other forms of wealth as well, so P is a variable affecting the "real" yield of each.

(ii) If we take the "standard" bond to be a claim to a perpetual income stream of constant nominal amount, then the return to a holder of the bond can take two forms: one, the annual sum he receives—the "coupon"; the other, any change in the price of the bond over time, a return which may of course be positive or negative. If the price is expected to remain constant, then \$1.00 worth of a bond yields r_b per year, where r_b is simply the "coupon" sum divided by the market price of the bond, so $1/r_b$ is the price of a bond promising to pay \$1.00 per year. We shall call r_b the market bond interest rate. If the price is expected to change, then the yield cannot be calculated so simply, since it must take account of the return in the form of expected appreciation or depreciation of the bond, and it cannot, like r_b, be calculated directly from market prices (so long, at least, as the "standard" bond is the only one traded in).

The nominal income stream purchased for \$1.00 at time zero then consists of

$$r_b(0) + r_b(0)\,\frac{d\left(\dfrac{1}{r_b(t)}\right)}{dt} = r_b(0) - \frac{r_b(0)}{r_b^2(t)}\cdot\frac{d\,r_b(t)}{dt}, \tag{2}$$

where t stands for time. For simplicity, we can approximate this functional by its value at time zero, which is

$$r_b - \frac{1}{r_b}\frac{d\,r_b}{dt}. \tag{3}$$

This sum, together with P already introduced, defines the real return from holding \$1.00 of wealth in the form of bonds.

(iii) Analogously to our treatment of bonds, we may take the "standard" unit of equity to be a claim to a perpetual income stream of constant "real" amount; that is, to be a standard bond with a purchasing-power escalator clause, so that it promises a perpetual income stream equal in nominal units to a constant number times a price index, which we may, for convenience, take to be the same price index P introduced in (i).[1] The nominal return to the holder of the equity can then be regarded as taking three forms: the constant nominal amount he would receive per year in

1. This is an oversimplification, because it neglects "leverage" and therefore supposes that any monetary liabilities of an enterprise are balanced by monetary assets.

the absence of any change in P; the increment or decrement to this nominal amount to adjust for changes in P; and any change in the nominal price of the equity over time, which may of course arise from changes either in interest rates or in price levels. Let r_e be the market interest rate on equities defined analogously to r_b, namely, as the ratio of the "coupon" sum at any time (the first two items above) to the price of the equity, so $1/r_e$ is the price of an equity promising to pay \$1.00 per year if the price level does not change, or to pay

$$\frac{P(t)}{P(0)} \cdot 1$$

if the price level varies according to $P(t)$. If $r_e(t)$ is defined analogously, the price of the bond selling for $1/r_e(0)$ at time 0 will be

$$\frac{P(t)}{P(0)\, r_e(t)}$$

at time t, where the ratio of prices is required to adjust for any change in the price level. The nominal stream purchased for \$1.00 at time zero then consists of

$$\begin{aligned} r_e(0) \cdot \frac{P(t)}{P(0)} + \frac{r_e(0)}{P(0)} \cdot \frac{d\left[\dfrac{P(t)}{r_e(t)}\right]}{dt} &= r_e(0) \cdot \frac{P(t)}{P(0)} \\ &+ \frac{r_e(0)}{r_e(t)} \cdot \frac{1}{P(0)} \cdot \frac{dP(t)}{dt} - \frac{P(t)}{P(0)} \cdot \frac{r_e(0)}{r_e^2(t)} \cdot \frac{d\, r_e(t)}{dt}. \end{aligned} \tag{4}$$

Once again we can approximate this functional by its value at time zero, which is

$$r_e + \frac{1}{P}\frac{dP}{dt} - \frac{1}{r_e}\frac{d\, r_e}{dt}. \tag{5}$$

This sum, together with P already introduced, defines the "real" return from holding \$1.00 of wealth in the form of equities.

(iv) Physical goods held by ultimate wealth-owning units are similar to equities except that the annual stream they yield is in kind rather than in money. In terms of nominal units, this return, like that from equities, depends on the behavior of prices. In addition, like equities, physical goods must be regarded as yielding a nominal return in the form of appreciation or depreciation in money value. If we suppose the price level P, introduced earlier, to apply equally to the value of these physical goods, then, at time zero,

$$\frac{1}{P}\frac{dP}{dT} \tag{6}$$

is the size of this nominal return per $1.00 of physical goods.[2] Together with P, it defines the "real" return from holding $1.00 in the form of physical goods.

(v) Since there is only a limited market in human capital, at least in modern non-slave societies, we cannot very well define in market prices the terms of substitution of human capital for other forms of capital and so cannot define at any time the physical unit of capital corresponding to $1.00 of human capital. There are some possibilities of substituting non-human capital for human capital in an individual's wealth holdings, as, for example, when he enters into a contract to render personal services for a specified period in return for a definitely specified number of periodic payments, the number not depending on his being physically capable of rendering the services. But, in the main, shifts between human capital and other forms must take place through direct investment and disinvestment in the human agent, and we may as well treat this as if it were the only way. With respect to this form of capital, therefore, the restriction or obstacles affecting the alternative compositions of wealth available to the individual cannot be expressed in terms of market prices or rates of return. At any one point in time there is some division between human and non-human wealth in his portfolio of assets; he may be able to change this over time, but we shall treat it as given at a point in time. Let w be the ratio of non-human to human wealth or, equivalently, of income from non-human wealth to income from human wealth, which means that it is closely allied to what is usually defined as the ratio of wealth to income. This is, then, the variable that needs to be taken into account so far as human wealth is concerned.

6. The tastes and preferences of wealth-owning units for the service streams arising from different forms of wealth must in general simply be taken for granted as determining the form of the demand function. In order to give the theory empirical content, it will generally have to be supposed that tastes are constant over significant stretches of space and time. However, explicit allowance can be made for some changes in tastes in so far as such changes are linked with objective circumstances. For example, it seems reasonable that, other things the same, individuals want

2. In principle, it might be better to let P refer solely to the value of the services of physical goods, which is essentially what it refers to in the preceding cases, and to allow for the fact that the prices of the capital goods themselves must vary also with the rate of capitalization, so that the prices of services and their sources vary at the same rate only if the relevant interest rate is constant. I have neglected this refinement for simplicity; the neglect can perhaps be justified by the rapid depreciation of many of the physical goods held by final wealth-owning units.

to hold a larger fraction of their wealth in the form of money when they are moving around geographically or are subject to unusual uncertainty than otherwise. This is probably one of the major factors explaining a frequent tendency for money holdings to rise relative to income during wartime. But the extent of geographic movement, and perhaps of other kinds of uncertainty, can be represented by objective indexes, such as indexes of migration, miles of railroad travel, and the like. Let u stand for any such variables that can be expected to affect tastes and preferences (for "utility" determining variables).

7. Combining 4, 5, and 6 along the lines suggested by 3 yields the following demand function for money:

$$M = f\left(P,\ r_b - \frac{1}{r_b}\frac{dr_b}{dt},\ r_e + \frac{1}{P}\frac{dP}{dt} - \frac{1}{r_e}\frac{dr_e}{dt},\ \frac{1}{P}\frac{dP}{dt};\ w;\ \frac{Y}{r};\ u\right). \quad (7)$$

A number of observations are in order about this function.

(i) Even if we suppose prices and rates of interest unchanged, the function contains three rates of interest: two for specific types of assets, r_b and r_e, and one intended to apply to all types of assets, r. This general rate, r, is to be interpreted as something of a weighted average of the two special rates plus the rates applicable to human wealth and to physical goods. Since the latter two cannot be observed directly, it is perhaps best to regard them as varying in some systematic way with r_b and r_e. On this assumption, we can drop r as an additional explicit variable, treating its influence as fully taken into account by the inclusion of r_b and r_e.

(ii) If there were no differences of opinion about price movements and interest-rate movements, and bonds and equities were equivalent except that the former are expressed in nominal units, arbitrage would of course make

$$r_b - \frac{1}{r_b}\frac{dr_b}{dt} = r_e + \frac{1}{P}\frac{dP}{dt} - \frac{1}{r_e}\frac{dr_e}{dt}, \quad (8)$$

or, if we suppose rates of interest either stable or changing at the same percentage rate,

$$r_b = r_e + \frac{1}{P}\frac{dP}{dt}, \quad (9)$$

that is, the "money" interest rate equal to the "real" rate plus the percentage rate of change of prices. In application the rate of change of prices must be interpreted as an "expected" rate of change and differences of opinion cannot be neglected, so we cannot suppose (9) to hold; indeed, one of the most consistent features of inflation seems to be that it does not.[3]

(iii) If the range of assets were to be widened to include promises to pay specified sums for a finite number of time units—"short-term" securities as well as "consols"—the rates of change of r_b and r_e would be reflected in the difference between long and short rates of interest. Since at some stage it will doubtless be desirable to introduce securities of different time duration (see point 23 below), we may simplify the present exposition by restricting it to the case in which r_b and r_e are taken to be stable over time. Since the rate of change in prices is required separately in any event, this means that we can replace the cumbrous variables introduced to designate the nominal return on bonds and equities simply by r_b and r_e.

(iv) Y can be interpreted as including the return to all forms of wealth, including money and physical capital goods owned and held directly by ultimate wealth-owning units, and so Y/r can be interpreted as an estimate of total wealth, only if Y is regarded as including some imputed income from the stock of money and directly owned physical capital goods. For monetary analysis the simplest procedure is perhaps to regard Y as referring to the return to all forms of wealth other than the money held directly by ultimate wealth-owning units, and so Y/r as referring to total remaining wealth.

8. A more fundamental point is that, as in all demand analyses resting on maximization of a utility function defined in terms of "real" magnitudes, this demand equation must be considered independent in any essential way of the nominal units used to measure money variables. If the unit in which prices and money income are expressed is changed, the amount of money demanded should change proportionately. More technically, equation (7) must be regarded as homogeneous of the first degree in P and Y, so that

$$f\left(\lambda P,\ r_b,\ r_e,\ \frac{1}{P}\frac{dP}{dt};\ w;\ \lambda Y;\ u\right) = \lambda f\left(P,\ r_b,\ r_e,\ \frac{1}{P}\frac{dP}{dt};\ w;\ Y;\ u\right). \tag{10}$$

where the variables within the parentheses have been rewritten in simpler form in accordance with comments 7 (i) and 7 (iii).

3. See Reuben Kessel, "Inflation: Theory of Wealth Distribution and Application in Private Investment Policy" (unpublished doctoral dissertation, University of Chicago).

This characteristic of the function enables us to rewrite it in two alternative and more familiar ways.

(i) Let $\lambda = 1/P$. Equation (7) can then be written

$$\frac{M}{P} = f\left(r_b,\ r_e,\ \frac{1}{P}\frac{dP}{dt};\ w;\ \frac{Y}{P};\ u\right). \tag{11}$$

In this form the equation expresses the demand for real balances as a function of "real" variables independent of nominal monetary values.

(ii) Let $\lambda = 1/Y$. Equation (7) can then be written

$$\frac{M}{Y} = f\left(r_b,\ r_e,\ \frac{1}{P}\frac{dP}{dt},\ w,\ \frac{P}{Y},\ u\right) = \frac{1}{v\left(r_b,\ r_e,\ \frac{1}{P}\frac{dP}{dt},\ w,\ \frac{Y}{P},\ u\right)}, \tag{12}$$

or

$$Y = v\left(r_b,\ r_e,\ \frac{1}{P}\frac{dP}{dt},\ w,\ \frac{Y}{P},\ u\right)\cdot M. \tag{13}$$

In this form the equation is in the usual quantity theory form, where v is income velocity.

9. These equations are, to this point, solely for money held directly by ultimate wealth-owning units. As noted, money is also held by business enterprises as a productive resource. The counterpart to this business asset in the balance sheet of an ultimate wealth-owning unit is a claim other than money. For example, an individual may buy bonds from a corporation, and the corporation use the proceeds to finance the money holdings which it needs for its operations. Of course, the usual difficulties of separating the accounts of the business and its owner arise with unincorporated enterprises.

10. The amount of money that it pays business enterprises to hold depends, as for any other source of productive services, on the cost of the productive services, the cost of substitute productive services, and the value product yielded by the productive service. Per dollar of money held, the cost depends on how the corresponding capital is raised—whether by raising additional capital in the form of bonds or equities, by substituting cash for real capital goods, etc. These ways of financing money holdings are much the same as the alternative forms in which the ultimate wealth-owning unit can hold its non-human wealth, so that the variables r_b, r_e, P, and $(1/P)(dP/dt)$ introduced into (7) can be taken to represent the cost to the business enterprise of holding money. For some purposes, however, it may be desirable to distinguish between the rate of return re-

ceived by the lender and the rate paid by the borrower; in which case it would be necessary to introduce an additional set of variables.

Substitutes for money as a productive service are numerous and varied, including all ways of economizing on money holdings by using other resources to synchronize more closely payments and receipts, reduce payment periods, extend use of book credit, establish clearing arrangements, and so on in infinite variety. There seem no particularly close substitutes whose prices deserve to be singled out for inclusion in the business demand for money.

The value product yielded by the productive services of money per unit of output depends on production conditions: the production function. It is likely to be especially dependent on features of production conditions affecting the smoothness and regularity of operations as well as on those determining the size and scope of enterprises, degree of vertical integration, etc. Again there seem no variables that deserve to be singled out on the present level of abstraction for special attention; these factors can be taken into account by interpreting u as including variables affecting not only the tastes of wealth-owners but also the relevant technological conditions of production. Given the amount of money demanded per unit of output, the total amount demanded is proportional to total output, which can be represented by Y.

11. One variable that has traditionally been singled out in considering the demand for money on the part of business enterprises is the volume of transactions, or of transactions per dollar of final products; and, of course, emphasis on transactions has been carried over to the ultimate wealth-owning unit as well as to the business enterprise. The idea that renders this approach attractive is that there is a mechanical link between a dollar of payments per unit time and the average stock of money required to effect it—a fixed technical coefficient of production, as it were. It is clear that this mechanical approach is very different in spirit from the one we have been following. On our approach, the average amount of money held per dollar of transactions is itself to be regarded as a resultant of an economic equilibrating process, not as a physical datum. If, for whatever reason, it becomes more expensive to hold money, then it is worth devoting resources to effecting money transactions in less expensive ways or to reducing the volume of transactions per dollar of final output. In consequence, our ultimate demand function for money in its most general form does not contain as a variable the volume of transactions or of transactions per dollar of final output; it contains rather those more basic technical and cost conditions that affect the costs of conserving money, be it by changing the average amount of money held per dollar of transac-

tions per unit time or by changing the number of dollars of transactions per dollar of final output. This does not, of course, exclude the possibility that, for a particular problem, it may be useful to regard the transactions variables as given and not to dig beneath them and so to include the volume of transactions per dollar of final output as an explicit variable in a special variant of the demand function.

Similar remarks are relevant to various features of payment conditions, frequently described as "institutional conditions," affecting the velocity of circulation of money and taken as somehow mechanically determined—such items as whether workers are paid by the day, or week, or month; the use of book credit; and so on. On our approach these, too, are to be regarded as resultants of an economic equilibrating process, not as physical data. Lengthening the pay period, for example, may save book-keeping and other costs to the employer, who is therefore willing to pay somewhat more than in proportion for a longer than a shorter pay period; on the other hand, it imposes on employees the cost of holding larger cash balances or providing substitutes for cash, and they therefore want to be paid more than in proportion for a longer pay period. Where these will balance depends on how costs vary with length of pay period. The cost to the employee depends in considerable part on the factors entering into his demand curve for money for a fixed pay period. If he would in any event be holding relatively large average balances, the additional costs imposed by a lengthened pay period tend to be less than if he would be holding relatively small average balances, and so it will take less of an inducement to get him to accept a longer pay period. For given cost savings to the employer, therefore, the pay period can be expected to be longer in the first case than in the second. Surely, the increase in the average cash balance over the past century in this country that has occurred for other reasons has been a factor producing a lengthening of pay periods and not the other way around. Or, again, experience in hyperinflations shows how rapidly payment practices change under the impact of drastic changes in the cost of holding money.

12. The upshot of these considerations is that the demand for money on the part of business enterprises can be regarded as expressed by a function of the same kind as equation (7), with the same variables on the right-hand side. And, like (7), since the analysis is based on informed maximization of returns by enterprises, only "real" quantities matter, so it must be homogeneous of the first degree in Y and P. In consequence, we can interpret (7) and its variants (11) and (13) as describing the demand for money on the part of a business enterprise as well as on the part of an

ultimate wealth-owning unit, provided only that we broaden our interpretation of u.

13. Strictly speaking, the equations (7), (11), and (13) are for an individual wealth-owning unit or business enterprise. If we aggregate (7) for all wealth-owning units and business enterprises in the society, the result, in principle, depends on the distribution of the units by the several variables. This raises no serious problem about P, r_b, and r_e, for these can be taken as the same for all, or about u, for this is an unspecified portmanteau variable to be filled in as the occasion demands. We have been interpreting $(1/P)(dP/dt)$ as the expected rate of price rise, so there is no reason why this variable should be the same for all, and w and Y clearly differ substantially among units. An approximation is to neglect these difficulties and take (7) and the associated (11) and (13) as applying to the aggregate demand for money, with $(1/P)(dP/dt)$ interpreted as some kind of an average expected rate of change of prices, w as the ratio of total income from non-human wealth to income from human wealth, and Y as aggregate income. This is the procedure that has generally been followed, and it seems the right one until serious departures between this linear approximation and experience make it necessary to introduce measures of dispersion with respect to one or more of the variables.

14. It is perhaps worth noting explicitly that the model does not use the distinction between "active balances" and "idle balances" or the closely allied distinction between "transaction balances" and "speculative balances" that is so widely used in the literature. The distinction between money holdings of ultimate wealth-owners and of business enterprises is related to this distinction but only distantly so. Each of these categories of money-holders can be said to demand money partly from "transaction" motives, partly from "speculative" or "asset" motives, but dollars of money are not distinguished according as they are said to be held for one or the other purpose. Rather, each dollar is, as it were, regarded as rendering a variety of services, and the holder of money as altering his money holdings until the value to him of the addition to the total flow of services produced by adding a dollar to his money stock is equal to the reduction in the flow of services produced by subtracting a dollar from each of the other forms in which he holds assets.

15. Nothing has been said above about "banks" or producers of money. This is because their main role is in connection with the supply of money rather than the demand for it. Their introduction does, however, blur some of the points in the above analysis: the existence of banks enables productive enterprises to acquire money balances without raising capital from ultimate wealth-owners. Instead of selling claims (bonds or

equities) to them, it can sell its claims to banks, getting "money" in exchange: in the phrase that was once so common in textbooks on money, the bank coins specific liabilities into generally acceptable liabilities. But this possibility does not alter the preceding analysis in any essential way.

16. Suppose the supply of money in nominal units is regarded as fixed or more generally autonomously determined. Equation (13) then defines the conditions under which this nominal stock of money will be the amount demanded. Even under these conditions, equation (13) alone is not sufficient to determine money income. In order to have a complete model for the determination of money income, it would be necessary to specify the determinants of the structure of interest rates, of real income, and of the path of adjustment in the price level. Even if we suppose interest rates determined independently—by productivity, thrift, and the like—and real income as also given by other forces, equation (13) only determines a unique equilibrium level of money income if we mean by this the level at which prices are stable. More generally, it determines a time path of money income for given initial values of money income.

In order to convert equation (13) into a "complete" model of income determination, therefore, it is necessary to suppose either that the demand for money is highly inelastic with respect to the variables in v or that all these variables are to be taken as rigid and fixed.

17. Even under the most favorable conditions, for example, that the demand for money is quite inelastic with respect to the variables in v, equation (13) gives at most a theory of money income: it then says that changes in money income mirror changes in the nominal quantity of money. But it tells nothing about how much of any change in Y is reflected in real output and how much in prices. To infer this requires bringing in outside information, as, for example, that real output is at its feasible maximum, in which case any increase in money would produce the same or a larger percentage increase in prices; and so on.

18. In light of the preceding exposition, the question arises what it means to say that someone is or is not a "quantity theorist." Almost every economist will accept the general lines of the preceding analysis on a purely formal and abstract level, although each would doubtless choose to express it differently in detail. Yet there clearly are deep and fundamental differences about the importance of this analysis for the understanding of short- and long-term movements in general economic activity. This difference of opinion arises with respect to three different issues: (i) the stability and importance of the demand function for money; (ii) the independence of the factors affecting demand and supply; and (iii) the form of the demand function or related functions.

(i) The quantity theorist accepts the empirical hypothesis that the demand for money is highly stable—more stable than functions such as the consumption function that are offered as alternative key relations. This hypothesis needs to be hedged on both sides. On the one side, the quantity theorist need not, and generally does not, mean that the real quantity of money demanded per unit of output, or the velocity of circulation of money, is to be regarded as numerically constant over time; he does not, for example, regard it as a contradiction to the stability of the demand for money that the velocity of circulation of money rises drastically during hyperinflations. For the stability he expects is in the functional relation between the quantity of money demanded and the variables that determine it, and the sharp rise in the velocity of circulation of money during hyperinflations is entirely consistent with a stable functional relation, as Cagan so clearly demonstrates in his essay. On the other side, the quantity theorist must sharply limit, and be prepared to specify explicitly, the variables that it is empirically important to include in the function. For to expand the number of variables regarded as significant is to empty the hypothesis of its empirical content; there is indeed little if any difference between asserting that the demand for money is highly unstable and asserting that it is a perfectly stable function of an indefinitely large number of variables.

The quantity theorist not only regards the demand function for money as stable; he also regards it as playing a vital role in determining variables that he regards as of great importance for the analysis of the economy as a whole, such as the level of money income or of prices. It is this that leads him to put greater emphasis on the demand for money than on, let us say, the demand for pins, even though the latter might be as stable as the former. It is not easy to state this point precisely, and I cannot pretend to have done so. (See item [iii] below for an example of an argument against the quantity theorist along these lines.)

The reaction against the quantity theory in the 1930's came largely, I believe, under this head. The demand for money, it was asserted, is a will-o'-the-wisp, shifting erratically and unpredictably with every rumor and expectation; one cannot, it was asserted, reliably specify a limited number of variables on which it depends. However, although the reaction came under this head, it was largely rationalized under the two succeeding heads.

(ii) The quantity theorist also holds that there are important factors affecting the supply of money that do not affect the demand for money. Under some circumstances these are technical conditions affecting the supply of specie; under others, political or psychological conditions determining the policies of monetary authorities and the banking system. A stable demand function is useful precisely in order to trace out the effects of changes in supply, which means that it is useful only if supply is affected by at least some factors other than those regarded as affecting demand.

The classical version of the objection under this head to the quantity theory is the so-called real-bills doctrine: that changes in the demand for money call forth corresponding changes in supply and that supply cannot change otherwise, or at least cannot do so under specified institutional arrangements. The forms which this argument takes are legion and are still widespread. Another version is the argument that the "quantity theory" cannot "explain" large price rises, because the price rise produced both the increase in demand for nominal money holdings and the increase in supply of money to meet it; that is, implicitly that the same forces affect both the demand for and the supply of money, and in the same way.

(iii) The attack on the quantity theory associated with the Keynesian underemployment analysis is based primarily on an assertion about the form of (7) or (11). The demand for money, it is said, is infinitely elastic at a "small" positive interest rate. At this interest rate, which can be expected to prevail under underemployment conditions, changes in the real supply of money, whether produced by changes in prices or in the nominal stock of money, have no effect on anything. This is the famous "liquidity trap." A rather more complex version involves the shape of other functions as well: the magnitudes in (7) other than "the" interest rate, it is argued, enter into other relations in the economic system and can be regarded as determined there; the interest rate does not enter into these other functions; it can therefore be regarded as determined by this equation. So the only role of the stock of money and the demand for money is to determine the interest rate.

19. The proof of this pudding is in the eating; and the essays in this book contain much relevant food, of which I may perhaps mention three particularly juicy items.

On cannot read Lerner's description of the effects of monetary reform in the Confederacy in 1864 without recognizing that at least on occasion the supply of money can be a largely autonomous factor and the demand for money highly stable even under extraordinarily unstable circumstances. After three years of war, after widespread destruction and military reverses, in the face of impending defeat, a monetary reform that succeeded in reducing the stock of money halted and reversed for some months a rise in prices that had been going on at the rate of 10 per cent a month most of the war! It would be hard to construct a better controlled experiment to demonstrate the critical importance of the supply of money.

On the other hand, Klein's examination of German experience in World

War II is much less favorable to the stability and importance of the demand for money. Though he shows that defects in the figures account for a sizable part of the crude discrepancy between changes in the recorded stock of money and in recorded prices, correction of these defects still leaves a puzzlingly large discrepancy that it does not seem possible to account for in terms of the variables introduced into the above exposition of the theory. Klein examined German experience precisely because it seemed the most deviant on a casual examination. Both it and other wartime experience will clearly repay further examination.

Cagan's examination of hyperinflations is another important piece of evidence on the stability of the demand for money under highly unstable conditions. It is also an interesting example of the difference between a numerically stable velocity and a stable functional relation: the numerical value of the velocity varied enormously during the hyperinflations, but this was a predictable response to the changes in the expected rate of changes of prices.

20. Though the essays in this book contain evidence relevant to the issues discussed in point 18, this is a by-product rather than their main purpose, which is rather to add to our tested knowledge about the characteristics of the demand function for money. In the process of doing so, they also raise some questions about the theoretical formulation and suggest some modifications it might be desirable to introduce. I shall comment on a few of those without attempting to summarize at all fully the essays themselves.

21. Selden's material covers the longest period of time and the most "normal" conditions. This is at once a virtue and a vice—a virtue, because it means that his results may be applicable most directly to ordinary peacetime experience; a vice, because "normality" is likely to spell little variation in the fundamental variables and hence a small base from which to judge their effect. The one variable that covers a rather broad range is real income, thanks to the length of the period. The secular rise in real income has been accompanied by a rise in real cash balances per unit of output—a decline in velocity—from which Selden concludes that the income elasticity of the demand for real balances is greater than unity—cash balances are a "luxury" in the terminology generally adopted. This entirely plausible result seems to be confirmed by evidence for other countries as well.

22. Selden finds that for cyclical periods velocity rises during expansions and falls during contractions, a result that at first glance seems to contradict the secular result just cited. However, there is an alternative explanation entirely consistent with the secular result. It will be recalled

that Y was introduced into equation (7) as an index of wealth. This has important implications for the measure or concept of income that is relevant. What is required by the theoretical analysis is not usual measured income—which in the main corresponds to current receipts corrected for double counting—but a longer term concept, "expected income," or what I have elsewhere called "permanent income."[4] Now suppose that the variables in the v function of (13) are unchanged for a period. The ratio of Y to M would then be unchanged, provided Y is *permanent* income. Velocity as Selden computes it is the ratio of *measured* income to the stock of money and would not be unchanged. When measured income was above permanent income, measured velocity would be relatively high, and conversely. Now measured income is presumably above permanent income at cyclical peaks and below permanent income at cyclical troughs. The observed positive conformity of measured velocity to cyclical changes of income may therefore reflect simply the difference between measured income and the concept relevant to equation (13).

23. Another point that is raised by Selden's work is the appropriate division of wealth into forms of assets. The division suggested above is, of course, only suggestive. Selden finds more useful the distinction between "short-term" and "long-term" bonds; he treats the former as "substitutes for money" and calls the return on the latter "the cost of holding money." He finds both to be significantly related to the quantity of money demanded. It was suggested above that this is also a way to take into account expectations about changes in interest rates.

Similarly, there is no hard-and-fast line between "money" and other assets, and for some purposes it may be desirable to distinguish between different forms of "money" (e.g., between currency and deposits). Some of these forms of money may pay interest or may involve service charges, in which case the positive or negative return will be a relevant variable in determining the division of money holdings among various forms.

24. By concentrating on hyperinflations, Cagan was able to bring into sharp relief a variable whose effect is generally hard to evaluate, namely, the rate of change of prices. The other side of this coin is the necessity of neglecting practically all the remaining variables. His device for estimating expected rates of change of prices from actual rates of change, which works so well for his data, can be carried over to other variables as well and so is likely to be important in fields other than money. I have already used it to estimate "expected income" as a determinant of consumption,[5]

4. See Milton Friedman, *A Theory of the Consumption Function*, forthcoming publition of the Princeton University Press for the National Bureau of Economic Research.

5. See *ibid.*

and Gary Becker has experimented with using this "expected income" series in a demand function for money along the lines suggested above (in point 22).

Cagan's results make it clear that changes in the rate of change of prices, or in the return to an alternative form of holding wealth, have the expected effect on the quantity of money demanded: the higher the rate of change of prices, and thus the more attractive the alternative, the less the quantity of money demanded. This result is important not only directly but also because it is indirectly relevant to the effect of changes in the returns to other alternatives, such as rates of interest on various kinds of bonds. Our evidence on these is in some way less satisfactory because they have varied over so much smaller a range; tentative findings that the effect of changes in them is in the expected direction are greatly strengthened by Cagan's results.

One point which is suggested by the inapplicability of Cagan's relations to the final stages of the hyperinflations he studies is that it may at times be undesirable to replace the whole expected pattern of price movements by the rate of change expected at the moment, as Cagan does and as is done in point 5 above. For example, a given rate of price rise, expected to continue, say, for only a day, and to be followed by price stability, will clearly mean a higher (real) demand for money than the same rate of price rise expected to continue indefinitely; it will be worth incurring greater costs to avoid paying the latter than the former price. This is the same complication as occurs in demand analysis for a consumer good when it is necessary to include not only the present price but also past prices or future expected prices. This point may help explain not only Cagan's findings for the terminal stages but also Selden's findings that the inclusion of the rate of change of prices as part of the cost of holding money worsened rather than improved his estimated relations, though it may be that this result arises from a different source, namely, that it takes substantial actual rates of price change to produce firm enough and uniform enough expectations about price behavior for this variable to play a crucial role.

Similar comments are clearly relevant for expected changes in interest rates.

25. One of the chief reproaches directed at economics as an allegedly empirical science is that it can offer so few numerical "constants," that it has isolated so few fundamental regularities. The field of money is the chief example one can offer in rebuttal: there is perhaps no other empirical relation in economics that has been observed to recur so uniformly under so wide a variety of circumstances as the relation between substantial

changes over short periods in the stock of money and in prices; the one is invariably linked with the other and is in the same direction; this uniformity is, I suspect, of the same order as many of the uniformities that form the basis of the physical sciences. And the uniformity is in more than direction. There is an extraordinary empirical stability and regularity to such magnitudes as income velocity that cannot but impress anyone who works extensively with monetary data. This very stability and regularity contributed to the downfall of the quantity theory, for it was overstated and expressed in unduly simple form; the numerical value of the velocity itself, whether income or transactions, was treated as a natural "constant." Now this it is not; and its failure to be so, first during and after World War I and then, to a lesser extent, after the crash of 1929, helped greatly to foster the reaction against the quantity theory. The studies in this volume are premised on a stability and regularity in monetary relations of a more sophisticated form than a numerically constant velocity. And they make, I believe, an important contribution toward extracting this stability and regularity, toward isolating the numerical "constants" of monetary behavior. It is by this criterion at any rate that I, and I believe also their authors, would wish them to be judged.

I began this Introduction by referring to the tradition in the field of money at Chicago and to the role of faculty members in promoting it. I think it is fitting to end the Introduction by emphasizing the part which students have played in keeping that tradition alive and vigorous. The essays that follow are one manifestation. Unpublished doctoral dissertations on money are another. In addition, I wish especially to express my own personal appreciation to the students who have participated with me in the Workshop in Money and Banking, of which this volume is the first published fruit. I owe a special debt to David I. Fand, Phillip Cagan, Gary Becker, David Meiselman, and Raymond Zelder, who have at various times helped me to conduct it.

We all of us are indebted also to the Rockefeller Foundation for financial assistance to the Workshop in Money and Banking. This assistance helped to finance some of the research reported in this book and has made possible its publication.

'The Monetary Theory and Policy of Henry Simons'

M. Friedman, 'The monetary theory and policy of Henry Simons', *Journal of Law and Economics*, X (October 1967), pp. 1–13.

The Journal of

LAW & ECONOMICS

VOLUME X OCTOBER 1967

THE MONETARY THEORY AND POLICY OF HENRY SIMONS*

MILTON FRIEDMAN
University of Chicago

IT is a great honor for me to give the Henry Simons Lecture. He was my teacher and my friend—and above all, a shaper of my ideas. No man can say precisely whence his beliefs and his values come—but there is no doubt that mine would be very different than they are if I had not had the good fortune to be exposed to Henry Simons. If, in this lecture, I express much disagreement with him, that, too, bespeaks his influence. He taught us that an objective, critical examination of a man's ideas is a truer tribute than slavish repetition of his formulas.

I am especially pleased to be giving this lecture under the auspices of the Law School. One of the unique advantages of the University of Chicago for economists has always been the close cooperation and interchange between economists and lawyers. Henry Simons was for many years on the Law School faculty, and Aaron Director and Ronald Coase have continued that fine tradition. *The Journal of Law and Economics* has set the seal on a happy affair.

On re-reading Henry Simons' work in preparation for this lecture, I was struck by the contrast between my reaction to his discussion of monetary theory, on the one hand, and to his proposals for monetary reform, on the

* The third Henry Simons lecture, delivered at the Law School, University of Chicago, May 5, 1967.

other. The monetary theory impressed me as sophisticated and correct; the proposals for reform as largely irrelevant and wrong. This contrast and how it can be explained are the themes of this lecture.

Though Simons nowhere set forth a consistent and comprehensive statement of his monetary theory, his views are implicit in his discussion of policy proposals, and explicit in many parenthetical remarks in his often lengthy and always penetrating footnotes.[1] I find myself, not only in full agreement with the views so revealed, but more important, enlightened by them and impressed by their sophistication.

Simons wrote on money mostly during the dozen years from 1933 to 1945. That was a period when, thanks to the Keynesian Revolution, the economics profession came to regard money—in the sense of currency, deposits, banking, and allied issues—as an unimportant and uninteresting subject. The fraction of the profession's attention devoted to this area probably reached an all time low from the late 'thirties to the early 'fifties. Since then there has been a tremendous revival of interest in this area, so that monetary theory is at the moment a dramatic growth industry. Recent developments have deepened and widened our understanding but they have cast no doubt on Simons' basic analysis of how money enters into the economic system or of the influence it exerts. Quite the contrary. These developments have produced a return to Simons' view that the quantity of money and its behavior play a central role in affecting the course of prices and of economic activity; that monetary stability is an essential prerequisite for economic stability.

Simons' policy proposals are a very different matter. They consist of two separable elements: (1) proposals for reforming the banking and financial structure—as he put it "transition to a less preposterous structure of private money contracts" (at 170), (2) proposals for "establishment of a simple, mechanical rule of monetary policy" (at 170). In his role as a monetary theorist, he clearly found the second much more intriguing and interesting. Yet he regarded it as the less important. The urgent and immediate task, the essential pre-condition for the satisfactory operation of any monetary rule, was, he believed, financial reform.

In Simons' view, the "financial good society" (at 239) required "financial reform . . . aiming at sharp differentiation between money and private obligations" (at 79). He viewed his well-known proposal for 100 per cent

[1] One partial exception to the statement that Simons nowhere set forth a consistent statement of his theory is an Appendix on Banking and Business Cycles in an unpublished and unsigned memorandum dated November, 1933, Banking and Currency Reform. In a footnote, Simons describes this memorandum as having been "prepared and circulated by several Chicago economists" but, according to Aaron Director, one of the group, it was written primarily by Simons. See Henry Simons, Economic Policy for a Free Society 326 n.2 (1948). All subsequent page references in the text are to this book.

reserve banking "only as the proper first step toward reconstruction of our whole financial organization. Standing by itself, as an isolated measure, it would promise little but evasion . . . and would deserve classification as merely another crank scheme" (at 331 n.17).[2] In addition to 100 per cent reserve banking, "Narrow limitation of the formal borrowing powers of other corporations would obviously be necessary . . . . Further limitations might also be necessary with respect to financing via the open account (book credit) and instalment sales" (at 171). For government, the debt structure should be drastically simplified, with all government obligations taking the form either of non-interest-bearing money or very long-term securities, ideally perpetuities (consols).

On monetary policy, Simons vacillated between favoring a rule expressed in terms of the quantity of money—for example, that the quantity of money be kept constant—and a rule expressed in terms of a price index—for example, that the authorities be instructed to keep the wholesale price index stable. His final position was, roughly, that the price-index rule was the only feasible rule pending a closer approximation to the "financial good society," but that the quantity of money rule was much preferable, when and if the "financial good society" was attained.

I would myself be inclined precisely to reverse Simons' priorities—and so, I believe would most other modern students of money, even those of us who share most completely Simons' basic objectives of social policy. Financial reform along his lines seems not only unnecessary but in the wrong direction.[3] Why should we not have variety and diversity in the market for borrowing and lending as in other markets? Is it not desirable that borrowers tailor their obligations to the demands of lenders? Is it not a sign of the ingenuity and efficiency of the free market that financial intermediaries develop which reconcile the needs of borrowers and lenders—providing funds on terms desired by borrowers and borrowing on terms desired by lenders? This simultaneously lowers the cost of capital to borrowers and raises the effective return on capital to lenders—thereby fostering a higher level of capital formation than would otherwise occur.

I agree with Simons on the desirability of 100 per cent reserve banking—but I regard it as less important and basic than he did and favor it in some

[2] His proposal involved separating existing commercial banks into two sets of institutions. One would be essentially a warehouse for money. It would accept demand deposits transferable by check but be required to keep a reserve in cash (or deposits at the Federal Reserve) of 100% of such deposits, and would get its income from service charges paid by depositors. The other would be an investment trust which would take over the lending activities of commercial banks, getting its capital by issuing securities to the public.

[3] Emphasis on this type of reform has almost disappeared from the literature. Its only counterpart was a temporary flurry of interest in non-bank financial intermediaries a few years ago.

ways for almost the opposite reasons. He viewed it as a step toward simplifying the structure of financial claims, as a step toward making effective the legislative limitations he favored on the terms on which people could borrow and lend. I view it as a step toward reducing government interference with lending and borrowing in order to permit a greater degree of freedom and variety in the arrangements for borrowing and lending.

Even on monetary policy, where the passage of time has only strengthened my belief in the lesson he taught me—that rules are greatly to be preferred to authorities, I am inclined to reverse his emphasis. A rule in terms of the quantity of money seems to me far superior, for both the short and the long-run, than a rule in terms of price-level stabilization.

What explains this contrast? How is it that I can admire so greatly Simons' grasp of monetary theory and disagree so completely with his proposals for reform?

We have all of us in our personal lives had the experience of coming on a fact that suddenly illuminated an issue in a flash, showing us how wrong we had been and leading us to a fresh and very different opinion. It is something of an oversimplification, but only a slight one, I believe, to say that that is the explanation of the contrast I have been stressing. A few facts, which we now know and he did not, have made all the difference.

The facts have to do primarily with the Great Depression of 1929-1933. Were I to interpret that episode as Simons did, I would agree with his recommendations. Had he interpreted that episode as I do, he would not have made the policy recommendations he did. And our differences of interpretation is not simply a difference of personality or taste. It reflects—or so I would like to believe—the accumulation of evidence through scientific study.

Needless to say, Simons' interpretation was not unique to him. On the contrary, it was widely shared by his contemporaries. In particular, I have been struck that the statements I have been making about Simons apply almost verbatim to John Maynard Keynes. He, too, was led to make policy recommendations that seem wrong now—and in his case that differed drastically from his own earlier views—because he accepted the same interpretation of 1929-1933 as did Henry Simons. In his case, too, I find his monetary theory sophisticated and modern, yet his policy recommendations unacceptable. As we shall see later, though some of his policy recommendations parallel Simons', in other respects they differ drastically. But they differ not because of a difference in monetary theory or a different interpretation of 1929-1933 but because of a different basic attitude toward social policy—Keynes was a reformer, Simons, a radical.

In exploring this thesis further, I shall outline Simons' interpretation of the 1930's and similar episodes, show how his policy recommendations follow from that interpretation, and contrast his policy recommendations with

Keynes'. I shall then indicate what our current interpretation of this episode is and suggest what policy views derive from that interpretation.

1. *Simons' Interpretation of Business Cycles in General and the Great Depression in Particular.* "The problem of synchronous industrial . . . fluctuations," wrote Simons, "is a problem (a) of rigidities in crucial areas of the price structure . . . and (b) of perverse flexibility in the total turnover (quantity and velocity) of effective money" (at 165).

The perverse flexibility in "total turnover"—Keynes' aggregate demand—was reinforced, Simons thought, but not essentially produced, by changes in the quantity of money. It reflected rather changes in "the speculative temper of the community."[4] Such changes, he argued, produce changes in velocity that can develop into "catastrophic disturbances as soon as short-term borrowing develops on a large scale. . . . Short-term obligations provide abundant money substitutes during booms, thus releasing money from cash reserves [that is, raising velocity]; and they precipitate hopeless efforts at liquidation during depressions [that is, lowering velocity]" (at 166).

These "cumulative maladjustments are likely to be peculiarly severe" "in an economy where most of the effective money is provided by private banks" because "the quantity of effective money, as well as its velocity, responds promptly and markedly to changes of business earnings."[5]

Widespread borrowing on short-term in order to finance long-term obligations is the key to instability because, in Simons' view, it makes the economy vulnerable to changes in confidence and hence in the desire for liquidity. Each individual separately may be in a position to convert his assets into cash but the economy as a whole is not. There is "shiftability" but not "liquidity." The commercial banking system makes this problem more serious not primarily as a creator of money, but because it fosters more widespread and extensive borrowing on demand and lending on time.

This vision undoubtedly was derived largely from the 1929-33 crash. Hence, Simons put special emphasis on the potentialities in such a system for deflation. ". . . [W]e evolved a fantastic financial structure and collections of enterprises for money-bootlegging, whose sanctimonious respectability and marble solidity only concealed a mass of current obligations and a shoestring of equity that would have been scandalous in any other type of business. . . . [W]e evaded long term deflation by continuously courting deflation catastrophe" (at 198-99).

Or again, "once a crisis has developed, and once earnings have begun to decline, the process is even more chaotic. Each bank seeks to contract its loans; but none augments its reserves unless it contracts more rapidly than the rest. Every reduction in bank loans means reduction in the community's

[4] Appendix to Banking and Currency Reform, *supra* note 1, at 2.

[5] *Id.* at 3.

effective money; and this in turn means lower prices, smaller volume of business, and still lower earnings. . . .

"It is more than an incidental aggravation that practically all the banks of necessity become insolvent in the process, and that large numbers are actually forced to close."[6]

For our purposes, the key feature of this interpretation is that the channel of influence runs from changes in business confidence to changes in velocity to changes in the quantity of money. For the depression, it is the collapse of confidence (Keynes' collapse of the marginal efficiency of investment) that sets off a demand for liquidity. This demand cannot be met but the attempt to meet it forces widespread liquidation, including the liquidation of bank loans with a resultant decline in the quantity of money and runs on banks.

Simons implicitly regarded the Great Depression as occurring despite not because of governmental monetary policy. Though he made no explicit statement to this effect, Simons' quite clearly accepted the official apologia of the Federal Reserve System—it had done its best but was powerless to stop the collapse, once private confidence was sapped, as it was by the stock-market crash. "Reflect casually," says Simons, "on what the thirties might have been if only we had not permitted the stock-market crash to initiate a long and precipitous deflation in the United States . . . ." (at 272).

2. *Simons' Theory of Cycles and His Policy Proposals.* It is clear how Simons' policy proposals derive from his interpretation of the Great Depression. It is the rigidity of prices that converts fluctuations in aggregate demand into fluctuations in output and employment. Hence, greater flexibility of prices is highly desirable, whatever else is done. This is the link between Simons' views on money, on the one hand, and on monopoly in industry and labor and government price-fixing, on the other. The way to make prices less rigid was by measures that are desirable in any event in order to make the economy more competitive. Hence, in his monetary writings, he only stated the objective of price flexibility, without a bill of particulars.

Since the inherent instability of the financial structure is the source of cumulative maladjustments, the *sine qua non* of stability in a free market economy is an improved financial structure. The "approximately ideal condition" would be one in which "there were no fixed money contracts at all—if all property were held in a residual-equity or common-stock form. With such a financial structure, no one would be in a position either to create effective money substitutes (whether for circulation or for hoarding) or to force enterprises into wholesale efforts at liquidation. Hoarding and dishoarding (changes in velocity) would, to be sure, still occur; but the dangers of cumulative maladjustment would be minimized" (at 165).

[6] *Id.* at 5.

In the absence of such financial reform, "The obvious weakness of fixed quantity [of money], as a sole rule of monetary policy, lies in the danger of sharp changes on the velocity side. . . . The fixing of the quantity of circulating media might merely serve to increase the perverse variability in the amounts of 'near moneys' and in the degree of their general acceptability . . . ." (at 164).

Hence, pending such financial reform, the theoretically attractive quantity of money criterion had to be relegated to the "more distant future" (at 183) despite its unique advantage of providing an objective rule and minimizing the role of discretion by monetary authorities. "For the present, we obviously must rely on a large measure of discretionary money management. . . ." (at 170). But this discretion should be guided by some definite policy objective, not be ". . . merely the composite of the uncertain daily actions of an indefinite number of agencies, governmental and private" (at 174). Simons was led by this route to endorse reluctantly the stabilization of a price index as the only feasible means of ". . . bringing the totality of monetary measures under the discipline of some rule. . . ." (at 174-75). "If price-level stabilization is a poor system," he wrote, "it is, still from a liberal viewpoint, infinitely better than no system at all. And it seems now highly questionable whether any better system is feasible or possible at all within the significant future" (at 174).

Finally, if, in the existing financial structure, the fluctuations in aggregate demand originate in the private sector and in turn affect the commercial banking system; if a major problem is the ease with which non-banks can create and destroy near-moneys, then the banking authorities, strictly interpreted, operate on too narrow a base to be able to control the price level. "Banking," Simons said, "is a pervasive phenomenon, not something to be dealt with merely by legislation directed at what we call banks" (at 172). Hence, "The task [of stabilizing the price level] is certainly not one to be intrusted to banking authorities, with their limited powers and restricted techniques, as should be abundantly evident from recent experience. Ultimate control over the value of money lies in fiscal practices—in the spending, taxing, and borrowing operations of the central government" (at 175).

3. *Simons and Keynes*. There is clearly great similarity between the views expressed by Simons and by Keynes—as to the causes of the Great Depression, the impotence of monetary policy, and the need to rely extensively on fiscal policy. Both men placed great emphasis on the state of business expectations and assigned a critical role to the desire for liquidity. Indeed, in many ways, the key novelty of Keynes' *General Theory* was the role he assigned to "absolute" liquidity preference under conditions of deep depression. It was this, in his view, that made it impossible for the monetary authorities to influence interest rates. It was this that meant that changes in

the quantity of money produced by the monetary authorities would simply be reflected in opposite movements in velocity and have no effect on income or employment.

Keynes had earlier been a strong champion of relying primarily on orthodox monetary policy to promote economic stability. He abandoned this position when he concluded that liquidity preference could frustrate central bank attempts to alter long-term interest rates. Like Simons, he turned instead to fiscal policy—changes in government expenditures and taxes—as his primary reliance.[7]

Despite the similarity between the views held by Simons and Keynes, Simons, as best I can determine, arrived at his views independently. My earlier quotation from Simons that "ultimate control over the value of money lies in fiscal practices" comes from an article published in February, 1936, or at roughly the same time as Keynes' *General Theory*. (The preface is dated December, 1935, and the book bears the publication date of 1936.) More important yet, Simons' basic ideas on both theory and policy are all contained in an unpublished mimeographed memorandum dated November, 1933. Already in that memorandum, Simons had written "at the present time, increase of expenditures or reduction of taxes would be far more immediately effective toward raising prices than conversion of the federal debt into the non-interest bearing form."[8] Indeed, I have always thought that it was because such ideas as these, and the earlier ones I have summarized, were in the air at the University of Chicago in the early and mid-1930's that the Chicago students were so much less susceptible to the

[7] In a letter commenting on this lecture, Friedrich A. Hayek writes: "I believe you are wrong in suggesting that the common element in the doctrines of Simons and Keynes was the influence of the Great Depression. We all held similar ideas in the 1920's. They had been most fully elaborated by R. G. Hawtrey who was all the time talking about the 'inherent instability of credit' but he was by no means the only one. . . . It seems to me that all the elements of the theories which were applied to the Great Depression had been developed during that great enthusiasm for 'business cycle theory' which preceded it."

No doubt the elements of the theories were all present and Hayek may be right that the Great Depression did not have the effect on Keynes' views that I attributed to it. However, the Great Depression surely produced a different emphasis. More important, my impression is that the Great Depression also produced an important difference in substance. Hawtrey and others emphasized the inherent instability of banking credit proper; their stress was on the forces that Simons described as explaining why these "cumulative maladjustments are likely to be peculiarly severe" "in an economy where most of the effective money is provided by private banks," not on the earlier effects to which Simons attributed the cumulative maladjustments themselves. The Great Depression led, I believe, Keynes and Simons to emphasize the inherent instability of the financial structure more generally—the effect of near-moneys rather than of money itself. Unfortunately, I have not had the opportunity to investigate this point at all fully, so this reaction to Hayek's comment is a tentative impression, not a documented conclusion.

[8] *Supra* note 4, at 13.

Keynesian virus than their contemporaries in London, England, and Cambridge, Massachusetts, who were taught that the Great Depression was a necessary and ultimately healthy purgative.

The major differences between Keynes and Simons on policy reflected their difference in temperament. To both, the financial structure threatened instability. To Keynes the reformer, with his emphasis on short-run problems —it was he, after all, who said, "in the long-run we are all dead," with his confidence in civil servants to control and regulate—he was himself, after all, in and out of the civil service, with his belief that we had seen "the end of laissez-faire," as he entitled a famous article, the solution was to substitute government intervention for market adjustment, to replace where necessary private investment by government spending. To Simons the radical, who always took the long view, who had the mid-westerner's suspicion of the bureaucrats in Washington, who regarded a large measure of laissez-faire as an essential requisite for the preservation of political liberty, the solution was to go to the root of the problem by reforming drastically the financial structure.

4. *The Key Facts as We Now Know Them.* The keystone of Simons' interpretation of 1929-1933 was that the trouble originated with business earnings and the shock to business confidence, documented or perhaps initiated by the stock-market crash. The subsequent widespread pressure for liquidation, on his interpretation, left the monetary authorities, narrowly defined, largely powerless. Once the scramble for liquidity was on, there was no way they could prevent a decline in the value of private claims and debts, which in turn rendered banks insolvent, and induced their depositors to try to withdraw deposits.

We now know that the critical relations ran precisely the other way. Beginning in mid-1928, the Federal Reserve System, concerned about stock market speculation, adopted a monetary policy of nearly continuous restraint, despite its desire to foster business expansion. The result was a policy that was ". . . not restrictive enough to halt the bull market yet too restrictive to foster vigorous business expansion."[9] The stock of money failed to rise and even fell slightly during most of the cyclical expansion from November, 1927 to August, 1929—a phenomenon not matched in any prior or subsequent cyclical expansion.

Cyclical contraction began in August, 1929, well before the stock-market crash in October, 1929. That crash no doubt did shake business confidence and may well have produced a rise in liquidity preference (that is, a decline in velocity). But there is no sign that it produced any panicky pressure for liquidation, any tendency for bankers to call loans, any concern about

[9] M. Friedman and A. Schwartz, A Monetary History of the United States, 1867-1960, 298 (1963).

the safety of banks, or any widespread deterioration in the value of bank assets—on the contrary, the prices of the kinds of bonds banks held initially went up rather than down.

The downward pressure on velocity produced by the reaction to the stock-market crash was strongly reinforced by the behavior of the quantity of money, which fell by 2.6 per cent from August, 1929 to October, 1930. This may seem like a small decline—and it is, compared to the total decline of over 30 per cent that occurred before the depression was over. But the decline should be interpreted in the light of prior and subsequent experience. Because of the long-term growth in the quantity of money, there are only four earlier cyclical contractions and no later ones in which the quantity of money declined as much—and all of these earlier exceptions were also unusually severe contractions.

For our purposes, the source of the decline in the quantity of money is even more important than its magnitude. It was produced entirely by a decline in Federal Reserve credit outstanding. No part whatever was played by weakness in the banking structure, attempted liquidation of loans by banks, or an attempt by depositors to convert deposits to currency. On the contrary, the banks' willingness to reduce reserves and the public's willingness to hold more deposits relative to currency offset half of the decline in Federal Reserve credit. The monetary authorities, not the private economy, were the major source of deflationary pressure.

The character of the contraction changed drastically in December, 1930 when a series of scattered bank failures culminated in the dramatic failure of the Bank of the United States in New York—the largest single bank failure in the United States up to that time. For the first time, there was widespread distrust of banks and runs on banks. But again the sequence was the opposite of that which Simons postulated. The runs on banks produced pressure on banks to liquidate. This did lower the market value of their assets and so gave substance to the initially unfounded fears of the safety of the banks. But their position was not weakened by declines in the value of their assets originating in the rest of the financial structure.

A major objective in establishing the Federal Reserve System in 1913 was to meet precisely this kind of situation—to serve as a "lender of last resort" in order to enable banks to meet the demands of depositors without having to dump assets. In the immediate month of December, 1930, the Reserve System behaved to some extent as initially intended. But no sooner was the immediate crisis over than it retreated back to its earlier position and renewed its deflationary pressure on the money supply.

When a second banking crisis began in March, 1931, the Reserve System did not even temporarily step in to ease the situation. The only relief came from gold imports. The Reserve System renounced its heritage and treated the banking crisis as something outside its sphere of competence.

But worse was yet to come. When Britain left gold in September, 1931, the Reserve System embarked on an active deflationary policy—taking the most extreme deflationary measures in its history before or since. The result was to turn a crisis into a catastrophe. The quantity of money had fallen at an annual rate of 13 per cent from March, 1931 to August, 1931. It fell at the incredible annual rate of 31 per cent in the five months from August, 1931 to January, 1932.

One fact during this episode highlights the error in Simons' interpretation. The chief problem confronting banks was not the collectibility of their commercial loans but the decline in the prices of the bonds they held in their portfolios. Among the prices that declined was the price of U.S. government bonds, which fell by 10 per cent. This price decline clearly did not reflect a scramble for liquidity on the part of the community at large or the decline in earnings of business enterprises or a fear about the safety of the bonds. Like the accompanying decline of 20 per cent in the price of high grade corporate bonds, it reflected the inevitable effect of the dumping of bonds by banks which was enforced by the failure of the Federal Reserve System to provide sufficient liquidity to enable banks to meet the demands of their customers.

In our ***Monetary History***, Anna Schwartz and I summarized the role of the Reserve System in the great contraction from 1929-1933 as follows:

"The System pleaded impotence, arguing explicitly that the non-monetary forces making for contraction were so strong and violent that it was powerless to stem the tide, and implicitly that the depth of the decline in the money stock was due to the depth of the decline in business activity, rather than . . . the reverse. Many others, recognizing the good intentions of the monetary authorities and the ability of many individuals in the System, while independently holding a wide variety of views about the role of money in economic affairs, accepted the System's plea"—as we have seen, Simons and Keynes were in this company.

Evaluating the claim of impotence, we concluded that "At all times throughout the 1929-33 contraction, alternative policies were available to the System by which it could have kept the stock of money from falling, and indeed could have increased it at almost any desired rate. These policies did not involve radical innovations. They involved measures of a kind the System had taken in earlier years, of a kind explicitly contemplated by the founders of the System to meet precisely the kind of banking crisis that developed in late 1930 and persisted thereafter. They involved measures that were actually proposed and very likely would have been adopted under a slightly different bureaucratic structure or distribution of power, or even if the men in power had had somwhat different personalities. Until late 1931—and we believe not even then—the alternative policies involved no conflict with the maintenance of the gold standard. Until September, 1931, the problem that recurrently troubled the System was how to keep the gold inflows under control, not the reverse."[10]

I have stressed the Great Depression because this climactic episode clearly played a key role in leading Simons—and also Keynes—to believe that the orthodox powers of the monetary authorities were too weak to cope with disorders arising in the private financial markets. In fact, as I have emphasized, the private financial markets displayed extraordinary resilience and stability—but not enough to cope with the disorders arising from the actions—and inaction—of the monetary authorities.

An enormous amount of evidence has accumulated since Simons wrote that bears not only on these few years but also on a far wider range of economic history. This evidence, too, contradicts Simons' interpretation of the source of instability. It turns out that the rate of growth of the quantity of money has systematically tapered off well before the economy in general slows down, and has speeded up well before the economy speeds up. The movements in velocity—which Simons took as an independent source of instability—come later than the movements in the quantity of money and are mild when the movements in the quantity of money are mild. They have been sharp only when there have been sharp movements in the quantity of money. There is no evidence to support Simons' fear that a fixed quantity of money might involve "the danger of sharp changes on the velocity side." On the contrary, the evidence is precisely the reverse—that it would lessen the danger of sharp changes in velocity.

5. *Policy Implications.* Had Simons known the facts as we now know them, he would, I believe, have been confirmed in "his earlier persuasion as to the merits of the rule of a fixed quantity of money. . . ." (at 170)[11] rather

[10] *Supra* note 8, at 691, 693.

[11] To avoid misunderstanding, I should note explicitly that Simons' rule is not identical with the rule I have come to favor. Simons proposed that the quantity of money be held constant in amount. I propose that it grow at a fixed rate year after year, the rate of growth being designed to produce roughly stable final product prices.

Simons explicitly rejected the rule of a constant rate of growth. He recognized that his rule of a constant money supply involved a secular decline in final product prices. His basic reason for favoring it nonetheless was that the sticky and inflexible prices were factor prices, especially wages, and that a constant quantity of money would (aside from growth of population, which he thought would decline and might disappear, and aside from secular changes in velocity, which he ignored) mean stability in these prices and hence would minimize the necessity for changes in the sticky prices. Supplementary reasons were the greater ease of public understanding of a constant quantity of money than of a necessarily arbitrary rate of growth and the greater pressure for fiscal discipline it would impose on legislators.

than have accepted, albeit with great reluctance, stabilization of a price level as at least a temporary objective pending the establishment of the "financial good society." He would not have felt constrained to denigrate monetary powers narrowly conceived and to elevate fiscal powers to the forefront as the major weapon of monetary policy.

In short, as it happens, a correct view of the facts would have strengthened his basic intiuitions, would have reinforced his confidence in policies fully consistent with his central belief in laissez-faire for the private economy and the rule of law for governmental bodies.

Instead, because of a misconception of the facts, he was led to compromise for the short run and to propose radical reform for the long-run.

Is it just a happy accident that a fuller study of the facts would have led Henry Simons to compromise less with his basic intuitions, would have supported the conclusions to which he was drawn by his economic theorizing? I believe not. Those intuitions, those conclusions were derived from a sophisticated body of economic theory that had developed over centuries. Such a body of theory has implicit in it a set of empirical judgments about the character of the world. It survives if and only if those implicit judgments are vindicated by experience. It may go into temporary eclipse when casual empiricism seems to run counter to it. That is what happened during the 'thirties. But the sign that it is a good theory is that it will revive and be restored to grace as emerging evidence vindicates it. That is what has been happening in the past decade. That is why Simons' keen theoretical understanding has proved more permanent than his empirical compromises.

'The Quantity Theory of Money'

M. Friedman, 'The quantity theory of money', in D. L. Sills (ed.), *International Encyclopedia of the Social Sciences* (New York, Macmillan, 1968), pp. 432–46.

II
QUANTITY THEORY

Since men first began to write systematically about economic matters they have devoted special attention to the wide movements in the general level of prices that have intermittently occurred. Two alternative explanations have usually been offered. One has attributed the changes in prices to changes in the quantity of money. The other has attributed the changes in prices to war or to profiteers or to rises in wages or to some other special circumstance of the particular time and place and has regarded any accompanying change in the quantity of money as a common consequence of the same special circumstance. The first explanation has generally been referred to as the quantity theory of money, although that designation conceals the variety of forms the explanation has taken, the different levels of sophistication on which it has been developed, and the wide range of the claims that have been made for its applicability.

The broad outlines of the quantity theory of money were fully developed by the eighteenth century. The contemporary economist can still read David Hume's essay "Of Money" (1752) with pleasure and profit and find few if any errors of commission. Reasonably satisfactory attempts at mathematical formulation have been traced back to the eighteenth century (see the references in Marget 1938). And certainly the mathematical formulation given by Simon Newcomb, the eminent astronomer, in 1886 is entirely modern, excepting only the particular symbols used. Knut Wicksell published a highly sophisticated analysis in 1898 that, because it was written in German, had less influence than its excellence justified. The two formulations of the quantity theory that have most influenced modern thinking both date from the end of the nineteenth century (although the dates of their publication are later): Irving Fisher's transactions version (1911) and the Cambridge cash-balances version, attributed to Alfred Marshall (1923) and Arthur C. Pigou (1917). After some introductory remarks, this article discusses these two versions and then examines the Keynesian attack on the quantity theory, the post-Keynesian reformulation, empirical evidence bearing on the quantity theory, and finally some policy implications of the quantity theory.

In its most rigid and unqualified form the quantity theory asserts strict proportionality between the quantity of what is regarded as money and the level of prices. Hardly anyone has held the theory in that form, although statements capable of being so interpreted have often been made in the heat of argument or for expository simplicity. Virtually every quantity theorist has recognized that changes in the quantity of money that correspond to changes in the volume of trade or of output have no tendency to produce changes in prices. Nearly as many have recognized also that changes in the willingness of the community to hold money can occur for a variety of reasons and can introduce disparities between changes in the quantity of money per unit of trade or of output and changes in prices. What quantity theorists have held in common is the belief that these qualifications are of secondary importance for substantial changes in either prices or the quantity of money, so that the one will not in fact occur without the other.

The quantity theory in all its versions rests on a distinction between the *nominal* quantity of money and the *real* quantity of money. The nominal quantity of money is the quantity expressed in whatever units are used to designate money—talents, shekels, pounds, francs, lire, drachmas, dollars, and so on. The real quantity of money is the quantity expressed in terms of the volume of goods and services that the money will purchase.

There is no unique way to express the real quantity of money. One way of expressing it, one that is widely used, is in terms of some specified standard basket of goods and services. That is what is implicitly done when the real quantity of money is calculated by dividing the nominal quantity by a price index. The standard basket is then the basket whose components are used as weights in computing the price index—generally the basket purchased by some reference group in a base year.

Another way of expressing the real quantity of money is in terms of the time duration of the flows of goods and services the money could purchase. For a household, for example, the real quantity of money can be expressed in terms of the number of weeks of the household's average level of consumption that it could finance with its money balances or, alternatively, in terms of the number of weeks of its average income to which its money balances are equal. For a business enterprise, the real quantity of money it holds can be expressed in terms of the number of weeks of its average purchases or of its average sales or of its average expenditures on final productive services (net value added) to which its money balances are equal. For the community as a whole, the real quantity of money can be expressed in terms of the number of weeks of aggregate transactions of the community or aggregate net output of the community to which it is equal.

For the community, attention has generally centered not on the real quantity of money but on a velocity of circulation—which can be regarded as the reciprocal of a particular expression of the real quantity of money. The ratio, for example, of the aggregate annual transactions of a community to its stock of money is termed the "transactions velocity of circulation of money," since it gives the number of times the stock of money would have to "turn over" in a year to accomplish all transactions; similarly, the ratio of annual income to the stock of money is termed "income velocity." In every case the calculation of the real quantity of money or of velocity is made at the set of prices prevailing at the date to which the calculation refers. These prices are the bridge between the nominal and the real quantity of money.

The quantity theory takes for granted that what ultimately matters to holders of money is the real quantity rather than the nominal quantity of money they hold and that there is some fairly definite real quantity of money that people wish to hold under any given circumstances. Suppose the nominal quantity that people hold happens to correspond at current prices to a real quantity larger than that which they wish to hold. Individuals will then seek to dispose of what they regard as their excess money balances, they will try to pay out a larger sum for the purchase of securities, goods, and services, for the repayment of debts, and as gifts than they are receiving from the corresponding sources. However, one man's expenditures are another's receipts. One man can reduce his nominal money balances only by persuading someone else to increase his. The community as a whole cannot in general spend more than it receives.

The community's attempt to do so will nonetheless have important effects. If prices and income are free to change, the attempt to spend more will raise the nominal volume of expenditures and receipts, which will lead to a bidding up of prices and perhaps also to an increase in output. If prices are fixed by custom or by government edict, the attempt to spend more either will be matched by an increase in goods and services or will produce "shortages" and "queues." These in turn will raise the effective prices and are likely sooner or later to force changes in official prices. The initial excess of money balances will therefore tend to be eliminated, even though there is no change in the nominal quantity, by either a reduction in the real quantity held through price rises or an increase in the real quantity desired through output increases. Conversely, if nominal balances happen to correspond to a smaller real quantity at current prices than people wish to hold, people will seek to spend less than they are receiving. They cannot in the aggregate do so. But their attempt will in the process lower nominal expenditures and receipts, driving down prices or output and either raising the real balances held or lowering the real balances desired.

It is clear from this discussion that changes in prices and nominal income can be produced either by changes in the real balances that people wish to hold or by changes in the nominal balances available for them to hold. Indeed it is a tautology, summarized in the famous quantity equation (to which we shall return) that all changes in nominal income can be attributed to one or the other—just as a change in the price of any good can always be attributed to a change in either demand or supply. The quantity theory is not, however, this tautology. It is, rather, the empirical generalization that changes in desired real balances (in the demand for money) tend to proceed slowly and gradually or to be the result of events set in train by prior changes in supply, whereas, in contrast, substantial changes in the supply of nominal balances can and frequently do occur independently of any changes in demand. The conclusion is that substantial changes in prices or nominal income are almost invariably the result of changes in the nominal supply of money.

Variants of the quantity theory of money are distinguished by the variables that are regarded as most important in determining the real quantity of money that people desire to hold and by the analysis of the process whereby any discrepancy between actual and desired real balances works itself out. The chief issues that have occasioned controversy and conflict are perhaps the definition of money, the importance of transactions motives versus asset motives in the holding of money; the importance of substitution between money and other assets expressed in nominal terms as compared with substitution between money and real goods and services, and the speed and character of the dynamic process of adjustment. We shall have occasion to comment on these below.

Fisher's transactions approach

The quantity equation in transactions form. Every payment made by one economic unit in an economy—household, business enterprise, or governmental organization—to another can be regarded as the product of a price and a quantity: wage per week times number of weeks, price of a good times number of units of the good, dividend per share times number of shares, and so on. The total volume of transactions during a period of time can thus be regarded as equal to the sum of a large number of such products, say $\sum p_i t_i$, where p_i is the price and t_i the quantity for the ith transaction. Let P be a suitably chosen average of the prices, and let T be a suitably chosen aggregate of the quantities. We then have

(1) Total volume of transactions $= PT = \sum p_i t_i$.

The total volume of transactions can also be viewed in terms of the medium of exchange used to effectuate them. Let M be the total quantity of money in the economy and V the average number of times each unit of money is used to effectuate a transaction during the year (the transactions velocity). We then have

$$(2) \qquad \text{Total volume of transactions} = MV,$$

or, putting (1) and (2) together, the famous quantity equation

$$(3) \qquad MV = PT.$$

Each side of this equation can be broken into subcategories. the right-hand side into different categories of transactions and the left-hand side into payments in different form. Fisher and later writers emphasized in particular the subdivision of the left-hand side into two categories of payments, those effected by the transfer of hand-to-hand currency (including coin) and those effected by the transfer of deposits. Let M stand solely for the volume of currency and V for the velocity of currency, M' for the volume of deposits and V' for the velocity of deposits. We then can write

$$(4) \qquad MV + M'V' = PT.$$

One reason for the emphasis on this division was the persistent dispute about whether the term "money" should include only currency or deposits as well—this dispute was at the center of the banking school–currency school controversy that raged in England in the nineteenth century. Another reason was the direct availability of figures on $M'V'$ from bank records of clearings or of debits to accounts so that it was and is possible to calculate V' in a way that it is not possible to calculate V.

As they stand, equations (3) and (4) are identities: The V of (3) or the V and V' of (4) are defined as the numbers having the property that they render the equations correct. If P changes from one time period to the next, then so must one or more of the other terms in the equations. That is an arithmetic necessity, not an economic proposition. The identities are useful for economic analysis because they offer a useful classification of the factors at work, a classification into categories each of which contains factors largely independent of those in the other categories.

The categories in the quantity equation. Consider the fourfold classification in equation (3).

Transactions. The physical volume of transactions is denoted by T It is determined by the resources available to the economy, the efficiency with which they are used, the degree of integration or disintegration of the economy (which determines the number of transactions involved in the production and sale of final goods), and so on. These are the basic physical and operational characteristics of the economy. All quantity theorists, at least since Hume, have recognized that changes in the stock of money may have transitional effects on T. However, they have generally regarded the average level of T and long-run changes in T as largely independent of the quantity of money, although not of the existence of a money economy.

Price level The price level, which is the object of investigation, is denoted by P It has generally been regarded as the resultant of other forces rather than as itself having any important element of autonomy. Cost-push or profit-push theories of inflation treat it as being to some extent independently determined. Under a regime of widespread government price fixing, it clearly does have some measure of autonomy.

Stock of money. The stock of money in nominal units is denoted by M. Its precise definition, as noted before, has been the subject of much controversy. The transactions approach makes it seem natural to define money in terms of its function as a medium of exchange and to include only those means of payments generally acceptable in discharge of debts. Under a gold standard, specie was regarded as money par excellence, and questions were raised about extending the definition to include paper money and then demand deposits transferable by check. Today these would generally be included in the definitions, but there is much controversy about the treatment of other deposits, such as time deposits and savings deposits. On transactions lines, it is argued that such deposits cannot be used to discharge debts without first being converted into either currency or demand deposits. One answer to this argument is that it is also true of some items that all are willing to regard as money. For example, in the United States, \$10,000 is the largest denomination of currency. Such a currency note can be used to effectuate few transactions without first being converted into smaller denominations. No issue of principle is involved. However M is defined, equation (3) remains valid, provided V is appropriately defined. The issue is one of the usefulness of one or another definition. what definition of M will have the empirical property of rendering the forces determining the other symbols in the equation as nearly independent as possible of those determining M?

Whatever the precise definition of M, the factors determining it depend critically on the monetary system and are largely independent of the forces determining T Two main cases should be distinguished: a commodity standard, of which a gold standard is the most important historical example, and a fiduciary standard.

Under a gold standard the amount of money in the gold standard world is determined by the total existing amount of gold, the fraction used as money, and the institutional arrangements determining the superstructure of claims to gold, in the form of currency or deposits, that can be erected on any given stock of gold. Changes in the amount of money depend on costs of producing various quantities of gold, the demand for gold for nonmonetary purposes, and the financial arrangements for issuing fiduciary claims to gold. For any one country the situation is somewhat different: the quantity of money is a dependent rather than an independent variable. It must be whatever quantity is consistent with levels of prices and incomes that will maintain balance in its international payments. Gold inflows or outflows tend to keep it at that quantity.

Under a fiduciary standard the amount of money is ultimately under the control of the monetary authorities. In practice these authorities have always been governmental agencies. Although they have had the power to control the stock of money, they frequently have not stated their objectives in these terms but have let the stock of money be whatever was consistent with some alternative objective (e.g., given exchange rates or given interest rates).

Under either the gold or the fiduciary standard the factors determining M are connected only loosely, if at all, with those we have considered as affecting directly either P or T. It is precisely this clearly perceived independence of the factors determining the quantity of money that has rendered the quantity theory so attractive to economists.

Velocity of circulation. We now come to V, the velocity of circulation. This is the core of the quantity theory. It is determined by whatever factors affect, on the one hand, the amount of money people want to hold and, on the other, their ability to make their actual money balances equal their desired balances.

The transactions approach makes it natural to emphasize payment practices: the frequency with which people are paid, the irregularity of receipts and payments, and so on. However, such payment practices themselves seem to be largely explained by the willingness of people to hold money. For example, during periods of rapid inflation, when it is costly to hold money, pay periods consistently tend to become more frequent.

It is convenient to postpone a fuller consideration of the factors determining velocity until we discuss the post-Keynesian formulation in terms of the demand for money. Here it suffices to point out that Fisher and other earlier quantity theorists explicitly recognized that velocity would be affected by, among other factors, the rate of interest and also the rate of change of prices. They recognized that both high rates of interest and rapidly rising prices would give people an incentive to economize on money balances and so tend to raise velocity and that low rates of interest and falling prices would have the opposite effect. They were never guilty of the crude fallacy—with which critics have often charged them—of regarding velocity as something of a natural constant.

The quantity equation in income form. One difficulty with equations (3) and (4) is that the magnitudes designated "transactions" and the associated "general price level" proved conceptually ambiguous and difficult to measure with available data. Despite the large amount of empirical work done on these equations, notably by Fisher and Carl Snyder, these ambiguities and deficiencies of data have never been satisfactorily resolved. Should capital transfers, such as purchases and sales of real estate and securities, be included? What about gifts? Money-changing transactions? What is the relevant price and quantity in these transactions?

As noted before, the data on volume of transactions have been satisfactory only for transactions effected by check. For these, debits to bank accounts (or bank clearings) provide a statistically reliable total, although even then there are problems involved in separating out money-changing transactions. Average deposits give a statistically reliable estimate of M', so that estimates of V' can be and are readily calculated for frequent time intervals and for many different geographical areas. However, even for check transactions, there is no satisfactory way to break down the other side of the equation into price and quantity components.

With the development of national or social accounting, which has stressed income transactions rather than gross transactions and which has explicitly and satisfactorily dealt with the conceptual and statistical problems of distinguishing between changes in prices and changes in quantities, there has been a tendency to express the quantity equation in terms of income rather than of transactions. Let Y be money national income, P the price index implicit in estimating national income at constant prices, and y national income in constant prices, so that

$$Y = Py. \tag{5}$$

Let M represent, as before, the stock of money, but define V as the average number of times per year that the money stock is used in making *income* transactions (that is, payments for final productive services) rather than all transactions. We then can write the quantity equation in income form as

$$MV = Py. \tag{6}$$

Although the symbols P and V are used both in eqs. (5) and (6) and in eqs. (1) through (4), they stand for different concepts in each group.

Equation (6) is both conceptually and empirically more satisfactory than equation (3). Nonetheless, the earlier discussion of the fourfold classification implicit in the quantity equation applies, except for changes that are nearly self-evident, such as the very different relevance for y than for T of the degree of integration or disintegration of industry. Equation (6) is also closer in conception to the Cambridge approach, to which we now turn.

The Cambridge cash-balances approach

The essential feature of a money economy is that it enables the act of purchase to be separated from the act of sale. An individual who has something to exchange need not seek out the double coincidence—someone who both wants what he has and offers in exchange what he wants. He need only find someone who wants what he has, sell it to him for general purchasing power, and then find someone else who has what he wants and buy it with general purchasing power.

In order for the act of purchase to be separated from the act of sale, there must be something which can serve as a temporary abode of purchasing power in the interim. It is this aspect of money which is emphasized in the cash-balances approach.

How much money will people or enterprises want to hold for this purpose? As a first approximation we may suppose that the amount one wants to hold bears some relation to one's income, since that determines the volume of purchases and sales in which one is engaged. We then add up the cash balances held by all holders of money in the community and express the total as a fraction of their total income. We can then write

$$M = kPy, \tag{7}$$

where M, P, and y are defined as in equation (6) and k is the ratio of the money stock to income. We can regard k either as a constant so calculated as to make (7) an identity, or as the "desired" ratio, so that M is the "desired" amount of money, which need not be equal to the actual amount. In either case, k is clearly equal numerically to the reciprocal of the V of equation (6), the V in one case being interpreted as measured velocity and in the other as desired velocity.

Formally the Cambridge equation (7) is simply a transformation of Fisher's equation (6). Most writers who have used one of the two approaches regarded them in this way and tended to cover much the same ground. Yet to a far greater extent than is reflected in the writings of the early expositors, the two approaches stress different aspects of money, make different definitions of money seem natural, and lead to emphasis being placed on different variables and analytical techniques.

Consider the definition of money. The transactions approach makes it natural to define money in terms of whatever serves as the medium of exchange in discharging obligations. By stressing the function of money as a temporary abode of purchasing power the cash-balances approach makes it seem entirely appropriate to include also such stores of value as demand and time deposits not transferable by check, although it clearly does not require their inclusion.

Similarly, the transactions approach leads to stress being placed on such variables as payments practices, the financial and economic arrangements for effecting transactions, and the speed of communication and transportation as it affects the time required to make a payment—essentially, that is, to emphasis on the mechanical aspects of the payments process. The cash-balances approach, on the other hand, leads to stress being placed on variables affecting the usefulness of money as an asset: the costs and returns from holding money instead of other assets, the uncertainty of the future, and so on.

Stress on the first set of variables led most early writers—both those using the Fisher equation and those using the Cambridge equation—to predict that velocity would increase over time as a result of technological improvements in transportation and communication, which would facilitate the payments process. In fact, velocity has shown no tendency to rise over time. If anything it has rather tended to decline in economically progressive countries along with rises in real income, although this tendency is less pronounced when money is defined narrowly than when it is defined to include some deposits not transferable by check. The tendency for velocity to decline, along with the very size of money balances (equal in 1960 in the United States to about one month's income for currency outside banks alone, to nearly five months' income for currency plus adjusted demand deposits, and to about seven months' income for currency and all deposits at commercial banks) has contributed to a shift of emphasis from the function of money as a medium of exchange to its function as a temporary abode of purchasing power.

Finally, with regard to analytical techniques, the cash-balances approach fits in much more readily with the general Marshallian demand–supply apparatus than the transactions approach does. Equation (7) can be regarded as a demand function for money, with P and y on the right-hand side being two of the variables on which demand for money depends, and with k symbolizing all the other variables, so that k is to be regarded not as a numerical constant but as itself a function of still other variables. For completion the analysis requires another equation showing the supply of money as a function of other variables. The price level is then the resultant of the interaction of the demand and supply functions. From this point of view the quantity theory of money as embodied in equation (7) is a theory of the demand for money, not a theory of the price level or of money income.

The Keynesian attack

The Keynesian income–expenditure analysis developed in the *General Theory of Employment, Interest and Money* (1936) offered an alternative approach to the interpretation of changes in money income that emphasized the relation between money income and investment or autonomous expenditures rather than the relation between money income and the stock of money. The success of the Keynesian revolution in economic thought led to a temporary eclipse of the quantity theory of money and to perhaps an all-time low in the amount of economic research and writing devoted to monetary theory and analysis, narrowly interpreted. It became a widely accepted view that money does not matter, or, at any rate, that it does not matter very much, and that policy and theory alike should concentrate on investment, government fiscal policy, and the relation between consumer expenditures and income.

Keynes did not, of course, deny the validity of the quantity equation. What he did was something very different. He argued that *under conditions of underemployment equilibrium* the V in equation (6) and the k in equation (7) were highly unstable and would, for the most part, passively adapt to whatever changes independently occurred in money income or the stock of money. Hence, under such conditions these equations, although entirely valid, were largely useless for policy or prediction. Moreover, he regarded such conditions as prevailing much, if not most, of the time.

Keynes reached this conclusion by giving a highly specific form to equation (7). The quantity of money demanded, he argued, could be treated as if it were divided into two parts, one part, M_1, "held to satisfy the transactions- and precautionary-motives," the other, M_2, "held to satisfy the speculative-motive" (1936, p. 199). He regarded M_1 as a roughly constant fraction of income. He regarded the demand for M_2 as arising from "*uncertainty* as to the future course of the rate of interest" and the amount demanded as depending on the relation between current rates of interest and the rates of interest expected to prevail in the future. (Keynes, of course, emphasized that there was a whole complex of interest rates. However, for simplicity, he spoke in terms of "the rate of interest," usually meaning by that the rate on long-term securities that were fixed in nominal value and that involved minimal risks of default—for example, government bonds.) In a "given state of expectations," the higher the current rate of interest, the lower would be the (real) amount of money people would want to hold for speculative motives for two reasons: first, the greater would be the cost in terms of current earnings sacrificed by holding money instead of securities, and, second, the more likely it would be that interest rates would fall, and hence bond prices rise, and so the greater would be the cost in terms of capital gains sacrificed by holding money instead of securities.

Although expectations are given great prominence in developing the liquidity function expressing the demand for M_2, they do not enter explicitly into that function. For the most part, Keynes and his followers in practice treated the amount of M_2 demanded simply as a function of the current interest rate, the emphasis on expectations serving only as a reason for their attribution of instability to the liquidity function.

Except for somewhat different language, the analysis up to this point differs from that of earlier quantity theorists, such as Fisher, only by its subtle analysis of the role of expectations about future interest rates and its greater emphasis on current interest rates and by restricting more narrowly the variables explicitly considered as affecting the amount of money demanded.

Keynes's special twist concerned the empirical form of the liquidity-preference function at the low interest rates that he believed would prevail under conditions of underemployment equilibrium. Let the interest rate fall sufficiently low, he argued, and money and bonds would become perfect substitutes for one another, liquidity preference, as he put it, would become absolute. The liquidity-preference function, expressing the quantity of M_2 demanded as a function of the rate of interest, would become horizontal at some low but finite rate of interest. Under such circumstances, he held, if the amount of money is increased by whatever means, the holders of money might seek to convert the additional cash balances into bonds. This would, however, tend to lower the rate of return on bonds. Even the slightest lowering would, he argued, lead holders of money to desist from trying to convert it into bonds. The result would simply be that people would be willing to hold the increased quantity of money, k would be higher and V lower. Conversely, if the amount of money were decreased, holders of bonds would seek to convert them into money, but this would tend to raise the rate of interest, and even the slightest rise would reconcile them to holding the bonds instead of the money. Or, again, suppose there is an increase in money income for whatever reason. That will require an increase in M_1, which can come out of M_2 without any further effects. Conversely, any decline in M_1 can be added to M_2 without any further effects. The conclusion is that *under circumstances of absolute liquidity preference* income can change without a change in M and M can change without a change in income. The holders of money are in metastable equilibrium, like a tumbler on its side on a flat surface; they will be satisfied with whatever the amount of money happens to be.

Keynes regarded absolute liquidity preference as a strictly "limiting case" of which, though it "might become practically important in future," he knew "of no example . . . hitherto" (1936, p. 207). But, since he regarded interest rates as frequently being not far above the level at which liquidity preference would become absolute, he treated velocity as if in practice its behavior frequently approximated that which would prevail in this limiting case.

Keynes's disciples went much farther than Keynes himself. They were readier than he was to accept absolute liquidity preference as the actual state of affairs. More important, many argued that when liquidity preference was not absolute, changes in the quantity of money would affect only the interest rate on bonds and that changes in this interest rate in turn would have little further effect. They argued that both consumption expenditures and investment expenditures were nearly completely insensitive to changes in interest rates, so that a change in M would merely be offset by an opposite and compensatory change in V (or a change in the same direction in k), leaving P and y almost completely unaffected. In essence their argument consists in asserting that only paper securities are substitutes for money balances—that real assets never are (see Tobin 1961).

The issues raised for the quantity theory by the Keynesian analysis are clearly empirical rather than theoretical. Is it a fact that the quantity of money demanded is a function primarily of current income and of the rate of interest on fixed-money-value securities? Is it a fact that the amount demanded is highly elastic with respect to the rate of interest on such securities at a low but finite rate of interest? Is it a fact that expenditures are highly inelastic with respect to such a rate of interest? Or, to put the issue in an equivalent but more readily observable form, is it a fact that velocity is a highly unstable and unpredictable magnitude that generally varies in a direction opposite to that of the quantity of money?

The post-Keynesian reformulation

Experience with monetary policy after World War II very quickly produced a renewed interest in money and a renewed belief that money matters. Under the influence of Keynesian ideas, country after country followed an easy-money policy designed to keep interest rates low in order to stimulate, if only slightly, the investment regarded as needed to offset the shortage of demand that was universally feared. The result was an intensification of the strong inflationary pressure inherited from the war, a pressure that was brought under control only when countries undertook so-called orthodox measures to restrain the growth in the stock of money, as in Italy, beginning in August 1947, in Germany in June 1948, in the United States in March 1951, in Great Britain in November 1951, and in France in January 1960.

The effect of experience was reinforced by developments in economic theory, especially by the explicit analysis of the so-called real-balance effect as a channel through which changes in prices and in the quantity of money could affect income, even when investment and consumption were insensitive to changes in interest rates or when absolute liquidity preference prevented changes in interest rates (see Haberler 1937, Tobin 1947; Pigou 1943; 1947, Patinkin 1948).

Many economists continue to use Keynesian analysis but have revised their empirical presumptions. They grant that liquidity preference is not absolute and that investment does have a sizable elasticity with respect to interest rates. They continue, however, to regard analysis in terms of the quantity equation as less useful and meaningful than analysis in terms of autonomous expenditures and the multiplier, with monetary changes being taken into account as one factor among many that can affect these magnitudes.

The postwar period has also seen a return to analysis in terms of the quantity equation accompanied by a reformulation of the quantity theory that has been strongly affected by the Keynesian analysis of liquidity preference (Johnson 1962). The reformulation emphasizes the role of money as an asset and hence treats the demand for money as part of capital or wealth theory, concerned with the composition of the balance sheet or portfolio of assets.

From this point of view, it is important to distinguish between ultimate wealth-holders, to whom money is one form in which they choose to hold their wealth, and enterprises, to whom money is a producer's good like machinery or inventories.

Demand by ultimate wealth-holders. For ultimate wealth-holders the demand for money, in real terms, may be expected to be a function of the following variables.

(*a*) Total wealth. This is the analogue of the budget constraint in the usual theory of consumer choice. It is the total that must be divided among various forms of assets. In practice, estimates of total wealth are seldom available. Instead, income may serve as an index of wealth. However, it should be recognized that income as measured by statisticians may be a defective index of wealth because it is subject to erratic year-to-year fluctuations and that a longer term concept, like the concept of permanent income developed in connection with the theory of consumption, may be more useful. (Friedman 1957; 1959, p. 7; Meltzer 1963; Brunner & Meltzer 1963).

The emphasis on income as a surrogate for wealth, rather than as a measure of the "work" to be done by money, is conceptually perhaps the basic difference between the reformulation and the earlier versions of quantity theory.

(*b*) The division of wealth between human and nonhuman forms. The major asset of most wealth-holders is their personal earning capacity, but the conversion of human into nonhuman wealth or the reverse is subject to narrow limits because of institutional constraints. It can be done by using current earnings to purchase nonhuman wealth or by using nonhuman wealth to finance the acquisition of skills but not by purchase or sale and to only a limited extent by borrowing on the collateral of earning power. Hence, the fraction of total wealth that is in the form of nonhuman wealth may be an additional important variable.

(*c*) The expected rates of return on money and other assets. This is the analogue of the prices of a commodity and its substitutes and complements in the usual theory of consumer demand. The nominal rate of return on money may be zero, as it generally is on currency, or negative, as it sometimes is on demand deposits subject to net service charges, or positive, as it sometimes is on demand deposits on which interest is paid and generally is on time deposits. The nominal rate of return on other assets consists of two parts; first, any currently paid yield or cost, such as interest on bonds, dividends on equities, and storage costs on physical assets, and, second, changes in their nominal prices. The second part will, of course, be especially important under conditions of inflation or deflation.

(*d*) Other variables determining the utility attached to the services rendered by money relative to those rendered by other assets—in Keynesian terminology, determining the value attached to liquidity proper. One such variable may be one already considered—namely, real wealth or income, since the services rendered by money may in principle be regarded by wealth-holders as a "necessity," like bread, the consumption of which increases less than in proportion to any increase in income, or as a "luxury," like recreation, the consumption of which increases more than in proportion to any increase in income.

Another variable, one that is likely to be important empirically, is the degree of economic stability expected to prevail in the future. Wealth-holders are likely to attach considerably more value to liquidity when they expect economic conditions to be unstable than when they expect them to be highly stable. This variable is likely to be difficult to express quantitatively even though the direction of change may be clear from qualitative information. For example, the outbreak of war clearly produces expectations of instability, which is one reason why war is often accompanied by a notable increase in real balances—that is, a notable decline in velocity.

We can symbolize this analysis in terms of the following demand function for money for an individual wealth-holder:

$$\frac{M}{P} = f\left(y, w; r_m, r_b, r_e, \frac{1}{P}\frac{dP}{dt}; u\right), \tag{8}$$

where M, P, and y have the same meaning as in equation (7) except that they relate to a single wealth-holder; w is the fraction of wealth in nonhuman form (or, alternatively, the fraction of income derived from property), r_m is the expected rate of return on money; r_b is the expected rate of return on fixed-value securities, including expected changes in their prices, r_e is the expected rate of return on equities, including expected changes in their prices, $(1/P)(dP/dt)$ is the expected rate of change of prices of goods and hence the expected rate of return on real assets; and u is a portmanteau symbol standing for whatever variables other than income may affect the utility attached to the services of money. Each of the four rates of return stands, of course, for a set of rates of return, and for some purposes it may be important to classify assets still more finely—for example, to distinguish currency from deposits, long-term from short-term fixed-value securities, risky from relatively safe equities, and different kinds of physical assets from one another.

The usual problems of aggregation arise in passing from equation (8) to a corresponding equation for the economy as a whole—in particular, they arise from the possibility that the amount of money demanded may depend on the distribution of such variables as y and w and not merely on their aggregate or average value. If we neglect these distributional effects, (8) can be regarded as applying to the community as a whole, with M and y referring to per capita money holdings and per capita real income, respectively, and w to the fraction of aggregate wealth in nonhuman form.

The major problems that arise in practice in applying (8) are the precise definitions of y and w, the estimation of *expected* rates of return as contrasted with actual rates of return, and the quantitative specification of the variables designated by u.

Demand by business enterprises. Business enterprises are not subject to a constraint comparable to that imposed by the total wealth of the ultimate wealth-holder. The total amount of capital embodied in productive assets, including money, is a variable that can be determined by the enterprise to maximize returns, since it can acquire additional capital through the capital market. Hence, there is no reason on this ground to include total wealth, or y as a surrogate for total wealth, as a variable in their demand function for money.

It may, however, be desirable to include a somewhat similar variable defining the "scale" of the enterprise on different grounds—namely, as an index of the productive value of different quantities of money to the enterprise. This is more nearly in line with the earlier transactions approach emphasizing the "work" to be done by money. It is by no means clear what the appropriate variable is: total transactions, net value added, net income, total capital in nonmoney form, or net worth. The lack of availability of data has meant that much less empirical work has been done on the business demand for money than on an aggregate demand curve encompassing both ultimate wealth-holders and business enterprises. As a result there are as yet only faint indications about the best variable to use.

The division of wealth between human and nonhuman form has no special relevance to business enterprises, since they are likely to buy the services of both forms on the market.

Rates of return on money and on alternative assets are, of course, highly relevant to business enterprises. These rates determine the net cost to them of holding the money balances. However, the particular rates that are relevant may be quite different from those that are relevant for ultimate wealth-holders. For example, rates charged by banks on loans are of minor importance for wealth-holders yet may be extremely important for businesses, since bank loans may be a way in which they can acquire the capital embodied in money balances.

The counterpart for business enterprises of the variable u in (8) is the set of variables other than scale affecting the productivity of money balances. At least one of these—namely, expectations about economic stability—is likely to be common to business enterprises and ultimate wealth-holders.

With these interpretations of the variables, equation (8), with w excluded, can be regarded as symbolizing the business demand for money and, as it stands, symbolizing aggregate demand for money, although with even more serious qualifications about the ambiguities introduced by aggregation.

The process of adjustment. Emphasis on the role of money as a component of wealth is important because of the variables to which it directs attention. It is important also for its implications about the process of adjustment to a difference between actual and desired stocks of money. Any such discrepancy is a disturbance in a balance sheet. As such it can be corrected in either of two ways: by a rearrangement of assets and liabilities through purchase, sale, borrowing, and lending or by the use of current flows of income and expenditure to add to or subtract from some assets and liabilities. The Keynesian liquidity-preference analysis stressed the first and, in its most rigid form, only one specific rearrangement: that between money and bonds. The earlier quantity theory stressed the second to the almost complete exclusion of the first. The reformulation enforces consideration of both.

The process of adjustment is important in particular for its implications about the time that readjustment may be expected to take. Balance-sheet adjustments can in general be expected to take considerable time, especially when they take the form of adjustments through alterations in flows and especially when they concern the money balance, M, whose function is precisely that of serving as a temporary abode of purchasing power, thereby permitting purchases to be separated from sales.

It is plausible that any widespread disturbance in money balances—through, say, an unanticipated increase or decrease in the quantity of money by the actions of monetary authorities—will initially be met by an attempted readjustment of assets and liabilities through purchase or sale. But such attempted readjustments will alter the prices of assets and liabilities, leading to the spread of the adjustment from one asset or liability to another. Such changes in prices will also alter the relative prices of capital items and the services they yield and so establish incentives to alter flows of receipts and expenditures. If the monetary change has altered the total nominal value of wealth, not simply its composition, this will introduce an additional reason to change flows. The effect of any monetary disturbance will thus spread in ever-widening ripples, and some of its most important effects may not be manifest for many months after the initial disturbance.

Empirical evidence

Empirical evidence about the relation between changes in the quantity of money and in prices, although it was sufficiently extensive to produce a widespread belief in the quantity theory, has seldom been systematically collated and organized. Until modern times, money was mostly metallic—copper, brass, silver, gold. The most notable changes in its nominal quantity under such circumstances were produced by sweating and clipping, by governmental edicts changing the nominal values attached to specified physical quantities of the metal, or by great discoveries of new sources of specie. Economic history is replete with examples of the first two and their coincidence with corresponding changes in nominal prices (see Cipolla 1956, Feavearyear 1931). The most important example of the third is the great specie discoveries in the New World in the sixteenth century. The association between this increase in the quantity of money and the price revolution of the sixteenth and seventeenth centuries has been well documented (see Hamilton 1934).

The nineteenth and early twentieth centuries offer another striking example, despite the much greater development of deposit money and paper money. The gold discoveries in Australia and the United States in the 1840s were followed by substantial price rises in the 1850s. When the rate of growth of the gold stock slowed down, and especially when country after country shifted from silver to gold (Germany in 1871–1873, the Latin Monetary Union in 1873, the Netherlands in 1875–1876) or returned to gold (the United States in 1879), world prices in terms of gold fell slowly but fairly steadily for about three decades. New gold discoveries in the 1880s and 1890s, powerfully reinforced by the development of improved methods of mining and refining, particularly the development of commercially feasible methods of using the cyanide process to extract gold from low-grade ore, reversed the trend. The world gold stock started to grow at a much more rapid rate, and no additional important countries shifted to gold, so there was no increase in demand from this source. The price trend also reversed itself. From the mid-1890s to 1914, world prices in terms of gold rose by 25 to 50 per cent, depending on the index used.

Evidence from great inflations. The most dramatic evidence about the role of the quantity of money comes from periods of great monetary disturbances, and among these the most striking are the periods of extremely rapid price rise, such as the hyperinflations after World War I in Germany, Austria, and Russia, those after World War II in Hungary and Greece, and the rapid rises, if not hyperinflations, in many South American and some other countries both before and after World War II. These twentieth-century episodes have been rather more systematically studied than earlier ones. The studies demonstrate almost conclusively the critical role of changes in the quantity of money (the most important study is Cagan 1956).

These studies also enable us to sketch with considerable accuracy a rather typical profile of an inflation that follows a period of fairly stable prices. The inflation often has its start in a period of war, but it need not. What is important is that something, generally the financing of extraordinary governmental expenditures, produces a much more rapid rate of growth of the money stock. Prices start to rise, but at a slower pace than the money stock, so that for a time the real stock of money increases. The reason for this is twofold. First, it takes time for people to readjust their money balances. Second, initially there is a general expectation that what goes up will come down, that the rise in prices is temporary and will be followed by a decline. Such expectations make money seem to be a desirable form in which to hold assets, and therefore they lead to an increase in desired money balances in real terms.

As prices continue to rise, expectations are revised. People come to expect prices to continue to rise. Desired balances decline. People also take more active measures to eliminate the discrepancy between actual and desired balances. The result is that prices start to rise faster than the stock of money, and real balances start to decline (that is, velocity starts to rise). How far this process continues depends on the rate of rise in the stock of money. If it remains fairly stable, real balances settle down to a level that is lower than the initial level but roughly constant—for a constant expected rate of rise in prices there will be a roughly constant level of desired real balances, in this case, prices ultimately rise at the same rate as the stock of money. A decline in the rate of rise in the stock of money is followed by a decline in the rate of rise in prices, and this is followed in turn by an increase in actual and desired real balances as people readjust their expectations, the converse also holds. The result is that once the process is in full swing, changes in real balances follow with a lag changes in the rate of change of the stock of money. The lag reflects the fact that people apparently base their expectations of future rates of price change on an average of experience over the preceding several years, the period of averaging being shorter the more rapid the inflation.

In the extreme cases, those which have degenerated into hyperinflation and a complete breakdown of the medium of exchange, rates of price change have been so high and real balances have been driven down so low as to lead to the widespread introduction of substitute moneys, usually foreign currencies. At that point completely new monetary systems have had to be introduced.

A similar phenomenon has occurred when inflation has been effectively suppressed by price controls, so that there is a substantial gap between the prices that would prevail in the absence of controls and the legally permitted prices This gap prevents money from functioning as an effective medium of exchange and also leads to the introduction of substitute moneys, sometimes rather bizarre ones like the cigarettes and cognac used in post-World War II Germany.

Evidence from the United States. Recent studies of the monetary history of the United States provide an especially full documentation of monetary relations (see especially Friedman & Schwartz 1963*a*). Some of the salient findings may be summarized briefly.

(*a*) The real stock of money, expressed in terms of months of income, has risen from about 3½ months' income at the end of the Civil War in 1865 to over 7 months' income by 1960—that is, velocity has fallen (money is defined as currency held by the public plus all adjusted deposits in commercial banks, income is defined as net national product). One interpretation of this trend is that the rise in real balances reflects the contemporaneous rise in real income per capita. From the end of World War II to almost 1960, velocity rose rather than fell. It is not yet clear whether this was a temporary interruption or a change of trend.

(*b*) If allowance is made for the trend in velocity, there has been a very close connection between the stock of money per unit of output and prices. This is brought out clearly by Figure 1, which, to eliminate short-period fluctuations, plots the average stock of money per unit of output and average prices in successive reference-cycle phases.

(*c*) In the course of business cycles the stock of money has slowed up its rate of growth well before the date designated by National Bureau of Economic Research reference-cycle dates as the peak of the cycle and has increased its rate of growth well before the trough. In mild contractions these decelerations have generally produced not an absolute decline in the stock of money but only a lower rate of growth. Every severe contraction has been accompanied by an absolute decline in the stock of money, and the severity of the contrac-

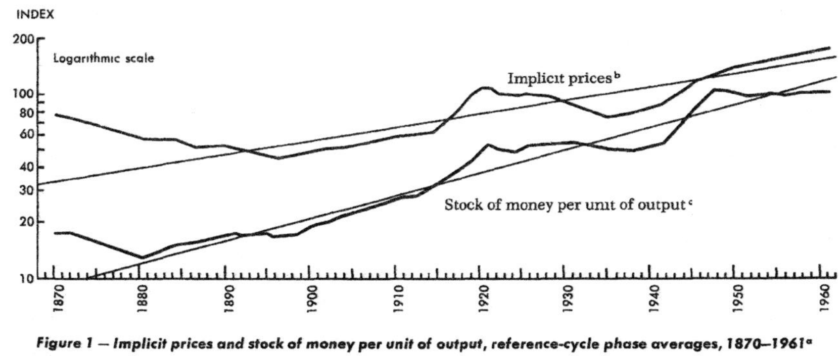

Figure 1 — Implicit prices and stock of money per unit of output, reference-cycle phase averages, 1870–1961[a]

a. A phase is the trough-to-peak or peak-to-trough interval between reference-cycle turning points (For a discussion of reference cycles, see Moore 1961) Phase averages are computed by weighting initial and terminal years each at one-half and intervening years at unity The trend lines are computed regressions based on phase-average values, 1882–1961

b The index of implicit prices is based on 1929 = 100. For the underlying figures, see Friedman and Schwartz (1963*a*, chart 62).

c. Stock of money per unit of output is the ratio of the money stock to real income, expressed as an index. For the underlying figures, see Friedman and Schwartz (1963*a*, table A-1, col. 8, and source notes to chart 62).

tion has been in roughly the same order as the size of the decline in the stock of money. Although changes in the rate of growth of the stock of money have to some extent reflected the contemporaneous course of business, on many occasions they have quite clearly been the result of independent forces, such as the deliberate decisions of monetary authorities. The clearest examples are probably the wartime increases and the decreases from 1920 to 1921, 1929 to 1933, and 1937 to 1938.

(*d*) Velocity as usually measured has tended to rise during business expansions and decline during business contractions. One explanation offered is that this pattern reflects the use of measured income in computing velocity rather than a longer term concept, such as permanent income (Friedman 1959). Another explanation offered is that it reflects the effect of interest rates.

(*e*) It is agreed that velocity is related to interest rates, higher interest rates being associated with higher velocity, and conversely, but there is wide disagreement about the magnitude and significance of the relation. One view is that changes in interest rates are either the primary or a major source of all cyclical and secular changes in velocity (Latané 1954, 1960, Brunner & Meltzer 1963). Another view is that changes in interest rates have been a minor factor, much less important than changes in real per capita income for secular changes in velocity and much less important than differences between measured and permanent income for cyclical changes (Friedman 1959, Friedman & Schwartz 1963*a*).

Evidence from underdeveloped countries. A few scattered figures for some of the less developed countries may help to indicate the broad range of applicability of the quantity theory of money.

Real balances of currency. In less developed countries, currency is often a more meaningful total than currency plus deposits for two reasons. One is that deposits are often used to a very limited extent and by highly selected groups in the population. The other is that governmental monetary intervention is more frequent and more important with respect to deposits, so that an erratic element is introduced into the conditions of supply of deposits.

Table 1 gives estimates for a recent year of the stock of currency expressed in number of weeks of personal disposable income for less developed countries and, for comparison, for the United States. These figures are subject to very wide margins of error, particularly because of the unreliability of income estimates for the less developed countries. It is, therefore, all the more striking that for countries for which methods of economic organization vary so greatly and for which real income per capita must vary over a range of something well in excess of 20 to 1, real balances vary over a range of decidedly less than 2 to 1. And much of that variation is readily explained by different degrees of financial development: deposits are least widely used in India, Greece, and Yugoslavia, most widely used in Israel and the United States, and used to an intermediate extent in Turkey. Clearly, money-holding propensities have a great degree of uniformity under a wide range of circumstances.

Table 1 — International comparison of real balances

	Year	Number of weeks of personal disposable income held in currency
India	1958–1959	6.9
Greece	1960	6.3
Yugoslavia	1960	6 2
Turkey	1961	5 2
Israel	1961	4.4
United States	1960	4.3

Changes in quantity of money and in prices. If data like those in Table 1 are of questionable accuracy, year-to-year data are even more dubious for the underdeveloped countries. A recent study that was confined to the Middle East shows a variety of relations. In Egypt and Turkey the data for wholesale prices show the kind of close relationship between money supply and price changes that other experiences would lead one to expect. For the other countries the relation is loose or nonexistent (Penrose 1962). Rises in output may explain some part of the discrepancy. Much more likely explanations are the following: (*a*) The inclusion of rapidly expanding deposits whose significance is questionable. Currency figures alone show much less of a discrepancy. (*b*) Major defects in the price indexes. The countries have sought to suppress price increases, often have legal prices that are honored more in the breach than in the observance, and calculate price indexes in ways that understate the actual price rise. It is highly likely that revised and improved figures will remove much of the apparent discrepancy.

Stability of velocity and the multiplier. As pointed out above, the challenge to the quantity theory offered by Keynes rested entirely on differences in empirical presumptions, which can be summarized in terms of the stability attributed to the velocity of circulation, on the one hand, and the Keynesian multiplier (the ratio of changes in income to changes in autonomous expenditures), on the other.

A systematic comparison of the relative stability of velocity and the multiplier has been made for the United States from 1896 to 1958 (Friedman & Meiselman 1964*a*; 1964*b*, 1965). The results are striking: velocity is consistently more stable than the multiplier. These results have been challenged by other writers (Hester 1964, Ando & Modigliani 1965, DePrano & Mayer 1965), showing that this question is still far from settled.

Policy implications

On a very general level the implications of the quantity theory for economic policy are straightforward and clear. On a more precise and detailed level they are not.

Acceptance of the quantity theory clearly means that the stock of money is a key variable in policies directed at the control of the level of prices or of money income. Inflation can be prevented if and only if the stock of money per unit of output can be kept from increasing appreciably. Deflation can be prevented if and only if the stock of money per unit of output can be kept from decreasing appreciably. This implication is by no means a trivial one. Monetary authorities have more frequently than not taken conditions in the credit market—rates of interest, availability of loans, and so on—as criteria of policy and have paid little or no attention to the stock of money per se. This emphasis on credit as opposed to monetary policy accounts both for the great depression in the United States from 1929 to 1933, when the Federal Reserve System allowed the stock of money to decline by one-third, and for many of the post-World War II inflations.

The quantity theory has no such clear implication, even on this general level, about policies concerned with the growth of real income. Both inflation and deflation have proved consistent with growth, stagnation, or decline.

Passing from these general and vague statements to specific prescriptions for policy is difficult. It is tempting to conclude from the close average relation between changes in the stock of money and changes in money income that control over the stock of money can be used as a precision instrument for offsetting other forces making for instability in money income. Unfortunately there are many slips between this cup and this lip.

One slip is that a very close relationship *on the average* is consistent with much variation in the individual instance. A high correlation between changes relative to trend in the stock of money and in money income over many business cycles—involving, say, an average increase of 2 per cent in money income for every 1 per cent increase in money—is entirely consistent with the corresponding ratio varying in individual years or over single cycles from zero or a negative number to, say, 4 or 5 But for policy in a particular cycle, what is important is the relation in that cycle, not the relation on the average.

A second slip is the length of time it takes for changes in the stock of money to have their effect—this is one of the reasons for the variability that constitutes the first slip. A change in the stock of money today will have most of its effects some months from now, perhaps on the average as much as 12 to 15 months from now. A policy of using monetary changes to offset other forces making for instability therefore requires an ability to forecast a considerable time in advance what those forces will be—an ability that has so far been conspicuous by its absence. Moreover, the time it takes for monetary changes to be effective undoubtedly varies rather considerably. Hence it would also be necessary to forecast how long the lag would be in the specific instance.

These two slips mean that monetary changes intended to be stabilizing may in fact be destabilizing, they may introduce a random and erratic influence into economic affairs. It is a sobering thought that both the stock of money and economic activity displayed greater instability in the first two peacetime decades after the establishment of the Federal Reserve System (1919 to 1939) than in any other pair of decades in the whole of United States history. The blind, quasi-automatic forces that controlled monetary matters in earlier decades produced a higher degree of stability than a system specifically established to promote monetary and economic stability. The greater stability of prices and employment since the end of World War II may be a sign that we have learned how to avoid the mistakes of the interwar decades, but it is much too soon to have any confidence in that comfortable conclusion.

Other slips have to do with the indirect effects of methods used to control the stock of money; with possible conflicts between the objective of stable prices and such other objectives as stable exchange rates, stable employment at a high level, and low interest rates on government borrowing; and with the possible desire to use inflation as a means of imposing a tax on money balances.

One negative implication of the quantity theory, implicit in the above, is worth spelling out because of the continued widespread acceptance of the belief that fiscal policy is the key to control of the level of money income. The quantity theory implies that the effect of government deficits or surpluses depends critically on how they are financed. If a deficit is financed by borrowing from the public without an increase in the quantity of money, the direct expansionary effect of the excess of government spending over receipts will be offset to some extent, and possibly to a very great extent, by the indirect contractionary effect of the transfer of funds to the government through borrowing. Furthermore, the deficit will primarily affect income only while it lasts, a cessation of the deficit will mean a cessation of its effects. If a deficit is financed by printing money, there will be no offset, and the enlarged stock of money will continue to exert an effect after the deficit is terminated. What matters most is the behavior of the stock of money, and government deficits are expansionary primarily if they serve as the means of increasing the stock of money; other means of increasing the stock of money will have closely similar effects.

MILTON FRIEDMAN

'The Chicago Tradition, the Quantity Theory and Friedman'

D. Patinkin, 'The Chicago Tradition, the Quantity Theory and Friedman' (1969), reprinted in Patinkin, *Essays on and in the Chicago Tradition* (Durham, North Carolina, Duke UP, 1981), pp. 241–74.

10. The Chicago Tradition, the Quantity Theory, and Friedman*[1]

I must begin this paper with an apology for being over a decade late; for I should have written it as an immediate reaction to Milton Friedman's by now well-known 1956 essay on "The Quantity Theory of Money—A Restatement." [2, 3] But the recent appearance of Friedman's *International Encyclopedia* article on the quantity theory[4] (though, as will be shown in Part IV below, it differs significantly in its doctrinal aspects from the earlier paper) provides an appropriate, if tardy, occasion to raise some basic questions—from the viewpoint of the history of monetary doctrine—about the validity of Friedman's interpretation of the quantity theory of money, and of its Chicago version in particular.

Reprinted by permission from *Journal of Money, Credit and Banking*, Vol. 1 (February 1969), 46–70. Appears here with the minor modifications and additions with which it was reprinted in my *Studies in Monetary Economics*, New York, 1972.

*This paper was written during 1968 while I was visiting at M.I.T. under a research grant from the National Science Foundation (NSF Grant GS 1812). I am grateful to both institutions for making this work possible.

I am happy to express my deep appreciation to Mr. Stanley Fischer of M.I.T. for his invaluable assistance at all stages of the preparation of this paper—and particularly in the examination of the relevant literature. In addition, I have benefited from discussions with him and from his criticisms of earlier drafts.

I am also indebted to my Jerusalem colleagues Yosef Attiyeh, Yoram Ben-Porath, and Giora Hanoch whose thoughtful suggestions have greatly improved the general organization of this paper, as well as the discussion of specific points.

As usual, it is a pleasure to thank Miss Susanne Freund for her careful and conscientious checking of the final manuscript and its references.

Because of its concern with historical questions, this paper refers to reprinted works by the date of original publication; for convenience, however, the page references themselves follow the pagination of the reprinted form as indicated in the bibliography.

Needless to say, responsibility for the interpretations and views presented in this paper remain entirely my own.

1. I would like to dedicate this paper to the memory of Miguel Sidrauski. His untimely death in August 1968 was a great loss, not only to his family and friends, but to the economics profession in general—and particularly to the development of monetary theory. Though I do not think Miguel had a strong interest in the history of doctrine, I hope that—as a Chicago graduate—he would have been interested in reading the final product of a work whose beginnings he witnessed.

2. In *Studies in the Quantity Theory of Money*, ed. M. Friedman (1956), pp. 3–21.; referred to henceforth as "Quantity Theory I."

3. In self-defense, I might, however, note that I have on previous occasions discussed in passing some of the points presented below—and have also emphasized the Keynesian nature of Friedman's essay. Thus see my "Indirect-Utility Approach to the Theory of Money, Assets, and Savings" (1965a), p. 54, note 5 (this is the proceedings volume of an International Economic Association Conference held at Royaumont in March 1962); and *Money, Interest, and Prices*, 2nd ed. (1965b), p. 81, note 8. See also the implicit criticism contained in my *International Encyclopedia* article on "Interest" (1968), p. 480b. See also below, p. 255.

4. "Money: Quantity Theory" in (1968), pp. 432–47; referred to henceforth as "Quantity Theory II."

The argument of the present paper is as follows: In both of the foregoing articles, Friedman presents what he calls a "reformulation of the quantity theory of money." In Part IV, I shall show that this is a misleading designation and that what Friedman has actually presented is an elegant exposition of the modern portfolio approach to the demand for money which, though it has some well-known (albeit largely undeveloped) antecedents in the traditional theory, can only be seen as a continuation of the Keynesian theory of liquidity preference.

The main purpose of this paper, however, is to describe (in Parts II and III) the true nature of the Chicago monetary tradition. In this way I shall also demonstrate the invalidity of Friedman's contention (in his 1956 essay) that this tradition is represented by his "reformulation of the quantity theory." As a minimum statement let me say that though I shared with Friedman—albeit, almost a decade later—the teachers at Chicago whom he mentions (namely, Knight, Viner, Simons, and Mints), his description of the "flavor of the oral tradition" which they were supposed to have imparted strikes no responsive chord in my memory.

Friedman offers no supporting evidence for his interpretation of the Chicago tradition. This is unfortunate. For questions about the history of economic doctrine are empirical questions. And the universe from which the relevant empirical evidence must be drawn is that of the writings and teachings of the economists in question. No operational meaning can be attached to the existence of a "tradition" which does not manifest itself in at least one of these ways.

From this it will be clear that my examination of this evidence in what follows should not be interpreted as a criticism of the individuals involved. On the contrary, I would consider it unjustified to criticize them for not having fully understood and integrated into their thinking what we have succeeded in learning only in the course of the subsequent development of Keynesian monetary theory. My quarrel is only with those who imply that such an understanding and integration existed before, or independently of, this development.

I would like finally to emphasize that my concern in this chapter is with the analytical framework of the Chicago monetary tradition, and not with its policy proposals as such. Correspondingly, I shall not—except incidentally—discuss the relation between these proposals and those of Friedman. Let me, however, note that though there are, of course, basic similarities, there are also significant differences—particularly about the degree of discretion to be exercised by the monetary authorities.[5]

5. This will become clear from a comparison of Friedman's policy (namely, expanding the quantity of money at a constant rate) with the contracyclical monetary policy advocated by Simons and Mints (see Propositions (4) and (5) on p 246 below; see also p. 247 and especially fn. 19). One might also note Jacob Viner's criticism of Friedman's policy proposals in his (Viner's) "The Necessary and the Desirable Range of Discretion to be Allowed to a Monetary Authority" (1962), pp. 244–74.

Friedman himself discusses some of these differences explicitly in his paper on Simons referred to in fn. 22 below—and implicitly in his *Program for Monetary Stability* (1960), pp. 86–90. See also M. Bronfenbrenner, "Observations on the 'Chicago School(s)' " (1962), pp. 72–73.

Another interesting question which lies beyond the scope of the present paper is the extent to which the policy views of the Chicago school in the 1930s represented those of other quantity theorists of the period. {See next chapter.}

I. Friedman's Chicago

Friedman begins his 1956 essay with the explanation that (1956, pp. 3–4):

> Chicago was one of the few academic centers at which the quantity theory continued to be a central and vigorous part of the oral tradition throughout the 1930's and 1940's, where students continued to study monetary theory and to write theses on monetary problems. The quantity theory that retained this role differed sharply from the atrophied and rigid caricature that is so frequently described by the proponents of the new income-expenditure approach—and with some justice, to judge by much of the literature on policy that was spawned by quantity theorists. At Chicago, Henry Simons and Lloyd Mints directly, Frank Knight and Jacob Viner at one remove, taught and developed a more subtle and relevant version, one in which the quantity theory was connected and integrated with general price theory and became a flexible and sensitive tool for interpreting movements in aggregate economic activity and for developing relevant policy prescriptions.
>
> To the best of my knowledge, no systematic statement of this theory as developed at Chicago exists, though much can be read between the lines of Simons' and Mints' writings. . . . It was a theoretical approach that insisted that money does matter. . . .
>
> The purpose of this introduction is not to enshrine—or, should I say, inter—a definitive version of the Chicago tradition. . . . The purpose is rather to set down a particular "model" of a quantity theory in an attempt to convey the flavor of the oral tradition. . . .

Friedman then goes on to present this model. Since I am interested only in the doctrinal aspects of the question, it is sufficient to cite the model's basic features. In Friedman's words (1956, p. 4, italics in original):

> 1. The quantity theory is in the first instance a theory of the *demand* for money. It is not a theory of output, or of money income, or of the price level. Any statement about these variables requires combining the quantity theory with some specifications about the conditions of supply of money and perhaps about other variables as well.
> 2. To the ultimate wealth-owning units in the economy, money is one kind of asset, one way of holding wealth. . . .
> 3. The analysis of the demand for money on the part of the ultimate wealth-owning units in the society can be made formally identical with that of the demand for a consumption service. As in the usual theory of consumer choice, the demand for money (or any other particular asset) depends on three major sets of factors: (a) the total wealth to be held in various forms—the analogue of the budget restraint; (b) the price of and return on this form of wealth and alternative forms; and (c) the tastes and preferences of the wealth-owning units.

From these and other considerations Friedman arrives at a demand function for money of the form

$$M = g\left(P, r_b, r_e, \frac{1}{P}\frac{dP}{dt}, w, Y; u\right), \tag{1}$$

where M is the nominal quantity of money; P, the price level; r_b is the interest rate on bonds; r_e, the interest rate on equities; $(1/P)\,(dP/dt)$, the rate of change of prices—and hence the negative of the rate of return on money balances; w, the ratio of nonhuman to human wealth; Y, money income; and u, "variables that can be expected to affect tastes and preferences."[6] Friedman then makes the familiar assumption that this function is homogeneous of degree one in P and Y, and hence rewrites it as (1956, p. 11, equation 11):

$$\frac{M}{P} = f\left(r_b, r_e, \frac{1}{P}\frac{dP}{dt}, w; \frac{Y}{P}; u\right). \tag{2}$$

Alternatively, dividing (1) through by Y, he obtains

$$Y = v\left(r_b, r_e, \frac{1}{P}\frac{dP}{dt}, w, \frac{Y}{P}; u\right) \cdot M. \tag{3}$$

"In this form the equation is in the usual quantity theory form, where v is income velocity" (1956, p. 11).

As an aside, I might note that at no point in the foregoing exposition does Friedman mention the name of Keynes. Indeed, one cannot escape the impression that even the term "liquidity" is being avoided.[7]

Friedman does recognize that "almost every economist will accept the general lines of the preceding analysis on a purely formal and abstract level." But Friedman defines three distinguishing features of the quantity theorist, of which the first is that the quantity theorist

> accepts the empirical hypothesis that the demand for money is highly stable. . . . The quantity theorist need not, and generally does not, mean that the . . . velocity of circulation of money is to be regarded as numerically constant over time. . . . For the stability he expects is in the functional relation between the quantity of money demanded and the variables that determine it. . . .

The other two features are that the quantity theorist believes that "there are important factors affecting the supply of money that do not affect the demand for money" and that the demand for money does not become infinitely elastic (viz., absence of a "liquidity trap") (1956, pp. 15–16).

There is no question that these last two features are generally found (either explicitly or implicitly) in presentations of the quantity theory. But it is equally clear to me that the first—which is crucial to Friedman's interpretation—is not. Correspondingly, one of the basic points that will be examined in the following discussion

6. Friedman (1956), pp. 4–10; the quotation is from p. 9.

7. Cf., e.g., *ibid.*, pp. 5, 14, and 19.

of the Chicago economists is whether they did indeed think in terms of a stable velocity in Friedman's functional sense.

II. The Other Chicago

As against the foregoing, let me now describe a Chicago tradition of monetary theory whose approach, contents, and language can be represented by the following summary-propositions.[8]

1. The quantity theory is, first and foremost, not a theory of the demand for money, but a theory which relates the quantity of money (*M*) to the aggregate demand for goods and services (*MV*), and thence to the price level (*P*) and/or level of output (*T*); all this in accordance with Fisher's $MV = PT$.

2. *V* is not constant; on the contrary, a basic feature of economic life is the "danger of sharp changes on the velocity side"; or in other words, the danger "of extreme alternations of hoarding and dishoarding." [9] These "sharp changes" in turn are due to anticipations of changing price levels, as well as to the changing state of business confidence as determined by earnings.[10] Thus if individuals expect prices to rise and earnings to be good, they will dishoard—that is, increase the velocity of circulation. But the crucial point here is that these expectations will be self-justifying: for the very act of dishoarding will cause prices to rise even further, thus leading to further dishoarding, and so on. In this way a "cumulative process" of expansion is set into operation which "feeds upon itself" and which has no "natural" limit.[11] Conversely, an indefinite "cumulative process" of hoarding, price declines and depression, and further hoarding is set into operation by the expectation that the price level will fall and/or that earnings will be poor. Thus the economic system is essentially unstable.[12]

3. Such a cumulative process might possibly take place—albeit in a much less severe form—even if the quantity of money in the economy were to remain constant.[13] In the actual world, however, the process is highly exacerbated by the

8. The following is primarily a summary of Simons' views, which were largely accepted by Mints. Knight's analysis is the same, though—quite characteristically—he seems to have had less faith than did Simons and Mints in the policy proposals. For Viner, I have been able to find clear evidence only on the first proposition. Nevertheless, Viner (together with his colleagues) did advocate government deficit financing as a means of combating unemployment.

For references to the relevant writings of the foregoing (as well as further comments on Viner's position) see Appendix I below. Cf. also J. R. Davis, "Chicago Economists, Deficit Budgets, and the Early 1930s" (1968), pp. 476–82.

9. Simons, "Rule versus Authorities in Monetary Policy" (1936), p. 164 (this passage is cited in full in Appendix I below). That by "hoarding and dishoarding" Simons means changes in velocity is clear from p. 165; see also the reference cited in the next footnote.

10. See Simons, "Banking and Currency Reform" (1933), as quoted in Appendix I below

11 Knight, "The Business Cycle, Interest, and Money: A Methodological Approach" (1941), pp. 210–11, 223–24.

12. See Appendix I for supporting quotations from Simons, *Personal Income Taxation* (1938), p 222, and "Hansen on Fiscal Policy" (1942), p. 188, and from Knight's "The Business Cycle, Interest, and Money" (1941), pp. 211 and 224.

13. See the quotation from Simons, "Rules versus Authorities in Monetary Policy" (1936) p 164, reproduced in Appendix I below. See also *ibid.*, p. 331, footnote 16, and Mints, *Monetary Policy for a Competitive Society* (1950), pp. 120–22.

"perverse" behavior of the banking system, which expands credit in booms and contracts it in depressions. As a result the quantity of money (*M*) and near-moneys (and hence *V*) increases in booms, and decreases in depressions.

4. In accordance with (2) and (3), the government has an obligation to undertake a contracyclical policy. The guiding principle of this policy is to change *M* so as to offset changes in *V*, and thus generate the full-employment level of aggregate demand *MV*. If prices are downwardly flexible, the operational rule which will assure the proper variation in *M* is that of increasing *M* when *P* falls, and decreasing it when *P* rises. In any event, it is "inconceivable" that a sufficiently vigorous policy of (say) expanding *M* in a period of depression would not ultimately affect aggregate spending in the required manner.

5. The necessary variations in *M* can be generated either by open-market operations or by budgetary deficits. The latter method is more efficient, and in some cases might even be necessary. Budgetary deficits, in turn, can be generated by varying either government expenditures or tax receipts. From the viewpoint of contracyclical policy, this makes no difference—for either method changes *M*; but from the viewpoint of the general philosophy of the proper role of government in economic life, the variation of tax receipts is definitely preferable. Hence, a tax system which depends heavily on the income tax is desirable not only from the viewpoint of distributive justice, but also from the viewpoint of automatically providing proper cyclical variations in tax receipts.

Before going on to bring out the flavor of these propositions as contrasted with that of Friedman's presentation, I would like briefly to indicate three reasons for the emphasis I have given in the foregoing to the writings of Simons. First, at the Chicago which concerns us, Simons was undoubtedly the dominant figure in discussions of monetary and fiscal policy. (In Friedman's presentation too there is more emphasis on the writings of Simons and Mints than on those of Knight and Viner.) Second, Simons' writings on these questions were the earliest by far of the writers here considered. And, third, they were sufficiently early to represent the Chicago tradition in its pristine—and pre-Keynesian—form.

The significance of this last point will become clear from our discussion of Mints at the end of this part. In connection with the first reason, I might note that Mints repeatedly makes clear his indebtedness to Simons.[14] Again, I would conjecture that Knight's writings referred to above also reflect Simons' influence. Similarly, in my recollections of student days at Chicago—and I think I can safely speak for my fellow students at the time—it is Simons who stands out sharply as the major source of intellectual stimulation and influence in all that regards monetary and fiscal policy. In the slang of those days, most of us were "simonized" to some degree or other.[15]

14. Cf., e.g., *Monetary Policy for a Competitive Society* (1950), p. vii. {Cf. also Mints' letter to me reproduced on p. 285 below.}

15. In a letter to me commenting on this paper, Martin Bronfenbrenner disagrees with this evaluation of Simons' influence and states that "Simons was wasted on the undergraduates; few graduate students other than tax technicians took his 'Fiscal Policy' course, 361."

My opinion is still that expressed in the text. But I must admit that—in contrast with most graduate students—I also did my undergraduate work at Chicago, and that my first impressions of Simons were accordingly formed in that context. I should also note (though again I am not sure that it is relevant) that Bronfenbrenner's recollections refer to the period 1934–36 whereas mine are for 1941–46.

Let me turn now to the propositions themselves. The contrast drawn by Proposition (1) is that between the transactions approach to the quantity theory and the cash-balance approach emphasized by Friedman. Now, it is a commonplace of monetary theory that these two approaches can be made analytically equivalent. Indeed in his general discussion of monetary influences, Fisher himself vividly shows (1913, pp. 153–54) that he was thinking in terms of a demand for money. Nevertheless, if we consistently find a treatment in terms of the transactions approach, we can take this as some indication that the economists in question did not primarily approach monetary theory from the viewpoint of the demand for money. Or at least we cannot take it as an indication that they did![16]

Indeed, it is a much closer approximation to the flavor of the Chicago tradition to say that basically it was not interested in a systematic analysis of the demand for money:[17] for it believed so strongly that "the supply of money matters" that—for the policy purposes which were its main concern—the exact form of the demand function for money did not matter at all, aside from the critical (though sometimes implicit) assumption "that additional money in unlimited amounts would [not] be hoarded in its entirety." For then no matter what the demand for money—in the language of Simons and Mints, no matter what the extent of hoarding—its adverse effects could be offset by a sufficient increase in M. "Much hoarding would simply require a larger addition to the stock of money." [18] The possibility that destabilizing lags could interfere with the efficacy of such a monetary policy—a problem which has received so much attention in recent years—was either not seen (Simons) or not given much weight (Mints [19]).

It should therefore not surprise us that Simons did not present a detailed analysis of the demand for money. Indeed, despite his frequent references to "hoarding," there does not seem to be any point in his writings in which he even uses the term "demand for money." Another, and related, manifestation of the lack of interest in such an analysis is the fact that Simons did not spell out the details of the mechanism by which an increase in the quantity of money was supposed to increase the volume of spending on goods and services. Instead, he sufficed with the simple, sometimes implicit, and frequently mechanical statement that an increase in M increased aggregate demand MV.

Again, even the influence of the rate of interest on the demand for money was not

16. Actually, Friedman draws a sharper distinction on this score between the transactions and cash-balance approaches than I would; thus compare his "Quantity Theory II" (1968), pp. 437–38 with my *Money, Interest, and Prices*, (1965b), pp. 166–67.

17 It is noteworthy that the work on the empirical nature of the demand function for money that was done at Chicago during the 1940s was carried out under the inspiration not of the "Chicago oral tradition," but of the Keynesian model builders at the Cowles Commission, which was then located at the University of Chicago See in particular Lawrence Klein, "The Use of Econometric Models as a Guide to Economic Policy" (1947), p. 125 ff., and *Economic Fluctuation in the United States, 1921–1941* (1950), pp 95–101.

18. The last two quotations in this paragraph are from Mints, "Monetary Policy," (1946), p. 67. See also *ibid* , p. 61 and *Monetary Policy for a Competitive Society* (1950), pp 48–49 Cf in this connection the quotation (given in Appendix I below) from Viner's "Schumpeter's *History of Economic Analysis*" (1954), as reprinted in *The Long View and the Short* (1958), p 365.

19. Mints, *Monetary Policy for a Competitive Society*, (1950), pp. 138 ff Mints ascribes the suggestion that such a destabilizing influence might occur to Milton Friedman, who by then was his colleague (*ibid.*, p. 138, fn. 8).

consistently recognized by the Chicago school of the 1930s and 1940s. Thus even though Knight discussed cyclical variations in the rate of interest, he did not take account of the possible influence of such variations on the velocity of circulation.[20] Similarly, though (as indicated in Proposition (3)) Simons and Mints did emphasize the influence of near-moneys on velocity, it was the *volume* of these money substitutes to which they referred, not to the *rate of interest* upon them.

Let me turn now to the "extreme alternations" in velocity described in Proposition (2). It is not clear from the writings of the Chicago school whether it believed that the very fact that prices were, say, increasing would cause an indeterminate flight from money—so that there could exist no stable functional relationship between velocity and the anticipated rate of change of prices; or whether velocity was unstable because of the nature of the expectations function which generated a sequence of ever-increasing anticipated rates of price changes which operated through a stable demand function to generate ever-increasing (or decreasing) changes in the quantity of money demanded; or whether there were other forces in the economy (of which those described in Proposition (3) are an example) which generated such a divergent sequence—or whether it believed that a combination of some or all of these factors was at work. But in any event one point is clear: there is no place in their writings in which the aforementioned Chicago economists even hint that they were thinking in terms of Friedman's crucial assumption of a velocity which is a stable function of (among other variables) the anticipated rate of change of prices.[21, 22]

There were other respects in which the Chicago tradition lacked some of the basic ingredients of the flavor of the "model" which Friedman has presented of it. In particular, whereas (as indicated above) this tradition was primarily concerned with the relation between the stock of money and the flow of expenditures, Friedman's primary concern is with the relation between the stock of money and the stocks of other assets. I shall return to this point in Part IV below. But let me now admit that with respect to this comment—and, even more so, with respect to much of what has

20. See the discussion of Knight in Appendix I below

21. See in this context the statement by Frank Knight (from his *Risk, Uncertainty and Profit*, (1957), p. xlv) quoted in full Appendix I.

22. I might at this point note that in his recent paper on Simons, Friedman cites the passage referred to in footnote 13 above and then concludes that:

> There is clearly great similarity between the views expressed by Simons and by Keynes—as to the causes of the Great Depression, the impotence of monetary policy, and the need to rely extensively on fiscal policy. Both men placed great emphasis on the state of business expectations and assigned a critical role to the desire for liquidity. Indeed, in many ways, the key novelty of Keynes' *General Theory* was the role he assigned to "absolute" liquidity preference under conditions of deep depression [1967, p. 7].

But Friedman gives no indication of the fact that this interpretation of Simons is hardly consistent with that of his 1956 essay, with its emphasis on the functional stability of V and, even more to the point, on the absence of a "liquidity trap" (cf. pp. 244–45 above).

In this paper, Friedman also contends that "had Simons known the facts as we now know them [about the monetary history of the U.S. during the Great Depression], he would, I believe," have been less concerned with " 'the danger of sharp changes on the velocity side' " (ibid., p. 12). Without discussing the validity of this conjecture {cf., however, below, ch. 12, pp. 295–97}, I shall merely note that it is not relevant to the question which concerns me here—namely, Simons' actual approach to the quantity theory.

been said above about the lack of interest at Chicago in the demand for money—Lloyd Mints was at least a partial exception. Thus even though it is not at all comparable—in either detail or precision—with Friedman's exposition, Mints' *Monetary Policy for a Competitive Society* contains a more explicit analysis of the asset-demand for money than any earlier Chicago discussion.[23] But it is highly significant that the chapter in which this analysis is presented (Chapter 3) is followed by a special appendix on Keynes' theory of liquidity preference. Similarly, as shown in Appendix II, it was in this context (and not in that of the quantity theory of money) that Mints' lectures on the asset-demand for money were given. It is also noteworthy that the few Chicago doctoral theses of the period 1939–1950 that were concerned with the choice of money as a component of a portfolio of assets generally took Keynes as their point of departure and gave no indication that they saw this approach as stemming from the Chicago tradition (see Part III below).

Thus the picture which emerges from all this is that by the 1940s the Chicago School itself had—quite understandably—been influenced by Keynesian monetary theory. Accordingly, not only did it begin to evince an interest in a systematic analysis of the demand for money, but it frequently did so from the Keynesian viewpoint of money as one component of an optimally chosen portfolio of assets. Indeed, it had to use this viewpoint in order to explain why it rejected some aspects of the Keynesian theory: namely, the Keynesian concentration on the choice between money and bonds, and the related interpretation of interest as a monetary phenomenon; and the emphasis on the possibility of indefinite hoarding (the "liquidity trap"), and the related Keynesian conclusion that money could not matter enough, so that only a policy of increased government expenditures could deal adequately with the problem of unemployment.[24]

III. The Oral Tradition of Chicago

The preceding discussion of the Chicago School has been based on its writings. It is, however, the "oral tradition of Chicago" which Friedman primarily claims to represent—and to which, accordingly, I shall now turn.

A priori it seems unlikely that scholars who had presented a consistent—and sometimes lengthy—statement of their views in print would have provided a significantly different presentation in their classroom discussions. Fortunately, there is no need to rely solely on such a priori considerations—or even on my memories of these classroom discussions as contrasted with those of Friedman. For there is concrete evidence on their nature in the form of lecture notes which I took during my graduate studies at Chicago in the period 1943–1945.

Of course, these lecture notes are subject to all of the standard reservations about the accuracy with which students understand their teachers. Furthermore, they constitute only one observation on these teachings. But at the present moment this is

23. Mints (1950), ch. 3; see also ch. 9 and especially pp. 210–11 See also Mints' *History of Banking* Theory (1945), pp. 219–22, and Mints (1946), pp. 63 *et passim*

24. See again the references to Mints in the preceding footnote See also the discussion of Knight in Appendix I.

one more than has yet been provided on the question. It should also be noted that if we accept (as I do) the fact that there was a "tradition" at Chicago, then we can also assume that there was a high degree of continuity between what was taught in my student days and what was taught before.

Mints devoted several lectures to the quantity theory at the beginning of his course on "Money." After presenting Fisher's equation of exchange (with no discussion of the determinants of V—or of the Cambridge K, to which he also referred), Mints went on to formulate the quantity theory of money in a way which has remained sharply etched in my memory—and which has always represented for me "the flavor of the Chicago tradition":

> Some attempts [have been made statistically] to verify quantity theory by showing that $MV + M'V' = PT$ is true. But quantity theory says that P *is the dependent variable*. So [in order to verify theory] would have to show that exist consistent time lags. Have to establish *causal relationship*. Formula itself is a truism—doesn't need verification. Formula $\neq$quantity theory.
>
> . . . .
>
> Mints prefers following statement of quantity theory: P is the dependent variable (in the long run) of the equation $MV = PT$. But in the short run all the variables tend to move together. [Classnotes, Econ. 330, June 28 and July 3, 1944; italics in original.] [25]

For our purposes (see end of preceding part), it is also most significant that Mints' discussion of the demand for money from a viewpoint which is closer to the portfolio approach did not occur in his lectures on the quantity theory, but a month later in the context of his discussion of Keynes' theory of liquidity preference. Here Mints said:

> Really four factors to be kept in equilibrium: (1) price level (2) rate of interest (3) demand for cash (liquidity preferences) and (4) quantity of money.
>
> Methods of disposing of cash:
> (1) Hold in cash
> (2) Purchase consumer's goods
> (3) Purchase producer's goods
> (4) Lend on short term
> (5) Purchase long-term bonds
> (6) Purchase corporation shares.
>
> Keynes assumes that doubts about the future affect only (5).
>
> But uncertainties affect (2) and especially (3). Demand will fall off for these, prices there will fall, profits decrease, and [hence] beginning of unemployment, etc. [Classnotes, Econ. 330, Aug. 4, 1944.]

25. It is noteworthy that this distinction between the quantity theory and the identity $MV + M'V' = PT$ is also emphasized by Friedman in his encyclopedia article; see Friedman (1968), pp. 434–36.

Mints then went on to present a discussion which closely parallels that of the first part of Chapter 3 of his *Monetary Policy for a Competitive Society* (1950).

Some other notes from Mints' lectures, as well as relevant notes from the lectures of Knight and Simons, are reproduced in Appendix II. The evidence of these notes leads unmistakably to one simple and unsurprising conclusion: the oral tradition of the Chicago School of monetary theory was entirely reflected in its written tradition; whatever was not in the latter was also not in the former.

Let me turn now to the doctoral theses written at Chicago during the period in question.[26] As we all know, students' theses reflect the interests, approach, and all too frequently even the views of their teachers. It is therefore interesting to see what we can learn about the Chicago tradition from this source. This is all the more legitimate in the present context in view of Friedman's assertion (1956, p.3) that "Chicago was one of the few academic centers at which the quantity theory continued to be a central and vigorous part of the oral tradition throughout the 1930s and 1940s, whose students continued to study monetary theory and to write theses on monetary problems."

The list of relevant theses is presented in Appendix III. Even after taking account of the small number of theses which were being submitted in those days (a total of 46 for the 1930s and 52 for the 1940s), one is struck by the paucity of monetary theses written at Chicago during the 1930s. The fact that from 1931 through 1938 only one such thesis was submitted speaks for itself. The number is decidedly greater for the 1940s. Nevertheless, a casual comparison with the list of doctoral theses submitted at Harvard shows that even during the 1940s there were at least as many monetary theses being submitted at Harvard as at Chicago (though admittedly the total number of theses submitted at the former was three times as large).

Let me turn now to the far more important question as to the contents of the Chicago theses. The situation can be described quite simply: several of the theses are primarily descriptive and contain little, if any, analysis. To the extent that the theses refer to the quantity theory of money, they do so in terms of Proposition (1) on p. 245 above;[27] none of them do so in terms reminiscent of Friedman's "reformulation." Few theses even reflect a portfolio approach to the demand for money. Furthermore, those that do, draw their primary inspiration from Keynes or his supporters.[28] Similarly, the influence of the rate of interest on the demand for money is rarely mentioned, even in

26. Without disclaiming any responsibility for what follows, I would like to express my appreciation to my assistant, Mr. Stanley Fischer, who has carefully gone through the monetary theses written at Chicago during the period 1930–50—and on whose excellent notes I have relied heavily.

I would also like to thank Professor Lester Telser of the Department of Economics at the University of Chicago and his secretary Mrs. Hazel Bowdry for their help in obtaining a complete list of Chicago theses and microfilms of those discussed here, as well as information about theses committees

27 Thus see, e.g , Benjamin F Brooks, "A History of Banking Theory in the United States Before 1860" (1939), p. 354; Marion R. Daugherty, "The Currency School-Banking School Controversy" (1941), p. 54; Roland N. McKean, "Fluctuations in Our Private Claim-Debt Structure and Monetary Policy" (1948), pp. 51, 98, and 103 See also the references to Leland Bach's thesis in fn. 31

28. Thus see, e.g , Martin Bronfenbrenner, "Monetary Theory and General Equilibrium" (1939), pp. iii, 43, 45, 156–57, McKean (1948), ch. 4, and especially pp. 52, fn. 5, and 57–59; and William W. Tongue, "Money, Capital and the Business Cycle" (1947), chs. 1 and 2.

appropriate contexts,[29] and when there is a mention, it is again largely inspired by Keynesian monetary theory.[30]

Of particular interest in the present context is Leland Bach's thesis on "Price Level Stabilization: Some Theoretical and Practical Considerations" (1940). In his general analysis and policy proposals, Bach presents the position of the Chicago School as summarized in the five propositions of Part II above.[31] Furthermore, in the process of so doing he refers explicitly (on pp. 35–36) to an "oral tradition" at Chicago which he describes in the following terms:

> The explanation of the cycle may, for our purposes, be ultimately reduced to the existence of two basic factors, the first redivisible into two more or less separate elements. These two sub-factors in the first are (a) psychological shifts by consumers, entrepreneurs, and investors, leading to changes in the propensities to hoard, consume, and invest, and (b) perverse fluctuations in the volume of money in the system (*M* plus *M′* in the Fisherian notation). The second basic factor is the existence of "sticky" prices throughout large sectors of the economy, of which many are cost-prices, so that costs have a tendency to move more slowly than do the more flexible selling prices.*
>
> *On this reduction to essentials I am indebted to Professor Mints, although it has been in the nature of an "oral tradition" at Chicago for some time and can be found in many writers, but only more or less obscured.

It might be noted that at the time Bach wrote this footnote, the tradition was indeed largely oral: for all that then existed in print was Simons' brief discussions; the writings of Knight and Mints had yet to appear (see Appendix I).

In concluding this discussion of the Chicago School, I would like to emphasize once again that its purpose has not been either to praise or to criticize—and surely not to criticize the writers of the theses—but only to convey the flavor of the Chicago tradition as it really was.

29. Cf., e.g., Arthur I. Bloomfield, "International Capital Movements and the American Balance of Payments, 1929–40" (1942), pp. 578–79; McKean (1948), p. 80.

In all but the last chapter of his thesis (see especially ch. 4), McKean follows Simons (to whom he repeatedly refers—pp. 3, 32, 52, 68, *et passim*), in being concerned with the volume of liquid assets and debts, and not the rates of return upon them (cf. above, p. 248). On the other hand, his discussion of 100 percent money in the last chapter (see especially pp. 174–77) explicitly takes account of the effect on the demand for money (and hence velocity) of changes in the rates of interest on money substitutes.

30. See again the references cited in fn. 28. See also McKean (1948), p. 100, who, however, refers to the influence of the quantity of money on the interest rate as "the very old argument, revived in the thirties" (*ibid.*, p. 99).

It might be noted that at some points McKean's thesis also reflects the influence of Milton Friedman, who had joined the Chicago staff in 1946. Thus see the reference to Friedman in McKean's discussion of the simultaneous influence of the interest rate on the demand for money and on savings (p. 101, fn. 1). Somewhat less relevant for our present purpose are McKean's many references in chs. 1–2 and on p. 191 to Friedman's discussions of the problem of lags in monetary policy and of the proper framework for monetary and fiscal policy.

31. See especially pp. 42–45 and 72–75 of Bach's thesis.

IV. The Quantity Theory, Friedman, and Keynesian Economics

As indicated in my opening remarks, the nominal occasion for the appearance of this paper is the recent publication in the *International Encyclopedia of the Social Sciences* of Friedman's article on the "Quantity Theory." From the substantive viewpoint, the "reformulation of the quantity theory" which Friedman presents on pp. 439–42 of this article is essentially the same as the one he presented in his 1956 essay (see Part I above). But from the doctrinal viewpoint which engrossed us in Parts II and III, there is a fundamental difference: for Friedman now makes no attempt to present this reformulation as a "model of the oral tradition of Chicago." Indeed, neither the Chicago School nor its individual members are even mentioned.

On the other hand, as just indicated, Friedman does continue to denote his presentation as a "reformulation of the quantity theory." The only support he adduces for this nomenclature is that "Fisher and other earlier quantity theorists explicitly recognized that velocity would be affected by, among other factors, the rate of interest and also the rate of change of prices" (1968, p. 436b).

That such a recognition existed, there can be no doubt.[32] But—as I have indicated elsewhere (1968, p. 480b) [33]—the real question is the extent to which the "earlier quantity theorists" recognized the full and precise implications of these effects: the extent to which they consistently took account of these effects at the appropriate points in their discussions. For one of the fundamental facts of the history of ideas is that in general the full implications of a set of ideas are not immediately seen. Indeed—as has been frequently noted—if they were, then all mathematics would be a tautology; for its theorems are implicit in the assumptions made. The failure to see such implications is also familiar from many episodes in the history of economic doctrine: for example, from the tortuous and faltering manner in which the full implications of the marginal productivity theory were developed.[34]

Thus there is indeed a striking passage in Fisher's *Rate of Interest* (1907, p. 212) about the "convenience" of money holdings which makes an individual willing to forgo the interest that he could earn.[35] But the only echo of this passage in *The Purchasing Power of Money* is a passing reference (1913, p. 152) to the influence of the "waste of interest" on velocity. Furthermore, it is clear that Fisher did not integrate this influence into the general analysis of this book. Indeed, this influence is not mentioned at any other point in it: neither in the analysis of the effects of the higher interest rates which mark the "transition period" (Chapter IV), nor in the detailed

32. For specific references to writings of Walras, Wicksell, the much neglected Karl Schlesinger, Fisher, and the Cambridge school (Marshall, Pigou, and especially Lavington) which discuss or at the least refer to the influence of interest on the demand for money, see my *Money, Interest, and Prices* (1965) pp. 372, 545, 556, and 576–80.

33. Cf. also my *Money, Interest, and Prices*, (1965b), p. 372

34. See G. J. Stigler, *Production and Distribution Theories* (1941).

35. This passage is slightly elaborated upon in *The Theory of Interest* (1930), p 216, where Fisher refers to the "liquidity of our cash balances [which] takes the place of any rate of interest in the ordinary sense of the term."

description of the determinants of the velocity of circulation (Chapter V),[36] nor finally in the statistical investigation of the theory, with its description of how velocity varied during the periods examined (Chapters XI–XII).

I find this last omission particularly significant. For the empirical investigator is confronted with a concrete situation in which he is called upon to take account of the major theoretical variables which might explain the data (even if some of these variables will subsequently be rejected as statistically insignificant); hence this situation provides a proper and operationally meaningful test of whether the influence of a variable has been "fully recognized." It should therefore be emphasized that the failure even to mention the rate of interest as a possible explanation of the observed variations in the velocity of circulation also characterizes the writings of Carl Snyder (1924, 1925, 1935), to whose empirical work (as well as that of Fisher) Friedman refers (1968, p. 436b). And a similar picture obtains for the earlier studies by James W. Angell (1933, 1936) [37] and Clark Warburton[38] (1945, 1946) to which Selden refers (1956, pp. 184–85) in his survey of empirical investigations of the income velocity of circulation in the United States.[39] Furthermore, the fact that Angell and Warburton mention the influence of interest only in their later studies—and in explicit response to issues raised by Keynesian monetary theory[40]—reinforces my basic contention that the "early quantity theorists" did not of themselves fully recognize this influence.

It is true that the aforementioned empirical studies were primarily concerned with explaining the observed price level in the market, and not the demand function for money. But to press this point too far in the present context is to admit that these "early quantity theorists" did not really have a major concern with the properties of this demand function. Furthermore, even within the context of these empirical studies it is quite appropriate to investigate the possibility that observed deviations from the hypothesized V (whether assumed constant or secularly declining) can be explained in terms of changes in the interest rate—provided the observed V is assumed to equal the

36. Fisher's discussion here is in terms of the "habits of the individual," the "systems of payments in the community," and "general causes"—by which he means "density of population" and "rapidity of transportation" (*ibid.*, p. 79).

37. Angell's detailed and systematic analysis of the velocity of circulation is almost entirely in terms of the timing and mechanics of the payment process. The passing references to interest on pp. 57–58 of the article and pp. 164–65 of the book do not change this basic picture. Note too the discussion of "idle balances" on pp. 140 ff. of the book, which is devoid of any reference to the interest rate.

38. Warburton's primary concern is with the secular trend in velocity, which he explains in terms of the mechanism of the payment process and a greater-than-unity income elasticity of demand for cash balances (1946, pp. 443–44); see also pp. 86–90 of his 1949 article cited in fn. 40 below.

39. Nearly half of the studies surveyed by Selden are by Angell and Warburton.

40. Thus see James W. Angell, *Investment and Business Cycles* (1941), chs. 6 and 9. Similarly, Warburton first deals with this influence in his reply to Tobin's criticism (from the viewpoint of Keynes' liquidity-preference theory) of his (Warburton's) earlier work; see Clark Warburton, "Monetary Velocity and Monetary Policy" (1948), pp. 304–14 It is against this background that one must also read Warburton's discussion of the rate of interest in his later "Secular Trend in Monetary Velocity" (1949), pp 89–90.

desired V. In fact, this is what Warburton did in his later (1949) study, though he concluded that this possibility should be rejected.

In any event, it is significant that the first empirical study (to the best of my knowledge) which explicitly deals with the influence of interest on the demand for money is the 1939 Keynesian-inspired study by A. J. Brown on "Interest, Prices, and the Demand Schedule for Idle Money." [41] I might also add that this is the first such study which discusses a *functional relationship* between the demand for money and "the rate at which the general price-level has lately been changing." [42] This discussion can well be contrasted with Fisher's imprecise statement (1913, p. 63) that when money "is depreciating, holders will get rid of it as fast as possible." Furthermore, Fisher sees this as an unstable process which will cause a further rise in prices which will again increase V "and so on" (1913, p. 63). In my discussion of the Chicago quantity theorists (above, p. 248), I have already stressed the difference between this view and the stable relationship between the demand for money and rate of change of prices described by Friedman—and by Brown.

I have dwelt at length on the treatment of the rate of interest in Friedman's "reformulation" as compared with the actual writings of the quantity-theorists because this difference can be well defined and hence clearly observed in the literature. But I attach no less significance to other—and more subtle—differences, which also characterize Friedman's 1956 essay. Thus Friedman's presentation (1968, p. 440a) of the demand for money is first and foremost in terms of the demand for an asset; for him the income variable in the demand function is primarily "a surrogate for wealth, rather than [as in the quantity theory] a measure of the 'work' to be done by money." Correspondingly, as I have noted elsewhere (see note 3 above), Friedman is primarily concerned with the optimal relationship between the stock of money and the stocks of other assets, whereas the quantity theorists were primarily concerned with the relationship between the stock of money and the flow of spending on goods and services. Furthermore, their discussions of this relationship either did not make the distinction between stocks and flows—or at least were imprecise about it. Similarly, quantity theorists paid little, if any, attention to the effects on the rate of interest and other variables of shifts in tastes as to the form in which individuals wished to hold their assets.[43]

And now to our main point: all of the foregoing are precisely the differentia of Keynesian monetary theory as compared with the traditional quantity theory. They are the basic components of a theory of portfolio choice of which there are undoubtedly antecedents in the Cambridge cash-balance school (particularly as represented by Lavington) and before, but whose analytical structure as it now exists stems from the publication during the 1930s of Keynes' *Treatise on Money* (vol. 1, pp. 140–46),

41. As reprinted in T. Wilson and P. W. S. Andrews (eds.), *Oxford Studies in the Price Mechanism* (1951), pp. 31–51.

42. *Ibid.*, p. 34; unfortunately, Brown goes on to represent this rate by the absolute difference $p_t - p_{t-1}$ instead of the ratio of this difference to p_t (or p_{t-1}), where p_t represents the price level p at time t.

43. These differences also prevail between Friedman and the Chicago tradition; see above, pp. 248–49.

Hicks' "Suggestion for Simplifying the Theory of Money" (1935, pp. 13–32), and Keynes' *General Theory* (1936, pp. 166–72, 222–29). Subsequent valuable contributions to this analysis were made—during the 1940s and early 1950s—by, among others, H. Makower and J. Marschak (1938), Franco Modligliani (1944, especially pp. 190–201), R. F. Kahn (1954, especially pp. 236–43), Joan Robinson (1951), Harry Markowitz (1952, pp. 77–91), and James Tobin (1955, especially pp. 104–7). And in direct continuation of this intellectual line of descent, Milton Friedman provided us in 1956 with a most elegant and sophisticated statement of modern Keynesian monetary theory—misleadingly entitled "The Quantity Theory of Money—A Restatement." [44]

Actually, a careful reading of Friedman's encyclopedia article would seem to indicate that he has taken account of criticisms of his earlier exposition and that—at least in part—he himself now recognizes this intellectual indebtedness. Thus, first of all, he now describes (1968, p. 439b) his reformulation as one "that has been strongly influenced by the Keynesian analysis of liquidity preference." [45] Similarly, the term "liquidity"—which had been avoided in the 1956 essay—is now used.[46] Second, he admits (1968, p. 438b) that the Keynesian analysis of the demand for money lays "greater emphasis on current interest rates" than did the "earlier quantity theorists." Third, Friedman now recognizes (1968, p. 441b) that the "earlier quantity theory" envisaged the process of monetary adjustment in terms of the relation between the stock of money and the flow of expenditures—"to the almost complete exclusion" of the Keynesian approach, which envisages it in terms of the relation between the stock of money and other assets, particularly bonds. Furthermore, Friedman himself accepts (1968, pp. 441b–42a) as "plausible" the Keynesian approach that "any widespread disturbance in money balances . . . will initially be met by an attempted readjustment of assets and liabilities, through purchase and sale"—though he goes on to explain how the resulting change in prices will also "establish incentives to alter flows of receipts and expenditures." [47]

In view of all this, one can only regret that Friedman has persisted—even within the confines of an international encyclopedia—in presenting his exposition of the demand function for money as a "reformulation of the quantity theory."

44. For a somewhat more detailed account of this intellectual genealogy, see again the references cited in fn. 3 above.

45. Although Friedman refers to Johnson's 1962 *American Economic Review* survey article immediately after this statement, I think that it can safely be assumed to reflect his own view as well.

46. " . . . the services rendered by money relative to those rendered by other assets—in Keynesian terminology . . . liquidity proper" (Friedman, 1968, p. 460b).

Compare this with the corresponding passage on p. 14 of the 1956 essay, cited in fn. 7 above.

47. Though he does not refer to it at this point, Friedman's discussion here essentially summarizes the analysis presented in his and Meiselman's paper on "Relative Stability of Monetary Velocity and the Investment Multiplier in the United States, 1897–1958," (1963), pp. 217–22. In this analysis, Friedman and Meiselman distinguish their approach from the Keynesian one in terms of the range of assets involved in the monetary adjustment.

Appendix: The Empirical Evidence

I. The Writings[1]

The sources for the first four[2] summary-propositions at the beginning of Part II are as follows:

Henry C. Simons

A Positive Program for Laissez Faire (1934). As reprinted in *Economic Policy for a Free Society* (1948), p. 64.

"Rules versus Authorities in Monetary Policy" (1936). As reprinted in *Economic Policy for a Free Society* (1948). Pp. 164–66, 170–72, 326 (fn. 5), 331 (fn. 16).

Personal Income Taxation (1938), p. 222.

"Hansen on Fiscal Policy" (1942). As reprinted in *Economic Policy for a Free Society* (1948), p. 188.

"Banking and Currency Reform" (1933), p. 3 and Appendix, p. 2.[3]

The passage from the Appendix to "Banking and Currency Reform" reads:

> But any general change in business earnings will affect promptly the speculative temper of the community. Larger profits breed optimism; they stimulate investment and induce dishoarding (reduction of idle cash reserves). Producers will become more anxious to borrow for purposes of increasing inventories, expanding production, and increasing plant capacity. Lenders will have fewer misgivings about the ability of borrowers to repay. People generally will increase their lending and investment at the expense of their idle reserves of cash. In a word, the velocity of circulation will increase. But this change, in turn, means a larger volume of business and higher product-prices, and thus still larger earnings. The further increase of earnings, moreover, will induce further increase in the velocity of money. And so on and on, until the initially sticky prices which govern costs do finally move upward markedly and rapidly—or until some fortuitous disturbance (perhaps a mere speculative scare) happens to establish a sharp reversal of the trend in product prices. On the other hand, once earnings

1. See fns 8 and 10 on p. 245 above.

2. I have not provided specific sources for Proposition (5)—which does not really bear on the issue at hand, and which has been included in the text only for the sake of completeness {Documentation for this proposition is, however, provided in ch. 12 below (pp. 302–3).}

3. "Banking and Currency Reform" is an unpublished and unsigned memorandum dated by Aaron Director as November 1933 and ascribed by him largely to Simons; see the Bibliography in Simons (1948), p. 313. See also Friedman (1967), p 2, fn. 1 and Reeve (1943), p. 317, fn. 45. (I am greatly indebted to Friedman and Director for providing me with a copy of this memorandum.)

Actually, the date which appears at the end of the memorandum (p 15) is "November 17, 1953", this is clearly an error.

Friedman (1967, p. 2, fn. 1) describes the Appendix to the memorandum as a "partial exception to the statement that Simons nowhere set forth a consistent statement of his theory." However, except for its explicit relating of velocity to business earnings (see the passage which follows immediately) the theoretical presentation of the Appendix to this memorandum seems to me to be no more detailed or systematic than Simons' other writings.

begin to decline, forces will be set in motion to continue and accelerate the trend—and perhaps with more striking results, for the crucial, sticky prices are peculiarly resistant to downward pressure.

The passages from Simons' writings referred to in fns. 9, 12, and 13 above are as follows:

> Once a deflation has gotten under way, in a large modern economy, there is no significant limit which the decline of prices and employment cannot exceed, if the central government fails to use its fiscal powers generously and deliberately to stop that decline. Only great government deficits can check the hoarding of lawful money and the destruction of money substitutes once a general movement has gotten under way. [*Personal Income Taxation,* 1938, p. 222.]

> The bottom of an uncontrolled deflation, for all practical purposes, is nonexistent—with adverse expectations causing price declines and with the actual declines aggravating expectations, etc. [''Hansen on Fiscal Policy,'' 1942, p. 188.]

> With all its merits, however, this rule [of holding the quantity of money constant] cannot now be recommended as a basis for monetary reform. The obvious weakness of fixed quantity, as a sole rule of monetary policy, lies in the danger of sharp changes on the velocity side, for no monetary system can function effectively or survive politically in the face of extreme alternations of hoarding and dishoarding. It is easy to argue that something would be gained in any event if perverse changes were prevented merely as to quantity, but the argument is unconvincing. The fixing of the quantity of circulation media might merely serve to increase the perverse variability in the amounts of ''near moneys'' and in the degree of their general acceptability, just as the restrictions on the issue of bank notes presumably served to hasten the development of deposit (checking-account) banking. [''Rules versus Authorities in Monetary Policy,'' 1936, p. 164.]

Lloyd W. Mints

A History of Banking Theory (1945), pp. 218–22.

''Monetary Policy'' (1946), especially pp. 61, 63, 67.

Monetary Policy for a Competitive Society (1950). Ch. 3 (especially pp. 29, 32–35, 39–41, 48–49, 69–70), ch. 6 (especially pp. 120–22, 138–42), and ch. 9 (especially pp. 194, 202–3, 207, 210–11, 227).

Frank H. Knight

''Economics'' (1951). As reprinted in *On the History and Method of Economics* (1956), pp. 15, 30.

''The Business Cycle, Interest, and Money: A Methodological Approach'' (1941). As reprinted in *On The History and Method of Economics* (1956), pp. 210–11, 213, 223–24.

Preface to 1948 reprint of *Risk, Uncertainty and Profit*, pp. xlii–xlv.

The passages from Knight referred to in footnotes 12 and 21 are as follows:

> . . . in the case of money, just what does set a boundary to a movement of general prices in either direction, and especially the downward movement, becomes something of a mystery. [''The Business Cycle, Interest, and Money,'' 1941, p. 211.]

> Up to a point, socialist critics have been right in regarding cycles and depressions as an inherent feature of ''capitalism.'' Such a system must use money, and the circulation of money is not a phenomenon which naturally tends to establish and maintain an equilibrium level. Its equilibrium is vague and highly unstable. Its natural tendency is to oscillate over a fairly long period and wide range, between limits which are rather indeterminate. [*Ibid.*, p. 224.]

> My chief ground for disagreement with the Keynesian theory of money is the belief that in view of these facts, [viz., the instability of *V*]—some, or most, or all of them well recognized by Keynes as well as others—supply and demand curves for ''liquidity'' have no solid foundation and are not a sound basis for action but are ''theoretical'' in the bad and misleading sense. [*Risk, Uncertainty and Profit*, 1948, p. xlv.]

It might be noted that in his discussion of Keynes' theory of liquidity preference in his 1941 article, Knight readily recognizes that the rate of interest ''must equalize the attractiveness of bonds and of money for holding'' (p. 221), and earlier in this article he also describes the holding of money as an alternative to the holding of other assets (p. 210). Knight does not, however, take this dependence of the demand for money on the rate of interest into account in his discussion of variations in the velocity of circulation during the course of the business cycle—despite his discussion of the cyclical changes in the rate of interest (pp. 219–20).[4] All that is discussed in this context is the influence of price expectations.

Jacob Viner[5]

Studies in the Theory of International Trade (1937), pp. 40–45, 131, *et passim.*

''Schumpeter's *History of Economic Analysis*'' (1954). As reprinted in *The Long View and the Short* (1958), 365.

4. On p 223, Knight does refer to high ''liquidity preference'' and low interest rates in depressions, but he does not refer to a causal relationship between these two phenomena (i.e., to a movement along a demand curve for money), and instead presents them as parallel consequences of the same cause—namely, the depression.

5. For methodological reasons, I have restricted myself to writings of the period in question (1930–50)—or at least not too long afterward, hence I have not taken account of Viner's 1962 article on monetary policy cited above in note 5 of the text.

"International Aspects of the Gold Standard" (1932). As reprinted in *International Economics* (1951), pp. 137–40.

The discussion on pp. 40–45 of the *Studies* shows that Viner thought of the quantity theory as specifying a causal relationship between the quantity of money and its value. The effect of anticipations of price increases in increasing the velocity of circulation is indicated on p. 131.

The passage from Viner's review of Schumpeter is an instance in which it would have been most appropriate for Viner to have indicated (if he had so believed) that the quantity theory specified not the constancy of the velocity of circulation, but the constancy of the functional relationship between this velocity and the variables that determine it. Instead, he merely emphasizes that exponents of the quantity theory

> would not find variability of velocity disturbing for their theory, provided the variations in velocity were not inverse to those in quantity—or, perhaps, even if they were, provided the amplitude of variation of velocity was less than that of quantity.

It is also interesting to note that Viner goes on in this passage to say that

> the quantity theory of money [can be] understood as holding only: (1) that an authority powerful enough to make the quantity of money what it pleases can so regulate that quantity as to make the price level approximate to what it pleases, and (2) that the possibility of existence of such power is not inconceivable *a priori*.

The foregoing writings thus reflect Viner's agreement with Proposition (1) in the text as well as his rejection of the constancy of *V*. At the same time, Viner did not develop the inconstancy of *V* into the cyclical theory presented by Proposition (2).

I might also note that in his 1932 Harris Foundation lecture on the gold standard Viner discussed the problem of price stablization in the following terms:

> A country on the gold standard binds itself to all the vagaries of gold as a standard of value. . . . A standard of value fluctuating erratically in its own value must be an important factor in initiating and in accentuating the recurrent cycles of expansion and depression from which the modern world has suffered. [pp. 137–38.]

He then went on to

> express [the] individual view [that] we know too little as yet of the possibilities of [price] stabilization to take immediately any major steps in that direction. [pp. 138–39.]

What Viner did, however, advocate was "continuous experimentation . . . with the possibilities of stabilization . . . in the hope that something can still be made of the gold standard" (p. 139).

II. The Lectures[6]

The only relevant passage I have been able to find in my notes from Simons' lectures are from his course on "Economics of Fiscal Policy." This passage reads:

> Only thing that has stopped deflationary movement is that government begins to get insolvent too. (Fears that cheap money really would set in.) So inevitably get government deficit which works to stop deflation. No automatic recovery—nothing in system to bring this about. This Simons' theory of business cycles: deflation [continues] until government action. No stability in economy—so that's why have fluctuations to begin with.
>
> Should we obtain deficits by (1) revenue changes or (2) spending changes? Simons in favor of (1). [Classnotes, Econ. 361, Apr. 20, 1945.]

My lecture notes from Mints' courses contain the following additional relevant passage, taken from his discussion of the Cambridge cash-balance approach:

> In modern theory, demand for money said to have unitary elasticity. Assume that *V* and *T* constant. Then *P* changes directly proportionate with *M*. [Real] value of total money remains the same. [A diagram of a rectangular hyperbola appears at this point].
>
> Some have said on basis of postwar I experience that η for money $\neq 1$. E.g., total quantity of money increased 10 times, while goods that could be purchased with this [i.e., a unit of money] decreased 1/15 (?). But in this case have been changes in *V* and *T*—contrary to our assumptions. So assume that has been shift from one demand curve to another (also with $\eta = 1$) according as *V* and *T* change. [More diagrams follow here]. [Classnotes, Econ. 330, June 30, 1944.]

Mints concluded his course on "Money" with a discussion of policy, in which (among other things) he stated:

> If [government] stabilizes price level, will stabilize aggregate demand and thus prevent unemployment. Inconceivable that federal government couldn't so increase cash balances of public that it wouldn't want to purchase goods. [Classnotes, Econ. 330, Aug. 11, 1944.]

Most of Mints' discussions of policy matters were, however, contained in his course on "Banking Theory and Monetary Policy" (Economics 331). The material presented here closely paralleled the corresponding discussions in his books on *A History of Banking Theory* (1945) and *Monetary Policy for a Competitive Society* (1950).

There is nothing of relevance in my lecture notes from Viner's courses (economic theory, international trade). In my notes from Knight's lectures on economic theory there is a passage that repeats the analysis of his article on "The Business Cycle, Interest, and Money: A Methodological Approach" which had appeared a few years before (see Appendix I). Indeed, the notes refer explicitly to this article and read:

6. See Part III above.

III. Doctoral Theses on Monetary Problems Submitted to The University

Author	Title of thesis
Ernest R. Shaw	The Investment and Secondary Reserve Policy of Commercial Banks
Francis A. Linville	Central Bank Cooperation
Benjamin F. Brooks	A History of Banking Theory in the United States Before 1860
Martin Bronfenbrenner	Monetary Theory and General Equilibrium
Joseph E. Reeve	Monetary Proposals for Curing the Depression in the United States, 1929–1935
George Leland Bach	Price Level Stabilization: Some Theoretical and Practical Considerations
Mrs. Marion R. Daugherty	The Currency School-Banking School Controversy
Benjamin Caplan	The Wicksellian School—A Critical Study of the Development of Swedish Monetary Theory, 1898–1932
Arthur I. Bloomfield	International Capital Movements and the American Balance of Payments, 1929–1940
R. Craig McIvor	Monetary Expansion in Canadian War Finance, 1939–1945
Don Patinkin	On the Inconsistency of Economic Models: A Theory of Involuntary Unemployment
William W. Tongue	Money, Capital and the Business Cycle
Roland N. McKean	Fluctuations in Our Private Claim-Debt Structure and Monetary Policy
Joel W. Harper	Scrip and Other Forms of Local Money
Raymond H. McEvoy	The Effects of Federal Reserve Operations, 1929–1936

of Chicago: 1930–1950

Thesis committee[7]	Date of submission
L. D. Edie,* S. P. Meech, L. W. Mints	1930
H. D. Gideonse (?), L. W. Mints, J. Viner	1937
F. H. Knight, L. W. Mints,* J. Viner	1939
F. H. Knight, L. W. Mints, H. Schultz,* J. Viner	1939
G. V. Cox, L. W. Mints,* J. Viner	1939
L. W. Mints, H. C. Simons, J. Viner	1940
G. V. Cox, L. W. Mints, J. Viner*	1941
O. Lange, H. C. Simons, J. Viner	1942
O. Lange, L. W. Mints, J. Viner*	1942
R. Blough,* J. K. Langum, L. W. Mints	1947
P. Douglas, H. G. Lewis, J. Marschak,* T. Yntema	1947
O. Lange (?), H. G. Lewis, F. H. Knight, L. W. Mints*	1947
A. Director, E. J. Hamilton, L. A. Metzler, L. W. Mints*	1948
S. E. Leland,* L. W. Mints, H. C. Simons (?)	1948
E. J. Hamilton, L. A. Metzler, L. W. Mints*	1950

7. Where known, the committee chairman is designated by an asterisk attached to his name.

> Keynesian economics. The older viewpoint assumed ideal neutral money: money only an intermediary, so really have barter [economy]. Say's law—*loi des debouchés*. Under ideal competition [conditions?] wouldn't have any money used as medium of exchange—just as unit of account.
>
> Keynes didn't do anything not adumbrated in previous writings. Instead of saying: "Every supply of goods a demand for other goods"—said: "Every supply of goods a demand for money." [Keynes] hypostatizes money under name "liquidity preference." People want money as such—for its own sake—not as immediate purchasing power.
>
> Knight says demand for money highly speculative—especially in investors' market and even in consumers' market. If consider changes in prices relative to changes in interest rate—former much greater than latter. So if foresee rising prices will borrow money to buy goods; and when foresee lower prices will hurry to sell now. And the anticipation itself will create the price change—and this is cumulative. "Every speculation on the future value of goods is a speculation on the future value of money." Essential fact in slump is just that. In a boom everybody begins to realize that prices are really too high—overcapitalization. All changes in the value of money tend to be cumulative—an unstable equilibrium.
>
> In wheat futures markets have same thing—anticipation creates changes. But there, there is an equilibrium dependent on well-known objective facts. So damped oscillations. But no definite known equilibrium value of money. Everyone might know that [value of] money is too high—but question is whether it will continue to rise—don't know where the breaking point is.
>
> Knight doesn't know how to stabilize price level—and at what height to stabilize it. [Classnotes, Econ. 301, July 24, 1945.]

I cannot resist citing in addition the following typical Knightian remark, which occurred at a later point:

> In medieval times [men] didn't look for remedies since thought everything from God who was good—so everything good. Now science is the God—and we think that must be remedy for every disease. Maybe there is no answer to the business cycle: [maybe] have to let it take its course. [Classnotes, Econ. 301, July 26, 1945.]

Postscript

(i) Further Comment on Friedman

Friedman's reaction to the article reprinted in this chapter has been ambivalent. Thus in his concluding comments in a subsequent symposium in which I also participated (Patinkin 1972), Friedman (1972, p. 941) refers at one point to the article and states that "Patinkin has made a real contribution to the history of thought by examining and presenting the detailed theoretical teachings of Simons and Mints, and I have little quarrel with his presentation.'' Now, the correct presentation of these ''theoretical teachings'' is precisely the major purpose of the foregoing article; it is accordingly puzzling that at other points in his concluding comments Friedman (1972, pp. 907 and 930–33) alleges that my article gives a ''misleading,'' if not ''highly misleading,'' impression of the Chicago tradition. Furthermore, and more important, the evidence with which Friedman attempts to support this allegation is irrelevant. For this evidence consists primarily of the detailed documentation (*ibid.*, pp. 939–40) of a point which was never in question, and which is indeed subsumed under my Propositions 4 and 5 above: namely, the fact that in the early 1930s Jacob Viner advocated a highly activist central-bank and fiscal policy as the means of dealing with unemployment. More generally, Friedman's implications to the contrary notwithstanding, his description of the Chicago policy position (*ibid.*, pp. 936–41) is basically the same as the one summarized on p. 246 above.

(ii) Correspondence with Jacob Viner

In November 1968 I sent a draft of the preceding paper to Frank Knight, Lloyd Mints, and Jacob Viner, respectively, with a request for comments. Mints did not reply. From Knight I received a brief though warm note (dated March 19, 1969) declining comment, and adding: ''. . . to be frank, I'm very definitely 'retired' from economics—in fact from any serious 'work,' beyond fairly light reading'' (see above, p. 44, fn. 25). From Viner, I at first did not hear; but some months later, after sending him a reprint of the published article, I received a long letter which led to the following correspondence (all of which was typewritten). This correspondence is reproduced here with the kind permission of the late Mrs. Jacob Viner. Some explanatory footnotes have been added:

Princeton, November 24, 1969.

Dear Patinkin,

Many thanks for the copy of your article on ''The Chicago Tradition.'' Perhaps I should apologize for not acknowledging receipt of your earlier draft. If so, here goes. Physical circumstances oblige me to ration strictly expenditure of energy even on correspondence. The issue you raised was one that I never was interested in, nor even knew much about, nor could contribute anything really significant to, from either my fallible memory or my disordered records.

At Chicago, from late in 1929 to early 1933 I was, for me, fairly deeply engaged in policy promotion, but that is not what your piece is about. In this area, both my memory and my records indicate that the Department was in practically perfect accord. As far as my teaching at Chicago was concerned, as the Department operated throughout my membership in it, graduate courses were as narrowly specialized as the members chose to make them. I chose to exclude from my courses consideration of monetary-fiscal doctrine, of business cycles, of what we now call ''economic development,'' except as such consideration was unavoidable when I was dealing with the early history of international trade theorizing. I fear I even excluded them from my thinking. Such specialization as I practised I would have regarded then—as I do even more so now—as foolish or even immoral if practised on undergraduates, or in contacts with the lay world, but I neither taught undergraduates nor wrote textbooks. What went on in other courses than my own I neither knew nor sought to know.

It was not until after I left Chicago in 1946 that I began to hear rumors about a "Chicago School" which was engaged in *organized* battle for laissez faire and "quantity theory of money" and against "imperfect competition" theorizing and "Keynsianism." I remained sceptical about this until I attended a conference sponsored by University of Chicago professors in 1951. The invited participants were a varied lot of academics, bureaucrats, businessmen, etc., but the program for discussion, the selection of chairmen, and everything about the conference except the unscheduled statements and protests from individual participants were so patently rigidly structured, so loaded, that I got more amusement from the conference than from any other I ever attended. Even the source of the financing of the Conference, as I found out later, was ideologically loaded. There is a published account of the proceedings of the Conference,[a] but it does not include the program, etc. as presented to the participants to direct their discussion. From then on, I was willing to consider the existence of a "Chicago School" (but one not confined to the economics department and not embracing all of the department) and that this "School" had been in operation, and had won many able disciples, for years before I left Chicago. But at no time was I consciously a member of it, and it is my vague impression that if there was such a school it did not regard me as a member, or at least as a loyal and qualified member. In any case, I am not well-informed about the past or the present of such a "school," and therefore I have had nothing to contribute to the recent inquirers about the intellectual history of this putative "school."

Whatever may be the proper evaluation of my outside-the-battle record in this respect, it did quite probably contribute substantially to the fact, whose memory I cherish deeply, that in my thirty years at Chicago my personal relations with my economist colleagues were on my part, and as far as I know mutually, uninterruptedly marked by mutual affection and respect.

With best wishes,
Cordially yours,
[signed] Jacob Viner

Jerusalem, December 21, 1969

Dear Viner:

I greatly appreciate your taking the time and energy to write me your recollections of the "Chicago School."

Your letter is indeed most interesting. I might also add that since writing the

a. This is presumably a reference to *Defense, Controls, and Inflation: A Conference Sponsored by The University of Chicago Law School*, ed. Aaron Director, Chicago, 1952. This contains the proceedings of a conference that took place in 1951 and included Viner among its participants (*ibid.*, p.x).

article, I came across your paper in the volume edited by Leland Yeager, *In Search of a Monetary Institution*—which also makes your position on the "Chicago School" quite clear.

It may be that I shall be reprinting my article in a collection of essays that I am planning to put out.[b] In this connection, I would like very much to be able to add a footnote citing various passages from your letter, in order to present your view of the "school" and your relationship to it. I would greatly appreciate it if you could let me know if you agree to this.

Sincerely yours,
[signed] Don Patinkin

Princeton, January 15, 1970.

Dear Patinkin,

I dislike being difficult, but I have misgivings as to authorizing quotations from my letter which in the context which you may put them could seem to assert or suggest that as an individual or in concert with others at Chicago or elsewhere I was a participant in controversy against what I ever consciously regarded or publicly or privately labelled as existentially a "Chicago school." I am perfectly happy to have my past views on monetary theory on record. But I don't trust my unaided memory and my manuscript papers are at present not in completely chronological arrangement. Perhaps I can best comply with your wishes if you let me see in advance what references you propose to make to my letter.

Except for Knight, I don't think your bibliography touches anything pre-1933. But "money", of course, was referred to in courses at Chicago (including the business school) before 1933. In your article, I miss references to Angell as (for a year, I think) teaching assistant—for me—and perhaps also as graduate student at Chicago, with the possibility, therefore, of "Chicago" influence on him or of his influence on Chicago. Carl Snyder participated in at least one conference on monetary policy at Chicago,[c] and I still remember the inside information he gave us (in 1931?) on the issues and the facts as to "money" supply as seen at the Federal Reserve Bank of New York—facts which clash with those postulated for the period by Friedman. You should also look at '*A Memorandum Presented To A Member Of The House Committee On Military Affairs, April 26, 1932*' (mimeographed) which was wholly on monetary and fiscal policy. The signatures will, I think, interest you: Cox, Director, Douglas, Gideonse, Knight, Millis, Mints, Schultz (Henry), Simons, Viner, [Chester] Wright, Yntema.

I gather that the concept of 'liquidity' is for you a key concept in distinguishing schools of monetary theory. I don't know the history of the *term* and I

b Ultimately published as *Studies in Monetary Economics*, New York, 1972.

c. This is presumably a reference to the Harris Foundation Lectures of 1932, in which both Snyder and Viner participated; see Harris Memorial Foundation, *Gold and Monetary Stabilization*, ed. Q. Wright (Chicago, 1932), p. 166.

have what is undoubtedly only a very sketchy notion of the history of the *idea*. I don't know whether I have ever used the term in print, but my concern with the idea goes back to my undergraduate days in Montreal. I then constituted the accounting staff of a small manufacturing concern and handled its credit relations with its bank. (Incidentally, bank rates of interest in Canada were invariable, and negotiations with banks related only to the size of the "line of credit"). From that time on I was conditioned to regard all macro-statistics of 'money' I might encounter as "promiscuous aggregates". When I came back to Chicago in 1919, I was strengthened in this by my colleage, J. O. McKinsey, who talked and wrote from a very realistic managerial point of view on the importance of "cash budgeting", and, in effect, on the importance of "liquidity", to a business firm. When I went to the Treasury in 1934 I encountered Lauchlin Currie and found we shared some views in common on the complex nature of, in effect, "liquidity". Later, when he left the Treasury for the Federal Reserve Board he followed a suggestion of mine on the accumulation of statistical data relating to the effect of the financial activities of government on the "liquidity" of the economy. I am sure that in my correspondence files there is material relevant to all this,[d] and also that he then published some of his findings.

As further bits of evidence relating to my own monetary notions, I enclose (1) a Xerox of a page from the original of my contribution to the Wieser Festschrift (*Die Wirtschaftstheorie der Gegenwart,* Vienna, 1928, vol. iv), (this page has never appeared in print in its English version); (2) a recent letter of mine to the *New York Times,* which relates to some activity of mine some fifteen years or so ago whose circumstances I still appear to be bound to keep confidential. The present relevance of these items, I take it, is to the imprecision of the concept of "money," as used in current and ancient theorizing and in all statistical series I know about, as potentially a simple statistical quantity.

I have turned over all my books to the Princeton University Library, but some day in the near future I hope to go to the Library to explore what Patinkin and Keynes mean by "money" and "liquidity" and how, *if at all,* they construct their own promiscuous aggregates to represent them quantitatively.

Sincerely yours,
[signed] Jacob Viner

The following are, respectively, (1) the page from the Wieser *festschrift* and (2) the letter to *The New York Times* which Viner enclosed with his letter:

(1) It would be regrettable if the foreign reader were to get the impression that there is on all of these questions a perfect unanimity of opinion among American economists. Some American economists have been hostile to this mode of explanation of the mechanism of adjustment of international balances, because it seems to involve acceptance of the quantity theory of the value of money. But

d. There is indeed a voluminous correspondence with Currie in The Jacob Viner Papers at Princeton University Library; I am indebted to Shlomo Maital for this information.

although the classical economists did expound the theory of international trade in terms of a rigid quantity theory of money, the modern American expositions of the theory of international trade make little or no appeal to the quantity theory of money. They merely take for granted, on *a priori* grounds, or they demonstrate inductively, that price levels do tend to reflect in some degree changes in the stock of gold. They grant freely that by deliberate banking policy, or as the result of cyclical variations in business conditions, the influence of gold movements on price levels may for a time be neutralized by counter-movements in the volume of bank deposits and bank-note circulation, or in the rapidity of circulation of money, and that the influence of gold movements on price levels can be clearly traced only if proper allowance is previously made for the influence on price levels of changes in banking policy, banking methods, or business conditions other than those which are themselves the results of the gold movements.

(2) Bank Commitments [e]

To the Editor:

Officers of the Federal Reserve System are complaining that the American banking system is making too slow and too small a contribution to the fight against inflation. Some American bankers are saying that their hands are tied by outstanding "commitments to lend" which their customers are currently calling upon them to meet.

If this is true, it is important, and information as to the extent of and behavior through time of such aggregate commitments could conceivably be of considerable value both to the monetary authorities and to the professional and academic interpreters in terms of the state of the national economy. But no public source exists today where statistics as to commitments to lend are obtainable.

Some years ago, the staff of the Board of Governors of the Federal Reserve System did attempt a spot survey of the commitment-to-lend situation in the New York money market, including total commitments per bank and total receipts per bank from fees charged for the commitments.

Since, however the inquiry was on a strictly voluntary basis and many banks were noncooperative, the results were inconclusive except as to the one fact that commitments to lend were not an unusual phenomenon in the New York money market. Presumably for this reason, the report containing the results of the inquiry never emerged from the printers'-proof stage.

Today an inquiry of the same sort would not need to be on so purely voluntary a basis. Even if each bank were required only to report on a periodic basis its receipts from commitment fees, and if the Federal Reserve were to make public only its summation by regions of the amounts of such receipts, this of itself would serve to provide a good statistical basis for estimating the aggregate size and behavior through time of outstanding commitments.

Banks of course have obligations to their customers extending beyond their

e. Appeared with this caption in Letters to the Editor in *The New York Times* of July 6, 1969.

commitments to lend and their deposit liabilities, such as agreed-upon ''lines of credit'' and tacit understandings that the ''needs'' of their customers for loans will be reasonably taken care of. As compared to commitments, however, lines of credit and tacit understandings, dollar for dollar and probably also over-all, have much less power to ''tie the hands'' of bankers who wish to cooperate with the efforts of monetary authorities to check inflation by checking the expansion of credit.

For instance, lines of credit and tacit understandings are less susceptible to legal enforcement, are more subject to elastic interpretation at the discretion of the banker, and are ordinarily applicable in the absence of renewal for shorter periods of time.

Jacob Viner
Princeton, N.J., June 28, 1969

Jerusalem, February 9, 1970

Dear Viner:

Thank you very much for your letter of January 15, and the additional information which it contains.

I can well understand your interest in seeing whatever quotation I may from your earlier letter. I am, therefore, enclosing Footnote 13 of my paper with the additional paragraph, which I would now like to add.[f]

Also enclosed is a revised version of Footnote 5,[g] in which I refer to the article you wrote, edited by Yeager, and which is referred to in Footnote 13.

I would greatly appreciate hearing from you as to whether you agree to letting me quote you in this manner.

Thank you once again for your interest and help.

Sincerely yours,
[signed] Don

Princeton, Feb. 23, 1970.

Dear Patinkin,

I have no comment to make on your note 5.

In your note 13, you say: ''For Viner, I have been able to find evidence only on the first proposition. It should, however, be noted that he did not take a position on the policy of price stabilization, . . .''

I am not at all sure that I know what you are attributing, or denying, to me here. I feel fairly confident, however, that what you say is not confirmed by the items of mine to which J. R. Davis [1968] refers and by the following items to which he does not refer:

f. As a result of subsequent changes, this paragraph did not appear in fn. 13 (which corresponds to fn. 8 on p. 245 above) of the reprinted article, but at the end of Appendix I there (*Studies in Monetary Economics* (1972), p. 113). The paragraph cited three sentences from the third paragraph of Viner's first letter to me; since this letter has been reproduced here in its entirety, this paragraph has not been included in Appendix I above.

g. This version more or less coincided with fn. 5 on p. 242 above.

Review of P. W. Martin, *The Problem of Maintaining Purchasing Power*, 1931, *J.P.E.*, June, 1932, pp. 418–419.

"International Aspects of the Gold Standard," in Harris Foundation Lectures, *Gold and Monetary Stabilization*, Chicago, 1932, reprinted in my *International Economics, Studies*, Free Press, Glencoe Ill., pp. 123–140.

I expressly indicated in one or more of these items, that I did not regard velocity as stable, and I hope I never said or implied that I did not accept price-level stabilization as in the long run *an* appropriate and major objective.

Your quotation from my letter is O.K. But could you add that the emphasis on "organized" was in the original letter, (if it was)?

I trust that my comments will not cause you any trouble.

With best wishes,
Sincerely yours,
[signed] Jacob Viner

As a result of this letter, I added the references to Viner's Harris Foundation Lectures at the end of Appendix I above. For some reason, however, I did not add any reference to Viner's review of Martin's book. The most relevant passages here are the following:

> Mr. Martin criticizes at some length the doctrine expounded by many of the classical economists, and especially by J. B. Say, that since goods themselves constitute the demand for goods, general overproduction is impossible. He uses general overproduction to mean either (1) output or (2) capacity for production in excess of the amounts which the available amounts of purchasing power can absorb at remunerative prices. No one who had lived through any period of widespread business depression and unemployment could possibly have denied the existence of "general overproduction" when so defined. . . .
>
> In the author's own account there is perhaps undue emphasis on the significance for control of manipulation of the volume of purchasing power. There is ground for maintaining that, given the prejudices and the obsessions of statesmen, bankers, and economists, the problem of unemployment is as much a problem of regulating wage rates, interest rates, rents, and the prices of monopoly commodities as one of regulating the amount of purchasing power. For a single country under the gold standard and suffering from severe unemployment, deflation of monopoly prices and of money costs may be the only way out. And for unemployment due to maladjustments in relative prices rather than to falling price levels as a whole, an artificially stimulated expansion of purchasing power may accentuate instead of remedy the evil if the elements which had superior price-bargaining power before the inflation still retain it under the inflation and employ it to intensify the non-equilibrium divergences in relative prices. In any case, both the purchasing power and the price sides of the picture call for analysis, whereas only one side receives it here. But this book embodies an important contribution, of whose timeliness and thought-provoking quality there can be no question.

Bibliography*

J. W. Angell. "Money, Prices and Production: Some Fundamental Concepts." *Quarterly Journal of Economics*, Nov. 1933, *48*, 39–76.

———. *The Behavior of Money*. New York, 1936.

———. *Investment and Business Cycles*. New York, 1941.

M. Bronfenbrenner. "Observations on the 'Chicago School(s).' " *Journal of Political Economy*, Feb. 1962, *70*, 72–75.

A. J. Brown. "Interest, Prices, and the Demand Schedule for Idle Money." *Oxford Economic Papers*, May 1939, *2*, 46–69. Reprinted in *Oxford Studies in the Price Mechanism*, ed. T. Wilson and P. W. S. Andrews. Oxford, 1951. Pp. 31–51.

J. R. Davis. "Chicago Economists, Deficit Budgets, and the Early 1930's." *American Economic Review*, June 1968, *58*, 476–82.

†A. Director, ed. *Defense, Controls, and Inflation: A Conference Sponsored by The University of Chicago Law School*. Chicago, 1952.

I. Fisher. *The Rate of Interest*. New York, 1907.

———. *The Purchasing Power of Money*, rev. ed. New York, 1913 (reprinted New York, 1963).

———. *The Theory of Interest* (1930). New York, 1954.

M. Friedman. "The Quantity Theory of Money—A Restatement." In *Studies in the Quantity Theory of Money*, ed. M. Friedman. Chicago, 1956. Pp. 3–21.

———. *A Program for Monetary Stability*. New York, 1960.

———. "The Monetary Theory and Policy of Henry Simons." *Journal of Law and Economics*, Oct. 1967, *10*, 1–13.

———. "Money: Quantity Theory." In *International Encyclopedia of the Social Sciences*. New York, 1968. Vol. 10, pp. 432–47.

†———. "Comments on the Critics." *Journal of Political Economy*, Sept./Oct. 1972, *80*, 906–50.

——— and D. Meiselman. "The Relative Stability of Monetary Velocity and the Investment Multiplier in the United States, 1897–1958." In *Stabilization Policies* (Commission on Money and Credit). Englewood Cliffs, N.J., 1963.

†Harris Memorial Foundation. *Gold and Monetary Stabilization*, ed. Q. Wright. Chicago, 1932.

J. R. Hicks. "A Suggestion for Simplifying the Theory of Money." *Economica*, Feb. 1935, *2*, 1–19. Reprinted in *Readings in Monetary Theory*, ed., F. A. Lutz and L. W. Mints. Philadelphia, 1951. Pp. 13–32.

H. G. Johnson. "Monetary Theory and Policy." *American Economic Review*, June 1962, *52*, 335–84.

R. F. Kahn. "Some Notes on Liquidity Preference." *The Manchester School*, Sept. 1954, *22*, 229–57.

J. M. Keynes. *A Treatise on Money*. London, 1930.

———. *The General Theory of Employment, Interest and Money*. New York, 1936.

L. R. Klein. "The Use of Econometric Models as a Guide to Economic Policy." *Econometrica*, Apr. 1947, *15*, 111–51.

*References in text to works listed here as reprinted are to the date of original publication; the page references, however, follow the pagination of the reprinted form.

Items marked with a dagger appear only in Postscript

______. *Ecomonic Fluctuations in the United States*, 1921–41. New York, 1950 (Cowles Commission Monograph No. 11).

F. H. Knight. "The Business Cycle, Interest, and Money: A Methodological Approach." *Review of Economic Statistics*, May 1941, *23*, 53–67. Reprinted in *On the History and Method of Economics*. Chicago, 1956. Pp. 202–26.

______. "Economics." *Encyclopedia Britannica*, 1951. Reprinted in *On the History and Method of Economics*. Chicago, 1956. Pp. 3–33.

______. *On the History and Method of Economics*. Chicago, 1956.

______. *Risk, Uncertainty and Profit*. New York, 1948 (reprinted New York, 1957).

H. Makower and J. Marschak. "Assets, Prices and Monetary Theory." *Economica*, Aug. 1938, *5*, 261–88. Reprinted in *Readings in Price Theory*, ed. G. J. Stigler and K E. Boulding, Chicago, 1952. Pp. 283–310.

H. Markowitz. "Portfolio Selection." *Journal of Finance*, Mar. 1952, *7*, 77–91.

L. W. Mints. *A History of Banking Theory*. Chicago, 1945.

______. "Monetary Policy." *Review of Economic Statistics*, May 1946, *28*, 60–69.

______. *Monetary Policy for a Competitive Society*. New York, 1950.

F. Modigliani. "Liquidity Preference and the Theory of Interest and Money." *Econometrica*, Jan. 1944, *12*, 45–88. Reprinted in *Readings in Monetary Theory*, ed. F. A. Lutz and L. W. Mints. Philadelphia, 1951. Pp. 186–239.

D. Patinkin. "An Indirect-Utility Approach to the Theory of Money, Assets, and Savings " In *The Theory of Interest Rates*, ed. F. H. Hahn and F. P. R. Breckling. London, 1965. Pp. 52–79. (a)

______. *Money, Interest, and Prices*, 2nd ed. New York, 1965. (b)

______. "Interest." In *International Encyclopedia of the Social Sciences*. New York, 1968. Vol. 7. Pp. 471–85.

†______. "Friedman on the Quantity Theory and Keynesian Economics." *Journal of Political Economy*, Sept./Oct. 1972, *80*, 883–905.

†______. *Studies in Monetary Economics*. New York, 1972.

J. E. Reeve. *Monetary Reform Movements*. Washington, D.C., 1943.

J. Robinson. "The Rate of Interest." *Econometrica*, Apr. 1951, *19*, 92–111.

R. T. Selden. "Monetary Velocity in the United States." In *Studies in the Quantity Theory of Money*, ed. M. Friedman. Chicago, 1956. Pp. 179–257.

H. C. Simons. *Personal Income Taxation*. Chicago, 1938.

______. *A Positive Program for Laissez Faire*. Public Policy Pamphlet No. 15, ed. Harry D. Gideonse. Chicago, 1934. Reprinted in Simons (1948), pp. 40–77.

______. "Rules versus Authorities in Monetary Policy." *Journal of Political Economy*, Feb. 1936, *44*, 1–30. Reprinted in Simons (1948), pp. 160–83.

______. "Hansen on Fiscal Policy." *Journal of Political Economy*, Apr. 1942, *50*, 161–96. Reprinted in Simons (1948), pp. 184–219.

______. *Economic Policy for a Free Society*. Chicago, 1948.

C. Snyder. "New Measures in the Equation of Exchange." *American Economic Review*, Dec. 1924, *14*, 699–713.

______. "The Influence of the Interest Rate on the Business Cycle." *American Economic Review*, Dec. 1925, *15*, 684–99.

______. "The Problem of Monetary and Economic Stability." *Quarterly Journal of Economics*, Feb. 1935, *49*, 173–205.

G. J. Stigler. *Production and Distribution Theories*. New York, 1941.

J. Tobin. "A Dynamic Aggregative Model." *Journal of Political Economy*, Apr. 1955, *63*, 103–15.

†J. Viner. "Die Theorie des auswärtigen Handels." In *Die Wirtschaftstheorie der Gegenwart* [Wieser *Festschrift*], IV, 1928. Pp. 106–25 [Part III of this article appears in the original English version in Viner (1951), pp. 40–48.]

†———. Review of *The Problem of Maintaining Purchasing Power* by P. W. Martin. *Journal of Political Economy*, June 1932, *40*, 418–19.

———. "International Aspects of the Gold Standard." In Harris Memorial Foundation, *Gold and Monetary Stabilization*, ed. Q. Wright, 1932. Reprinted in Viner (1951), pp. 123–40.

———. *Studies in the Theory of International Trade*. New York, 1937.

———. *International Economics*. Glencoe, Ill., 1951.

———. "Schumpeter's *History of Economic Analysis*." *American Economic Review*, Dec. 1954, *44*, 894–910. Reprinted in Viner (1958), pp. 343–65.

———. *The Long View and the Short*. Glencoe, Ill., 1958.

———. "The Necessary and the Desirable Range of Discretion to be Allowed to a Monetary Authority." In *In Search of a Monetary Constitution*, ed. L. B. Yeager. Cambridge, Mass., 1962. Pp. 244–74.

C. Warburton. "The Volume of Money and the Price Level Between the World Wars." *Journal of Political Economy*, June 1945, *53*, 150–63.

———. "Quantity and Frequency of Use of Money in the United States, 1919–45." *Journal of Political Economy*, Oct. 1946, *54*, 436–50.

———. "Monetary Velocity and Monetary Policy." *Review of Economics and Statistics*, Nov. 1948, *30*, 304–14.

———. "The Secular Trend in Monetary Velocity." *Quarterly Journal of Economics*, Feb. 1949, *63*, 68–91.

†Q. Wright. See Harris Memorial Foundation.

Unpublished Materials

Author's Lecture Notes of Following Courses:

Frank H. Knight:

Economics 301: "Price and Distribution Theory." Summer 1945.

Lloyd W. Mints:

Economics 330: "Money." Summer 1944.

Economics 331: "Banking Theory and Monetary Policy." Winter 1944.

Henry C. Simons:

Economics 361: "Economics of Fiscal Policy." Spring 1945.

[H. C. Simons]. "Banking and Currency Reform." [Chicago, 1933] [See p. 257, fn. 3, above.]

University of Chicago Ph.D. Dissertations as listed in Appendix III.

'Friedman on the Quantity Theory and Keynesian Economics'

D. Patinkin, 'Friedman on the Quantity Theory and Keynesian Economics', in R. J. Gordon (ed.), *Milton Friedman's Monetary Framework: A Debate with his Critics* (Chicago, Chicago UP, 1974), pp. 111–31.

Friedman on the Quantity Theory and Keynesian Economics

Don Patinkin

> "When *I* use a word," Humpty Dumpty said, in rather a scornful tone, "it means just what I choose it to mean—neither more nor less."
>
> "The question is," said Alice, "whether you *can* make words mean so many different things."
>
> "The question is," said Humpty Dumpty, "which is to be master—that's all." [LEWIS CARROLL, *Through the Looking Glass*]

Milton Friedman's article on "A Theoretical Framework for Monetary Analysis" has two concerns. The first and—from the viewpoint of the space devoted to it—major one is the chapter in the history of monetary doctrine which deals with the nature of—and interrelationships between—the quantity theory and Keynesian monetary theory. The second concern is to present an analytical framework to analyze the dynamics of monetary adjustment. In this paper I shall concentrate primarily on the doctrinal aspects of Friedman's paper.[1]

Clearly, questions about the history of economic doctrine are empirical questions which can be answered only on the basis of evidence cited from

I am indebted to my colleagues Yoram Ben-Porath, Yoel Haitovsky, Giora Hanoch, Ephraim Kleiman, and Josef May, and to Stanley Fischer of the University of Chicago for helpful criticisms of early drafts of this paper.

[1] In the form in which Friedman's subsequent paper (Friedman 1971) was incorporated into the version reproduced above, the "monetary theory of nominal income" described in this paper is referred to as "an alternative version of the quantity theory" (p. 31 above). But Friedman goes on immediately to say that this theory "is implicit in much recent literature but has not heretofore been made explicit." And in his orginal paper, Friedman states that the "monetary theory of nominal income is not new. It is implicit and parts of it explicit in much work in the field of money *of the past two decades*" (Friedman 1971, p. 336; italics added). From this I infer that Friedman does not present his monetary theory of nominal income as a representation of the traditional quantity theory. Correspondingly, since my major concern in the section which follows is with the true nature of this traditional theory, I have not found it necessary to discuss Friedman's monetary theory of nominal income in this context.

the relevant literature. Indeed, the "elementary canons of scholarship call for [such] documentation" (Friedman 1970*c*, p. 318). My criticism of Friedman is, accordingly, that on many occasions he has not provided such evidence; that, indeed, on some occasions he has ignored the detailed evidence which has been adduced against the views he expresses; and that on still other occasions he has indulged in casual empiricism in the attempt to support his doctrinal interpretations. These criticisms will be documented in what follows.

I. Friedman on the Quantity Theory: The Doctrinal-History Aspects

In the paper under discussion, Friedman once again (see Friedman 1956, 1968) presents a theory of money whose central feature is a demand function for money, where this demand is treated "as part of capital or wealth theory, concerned with the composition of the balance sheet or portfolio of assets" (p. 11). Accordingly, his demand function depends on wealth and the alternative rates of return on money and other assets (pp. 11–14).

If Friedman had simply presented this as a conceptual framework to be used for monetary analysis, then few would have disagreed with him. On the contrary, most of us would have enjoyed the systematic clarity of the exposition; would have considered the suggested influence on the demand for money of the division between human and nonhuman wealth (which Friedman carries over from his well-known work on the consumption function) to be a fruitful one, well worth exploring; and would also have benefited from the insightful presentation of the rate of change of the price level as one of the alternative rates of return which affect the demand for money. For though this last factor has been referred to in both the quantity-theory and Keynesian literature (Fisher 1922, p. 63; Brown 1939, p. 34), it was not systematically integrated into our thinking until the work of Friedman and his associates, particularly Cagan (1956).

But, as indicated in my introductory remarks, Friedman is not concerned solely with substantive analytical matters but has a major concern with the doctrinal-history aspects of monetary theory. Once again, few would have disagreed if Friedman had described his conceptual framework as being a particular instance of the Keynesian liquidity-preference theory, while noting the specific contributions indicated in the preceding paragraph. This, however, is not Friedman's way. Instead he tells us that "the general theoretical framework that underlies" his empirical studies—and which has been referred to at the beginning of this section—is that of "the quantity theory of money" (p. 1). Accordingly, he presents this framework as the sequel to a fairly detailed presentation, first of Fisher's transactions equation, $MV=PT$ (which Friedman describes as being primarily concerned with "the mechanical aspects of the payments process");[2] then of the income form of this equation, $MV=Py$; and finally of the Cambridge cash-balance equation, $M=kPy$ (with which Friedman claims the closest affinity) (pp. 1–10).

What, then, does this leave as Keynes's contribution to his theoretical framework? Friedman's answer to this question is expressed in the following passage:

> J. M. Keynes's liquidity preference analysis (discussed further in section 5, below) reinforced the shift of emphasis from the transactions version of the quantity equation to the cash-balances version—a shift of emphasis from mechanical aspects of the payments process to the qualities of money as an asset.[3] Keynes's analysis, though strictly in the Cambridge cash-balances tradition, was much more explicit in stressing the role of money as one among many assets, and of interest rates as the relevant cost of holding money. [P. 11]

In his subsequent discussion of the demand function for money in section 5—entitled "The Keynesian Challenge to the Quantity Theory"—Friedman goes on to say:

> Keynes's basic challenge to the reigning theory [was in his proposition that the] . . . demand function for money has a particular empirical form—corresponding to absolute liquidity preference—that makes velocity highly unstable much of the time, so that changes in the quantity of money would, in the main, simply produce changes in V in the opposite direction. [P. 15]

Thus the picture which Friedman attempts to create is clear: namely, the conceptual framework he uses for monetary analysis is that of the quantity theory; its basic difference from the Keynesian theory lies in the fact that the latter assumed the demand function for money to become highly (infinitely) interest elastic. As against this picture, I would like to present the following one: the conceptual framework which Friedman uses to

[2] As a general characterization, this is somewhat unfair; for, as I have shown elsewhere, Fisher's analysis of the effects of a monetary change is actually far less mechanical than that of the Cambridge school (Patinkin 1965, pp. 166–67).

[3] From much the same viewpoint, one could say that Newton's theory reinforced the shift from Ptolemaic to Copernican astronomy.

analyze the demand for money is that of the Keynesian theory of liquidity preference—with Friedman's addendum that empirically this demand does not become highly (infinitely) elastic, and is indeed relatively inelastic. And, as important as are the policy implications of this addendum, we should not let it wag the theory.

It is obviously no criticism of Friedman—nor does it derogate from his stature as a monetary economist— to say that his analytical framework is Keynesian. All that is being criticized is Friedman's persistent refusal to recognize this is so.

Let me also say that to accept the Keynesian conceptual framework for the analysis of the demand for money does not imply that one must reject the quantity-theory conclusions about the long-run impact of monetary changes on the economy. This is a proposition which has been emphasized for many years in the literature (Modigliani 1944, sec. 14; Patinkin 1949, pp. 23-26; 1954; 1965, chaps. 10-11). But the converse of this proposition is also true: namely, that there is no need for modern-day quantity theorists to attempt to reinterpret the history of monetary doctrine so as to minimize the Keynesian nature of their analytical framework.

As I have shown elsewhere (Patinkin 1969*a*, pp. 58-61), there are two (related) justifications for the usual practice of treating the Keynesian theory as a distinct one, and not simply as a variation of the Cambridge cash-balance theory. The first is the different relationship of these two theories to one of the central distinctions of economic analysis—that between stocks and flows. In particular, Keynesian liquidity-preference theory is concerned with the optimal relationship between the stock of money and the stocks of other assets, whereas the quantity theory (including the Cambridge school) was primarily concerned with the direct relationship between the stock of money and the flow of spending on goods and services. Furthermore, the quantity-theory discussion of this relationship either did not make the distinction between stocks and flows—or at least was imprecise about it. This stands in sharp contrast with the Keynesian analysis of the effect of monetary changes in terms of initial balance-sheet adjustments among assets which generate changes in their relative yields, which in turn ultimately affect the flows of expenditures and receipts. Similarly, quantity theorists paid little, if any, attention to the effects on the rate of interest and other variables of shifts in the tastes of individuals as to the form in which they wish to hold their assets.

The second justification lies in the different treatment by these two theories of what continues to be[4] one of the central issues of monetary

[4] As attested particularly by the extensive empirical literature of the past fifteen years; see

economics—the influence of the rate of interest on the demand for money. For, though quantity theorists did frequently recognize this influence,[5] they did not fully integrate it into their thinking. Most revealingly, they failed to do so in their empirical work—which, by its very nature, confronted them with a concrete situation in which they were called upon to list the major theoretical variables which might explain the data, even if some of the variables might subsequently be rejected as statistically unimportant. It is therefore significant that the first empirical study (to the best of my knowledge) which explicitly deals with the influence of interest on the demand for money is the 1939 Keynesian-inspired study by A. J. Brown.[6]

These hallmarks of the Keynesian liquidity-preference theory also characterize Friedman's exposition. It should be said that Friedman has taken some account of criticisms and has in recent years partly acknowledged this intellectual indebtedness. Thus in his 1956 essay Friedman presented his analytical framework as one that "conveys the flavor" of the Chicago quantity-theory tradition of Simons, Mints, Knight, and Viner—and did not even mention Keynes or the liquidity-preference theory (Friedman 1956, pp. 3–4). In contrast, in his 1968 paper and the current essay he does not mention either the Chicago school or its individual members—and he describes his framework as "a reformulation of the quantity theory that has been strongly affected by the Keynesian analysis of liquidity preference" (Friedman 1968*a*, p. 439*b*).

At the same time, Friedman has not yet faced up to the implications of the fact[7] that whatever the similarities in policy proposals (and there are significant differences here too [Patinkin 1969*a*, p. 47]), the theoretical framework of the Chicago school of the 1930s and 1940s—a major center of the quantity theory at the time—differed fundamentally from his. In particular, the Chicago school—as exemplified especially by Henry Simons—was basically not interested in the demand function for money (Simons never even mentioned this concept!) and carried out its analysis instead in terms of Fisher's $MV=PT$ equation. Furthermore (and in marked contrast with Friedman) the basic assumption of the Chicago

---

the convenient summary in Laidler (1970, chap. 8), noting especially the questions relating to the rate of interest listed on p. 89.

[5] For specific references to the writings of Walras, Wicksell, the much-neglected Karl Schlesinger, Fisher, and the Cambridge school (Marshall, Pigou, and especially Lavington), see Patinkin (1965, p. 372 and supplementary notes *C, D*).

[6] For supporting documentation and fuller discussion of this and the preceding paragraph, see Patinkin (1969*a*, sec. 4).

For a more systematic and detailed treatment of the questions at issue here, see my paper on "Keynesian Monetary Theory and the Cambridge School" (1972*b*).

[7] Demonstrated in Patinkin (1969*a*, secs. 2, 3).

school analysis was that the velocity of circulation is unstable. Correspondingly, it considered sharp changes in this velocity to be a major source of instability in the economy.

Similarly, Friedman has not changed his basic contention that his conceptual framework is that of the quantity theory. Indeed, he includes a further misinterpretation of the nature of this theory. In particular, in his discussion of the transactions approach to the quantity theory, Friedman makes the familiar distinction between the Fisherine equation $MV=PT$ and the "income form of the quantity equation," $MV=Py$, where y is real national income and V accordingly represents the income velocity of circulation. He then goes on to say:

> Clearly, the transactions and income versions of the quantity theory involve very different conceptions of the role of money. For the transactions version, the most important thing about money is that it is transferred. For the income version, the most important thing is that it is held. This difference is even more obvious from the Cambridge cash-balances version of the quantity equation. Indeed, the income version can perhaps best be regarded as a way station between the Fisher and the Cambridge versions. [P. 8]

No evidence is given in support of this assertion about the nature of the income version of the transactions approach—which, if true, would obviously increase the possible relevance of Friedman's interpretation of the quantity theory in terms of the individual's demand to hold money as a component of a portfolio of assets. This is not the occasion to undertake a full-scale study of the development of the income-velocity form of the quantity theory. Let me only say that a brief examination of the interwar quantity-theory literature shows that the income-velocity approach was used as a variant of the transactions approach—and involved no more emphasis on the *holding* of money (as contrasted with its being *transferred*) than did the latter. The reasons for using income velocity were either considerations of data availability or the feeling that the volume of final output and/or the price level of this output were more meaningful economic variables than the gross volume of transactions and/or its price level (to use modern terms, more strategic variables). To the extent that the income-velocity approach constituted a "way station," it was one on the road between the Fisherine quantity theory and the Keynesian income-expenditure approach. It was not one on the road to the Cambridge cash-balance approach.[8]

[8] This paragraph is based on Robertson (1948, pp. 33, 38), Angell (1933, pp. 43–46), Warburton (1945, p. 161), and Chandler (1940, pp. 71–72; 1953, p. 543). I hope on some

I have so far criticized Friedman for claiming too much for the quantity theory; let me now indicate one direction in which he has claimed too little. This occurs in the context of his identification of the quantity theory with the short-run assumption that real income is constant, while only the price level changes (for details, see the next section). Here Friedman states:

> There is nothing in the logic of the quantity theory that specifies the dynamic path of adjustment, nothing that requires the whole adjustment to take place through P rather than through k or y. It was widely recognized that the adjustment during what Fisher, for example, called "transition periods" would in practice be partly in k and in y as well as in P. *Yet this recognition was not incorporated in formal theoretical analysis.* [Pp. 17–18; italics added]

The facts of the case, however, are quite different. Thus Fisher's analysis of the "transition period"—which was assumed to last ten years on the average, and during which both the level of real output and the velocity of circulation were changing—assigned a critical role to the difference between the money and real rates of interest. In this way Fisher integrated his analysis of the "transition period" into his formal theoretical analysis of the distinction between these two rates of interest—a distinction that was a basic component of his theoretical framework even before he turned to monetary problems. It might also be noted that Fisher wrote incomparably more on his monetary proposals for mitigating the cyclical problems of the "transition period" than on the long-run proportionality of prices to money. This concentration on short-run analysis was even more true of the policy-oriented Chicago quantity-theory school of the 1930s and 1940s: indeed, Simons and Mints showed little, if any, interest in the long-run aspects of the quantity theory. Again, representatives of the Cambridge school such as Lavington, Pigou, and Robertson wrote entire monographs on the problems of the "trade cycle" and of "industrial fluctuations"—and devoted substantial parts of these monographs to the analysis of the role of money in these fluctuations. Needless to say, this role was also a primary concern of Wicksell and Hawtrey. Thus, far from being a question dealt with in "asides," the systematic analysis of the short-run variations in output and velocity generated by monetary changes was a major concern of the pre-Keynesian quantity theorists.[9]

---

future occasion to deal more fully with this question, as well as the general question of the relations between the three forms of the quantity theory.

[9] See Fisher (1896; 1907; 1922, chap. 4). For a detailed description of Fisher's voluminous

In order to avoid any possible misunderstanding, I wish to emphasize that Friedman in his own application of his "modern quantity theory" obviously assigns a central role to the short-run effects of changes in the quantity of money on k and y; what I am criticizing here, however, is Friedman's contention that the traditional quantity theorists themselves did not recognize this role in their "formal theoretical analysis."

II. Friedman on the Quantity Theory: Some Analytical Issues

In the preceding section I have dealt with the history of doctrine. In the present section I shall turn briefly to analytical issues and again criticize Friedman for claiming too little: namely, for not presenting the long-run quantity theory in the most general way that one can, once one has decided to reformulate it. To a large extent, what is involved here is a question of tastes. My own are for introducing explicitly into the mathematical model the assumptions of the text—particularly when this yields (without much inconvenience) a more general model.

Friedman's presentation of the "simple quantity theory" is in terms of the following general equilibrium model which, "in Keynes's spirit, . . . refers to a short period in which the capital stock can be regarded as fixed" (p. 30):

$$f(y, r)+g(r)=y, \tag{1}$$

$$l(y, r)=\frac{M_0}{P}, \tag{2}$$

where y is real national income, r is the rate of interest, and M_0 is the fixed quantity of money; and where the left-hand side of (1) consists respectively of the consumption and investment functions, while the left-hand side of (2) consists of the demand function for money—all expressed in real terms (pp. 29–30, 32).

This is a system of two equations in three variables: y, P, and r. Hence, continues Friedman,

> there is a missing equation. Some one of these variables must be determined by relationships outside this system. . . . The simple quantity theory adds the equation

---

writings on his policy proposals (the main one of which was to stabilize the price level), see Reeve (1943, chap. 11). On the Chicago school, see Patinkin (1969*a*, secs. 2, 3). This question is discussed in greater detail in my paper "On the Short-Run Non-Neutrality of Money in the Quantity Theory" (Patinkin 1972*a*).

$$y = y_0; \tag{3}$$

> that is, real income is determined outside the system. In effect, it appends to this system the Walrasian equations of general equilibrium, regards them as independent of these equations defining the aggregates, and as giving the value of [y], and thereby reduces this system to one of [two] equations determining [two] unknowns. [Pp. 31–32]

Equation (3) then permits "a sequential solution" of system (1)–(2). In particular, substituting from (3) into (1), we can solve for $r = r_0$. Substitution of this value into (2) then yields the "classical quantity equation"

$$M_0 = Pl(y_0, r_0) = P\frac{l(y_0, r_0)}{y_0}y_0 = \frac{Py_0}{V}, \tag{4}$$

which then determines P (pp. 32–33).

Instead of initially creating a problem of a "missing equation" which is then solved by determining y "outside the system," I would prefer including in the model from the very beginning that part of the "Walrasian equations of general equilibrium" needed to determine y endogenously. This preference is reinforced by the fact that all that need be added to the model for this purpose are the production function and the excess-demand equation in the labor market. For the assumption of wage and price flexibility (which, in the context of the quantity theory, is in any event being made) assures that the equilibrium level of employment will be achieved in the labor market. And since the capital stock is fixed, the production function then determines the equilibrium level of real output, y, corresponding to this level of employment. Indeed, this procedure has been the standard one in the literature since Modigliani (1944).

Again, in view of the crucial role that Friedman assigns to the real-balance effect in assuring the long-run equilibrium of the system (pp. 16, 25), I would prefer introducing this effect explicitly into the commodity-demand functions. This would also seem to provide an expression of Friedman's view that

> the key insight of the quantity-theory approach is that such a discrepancy [that is, between the nominal quantity of money demanded and supplied] will be manifested primarily in attempted spending. [P. 51]

It will not come as a surprise to the reader that these modifications yield a model which I have developed at length elsewhere (Patinkin 1954; 1965, chaps. 9–10). The long-run proportionality of P to M specified by the quantity theory holds true in this model even though it cannot, in Friedman's terms, be "solved sequentially" (or, to use the more usual term, it cannot be dichotomized), so as to reduce it to one equation (that for money) in one variable (the price level). Thus this model requires us to abandon the traditional single-equation form of the quantity theory which Friedman apparently prefers. On the other hand, the model has what is for me the more than compensating advantage of demonstrating that the long-run validity of the quantity theory does not (as it was at one time thought—and as might mistakenly be inferred from Friedman's presentation) depend on the restrictive assumption that the system can be dichotomized in the foregoing manner (Patinkin 1965, p. 175).

III. Friedman on Keynesian Economics

A Keynesian, according to Friedman, is one who makes the above system (1)-(2) determinate in the short run by adding the equation

$$P = P_0 \tag{5}$$

instead of equation (3), $y = y_0$ (pp. 15, 32). Thus, the contrast that Friedman tries to draw is between the quantity theorists—who assume real income constant and prices flexible, and indeed changing in direct proportion to changes in the money supply—and the Keynesians—who make the opposite assumptions about real income and prices.[10]

Let me first of all point out that this description of the quantity theory is misleading. For, though Friedman presents both of the foregoing positions as referring to the short run (pp. 15, 44), quantity theorists did not actually assume real income to remain constant—and the price level to change proportionately with the quantity of money—except in the long run. In the short run (as shown at the end of Section I above) they believed that a (say) decrease in the quantity of money would decrease both the velocity of circulation and the level of real output as well as the price level. Thus part of what Friedman presents as a difference between Keynes and the quantity theory is really a difference between these "runs."

Let me also say that presentations of the Keynesian theory of unemployment usually begin with an analysis based on the assumption of absolute wage and price rigidity. However, the basic question here at issue is whether these presentations have gone on to generalize the theory to the case of wage and price flexibility.

[10] In Friedman's n. 20, this interpretation of Keynes is slightly modified—but not in a way that really affects the following criticism.

The clear implication of Friedman's interpretation (esp. pp. 15, 18–21) is that Keynesian economics provided no such generalization. But Friedman achieves this interpretation only by overlooking the chapter in the *General Theory* devoted to—and indeed, entitled—"Changes in Money Wages,"[11] by overlooking those portions of interpretations of Keynes that he does cite in which the implications of wage and price flexibility are analyzed within the Keynesian system (for example, Tobin 1947, pp. 585–86;[12] Patinkin 1951, sec. 14; Leijonhufvud 1968, pp. 319 ff., 340 ff.),[13] and, finally, by overlooking entirely the classic interpretation of Keynes by Modigliani, which has provided the basis for so many textbook expositions. Indeed, in this interpretation the case of downward wage and price flexibility that depresses the rate of interest until it ultimately pushes the economy into the "liquidity trap" is even singled out for designation as "the Keynesian case" (Modigliani 1944, sec. 16[A]).[14]

[11] I have long considered this chapter to be the apex of Keynes's analysis (Patinkin 1951, p. 283, n. 38). In support of this interpretation let me cite its opening paragraphs: "It would have been an advantage if the effects of a change in money-wages could have been discussed in an earlier chapter. For the Classical Theory has been accustomed to rest the supposedly self-adjusting character of the economic system on an assumed fluidity of money-wages; and, when there is rigidity, to lay on this rigidity the blame of maladjustment. It was not possible, however, to discuss this matter fully until our own theory had been developed. For the consequences of a change in money-wages are complicated. A reduction in money-wages is quite capable in certain circumstances of affording a stimulus to output, as the classical theory supposes. My difference from this theory is primarily a difference of analysis; so that it could not be set forth clearly until the reader was acquainted with my own methods" (Keynes 1936, p. 257; see also pp. 231–34).

[12] Again, the opening paragraph of this article—entitled "Money Wage Rates and Employment"—indicates the perspective from which the writer approaches the question: "What is the effect of a general change in money wage rates on aggregate employment and output? To this question, crucial both for theory and for policy, the answers of economists are as unsatisfactory as they are divergent. A decade of Keynesian economics has not solved the problem, but it has made clearer the assumptions concerning economic behavior on which the answer depends. In this field, perhaps even more than in other aspects of the *General Theory*, Keynes' contribution lies in clarifying the theoretical issues at stake rather than in providing an ultimate solution" (Tobin 1947, p. 572).

[13] In presenting his interpretation of Keynes, Friedman (n. 7) expresses his indebtedness to Leijonhufvud's book. One might therefore note Leijonhufvud's view that "the most common interpretation is perhaps that, once having adopted the assumption of 'wage-rigidity' and built his model on this assumption, Keynes had little further interest in questions relating to money price flexibility. That this is a superficial explanation is apparent both from our discussion in Chapter II and from the fact that Keynes devoted a large portion of the latter half of the *General Theory* to these problems" (Leijonhufvud 1968, p. 332). One might also note that Leijonhufvud (1968, p. 332, n. 1) supports this view with a reference to my 1951 article, which, as just noted, is also referred to by Friedman.

[14] For reasons elsewhere presented (Patinkin 1965, chap. 14, sec. 3), I do not agree with this identification of Keynesian economics with the "liquidity trap"—an identification which has also been followed by Friedman (pp. 15, 21 ff.). This point is further discussed in the next section.

Friedman (p. 15) identifies Keynesian economics with price rigidity as well as the "liquidity

More specifically, in chapter 19 of the *General Theory*, Keynes analyzes in detail the ways in which a decrease in the wage rate caused by the pressure of unemployment might be expected to increase the level of employment. He argues that the main way is by the reduction in interest caused by the increase in the real quantity of money thus generated—and the consequent increase in investment. After discussing the limitations of this mechanism he concludes:

> There is, therefore, no ground for the belief that a flexible wage policy is capable of maintaining a state of continuous full employment;—any more than for the belief that an open-market monetary policy is capable, unaided, of achieving this result. The economic system cannot be made self-adjusting along these lines. [Keynes 1936, p. 267]

Thus wage rigidities in this chapter are not an *assumption* of the analysis but the *policy conclusion* which Keynes reaches after investigating the results to be expected from wage flexibility.

Let me note that Friedman does state that Keynes qualified his assumption of price rigidity by

> assuming it to apply only to conditions of underemployment. At "full" employment, he shifted to the quantity-theory model and asserted that all adjustment would be in price—he designated this a situation of "true inflation." However, Keynes paid no more than lip service to this possibility, and his disciples have done the same; so it does not misrepresent the body of his analysis largely to neglect the qualification. [P. 19]

Surely, "lip service" is hardly the term to use to describe the detailed analysis of full employment—and the consequent upward wage and price

---

trap." Actually, however, the "liquidity trap" assumes its critical role in Keynesian economics only in the case of price flexibility.

For examples of Keynesian macroeconomic-textbook analyses of wage and price flexibility under conditions of unemployment, see Klein (1947, pp. 87-90), Dillard (1948, chap. 9), Hansen (1949, pp. 122-29), McKenna (1955, chap. 12), Dernburg and McDougall (1960, pp. 144-47), Siegel (1960, pp. 225-31), Ackley (1961, pp. 191-98, 377-93), and Shapiro (1966, pp. 477-87). These discussions refer not only to the indirect effect of a wage decrease on the demand for commodities via the rate of interest but also to the direct (Pigou or real-balance) effect. Needless to say, my own discussions of these problems have included both of these effects of wage and price flexibility—and have interpreted the difference between Keynesian and classical economics within this context (see the next section). I might, however, note that I have also analyzed the case of absolute wage and price rigidity and have—for this case—drawn the contrast between Keynes and the classics in terms of the "reversal of roles" of y and p with respect to the question as to which is constant and which is variable (Patinkin 1965, chap. 13, sec. 4, esp. p. 331).

movement—which Keynes provides in the *General Theory* (1936, pp. 295–306; see also pp. 118–19, 171–74, 239–41, 289–91, 328). Indeed, despite the fact that he wrote during a period of mass unemployment, Keynes warns of the danger that wages will begin to rise with increasing unemployment even before full employment is reached (1936, p. 301). Furthermore, the upward flexibility of the wage rate under conditions of full employment is one that is basic to Modigliani's interpretation of Keynes (1944, pp. 189, 201–2)—and indeed to the standard textbook expositions of Keynesian economics. For obvious reasons, the case of full employment has concerned Keynesian economics much more since World War II than before. But to write today and "neglect as a qualification" the extensive Keynesian literature (particularly during World War II) on the inflationary gap—and the upward price movements it generates—is indeed to misrepresent the nature of this analysis.[15]

I think I can best summarize Keynes's own view of the role of price—and output—variations in his system by citing the paragraph with which he ends chapter 20 ("The Employment Function") of the *General Theory*:

> There is, perhaps, something a little perplexing in the apparent asymmetry between Inflation and Deflation. For whilst a deflation of effective demand below the level required for full employment will diminish employment as well as prices, an inflation of it above this level will merely affect prices. This asymmetry is, however, merely a reflection of the fact that, whilst labour is always in a position to refuse to work on a scale involving a real wage which is less than the marginal disutility of that amount of employment, it is not in a position to insist on being offered work on a scale involving a real wage which is not greater than the marginal disutility of that amount of employment. [Keynes 1936, p. 291]

Returning to the case of unemployment, let me now examine the evidence Friedman adduces in support of his interpretation of the role of price and wage rigidity in the Keynesian system. In this context Friedman writes:

> Keynes embodied this assumption [of wage rigidity] in his formal

[15] On Keynes's own contributions to this literature, see Klein (1947, chap. 6). Friedman (n. 11) claims to find support for his interpretation in Holzman and Bronfenbrenner's survey article (1963) in which (contends Friedman) "theories of inflation stemming from the Keynesian approach stress institutional, not monetary, factors." This contention is hardly consistent with Holzman and Bronfenbrenner's discussion (under the heading of "Demand Inflation") of "Keynesian inflation theory" in terms of the inflationary gap of the "Keynesian cross" diagram (1963, p. 53)—or with their detailed description of the literature which subsequently developed on this question (1963, pp. 55–59).

> model by expressing all variables in wage units, so that his formal analysis—aside from a few passing references to a situation of "true" inflation—dealt with "real" magnitudes, not "nominal" magnitudes (Keynes 1936, pp. 119, 301, 303). [P. 18][16]

This passage reflects two basic and related misunderstandings. First, to "express all variables in wage units"—that is, to deflate nominal quantities by the wage rate—is surely not to assume that this unit is constant! This is clear from such passages in the *General Theory* as the following:

> Consumption is obviously much more a function of (in some sense) *real* income than of money income. . . . A man's real income will rise and fall . . . with the amount of his income measured in wage-units. . . . As a first approximation, therefore, we can reasonably assume that if the wage-unit changes, the expenditure on consumption corresponding to a given level of employment will, like prices, change in the same proportion. [Keynes 1936, p. 91; italics in original]

In a similar vein we find:

> Unless we measure liquidity-preference in terms of wage-units rather than that of money (which is convenient in some contexts), similar results [that is, the increased demand for nominal transactions balances] follow if the increased employment ensuing on a fall in the rate of interest leads to an increase in wages, *i.e.*, to an increase in the money value of the wage-unit. [1936, p. 172; see also pp. 248–49]

As a final example, let me cite the following:

> But if the quantity of money is virtually fixed, it is evident that its quantity in terms of wage-units can be indefinitely increased by a sufficient reduction in money-wages. [1936, p. 266]

And to those passages can be added all those cited above in which Keynes discusses the effect of full employment—and the approach thereto—on the wage unit.

Similarly, to express a model in "real magnitudes" does not mean to assume that wages and prices are rigid or exogenously determined. It is, instead, simply to assume that there is no money illusion in the system

[16] The references to the *General Theory* provided here by Friedman are not to passages dealing primarily with the procedure of measuring variables in terms of wage units, but to the allegedly "few passing references to a situation of . . . inflation."

(Patinkin 1954, 1965). Indeed, for this reason I would consider as a priori implausible any model which is *not* expressed in "real magnitudes."[17] Furthermore, this absence-of-money illusion is a necessary condition for the validity of the quantity theory. Thus, both of the quantity-theory models discussed in the preceding section—Friedman's as well as my own—are concerned solely with real variables, including real money balances. But since the nominal quantity of money is given, there is an inverse one-to-one correspondence between the level of these balances and the price level.

The major piece of additional evidence which Friedman brings in support of his interpretation of Keynesian economics is the following:

> A striking illustration [of the treatment of the price level as an institutional datum] is provided in a recent Cowles Foundation Monograph, edited by Donald Hester and James Tobin, on *Financial Markets and Economic Activity* (Hester and Tobin 1967). A key essay in that book presents a comparative static analysis of the general equilibrium adjustment of stocks of assets. Yet the distinction between nominal and real magnitudes is not even discussed. The entire analysis is valid only on the implicit assumption that nominal prices of goods and services are completely rigid, although interest rates and real magnitudes are flexible. [P. 21][18]

[17] Correspondingly, my criticism of Goldfeld (1966) on this issue would be exactly the opposite of Friedman's. Thus, compare my criticism of Arena (1963) in Patinkin (1965, p. 660) with Friedman's (n. 11) criticism of Goldfeld.

[18] In the footnote attached to this passage, Friedman cites—as an example documenting his last sentence—Tobin and Brainard's assumption "that central banks can determine the ratio of currency (or high-powered money) to total wealth including real assets"—and he contends that "if prices are flexible, the central bank can determine only nominal magnitudes, not such a real ratio." In this contention, however, Friedman is not correct. For as I have shown elsewhere, even if prices are flexible, an open-market operation by the central bank will affect the rate of interest—and hence the optimum ratio of money balances to total wealth. The reason the equilibrium rate of interest is affected in such a case—as contrasted with the case in which the quantity of money changes as a result of deficit financing—is that an open-market operation causes a change in the relative quantities of financial assets (measured in real terms) in the equilibrium portfolios of individuals. Now, a change in the price level affects the real value of nominal financial assets in an equiproportionate manner and hence cannot effect such relative changes. Correspondingly, equilibrium can be restored in this case only by variations in the relative rates of return on the various assets so as to make individuals willing to hold them in their changed proportions. The price movement which simultaneously takes place does indeed dampen the extent of the changes in the equilibrium rate(s) of interest, but, for the reasons just explained, it cannot eliminate them entirely. This argument also holds for shifts in liquidity preference as well as for the introduction of financial intermediaries or of new types of financial assets. For further details, see Patinkin (1961, pp. 109–16; 1965, chap. 10, secs. 3-4, chap. 12, secs. 4–6).

Of the five articles which Friedman cites in support of this interpretation of the Keynesian literature (n. 11), three are not relevant to the question at issue, one is relevant but not for the reason adduced by Friedman,[19] and only one is validly cited.

In particular, the three articles by Tobin and Brainard (1967), Brainard (1967), and Gramley and Chase (1965) all explicitly restrict themselves to an analysis of the nature of the stock (or balance-sheet, or asset-portfolio-composition) equilibrium achieved under the assumption that the situation in the market for the flow of current output is taken as given; correspondingly, the assumption of this analysis is not (as Friedman would have us believe) that prices are rigid while real income varies, but that—at the stage of the analysis being presented—both prices *and the flow of current income* are assumed to be held constant.[20] In the illuminating words of Brainard, the concern of these articles can be described as being "analogous to exploring the vertical displacements of the '*LM*' curve which result from monetary actions" (Brainard 1967, p. 99).

On the other hand, a valid criticism can be made of Brainard and Tobin (1968). For though most of this article is devoted to the kind of analysis described in the preceding paragraph, it does contain a section which provides for the endogenous determination of income but not of prices (pp. 112-13). And if it is this section that Friedman has in mind (he provides no specific page references), then he has a point—but only a point. For Brainard and Tobin themselves describe this section as a "primitive extension of the model" (1968, p. 112). A more basic extension—to include the production function and labor market—is not provided; and, as will be shown in the following discussion, it is these which play a vital role in the determination of absolute wages and prices in the Keynesian system.

I definitely agree that Tobin and his colleagues are to be criticized for not having made such an extension in these articles—for one of the primary

[19] I am referring here to Friedman's criticism of Goldfeld (1966); see n. 17 above. What Friedman does not, however, point out—and what is the relevant point—is that Goldfeld's study does not include the price level as an endogenous variable (Goldfeld 1966, p. 136). It should, however, be noted that one of the directions in which Goldfeld indicates that this model might be refined is that "the wage-price nexus might be introduced. This would bring in supply considerations and make the price level endogenous" (1966, p. 197). This point will be further discussed at the end of this section.

[20] See Tobin and Brainard (1967, pp. 59-60), Brainard (1967, pp. 98-100), Gramley and Chase (1965, pp. 221-22). Note also the inclusion of Y as an exogenous variable in Brainard and Tobin (1968, p. 102), in addition to the assumption of a given commodity price level (1968, p. 105). The holding of both Y and p constant at this stage of his analysis is most clear from the methodological discussion in Tobin (1969*a*, pp. 15-16); see also Tobin's listing of the exogenous variables in the various models he presents here (1969*a*, pp. 21, 24, 28). As will, however, be shown in the next paragraph, these last two articles are subject to criticism on the point at issue.

tasks of monetary theory is indeed to explain the determination of the wage and price levels.[21] But a far more important question in the present context is whether those Keynesian discussions that do extend the analysis to the labor market assumed (as Friedman contends they did) that the wage and price levels are exogenously determined.

I have already cited the contrary evidence of the analysis of the effects of wage and price flexibility in the theoretical discussions of Keynes and the Keynesians (see above). But, as before, it seems to me that the best way to answer such questions is to examine the empirical writings of the economists involved. In particular, let us see how Keynesian economists treated the wage and price level in their econometric models of the economy as a whole, for the methodology of model building requires the specification of the variables as endogenous or exogenous.

Of particular interest in this context is the work of Lawrence R. Klein, both because of its relative earliness and because of its being explicitly motivated by the desire to provide an empirical expression of the Keynesian system. The first large model (for the United States, 1921-41) constructed by Klein (in the late 1940s) does provide some support for Friedman's contention. For in analyzing the market as a whole, Klein assumes that —because of the lack of competition—"instead of taking price as the adjustment variable here, we take output" (Klein 1950, p. 102; see also pp. 50-57, 85). Nevertheless, the adjustment equation which Klein actually presents is one in which the change in the price level also appears as a variable (1950, p. 102). Furthermore, Klein explicitly treats this price level as an endogenous variable of the system as a whole (1950, p. 105).

In his subsequent work—in the early 1950s—Klein himself criticized the preceding model for giving "inadequate treatment to prices and wages, both absolute and real" and noted that "the postwar inflation showed this deficiency in a striking manner" (Klein and Goldberger 1955, p. 2). Correspondingly, in the model which they proceeded to construct (for the United States, 1929-52) Klein and Goldberger presented a "labor market adjustment equation" which is

[21] However, to maintain a proper perspective on this criticism one should remember that this, after all, is the same Tobin whom Friedman himself (n. 5) cites as being one of the first to point out the key role of the real-balance effect generated by a downward price movement in assuring the existence of a long-run equilibrium position. A characteristic of Friedman's present exposition which may partially explain his losing sight of this aspect of Tobin's work is the fact that Friedman never explicitly refers to the role of the movement of the price level in this equilibrating process; thus see Friedman (pp. 16, 25).

It is also the same Tobin who—in one of his few analyses of a model with a production function and labor market—explains that the "equilibrium absolute price level" is determined at that level "that provides the appropriate amount of real wealth in liquid form" (Tobin 1955, p. 107).

> the strategic equation for determining the level of absolute wages and prices in the system. . . .
>
> The main reasoning behind this equation is that of the law of supply and demand. Money wage rates move in response to excess supply or excess demand on the labor market. High unemployment represents high excess supply, and low unemployment below customary frictional levels represents excess demand. [1955, p. 18]

Another relevant factor is the rate of change of prices, for workers take this into account when they bargain for money wages. Thus, the rate of change of the wage rate depends on the volume of unemployment and the rate of change of the price level; and the volume of unemployment, in turn, is essentially determined as the difference between the number of people in the labor force and the input of labor as endogenously determined by the production function. Needless to say, both the wage rate and the price level are endogenous variables of this model (Klein and Goldberger 1955, pp. 17, 34–35, 37, 41, 52).

This theory of wage determination has characterized all of Klein's later work. In the revised version of the Klein-Goldberger model, much the same wage-adjustment equation is associated with the Phillips curve (Klein 1966, p. 239). In the subsequent Wharton model there is a further elaboration on the wage equation, as well as the introduction of a markup equation (which also reflects the demand situation in the market) to explain the movements of the price level (Evans, Klein, and Schink 1967, pp. 33–36). And this is carried over to the Brookings model as well (Duesenberry et al. 1965, pp. 284–85, 311). Thus in all of these models the wage rate and price level continue to be treated as endogenous variables.

That this is true not only of Klein's work can be seen most easily from the tabular survey of macroeconometric models prepared by Nerlove (1966). Of the twenty-five models there described (including the preceding four) the great majority provide for the endogenous determination of the wage and price levels.

I can most easily summarize the findings of this section by noting that they show how misleading is Friedman's contention that

> initially, the set of forces determining prices was treated [by Keynesian economics] as not being incorporated in any formal body of economic analysis. More recently, the developments symbolized by the "Phillips curve" reflect attempts to bring the determination of prices back into the body of economic analysis, to establish a link between real magnitudes and the rate at which prices change from their initial historically determined level (Phillips 1958). [P. 32]

First of all, an economic analysis of wage movements was already provided by the *General Theory*. Indeed, the Phillips-curve theory itself is foreshadowed in chapters 19 and 21 of this book. Second, even before the flourishing of the Phillips curve, Keynesian econometric models generally treated the wage rate and price level as endogenous variables of the system. And this has continued to be the case.

One final observation should be made. It has already been indicated in this section that Keynesian economics is concerned with disequilibrium states, with the principal market in disequilibrium being that for labor. Correspondingly, in the Keynesian system—and particularly in the econometric expressions thereof—there is no equilibrium equation for the labor market but rather a dynamic wage-adjustment equation determining the rate of change of the nominal wage rate in response to the state of excess supply in this market. And, as we have seen, it is this equation which plays a vital role in the endogenous determination of nominal wages and prices.

It is, therefore, not surprising that an equilibrium model, without a labor market—and this is the nature of Friedman's model—does not reveal the nature of the endogenous dynamic process by which the time paths of the nominal wage rate and price level have been analyzed in the Keynesian literature.

IV. Concluding Remarks

The standard interpretation of Keynesian economics as developed by Hicks, Modigliani, and Hansen presents as its central message—and basic differentia from classical economics—the possible existence of a position of "unemployment equilibrium." Correspondingly—in order to explain how the level of unemployment remains unchanged in such a position—this interpretation assigns a crucial role to the "liquidity trap." For it is this "trap" that keeps constant the rate of interest, hence the level of aggregate demand, and hence the levels of output and employment in the economy.

Friedman follows this standard textbook interpretation in presenting the "trap"—or, to use (as Friedman does) Keynes's term, the case of "absolute liquidity preference"—as part of "Keynes's basic challenge to the reigning theory" (pp. 15, 21 ff.).[22] All this, it might be noted, is in contrast with

[22] Once again (see n. 12 above) Friedman (n. 7) cites "Leijonhufvud's penetrating analysis" in support of his (Friedman's) view—even though Leijonhufvud's actual position is exactly the opposite! Thus Leijonhufvud writes: "The 'Liquidity Trap' notion is anti-Keynesian not only in that Keynes explicitly rejected the idea that the money-demand function would be perfectly interest-elastic within any range that we would possibly be interested in, but also in its neglect of the downward shift of the entire schedule that, in a continuing state of depression, 'at long last . . . will doubtless come by itself.' Cf. *Treatise, loc. cit.*" (1968, p. 202, n. 26). Similarly, on pp. 160-61 Leijonhufvud rejects interpretations of Keynes that are based on the "liquidity trap."

Keynes's own statement that "whilst this limiting case might become practically important in the future," he knew "of no example of it hitherto" (1936, p. 207).[23]

An alternative interpretation that I have elsewhere developed[24]—and of which I have made use in the preceding section—presents Keynesian economics as the economics of unemployment *dis*equilibrium. More specifically, the fundamental issue raised by Keynesian economics is the stability of the dynamic system: its ability to return automatically to full-employment equilibrium within a reasonable time (say, a year) if it is subjected to the customary shocks and disturbances of a peacetime economy. In this context Keynesian economics contends that as a result of high interest elasticity of the demand for money and low interest elasticity of investment, on the one hand, and distribution and expectation effects, on the other, the automatic adjustment process of the market—even when aided by a monetary policy that pushes the rate of interest down—is unlikely to converge either smoothly or rapidly to the full-employment equilibrium position. And since this interpretation thus frees Keynesian economics from the confines of an equilibrium system, it also frees it from any logical dependence on the existence of a "liquidity trap."

In brief, even if monetary policy could be depended upon to ultimately restore the economy to full employment, there would still remain the crucial question of the length of time it would need. There would still remain the very real possibility that it would necessitate subjecting the economy to an intolerably long period of dynamic adjustment: a period during which wages, prices, and interest would continue to fall, and—what is most important—a period during which varying numbers of workers would continue to suffer from involuntary unemployment. Though I am not aware that he expressed himself in this way, this is the essence of Keynes's position. This is all that need be established in order to justify his fundamental policy conclusion that the "self-adjusting quality of the economic system"—even when reinforced by central-bank policy—is not enough, and that resort must also be had to fiscal policy.

Thus this interpretation takes the debate on the degree of government intervention necessary for a practicable full-employment policy—which is the basic policy debate between Keynes and the classics—out of the realm of those questions that can be decided by a priori considerations of internal

[23] This contrast—as well as the passage from Keynes just cited in the text—is further discussed in Patinkin (1965, pp. 349, 352–54, esp. n. 29). This passage is also referred to by Friedman (pp. 25–26).

[24] The following three paragraphs draw freely on the discussions in Patinkin (1951, sec. 14; 1965, chap. 14 and suppl. n. K:3).

consistency and logical validity, and into the realm of those questions that can be decided only by empirical considerations of the actual magnitudes of the relevant economic parameters.

Friedman can undoubtedly point to passages in his article which agree with this last sentence (for example, p. 61). The trouble is that there are many more passages in which he presents quite a different interpretation of the relations between Keynes and the classics. It is these other passages which constitute the major part of his article—and to which, accordingly, my own has been devoted.

I would like to conclude this paper with one observation of an analytical nature on the dynamic equations which Friedman presents in his paper (p. 49). These, unfortunately, are not the structural equations that one might have expected from Friedman's opening statement that the purpose of this paper is to present the theoretical framework implicit in his and Anna Schwartz's book on *A Monetary History of the United States* (1963*b*).[25] Instead, they are essentially reduced-form equations. The coefficients of these equations are undoubtedly dependent on the elasticities of the structural equations, as well as on their respective speed-of-adjustment parameters. But since Friedman does not specify the nature of this dependence, his dynamic equations do not enable us to investigate what is, after all, one of the basic questions at issue: namely, the way in which—in a given policy context—different assumptions about the various elasticities of demand and dynamic parameters affect the respective time paths of price and output in the system.

[25] Nor, correspondingly, does Friedman's present discussion provide any additional details about the admittedly "tentative" dynamic analysis which he sketched in Friedman and Meiselman (1963, pp. 217–22) and Friedman and Schwartz (1963*a*, sec. 3). The main point of this analysis is that monetary changes initially generate portfolio-composition (balance-sheet) adjustments, and hence changes in the prices (and hence rates of return) of the assets (including consumer durables) held in the portfolio; these, in turn, generate changes in the demands for commodity flows and hence in their prices and/or output.

In the revised version of his *JPE* papers as reprinted above, Friedman added four paragraphs at the end of section 5 in which he summarizes—without further elaboration—his earlier analysis referred to in the preceding paragraph of this footnote. As in this earlier analysis, Friedman emphasizes that the range of assets over which he carries out his analysis of balance-sheet adjustments is broader than that of Keynesian economics. With this there can be no disagreement. Nor, obviously, would I disagree with the contention that the quantity theorists assumed that a monetary increase increases the demand for commodities even without a prior decrease in the rate of interest on bonds, for this contention can (pragmatically speaking) simply be interpreted as an alternative statement of the real-balance effect (cf. Patinkin [1965, p. 664, n. 44] for an interpretation of Friedman's analysis here in precisely these terms). But what cannot be accepted—for the reasons discussed in Section I above—is any implication that Friedman's analysis here is a proper representation of the traditional quantity theory. On the contrary (as indicated above), this highly sophisticated stock-flow analysis of Friedman's is far closer in its conceptual framework to that of Keynesian monetary theory than to that of the quantity theory.

‘Comments on the Critics’

M. Friedman, ‘Comments on the critics: Patinkin’, in R. J. Gordon (ed.), *Milton Friedman's Monetary Framework: A Debate with his Critics* (Chicago, Chicago UP, 1974), pp. 158–77.

Patinkin

Patinkin's (1969*a*) article on "The Chicago Tradition, the Quantity Theory, and Friedman" served as an important source for Harry Johnson's 1970 Richard T. Ely lecture (Johnson 1971). Patinkin—both in his 1969 article and in the present comments—and Johnson criticize me for linking my work to a "Chicago tradition" rather than recognizing that, as they see it, my work is Keynesian. In the course of their criticism, they give a highly misleading impression of the Chicago tradition. Grant for the sake of the argument—as I do not in fact grant—that my 1956 "Restatement" (see "The Quantity Theory of Money—a Restatement," in Friedman 1956; reprinted in Friedman 1969, pp. 51-67), which is the main object of criticism in Patinkin's 1969 article, had nothing whatsoever of the flavor of the Chicago tradition. That would indict my perception, or integrity, or scholarship, but it would in no way contradict the existence of an important Chicago tradition in the field of money that had a great influence on subsequent work in monetary economics and on my own work in particular. Similarly, it might justify Johnson's charge that I engaged in "scholarly chicanery," but it would not justify his charge that the "University of Chicago oral tradition" was my "invention."

Whether I conveyed the flavor of that tradition or not, there was such a tradition; it was significantly different from the quantity theory tradition that prevailed at other institutions of learning, notably the London School of Economics; that Chicago tradition had a great deal to do with the differential impact of Keynes's *General Theory* on economists at Chicago and elsewhere; and it was responsible for the maintenance of interest in the quantity theory at Chicago. My restatement *is* a restatement of the quantity theory and is not Keynesian in any meaningful sense of that term.

One reason Patinkin gives such a misleading view of both the Chicago school tradition and of my theoretical framework is his propensity to take the "quantity theory" to mean one thing and one thing only, namely, the long-run proposition that money is neutral, even though he fully recognizes, indeed insists, that the quantity theorists (myself included) were concerned mostly with short-run fluctuations. My explicit statement of what I mean by the quantity theory (quoted in my reply to Tobin, p. 145) is not referred to by Patinkin; he interprets almost all my references to the quantity theory as if I meant by it what he means by it. For example, he criticizes me for "not presenting the long-run quantity theory in the most general way that one can, once one has decided to reformulate it" and proceeds in the very next paragraph to document this criticism by referring to a model which I said—and he even quotes this statement—"refers to a short period"![17]

A second, and closely related, reason why Patinkin gives a misleading view of both the Chicago school tradition and of my framework is his emphasis on the role of the interest rate in the demand function for money as "one of the central issues of monetary economics." He regards the inclusion of the interest rate in the demand function for money as distinctively Keynesian and its neglect as a key omission in pre-Keynesian monetary theory. The contrast between that alleged omission and my inclusion of the interest rate in the demand function for money is a major ground on which he criticizes my "persistent refusal to recognize" that my "analytical framework is Keynesian." As I show below, the inclusion of the interest rate in the demand for money is not distinctively Keynesian. But, far more important for the present purpose, the inclusion of the interest rate is a minor feature of my framework, and its exclusion would have been a minor feature of pre-Keynesian monetary theory. As I also show below, the inclusion or exclusion of the interest rate in the demand function for money is not the respect in which my work is in the Chicago tradition. That tradition influenced my work primarily with respect to the interpretation of short-run movements, the reasons for the Great Depression, and the role of monetary and fiscal policies.

In arguing that inclusion of the interest rate in the demand for money is "Keynesian," Patinkin implicitly takes everything in the *General Theory* as *ipso facto* "Keynesian," as we use that term. Keynes was a quantity theorist long before he was a Keynesian, and he continued to be one after he became a Keynesian. Many parts of the *General Theory* are a continuation of his earlier interests and beliefs. The fact that Patinkin can find parallels between some of my discussion of the demand for money and Keynes's discussion in the *General Theory* does not establish that my discussion is therefore Keynesian. I shall argue, rather, that those parts of the *General Theory* are a direct outgrowth of Keynes's earlier quantity-theory views.

A more fundamental reason for Patinkin's emphasis on long-run "neutrality," the interest rate, and the real balance effect, and for his slighting the short-run context of most of my framework is that Patinkin, even more than Tobin, is Walrasian, concerned with abstract complete-

[17] For another striking example, see his discussion of the comment he quotes from my article (p. 51), in which he regards as an advantage of his own model that it demonstrates "the validity of the quantity theory," meaning by that simply the long-run neutrality of money, a result that is wholly irrelevant to my quotation in which I used "quantity-theory approach" in my sense, not his.

ness, rather than Marshallian, concerned with the construction of special tools for special problems.

In a recent article, "On the Short-Run Non-Neutrality of Money in the Quantity Theory," Patinkin (1972*a*) cites evidence that he regards as decisively contradicting my interpretation that Fisher and quantity theorists "simply took over Marshall's assumption" that "prices adjust more rapidly than quantities." Yet I regard the evidence he cites as strikingly confirming my interpretation. One sample of his evidence will do:

"The sequence of effects visualized by Fisher" after an increase in the quantity of money is "as follows:

"1. Prices rise.

"2. Velocities of circulation (V and V') increase; the rate of interest rises, but not sufficiently.

"3. Profits increase, loans expand, and the Q's [i.e., the real volume of trade] increase.

"4. Deposit currency (M') expands relatively to money (M).

"5. Prices continue to rise; that is, phenomenon No. 1 is repeated. Then No. 2 is repeated, and so on."

I described Marshall's assumption as being "that prices adjust more rapidly than quantities, indeed, so rapidly that the price adjustment can be regarded as instantaneous. An increase in demand (a shift to the right of the long-run demand curve) will produce a new market equilibrium involving a higher price but the same quantity. The higher price will, in the short run, encourage existing producers to produce more with their existing plants, thus raising quantity and bringing prices back down toward their original level, and, in the long run attract new producers and encourage existing producers to expand their plants, still further raising quantities and lowering prices. Throughout the process, it takes time for output to adjust but no time for prices to do so" (p. 17). Is not Fisher's sequence precisely the counterpart for the aggregate to this analysis for a particular product?

Further proof is that just prior to listing the five steps that Patinkin quotes, Fisher states that "an increase in currency cannot, even temporarily, very greatly increase trade. . . . [A]lmost the entire effect of an increase of deposits must be seen in a change of prices" (Fisher 1911, pp. 62–63).

Consider how a Keynesian would describe the effects of an increase in the quantity of money. It would go:

1. Interest rates fall.
2. Investment increases.

3. Output and real income increase.
4. Consumption increases.

It is not clear when he would come to the statement "prices rise," but it would surely be late in his list. Moreover, his step number 1 implies that velocity falls, but he would be most unlikely ever to refer to that phenomenon.

Is this not precisely the contrast that I drew between the quantity theorists and the Keynesians when I said that Keynes "deviated from Marshall . . . in reversing the roles assigned to price and quantity" (p. 18)?[18]

I must plead guilty to one careless expression that Patinkin quotes and that does lend itself to the interpretation that I was accusing the quantity theorists of assuming strict neutrality in the short run. This was my statement: "There is nothing in the logic of the quantity theory that specifies the dynamic path of adjustment, nothing that requires the whole adjustment to take place through *P* rather than through *k* or *y*." In light of my quotation above about Marshall's assumption (which is separated from the prior sentence by only one paragraph), I intended this sentence to refer to the instantaneous market equilibrium and to the assertion that "throughout the process, it takes time for output to adjust but no time for prices to do so"; it is not intended to mean that there are no effects on output during the process. But my wording is ambiguous and I should have been more careful.

Patinkin goes on also to quote my statement: "It was widely recognized that the adjustment during what Fisher, for example, called 'transition periods' would in practice be partly in *k* and in *y* as well as in *P*. Yet this recognition was not incorporated in formal theoretical analysis." He italicizes the last sentence for emphasis and asserts, "The facts of the case, however, are quite different," giving as evidence that "Fisher wrote incomparably more on his monetary proposals for mitigating the cyclical problems of the 'transition period' than on the long-run proportionality of prices to money. This concentration on short-run analysis was even more true for the policy-oriented Chicago quantity-theory school of the 1930s and 1940s."

The issue here is one that we have already encountered in my replies to Tobin and Davidson (and that is discussed also in points 7 and 11 of Appendix 2 below). There can be a great difference between what is implied by or contained in a formal theory, what proponents of the theory

[18] The references in Patinkin's article to statements by Chicago economists, Pigou, Keynes, Robertson, and Lavington, all equally strike me as clearly confirming my interpretation.

may believe it implies or contains, and what they write about. Of course, Fisher, the Chicago monetary economists, and the host of other economists who studied business cycles wrote a great deal about short-run movements and constructed many ingenious theories about business cycles that have much to teach us. In particular, Fisher's distinction between nominal and real interest rates, which dates back to some of his earliest writing, remains a seminal and penetrating insight. Yet, so far as I know, none of this voluminous writing and none of these theories provide a formal theoretical extension of the quantity theory to explain the division of changes in nominal income between changes in prices and in output or of changes in the quantity of money between changes in velocity, in prices, and in output, just as none of Keynes's extensive discussion of changes in money-wage rates prior to the point of full employment provides a formal theoretical analysis of such changes.

Rather than continuing to examine Patinkin's remarks in detail, I believe it will contribute more to clarify the issues raised by Patinkin if I address myself directly to the two key questions: (1) What was the distinctive quality of the Chicago tradition as it affected my own writings? (2) What are the quantity theory antecedents of Keynes's and my writings on the demand for money? I shall therefore relegate further detailed comments on those of Patinkin's statements that do not bear directly on these two issues to Appendix 2.

1. *The Chicago Tradition*

I was myself first strongly impressed with the importance of the Chicago tradition during a debate on Keynes between Abba P. Lerner and myself before a student-faculty seminar at the University of Chicago sometime in the late 1940s (or perhaps early 1950s). Lerner and I were graduate students during the early 1930s, pre-*General Theory*; we have a somewhat similar Talmudic cast of mind and a similar willingness to follow our analysis to its logical conclusion. These have led us to agree on a large number of issues—from flexible exchange rates to the volunteer army. Yet we were affected very differently by the Keynesian revolution—Lerner becoming an enthusiastic convert and one of the most effective expositors and interpreters of Keynes, I remaining largely unaffected and if anything somewhat hostile.

During the course of the debate, the explanation became crystal clear. Lerner was trained at the London School of Economics, where the dominant view was that the depression was an inevitable result of the prior boom, that it was deepened by the attempts to prevent prices and wages from falling and firms from going bankrupt, that the monetary authorities had brought on the depression by inflationary policies before the crash and had prolonged it by "easy money" policies thereafter; that the only sound policy was to let the depression run its course, bring down money costs, and eliminate weak and unsound firms.

By contrast with this dismal picture, the news seeping out of Cambridge (England) about Keynes's interpretation of the depression and of the right policy to cure it must have come like a flash of light on a dark night. It offered a far less hopeless diagnosis of the disease. More important, it offered a more immediate, less painful, and more effective cure in the form of budget deficits. It is easy to see how a young, vigorous, and generous mind would have been attracted to it.

It was the London School (really Austrian) view that I referred to in my "Restatement" when I spoke of "the atrophied and rigid caricature [of the quantity theory] that is so frequently described by the proponents of the new income-expenditure approach—and with some justice, to judge by much of the literature on policy that was spawned by the quantity theorists" (Friedman 1969, p. 51).

The intellectual climate at Chicago had been wholly different. My teachers regarded the depression as largely the product of misguided governmental policy—or at least as greatly intensified by such policies. They blamed the monetary and fiscal authorities for permitting banks to fail and the quantity of deposits to decline. Far from preaching the need to let deflation and bankruptcy run their course, they issued repeated pronunciamentos calling for governmental action to stem the deflation—as J. Rennie Davis put it, "Frank H. Knight, Henry Simons, Jacob Viner, and their Chicago colleagues argued throughout the early 1930's for the use of large and continuous deficit budgets to combat the mass unemployment and deflation of the times" (Davis 1968, p. 476).

They recommended also "that the Federal Reserve banks systematically pursue open-market operations with the double aim of facilitating necessary government financing and increasing the liquidity of the banking sructure" (Wright 1932, p. 162). There was nothing in these views to repel a student; or to make Keynes attractive. On the contrary, so far as policy was concerned, Keynes had nothing to offer those of us who had sat at the feet of Simons, Mints, Knight, and Viner.

It was this view of the quantity theory that I referred to in my "Restatement" as "a more subtle and relevant version, one in which the quantity theory was connected and integrated with general price theory and became a flexible and sensitive tool for interpreting movements in aggregate economic activity and for developing relevant policy prescriptions" (Friedman 1969, p. 52).

I do not claim that this more hopeful and "relevant" view was restricted to Chicago. The manifesto from which I have quoted the recommendation for open-market operations was issued at the Harris Foundation lectures held at the University of Chicago in January 1932 and was signed by twelve University of Chicago economists. But there were twelve other signers (including Irving Fisher of Yale, Alvin Hansen of Minnesota, and John H. Williams of Harvard) from nine other institutions.[19] I have done no exhaustive research on the policy views at the time of economists at other institutions. But we do know that the London School view, really the Austrian view of Ludwig von Mises, had many adherents—including Gottfried Haberler, who was at the time a visiting lecturer in economics at Harvard and who gave a talk on "Money and the Business Cycle" at the same Harris Foundation lectures.

To assure you (and myself) that this is not simply hindsight, let me quote from pre-Keynesian publications about the depression, reflecting the London-Austrian view and the Chicago view.

Lionel Robbins's *The Great Depression* (1934) is an extraordinarily lucid and penetrating analysis of the depression from the Austrian point of view.[20] Published in 1934, large stretches of it make instructive reading today, especially the analysis of the consequences of restrictive foreign and domestic policies. But when it comes to the role of money and to causes and cures of the depression, here is what he has to say:

"If we take deflation to mean a deliberate curtailment of the supply of money, there seems to be no evidence of its existence on a large scale either before or since the slump commenced. . . . Since the slump, Central Banks and Governments have vied with each other in promoting policies calculated to bring about easy money conditions" (p. 17).

"It is clear that the authorities of the Federal Reserve Bank and the Bank of France did nothing to prevent their increased reserves [as a result of gold inflows during the depression] from becoming effective. It is not really sensible, therefore, to attribute what happened after 1929 to their policy" (p. 23).

"A fluctuation of the kind described in the last chapter [the alleged inflation of the twenties] is bound to be followed by a period of extensive depression" (p. 55). But it "does not explain why [the slump] has been so severe." Robbins goes on to argue that "no single explanation of this phenomenon will be sufficient" (p. 56), gives a long catalog of special

[19] However, several of these were Chicagoans at one remove, for example, Charles D. Hardy and Harold G. Moulton of Brookings Institution.

[20] Compare the footnote in the *General Theory*, "It is the distinction of Prof. Robbins that he, almost alone, continues to maintain a consistent scheme of thought, his practical recommendations belonging to the same system as his theory" (Keynes 1936, p. 20).

factors intensifying the depression, and turns to "certain tendencies of policy . . . which have greatly enhanced these difficulties" (p. 65). After stressing restrictions on international trade, he turns to wage policy. "If profitability is to be restored, costs must be cut and the capital resources rehabilitated" (p. 69).

"In earlier depressions this has been the rule. . . . But at the outset of this depression other measures were adopted" (p. 69) to keep up wage rates.

"Now this policy was the reverse of what was needed. . . . The maintenance of wage rates and dividends was at the expense of capital. . . . Consumption is maintained at the expense of capital. . ." (p. 71).

"In the present depression . . . we eschew the sharp purge. We prefer the lingering disease. . . .

"The moment the boom broke in 1929, the Central Banks of the world, acting obviously in concert, set to work to create a condition of easy money, quite out of relation to the general conditions of the money market. . . . The process of liquidation was arrested" (p. 73).

"It is agreed that to prevent the depression the only effective method is to prevent the boom" (p. 171). There is needed "a greater flexibility of wage rates" (p. 186). "Our main contention [is] the necessity for the elimination of all kinds of inflexibility" (p. 189).

Compare this with what Jacob Viner said in early 1932 in his Harris Foundation lecture:

"The Federal Reserve Board has revealed to the outsider no greater capacity [than other Central Banks] to formulate a consistent policy, unless a program of drift, punctuated at intervals by homeopathic doses of belated inflation and deflation and rationalized by declarations of impotence, can be accepted as the proper constituents of central bank policy. While the New York Federal Reserve Bank has made more effort than any other central banking institution to develop a program and a technique of credit control with a view to stabilization, it has at critical moments found itself at cross-purposes with, and inhibited from action by, a Federal Reserve Board with an attitude toward its functions resembling with almost miraculous closeness that of the Bank of England during its worst period" (Wright 1932, p. 28).

Even more pertinent is a talk Viner delivered in Minneapolis on February 20, 1933, on "Balanced Deflation, Inflation, or More Depression" (Viner 1933). While agreeing with Robbins on the harm done by wage and price rigidity, and in particular by the Hoover Administration pressure against wage reductions, he also spoke vigorously against letting the cure take its course:

"We have already had three years of patient waiting, probably three years too much. It is arguable that even dangerous remedies now threaten less risk of disaster than does continuance of inaction" (p. 10).

"Had it not been for this campaign of fear . . . it would have been sound policy on the part of the federal government deliberately to permit a deficit to accumulate during depression years, to be liquidated during prosperity years. . . . The outstanding though unintentional achievement of the Hoover Administration in counteracting the depression has in fact been its deficits of the last two years, and it was only its own alleged fears as to the ill effects of these deficits, and the panic which the big business world professed to foresee if these deficits should recur, which have made this method of depression finance seriously risky" (pp. 18–19).

"I will use the term inflation to mean an increase in the total amount of spendable funds, whether consisting of coin, paper money, or bank deposits subject to check.

"The basic argument for inflation is that it would operate to raise product-prices more than cost-prices, would in this way restore a profit margin for business, and thus would bring about an increased volume of production and of employment. Against inflation many things are urged. . . .

"I can see little force in most of these objections. . . " (p. 20).

"It is often said that the federal government and the Federal Reserve system have practiced inflation during this depression and that no beneficial effects resulted from it. What in fact happened was that they made mild motions in the direction of inflation, which did not succeed in achieving it, did not succeed even in accomplishing 'reflation'; but which probably did slow up somewhat the rate of price decline . . . [p. 21]. At no time . . . since the beginning of the depression has there been for so long as four months a net increase in the total volume of bank credit outstanding. On the contrary, the government and Federal Reserve bank operations have not nearly sufficed to countervail the contraction of credit on the part of the member and non-member banks. There has been no net inflation of bank credit since the end of 1929. There has been instead a fairly continuous and unprecedentedly great contraction of credit during this entire period" (p. 22).

"Assuming for the moment that a deliberate policy of inflation should be adopted, the simplest and least objectionable procedure would be for the federal government to increase its expenditures or to decrease its taxes, and to finance the resultant excess of expenditures over tax revenues either by the issue of legal tender greenbacks or by borrowing from the banks" (p. 24).

However, Viner adds, such a policy might be vitiated by "general fear of an early departure from the gold standard and therefore a flight from the dollar." In light of this, "if going off the gold standard were as simple a matter for us as for England and Canada, I would not only advocate it, but if the mere cessation of gold payments did not suffice to lower substantially the internal purchasing power of the dollar I would recommend its accompaniment by increased government expenditures financed by the printing press or by loans" (p. 25).

However, "the actual process of going off the gold standard, while it is under way, is extremely painful, costly, panic-breeding. . . . In this country, it would undoubtedly require weeks, if not months, of public and congressional debate, during which utter confusion would be likely to prevail. . . .

"If we are to have inflation, therefore, we must have it within the gold standard" (p. 27).

Two weeks after Viner spoke these words, the United States was off the gold standard! Another graphic illustration of why economists should not let their amateur judgments of political feasibility overrule their professional judgments of economic desirability.[21]

But this is a digression. My main point is different. What, in the field of interpretation and policy, did Keynes have to offer those of us who learned their economics at a Chicago that was filled with these views? Can anyone who knows my work read Viner's comments and not see the direct links between them and Anna Schwartz's and my *Monetary History* (1963*b*), or between them and the empirical *Studies in the Quantity Theory of Money* (1956)? Indeed, as I have read Viner's talk for the purposes of this paper, I have myself been amazed to discover how precisely it foreshadows the main thesis of our *Monetary History* for the depression period, and have been embarrassed that we made no reference to it in our account. Can you find any similar link between Robbins's comments and our work?

I shall not defend my "Restatement" as giving the "flavor of the oral tradition" at Chicago in the sense that the details of my formal structure have precise counterparts in the teachings of Simons and Mints. After all, I am not unwilling to accept some credit for the theoretical analysis in that article. Patinkin has made a real contribution to the history of thought by examining and presenting the detailed theoretical teachings of Simons and Mints, and I have little quarrel with his presentation. But I certainly do defend my "Restatement" as giving the "flavor of the oral tradition" at

[21] The other famous example, of course, is Keynes's advocacy of a tariff in 1931 as a second-best solution to Britain's departure from the gold standard, which he ruled out as not feasible politically, only to see it happen very shortly.

Chicago in what seems so me the much more important sense in which, as I said, the oral tradition "nurtured the remaining essays in" ***Studies in the Quantity Theory of Money***, and my own subsequent work. And, in any event, it is clearly not a tradition that, as Johnson charges, I "invented" for some noble or nefarious purpose.

2. *Keynes and the Quantity Theory*

Is everything in the *General Theory* Keynesian? Obviously yes, in the trivial sense that the words were set down on paper by John Maynard Keynes. Obviously no, in the more important sense that the term Keynesian has come to refer to a theory of short-term economic change—or a way of analyzing such change—presented in the *General Theory* and distinctively different from the theory that preceded it. To take a noncontroversial example: in his chapter 20 on "The Employment Function" and elsewhere, Keynes uses the law of diminishing returns to conclude that an increase of employment requires a decline in real-wage rates. Clearly that does not make the "law of diminishing returns" Keynesian or justify describing the "analytical framework" of someone who embodies the law of diminishing returns in his theoretical structure as Keynesian.

In just the same sense, I maintain that Keynes's discussion of the demand curve for money in the *General Theory* is for the most part a continuation of earlier quantity theory approaches, improved and refined but not basically modified. As evidence, I shall cite Keynes's own writings in the *Tract on Monetary Reform* (1923)—long before he became a Keynesian in the present sense.

a) Absolute Liquidity Preference

There is one respect—and I believe only one—in which the discussion of the demand curve for money in the *General Theory* is distinctively Keynesian and that is the importance attached to "absolute liquidity preference" or a high-interest elasticity of the demand for money. This element is distinctively Keynesian in the double sense that it is, so far as I know, introduced for the first time in the *General Theory* and also, as I stated in the "Theoretical Framework," that it can "be regarded as a direct consequence of his assumption about the relative speed of adjustment of price and quantity" (p. 20).

Patinkin objects to my treating "the case of 'absolute liquidity preference'—as part of 'Keynes's basic challenge to the reigning theory.' " He cites as counterevidence Keynes's own statement (which I also quoted) that "whilst this limiting case might become practically important in the future" he knew "of no example of it hitherto." However, the right hand apparently knows not what the left does. In the very next paragraph, Patinkin says, "Keynesian economics contends that as a result of high-interest elasticity of the demand for money. . . ." Pray tell how that statement differs from mine that Keynes "treated velocity as if in practice its behavior frequently approximated that which would prevail in this limiting case" (p. 26)?

More important, Patinkin does not quote the sentence immediately following Keynes's disclaimer, to wit, "Indeed, owing to the unwillingness of most monetary authorities to deal boldly in debts of long term, there has not been much opportunity for a test" (Keynes 1936, p. 207).[22] Neither does Patinkin note that, so far as I can discover, this is the only disclaimer in the *General Theory;* while there are repeated statements in the opposite direction, such as, to pick only one, "The most stable, and the least easily shifted element in our contemporary economy has been hitherto, and may prove to be in the future, the minimum rate of interest acceptable to the generality of wealth-owners" (Keynes 1936, p. 309).

One consequence of my rereading large parts of the *General Theory* in the course of writing this reply has been to reinforce my view that absolute liquidity preference plays a key role. Time and again when Keynes must face up to precisely what it is that prevents a full-employment equilibrium, his final line of defense is absolute liquidity preference. To document this point, I have assembled the relevant quotations in Appendix 1. The first quotation is from page 172 because Keynes does not introduce liquidity preference or the quantity of money, with only trivial exceptions, until page 166. I do not see how anyone can read through these quotations and come to any other conclusion than that his "special twist" was highly elastic liquidity preference and that this "was a key element in Keynes's proposition" about the possibility that there might not be a

[22] As Allan Meltzer points out, this comment was in line with views that had long been held by Keynes.

"Keynes of the *Treatise* and even more Keynes of the *Essays in Persuasion* was scornful of the analysis and policies of bankers, central as well as private. In the *Treatise*, Keynes talked repeatedly and at length about the inadequacies of monetary policy during the interwar period and the limitations imposed by bankers. . . .

"Keynes's views on the subject of monetary policy, central banks, and the liquidity trap were much the same when he wrote the *General Theory*. The main point Keynes makes about the possibility of a liquidity trap and the breakdown of monetary policy is sandwiched between two statements that are critical of central bankers for not acting boldly and for not dealing in long-run debts" (Meltzer 1970, pp. 46–47).

full-employment equilibrium even with flexible prices. Patinkin sees the fly on the barn door but not the door!

b) Stocks versus Flows and Interest-Rate Effects

Patinkin argues that the liquidity-preference analysis of the *General Theory* differs from the earlier quantity-theory approach in two key respects: first, that it "is concerned with the optimal relationship between the stock of money and the stocks of other assets, whereas the quantity theory . . . was primarily concerned with the direct relationship between the stock of money and the flow of spending on goods and services."

Second, the two theories treated differently "the influence of the rate of interest on the demand for money. For, though quantity theorists did frequently recognize this influence, they did not fully integrate it into their thinking."

With respect to the first point, Patinkin does not correctly describe the analysis in the *General Theory.* The liquidity function includes both M_1, which is treated as strictly a function of "the flow of spending on goods and services," as well as M_2, which is treated as related to the stock of other assets.

In his *Tract on Monetary Reform* (1923), Keynes discusses the amount of cash people wish to hold, saying that it "depends partly on the wealth of the community, partly on its habits. Its habits are fixed by its estimation of the extra convenience of having more cash in hand as compared with the advantages to be got from spending the cash or investing it. . . . The matter cannot be summed up better than in the words of Dr. Marshall." There follows a lengthy quotation from Alfred Marshall's *Money, Credit, and Commerce,* including: "Let us suppose that the inhabitants of a country . . . find it just worth their while to keep by them on the average ready purchasing power to the extent of a tenth part of their annual income, together with a fiftieth part of their property" (Keynes 1923, pp. 78–79).

This is precisely the liquidity preference function of the *General Theory* (p. 199):

$$M = M_1 + M_2 = L_1(Y) + L_2(r),$$

except that Marshall expressed the M_2 part as a fraction of wealth, whereas Keynes expresses it as a function of the interest rate. So Patinkin's first point reduces to his second.

With respect to the second, Patinkin states that the "rate of change of the price level as one of the alternative rates of return which affect the demand for money . . . was not systematically integrated into our thinking until the work of Friedman and his associates, particularly Cagan (1956)." Patinkin is clearly wrong, at least if "our" includes the Keynes of *Monetary Reform*. Keynes has an excellent and explicit discussion of inflation as a tax and of the effect of the tax on the quantity of real balances demanded. "The public," he writes, "discover that it is the holders of notes who suffer taxation . . . and they begin to change their habits and to economize in their holding of notes" (Keynes 1923, p. 51).

Keynes also uses Germany as "an illustration of the extraordinary degree in which the money rate of interest can rise in its endeavor to keep up with the real rate, when prices have continued to rise for so long and with such volume that, rightly or wrongly, everyone believes that they will continue to rise further" (Keynes 1923, p. 26). The remark already quoted about "the advantages to be got from . . . investing" cash is further evidence that he recognized the role of the interest rate. True, he discussed the role of the rate of inflation explicitly, and of the interest rate only implicitly, but that was because his book was so largely devoted to an analysis of post-World War I inflations and their implications for exchange rates. True, also, he did not write down an explicit demand function with the rate of interest as an argument, but neither did he write one down with the anticipated rate of inflation as an argument.

Patinkin is correct when he says "quantity theorists paid little, if any, attention to the effects on the rate of interest . . . of shifts in the tastes of individuals as to the form in which they wish to hold their assets." This indeed was a Keynesian development that reflected what I regard as Keynes's critical assumption that prices were an institutional datum. The quantity theorists (including Keynes in *Monetary Reform*) found it natural to regard changes in the quantity of money as affecting prices in the first instance, and to regard the interest rate as determined by saving and investment or lending and borrowing. Monetary changes affected the interest rate by producing inflation (or deflation), which shifted the saving and investment functions by leading lenders to demand higher (or lower) nominal rates and borrowers to be willing to pay higher (or lower) nominal rates. Because the Keynesians take the price level as an institutional datum, they regard a change in the interest rate as the means whereby people are induced to hold a larger or smaller quantity of money. Hence the Keynesians were led to place greater importance than the quantity theorists on the role of changes in the interest rate in the economy's adjustment to monetary change.

But this valid point is a final, and decisive, piece of evidence against Patinkin's claim that my "analytical framework is Keynesian." For in this respect the treatment in my "Restatement" and in my "Theoretical Framework" (except where I am discussing the Keynesian theory) is the quantity-theory treatment. I too pay no attention to "the effects on the rate of interest" of shifts in the demand function for money. I too tend to minimize changes in market interest rates as the primary channel through which changes in the quantity of money affect spending, output, and prices. To go further, in the "Restatement" I do not even consider the effect of changes in the quantity of money on interest rates. In the "Theoretical Framework" I do, but only (in the passage I added to the NBER version that is referred to in my reply to Brunner and Meltzer) to show how the quantity-theory and income-expenditure approaches "can be readily reconciled on a formal level" (p. 28).

I conjecture that Patinkins's insistence on labeling my analytical framework Keynesian ultimately reflects his concentration on "neutrality." For if he interprets my framework as in the "quantity-theory" tradition, he cannot continue to regard "the quantity theory" as synonymous with the long-run neutrality of money, since my framework is clearly and obviously not about that—just as I believe the writings of earlier quantity theorists, from Ricardo and Thornton to Keynes, were not about that either. So cut down the forest to let the "neutrality tree" stand proud and tall.

Appendix 1

Quotations from the *General Theory* Related to Absolute Liquidity Preference

1. "Circumstances can develop in which even a large increase in the quantity of money may exert a comparatively small influence on the rate of interest" (p. 172).

2. "In the extreme case where money-wages are assumed to fall without limit in face of involuntary unemployment through a futile competition for employment between the unemployed labourers, there will, it is true, be only two possible long-period positions—full employment and the level of employment corresponding to the rate of interest at which liquidity-preference becomes absolute (in the event of this being less than full employment)" (p. 191).

3. "This, indeed, is perhaps the chief obstacle to a fall in the rate of interest to a very low level" (p. 202).

4. "The long term rate may be more recalcitrant when once it has fallen to a level which . . . is considered 'unsafe' by representative opinion. . . . [A] domestic rate of interest dragged up to a parity with the *highest* rate . . . prevailing in any country belonging to the international system may be much higher than is consistent with domestic full employment. . . .

"M_2 may tend to increase almost without limit in response to a reduction of r below a certain figure. . . .

"*Any* level of interest which is accepted with sufficient conviction as *likely* to be durable will be durable. . . .

"[I]t may fluctuate for decades about a level which is chronically too high for full employment. . . .

"The difficulties in the way of maintaining effective demand at a level high enough to provide full employment, which ensue from the association of a conventional and fairly stable long-term rate of interest with a fickle and highly unstable marginal efficiency of capital, should be, by now, obvious to the reader" (pp. 203-4).

5. "There is the possibility, for the reasons discussed above, that, after the rate of interest has fallen to a certain level, liquidity-preference may become virtually absolute. . . . In this event the monetary authority would have lost effective control over the rate of interest. But whilst this limiting case might become practically important in future, I know of no example of it hitherto. Indeed, owing to the unwillingness of most monetary authorities to deal boldly in debts of long term, there has not been much opportunity for a test" (p. 207).

6. "What would this involve for a society which finds itself so well equipped with capital that its marginal efficiency is zero and would be negative with any additional investment; yet possessing a monetary system, such that money will 'keep' and involves negligible costs of storage and safe custody, with the result that in practice interest cannot be negative; and, in conditions of full employment, disposed to save?

". . . the position of equilibrium, under conditions of *laissez faire*, will be one in which employment is low enough and the standard of life sufficiently miserable to bring savings to zero" (pp. 217-18).

7. "We have assumed so far an institutional factor which prevents the rate of interest from being negative. . . . In fact, however, institutional and psychological factors are present which set a limit much above zero to the practicable decline in

the rate of interest . . . , which in present circumstances may perhaps be as high as 2 or 2½ percent on long term" (pp. 218–19). (At the time Keynes wrote, consol yields in the United Kingdom were around 3 percent.)

8. "It seems, then, that the *rate of interest on money* plays a peculiar part in setting a limit to the level of employment" (p. 222).

9. "We come to what is the most fundamental consideration in this context, namely, the characteristics of money which satisfy liquidity-preference. For, in certain circumstances such as will often occur, these will cause the rate of interest to be insensitive, particularly below a certain figure, even to a substantial increase in the quantity of money in proportion to other forms of wealth" (p. 233).

10. "The significance of the money-rate of interest arises, therefore, out of the combination of the characteristics that, through the working of the liquidity-motive, this rate of interest may be somewhat unresponsive to a change in the proportion which the quantity of money bears to other forms of wealth measured in money. . ." (p. 234).

11. "If . . . money wages were to fall without limit whenever there was a tendency for less than full employment . . . there would be no resting place below full employment until either the rate of interest was incapable of falling further or wages were zero" (pp. 303–4).

12. "The most stable, and the least easily shifted, element in our contemporary economy has been hitherto, and may prove to be in future, the minimum rate of interest acceptable to the generality of wealth owners" (p. 309).

13. "The destruction of the inducement to invest by an excessive liquidity-preference was the outstanding evil, the prime impediment to the growth of wealth, in the ancient and medieval worlds" (p. 351).

Appendix 2

Comments on Some of Patinkin's Other Detailed Criticisms

Except where otherwise indicated, all quotations are from Patinkin's comment.

1. "Milton Friedman's article . . . has two concerns. The first and—from the viewpoint of the space devoted to it—major one is the chapter in the history of monetary doctrine which deals with . . . the quantity theory and Keynesian monetary theory."

That was not my intention in the article under discussion, and I made no attempt to survey the relevant literature exhaustively. I was, and am, interested primarily in the analytical differences between the two approaches, and used references to literature to illuminate them. That is, I was concerned with "doctrinal aspects of monetary theory" but not with "the history of monetary doctrine"—though Patinkin treats these terms as synonymous.

2. Patinkin sees confession of error in my failure in the 1968 and 1970 essays to "mention either the Chicago school or its individual members."

No such thing. The 1956 essay was the introduction to a series of studies done as Ph.D. theses at Chicago. The Chicago background was relevant. It was not relevant to the later articles.

3. "No evidence is given in support of this assertion about the nature of the income version of the transactions approach"—that it stresses that money is held and can be regarded as a way station between the Fisher and the Cambridge version.

In line with point 1, I did not intend this to be a statement about the history of doctrine. Clearly, as an analytical matter, it can be regarded as a way station.

4. "Friedman . . . has claimed too little . . . in the context of his identification of the quantity theory with the short-run assumption that real income is constant."

As already explained, I identified the quantity theory rather with the assumption that prices react more rapidly than output. The assumption Patinkin attributes to me, I introduced only in the "simple model" designed to highlight the problem of the missing equation.

5. "In view of the crucial role that Friedman assigns to the real-balance effect in assuring the long-run equilibrium of the system, I would prefer introducing this effect explicitly into the commodity-demand functions."

But for the most part I was concerned with the short run, not the long run, and I never have believed that the real balance effect is of much empirical significance for the short run.

6. (Continuation of quotation in point 5.) "This would also seem to provide an expression of Friedman's view that 'the key insight of the quantity-theory approach is that such a discrepancy [that is, between the nominal quantity of money demanded and supplied] will be manifested primarily in attempted spending.' "

It would provide an erroneous expression, in my opinion. I believe the real balance effect plays a negligible role in this process. The substitution effect between money and other assets is, I believe, the key factor. This is a particularly clear example of Patinkin's propensity to identify the quantity theory with long-run neutrality.

7. "Friedman achieves this interpretation [that Keynes assumed rigid wages

and prices and did not generalize the theory to the case of wage and price flexibility] only by overlooking the chapter [chap. 19] in the *General Theory* . . . entitled 'Changes in Money Wages' " which "I [Patinkin] have long considered . . . to be the apex of Keynes's analysis" and in which Patinkin believes an economic analysis of wage movements was already provided.

Chapter 19 of the *General Theory* correctly points out that the argument that wage cuts will increase employment cannot be generalized directly from a single industry to the economy as a whole without taking into account effects on demand. It then lists various possible effects of wage cuts on the propensity to consume, the marginal efficiency of capital, and the rate of interest, stresses that the only significant positive effect (in Keynes's system) is by increasing the real quantity of money and thereby lowering the rate of interest, and points out that this is subject to the same limitations as monetary policy—that is, the liquidity trap. It ends with some reflections on the appropriate policy, which Keynes concludes to be rigid wages.

There are intelligent, thoughtful comments in the chapter, but to call it "the apex of Keynes's analysis" is an insult to Keynes. The chapter adds nothing important to the rest of the Keynesian apparatus; it rather illustrates how that apparatus can be applied to a particular problem and gives a basis for regarding rigid wages as not only an observable phenomenon but also a desirable policy. (See also my reply to Davidson.)

8. "Thus wage rigidities in this chapter [chap. 19 of the *General Theory*] are not an *assumption* of the analysis but the *policy conclusion* which Keynes reaches after investigating the results to be expected from wage flexibility."

Agreed. That is precisely what I said: "When there was no full-employment equilibrium, there was also no equilibrium nominal price level; something had to be brought in from outside to fix the price level; it might as well be institutional wage rigidity. Put differently, flexible nominal wages under such circumstances had no economic function to perform; hence they might as well be made rigid" (pp. 18–19).

9. "To 'express all variables in wage units' . . . is surely not to assume that this unit is constant."

Of course not. But it does mean that the system of equations or relations expressed in wage units provides no information on the money value of the wage unit. That has to be brought in from outside, which is precisely my point. (See also section 1 of my reply to Tobin.)

10. "Furthermore, this absence-of-money illusion is a necessary condition for the validity of the quantity theory."

Only in Patinkin's sense of that term, not my sense.

11. "Even before the flourishing of the Phillips curve, Keynesian econometric models generally treated the wage rate and price level as endogenous variables of the system," which, in Patinkin's view, contradicts my interpretation of Keynes as assuming wage rigidity.

The crucial question is not whether such equations are included in the models but whether they are ad hoc or derivable from Keynes's theoretical system. The price equations generally simply link prices to costs, mainly wages. This equation can be regarded as derivable from Keynes's system. But the wage equations are either purely ad hoc or, insofar as they are derivable from any theoretical system, it is the pre-Keynes classical system rather than Keynes's. For example, Patinkin refers approvingly to Klein's comment that "the main reasoning behind this equation is that of the law of supply and demand. Money wage rates move in response to excess demand on the labor market." The "law of supply and demand" is hardly Keynesian! More important, Klein misapplies it. The "classical law," *as taken over by Keynes*, would connect *real-wage rates*, not *money-wage rates*, with excess supply or demand. Klein's inclusion of the rate of change of prices in the equation, which Patinkin cites, is a move toward the correct classical inclusion of real wages, but if it went wholly in that direction it would leave money wages and money prices either undetermined or a simple inheritance from past history—which is precisely what I say Keynes's system assumes.

12. "Friedman cites 'Leijonhufvud's penetrating analysis' in support of his (Friedman's) view [that the liquidity trap plays a crucial role in Keynes's system]—even though Leijonhufvud's actual position is exactly the opposite."

This is careless textual interpretation. What I actually said in the footnote to which Patinkin refers was, "I am indebted to a brilliant book by Leijonhufvud (1968) for a full appreciation of the importance of this proposition [that, 'as an empirical matter, prices can be regarded as rigid—an institutional datum—for *short-run economic fluctuations*'] in Keynes's system. This subsection and the one that follows, on the liquidity preference function, owe much to Leijonhufvud's penetrating analysis."

That is literally true and in no way whatsoever implies either that I agree with every conclusion Leijonhufvud reaches or that he agrees with my conclusions. In fact, I believe that Leijonhufvud's "penetrating analysis" justifies a different conclusion about the role of absolute liquidity preference in Keynes's system than the one Leijonhufvud reaches (that it plays no important role), and I am strongly confirmed in that conclusion by my rereading of Keynes (see quotations in Appendix 1).

'The Keynesian Revolution and the Monetarist Counter-Revolution'

H. G. Johnson, 'The Keynesian Revolution and the Monetarist Counter-Revolution', *American Economic Review* 61 (May 1971), pp. 1–14.

RICHARD T. ELY LECTURE

The Keynesian Revolution and the Monetarist Counter-Revolution

By HARRY G. JOHNSON
The London School of Economics and Political Science and The University of Chicago

When James Tobin and I agreed on the subject of this lecture last spring, it appeared to be a highly topical subject that would command widespread interest among the membership of this Association. Unfortunately, as so often happens with forward planning for academic purposes, others have also been alert to topicality, and have undermined our forward planning by getting in earlier with their version of the theme. Thus Milton Friedman himself gave a widely publicized lecture on "The Counter-Revolution in Monetary Theory" last September in London, which lecture has recently been published by the Institute of Economic Affairs, [4]; Karl Brunner has recently circulated a typically scholarly paper on "The 'Monetarist Revolution' In Monetary Theory" [1]; and undoubtedly many others have been writing and publishing on the same subject. My treatment of this beginning-to-be-well-worn theme today will, I hope, still retain some novelty, inasmuch as I shall be primarily concerned, not with the scientific issues in dispute in the monetarist counter-revolution against the Keynesian revolution, but with the social and intellectual conditions that make a revolution or counter-revolution possible in our profession. This lecture is therefore an excursion—amateurish, I must confess—into the economics and sociology of intellectual change.

As is well known from the field of economic history, the concept of revolution is difficult to transfer from its origins in politics to other fields of social science. Its essence is unexpected speed of change, and this requires a judgment of speed in the context of a longer perspective of historical change, the choice of which is likely to be debatable in the extreme. Leaving the judgmental issue aside for the moment, one could characterize the history of our subject in terms of a series of "revolutions," very broadly defined, as follows. Economics as we know it began with what might be called the "Smithian Revolution" against the established body of doctrines generically described as "mercantilism," a revolution which changed ideas on the nature and sources of the wealth of nations and the policies required to promote the growth of what we now call "affluence." The Ricardian revolution turned the attention of economists from concern with national wealth and its growth to the distribution of income among social classes and the interactions of growth and income distribution. The marginalist revolution of the 1870's essentially introduced a new and superior analytical technology for dealing with Ricardo's distribution problem, in the process gradually depriving Ricardian economics of its social content; hence, the results of that revolution have been described as neo-Ricardian or more commonly neoclassical economics.

Contemporary economics is based on this development and on at least four discernible "revolutions" that occurred in the late 1920's and in the 1930's. One was the imperfect-monopolistic competition revolution, which challenged the validity of the assumption of perfect competition on which value theory had come to be built following the marginalist revolution, and particularly the conclusions about the welfare effects of competition to which that theory led. This revolution has more or less fizzled out, though its fossilized remnants continue to plague both students and their instructors in elementary courses. Another was the empirical or econometric revolution, with its insistence initially on the measurement of economic relationships and, subsequently and more ambitiously, on the testing of economic hypotheses—though the "testing of hypotheses" is frequently merely a euphemism for obtaining plausible numbers to provide ceremonial adequacy for a theory chosen and defended on *a priori* grounds. The third was the general equilibrium revolution, based on the introduction by Hicks and Allen of the continental Walrasian-Paretoan approach into the Anglo-Saxon tradition in replacement of the then-dominant Marshallian partial-equilibrium approach. Finally, and most sweeping in its effects, there was the Keynesian Revolution in monetary theory.

By contrast with the abundance of revolutions, counter-revolutions are hard to find in the development of economic thought. About the closest one can come to a counter-revolution in the history of economic thought is to interpret the development of the Austrian theory of value as a counter-revolution against the socialist, and especially the Marxist, tradition of economic theorizing; and that aspect of the work of the Austrian school was a side issue in the marginalist revolution. The monetarist counter-revolution of contemporary times is probably the first significant counter-revolution in the development of our subject. In venturing this judgment, however, I should note that the disrepute into which the theories of imperfect and monopolistic competition have fallen, as theories of contemporary industrial competition, in the period since the second world war could be described as the result of an intellectual counter-revolution, based on a combination of faith in the preexisting theory of competition and devotion to the empirical revolution; and also that, if one is prepared to disregard the political labels that people choose to attach to themselves, the left-wing student and faculty demand for a politically and socially relevant "radical" economics and protest against emphasis on mathematical and econometric quantification can be classed as counter-revolutionary, inasmuch as it seeks to revert to the pre-marginalist-revolution concern with the economic system as a system of relationships among social classes.

As I have already mentioned, the chief problem in identifying revolutions and counter-revolutions and distinguishing them from slower and more comprehensible and rational processes of change in economic thought is to arrive at a judgment of the relative speed of change and the degree to which the speed is justifiable. From this point of view, some of what I have just now described as revolutions were not really revolutionary—notably the Smithian and marginalist revolutions, the imperfect-monopolistic competition revolution, and the general equilibrium and empirical revolutions. The Smithian and marginalist revolutions spread relatively slowly, through the force of their scientific superiority and intellectual appeal and the process of natural wastage of their opponents. The imperfect-monopolistic competition revolution was the end result of puzzling by many minds over a problem that Marshall had stated but had been unable to solve satisfactorily—the existence of downward-sloping cost curves for individual firms. The general equilibrium revolution was a result of the delayed appreciation by economists of the need for a better command of mathematical techniques, the delay being occasioned by the long association of the subject with philosophy in the English academic tradition and its continuing association with law in the continental tradition. And the empirical revolution depended on the development of the techniques of statistical inference—most of the historically great economists were quantitatively oriented, or at least paid lip service to the need for quantitative work, but lacked the requisite tools to carry out such work themselves. For real intellectual revolutions, we are left with three major examples: the Ricardian revolution, the reasons for whose rapid propagation were examined some twenty years ago by S. G. Checkland [2], the Keynesian revolution, and the monetarist counter-revolution. These last two are the subject of my lecture today.

My concern, specifically, is with the reasons for the speed of propagation of the monetarist counter-revolution; but I cannot approach this subject without reference to the reasons for the speed of propagation of the Keynesian revolution, since the two are interrelated. Indeed, I find it useful in posing and treating the problem to adopt the "as if" approach of positive economics, as expounded by the chief protagonist of the monetarist counter-revolution, Milton Friedman, and to ask: suppose I wished to start a counter-revolution against the Keynesian revolution in monetary theory, how would I go about it—and specifically, what could I learn about the technique from the revolution itself? To pose the question in this way is, of course, to fly in the face of currently accepted professional ethics, according to which purely scientific considerations and not political considerations are presumed to motivate scientific work; but I can claim the protection of the "as if" methodology against any implication of a slur on individual character or a denigration of scientific work.

From this point of view, obviously, the first problem is to identify the elements in the situation at the time of the *General Theory* that accounted for its rapid acceptance and propagation among professional economists. Such elements are of two types, one relating to the objective social situation in which the new theory was produced, the other relating to the scientific characteristics of the new theory itself.

As regards the objective social situation, by far the most helpful circumstance for the rapid propagation of a new and revolutionary theory is the existence of an established orthodoxy which is clearly inconsistent with the most salient facts of reality, and yet is sufficiently confident of its intellectual power to attempt to explain those facts, and in its efforts to do so exposes its incompetence in a ludicrous fashion (on this see [8]). Orthodoxy is, of course, always vulnerable to radical challenge: the essence of an orthodoxy of any kind is to reduce the subtle and sophisticated thoughts of great men to a set of simple principles and straightforward slogans that more mediocre brains can think they understand well enough to live by—but for that very reason orthodoxy is most vulnerable to challenge when its principles and slogans are demonstrably in conflict with the facts of everyday experience.

So it was in the 1930's, and particularly in the 1930's in Britain, which had already experienced a decade of mass unemployment associated with industrial senescence and an overvalued exchange rate, mass unemployment which the prevailing orthodoxy could neither explain nor cope with. This, it may be noted, was in large part the fault of the economists themselves. There existed already a body of monetary analysis that was quite capable of explaining both Britain's and the industrial world's unemployment problems as a consequence of monetary mismanagement. But, hypnotized by the notion that money is merely a veil cast over real phenomena—the homogeneity postulate of contemporary monetary theory—the economists of the time attempted to explain what were essentially monetary phenomena by real causes. Eminent British economists sought to explain mass unemployment as a consequence of the satiation of real human wants, a satiation that should have produced a general reduction in working hours but unfortunately and inexplicably operated instead differentially to reduce the working hours of a substantial part of the population to absolute zero. Other economists viewed the depression as a punishment justly visited upon enterprises and individuals for past sins of speculation and erroneous microeconomic decision-taking. The concern for microeconomic explanations diverted attention from what the available macroeconomic analysis could have said about the problem; it also led to the recommendation of *ad hoc* remedies such as public works that lacked any firm grounding in theory as generally understood.

In this situation of general confusion and obvious irrelevance of orthodox economics to real problems, the way was open for a new theory that offered a convincing explanation of the nature of the problem and a set of policy prescriptions based on that explanation. Such a theory, however, would have to possess certain characteristics if it were to win intellectual acceptance and political success. In particular, it would have to come from within yet offer liberation from the established orthodoxy—for one must remember that orthodoxy includes both an established conservative orthodoxy and an established self-termed "radical" orthodoxy, and, since each recognizes and accommodates the other's arguments, there is no real hope of progress being achieved by a switch from one position to the other.

To be more specific, a revolutionary theory had to depend for its success on five main characteristics—here I must admit that I am conducting my analysis in the blinding light of hindsight. First, it had to attack the central proposition of conservative orthodoxy—the assumed or inferred tendency of the economy to full employment—with a new but academically acceptable analysis that reversed the proposition. This Keynes did with the help of Kahn's concept of the multiplier and his own invention of the propensity to consume. Second, the theory had to appear to be new, yet absorb as much as possible of the valid or at least not readily disputable components of existing orthodox theory. In this process, it helps greatly to give old concepts new and confusing names, and to emphasize as crucial analytical steps that have previously been taken as platitudinous; hence, in the *General Theory*, the marginal productivity of capital became the marginal efficiency of capital; the desired ratio of money to income, the *k* of the Cambridge tradition, became a minor constituent of the new theory of "liquidity preference;" and the *ex post* identity of savings and investment, which previous theorists including Keynes himself had rightly recognized as unhelpful to dynamic analysis, became the *sine qua non* of right reasoning.

Third, the new theory had to have the appropriate degree of difficulty to understand. This is a complex problem in the design of new theories. The new theory had to be so difficult to understand that senior academic colleagues would find it neither easy nor worth while to study, so that they would waste their efforts on peripheral theoretical issues, and so offer themselves as easy marks for criticism and dismissal by their younger and hungrier colleagues. At the same time, the new theory had to appear both difficult enough to challenge the intellectual interest of younger colleagues and students, but actually easy enough for them to master adequately with a sufficient investment of intellectual endeavour. These objectives Keynes's *General Theory* managed to achieve: it neatly shelved the old and established scholars, like Pigou and Robertson, enabled the more enterprising middle- and lower-middle-aged like Hansen, Hicks, and Joan Robinson to jump on and drive the bandwagon, and permitted a whole generation of students (as Samuelson has recorded) to escape from the slow and soul-destroying process of acquiring wisdom by osmosis from their elders and the literature into an intellectual realm in which youthful iconoclasm could quickly earn its just reward (in its own eyes at least) by the demolition of the intellectual pretensions of its academic seniors and predecessors. Economics, delightfully, could be reconstructed from scratch on the basis of a little Keynesian understanding and a lofty contempt for the existing literature—and so it was.

Fourth, the new theory had to offer to the more gifted and less opportunistic scholars a new methodology more appealing than those currently available. In this respect, Keynes was lucky both in having a receptive audience available, and to hit somewhere conveniently between the old and the newly emerging styles of economic theorizing. The prevailing methodological orthodoxy was that of Marshall—a partial-equilibrium approach set within a clear appreciation of the two complex problems of general equilibrium and of historical change, and hence both unsatisfactory at the simple level of partial-equilibrium analysis taken by itself, and extremely difficult to apply skillfully in a broader analytical and social context. The new methodological challenge was coming from the explicitly mathematical general-equilibrium approach of Hicks and Allen, an approach whose empirically and historically almost empty generality was of little general appeal. The *General Theory* found a middle ground in an aggregated general-equilibrium system which was not too difficult or complicated to work with—though it demanded a substantial step forward in mathematical competence—and which offered a high degree of apparent empirical relevance to those who took the trouble to understand it.

Finally, the *General Theory* offered an important empirical relationship for the emerging tribe of econometricians to measure—the consumption function, a far more challenging relationship than the demand for sugar, a relationship for which the development of national income statistics provided the raw material needed for estimation, and which could be estimated with surprising success given the limitation of the available data to approximately a single business cycle.

In my judgment, these factors accounted for the success of the Keynesian revolution: on the one hand, the existence of an important social and economic problem with which the prevailing orthodoxy was unable to cope; on the other hand, a variety of characteristics that appealed to the younger generation of that period—notably the claim of the new theory to superior social relevance and intellectual distinction, its incorporation in a novel and confusing fashion of the valid elements of traditional theory, the opportunity it offered to bypass the system of academic seniority by challenging senior colleagues with a new and self-announcedly superior scientific approach, the presentation of a new methodology that made general-equilibrium theory both manageable and socially relevant, and the advancement of a new empirical relationship challenging for econometricians to estimate.

The very success of the Keynesian revolution, however, ensured that it would in its turn become the established orthodoxy, and as such be as vulnerable as the old to revolutionary attack—which would necessarily have to be a counter-revolutionary attack. Keynes himself, as Leijonhufvud's monumental reinterpretation of his thought [9] has reminded us, had a seasoned and subtle mind, conscious both of the flow of economic history and of the role of theory as an adjunct to policy-making in a given set of historical circumstances. His followers—which means the profession at large— elaborated his history-bound analysis into a timeless and spaceless set of universal principles, sacrificing in the process much of his subtlety, and so established Keynesianism as an orthodoxy ripe for counter-attack.

There are several factors in this transmogrification worthy of note. The first, and probably most important, has been the conviction of Keynesians that the mass unemployment of the 1930's represents the normal state of capitalist society —more accurately, of capitalist society unaided by Keynesian management—and that unemployment is always the most urgent social problem. This view was elevated into a dogma in the United States under the leadership of Alvin Hansen, whose theory of secular stagnation was the subject of his Presidential Address to this Association [6]. While that theory has been quietly forgotten, or frugally converted into a theory applicable to the underdeveloped countries, vestiges of it linger on in the thinking of American Keynesians. The view that unemployment is the overriding social problem also lingers on among British Keynesians such as Joan Robinson, Roy Harrod, and Thomas Balogh, though I should note that Nicholas Kaldor has for many years taken a much more optimistic view of the resilience of capitalism. The corollary of the Keynesian view of the primacy of the unemployment problem has been a pronounced tendency to play down the adverse economic consequences of inflation, and to assume that, if only the unemployment consequences of anti-inflationary policies were properly understood, society would cheerfully agree to adopt and implement an incomes policy instead.

A second factor in the transformation of Keynesianism into an orthodoxy has been that people who made their academic reputations and earned their present status on the basis of an early and enthusiastic conversion to Keynesianism in the late 1930's and early 1940's have continued to trade on their foresight, to the academic detriment of their juniors, who have never had the same chance to jump onto the front—and not the rear—of an academic bandwagon. This factor has been far more effective in paving the way for a monetarist counter-revolution in the United States, where institutional competition prevents centralized control of professional advancement, than in the United Kingdom, where Oxbridge continues to dominate the academic scene.

A third factor has been that, while the Keynesian revolution in its time offered a tremendous liberation to the energies of young economists in the fields of pure theorizing about concepts, the construction of macroeconomic general-equilibrium models, and the estimation of econometric models of the economy, these activities have run into diminishing returns so rapidly that they have ceased to be appealing to young and ambitious economists.

The result has been that—beginning perhaps sometime in the mid-1950's—Keynesianism has become itself an established orthodoxy, ripe for attack in exactly the same way as what Keynes chose to call "classical economics" and to attack in the 1930's. It has had the same two vulnerable characteristics: inability to prescribe for what has come to be considered a major social problem—inflation, in contrast to the unemployment of Keynes's time—and a dependence on the authority and prestige of senior scholars which is oppressive to the young. Also, ironically enough in view of Keynes's own long concern with the influence of money on the economy, it has suffered from the same major defect as the orthodoxy Keynes attacked—the attempt to explain essentially monetary phenomena in terms of a mixture of real theory and *ad-hoc*-ery, and specifically to explain inflation in terms of real effective demand and the Phillips curve. The fact that Keynesian economics has stumbled into the same pitfall as the "classical" orthodoxy it succeeded is, perhaps, an indication of the difficulty of monetary theory as contrasted with value theory, as well as of the perils of abandoning monetary theory in favor of what appears seductively to be more reasonable common sense.

If, in accordance with the "as if" methodology of positive economics that I adopted earlier in this lecture, one posed the question of how to mount a counter-revolution against Keynesian orthodoxy, and considered the question in the light of the factors that contributed to the success of the Keynesian revolution, one would, I think, be driven inescapably to two sets of conclusions.

The first would be the need to find an important social problem that the established orthodoxy is incapable of dealing with, even though it tries its best and claims to be successful. The second would be the need to develop a counter-revolutionary theory that had the requisite characteristics to be academically and professionally successful in replacing the previous revolutionary theory.

The obvious answer to the first problem —finding an important social problem that orthodox theory cannot solve—is to concentrate on the issue of inflation, the issue that Keynesian theory was least well designed to deal with. The trouble with that answer has been that, under the influence of both experienced inflation and Keynesian theory, the public has for the most part not been much concerned about the economic evils of inflation, and so has not regarded inflation as an important test of the intellectual strength of Keynesian orthodoxy. The history of the monetarist counter-revolution has, in fact, been characterized by a series of mostly vain efforts to convince the profession and the public (a) that inflation is an important question and (b) that monetarism can provide an explanation and a policy whereas Keynesianism cannot. Proposition (b) is eminently plausible; but it can only get a hearing if proposition (a) is accepted first; and, aside from a brief interlude in the late 1950's, the public has become convinced of proposition (a) only very recently. It is no accident that the appearance of monetarism as a strong intellectual movement has had to wait until the aftermath of the escalation of the war in Viet Nam in 1965. It is even less of an accident that its current success has depended on a prior Keynesian claim to, and acceptance of, responsibility for efforts to stop inflation by Keynesian fiscal means, under the auspices of the "New Economics." Monetarism has until the past few years been in the position of investing a great deal of intellectual ability in analyzing problems and producing solutions that no one else has considered worth the effort involved. It has eventually become a public force less by its own efforts than as a consequence of the "New Economics" overreaching itself when it was riding high in the formation of national economic policy. The "New Economics" was favored by the opportunity to sell Keynesian policies to meet a Keynesian problem; it encountered disaster when it tried to sell reverse Keynesian policies to meet a non-Keynesian problem. And the monetarist counter-revolution has been cashing in on that mistake of intellectual strategy.

Nevertheless, on this score of social relevance, the monetarist counter-revolution has had certain factors working in its favor which have enabled it to survive and prosper despite the absence of an overwhelmingly obvious inadequacy of the established Keynesian orthodoxy, for most of the postwar period. One has been that, with the growing professionalization of economics and the expansion of academic support of interest in it, it has become increasingly possible for an issue to be deemed scientifically interesting and worthy of investigation even if the general public displays no visible interest in it. Another has been the rise of the United States to the position of a world power, which has made the exploration of issues of no direct relevance to the economic interests of the United States nevertheless worth pursuing as potentially matters of the national interest in the world economy. Both the hyper-inflations in Europe and elsewhere that followed the two world wars, and the strong inflations that have characterized Latin American economic history, have lent themselves to investigation with the aid of the quantity theory as matters of potential relevance to U.S. economic policy. But, as already mentioned, while these foreign experiences have provided fodder for monetarism, and in the course of time support for the contention that monetarism rests on a far wider base of empirical investigation than Keynesianism, the real counter-revolutionary thrust of monetarism has only developed since inflation became a major problem for the United States itself. Further, it is only since that event—which, given the world importance of the United States, has meant the emergence of inflation as a worldwide problem—that monetarism has been taken seriously by academic and public opinion in other countries.

Practical social relevance apart, the question of success for a new theory, whether revolutionary or counter-revolutionary, depends on its fitting appropriately into the intellectual climate of its time. Here we may apply what has already been said about the reasons for the successful rapid propagation of the Keynesian revolution to the "as if" question of how to proceed to mount a quantity-theory counter-revolution. There were, I trust you will remember, five elements in the success of the Keynesian revolution, and I shall take them in turn.

The first was a central attack, on theoretically persuasive grounds, on the central proposition of the orthodoxy of the time. In the case of the Keynesian revolution, that proposition was the automatic tendency of the economy to full employment. In the case of the counter-revolution, the obvious point of attack, in a world characterized by high employment and inflationary tendencies, was the vulgar Keynesian orthodox position that "money does not matter." As James Tobin has pointed out, there is a world of difference between two alternatives to this proposition, namely, one, "money does too matter," and, two, "money is all that matters." But this difference was easily and conveniently blurred, to the benefit of the counter-revolution, by seizing on the extreme Keynesian position that money does not matter at all as the essence of the prevailing orthodoxy.

The second aspect of Keynesian success was the production of an apparently new theory that nevertheless absorbed all that was valid in the existing theory while so far as possible giving these valid concepts confusing new names. This was the technique followed—again I would emphasize the "as if" character of my interpretation —in Friedman's classic restatement of the quantity theory of money [3]. The restated quantity theory is, as Patinkin has recently pointed out, essentially a generalization of Keynes's theory of liquidity preference on the basis of a more sophisticated analysis of the nature of wealth and the relation of wealth to income. Novelty and the requisite intellectual confusion were provided by the substitution of the concept of "permanent income" for that of wealth, and the dragging across the trail of the red herring of human capital that was emerging from other work being conducted at Chicago at that time. Nevertheless, the restatement of the quantity theory of money did include one important and genuinely novel element, drawn not from Keynes but from his predecessors in monetary theory, which was highly relevant to the problem of inflation and which continues to distinguish quantity theorists from Keynesians; this consisted in its emphasis on the Fisherian distinction between the real and the money rate of interest and on the expected rate of price inflation or deflation as determining the difference between the two.

For the reasons just given, the restatement of the quantity theory provided a new theory meeting the third criterion for success, a degree of difficulty of understanding just sufficient to deter the old and to challenge and reward the young, and hence to reopen the avenues of professional opportunity for the ambitious.

The fourth criterion for success was a new and appealing methodology. Here the counter-revolutionary theory could appeal against the tendency of Keynesian economics to proliferate into larger and yet larger models of the economic system, a tendency which sacrificed theoretical insights to the cause of descriptive realism and which had the incidental but important detractions of demanding large sums of scarce research money available only to senior economists and of turning young economists into intellectual mechanics whose function was to tighten one bolt only on a vast statistical assembly line, the end product of which would contain nothing that could be visibly identified as their own work. In place of this approach, the counter-revolution set up the methodology of positive economics, the essence of which is not to pursue descriptive realism as represented by the largest possible system of general equilibrium equations, but to select the crucial relationships that permit one to predict something large from something small, regardless of the intervening chain of causation. This methodology obviously offered liberation to the small-scale intellectual, since it freed his mind from dependence on the large-scale research team and the large and expensive computer program.

The fifth criterion for success was the advancement of a new and important empirical relationship, suitable for determined estimation by the budding econometrician. That relationship was found in the demand function for money, the stability of which was claimed to be the essence of the traditional quantity theory of money. Presentation of the stable demand function for money as the essence of the quantity theory offered a close parallel to the Keynesian consumption function of the 1930's—a statistical relationship simple to understand theoretically and not too hard to estimate statistically, which promised, nonetheless, to contribute importantly to the resolution of central theoretical issues. Moreover, since intelligent and gifted young men and women will persevere until they succeed in finding statistical validation of an allegedly important theoretical relationship, and will then interpret their results as evidence in favor of the theory that originally suggested the relationship, their efforts will inevitably be extremely favorable to the theory in question. And so it has proved. A stable demand function for money is by no means inconsistent with the Keynesian macroeconomic general equilibrium model, and indeed is presumed to exist in the construction of the standard IS-LM diagram. But the empirical finding of the existence of such a function has been widely adduced in support of the quantity theory as against the rival Keynesian theory, a procedure justified only by the identification of the Keynesian orthodoxy with the proposition that money does not matter and that velocity is either highly unstable or infinitely interest-elastic.

The quantity-theory counter-revolution could therefore make use of the same factors as facilitated the rapid propagation of Keynesian economics—the attack on a central and widely held theoretical proposition, the development of a new theory that absorbed and rechristened the best of the old, the formulation of that theory in terms that challenged the young and enabled them to leapfrog over the old, the presentation of a new methodology that made more immediate sense than the prevailing methodology, especially in terms of accessibility to the young and to those outside the established centers of academic excellence, and a new and presumptively crucial empirical relationship suitable for relatively small-scale econometric testing.

A counter-revolution, however, has to cope somehow with a problem that a revolution by definition can ignore—though it can trade on it in its propaganda—the problem of establishing some sort of continuity with the orthodoxy of the past. Specifically, the monetarist counter-revolutionaries were burdened with the task of somehow escaping from the valid criticisms of the traditional quantity theory, which the Keynesian revolution had elevated into articles of dogma and self-justification. These criticisms were, first, that the quantity theory had assumed an automatic tendency to full employment, which was manifestly in conflict with the facts of experience; and, second, that velocity was a highly unstable variable, useful, if at all, only for the *ex post* description of historical events. The restatement of the quantity theory met these criticisms by two counter-contentions: that the question of whether the economy responds to monetary impulses by price-level or by output changes is an empirical question falling outside the domain of monetary theory properly defined, because the quantity theory is a theory of the demand for money and not a theory of aggregate response to monetary change; and that the essence of the quantity theory as a theory of the demand for money is not presumptive constancy of velocity but the stable functional dependence of velocity on a few major variables. The former counter-contention freed the quantity theory from the charge that it was too silly to be worth considering, and opened the way for fruitful scientific controversy and development in monetary theory—though, as I shall explain later, the abnegation of responsibility for explaining the division of the effects of monetary change between price and quantity movements has subsequently proved a serious short-coming of the counter-revolution, now that the counter-revolution has come to be taken seriously. The latter counter-contention, involving emphasis on the existence of a stable demand function for money, permitted the absorption of the best of Keynesian ideas into the quantity theory cause, without any recognized need for acknowledgment of their source. The problem in the case of both counter-contentions was to establish a plausible linkage with pre-Keynesian orthodoxy.

The solution to this problem was found along two lines. The first was the invention of a University of Chicago oral tradition that was alleged to have preserved understanding of the fundamental truth among a small band of the initiated through the dark years of the Keynesian despotism. The second was a careful combing of the *obiter dicta* of the great neo-classical quantity theorists for any bits of evidence that showed recognition (or could be interpreted to show recognition) of the fact that the decision to hold money involves a choice between holding money and holding wealth in other forms, and is conditioned by the rates of return available on other assets.

Don Patinkin has very recently—and over-belatedly, from the standpoint of the history of economic thought—exploded these efforts to provide bridges between the pre-Keynesian orthodoxy and the monetarist counter-revolution [10]. He demonstrates conclusively that in their theorizing the neo-classical theorists did assume a tendency to automatic full employment, and that in their analyses of practical policy problems they regarded the inherent instability of velocity as a major disturbing element and made no use whatever of the functional relationship between velocity and other aggregate variables implied by their own *obiter dicta*. And he shows specifically that the Chicago quantity theorists—Simons and Mints—were no different from their quantity theory colleagues elsewhere in these respects. There was no lonely light constantly burning in a secret shrine on the Midway, encouraging the faithful to assemble in waiting for the day when the truth could safely be revealed to the masses; that candle was made, and not merely lit, only when its light had a chance of penetrating far and wide and attracting new converts to the old-time religion.

Nevertheless, one should not be too fastidious in condemnation of the techniques of scholarly chicanery used to promote a revolution or a counter-revolution in economic theory. The Keynesian revolution derived a large part of its intellectual appeal from the deliberate caricaturing and denigration of honest and humble scholars, whose only real crime was that they happened to exist and stand in the way of the success of the revolution. The counter-revolution had to endow these scholars, or at least their intellectual successors, with a wisdom vastly superior to what their opponents had credited them with. *Obiter dicta* and an oral tradition are at least semilegitimate scholarly means to this polemical end. Moreover, as time has passed and the counter-revolution has acquired increasing academic respectability, it has become increasingly possible to admit, and even to brag, that the useful ideas have been drawn from the revolution and not from the preexisting orthodoxy. Indeed, this is a necessary element in a successful counter-revolution, an element for which a previously successful revolution inevitably provides the foundations—because it ultimately becomes possible to draw an intellectually acceptable distinction between the sophisticated ideas of the revolutionary leader and the unsophisticated ideas of the revolutionary followers and executors, and to absorb the former into the counter-revolutionary ideology while discarding the latter as beneath intellectual contempt. The service of drawing this distinction in intellectually acceptable terms has been performed for the monetarist counter-revolution with great scholarly distinction by Axel Leijonhufvud's book on Keynesian economics and the economics of Keynes.

I have in this lecture been concerned primarily with the intellectual and social factors that make it possible to launch a successful revolution or counter-revolution in economic theory. However, I would judge that the key determinant of success or failure lies, not in the academic sphere, but in the realm of policy. New ideas win a public and a professional hearing, not on their scientific merits, but on whether or not they promise a solution to important problems that the established orthodoxy has proved itself incapable of solving. Keynes, and many other economists in Britain and elsewhere, spent much time in the 1920's and 1930's advocating public works as a cure for unemployment—a cure that, because it conflicted with prevailing orthodoxy, was unacceptable. The *General Theory* was successful, precisely because, by providing an alternative theory to the prevailing orthodoxy, it rationalized a sensible policy that had hitherto been resisted on purely dogmatic grounds. Similarly, the monetarist counter-revolution has ultimately been successful because it has encountered a policy problem—inflation—for which the prevailing Keynesian orthodoxy has been able to prescribe only policies of proven or presumptive incompetence, in the form of incomes or guidelines policy, but for which the monetarist counter-revolution has both a theory and a policy solution.

No particular point would be served in a lecture of this kind by recounting the stages of accomplishment in the monetarist counter-revolution (see [7]). The advance from strength to strength is summarizable in a few key phrases: the restatement of the quantity theory, a statistical illusion in the judging of Keynesian models, velocity versus the multipler in U.S. monetary history, monetarism versus fiscalism, and "the new new economics." The question of interest is whether the monetarist counter-revolution will sweep the board and become the orthodoxy of the future, itself ripe for attack by a new revolution, or whether it will gradually peter out.

Personally, I expect it to peter out, for two reasons. The first, and most important, is that I believe the Keynesians are right in their view that inflation is a far less serious social problem than mass unemployment. Either we will vanquish inflation at relatively little cost, or we will get used to it. The odds at present are that we will accept it as a necessary price of solving other pressing domestic issues—this seems to be the current view of the present Administration—and in that case monetarism will again be reduced to attempting to convince the public of the importance of the problem it is equipped to solve before it can start arguing about the scientific superiority of its proposed solution to the problem. The second reason is that monetarism is seriously inadequate as an approach to monetary theory, judged by prevailing standards of academic economics, and in the course of repairing its intellectual fences and achieving full scientific respectability it will have to compromise irretrievably with its Keynesian opposition.

The most serious defects of the monetarist counter-revolution from the academic point of view are, on the one hand, the abnegation of the restated quantity theory of money from the responsibility of providing a theory of the determination of prices and of output, and, on the other hand, its continuing reliance on the methodology of positive economics. Abnegation of responsibility for analyzing the supply response of the economy to monetary impulses, and particularly the disclaiming of the need for an analysis of whether monetary changes affected prices or quantities, was, as I have explained earlier, necessary to the restoration of the quantity theory to a position of academic respectability. But this need was transitory: once the quantity theory regained academic respectability, it was obliged to resume responsibility for the short-run forecasting of aggregate movements of prices and quantities (see [5]). This it has begun to do, most importantly through the research work of the Federal Reserve Bank of St. Louis, and with appreciable success; but it has been lured into playing in a new ballpark, and playing according to a different set of rules than it initially established for itself.

In similar fashion, the methodology of positive economics was an ideal methodology for justifying work that produced apparently surprising results without feeling obliged to explain just why they occurred, and in so doing mystifying and exciting the interest of noncommitted economists and wavering Keynesians. But the general equilibrium and empirical revolutions of the recent past have taught economists to ask for explicit specification of the full general equilibrium system with which the theorist or empiricist is working, and to distrust results that appear like rabbits out of a conjurer's hat—and an old-fashioned top hat at that. The demand for clarification of the mechanism by which results can be explained is contrary to the methodology of positive economics, with its reliance on the "as if" approach. But it will have to be answered satisfactorily if the monetarist counter-revolution is to win general acceptance among the profession; and the attempt to answer it will necessarily involve the counter-revolutionaries in the opposing methodology of general-equilibrium systems and multi-equation econometric models. The quantity theorists have already begun to extend their efforts into simultaneous-equation formulations and estimations of economic relationships. In so doing, they have been making important methodological compromises with the Keynesian opposition—or, to put it another way, reaching out for a synthesis between the revolution and the counter-revolution.

In summary, it seems to me that the monetarist counter-revolution has served a useful scientific purpose, in challenging and disposing of a great deal of the intellectual nonsense that accumulates after a successful ideological revolution. But its own success is likely to be transitory, precisely because it has relied on the same mechanisms of intellectual conquest as the revolution itself, but has been forced by the nature of the case to choose a less important political issue—inflation—to stand on than the unemployment that provided the Keynesian revolution with its political talking point, and has also espoused a methodology that has put it in conflict with long-run trends in the development of the subject. If we are lucky, we shall be forced as a result of the counter-revolution to be both more conscious of monetary influences on the economy and more careful in our assessment of their importance. If we are unlucky (those of us who are not good at jumping on bandwagons) we shall have to go through a post-counter-revolution revolution as the price of further progress on the monetary side of our science.

REFERENCES

1. **Brunner, Karl,** "The 'Monetarist Revolution' in Monetary Theory," (mimeographed, 1970).
2. **Checkland, S. G.,** "The Propagation of Ricardian Economics in England," *Economica,* New Series, Vol. 16, No. 61 (February 1949), pp. 40–52.
3. **Friedman, Milton,** "The Quantity Theory of Money—A Restatement," in M. Friedman (ed.), *Studies in the Quantity Theory of Money* Chicago 1956, pp. 3–21.
4. ———. *The Counter-Revolution in Monetary Theory,* London 1970.
5. ———. "A Theoretical Framework for Monetary Analysis," *Jour. P. Econ.,* 78, No. 2 (March-April 1970), pp. 193–238.
6. **Hansen, Alvin,** "Economic Progress and Declining Population Growth," *A.E.R.,* March 1939, 29, pp. 1–15.

7. **Johnson, Harry G.**, "Recent Developments in Monetary Theory—A Commentary," David R. Croome and Harry G. Johnson (eds.), *Money in Britain, 1959–1969* London 1970, pp. 83–114.
8. ———, "Monetary Theory and Monetary Policy," *Euromoney*, December 1970, 2, pp. 16–20.
9. **Leijonhufvud, Axel**, *On Keynesian Economics and the Economics of Keynes*, New York 1968.
10. **Patinkin, Don**, "The Chicago Tradition, The Quantity Theory, and Friedman," *Journal of Money, Credit and Banking*, February 1969, 1, pp. 46–70.

'Monetarism: An Interpretation and an Assessment'

D. Laidler, 'Monetarism: An interpretation and an assessment', *Economic Journal* (March 1981), pp. 1–28.

EDITORIAL NOTE

The papers which follow by Professor David Laidler and James Tobin and the comments on these papers by Professor R. C. O. Matthews and Professor James E. Meade were initially prepared for presentation at a Conference on 'Monetarism – An Appraisal' organised by the Royal Economic Society in London in July 1980.

MONETARISM: AN INTERPRETATION AND AN ASSESSMENT*

Like beauty, 'monetarism' tends to lie in the eye of the beholder, and before it can be assessed it must be defined. Though there have been several valuable attempts over the years to specify monetarism's key characteristics,[1] I shall not rely upon them in this essay. Each of them has been heavily conditioned by its time and place of writing, and monetarism has evolved over the years in response to changing circumstances, and in different ways in different places, as new hypotheses have either been developed or absorbed. Thus, I will begin this paper with my own characterisation of monetarism. In my view, the key characteristics of monetarism are as follows:

(I) A 'quantity theory' approach to macroeconomic analysis in two distinct senses: (*a*) that used by Milton Friedman (1956) to describe a theory of the demand for money, and (*b*) the more traditional sense of a view that fluctuations in the quantity of money are the dominant cause of fluctuations in money income.

(II) The analysis of the division of money income fluctuations between the price level and real income in terms of an expectations augmented Phillips curve whose structure rules out an economically significant long-run inverse trade off between the variables.

(III) A monetary approach to balance-of-payments and exchange-rate theory.

(IV) (*a*) Antipathy to activist stabilisation policy, either monetary or fiscal, and to wage and price controls, and (*b*) support for long-run monetary policy 'rules' or at least prestated 'targets', cast in terms of the behaviour of some monetary aggregate rather than of the level of interest rates.

(I) Categorises the theoretical core of monetarism as it developed in the 1950s and 60s, (II) and (III) represent theory developed or absorbed by

* I have benefited greatly from the extensive comments of John Foster, Milton Friedman, John Helliwell, Geoffrey Kingston, Clark Leith, Thomas Mayer, Ronald Shearer and George Zis, none of whom is to be held responsible for the views that I espouse. The financial support of the Social Science and Humanities Research Council of Canada is gratefully acknowledged.

[1] See, for example, James Boughton (1977), Karl Brunner (1970), Nicholas Kaldor (1971), Harry Johnson (1972), Franco Modigliani (1977), Thomas Mayer (1978), Douglas Purvis (1980). This list is far from exhaustive.

monetarists since the mid-1960s, while (IV) summarises a view of macro-economic policy issues which, even though it is neither logically implicit in their positive analysis, nor their exclusive property, has remained reasonably constant among monetarists for the last quarter century.

Before discussing these characteristics of monetarism in detail let me deal briefly with two propositions that some might feel should be included in the above list. First, on the one hand monetarists have frequently been accused of failing to give any account of the transmission mechanism of monetary policy, and have had attributed to them a belief in some mysterious 'direct' influence of money on expenditure; on the other hand they have themselves sometimes referred to a characteristically 'monetarist model' of that same transmission mechanism cast in terms of portfolio substitution among a wide variety of assets including reproducible capital, and even perhaps non-durable consumption goods. I believe that this is and always has been a non-issue. The claim that monetarists have failed to specify their transmission mechanism has been untrue from the very outset (see, for example, Brunner (1961), Friedman and David Meiselman (1963), Friedman and Anna Schwartz (1963*b*)), and although the mechanism propounded in those papers is a good deal more sophisticated and better grounded in relative price theory than that embodied in the textbook macro-economic models of the 1950s, or in the econometric models of that vintage, there is no essential difference between it and that analysed for example by James Tobin and his associates.[1]

Second, monetarists are often said to prefer 'small' to 'big' econometric models, and their views about the importance of the quantity of money for the determination of the general price level have undoubtedly led them to take highly aggregated systems seriously. Moreover, early large-scale econometric models were not constructed so as to highlight any strong effects of money on economic activity. Monetarists criticised them, as much for being Keynesian, as for being 'big'. Even so, subsequent developments have clearly shown that 'big' models can easily take on some very monetarist characteristics, while the Albert Ando and Franco Modigliani (1965) and Michael De Prano and Mayer (1965) papers demonstrate that single equation reduced form techniques can as well produce 'Keynesian' as 'monetarist' results.[2] Empirical analysis of all sorts has been used by both sides in the monetarist controversy, and if there is a method of empirical research more frequently associated with monetarist work than Keynesian, it is not small model or single equation econometrics, but National Bureau techniques of business cycle analysis.[3] Thus though empirical techniques have in specific instances, provided something to argue about, there seems to me to be no clear dividing line between the statistical methodology of monetarists and their opponents about which one can usefully generalise.

[1] This is the judgment of Johnson (1962) and Brunner (1970), among others.

[2] Consider, for example, the London Business School model of the U.K. economy (see Jim Ball and Terry Burns (1976)). The Canadian RDX2 model also seems to me to fall into this category.

[3] See, for example, Friedman and Schwartz (1963*a*), Philip Cagan (1979). Note that such monetarists as Brunner and Meltzer, however, do not use National Bureau techniques. They are mainly associated with the Chicago branch of monetarism.

I. THE QUANTITY THEORY OF MONEY

It has often been said that Friedman's celebrated essay on the Quantity Theory could just as well have been called 'The Theory of Liquidity Preference – a Restatement'. Harry Johnson (1962) argued that Friedman's work on the demand for money should be viewed as a development of a fundamentally Keynesian capital theoretic approach to monetary theory and Don Patinkin (1969) later documented that it was indeed just that. However, I would stress the word *development* here, for 'Keynesian' though Friedman's model is, it is no more *Keynes*' model than Keynes' 'Marshallian' theory of income determination is Marshall's theory; and it differed from other developments of Keynes' theory of liquidity preference that appeared at about the same time in a number of ways.

First it abstracted from any specific characteristics that money might have because it is a financial asset; Friedman treated money instead 'as if' a service-yielding consumer durable to which the permanent income hypothesis of consumption could be applied, just as Margaret Reid (1962) applied it to housing, or the contributors to Arnold Harberger (1960) did to a variety of other durable goods. In this respect Friedman's approach stands in sharp contrast to the analyses of William Baumol (1952) and Tobin (1956) (1958) as it does in its claim to be a theory of the total demand for money in the macro-economy rather than of some component of that demand. Second, Friedman explicitly recognised inflation as an own rate of return on money and postulated a well determined functional relationship between the expected inflation rate and the demand for money, a relationship whose existence Maynard Keynes (and some of his disciples) explicitly denied. (See Roy Harrod (1971).)

Finally, and so obviously that the matter is usually overlooked, Friedman asserted that the demand for money was, *as an empirical matter*, a stable function of a few measurable arguments. Keynes did not believe that – his empirically stable relationship was the consumption function – and nor did (or perhaps do) many of his British followers.[1] Moreover, pre-Keynesian monetary theorists did not believe in an empirically stable demand for money function either. Though they often enough assumed a constant velocity of circulation that is by no means the same thing, and in any event, they typically did so in order to make their analytic points with the maximum of clarity, and not with the intention of stating a belief about the nature of the real world. It is only with the publication of Friedman's essay that statements to the effect that the velocity of circulation is, *as a practical matter*, a stable function of a few arguments become central to debates about monetary economics. Its stress on this hypothesis makes monetarism a very different doctrine from Classical and Neoclassical economics, no matter what other similarities there may be, though it should be noted explicitly that the econometricians among American Keynesians

[1] The Radcliffe Report (1959) is based on the proposition that the demand for money function is essentially nonexistent as a stable relationship. For a later statement of the same point of view see Kaldor (1971), or Joan Robinson (1970).

have not found it necessary to adopt a monetarist label as a result of contemplating the possibility of the empirical stability of the relationship.[1]

Ten years ago it was possible to argue that this characteristic monetarist belief in a stable demand for money function was well supported by empirical evidence as I did in Laidler (1971). However, the last decade has produced a good deal of evidence to suggest that the relationship has shifted in an unpredicted way in a number of countries. There is not space to go into details here, but I would be willing to defend the following assertions.[2]

First the instability in question is often presented, particularly in the United States, as a matter of a cumulative deterioration in the ability of the function to track data. This cumulative deterioration is largely an illusion stemming from the use of dynamic simulations of relationships containing a lagged dependent variable. A *one-time shift* of such a function will, as a matter of arithmetic, lead to a *cumulative deterioration* of its dynamic simulation goodness of fit that should not be read as implying a *continuous* tendency of the relationship to shift. On the other hand, I do not believe we can safely conclude that such one-time shifts in the demand for money function have not occurred, despite the fact, again particularly in the United States, that some formulations of the relationship turn out to deteriorate significantly less than others during the 1970s. When important issues like the stability of the demand for money function begin to depend, for example, on just which interest rate or rates one uses to proxy the opportunity cost of holding money, I believe that the correct conclusion is not that the variable which provides the best fit this time around is the 'right' one, but that our knowledge of the details of the relationship is more fragile than we thought. Finally, arguments to the effect that the demand for money function has not 'really' shifted, that we can restore its stability by taking note of institutional change and redefining 'money' so as to take account of its effects, need to be handled carefully. They are relevant to the interpretation of economic history, but the successful conduct of policy requires that specific actions be taken *vis à vis* precisely defined aggregates in order to achieve particular policy goals. To say, after the event, that our policy did not work because new assets evolved whose existence affected the outcome of our policies in a way that we could have forecast had we only been able to foresee their invention, may be true, but it is not very helpful in enabling us to do better next time, unless the evolution in question was, as it sometimes can be, the predictable outcome of some policy action or other.

Shifts in the demand measured for money function are not a new phenomenon. Evidence drawn from more than one country shows that the demand for money function shifted as the institutional framework evolved long before 1974. To cite but four examples: the income elasticities of demand for money seem to have fallen significantly in both the United States and Britain in the

[1] Note in particular that the Keynesian James Tobin was the author of a pioneering econometric study of the demand for money function. See Tobin (1947). See also his review of Friedman and Schwartz (1963*a*), Tobin (1965), where further econometric estimates of the demand for money function are presented.

[2] I have dealt with the matters taken up here in much greater length in Laidler (1980).

20th century (see Laidler, 1971), the abolition of interest payments on demand deposits in the United States in 1933 was associated with a change in the nature of the demand function for narrow money (see Charles Lieberman, 1980), as was the growth of Savings and Loan Associations in the 1940s (see Cagan and Schwartz, 1975), or in Britain, the introduction of 'Competition and Credit Control' in 1971. Such shifts in the demand for money function are not new, then, but they are important. Though two of the above examples were the result of policy changes and might have been predicted *ex ante*, two were not. In any event these effects of institutional change on the demand for money function have important implications for our views on the proper conduct of monetary policy, as I shall argue in Section IV below.

In the traditional vocabulary of economics, the phrase 'quantity theory of money' referred to a theory of (or better an approach to the analysis of) the relationship between the supply of money and the general price level. The characteristic monetarist belief that variations in the supply of money are the 'dominant impulse' (to borrow Brunner's phrase) causing fluctuations in money income is clearly related to this traditional version of the quantity theory, but modern monetarists are more clearcut in their attribution of a dominant causative role to the money supply than were quantity theorists of earlier vintages.[1] The difference here is surely attributable to monetarists' belief in a stable demand for money function, because earlier quantity theorists spent much of their time contemplating the empirical possibility of autonomous shifts in velocity. However, it takes more than a belief in a stable demand for money function to yield the monetarist view of these matters.

Setting aside the important complications that arise in the open economy, there are two ways in which a conventional analytic model of the IS-LM variety can be made to produce 'monetarist' results. First in its under-employment form, if, relative to expenditure, the demand for money is insensitive to interest rates then the quantity of money comes to dominate the determination of the level of real income. Now obviously a monetarist must deny that the interest elasticity of demand for money is infinite, and this has been done often and explicitly, but it is mainly in Britain that such a denial has been thought to amount to a distinctively monetarist statement. A number of textbook writers (including myself) have gone to the other extreme and used the assumption of a zero interest elasticity of demand for money to generate monetarist propositions from an under-employment IS-LM model. However, Friedman's (1959) study of the United States function is a notable exception to the general tendency of demand for money studies – including those of such monetarists as Brunner and Meltzer (e.g. (1963)) – to find a significant interest elasticity of demand for money, and his inability to find a relationship turned out to be the result of faulty statistical method (see Laidler, 1966, and Friedman, 1966). Thus, the existence or non-existence of a statistically significant interest elasticity of demand for money has not been a serious

[1] But as with all such blanket judgments as this there are important exceptions. Irving Fisher's empirical work on the relationship between money and prices presented in *The Purchasing Power of Money* (1911) is not so far removed from modern monetarism.

issue between monetarists and their opponents for at least fifteen years. If it had been, it is hard to see how monetarists, not least Friedman could have contributed to the analysis of the welfare costs of inflation, or how Friedman and Meiselman could have accepted their own evidence of the importance of autonomous expenditure as an influence on money income during the depression years with such equanimity.[1]

If we rule out the vertical LM curve, we can still get an IS-LM model to produce monetarist results if we assume full employment, and then postulate that the major source of disturbance is variations in the level – or rate of change of – the nominal money supply. With the determinants of velocity, except the expected rate of inflation, thus pinned down at full employment, and with fluctuations in money income thus reduced to fluctuations in the price level, the characteristics of the demand for money function – other than its stability and homogeneity in the general price level and its sensitivity to fluctuations in the expected inflation rate – become quite irrelevant to the relationship between the quantity of money and money income. A Keynesian of course would agree, as an analytic matter, with this proposition, but would probably deny what the monetarist would claim: namely that, if the IS-LM model is to be used as a framework for discussion at all – and there are some monetarists, notably Brunner and Meltzer, who would not want to use it at any price – then this full employment version of it is frequently the empirically relevant one.

To put matters this way is, in effect, to say that monetarists' belief in the quantity theory as a theory of money income boils down to the view that sustained inflation is caused by an expanding money supply. This is not too far from the mark, and much of the spread of monetarism in the last fifteen years stems from its ability to provide a readily comprehensible explanation of inflation along these lines. However, to cast the monetarist approach to the analysis of inflation in terms of a 'full employment' IS-LM model is difficult to justify except as a very first approximation. Though monetarists are among those who have written at considerable length about the interaction of the quantity of money and the price level in models where 'full employment' is the rule, the models in question have been long-run equilibrium growth models, not versions of short-run IS-LM analysis; in any event the 'money and growth' literature and, to a lesser extent, that dealing with 'money and welfare', even though it builds on Friedman's formulation of the relationship between the demand for real balances and the expected rate of inflation as a well defined inverse function, is properly viewed, not as an offshoot of monetarism, but as an extension of Patinkin's (1956) theoretical analysis of the classical dichotomy and the neutrality of money to deal with the *long-run* properties of a *growing* economy, in the presence of variations in the *rate of change* of the nominal

[1] But this of course is not to say that Friedman has always paid as much attention to the interest elasticity of the demand for money as his critics might have wished. See for example the various reviews of the monetary history of the United States, but note that the monetarist Allan Meltzer (1965) was as critical on this score as any other reviewer. What we are here dealing with is a characteristic of some of the work of one, albeit the most important, monetarist rather than of monetarism in general.

money supply.[1] In dealing with the interaction of the quantity of money, money income, and prices, the essential monetarist contribution has been to postulate the existence of stable relationships among these variables as an *empirical* matter, and to draw *practical* conclusions about the proper conduct of *short-run* stabilisation policy from studying their nature, and the 'money, growth and welfare' literature has next to nothing to say about these matters.

When it comes to empirical propositions about the relationship between money and money income, what was once monetarist heresy is now close to being received orthodoxy. In this respect monetarism has made an important positive contribution to macroeconomics. In the United States it seems now to be widely accepted that the correlation between the quantity of money and money income that long runs of time series data display is not just the result of coincidence, but does in fact constitute evidence for the existence of a causative relationship that has run primarily from money to money income rather than vice versa. The weight of the evidence produced by Friedman and his various collaborators (not to mention predecessors) and the persuasiveness of their arguments, has changed enough minds to warrant the conclusion that, in an important sense, 'we are all monetarists' now. Elsewhere in the world, not least in Britain, there has been a similar movement of opinion. Certainly one no longer hears much about velocity being variable 'almost without limit'. However, one does hear more about 'reverse causation' in Britain as an explanation of the correlation between money and money income than one does in the United States (I shall take this matter up below).

Even so, monetarist doctrine asserts not just that variations in the quantity of money lead to systematic variations in money income, but also, that those variations are primarily in prices rather than real income. Although, as I have already noted, much of monetarism's popular appeal stems from its claim to provide an easily comprehensible theory of inflation, that theory of inflation is by no means universally accepted. The view that the influence of money on money income falls on its real income component and not on prices has constituted a 'Keynesian' alternative to the monetarist position on these matters and the 'expectations augmented Phillips Curve' has provided a focus for debate about them.[2] That is why a particular set of beliefs about its nature is a vital ingredient of monetarist doctrine.

II. THE EXPECTATIONS AUGMENTED PHILLIPS CURVE

The notion of a trade off between inflation and unemployment was widely prevalent in Keynesian literature even before Arthur Brown (1955), William Phillips (1958) and Richard Lipsey (1960) formalised it in terms of what seemed

[1] Mayer (1978) argues, correctly I believe, that Patinkin should not be regarded as a monetarist. This of course is not to deny the important influence that Patinkin's work had on subsequent monetary analysis. See, for example, Jonson (1976*b*).

[2] There seems to have been a systematic shift in British opinion from the Radcliffe view that money does not matter at all, to the view that money matters for real income but not for prices. To trace this development is beyond the scope of this paper. However, the work of Richard Kahn shows clearly that it has taken place. Compare his evidence to the Radcliffe Committee with, for example, Kahn (1976).

to be an empirically stable functional relationship. Monetarists have long doubted its existence, instead asserting a belief in the 'inherent stability' of the private sector in the absence of policy induced monetary disturbances, by which they have usually meant nothing more complex than that the system tends in and of itself to operate at or near 'full employment', regardless of the inflation rate, if policy makers do not upset matters. The papers of Edmund Phelps (1967) and Friedman (1968) provided a framework in terms of which differences of opinion about these matters could be stated sharply enough to be confronted with empirical evidence. Although some commentators (e.g. Helmut Frisch, 1978) treat the Phillips curve as providing an alternative theory of inflation to the monetarist approach, this is surely a mistake. In its expectations augmented form, it emerged at the turn of the decade to provide what Friedman (1970) called 'the missing equation' in the monetarist model of inflation.

It is possible to derive this 'missing equation' from two very different theoretical bases, and disagreements here are of quite fundamental importance for macroeconomics, but the first round in the debate about the expectations augmented Phillips curve, and the one that was crucially relevant to monetarism, paid little attention to these matters. It was almost entirely empirical because the relationship in question enabled alternative viewpoints about important and pressing policy issues to be formulated and investigated in an easily manageable way. With Δp the inflation rate, Δp^e the expected inflation rate, and y some measure, either direct or indirect, of the deviation of output from its 'full employment' level, and v a 'catchall' vector of other influences, systematic as well as random, the general form of the relationship may be written as follows:

$$\Delta p = gy + b\Delta p^e + v. \tag{1}$$

A whole spectrum of beliefs about the nature of inflation may be expressed in terms of this simple equation, depending upon the values assigned to its parameters. Thus, the extreme 'sociological' view of the determination of the price level, that was widely prevalent in Britain in the early 1970s, would predict that the parameters g and b were essentially equal to zero, implying that monetary policies, if they had any effect on money income, would influence real income alone.[1] The behaviour of prices, in this view, was determined by exogenous factors that would all go into the catchall vector v. At the other extreme, the typical monetarist of the early 1970s would argue that g was positive, so that inflation would, relative to expectations, be low in a depressed economy, and high in an over-expanded one. He would also argue that the coefficient b on expected inflation would be equal to unity, and would supplement equation (1) with some formula for the formation of expectations, typically based on the error learning hypothesis, that ensured that, eventually, any constant actual inflation rate would come to be fully anticipated. For him, therefore, any trade off between inflation and deviations of output from full employment was a temporary one which vanished in the long run. The typical 'American Keynesian' of the same vintage would agree with the monetarist about the parameter g, and about the reasonableness of assuming that expecta-

[1] See Peter Wiles (1973) for a particularly extreme version of the sociological approach to inflation.

tions would eventually catch up with experience, but would assign a value of less than unity to the parameter *b*, thus ensuring that though the price in terms of inflation of increasing output was higher in the long run than in the short run, it did not, as the monetarist asserted, ever become infinitely high.[1] He might also argue that equation (1) omitted to mention explicitly many factors that in particular times and places might have an important influence on the inflation rate, and which it will suffice here to think of as being captured in *v*.

There is not space here to survey the extensive empirical literature that these issues generated, but its upshot may be summarised easily enough. The evidence that, other things equal, inflation varies with the level of aggregate demand is overwhelming. To the extent that differences of opinion here ever set monetarism apart from other points of view – and I think they probably did in Britain, though not in North America – then surely we have here another case of 'we are all monetarists now'.[2] There has also been a swing towards the typically monetarist belief that in the long run there is no economically significant inflation–output trade off. The more rapid inflation of the 1970s and the more sophisticated methods of modelling expectations developed over the same period have provided empirical evidence of a type that we did not have a decade ago to support this belief. There is still substantial disagreement though on the question of how fast the economy converges on the long-run solution. Finally there is more of a consensus about the importance of the influence of 'other' factors on the inflation rate than there was. Monetarists are willing to agree that factors such as the activities of OPEC, unexpected real shocks, or sudden changes in the level of indirect taxes, can affect the behaviour of the price level 'temporarily' against the background of long-run trends determined by monetary factors; Keynesians, particularly American ones, in their turn are now willing to agree that the long-run trend of inflation may well be determined by monetary factors while continuing to stress the importance of special factors for the short run. However, as we shall now see, there is much less of a consensus about the theoretical basis of the Phillips curve than there is about its empirical properties.

As originally analysed by Lipsey, the Phillips curve dealt with the reaction of the money wage to the existence of a general condition of excess demand for labour in the economy, and therefore of the general price level to the excess demand for goods. Excess demand was conceived of, not as a purely *ex ante* notion such as we meet in theoretical analyses of Walrasian tâtonnement, but as a realised quantity such as appears in models of economies made up of markets characterised by sticky prices. In their original critiques of the Phillips curve. Friedman (1968) and Phelps (1967) both concentrated on the point that disequilibrium in the labour market might be expected to bring pressure to bear on real wages rather than on money wages *per se*, and that what would happen to the latter would therefore be critically influenced by what was thought to be happening to the general price level. Each of them, though Phelps more explicitly so than Friedman, treated unemployment as a quantity

[1] I have in mind here, in particular, the work of Robert Solow (1969) and James Tobin (1972).

[2] See Anthony Santomero and John Seater (1979) for a recent and well-balanced survey of the evidence on these matters.

signal that conveyed to economic agents the desirability of varying prices, and hence seemed to be providing a crucial correction to what remained a fundamentally Keynesian approach to the analysis of wage and price stickiness.[1]

On the other hand, most of the contributors to the well-known Phelps (1969) volume started from a very different theoretical basis to provide an explanation of the interaction of output and prices, though the similarity of their conclusions to those stated by Phelps and Friedman at first distracted attention from what in retrospect was the much more important theoretical matter of different premises.[2] According to this alternative approach, which was anticipated by Irving Fisher (1911), the expectations augmented Phillips curve is in fact an aggregate supply curve. Equation (1) is derived from

$$y = (1/g)(p - p^e) \tag{2}$$

combined with the following definition of the expected rate of inflation

$$\Delta p^e \equiv p^e - p_{-1}. \tag{3}$$

Brunner and Meltzer were quick to adopt this interpretation of the expectations augmented Phillips curve. They had already developed a view of the transmission of monetary impulses in asset markets that stressed the role of relative prices as signalling devices, and found it easy enough to extend that line of reasoning to the markets for output and labour services as well (see Meltzer, 1969).[3] By now there can be no doubt that this aggregate supply curve interpretation of inflation employment interaction is the dominant one among monetarists. However, not all monetarists have accepted it (see, for example, Cagan, 1979), and as I shall now argue, it raises issues that go well beyond the traditional subject matter of the monetarist debate.

To say that the Phillips curve is an aggregate supply curve is to say that fluctuations in output and employment in response to price level variations represent the voluntary choices of individuals operating in markets which are continually clearing. Since voluntary choices made on the basis of erroneous expectations are by no means the same thing as choices that lead to the outcome which agents would have desired, this is not to deny that deviations of output and unemployment from the 'natural' levels they would attain if expectations were fulfilled represent a serious problem.[4] However, it is to

[1] Notice that in some of his subsequent writings on inflation-unemployment interaction Friedman adopts an aggregate supply curve interpretation of the Phillips curve. See, for example, Friedman (1975).

[2] See the papers by Armen Alchian, Robert E. Lucas and Leonard Rapping, Donald Gordon and Alan Hynes, and Dale Mortensen, all in the Phelps (1969) volume.

[3] In later work carried out by Brunner and Meltzer and their associates, a version of the aggregate supply curve in which the rate of change of output rather than the level of output affects the rate of inflation appears. This form of the relationship appears to stem from their tendency to treat the expected inflation rate as synonymous with the rate of change of the expected price level. See Brunner and Meltzer (eds.) (1978) and particularly the comments there by Bennett McCallum.

[4] Thus, though I agree with much of what Willem Buiter (1980) has to say about this theory of employment, I cannot accept his characterisation of it as 'The Macroeconomics of Dr. Pangloss'. It might be noted that in the aggregate supply curve interpretation of the Phillips curve, the natural unemployment rate becomes a long-run equilibrium concept. In the price reaction function interpretation of the relationship it seems to me to be synonymous with the Keynesian concept of the minimum feasible unemployment rate. For a perceptive discussion of some of the issues involved here see Thomas Wilson (1976).

locate the cause of unemployment, not in the failure of markets to bring together all willing buyers and sellers in *ex ante* mutually satisfactory trades, but rather in a failure of markets (and other social institutions as well perhaps) to convey sufficient information to enable the expectations upon which those trades are based to be formed accurately in an economy subjected to stochastic shocks.

If fluctuations in output and employment about their natural rates are the result of the failure of expectations to be realised, the manner in which expectations are formed must play a vital role in their analysis. That is why the "rational expectations" hypothesis is a natural supplement to the aggregate supply curve interpretation of the Phillips curve. If agents suffer losses in utility as a result of making expectational errors, they have an incentive to use all available information in forming their expectations up to the point at which the marginal benefit from improving their accuracy equals the marginal cost of doing so. The rational expectations hypothesis does *not* say that every agent's expectations are always as accurate (i.e. have as small a variance) as they would be if he were equipped with a 'true' econometric model of the economy in which he operates (though it is sometimes convenient to formulate it that way in analytic and empirical exercises), but it does say that his expectations will not be wrong *systematically* over time and to that extent will resemble those generated by such a 'true' model in being unbiased and serially uncorrelated. An agent who forms expectations in a manner that leads to systematic error will find himself persistently making the wrong choices; hence in the very course of his market activities, he will be provided *gratis* with the information necessary to eliminate that systematic error.

If each individual makes only random errors in forming expectations, two questions naturally arise: how does it happen that at a particular moment the expectations of a predominant number of agents in the economy should be in error in one particular direction so that aggregate output and employment come to deviate from their 'natural rates', and how does it happen that the fluctuations in output and employment which are observed in any actual economy come to display that pattern of serial correlation summarised in the term 'business cycle'? The answer to the first question given by Lucas (1972) is by now well known. If individuals have more up-to-date information about the money prices that rule in the markets in which they operate as sellers than about others, then in order to assess the pattern of relative prices upon which their quantity decisions rest, they must form expectations about the behaviour of other money prices. An unforeseen shock affecting the whole economy which leads to a change in the general price level will influence individual money prices, and will have its consequences everywhere misread as reflecting relative price changes. Hence quantities supplied will everywhere change.

If that was all there was to it, output and employment fluctuations would be random over time. However, if there are time delays in getting information to agents, if there are costs of adjusting output decisions once taken, or if some of the goods over-produced in error in the face of a positive unexpected shock to the price level are durable, then the effects of that shock will persist over time.[1] By the time its effects on output have petered out there will be too many durable goods in the economy – capital will be 'too deep' – and the marginal productivity of labour in terms of consumption in industries producing durable goods will fall. If workers prefer to take extra leisure when their marginal productivity is low, and if the price system operates so as to inform them of when that is the case, there will be a voluntary fall in the level of employment that will persist until the structure of the economy's capital stock is restored. The objection to this explanation of the cycle, that it predicts more wage variability than we observe in the real world, can be countered by arguments to the effect that firms and households find it mutually beneficial to enter into wage contracts under which wages do not instantaneously fluctuate in tune with the marginal productivity of labour, but under which firms are permitted to lay off workers in such a way that the latter still take more leisure at times when their marginal productivity is unusually low, even though the behaviour of wages no longer signals the fact.

Readers will find the last paragraph reminiscent of the Austrian business cycle theory of the 1920s and 1930s, and that is no accident. It is the Austrians, and not, as Solow (1980) has suggested, Pigou, who are the predecessors of Lucas, Sargent and their associates. Like Ludwig von Mises and Friedrich von Hayek, they have set themselves the task of producing a theory of the business cycle that is firmly based on the notion that all market phenomena represent the harmonious outcome of the voluntary choices of maximising individuals. However these neo-Austrians have gone beyond their predecessors to produce a theory in which output and employment as well as prices fluctuate as a result of such voluntary choices. Whatever we may think of the empirical relevance of that theory, and its proponents show an admirable, and un-Austrian, willingness to submit their ideas to empirical tests,[2] we must surely agree that its very construction represents an intellectual achievement of the highest order.

One can admire a theory without agreeing with it, and there are many including myself who would challenge the basic assumption upon which the analysis just discussed is based, namely that it is legitimate to model the economy 'as if' markets always clear. It is one thing to agree that commodity and asset markets dominated by specialist traders ought, and indeed do,

[1] I base the following arguments on the papers of Lucas (1975), Thomas Sargent (1976) and Lucas (1977). The first two of these papers are extremely technical and I am by no means sure that I am doing justice to them in the discussion that follows. Milton Friedman has pointed out to me that one can only say that errors are random or systematic if one is also specific about both the *time at* which expectations are formed, and the *period for* which they are formed. If one is now planning for, say a five-year horizon, then the rational expectations hypothesis permits the actual value of any variable to deviate systematically from its *ex ante* expected value over any interval of less than five years. This matter is clearly related to questions raised by adjustment lags, the durability of certain goods, and so on, since the horizon over which a decision taken now is likely to be binding is also presumably the horizon over which a rational agent would seek to form expectations about relevant variables. To the best of my knowledge, the published literature has not recognised this point explicitly, and it deserves much more attention than I have space to give it here.

[2] To comment on the empirical work in question, notably that of Robert J. Barro (1978), would take us beyond the scope of this essay.

display the characteristics associated with continuous clearing and rational expectations, and quite another to attribute similar characteristics to the markets for many components of final output, and above all to the labour market. One may follow Hicks (1974) in distinguishing between 'flexprice' and 'fixprice' markets, assign the labour market to the latter category, and argue that the interaction of inflation and unemployment is best analysed on the premise that the Phillips curve represents the disequilibrium response of prices to a mismatching of supply and demand.

Of course the 'neo-Austrians' are well aware that there is no Walrasian auctioneer to set prices, and no recontracting to ensure that trade only takes place at market clearing prices; but they do assert that individual agents – or their representatives – are acute enough in their bargaining to ensure that money wages and prices universally behave 'as if' markets operated along such Walrasian lines, that they perceive the possibility of realising mutual gains by adjusting wages downward when excess supply turns up in the market in which they are operating, and act upon that perception.[1] However one can have no difficulty accepting the proposition that, even in labour markets, if it is mutually beneficial to lower money wages (or their rate of change), agents will discover this and will agree to do so, but still find it hard to understand how the relevant information is conveyed to the agents in question without the intervention of quantity signals. In a Walrasian market, the auctioneer can discover that the price is too high by adding up notional supplies and finding out that they exceed notional demands, to use Robert Clower's (1965) terms, but how can participants in any actual labour market find out that money wages there are too high without some of them discovering first that they are unable to sell all the services that they would like at the going rate?

If adjustments in the level (or rate of change) of money wages and prices to aggregate demand shocks are anything other than instantaneous, then markets fail to clear, trade takes place at false prices, and quantity signals, perhaps amplified by multiplier effects, become an integral part of the mechanism whereby monetary changes are transmitted to the behaviour of the price level. This line of analysis is as 'Keynesian' in spirit as the clearing market approach is 'Austrian', and its existence permits one to subscribe to the expectations augmented Phillips curve without also being committed to a clearing market rational expectations approach to the analysis of economic fluctuations. Moreover, the approach in question does *not* differ from the clearing market view in denying that individuals perceive and then engage in all available mutually beneficial trades. It simply denies that they do so infinitely rapidly. I do not see why, as for example Barro (1979) has recently suggested, to postulate an infinite speed of price adjustment in the face of excess demand or supply is to conform to sound microeconomic principles,

[1] Robert J. Barro (1979) presents a particularly forceful and clearcut statement of what I am calling the 'neo-Austrian' view on these matters. Robert Solow (1979) might be regarded as providing a traditional Keynesian rebuttal of this line of argument. Note that questions of the relevant time horizon, raised in footnote 1, p. 12, are again relevant here.

and to postulate anything significantly slower is to propose an '*ad hoc* non-theory'.

The non-clearing market approach to analysing inflation employment interaction is not obviously incompatible with the notion of rational expectations. If output fluctuations convey information about the appropriate behaviour concerning price setting as this approach suggests, they can be regarded as constituting one of the ingredients of the expectations upon which such behaviour is based. In that case the term Δp^e in equation (1) can be thought of as summarising influences upon expectations *other than quantity signals*.[1] To say this begs the question of what those 'other influences' on expectations might be, but leaves open the possibility that the same type of information to which the rational expectations hypothesis draws our attention could be incorporated without difficulty into models based on the non-clearing market approach. Observations on the past behaviour of the money supply, for example, might well provide agents with information about the appropriate way to set prices, and might be included among those 'other' influences, as might, in an open economy, variations in prices ruling elsewhere in the world economy, variations in exchange rates, and so on.[2]

The non clearing-market interpretation of the Phillips curve needs to be reconciled with the basic facts of the business cycle. Once given, why do output signals not result in an immediate adjustment of prices to a market clearing level? The answer here is straightforward – a quantity signal will lead to a response in price behaviour only to the extent that agents believe that the shock which gave rise to it will persist into the future. Inability to disentangle short-term from persistent shocks will lead to a tendency to under-react to quantity signals, and hence to cause them to be drawn out over time. I would conjecture that the Austrian-style arguments about the role of errors made with respect to the production of durable goods in the business cycle can be superimposed upon this fundamentally Keynesian explanation of the persistence of output fluctuations should anyone wish to do so.[3]

Although theoretical analysis of the interaction of output, employment and prices in terms of an expectations augmented Phillips curve can thus proceed along two very different lines, it is a mistake to treat debate about these issues as simply the latest round in the monetarist controversy. Though monetarists and Keynesians are in much closer agreement than they were about the empirical stability of the demand for money function, and about the empirical nature of output-inflation interaction, they still take the same diametrically

[1] Alternatively, as Michael Wickens has suggested to me, we may think of Δp^e as being a rational expectation of inflation conditional upon information available at an earlier time than that at which the quantity signal is received.

[2] I base the foregoing discussion on conversations and correspondence that I have had with Marcus Miller and Peter Jonson on various occasions. See also Clements and Jonson (1979).

[3] A more extensive account of these matters is given in Laidler (1975), chapter 1. Note that Brunner, Alex Cuckeirman and Meltzer (1979) provide an analysis of persistent shocks within an aggregate supply curve framework. Note also that Peter Howitt (1979) argues that, once explicit attention is paid to the role of inventories in the price setting process, the contrast between clearing-market and non-clearing-market approaches to economic modelling becomes blurred, and to some extent semantic rather than substantive in nature.

opposed views on the proper conduct of macroeconomic policy that they did a quarter century ago, and divisions of opinion here do not, as I shall argue below, depend upon differences of views about the theoretical basis of price-output interaction. Since the policy debate is undoubtedly a continuation of the monetarist controversy, and since disputes about the theoretical basis of the Phillips curve clearly deal with a new set of issues, it seems to me to be misleading to treat what I have here termed the neo-Austrian view as synonymous with monetarism, as for example Frank Hahn (1980) does. I shall discuss the policy aspects of the monetarist controversy in Section IV, but before I do so, it will be convenient to discuss the place of the monetary approach to balance of payments and exchange rate theory in monetarist doctrine.

III. THE MONETARY APPROACH TO BALANCE OF PAYMENTS AND EXCHANGE RATE ANALYSIS

The monetary approach to balance of payments and exchange rate analysis represents in some respects a revival of the English Classical approach to these problem areas. However, the monetary approach differs in important ways from Classical analysis, and the very characteristics that thus distinguish it are borrowed from closed economy monetarism.[1] Most important, advocates of the monetary approach postulate the existence of a stable demand for money function, not just as a working simplification, but as an empirical hypothesis; it is this hypothesis that transforms the approach from an accounting framework into a body of substantive theory. Furthermore, in early statements of the doctrine, its proponents tied down the real income argument of that function by assuming full employment but they soon learned how to replace this assumption with an expectations-augmented Phillips curve approach to price-output interaction.[2] In effect the monetary approach to balance of payments and exchange rate analysis provided the means whereby these characteristically monetarist hypotheses were made relevant to economies other than the United States which, under the Bretton Woods system, was about as close an approximation to a closed economy that was also a separate political entity as the world has ever seen. Monetarism thus only came to be important outside the United States, not least in Britain, in alliance with the monetary approach to balance of payments and exchange rate analysis.

Until 1971 the world was on a system of fixed exchange rates against the United States dollar. Under such a system the existence of a stable demand for money function, whose arguments are beyond the direct control of the domestic authorities, implies that the money supply is an endogenous variable that must adjust to demand. Given this insight, evidence that suggests, for example in the United Kingdom in the 1950s and 1960s, that causation seems to have run predominantly from money income to money, rather than vice

[1] The locus classicus for pioneering work on the monetary approach to balance of payments analysis is, of course, Frenkel and Johnson (1975).

[2] See, for example, Laidler (1975), chapter 9, and Jonson (1976*a*).

versa, is no embarrassment to a monetarist provided that he is also willing to attribute most of the variation in money income to causative factors originating abroad. Moreover, although the expectations augmented Phillips curve tells us that in general we should expect to find no stable inverse trade off between inflation and unemployment, post-war United Kingdom data do display just such a well determined relationship down to 1967, and this fact needs explaining. The monetary approach to balance of payments analysis suggests two complementary reasons why this should be the case. First it notes that, so long as a fixed exchange rate is to be maintained, the prices of tradable goods sold domestically are going to be determined in the long run, not domestically, but on world markets, and from this it follows that the domestic price level's long-run behaviour is going to be constrained by the behaviour of prices in the world at large. Economic agents do not have to be more than merely sensible to perceive this fact and to incorporate it into their expectations. If world prices are relatively stable, and they were until the late 1960s, then so are inflation expectations, and our expectations augmented Phillips curve, equation (1), no matter how we interpret its microeconomic origins, will predict that the data will generate a stable inflation–unemployment trade-off.

This explanation of the existence of a stable inflation–unemployment trade-off in post-war Britain is an important component of what may fairly be called monetarist hypotheses, about the nature of the stop-go cycle in the 1950s and 1960s and about the degeneration of that economy's performance in the 1970s, which contrast strongly with conventional 'Keynesian' accounts of the same phenomena. The latter begin from the proposition that Britain has a peculiarly high marginal propensity to import, so that, under the Bretton Woods system, attempts to run the economy at a high degree of capacity utilisation, though they produced only a small and on the whole acceptable amount of inflation, were frustrated by balance of payments pressure which forced a reversal of policy. The monetarist hypothesis about stop-go, on the other hand, has it that high levels of demand were associated with high rates of domestic credit expansion which, under fixed exchange rates, generated balance of payments problems in large measure as an *alternative* to domestic inflationary pressure. The conventional view seemed to imply that Britain's economic performance could be improved by adopting exchange rate flexibility and allowing a depreciating currency to offset the balance of payments effects of a high propensity to import. With a flexible exchange rate, the economy could be run at a higher level of capacity utilisation and could grow more rapidly without interference from a balance of payments 'constraint'. According to this view a series of exogenous shocks and the autonomous activities of trade unions undermined a basically well-founded strategy when it was adopted in the 1970s. The monetarist view, on the other hand, argues that the adoption of exchange rate flexibility replaced a balance of payments problem with a domestic inflation problem when expansionary policies were pursued, and did nothing to influence the economy's ability to sustain either a higher level or rate of growth of real income. For the monetarist, therefore, the deterioration of British economic performance after 1972 was the predictable (and predicted) consequence of a policy of expanding aggregate demand against a background of exchange rate flexibility.[1]

Now the monetary approach to balance of payments analysis does far more than make monetarist analysis relevant to Britain. It also permits the explanation of the international spread of inflation in the late 1960s in terms of the repercussions in the world economy of United States monetary expansion, and it treats the breakdown of the Bretton Woods system as the culmination of this process. However, it is only fair to note that such analysis performs less well in the face of the behaviour displayed by the international monetary system since exchange rates began to float in the early 1970s. The prediction that the behaviour of exchange rates can be analysed fruitfully as if determined in efficient asset markets does seem to be supported by the data. However, a basic postulate of the monetary approach is that the equilibrium value of the exchange rate between any two currencies reflects purchasing power parity. Just as data generated under fixed rates show that the price levels of particular economies can display considerable autonomy for substantial periods of time, so under flexible exchange rates systematic and persistent deviations of exchange rates from purchasing power parity do seem to be possible. Though purchasing power parity considerations underlie the behaviour of long period averages of data, implying that, ultimately the terms of trade between countries are independent of monetary factors, there seems to be ample room for short run deviations from the long run pattern. Just why this should be the case, and what explains the patterns of such deviations as we observe, are important and, at the moment, open questions.[2]

Be all that as it may, the present regime of flexible exchange rates came into being because the authorities in various countries learned that they could not control such politically important variables as domestic inflation and unemployment while continuing to adhere to the Bretton Woods arrangements. The diversity of inflation rates among countries since 1971 supports the view that the adoption of flexible rates allows such variables to have their behaviour predominantly determined at home; and long before the 1970s, monetarists, not least of course Friedman, argued that the adoption of exchange rate flexibility was a necessary prerequisite to the pursuit of monetarist policies in individual countries. In the 1970s we have seen the emergence of conditions under which individual countries could implement independent monetary policies, and as I have suggested above, it is mainly on the matter of policy prescriptions that sharp differences between monetarists and their opponents persist. I shall therefore devote the penultimate section of this paper to a discussion of these matters.

[1] It is worth pointing out that I set out much of the foregoing argument in my 1972 Lister Lecture. See Laidler (1975), chapter 10, where the lecture is reprinted. The argument is developed in further detail in Laidler (1976*a*).

[2] Frenkel (1980) provides a useful and accessible overview of the issues involved here and the evidence on them.

IV. POLICY ISSUES

As we have seen, when it comes to propositions about the demand for money function, the relationship between money and money income, and output inflation interaction, there is a real sense in which 'we are all monetarists now'. The issues that nowadays distinguish monetarists from their opponents concern the conduct of economic policy. As he did in the 1950s the monetarist still wants fiscal policy to stick mainly to its traditional tasks of influencing resource allocation and the distribution of income and wealth, and monetary policy to adhere to some simple rule under which the monetary aggregates do not react to short-run fluctuations either in real output or prices; the Keynesian on the other hand is still a proponent of activist stabilisation policy.

These policy issues are not independent of the theoretical questions that we have discussed earlier, and indeed, much of the current popularity among monetarists of the neo-Austrian approach to the analysis of price-output interaction stems from the erroneous belief that it provides the only sound basis for scepticism about the effectiveness of activist stabilisation policies. Many Keynesians focus their attacks on that same piece of analysis in the belief, just as erroneous, that if they succeed in refuting it, they also succeed in restoring the case for activist stabilisation policy. Now the approach in question does indeed imply that output and employment can be influenced by policy only to the extent that it causes prices to vary in a way that agents in the private sector do not forsee, while the rational expectations hypothesis tells us that if such effects were systematic, the private sector would discover the fact, adapt to it, and thereby render policy ineffective. It follows at once that the only macroeconomic policy that can influence income and employment is a purely random one, and no supporter of 'fine tuning' could possibly recommend that.

The argument just sketched out is logically watertight. So is this counter-argument: if inflation–output interaction reflects the role of quantity signals in the mechanism whereby various shocks, including those imparted by policy, have their effects transmitted to prices, the way is opened for monetary and fiscal policy to exert a systematic influence upon output and employment. However, there is much more than this to be said about the feasibility and desirability of activist policies. If there was not, how could it be that Friedman (1960) was able systematically to state his views on policy more than a decade before Lucas (1976) and Sargent and Neil Wallace (1975) developed the theoretical arguments that are now so widely regarded as the only logical underpinning of those views? The Lucas–Sargent–Wallace analysis certainly provides a *sufficient* basis for monetarist policy prescriptions, but it is not a *necessary* basis for them: it is one thing to say that the world is so structured that policy can systematically influence output and employment in the short run, and another thing altogether to say that policy makers have enough knowledge to use that ability in a way that will be beneficial.

If it is agreed that in the long run the Phillips curve is essentially vertical – or perhaps even positively sloped if allowance is made for super-non-neutralities

– then that certainly does not rule out the possibility of the economy slipping below its natural rate of output in a short run that may be of considerable duration, or the possibility that there exists an appropriate menu of monetary and fiscal policies that might hasten its return to that natural rate without generating any serious costs during the transition. As a first step to exploiting this possibility though, those in charge of policy would need to know what the natural rates of output and employment actually are. As a second step, they would need accurate information upon where the economy actually is, and where it would move in the absence of a policy change, not to mention at what pace. Armed with this not inconsiderable amount of information, policy makers would know that they were in a position where it might be useful to deploy some policy measure or other. To design the policy would of course require them to know about the size and time path of the economy's response to the measures they might take, factors which even the loosest application of the rational expectations idea tells us are likely to be influenced by the policy measures themselves.

Now I will readily agree that we have the mathematical and statistical tools available for tackling the design of stabilisation policy along the foregoing lines, and I also agree that our econometric models contain answers to all the quantitative questions that I have just raised. However the conclusion that I draw from all this is that we are probably rather good at fine-tuning econometric models.[1] One can rest the monetarist case against activist policy on the proposition that markets always clear and that expectations are rational, but one can also rest it on the much more down-to-earth proposition that we are too ignorant of the structure of the economies we live in and of the manner in which that structure is changing to be able safely to implement activist stabilisation policy in the present environment, or in the foreseeable future.

Among the penalties for making errors in fine tuning that concern monetarists are those that come in the form of uncomfortably high and perhaps accelerating inflation that would result from setting over-optimistic targets for employment and output. Thus, if there is something in the policy environment that weakens the ability of the inflation rate to accelerate, the penalties for such errors are milder, and the case against fine tuning developed above can be softened a little. In the 1950s and 1960s, there can be little doubt that the British authorities did succeed in fine tuning income and employment variables within the rather narrow bounds laid down by what then appeared to be balance of payments constraints. The monetarist interpretation of that period implies that the background of monetary stability implicit in the commitment to a fixed exchange rate was the real constraint on how far fine-tuning policy could be pushed and also that it provided the necessary conditions for its limited success. However the fact remains that the experience in question does show that a limited degree of fine tuning is feasible if only a background of long-run price stability is assured, and is seen to be assured.

It is hard for a monetarist to see how one could avoid assigning to monetary

[1] John Helliwell has suggested to me that the application of policy optimisation techniques to such models is better regarded as a test of their validity than as a preliminary to actual policy making.

policy the role of providing that necessary assurance.[1] A fixed exchange rate regime is one way of tying down monetary policy, and the adoption of some sort of a money supply growth rule would be an alternative. But this means that fine tuning would have to be by fiscal policy. Such a conclusion will be of little consolation to American Keynesians who are forced by the inability of American institutions to deliver rapid changes reliably in fiscal variables to assign to monetary variables a far more important role in stabilisation policy than their British counterparts ever did. However it may do a little to cheer up the British, for whom a return to the days of 'never had it so good' might be a welcome relief from the consequences of 'going for growth'.

As should be apparent from the last few paragraphs, I regard the question of whether governments should or should not indulge in a limited amount of fiscal fine tuning as a secondary issue for monetarists.[2] Related questions concerning public sector borrowing and the share of the public sector in National Income are even more peripheral to the monetarist debate. No matter what the public perception of these matters might be, I insist that monetarist doctrine tells one that there are severe limits to the extent to which public sector borrowing can be financed by money creation, and beyond that has nothing to say about whether a 'high' or 'low' level of such borrowing is in and of itself desirable. Similarly monetarism offers no guidance as to how big the public sector of any economy ought to be. It is a macroeconomic doctrine and the issues at stake in debates about the size of the public sector, the welfare state, and so on are fundamentally microeconomic in nature.

Monetarism however has had a good deal to say about wage and price control policies. It has opposed them, not just for ideological reasons, but for the much more down to earth reason that they have not been expected to work.[3] This position has been mainly and justifiably defended on the basis

[1] It is worth noting that the Radcliffe Committee (1959) regarded the task of monetary policy to be the achievement of background stability for the economy. Their view differed from the monetarist approach to the same issue in putting interest rates at the centre of the policy making process rather than any monetary aggregate. In the kind of sociological theorising about inflation that was particularly popular in Britain in the early 1970s incomes policy was to be assigned the task of stabilising prices and expectations.

[2] I would emphasise that this is not a new position on my part. It is one that I have consistently taken. Of course the questions about the effectiveness of fiscal policy are important ones for macro-economists, and the Brown Univesity Conference on Monetarism (see Jerome Stein, 1975) dealt almost exclusively with such issues. I accept Purvis' (1980) judgment that the outcome of that conference was to show beyond a reasonable doubt that 'fiscal policy matters' but also his judgment that in retrospect the debate about the effectiveness of fiscal policy has not been the most important one in the monetarist debate, however important an issue it might be in its own right for macro-economics.

Finally note that the foregoing discussion ignores the question as to whether, even if we had enough knowledge to ensure that fine tuning could be used beneficially, the political process would permit it to be used in that way. This question, as Milton Friedman has pointed out to me, is a vital one in any practical debate about activist policies.

[3] Of course there has been a considerable ideological content to the monetarist debate and I would not deny that for a moment. Nor would I take the position that there is anything reprehensible about ideological debates *per se*. I play these issues down in this paper not because, from a broader perspective I would regard them as unimportant, but because my expertise as an economist does not put me in a position to say anything very useful about them.

of empirical evidence: in the post-Korean war period it is hard indeed to find any wage-price control scheme that has not produced disappointing results over any period longer than a few months. However monetarists have also sometimes opposed controls on theoretical grounds, particularly in the context of open economies. They have noted that under fixed exchange rates the behaviour of world prices and hence the domestic prices of traded goods cannot be controlled by domestic regulations, any more than can the money supply. They have also pointed out that under flexible rates, though the money supply is under control, neither the exchange rate nor world prices can be regulated separately. In either case in an open economy wage and price controls inevitably impinge upon 'the domestic component' of the price level and are hence policies towards relative prices. For that reason, they cannot for long influence the behaviour of the general price level, unless they are accompanied by a battery of quantitative restrictions, not least on foreign trade, that very few of their advocates have been willing to contemplate.

In the 1960s wage and price controls came to be regarded as an alternative to monetary policy in the control of inflation, and in the early 1970s serious attempts were made in both Britain and the United States to use them as such. In both cases the attempts failed sufficiently dramatically that the proponents of controls now regard them at best as supplementary devices to be deployed in harmony with more traditional demand side policies rather than as a serious alternative to such measures. Though such a viewpoint stops short of the blanket opposition to controls that, along with other monetarists, I would still be willing to defend, it does represent a substantial move in a monetarist direction from positions taken a decade ago. Here, as in other instances, much of the heat has gone out of the monetarist controversy.[1]

There is more to practical monetarism than scepticism about fiscal fine tuning and opposition to wage and price controls. Its key positive tenet is that monetary weapons should be assigned to the attainment and maintenance of long-run price stability, and hence that those same monetary weapons not be used for fine tuning purposes. In this respect, as with the other components of the doctrine which we considered earlier, there has been a considerable growth in the acceptance of monetarism. Propositions about the desirability of setting rules and targets for the growth of monetary aggregates are now commonplace in the statements of Central Banks. If monetarists complain – and they do – about the failure of Keynesian policies since the mid 1960s, then simple fairness requires them to say something about the lessons that they have learned about the viability of their own policy proposals from what many observers believe to have been widespread and sustained efforts to apply them during the 1970s.

[1] Michael Parkin, Michael Sumner and Robert Jones (1973) is still an admirable source of information about wage and price controls in the British economy. Michael Walker (ed.) (1976) contains much useful information on other countries. Note that the views that I state here about the importance of using wage and price controls, if they are to be used, in conjunction with monetary and fiscal policy, rather than instead of such policies, are those of the McCracken Committee. See McCracken *et al.* (1978).

The first thing to be said on this score is that the case for monetary growth-rate rules, as initially stated by Friedman (and Edward Shaw) was put in terms of the capacity of such a policy to *maintain* stability in an already stable economy – it was a policy prescription for *staying out* of trouble. However it has been only since our economies have found themselves deeply *in trouble* that monetarist policy proposals have attracted the attention of policy makers. There is much less unanimity among monetarists about how to tackle the problem of restoring stability than there is about how to maintain it. Though all monetarists would agree that a return to a modest growth rate of some monetary aggregate or other is the long-run goal, the neo-Austrians would favour a rapid return to such a rule, while those of us who take a more traditional view of the nature of the Phillips trade-off have advocated 'gradualism'.

Unless we take the cynical view that the rhetoric of central bankers bears no relationship to their intentions, we must conclude that in a number of places attempts have been made to implement gradualist policies. There are two questions to be asked about those attempts: first, is it the case that those attempts have resulted in a systematic and gradual reduction in the rate of growth of any monetary aggregate? and second, if such attempts have anywhere been successful, did that success lead to a reduction in the inflation rate? As is well known, policy has in the main failed on the first count. Only in Canada, to the best of my knowledge, have the authorities set, and on the whole succeeded in achieving, pre-stated monetary growth targets over an extended period. It is equally well known that the single most important reason for this failure, at least in the United States and Britain, has been the unwillingness of those in charge of monetary policy to give up setting interest rate targets when they adopted targets for the money supply, combined with a proclivity to stick with the interest rate target when the two came into conflict, as they inevitably had to sooner or later. This was not been universally the case, however. Germany and Switzerland have had difficulty sticking to money supply targets because of concern with the behaviour of the exchange rates rather than interest rates, as Sumner (1979) has noted, while political concern over the exchange rate and interest rates during the winter of 1979–80 posed a serious threat to the continuation of the Canadian experiment.

It would be easy enough to argue in the light of all this that recent experience offers essentially no test of monetarist gradualism, but that seems to be going too far. Monetarists have usually treated questions of income distribution and resource allocation as separate and distinct from those of monetary policy. This dichotomy is a useful one when the problem for monetary policy is to *maintain* already existing stability, but can all too easily lead one to neglect the way in which monetary policy interacts with allocation and distribution when its implementation requires sharp (albeit temporary) increases in interest rates. A key factor here is of course the political importance of the housing market, and of the behaviour of mortgage interest rates. In retrospect, it is clear that monetarists did not do a very good job of educating policy makers – both elected and otherwise – about the problems that adopting monetarist policies would generate in this area. Some of us did raise these matters, but apparently not loudly enough.[1] High interest rates have turned out to be more difficult for politicians to face up to than high unemployment rates, and that was not foreseen.

There are also technical problems with implementing monetarist policies. The manipulation of interest rates as the centrepiece of monetary policy long antedates the Keynesian revolution, and was quite appropriate in economies whose monetary rule was to maintain convertibility into gold or some other currency at a fixed price. However the day-to-day operating procedures of central banks, the very organisation of their decision making processes, not to mention the structure of the private markets in which they operate are all geared by force of tradition to making and implementing decisions about interest rates. Although monetarists have done a great deal of work on the basic economics of the money supply process under different policy regimes, and though some of them, notably Brunner and Meltzer, have frequently scolded their colleagues for neglect of these issues, hindsight suggests that they did not recognise the extent to which the problem of implementing a different monetary policy might require a basic overhaul of institutions if it was to be solved, an overhaul that might involve a considerable break with traditional practices, and hence be hard to implement, or that, if they did, they were unable to convince policy-makers to undertake that overhaul at the same time as they adopted monetarist rhetoric.

If central banks, apart from the Bank of Canada, have not in fact succeeded in smoothly slowing down monetary expansion rates in a sustained way, a number of them have nevertheless managed to create contractions in monetary growth rates that have been sharp and persistent enough to bite. Associated with these contractions, have been the 'shifts' of the demand for money function that I discussed earlier in this paper. As the reader will recall, I argued that these shifts were, in all probability, real phenomena, and not statistical artifacts, that such shifts were nothing new, and that they were probably to be explained, at least in part, by institutional changes which themselves might plausibly be interpreted as a response to monetary policy. I believe that these shifts of the demand for money function, relatively small though they have been, force us to reassess a fundamental tenet of practical monetarism, namely the injunction to fix *ex ante* a growth rate rule for the money supply, and then ensure adherence to it by taking away from the monetary authorities the discretion to do otherwise.

Objections to such a proposal have frequently been cast in terms of the question 'How are you going to define the money supply for purposes of implementing this policy?' The answer typically given has been that it does not much matter, because if the rate of growth of one monetary aggregate is pinned down, all the others will end up behaving consistently, at least on average over the kind of time periods for which stability in monetary policy is really important. That answer is surely valid if one is dealing with an

[1] See Laidler (ed.) (1976*b*), particularly chapters 7 and 9, for an earlier statement of my own views on the role of the housing market and its interaction with monetary policy and inflation. I readily acknowledge that the source is an obscure one.

economy in which there is no institutional change in the private sector, but that does not make it as adequate a response to the question as I once thought it did. Suppose we agreed to set a rule for the growth rate of M1 and that initially we could agree on what assets to include in that aggregate. What if after the rule had been implemented some new asset, for example a new kind of chequing account, evolved? Perhaps the demand function for M1 as initially defined would then shift, but if *ex post* we included the new asset in our definition of M1 we might still be able to show that the demand for narrow money had not 'really' shifted, after all.

Such problems would not arise if we were not too specific in laying down the precise definition of money that was to bind policy makers in the future. However, to do that would leave it open to the discretion of someone at some time in the future to decide just how to define the monetary aggregate whose rate of growth was tied down with a rule, and that amounts to giving them the discretion to ignore the rule in question. It is hard to resist the implication that it does not seem to be possible, let alone desirable, to eliminate all scope for discretionary policy in a world in which the monetary system is in a state of evolution. I hasten to add that this does not imply that attempts to implement short-run fine tuning of the economy by way of manipulating interest rates are all of a sudden alright, or that it is fruitless to require central banks to announce target ranges for monetary expansion over, say, one or two year time horizons. However it does imply that it is as a practical matter impossible to prevent policy makers doing the wrong things if they so wish by tying them down to a monetary growth-rate rule. Unless we can accurately foresee the path that innovations in the financial sector are going to take, someone somewhere is going to have to be granted the discretion to deal with them when they arise. The monetarist injunction not to use monetary policy for fine tuning is not affected by these considerations, but the proposal that the once and for all enactment of a simple rule can lead to that injunction being implemented is undermined. That seems to me to be a rather severe criticism of monetarist policy doctrine.

V. CONCLUDING COMMENTS

As the reader will by now have seen, it is my view that the core of monetarism has consisted of a series of empirical propositions and policy prescriptions, all of which are quite consistent with mainstream economic theory. One can approach the analysis of social questions in terms of the maximising behaviour of individual agents without believing in a stable demand for money function, or a vertical long-run Phillips curve, but evidence that such relationships exist need in no way disturb one's theoretical preconceptions. Although there have been episodes in the monetarist debate where the relevance of mainstream economics to the analysis of such social questions as inflation and unemployment has been vigorously questioned, particularly in Britain, it has mainly been about questions amenable to being settled with reference to empirical evidence, as Mayer (1978) has also argued.

Viewed in this light, I would suggest that, in all but one aspect, the monetarist debate is as close to being over as an economic controversy ever is. The demand for money function does seem to be more stable over time than the early critics of monetarism suggested, while shifts in it have been neither new phenomena, nor of sufficient magnitude seriously to undermine long-run relationships between money and money income. Puzzles about 'reverse causation' in the data for countries such as Britain cease to be puzzles when the openness of the economy and the nature of the exchange-rate regime are taken account of. There is now much less disagreement about the empirical nature of the interaction of real income and inflation: there is a short-run trade off between inflation and unemployment and it does seem to vanish in the long run. Though we should not under-rate the importance of the consensus that has been achieved on the foregoing issues – or neglect to mention explicitly that the consensus in question is not universal – this does not mean that there is now no controversy in macroeconomics. As we have seen two areas remain contentious.

First, one aspect of the monetarist debate remains alive, and that concerns the proper conduct of monetary policy. I doubt that my own view, that the case for governing monetary policy by rules is impossible to sustain in the face of careful consideration of the influence of institutional change on the behaviour over time of the demand for money function, will find a great deal of support among monetarists at present, while I would be surprised to find it regarded as sufficient of a concession to 'fine tuning', and it really is no such thing, to satisfy the Keynesians. Thus, I would expect debates about this matter to keep the monetarist controversy alive for a while yet.

The other, and in my view far more important, issue has to do with the market-theoretic foundations of macroeconomics. The issues raised by Lucas and his collaborators are not the issues that have traditionally concerned participants in the monetarist debate and it is misleading to approach them as if they were. The debate about the assumptions of clearing markets and rational expectations as a basis for macroeconomics is a new one, and as Brian Kantor (1979) has suggested is really about whether Keynes' *General Theory* carried economics forward or took it on a fruitless detour. Though it has very little to do with monetarism, it nevertheless concerns issues of fundamental theoretical importance for macroeconomics. Let us hope that this new controversy proves to be as fruitful as the monetarist controversy has been.

University of Western Ontario D. LAIDLER

Date of receipt of final typescript: August 1980

References

Ando, A. and Modigliani, F. (1965). 'The relative stability of monetary velocity and the investment multiplier.' *American Economic Review*, vol. 55 (September), pp. 693–728.

Ball, R. J. and Burns, T. (1976). 'The inflationary mechanism in the U.K. economy.' *American Economic Review*, vol. 66 (September), pp. 478–84.

Barro, R. J. (1978). 'Unanticipated money, output and the price level in the United States.' *Journal of Political Economy*, vol. 86 (August), pp. 549–81.

—— (1979). 'Second thoughts on Keynesian economics.' *American Economic Review*, vol. 69 (May), papers and proceedings, pp. 54–9.

Baumol, W. J. (1952). 'The transactions demand for cash: an inventory theoretic approach.' *Quarterly Journal of Economics*, vol. 66 (November), pp. 545–56.

Boughton, James M. (1977). 'Does Monetarism Matter' in Elmus Wicker (ed.). *Lilley Conference on Recent Developments in Economics April 21–23*. Bloomington, Indiana, Indiana University.

Brown, Arthur J. (1955). *The Great Inflation 1939–1951*. London: Oxford University Press.

Brunner, K. (1961). 'The report of the Commission on money and credit.' *Journal of Political Economy*, vol. 69 (December), pp. 605–20.

—— (1970). 'The monetarist revolution in monetary theory.' *Weltwirtschaftliches Archiv*, vol. 105, pp. 1–30.

—— (1978). 'Issues of post-Keynesian monetary analysis.' In Thomas Mayer (1978).

—— Cukierman, A. and Meltzer, A. H. (1979). 'Stagflation, persistent unemployment and the permanence of economic shocks.' Carnegie–Mellon University (mimeo).

—— and Meltzer, A. H. (1963). 'Predicting velocity: implications for theory and policy.' *Journal of Finance*, vol. 18 (May), pp. 319–54.

—— —— (eds.) (1978). *The Inflation Problem*. Carnegie–Rochester Public Policy Conference Series. Amsterdam: North-Holland.

Buiter, W. H. (1980). 'The macroeconomics of Dr. Pangloss: a critical survey of the New Classical Macroeconomics.' ECONOMIC JOURNAL, vol. 90 (March), pp. 34–50.

Cagan, P. (1978). 'Monetarism in historical perspective.' In Thomas Mayer (1978).

—— (1979). *Persistent Inflation*. New York: Columbia University Press.

—— and Schwartz, A. J. (1975). 'Has the growth of money substitutes hindered monetary policy?' *Journal of Money, Credit and Banking*, vol. 7 (May), pp. 137–60.

Clements, K. W. and Jonson, P. D. (1979). 'Unanticipated money, disequilibrium modelling and rational expectations.' *Economic Letters*, vol. 2, pp. 303–8.

Clower, R. W. (1965). 'The Keynesian counterrevolution: a theoretical appraisal.' *The Theory of Interest Rates* (ed. F. H. Hahn and F. P. R. Brechling). London: Macmillan.

De Prano, M. and Mayer, T. (1965). 'Tests of the relative importance of autonomous expenditure and money.' *American Economic Review*, vol. 55 (September), pp. 729–52.

Fisher, I. (1911). *The Purchasing Power of Money*. New York.

Frenkel, J. (1980). 'Flexible Exchange Rates in the 1970s', in Laurence H. Meyer (ed.). *Stabilisation Policies Lessons from the 70s and Implications for the 80s*. St. Louis, Washington University and Federal Reserve Bank of St. Louis.

—— and Johnson, H. G. (1976). *The Monetary Approach to Balance of Payments Theory*. London: George Allen and Unwin.

Friedman, M. (1956). 'The quantity theory of money: a restatement.' In *Studies in the Quantity Theory of Money* (ed. M. Friedman). Chicago: University of Chicago Press.

—— (1959). 'The demand for money: some theoretical and empirical results.' *Journal of Political Economy*, vol. 67 (June), pp. 327–51.

—— (1960). *A Program for Monetary Stability*. New York: Fordham University Press.

—— (1966). 'Interest rates and the demand for money.' *Journal of Law and Economics*, vol. 9 (October).

—— (1968). 'The role of monetary policy.' *American Economic Review*, vol. 58 (March), pp. 1–17.

—— (1970). 'A theoretical framework for monetary analysis.' *Journal of Political Economy*, vol. 78 (March–April), pp. 193–238.

—— (1975). *Unemployment Versus Inflation*. London: Institute of Economic Affairs.

—— and Meiselman, D. (1963). 'The relative stability of monetary velocity and the investment multiplier in the United States, 1898–1958. Commission on Money and Credit. *Stabilization Policies*. Englewood Cliffs, New Jersey: Prentice-Hall.

—— and Schwartz, A. J. (1963*a*). *A Monetary History of the United States, 1867–1960*. Princeton, New Jersey: Princeton University Press for the NBER.

—— —— (1963*b*). 'Money and business cycles.' *Review of Economics and Statistics*, vol. 45 (February), supplement, pp. 32–64.

Frisch, H. (1977). 'Inflation theory 1963–1975: a second generation survey.' *Journal of Economic Literature*, vol. 15 (December), pp. 1289–317.

Hahn, F. H. (1980). 'Monetarism and Economic Theory'. *Economica* NS 47 (February), pp. 1–18.

Harberger, A. C. (ed.) (1960). *The Demand for Durable Goods*. Chicago: University of Chicago Press.

Harrod, R. F. (1971). 'Discussion paper.' In *Monetary Theory and Monetary Policy in the 1970's*. (ed. G. Clayton, J. C. Gilbert and R. Sedgewick). London: Oxford University Press.

Hicks, J. R. (1974). *The Crisis in Keynesian Economics*. Oxford: Basil Blackwell.

Howitt, P. W. (1979). 'Evaluating the non-market-clearing approach.' *American Economic Review*, vol. 69 (May), Papers and Proceedings, pp. 60–4.

Johnson, H. G. (1962). 'Monetary theory and policy.' *American Economic Review*, vol. 52 (June), pp. 335–84.

—— (1972). *Inflation and the Monetarist Controversy*. DeVries Lectures, 1971. Amsterdam: North Holland.

Jonson, P. D. (1976*a*). 'Money and economic activity in the open economy, the United Kingdom 1880–1970.' *Journal of Political Economy*, vol. 84 (October), pp. 979–1012.

—— (1976*b*). 'Money, prices and output: an integrative essay.' *Kredit und Kapital*, vol. 9, pp. 499–518.

Kahn, R. F. (1976). 'Inflation: a Keynesian view.' *Scottish Journal of Political Economy*, vol. 23 (February), pp. 11–5.

Kaldor, N. (1970). 'The new monetarism.' *Lloyd's Bank Review* (July), pp. 1–18.

Kantor, B. (1979). 'Rational expectations and economic thought.' *Journal of Economic Literature*, vol. 17 (December), pp. 1422–75.

Laidler, D. (1966). 'The rate of interest and the demand for money: some empirical evidence.' *Journal of Political Economy*, vol. 74 (December), pp. 545–55.

—— (1971). 'The influence of money on economic activity: a survey of some current problems.' In *Monetary Theory and Monetary Policy in the 1970's* (ed. G. Clayton, J. C. Gilbert and R. Sedgwick). London: Oxford University Press.

—— (1975). *Essays on Money and Inflation*. Manchester: University of Manchester Press; Chicago: University of Chicago Press.

—— (1976*a*). 'Inflation in Britain: a monetarist analysis.' *American Economic Review*, vol. 76 (September), pp. 485–500.

—— (1980). 'The demand for money in the United States: yet again' (ed. K. Brunner and A. H. Meltzer). Carnegie-Rochester Conference Series. *The State of Macroeconomics*. Amsterdam: North Holland.

—— (*et al.*) (1976*b*). *Study on the Possible Part Played by Certain Primary Non-employment Incomes in the Inflationary Process in the United Kingdom*. Commission of the European Communities, Brussels.

Lieberman, C. (1980). 'The long-run and short-run demand for money revisited.' *Journal of Money, Credit and Banking*.

Lipsey, R. G. (1960). 'The relationship between unemployment and the rate of change of money wage rates in the United Kingdom, 1862–1957.' *Economica*, vol. 27, pp. 1–31.

Lucas, R. E., Jr. (1972). 'Expectations and the neutrality of money.' *Journal of Economic Theory*, vol. 4, pp. 103–24.

—— (1975). 'An equilibrium model of the business cycle.' *Journal of Political Economy*, vol. 83 (November–December), pp. 1113–44.

—— (1976). 'Econometric policy evaluation: a critique.' *The Phillips Curve and Labour Markets* (ed. K. Brunner and A. H. Meltzer). Carnegie-Rochester Conference Series. Amsterdam: North Holland.

—— (1977). 'Understanding business cycles.' In *Stabilization of the Domestic and International Economy* (ed. K. Brunner and A. H. Meltzer). Carnegie–Rochester Conference Series. Amsterdam: North Holland.

Mayer, T. (1978). *The Structure of Monetarism*. New York: W. W. Norton.

McCracken, P. *et al.* (1977). *Towards Full Employment and Price Stability*. (The McCracken Report.) Paris: OECD.

Meltzer, A. H. (1965). 'Monetary theory and monetary history.' *Schweizerische Zeitschrift Volkswirtschaft und Statistik*, (spring), pp. 409–22.

—— (1969). 'Money intermediation and growth.' *Journal of Economic Literature*, vol. 7 (March), pp. 27–56.

Modigliani, F. (1977). 'The monetarist controversy, or should we forsake stabilization policies?' *American Economic Review*, vol. 67 (March), pp. 1–19.

Parkin, J. M., Sumner, M. T. and Jones, R. A. (1972). 'A survey of the econometric evidence on the effects of incomes policy on the rate of inflation.' In *Incomes Policy and Inflation* (ed. J. M. Parkin and M. T. Sumner). Manchester: University of Manchester Press.

Patinkin, D. (1965). *Money, Interest and Prices*, 2nd ed. New York: Harper Rowe.

—— (1969). 'The Chicago tradition the quantity theory and Friedman.' *Journal of Money, Credit and Banking*, vol. 1 (February), pp. 46–70.

Phelps, E. (1967). 'Phillips curves expectations of inflation and optimal unemployment over time.' *Economica*, N.S., vol. 34 (August), pp. 254–81.

—— (*et al.*) (1969). *Microeconomic Foundations of Employment and Inflation Theory*. New York: W. W. Norton.

Phillips, A. W. (1958). 'The relation between unemployment and the rate of change of money wage rates in the United Kingdom, 1861–1957.' *Economica*, N.S., vol. 25 (November), pp. 283–99.

Purvis, D. D. (1980). 'Monetarism – a review.' *Canadian Journal of Economics*, vol. 1 (February), pp. 96–121.

Radcliffe Committee (Committee on the Working of the Monetary System) (1959). *Report*. London: HMSO.

Reid, M. (1962). *Housing and Income*. Chicago: University of Chicago Press.

Robinson, J. (1970). 'Quantity theories old and new.' *Journal of Money, Credit and Banking*, vol. 2 (November), pp. 504–12.
Santomero, A. M. and Seater, J. J. (1978). 'The inflation–unemployment trade-off: a critique of the literature.' *Journal of Economic Literature*, vol. 16 (June), pp. 499–544.
Sargent, T. J. (1976). 'A classical macroeconomic model for the United States'. *Journal of Political Economy*, vol. 84 (April), pp. 207–38.
—— and Wallace, N. (1975). 'Rational expectations, the optimal monetary instrument and the optimal money supply rule.' *Journal of Political Economy*, vol. 83 (April), pp. 241–54.
Solow, R. M. (1968). Recent controversies on the theory of inflation: an eclectic view.' In *Symposium on Inflation – Its Causes, Consequences and Control* (ed. S. Rousseas). New York: The Calvin K. Kazanjian Economics Foundation.
—— (1979). Alternative approaches to macroeconomic theory: a partial view.' *Canadian Journal of Economics*, vol. 12 (August), pp. 339–54.
—— (1980). On theories of unemployment.' *American Economic Review*, vol. 70 (March), pp. 1–11.
Sumner, M. T. (1980). The operation of monetary targets.' In K. Brunner and A. H. Meltzer (eds.): *Monetary Institutions and the Policy Process*. Carnegie-Rochester Public Policy Conference Series. Amsterdam: North-Holland.
Stein, J. (1976). *Monetarism*. Amsterdam: North-Holland.
Tobin, J. (1947). Liquidity preference and monetary policy.' *Review of Economics and Statistics*, vol. 29 (May), pp. 124–31.
—— (1956). The interest elasticity of transactions demand for cash.' *Review of Economics and Statistics*, vol. 38 (August), pp. 241–7.
—— (1958). Liquidity preference as behaviour towards risk.' *Review of Economic Studies*, vol. 25 (February), pp. 65–86.
—— (1965). 'The monetary interpretation of history.' *American Economic Review*, vol. 55 (June), pp. 464–85.
—— (1972). 'Inflation and unemployment.' *American Economic Review*, vol. 62 (March), pp. 1–18.
Walker, M. (ed.) (1976). *The Illusion of Wage and Price Control*. Vancouver, B.C.: Fraser Institute.
Wiles, P. (1973). 'Cost inflation and the state of economic theory.' ECONOMIC JOURNAL, vol. 83, pp. 377–98.
Wilson, T. (1976). 'The natural rate of unemployment.' *Scottish Journal of Political Economy*, vol. 23 (February), pp. 99 107.

'The Monetarist Counter-Revolution Today – An Appraisal'

J. Tobin, 'The Monetarist Counter-Revolution today – an appraisal', *Economic Journal* (March 1981), pp. 29–42.

THE MONETARIST COUNTER-REVOLUTION TODAY – AN APPRAISAL

The oft-quoted concluding note of Keynes' *General Theory* sings of the power of 'the ideas of economists and political philosophers, both when they are right and when they are wrong'. 'Practical men', 'madmen in authority', 'civil servants and politicians and even agitators' – all are unconscious 'slaves of some defunct economist' or 'academic scribbler of a few years back'. The power of his own ideas fulfilled his prophecy, and he was right too that 'the gradual encroachment of ideas' 'came not immediately', but 'after a certain interval'. The monetarist counter to his own revolution is another confirmation. But the transmission of ideas to the world of affairs has speeded up, like so many communications in modern society. The insatiable appetite of the media for novelty assures an audience for intellectual revolutionaries who can convey their ideas in plausible and homely language. The monetarist economists and 'scribblers' whose theories are coming to rule the world are by no means defunct.

Another giant of a generation past, Joseph Schumpeter, reassured our profession about its inevitable compound of 'Science and Ideology'.[1] 'Vision or Intuition' guides the observations and interests that motivate our work, and is inherently ideological. Though the economist cannot purge his own scientific work of the ideological bias stemming from his initial vision, Schumpeter was optimistic that the collective intercourse of scientists gradually cumulates the durable truths distilled from successive waves of ideologically contaminated inquiries. He concludes, 'That prescientific cognitive act which is the source of our ideologies is also the prerequisite of our scientific work. No new departure in any science is possible without it. Through it we acquire new material for our scientific endeavours and something to formulate, to defend, to attack. Our stock of facts and tools grows and rejuvenates itself in the process. And so – though we proceed slowly because of our ideologies, we might not proceed at all without them'. Schumpeter's address takes Smith, Marx and Keynes as examples. Following his precedent, I intend nothing pejorative in stressing that monetarism is both science and ideology.

That point was made with characteristic eloquence and perception by Harry Johnson ten years ago in his Ely Lecture to the American Economic Association.[2] He observed that the Keynesian revolution and the monetarist counter-revolution shared characteristics essential for the success of revolutionary theory: a vulnerable orthodoxy to attack and to blame for contemporary economic reverses and policy failures; novel socially relevant conclusions

[1] The title of his 1948 Presidential address to the American Economic Association, *American Economic Review* (March 1949), pp. 345–59.

[2] The Keynesian revolution and the monetarist counter-revolution, *American Economic Review* (May 1971), pp. 1–14.

reached by professionally respectable techniques; focus on the salient economic evil of the era; intellectual and methodological excitement for the most talented young scientists and plenty of applied work for the journeymen. The forms these conditions took in the two cases are pretty obvious: I will not repeat or update Johnson's descriptions.

Johnson's 1970 prediction that monetarism will 'peter out' – the same words as Schumpeter's 1948 judgement of Keynesianism – was premature at best. Today it is interesting to see why. He gave two reasons. One was that the monetarists' Evil, inflation, 'is far less a serious problem than mass unemployment', the Evil of Keynesian ideology. But in the 1970s prevailing professional and lay opinion has not rendered this verdict.

Johnson's second reason was 'that monetarism is seriously inadequate as an approach to monetary theory, judged by prevailing standards of academic economics, and in the course of repairing its intellectual fences and achieving full scientific respectability it will have to compromise irretrievably with its Keynesian opposition'. His indictment made two specific charges. One was 'the abnegation of the restated quantity theory of money from the responsibility of providing a theory of the determination of prices and of output,' i.e. 'for analysing the supply response of the economy to monetary impulses, ... whether monetary changes affected prices or quantities.' The second was 'reliance on the methodology of positive economics', i.e. the appeal to simple reduced-form statistical correlations that do not contradict the theory, without specification of the structural mechanisms that could have produced them. Johnson predicted that to maintain academic respectability, and therefore ultimately public influence, monetarists would have to grapple with hard theoretical and empirical questions, losing in the process their sharp differentiation from mainstream Keynesians and eclectics.

The flaws Johnson detected have not yet proved fatal. The problems remain, but the failure to solve them has never been an embarrassment. To the contrary, it has become a virtue. In the ten-year interim monetarists, instead of being absorbed into a bland and messy synthesis, have pulled the centre of gravity of the profession toward their positions and their methodology. The credit goes to a second wave of monetarism, a second counter-revolution that has absorbed and breathed new life into the first, a movement both more reactionary and more revolutionary than its precursor. I shall return to this development, the new classical macroeconomics, later in my talk. It is very much an academic and intellectual development, and first I want to review the triumphs and trials of monetarism in the public arena since Harry Johnson's lecture.

I. MONETARISM, POLICY, AND PERFORMANCE IN THE 1970S

It is not surprising that the central banking fraternity embraced monetarism. Central bankers feel the need of an orthodoxy to which they can appeal in defence against the pressures of Presidents and Prime Ministers, Congresses and Parliaments. With the gold standard long gone and Bretton Woods moribund, money stock targets – their legitimacy and necessity scientifically attested – became the vehicles of discipline.

In the United States, the Federal Reserve began formulating its policies in these terms in 1970. The monetary oversight Committees in both Houses of Congress, influenced by monetarist staff, insisted on targets for monetary aggregates. These Committees examine the 'Fed' Chairman quarterly and grade him on his marksmanship. Elsewhere in the Capitol other Committees struggle, along with the President's agents, with the budget. The operations are

Table 1

U.S. Monetary Aggregates and Measures of Macroeconomic Performance 1951–1979
Means and Standard Deviations for Selected Periods

	Quarterly Changes of Seasonally Adjusted Series at Annual Percentage Rate					
	Monetary aggregates			Macroeconomic outcomes		
	Base	M1	M1B	Real GNP (1972 dollars)	GNP price Defla-tor	Unemploy-ment rate quarterly average Percen-tage of Labour Force)
Means						
(1) 1951:1 to 1960:4	1·71	2·20	n.a.	2·81	2·24	4·55
(2) 1961:1 to 1969:4	5·10	4·14	4·10	4·32	2·79	4·69
(3) 1970:1 to 1979:4	7·97	6·06	6·40	2·94	6·63	6·19
(4) 1951:1 to 1979:4	4·92	4·13	n.a.	3·33	3·92	5·16
Standard deviations						
(5) 1951:1 to 1960:4	1·80	2·27	n.a.	4·76	2·32	1·28
(6) 1961:1 to 1969:4	1·66	2·40	2·42	2·57	1·68	1·09
(7) 1970:1 to 1979:4	1·36	2·31	2·14	4·50	2·35	1·17
(8) 1951:1 to 1979:4 from grand means, row 4	3·07	2·82	n.a.	4.13	2·91	1·40
(9) 1951:1 to 1979:4 from decade means, rows 1–3	1·62	2·33	n.a.	4.11	2.15	1·19

Note: 1961:1 and 1970:1 were chosen as beginnings of periods with explicitly different macroeconomic policies

disjoint, in keeping with monetarist premises. That monetary policy should be different with different budgets, that fiscal and monetary policies should be concerted for common macro-economic objectives – these ideas are not effectively entertained.

What have been the results of the monetarist turn in U.S. demand-management policies? Following the reduced-form methodology to which Johnson alluded, we may seek proof of the pudding in the eating. As we all know, real outcomes have been less satisfactory on average than in the two previous decades and less stable than in the 1960s. Inflation has accelerated and its variance has risen too. After a decade without recession, we have suffered three in the last ten years, including the one now in progress. The two most recent recessions are the most severe of post-war history. All three recessions were deliberate acts of policy, especially monetary policy. As Table 1 indicates, there was somewhat greater stability in monetary growth rates in the 1970s, but considerably less stability in the macro variables of real importance. The decade of activist policy, the 1960s, looks better than the years before or after.[1]

Monetarists complain, of course, that the players on the field did not faithfully follow their coaches' game plan. True enough, and quite normal. Neither did Lyndon Johnson follow his 'Keynesian' coaches' game plan when he escalated the Vietnam war without raising taxes in 1966, but the 'New Economics' of the period has not thereby escaped blame for the resulting inflation. The Federal Reserve has not been wholly monetarist since the 1970 conversion. The 'Fed' moved its short-run money growth targets with eyes on national and international economic variables, actual and projected, and did not completely abandon its old strategy of 'leaning against the wind' but not too hard.

The 'Fed's' imperfect marksmanship did not prevent strong swings in demands for money and credit from showing up in money supplies. Sometimes these were 'IS' shocks whose accommodation intensified boom or recession. Sometimes they were 'LM' shocks that, according to William Poole's paradigm[2], should be accommodated. By the same principles, the Fed's corrective responses to errors of marksmanship were sometimes stabilising and sometimes not. Lacking any levers at its operations desk marked M_1 or M_2, the 'Fed' has to control these quantities indirectly, by reference to a related variable it can control. Until recently, this was the market interest rate on overnight interbank loans, 'Federal Funds'. Every month, sometimes more frequently, the Federal Open Market Committee reconsidered its Funds rate target and moved it up or down as thought necessary to return money stocks to the desired track or keep them there.

Monetarists criticised this procedure – pegging nominal interest rates! – for allowing excessive swings in money supplies. The Federal Open Market Committee, the critics said, adjusted the instrumental Funds rate target too little and too late. In October 1979 the Fed surrendered, announcing that henceforth its week-to-week operations would be guided by quantitative targets for bank reserves, subject to broad and adjustable interest rate limits. Unfortunately the short run relation of Ms and MVs to reserve stocks is, as subsequent events illustrate, no tighter than their relation to the Federal Funds rate.

More basic practical difficulties of single-minded monetarism were exemplified in the summer of 1980 by the dilemma of the American central bank. Demand for new bank credit had dwindled, and for the time being the 'Fed's' money growth targets seemed unattainable without short-term rates so low compared to those

[1] See also M. N. Baily, 'Stabilisation policy and private economic behaviour,' *Brookings Papers on Economic Activity* (1: 1978), pp. 11–50.

[2] W. Poole, 'Optimal choice of monetary policy instruments in a simple stochastic macro model, *Quarterly Journal of Economics* (May 1970), pp. 197–216.

on this side of the Atlantic that the dollar would plummet once again. Apparently this pragmatic consideration prevailed over faithful pursuit of the targets.

Though not purely monetarist, demand management policies in the 1970s have been increasingly influenced by monetarist principles and sensitive to monetarist criticisms. Real outcomes have not been good, and might well have been worse if the authorities had followed less compensatory and accommodative policies. The 1970s were tough for demand management of any brand. But monetarists are in a poor position to shift blame to the inflationary legacy of the 1960s, or to OPEC, or to fiscal policies. Their own doctrines – stressing sharp dichotomies between real and monetary shocks, between relative and absolute prices, and between past trends and future expectations – disqualify as vulgar fallacies these popular explanations of inflation and stagflation.

The dismal record has not yet appreciably diminished the appeal of monetarism to central bankers, statesmen, and influential citizens. The doctrine has survived recent economic reverses much better than the so-called New Economics of the early 1960s weathered the failures for which it was, rightly or wrongly, held responsible at the end of that decade. The claim that current travails are the fault of the old orthodoxy, indeed further proof of its errors and dangers, has not lost credibility. Monetarism gains still from poor economic performance. Moreover, the inevitable short-run pro-cyclical elasticity of money supplies gives ready alibis to those monetarists who are not actually running central banks. Having defined policy by stochastic endogenous variables rather than by operationally controllable instruments, monetarist critics can always complain that 'policy' has been too unstable and accommodative. The more wilful deviations of practical central bankers, previously noted, add to the credence of these criticisms.

But there are signs that the honeymoon is coming to an end. The redefinition of monetary aggregates to catch up to financial innovations and substitutions, the persistence of endogenous swings in the aggregates after the authorities abandoned even temporary stabilisation of overnight interest rates, and recent gyrations of other interest rates inspire critical questions even within the naturally loyal financial constituencies of the central bank. As Johnson observed intellectual and operational responses to such questions are bound to impair the appealing simplicity of monetarist doctrine and policy.

II. MONETARISM AS CONSERVATIVE IDEOLOGY

In public political and economic debate, monetarism has become a central part of conservative, that is to say nineteenth-century liberal, ideology. These days the other principal elements are most easily summarised as oppositions to Government: to public operation or regulation of economic activities, to redistributions of income and wealth, to collective consumption and investment, and to budget deficits. 'Supply-side economics' is a more positive theme of contemporary right-wing ideology, stressing tax reductions and deregulation as incentives for work, saving, enterprise and efficiency.

The logical connections of the monetarism of the 1960s to its ideological partners remain obscure. Their unity was less in logic than in the person of Milton Friedman, the powerful and persuasive protagonist of the several ideas. In principle a monetarist could favour big and active government, advocate public interventions to correct market failures, or – like Friedman's Chicago precursor Henry Simons – urge redistribution by progressive taxation.

In principle monetarism provides no support for the traditional and ever-popular conservative warning that deficit spending is inflationary. Monetarist doctrine says that deficits increase aggregate nominal spending only as they lead to increases of money supply. In countries with underdeveloped financial systems, printing money may be the only feasible way to finance deficits. But in countries like the United States and United Kingdom, any linkage must be political choice rather than technical necessity. The allegation that political pressure forces the central bank to monetise deficits has dubious empirical foundation, especially in recent years. Some non-causal correlation between base money growth and deficits will be observed when both move counter-cyclically, money for policy reasons, deficits endogenously.

Monetarists frequently charge deficit spending with 'crowding out' productive private investment. Popular versions of this charge are particularly disingenuous in failing to distinguish cases in which real output is supply-constrained from those in which it is merely money-constrained. In the former cases, any new draft on resources, however financed, is bound to crowd out other uses. Allocational priorities are an important consideration in the mix of monetary and fiscal policies, but judgement about them is not a specifically monetarist issue. In cases of the second kind, to crowd out or not to crowd out is a choice of monetary policy. With employable resources available, deficit-financed demands could be accommodated by money supply to the degree they are not naturally accommodated by velocity.

Professional debate on the macro-economic efficacies of fiscal and monetary policies contains, after all, little ideological excitement. First principles of free enterprise do not say which will be the more effective or useful or hazardous. Both public finance and monetary management are embarrassing exceptions to the ideological rule that competitive pursuit of private interests will handle all society's economic problems. For just that reason many conservatives find the unmanaged gold standard more congenial than the controlled fiat money of the monetarists.

Monetarism is more in tune with the wider ideology in its insistence on stability in macro-economic policy. Activist demand management, 'fine tuning' compensatory counter-cyclical policies – monetarists identify these as the sources of instability in overall economic performance. With stable policies, they say, the economy itself will be stable. Exogenous non-policy shocks, including entrepreneurial expectations and spirits, are assigned comparatively little empirical importance. To those shocks that do occur market adjustments are swift and convergent. Policy variations are more likely to amplify than to dampen natural fluctuations, misallocating resources in the process. The logic of this view applies to all policy instruments, fiscal as well as monetary. Friedman himself so applied it, before he became so exclusively monetarist, in his 'Fiscal and Monetary Framework for Economic Stability'.[1]

This is a more fundamental theme than the technical sovereignty of any monetary aggregate and it is more congenial to free enterprise ideology. It is also the theme of the second wave of the monetarist counter-revolution, the new classical macro-economics. The new doctrine has given a theroetical rationale for propositions that were previously matters of faith and empirical judgement. The grasp of the Invisible Hand is extended beyond micro-economic resource allocation to macro-economic optimality – market competition produces not just a tendency towards long-run optima but a continuous sequence of equilibria. Friedman himself is the link between the old monetarism and the new. The 1968 message of his 'natural rate of unemployment'[2] was that demand management policies can only temporarily alter real economic outcomes, that under stable policies the economy will reach equilibrium employment on its own.

Nevertheless I doubt that the new wave will establish a permanent place for monetarism in conservative ideology. The popular success of monetarism arose along with Inflation, the Evil that could be plausibly blamed on the errors and excesses of the reigning orthodoxy, the Evil for which monetarist rules of policy were the specific remedy. As ideology monetarism profited from the substantial real disappointments of the decade, notably OPEC shocks, because the public identified all personal, national, and worldwide reverses of economic fortune in the 1970s as ravages of Inflation. Professional economists of all schools know that such disappointments and reverses could not be avoided by less accommodative monetary policies, any more than their first-order costs could be escaped by more accommodative policies. Printing money does not produce oil, and neither does not printing it.

There has always been tension between ideological monetarism, which promises to rescue us from Inflation, and theoretical monetarism, which says that Inflation has little or no effect on the real performance of the economy. The tension is accentuated in monetarism mark II, which relies heavily on the neutrality of money, even on super-neutrality, and applies the 'classical dichotomy' to continuously moving equilibrium. The message of the new classical macro-economics is not so much that Keynesian policies do Evil as that they do Nothing. Not quite: an alleged evil is that capricious shifts in policy rules confuse private agents and cause allocational distortions. Whatever its intrinsic merit, this point is not the stuff of ideology; its lay appeal is as limited as that of the 'shoe-leather' costs of economising cash during anticipated inflations.

The tension is likely in time to become a telling weakness in monetarism as conservative ideology, if only because it attenuates the evangelical fervour of leading new classical theorists. In the face of monetarism II, some more old-fashioned conservative economists steadfastly maintain that deficits, debt, easy money, and inflation do serious positive harm.

Both wings can agree on macro-economic policies. It is therefore likely that

[1] *American Economic Review* (June 1948), pp. 265–74.

[2] 'The role of monetary policy', *American Economic Review* (March 1968), pp. 1–17.

the public focus of conservative political economy will shift away from macro concerns to the size of government, regulation, progressive taxation, the welfare state, and related 'supply-side' issues. Government is a currently popular Evil, and probably an easier target than Inflation.

III MONETARISM AS PROFESSIONAL ECONOMICS

I return now to the intellectual inadequacies that Harry Johnson detected in monetarism in 1970. Why have they not proved as damaging as he predicted? How have the monetarists, especially those riding the second wave, handled them? Where does the professional debate between the old Keynesian revolution and the counter-revolution stand today? Johnson mentioned two problems, which I paraphrase as the output-price responses of the economy to variations of monetary demand, and the structure of the process by which measures of monetary control are transmitted to aggregate demand. I shall discuss them in turn.

The 'missing equation': money, output, and prices. 'The supply response of the economy to monetary impulses' is still the central issue, for both theory and policy. A monetary impulse can be regarded as a change, however generated, in the nominal rate of spending on final goods and services – nominal GNP or M times V. The roles of monetary policies and aggregates, fiscal policies, and velocity shocks in determining the path of MV are separable and secondary questions, deferred to the second part of this section. The division of monetary impulses between prices and quantities is the crucial matter today in assessing the real consequences and counter-inflationary prospects of the restrictive macro-economic policies your government and mine are pursuing.

In his 'Theoretical Framework'[1] Friedman referred to this division as the 'missing equation' of short-run models. He claimed that both Keynes and the classics relied on arbitrarily assumed rigidities, at one pole the money wage and at the other aggregate supply. His own candidate, a short-run adjustment equation, was not different in spirit from the wage/price/output mechanisms of mainstream eclectic Keynesian theory and econometrics. These included Okun's Law and Phillips-type equations for money wages and mark-ups, along with competitive pricing in 'flex-price' sectors.

The salient proposition underlying this approach is that labour and product markets in the dominant 'fixprice' sectors are in disequilibrium most of the time. That is, they are characterised by excess supply or demand at existing wages and prices. A large share of short-run adjustment occurs via quantities rather than prices. Wages and prices are insufficiently flexible to keep markets continuously cleared.

The adjustment process itself has not, in general, been successfully described as optimising behaviour, the only paradigm that carries theoretical conviction in our profession. This failure, neither surprising nor discreditable in view of the

[1] 'A theoretical framework for monetary analysis', *Journal of Political Economy* (March/April 1970) pp. 193–238.

intrinsic difficulties of the task, is the root of the chronic crisis in macro-economics.

Monetarism II has not solved this problem, but has evaded it. The new classical macro-economists,[1] bolder than their pre-Keynesian forebears, just assume that product and labour markets are continuously in supply–demand equilibrium. They know and admit, of course, that this is not literally true. But the 'methodology of positive economics' protects them from empirical examination of their premises: let's see, they say in effect, if macroeconomic observations behave 'as if' generated by price-cleared markets.

They further assume, of course, that participants in those markets make future-oriented decisions on the basis of rational expectations of relevant variables, including government policies. The substantive thrust of this important assumption is to eliminate the inertia that adaptive expectations imparted to earlier models of wage and price adjustments. The implication is that real outcomes will be invariant to anticipated monetary policies, as indeed to any events that do not change real endowments, current and expected.

By defining away the problem of the 'missing equation', the monetarists have escaped the messy grubwork in which Johnson expected them to lose their identity. Thus liberated, Monetarism II mobilises the power of general equilibrium theory and the eager young talent its apparatus naturally attracts.

But the facts of business fluctuations remain, challenging the theorists to explain in their equilibrium terms the cyclical variability of real macro-economic variables. I find neither of the two lines of explanation so far advanced convincing. One is to attribute cyclical swings to basic real data: tastes, technologies, resource endowments. For example, swings in employment could reflect intertemporal choices between leisure and other consumption. Besides being an inherently implausible account of the variations of unemployment of labour and capital capacity since 1946, not to mention pre-war experience, this version of equilibrium theory omits monetary variables altogether.

The second approach attempts to explain the well-documented short-run positive association of nominal prices and real quantities. Superficially this correlation appears to refute the asserted neutrality of monetary policy. Robert Lucas's celebrated reconciliation[2] is that the correlated observations arise wholly from monetary surprises – for example, suppliers mistakenly interpret an economy-wide increase in absolute prices as a rise in their own relative prices. This theory invites two decisive objections. First, it requires, in addition

[1] The leading protagonists are Robert Lucas, Thomas Sargent, and Robert Barro. See, for example, Lucas and Sargent, 'After Keynesian macroeconomics', in *After the Phillips Curve* (Federal Reserve Bank of Boston Conference Series 19, June 1978); Lucas, 'Understanding business cycles', in Brunner and Meltzer, eds., *Stabilization of the Domestic and International Economy*, *Journal of Monetary Economics Supplement* (1977). T. Sargent and Neil Wallace, 'Rational Expectations, the optimal monetary instrument, and the optimal money supply rule,' *Journal of Political Economy* (April 1975), pp. 241–54. For a critique of these developments see my Jahnsson lectures: Tobin, *Asset Accumulation and Economic Activity: Reflections on Contemporary Macroeconomic Theory* (London: Blackwell, 1980) chapter 2; also, 'How dead is Keynes?', *Economic Inquiry* vol. XV, no. 4 (October 1977), pp. 459–68.

[2] Robert E. Lucas, Jr, 'Econometric testing of the natural rate hypothesis', in Otto Eckstein, ed., *The Econometrics of Price Determination Conference*, sponsored by the Board of Governors of the Federal Reserve System and the Social Science Research Council (Washington: Federal Reserve System, 1972).

to the basic assumptions of market-clearing and rational expectations, an arbitrary and empirically far-fetched specification of imperfections and asymmetries in the information available to various economic agents, for example sellers and buyers.

Second, the theory fails to account for many observed regularities of cyclical fluctuations. I do not have time to catalogue them here. My dear friend Arthur Okun, in a paper I heard him give only a couple of weeks before his tragic death, gave a thorough and admirable list[1]. These phenomena are quite consistent with the modern Keynesian view, and indeed the old monetarist view as well, that unemployment and idle capacity reflect excess supply in non-cleared markets. They are not consistent with the new classical view.

Inertia of wage and price paths could be attributed either to sluggishness in adaptation of expectations or to institutional rigidities. The rational expectations revolution, discrediting adaptive expectations, has focused the profession's attention on the second source of inertia. Contracts, explicit and implicit, are an obvious institutional rigidity. They are particularly important in United States labour relations, where collective bargaining contracts are made for as long as three years. Workers' concern for relative status is, as Keynes argued, another important factor, again especially in the United States, where collective bargaining is both decentralised and unsynchronised in time. Since contracts do not cover all contingencies, as they would if made by Arrow and Debreu, it is possible for compensatory policies following well-understood rules to be effective for good or ill by responding to macro-economic information that becomes available during the tenure of contracts.

The big policy debate today, certainly in our two countries, concerns the effectiveness and the side effects of a sustained and determined programme of monetary disinflation.[2] Will such a programme succeed in eliminating or significantly reducing our current inflations, and if so how fast? How much damage to real economic variables, employment, output, and investment, will occur in the process? How rapidly will local prices adjust downward if the monetary authorities resolutely refuse to accommodate OPEC boosts and other specific price shocks?

Past experience, including the previous recession and the current one, yields pessimistic answers. In the United States, up to 90% of reductions in monetary spending for a year goes into output rather than prices. Two or three point-years of extra unemployment bring down the inertial core inflation by only one point.

Monetarists contend that the observations that generated these unpromising estimates of short-run trade-offs were coloured by the expectations of private agents – workers, unions, managements – that compensatory policies would relieve them of the necessity to lower money wages and prices to restore normal employment and sales volumes. Consequently, they contend, disin-

[1] A. M. Okun, 'Rational-expectations-with-misperceptions as a theory of the business cycle,' prepared for the American Enterprise Institute Seminar on Rational Expectations (February 1980).

[2] I have discussed the issues at more length in 'Stabilization policy ten years after', *Brookings Papers on Economic Activity* (1:1980), pp. 19–72.

flation will occur much more rapidly, and with much less real transitional damage, if the determination of the authorities to 'stay the course' this time is well advertised and well understood.[1]

This is a highly speculative prospect to bet on. Can such a threat really be credible in a democracy, where governments cannot bind their successors? Perhaps the chances of policy reversal are, and will be perceived to be, less in a Parliamentary system like your own than in our Congressional–Presidential structure. Even if the threat is credible, how will it be read by individual workers, unions, and enterprises? Each group might well prefer to let the rest of the economy do the disinflating, thus making sure that its relative status is protected whatever the other groups do. Unfortunately, monetarist propaganda has undermined the monetarist programme, by spreading the notions that inflation is wholly the responsibility of government and that disinflation can be achieved solely and costlessly by governmental financial reform while private agents conduct business as usual.

The main point is that the experiment is novel, the subjects are national and world economies, and the stakes are very high. For this reason, I personally think it would be only prudent to coordinate monetary disinflation with an incomes policy designed to disinflate nominal income claims at a pace consistent with the deceleration of aggregate monetary demand. A coordinated programme would combine threat with promise – promise that jobs and sales will be maintained and promise that no union or other interest will be going it alone. Given mutual consistency of the policies, wage/price controls would not be trying to hold the lid on a kettle boiling with excess demand. At the end of several transitional years, the inflationary legacy of existing contracts and status comparisons would have been overcome. Both expectations and policies would then support the continuation of less inflationary patterns without controls.

A coordinated programme of this kind presumes that the society enjoys or can reach rough basic consensus on division of the social product. If there is irreconcilable conflict, the society's maladies are deeper than their inflationary symptoms and certainly beyond the reach of any central bank. And it is gratuitously optimistic to think that fundamental distributional conflict can be resolved by shrinking the pie over which the parties are contesting.

Monetarists, of course, fervently oppose controls of any kind, even flexible varieties based on tax penalities or rewards or on the negotiable ration tickets devised by the ever-inventive Abba Lerner.[2] Monetarists commonly say that incomes policies are not sufficient, which is true; they must be accompanied by suitably disinflationary demand management. They commonly say that they were not necessary, which is a highly debatable assertion of faith. They always say they are allocationally inefficient, which is true as far as it goes. But these inefficiencies must be compared with the real costs of recession and stagflation

[1] William Fellner, *Towards a Reconstruction of Macroeconomics* (Washington: American Enterprise Institute, 1976).

[2] See Arthur M. Okun and George L. Perry (eds.), *Curing Chronic Inflation* (The Brookings Institution, 1978). For an elegant alternative with the same properties of flexibility, see Abba P. Lerner, 'A wage-increase permit plan to stop inflation,' *Brookings Papers on Economic Activity* (2: 1978), pp. 491–505.

resulting from unassisted monetary disinflation. Ultimately, I suspect, monetarist objection to controls is based not on such cost-benefit analysis but on ideological preference for a 'free' economy however badly it may perform. But if the monetarist prescription exhausts the public's tolerance of real hardships without visible abatement of inflation, the reaction will damage not only the credibility of monetarism and the economy's freedom from controls but also some more important social values.

Structural modelling of money and monetary policy. The second scientific deficiency mentioned by Johnson in 1970 was the failure to provide structural models, either theoretical or econometric. Johnson attributed this failure to excessive reliance on the 'as if' methodology of positive economics.

For example, Friedman and other monetarists were impatient with requests to define conceptually the 'money' whose quantity was the alleged fulcrum of the economy. What properties of liabilities payable in the unit of account are essentially monetary? What characteristics matter? The identity of the debtor – government, commercial banks, other intermediaries? The term of the liability – demand, notice, term? The bearing of nominal interest – zero, otherwise fixed, market-determined? Transferability and acceptability in transactions? Safety and predictability of nominal value? Monetarists have preferred not to hear these questions but to reason in theoretical models 'as if' there were an unambiguous unique monetary store of value, and to identify as its real world counterpart whatever aggregate correlated best with nominal GNP. However persuasive the R^2s of these simple regressions were to laymen, Johnson was right that neither the theory nor the statistics satisfied the canons of the profession as of 1970.

On the theoretical side, it seemed to critics, myself included, that monetarists made quantum leaps from general asset preference theory to special monetarist propositions. However stable 'the' money demand function may be, equating it to money supply cannot describe the whole economy if the function contains more than one endogenous variable. How Friedman and Brunner–Meltzer[1] could turn multi-asset systems of equations into single equation monetarism remains a mystery I do not fathom. Nor did Friedman's 'Theoretical Framework', evidently written in belated response to complaints of this genre, provide a structural model supporting his strong propositions and policy recommendations. Certainly that work has not proved nearly so seminal and influential as his 'natural rate' Presidential address.

However, on this score too the second wave of the counter-revolution has saved monetarism from much of the embarrassment and absorption Johnson foresaw. For example, Barro's revival of the Ricardian theorem[2] of the equivalence of public borrowing and taxation has provided an intellectually tight, if

[1] For an exposition of their monetary theory, see K. Brunner and A. Meltzer, 'An aggregate theory for a closed economy', in J. Stein, ed., *Monetarism* (Amsterdam: North Holland, 1976), ch. 2. Benjamin Friedman points out that the model does not differ significantly in its structure from other macro models of asset stocks and flows: B. Friedman, 'The theoretical non-debate about monetarism', in T. Mayer, ed., *The Structure of Monetarism* (New York: Norton, 1978), pp. 94–112.

[2] Robert Barro, 'Are government bonds net wealth?', *Journal of Political Economy*, vol. 82 (November/December 1974), pp. 1095–117.

empirically implausible, rationale for monetarist dismissals of the macro-economic importance of fiscal policies. (At the same time, however, it exonerates government borrowing of the charge of crowding out private investment.) On the empirical front, Lucas's critique of econometric policy evaluation[1] has called existing structural models into question, on the ground that their behavioural equations will not be invariant to policy rules and regimes. Given the hazards of *a priori* classification of variables as exogenous or endogenous, Sims and others seek to infer causation from nonstructural systems.[2] So the pseudo-reduced-form empiricism of Monetarism I seems less illegitimate now than it did ten years ago. In any event, the question whether money causes income or income money or both is still undecided.

In some respects the new monetarism is as vulnerable to Johnson's objection as the old. Popular rational expectations macro-models, from which strong propositions about policy are derived, are underdeveloped on the financial side. They too neglect to describe the monetary transmission process. They assume a single sovereign M, unspecified as to concept, properties, and measure. They assume it to be directly controllable by the authorities; they do not explicitly relate it to instruments of monetary control, government budgets, or financial institutions and markets. They assume neutralities that would not survive in richer models, which would take account of such phenomena as rigidities of nominal interest rates on currency, deposits, and central bank discounts and as the different wealth and portfolio effects of monetisation of government deficits, central bank open-market operations, credit creation by financial intermediaries, and other money-supply processes. A related monetarist oversimplification is the common two-way classification of shocks as monetary or real, ignoring the monetary–real combination in a shock, for example, to the marginal efficiency of capital. These deficiencies are remediable as the new monetarism drops the primitive dogmas of the old, but as Johnson said, the process will involve some loss of distinctive identity.

The synthesis of revolution and counter-revolution that Harry Johnson expected in 1970 has not yet occurred. Instead the gulf has widened, as the advent of Monetarism II prolonged the life of the counter-revolution. I think nonetheless that the synthetic phase of the dialectic is beginning. The synthesis will not be, to the extent that Johnson predicted, the disappearance of monetarism into an eclectic neoclassical neo-Keynesian mainstream. The ideas of the second counter-revolution are too distinctive and too powerful to be lost in the shuffle. They are bound to shape whatever orthodoxy emerges. The durable ideas are more methodological than substantive – internally consistent derivation of rational expectations and rational behaviour, embodied in the structural equations of a general equilibrium macro-economic model. These ideas are already being mobilised not just to exalt the Invisible Hand but to explain the

[1] Robert E. Lucas, 'Econometric policy evaluation: a critique', in Karl Brunner and Allan H. Meltzer (eds.), *The Phillips Curve and Labor Markets*, Carnegie-Rochester Conference Series on Public Policy, vol. 1 (Amsterdam: North-Holland, 1976), pp. 19–46.

[2] Christopher Sims, 'Macroeconomics and reality', *Econometrica*, (January 1980), pp. 1–48.

causes and effects of informational imperfections, long-term contracts and other commitments, incompleteness of capital markets, liquidity constraints, and many other phenomena of common observation. As the process bears fruit, Keynesian problems will be interpreted in a new light but will not disappear or be dismissed as theoretical impossibilities. There will be plenty of room for compensatory demand management, both in theoretical models and in real economies, and improved understanding how to use it. As this scientific synthesis proceeds, monetarism will lose the polar simplicity essential to its ideological appeal, which will in any case be eroded by disillusionment with the results of policies identified with monetarism. If I am right in these guesses, Joseph Schumpeter's faith in the fruitful interaction of science and ideology will be once more vindicated.

Yale University JAMES TOBIN

Date of receipt of final typescript: September 1980

‘Early Patinkin–Friedman Correspondence’

R. Leeson, ‘The early Patinkin–Friedman correspondence’, *Journal of the History of Economic Thought*, 20:4 (December 1998), pp. 433–48.

THE EARLY PATINKIN—FRIEDMAN CORRESPONDENCE

BY

ROBERT LEESON

I. INTRODUCTION

Don Patinkin (1922–95) was a co-author of the Keynesian neoclassical synthesis, and became engaged in several important controversies. One of them involved Milton Friedman's (1956) assertion about a supposed Chicago quantity theory "oral tradition." From 1968 until his death, Patinkin hardly seemed to miss an opportunity of denigrating what he regarded as Friedman's "invention." This controversy was taken to the 1970 American Economic Association (AEA) meeting by Harry Johnson (1971), and divided at least two economics departments, Chicago and the University of Western Ontario, where Patinkin and Johnson were frequent visitors, and where two influential monetarists, David Laidler and Michael Parkin, had migrated from Britain (Parkin, 1986; Patinkin, 1986).

Milton Friedman's star rose to spectacular heights following his successful AEA presidential prediction of the breakdown of the Phillips curve trade-off, using his own methodology of positive economics (Friedman, 1968a; 1953). Almost immediately after his AEA address (and, therefore, just before the start of the monetarist decade), Friedman felt that he had been libeled by Patinkin and Johnson. Specifically, Patinkin's charge was that Friedman's 1956 essay on "The Quantity Theory of Money—A Restatement" should have been entitled "The Theory of Liquidity Preference—A Restatement."[1] Friedman, Patinkin argued, had "invented" a bogus Chicago oral tradition. Patinkin's (1981) assault on Friedman appeared in the first issue of the first edition (1969) of the *Journal of Money Credit and Banking* (*JMCB*) which had been founded and edited by a

---

Murdoch University, Perth, Western Australia.

This essay (and especially my understanding of Don Patinkin) has been improved by comments and information provided by Robert Dimand, Graeme Dorrance, Paul Evans, Stanley Fischer, Milton Friedman, Craufurd Goodwin, Daniel Hammond, David Laidler, Richard Lipsey, Donald Moggridge, Michael Parkin, Mark Perlman, Paul Samuelson, Winton Solberg, Frank Steindl, James Tobin, Haim Barkai and his colleagues at the Hebrew University of Jerusalem, and three referees from this journal. I am also grateful to the staff of the Special Collections Library, Duke University, for their assistance and for their permission to quote material from the Special Collections Library.

[1] This phrase was used by David Laidler (1980, p. 3), although not specifically in connection with Patinkin's assault on Friedman.

1042-7716/98/030433-16

monetarist, Karl Brunner, who had apparently just invented the word "monetarism."

This essay describes the early correspondence between Patinkin and Friedman prior to Patinkin's *JMCB* essay. The correspondence is affectionate and, at times, amusing, although the public tensions that boiled over in 1969 were present in this early private correspondence. Patinkin left the University of Chicago in 1948 and migrated to Israel in 1949, but was a frequent visitor to Chicago. He continued to regard himself, and was regarded by others, as being ... *In The Chicago Tradition* (Patinkin, 1981, p. xii).[2] Policy disputes in Israel about the appropriate use of the price mechanism as opposed to administrative judgment resulted in what was perceived as a "victory for ... the 'Chicago' economists in the Hebrew University" (Pomphret, 1976, pp. 26–27, 170). Patinkin and (to a lesser extent) Friedman were involved in these policy disputes. A common (if exaggerated) perception was "that Don's message, and that of Economics as a whole, was that of 'The Gospel According to Chicago'" (Barkai *et al.*, 1993, p. 6).[3]

One of the interesting aspects of Patinkin's reply to Friedman was that it took him twelve years (1956–68) to respond. If Patinkin were *solely* interested in correcting an historical "error," it seems likely that he would have done the correcting in the 1950s and not the late 1960s. The 1969 *JMCB* article began as "an aside" in a letter to Friedman in 1959. After Friedman's (1968b) *Encyclopedia* entry on the quantity theory, Patinkin wrote up his "aside" and apologized to his readers for not having done so years earlier. It is therefore worth investigating the reasons why Patinkin was prepared to launch an attack on Friedman in the late 1960s and not in 1956. Patinkin's response to Friedman's 1968 entry reflected, in part, changes in his relationship with Friedman, and in part, perhaps, a change in the degree of influence that Friedman exerted. These changes are documented in their correspondence.

This essay describes the early personal relations between Patinkin and Friedman and their discussions about Israeli policy disputes (section II); Patinkin's response to warfare—hot, cold and scholarly (section III); their exchanges about Alfred Marshall (section IV); Patinkin's influence on the development of Friedman's methodology of positive economics (section V); and Frank Knight's suspicions that Friedman's views on capitalism were oversimplified (section VI). Concluding comments are provided in section VII.

II. PERSONAL RELATIONS

Patinkin

Patinkin was born and educated in Chicago, taking a B.A. (1943), an M.A. (1945) and a Ph.D. (1947) from the University, after having spent two years at

[2] Robert Lucas (1980, p. 696, n.) developed part of his approach to business cycles after attending Patinkin's 1979 course on the history of monetary thought.

[3] Patinkin was a member of the Foreign Currency Committee (1953–54) and sided with the majority position, which rejected the "free market" proposal immediately to abolish currency controls (correspondence from Barkai, January 11, 1998).

Central YMCA College, which subsequently evolved into Roosevelt University (Patinkin, 1981, p. 3, n. 2). Chicago was one of the cities with a high concentration of Jewish people, with a proportion of Jews to Gentiles roughly similar to the proportion of Jews to Arabs in Palestine. Very few (only 494) American Jews migrated to Palestine in the period 1936 to 1945. Until the period of mass migration following the establishment of the state of Israel (May 14, 1948) and The Law of Return (1950) many of the migrants were Socialist-Zionists (Patinkin, 1956a, p. 22; Crossman, 1946, pp. 37, 39, 176, 170; Rubner, 1960, p. xvii, 3, 67, 89; Donovan, 1967; Halevi and Klinov-Malul, 1968, p. 41).

Israel's stock of human capital may have been the highest in the world, with unparalleled levels of X-efficiency. Patinkin must have been struck by the contrast between the economics he had been taught at Chicago and the quasi-socialist policies pursued by the new Israeli state. The government played a very large role in resource allocation and capital formation, and in keeping wage differentials and income inequality low (Patinkin, 1974, p. 6; Easterlin, 1961, pp. 71, 76–81; Pomphret, 1976, p. 5; Lerner and Ben-Shahar, 1975, p. 146; Halevi and Klinov-Malul, 1968, p. 4). Crossman thought that he had witnessed the construction of a "socialist commonwealth ... just as the Americans became a nation through the blood shed in the War of Independence," with labor leaders "fanatically building what they believe will be the only free socialist society in the world." The Interest Law, inherited from the Ottoman period, imposed heavy fines on those charging interest rates in excess of the legal maximum. It was supported by the three socialist parties, but opposed by the Governor of the Bank of Israel, and most economists (Halevi, 1969, p. 100). In the early years, prices were strictly controlled. Food, clothing, building material and foreign exchange were all rationed, until the rampant black market disintegrated the price-fixing system (Patinkin, 1960, pp. 108–9). A relatively small percentage of Israel's national product was generated in the private sector; and a relatively large proportion of investment volume was directed by government officials (Patinkin, 1974, p. 7; Rubner, 1960–61, pp. 69–70). The United States Joint Chief of Staff, the State Department and the British Foreign Office all came to believe that Israel was in danger of becoming a communist state, aided by Soviet penetration (Bullock, 1985, p. 648). Patinkin and his wife and young daughter migrated into this turmoil, being employed at the Hebrew University.

Until his departure for Israel, Patinkin was closely involved with both the Chicago Department of Economics and the Cowles Commission, where a large number of "giants" stalked the corridors. It must have been an extraordinarily exciting period to be a student, with all sorts of interconnections with world history. One of these "giants," Oskar Lange, failed to turn up for lectures for a while (enlisting Leonid Hurwicz as a stand in); he reappeared shortly afterwards on the front page of the newspapers having an audience with Stalin in Moscow. Likewise, Patinkin's squash games with Lawrence Klein under the West Stands of Stagg Field were suddenly interrupted by the mysterious closure of the courts (Patinkin, 1981, pp. 3–17). Only later was it revealed that Enrico Fermi had started the first primitive uranium reactor in the windowless cellars beneath the grandstands of Stagg Field.[4]

As a twenty-four year old, Patinkin was moving in some high-powered circles at Cowles and Chicago: Klein, Hurwicz, Jacob Marschak, Tjalling Koopmans, Trygve Haavelmo and Ragnar Frisch attended the staff seminar on his essay on "Unemployment in Keynesian Economics" (February 1947). In his early thirties, Patinkin was a valued adviser to David Ben-Gurion and the Israeli Minister of Finance (Arnon, 1974, p. 22). At this age, he was more influential than Friedman was at a comparable age. In the same year as Friedman's (1956) revival of the quantity theory (a revival that would undermine the post-war economic consensus) Patinkin (1956b) attempted to consolidate that consensus by integrating monetary and value theory, thus resolving the Keynes-Classics dichotomy by redefining Keynes's contribution as the unemployment economics of disequilibrium, not equilibrium as previously maintained by John Hicks and others.[5]

Patinkin and Friedman

Friedman was ten years Patinkin's senior, and returned to Chicago only in 1946. In spite of the relatively brief period of their time as Chicago colleagues (approximately two years), they became close personal friends. Friedman visited the Hebrew University in 1969, spring 1972, summer 1977 and 1990 and spent a semester there in 1963: "The time went very quickly and we were very reluctant to leave" (Rose Friedman, 1976a, p. 26; 1977, p. 26).[6] Patinkin's article on "The Chicago Tradition, the Quantity Theory and Friedman" was published in the February 1969 issue of the *JMCB*, just prior to the Friedmans' visit to Israel at the invitation of the Israeli government (Rose Friedman, 1976b, p. 31).[7]

Patinkin was a member of the Cowles Commission between May 1946 and June 1948 (Debreu, 1991, p. 34). On June 21, 1948, he was offered a two-year position as Associate Professor at the University of Illinois. He took up the position on September 1, 1948, but resigned, effective from February 28, 1949, and migrated to Israel.[8] Shortly afterwards (March 16, 1949) Israel and Jordan signed an agreement accepting the armistice lines as the official borders between the two states. The Mount Scopus campus of the National Library and the Hebrew University became Jewish enclaves in Jordanian Jerusalem; snipers shot

[4] Some of the atomic scientists at the University of Chicago became alarmed about the perils of the new discoveries. In June 1945, seven of them unsuccessfully petitioned the United States Secretary of War; two then founded *The Bulletin of the Atomic Scientists*, which acquired a large influence on intellectual life in America (Jungk, 1970, pp. 145, 169, 224). Later, some of Patinkin's correspondence came from the Israel Academy of Sciences and Humanities, Albert Einstein Square.

[5] This led to a *Review of Economic Studies* symposium on "The Patinkin Controversy" (Hahn, 1960–61) in which Patinkin refused to participate because the editors sought to restrict the length of his reply (Editorial Note, 1960–61, p. 29; Archibald and Lipsey, 1958, 1960–61; Hicks, 1957).

[6] I am grateful to Haim Barkai for providing me with this information.

[7] Their visit took place amid an intense terror campaign: a bomb injured twenty-six people in the cafeteria of the National Library of the Hebrew University (Armstrong, 1997, p. 412).

[8] I am grateful to Winton Solberg (correspondence, November 24, 1997) for this information, which came from the University of Illinois Transactions of the Board of Trustees, 45th Report. Thus, Patinkin was not lost to the University of Illinois because of the Bowen controversy, as implied by W. Solberg and R. Tomlinson (1997, p. 80).

into "enemy" territory on the other side of the highly fortified No Man's Land (Armstrong, 1997, pp. 389, 393, 395). In May 1949 the Hebrew University Department of Economics was established (Barkai, 1993, pp. 3–4). The Patinkins were initially housed in a Hebrew University flat with no water (which as Patinkin explained to Friedman, made cleaning diapers difficult!), and their electric stove was too expensive to use except for "Special Occasions." Patinkin found that "The time is going by at a terrific pace" (February 4, 1950). His daughter Na'ama was "growing. Too fast for me—for now she's started eating her rations of banana and eggs on which we've been feasting for the past seven months" (February 4, 1950).

Patinkin asked Friedman for advice about outlets for publications: "I have the feeling that stuff published in *Econometrica* is pretty much lost as far as any effect goes on economists as a whole" (November 7, 1949). He obviously missed his Chicago colleagues: frequently his letters would end with "Best regards to all the people on the staff" (November 10, 1948); sometimes with specific requests: "Please go next door and give my best regards to Gregg" (presumably Gregg Lewis). Friedman inquired about Patinkin's "present feelings and views about remaining in Israel? Do you like it well enough so that you are really going to become permanent residents or are you now thinking in terms of possibly returning to the United States? Best regards to all of you from all of us" (December 9, 1949).

Patinkin appeared to be exasperated by the time it took Friedman to reply to his letters. Sometimes his own letters would take him a month or more to finish: "My God! Is that how long this letter has been lying here unfinished" (March 5, 1950). Mail to Israel was slow and uncertain: "Your JPE article still hasn't shown up yet—though I hope it will within the next week or so" (February 4, 1950); and the arrival of academic journals were "awaited with the same anticipation usually reserved for serial magazines ... in these isolated parts" (November 7, 1949). Patinkin told Friedman that he would greatly appreciate receiving copies of problems and examinations: "(Suggestion: send these on immediately without any letter; why should I wait two months?)."[9]

Friedman provided Patinkin with extremely detailed ("early and often") comments on various drafts of his papers. In November 1947, Friedman scribbled comments all over Patinkin's "Price Flexibility and Unemployment"; repeating the exercise two months later on the revised version entitled "Price Flexibility and Full Employment." Patinkin told Friedman that "you are a wonderful conscience for me" (February 4, 1950).[10] Patinkin felt that Friedman had great expectations of him: "One of the things that has kept me back from writing this letter is the feeling that sooner or later I shall be expected to deal with some of the Great Problems here; to make some observation on the Way of Life; to indicate Our State of Mind and General Reaction. And the truth is that I have very little to say on any of these subjects." He was simply too busy

[9] Even to the University of Illinois, to ensure that his correspondence got through, Friedman thought it wise to address his letter to "Professor" Patinkin: "then the mail people know that they're dealing with the faculty and not with students" (November 8, 1948).

[10] Patinkin was referring to Friedman's insistence that he rewrite an article for the *AER* two or three times to improve the quality.

dealing with administrative tasks to "do the thing I really want to: get my teeth into some of the practical economic problems facing the country" (November 7, 1949).

Friedman took a guiding interest in Patinkin's career. He advised Patinkin against studying the relationship between liquid assets and consumption in favor of studying the relationship between total asset holdings and consumption (November 8, 1948). Later (December 9, 1949), he expressed the hope that "by this time you have gotten involved in some of the practical problems of the Israeli government. It seems to me that your education would be greatly furthered by that, and that you would benefit by allowing yourself to get mixed up in it." In 1952, Friedman was approached by the State Department to join a "point 4 tax reform" mission to Israel: "it broke my heart to refuse the request, since I would love personally to spend a few months in Israel for all kinds of reasons that you can readily understand .... In talking to the people in Washington, I mentioned your being there, which they knew about, and urged them strongly to be sure to make every effort to draw you into the mission's work in an active fashion .... Let me urge you strongly to do anything you can to permit yourself to be drawn in, and I do so, not primarily for the benefits to the mission–which I know would be very great–but because of what I think would be the benefits to you. I can think of no activity which would be of as much marginal value in adding to your background and experience and understanding of Israel's problems .... I am by no means sure that I didn't make a mistake in not accepting myself" (April 2, 1952).

Patinkin also asked Friedman for advice about teaching. Economists entering the public service soon became known as "Patinkin's Boys" (Kleiman, 1981, p. 215; Halevi, 1969, p. 101; Barkai, 1993, p. 7); but their "father" confessed to Friedman that he felt "nervous" about his responsibility for training Israeli economists. He explained that most of the country's economists had been trained in the German historical tradition and possessed little neoclassical or Keynesian apparatus. In addition, the choice of visiting experts tended in the early years to be quite left-wing (these included Michal Kalecki, Harry Dexter White and Abba P. Lerner). Even when the economy was liberalized in 1952, a Soviet name (New Economic Policy) was used to describe the changes (Kleiman, 1981, pp. 211, 214, 216; Rubner, 1960, p. 25; Pomphret, 1976, pp. 26–43; Halevi, 1969, p. 96; Halevi and Klinov-Malul, 1968, pp. 7–8; Barkai, 1993, p. 5). Indeed, one of the first Hebrew economic textbooks, which influenced many early Israeli leaders, presented a Marxist theory of value (Kleiman, 1973).

Economic Policy Disputes in Israel

Economic policy disputes in Israel (especially in the early period) tended to involve all sorts of passions. An Australian participant at a recent central banking conference in Israel informed me that he had never seen economic policy disputes take on such personal tones. This type of apocalyptic passion is perhaps not surprising in a country where the survival of the state is apparently at stake. In a country such as Australia (which is surrounded by water) insightful paradoxes about water and diamonds generate less passions than the never-ending dispute in Israel (which is surrounded by enemies) about the pricing of water.[11] For example, when Israel became Independent, and excluded from the sterling area, passions were aroused over the desirability of floating the exchange rate and abolishing exchange controls. Initially, Kalecki's advice was sought; he not only recommended that controls be retained, but advocated that prices should also continue to be controlled (Halevi, 1969, p. 97). Patinkin (1960, pp. 138–40), tentatively suggested that "The market mechanism could probably be used here to greater advantage than it has been hitherto." In his second Horowitz Lecture in Israel, Friedman (1972, pp. 54–55) argued that: "Who do you suppose invented the modern system of exchange controls? It was Hjalmar Schacht in 1934 in Germany. What did he invent it for? He invented it primarily in order to despoil the Jews .... As a Jew, rather than an economist, I say to you, why don't you get rid of the false appearance, why don't you abolish the exchange controls and make your practice conform to your values. Set your people free."[12]

Friedman was famous (or notorious) for seeing a reasonable approximation to perfect competition breaking out wherever he looked, restrained (only temporarily) by the foolish and misguided interventions of governments. In his *Newsweek* column, (May 5, 1969, p. 44), after a visit to Israel, and immediately after the publication of Patinkin's *JMCB* article (February 1969), he reflected on an excursion to the occupied west bank territory and on Moshe Dayan's political "policy of laissez faire ... [and] almost literal policy of laissez faire in the economic sphere .... [T]he military, who generally favor running things by direct orders coming down a chain of command, are in Israel the strongest supporters of free markets and non intervention .... To the casual observer the area appears to be prospering." In this free trade induced harmony, "the Jordanian Arabs were peacefully going about their business. I had no feeling whatsoever of being in an occupied territory."

According to Friedman (1972, pp. 56–57) this was part of a 2000 year "tradition that had enabled the Jews to survive in the Diaspora", which competed against "a tradition of a hundred years, a tradition of socialism." But, at least at an earlier stage of Israel's history, markets and economists were suspect; the state was built by enthusiasts and visionaries to whom economic calculation meant little (Kleiman, 1981, p. 224). Patinkin had previously reflected on this theme to Friedman: "One of the fundamental things is that Israel would never have been built up if the people had listened to economists. They would never have dared and succeeded in doing what they have done. Now I know you are going to tell me this is all silly; so I won't continue. But you're wrong" (November 7, 1949). This private type of disagreement contrasts with their very public dispute over the quantity theory. Indeed, after 1969, Patinkin seemed

[11] In 1958, for example, a proposal to export small arms to West Germany (beneficial to Israel and therefore productive of an increased defensive capacity against the nation's current enemies) was vehemently opposed, and led to a governmental crisis (Easterlin, 1961, p. 84).

[12] Later, after the unexpected defeat of the Labor Party in May 1977, Milton Friedman (who had just been awarded a Nobel Prize and was in Israel to receive an honorary doctorate from the Hebrew University) had a meeting with the new Minister of Finance. In October 1977, Israel adopted a floating exchange rate and abolished exchange controls on current account transactions (Halevi, 1979, pp. 11–12, 16, 25; Rubner, 1960, p. 129). Politicians, of course, seek advice from economists for a variety of motives. For an Israeli example, see Kochav, 1974, p. 16.

determined to refer to this dispute as often as possible. For example, the Israeli 1985 stabilization policy illustrated "Some Simple Truths of Monetary Theory" as opposed to "Milton Friedman's well known dictum that 'inflation is always and everywhere a monetary phenomenon"' (Patinkin, 1993, pp. 103–5).[13]

III. WARFARE: HOT, COLD AND SCHOLARLY

Like other Israelis of his generation, Patinkin lived through the Second World War, plus the Arab-Israeli conflicts of 1948–49, 1956, 1967, and 1973. One of his last letters to Paul Samuelson was written during the Gulf War: "As you can well imagine, the situation here is very quite tense, but except for a minority of extremists, we are keeping our calm. And the most important condition for doing so is to continue with our work as usual—no matter how removed it is from our present threatening position: work therapy" (August 28, 1990). Patinkin contributed as much as anybody to the development of Israel; at the time of his public dispute with Friedman, he also became an intense critic of government economic, foreign and defense policy, expressed through the public medium of a newspaper column. Despite his rage, "Don's message ... failed to prevent Israel's Great Inflation" (Barkai, 1993, pp. 12–13).

On February 4, 1950, Patinkin informed Friedman that he had been lecturing on "my favourite topic—the Marshall Plan. The reason for this favoritism is that here I have found an opening wedge into the doctrinaire socialist thinking that is all too frequent in Israel. According to this commonly accepted interpretation, the only reason for the Marshall Plan is the necessity of the U.S. to eliminate unemployment in its economy. For me the ERP [Economic Recovery Program] is a made-to-order counterexample .... I have found nothing quite as successful as statistics in cutting short political diatribes. Sometimes I run into trouble. I always make it clear that individual interest groups in the U.S. have attempted and in some cases succeeded in exploiting the program as a means of dumping. But I insist that quantitatively this element has not been very strong. This was

[13] The Israeli authorities had self-consciously pursued an ambitious program of economic development and full employment, financed in an inflationary fashion (Halevi, 1969, p. 75). In 1985, a group of eight economists formulated and implemented an anti-inflation stabilization program, which reduced the annual rate of inflation from 500% to less than 20% with minimal adverse effects on employment. Friedman (1992, pp. 234–48) reflected on the success of this operation in comparison to a similar, but disastrous strategy pursued by another group of Chicago-trained economists in Chile. Samuelson (August 9, 1993) informed Patinkin that "I found your piece on the Israel inflation and stabilization [Patinkin, 1993] fascinating from beginning to end. Somewhere in my writings I mentioned that around 1939 Stan (islaus) Ulam, already a *great* young mathematician and later to become (with Teller) the inventor of the hydrogen bomb, challenged me: 'Name one theory in economics that is neither trivial nor obvious.' I muttered: 'The theory of comparative advantage.' Now in 1993 I can tell him (in Valhalla), 'The predictable and documented change in behavior during the frictionless inflation and its stabilization."' One implication of Samuelson's letter is that if the Israeli stabilization experience had been available and documented in the 1970s, then the monetarist anti-Keynesian counter-revolution need never have happened. Whether the experience of the Israeli economy (which is based on a permanent semi-war footing) is generalizable to the inflation and strike-torn Western economies of the 1970s is, of course, another matter. Patinkin (1993, pp. 120–21) clearly spelt out the special forces at work in Israel at that time (which included a coalition of the two major parties).

the line I took in a series of lectures I gave to some high school graduates from the collective settlements. These kids have all grown up in these settlements and have received all their education there. As usual, their economic training was straight and unadulterated Rosa Luxembourg. I found myself not making much progress with them: to be frank it was like talking to a stone wall."

Some of his most passionately felt academic controversies took place against the background of military threat; and on at least one occasion, Patinkin turned to Friedman for moral support, displaying signs of over-sensitivity. In January 1950, *Econometrica* published rejoinders to Patinkin's essay on "The Indeterminancy of Absolute Prices in Classical Economic Theory" (1949) by W. B. Hickman, C. C. Phipps and Wassily Leontief without an immediate reply from Patinkin. Hickman (1950, p. 20) purported to find a "basic methodological flaw" in Patinkin's argument; Leontief (1950, p. 21) found Patinkin's argument and conclusions to be "erroneous"; Phipps (1950, p. 26) doubted that Patinkin had correctly specified a classical model. Patinkin asked Friedman to get hold of the offending issue, "clip out the pages of the Phipps-Hickman-Leontief articles and airmail them to me as soon as possible." Patinkin also asked Friedman to do the proof reading in case there was insufficient time to get the galleys to Israel; and, not for the last time, to "find out who did the refereeing on the Hickman paper" (February 4, 1950). Patinkin (1972, pp. 282–83) was still sensitive about this criticism more than twenty years later.[14]

During this controversy, Patinkin reflected that "it's characteristic of human nature that I should be troubled by this matter at the same time when the world seems to have a pretty good chance of going to pot in Korea. If only the U.S. could have wiped out the North Koreans within a few days .... But the longer this drags on the more dangerous it becomes. Furthermore, the origins of the fighting in Korea are now back in the distant irrelevant past .... Now all the people see are Americans fighting Koreans and their lineup on that question is the same as their lineup on America vs. Russia .... I'm becoming more and more convinced that the U.S. is losing badly on the propaganda front—and I'm taking Israel as an example. There are few communists here—there is a larger party of communist sympathizers—and every one of them is an ardent and vociferous advocate of Russia's case in any conflict. They never miss an opportunity to accuse America, to distort facts, to smear. The propaganda they have built up about an imperialist U.S. forcing Marshall aid on an enslaved Europe is a case in point. You would think that with something like this the U.S. would have succeeded in making the purposes of its program clear. But that just isn't so .... The U.S. doesn't have the army of *unpaid* and intense sympathizers that Russia does; and from what I have seen here I am convinced that this places it at a serious disadvantage. It has placed too much emphasis on military strength; not enough on pleading—and making—its case before world public opinion" (July 15, 1950).

In 1950, Friedman (1992, p. 248) was a consultant to the Marshall Plan

[14] In other disputes, Patinkin sought to discover the identity of referees and sometimes attempted to persuade editors to reveal the names of anonymous referees by stating that the referee appears to have been a specific person.

agency, analyzing the Schuman Coal and Steel Community, which later became the Common Market. Friedman (November 6, 1950) wrote from Paris about his experiences with the Economic Cooperation Administration: "on coming into Germany, Rose and I had a tremendous feeling of revulsion, the hatred of years came to the surface and we saw a Nazi in every German face. That softened a bit but did not disappear in a few days .... Industrially, Europe is a mess. By comparison, the U.S. is the purest of pure competitive economies. Everything here is rigid and controlled and competition almost nonexistent. God knows what can be done about it."

IV. THE OTHER MARSHALL

Two Marshalls (General, cum Secretary of State, and Alfred) figure prominently in the correspondence. There are detailed and protracted discussions about the Marshallian demand curve (Friedman, 1949a). Patinkin was ambivalent about Alfred Marshall's qualities. In deciding to recommend that his students use Stigler's *Price Theory* ("it's neat and precise") he informed Friedman that "I shall also assign Marshall, altho I'm not sure why. It's primarily the force of tradition. Or maybe when I reread it now I'll find out why you think so highly of him. (Incidentally, I wonder how your opinion of Marshall as an economist with a healthy empirical bent stands up against the description of the method he used in one of his studies. See his preface to Industry and Trade (1919), p. vii third paragraph–the one beginning with 'In pursuit ....')."

In contrast, Friedman (1996, p. 1989) was "a long-time Marshallian." In *A Theoretical Framework For Monetary Analysis*, he (1974, p. 18) wrote that "Keynes was a true Marshallian in method .... Where he deviated from Marshall, and it was a momentous deviation, was in reversing the roles assigned to prices and quantities. He assumed that, at least for changes in aggregate demand, quantity was the variable that adjusts rapidly, while prices was the variable that adjusts slowly, at least in a downwards direction." Earlier, he had told Patinkin that he was surprised to find in Marshall the statement that for "more complex problems" it was desirable to take quantities rather than prices as the independent variable: "as I write I find myself very confused about what it does all mean and portend, and I have pages and pages of scribblings in my notes that I can't now understand .... This is so darn intriguing that I have already spent more time on this now than I can afford" (April 2, 1952).

Patinkin questioned the accuracy of Friedman's interpretation of Marshall. Friedman held a social gathering for the Patinkins before they left Chicago, and years later, Patinkin wrote that he had "been meaning to write for some time .... You said then that Marshall was an anti-Semite, and that all you had to do was look up the reference to "Jew" in his Principles. I didn't get a chance to do this then but your statement stuck in my mind and when I got back to Jerusalem I did just that. I also looked in all his other books. To my great surprise I found nothing corresponding to your accusation; on the contrary I was left with the distinct impression that he had a great admiration for what he called the economic and financial capabilities of the Jews" (March 20, 1952). Patinkin detected in Friedman what he regarded as a tendency to reconstruct history in an unreliable fashion. Their correspondence reveals that the *JMCB* essay had a history of disputes over historical accuracy, discussed in less public domains.

V. AN INFLUENCE ON FRIEDMAN'S METHOD OF POSITIVE ECONOMICS?

Even though Friedman was an accomplished statistician and had extensive experience with the National Bureau of Economic Research statistical investigations, Patinkin adopted an aggressively missionary posture with respect to the overriding importance of empirical work; hovering on the brink of accusing Friedman of methodological inconsistency. Friedman told Patinkin (November 8, 1948) that he had been disappointed with the "very little violent criticism" of his "Monetary and Fiscal Framework for Economic Stability" (Friedman, 1948): I, too, have been expecting that someone would take a crack at it .... I shall certainly be disappointed if someone doesn't write a rejoinder to it." Commenting on Friedman's (1949b) subsequent rejoinder to Neff's "crack" (1949a, 1949b), Patinkin told Friedman that his position "represents a basic departure from the empirical verification you usually demand from others. You base your whole scheme on the sensitivity of the expenditure function to changes in real balances; and if your scheme is to be practical this sensitivity must be strong enough to bring the system back to full employment within an acceptable (one year?) interval. What empirical evidence can you adduce in support of such a faith?... . [T]here is a burden of proof upon you, one that you have never recognized" (November 7, 1949).

Stigler's approach to empirical evidence was also criticized: it "sent shudders" through Patinkin (February 4, 1950). Reviewing the Stigler (1947)-Lester (1947)-Machlup (1947) controversy on marginal productivity, Patinkin (February 4, 1950) complained that "Machlup and Stigler dispense with [Lester's] findings much too glibly .... I would like to ask Machlup your question: under what circumstances would you reject the marginal productivity theory. I don't know if he can produce any (can you?); but even if he did, I would be willing to bet that faced with such circumstances, he would plead "special factors." The damned thing is that it's almost impossible to set up a critical experiment in economics." Stigler, he thought, was guilty of dismissing observations on *a priori* grounds: "it does seem to me that Stigler must present some empirical evidence before sounding off like that. Isn't it a sad reflection on the sad state of economics that Stigler can write a straight textbook analysis of minimum wage legislation without even feeling himself obliged to make any empirical surveys. Stigler is just an example of what everybody does—including yours truly. I am merely bemoaning the type of training we receive that doesn't make us horrified at 'casual empiricism' ... I'd like to get your reaction" (March 5, 1950).

Patinkin never seemed to miss an opportunity to reinforce this message: "I understand that the A.E.R. pays something for major articles. Is this correct? Please answer on the basis of your own experience. After all, we must be empirical" (November 10, 1948). In reply to these strictures, Friedman informed

Patinkin that "I have been trying to write some kind of article on the general methodological problem you raise" (November 8, 1948).[15]

VI. KNIGHT AND FRIEDMAN

The Patinkin Archives reveal fresh evidence about Frank Knight's (1885–1972) suspicions about Friedman's counter-revolution. These supplement Jacob Viner's (1882–1970) suspicions, which have already been documented by Patinkin. In defending himself against Patinkin's accusations, Friedman (1974, pp. 165–167) referred to Viner's writings in the 1930s. Patinkin responded by enlisting Viner in support of his suspicions about the Chicago counter-revolution: "It was not until after I left Chicago in 1946," Viner wrote, "that I began to hear rumours about a 'Chicago School' which was engaged in *organised* battle for laissez faire and 'quantity theory of money' and against 'imperfect competition' theorizing and 'Keynesianism."' Viner went on to recount his experiences of an "ideologically loaded" conference at Chicago in 1951 (Viner cited by Patinkin, 1981, p. 266).

Meyer Burstein[16] informed Patinkin of Knight's "enormous" admiration for Friedman: "I remember a Kaldor seminar at UC. Kaldor was killing the Defenders of the Local Faith. FHK was no longer up to it (1956). He summoned a student. 'Get Milton! Bring Milton here at once!' Milton came. Kaldor survived but some local pride was salvaged." In 1968, Patinkin sent Knight an early version of his *JMCB* essay. Patinkin (1981, 44, n25, 265) referred to Knight's "warm" reply (dated March 19, 1969) "declining comment," stating that Knight "went on to write briefly about other matters." These "other matters" involved an assessment of contemporary developments at Chicago, which Patinkin, for whatever reason, declined to report. Writing on University of Chicago, Department of Economics notepaper, Knight concluded that "I simply can't work in the spiritual atmosphere of the world right now, and of this university community in particular" (March 19, 1969). Patinkin asked Roger Weiss for his assessment (which he recorded in a conversation, dated December 6, 1972): "Knight very critical of Friedman's views on capitalism: oversimplified. Very much alone in last years. Stigler remained very close to Knight—tho now trying to say that Knight did not do anything new after early 1930s."

VII. CONCLUDING REMARKS

Reading and reporting private correspondence can be fascinating; it can also amuse the prurient, as Donald Moggridge (1992, p. 839) pointed out. Patinkin (March 6, 1992), in this vein, told Samuelson that "one of the advantages of working in the history of thought is that we can indulge in gossip and present

[15] Friedman was specifically referring to philosophical disputes about public works, "unborne costs and unappropriable benefits" which had to be resolved on "empirical grounds."

[16] There is no date visible on my photocopy of the letter, but it appears to have been written immediately after Patinkin's December 1973 *AER* essay on Knight.

ourselves as being engaged in scholarship."[17] But several points of genuine historical interest emerge from the early Friedman-Patinkin correspondence. Patinkin several times confronted Friedman (and indirectly, Stigler) with the charge of methodological inconsistency in their approach to empirical evidence. Patinkin's dissatisfaction with the prevailing climate of casual empiricism also provides an important illustration of the motive behind the desire to increase the rigor of theoretical and empirical economics (sometimes described as the formalist revolution). Patinkin (1981, pp. 16–17) found the fruit of the formalist revolution a little disappointing, and turned instead to a study of rhetoric. At the start of his publishing career, Patinkin (November 7, 1949) asked Friedman whether his *Econometrica* articles (1948; 1949) "deserve translation into English .... Query: do you think I should do this. I don't have to add that I want a frank answer; I know I will get one." Towards the end of his life, Patinkin moved away from this post-war methodological focus: his interests had "to a certain extent led me into the sociology of knowledge and more recently into literary criticism and hermeneutics" (to Samuelson, August 28, 1990).[18]

Friedman's hostile questioning of the Cowles econometricians led to the creation of an oral tradition known as "the Friedman critique." In response to Friedman, Koopmans asked him: "But what if the investigator is honest?" (cited by Epstein, 1987, p. 107). The Patinkin-Friedman correspondence reveals the existence of another oral tradition: "the Friedman question": "under what circumstances would you abandon your pet theory?" (February 4, 1950).

Friedman (1953, p. 5) wrote that "the progress of positive economics" could lead to differences being "eliminated"; leaving only differences in basic values "about which men can ultimately only fight." Friedman (1974, p. 159) suggested that the "fundamental reason ... for his slighting the short-run context of most of my framework is that Patinkin, even more than Tobin, is Walrasian, concerned with abstract completeness, rather than Marshallian, concerned with the construction of special tools for special problems." Far from eliminating differences, Friedman's counter-revolution produced an enormous amount of heat in addition to some light. No dispute of the period was more heated than the Patinkin-Friedman controversy over the Chicago oral tradition.

The Patinkin Archives document the extraordinary influence that Friedman exerted on his colleagues and students. Gary Becker, for example, reflected to Patinkin (April 6, 1979) on Friedman's influence in the 1950s: "I did not fully appreciate the power of Cowles at that time because of the great influence on me exerted by Milton Friedman. In my judgment, he was by far the most dominating and most interesting person in the department, and I abandoned my affiliation

---

[17] One Nobel prize winner (October 21, 1991) was not averse to gossiping with Patinkin about an ex-student (who later won a Nobel prize): "just between us two girls, much in that thesis paralleled my views of the time—including the ultimate title which I knew would catch on." These scandalous sentiments were prefaced by the words, "For your eyes only."

[18] Others, such as Klein (who became co-ordinator of President-elect Carter's economic task force), objected to Patinkin's skepticism about econometrics: "I don't really like or appreciate your final three sentences .... We are a force (with models) in policy making at the very highest levels of government and enterprise .... I think you have the wrong pitch on these points; we definitely over-fulfilled the C.C. [Cowles Commission] visions" (to Patinkin, April 2, 1979).

with Marschak and Cowles to pursue further my contacts with Friedman." Friedman exerted an enormous influence on Patinkin also. They argued passionately, but privately, initially with undiminished affection. As both reached the pinnacle of their influence, this affection soured, and Patinkin devoted an extraordinary proportion of his professional energy to publicly questioning Friedman's reliability as a source of historical knowledge. Harry Johnson (1971) became involved in what was virtually a coordinated attack on Friedman. The dispute over the historical accuracy of a 1956 introductory essay escalated into the charge that Friedman was "a crook" (Johnson to Patinkin, September 29, 1969). Friedman's increasing influence (especially after his 1967 Presidential Address), exerted over a wider professional and political landscape, provoked Patinkin to launch an extraordinarily vitriolic attack on his friend and colleague; an episode that is examined in the sequel to this essay (Leeson, 1998).

REFERENCES

Archibald, C. and R. Lipsey. 1958. "Monetary and Value Theory: A Critique of Lange and Patinkin," *Review of Economic Studies*, *26*, 1–22.

Archibald, C. and R. Lipsey. 1960–61. "Monetary and Value Theory: Further Comment," *Review of Economic Studies*, *28*, 50–56.

Armstrong, K. 1997. *A History of Jerusalem*, Harper Collins, London.

Arnon, J. 1974. "The Economist's Task in Government," in N. Halevi and Y. Kupps, eds., *Issues in the Economy of Israel*, Falk Institute, Jerusalem.

Barkai, H. 1993. "Don Patinkin's Contribution to Economics in Israel," in Barkai *et al.*, ed., 1993.

Barkai, H., S. Fischer and N. Liviatan, eds. 1993. *Monetary Theory and Thought: Essays in Honour of Don Patinkin*, Macmillan, London.

Bullock, A. 1985. *Ernest Bevin, Foreign Secretary*, Oxford University Press, Oxford.

Crossman, R. 1946. *Palestine Mission*, Hamish Hamilton, London.

Debreu, G. 1991. "Mathematical Economics at Cowles," in K. J. Arrow, G. Debreu, E. Malinvaud and R. Solow, eds., *Cowles Fiftieth Anniversary: Four Essays and an Index of Publications*, Cowles, Yale University Printing.

Donovan, R. J. 1967. *Israel's Fight for Survival*, Signet, New York.

Easterlin, R. 1961. "Israel's Development, Past Accomplishments and Future Problems," *Quarterly Journal of Economics*, *75*, 63–86.

Editorial Note. 1960–61. *Review of Economic Studies*, *28*, 29.

Epstein, R. 1987. *A History of Econometrics*, North Holland, Amsterdam.

Friedman, M. 1948. "A Monetary and Fiscal Framework for Economic Stability," *American Economic Review*, *38*, 245–64.

Friedman, M. 1949a. "The Marshallian Demand Curve," *Journal of Political Economy*, *57*, December, 463–95.

Friedman, M. 1949b. "Rejoinder," *American Economic Review*, *39*, 949–55.

Friedman, M. 1953. *Essays in Positive Economics*, University of Chicago Press, Chicago.

Friedman, M., ed. 1956. *Studies in the Quantity Theory of Money*, University of Chicago Press, Chicago.

Friedman, M. 1968a. The Role of Monetary Policy, *American Economic Review*, *58*, May, 1–17.

Friedman, M. 1968b. "Money: Quantity Theory," in *International Encyclopedia of the Social Sciences*, *9*, 432–47.

Friedman, M. 1969. "Invisible Occupation," *Newsweek*, May 5, 44.

Friedman, M. 1972. *Money and Economic Development*, Praeger, New York.

Friedman, M. 1974. "A Theoretical Framework for Monetary Analysis," and "Comments on the Critics," in R. J. Gordon, ed., *Milton Friedman's Monetary Framework: A Debate with his Critics*, University of Chicago Press, Chicago.

Friedman, M. 1992. *Money Mischief: Episodes in Monetary History*, Harcourt Brace Jovanovich, New York.
Friedman, M. 1996. "Review of Groenewegen's *A Soaring Eagle: Alfred Marshall 1842–1924*," *Journal of Economic Literature*, December, 1989–91.
Friedman, R. 1976a. "Milton Friedman: Husband and Colleague (6)," *Oriental Economist*, October, 22–26.
Friedman, R. 1976b. "Milton Friedman: Husband and Colleague (8)," *Oriental Economist*, December, 26–33.
Friedman, R. 1977. "Milton Friedman: Husband and Colleague (9)," *Oriental Economist*, January, 24–32.
Hahn, F. 1960–61. "The Patinkin Controversy," *Review of Economic Studies*, *28*, 37–43.
Halevi, N. 1969. "Economic Policy Discussion and Research in Israel," *American Economic Review*, *59*, 75–118.
Halevi, N. 1979. "The Exchange Rate in Israel," *Revue Economique*, *1*, January, 10–30.
Halevi, N. and R. Klinov-Malul. 1968. *The Economic Development of Israel*, Praeger, New York.
Hickman, W. B. 1950. "The Indeterminacy of Absolute Prices in Classical Economic Theory," *Econometrica*, *18*, January, 9–20.
Hicks, J. R. 1957. "A Rehabilitation of 'Classical' Economics," *Economic Journal*, *67*, 278–89.
Johnson, H. G. 1971. "The Keynesian Revolution and the Monetarist Counter-Revolution," *American Economic Review*, *61*, May, 91–106.
Jungk, R. 1970. *Brighter than a Thousands Suns*, Pelican, London.
Kleiman, E. 1973. "An Early Modern Hebrew Textbook of Economics," *History of Political Economy*, *5*, 339–58.
Kleiman, E. 1981. "Israel: Economists in a New State," in A. W. Coats, ed., *Economists in Government: An International Comparative Study*, Duke University Press, Durham.
Kochav, D. 1974. "The Economist's Task in Government," in N. Halevi and Y. Kupps, eds., *Issues in the Economy of Israel*, Falk Institute, Jerusalem.
Laidler, D. 1980. "Monetarism: An Interpretation and an Assessment," *Economic Journal*, *91*, March, 1–28.
Leeson, R. 1998. "Patinkin, Johnson and 'The Shadow of Friedman'," mimeo work-in-progress.
Leontief, W. 1950. "The Consistency of the Classical Theory of Money and Prices," *Econometrica*, *18*, January, 21–24.
Lerner, A. P. and H. Ben-Shahar. 1975. *The Economics of Efficiency and Growth: Lessons from Israel and the West Bank*, Ballinger, Cambridge, MA.
Lester, R. 1947. "Marginalism, Minimum Wages and Labor Markets," *American Economic Review*, March, 135–48.
Lucas, R. E. 1980. "Methods and Problems in Business Cycle Theory," *Journal of Money Credit and Banking*, *12*, November, 696–715.
Machlup, F. 1947. "Rejoinder to an Antimarginalist," *American Economic Review*, March, 148–54.
Moggridge, D. 1992. *Maynard Keynes: An Economist's Biography*, Routledge, London.
Neff, P. 1949a. "Professor Friedman's Proposal: A Comment," *American Economic Review*, *39*, 946–49.
Neff, P. 1949b. "Final Comment," *American Economic Review*, *39*, 955–56.
Parkin, M. 1986. "Essays On and In the Chicago Tradition: A Review Essay," *Journal of Money Credit and Banking*, *18*, February, 104–116.
Patinkin, D. 1949. "The Indeterminacy of Absolute Prices in Classical Economic Theory," *Econometrica*, *17*, January, 1–27.
Patinkin D. 1956a. "Money and Price Developments in Israel: 1949–53," in R. Bachi, ed., *Scripta Hierosolymitana: Studies in Economic and Social Science*, *3*, Magnes Press, Hebrew University, Jerusalem, 22–52.
Patinkin, D. 1956b. *Money, Interest and Prices: An Integration of Monetary and Value Theory*, Row Peterson, Evanston.
Patinkin, D. 1960. *The Israel Economy: The First Decade*, Jerusalem Post Press, Jerusalem.Patinkin, D. 1972. "Samuelson on the Neoclassical Dichotomy," *Canadian Journal of Economics*, *5*, May, 279–83.
Patinkin, D. 1974. "Economic Research in Israel," in N. Halevi and Y. Kupps, ed., *Issues in the Economy of Israel*, Falk Institute, Jerusalem.

Patinkin, D. 1981. *Essays in and in the Chicago Tradition*, Duke University Press, Durham.
Patinkin, D. 1986. "A Reply," *Journal of Money Credit and Banking*, *18*, February, 116–21.
Patinkin, D. 1993. "Israel's Stabilization Program of 1985, or Some Simple Truths of Monetary Theory," *Economic Perspectives*, Spring, 103–28.
Phipps, C. G. 1950. "A Note on Patinkin's 'Relative Prices'," *Econometrica*, January, *18*, 25–26.
Pomphret, R. 1976. *Trade Policies and Industrialisation in a Small Country: The Case of Israel*, University of Keil, Lubingen.
Rubner, A. 1960. *The Economy of Israel: A Critical Account of the First Ten Years*, Cass, London.
Solberg, W. U. and R. W. Tomlinson. 1997. "Academic McCarthyism and Keynesian Economics: The Bowen Controversy at the University of Illinois," *History of Political Economy*, *29*, Spring, 55–81.
Stigler, G. 1947. "Professor Lester and the Marginalists," *American Economic Review*, March, 154–57.

'Patinkin, Johnson and the Shadow of Friedman'

R. Leeson, 'Patinkin, Johnson and the shadow of Friedman', *History of Political Economy,* 32:4 (Winter 2000), pp. 733–63.

Patinkin, Johnson, and the Shadow of Friedman

Robert Leeson

George Stigler (1987, 311) concluded that his friend and Chicago colleague, Milton Friedman, had "established (to my complete satisfaction) his claim as the best debater in a profession that likes to debate." Since Friedman (like Stigler) set out to change the direction of economic policy and research he could not have been surprised by the controversy his efforts elicited. Indeed, he courted controversy to further his counterrevolution. He informed Don Patinkin (8 November 1948) that he had been disappointed with the "very little violent criticism" of his "Monetary and Fiscal Framework for Economic Stability" ([1948] 1953): "I, too, have been expecting that someone would take a crack

Correspondence may be addressed to Robert Leeson, School of Economics, Murdoch University, WA 6150, Australia. I am grateful to the staff of the Special Collections Library, Duke University, for their assistance in writing this essay and for their permission to quote material from the Patinkin Archives. This essay has been improved by comments and information provided by an extremely diligent referee plus Bob Dimand, Bernard Corry, Graeme Dorrance, Paul Evans, Dietrich Fausten, Stanley Fischer, Milton Friedman, Craufurd Goodwin, Dan Hammond, David Laidler, Richard Lipsey, Donald Moggridge, Michael Parkin, Mark Perlman, Paul Samuelson, Roger Sandilands, Frank Steindl, James Tobin, Winton Solberg, and Richard Watson. Haim Barkai very kindly circulated this article to his colleagues at the Hebrew University of Jerusalem; their collective response was very helpful to me The early Patinkin-Friedman relationship is discussed in Leeson 1998. This essay was partly written when I was the Bradley Fellow at the University of Western Ontario. I am most grateful to the Bradley Foundation for this support. The title of this essay is inspired by the title of Harry and Elizabeth Johnson's book *The Shadow of Keynes*.

History of Political Economy 32:4 © 2000 by Duke University Press at it. . . . I shall certainly be disappointed if someone doesn't write a rejoinder to it."[1]

Some of his opponents reacted more strongly than perhaps he had bargained for. Toward the end of the "monetarist decade" (1975–84), David Hendry and Neil Ericsson presented an explosive critique of Friedman and Anna Schwartz's *Monetary Trends* (1982). Titled "Assertion without Empirical Basis," they concluded that Friedman and Schwartz's "assertions" were "devoid of credibility. . . . rigorous evaluation of empirical claims seems a necessary first step towards taking the con out of economics" (1983, 82; 1991). The London *Guardian* of 15 December 1983 reported the Hendry and Ericsson paper under the title "Monetarist's guru 'distorts his evidence.'" Friedman was incensed and wrote to Hendry requesting that he disown the account in the *Guardian*. But Hendry replied that "if your assertion is true that newspapers have produced 'a spate of libellous and slanderous' articles 'impugning Anna Schwartz's and [your] honesty and integrity' then you must have ready recourse to a legal solution" (letter from Hendry to Friedman, 13 July 1984, quoted in Hammond 1996, 199).

Friedman's star rose to spectacular heights following his successful American Economic Association (AEA) presidential prediction of the breakdown of the Phillips curve trade-off (the applied policy framework of the Keynesian neoclassical synthesis) using his own methodology of positive economics (1968c; 1953). Almost immediately after his AEA address Friedman felt that he had been libeled by two friends and Chicago colleagues, Don Patinkin and Harry Johnson, who had both made major contributions to the postwar consensus. They effectively accused him (to paraphrase) of assertion without historical basis. Specifically, the charge was that Friedman's 1956 essay, "The Quantity Theory of Money—A Restatement," should have been titled "The Theory of Liquidity Preference—A Restatement." Friedman, they argued, had invented a bogus Chicago oral tradition. This was the primary accusation, but there was also the accusation that Friedman's monetarism consisted of (paraphrasing again) policy assertion without empirical or theoretical basis (see, for example, Johnson 1971a). Patinkin (1972, 1987) was determined to demonstrate "the short-run nonneutrality of money in the quantity theory" and to highlight Friedman's "misleading"

1. All correspondence is from the Don Patinkin Papers in the Special Collections Library at Duke University, unless otherwise indicated.

discussion of the quantity theory. The disputed historical evidence appears, in part, to have been a surrogate for the policy implications of Friedman's monetarism and his unspecific discussion about how disinflation would affect output and employment. Friedman (1968c, 5) suspected that the "pendulum may well have swung too far" with respect to the perceived influence of money; Patinkin and Johnson appeared to suspect that the pendulum had swung too far with respect to Friedman's influence.

It took Patinkin twelve years to reply to Friedman's 1956 essay, although earlier he had displayed signs of wishing to rush into print with his essays. Thus, if Patinkin were *solely* interested in correcting a historical error, it seems likely that he would have done the correcting in the 1950s, and not in the late 1960s. Patinkin's 1969 *Journal of Money, Credit, and Banking* essay began as "an aside" in a 1959 letter to Friedman. After Friedman's (1968b) *Encyclopedia* entry on the quantity theory, Patinkin wrote his "aside" and apologized for not having done so years earlier. Patinkin's ([1962] 1965, 54–55 n. 5) earlier criticism of Friedman's "somewhat mislabelled" essay was mild in comparison: "The true relationship of Friedman's exposition to Keynesian theory would have been somewhat clearer if only he had explicitly used the term 'liquidity.'" On at least four occasions, including his *Encyclopedia* entry, Friedman retracted his assertion: his reformulation had been "strongly influenced by the Keynesian theory of liquidity preference" (1968b, 439; 1963b, 1; 1964, 4; 1969, 73). But the retraction failed to satisfy the inquisitors: "As time has passed and the counter revolution has acquired increasing academic respectability, it has been increasingly possible to admit, and even to brag, that the useful ideas have been drawn from the revolution and not from the pre existing orthodoxy" (Johnson 1971a, 11).

This controversy has all the ingredients of a fascinating dispute involving evidence, egos, and jealousy among colleagues who, for the most part, remained cordial throughout.[2] Johnson's animosity toward

2. The dispute did not end their professional connections; indeed, in a sequel, Patinkin (1981a, 281) somewhat retreated from his previous position: "Thus contrary to Friedman's implication, the Chicago School of that time cannot be represented as an isolated center of monetary studies and of belief in the importance of money. What seems, however, to be true is that in some important respects it behaved as if it were." Barkai (personal correspondence, 11 January 1998) confirms that Patinkin and Friedman remained on cordial terms, although Patinkin (10 March 1993) told Laidler that he was "very sensitive" about his dispute with Friedman, "a sensitivity that results from both his misrepresentation and corresponding evasion

Friedman increased noticeably toward the end of the 1960s. He wrote to Patinkin (29 September 1969): "I've just read your JMC hatchet job on Milton. I recall our talk about it in '63 on the plane from Pittsburgh. . . . You have shown him to be a crook, and I accept that, but I can't help thinking he has not only been clever but also useful."[3] Earlier, Johnson ([1962] 1969, 20 n. 1, 30–33) had published two passing remarks that were later to form the basis of the charge that Friedman was a "crook": Friedman's money demand function was "hard to distinguish from a modern Keynesian formulation" and he was "claiming allegiance to the quantity theory as handed down in the oral tradition" at Chicago.[4] These passing remarks were soon augmented by attempts to undermine Friedman's credibility. This period coincided with Friedman's meteoric rise to influence.

Friedman (1968b) emphasized that the quantity theory had a distinguished lineage; there was obviously some rhetorical mileage in discovering a specifically Chicago lineage. The policy attractiveness of both the quantity theory and the original Phillips curve was considerably enhanced by statistical historical evidence; Friedman was adducing oral

---

of my criticisms of his 1956 paper . . and even more so from his continued attempts to rewrite the history of the quantity theory, as he has once again done in his *New Palgrave* article." Patinkin referred Laidler to Friedman's "evasive way of dealing with criticism and inability to admit error" (9 October 1994): "It is admittedly difficult for any one of us to admit error, but as economists we should also take quantitative account of the degree of such unwillingness—and in that Milton's score is among the highest" (18 November 1994). Patinkin asked Laidler to send him a copy of Friedman's mea culpa letter referred to in Laidler 1993, 1077–78 n. 12. Patinkin then informed Laidler (9 October 1994) that "I would also need Milton's permission to quote directly from his letter—which makes it even less likely that I should ever want to do so."

3. In 1969–70, Johnson (1971b, 96, 122) told his LSE graduate students that Friedman's assertions about the Chicago oral tradition "will not do"; his quantity theory was Keynesian economics "writ in another language . . . [with] strategic value in then allowing him to cite any stable demand for money equation as proof of the quantity theory." Finding empirically that the demand for money is not interest elastic, thus justifying a vertical LM curve, "Friedman is then free to advise policy makers to increase money [at] a certain rate each year, believing that fluctuations in the IS curve will cause changes in interest rates, but not in employment or output."

4. Johnson's (1965) review of Friedman and Schwartz's *Monetary History* (1963) had been quite enthusiastic and contained only comparatively mild criticisms of Friedman's style of operation. Friedman (1966, 71, 85) responded by stating that Johnson and other critics were committing errors akin to confusing nominal and real variables and shifts of, and along, a function. Johnson corresponded extensively with Friedman over this reply, but would not have been impressed with the outcome, especially Friedman's reference to the consensus-concealing but "natural tendency for writers to differentiate their products."

historical evidence that was intended to elevate interwar Chicago "wisdom." The probability of a Chicago graduate of the 1930s or 1940s, with detailed textual evidence in the form of meticulous lecture notes, having both the motive and the historical competence to engage Friedman (and thus damage the Chicago "cause"), must have seemed, *ex ante*, rather low, if not disjoint. *Ex post*, the set was found to include one member, although it took Patinkin a dozen years to acquire a sufficient motive. One other potential candidate for inclusion in this tiny set was Paul Samuelson; in fact Patinkin's essay was written during a sabbatical at MIT, where he had the opportunity to run his thoughts past Samuelson. Earlier, Patinkin (11 January 1949) had indicated that his disagreements with Friedman could be "recorded" through private correspondence: "I am still not satisfied with your treatment of the experiment I suggested to test out the theory of maximising profit. I am sure it will make no difference to you but let me put it on the record anyway." Patinkin (4 February 1950) had earlier referred to Friedman as a "wonderful conscience for me," but was dissatisfied by the outcome of the role reversal. After 1968, like Johnson, he expressed his disagreements very publicly.

The Patinkin-Johnson attacks were not just about precise historical accuracy, although that was the vehicle for their animosity. Their implication was that Friedman was guilty of more than overstatement: he had, they implied, distorted evidence to serve his own agenda. These assaults involved a degree of venom and ridicule that requires a special explanation: "I have never found the familiar statement that inflation is everywhere and at all times a monetary phenomenon to be a very edifying one: for the price level is the inverse of the purchasing power of money, so that by the same token one can say that the price of potatoes is everywhere and at all times a potato phenomenon. The real question is whether the quantity of money is an exogenous variable or an endogenous one" (Patinkin 1981b, 31). This explanation must address the *timing* of Patinkin's newly discovered determination to destroy Friedman's reputation as a reliable source of historical knowledge. Patinkin's 1967 Wicksell lectures on the nature of the money mechanism provided all the opportunities to refute Friedman's oral tradition; but Patinkin did not repeat his earlier passing criticism ([1962] 1965, 54–55 n. 5). After Friedman's AEA presidential prediction, Patinkin and Johnson rarely missed an opportunity to ridicule Friedman's account of the oral tradition.

If Friedman had been an obscure scholar, passionately beavering away on some peripheral topic, then friends and colleagues might have taken a more lenient approach, valuing Friedman's friendship and reputation above some minor exaggeration of an oral tradition. But Friedman was spearheading a counterrevolution and acquiring a status much higher than that achieved by either Patinkin or Johnson (or any other economist since Keynes). The disputants were playing for higher stakes than the subject matter of their essays might suggest, and Patinkin and Johnson chose to play the role of the profession's Torquemada. From the late 1960s (until their deaths) both were highly agitated about a one-page section in a 1956 essay: this can only adequately be explained by Friedman's increasing influence over policy, their jealousy, the competition for Nobel Prizes, and their sense of being oppressed by the shadow of Friedman.

Patinkin and Johnson versus Friedman

Patinkin

"The Quantity Theory of Money—A Restatement" was an editorial introduction to a volume of essays written by Friedman's students at his Chicago workshop on money and banking. After 1929, according to Friedman (1956, 3–4), the quantity theory had fallen into disrepute, except at Chicago, where Henry Simons, Lloyd Mints, and, "at one remove," Frank Knight and Jacob Viner continued this "aberrant tradition." It "continued to be a central and vigorous part of the oral tradition throughout the 1930s and 1940s, where students continued to study monetary theory and to write theses on monetary problems." Friedman's introduction was designed to convey the "flavor" of this oral tradition. This tradition, according to Friedman, had achieved the task that Patinkin (1956a) had set himself: integrating monetary and value theory. The volume was a "symptom" of the slow reemergence of the quantity theory into "professional respectability."

Patinkin stated that it was Friedman's 1968 *Encyclopedia* entry on the quantity theory that had stimulated his rebuttal. But the "main purpose" of Patinkin's essay was to describe the "true nature of the Chicago monetary tradition" in contrast to Friedman's 1956 historical reconstruction—*a tradition that Friedman did not refer to in his 1968 entry*. In Patinkin's twenty-four page attack, only four pages are devoted to the 1968 *Encyclopedia* entry and its overlap with the 1956 essay (1969, 58–62). Of those four pages, half a page is devoted to documenting the changes that Friedman made following "criticisms of his earlier exposition." It seems likely that Patinkin's response reflected, in part, changes in his relationship with Friedman and in the degree of influence that Friedman was beginning to exert.[5]

Patinkin's attack began with an apology for not having debunked Friedman in 1956. He contrasted "Friedman's Chicago" with "the other Chicago" in which the quantity theory was "first and foremost, not a theory of the demand for money"; velocity was not constant and government had an obligation to conduct contra-cyclical policies. "The other Chicago" was supported by published material, lecture notes, and a list of theses from the relevant period. Patinkin made two charges: first that Friedman had misrepresented the "flavour" of the Chicago monetary tradition, claiming a Chicago interwar lineage that was not supported by the evidence; and second that Friedman's reformulation was highly Keynesian in origin. Patinkin (1969, 46 n. 3; 1981a, 241) dated his own first "in passing" discussion of the Keynesian nature of Friedman's essay to a 1962 conference (Patinkin [1962] 1965, 54–55 n. 5). Certainly, an air of formality enters their correspondence at the end of the 1950s. Patinkin began reporting in note form not only fresh points but summaries of conversations between them (28 October 1965).[6]

On 16 November 1959, Patinkin wrote a strongly worded letter to Friedman: "Most of the issues revolve around your assertion on page 2 that you will accept fully my assumptions and framework of analysis—and you will demonstrate the existence of error. But this is exactly what you have not done. . . . This failure begins with the main issue itself:

5. What may seem as anger to some was seen by Stanley Fischer as "a very strong stand on matters of intellectual honesty" (personal correspondence, 3 September 1997). The two are, of course, not inconsistent. On at least one occasion, Patinkin's strong stand led to bizarre results. According to Nicholas Georgescu-Roegen (1992, 140–41), Patinkin was scheduled to act as discussant of his 1965 International Economics Association conference paper on production functions and scale. But Patinkin stated that he "could not introduce a paper vitiated by a 'fundamental mathematical error' and simply sat down." After the conference, Patinkin realized that he had been wrong and attempted to persuade the IEA not to publish his criticism in the *Proceedings*.

6. Patinkin must have felt that he needed to document his steps, recording by hand at the top of this "documentary" letter that it had been written during a visit to Johns Hopkins

the nature of the long run demand curve for money."[7] Patinkin objected that

> in an introductory essay to an empirical volume dealing with historical data, should there not have been at least a mention of the real balance effect as a possible factor in the demand curve for money? It seems to me that the answer is clearly in the positive. . . . As an aside, I might add that my only other objection to your essay is its refusal to recognise the strongly Keynesian flavour of the analysis it presents. I don't think you could find support in the literature for your insistence on presenting this exposition—and particularly the detailed discussion on alternative rates of return on the different forms of holding wealth—as if it were close to the surface of the traditional quantity theory. On the contrary, to me it seems that with perhaps one exception (Karl Schlesinger) an exposition with the contents and spirit of yours could not have been written (and was not written) before Keynes. I find it particularly difficult to accept your implication that your essay represents the kind of thing that was taught at Chicago by Knight, Viner, Simons and Mints. My own recollections are different.[8]

Patinkin (1968) contributed an *Encyclopedia* entry on interest and commented on an early draft of Friedman's entry. Patinkin (28 October 1965) informed Friedman that

> I don't think it is correct to represent [Irving] Fisher as being more mechanical in his approach—and less related to ordinary supply and demand analysis—than the Cambridge economists. . . . I still think it is inappropriate to include in an encyclopedia article on the quantity theory the section entitled "Post Keynesian Reformulation." For this is more Keynesian in its formulation than "quantity theoretic." But if

7. Friedman (personal correspondence, 19 September 1997) believes that Patinkin was referring to a letter: "I have no recollection of ever publishing anything that constituted a criticism of Patinkin, but I might well have done so in a letter."

8. Shortly after this exchange of letters, Christopher Archibald (1961, 1963) invited Chicago to take part in the kind of microeconomic statistical race that they had successfully engaged their macroeconomic opponents in—an invitation that, he thought, "should commend itself to Chicago methodologists." Given that Stigler's approach to empirical evidence "sent shudders" through Patinkin (to Friedman, 4 February 1950), it is likely that Patinkin was irritated by the Chicago response: "there is a real doubt that any communication between Archibald and me is possible" (Friedman 1963a, 66). Patinkin took an exceptional interest in this exchange: Archibald's essay is among the most heavily annotated articles in his archives; his comments (atypically) were in Hebrew.

> you have decided to go in this direction . . . then the question must be asked why have you almost entirely restricted the discussion in this section to your own reformulation? In this connection I must emphasise once again (see *Money, Interest and Prices* p. 644 footnote 44) that the empirical work you have done on the quantity theory—and to which you refer at the end of your article—gives support to other reformulations of the quantity theory as well.

Previously, his disagreements with Friedman had first been discussed in correspondence; now Patinkin wrote his essay and sent it to Friedman (27 November 1968). Patinkin's draft bounced from Chicago to the Friedman's holiday home in Ely, Vermont, from where Friedman replied on 5 December 1968. Friedman complained that he had revised the entry as Patinkin suggested and had included a reference to Knut Wicksell and made a greater acknowledgment of Keynes's influence. He objected to Patinkin's insinuation that "there had been no change in my knowledge but only in my willingness to be honest about it." Friedman suspected that Patinkin was making a broader attack on his honesty. On rereading his letter, Friedman wrote alongside these words that "this I fear is a characteristic of your presentation that has broader relevance." Friedman informed Patinkin that "I continue to regard what I wrote as a reformulation of the quantity theory of money, just as I continue to regard Keynes' Monetary Reform, and large parts of his Treatise, and some parts of his Gen. Theory, as the writings of a quantity theorist. I have increasingly become persuaded that the really Keynesian element (this I have had impressed on me mostly by [Axel] Leijonhufvud) in the Gen. Theory is the treatment of prices as institutional datum." But he accepted Patinkin's major criticism: "I find your description of the oral tradition entirely acceptable and much better and more acceptable than mine. In extenuation, I can only say that the 1956 essay did not set out to be an essay in the history of thought but an introduction to a collection of studies."

Friedman (personal correspondence, 19 September 1997) recalled that he "was puzzled at the time about why Don was getting agitated when I had leaned over backwards trying to accommodate his criticisms. . . . I don't believe that either Patinkin or Johnson in 1971 were venomous, though perhaps both were ungenerous. I believe that their objective was much less to embarrass me than to elevate themselves. After all, they were following a very well trodden path." But in response to Friedman,

Patinkin composed one of the most intensely thought-out letters of his career. His reply to Friedman was first composed in longhand (headed "draft for letter Dec. 1968"), followed by a "1st typed draft—not [underlined three times] sent," dated 26 December 1968; then the final letter, which was dated 31 December 1968. Patinkin typed Friedman's handwritten letter of 5 December 1968 and enclosed it with his reply to Friedman.

In the draft that was not sent, Patinkin wrote that "the categories of 'honest' and 'dishonest' are quite irrelevant. What is instead relevant is the far more subtle phenomenon involved in human failing (to which we are all subject) of sometimes suppressing that which it would be more convenient for us not to note or remember—with reference to questions to which we are strongly involved." Patinkin preferred to leave "it to the reader to decide on the nature of the change in [Friedman's] views." In the letter that Patinkin did send, the psychological analysis became less specific: "the categories of 'honest' and 'dishonest' are quite irrelevant—and what are instead involved are far more subtle processes."

It might be uncharitable to suggest that there was a catering aspect to these deliberations (besides, Friedman was probably "a man more dined against than dining"). But on 16 March 1971, the Friedmans held a party at which the Patinkin-Johnson assaults were discussed. (Friedman had apparently just heard that Johnson's Ely lecture was to be published in both *Encounter* and the *American Economic Association Papers and Proceedings*.) Homer Jones, who had taught at Chicago in the 1930s, was invited, as was Robert Gordon (the editor of the *JPE*), Gary Becker, David Meiselman, and Stanley Fischer. Fischer had assisted Patinkin in his *JCMB* essay, and when he returned home from the party he immediately sent a report to Patinkin. If this meeting were interpreted *as if* it were Friedman's intention to plan his counterattack at this party (a potentially ungenerous interpretation of a possibly coincidental social gathering), then he was unaware of Fischer's role: "By the way, Milton did not know that I had been the research assistant for the article. I suspect we'll discuss it again" (Fischer to Patinkin, 16 March 1971).[9]

9. Fischer reported that Friedman complained that he didn't "have the time to be involved in polemics"; but Friedman took Johnson's accusation about the "planned" nature of the counterrevolution "as a compliment." Becker and Meiselman supported Friedman's account of the oral tradition, stating that "Mints of the early 1950s did not believe that velocity was unstable, and Homer Jones said that Mints of the late 20s also emphasised the stability of velocity." Meiselman suggested that "there was an oral tradition independent of Milton." Friedman was more cautious than his supporters: "he seemed to argue that the only statements about the oral

Patinkin's essay was written during his visit to MIT, where combating Friedman had become an obsession. Fischer (personal correspondence, 3 September 1997) is "certain no-one at MIT pushed [Patinkin] to write the essay." Samuelson (personal correspondence, 25 September 1997), however, has memories of seeing and approving Patinkin's evidence: "In the privacy of my study I silently nodded."[10] When *Studies in the Quantity Theory of Money* (1956) was published, the velocity of circulation was regarded in Cambridge, Massachusetts, as "a mere residual . . . [to be] forced back into oblivion where it belongs" (Hansen 1957, 50). One month after Friedman's 1968 AEA presidential prediction, Robert Solow (1968, 3) maintained that the quantity theory got "more publicity than its intrinsic interest or importance would require." But northeasterly movements of inflation-unemployment observations (widely interpreted as a vindication of Friedman's prediction) shattered that complacency, and the Patinkin-Johnson animosity became intensely vehement from that point on.

When Samuelson (to Patinkin, 5 July 1995) heard from Fischer of the seriousness of Patinkin's health problems, he wrote of his "immortality" as a scholar and of his own "great affection" and "love": "Few countries have had an Abraham that all see as the Father of their nation's science. You are the Adam of Israeli economics and economists—and what Isaacs, Jacobs, and Josephs have graced your seminar rooms. In your own right, and for all the world, it was you who (as it is said) *rediscovered money*—as if it was previously perfected, was then lost, and had to be found again. In fact it was you who first discovered the first complete theory of money." The first edition of Patinkin's *Money,*

---

tradition which are to be taken seriously are those at the beginning of the article, before he begins to number points." Patinkin and Fischer had tracked down thesis titles to support their argument: "Milton said that the fact that he had said the 'thirties and forties' in his article covers him for the dearth in the 30s. At which stage, Bob Gordon said 'You always have some qualification which saves you,' or words to that effect" (Fischer to Patinkin, 16 March 1971).

10. "That Friedman account did not accord with the detailed experience I had as a Chicago undergraduate, both before and after Milton's overlap with me there as a graduate student. It also did not accord with what I experienced first hand in my many visits to the University of Chicago in the period 1935–1946. . . . Therefore, when Patinkin pointed out the evidence in his student notes on lectures of discrepancies with the Friedman account, in the privacy of my study I silently nodded. And added that my testimony of the period *before* Patinkin's arrival on the Midway agreed with his memory and testimony and with his critiques of the Friedman memoir" (personal correspondence from Samuelson, 25 September 1997). Samuelson (1985, 7; 1996, 148) concluded that Friedman's assertion had been "amply debunked. . . . There was no such oral tradition at Chicago."

Interest, and Prices: An Integration of Monetary and Value Theory was published in 1956, the same year as *Studies in the Quantity Theory of Money*.

Money, Interest, and Prices completed the Keynesian neoclassical synthesis, and Patinkin believed that he had laid out a framework for macroeconomics whereby the low level equilibrium trap was ruled out on theoretical grounds, leaving a role for fiscal policy to speed up the adjustment toward full employment.[11] But monetary economics became "a dramatic growth industry" (Friedman 1969, 82), and it was Friedman's rediscovery of money that dominated the profession. In the introduction to the second abridged edition, Patinkin (1989, xv, liii, xvii, xx) wrote that he "had little to add or change" except to denigrate Friedman's (1956) quantity theory "misnomer" and to point out the "misleading nature" of Friedman's "natural rate of unemployment [which] begs the basic policy question that Keynes raised . . . whether one can rely on the 'self-adjusting character of the economic system' for the achievement of full employment." Patinkin (1959, 586; 1974a, 130) believed that he had refocused attention away "from underemployment equilibrium . . . to unemployment disequilibrium." But after Friedman's AEA presidential address, "the concept of 'underemployment equilibrium' [had] been replaced by the concept of a 'natural' rate of unemployment" (Friedman 1987, 12). As a controversialist Friedman had overtaken Patinkin.

Johnson

Despite being the coauthor of *The Shadow of Keynes* (Johnson and Johnson 1978), Harry Johnson was regarded by many as a Keynesian. But "in Britain, a Keynesian of Harry's type found himself labelled a monetarist whether he liked it or not" (Laidler 1984, 604). In fact, Johnson was, by temperament, an iconoclast, and he was not inclined to be anybody's second-in-command. Perhaps he also became aware of straws in the wind with respect to judgments formed by those who had once looked to him for intellectual leadership: "Much of what his later writings contain was without a doubt 'well known at Chicago' when it was published" (Laidler 1984, 592). The revival of interest in monetary issues was associated with Friedman's name, and Johnson (1977, 4) was

11. Solow (1991, 88) emphasized Patinkin's role in formulating Keynesian economics as the economics of "slow, even if ultimately stabilizing, disequilibrium motion."

irked to be "identified by the unthinking as [one of the] lesser lights in the contemporary 'Chicago School' led by Milton Friedman." Likewise, Patinkin was the victim of a "gross caricature . . . often presented as a brilliant but wrong-headed exponent of some 'Classical' tradition that perceptive and disinterested men abandoned in 1936—except at the University of Chicago! Perhaps indeed he was the principal victim of Friedman's myth about the Chicago tradition" (Laidler 1973, 263).[12] Israeli policy disputes about the appropriate use of the price mechanism as opposed to administrative judgment resulted in "victory for . . . the 'Chicago' economists in the Hebrew University" (Pomphret 1976, 26–27, 170). Patinkin was closely involved in these policy disputes; the common (if exaggerated) perception was "that Don's message, and that of Economics as a whole, was that of 'The Gospel According to Chicago'" (Barkai 1993, 6). Patinkin would have resented as much as Johnson the implication that he was merely peddling someone else's economics.

Johnson was simultaneously pioneering the monetary approach to the balance of payments, regarded by some as "international monetarism" (Johnson 1972b; Mundell 1971). He also became the intellectual leader of a group of energetic monetarists who sought to convert British policy makers. Johnson (1971a) implied that Friedman had planned his monetarist counterrevolution by imitating the tactics of the Keynesian revolution. Toward the end of his life, Johnson appeared to have forgotten the details of some old animosities. Thus, Johnson (1976a, 591) thought that Joan Robinson's (1962, 690–91) first use of the term *bastard Keynesianism* was in 1975—although her first use of the term had been in reference to him.[13] But other animosities still rankled. Immediately after Friedman was awarded the Nobel Prize, Johnson (1976b, 95) complained that Friedman "has frequently trapped and sandbagged critics of reputation and integrity by the technique of under-disclosure of analysis and evidence and apparent overstatements of the strength of his results." At the time of his death Johnson left, at the galley stage, a review of monetarism from a historic-theoretic perspective in which he adjudicated the Patinkin-Friedman dispute in favor of Patinkin (Nobay

12. Laidler (personal correspondence, 16 February 1999) informs me that Patinkin remained highly sensitive about this suggestion throughout his life.

13. The Patinkin-Johnson critique was embraced by Joan Robinson (1970, 510), who nevertheless regarded both Johnson and Patinkin as the propagators of a "bastard" Keynesian tradition: "There is an unearthly, mystical element in Friedman's thought. . . . in so far as he offers an intelligible theory, it is made up of elements borrowed from Keynes (Patinkin 1969)."

and Johnson 1977, 478). Likewise, Patinkin (1995a, 127–28; see also 1995b, 361–62), at the time of his death, left a chapter in press for the History of Economics Society in which he berated a fellow contributor who suggested that Friedman's "restatement" was less sophisticated than earlier versions of the quantity theory (Patinkin's point, once again, was that Friedman's work was not really in the tradition of the quantity theory at all).[14] Thus Patinkin and Johnson continued, in effect, to harass Friedman from beyond the grave. Friedman (1974, 158, 168) felt that his "perception, or integrity, or scholarship" had been impugned by his two Chicago colleagues; but he was not sure whether he was supposed to have invented this evidence for some "noble or nefarious purpose." Either way, Friedman was in no way deflected from his mission to change the direction of economic policy.[15]

Johnson had been at Chicago since 1959. Although he had been hired to form a Keynesian counterweight to Friedman, his views changed with time: "Harry was originally a very strong Keynesian who was converted to monetarism" (Friedman Collection, correspondence from Friedman, 18 April 1995; see also Frenkel 1987, 1023). Nevertheless, there were considerable tensions between the two. After listening to Friedman's address, James Tobin (1968, 49) noted the power of sermons from "the pulpit" of the AEA presidency. Johnson did not live long enough to become AEA president; but Tobin used his presidential prerogative to invite him to deliver the 1970 Ely lecture. Tobin chaired this eagerly

14. "The truth of the matter (as I documented in detail long ago, 1969, 1972[a] and 1974[a]) is exactly the opposite: Friedman's optimum-portfolio approach to the quantity theory is far more sophisticated than—and significantly different from—the approach of the Cambridge School and *a fortiori* that of Fisher. To repeat the conclusion of my 1969 paper . . . " (Patinkin 1995a).

15. This episode may also cast some light on the nature of the information flows from academia to the policy-making process. Despite all this sound and fury, hostile critics of monetarism, such as the economics correspondent of the London *Times* and the author of *The Rise and Fall of Monetarism*, uncritically reported Friedman's oral tradition assertion without mention of the Patinkin-Johnson critique: "Friedman set himself the task of capturing this oral tradition on paper" (Smith 1987, 12). The economics editor of the London *Observer* also failed to notice the Patinkin-Johnson critiques, despite believing that monetarism was "a defunct economic doctrine. . . . Just as there are always confident tricksters ready to part people from their money, so there are always intellectual deceivers ready to fill a vacuum and capitalise on people's innate sense of guilt" (Keegan 1984, 207). The editor of the political section of the London *Sunday Times* also failed in this regard despite having mustered other evidence against monetarism (Young 1989). Patinkin (5 December 1994) complained to David Laidler that future students will learn about the "modern quantity theory" from the textbooks and then "turn to Milton's article in the *New Palgrave*, which will undoubtedly serve as the standard reference book in economics for a generation."

anticipated session and remembers that Johnson's lecture "created quite a stir" (1968, 49). It appeared to be a *deliberate* attempt to shoot Friedman down in flames (see also Laidler 1984, 609).[16] Johnson (1971a, 11) devoted his Ely lecture to the accusation that Friedman had engaged in "scholarly chicanery" in both his "invention" of a Chicago oral tradition and in his promotion of monetarism. The first "invention" had been "exploded" by Patinkin's *JMCB* article: "There was no lonely light constantly burning in a secret shrine on the Midway, encouraging the faithful to assemble in waiting for the day when the truth could be safely revealed to the masses; that candle was made, and not merely lit, only when its light had a chance of penetrating far and wide and attracting new converts to the old time religion" (Johnson 1971a, 11)

On 7 April 1970, Johnson, as chairman of the Association of University Teachers of Economics (AUTE), delivered an early version of his Ely lecture, titled "The Monetarist Revolution," to the Belfast AUTE meeting. News about the contents of the forthcoming Ely lecture must have filtered out along University of Chicago corridors, because Johnson (1971a, 1) began by complaining that Friedman (and Allan Meltzer) had "undermined our [Tobin and Johnson's] forward planning by getting in earlier with their version of the theme." Friedman's "version of the theme" was delivered three months before Johnson's Ely lecture. In *The Counter-Revolution in Monetary Theory*, Friedman (1970, 7–8, 21, 26) referred to monetarism as "a scientific development that has little ideological or political content." Not only had it been "strongly influenced" by the Keynesian revolution, but "if Keynes were alive today he would no doubt be at the forefront of the counter-revolution. You must never judge a master by his disciples." Friedman stated that "our present understanding of the relation between money, prices and output is so meagre"; he also clearly identified the revival of interest in money with himself: "*This is where I came in.*" Friedman continued to retreat from the 1956 position that had enabled Patinkin to make his specific charges.

16. When invited to be the chief critic of monetarism, Tobin (1980) structured his assault around Johnson's Ely lecture. Tobin (personal correspondence, 15 October 1997) recalled that "Johnson thought Friedman was playing unfairly, not only in monetarism but in other contexts (speculation, exchange rates). I don't think Johnson was so concerned about the unemployment consequences of monetarist disinflation. Patinkin, however, was (like me) much concerned about that. And Patinkin also thought that Friedman was inventing history and thus happened to give Johnson ammunition for his view."

The Money Study Group

The dispute then shifted across the Atlantic, where Patinkin delivered the first (and only) Sir Dennis Robertson Lecture to Johnson's 1972 money study group. Johnson (1972a, 60, 64, 67) believed (or hoped) that the monetarist "mantle of leadership" had passed from Friedman to (at a theoretical level) Karl Brunner and Meltzer and Armen Alchian, and (at an empirical level) to Leonall Anderson and coworkers at the Federal Reserve Bank of St. Louis. He also sought to "free both Keynesians and Friedmanians from the obligation of loyalty to what they believe to have been their master's words."

Presumably with these goals at least partly in mind, Johnson assembled over one hundred of the world's leading monetary economists (twenty-seven international visitors, including Robert Barro from Chicago, but not Friedman, plus all the leaders of British monetarism) to hear Patinkin berate Friedman. Although the title of his Robertson lecture was "Keynesian Monetary Theory and the Cambridge School," Patinkin (1974b, 3–7) devoted his introduction to Friedman:

> The exaggerated claims for the quantity theory have expressed themselves in the attempt (especially by Milton Friedman) to present Keynes's monetary theory not as a new theory, but as a variation on the Cambridge cash-balance theory. . . . I do not want right at the beginning of this conference to run the risk of setting off a violent argument. Nor do I want to offend the man who is really responsible for my being here this evening; for surely you would not have brought me all the way from Israel to speak on this antiquarian subject in a conference devoted to such currently pressing matters as European monetary integration, commercial bank behaviour, and U.K. monetary policy in the 1970s, were it not for the reawakened interest in the doctrinal history of the quantity theory that has been sparked in recent years by Friedman's repeated and provocative assertions about its alleged nature.[17]

17. Patinkin continued: "As an aside, I might quite frankly note that what generates in me a great deal of scepticism about the state of our discipline is the high positive correlation between the policy views of a researcher (or, what is worse, of his thesis director) and his empirical findings. I will begin to believe in economics as a science when out of Yale there comes an empirical Ph.D. thesis demonstrating the superiority of monetary policy in some historical episode—and out of Chicago, one demonstrating the superiority of fiscal policy."

Johnson (1972a, 41, 44, 49, 61, 65, 67, 68 n. 7) also became repetitive, continuing to berate Friedman on three interrelated counts. First, Johnson emphasized "the practically important question, left open (deliberately) by Friedman's restatement of the quantity theory, of how the effect of a monetary impulse is divided between price level changes and output quantity changes" (65). Debunking Friedman was a necessary preliminary to "the understanding of the pressing problems that confront us—which concern the short-run dynamics of an economic system in which money has an undeniable long-run determining influence" (67). Second, Johnson emphasized Friedman's tactical "trickery": Friedman's empirical work "guaranteed the victory of the quantity theory over the Keynesian in terms of the chosen test procedure and thoroughly confused and confounded the Keynesian opposition, which instead of ridiculing and dismissing the methodology attempted to prove that despite its ridiculousness it yielded results favouring Keynesianism when properly interpreted and applied—and so fell into a series of traps laid by the unfamiliarity of the methodological ground-rules" (61). Third, Johnson repeated Patinkin's specific charge: Friedman's restatement "is a much clearer and more enlightening statement of Keynes's essential contribution to the development of monetary theory than the statements of Keynes and his followers" (68 n. 7).

In terms of space and practical importance, the first assault dominated. It seems likely that the passion engendered by the third assault can only adequately be explained by the desire to undermine Friedman's ability to dominate the agenda with respect to the first two. Otherwise, Johnson could have devoted at least part of his invited 1960 AEA commemorative lecture or his 1962 AEA survey article on monetary theory and policy to Friedman's "invention." But prior to Friedman's polemical success, Johnson (1962b, 137) made only a somewhat flattering remark about the third charge: "Friedman's restatement of the quantity theory of money goes far towards providing a synthesis of Keynesian and classical approaches to the demand for money in capital theory terms." At the 1969 conference titled "The Radcliffe Report: Ten Years After," Johnson (1970, 85–86, 107 n. 48), despite the topic of the conference, launched immediately into a discussion of the "motivational construction" behind Friedman's monetarist counterrevolution: "My personal hypothesis is that, as a result of his studies of the Marshallian demand curve and his year as a visitor at Cambridge, Friedman became enamoured of the 'Cambridge oral tradition' as a concept permitting the attribution to an institution of a wisdom exceeding that displayed in its published work, and unconsciously stole a leaf from Cambridge's book for the benefit of his own institution."[18] Patinkin's debunking was described as "conclusive."

The Output and Unemployment Costs of Monetary Disinflation

Patinkin (1948, 560) emphasized that "the fundamental issue raised by Keynesian economics is the *stability of the dynamic system*: its ability to return automatically to a full employment equilibrium within a reasonable time (say, a year)." His contribution to the Keynesian neoclassical synthesis had, he thought, made "unmistakably clear—what should always have been clear—that the involuntary unemployment of the *General Theory* need *not* have its origins in wage rigidities. . . . even if monetary policy could definitely restore the economy to full employment, there would still remain the crucial question of the length of time it would need. There would still remain the very real possibility that it would necessitate subjecting the economy to an intolerably long period of dynamic adjustment . . . a period during which varying numbers of workers would continue to suffer from involuntary unemployment" (1965, 339–40). Patinkin's (1971, 6, 11; 1995a, 121) animosity was fueled by Friedman's success in redirecting macroeconomic policy discussions. In the previous "five, maybe eight years," Friedman had destroyed "the consensus of the profession" about the nature of Keynesian economics and the quantity theory: there were now too many "very impressionistic type of statements which really have no foundation in the literature. . . . There has been a lot of rewriting of the history of economic doctrines to fit in with the present conceptions. . . . I do not think it is a proper kind of pursuit for intellectual endeavours."[19]

18. Johnson was presumably referring to Keynes's (1983, 11:375–76) assertion that "the theory of money, as it has been ordinarily understood and taught by academic economists in England for some time past, is considerably in advance of any published account of it. It is hardly an exaggeration to say that monetary theory, in its most accurate form, has become in England a matter of oral tradition. These preliminary remarks are necessary in order to explain that it is from the standpoint of this oral tradition, rather than from that of any printed book, that an English economist must approach Professor Fisher's very important contribution to the subject."

19. Patinkin (1995a, 121) was "in complete disagreement" with Friedman's representation of the interwar Chicago school: "I did not quite hear those words" from his teachers at Chicago. Patinkin (1971, 14) informed a prerevolutionary Iranian audience (the Iran-American Society)

The ambiguous consequences for output and unemployment resulting from Friedman's proposed monetary disinflation appeared to concern both Patinkin and Johnson. Patinkin's interest was informed by Israeli experience, in which the survival of the state was at issue.[20]

Friedman (1980, 61, 56) was quite specific before the House of Commons Select Committee on Monetary Policy: from "the best evidence . . . (a) only a modest reduction in output and employment will be a side effect of reducing inflation to single figures by 1982 and (b) the effect on investment and the potential for future growth will be highly favourable." Unemployment was "an unfortunate side effect of reducing inflation" involving "a temporary retardation in economic growth." Earlier Friedman had been much less specific. When asked for his definition, he replied, "I do not know what the long run is" (1965, 56); "the weakest and least satisfactory part of current economic theory seems to me to be in the field of monetary dynamics, which is concerned with . . . short-period fluctuations in aggregate activity" (1953, 42). With respect to the division between price changes and real income changes, following a change in money income there were only "*obiter dicta* arbitrarily attached to the theories" by both quantity theorists and Keynesians (1963b, 15). With respect to the equilibrating mechanism of the natural-rate model, the "price expectation effect is slow to develop and also slow to disappear.

---

that he found it "somewhat objectionable" that economists had been seduced by Friedman into perceiving macroeconomic policy as "a competitive game: either you believe in monetary policy or you believe in fiscal policy, that there is only one Allah and you cannot believe in more than one at the same time."

20. His conclusions differed from Friedman's: the existence of a close relationship between money and prices did not rule out a cost-push causal sequence with money being the dependent policy variable. His causal sequence for the relationship between money and prices after July 1952 consisted of the rise in the price level causing an increased demand for credit and therefore an increase in the money supply. This was a private-sector response: the banks expanded their credit at the expense of their reserve ratios. In the 1950s, the Israeli economy had got stuck in an inflation-devaluation "cost-price-credit" spiral, with the government absorbing the excess demand with imported goods, financed by grants and loans from abroad (Patinkin 1960, 117–18, 125; 1956b). These debates intensified during and after the 1965–67 anti-inflationary "restraint policy." But the Israeli government failed to correctly estimate the output and unemployment costs of this disinflationary exercise; the costs of moving out along a Phillips curve were perceived to be too high for the Israeli nation to bear (Halevi 1969). Indeed, Abba Lerner and H Ben-Shahar (1975, xiv, 70, 134) calculated that if Israeli economic growth had been 5 percent instead of 10.5 percent per year, "total GNP would not have covered the 1974 defence expenditures." Yet just before the June 1967 Six Day War, this policy-induced disinflation reduced investment by more than 40 percent, unemployment increased, and "economic growth stopped." The reduction in inflation and the import surplus came at "a great social cost. . . . The price paid for these achievements was too high."

Fisher estimated that it took several decades for a full adjustment and recent work is consistent with his estimate. . . . I do not want to pretend for a moment that we have done more than scratch the surface" (1968c, 6; 1968a, 21, 45, 54). Friedman (1974, 61–62) presented his reformulation of the quantity theory as an empirical research agenda, appealing for a "more subtle examination of the record" to illuminate the all-important question of what would happen to the economy following "monetary disturbances." He stated that "there is no way of stopping an inflation without a recession," but the precise short-run consequences for output and employment of a monetary shock (and how long that monetary shock would last) still needed to be investigated: "I have myself tended in the past few years to stress that one shouldn't overstate the case for monetarism" (1972, 34, 36).

Patinkin (1995a, 127) sought to distance Friedman's monetarism from David Hume, whose policy recommendations "stand in direct contradiction to the basic monetarist tenet that the long-run Phillips curve is vertical." Patinkin (1974a, 131) also criticized Friedman on the grounds that his unspecific discussion did "not enable us to investigate what is, after all, one of the basic questions at issue: namely the way in which—in a given policy context—different assumptions about the various elasticities of demand and dynamic parameters affect the respective time paths of price and output in the system." Using virtually identical language, Johnson (1971a, 12) complained that one of "the most serious defects of the Monetarist counter-revolution . . . [is] the abnegation of the restated quantity theory of money from the responsibility of providing a theory of the determination of prices and of output . . . [and from the responsibility of] *analysing the supply response of the economy to monetary impulses . . . whether monetary changes affected prices or quantities*" (emphasis added). A few paragraphs earlier he had stated, "Personally, I expect [monetarism] to peter out" (12).

Johnson (e.g., [1963] 1969, 141; 1970, 110–12) used his considerable influence to propagate the Phillips curve trade-off, which he described as "the only significant contribution to emerge from post-Keynesian theorizing" (see Laidler 1997). Citing Solow's empirical evidence that appeared to refute Friedman's AEA presidential prediction, Johnson suggested that "a 'sophisticated' Phillips curve, based on a dynamic version of 'money illusion' . . . still offers a trade-off to the policy-maker, though its slope is steeper than that implied by the 'naive' Phillips curve. . . . Tobin's [1968] comment is especially apposite."[21] For Tobin, "living with inflation" was a moral imperative, because the unemployment costs of disinflation were excessive (Tobin and Ross 1971, 1972). Likewise, Johnson (1971a, 12) argued that "either we will vanquish inflation at relatively little cost, or we will get used to it. The odds are at present that we will accept it as a necessary price of solving other pressing domestic issues." It seems plausible that Johnson's hostility to Friedman's discussion of an oral tradition was directly proportional to the influence of Friedman's policy recommendations.

The Struggle for Influence

The debate then moved onto the pages of the *JPE* where the September–October 1972 issue was devoted to a symposium on Friedman and his critics (Gordon 1974). In an early draft of his contribution to this debate, Friedman angrily wrote that he was "very glad" to respond to Patinkin and "the libels erected on that shaky foundation [provided by Patinkin's 1969 article] by Harry Johnson." An anonymous referee informed Friedman that "I cannot see that anything constructive is accomplished by the sentence on p.36 which calls Patinkin a 'heartstruck swain.' This comes across with the implication that the macroeconomic analysis in Patinkin's book was not worth the time invested, and it is an unnecessarily personal insult. . . . Finally, 'libel' is too strong a word for Harry's piece."

As that issue of the *JPE* was being printed, Friedman (whose father had died prematurely of heart disease) complained to his wife of anginal pains during the night. The press then reported that America's most famous living economist had undergone open-heart surgery (Rose Friedman 1977, 30; Friedman and Friedman 1998, 23–24, 420–23). Friedman was "deeply hurt" by Johnson's criticisms (personal correspondence from David Laidler, 18 September 1997); Johnson (whose own health was about to break; two more strokes killed him in 1977 at the age of fifty-three) was visibly upset by Friedman's heart problems (personal conversation with Graeme Dorrance, 11 September 1997). In an unpublished and repetitive note titled "Friedman on the Quantity Theory and

21. Tobin (1968, 53) argued that the coefficient on inflationary expectations was less than 1: the worst outcome was that when inflationary expectations caught up with actual experience, unemployment would rise to its natural level.

Keynesian Economics Continued" (dated 19 October 1972) Patinkin declared his intention of shortly "withdrawing from this debate once and for all."

But Friedman ended the year recuperating in Palm Springs, California, where he became closely involved in Governor Ronald Reagan's plan for a referendum to limit state expenditure by constitutional amendment. In February 1973, Friedman was fit enough to appear on a television program with Reagan to support the amendment (Rose Friedman 1977, 30; Friedman and Friedman 1998, 389). Johnson's Ely lecture must have caused a sensation among the academic economists present; Friedman's unrelenting advocacy of free market economics in the face of such hostility probably *increased* his credibility in the eyes of politicians such as Margaret Thatcher and Reagan. Friedman's monetarism was about to enter its period of maximum influence.

Friedman's (1978) preface to William Simon's *A Time For Truth* may display signs of scar tissue left by his academic encounters with Johnson, Patinkin, and others. Friedman was concerned to "strongly reinforce a change in philosophical views towards individualism that to my perhaps overoptimistic and biased eyes has already set in." In the three-page preface, there appears to be an extraordinary number of hostile references toward intellectuals:

> I know from long experience with my fellow intellectuals that many of them will fail to be [persuaded by this book]. . . . I have discovered repeatedly [that] the successful businessman is far more open-minded with respect to new ideas . . . than the academic intellectual who prides himself on his alleged independence of thought. . . . the intellectual architects of our suicidal course have found a profitable market for their views and might well be hard put to develop an equally saleable new product. . . . Self-interest is no less powerful in the intellectual market-place than in the narrowly economic market-place. Self-interest has been reinforced by the herdlike instinct of so many intellectuals, by their sheltered environments, in which they tend to talk only to one another, to reinforce their prejudices, and to know little of the arguments on the other side. The result has been an incredible homogeneity of views among intellectuals.

Friedman even referred to the intellectuals' "just retribution" and predicted that "the prison, the insane asylum, or the graveyard would be the fate . . . of the intellectuals who have done so much to drive us down this path." He also complained that "the market has no press agents who will trumpet its successes and gloss over its failures; the bureaucracy does" (1978; see also 1965, 27–29). Within months, the market acquired such a press agent in Friedman's influential television series and book, *Free to Choose* (Friedman and Friedman 1980).

Friedman's ex-Chicago colleague, Donald McCloskey, placed a picture of Friedman on the front cover of his *Rhetoric of Economics* (1986). Opponents, such as Paul Samuelson, were convinced that Friedman was an "eel" introduced into the barrel to keep economics "lively and fresh" ("Intellectual Provocateur" 1969, 71). According to Friedman, the monetarist counterrevolution and the reaction it generated was like a play with four acts ("Intellectual Provocateur" 1969, 71). Economists occasionally use rhetorical analogies; Samuelson (1972) described Frank Knight as the Abraham of the Chicago school and Friedman as the Jacob. But Friedman was more like Joshua with his trumpet, searching for the chords that would bring down the Keynesian walls. His Keynesian adversaries with their faith in econometric estimation, and Johnson and Patinkin with their passionate denunciations of what they regarded as "scholarly chicanery," were angry choruses in Friedman's four-act drama, abetting his tendency to be deliberately shocking in pronouncing his ideas: "an effective device to get people's attention, Friedman said of his proclivity to be extreme." ("Intellectual Provocateur" 1969, 71). The adversaries served to increase the intellectual excitement of the monetarist counterrevolution—their public anger contrasting unfavorably with Friedman's public geniality: "I often tease my husband by telling him that he wins arguments with his smile as much as with his logic" (Rose Friedman 1976, 22).

Friedman (1974, 16 n. 6) highlighted the potency of the Keynesian analytical system, which, "once mastered, appeared highly mechanical and capable of yielding far-reaching and important conclusions with a minimal of input," especially when those conclusions were "highly congenial to opponents of the market system." Friedman was impressed with Mrs. Thatcher's economic literacy: "She recognised very clearly the relationship between monetary policy on the one hand and inflation on the other" (cited by Smith 1987, 74). But Mrs. Thatcher (1995, 97, 126, 417) appeared to have learned how to "control the money supply through interest rates," and then proceeded to undertake a major social and economic experiment underpinned by monetary targeting.[22] This was, in part, because monetarism yielded far-reaching and important conclusions with a minimum of input, and its conclusions were highly congenial to supporters of the market system.

Friedman went on to achieve a Nobel Prize and unparalleled policy influence; in fact one of the first countries to seek his advice after the prize was Israel in 1977 (Halevi 1979, 11–12, 16, 25). The controversy over the 1968 *Encyclopedia* entry did not diminish his credentials; indeed, he was asked to write the *New Palgrave* entry on the quantity theory, which concluded with a statement about his overwhelming concern with policy influence. As a methodologist, Friedman (1953) argued that the input side of economic theory (assumptions) was irrelevant; what mattered was the persuasiveness of the output (predictions). The disputes in which he engaged were an interesting mirror image of that view: precisely because the output side (influence on policy makers) mattered, the input side was more of a private conversation between ill-tempered advocates.[23]

Concluding Remarks

Johnson and Patinkin are barely mentioned in Friedman's autobiography, and his side of the (apparently anonymous) "scholarly chicanery" accusation is accorded less than two pages. But there is a reference to jealousy between academic colleagues: "Envy is the least relevant motive; malice the most. What matters is the invidious distinction that is perceived between him and them. They will feel demeaned" (Friedman and Friedman 1998, 40, 103).

22. With this sense of certainty, monetarism was embraced with no accompanying evidence about the potency of monetary targeting (its central policy message). In 1984, after monetary targeting lost credibility, Mrs. Thatcher (in a television interview with an "incredulous" Peter Jay) appeared to run for cover: monetarism was "not a doctrine to which I've subscribed. It's one that came in with Milton Friedman. I used to look at it, I used to look at it and not adopt it. It's a theory to which I've never subscribed. At the moment in spite of three and a quarter million unemployed, we have a current-account surplus—we've had a current-account surplus for five years in a row" (cited by Smith 1987, 122). Monetary targeting *appeared* to transfer the primary location of incompetence away from the political marketplace (which had previously been incapable of producing satisfactory inflation-unemployment outcomes) to central bankers (who appeared to be incapable of hitting monetary targets).

23. "One thing is certain: the quantity theory of money will continue to generate agreement, controversy, repudiation, and scientific analysis, and will continue to play a role in government policy during the next century as it has for the past three" (Friedman 1987, 19, final sentence).

In 1968, the year after Patinkin's Wicksell lectures in Stockholm, the Central Bank of Sweden guaranteed that economists would now compete for immortality (in addition to fame and policy influence). The first corecipient (1969) of the Nobel Prize was Patinkin's Cowles colleague, Ragnar Frisch.[24] On any criterion, Patinkin must have been a strong candidate for a prize. Johnson (1968) followed Patinkin to Stockholm to deliver the 1968 Wicksell lectures; he was "the people's choice within the profession" for a Nobel Prize (Tobin 1978, 457). It seems likely that some leading economists became at this time even more than usually concerned about the pecking order and the importance of their relative contributions.[25]

Patinkin and Johnson sought to turn Friedman into a pillar of salt for "looking back" through rose-colored[26] quantity theory spectacles. In

24. It is possible that Patinkin felt an additional affinity with Frisch, given his wartime imprisonment at the hands of the German occupiers of Norway.

25. Johnson (1971a, 7), having "posed the question of how to mount a counter revolution," may have learned how to propagate international monetarism while denigrating Friedman's domestic version. Johnson was the "Surveyor General" of economics; but immortality is achieved, and Nobel Prizes are awarded, for more lasting contributions. Indeed, many economists are astonished at the speed at which Johnson's work disappeared from the literature. Like Edward Chamberlin (with respect to Joan Robinson), Johnson was keen to differentiate his monetarist product from Friedman's: the evolution of the monetary approach to the balance of payments had, he argued, "proceeded independently of the debates between monetarists and Keynesians" (Nobay and Johnson 1977, 480; Frenkel and Johnson 1976, 24). Like Friedman, Johnson concluded that only "the 'Chicago' approach" of "empirical testing and verification" could "challenge the theories accepted in policy-making circles. . . . empirical studies based on the monetary approach to the balance of payments are at about the same stage as were empirical studies of the domestic demand for money some twenty years ago" (Frenkel and Johnson 1976, 12). Like Friedman, Johnson published a collection of essays from students in his Chicago workshop. Like Friedman, Johnson introduced these essays with the assertion that his (international) version of monetarism had "a long, solid and academically overwhelmingly respectable history" going back to David Hume (Frenkel and Johnson 1976, 9; Johnson 1977, 3–7), an historical account regarded by Dietrich Fausten (1979, 1980) as suspect Like Friedman, Johnson (1975, 254, 256, 348 n. 3) found an influential ally in Henry Simons. "there were a mere handful of monetarists, centred on the University of Chicago and represented by Henry Simons." Johnson also asserted that "trained economists are usually clever enough at concealing their emotions within the trappings of scientific analysis to pass for dispassionate experts." Johnson was obliged to add a footnote: "The points of view described in this paragraph may seem bizarre to many readers; so much so that some readers have asked for references. Unfortunately, useful references are hard to provide. . . . Readers will have to be satisfied by the writer's assurance that there is such a tradition, though much of it oral." David Laidler (personal correspondence, 16 February 1999) recalls his Manchester colleague Dennis Coppock offering a similar interpretation in the mid-1970s, but does not know whether it was sufficiently widely held or discussed to constitute a Manchester "oral tradition."

26. No pun intended on Mrs. Friedman's first name.

their eyes, Friedman was guilty of inventing bogus historical evidence to increase the appeal of his version of the quantity theory. Friedman (1974, 133) regarded the historical evidence under discussion as "expository devices to bring out analytical points rather than for their own sake." The repetitive nature of the Patinkin-Johnson assaults suggests that they wished to cast doubt on something larger than a 1956 introductory essay.

Some (such as Samuelson [1996], 148–49], Fischer, David Laidler [1993], and Haim Barkai) remain convinced by Patinkin's side of the evidence. Barkai, for example, translated for me the relevant sections from Patinkin's 1953 lectures to his introductory economics courses to confirm Patinkin's version. Others (such as Michael Parkin [1986], Frank Steindl [1990], and George Tavlas [1998]) remain convinced that Friedman's account is more authentic. Still others were caught uneasily between feuding colleagues. This essay has not attempted to adjudicate between Patinkin and Friedman, but to reconstruct the dispute and to explain the behavior of the combatants. Patinkin and Johnson did feel passionately about the strength of the evidence against Friedman's account of the oral tradition. It also seems clear that they felt both apprehensive about, and demeaned by, the lengthening shadow of Friedman.

References

Archibald, C. G. 1961. Chamberlin versus Chicago. *Review of Economics and Statistics* 28 (October): 2–28.

———. 1963. Reply to Chicago. *Review of Economics and Statistics* 30:68–71.

Arrow, K. J., G. Debreu, E. Malinvaud, and R. Solow. 1991. *Cowles Fiftieth Anniversary: Four Essays and an Index of Publications*. New Haven, Conn.: Cowles Foundation for Research in Economics at Yale University.

Barkai, H. 1993. Don Patinkin's Contribution to Economics in Israel. In *Monetary Theory and Thought: Essays in Honour of Don Patinkin*, edited by H. Barkai, S. Fischer, and N. Liviatan. London: Macmillan.

Fausten, D. 1979. The Humean Origin of the Contemporary Monetary Approach to the Balance of Payments. *Quarterly Journal of Economics* 93.4:655–73.

———. 1980. Beyond the Analytics of the Monetary Approach to the Balance of Payments: Methodology, Innovation, and Monetarism. *Kredit and Kapital* 13.1:66–82.

Frenkel, J. A. 1987. Harry G. Johnson. In *The New Palgrave: A Dictionary of Economics*, edited by J. Eatwell, M. Milgate, and P. Newman. London: Macmillan.

Frenkel, J. A., and H. G. Johnson, eds. 1976. *The Monetary Approach to the Balance of Payments*. London: George Allen & Unwin.

Friedman, M. Milton Friedman Collection, Hoover Institution Archives, Stanford University.

———. [1948] 1953. Monetary and Fiscal Framework for Economic Stability. In *Essays in Positive Economics*. Chicago: University of Chicago Press.

———. 1953. *Essays in Positive Economics*. Chicago: University of Chicago Press.

———. 1956. The Quantity Theory of Money—A Restatement. In *Studies in the Quantity Theory of Money*. Chicago: University of Chicago Press.

———. 1963a. More on Archibald versus Chicago. *Review of Economics and Statistics* 30:65–67.

———. 1963b. The Present State of Monetary Theory. *Economic Studies Quarterly* 14.1:1–15.

———. 1964. Post War Trends in Monetary Theory and Policy. *National Banking Review* 2 (September): 1–9.

———. 1965. Discussion. In *Conference on Savings and Residential Finance*, edited by M. D. Ketchum and N. Strunk. Chicago: U.S. Savings and Loan League.

———. 1966. Interest Rates and the Demand for Money. *Journal of Law and Economics* 9 (October): 71–85.

———. 1968a. Factors Affecting the Level of Interest Rates. In *Savings and Residential Financing*, edited by D. P. Jacobs and R. T. Pratt. Chicago: U.S. Savings and Loan League.

———. 1968b. Money: Quantity Theory. In *International Encyclopedia of the Social Sciences*, edited by David L. Sills, 10:432–47. New York: Macmillan.

———. 1968c. The Role of Monetary Policy. *American Economic Review* 58 (May): 1–17.

———. 1969. *The Optimum Quantity of Money and Other Essays*. London: Macmillan.

———. 1970. *The Counter-Revolution in Monetary Theory*. London: Institute of Economic Affairs.

———. 1972. *Money and Economic Development*. New York: Praeger.

———. 1974. A Theoretical Framework for Monetary Analysis. And Comments on the Critics. In *Milton Friedman's Monetary Framework: A Debate with His Critics*, edited by R. J. Gordon. Chicago: University of Chicago Press.

———. 1978. Preface to *A Time For Truth*, by William Simon. Sydney: McGraw-Hill.

———. 1980. Evidence. In *The House of Commons Treasury and Civil Service Committee: Memoranda on Monetary Policy*. London: HMSO.

———. 1987. The Quantity Theory of Money. In *The New Palgrave: A Dictionary of Economics*, edited by J. Eatwell, M. Milgate, and P. Newman. London. Macmillan.

———, ed. 1956. *Studies in the Quantity Theory of Money*. Chicago: University of Chicago Press.

Friedman, M., and R. Friedman. 1980. *Free to Choose: A Personal Statement*. New York: Harcourt Brace Jovanovich.

———. 1998. *Two Lucky People*. Chicago: University of Chicago Press.

Friedman, M., and A. Schwartz. 1963. *A Monetary History of the United States, 1867–1960*. Princeton: Princeton University Press.

———. 1982. *Monetary Trends in the United States and the United Kingdom*. Chicago: University of Chicago Press.

Friedman, R. 1976. Milton Friedman: Husband and Colleague. [No. 1 of 12.] *Oriental Economist* April: 22–26.

———. 1977. Milton Friedman: Husband and Colleague. [No. 9 of 12.] *Oriental Economist* January: 24–32.

Georgescu-Roegen, N. 1992. Nicholas Georgescu-Roegen about Himself. In *Eminent Economists: Their Life Philosophies*, edited by N. Szenberg. Cambridge: Cambridge University Press.

Gordon, R. J, ed. 1974. *Milton Friedman's Monetary Framework: A Debate with His Critics*. Chicago: University of Chicago Press.

Halevi, N. 1969. Economic Policy Discussion and Research in Israel. *American Economic Review* 59.2:75–118.

———. 1979. The Exchange Rate in Israel. *Revue Economique* 1 (January): 10–30.

Hammond, J. D. 1996. *Theory and Measurement: Causality Issues in Milton Friedman's Monetary History*. Cambridge: Cambridge University Press.

Hansen, A. 1957. *The American Economy*. New York: McGraw-Hill.

Hendry, D., and N. R. Ericsson. 1983. Assertion without Empirical Basis: An Econometric Appraisal of *Monetary Trends . . . in the United Kingdom* by Milton Friedman and Anna Schwartz. London: Bank of England.

———. 1991. An Econometric Analysis of U.K. Money Demand in Monetary Trends in the United States and the United Kingdom. *American Economic Review* 81 (March): 8–38.

Intellectual Provocateur. 1969. *Time*, 19 December, 71.

Johnson, E. S., and H. G. Johnson. 1978. *The Shadow of Keynes*. Oxford: Basil Blackwell.

Johnson, H. G. 1962a. Monetary Theory and Policy. *American Economic Review* 52 (June): 335–84.

———. 1962b. *Money, Trade, and Economic Growth*. London: George Allen & Unwin.

———. [1962] 1969. Monetary Theory and Policy. In Johnson 1969.

———. [1963] 1969. World Inflation: A Monetarist View. In Johnson 1969.

———. 1965. A Quantity Theorist's Monetary History of the United States. *Economic Journal* 75 (June): 388–96.

———. 1968. *Comparative Cost and Commercial Policy Theory for a Developing World Economy*. Stockholm: Almqvist and Wicksell.

———. 1969. *Essays in Monetary Economics*. 2d ed. London: George Allen & Unwin.

———. 1970. Recent Developments in Monetary Theory—A Commentary. In *Money in Britain 1959–1969*, edited by D. R. Croome and H. G. Johnson. London: Oxford University Press.

———. 1971a. The Keynesian Revolution and the Monetarist Counter-Revolution. *American Economic Review* 61 (May): 1–14.

———. 1971b. *Macroeconomics and Monetary Theory*. London: Gray-Mills.

———. 1972a. *Inflation and the Monetarist Controversy*. Amsterdam: North Holland.

———. 1972b. The Monetary Approach to the Balance of Payments. In *Further Essays in Monetary Economics*. London: Allen & Unwin.

———. 1975. *On Economics and Society*. Chicago: University of Chicago Press.

———. 1976a. Keynes' General Theory: Revolution or War of Independence? *Canadian Journal of Economics* 9.4:580–94.

———. 1976b. The Nobel Milton. *Economist* 23 (October): 95.

———. 1977. Money, Balance of Payments Theory, and the International Monetary Problem. Essays in International Finance, no. 124, Princeton University.

Keegan, W. 1984. *Mrs Thatcher's Economic Experiment*. London: Penguin.

Keynes, J. M. 1983. *The Collected Writings of John Maynard Keynes*. Vol. 11. London: Macmillan.

Laidler, D. 1973. Review of Patinkin's *Studies in Monetary Economics*. *Economic Journal* 83.329:262–64.

———. 1984. Harry Johnson as a Macroeconomist. *Journal of Political Economy* 92.4:592–615.

———. 1993. Hawtrey, Harvard, and the Origins of the Chicago Tradition. *Journal of Political Economy* 101 (December): 1068–1103.

———. 1997. The Emergence of the Phillips Curve as a Policy Menu. In *Trade Technology and Economics: Essays in Honour of Richard G. Lipsey*, edited by B. C. Eaton and R. G. Harris, Cheltenham, U.K.: Edward Elgar

Leeson, R. 1998. The Early Patinkin-Friedman Correspondence. *Journal of the History of Economic Thought* 20.4:433–48.

Lerner, A. P., and H. Ben-Shahar. 1975. *The Economics of Efficiency and Growth: Lessons from Israel and the West Bank*. Cambridge, Mass.: Ballinger.

McCloskey, D. 1986. *The Rhetoric of Economics*. Madison: University of Wisconsin Press.

Mundell, R. 1971. *Monetary Theory*. Pacific Palisades, Calif.: Goodyear.

Nobay, R., and H. G. Johnson. 1977. Monetarism: A Historic-Theoretic Perspective. *Journal of Economic Literature* 15 (June): 470–85.

Parkin, M. 1986. *Essays on and in the Chicago Tradition*: A Review Essay. *Journal of Money Credit and Banking* 18.1:104–16.

Patinkin, D. 1948. Price Flexibility and Full Employment. *American Economic Review* 38:543–64.

———. 1956a. *Money, Interest, and Prices: An Integration of Monetary and Value Theory*. Evanston, Ill.: Row Peterson.

———. 1956b. Money and Price Developments in Israel: 1949–53. In vol. 3 of *Scripta Hierosolymitana: Studies in Economic and Social Science*, edited by R. Bachi, 22–52. Jerusalem: Magnes Press.

———. 1959. Keynesian Economics Rehabilitated: A Rejoinder to Professor Hicks. *Economic Journal* 69:582–87.

———. 1960. *The Israel Economy: The First Decade*. Jerusalem: Jerusalem Post Press.

———. [1962] 1965. An Indirect-Utility Approach to the Theory of Money, Assets, and Savings. In *The Theory of Interest Rates*, edited by F. Hahn and F. Brechling. London: Macmillan.

———. 1965. *Money, Interest, and Prices: An Integration of Monetary and Value Theory*. 2d ed. Cambridge: MIT Press.

———. 1967. *On the Nature of the Monetary Mechanism*. Stockholm: Almqvist and Wicksells.

———. 1968. Interest. In *International Encyclopedia of the Social Sciences*, edited by David L. Sills, 7:471–85. New York: Macmillan.

———. 1969. The Chicago Tradition, the Quantity Theory, and Friedman. *Journal of Money Credit and Banking* 1 (February): 46–70.

———. 1971. Keynesian Economics versus the Quantity Theory. *Bulletin Bank Markazi Iran* 55 (May–June): 6–14.

———. 1972. On the Non-Neutrality of Money in the Quantity Theory. *Banca Nazionale del Lavoro Quarterly Review* 100 (March): 3–22.

———. 1974a. Friedman on the Quantity Theory and Keynesian Economics. In *Milton Friedman's Monetary Framework: A Debate with His Critics,* edited by R. J. Gordon. Chicago: University of Chicago Press.

———. 1974b. Keynesian Monetary Theory and the Cambridge School. In *Issues in Monetary Economics,* edited by H. G. Johnson and A. R. Nobay. London: Oxford University Press.

———. 1981a. *Essays on and in the Chicago Tradition*. Durham, N.C.: Duke University Press.

———. 1981b. Some Observations on the Inflationary Process. In *Developments in an Inflationary World*, edited by J. Flanders and A. Razin. New York: Academic Press.

———. 1987. Neutrality of Money. In *The New Palgrave: A Dictionary of Economics*, edited by J. Eatwell, M. Milgate, and P. Newman. London: Macmillan.

———. 1989. *Money, Interest, and Prices: An Integration of Monetary and Value Theory*. 2d ed., abridged. Cambridge: MIT Press.

———. 1995a. Concluding Comments on the Quantity Theory. In *The Quantity Theory of Money: From Locke to Keynes and Friedman*, edited by M. Blaug, W. Eltis, D. O'Brien, D. Patinkin, R. Skidelsky, and G. Wood. Cheltenham, U.K.: Edward Elgar.

———. 1995b. The Training of an Economist. *Banca Nazionale del Lavoro Quarterly Review* 195 (December): 359–95.

Pomphret, R. 1976. *Trade Policies and Industrialisation in a Small Country: The Case of Israel*. Lubingen: University of Keil.

Robinson, J. 1962. Review of H.G. Johnson's *Money, Trade, and Economic Growth*. *Economic Journal* 72.287:690–92.

———. 1970. Quantity Theory Old and New. *Journal of Money Credit and Banking* 2:504–12.

Samuelson, P A. 1972. Frank Knight, 1885–1972. *Newsweek* 31 July, 55.

———. 1985. Succumbing to Keynesianism. *Challenge* 28 (January–February): 4–11.

———. 1996. Paul Anthony Samuelson. In *The Coming of Keynesianism to America: Conversations with the Founders of Keynesian Economics*, edited by D. C. Colander and H. Landreth. Cheltenham, U.K.: Edward Elgar.

Smith, D. 1987. *The Rise and Fall of Monetarism*. London: Penguin.

Solow, R. 1968. Discussion. In *Inflation: Its Causes, Consequences, and Control*, edited by S. W. Rousseas. Wilton, Conn.: Calvin K. Kazanjian Economics Foundation.

———. 1991. Cowles and the Tradition of Macroeconomics. In *Cowles Fiftieth Anniversary: Four Essays and an Index of Publications*, edited by K. J. Arrow, G. Debreu, E. Malinvaud, and R. Solow. New Haven, Conn.: Cowles Foundation for Research in Economics at Yale University.

Steindl, F. G. 1990. The "Oral Tradition" at Chicago in the 1930s. *Journal of Political Economy* 96.2:430–32.

Stigler, G. 1987. *The Theory of Price*. New York: Macmillan.

Tavlas, G. 1998. Was the Monetarist Tradition Invented? *Journal of Economic Perspectives* 12.4:211–22.

Thatcher, M. 1995. *Margaret Thatcher: The Downing Street Years*. London: Harper Collins.

Tobin, J. 1968. Discussion. In *Inflation: Its Causes, Consequences, and Control*, edited by S. W. Rousseas. Wilton, Conn.: Calvin K. Kazanjian Economics Foundation.

———. 1978. Harry Gordon Johnson. *Proceedings of the British Academy* 80:442–58.

———. 1980. The Monetarist Counter-Revolution Today—An Appraisal. *Economic Journal* 91.361:29–42.

Tobin, J., and L. Ross. 1971. Living with Inflation. *New York Review of Books* 6 May, 23–26.

———. 1972. A Reply to Gordon Tullock. *Journal of Money Credit and Banking* 3:431–36.

Young, H. 1989. *One of Us*. London: Macmillan.

Part Two

The Debate Widens

The Debate Widens

Shortly after Don Patinkin's initial assault on Milton Friedman, Thomas Humphrey (pp. 313–19 [1971], 313) highlighted the importance of the contributions ('overlooked by both Patinkin and Friedman') made to the quantity theory between 1930–50 by four non-Chicagoan economists: Carl Synder,[1] Lionel Edie,[2] Lauchlin Currie and Clark Warburton. There are similarities between Friedman's version of the Chicago monetary tradition and Currie's *Supply and Control of Money in the United States* (1934). Also, Currie's (1962 [1934]) essay on 'The Failure of Monetary Policy to Prevent the Depression of 1929–32' interpreted the Great Depression as a Great Contraction in a manner which foreshadowed the later work by Friedman and Anna Schwartz (1963). Humphrey commented that 'oddly enough, however, [Lloyd] Mints and Friedman do not seem to be aware of the extent to which their criticisms were anticipated by Currie, for they cite him infrequently'. In the exchange that followed two further names were added to the list of overlooked quantity theorists: Arthur Marget[3] and James Angell (Patinkin, Vol. 2, pp. 317–44 [1974], 344; Humphrey, pp. 345–8 [1973], 347).[4] Both Patinkin and Humphrey expressed curiosity about these omissions. Currie (pp. 323–6 [1972]) provides an additional perspective on Humphrey's contribution in a note that is published here for the first time.

It seems unlikely that Friedman was unaware of Currie's April 1934 *Journal of Political Economy* (*JPE*) essay since it was reprinted, at Harry Johnson's insistence, in 1962 as one of the *JPE Landmarks in Political Economy*; the selection criteria of which included 'impact upon professional economists'.[5] The editor of that volume noted that the load 'borne by … Milton Friedman' in the production of that volume had been 'disproportionately heavy' (Hamilton 1962, ix–x). There are several references to Warburton's 'important papers' in Friedman and Schwartz (1963, 301, n. 2, 359, n. 71) *Monetary History*, but Currie's name is not listed in their bibliography. Indeed, Currie (correspondence 29 November 1972) informed Patinkin that he had been informed by Harry Johnson that

Friedman had 'nothing to do with the selection of my paper in the *Landmarks of Political Economy*'.[6]

This introductory chapter contrasts Friedman's endorsement of Warburton as a pioneer monetarist and his initial reluctance to mention Currie and Angell in this context. It also examines some previously unpublished archival evidence highlighting the intensity of some of the passions engendered by this debate.

Warburton

Without specifically referring to his own work, Warburton (1963, 77) noted that the conclusions derived by Friedman and Schwartz (1963) 'should come as no surprise to anyone who has surveyed the history of business-fluctuation theory'. The 'most continuous' component of the existing literature was to attribute 'a dominant causal' role to 'misbehavior of the monetary and banking system'. Warburton (1952, 292–3) reported that 'the most remarkable theory feature of contemporary business-fluctuation theory is the unanimity with which economists have ignored the timing and amplitude of changes in the quantity of money in the United States relative to changes in population, output, consumer spending, prices and employment'. The first three 'villains' in Warburton's list were John Maynard Keynes, Alvin Hansen and Frank Knight. Mints and Henry Simons apparently approved of Warburton's work. Mints recalled that (presumably in the 1930s) 'I remember distinctly (I think!) that after a talk by Warburton at the University [of Chicago] both Simons and I were greatly pleased by what Warburton had said. I even gained the impression that Warburton was grateful for our approval' (cited by Patinkin, pp. 329–41 [1979/1981], 338–9).

Warburton was a monetarist while Friedman was still a wartime Keynesian.[7] Friedman and Warburton contributed to the same wartime debate on the Inflationary Gap in the *American Economic Review* (*AER*). Friedman criticised Walter Salant's (1941) essay on 'The Inflationary Gap: Meaning and Significance for Policy Making'. But when his *AER* critique was reprinted, Friedman (1953, 253, n. 2, 251, n.) was obliged to add a footnote: 'The next seven paragraphs and the subsequent material inclosed in brackets are additions to the article as originally published. As I trust the new material makes clear, the omission from that version of monetary effects is a serious error which is not excused but may perhaps be explained by the prevailing temper of the times'. This was 'a serious error of omission'.

Warburton continued the debate with 'Measuring the Inflationary Gap' (1943) and 'Monetary Expansion and the Inflationary Gap' (1944). Warburton (1944, 303, 318, 323, 325–6) argued that the first 'gap' that required filling was 'the gap between those economists who approach the problem of price inflation from analysis of the use of income and those who approach it from monetary theory and the analysis of monetary statistics ... Monetary theory has also long had an answer to the next question in the exploration of the causes of price fluctuations: How much pressure on prices is exerted by monetary expansion or monetary contraction? ... This commonsense view is an application to money of the general economic principle known as the law of supply and demand. The refinement of this view which has long been made by monetary theory is often spoken of as the quantity theory of money'. Warburton believed that his statistical analysis demonstrated that 'These facts are in perfect accord with the quantity theory of money, defined as the belief that changes in the price level are primarily due to changes in the volume of money relative to the need for money ... Modern economists who observe the facts around them have no ... reason to disavow this old-fashioned theory'. For Warburton the 'cause of the great depression of the early 1930s was monetary deficiency' and 'the greater part of the amplitude of business fluctuations could be eliminated by ... monetary policy'.

Although Warburton was not a full member of the Chicago School, several of his articles appeared in Chicago journals.[8] The *JPE* published Warburton's 'The Trend of Savings' (1935), 'The Volume of Money and the Price Level Between the World Wars' (1945), 'Quantity and Frequency of Use of Money in the United States, 1919–45' (1946), 'Volume of Savings, Quantity of Money and Business Instability' (1947) and 'Money and Business Fluctuations in the Schumpeterian System' (1953). Also, the *Journal of Business of the University of Chicago* published Warburton's 'Monetary Policy and Business Forecasting' (1949) and his 'Misplaced Emphasis in Contemporary Business-Fluctuation Theory' (1952 [1946]). This later essay – 'his best known and most important contribution' – was reprinted in the AEA *Readings in Monetary Theory* co-edited by Mints (Lutz and Mints, 1952). According to Michael Bordo and Anna Schwartz (1987 [1979], 236–7) this essay provided evidence that Warburton 'anticipated the Keynesian-monetarist debate of the 1960s by a decade or more'. Warburton's (1952 [1946], 284, 317) purpose was to point out that 'a far more potent force of economic instability in recent years, namely, erratic variations in the quantity of money, has been ignored' in Keynesian analysis. There would be no progress in business cycle theory without the 'elimination of its misplaced emphasis on savings-investment relationships and a re-examination of the significance of changes in the money supply'.

Warburton (6 January 1968) wrote to Friedman to congratulate him on his AEA Presidential Address: 'it was a very well-developed exposition of the view *both of us* [emphasis added] have reached from our studies of the factual record and the reasoning and hypotheses of our predecessors. I still find it amazing that the factual data available and the views of earlier economists on the role of money were so largely ignored during the "Keynesian revolution" ... your eloquent statement of *our case* [emphasis added] before today's professional audience, young and old, will bear fruits I am sure'.[9] Friedman (20 January 1966) informed Charles Golembe of the American Bankers Association that Warburton 'is now, we are all glad to say, no longer so lonely in his intellectual companionship'.[10]

From 1934 until his retirement in 1965, Warburton (1981, 293) was employed at the Federal Deposit Insurance Commission (FDIC) which was not, he recalled, an 'academic center' (it was established in 1933 to prevent another collapse of the banking system).[11] In July 1951, Friedman wrote to Warburton urging him to write a 'substantial monograph' so as to maximise the impact of his work. Warburton thought it was unwise for him to do so. Warburton (6 January 1968) recalled to Friedman that in 1955 John Black, the AEA president had invited him to participate in an AEA panel discussion on 'The Monetary Role in Balanced Economic Growth'. Since 1953, Warburton had 'been prohibited by FDIC from publishing articles or participating in public discussions on monetary problems or policies'. His employers led him to believe that his 'job would be at stake' if he accepted Black's invitation: 'With real regret, I declined, deciding to play by the rules of the 'game' in which I was involved, but hoping to extract myself or that a new breeze would blow soon in Washington. The ban was in effect for several years' (see also Yeager, 1981, 280; Cargill, 1979, 445; Bordo and Schwartz, 1987 [1979], 235; Steindl, 1995, 160, n. 5, 159, n. 1).[12]

Currie

Unlike Warburton, Friedman did not initially embrace Currie as an intellectual predecessor.[13] In his study of the causes of the Depression, Hans Neisser (1936, 116, n. 14) interpreted Currie and Ralph Hawtrey as having placed the 'responsibility entirely upon the credit policy of the Federal Reserve System'.[14] In the 1930s, Currie's work was well known to Chicago economists (Laidler, Vol. 2, pp. 137–72 [1993], 160; Samuelson, 1996,

150; Bach, 1940, 76, n. 1; Reeve, 1943). Jacob Viner befriended Currie whilst visiting Harvard in November 1932.[15] At Harvard in 1933, Erik Lundberg (1994 [1934], 62) learnt that the depression had been caused by 'a lack of money rather than an abundance ... It was certainly stimulating though a sad bankruptcy in economic theory, to now learn the exact opposite of what I had learnt before ... Professor Currie was the most eager advocate of this theory'.[16]

When Viner was asked by Henry Morgenthau, President Roosevelt's Treasury Secretary to assemble a 'monetary Brain Trust', among his early recruits were Currie and Harry Dexter White (Sandilands, 1990, 56–7; Rees 1973, 40; Laidler and Sandilands, Vol. 2, pp. 253–70 [2002]). The 1935 banking bill was described by James Warburg (1969, 2944) as 'Curried Keynes'.[17] When Herbert Stein (1995, 216) arrived in Washington in 1938 he regarded Currie as 'the most important economist in Washington'. In the 1930s, Currie attempted to recruit both Friedman and Arthur F. Burns to the Federal Reserve (Currie, 1978, 547; Steindl, 1995, 73, n. 14; correspondence from Friedman 13 September 2000).

In his *The Quantity Theory of Money: A Critical Study of its Historical Development and Interpretation and a Restatement*, Hugo Hegeland (1969 [1951], 3) observed that 'the interpretations of the quantity theory shows almost as many variations as the number of its adherents'.[18] But Friedman (pp. 33–51 [1956], 45–7) expropriated the quantity theory for monetarist purposes: 'the question arises what it means to say someone is or is not a "quantity theorist"'. Friedman then went on to delineate the set of 'deep and fundamental' demarcation rules which had to be accepted before one could be treated as a member of the quantity theorist 'crusade'.[19] In particular, Friedman asserted that the quantity theorist 'accepts the empirical hypothesis that the demand for money is highly stable – more stable than functions such as the consumption function that are offered as alternative key relations'.

Roger Sandilands (1990, 38, 96, 55–6, 156–7) speculated that underpinning Friedman's neglect of Currie might have been the view that 'one cannot be a bona fide monetarist if one is also a New Dealer'. Currie recalled that 'in the early days, the New Deal was in the nature of a crusade' (see also Green, 1981, 231–2). Currie became the victim of another crusade. In testimony to the 1948 House Committee on Un-American Activities, the self-confessed Soviet agent, Elizabeth Bentley, stated that in 1935 she 'met Communists, both in Columbia and downtown, and gradually my ideas began to change'. Although she had never met him, she named Currie as someone who had passed information to a wartime spy ring that reported to her during Currie's tenure as adviser to President Roosevelt (Carr, 1952, 90–1, 241). In 1948, Currie and his old Harvard friend, Harry Dexter White, were obliged to appear before the House Committee on Un-American Activities to defend themselves against her allegations (White died of a heart attack immediately after these proceedings). No charges were ever brought against Currie, and in 1949 he was chosen to head a World Bank mission to Colombia and later to help administer President Harry Truman's 'Point Four' development programme there (Sandilands, 1990, 156). During the McCarthy era, however, an unjustified cloud of suspicion hung heavily over Currie and he chose to settle permanently in Colombia where he developed a highly successful career as a top-level presidential adviser and development economist, noted for his sustained work on monetary theory and policy that paralleled his 1930s work in the United States.

The *Chicago Tribune* was a primary vehicle for the dissemination of these jaundiced opinions about Currie. Friedman (1983, 178) calculated that by 1934 'close to a majority' of faculty and students within the social sciences at the University of Chicago were 'either members of the Communist party or very close to it'. The *Chicago Tribune* fanned anti-communist flames and the Illinois State Senate established a committee to investigate subversive influences in the educational system (Schlesinger, 1960, 604, 607, 529, 88, 94; Stigler, 1988, 157; Ickes, 1953, 368, 376).[20] In February 1950, Senator Joseph McCarthy's 'first important blow' against supposed communists in the State Department was reported the following day in only two newspapers, one of which was the *Chicago Tribune* (Buckley and Bozell, 1954, 160, n., 50–1). Later, McCarthy received financial backing from Colonel Robert McCormick, the publisher of the *Chicago Tribune* (Revere, 1959, 115).

The *Chicago Tribune* produced what Herbert Simon (1991, 121) regarded as a 'thick stream of bile' in its battle to save what it regarded as the American way of life against the New Deal. According to Rexford Tugwell (1972, 169), the *Chicago Tribune* continued to print stories that were 'straight Hoover. It might have been culled from the Memoirs'. In 1961, the *Chicago Tribune* described Currie as a Soviet spy 'who is planning how the dollars provided by a country which has stripped him of citizenship are to be employed in Colombia. It will be surprising if President Kennedy doesn't find out he has made an alliance for Communist progress in that country' (cited by Stormer, 1964, 72).[21] In reality, Currie was not involved in Kennedy's Alliance for Progress. Indeed, in 1961, he travelled to Washington to enlist the support of White House adviser Walt Rostow for an alternative national urbanisation programme for Colombia (Sandilands, 1990, 157).[22]

In the introduction to the second edition of Currie's *Supply and Control of Money in the United States*, Karl Brunner (1968) highlighted the many unacknowledged similarities between Currie's work in the 1930s and subsequent monetary analysis. In 1966, as Brunner was preparing the reprint, Friedman informed him that 'Currie is a fugitive from justice somewhere in South America' (cited by Sandilands, 1990, 157; correspondence from Sandilands, 15 March 2002). Citing Currie's (1934) book, Anna Schwartz (1981, 6) explained that she and Friedman 'did, of course, have at hand' a variety of measures of monetary variables for the period of the Great Depression. But Friedman did not initially acknowledge Currie's contribution. Currie (29 November 1972) wrote to Patinkin: 'I know that both Karl Brunner and Lowell Harriss wrote to Friedman over his lack of mention of my work in his book but I never heard that he replied. I suspect that he disapproves of me strongly'.[23] But Friedman made reparations: Currie (14 November 1979) wrote to Albert Lepawsky explaining that in the 1970s Friedman sent him a copy of *Monetary Statistics of the United States* (Friedman and Schwartz, 1970) inscribed 'to a pioneer in the field'.[24] In addition, he has now issued a specific 'mea culpa' (Laidler, Vol. 2, pp. 137–72 [1993], 148, n. 12).

Angell

In launching the monetarist counter-revolution, Friedman characterised Chicago as the early intellectual home of the modern quantity theory. He spent his second graduate year (1933–4) at Columbia: 'the early intellectual home of the New Deal' (Adolf Berle, cited by Schlesinger, 1960, 393). At Columbia, Friedman was taught by Angell, who served on the front line of Roosevelt's brains trust as a monetary expert and speechwriter (Moley, 1939, 15, 18, 22; Berle, 1973, 51, 32, 45, 50–1).[25] Angell was one of the *Men Around the President* (Alsop and Kintner, 1939, 21).

The policy conclusions in Angell's *The Behaviour of Money: Exploratory Studies* (1936) appear to have a monetarist ring about them (Lee and Wellington, 1984; Milgate and Levy, 1987; Steindl, 1995). Angell (1936, 144–5, 161–4, 61, 159) sought to provide the groundwork to 'test' the relevant parts of existing theories. He concluded that the circular velocity had been very stable between 1909–30, but had fallen after 1930. Thus the large increase in national income prior to 1930 'must have been chiefly associated with increases in the money stock'. Although Angell doubted that there was a close relation between the quantity of deposits and the level of prices, he opposed the counter-cyclical manipulation of the money supply. He concluded that 'the most effective procedure is to stabilise the quantity of money itself' allowing it to change 'only gradually and evenly'. Although he was wary of dogmatic conclusions about causality, he suggested that an increase in business activity would cause 'a subsequent expansion of (particularly) deposits, which our type of banking system permits and usually encourages, will in turn support or even induce a further increase in business activity. A rising spiral of mutually aggravating actions and reactions may thus be set up, which may persist for a considerable time'.[26]

Angell (1933a, 225, 207) used the quantity theory to advance the proposition that the principal cause of unemployment was 'excessive variations in the volume of bank credit'. Angell also prefaced his analysis with a statement about his preference for 'planned economies ... With these proposals I have great sympathy, and I think the adoption of almost any one of them would be an improvement over our present forms of business organisation'. Angell (1933b, 56, 70) also explained that 'a solution through explicit socialisation or collectivisation may be debarred here by hypothesis' because 'intelligent systems of planning' were too far in advance of American opinion: 'In a society where laws and the prevailing social and economic philosophy make deliberate control easier than it is now in the United States, this type of planning and the monetary measures outlined above would presumably go hand-in-hand'.

In his *Memoirs*, Friedman recalled that he thought that he had attended Angell's course on international economics, which he found to be 'most valuable' (Friedman and Friedman, 1998, 44, 46).[27] In a letter to Patinkin (19 July 1972) Friedman explained that the reason he had subsequently paid 'little or no attention' to Angell was 'very simple: his theoretical work in my opinion was very pedestrian and superficial. Let me say that I was a graduate student Colombia in the year 1933–34 and took Angell's course. I started to dictate that I took his course in monetary analysis, but I'm not sure whether it was that which I took or his course in international theory which he also gave. In any event I recall very well that I was unenthusiastic to put it mildly – contemptuous would be a better word – at the theoretical level of the analysis. The same thing goes for Angell's [1936] book. I believe the theoretical analysis in it adds very little to our understanding. It is a highly mechanical approach. On the other hand Angell was responsible for a good deal of empirical work. He was very much a pioneer in that area'.[28]

Friedman's first recollection was more accurate than his second: in spring semester 1934 he attended Angell's 'Economics 128 Currency and Credit'.[29] Thirty of Friedman's forty-six pages of lecture notes from Angell's course relate to Keynes' *Treatise*. This section of the course began with 'Keynes: "Treatise on Money" great "tour de force" says Angell'. Friedman may well have been 'contemptuous' because he had already been thoroughly exposed to the *Treatise* in Chicago the previous year in Mints' Economics 330 (see Vol. 2, pp. 483–525). Perhaps there were other factors, too. George Tavlas (Vol. 2, pp. 175–99 [1997], 197) recounts the information (provided to him by Peter Kenen and Benjamin Cohen) that by the 1950s, Angell devoted much of his teaching to defending the *General Theory* against the Keynesian Neoclassical Synthesis.[30]

Stigler

In addition to the Patinkin-Humphrey exchange there were eight other occasions in which pairs of economists debated the validity of Friedman's claim. The original pair were Friedman (pp. 33–51 [1956]) and Patinkin (pp. 87–120 [1969/1981]). A second bout was arranged between Friedman (pp. 147–66 [1972/1974]) and Patinkin (pp. 123–43 [1972/1974]) in a *JPE* symposium. In the third and fourth bouts George Tavlas engaged J. Ronnie Davis and Tom Cate in the *Southern Economic Journal* (Vol. 2, pp. 49–55 [1979]; Vol. 2, pp. 58–63 [1979]; Vol. 2, pp. 65–9 [1981]; Vol. 2, pp. 70–5 [1981]). The fifth bout occurred in the *JMCB* in February 1986 between Michael Parkin (pp. 351–63 [1986]) and Patinkin (pp. 363–8 [1986]).

The Parkin-Patinkin exchange illustrates some of the cross-cutting cleavages generated by the dispute over the Chicago tradition. Parkin and David Laidler are fellow monetarists who estimated the 'Demand for Money in the United Kingdom, 1956–1967' (Laidler and Parkin, 1970). Their establishment of the Manchester University Inflation Workshop in July 1971 contributed to the monetarist explanation of inflation (Congdon 1978, 20). They joined the University of Western Ontario, where Patinkin held a visiting appointment and where Johnson was a regular visitor. Simultaneously, Parkin (1986) implicitly used the Chicago 'sticky price' oral tradition located by Patinkin and Stanley Fischer (Patinkin, pp. 87–120 [1969/1981]) to analyse the output-inflation trade-off. This type of research became an important component of the New Keynesian response to the New Classical third generation Chicago School version of Simons' 'rules party' (Fischer, 1977; Taylor, 1979; Mankiw, 1985; Akerlof and Yellen, 1985).

Parkin (pp. 351–63 [1986], 353–4) interpreted Patinkin (Vol. 2, pp. 317–44 [1974], 320) as having defined Keynesian monetary theory as being primarily concerned with 'details concerning the demand for money function ... a direct outgrowth of the *Treatise*'. Parkin noted that between 1917–30, A. C. Pigou, R. G. Hawtrey, Edward Cannan, Lionel Edie and Cyril James all appeared to recognise that the quantity theory could be formulated in terms of the demand for money and that 'such a formulation was explicitly a portfolio analysis – an analysis of substitution between money and goods'. Moreover, Simons, Mints and Knight appeared also to be in this tradition. Thus 'Friedman's identification of the quantity theory as being first and foremost a theory of the demand for money is entirely in line with the writings of all the major quantity theorists of the 1930s'.

Parkin examined Patinkin's method of historical research and found that he had fallen into the 'dangerous pitfall' which he cautioned others about: that of 'reading things out of context'. In particular, Patinkin 'misquoted and misunderstood' Friedman's reasoning. In reply, Patinkin (pp. 363–8 [1986]) argued that Parkin had not distinguished between a writer's 'basic analytical framework' and occasional references to other frameworks: 'Parkin is repeatedly guilty of the basic methodological fallacy of reading meaning into texts'. Moreover, Parkin had not, as purported, written a review of *Essays On and In the Chicago Tradition*, but instead after seventeen years provided a 'belated criticism' of 'my 1969 article' (pp. 87–120 [1969/1981]).[31]

Following Patinkin and Parkin, the next combatants were Laidler (Vol. 2, pp. 137–72 [1993]) and George Tavlas (Vol. 2, pp. 175–99 [1997]) in the *JPE*. Following the commonly accepted rules of scholarly engagement, the editors of the *JPE* offered Laidler a brief right of reply. This constraint (a two page rejoinder) was, however, ill suited to the nature of the evidence in dispute and so a seventh bout was arranged in the *Journal of Economic Studies* (Laidler, Vol. 2, pp. 241–3 [1998]; Tavlas, Vol. 2, pp. 233–7 [1998]).[32] This was followed by a further exchange of letters in the *Journal of Economic Perspectives* (Vol. 2, pp. 247–9 [1999]). Patinkin was Friedman's major critic; now Tavlas emerged to defend Friedman's assertion.[33] It seems unlikely that Laidler's further contribution with Sandilands (Vol. 2, pp. 253–70 [2002] and Vol. 2, 271–90 [1932]) will pass without a rejoinder.

Yet there is an exception to this sequence of seven pairs: when the *JPE* published Frank Steindl's (pp. 377–9 [1990]) essay on 'The "Oral Tradition" at Chicago in the 1930s' without Patinkin's brief rejoinder, which is published here for the first time (p. 381 [1991]). Stigler was the *JPE* editor dealing with both Steindl's essay and Patinkin's rejoinder. The archival evidence cast some light on the passions engendered by the dispute over the authentic Chicago lineage.[34]

Steindl (pp. 377–9 [1990], 377–8) briefly summarised Patinkin's accusations and then posed the question: 'Was there an oral tradition of the quantity theory at Chicago or not? One important piece of evidence in support of such a tradition is Henry Simons' enthusiastic review (pp. 371–4 [1935]) of Lauchlin Currie's *Supply and Control of Money in the United States* (1934)'. Steindl continued: 'the quantity theory is an essential component of Currie's analysis ... The existence of a Chicago oral tradition can be seen in Simons' four page review, which begins "This book should have a significant and salutary effect, both on professional opinion and on college teaching. It ... expounds clearly a set of views which, while firmly established in the 'oral tradition' of some schools [leaving little doubt that Chicago is one of them], are [*sic*] meagerly represented in the accessible literature"'.

The plurality of the 'schools' mentioned by Simons suggests a lack of uniqueness.[35] Indeed, Currie (1934, ix) explained that 'most of the subject matter' of his book had 'been taught [by Currie] in the first half of the money and banking courses at Harvard for some years'. Nevertheless, Steindl's evidence was relevant to the debate and deserved to be published. Tavlas (Vol. 2, pp. 203–14 [1998], 209) regarded it as a significant, possibly even a clinching contribution. Patinkin's (p. 381 [1991]) response was that Steindl's evidence failed to support Friedman's propositions about the *specific* contents of the oral tradition.

According to Patinkin (pp. 87–120 [1969/1981], 95) the dispute over the oral tradition did not revolve around fallible memories since he, unlike his rival, had the 'concrete evidence' of lecture notes. Patinkin also took his stand not only on the basis of his superior mastery of the relevant historical literature. Patinkin (pp. 329–41 [1973/1981], 337) referred to Simons' 1935 review of Currie's *Supply and Control of Money in the United States*; he left no doubt that he was claiming to have exhaustively searched the Simons literature. But Steindl appeared to have resolved the Patinkin-Friedman dispute in favour of Friedman, using evidence that Patinkin must have been aware of. This must have been especially stinging for Patinkin (pp. 123–43 [1972/1974], 124) given that his accusation against

Friedman was that he had 'ignored the detailed evidence which has been adduced against the views he expresses' and had 'indulged in casual empiricism in the attempt to support his doctrinal interpretations'. Friedman (pp. 147–66 [1972/1974], 166) believed he had refuted Patinkin's claims, and in return accused him of 'careless textual interpretation'.

Stigler had a 'mordant' sense of humour (McCann and Perlman, 1993, 994, 1012); and Patinkin believed that Stigler was attempting to ensure that Friedman got the last laugh with respect to the Chicago monetary tradition. Patinkin (to Stigler, 31 January 1990) was cross with Stigler for not reviewing Thomas K. Rymes' (1988) *Keynes's Lectures, 1932–35: Notes of a Representative Student*; but he was livid when the *JPE* published Steindl's note. In his reply, Patinkin (p. 381 [1991]) stated that Steindl's note completely misrepresented the debate. He had never denied the existence of a Chicago monetary oral tradition; it was Friedman's interpretation of that tradition that was the subject at issue.[36] In correspondence, Patinkin (18 June 1991) reminded Stigler of sentiments that he (Patinkin) had expressed in an earlier letter, about the 'fallacious nature' and the 'demonstrably false statements' contained in Steindl's essay. Stigler had replied to Patinkin, apparently sympathetically, bemoaning the 'shocking ... lack of care of people in reading and reporting on the literature'.[37] It seems likely that Patinkin interpreted Stigler's letter as an indication that his rejoinder to Steindl would be sympathetically considered. But Stigler, who apparently accepted Steindl's note without subjecting it to the usual refereeing process, unceremoniously rejected Patinkin's reply. Friedman (correspondence to the author, 19 September 1997) recalls that he 'was very appreciative of Steindl's piece'. Patinkin was certainly not and was outraged by Stigler's behaviour. He insisted that Stigler reconsider the matter with his three co-editors. But Stigler (6 August 1991) replied that he and his fellow *JPE* editors regarded Patinkin's rejoinder as 'simply too unimportant to be published'.[38]

The Patinkin-Stigler relationship was different from the Patinkin-Friedman relationship. In particular, Stigler, unlike Friedman, was an historian of economic thought. In this context Stigler (3 July 1972) advised Patinkin that in his research on Chicago monetary history he was 'as mistaken as you can be'. Stigler appeared to be pulling rank in his efforts to discourage Patinkin: 'As a historian of economics I have come more and more to view science as a social institution and process, not as intellectual acrobatics by individual good and bad guys. I commend that viewpoint to you'.[39]

Patinkin spent autumn 1972 at Chicago where he pursued his interest in what he regarded as the authentic Chicago tradition.[40] He could have used the opportunity to launch a parallel attack on Stigler's version of the Chicago tradition. 'The Chicago School of Anti-Monopolistic Competition' was first explicitly defined and described by Edward Chamberlin (1957, 296). According to Stigler (1988, 150), only then did economists begin to refer to Chicago as a 'School'.[41] Chamberlin (1957, 13–5, 17, 26, 300, 305, 24, 43, 70–91, 226–49, 305–6) sought to direct microeconomists *Towards a More General Theory of Value*. He felt himself to be confronted by the 'right wing orthodoxy' of the Chicago School who 'cling desperately to perfect competition' and could offer only a 'jumble of reasons ... a cloud of dust' to defend the status quo: 'mere tricks to bolster up what is at bottom an emotional position ... surely better sticks than this could be found ... people who live in *ad hoc* houses should be more indulgent'. Chamberlin sought to overcome this 'heavy' legacy by reformulating his theory to assist the process of measurement. He concluded that his hypothesis had come into existence following the 'classical' scientific process outlined in Friedman's (1953) 'Methodology of Positive Economics'.

With respect to this second generation Chicago School methodology, Patinkin accused Friedman and Stigler of inconsistency, if not hypocrisy. In particular, Stigler's approach to empirical work 'sent shudders' through him (cited by Leeson [1998], pp. 231–46). In 1963, Friedman and Stigler stood accused on identical grounds by refusing to debate the empirical merits of the theory of monopolistic competition. Patinkin apparently took a keen interest in this exchange between Christopher Archibald (1961; 1963) and Friedman (1963) and Stigler (1963). Stigler (1963, 63) ridiculed Archibald's discussion of Chicago as a 'detour ... The methodological discussion is a detour on the detour'. In 'Reply to Chicago' Archibald (1963, 69) repeated his complaint about the methodological 'inconsistency in Friedman's and Stigler's dismissal of monopolistic competition on apparently *a priori* grounds'. They were, he stated, guilty of 'a shocking piece of obscurantism, and an indefensible attempt to close discussion'.[42]

Patinkin and Stigler presented differing assessments about the extent to which monopolistic competition had been discussed in Chicago. Citing this exchange between Chicago and its critics, and using his 1942 Economics 301 class notes, Patinkin (1981 [1973], 31) concluded that Knight had discussed monopolistic competition and had referred his students to the relevant readings 'to an extent greater than one might infer from some of the things that have been written on the attitude of the Chicago school to this theory'.[43] This contradicted Stigler's view, which was that Knight (his PhD supervisor) 'devoted even less time than compliments to Chamberlin so students had to read the book on their own' (Stigler and Friedland, 1975, 497, n. 23).[44] But for whatever reason, this skirmish with Stigler did not escalate as his private skirmish had with Friedman.

Both Patinkin and Stigler were stern 'gate-keepers' of their respective disciplines. With respect to the Keynesian literature, Patinkin had a well-deserved reputation for rejecting an astonishingly high proportion of essays that he was asked to referee. Between 1976-95, Patinkin wrote sixty-nine referees reports for the *History of Political Economy*; fifty-six he rejected outright, three he accepted outright (Saunders, 2001).[45] Referring to 'committee meetings and journal editing', Stigler (1969, 229) argued that it was both 'true, and necessary to their survival' that 'learned bodies are each run by a self perpetuating inner clique'. Citing *The Devil's Dictionary*, Stigler defined an incumbent as 'A person of the liveliest interest to the outcumbents'. Referring to the dispute over the oral tradition, Stigler (1988, 153–4) pointed out that Friedman used the quantity theory 'as a powerful weapon to attack the Keynesian theory' and was 'quite talented in outraging his intellectual opponents'. Stigler outraged Patinkin by refusing to publish his rejoinder to Steindl.

On another occasion Stigler (2 April 1979) had advised Patinkin: 'Why be so polite?'[46] Certainly, Stigler could not be accused of handling Patinkin with excessive tact over his rejoinder to Steindl. In a letter to all four editors, Patinkin maintained his rage about Steindl's 'egregious misinterpretation of this disagreement'. It was, he explained, troubling to see the *JPE* 'with which for obvious reasons I feel a close connection – fail to fulfill its obligations as a scholarly journal'. Patinkin's letter was dated 19 September 1991, but Stigler's death (1 December 1991) did not diminish his anger. Samuelson (12 February 1992) tried to console him with similar stories about Stigler's behaviour. To which Patinkin (6 March 1992) replied that 'In my case, it was even worse …'.[47]

Patinkin proceeded to question Stigler's credentials as an historian.[48] He informed Laidler (correspondence, 9 October 1994) that Friedman's attempt to defend himself against the criticisms contained in the original *JMCB* essay 'by expounding at length on the Chicago advocacy in the 1930s of an activist monetary and [sic] policy' was irrelevant because the point was 'never in question'. Patinkin continued: 'Unfortunately – for we would expect that a leading historian of thought would base his views on a careful reading of texts – Stigler in his autobiography attempts to defend Friedman with the same irrelevant argument'.[49]

However, despite the relatively high heat-to-light ratio, the debate over the Chicago tradition revealed a vibrant sub-culture in the economics profession. Patinkin, Johnson (and Stigler) were pre-eminent theorists, fully aware of the important role that history can play in the analysis of contemporary issues (Laidler, 2003).[50] One of the consequences of the formalist revolution has been to leech this 'dynamic framework' out of economic analysis (Leeson, 2000a). A quarter of a century ago, Lionel Robbins (1976, 39) himself a pre-eminent theorist, denigrated 'the extraordinary provincialism in time of much contemporary professional literature' – a trend which has continued. As a result many contemporary theorists (many of whom are historically untrained) typically deny their students an opportunity to acquire historical erudition by denigrating the subject and by deleting history of thought courses (Rosen, 1993, 811).[51] History continues to be used by theorists as a potent rhetorical weapon – a rhetorical flourish sustained by an intellectual monopoly (Laidler, 2003). Moreover, the formalist revolution has begun to devour its own children: as the demand to study economics falls, so the supply of academic positions dries up.

Notes

[1] Frank Knight would not have appreciated Carl Snyder's (1927) *Business cycles and business measurements: studies in quantitative economics*, with its emphasis on empirical economics and its frontispiece quotation from Lord Kelvin extolling the empirical approach. When in 1929 the University of Chicago Social Science Research Building was dedicated, the Committee of Symbolism chose as the building's inscription another quotation supposedly from Kelvin: 'When you cannot measure your knowledge is meagre and unsatisfactory' (Cate 1956, 426–7). In his *JPE* analysis of 'Truth in Economics' Knight (1940, 18, n. 10, 30, n. 17) stated that Kelvin's dictum was a perversion of the social sciences: 'misleading and pernicious … In this field, the Kelvin dictum very largely means in practice "if you cannot measure, measure anyhow!" … To call averaging estimates, or guesses, measurement seems to merely embezzling a word for its prestige value'. In contrast, Paul Douglas (1930, 4) used Kelvin's dictum to 'remind … objectors' of the importance of empirical work. For Douglas (1934, xii) this was an antidote to the 'sterile shadow boxing which has characterised so much of dialectical economics'. This dispute was part of the ongoing warfare between Douglas and Knight (and his disciples) that characterised Chicago in the 1930s (Leeson, forthcoming).

[2] Fisher (1933, 124) associated the idea that the supply of money should grow at 3 per cent per year (in line with the growth of trade) with Snyder, Edie and James Harvey Rogers.

[3] Friedman was at the University of Minnesota in the year before his return to Chicago; as was Stigler from 1938–46, with a three-year break (Stigler, 1988, 39–40; Friedman and Friedman, 1998, 148–9). Marget (1938), one of their Minnesota colleagues, published a two-volume 'monetarist', *Theory of Prices: a Re-examination of the Central Problems of Monetary Theory.* In the *AER* review of 'Monetary Theory at the Textbook Level' Marget (1942, 781, 787) noted that it 'can hardly escape even those who will not go beyond the titles of the chapters' that the authors of the textbooks under review had 'unashamedly accepted ... the "*equation of exchange*" [emphasis in original] as an organising device' and were 'unrepentant users of the Fisherine equations as their formal framework'. The two books reviewed by Marget were Harold Reed's (1942) *Money, Currency and Banking* and George Halm's (1942) *Monetary Theory: A Modern Treatment of the Essentials of Money and Banking.* Friedman used Reed's (1942) text for his Economics 230 course at Chicago and a number of Reed's judgments 'align remarkably closely' with the some of Friedman's macroeconomic judgments (Hammond, 1999, 462–3). Referring to the word 'money' Reed (1950, 210) explained that he 'agree[d] with Mr Homer Jones that the word should be dropped from scientific terminology'. Currie (1933, 79) suggested that 'the continued use of the term "credit" appears to be an obstacle both to the advancement of monetary science and its application to current problems'. One alternative was to 'drop the word entirely on the grounds that its ambiguity renders it unsuitable for scientific purposes'.

[4] Angell's father, James R. Angell, was President of Yale University, and was described by William O. Douglas (1974, 164) as 'broad-gauged, tolerant and fastidious when it came to academic freedom'. Angell and Nicholas Murray Butler, the President of Columbia, received unfavourable comment in President Roosevelt's ([1937] 1950, 650) private correspondence for 'howling their heads off' against the new income and inheritance taxes which they believed would dry up the flow of new contributions to the universities. After the First World War, Angell Sr as Acting President of Chicago, recruited the twenty-four year old Robert Hutchins (the future President of Chicago) as University Secretary (Reagan, 1982, 221; *Time,* 1967, 183). James W. Angell was born in Chicago, graduated from Harvard, and spent 1919–20 as Viner's teaching assistant at Chicago (Patinkin, pp. 87–120 [1969/1981], 113; pp. 329–41 [1973/1981], 334, n. 7). Angell taught at Columbia from 1924, as Full Professor, 1931–66, and Emeritus Professor after 1966 (American Men of Science 1968). He was vice president of the American Economic Association (1940) and was part of the US delegation to the Bretton Woods conference.

[5] The *JPE* also published Currie's (1933) 'The Treatment of Credit in Contemporary Monetary Theory'.

[6] Don Patinkin Papers, Box 44.

[7] In 'The Spending Tax as a Wartime Fiscal Measure' Friedman (1943, 51, n. 3) explained that his analysis offered 'no judgment ... on the critical issue separating the 'Keynesians' and 'anti Keynesians'.

[8] He obtained his doctorate on *The Economic Results of Prohibition* from Columbia (Warburton 1932).

[9] Milton Friedman Papers, Correspondence, Warburton file.

[10] Milton Friedman Papers, Correspondence, Golembe file. In conversation with Warburton, Leland Yeager (1981, 280, 284) reflected on his 'puzzlement' over the relative lack of influence that Warburton achieved. Academic 'gamesmanship' was advanced as a potential explanatory factor.

[11] In the 1930s both Friedman's wife and one of his mentors (Homer Jones) were employed in the Division of Research and Statistics within the FDIC (Friedman and Friedman 1998, 65).

[12] Milton Friedman Papers, Correspondence, Warburton file.

[13] In contrast, Arthur Kemp (1979, 11), the Treasurer of the Mt Pelerin Society (1969–79), characterised Currie as 'a classic figure among the early members of the Chicago School'. Kemp does not explain where this information is derived from, but presumably he had recently been in close contact with Stigler, the 1976–8 President of the Mt Pelerin Society (Hartwell, 1995, 78). At a 1977 seminar at the University of Toronto, John Scadding, the seminar chairman and a Chicago graduate, asked Currie what was the price of money. Currie replied 'the price level'. 'Congratulations!' shot back the chairman, 'you pass the test' (correspondence from Sandilands, 15 March 2002).

[14] Neisser was Professor of Monetary Theory at the Wharton School of Finance and Commerce, University of Pennsylvania.

[15] Friedman (pp. 147–66 [1972/1974], 156) was 'amazed' to discover how 'precisely' Viner's account of the Depression 'foreshadows' the interpretation contained in his *Monetary History* (Friedman and Schwartz, 1963).

[16] Currie's *Supply and Control of Money in the United States* (1934) was described in a Chicago Public Policy Pamphlet as 'An extremely valuable analysis ... carefully and logically presented' (Whittlesey, 1935, 25).

[17] Warburg (1969, 2944) described the bill as 'Curried Keynes' a 'large half-cooked lump of J. Maynard Keynes ... liberally seasoned with a sauce prepared by Prof. Laughlin [sic] Currie' (see also Egbert, 1967, 122).

[18] Hegeland (1969 [1951], x, 96) spent two years in the United States researching his 1951 history, but reported no mention of a Chicago quantity theory tradition.

[19] Friedman (pp. 33–51 [1956], 46) stated that: 'The quantity theorist must sharply limit, and be prepared to specify explicitly, the variables that it is empirically important to include in this function ... the quantity theorist not only regards the demand for money function as stable; he also regards it as playing a vital role in determining variables that he regards as of great importance for the analysis of the economy as a whole ...The quantity theorist also holds that there are important factors affecting the supply of money that do not affect the demand for money'.

[20] The owner of the *Chicago Daily News*, Colonel Frank Knox, who had previously been general manager of Hearst's newspapers, and was Alfred Landon's Republican vice presidential running mate in 1936, declared that 'the new deal candidate has been leading us towards Moscow'. During this 1930s 'red scare', Charles Walgreen, a prominent drug store owner, withdrew his niece from the University of Chicago believing that she had been exposed to the doctrines of free love and communism.

Finally, Walgreen was persuaded to donate funds to establish the professorship at Chicago which Allen Wallis successfully offered to Stigler in 1958.

[21] For a more balanced assessment, see Sandilands (2000) and Boughton and Sandilands (2002). Also see Sandilands' online biography of Currie on American National biography On-line at www.anb.org.

[22] I am most grateful to Roger Sandilands for supplying me with this information.

[23] Don Patinkin Papers, Box 44.

[24] Lauchlin Currie Papers, Correspondence, Lepawsky file.

[25] 'Jimmy Angell contributed ideas on prices and money' (Moley 1939, 15, 18, 22).

[26] In his review, Dennis Robertson (1937, 330) noted that Angell's policy proposal was to keep '*national income* relatively stable ... by stabilising the quantity of circulating money' [emphasis in original].

[27] In the Friedman Papers there is a 'Reading List in International Trade Economics 125–6 ... (Revised: 1933)'. A tick appears alongside a 1931 essay by Angell on 'foreign exchange' for the encyclopedia of the social sciences. However, there is no record on Friedman's Columbia academic transcript of him attending this two-semester course. (At the bottom of his transcript three courses are listed as having been 'visited': social economics given by J. M. Clark, one in Labor given by Leo Wolman and one in theory given by R. W. Souter). Milton Friedman Papers, Box 5.

[28] Patinkin (6 August 1972) replied: 'On Angell, I won't argue with you about his theoretical abilities, (though a letter I received from Viner would seem to indicate a somewhat higher estimation). However, as I recall, Angell did emphasise one empirical finding (namely, that monetary changes followed those in prices, instead of preceding them) that I think should have been dealt with by the Chicago School'. Don Patinkin Papers, Box 32. In 1934, Angell and Currie engaged in dispute over their early separate estimates of the income velocity of money. Their estimates of the course of money's 'income velocity' in the 1920s differed widely and made for very different interpretations of Fed policy at that time. The dispute essentially revolved around their different definitions of 'money', Currie preferring a narrower, means-of-payments definition (see Sandilands, 1990, 41).

[29] In Friedman's Papers (Box 5) archives is a ten page 'Reading List in Money and Banking Economics 127–8 (J. W. Angell) Revised: 1933'. Section three of the course on 'The General Theory of Money, Banking and Prices' has seventy-two books or articles listed for reading. Items marked '##' were described as 'Required Reading, to be prepared for class-room discussion'. Among such items were Fisher's 'The Purchasing Power of Money (1911)', Keynes' 'Monetary Reform (1924), pp. 1–95' and 'Treaties [sic] on Money (2 vols., 1930)' and Angell's 'Theory of International Prices (1926), pp. 116–135, 178–186, 274–280, 308–312, 324–331'.

[30] Alan D. Whitney (21 August 1976) recalled in a letter to Friedman that 'Angell was a fascinating personality' (Milton Friedman Papers, Correspondence, Whitney file). While some detected misanthropic tendencies in Angell's personality, others, such as Kenen (a young departmental chair dealing with older and more senior colleagues) recalled that Angell was most helpful. Stigler (1988, 43) was Angell's Columbia colleague for eleven post-war years but the only 'oral ... legend' that he

associated with Angell was his displeasure when Arthur F. Burns (then a PhD candidate) declined to answer a role-playing question about how he (as Treasury Secretary) would respond to a financial panic. Anna Schwartz sought to submit *A Monetary History of the United States* (Friedman and Schwartz 1963) as her Columbia PhD thesis. Burns, the Director of the National Bureau of Economic Research (NBER), may have contributed to the delay she experienced in having her dissertation approved by questioning whether her individual contribution to the Friedman–Schwartz NBER project was sufficient to warrant acceptance. If Angell was a difficult thesis committee member, this may have increased Friedman's contempt for Angell. On 22 October 1958, Friedman (with a copy to Angell) wrote to Albert Hart at Columbia about 'a matter that is strictly speaking on my business, namely, Anna Schwartz's thesis problem … the report of her conversations with you and Angell suggest to me that, she must have presented the case very badly indeed … it is incumbent on us to keep our requirements from being meaningless hurdles, and to adapt them to the particular situation … the fundamental problem is how to satisfy formal requirements without imposing "make-work". If I may again cite our own experience, we have had the same problem here in the past few years in connection to other mature scholars, Homer Jones and Herbert Stein'. Six years later Friedman (7 January 1964) wrote to Barger explaining that he had tried to contact him by phone to 'talk over with you the problems connected with Mrs Schwartz finally getting her degree. She tells me that there has been some question raised over using *A Monetary History* because it is in printed form and this limits the possibility of people on the committee making suggestions for change … it would be a shame to let technicalities of any kind play an important role in the process … I would much prefer to talk to you about this than to write about it because clearly I am very much misinformed and there is some misunderstanding about it on her part'. Barger immediately (16 January 1964) wrote a sympathetic letter to Schwartz explaining that he did not know 'how much trouble [the committee] may cause you about revisions' (her thesis was finally approved later in the year). Milton Friedman Papers, Correspondence, Schwartz file.

[31] Patinkin's original essay (pp. 87–120 [1969/1981]) was published thirteen years after Friedman's essay (pp. 33–51 [1956]).

[32] Sandilands suggested the *JES* as an outlet for Laidler's reply; Laidler suggested that Tavlas be invited to respond.

[33] Patinkin (24 January, 1994) wrote to Sandilands to say how pleased he was 'for more reasons than one' to see Laidler's (Vol. 2, pp. 137–72 [1993]) essay in the *JPE*. Don Patinkin Papers, Box 66.

[34] Not only was Patinkin a gatekeeper with respect to the journals, he played a similar role with respect to application for funding from research foundations. Patinkin did not support Steindl's request for financial assistance to support his monetary research.

[35] Another book review casts further doubt about Simons' supposed commitment to analysing the economy through the quantity theory. Edwin Nourse (1933, ix–x) of the Brookings Institution in his Director's preface to Leo Pasvolsky's *Current Monetary Issues* explained that Pasvolsky's objective was to present 'a general survey of the monetary issues which have dominated world economic discussions during the past year.

After showing the divergence of opinion between various groups and nations participating in international discussions and negotiations during the course of the year, it sets forth the trend of monetary developments in the United States'. But Pasvolsky confined his attention to 'the vital relationship of present monetary policies to economic recovery'. Pasvolsky did not mention the quantity theory and neither did Simons in his February 1934 review. Instead, Simons (1934, 53) stated that he was 'impressed throughout with his fairness and competence in the analysis of issues and in the interpretation of conflicting positions'.

[36] This was the position he had maintained in a letter to Steindl (7 August 1989). Don Patinkin Papers, Box 62.

[37] I was unable to find Stigler's letter and so I am relying on Patinkin's report of it (to Stigler, 18 June 1991). Don Patinkin Papers, Box 62.

[38] Don Patinkin Papers, Box 62.

[39] Don Patinkin Papers, Box 37.

[40] In the resulting essay, Patinkin (1981 [1973], 40, n. 19) tentatively attributed to Knight the second generation Chicago tradition that 'there is no such thing as a free lunch'. Knight (1935 [1932], 251–76) wrote the entry on 'Interest' in the *Encyclopaedia of the Social Sciences*; Patinkin (1968) wrote the equivalent entry in the *Encyclopaedia* alongside Friedman's *Encyclopaedia* entry on the quantity theory (pp. 71–84 [1968]) which was the 'nominal' reason for Patinkin's initial assault (pp. 87–120 [1969/1981]).

[41] Chamberlin (1957, 13–5, 17, 26, 300, 305 In 'Comment on the Chicago School', Stigler (1962, 71) asserted that the title invited a 'slovenly stereotype'.

[42] For a detailed discussion of this controversy, see Leeson (2000b, chapter 3).

[43] Patinkin (1981, 8) also attended Oskar Lange's 1944 Economics 307 lectures on Imperfect Competition and A. J. Nicholl's course on Imperfect Competition. In an article published while he was still at the University of Chicago, Patinkin (1981 [1947], 91, n.) proposed to use empirical evidence to improve the theory of imperfect competition. Moreover, Patinkin acknowledged that 'I cannot overemphasize my debt to Professor Henry C. Simons, on whose Economics 201 Syllabus ... this article is so largely based'. Stigler (1974, 2–3) acknowledged that Patinkin had 'elaborated' upon Simons' analysis of cartels.

[44] Wallis' (1993, 776) recollections supported Stigler's: the Chicago faculty of the 1930s gave Chamberlin's work 'no attention: literally none'. However, Albert Hart's (1936, iii, 151) Chicago dissertation (supervised by Knight, Viner, Henry Schultz and Theodore Yntema) had been 'very profoundly ... influenced' by the 'recent writings on "imperfect competition" (especially those of Mrs Robinson, and Drs. Hicks, Chamberlin and Kaldor)'. Hart also recalled that Simons' and Aaron Director's undergraduate teaching material had been 'freely cribbed by George Stigler and others'. Paul Douglas (1972, 351, n.) explained that he been 'strongly influenced by Joan Robinson's The Economics of Imperfect Competition ... After nearly forty years I still think Mrs. Robinson's book was the best in my generation'.

[45] Patinkin took a very jaundiced view of a paper submitted to the *JPE* by one of his opponents in the dispute over the Chicago tradition. Patinkin (11 June 1982)

informed Stigler, that with respect to his role as a referee 'it was a serious misallocation of my resources to have spent so much time on a paper that is superficial, unscholarly and carelessly written – and whose rejection I accordingly unhesitatingly recommend'. The report sent to the author appeared to be quite neutral – but the *JPE* editors were left in no doubt about Patinkin's determination to see the paper rejected: 'Despite the concluding sentence of my report, I have strong doubts whether [the author] has the necessary scholarly qualifications for carrying out the proper study ... and so I do not think you should ask him to resubmit it after revision'. Don Patinkin Papers, Box 51.

[46] Don Patinkin Papers, Box 48. According to one of his Chicago colleagues, verbal disputes with Stigler were 'likely to be terminated by a positivist edict and a sneer' (McCloskey, 1994, 14).

[47] Don Patinkin Papers, Box 61.

[48] On other occasions Patinkin appeared to resort to ridicule when challenged. Patinkin (pp. 363–8 [1986], 367) criticised Parkin for being 'more Friedmanian than Friedman' because Friedman had 'subsequently admitted' the Keynesian influence, but 'there is barely a hint of this fact in Parkin's paper'. Parkin (correspondence to the author, 24 October 1997) recalled that 'Patinkin seemed angered and seemed to take my critique personally. He insulted me personally in his published response. I thought about rejoining but decided not to after talking with Milton'. Laidler (correspondence to the author, 4 November 1997) recalled that 'Patinkin was contemptuous of Parkin's *JMCB* piece'. See also Patinkin's (1978, 577) patronising 'plea for common sense' to counteract the basic illogical fallacies (christened 'Jacob's Principle') which he detected in David Roberts' (1978) critique of his analysis of *Keynes' Monetary Thought* (1976).

[49] Don Patinkin Papers, Box 57.

[50] In a review of the AEA *Survey of Contemporary Economics*, Stigler (1949, 101, 98, 102) noted that the collection 'demonstrates anew that interest in the history of thought has languished mightily'. This had impoverished the 'scope and depth' of the essays in the volume and also 'contemporary economics' in general. This concerned Stigler because it was 'easy to show that the neglect of doctrinal history has led the contributors to exaggerate the recent advances in theory'. Also, a 'second characteristic of recent economics documented by the *Survey* is the triumph of statistics over history as the source of empirical knowledge'. This was lamentable because the 'historical method ... has the obvious advantage of making available a long sweep of experience unrecorded in statistics. This alone is ample reason for exploiting it: we *are* [emphasis in original] interested in the long run. The historical method has also the advantage ... of yielding information on a much wider range of problems than one can illuminate with quantitative studies'. As Chicago lost its 'outcumbent' status, Stigler's views about the role of historical studies appeared to have changed. Stigler (1988, 214–15) concluded that 'I cannot be confident that it would be profitable for a young scholar to study the history of his subject'. Stigler (1969, 217–18, 230) defined 'the subject matter of the history of economics to be economics which is not read to master present day economics'. In other words, the history of thought was a largely redundant subject: 'one need not read in the history of economics – that is, past economics – to master present economics'. Stigler predicted that 'the young economist

will increasingly share the view of the more advanced formal sciences that the history of the discipline is best left to those underendowed for fully professional work at the modern level ... it remains the unfulfilled task of the historians of economics to show that their subject is worth the cost'.

[51] In 1972, Stigler successfully proposed that the history of economic thought requirement be dropped at the University of Chicago. Most other economics departments later followed suit (Rosen 1993, 811). Deirdre McCloskey (correspondence to the author, 2 June 1997) recalls that at the same meeting Stigler unsuccessfully proposed that the economic history requirement also be dropped.

Bibliography

Akerlof, G. A. and J. L. Yellen, 'A Near-Rational Model of the Business Cycle with Wage and Price Inertia', *Quarterly Journal of Economics*, 100 supplement (1985), pp. 823–38.

Alsop, J. and Kintner, R., *Men Around the President* (New York, Doubleday, 1939).

'American Men of Science: A Biographical Directory', ed. Jacques Cattell Press, *The Social and Behavioural Sciences* (New York, Bowker, 1968).

Anderson, B. M., *Economics and the Public Welfare: A Financial and Economic History of the United States 1914–46*, 1st edn 1949 (Indianapolis, Liberty Press, 1979).

Angell, J. W., 'Monetary Prerequisites for Employment Stabilisation' in Roos (ed.), *Stabilisation of Employment* (Bloomington, Indiana, Principia, 1933a).

——, 'Monetary Control and General Business Stabilisation' in *Economic Essays in Honour of Gustav Cassel* (London, Allen and Unwin, 1933b).

——, *The Behaviour of Money: Exploratory Studies* (London, McGraw Hill, 1936).

Archibald, C. G., 'Chamberlin versus Chicago', *Review of Economics and Statistics*, 28 (October 1961), pp. 2–28.

——, 'Reply to Chicago', *Review of Economics and Statistics*, 30 (1963), pp. 68–71.

Bach, G. L., 'Price Level Stabilisation: Some Theoretical and Practical Considerations' (unpublished dissertation University of Chicago, 1940).

Berle, A. A., *Navigating the Rapids, 1918–71*, ed. B. Berle and T. Jacobs (New York, Harcourt Brace, 1973).

Bordo, M. D. and A. Schwartz, 'Clark Warburton: Pioneer Monetarist', *Journal of Monetary Economics*, 5 (January 1987), pp. 43–66.

Boughton, J. M. and R. Sandilands, 'Politics and the Attack on FDR's Economists: From Grand Alliance to Cold War', *Intelligence and National Security*, 17:2 (forthcoming).

Brunner, K., 'On Lauchlin Currie's Contribution to Monetary Theory' in Currie (ed.), *Supply and Control of Money in the United States ...* (New York, Russell and Russell, 1968).

—— (ed.), *The Great Depression Revisited* (Boston, Kluwer, 1981).

Buckley, W. F. Jr, and Bozell, L. B., *McCarthy and his Enemies: the Record and its Meaning* (Chicago, Henry Regnery, 1954).

Cargill, T. F., 'Clark Warburton and the Development of Monetarism since the Great Depression', *History of Political Economy*, 11:3 (1979), pp. 425–49.

Carr, R., *The House Committee on Un-American Activities* (Ithaca, New York, Cornell UP, 1952).

Cate, J. L., 'Humanism and the Social Sciences: But what about John de Neushom?' in D. White (ed.), *The State of the Social Sciences* (Chicago, Chicago UP, 1956).

Chamberlin, E., *Towards a More General Theory of Value* (New York, Oxford UP, 1957).

Colander, D. and Landreth, H. (eds), *The Coming of Keynesianism to America* (Cheltenham, England, Edward Elgar, 1996).

Congdon, T., *Monetarism: An Essay in Definition* (London, Centre for Policy Studies, 1978).

Currie, L., 'The Treatment of Credit in Contemporary Monetary Theory', *Journal of Political Economy*, (1933), pp. 58–79.

——, *Supply and Control of Money in the United States*, 1st edn (Cambridge, Mass., Harvard UP, 1934).

——, 'The Failure of Monetary Policy to Prevent the Depression of 1929–32', reprinted in Hamilton *et al.* (eds), *Landmarks in Political Economy* (Chicago, Chicago UP, 1962).

——, *Supply and Control of Money in the United States together with A Proposed Revision of the Monetary System of the United States* (New York, Russell and Russell, 1968).

——, 'Comments and Observations', *History of Political Economy*, 10:4 (1978), pp. 541–8.

Douglas, P., *Real Wages in the United States 1890–1926* (Boston, Houghton Mifflin, 1930).

——, *The Theory of Wages* (New York, Macmillan, 1934).

——, *In the Fullness of Time* (New York, Harcourt Brace Jovanovich, 1972).

Douglas, W. O., *Go East, Young Man* (New York, Random House, 1974).

Eatwell, J., Milgate, M. and Newman, P. (eds), *The New Palgrave A Dictionary of Economics* (London, Macmillan, 1987).

Egbert, A. O., 'Marriner S. Eccles and the Banking Act of 1935' (PhD, Brigham Young University, 1967).

Fischer, S., 'Long-Term Contracts, Rational Expectations, and the Optimal Money Supply Rule', *Journal of Political Economy*, 85:1 (1977), pp. 191–205.

Fisher, I., *Booms and Depressions: Some First Principles* (London, George Allen & Unwin, 1933).

Friedman, M., 'The Spending Tax as a Wartime Fiscal Measure', *American Economic Review*, (March 1943), pp. 50–62.

——, *Essays in Positive Economics* (Chicago, Chicago UP, 1953).

——, 'More on Archibald versus Chicago', *Review of Economics and Statistics*, 30 (1963), pp. 65–7.

——, In Kitch, *Journal of Law and Economics*, XXVI (April 1983), pp. 163–234.

Friedman, M. and Friedman, R., *Two Lucky People: Memoirs* (Chicago, Chicago UP, 1998).

Friedman, M. and Schwartz, A., *A Monetary History of the United States* (Princeton, Princeton UP, 1963).

——, *Monetary Statistics of the United States* (New York, Columbia UP, 1970).

Green, G. D., 'The Ideological Origins of the Revolution in American Financial Policies' in K. Brunner (ed.), *The Great Depression Revisited* (Boston, Kluwer, 1981).

Halm, G., *Monetary Theory: A Modern Treatment of the Essentials of Money and Banking* (Philidelphia, Blackiston, 1942).

Hamilton, E. J., 'Preface' in Hamilton *et al.* (eds), *Landmarks in Political Economy* (Chicago, Chicago UP, 1962).

Hamilton, E. J., Rees, A. and Johnson, H. G. (eds), *Landmarks in Political Economy* (Chicago, Chicago, UP, 1962).

Hammond, J. D., 'Labels and Substance: Friedman's Restatement of the Quantity Theory', *History of Political Economy*, 31:3 (Fall 1999), pp. 449–71.

Hart, A., 'Anticipations, Business Planning and the Cycle' (unpublished University of Chicago dissertation, 1936).

Hartwell, R. M., *A History of the Mont Pelerin Society* (Indianapolis, Liberty Fund, 1995).

Hegeland, H., *The Quantity Theory of Money: A Critical Study of its Historical Development and Interpretation and a Restatement*, 1st edn 1951 (New York, Augustus Kelley Reprints, 1969).

Ickes, H. L., *The Secret Diary of Harold L. Ickes: The First Thousand Days* (New York, Simon and Schuster, 1953).

Kemp, J., 'Foreword' in Anderson, *Economics and the Public Welfare* (Indianapolis, Liberty Press, 1979).

Kitch, E. W., 'The Fire of Truth: A Remembrance of Law and Economics at Chicago, 1932–1970', *Journal of Law and Economics*, XXVI (April 1983), pp. 163–234.

Knight, F., *The Ethics of Competition and Other Essays* (London, George Allen and Unwin, 1935).

——, '"What is Truth" in Economics?', *Journal of Political Economy*, XLVIII:1 (February 1940), pp. 1–32.

Krooss, H. E. (ed.), *Documentary History of Banking and Currency in the United States* (New York, McGraw Hill, 1969), vols 1 and 4.

Laidler, D., 'The Role of the History of Economic Thought in Modern Macroeconomics', in P. Mizen (ed.), *Monetary History, Exchange Rates and Financial Markets: Essays in Honour of Charles Goodhart* (Aldershot, UK and Northampton MA, Edward Elgar Publishing, 2003), Vol. 2, pp. 12–29.

Laidler, D. and M. Parkin, 'Demand for Money in the United Kingdom, 1956–1967 Some Preliminary Estimates', *Manchester School*, 38 (September 1970), pp. 187–208.

Lee, J-K. and D. C. Wellington, 'Angell and the Stable Money Rule', *Journal of Political Economy*, 92:5 (1984), pp. 972–8.

Leeson, R., 'Inflation, Disinflation and the Natural Rate of Unemployment: A Dynamic Framework for Policy Analysis' in *The Australian Economy in the 1990s* (Sydney, Reserve Bank of Australia, 2000a).

——, *The Eclipse of Keynesianism: The Political Economy of the Chicago Counter Revolution* (New York, Palgrave Macmillan, 2000b).

——, *Economics: Origins of the Modern Configuration*, forthcoming.

Lundberg, E., *Studies in Economic Instability and Change*, ed. R. Henriksson (Stockholm, SNS Forlag, 1994).

Lutz, F. and Mints, L. (eds), *Readings in Monetary Theory* (American Economic Association, London, George Allen and Unwin, 1952).

Mankiw, N. G., 'Small Menu Costs and Large Business Cycles: A Macroeconomic Model of Monopoly', *Quarterly Journal of Economics*, 100, (May 1985), pp. 529–39.

Marget, A. W., *The Theory of Prices: A Re-examination of the Central Problems of Monetary Theory* (New York, Prentice-Hall, 1938).

——, 'Monetary Theory at the Textbook Level', *American Economic Review*, (December 1942), pp. 775–90.

McCann, C. R. and Perlman, M., 'On Thinking about George Stigler', *Economic Journal*, 103:419 (1993), pp. 994–1014.

McCloskey, D., *Knowledge and Persuasion in Economics* (Cambridge, Cambridge UP, 1994).

Milgate, M. and Levy, A., 'James Waterhouse Angell' in Eatwell *et al.* (eds), *The New Palgrave: A Dictionary of Economics* (London, Macmillan, 1987), Vol. 1, pp. 94–5.

Moggridge, D., *Maynard Keynes: An Economist's Biography* (London, Routledge, 1992).

Moley, R., *After Seven Years* (New York, Harper, 1939).

Neisser, H., *Some International Aspects of the Business Cycle* (Philadelphia, Pennsylvania UP, 1936).

Nourse, E., 'Director's Preface' in Pasvolsky, *Current Monetary Issues* (Washington DC, Brookings Institution, 1933).

Parkin. M., 'The Output-Inflation Trade-Off When Prices are Costly to Change', *Journal of Political Economy*, (February 1986).

Pasvolsky, L., *Current Monetary Issues* (Washington, DC, Brookings Institution, 1933).

Patinkin, D., 'Interest' in *International Encyclopedia of the Social Sciences* (New York, Macmillan and Free Press, 1968).

——, *Keynes' Monetary Thought: A Study of its Development* (Durham, North Carolina, Duke UP, 1976).

——, 'Keynes' aggregate supply function: a plea for common sense', *History of Political Economy*, 10:4 (1978), pp. 577–96.

——, *Essays on and in the Chicago Tradition* (Durham, North Carolina, Duke UP, 1981).

Reagan, P. D., *The Architects of Modern American National Planning* (PhD, Ohio State University, 1982).

Reed, H., *Money, Currency and Banking* (New York, McGraw Hill, 1942).

——, 'Review of Goldenweiser's *Monetary Management*', *American Economic Review*, (1950), pp. 208–11.

Rees, D., *Harry Dexter White: A Study in Paradox* (London, Macmillan, 1973).

Reeve, J. E., *Monetary Reform Movements: A Survey of Recent Plans and Panaceas* (Washington, American Council on Public Affairs, 1943).

Revere, R. H., *Senator Joe McCarthy* (London, Methuen, 1959).

Roberts, D., 'Patinkin, Keynes and Aggregate Demand and Supply Analysis', *History of Political Economy*, 10:4 (1978), pp. 549–76.

Robertson, D. H., 'Review of Angell's *The Behaviour of Money: Exploratory Studies*', *Economic Journal*, (June, 1937), pp. 330–3.

Roos, C. F. (ed.), *Stabilisation of Employment* (Bloomington, Indiana, Principia, 1933).

Roosevelt, F. D., *F. D. R.: His Personal Letters* (New York: Dual, Sloan and Pearce, 1950).

Rosen, S., 'George J. Stigler and the Industrial Organization of Economic Thought', *Journal of Political Economy*, 101:5 (October 1993), pp. 809–17.

Rymes, T. K. (ed.), *Keynes's Lectures, 1932–35: Notes of a Representative Student* (London, Macmillan, 1988).

Salant, W. S., 'The Inflationary Gap: Meaning and Significance for Policy Making', *American Economic Review*, XXXII (June 1942), pp. 308–14.

Samuelson, P. A., 'Paul Anthony Samuelson (b. 1915)' in Colander and Landreth (eds), *The Coming of Keynesianism to America* (Cheltenham, England, Edward Elgar, 1996).

Sandilands, R., *The Life and Political Economy of Lauchlin Currie: New Dealer, Presidential Adviser and Development Economist* (Durham, Duke UP, 1990).

——, 'Guilt by Association? Lauchlin Currie's Alleged Involvement with Washington Economists in Soviet Espionage', *History of Political Economy*, 32:3 (Fall 2000), pp. 473–515.

Saunders, S., 'Patinkin and Talmudic Readings in the History of Economics' (paper presented to the Patinkin conference, Lausanne, September 2001).

Schlesinger, A. M., *The Politics of Upheaval* (Boston, Houghton Mifflin, 1960).

Schwartz, A. J., 'Understanding 1929–33' in K. Brunner (ed.), *The Great Depression Revisited* (Boston, Kluwer, 19981).

Simon, H. A., *Models of my Life* (USA, Basic Books, 1991).

Simons, H. C., 'Money and the New Deal: Review of Pasvolsky's *Current Monetary Issues*', *New Republic*, 21 (February 1934), pp. 53–4.

Snyder, C., *Business Cycles and Business Measurements: Studies in Quantitative Economics* (New York, Macmillan, 1927).

Stein, H., *On the other Hand … Essays on Economics, Economists, and Politics* (Washington DC, AEI Press, 1995).

Steindl, F. G., *Monetary Interpretations of the Great Depression* (Ann Arbor, Michigan UP, 1995).

Stigler, G., 'Comment on the Chicago School', *Journal of Political Economy*, 70 (February 1962) pp. 70–1.

——, 'Archibald Versus Chicago', *Review of Economics and Statistics*, 30 (1963), pp. 63–4.

——, 'Does Economics Have a Useful Past?', *History of Political Economy*, 1:2 (Fall 1969), pp. 217–30.

——, 'A Survey of Contemporary Economics', *Journal of Political Economy*, LVII:2 (April 1974), pp. 93–105.

——, 'Henry Calvert Simons', *Journal of Law and Economics*, (April 1974), pp. 1–5.

——, *Memoirs of an Unregulated Economist* (New York, Basic Books, 1988).

Stigler, G. and C. Friedland, 'The Citation Practices of Doctorates in Economics', *Journal of Political Economy*, 83:3 (1975) pp. 477–507.

Stormer, J. A., *None Dare Call it Treason* (Florissant, Missouri, Liberty Bell, 1964).

Taylor, J. B., 'Staggered Wage Setting in a Macro Model', *American Economic Review*, 69 (May 1979), pp. 108–13.

Time, *Time Capsule 1929: A History of the Year Condensed From the Pages of Time* (New York, Time, 1967).

Tugwell, R., *In Search of Roosevelt* (Cambridge, Mass., Harvard UP, 1972).

Wallis, W. A., 'George J. Stigler: In Memorandum', *Journal of Political Economy*, 101:5 (October 1993), pp. 774–89.

Warburg, P., 'Testimony' in Krooss (ed.), *Documentary History of Banking and Currency in the United States* (New York, McGraw Hill, 1969), vol. 4.

Warburton, C., *The Economic Results of Prohibition* (New York, Columbia UP, 1932).

——, 'The Trend of Savings', *Journal of Political Economy*, 43 (1935), pp. 84–101.

——, 'Measuring the Inflationary Gap', *American Economic Review*, 33 (1943), pp. 303–69.

——, 'Monetary Expansion and the Inflationary Gap', *American Economic Review*, (June 1944), pp. 303–27.

——, 'The Volume of Money and the Price Level between the World Wars', *Journal of Political Economy*, LIII (1945), pp. 150–63.

——, 'Quantity and Frequency of Use of Money in the United States, 1919–45', *Journal of Political Economy*, (October 1946), pp. 442–50.

——, 'Volume of Savings, Quantity of Money and Business Instability' *Journal of Political Economy*, LV (June 1947), pp. 222–33.

——, 'Hansen and Fellner on Full Employment Policy', *American Economic Review*, XXXVIII:1 (March 1948), pp. 128–34.

——, 'Monetary Policy and Business Forecasting, Parts I and II', *Journal of Business of the University of Chicago*, 22 (1949), pp. 71–82, 178–87.

——, 'Misplaced Emphasis in Contemporary Business-Fluctuation Theory' reprinted in Lutz and Mints (eds), *Readings in Monetary Theory* (American Economic Association; London, George Allen and Unwin, 1952).

——, 'Money and Business Fluctuations in the Schumpeterian System', *Journal of Political Economy*, 61 (1953), pp. 509–22.

——, 'Money and Business Cycles', *Review of Economics and Statistics*, (February 1963), pp. 77–8.

——, 'Monetary Disequilibrium Theories in the First Half of the Twentieth Century', *History of Political Economy*, 13:2 (1981), pp. 285–99.

White, D. (ed.), *The State of the Social Sciences* (Chicago, Chicago UP, 1956).

Whittlesey, C. R., *Banking and the New Deal*, Public Policy Pamphlet No. 16 (Chicago, Chicago UP, 1935).

Yeager, L. B., 'Clark Warburton, 1896–1979', *History of Political Economy*, 13:2 (1981), pp. 279–84.

'Role of non-Chicagoan Economists'

T. M. Humphrey, 'Role of non-Chicagoan economists in the evolution of the Quantity Theory in America', *Southern Economic Journal*, 38 (July 1971), pp. 12–18.

ROLE OF NON-CHICAGO ECONOMISTS IN THE EVOLUTION OF THE QUANTITY THEORY IN AMERICA 1930–1950*

THOMAS M. HUMPHREY

Federal Reserve Bank of Richmond

In his famous restatement of the quantity theory Milton Friedman observes that, while the quantity theory approach generally fell into disrepute after 1929,

> Chicago was one of the few academic centers at which the quantity theory continued to be a central and vigorous part of the oral tradition throughout the 1930's and 1940's ... The quantity theory that retained this role differed sharply from the atrophied and rigid caricature that is so frequently described by proponents of the new income-expenditure approach—and with some justice to judge by much of the literature on policy that was spawned by quantity theorists. At Chicago Henry Simons and Lloyd Mints directly, Frank Knight and Jacob Viner at one remove, developed a more subtle and relevant version.... [6, 3].

Although this statement sharply distinguishes between the Chicago approach (the "more subtle and relevant version") and the constant-velocity quantity theory extant in the 1930's, it omits possible connections between the Chicago version and the earlier (Fisherine) quantity theory tradition in the U. S. It also implies that the contemporary Chicago version had its roots primarily in the teachings and doctrines of an earlier generation of Chicago economists. The modern quantity theory, it seems to say, was born at Chicago and developed there largely in isolation from the rest of the profession. In short, Friedman's statement suggests that the modern Chicago approach is separate and distinct from the earlier Fisherine tradition, that it has but few links with that tradition and cannot be viewed as evolving out of it.

Recently, Patinkin has criticized Friedman's interpretation of the role of his Chicago predecessors in shaping his monetary views. Patinkin [13, 50–58] argues that, far from originating a radically new approach to the quantity theory, Friedman's mentors largely adhered to the established Fisherine transaction velocity framework. Patinkin [13, 47, 61] states further that the origins of Friedman's portfolio demand-for-cash approach to monetary theory are to be found in the Keynesian analysis of liquidity preference, and not in the doctrines of Mints and Simons.

Overlooked by both Patinkin and Friedman is another significant influence on modern Chicago monetary thought, namely, the writings of American quantity theorists outside the University of Chicago. The work of these non-Chicago economists has its roots in and emanates from the earlier Fisherine tradition and thus represents a clear and direct line of development from the earlier approach to the contemporary one. In fact, several of the doctrines currently espoused by Chicago monetary economists orginated *not* with Friedman's mentors, but with these non-Chicago quantity theorists. It is odd that Friedman overlooked these other writers, because their work was so conspicuous in the 30's and 40's, when so few economists were arguing that "money matters."

This paper outlines the contributions of those writers who represent the bridge between the earlier and newer versions of the quantity theory. Special attention is given to the innovations of this group which have been adopted in the contemporary Chicago version. This evaluation is to dispel the impression that the modern Chicago quan-

* I am indebted to James Parthemos, Aubrey N. Snellings and Richard H. Timberlake, Jr. for their helpful comments

tity theory is largely divorced from the earlier Fisherine tradition.

EXTRA-CHICAGO INNOVATIONS

The most important non-Chicago quantity theorists bridging the interval 1930–1950 were Carl Snyder, Lionel Edie, Lauchlin Currie, and Clark Warburton.

In the 1920's Snyder[1] offered an empirical reconciliation of Irving Fisher's long-run, secular quantity theory with the short-run cyclical behavior of money and prices. Fisher's contemporaries thought him unable or unwilling to reconcile his secular quantity theory with his theory of credit cycles, and most of his critics had concentrated on this point. Snyder [16] demonstrated that in the short run, oscillations in velocity are accompanied by similar short run fluctuations in trade. Hence, over the cycle, the ratio V/T is roughly constant, giving a proportional relation between money and the price level. Secularly, however, the ratio V/T showed a downward trend. While there were weaknesses in Snyder's work—particularly his exclusive focus on the transaction velocity of demand deposits—his work must be recognized as a pioneer attempt to reconcile within the framework of a single empirical model both the secular and cyclical behavior of money and prices. Friedman's work today likewise makes many attempts to reconcile secular and cyclical behavior of quantity theory variables.

Snyder argued that the ratio V/T, though relatively constant in the short run, exhibited a downward secular trend due solely to the trend growth rate of T which Snyder estimated to be 4 per cent annually.[2] Since $P = (V/T)\,M$, Snyder [16, 712–3; 17, 197–8] suggested that the money supply should expand by 4 per cent annually to compensate for the 4 per cent fall in the (V/T) ratio in order to maintain price-level stability. Lionel Edie [4, 47–8, 117–18] in the late 20's and early 30's urged that this constant 4 per cent growth rate of the money supply be instituted as the sole policy guide for the monetary authority. Edie had examined the growth rate rule along with other stabilization criteria and found it to be the most satisfactory. In his examination Edie developed several points identical to those now associated with Friedman. Edie judged the other stabilization criteria deficient because of their ambiguity and because they relied upon imperfectly understood links between policy guides and policy goals. He was opposed to cyclical and seasonal variations in the growth of the money stock [4, 119–23]. He thought price-level stabilization a desirable goal, but he felt it could be better attained indirectly via the growth-rate rule than via direct stabilization of a price index. The latter policy, he felt, was handicapped by the existence of imperfectly understood links as well as variable lags and required too much discretion (choice of the index) to be left with the monetary authority [4, 29–30, 42–3, 114–5]. He stated that a boom could be halted by a cessation in the *growth* of the money stock, *i.e.*, an absolute contraction of the money supply was not necessary to cause a downturn [4, 120]. Other economists—including Harold Reed [14, 81–2] and James Harvey Rogers—followed Edie in advocating the constant growth rate rule. Thus, the fixed growth rate rule that Friedman now advocates originated with Snyder and Edie and *not* with his Chicago mentors. Friedman's teachers at Chicago—Simons and Mints—were, in fact, exponents of price index stabilization rather than a money-growth rate rule as a policy guide.

Lauchlin Currie's contributions to the evolution of the quantity theory were of great significance. Currie was the first American economist to replace the transaction velocity concept with the income velocity concept. Although the income velocity concept itself was used by A. C. Pigou in 1927, it was ignored by American economists until

[1] Snyder [17; 18] summarizes his earlier studies and the conclusions he had already reached in the 1920's.

[2] Snyder thought the trend of V to be horizontal.

Currie used it in his analysis in the 1930's.[3] Thereafter, the concept was almost exclusively employed, replacing the Fisherine transaction velocity concept in most analyses. Currie thus 1) transformed the quantity theory into a relation between money supply and the national income (instead of prices) and 2) made the equation of exchange more operational (national income is more easily estimated than the total volume of transactions.)

Currie's second contribution was his trenchant criticism of Federal Reserve theory and policy [3, 34–62]. He pointed out the failure of the Reserve Administration to appreciate the connection between the money supply and the level of economic activity, and he called attention to the inappropriate policies adopted as a consequence. Currie attributed the impotence of monetary policy in the 1930's to Reserve officials' philosophy, attitudes, and misconceptions of their role rather than to the weaknesses of the technical links between monetary policy and real income. He argued convincingly that a philosophy of credit policy (instead of monetary policy) had thoroughly permeated Federal Reserve thinking. He contended that the administration's commitment to the objective of controlling the use of credit and the quality of bank assets rendered it incapable of discerning or implementing proper counter-cyclical monetary policy. All of the specific criticisms that Currie voiced in the mid-1930's were later echoed in the writings of the Chicago economists, Mints and Friedman. Oddly enough, however, Mints and Friedman do not seem to be aware of the extent to which their criticisms were anticipated by Currie, for they cite him infrequently.[4]

Currie was the *only* American monetary theorist in the early 1930's to hold the Federal Reserve authorities responsible for precipitating the Great Depression.

> The policy followed throughout 1929, so far from tending to prevent the depression, actually operated . . . to bring it on. There is no justification, therefore, for the frequent citation of the monetary and business developments of 1929 and 1930 as evidence of the *inability* of the Reserve administration to prevent the depression [2, 176].

This same view—holding the central bank largely responsible for the depression because of its inept policies—is now part of the current Chicago interpretation of American financial history. But, as Friedman [8] himself points out, it was *not* the interpretation of events adopted by his mentors—those who supposedly fathered the Chicago quantity theory. At the same time that Currie was blaming the Reserve administration for causing the depression, Simons was agreeing with the official Reserve explanation that the depression was initiated not by a reduction in the money supply's growth rate, but by a deterioration of confidence, a panic-induced rise in the demand for cash (fall in velocity) and the consequent collapse of the inherently unstable banking structure—forces that the Federal Reserve System was powerless to prevent.

Contrary to Simons' interpretation, the variability of velocity played no role in Currie's explanation. As Currie saw it, the downswing in business activity was preceded by high interest rates and inadequate growth of the money supply rather than a fall in velocity. Currie argued that business activity had reached its peak in mid-1929. The stabilization of activity at this level (transforming the peak into a plateau) required reduction in interest rates to stimulate new investment to offset savings forthcoming at this high income level.[5] But the Federal

[3] The income velocity concept was, of course, implied in earlier work of Marshall, Wicksell, and Pigou, but, as Joseph Schumpeter has said, "It was not before the publication of Pigou's *Industrial Fluctuations* that the various types of velocity were clearly distinguished and that most important of them . . . Income Velocity was brought home to the profession at large" [15, 1098].

[4] Currie is never mentioned in Friedman's and Schwartz's *Monetary History of the United States*, and he is referred to only three times in Lloyd Mints, *A History of Banking Theory*.

[5] The appearance of interest rate effects in Currie's analysis is not quite in line with the quantity

Reserve, preoccupied with the dominant objective of checking stock market speculation, actually *raised* interest rates. (Currie said that the higher interest rates were chiefly attributable to the Reserve's restrictive policies and not to the increased speculators' demand for loans.) The higher interest rate had no effect on stock speculation (stock speculation being insensitive to interest rate changes), but it did inhibit new investment spending required to offset saving and keep the economy operating close to capacity. Lower interest rates could have been attained easily had the Federal Reserve purchased sufficient volume of securities in the open market in early 1929. Currie argued that the stock market crash would have occurred anyway, regardless of Federal Reserve action. But he thought that the crash would have affected business activity only slightly had not restrictive Federal Reserve policy already permitted it to turn down from its trend.

> Although a break in the stock market should normally be expected to make for a decline in investment and an increase in saving, the net effect on business activity will be largely determined by the trend of business at the time of the break. Thus a break may merely moderate an upswing or it may accelerate a downswing. The depressing effect of the 1929 crash was due not so much to its violence as to its having occurred after business had turned downward [2, 176].

Had the Reserve administration acted, prior to the crash, to stimulate investment and real income, then the crash itself would have exerted but little adverse impact on the level of national income.

Currie's interpretation is remarkable for several reasons: 1) he skillfully combines the quantity theory with a pre-Keynesian saving-investment analysis, yet eschews the notion of unstable velocity. 2) He places blame on the Federal Reserve for *causing* the depression. Other quantity theorists in the early 1930's, including Fisher [5, 347], W. I. King [9; 10], and H. G. Brown [1, 82, 107] were highly critical of the central bank for permitting the depression to *worsen*.[6] They did not, however, argue as Currie did that the Reserve was largely responsible for the initial downturn in business activity. It would appear that Friedman's criticism of Reserve policy of the late 20's and 30's can be traced to Currie (and also to Fisher's circle) before Henry Simons.

The last of the major "gap-bridgers" during the transition period was Clark Warburton. Warburton's work in the 1940's was essentially a project of meticulous empirical verification of the earlier suggestions of Fisher, Snyder, Edie, and Currie.[7] Warburton's analytical framework was the equation of exchange. Having available more detailed and elaborate time series of relevant data (some of these series constructed by Warburton himself) than his predecessors, he was able to demonstrate that their insights and conclusions about the importance of money were correct.

Like Snyder and Edie, Warburton believed that economic stability required price level stability and that price level stability in turn required that the money supply grow at a certain trend rate. In estimating this necessary trend rate, Warburton [19, 109–12, 163–7] started with the equation of exchange.

(1) $M_t = P_tQ_t/R_t$, where all of the items are index numbers, that is, ratios of magnitude at time t to base period magnitudes. The index of output in any year subsequent to the base year is expressed as

theory. However, his other arguments are certainly in line with the theory. They include the following: 1) Fluctuations of the money supply *precede* changes in the interest rate. Primacy of money over the interest rate is stressed. 2) The interest rate is a treacherous policy guide. 3) The money supply or its growth rate is the only suitable policy guide. 4) The Federal Reserve's use of the interest rate (reflecting its concern with credit policy rather than monetary policy) and stock speculation as policy guides resulted in the monetary disturbance which caused the downswing.

[6] Fisher, King and Brown repeatedly stated that the Federal Reserve could have halted the depression via open market operations.

[7] Warburton's important papers written in the 1940's and early 1950's are contained in [19].

(2) $Q_t = (1 + i)^t N_t H_o$, where t is number of years from the initial (base) period, i is the percentage growth rate of output per head due to technical progress, N_t is an index number of population size, relative to its base period size, and H_o is an index of output per capita in the base period. The base period selected is one in which output would be at its full potential. The index (R_t) of the rate of use of money relative to the base-year rate may be expressed as

(3) $R_t = 1/(1 + j)^t C_o$ where j is the percentage growth rate of the ratio of average cash balances to expenditure for final product and C_o is the base period index of that ratio. Assuming the price level to remain stable ($P_t = P_o$) and substituting (2) and (3) into (1), we get

(4) $M_t = [(1 + i)\ (1 + j)]^t P_o N_t H_o C_o$. As P_o, H_o, C_o—the base period index numbers —all equal unity, equation (4) reduces to

(5) $M_t = [(1 + i)\ (1 + j)]^t N_t$. If we further assume that population grows at k per cent annually, we get

(6) $M_t = [(1 + i)\ (1 + j)\ (1 + k)]^t N_o$,

or

(7) $M_t = [(1 + i)\ (1 + j)\ (1 + k)]^t M_o$ since $M_o = N_o = 1$.

Warburton [19, 154] estimated the trend growth rates to be $i = 2$ per cent, $j = 1.5$ per cent, and $k = 1.5$ per cent, thus requiring a growth rate of the money supply of approximately 5 per cent to attain both full capacity production and price level stability. His estimate of the necessary growth rate of M differed from Snyder's and Edie's. The latter economists detected no trend in velocity and thus thought that M would only have to grow as fast as output. Warburton's work came ten to fifteen years later during which time velocity suffered a marked decline. He therefore detected a downward trend in velocity and concluded that the money supply would have to grow at a rate sufficient to offset both the growth rate of output and the rate of decline of velocity.

In his analysis of the cyclical relation of the money stock and the level of national income, Warburton's standard procedure was first to estimate the trend values of the equation of exchange items and secondly to "remove the trend," observing the deviations from trend of the actual values of the items. For a growing economy, he said, the equation of exchange would have to be written as:

$$\{[(1 + i)(1 + j)]^t M'_t\}\{[1/(1 + j)^t]R'_t\} = P'_t\{(1 + i)^t Q'_t\}$$

where i is the trend growth rate of output, j the trend rate of decrease of velocity and M'_t, R'_t, P'_t, and Q'_t are the ratios of the index numbers of the exchange equation items relative to their trend values. Removing the trend (setting $i = j = 0$) gives the income-velocity version of the equation of exchange $M_t R_t = P_t Q_t = Y_t$.

Warburton's work on secular trends was but a prolegomena to his more important investigation of the cyclical behavior of the exchange equation variables, especially the lead-lag relation of those variables at cyclical turning points. Comparing series of deviations of M and V from their trend values with standard NBER reference dates of business cycle peaks and troughs, he found that the money supply changes consistently lead and velocity changes lag turning points in economic activity. Further investigation revealed that variations in the money supply (adjusted for trend) were preceded by or coincidental with, variation in bank reserves.

On the basis of his evidence, Warburton drew the following conclusions.

1. An erratic money supply is *the* main *cause* of a downturn in economic activity; that is, a significant departure of the money supply from its trend growth rate is the leading cause of the subsequent downturn in economic activity. Furthermore, the greater the departure of the money stock from its normal growth trend, the greater the length and severity of the depression.

2. A fall in velocity is a secondary force intensifying but not initiating a downswing. Velocity is an endogenous variable whose behavior depends upon prior changes in the money stock. Warburton was emphatic in his denial of the view expressed by Keynes and by Simons that velocity is an independent causal factor initiating a downswing.

3. The stock of money outstanding is determined by the availability of bank reserves and *not* by the actions (loan demands or loan repayments) of bank customers. The link between reserves and deposits is strong. Banks will normally be fully "loaned up." Hence, the quantity of money is dominated by central bank policies affecting bank reserves. In the final analysis, Federal Reserve actions are the main cause of changes in M.

These conclusions, substantiated by Warburton in the 1940's, have been accepted and confirmed by Friedman and Schwartz in their recent *Monetary History of the United States*. Of those economists mentioned in this paper, Friedman [7, 301, 320, 359, 406, 408, 525, 776] only acknowledges Warburton as an influence. But the presence of Warburton's influence in Friedman's work is enough to connect Friedman with both the earlier American tradition and the other authors of the transition period. For, as Warburton himself often points out, the hypotheses underlying his empirical work were derived from early twentieth century statements of the quantity theory, and his analyses parallel those of Snyder, Edie, and Currie. If Warburton influenced Friedman, then the latter is the intellectual heir of the equation of exchange theorists.

CONCLUSION

In summary, Friedman's implication that the contemporary version of the quantity theory was born and nurtured in the University of Chicago in the 30's and 40's, while the old version of the theory withered and died outside seems not to be an accurate evaluation. In fact, much the opposite seems to have happened. Non-Chicago economists continued in the 20's, 30's and 40's to make important improvements and extensions of the old theory—improvements and extensions which anticipated Friedman's modern version but which are not to be found in the published works of his mentors during that time.

When one compares doctrines, now embraced by Friedman, which were developed in the 30's and 40's by non-Chicago economists, with the doctrines then espoused by Friedman's teachers, one gains the impression that Friedman's quantity theory descends from the former rather than from the latter group. Non-Chicago economists investigated the necessary growth rate of the money supply for stabilizing P and stated the growth-rate rule while Friedman's Chicago forebears were advocating a rule in terms of stabilizing a price index. Non-Chicago economists were arguing that deviations of the money stock from its normal growth trend caused the depression at a time when Chicago economists were agreeing with Keynes that exogenous fluctuations of velocity were the basic cause. Non-Chicago economists were fixing blame squarely on the Federal Reserve System for initiating and aggravating the downswing, while Chicago economists were attributing the severity of the downswing and the accompanying rash of bank failures to the unstable structure of the banking system. In contrast to Chicago economists of this period, non-Chicago quantity theorists offered detailed empirical verification of their hypotheses. The type of painstaking analysis of data contributed by Snyder and Warburton was not forthcoming from the pens of Simons and Mints in the 30's and early 40's. In the late 40's Mints [12] offered a test to determine whether Federal Reserve action had been destabilizing and perverse (Currie's original argument). But Mints' test—which compared the extent and direction of change of Federal Reserve credit with changes in the wholesale price index—was far less sophisticated and detailed than the studies of Warburton.

The current notion of the 1930's and 1940's as the dark ages of the quantity theory also seems open to question. Dark ages they were if one judges by the sparse number of economists working to improve and extend the quantity theory. The number of economists, however, is not the appropriate criterion. Although the innovators themselves were few in number, the advances they made, primarily in the empirical verification and policy orientation of the quantity theory in the 30's and 40's would seem sufficient to mark those decades as an important transition era in the evolution of the American quantity theory.

REFERENCES

1. Brown, Harry G. *Economic Science and the Common Welfare*. 6th ed. Columbia, Missouri: Lucas Brothers, 1936.
2. Currie, Lauchlin, "The Failure of Monetary Policy to Prevent the Depression of 1929–1932," *The Journal of Political Economy*, April 1934, 145–77.
3. ———. *The Supply and Control of Money in the United States*. Cambridge: Harvard University Press, 1935.
4. Edie, Lionel. *The Banks and Prosperity*. New York: Harper, 1931.
5. Fisher, Irving, "The Debt-Deflation Theory of Great Depressions," *Econometrica*, October 1933, 337–57.
6. Friedman, Milton, "The Quantity Theory of Money—A Restatement," in *Studies in the Quantity Theory of Money*, edited by Milton Friedman. Chicago: University of Chicago Press, 1956.
7. ———, and Schwartz, Anna. *A Monetary History of the United States 1869–1960*. Princeton: Princeton University Press, 1963.
8. ———, "The Monetary Theory and Policy of Henry Simons," *Journal of Law and Economics*, October 1967, 1–13.
9. King, Willford I., "The Immediate Cause of the Business Cycle," Supplement, *Journal of the American Statistical Association*, March 1932, 229.
10. ———, Statement in U. S. Congress, House, Subcommittee of the Committee on Banking and Currency. *Hearings on H. R. 10517, Stabilization of Commodity Price*. 72nd Cong. 1st session, 1932, 187, 194.
11. Mints, Lloyd. *A History of Banking Theory*. Chicago: University of Chicago Press, 1945.
12. ———, "Monetary Policy and Stabilization," *American Economic Review*, May 1951, 188–93.
13. Patinkin, Don, "The Chicago Tradition, the Quantity Theory and Friedman," *Journal of Money, Credit, and Banking*, February 1969, 46–70.
14. Reed, Harold L., "Federal Reserve Policy and Broker's Loans," Supplement, *American Economic Review*, March 1929, 81–2.
15. Schumpeter, Joseph. *History of Economic Analysis*. London: George Allen and Unwin, 1954.
16. Snyder, Carl, "New Measures in the Equation of Exchange," *American Economic Review*, December 1924, 699–713.
17. ———, "The Problem of Monetary and Economic Stability." *Quarterly Journal of Economics*, February 1935, 173–205.
18. ———. *Capitalism the Creator*. New York: Macmillan, 1940.
19. Warburton, Clark. *Depression, Inflation, and Monetary Policy*. Baltimore: Johns Hopkins Press, 1967.

'A Note on Professor Humphrey's Article'

L. Currie, 'A note on Professor Humphrey's Article', unpublished.

November 28, 1972

A NOTE ON PROFESSOR HUMPHREY'S ARTICLE

Lauchlin Currie

The "Chicago School" of monetary theory, headed by Professor Milton Friedman, of the University of Chicago, has preached :

(a) – The importance of changes in the supply of money in accounting for changes in price levels, and

(b) – The advantages of a steady non-discretionary growth in the money supply over a discretionary, compensatory policy aimed at achieving price stability under conditions of full employment.

In the accompanying article, Professor Humphrey has challenged the pretensions of originality of the Chicago School, tracing its views back to some non-Chicago economists, including me.

Professor Humphrey's article recalls a period of intense activity in my first field, monetary theory. From 1928 to 1934 I had given some 1.000 Harvard undergraduates and graduates a fairly rigorous course on the supply and control of money and the significance of that control. Unorthodox fiscal policy was also taught unobstrusively by me in a course on money and banking, from 1930 to 1934.

At the Federal Reserve Board, from 1934 to 1939, where I was Deputy Director of Research, my work was more in what might be called today macroeconomics or "depression economics" than in monetary theory, though I

Deputy Director of Research, my work was more in what might be called today macroeconomics or "depression economics" than in monetary theory, though I was an author of the Banking Act of 1935. I had stressed the degree of member bank indebtedness to the Federal Reserve Banks as a general strategic factor explaining the growth of reserves and hence of means of payments. But in the years immediately following the publication of my book on The Supply and Control of Money, the banks remained out of debt to the Federal . Later, and today, my argument became again relevant, so this remains a valid description of the functioning of the system.

The concept of income velocity goes back at least to the Marshallian "k" – the demand for money. (It is the inverse of the demand for money, that is, an income velocity of 3 is another way of saying that the community holds purchasing power in the form of money over the value of four months' production). Probably the reason both James Angel of Columbia and I calculated this at the same time was because the gross and net income figures for the United States were just then becoming available.

The relative stability of "k" gives support to the significance of changes in the supply of money. Some people have tried to insist that the "quantity theory" means a direct and a proportional relation of changes in the quantity of money to changes in prices. If they do not find this relation, the "quantity theory" is, they say, wrong. This is fallacious reasoning. All that has to be demonstrated is that, over time, the income velocity is relatively stable in order to grasp the extreme importance of changes in the volume of the means of payment relative to output. If the means of payment are expanding at a rate of 15% and the producto bruto at 5% – 6% it is hardly necessary to conduct a search for speculators, hoarders and middlemen to discover the source of inflation !

My insistence, in my PhD thesis, on the profound difference between "credit" and "means of payment", if it had then been taken to heart, would have spared the English the ludicrous plight of having now no series of money. It might also have avoided the strenuous efforts to distinguish between "productive" and "unproductive" credit. I take some credit for not only starting the United States official series of means of payment but also for insisting that the line between checking accounts and time and saving deposits be kept clear, as a contribution to clear thinking.

In my study of the distribution of ownership of demand deposits I found that business is the owner of the bulk of money. Hence any explanation of changes in "k" or income velocity, must start with business motivations, as well as with variations in the money stock.

The 100% reserve system was another simultaneous discovery -- this time with Henry Simons of Chicago University. However, his publication predated the appearance of my book by several months. In the same year, 1934, for the United States Treasury, I elaborated the system and set myself the exercise of suggesting how it might be grafted onto an existing fractional reserve system. It is interesting to note that the 100% tope occasionally used in Colombia is a modern variant of this system.

I was a little startled to find that I am credited by Professor Humphrey with being the only monetary theorist who held monetary policy "responsible" for the Great Depression. After this lapse of time the words must speak for themselves but my recollection, for what is worth, is that I did not intend to hold the Federal Reserve responsible for the Depression — many elements were necessary for that — but rather culpable for not pursuing a policy calculated to avoid or minimize, it but to precipitate the downturn and intensify its length and severity. In the passage cited "The policy ..... operated to bring it on" I suspect I was using the word "operated" in the sense of "tended". The distinction is perhaps subtle but I think important. It is more consistent with the long title of the piece "The Failure of Monetary Policy to Prevent the Depression of 1929-1932".

I differed from Milton Friedman in having much more faith in the possibility of discretionary, compensatory monetary policy than in a neutral policy. As I have gotten older, I am afraid that I have lost some of my optimism, as it was based on suppositions of knowledge and determination on the part of the money managers that have not always been in evidence. In all fairness, however, it must be admitted that cost - push inflation has taken much effective control out of the hands of the monetary authorities in economically advanced countries. The problem of price instability raised by exogenous price and income rises cannot be satisfactorily resolved through monetary means only without too great a cost in continuing unemployment.

'More on the Chicago Monetary Tradition'

D. Patinkin, 'More on the Chicago Monetary Tradition' (1973), reprinted in Patinkin, *Essays On and In the Chicago Tradition* (Durham, North Carolina, Duke UP, 1981), pp. 277–87.

11. More on the Chicago Monetary Tradition *

In a paper a few years ago on the nature of the Chicago School {see preceding chapter} I suggested that it would be interesting—though beyond the scope of that paper—to examine "the extent to which the policy views of the Chicago School in the 1930s represented those of the other quantity-theorists of the period" (above, p. 242, fn.5). Thomas Humphrey's recent note (1971) casts some interesting light upon this question, and I shall accordingly begin with some comments on it. I conclude with some general observations on the relations between the Chicago School of the 1930s and its contemporaries. I might note that the multifarious nature of these interrelationships raises the question of the proper basis of distinction between "Chicagoans" and "non-Chicagoans"—a question that I shall not, however, deal with here.

Humphrey's main point is that the present Chicago School as represented by Milton Friedman has been influenced by the work of American quantity theorists "outside The University of Chicago" during the 1930s and 1940s. More specifically:

> the work of these non-Chicago economists has its roots in and emanates from the earlier Fisherine tradition and thus represents a clear and direct line of development from the earlier approach to the contemporary one. In fact, several of the doctrines currently espoused by Chicago monetary economists originated not with Friedman's mentors, but with these non-Chicago quantity theorists (Humphrey 1971, p. 12).

In support of this contention, Humphrey cites evidence from the writings of Carl Snyder, Lionel Edie, Lauchlin Currie, and Clark Warburton—and states (1971, p.

Reprinted by permission from *Southern Economic Journal*, Jan. 1973, *39*, 454–59. Published originally under the title "On the Monetary Economics of Chicagoans and Non-Chicagoans: Comment." This was a comment on Thomas M. Humphrey's "Role of Non-Chicago Economists in the Evolution of the Quantity Theory in America 1930–1950" (1971). Slightly revised and expanded, in part by the reinsertion of material which was for various reasons deleted at the time.

* Work on this note was carried out in part while I was a Mills B. Lane Visiting Scholar at the University of Georgia in the fall of 1971. I am grateful to Robert R. Dince and Richard H Timberlake of the University of Georgia for helpful comments on an earlier draft I am also grateful to Martin Bronfenbrenner and Clarence E. Philbrook for their comments during a seminar at the University of North Carolina, Chapel Hill, where the latter part of this note was discussed I have also benefited from the criticisms of Milton Friedman and George Stigler Needless to say, none of the foregoing are to be held responsible for the views here expressed.

Finally—and with sadness—I express my deep indebtedness to the late Samuel H. Nerlove for his invaluable comments on an earlier draft of this note—comments which throw penetrating light on the respective roles of various economists at Chicago in the period under discussion. These comments are reproduced in the Appendix.

17) that only Warburton's influence is acknowledged by Friedman and Schwartz in their *Monetary History of the United States* (1963).[1]

Let me first of all say that Lionel Edie was not—strictly speaking—a "non-Chicagoan." In particular, the Annual Register of the University of Chicago for the academic years 1926/27–1928/29 (which in each case actually refers to the following academic year) list him as a professor of finance in what was then called the "School of Commerce and Administration" (and is now the Graduate School of Business).[2] During this period Frank H. Knight and Jacob Viner were full professors in the Department of Economics, Lloyd W. Mints, an assistant professor, and Henry C. Simons, first a lecturer and then an assistant professor. Indeed, according to the *Register*, in the academic year 1927–28 both Edie and Mints taught—in different quarters—the graduate course on "Money and Banking." Furthermore, in one case Edie was the chairman of a Ph.D. thesis committee of which Mints was a member (cf. p. 263 above).

It would nevertheless seem that from the viewpoint of the actual intellectual interaction between Edie and his colleagues in the Department of Economics, Humphrey is essentially correct in listing Edie as a "non-Chicagoan." For—as the late Samuel H. Nerlove (for many years Professor at The University of Chicago School of Business) wrote me [3]—"there was practically no real intellectual contact between Edie and the Economics Faculty during the short time he was in residence at Chicago." It is also noteworthy that Edie's many writings on monetary policy (1928, 1929, 1931, 1934, 1935) do not seem to contain any references to his colleagues in the economics department.[4]

In my opinion, however, Humphrey (1971, p. 13) is overstating the case when he writes that Edie preferred a policy of expanding bank credit at a steady rate to one directed at stabilizing the price index, on the grounds that the latter policy "was handicapped by the existence of imperfectly understood links as well as variable lags and required too much discretion (choice of the index) to be left with the monetary authority." I do not think that the pages of Edie's book (1931, pp. 29–30, 42–43, 114–15) on which Humphrey bases this statement can really be interpreted as referring to "imperfectly understood links" or to "variable lags"—certainly not in

1. Actually, Friedman and Schwartz do refer in this book to Carl Snyder (1963, pp. 252, 370, 374, 692). I should also note that in their subsequent volume on *Monetary Statistics of the United States*—which describes in detail the derivation of the series used in their *Monetary History*—Friedman and Schwartz do discuss the work of Currie (1970, pp. 268–70). They restrict themselves, however, to Currie's statistical work, and mention neither his monetary analysis nor his policy recommendations. Thus Humphrey's basic contention is unaffected. This is also the way in which Friedman and Schwartz (1970, pp. 270–71) treat the work of James Angell, mentioned below.

2. Note that the title page of the book by Edie (1931) that is cited by Humphrey (1971, p. 13) lists Edie's affiliations as "Vice-President, American Capital Corporation, Formerly Professor of Finance, University of Chicago."

3. In a letter commenting on an early draft of this note; reproduced in the Appendix.

4 It is true that Edie was one of those who gave a paper at the 1932 Harris Foundation Lectures on "Gold and Monetary Stabilization" which took place at The University of Chicago. But most of the participants in this conference (who included Angell and Snyder, as well as Irving Fisher) were non-Chicagoans—as was Edie at that time.

the sense that these terms are used today by Friedman and others to support their contention that the attempt to stabilize the price level might actually be destabilizing. Instead Edie's objections to price-level stabilization are stated in the following terms:

> Important as a stable unit is, the difficulties and dangers in attempting to attain it are great. Not least among these is the failure of economists to supply the scientific knowledge necessary for performance of the task. Economists have not agreed upon an index number to be used as a measure of the purchasing power of money. Although admitting that stabilization means *prevention* of undue fluctuations, and that prevention necessitates *forecasting*, nevertheless, they have been slow to develop a forecasting technique that can command confidence (1931, p. 30, italics in original).

I might also note that Edie did not seem to have too strong a preference for the growth-rate rule as against the price-stabilization rule. Thus in his earlier book on *Money, Bank Credit, and Prices* (1928, pp. 92, 470–93) he seems to be advocating the price stabilization policy—despite his many reservations about it. (It might be noted that Edie [1928, pp. 474–75] defines the central-bank policy necessary to achieve this stabilization not in terms of changes in the quantity of money or volume of credit, but in terms of the rediscount rate.) Again, in Edie's later book on *Dollars* (1934, pp. 278–79) he seems to be advocating the policy rule of price stabilization.

With reference to the other writers whom Humphrey cites (viz., Snyder, Currie, and Warburton), he [Humphrey] has little to say on what I would consider to be an even more interesting aspect of the question: namely, why the "original" Chicago school itself apparently did not refer to them? Insofar as Warburton is concerned, it is fair to say that this omission reflects the fact that his major studies (reprinted in Warburton, 1966) began appearing only in the mid-1940s—by which time Simons and other members of the Chicago School had long since formulated their position (see preceding chapter). Thus Reeve's (1943) comprehensive study of monetary discussions in the 1930s does not even contain a reference to Warburton.

This explanation may also hold—though with considerably less justification—for the case of Currie. For though Currie wrote some ten years before Warburton, his [Currie's] work appeared after the main features of the Chicago School position had been formulated. Indeed, in connection with his advocacy of "100% money" (which idea he apparently developed independently of the Chicago School), Currie himself referred (1934c, p. 156, fn.) to the 1933 Chicago memorandum on "Banking and Currency Reform" (cf. preceding chapter, p. 257). Similarly, Currie (1934b, p. 146, fn. 2) expressed his "substantial agreement" with C. O. Hardy (who was also connected with The University of Chicago, and who was indeed a teacher of Simons and Mints) [5] on the question of proper central-bank policy. Still, I agree with Humphrey's implication that the Chicago School should subsequently have taken

5. See again Professor Nerlove's letter in the Appendix.

more account of Currie's work.[6] And to this I would add that it should also have taken account of the work of Angell (1933, 1936).[7]

Though it does not bear on the present subject, there is one aspect of Humphrey's discussion of Currie which I would like to correct. This is Humphrey's statement (1971, p. 13) that "Currie was the first American economist to replace the transaction velocity concept with the income velocity concept." This is not the case. Currie's first published work making use of income velocity (a concept which he attributed to Schumpeter [1933, p. 91]) appeared in the same issue (November 1933) of the *Quarterly Journal of Economics* in which Angell (1933) employed the same concept, though denoting it as "circular velocity." Indeed, Currie subsequently wrote a note (1934a) to explain their different statistical findings. Furthermore, both Currie in his 1931 Ph.D. thesis (1931, p. 5, fn. 5) and Angell in the article just cited (1933, p. 43, fn. 5) refer to the use of the similar concept "circuit velocity" some ten years before by the American economists Foster and Catchings (1923, chapters 18–20, especially pp. 311–12). Similarly, Edie's 1928 textbook (pp. 395–98) includes a discussion of income velocity. Thus neither Angell nor Currie can be credited with having introduced this concept into the American scene.

There still remains the question as to why the original Chicago School did not refer to the work of Carl Snyder. And, frankly, what I find even more puzzling is a question which Humphrey does not discuss: namely why, in its policy discussions, the Chicago School of the 1930s and 1940s did not do justice to Irving Fisher—despite the fact that long before the Chicago School, Fisher had advocated the policy of stabilizing the price level as a means of mitigating—if not eliminating—cyclical fluctuations ("booms and depressions"). More specifically, ever since his *Purchasing Power of Money* (1911, chapter 4), if not before, Fisher had contended that business cycles were caused by the "dance of the dollar": by a changing price level which was not fully reflected in the nominal rate of interest, which failure therefore caused a change in the real rate of interest as perceived by entrepreneurs, and which change therefore caused them to undertake unwarranted expansions (or contractions) in their activities. Consequently, the way to prevent this succession of expansions and contractions was to stabilize the price level by means of a "compensated dollar." [8]

In the writings of Simons, I have not found any reference to these views of Fisher. And though Mints (1950, p. 10) did recognize that Fisher was "in more recent years . . . the strongest supporter of stabilizing the price level," he wrongly implied that this was only because of considerations of distributive justice to creditors and debtors, and not because price stability was "a necessary condition for the

6. On Currie's subsequent close connections with Viner, see pp. 268 above and 286 below. I might here also note that the index to Reeve's study (1943)—which had its origin as a Ph.D. thesis completed at Chicago in 1939 under a committee consisting of Mints (chairman), Viner, and G. V. Cox (above, p. 262)—has almost as many references to Currie as to Simons.

7. Who, incidentally, also studied at Chicago in the year (1919–20) between taking his A.B. degree at Harvard and beginning his graduate studies there. During that year, Angell served as Viner's teaching assistant (see above, p. 267).

8. Cf. Fisher (1920, 1923, 1925, 1932, and 1934). For a brief survey of Fisher's views on this point, see my "Non-Neutrality of Money in the Quantity Theory" (1972).

effective operation of a competitive system." As has just been emphasized, however—and as Mints himself had earlier recognized (1945, p. 272)—this was precisely Fisher's view of the matter. In contrast, Fisher (1935, p. ix) did refer to the Chicago School, and particularly Henry C. Simons, as being among the primary advocates of "100 percent money"—a proposal to which Fisher gave his unequivocal support.

In order to avoid any possible misunderstanding, I wish to emphasize that what I find puzzling here is the relation of the Chicago School to Fisher's policy views, as distinct from his theoretical contributions. Insofar as the latter are concerned, the theoretical framework of the Chicago School was explicitly based on Fisher's development of the quantity theory in terms of the equation of exchange, $MV + M'V' = PT$. Correspondingly, the chapters of Fisher's classic work on the *Purchasing Power of Money* (1911) in which this equation was explicated were required reading at Chicago (cf. above, pp. 5, 245, and 250).

Humphrey rightly notes (1971, p. 17) that the present Chicago School with its emphasis on the empirical verification of hypotheses is closer in spirit to the work of Snyder and Warburton than to the original Chicago School. To this observation I would add that it is also closer to Fisher—who devoted two chapters (11 and 12) of his *Purchasing Power of Money* to the statistical verification of his equation of exchange. Fisher also continued in later years to be concerned with empirical aspects of the economic problems he discussed.

The present Chicago School is also closer to Fisher in emphasizing his basic distinction between the nominal and the real rate of interest (Humphrey, 1971).[9] To the best of my knowledge, Simons did not explicitly refer to this distinction; nor did Mints, in his book on monetary policy (1950)—though he does mention it in passing in his history of banking theory (1945, pp. 53, 211). This is to be contrasted with the important role the distinction plays in the writings of Friedman and his associates (Friedman, 1956, 1971).

In conclusion, let me observe that the picture of monetary economics in the 1930s that emerges from Humphrey's note (1973) as well as from the foregoing discussion—and which accords with the larger picture that has been documented in the detailed studies of the period by Reeve (1943) and, more recently, Davis (1968, 1971)—is one of widespread ferment with respect to questions of both monetary theory and policy. Thus contrary to Friedman's implication,[10] the Chicago School of that time cannot be represented as an isolated center of monetary studies and of belief in the importance of money. What seems, however, to be true is that in some important respects it behaved as if it were—as is evidenced by the failure of Simons and Mints to refer in either their writings or their lectures (as reflected in my class

9. Fisher's deep conviction in the importance of this distinction is best demonstrated by the fact that in 1925 he persuaded the Rand-Kardex Company—of which he was a founder and major stockholder—to issue what he called (1934, p. 112) "the first 'Stabilized Bond' in history," or what we would today call an indexed bond. The index clause, however, was not to become operative unless the price level changed by more than 10% (Fisher, 1934, pp. 112, 387–89; Reeve, 1943, p. 164).

10. "Chicago was one of the few academic centers at which the quantity theory continued to be a central and vigorous part of the oral tradition throughout the 1930s and 1940s, where students continued to study monetary theory and to write theses on monetary problems" (Friedman, 1956, p. 3).

notes) to the work of their contemporaries, even when it bore them out on the importance of monetary factors, and even when it incorporated similar (if not identical) policy proposals. More specifically, Simons' writings in the first half of the 1930s give little, if any, indication that there was then and in earlier years a relatively high degree of agreement among economists from different backgrounds—and different countries [11]—in support of price stabilization as a contracyclical policy.

I strongly suspect, however, that the classroom teaching at Chicago during my student days (the early and mid-1940s) differed in this respect from that of a decade before. Specifically, I would not be surprised if in the early and mid-1930s these teachings contained many more references to the wider academic support for the kind of monetary policies taught at Chicago. Similarly, it may well be that the sense of isolation that I experienced during the early 1940s in part simply reflected the fact that at that time Chicago was indeed isolated in its continued advocacy of price stabilization as a contracyclical policy, by virtue of the fact that by then most of the leading academic centers (and Harvard in particular) had been converted to the advocacy of Keynesian fiscal policy for this purpose.

Obviously, none of this changes the basic fact that the Chicago School in the 1930s played a leading role in the realm of monetary-policy discussions. On the other hand, one thing is clear from the above: Chicago was not the center of empirical work on monetary economics in the 1930s; indeed, little, if any, such work was done then at Chicago. True, there was nowhere at that time a real ''center'' of empirical work in monetary economics. Nevertheless, the fact is that the major empirical work on monetary economics that was done during this period was carried out at Harvard (as represented by Currie 1931,[12] 1933, 1934b, 1934c) and Columbia (as represented by Angell 1933, 1936).

The failure of such empirical work to develop at Chicago in the 1930s stands in sharp contrast with the fact that Chicago was at that time the home of two outstanding empirical economists, both of whom had at least some interest in monetary matters: Henry Schultz, who participated in the 1932 Harris Foundation Lectures and was one of the signatories of its policy proposals (1932, p. 163), and Paul H. Douglas, who in 1935 wrote a book on *Controlling Depressions* whose policy proposals (pp. 277–81) were largely in accord with the ''traditional'' Chicago ones.

Still, the more relevant fact is that the people primarily responsible for the teaching of monetary and fiscal policy at Chicago during the 1930s, Simons and Mints, were themselves just not interested in empirical work—and the vital importance of such personal tastes in influencing the nature of the research carried out at an academic institution is something we have all experienced. Furthermore, we must remember the general intellectual atmosphere of the economics profession in the 1930s, which

11. Notably, Pigou and Keynes in England and Wicksell in Sweden; cf. Patinkin, 1972 and references there cited.

12. This was Currie's Ph.D. thesis on ''Bank Assets and Banking Theory'' carried out at Harvard under the direction of John H. Williams and S. E. Harris.

placed much less emphasis than it has come to place since the late 1940s on the obligation to subject hypotheses to empirical testing.[13]

I would, however, conjecture that the disinterest of Simons and Mints in empirical work also reflected the influence of a more specific factor: namely, the fact that they were so convinced on a priori grounds of the validity of their analysis and consequent policy proposals that they saw no need to subject these proposals to empirical study. This attitude is strikingly revealed in the following paragraph from Simons' 1935 review of Currie's *Supply and Control of Money in the United States* (1934):

> The study reflects a rare combination of penetrating theoretical insights and patient competence in the analysis of banking statistics. The highly realistic treatment will make the author's argument convincing, or at least disturbing, to many readers who would be unimpressed by "mere theory." For critical students, however, Dr. Currie's inductive verifications will be largely gratuitous—although everyone will be grateful for the excellent statistical compilation and analysis. In general, the author's fundamental insights are so sound that failure of statistical confirmation would only indicate error or inadequacy in the statistics [Simons, 1935, p. 556].

Reflecting a similar conviction, Mints in his lectures (according to my notes) said: "If [government] stabilizes price level, will stabilize aggregate demand and thus prevent unemployment. Inconceivable that federal government couldn't so increase cash balances of public that it wouldn't want to purchase goods" (cited in the preceding chapter, p. 261; cf. also Mints, 1946, p. 67). What we have since learned (in large measure, due to Friedman's own seminal contributions (1961, and references there cited)) about the fundamental problem of lags—and particularly about the implications of possibly destabilizing lags for such a policy—was either not seen (Simons) or not given much weight (Mints) (p. 247 above). So I find it highly significant that it is precisely this question of lags that has raised doubts about the efficacy of (*inter alia*) the monetary policy espoused by the original Chicago School—and has stimulated so much empirical work since the early 1960s in the effort to determine (if possible) a more optimal policy.

Appendix

At the end of October 1971 I sent a draft of this note to Professor Samuel H. Nerlove, asking him for his comments, and particularly for information on the extent of intellectual interaction between Edie and the Department of Economics, as well as on the role that Charles O. Hardy played in the development of the Chicago School. (Professor Nerlove took his M.A. degree at Chicago in 1923, and served there on the staff of the School of Business from that time and until his retirement in 1965. I regret

13. Cf. also Humphrey (1973).

to say that Professor Nerlove died on February 13, 1972.) To this request Professor Nerlove replied in a letter dated December 5, 1971, the main parts of which are reproduced here with his permission:

> Getting at an accurate statement of the intellectual development and implementation of a set of ideas is obviously exceedingly difficult, especially in relation to the development of such a complicated set of ideas as are involved in the evolution of the Quantity Theory in this country during a 20 year period, 1930–1950.
>
> Nevertheless, here are my recollections about Edie and Hardy—and as I approach three score and ten—I find that I have total recall of past events, so perhaps the following is "more accurate" rather than less accurate.
>
> Hardy was much more influential than Edie. His influence on Mints and Simons was exceedingly significant, and therefore some reference should be made to his work when he was at the Institute of Economics in Washington (now Brookings) in the so-called money and banking area. Indeed, he had an important impact on Warburton's work. Hardy was Simons' teacher (as well as Angell's and Mints' teacher) and was influential in getting him to "respect" Currie's work on the "Supply and Control of Money," as it was being developed at Harvard as a Ph.D thesis.
>
> Edie had very little "real" contact with the Economics Faculty. He was brought to Chicago, over the negative reactions of the Economics group, by L. C. Marshall primarily because he had a manuscript of his forthcoming text book on "Money, Bank Credit and Prices". The Economics group did not think well of the book. . . . My distinct impression is that Edie was so uncomfortable at Chicago that at the first opportunity, and shortly after he came to Chicago, he left for a job in Detroit with an investment trust. In short, there was practically no real intellectual contact between Edie and the Economics Faculty during the short time he was in residence at Chicago. . . .

Postscript

In June 1972, I sent Lloyd Mints a draft of the foregoing article and this time (see above, p. 265) received a reply, reproduced here with his permission:

Ft. Collins, Colorado,
Sept. 21, 1972

Dear Don:

I make no claim to an infallible memory such as Sam Nerlove claimed to have had (in your quotation from him), but as I recollect the situation during the 1930's it was as follows. The primary interest of several of us at Chicago, in such public statements as were made, was in monetary policy and its relation to economic activity. We tacitly assumed that monetary behavior had an important influence on economic activity. It was the era of the great depression, and we believed that the actions of the Federal Reserve System and of the government were woefully wrong. We therefore proposed monetary actions which we believed would facilitate a return to better economic conditions. We were not concerned with the question of who should be given credit for any particular monetary theory or policy. We merely wanted to do what little we possibly could to improve economic conditions in the country.

I have always had the greatest respect for Irving Fisher. Whether I sufficiently indicated that fact in what I said or wrote I don't know. I remember distinctly (I think!) that after a talk by Warburton at the University both Simons and I were greatly pleased by what Warburton had said. I even had the impression that Warburton was grateful for our approval. I agree with Nerlove that Edie had little if any influence on the other members of the economics department at Chicago.

I was quite familiar with the writings of Angell and Currie, but whether I should have made that fact quite clear I don't know. All of us at Chicago had the greatest respect for Charles Hardy. Whether he had the extent of influence on some of us that Nerlove suggests I don't know. The one man who it is clear to me had a considerable influence on my thinking was Henry Simons. For a short time a small group of us had weekly (?) meetings at the home of Hardy. I am not sure who attended those meetings, but at least Knight, Hardy, Simons and myself must have been present. I don't remember whether Aaron Director was in Chicago at the time, but if he was he was surely present. There may have been a few others.

Sincerely,

[signed] L. Mints

I also sent a draft of the article to Lauchlin Currie and received a reply from which the following paragraphs are reproduced with his permission (footnotes added):

Bogota, Colombia
November 29, 1972

Dear Professor Patinkin,

I've been so busy defending and implementing a plan of development I developed, and this country adopted, that I couldn't get myself in a proper frame of mind to return to the distant past. But as a local journal is publishing (in Spanish) a translation of Humphrey's article and asked me to make a few comments on my early work, I was led to think a little about it.

I was a bit unlucky in both hitting on the 100% reserve idea a few months behind Simons and of working out a statistical series for the income velocity simultaneously with Angell. However, I hardly think this justifies your remark that my "work appeared after the main features of the Chicago school position had been formulated". I think I supplied the first explanation of the main factors governing the supply of money (which Humphrey did not mention) and my work on the ownership of demand deposits was certainly new and throws light on the demand for money (in *Journal of Amer. Stat. Ass.*, Dec. 1937 [*sic*]). I took a very strong line on the distinction between what is money and what is not. If you include savings deposits in commercial banks there is no logical place to stop. As Humphrey says, I took a highly critical line on Federal Reserve Policy, though I still defended discretionary policy.

On personal relations, I knew Simons but not well. My main link with Chicago was through Viner. (He had lectured a few times at Harvard and I got to know and respect him. I was an instructor while he had then an established reputation so our relationships was more like that of professor and student).[a]

I can't account for Nerlove's remark re Hardy's getting Simons to "respect" my work, except that I did respect Hardy. Nerlove made a little slip in connection with my Ph.D. thesis, which you may have noted.[b]

. . .

Yours sincerely,

[signed] Lauchlin Currie

Bibliography

J. W. Angell. "Money, Prices, and Production: Some Fundamental Concepts." *Quarterly Journal of Economics*, Nov. 1933, *48*, 39–76.

______. *The Behavior of Money*. New York, 1936.

L. Currie. "Bank Assets and Banking Theory." Unpublished Ph.D. thesis, Harvard University, 1931.

______. "Money, Gold, and Income." *Quarterly Journal of Economics*, Nov. 1933, *48*, 77–95.

______. "A Note on Income Velocities." *Quarterly Journal of Economics*, Feb. 1934a, *48*, 353–54.

______. "The Failure of Monetary Policy to Prevent the Depression of 1929–1932." *Journal of Political Economy*, Apr. 1934b, *42*, 145–77.

______. *The Supply and Control of Money in the United States*. Cambridge, Mass., 1934c.

†______. "The Economic Distribution of Demand Deposits." *Journal of the American Statistical Association*, June 1938, *33*, 319–26.

a. Cf. also Viner's letter above (p. 268) on his relations with Currie.

b. The slip—which I had not noticed—was that Currie's book on the *Supply and Control of Money* was a new work, and not a revised version of his thesis; see penultimate paragraph of Nerlove's letter and fn. 12 on p. 282 above.

†Cited only in Postscript.

J. R. Davis. "Chicago Economists, Deficit Budgets and the Early 1930's." *American Economic Review*, June 1968, *58*, 476–82.

———. *The New Economics and the Old Economists*. Ames, Iowa, 1971.

P. H. Douglas. *Controlling Depressions*. New York, 1935.

L. D. Edie. *Money, Bank Credit, and Prices*. New York, 1928.

———. "The 1928 Hearings on the Strong Bill." *Journal of Political Economy*, June 1929, *37*, 340–54.

———. *The Banks and Prosperity*. New York, 1931.

———. *Dollars*. New Haven, Conn., 1934.

———. "Monetary Stabilization from a National Point of View." *American Economic Review, Supplement*, Mar. 1935, *25*, 164–70.

I. Fisher. *The Purchasing Power of Money*. New York, 1911.

———. *Stabilizing the Dollar*. New York, 1920.

———. "The Business Cycle Largely a 'Dance of the Dollar.' " *Journal of the American Statistical Association*, Dec. 1923, *18*, 1024–28.

———. "Our Unstable Dollar and the So-Called Business Cycle." *Journal of the American Statistical Association*, June 1925, *20*, 179–202.

———. *Booms and Depressions*. New York, 1932.

———. *Stable Money*. New York, 1934.

———. *100% Money*. New York, 1935.

W. T. Foster and W. Catchings. *Money*. Boston, 1923.

M. Friedman, ed. *Studies in the Quantity Theory of Money*. Chicago, 1956.

———. "The Lag in Effect of Monetary Policy." *Journal of Political Economy*, Oct. 1961, *69*, 447–66. As reprinted in *The Optimum Quantity of Money and Other Essays*. Chicago, 1969. Pp. 237–60.

———. "A Monetary Theory of National Income." *Journal of Political Economy*, Mar./Apr. 1971, *79*, 323–37.

——— and A. J. Schwartz. *A Monetary History of the United States 1867–1960*. Princeton, N. J., 1963.

———. *Monetary Statistics of the United States: Estimates, Sources, Methods*. New York, 1970.

Harris Memorial Foundation. *Gold and Monetary Stabilization*, ed. Q. Wright. Chicago, 1932.

T. M. Humphrey. "Role of Non-Chicago Economists in the Evolution of the Quantity Theory in America 1930–1950." *Southern Economic Journal*, July 1971, *38*, 12–18.

———. "On the Monetary Economics of Chicagoans and Non-Chicagoans: Reply." *Southern Economic Journal*, Jan. 1973, *39*, 460–63.

L. W. Mints. *A History of Banking Theory*. Chicago, 1945.

———. "Monetary Policy." *Review of Economics and Statistics*, May 1946, *28*, 60–69.

———. *Monetary Policy for a Competitive Society*. New York, 1950.

D. Patinkin. "The Chicago Tradition, the Quantity Theory, and Friedman." *Journal of Money, Credit and Banking*, Feb. 1969, *1*, 46–70. [Reproduced as chap. 10 above]

———. "On the Short-Run Non-Neutrality of Money in the Quantity Theory." *Banca Nazionale del Lavoro: Quarterly Review*, Mar. 1972, *100*, 3–22.

J. E. Reeve. *Monetary Reform Movements*. Washington, D.C., 1943.

H. C. Simons. "Review of *The Supply and Control of Money in the United States*, by Lauchlin Currie." *Journal of Political Economy*, Aug. 1935, *43*, 555–58.

C. Warburton. *Depression, Inflation and Monetary Policy; Selected Papers, 1945–1953*. Baltimore, 1966.

Q. Wright. See Harris Memorial Foundation.

'Chicagoans and non-Chicagoans'

T. M. Humphrey, 'On the monetary economics of Chicagoans and non-Chicagoans: Reply', *Southern Economic Journal*, 39 (January 1973), pp. 460–3.

ON THE MONETARY ECONOMICS OF CHICAGOANS AND NON-CHICAGOANS: REPLY

Don Patinkin makes the following points in reference to my article: (1) that I neglected to show why members of the original Chicago school (Knight, Viner, Mints, Simons) did not refer more often to the work of Snyder, Currie, Fisher and other non-Chicago quantity theorists; (2) that I erred in stating that Currie was the first American economist to employ the income velocity concept; and (3) that my interpretation of Lionel Edie as a forerunner of modern advocates of the money-stock growth rate rule was too generous to Edie.

Although it was not the purpose of my article to determine why members of the original Chicago school did not refer to other quantity theorists, I believe their failure to do so indicated their negative reaction to the ultra-empirical orientation of economic research in the 1920's in general and to the studies conducted by Holbrook Working and Carl Snyder in particular. Synder's, and to a lesser extent Working's, investigations of the trend and cyclical movements of monetary variables [10; 11; 12; 17; 18] typified the "measurement without theory" approach to business cycle analysis which reached epidemic proportions in the 1920's. It seems probable that Frank Knight and Jacob Viner, the intellectual leaders at Chicago at the time, found these developments uncongenial. Knight eschewed empirical research completely. His approach to economic analysis was abstract, deductive, and philosophical—almost the antithesis of the empirical orientation of Working and Snyder. Viner, although not opposed to empirical research *per se* (one of his earliest books [13] was devoted to empirical testing of international trade theories), had become increasingly disenchanted with the disproportionate amount of effort devoted to statistical work in the 1920's. An advocate of a judicious mixture of theory and empiricism, Viner on several occasions voiced the opinion that the pendulum had swung too far in the direction of the latter [14; 15; 16].

Knight's and Viner's aversion to ultra-empiricism was probably accentuated by the extreme conclusions which Snyder and Working reached on the basis of their statistical research.[1] Each claimed to have

---

[1] Viner's negative reaction to ultra-empiricism was most vigorously expressed in his remarks made in December, 1927 at an American Economic Association round-table discussion on "The Present Status and Future Prospects of Quantitative Economics." Some of Viner's comments, while not directed specifically at Working and Snyder, nevertheless implied criticism both of their simplistic empirical model and of the techniques (curve fitting by least squares, correlation analysis, etc.) they employed in deriving their conclusions.

> I am completely skeptical as to the value of any purely empirical results of statistical analysis in economics, especially when by the mechanical application of statistical devices laws of striking simplicity and of fundamental importance are discovered to be ruling in the economic universe. Where the mind unaided by statistical analysis sees complexity everywhere ... statistical analysis unaided by the mind finds beautiful simplicity ... [16, 45].

It seems probable, moreover, that Viner would have been unimpressed by Snyder's celebrated empirical finding (and the basis of his money stock growth rate rule) of a constant four per cent secular increase in trade. Viner was especially critical of the tendency for statistically-oriented economists to proclaim, on the basis of trend lines fitted to historical data, the discovery of "economic laws."

> I do not believe that there are many economic time series which forecast their own future trend with sufficient accuracy to be much superior to the random guess as to future trends. That there is a law of the growth of population, which can be expressed in a simple algebraic equation; that there is a law of the growth of capital, namely, that it grows at the rate of 3 per cent a year; ... that the business cycle has a normal duration of thirty-seven months; that there is a fixed law governing the distribution of income which can be stated in arithmetical terms or shown graphically; such propositions ... seem to me to be purely fantastic [16, 45].

Incidentally, Viner's remarks indicate that he would have been less than enthusiastic about Paul Douglas' empirical work, initiated in the late 1920's, involving the statistical estimation of the Cobb-Douglas production function. This may partially explain Douglas' apparent lack of influence on Viner's proteges, Simons and Mints.

found evidence that short-run fluctuations in velocity and trade were mutually offsetting [10; 12; 17], suggesting that V and T could be disregarded in the equation of exchange and that the price level was related to the money supply by a constant. The Snyder-Working doctrine of neutralizing fluctuations in V and T came perilously close to the naive textbook version of the quantity theory (constancy of V and T) which the Chicago theorists would have found unpalatable.

The views of Viner and Knight could well have been transmitted to their younger colleagues, Simons and Mints, thereby accounting for the latter economists' apparent disregard for extra-Chicago empirical work. For example, Simons indicated the low value he placed on empirical research in a review of Currie's *The Supply and Control of Money in the United States*, one of the few occasions when a member of the Chicago school acknowledged the work of non-Chicago quantity theorists. In the course of the generally favorable review, Simons remarked that Currie's empirical work was unnecessary.

> For critical students, however, Dr. Currie's inductive verifications will be largely gratuitous.... In general, the author's fundamental insights are so sound that failure of statistical confirmation would only indicate error or inadequacy of the statistics [9].[3]

It is also possible that disenchantment with the ultra-empirical slant of economic research explains the Chicago economists' failure to do justice to Irving Fisher. During the second and third decades of the century, Fisher's interest in empirical work dominated his interest in pure theory. Schumpeter noted, for example, that Fisher's penchant for empirical verification apparently motivated his willingness to abandon the subtle and complex schema of his complete monetary theory for a simple, single-equation empirical model, namely the equation of exchange [7; 8]. Fisher was heavily engaged in statistical work in the 1920's [3; 4], and he cited Holbrook Working's findings in support of his own [3, 199]. The empirical thrust of Fisher's work may have biased Chicago economists against him, as may also the general decline of his professional reputation following the 1929 stock-market crash.

Patinkin is correct in his point concerning priority of introduction of the income velocity concept in the U.S. A distinction should be maintained, however, between those economists who merely stated the concept (Edie) or attempted a casual, single-year estimate of its magnitude (Foster and Catchings) and those who developed adequate measures of income velocity extending over several years, analyzed its behavior, and employed it as an integral part of their empirical research. As Patinkin rightly points out, James Angell, simultaneously with Currie, pioneered in the latter uses of the income velocity concept and thus deserves recognition as one of the important non-Chicago quantity theorists writing in the 30's.

Although objecting to my exclusion of James Angell, Patinkin failed to mention other important non-Chicago contributors to quantity theory research neglected in my earlier note. These include Holbrook Working of the University of Minnesota and Morris A. Copeland of Cornell University, both of whom employed correlation techniques in investigating lead-lag relationships between money supply changes and price level changes [1; 17; 18]. Also, James Harvey Rogers, a former student of Irving Fisher at Yale, investigated, in a study commissioned by Columbia University, the influence of price level changes on nominal interest rate levels and on changes in velocity [6]. The work of these economists is impressive additional testimony to the fact, noted by Patinkin, that the centers for em-

[3] I might note that on the issue of "rules vs. authorities" Simons and Currie were in opposition. Simons points out that, despite Currie's trenchant criticism of past Federal Reserve policy, Currie's notion of desirable reform was the augmentation of the discretionary power of the central bank [9, 558].

pirical work on monetary questions in the 20's and 30's were at institutions other than Chicago.

In the area of *theoretical* (as distinguished from empirical) research on the quantity theory conducted outside Chicago in the 30's, my most glaring omission, also overlooked by Patinkin, was the contribution of Arthur W. Marget of the University of Minnesota [5]. Marget ably defended Fisher's transaction-velocity equation against the criticisms of Keynes and demonstrated that, with proper interpretation, it could be a powerful analytical tool. Incidentally, it is ironic that the definitive history of the quantity theory was written by Marget at Minnesota rather than by someone at Chicago, where both history of economic thought and monetary theory were emphasized. These extra-Chicago empirical and theoretical contributions deny the myth that only at Chicago did the quantity theory flourish in the 1920's and survive in the 1930's.

Finally, in support of his third point, Patinkin cites writings by Edie other than the one cited in my article to show that Edie did not have a strong preference for the growth rate rule over price stabilization. Edie's ambivalence is, I agree, evident in those other works. However, in the work to which I referred, Edie's strong preference for the former rule is stated in unequivocal terms.

> Central banks should aim at so regulating the reserves of the banking system that the outstanding credit built upon those reserves will expand at the same rate as the long term growth of production. There is enough credit when the curves of credit growth and production growth parallel each other. More than this is too much. Less than this is too little.
> This criterion [rate of growth of production] is definite.... [It is estimated at] about 4 per cent per annum for the United States [2, 117–8].

Edie states that, if the central banks were following this criterion, "they would not be able to leap from a 6 per cent rate of growth one year to 2 per cent the next" [2, 118]. Edie emphatically rejects the price stabilization guide as "vague and ambiguous." He states that, although a stable price level is a worthy objective,

> it is not a definition of the type of credit curve which will help approximate that objective. By leaving this definition open, the price stabilizationists permit the credit authorities to treat each new situation that arises in a purely opportunist and makeshift spirit [2, 114].

Patinkin is correct in his claim that Edie did not explicitly discuss "variable lags" or "imperfectly understood links" in rejecting the price stabilization guide, but he is perhaps mistaken in implying that Edie did not, at one time, express a strong preference for the growth rate rule.

THOMAS M. HUMPHREY
Federal Reserve Bank of Richmond

REFERENCES

1. Copeland, Morris A., "Money, Trade and Prices—A Test of Causal Primacy," *Quarterly Journal of Economics*, August 1929, 648–66.
2. Edie, Lionel D. *The Banks and Prosperity*. New York: Harper, 1931.
3. Fisher, Irving, "Our Unstable Dollar and the So-Called Business Cycle," *Journal of the American Statistical Association*, June 1925, 179–202.
4. ———, "A Statistical Relation Between Unemployment and Price Changes," *International Labor Review*, June 1926, 785–92.
5. Marget, Arthur W. *The Theory of Prices*. New York: Prentice-Hall, Vol. I, 1938, Vol. II, 1942.
6. Rogers, James H. *The Process of Inflation in France*. New York: Columbia University Press, 1929, pp. 257–62, 297–325.
7. Schumpeter, J. A. *History of Economic Analysis*. London: George Allen and Unwin, 1954, pp. 1103–5.
8. ———. *Ten Great Economists: From Marx to Keynes*. New York: Oxford University Press, 1965, pp. 235–7.
9. Simons, Henry, "Review of Currie's *The Supply and Control of Money in the United States*," *Journal of Political Economy*, August 1935, 555–8.
10. Snyder, Carl, "New Measures in the Equation of Exchange," *American Economic Review*, December 1924, 699–713.
11. ———. *Business Cycles and Business Measurement*. New York: Macmillan, 1927.

12. ———, "The Problem of Monetary and Economic Stability," *Quarterly Journal of Economics*, February 1935, 173–205.
13. Viner, Jacob. *Canada's Balance of International Indebtedness, 1900–1913*. Cambridge: Harvard University Press, 1924.
14. ———, "Mills' *Behavior of Prices*," *Quarterly Journal of Economics*, February 1929, 349–52.
15. ———, "Review of M. K. Bennet's *Farm Cost Studies in the United States*," *Journal of the American Statistical Association*, 1930, 111.
16. ———, "The Present Status and Future Prospects of Quantitative Economics," *American Economic Review, Supplement*, March 1928 reprinted in J. Viner, *The Long View and the Short*. Glencoe: Free Press, 1958, pp. 45–7.
17. Working, Holbrook, "Prices and the Quantity of Circulating Medium, 1890–1921," *Quarterly Journal of Economics*, February 1923, 228–56.
18. ———, "Bank Deposits as a Forecaster of the General Wholesale Price Level," *Review of Economic Statistics*, July 1926, 120–33.

'Essays On and In the Chicago Tradition'

M. Parkin, 'Essays on and in the Chicago Tradition: a review essay', *Journal of Money Credit and Banking*, 18:1 (February 1986), pp. 104–16.

AND

'A Reply'

D. Patinkin, 'A Reply', *Journal of Money Credit and Banking*, 18:1 (February 1986), pp. 116–21.

BOOK REVIEWS

Essays On and In the Chicago Tradition

by Don Patinkin. Durham, N.C.: Duke University Press, 1981. xii + 315 pp. $29.75

A Review Essay by Michael Parkin

This is a collection of twelve essays (all published before), and a reminiscence of the Chicago that Patinkin knew as a student, enlivened with a series of photographs of some of the key members of the Chicago community of the 1940s. The range of the essays is considerable. Three are on price theory,[1] three on macroeconomics,[2] five on the history of thought and social history,[3] and one biographical—on Patinkin's most illustrious teacher, Frank Knight.

As the title of the collection implies, Patinkin portrays the Chicago tradition by the employment of two contrasting devices. The first device leaves the reader to infer what that tradition is from the sample of it presented—essays *In* the tradition. The second spells out and documents in varying detail Patinkin's perception of what the tradition actually was—essays *On* the tradition.

On my reading, two (but according to Patinkin three) Chicago traditions are portrayed in this book. First, there is "the traditional 'Chicago School'—that School which, with due regard to the differences among them, can be identified with the teaching of Frank H. Knight, Jacob Viner, Henry C. Simons, and Lloyd W. Mints"

The author is grateful to his colleagues Peter Howitt and David Laidler for their savage criticisms of a preliminary effort at this review, and to Milton Friedman and an anonymous referee for their most helpful comments on an earlier draft. I am also grateful to Roger Farmer (of the University of Pennsylvania) for helping me track down the first edition of a relatively obscure book that I read as shedding some light on traditional Chicago views concerning the theory of money. Finally, I wish to acknowledge that I have made some changes to the essay in response to comments by Don Patinkin. Naturally, I do not hold Patinkin responsible for what I have written here

[1]"Multiple-Plant Firms, Cartels, and Imperfect Competition"—*Quarterly Journal of Economics*, 1947; $Demand Curves and Consumer's Surplus"—*Measurement in Economics: Studies in Mathematical Economics and Econometrics in Memory of Yehuda Grunfeld*, 1963; "On the Economic Theory of Price Indexes"—*Economic Development and Cultural Change*, 1961 (with Nissan Liviatan).

[2]"The Indeterminacy of Absolute Prices in Classical Economic Theory"—*Econometrica*, 1949; "Reflections on the Neoclassical Dichotomy"—*Canadian Journal of Economics*, 1972; and "Involuntary Unemployment and the Keynesian Supply Function"—*Economic Journal*, 1949.

[3]"In Search of the 'Wheel of Wealth' . ."—*American Economic Review*, 1973; "Mercantalism and the Readmission of the Jews to England"—*Jewish Social Studies*, 1946; "The Chicago Tradition, the Quantity Theory, and Friedman"—*Journal of Money, Credit, and Banking*, 1969; "More on the Chicago Monetary Tradition"—*Southern Economic Journal*, 1973; and "Keynes and Chicago"—*Journal of Law and Economics*, 1979.

MICHAEL PARKIN *is professor of economics, University of Western Ontario.*

Journal of Money, Credit, and Banking, Vol. 18, No. 1 (February 1986)

(p. 3).[4] The second Chicago tradition is one that emerged when the above group was augmented by Oskar Lange (who arrived in 1939) and the members of the Cowles Commission, directed by Jacob Marschak (a group that began arriving in Chicago in 1943 and that included Ted Anderson, Trygve Haavelmo, Leo Hurwicz, Lawrence Klein, Tjalling Koopmans, Herman Rubin, and (later) Kenneth Arrow). Also, arriving in 1943, were the agricultural economists—Theodore W. Schultz, D. Gale Johnson, and William H. Nicholls—exiled from Iowa. H. Gregg Lewis should also be mentioned in connection with this strand of Chicago economics—a mathematical as well as econometric approach to the subject.

A third tradition identified—indeed highlighted—by Patinkin is one that emerged in the 1950s under the influence of the seminal contributions to macroeconomics and monetary theory of Milton Friedman. Whether or not that is a *separate* Chicago tradition is a matter in which I shall comment at some length in what follows.

Patinkin's essays *In* the Chicago tradition reflect, in part, both the traditional Chicago school and the new mathematical school of the 1940s. Of these, the doctrinal history essays, as well as those dealing with price theory, have clear origins in the scholarly traditions of Viner and the rigorous price theory of, in particular, Simons. The macroeconomics essays, like "Money, Interest and Prices," reflect something of the traditional school but are more obviously and directly works in that later mathematical tradition. None of the essays *In* the tradition provide examples of either the monetary theory or econometric traditions, though three of the essays *On* the tradition are explicitly about monetary doctrines.

It is this latter aspect of Patinkin's work that, for me at least—and as foreshadowed above—raises problems and puzzles. I will focus attention, therefore, in this area—that is, on Patinkin's "disquisition . . . on . . . the School's . . . monetary doctrines" (p. xi).

Patinkin's central message in this respect—well known and extensively debated in the subsequent literature (see, e.g., Friedman 1972; Patinkin 1972; Tavlas 1977a, 1977b)—is that what Milton Friedman wrote in 1956 ("The Quantity Theory of Money: A Restatement") was *not* in the Chicago tradition. Rather, it was Friedman's own invention and was heavily influenced by, and reflected the teachings of, not Friedman's Chicago mentors, but Keynes.

It is the essence of Patinkin's view that Friedman's restatement of the quantity theory may be summarized in two propositions: (i) the quantity theory of money is, first and foremost, a theory of the demand for money and (ii) the velocity of circulation is a stable function of a limited number of variables and particularly the nominal rate of interest. He contrasts the traditional Chicago view with Friedman's by summarizing that earlier view in two very different propositions, namely, (i) the quantity theory of money is, first and foremost, a theory of the determination of nominal income (or, equivalently, of MV) "in accordance with Fisher's $MV = PT$" (p. 245), and (ii) the velocity of circulation fluctuates considerably *and may be unstable*.

Friedman is contrasted with the traditional Chicago school on policy matters as well. In this regard, Friedman's well-known advocacy of a constant growth rate for the money stock is contrasted with the view of the Chicago scholars of the 1930s that

[4]The page references with no further qualification refer to the book under review. Others at Chicago when Patinkin arrived there in 1941 were Paul H. Douglas and John U. Nef.

fluctuations in the quantity of money may be required to offset fluctuations in velocity. The implication of these comparisons is that Friedman is not in the Chicago tradition. Indeed, pressing the matter harder, in the area of monetary theory, Friedman is a Keynesian. Further, in the area of policy, though not in the area of theory, the traditional Chicago school was closer to Keynes than to the position subsequently espoused by Friedman.

We can, of course, define words—even words such as *Chicago tradition* and *Keynesian*—to mean whatever we like, provided that we are explicit enough for the purpose at hand. Is it a convenient use of language to regard Friedman as being a Keynesian rather than being in the Chicago quantity theory tradition?

In summarizing his case, Patinkin writes:

> I have dwelt at length on the treatment of the rate of interest in Friedman's "reformulation" as compared with the actual writings of the quantity-theorists because this difference can be well defined and hence clearly observed in the literature. But I attach no less significance to other—and more subtle—differences, which also characterize Friedman's 1956 essay. Thus Friedman's presentation (1968, p. 440a) of the demand for money is first and foremost in terms of the demand for an asset; for him the income variable in the demand function is primarily "a surrogate for wealth, rather than [as in the quantity theory] a measure of the 'work' to be done by money." Correspondingly, as I have noted elsewhere, Friedman is primarily concerned with the optimal relationship between the stock of money and the stocks of other assets, whereas the quantity theorists were primarily concerned with the relationship between the stock of money and the flow of spending on goods and services. Furthermore, their discussions of this relationship either did not make the distinction between stocks and flows—or at least were imprecise about it. Similarly, quantity theorists paid little, if any, attention to the effects on the rate of interest and other variables of shifts in tastes as to the form in which individuals wished to hold their assets.
>
> And now to our main point: all of the foregoing are precisely the differentia of Keynesian monetary theory as compared with the traditional quantity theory. (p. 255)

It will be helpful first to clarify my understanding of what Patinkin means by the phrase "Keynesian monetary theory." I take it that "Keynesian monetary theory" is *not* the same thing as Keynes's *General Theory of . . . money,* but something narrower and having its origins in the *Treatise*. This interpretation seems natural in the light of Patinkin's own work on the *General Theory*. In that work, Patinkin argues that the "Central Message of the *General Theory* is the equilibrating role of changes in output generated by discrepancies between aggregate demand and aggregate supply" (Patinkin 1979, p. 175). This contrasts markedly with what Patinkin identifies as the differentia of Keynesian monetary theory—details concerning the demand for money function. It is of some importance, I think, to note that in establishing the essential contribution of the *General Theory* Patinkin demonstrates that, aside from seeing income as the equilibrating variable, all other aspects of the *General Theory* are to be found in the earlier writings of Keynes and others. In particular, the demand for money analysis is a direct outgrowth of the *Treatise* and has antecedents, as Patinkin recognizes, in the Cambridge cash balance school (see p. 255).

Was the Cambridge cash balance approach different from the quantity theory? As Patinkin himself notes: "Now it is a commonplace of monetary theory that these two approaches can be made analytically equivalent. Indeed, . . . , Fisher himself vividly shows (1913, pp. 153–54) that he was thinking in terms of a demand for money." Nevertheless, Patinkin goes on, "if we consistently find a treatment in terms of the transactions approach, we can take this as some indication that the economists in question did not primarily approach monetary theory from the viewpoint of the demand for money. Or at least we cannot take it as an indication that they did!" (p. 247).

Do we find that monetary economists in the pre-Keynesian age approached monetary theory consistently from the perspective of the Fisher equation and not "from the viewpoint of the demand for money"? Was the commonplace understanding of the *analytical* equivalence between the quantity theory approach and the Cambridge approach thoroughly appreciated in the pre-Keynesian period and did the monetary economists of that time "approach monetary theory from the viewpoint of the demand for money"?

There seems to be ample evidence from the literature of the period that the demand for money approach was well entrenched. Thus, for example, Pigou (1917) insisted that

> tho the machinery that I shall suggest in the following pages is quite different from that elaborated by Professor Irving Fisher in his admirable *Purchasing Power of Money*, and, as I think, more convenient, I am not in any sense an "opponent" of the "quantity theory" or a hostile critic of Professor Fisher's lucid analysis. He has painted his picture on one plan, and I paint mine on another. But the pictures that we both paint are of the same thing, and the witness of the two, as to what that thing in essentials is, substantially agrees. (rpt. 1951, p. 163)

Pigou goes on to show in explicit terms the formal equivalence between the demand for money and the velocity of circulation. He concludes this demonstration with,

> It is thus evident that there is no conflict between my formula and that embodied in the quantity theory But it does not follow that there is nothing to choose between them. Mine is not of course any "truer" than its rival. They are both equally true. The claim that I make on behalf of mine is merely that it is a somewhat more effective engine of analysis. It focusses attention on the proportion of their resources that people choose to keep in the form of [money] instead of focussing it on "velocity of circulation." This fact gives it, as I think, a real advantage, because it brings us at once into relation with volition — an ultimate cause of demand — instead of with something that seems at first sight accidental and arbitrary. But to argue in the air about the merits of a machine is always a waste of time. I offer this specification of it in order that those interested in monetary problems may test its powers in actual work upon concrete problems. (p. 174)

The above makes it clear that Pigou, at least, understood the formal equivalence between the quantity theory and the Cambridge cash balance approach. Did anyone else? It seems rather evident that Lionel Edie did. Having taken his reader through Irving Fisher's quantity equation he goes on "whether one adopts the quantity theory or some other causation theory of the value of money, one finds it necessary to have rather definite concepts of supply and demand factors in this special branch of value theory. The theory of the value of money is a particular application of value theory in general, and the exact nature of the manner in which general value theory applies to money in particular cannot be understood until adequate concepts of the demand and supply of money are understood" (Edie 1928, p. 191). As an aside, let me note the striking similarity in the language used here by Edie and that used by Friedman in 1956.

Another writer whose views on this matter are interesting (for a reason that will become apparent below) is a little known then assistant professor of finance in the

University of Pennsylvania, F. Cyril James. In 1930 Cyril James published his *The Economics of Money, Credit, and Banking*. Chapter 4 of that book—a general introductory text—deals with "the standard of value." It presents a brief but matter-of-fact exposition of Fisher's statement of the quantity theory. It then goes on to develop certain objections to the quantity theory and finally to some "modern formulations of the quantity theory" (James 1930, p. 54). Some of the material on "modern formulations" is worth reproducing. James writes as follows:

> On the whole, . . . economic opinion in the United States has tended to hold a version of the theory substantially similar to that of Professor Fisher, and for a complete restatement of the theory in satisfactory and convenient form, we must turn to the European writers who have been forced by the economic changes of the last two decades to reconstruct their exposition of the principles of monetary science.

James refers to R. G. Hawtrey (1919) as well as Edwin Cannan (1927) and develops the idea "that changes in the value of money will be proportional to changes in the willingness of people to hold *stocks of money*" (emphasis in original, p. 55). He goes on:

> Variations in the individual stocks of money are not . . . of primary importance, for it is the aggregate amount of all the individual stocks . . . which exercises an influence upon the general price level.
>
> The desire of people to hold stocks of money is not . . . a constant. . . .
>
> When . . . it is widely believed that the general level of prices will rise in the near future, the natural reaction will be for individuals to decrease the size of their stock of money in order to increase their stock of goods—and if there is a general feeling that prices are due to fall, there will be a tendency for the stock of money held by the community to increase.

Finally, James tells us that

> this formulation of the quantity theory of money receives support from the experiences in several of the countries of Europe during the period from 1914 to 1928.

It seems apparent from the passages quoted above that Cyril James certainly understood that the quantity theory of money could be formulated in terms of a theory of demand for money and, furthermore, that such a formulation was explicitly a portfolio analysis—an analysis of substitution between money and goods.

Although it is clear, from the above evidence, that Pigou, Edie, and a relatively obscure textbook writer all appreciated that the quantity theory of money was a theory that could only be given satisfactory content by organizing an analysis in terms of the demand for money, and solid though that evidence might be, it does not, of course, necessarily imply that the traditional Chicago scholars of the 1930s appreciated the equivalence. What is the evidence on this?

It seems (to me) hard to make any sense at all of the passage quoted by Patinkin from Henry Simons's "Banking and Currency Reform," unless it is imagined that Simons thought that he was talking equivalently about demand for money or velocity of circulation. Let me quote Simons (from Patinkin):

> Larger profits breed optimism; they stimulate investment and induce dishoarding (reduction of idle cash reserves). Producers will become more anxious to borrow for purposes of increasing inventories, expanding production, and increasing plant capacity. Lenders will have fewer misgivings about the ability of borrowers to repay. People generally will increase their lending and investment at the expense of their idle reserves of cash. In a word, the velocity of circulation will increase. (p. 257)

There is a certain lack of explicitness in the passage quoted concerning stocks and flows. But that Simons is talking about portfolio reallocations (away from idle cash and into inventories and plant capacity) as being the equivalent of a change in the velocity of circulation is transparent.

Simons was not alone (at Chicago) in viewing variations in velocity and variations in the demand for money as being equivalent. It is clear that Mints also shared that view. The best evidence supporting that conclusion that I know of is from Mints's review of Cyril James's work from which I provided some quotations above. (Indeed, the main reason for citing James is not to be able to establish what his views were — interesting though they are in and of themselves — but for the inferences that they enable us to make concerning the views of Mints.)

Mints reviewed that book in 1931 in the following terms:

> Mr. James has written an introductory text which possesses two points of merit in marked degree. The first relates to composition . . . the second . . . [to the fact that it] emphasizes . . . the significant economic problems which arise out of the functioning of monetary and commercial banking systems. . . .
>
> Approximately one-fourth of the book is devoted to the subject of money, and a fairly inclusive presentation is given. The discussion of the primitive theoretical aspects of the value of money is somewhat brief, even for an elementary text. A concise summary of Fisher's exposition of the quantity theory is given, and criticized upon the ground that it is inaccurate in a number of ways. Preference is given, therefore, to a presentation of the theory which emphasizes variations in the cash balances held by individuals. (p. 819)

In going on to evaluate this book, Mints raises many objections and criticisms but nowhere does he suggest that he finds it puzzling, objectionable, or in any other way disturbing to treat the theory of money as a "theory which emphasizes variations in the cash balances held by individuals" rather than in terms of Fisher's exposition.

Frank Knight also seems to share this same basic view. His most explicit and extensive writing on this topic from the period in question is "The Business Cycle, Interest, and Money: A Methodological Approach" (1941). Knight presents his views — relevant to the issue at hand — in the following terms:

> The economic process in a pecuniary economy involves the holding or owning, by somebody, of wealth — all the wealth in the economy — and also the entire stock of money. Hence every property owner has the alternative either of holding money up to the amount of his fortune or of choosing the concrete kind of wealth other than money that he will hold. . . . Any belief that the value of money will rise in the future, relative to real wealth, tends to lead men to hold money instead of real wealth, the natural effect of which is a fall in the money value of wealth, which tends to confirm the belief and aggravate the tendency, and so on cumulatively. . . .
>
> An incipient tendency of prices (of products in general) to rise creates the impression of an upward trend (a downward trend in the value of money). The root of the phenomena in this case is the fact that money, while not literally consumed, is in part effectively "used" — i.e., employed in a real, technical, or quasi-technical role in organized production and distribution — and in part it is held "idle." The motive for holding money idle, *or especially the main variable motive* [emphasis added] is speculation for a rise in its future value. (pp. 57–58)

It is clear from the above quotations that Knight is thinking in terms of a demand for money and in terms of a capital-theoretic approach to the theory of money. Further, he explicitly recognizes the role of the opportunity cost of holding money in influencing the demand for money.

Knight did say more, however, than the above. My purpose in citing that passage is simply to demonstrate that Knight was organizing his thinking in terms of a capital-theoretic demand for money framework. I do not want to assert that Knight had in mind a well-defined and stable demand for money function. The evidence clearly shows that he did not. Although Patinkin does cite passages from this work by Knight, he does not cite the one that provides the clearest evidence on this matter. In this regard Knight says,

> The tendency for increase and decrease in speculative holding of money to feed upon itself cumulatively is subject to no such effective check as results from the cumulation of a consumable commodity with a fairly definite demand curve, which is fairly well known, as is the stock held speculatively. Indeed, in the case of money, just what does set a boundary to a movement of general crisis in either direction and especially the downward movement, becomes something of a mystery. . . .
>
> That the division between active and idle funds is not definite or determinate goes without saying. (p. 59)

The evidence presented above seems to lead strongly to the conclusion that Friedman's identification of the quantity theory as being first and foremost a theory of the demand for money is entirely in line with the writings of all the major quantity theorists of the 1930s.

A further factor relevant to this matter concerns the historical context in which Friedman was writing as compared with his Chicago mentors. Viewed from a pre-*General Theory* perspective the Cambridge approach and the quantity theory were indeed different (though logically equivalent). Even Pigou was clear on this for, notwithstanding the passages quoted above, he ended his "Value of Money" essay by noting that

> the 'quantity theory' furnishes a tool which in the skilled hands of Professor Irving Fisher has accomplished great things. But less experienced craftsmen need, I think, a better—a more completely foolproof tool. It is this that, in the preceding pages, I have endeavored to provide. (rpt. 1951, p. 183)

Viewed from a post-*General Theory* perspective, however, and especially a post-bastardization perspective, the similarities between the quantity theory and cash balance approach dominate the distinctions between them especially when contrasted with the model of Keynes in the *General Theory*—a model which, if Patinkin's appraisal of it is correct, essentially amounts to an introduction into monetary theory of the notion that real income is the key equilibrating variable.

Perhaps the most thoroughly documented fact about the Chicago quantity theorists' writing in the 1930s is their neglect of the rate of interest as a factor upon which variations in velocity might depend. Patinkin takes this as evidence that these scholars did not have in mind the demand for money approach. That is clearly one way of reading the evidence. It does not, however, seem to be the most natural and obvious way. An alternative interpretation, if correct, would not lead to Patinkin's conclusion. Let me hasten to add that I am not claiming that the alternative (about to be suggested) is correct. I merely advance it as a hypothesis.

An alternative interpretation runs as follows. First, Chicago quantity theorists were aware of the weak procyclical co-movements of interest rates and velocity. They viewed each of these variables as, what we would today call, endogenous variables. Their monetary theory was couched in a language which, again using today's modes of expression, we would call reduced form analysis. That is, they did not set out explicit structural models (even in words) and proceed to analyze the effects of exogenous variables on endogenous variables by way of an explicit manipulation of such a model. Rather they conducted their analysis in terms of an attempt to sort out the effects of variables perceived as exogenous on endogenous variables with a less than fully articulated structural model and a good deal of what we might today call "arm waving."

Viewed from this perspective it would have struck a Chicago quantity theorist as quite *un*interesting to talk about the connection between the rate of interest and velocity. The data told him that such a relationship existed but, since both are simultaneously induced by some deeper and more primitive exogenous force, to emphasize the connection—even to mention it—would, from the perspective of that time, have seemed like superficial description.

The best documentary evidence that I can find supporting my hypothesis is in Knight's 1941 paper cited above. Towards the end of that article he notes that he has said very little about rates of interest and asks what role they play in the cycle. His answer is "very little." It is clear that he does not see interest rates as playing any role of prime mover and, therefore, sees little need to investigate their influence.

A view advanced strongly by Patinkin is that the traditional Chicago quantity theorists did not have in mind the existence of a *stable* demand for money (velocity) function. There is a feature of their writing, however, that raises questions (at least for me) about even that conclusion. This feature is the failure in those traditional writings recognized but not emphasized by Patinkin (see p. 248) to distinguish between stability in two senses: the stability of the functional relationship and the dynamic stability (or stationarity) of a difference or differential equation. One of the major contributions of Friedman (and Phillip Cagan 1956) was to emphasize the importance of this analytical distinction in the context of the demand for money. Asserting that the demand for money is a stable function of a limited number of variables (Friedman's position) does not imply that velocity may not be highly volatile or indeed dynamically unstable (nonstationary). Whether or not velocity is dynamically unstable will depend on the precise relationship between money, velocity, and prices on the one hand and the expected rate of inflation on the other. Although not devoid of analytical considerations, this will be primarily an empirical matter.

One passage from Simons quoted by Patinkin is certainly capable of being read as if Simons understoood this matter. Simons (1942, p. 188) writes,

> The bottom of an uncontrolled deflation, for all practical purposes, is nonexistent—with adverse expectations causing price declines and with the actual declines aggravating expectations, etc. (p. 258)

Simons is not here using the words "there is a stable functional relationship linking velocity to inflation and that relationship may be relied upon to generate a non-stationary price process." It is difficult to understand, however, how he could have talked about "adverse expectations causing price declines . . . with actual declines aggravating expectations, etc." if he was not thinking in those terms. I have no way of knowing whether Simons really understood that but his words are so clear that it is hard to see how else they may be interpreted. If this passage from Simons is read as saying that Simons did indeed appreciate the distinction between dynamic stability and stability of a functional relationship, it is the dynamic instability and not instability of the functional relationship to which he was drawing attention and from which he thought problems for price stability would arise. Interpreted in that way Friedman and Simons differ only in that one of Friedman's students[5] convinced Friedman that dynamic instability of the price process does not appear to occur as an empirical matter while Simons had no such empirical knowledge.

Patinkin's analysis of the distinctions between Friedman and the traditional Chicago approach extend beyond matters of theory and deal also with differences on policy. Patinkin documents the differences between Friedman and traditional Chicago and the quite remarkable similarities between that traditional Chicago view and the Keynes of the *General Theory* and beyond. Friedman advocates a fixed rule whilst his Chicago mentors advocated active variation in the quantity of money to offset fluctuations in velocity. There is one aspect, however, of the distinction between traditional Chicago and Keynes that Patinkin does not emphasize—but, in my view ought to have done. He says,

> I have already stressed the common view of Keynes and the Chicago School on the short-run instability of the economy. Another common feature was the fact that each chose what we today would call a discretionary policy to deal with this instability. (p. 303)

I believe that Patinkin is wrong to identify each school as choosing what we would today call a discretionary policy. On just one page earlier (p. 302) Patinkin quotes Simons's criticism of Keynes noting that

> he [Keynes] overlooks the need [clearly suggested by his own analysis] for the minimizing of monetary uncertainties and the achievement of a monetary system *based on definite and stable rules*. (emphasis added)

I view this statement by Simons as showing that he was not in favor of discretionary policies but rather the pursuit of explicitly stated and well understood rules.[6] It is interesting to note that this distinction between Keynes and traditional Chicago serves to emphasize a continuity between the Chicago school that extends well beyond that running from the 1930s to Friedman and coming all the way up to the current period. The emphasis on policy rules that arises out of the rational expectations framework developed by Robert E. Lucas, Jr. is the content of that continuity.

What is certainly true is that Friedman is a monetarist and traditional Chicago was not. Indeed, there is, on my reading, a remarkable similarity between traditional Chicago and those modern-day antimonetarists who worry about innovations and deregulation in the financial sector as sources of instability in the demand for money function and, therefore, as justifications for ad hoc discretionary variation in the supply of money. Friedman, in contrast, belittles the effects of these matters on the demand for money and emphasizes the importance of sticking to a steady and predictable behavior of the money supply. Based on their views, as reported by Patinkin, it is hard to resist the conclusion that had the deregulation and financial innovations of the past few years been occurring in the 1930s Simons and the others would have viewed them in much the same way as antimonetarists do today.

Friedman has suggested, however (in his Henry Simons lecture), that

> had Simons known the facts as we now know them, he would, I believe, have been

[5]I am referring here to the work of Phillip Cagan (1956).

[6]It must be admitted, however, that Simons advocated a fixed rule for the *price level* whereas Friedman proposed one for the money stock. With variable velocity, the pursuit of Simons's rule would require a *feedback* rule for the money stock.

> confirmed in "his earlier persuasion as to the merits of the rule of a fixed quantity of money . . . rather than have accepted . . . stabilization of the price level (rpt. 1969, p. 92)

Patinkin painstakingly rehearses the facts that were known to Simons and concludes that he was in possession of all the relevant facts and, despite this, and even more strongly despite having considered a fixed money stock as a possible rule, advocated variations in the quantity of money to achieve his price level target.

Patinkin has on occasion (and quite rightly) drawn attention to "one of the oldest and most dangerous pitfalls that lies along the path of those who venture into the history of doctrine." This is the pitfall of "reading things out of context" (1983, p. 48). There is a hint in Patinkin's treatment of Friedman's assertions concerning Simons's policy position that Patinkin has not completely avoided this "dangerous pitfall." Patinkin quotes Friedman as follows:

> Now, Friedman quite reasonably says that Simons' belief in the instability of velocity was based on his interpretation of the Great Depression; but Friedman goes on to contend that had Simons then known the "facts that we now know and he did not" (1967, p. 84), he would not have interpreted the Great Depression in terms of such an instability of V, and would accordingly have chosen instead of policy rules stated in terms of the quantity of money. (p. 296)

After this statement and after confessing that he (Patinkin) has some difficulty in understanding the operational meaning of such a statement he goes on to demonstrate that Simons knew the facts about the Great Depression as subsequently presented by Friedman and Schwartz in *A Monetary History of the United States* (1963) and also that Simons was familiar with the work of Lauchlin Currie which, in effect, provided a virtually identical interpretation of the Great Depression to that subsequently supplied by Friedman and Schwartz. Patinkin's implicit conclusion from all this is that Friedman is wrong. Simons was in possession of all the relevant facts and, despite that, he still reached the conclusion that a quantity of money rule would be inappropriate.

Before going on to consider what Friedman actually said let me note that, although the interpretation of the Great Depression provided by Currie was very similar to that subsequently supplied by Friedman and Schwartz, the basis for that interpretation was much less solid in Currie's paper. He provided an analysis of only ten years of data. This stands in marked contrast to Friedman and Schwartz who analyzed the Great Depression as one (albeit extreme) cycle in a ninety-three-year period of U.S. history.

Let me now turn however to what Friedman actually said in his Simons lecture and contrast that with Patinkin's out-of-context reading. What Friedman in fact said was this:

> Since Simons wrote, an enormous amount of evidence has accumulated that bears not only on these few years [i.e., the Great Depression] but also on a far wider range of economic history. This evidence . . . contradicts Simons' interpretation of the sources of instability. It turns out that the rate of growth of the quantity of money has systematically tapered off well before the economy in general slows down and has speeded up well before the economy speeds up. The movements in velocity—which Simons took as an independent source of instability—come later than the movements in the quantity of money and are mild when the movements in the quantity of money are mild. They have been sharp only when there have been sharp movements in the quantity of money. There is no evidence to support Simons' fear that a fixed quantity of money

> might involve "the danger of sharp changes on the velocity side." On the contrary the evidence is precisely the reverse — that it would lessen the danger of sharp changes in velocity. (rpt. 1969, pp. 91–92)

Read in context, it is clear that Friedman is not claiming that Simons did not know about the Great Depression. The facts of which Simons was ignorant were the facts that can only be discovered by a systematic investigation of a longer run of data than a single (albeit extreme) cyclical episode. In view of Patinkin's documentation of Simons's antiempirical approach, it is not clear whether Simons would have been as impressed with this evidence as Friedman is and as Friedman believes he would have been. It is clear, however, that Patinkin misquoted and misunderstood the reasoning that led Friedman to that conjecture.

Patinkin regards

> questions about the history of economic doctrine [as] empirical questions. And the universe from which the relevant empirical evidence must be drawn is that of the writings and teachings of the economists in question. (p. 242)

Subsequently, when studying Keynes, he went on to declare that

> I see it [the history of thought] as an empirical science in the broader sense that as historians of thought we are like econometricians fitting a multivariate regression equation to a man's writings: We are trying to pass a regression line through them that will best explain them. Now, one thing about a regression line is that there are always points off it, and then the question is whether they are random departures from the line, or whether they reflect a systematic influence that you have not taken account of. And the same is true when you pass a regression line through a man's writings: there will generally be some passages in his writings that you have not explained. And then you have to decide what is the true meaning of the man, what is his regression line and what is a chance phrase, a chance formulation, or perhaps even a mistake, whose departure from the regression line shouldn't make us change our view about the nature of the line. (Patinkin and Leith 1978, pp. 125–26)

Patinkin is here writing explicitly in the context of his work on Keynes and the *General Theory*. He does not, however, write in a way that invites us to regard him as restricting his attention only to that author and work. The passage that I have quoted sounds like a declaration of a general approach to the history of thought.

The analogy between texts and data and using texts to discern the true meaning of a writer and fitting a regression line is certainly a nice one. It invites an extension. Two aspects of inference have received a lot of attention at the hands of empirical (statistically oriented) economists, both of them appropriately at Chicago. One is the simultaneous equation problem[7] and the other is the sample selection bias problem.[8] The historian of thought needs to pay special attention to both of these problems in his "as if" regression running. A simultaneous equation problem arises for the historian of thought from the inevitable interaction between various traditions. Sample selection bias arises because scholars do not write down what seems to them to be obvious with the frequency that they write down those things with which they are wrestling. I would interpret some of my remarks in the foregoing as being an attempt to address the consequences of these two types of problems. I make no claim, however, to having invented a new estimator, or to having, in any adequate sense, solved these problems.

[7]The work of Haavelmo on this problem is referred to in Patinkin's reminiscence chapter.

[8]One of the early discoverers of this problem is even closer to home for Patinkin — see Reuben Gronau (1976). The name most associated with this matter is, however, James Heckman (1979).

Patinkin has provided us with an account of traditional Chicago monetary theory and of the work of Friedman that creates an overall picture which, in my view, puts the "regression line" in the wrong place and leaves too much in the error term. I have tried to show the essential continuity between the monetary theory of Milton Friedman and that of his Chicago precursors. There is, of course, also a continuity between the monetary theory of Keynes and that of Friedman. Keynes's monetary theory, however, is itself solidly in the Cambridge cash balance tradition—a tradition that is equivalent to the quantity theory approach.

Over and above all this (and not dealt with above because it is only tangential to Patinkin's treatment of the matter), Friedman seems to me to be in the Chicago tradition in a much more important way. That is, not only is Friedman a quantity theorist but also a quantitative quantity theorist. The quantitative tradition, eclipsed in Chicago with the death of Henry Schultz in 1938 but reestablished in 1943 with the arrival of the Cowles Commission, emerges as one of the clear Chicago antecedents of the careful systematic empirical investigations that Friedman subsequently undertook and inspired his students to pursue in establishing some of the propositions of monetary theory and policy that he (Friedman) sees as being distinctly in that earlier Chicago tradition.

LITERATURE CITED

Cagan, Phillip. "The Monetary Dynamics of Hyperinflation." In *Studies in the Quantity Theory of Money,* edited by Milton Friedman, pp. 25–117. Chicago: University of Chicago Press, 1956.

Cannan, Edwin. *An Economist's Protest.* London: P. S. King and Son, 1927.

Edie, Lionel D. *Money, Bank Credit, and Prices.* New York: Harper and Brothers, 1928.

Friedman, Milton. "The Quantity Theory of Money: A Restatement." In *Studies in the Quantity Theory of Money,* edited by Milton Friedman, pp. 3–21. Chicago: University of Chicago Press, 1956; reprinted in *The Optimum Quantity of Money and Other Essays,* by Milton Friedman, pp. 51–67. Chicago: Aldine, 1969.

———. "The Monetary Theory and Policy of Henry Simons." *Journal of Law and Economics* 10 (October 1967), 1–14; reprinted in *The Optimum Quantity of Money and Other Essays,* by Milton Friedman, pp. 81–93. Chicago: Aldine, 1969.

———. *The Optimum Quantity of Money and Other Essays.* Chicago: Aldine, 1969.

———. "Comments on the Critics." *Journal of Political Economy* 80 (September/October 1972), 906–50.

Friedman, Milton, and Anna J. Schwartz. *A Monetary History of the United States 1867–1960.* Princeton, N.J.: Princeton University Press, 1963.

Gronau, Reuben. "The Allocation of Time of Israeli Women" (*Essays in Labour Economics* in Honor of H. Gregg Lewis). *Journal of Political Economy* 84 (August 1976, Part 2), 201–20.

Hawtrey, Ralph George. *Currency and Credit.* London: Longmans, Green and Company, 1919.

Heckman, James J. "Sample Selection Bias as a Specification Error." *Econometrica* 47 (January 1979), 153–61.

James, F. Cyril. *The Economics of Money, Credit and Banking.* New York: The Ronald Press, 1930.

Knight, Frank H. "The Business Cycle, Interest, and Money: A Methodological Approach." *Review of Economics and Statistics* 23 (May 1941), 53–67.

Mints, Lloyd W. Review of *The Economics of Money, Credit and Banking by* F. Cyril James (New York: The Ronald Press, 1930). *Journal of Political Economy* 39 (December 1931), 819–22.

Patinkin, Don. "Friedman on the Quantity Theory and Keynesian Economics." *Journal of Political Economy* 80 (September/October 1972), 883–905.

———. "Keynes' Aggregate Supply Function: A Plea for Common Sense." *History of Political Economy* 10 (Winter 1978), 577–96.

———. "A Study of Keynes's Theory of Effective Demand." *Economic Inquiry* 17 (April 1979), 155–76.

———. "New Perspectives or Old Pitfalls? Some Comments on Allan Meltzer's Interpretation of the *General Theory*." *Journal of Economic Literature* 21 (March 1983), 47–51.

Patinkin, Don, and J. Clark Leith (eds.). *Keynes, Cambridge, and the General Theory*. London: Macmillan, 1978.

Pigou, A. C. "The Value of Money." *Quarterly Journal of Economics* 32 (1917), 38–65; reprinted in *Readings in Monetary Theory*, edited by Friedrich A. Lutz and Lloyd W. Mints, pp. 162–83. Homewood, Ill.: Richard D. Irwin, 1951.

Simons, Henry C. "Hansen on Fiscal Policy." *Journal of Political Economy* 50 (April 1942), 161–96.

Tavlas, George S. "Chicago Schools Old and New: On the Efficacy of Monetary Policy." *Banca Nazionale del Lavaro* 120 (March 1977), 51–73 (a).

———. "The Chicago Tradition Revisited: Some Neglected Monetary Contributions: Senator Paul Douglas (1892–1976)." *Journal of Money, Credit, and Banking* 9 (November 1977), 529–35 (b).

A Reply

by Don Patinkin

Though entitled "Essays On and In the Chicago Tradition: A Review Essay," Michael Parkin's essay (referred to henceforth as MP) is essentially not a review of my book of that title, but a criticism of one of the articles reprinted in it, namely my 1969 article on "The Chicago Tradition, the Quantity Theory, and Friedman" (henceforth CTF), which appeared in the maiden issue of this journal. This, accordingly, is a reply to Parkin's belated criticism.[1]

Parkin devotes a good part of his essay to establishing a point that was never at issue: namely, that the analytical equivalence between the transactions and demand-for-money approach to the quantity theory was recognized by monetary economists of the "pre-Keynesian period," including Chicago economists. Indeed, there is a strange inconsistency between Parkin's treatment of this point as if it were at issue,

[1]Since this article is concerned with the history of thought, all works are cited by the original year of publication. For the convenience of the reader, however, the page references of a reprinted work (as listed in the Literature Cited) are to the pages of the reprint in question.

DON PATINKIN *is professor of economics, Hebrew University of Jerusalem.*

Journal of Money, Credit, and Banking, Vol. 18, No. 1 (February 1986)

and the fact that he precedes his discussion with a quotation from my essay in which I state that this recognition was a "commonplace of monetary theory" and cite as supporting evidence not a post-Keynesian publication, but Irving Fisher's classic 1913 book *The Purchasing Power of Money* (CTF, p. 247).

Nor was it necessary for Parkin to seek supporting evidence for this recognition in obscure textbooks of the pre-Keynesian period. For in that most popular textbook of the period—one that was also in use at the University of Chicago[2]—Dennis Robertson's Cambridge Economic Handbook *Money* (1928, pp. 40–41), there is a lucid explanation (in Robertson's characteristically colorful language) of why the "Money-Sitting" (i.e., demand-for-money) approach and the "Money-on-the-Wing" (i.e., transactions) approach can be used interchangeably in analyzing the determination of the value of money. I might also note that another textbook that Mints used in the undergraduate course on "Money and Banking" that I took in 1943 was Lester Chandler's *An Introduction to Monetary Theory,* in which the equivalence of these two approaches was emphasized (1940, p. 40).[3]

What then, is the issue? Though quantity theorists recognized the analytical equivalence of the two approaches to the theory, they nevertheless—each to his own tastes—regarded one or the other of them as preferable. Thus, in a well-known passage,[4] Pigou (1917, p. 174) claims that his cash-balance approach is a "more effective engine of analysis" than Fisher's transactions approach "because it brings us at once into relation with volition—an ultimate cause of demand—instead of with something that seems at first sight accidental and arbitrary." Similarly, Keynes in *A Tract on Monetary Reform* (1923, p. 78, n. 1) states that his variation on Pigou's cash-balance equation "comes to the same thing in the end" as Fisher's transactions equation, but goes on to say that his equation "seems less artificial than Professor Fisher's." Correspondingly, the issue between Friedman and myself was—and is—which approach did the Chicago economists prefer? More specifically, is there any basis for Friedman's claim in his well-known 1956 essay "The Quantity Theory of Money—A Restatement" that in the Chicago tradition, "the quantity theory is *in the first instance* a theory of the *demand* for money," assumed to be functionally stable (Friedman 1956, p. 4, first set of italics added; cf. also CTF, p. 247)?

My 1969 paper provided evidence from the writings and lectures of the Chicago economists in question, as well as from the Ph.D. theses they directed, that *in the first instance* the traditional Chicago school (and Simons in particular) adopted

[2]See Paul Samuelson's recollections (1985, p. 6) of his student days at Chicago in the early 1930s. Robertson's textbook continued to be in use during my students days there a decade later.

[3]My lecture notes from Mints's 1944 graduate course on "Money" show that after presenting Fisher's transactions approach, Mints presented the cash-balance approach, and referred us to Pigou's classic 1917 article on the "Value of Money" (to which Parkin also refers), as well as to Keynes's 1923 *A Tract on Monetary Reform* (about which more in a moment). My notes on this subject conclude with the statement that "Mints doesn't see much choice between Fisher's transactions equation and [the] cash-balance equation."

It is, of course, nice to have Parkin's evidence (MP, p. 109) of Mints's expression of this opinion in his 1931 review of Cyril James's textbook as well Parkin, however, ignores the fact that this review provides further support for my proposition that, contrary to Friedman, the Chicago economists of the 1930s believed that the velocity of circulation (and hence the demand for money) was unstable. In particular, Mints refers here without objection to the possibility that an "increase in the quantity of money would be offset by an increase in the real value of the unspent margin [Hawtrey's term for cash balances held by individuals] and that consequently there would be no increase in the price level" (Mints 1931, p. 820)

[4]Which Parkin has even quoted (MP, p. 107). See also my *Money, Interest, and Prices* (1956), pp. 97, 100–101; 1965; pp. 163, 166–67).

the transactions approach to monetary theory, and that in this context it claimed that the velocity of circulation was unstable.

What contrary evidence does Parkin bring? He quotes again one of the passages that I have cited from Simons's writings, claims that it implicitly refers to the demand for money (MP, p. 108), and concludes his discussion of this passage (as well as similar ones from one of Knight's articles[5]) with the statement that "Friedman's identification of the quantity theory as being *first and foremost* a theory of the demand for money is entirely in line with all the major monetary theorists of the 1930s" (MP, p. 110, italics added). But this is surely a non sequitur: the same line of reasoning would lead us to conclude that since — as pointed out in my article and mentioned above — there is a passage in Fisher's *Purchasing Power of Money* (1913, pp. 153–54), which indicates that he was "thinking in terms of a demand for money" (CTF, p. 247), then that classic statement of the transactions approach to the quantity theory is "first and foremost" a theory of the demand for money! Similarly, Parkin's logic would lead us to conclude that since in one of his writings Pigou (1929, pp. 168–70) carried out his analysis in terms of changes in the velocity of circulation, Pigou was "first and foremost" an exponent of the transactions approach to monetary theory.

It is this failure to distinguish between a writer's basic analytical framework[6] and his occasional implicit or explicit recognition of other, analytically equivalent frameworks that vitiates Parkin's discussion of this point.

In subsequent parts of his essay, Parkin is repeatedly guilty of the basic methodological fallacy of reading meaning into texts. This is what he does in his attempt to deal with my demonstration that the traditional Chicago school did not take account of the influence of the rate of interest on the velocity of circulation. An even more extreme example occurs later in Parkin's essay. At no point in his writings does Simons ever explicitly refer to a functional relationship determining velocity or to a demand function for money; yet Parkin presents an interpretation which attributes to Simons not only such a notion, but even Friedman's highly sophisticated notion of a stable functional relationship between the velocity of circulation and the rate of change of prices. Surely that is farfetched.

Parkin's criticism of my later — and related — essay on "Keynes and Chicago" (1979) reflects the same failings as his criticism of my 1969 paper. Thus, he cites my statement that "a common feature [of Keynes and Chicago] was the fact that each chose what we today would call a discretionary policy to deal with instability" (ibid., p. 303) and criticizes it on the grounds that Simons "was not in favor of discretionary policies" (MP, p. 112). Here again Parkin fails to realize the nature of the point at issue. The key word in my statement is "today." Obviously, when in 1936 Simons wrote his celebrated essay on "Rules versus Authorities in Monetary Policy," he regarded his policy of varying the quantity of money so as to stabilize the price level as a rule. But today — as I go on to emphasize in the sentences following the one

[5]In my 1969 article, I noted that "by the 1940s the Chicago School itself had — quite understandably — been influenced by Keynesian monetary theory" (CTF, p. 249). This is particularly evident in the 1941 article by Knight which Parkin cites; for this is in part a criticism of Keynes's theory of liquidity preference (Knight 1941, pp. 63 ff.) and so naturally makes use of some of the concepts of this theory. Correspondingly, we cannot infer from this article that Knight also made use of these concepts before the appearance of the *General Theory* — and that is the point at issue. Parkin also ignores the fact that even in this article, Knight's " 'theory' of the behavior of money" is Fisher's $MV = PT$ transactions equation (ibid., p. 59).

[6]Which framework is a particular instance of what I have since denoted as the "central message" of a writer; see my *Anticipations of the General Theory?* (1982, pp. 17–18, 82–86).

that Parkin criticizes—because of what we have since learned about the difficulty of determining the "actual state of the world at any given time, compounded by the possibly destablizing effects of lags" (Patinkin 1979, p. 303)—we regard as discretionary what Simons regarded as a rule. Indeed, my view here is much the same as that expressed by Friedman in his 1960 *A Program for Monetary Stability* (pp. 84–89) in explaining why he rejected Simons's policy rule in favor of one specifying a constant rate of growth in the quantity of money.

Because he considered the economy to be characterized by "sharp changes on the velocity side . . . extreme alternations of hoarding and dishoarding," Simons (1936, p. 164)—a quarter of a century earlier—had made the opposite policy choice. In the introductory part of his 1967 Henry Simons lecture, Friedman discusses this difference and claims that "a few facts, which we now know and *he [i.e., Simons] did not,* have made all the difference. The facts have to do *primarily* with the Great Depression of 1929–1933. Were I to interpret that episode as Simons did, I would agree with his recommendations. Had he interpreted that episode as I do, he would not have made the policy recommendation he did" (Friedman 1967, p. 84, italics added). In section 1 of the paper, entitled "Simons' Interpretation of Business Cycles in General and the Great Depression in Particular," Friedman then states that Simons's interpretation "undoubtedly was *derived largely from the 1929–33 crash*" (ibid., p. 85, italics added). Friedman then begins section 2 of his paper—entitled "Simons' Theory of Cycles and his Policy Proposals"—with the statement that "it is clear how Simon's policy proposals *derive from his interpretation of the Great Depression*" (ibid., p. 86, italics added). A few pages later comes section 4, entitled "The Key Facts As We Now Know Them" (ibid., p. 89), whose second paragraph begins with the statement "We *now know* that the critical relation ran precisely the other way" (italics added). Then follows a three-page description of the key facts of the Great Depression as described in Friedman and Schwartz's *A Monetary History of the United States* (1963). This description concludes with the explanation that "I [Friedman] have stressed the Great Depression because this climactic episode clearly played a *key role* in leading Simons—and also Keynes—to believe that the orthodox powers of the monetary authorities were too weak to cope with disorders arising in the private financial markets" (Friedman 1967, p. 92, italics added). The final paragraph of section 4 then begins with the statement that "since Simons wrote, an enormous amount of evidence has accumulated that bears not only on these few years, but also on a far wider range of economic history. This evidence, too, contradicts Simons's interpretation of the source of instability" (ibid., p. 92).

In my 1979 paper "Keynes and Chicago" (which was also a Henry Simons lecture) I digressed briefly to show that here again Friedman's statements about the traditional Chicago School were in contradiction with the facts. In particular, I pointed out that when Simons chose his rule of varying the quantity of money so as to achieve a stable price level in preference to a constant-quantity-of-money rule, he had already published a review (Simons 1935) of Lauchlin Currie's book on *The Supply and Control of Money in the United States* (1934) which made "available to him [i.e., Simons] not only monetary data [about the Great Depression] that revealed roughly the same changes that Friedman has described in his lecture [on Simons], but even an alternative interpretation of these data which in its broad lines agreed with the one that Friedman was later to give" (Patinkin 1979, p. 297).

From all of Friedman's essay on Simons, Parkin refers only to the aforementioned last paragraph of section 4 (which he cites in full) and charges me with having read

Friedman out of context. In Parkin's words: "Read in context, it is clear that Friedman is not claiming that Simons did not know about the Great Depression [*sic*]. The facts of which Simons was ignorant were the facts that can only be discovered by a systematic investigation of a longer run of data than a single (albeit extreme) cyclical episode" (MP, p. 114).

Let the reader judge who is reading Friedman out of context.[7]

I conclude this discussion of the major deficiencies in Parkin's essay with two observations. First, Parkin is more Friedmanian than Friedman: for whereas (as stated on page 256 of my 1969 paper) Friedman subsequently admitted in his 1968 encyclopedia article on the quantity theory that his "reformulation" of that theory—which in his 1956 paper he had associated solely with the "Chicago tradition"—is one "that has been strongly influenced by the Keynesian theory of liquidity preference" (Friedman 1968a, p. 439), there is barely a hint of this fact in Parkin's paper.

Second, I began this note with the statement that Parkin's essay was not a review of my book of *Essays On and In the Chicago Tradition* (1981). I end it by expressing my regret that he did not indeed write one. As Parkin points out in his opening paragraph, the reprinted articles in my book fall into three categories: price theory, macroeconomics, and the history of thought. I regret accordingly that Parkin—a member of the new generation of economic theorists—did not make use of his expertise in these first two fields (and particularly in macroeconomics) to write a review that would, inter alia, give us his critical evaluation of the picture of those aspects of micro- and macroeconomics at the Chicago of forty years ago that are represented in my book.

LITERATURE CITED

Chandler, Lester W. *An Introduction to Monetary Theory*. New York: Harper & Bros, 1940.

Currie, Lauchlin. *The Supply and Control of Money in the United States*. Cambridge, Mass.: Harvard University Press, 1934.

Fisher, Irving. *The Purchasing Power of Money: Its Determination and Relation to Credit Interest and Crises*, rev. ed. New York: Macmillan, 1913. Reprinted, New York: Augustus M. Kelley.

Friedman, Milton. "The Quantity Theory of Money—A Restatement." In *Studies in the Quantity Theory of Money*, edited by Milton Friedman, pp. 3–21. Chicago: University of Chicago Press, 1956.

———. *A Program for Monetary Stability*. New York: Fordham University Press, 1960.

———. "The Monetary Theory and Policy of Henry Simons." *Journal of Law and Economics* 10 (October 1967), 1–13. As reprinted in Friedman (1969), pp. 81–93.

———. "Money: Quantity Theory." In *International Encyclopedia of the Social Sciences*, Vol. 10, edited by David L. Sills, pp. 432–47. New York: Macmillan and Free Press, 1968 (a).

———. "The Role of Monetary Policy." *American Economic Review* 58 (March 1968), 1–17 (b). As reprinted in Friedman (1969), pp. 95–110.

———. *The Optimum Quantity of Money and Other Essays*. Chicago: Aldine, 1969.

[7]The reader is also referred to note 1 on page 97 of Friedman's 1968 paper "The Role of Monetary Policy," which states that Simons's view of the Great Depression "accounts for the policy changes that he recommended."

Friedman, Milton, and Anna J. Schwartz. *A Monetary History of the United States. 1867–1960*. Princeton: Princeton University Press for the National Bureau of Economic Research, 1963.

Keynes, John Maynard. *A Tract on Monetary Reform*. London: Macmillan, 1923.

Knight, Frank H. "The Business Cycle, Interest, and Money: A Methodological Approach." *Review of Economics and Statistics* 23 (May 1941), 53–67.

Mints, Lloyd W. Review of *The Economics of Money, Credit, and Banking* by F. Cyril James. *Journal of Political Economy* 39 (December 1931), 819–22.

Parkin, Michael. "Essays On and In the Chicago Tradition: A Review Essay." *Journal of Money, Credit, and Banking* (this issue).

Patinkin, Don. *Money, Interest, and Prices*. Evanston, Ill.: Row, Peterson, 1956.

______. *Money, Interest and Prices*, 2nd ed. New York: Harper and Row, 1965.

______. "The Chicago Tradition, the Quantity Theory, and Friedman." *Journal of Money, Credit, and Banking* 1 (February 1969), 46–70. As reprinted with a postscript in Patinkin (1981), pp. 241–74.

______. "Keynes and Chicago." *Journal of Law and Economics* 22 (October 1979), 213–32. As reprinted with minor additions in Patinkin (1981), pp. 289–308.

______. *Essays On and In the Chicago Tradition*. Durham, N. C.: Duke University Press, 1981.

______. *Anticipations of the General Theory? And Other Essays on Keynes*. Chicago: University of Chicago Press, 1982.

Pigou, A. C. "The Value of Money." *Quarterly Journal of Economics* 32 (November 1917), 38–65. As reprinted in *Readings in Monetary Theory*. Selected by a Committee of the American Economic Association, pp. 162–83. Philadelphia: Blakiston, 1951.

______. *Industrial Fluctuations*, 2nd ed. London: Macmillan, 1929.

Robertson, Dennis Holme. *Money*, new ed., rev. Cambridge: Cambridge University Press, 1928.

Samuelson, Paul. "Succumbing to Keynesianism." *Challenge* 27 (January/February 1985), 4–11.

Simons, Henry C. Review of *The Supply and Control of Money in the United States* by Lauchlin Currie. *Journal of Political Economy* 43 (August 1935), 555–58.

______. "Rules versus Authorities in Monetary Policy." *Journal of Political Economy* 44 (February 1936), 1–30. As reprinted in Henry C. Simons, *Economic Policy for a Free Society*. pp. 160–83. Chicago: University of Chicago Press, 1948.

'Review of Currie's *Supply and Control of Money*'

H. Simons, 'Review of Currie's *Supply and Control of Money in the United States*', *Journal of Political Economy*, 43 (August 1935), pp. 555–8.

BOOK REVIEWS

VENETIAN SHIPS AND SHIPBUILDERS: A CORRECTION

A misapprehension may have been created by a passage in the very careful and sympathetic review of my *Venetian Ships and Shipbuilders* by Dr. S. H. Thomson.[1] I still maintain that the volume of the international trade of Venice was substantially stable between 1450 and 1560, and that "the Venetian merchant marine *employed in international commerce* appears not to have declined, but actually to have grown in cargo-carrying capacity during the sixteenth century." (Italics mine.) The two figures the comparison of which Dr. Thomson cites as being at variance with the above quotation are not comparable. One of them includes ships under 240 tons, the other does not. For reasons set forth at length in my book I consider that the figures concerning ships of 240 tons or more are those significant for the volume of international commerce. I certainly agree, however, with Dr. Thomson that Venice was not keeping pace with more rapidly expanding western trade centers, and I wished to emphasize, among the reasons why Venice fell behind, the decay of the shipbuilding industry at Venice.

FREDERIC C. LANE

Johns Hopkins University

The Supply and Control of Money in the United States. By LAUCHLIN CURRIE. "Harvard Economic Studies," Vol. XLVII. Cambridge: Harvard University Press, 1934. Pp. xvi+199. $2.50.

This book should have a significant and salutary effect, both on professional opinion, and on college teaching. It attacks, at critically weak points, a dominant and decadent tradition of American thinking on banking questions; and it expounds clearly a set of views which, while firmly established in the "oral tradition" of some schools, are meagerly represented in the accessible literature.

Dr. Currie's general position may be indicated by a sample of quotations:

> The truth is that the whole modern conception of the function of a central bank of controlling the community's money is lacking in the Federal Reserve Act. (P. 88.)

[1] *Journal of Political Economy*, April, 1935, pp. 265–67.

As long as the reserve administration conceives its task as that of the qualitative control of bank assets, the best work of the monetary theorists cannot fructify in actual banking policy, and it is futile to seek to enhance the effectiveness of central bank control over money. (P. 45.)

It may be objected that even though the reserve administration conceives that the primary function of a central bank is to enable member banks to supply at all times and at reasonable rates the needs of their commercial borrowers, there is no great harm in this theory so long as it is so interpreted as to call for an easy money policy in the downswing of business and a restrictive policy in the upswing. It is, however, dangerous to expect adherence to a wrong theory to lead to the adoption of correct policies. (P. 43.)

There is no theoretical justification for the attempt to tie notes to commercial loans, as was done in the Federal Reserve Act. (P. 36.)

If bank assets were confined to commercial loans, which some people think would be the ideal state of affairs, there would be no reason why the decline in loans and the contraction of money should ever cease in the downswing of business. (P. 121.)

The problem of note issue in this country is that of assuring that the changing requirements of the community for notes do not, in themselves, bring about changes in the total volume of money. (P. 110.)

If it is desired to impose a check upon central banks, it would appear to be much more desirable to base reserve requirements on something they can control. In any case there is no good reason for requiring a much *higher* gold reserve against notes than against demand deposits. They should, at the least, be equal. (P. 111.)

The study reflects a rare combination of penetrating theoretical insights and patient competence in the analysis of banking statistics. The highly realistic treatment will make the author's argument convincing, or at least disturbing, to many readers who would be unimpressed by "mere theory." For critical students, however, Dr. Currie's inductive verifications will be largely gratuitous—although everyone will be grateful for the excellent statistical compilation and analysis. In general, the author's fundamental insights are so sound that failure of statistical confirmation would only indicate error or inadequacy in the statistics.

On several crucial points, however, Dr. Currie's position is, to the reviewer, highly unsatisfactory. He contends that only actually circulating media should be regarded as money. "If we include with means of payment all factors which contribute to economy of means of payment," he says (p. 18), "it is difficult to see where we should stop, and the concept of money would become so broad as to be useless."

For quantitative study, of course, a line must be drawn somewhere; the author's distinction is both convenient and sound as a basis for his statistical analysis; but, carried over uncritically into discussion of matters of policy, it reveals an uninspired preoccupation with simple quantity theory and a tendency toward almost fallacious simplification of problems. In particular, the author's definitional reflections seem to account for his notion that changes in the volume of savings deposits, and possible conversions of demand deposits into the savings form, are of minor importance for central-bank policy.

More striking is the fact that Currie's narrow definition of money seems to explain his characterizing as ideal (chap. xv) a system which would represent only a small first step toward an ideal financial structure. The reviewer, while sharing the author's enthusiasm for abolition of banking on the fractional-reserve basis, is impressed with the probability that the fundamental faults of the present system would soon reappear (as with the development of checking accounts, after the strict limitations upon note issue), if reform were undertaken according to Currie's prescriptions. To argue that the functions of commercial banks might be assumed without much disturbance by savings banks, amounts almost to recommending drastic changes on the grounds that their intended effects would never be realized.

At all events, it seems likely that we shall make substantial progress toward understanding of monetary problems, and toward wise proposals for reform, only by facing squarely the task of working with that concept of money which Currie describes as "so broad as to be useless." We realize now that the currency problem has been swallowed up in the problem of commercial banking; but we must go further. We must see that there is little significant difference between demand deposits and savings accounts, and that all institutional borrowing and lending at short term presents the same problems and anomalies as does deposit banking. The criterion of "effective circulation," like legal tender and "general acceptability," must not be taken too seriously.

The effort to discuss banking policy, while only skirting and touching casually upon monetary problems, is not conducive to elegance or clarity. The book, in spite of its title, and in spite of its central thesis, deals almost exclusively with banking. There are a few remarks about the gold standard; and in many places the author impliedly approves of price-level stabilization. But nowhere does he face the fundamental questions as to the proper objectives or ideal rules of policy. Thus, he leaves himself open to the charge of defining error without defining truth—of criticizing other people's positions without taking a position himself.

Finally one note of emphatic dissent. Dr. Currie evidently is guided (against all experience, one might say) by a faith in monetary dictators—in authorities with large discretionary powers. His notions of desirable reforms run largely in terms of means for augmenting the powers of the Reserve Board. Here he has many writers and students on his side. Yet one may insist that the position is questionable empirically and, above all, that it is simply incompatible with a liberal, democratic faith. Managed currency without definite, stable, legislative rules is one of the most dangerous forms of "planning." A free enterprise economy can function only within a legal framework of rules; and no part of that framework is more important than the rules which define the monetary system. In the past those rules have been empty and inadequate; but there is no tolerable solution to be found in resort to the wisdom of "authorities." No liberal can contemplate with equanimity the prospect of an economy in which every investment and business venture is largely a speculation in the future actions of the Federal Reserve Board.

There is an unpardonable scarcity of punctuation in the volume. Dr. Currie's style is such as to require a generous sprinkling of commas and semicolons; and readers will resent the waste of time involved in rereading sentences repeatedly to discover their structure. While the discussion moves along briskly and concisely in the main, there are numerous protracted digressions on minutiae and elaborate arithmetic illustrations of points that needed only simple statement. With all its faults, however, this book is one of the few economics treatises of recent years which has left the reviewer genuinely grateful and indebted to its author.

HENRY C. SIMONS

University of Chicago

'The "Oral Tradition" at Chicago in the 1930s'

F. G. Steindl, 'The "Oral Tradition" at Chicago in the 1930s', *Journal of Political Economy*, 96:2 (1990), pp. 430–2.

The "Oral Tradition" at Chicago in the 1930s

Frank G. Steindl

Oklahoma State University

In "The Quantity Theory of Money—a Restatement" (1956), Friedman states that "Chicago was one of the few academic centers at which the quantity theory continued to be a central and vigorous part of the *oral tradition* throughout the 1930's and 1940's, where students continued to study monetary theory and to write theses on monetary problems" (p. 3; italics added).

In a celebrated article in the inaugural issue of the *Journal of Money, Credit and Banking,* Patinkin (1969) disputes the existence of the oral tradition, marshaling for his indictment a host of evidence—class notes, theses, and writings of Chicago students and faculty. Subsequently, Johnson in his Ely lecture (1971) charges Friedman with "the invention of a University of Chicago oral tradition that was alleged to have preserved understanding of the fundamental truth among a small band of the initiated through the dark years of the Keynesian despotism" (pp. 10–11).

The issue of the existence of an oral tradition was joined the following year by Patinkin and Friedman in this *Journal*'s special issue on monetary theory. Friedman (1972, p. 932) denied that there was no such tradition, namely,

> [Patinkin's and Johnson's charge] would indict my perception, or integrity, or scholarship, but it would in no way contradict the existence of an important Chicago tradition in the field of money that had a great influence on subsequent work in monetary economics and on my own work in particular. . . .
>
> Whether I conveyed the flavor of that tradition or not, there was such a tradition; it was significantly different from

[*Journal of Political Economy,* 1990, vol 98, no 2]

> the quantity theory tradition that prevailed at other institutions of learning.

Was there an oral tradition of the quantity theory at Chicago or not? One important piece of evidence in support of such a tradition is Henry Simons's enthusiastic review (1935) of Lauchlin Currie's *The Supply and Control of Money in the United States* (1934). First, it is important to note that the quantity theory is an essential component in Currie's analysis, as can be seen from his opening remarks: "To write a book at this time dealing primarily with the supply of money and touching only incidentally on the rate and character of spending of money is to invite hostile criticism. Even kindly disposed critics may be inclined to dub such a treatment inadequate and superficial, while those not so kindly disposed may be tempted to damn it with the deadly accusation 'quantity theory'" (p. 3). After stressing the importance of the behavior of the money stock, Currie presents his annual money stock estimates for 1921–33, which show a 24 percent decline for 1929–33.[1]

The existence of a Chicago oral tradition can be seen in Simons's four-page review, which begins, "This book should have a significant and salutary effect, both on professional opinion, and on college teaching. It . . . expounds clearly a set of views which, while firmly established in the 'oral tradition' of some schools [leaving little doubt that Chicago is one of them], are [*sic*] meagerly represented in the accessible literature" (1935, p. 555). His subsequent comments are clearly in the quantity theory framework, including the question of the definition of money and what he sees as Currie's implied approval of price-level stabilization.[2] He goes on to criticize Currie's empirical notion of money as being too narrow, for his failure to "face the fundamental questions as to the proper objectives or ideal rules of policy" (p. 557), and for his being "guided (against all experience, one might say) by a faith in monetary dictators—in authorities with large discretionary powers" (p. 558). Nonetheless he concludes that "this

[1] Currie's notion of money is a medium of exchange view—narrow money. Though markedly different in definition and construction from Friedman and Schwartz's M1, the two series are remarkably similar, as Patinkin (1979, p. 223) noted. The simple correlation coefficient between them is .89, and for annual *changes* it is .85. Remarkably, it is .93 for annual rates of growth!

[2] Simons's reading of Currie's implied approval of price-level stabilization as a proper goal of monetary policy underscores a classic problem in textual exegesis, which for want of a better term may be called the "believing is seeing" view. His review appeared three issues prior to his famous article "Rules versus Authorities in Monetary Policy," which of course favored a price-level stabilization rule. Robertson's (1935) review, on the other hand, has Currie's proposals "coloured by the inflation-bacillus whose presence one cannot help detecting in Mr. Currie's blood, and which leads him to assume that the Government action called for will almost always be in an expansory direction" (p. 130). Robertson's reading in fact more accurately reflects Currie's position.

book is one of the few economics treatises of recent years which has left the reviewer genuinely grateful and indebted to its author" (p. 558).

Simons's use of the phrase "oral tradition" and, more important, the tone of his review appear to be clear evidence that such a tradition existed at Chicago, at least in the first half of the 1930s. To be sure, that tradition, as Patinkin noted in his Simons lecture (1979, p. 224, n. 48), or at least Simons's perception of it, has little use for empirical work: "For critical students, however, Dr. Currie's inductive verifications will be largely gratuitous—although everyone will be grateful for the excellent statistical compilation and analysis. In general, the author's fundamental insights are so sound that failure of statistical confirmation would only indicate error or inadequacy in the statistics" (Simons 1935, p. 556). The nature of that tradition and whether it remained reasonably the same into the 1940s and 1950s is another issue, one on which there may be no reasonable consensus.[3]

References

Currie, Lauchlin B. *The Supply and Control of Money in the United States.* Cambridge, Mass.: Harvard Univ. Press, 1934.

Friedman, Milton. "The Quantity Theory of Money—a Restatement." In *Studies in the Quantity Theory of Money,* edited by Milton Friedman. Chicago: Univ. Chicago Press, 1956.

———. "Comments on the Critics." *J.P.E.* 80 (September/October 1972): 906–50.

Johnson, Harry G. "The Keynesian Revolution and the Monetarist Counter-Revolution." *A.E.R. Papers and Proc.* 61 (May 1971): 1–14.

McIvor, R. Craig. "A Note on the University of Chicago's 'Academic Scribblers.' " *J.P.E.* 91 (October 1983): 888–93.

Patinkin, Don. "The Chicago Tradition, the Quantity Theory, and Friedman." *J. Money, Credit and Banking* 1 (February 1969): 46–70.

———. "Friedman on the Quantity Theory and Keynesian Economics." *J.P.E.* 80 (September/October 1972): 883–905.

———. "Keynes and Chicago." *J. Law and Econ.* 22 (October 1979): 213–32.

Robertson, D. H. Review of *The Supply and Control of Money in the United States* by Lauchlin B. Currie. *Econ. J.* 45 (March 1935): 128–31.

Simons, Henry C. Review of *The Supply and Control of Money in the United States* by Lauchlin B. Currie. *J.P.E.* 43 (August 1935): 555–58.

[3] McIvor (1983) indicates that the tradition continued through the late 1930s, emphasizing especially the influence of Lloyd Mints. Inasmuch as Simons's monetary views remained essentially unchanged during his life, the oral tradition of which he wrote would have carried over into the 1940s.

'The Chicago Tradition: A Comment'

D. Patinkin, 'The Chicago Tradition: a comment', unpublished.

revised: 18 May 1991

The Chicago Tradition: A Comment

by

Don Patinkin

The Hebrew University of Jerusalem

Frank Steindl's recent note in this Journal on "The 'Oral Tradition' at Chicago in the 1930s" (1990) purports to deal with the disagreement between Milton Friedman (1956) and myself (1969) about this tradition – but is actually completely besides the point. For that disagreement was not (as Steindl presents it) about whether or not there was such an oral tradition, but what the nature of that tradition was. And far from my denying the existence of such a tradition (as Steindl repeatedly alleges), I devoted section III of my 1969 paper--which section was actually entitled "The Oral Tradition of Chicago"--to making use of my lecture notes from the courses I had with the same teachers (albeit, a decade apart) that Friedman and I both had at Chicago (viz., Knight, Viner, and especially Simons and Mints) to document a Chicago oral tradition of monetary theory (that was also expressed in their writings) which differs fundamentally from the picture that Friedman presents of it in his 1956 essay. On this – the only point at issue between Friedman and myself in this context – Steindl's note has nothing to say.

KEYNES, CHICAGO AND FRIEDMAN

VOLUME 2

Keynes, Chicago and Friedman

Volume 2

General Editor

ROBERT LEESON

LONDON

PICKERING & CHATTO

2003

Published by Pickering & Chatto (Publishers) Limited
21 Bloomsbury Way, London, WC1A 2TH

2252 Ridge Road, Brookfield, Vermont 05036, USA

www.pickeringchatto.com

BRITISH LIBRARY CATALOGUING IN PUBLICATION DATA

Keynes, Chicago and Friedman
1. Keynes, John Maynard, 1883–1946 2. Friedman, Milton
3. Chicago School of Economics 4. Keynesian economics
I. Leeson, Robert
330.1'5

ISBN 1851967672

LIBRARY OF CONGRESS CATALOGING-IN-PUBLICATION DATA

Keynes, Chicago and Friedman / general editor, Robert Leeson: preface by Milton Friedman
p. cm
Includes bibliographical references and index.
ISBN 1–85196–767–2 (alk. paper)
1. Friedman, Milton, 1912– 2. Chicago School of Economics 3. Keynes, John Maynard, 1883–1946. I. Leeson, Robert II. Friedman, Milton, 1912–

HB119 .F84 K49 2003
330.15--dc21 2002030351

∞

This publication is printed on acid-free paper that conforms to
the American National Standard for Permanence of Paper in Printed Library Materials.

Typeset by
P&C

Printed and bound in Great Britain

CONTENTS

PART FOUR: TOWARDS A RESOLUTION OF THE DISPUTE

Part Three

How Unique was the Chicago Tradition?

How Unique was the Chicago Tradition?

The first part of this introduction describes and elaborates upon the contributions made to this expanding literature by Tom Cate, J. Ronnie Davis, David Laidler and Joseph Aschheim and George Tavlas regarding the claim that inter-war Chicago exhibited unique quantity theory characteristics. The second part examines the so-called '"Chicago Plan" of Banking Reform', described by Albert Hart (1935), a Chicago graduate student of the 1930s. The Chicago Plan was a response to the Great Depression which required all banks to hold 100 per cent reserves against their deposits, thus eliminating the instability caused by fractional reserves.[1]

Tavlas versus Cate, Davis and Laidler

There are parallels between the somewhat heated exchanges between Tavlas and his critics and Don Patinkin's response to Michael Parkin. Also, there are similarities between aspects of Milton Friedman's limited response to Patinkin and Arthur Pigou's limited response to John Maynard Keynes. An analysis of these exchanges may also provide some wider insights into the nature of disputation in economics.

In the *General Theory*, Keynes (1936) assaulted the Marshallian tradition generally, and Pigou in particular. Pigou's loyalty lay with the social reforming ideology of the Marshallian School. On several occasions, Pigou (1936; 1945; 1946; 1950) reflected on the *General Theory*. He defended Alfred Marshall from Keynes' attacks but was less concerned for his own reputation.[2] Pigou (1935, 22–4; 1931, 544) objected to Keynes' 'Body-line bowling!' and regarded 'controversy for its own sake' as 'a prodigious waste of time'. Moreover, 'Controversies conducted in the manner of Kilkenny cats' undermined what he regarded as the potentially beneficial influence of economists. In consequence, Pigou became an involuntary accomplice in the cultivation of the ahistorical Keynes–Classics mythology.[3]

Friedman (Vol. 1, pp. 33–51 [1956]) launched the monetarist counter-revolution by minimising the originality of his own contribution and maximising the supposed contribution of the Chicago Fathers. When criticised privately by Patinkin, Friedman (Vol. 1, pp. 71–84 [1968]) deleted the references to Chicago in his encyclopaedia article on the quantity theory. When criticised publicly by Patinkin, Friedman (Vol. 1, pp. 147–66 [1972/1974], 156) responded: 'After all, I am not unwilling to accept some credit for the theoretical analysis in that article'. Patinkin devoted a considerable amount of time and energy to examining his 1944 Economics 330 notes. According to Stanley Fischer (to Patinkin, 16 March 1971), Friedman grumbled that he did not have 'the time to be involved in polemics'.[4] He either recalled, or examined his Archives, to provide David Laidler (1999, 239, n. 32) with information about Hawtrey's *Currency and Credit* being on Lloyd Mints' 330 reading list. But he did not examine his 1932 Economics 330 notes: 'It was indeed stupid of me in the early 70's not to go back to my notes, and as of this date I cannot really say why I did not think of doing so' (correspondence to the author, 29 November 2000). He thus directly contributed little to the debate (beyond the initial irritation to Patinkin, and the subsequent retraction of his assertion about Chicago uniqueness and immunity to the Keynesian virus).

For twenty-five years, Tavlas has been adding to the literature while providing stimulating irritation to those who believed that the evidence favoured Patinkin. He traced the money growth rule back to Jeremy Bentham, Henry Thornton and John Gray (1977) and contributed some 'notes' on Carl Snyder (1982). As a graduate student at New York University, Tavlas added 'some further observations' to the debate and analysed of the work of Senator Paul Douglas, an important Chicago economist of the 1930s and 1940s (pp. 29–36 [1976]; pp. 79–85 [1977]).

In conjunction with Aschheim, Tavlas explored the relationship between Monetarism and Ideology (pp. 115–34 [1979], 120). Whereas the *laissez faire* wing of the first generation Chicago School advocated discretionary changes in the money supply, Douglas, from the socialist-planning wing of the Chicago School, advocated a policy norm 'strikingly reminiscent of the monetary growth-rule advocated by contemporary monetarists'.

In his first contribution, Tavlas (pp. 29–36 [1976], 29–30, 36) argued that 'to [William] Foster and [Waddill] Catchings, and the Chicagoans, public works were a means of conducting monetary policy'. Keynes and his followers advocated budget deficits 'within a theoretical framework that featured the impotence of monetary policy during depressions'. In contrast, 'American economists – especially members of the Chicago School – advocated budget deficits precisely because monetary policy *did* matter' [emphasis in original].

Within the Keynesian framework, Y = C + I + G (where Y = national income, C = consumption, I = investment, and G = government expenditure), and there is a direct theoretical route whereby an increase in G can increase Y. Tavlas also demonstrated that within the Chicagoan quantity theory framework, MV = PT (where M = the quantity of money, V = the velocity of money, P = the price level, and T = the level of output), and an identical result could be achieved, with fiscal deficits increasing M. Hence, he argued, the immunity of Chicagoans from the influence of the *General Theory*.

This framework was also an important ingredient of Patinkin's (Vol. 1, pp. 87–120 [1969/1981], 91–2) 'Other Chicago' (as distinct from 'Friedman's Chicago' which Patinkin sought to debunk). The 'Other Chicago' was, according to Patinkin, 'primarily a summary of Simons' views, which were largely accepted by Mints' and to a lesser extent by Frank Knight and Jacob Viner. In what Patinkin regarded as this authentic Chicago tradition, 'the government had an obligation to undertake a contracyclical policy. The guiding principle of this policy is to change M so as to offset changes in V, and thus generate the full-employment level of aggregate demand MV ... The necessary variations in M can be generated either by open-market operations or by budgetary deficits. The latter method is more efficient, and in some cases might even be necessary. Budgetary deficits, in turn, can be generated by varying either government expenditure or tax receipts. From the point of view of contracyclical policy, this makes no difference – for either method changes M'. Patinkin contrasted 'his' Chicago with Friedman's, but not with other contemporaneous approaches to the business cycle.

Tavlas (pp. 203–14 [1998], 211–12) argued that Patinkin and Harry Johnson 'overlooked that lonely spot on the Midway that used the quantity theory to provide an alternative rationale for a policy of public works during the Depression'. Tavlas also argued that Friedman was 'expounding the old time-religion which insisted that money mattered'. Thus 'while some economists outside Chicago advocated the use of expansionary fiscal measures, only the Chicagoans used the quantity theory to rationalise such a policy. Only the Chicagoans identified the use of fiscal measures as a direct mechanism to effectuate an increase in the money supply'. This 1930s Chicago 'consensus' that 'fiscal measures are a way of conducting monetary policy' was, according to Tavlas, 'remarkable ... I am not aware of a single US economist during the early 1930s outside the University of Chicago who explicitly and consistently used the quantity theory framework in such a manner'.[5] Thus Tavlas identified a 'uniqueness' which is different from that initially identified by Friedman.

Aspects of Tavlas' work have been described as 'excellent' (Cate, pp. 65–9 [1981], 65). But Davis (pp. 49–55 [1979], 51) suggested that Tavlas appeared to be writing in ignorance of the literature he was criticising,[6] and Laidler (pp. 217–29 [1998]) suggested that he was writing in ignorance of the secondary literature. The conventional view is that underconsumptionists have typically confined their analysis to the real sector of the economy, and have thus, typically, downplayed the importance of monetary factors (see, for example, Schneider 1987, 742).[7] Conventional views are legitimate targets for scholars, although they have to be subjected to detailed criticism for any radical reinterpretation to have any chance of widespread acceptance. Laidler (1999, 211, n. 28; Laidler p. 227 [1998], n. 9) argued that Foster and Catchings, Douglas and John Gray were underconsumptionists and that Tavlas' attempts to portray them as quantity theorists 'seems quite indefensible in light of the textual evidence'. It was therefore 'utterly unhelpful' for Tavlas to 'gloss over' the division between underconsumptionism and the quantity theory: 'Perhaps other historians of economic thought will agree with me'.

Tavlas has, so far, engaged three opponents. The first, Davis (pp. 39–45 [1968]) provided a path breaking analysis of the Chicago economists of the 1930s, followed by an extensive analysis of *The New Economics and the Old Economists* (1971). Tavlas (pp. 29–36 [1976], 32) argued that Davis had blurred the 'very sharp differences between the U.S. economists, especially the residents at Chicago, and Keynes'. Moreover the work of Foster and Catchings had not been adequately appraised in this context.[8]

In response, Davis (pp. 49–55 [1979], 49, 51) concluded that Tavlas' 'corrective ... is itself adulterated'; Tavlas had committed 'a serious error' by 'misreading' his book. Davis titled his reply 'The Last Remake of the The New Economics and the Old Economists' but added that 'the character of the controversy' was unlikely to allow an immediate termination. Tavlas, in turn, suggested that Davis had 'failed to identify the Chicagoans of the 1930s as quantity theorists'. The monetary economics of Foster and Catching and the Chicagoans 'helped identify the historical foundations of the monetarist counter-revolution, including the reasons underlying the Chicago School's resistance to the Keynesian virus'.

Tom Cate (pp. 65–9 [1981], 65–6, 68–9) located what be believed to be 'a serious error' in Tavlas' argument which was based on an 'inaccurate reading of the *Treatise* and the *General Theory*'. According to Cate, the policy recommendations of the *Treatise* (which Keynes repeated in Chicago in

1931) were 'identical to the policies which he advocates in his earlier writings'. Thus the transformation in Keynes' analysis towards a loan-financed domestic investment program occurred after Keynes' visit to Chicago.

In response, Tavlas (pp. 70–5 [1981], 72) argued that Keynes' 'theoretical thinking had undergone a marked change' by the time of the publication of the *Treatise*. Thus by emphasing the continuity in Keynes' work between 1923 and 1931, Cate 'obscures the transformation of Keynes' own thinking on monetary economics and obviates one of the reasons why, in the initial stages, the monetarist counter-revolution was centred in Chicago. In particular, in the *Tract* Keynes expounded views on monetary theory similar to those which were later to categorise the 1930s Chicago School. Keynes' rejection of these views in the *Treatise* explains, in part, the Chicago School's resistance to the Keynesian revolution'.

According to Tavlas (pp. 70–5 [1981], 73), Pigou and Keynes of the *Tract* analysed the quantity theory using a choice theoretic demand for money approach, thus displaying a 'basic similarity with the macroeconomics of the Chicago school of the 1930s'. But in the *Treatise*, this approach had been replaced by 'the controversial and short-lived fundamental equations'. After his visit to Chicago in 1931, Keynes 'began to share the Chicago view that banking measures were insufficient in dealing with the 1930s depression. Moreover – and in accord with the Chicagoans – Keynes increasingly opted for budget deficits to combat the depression. Where he departs from the Chicagoans, however, is in his rejection regarding the compatibility of budget deficits within the framework of the quantity theory. Instead, Keynes elected to construct a new theoretical structure to support his practical recommendations of public works projects'.

Tavlas' next adversary was Laidler, the author of *The Golden Age of the Quantity Theory: the Development of Neoclassical Monetary Economics 1870–1914* (1991); *Fabricating the Keynesian Revolution: Studies of the Inter-War Literature on Money, the Cycle, and Unemployment* (1999); and *The Demand for Money: Theory and Evidence* (1969) which in its third edition became *The Demand for Money: Theory, Evidence and Problems* (1985).[9] Laidler's interest in the Chicago tradition presumably extends back to his experience of having been taught by Friedman at Chicago in the early 1960s. Laidler became a monetarist, albeit one critical of Friedman's formulation of the demand for money function (Laidler, 1966).

Tavlas (pp. 79–85 [1977]) argued that while Douglas is primarily remembered, at an academic level, for the Cobb-Douglas production function, he also utilised a monetary framework. Douglas was 'above all' a quantity theorist.[10] Tavlas concluded that Friedman was correct in delineating a unique Chicago quantity theory tradition. Moreover, Douglas' pre-1936 contribution 'was a major reason why Chicago became immune from the Keynesian virus'. Tavlas (pp. 70–5 [1981]) explored the evolution of two traditions: a cost-push explanation of inflation culminating in the Radcliffe Report and a Chicago quantity theory tradition culminating in monetarism. Friedman was the 'beneficiary' of this Chicago tradition; whereas the Keynesians had 'misconstrued' their 'master's message'.

In contrast, Laidler (pp. 137–72 [1993]) argued that some of the distinctive characteristics that Friedman attributed to Chicago in the 1930s were present in the work of two Harvard economists, Allyn Young and his student, Lauchlin Currie, and in the writings of the British Treasury economist, Ralph Hawtrey. Before his retirement, Hawtrey had only one academic appointment – at Harvard as Young's replacement (1928–9), with Currie as his assistant.[11] Judged by the citation count, Hawtrey and Young exerted an almost equivalent influence upon the first version of Currie's thesis. Young also taught James Angell, Edward Chamberlin, Frank Knight, Harold Reed and Arthur Marget and so exerted a considerable influence over interwar monetary economists (Blitch, 1995, 115; Laidler, 1999, 197, n. 14, 234, n. 24; Moggridge, 1992, 882; Bigg, 1987, 605).

Using Friedman's (1953) widely imitated methodological distinction, Laidler (pp. 137–72 [1993]) found the 'positive' theoretical content of the Chicago tradition to be essentially indistinguishable from this Harvard–Hawtrey tradition; whereas the 'distinctive feature of Chicagoan analysis was normative, namely to forge a link between a monetary explanation of the cycle and a liberal political agenda'.[12] Laidler provided support for Patinkin's conclusion: in inter-war Chicago in the 1930s and 1940s the quantity theory was not 'first and foremost' a theory of the demand for money.

Scholars are understandably irked when their hard-earned publications are not cited, even when no snub was intended. According to Tavlas (correspondence to the author, 9 May 2002), Laidler had committed 'preselection sample bias' by failing to cite his work.[13] Tavlas (pp. 248–9 [1999], 249) complained that 'Laidler does not even refer to [Tavlas, pp. 175–99, 1997] – but deflects attention away from it by diverting the reader to references that are not aimed at addressing the particular issues'.[14] Knight (1935, 355), the pre-eminent first generation Chicago sociologist of economic knowledge noted that 'we must recognise that there is in our field no objective test for separating either truth from opinion or the urge to promote an opinion "believed" to be true from the craving for personal aggrandisement'. George Stigler, the pre-eminent second generation Chicago sociologist of economic knowledge, noted that 'Even to be demolished is better for one's self-esteem than to be ignored'.[15] Tavlas, believing that his evidence had not been adequately treated, presented an uncompromising critique of Laidler's interpretation.[16]

Laidler and Roger Sandilands (pp. 253–70 [2002]) provide an introductory note to a 1932 Harvard *Memorandum* on anti-depression policy authored by Currie, Paul Theodore Ellsworthy and Harry Dexter White (pp. 271–90 [1932]).[17] They conclude that 'there was nothing unique about the Chicago tradition as it stood in early 1932'. Friedman acknowledged in correspondence to Laidler (Laidler and Sandilands, pp. 253–70 [2002]) that he has withdrawn his assertion about uniqueness: the *Memorandum* 'certainly supports your position that Chicago had no monopoly on the quantity theory approach to the Great Depression and to measures required to recover from it'.

With respect to the immunity argument, Tavlas provided evidence supporting Friedman's (Vol. 1, pp. 147–66 [1972/1974], 151) initial position about 'remaining largely unaffected and if anything somewhat hostile [to] ... the Keynesian revolution'. However, in his *Memoirs*, Friedman reversed his judgement about his own personal immunity from Keynesianism. He was 'shocked' to re-read his wartime essays with their unmistakably Keynesian taint. During the war, Friedman drafted speeches for the Secretary of the Treasury and made statements before congressional committees. In a statement in 1942 before the House Ways and Means Committee, Friedman declared that 'inflation ... must be neutralised by measures that restrict consumer spending. Taxation is the most important of those measures'. Looking back he was shocked: 'The most striking feature of this statement is how thoroughly Keynesian it is. I did not even mention "money" or "monetary policy"! The only "methods of avoiding inflation" I mentioned in addition to taxation were "price control and rationing, control of consumers" credit, reduction in government and war bond campaigns". Until I reread my statement to Congress in preparing this account, I had completely forgotten how thoroughly Keynesian I was then. I was apparently cured, some would say corrupted shortly after the end of the war' (Friedman and Friedman, 1998, 115, 123, 112).

The Chicago Plan of Banking Reform

Tavlas (pp. 233–7 [1998], 236; pp. 203–14 [1998], 207) cited the 'Chicago Plan of Banking reform' in support of his argument: 'At a minimum, the Chicago faculty seemed to believe that these elements added up to a cohesive and unique oral tradition'. One of the elements of this 'unique oral tradition' was 'support for 100 per cent reserve requirements for banks ... that was known as 'The "Chicago Plan" of Banking Reform' (Hart, 1934–5)'.

However, it is not clear that the Chicago Plan provides any compensating support for the uniqueness argument. The preamble to the Plan explained that its purpose was to contribute towards the construction of a *consensus* of academic opinion: 'it seems desirable that there should be some statement of opinion by academic economists, especially by *groups* [emphasis added] whose members hold substantially similar views' (cited by Phillips, 1995, 192; see also Simons, 1948 [1934], 76–7). Joseph Reeve (1943, 317, 191) in his history of the *Monetary Reform Movements* explained that the 100% money proposals appeared to have been 'largely independent reactions to the cataclysm'. In her study of *The Banking Crisis of 1933*, Susan Kennedy (1973, 166–7) noted that 'a host of academics bombarded' Roosevelt with reform proposals. These included proposals from John Dewey and the University of Minnesota, the University of Kansas and the University of Georgia. The Chicago plan was 'typical of the recommendations offered at this time ... Many of the proposals reiterated ideas submitted during the Glass bill debates'. Kennedy concluded that by the end of the 1930s a 'substantial minority of leading economists' had rallied behind the proposal. Irving Fisher (1934a, 157) credited Robert Hempell of the Federal Reserve Bank of Atlanta, not the Chicago economists, as the initial American advocate of the proposal. Fisher (1935, ix) also listed twenty-seven non-Chicago economists who supported *100% Money*.[18]

Albert Hart (1935, 104) described the Chicago Plan as coming from 'several quarters ... Simultaneously, and quite independently, the same notions were developed by Dr Laughlin [*sic*] Currie, of Harvard University.' In the footnote attached to that sentence, Hart referenced Currie's *Supply and Control of Money in the United States*. Hart had been one of Currie's students (Sandilands, 1990, 25) and had alerted Currie (1934, 156, n.) to the Chicago Plan as his book was in press. Indeed, the Chicago Plan outlined by Hart (1935, 104) was not actually derived from Chicago at all. In the opening paragraph Hart explained that 'Another independent inventor of very similar ideas was Mr Bostrom, now of the University of

Texas whose proposals are sketched below. From conversations with various Americans I am convinced that the same notion occurred to economists at several other centres of economics at the same time, although their findings have not happened to be published'.[19] One dissenting voice from the 'standard form of the "100% per cent scheme"' came in the form of a Chicago oral tradition. Hart (1935, 106, n. 1) explained that the dissenting voice 'which originates with Professor Frank Knight, has not – so far as I know – been advanced in any published writings'.

Henry Simons (1952 [1936], 356, n., 340–1, 358, n.) minimised the significance of the 100% reserve proposal: 'Standing by itself, as an isolated measure, it would promise little but evasion – small effects at the price of serious disturbance – and would deserve classification as merely another crank scheme'. Simons explained that the 'Chicago' reserve proposal was advanced together with the 'eventual fixing of the total quantity of circulating media'. This, Simons suggested, was initially found 'attractive' because it could 'provide the basis of a new "religion of money" around which might be regimented strong sentiments against tinkering with the currency'. But Simons emphasised that 'this rule cannot now be recommended as a basis for monetary reform. The obvious weakness of fixed quantity, as a sole rule for monetary policy, lies in the danger of sharp changes on the velocity side'. Moreover, Simons indicated that the proposal was not unique to Chicago: 'The so called 100 per cent scheme was suggested, at least by its Chicago proponents ...'.[20]

In his discussion of 100% money, Richard Lester (1939, 291–2) in his study of *Monetary Experiments*, directed readers to Fisher (1935), Currie (1934, Chapter XV), Hart (1935), Angell (1935), and Frank Graham (1936). The advocates of the Chicago Plan were seen as part of a wider constituency which included Currie, Angell and Fisher (Goldenweiser, 1951, 53).[21] Angell noted that the 100% reserve idea was 'not new either as theory or practice' (1935, 5; see also Lester, 1935, 34). Harold Reed (1942, 436–7) noted that Simons and Currie had independently espoused the Plan but that 'Angell's ingenuity in modifying the details of the plan has increased interest by lessening the force of some of the practical objections'. Fisher (1934–5, 410) also discussed Angell's implementation proposal in a favourable light. Leonard Watkins (1938, 22, 26–7) noted that Angell (unlike Frederick Soddy, Fisher or Simons) explicitly integrated his advocacy of the 100% proposal to his ultimate objective, in which he 'virtually urges' the 'stabilization of the total supply of money with an allowance for secular growth'.

Indeed, in his version of the 100% reserve Plan, Angell (1935, 17, n. 4, 27–8, n. 6) emphasised that his own development of the 'monetarist' component of the Plan predated and may have influenced the Chicago contribution. Angell criticised as 'inadequate' the 'Chicago group's explanation of banking and business cycles, running chiefly in terms of "sticky" prices'. Instead, he found 'much more attractive' the idea of 'keeping the quantity of money fairly stable over time, as there proposed (constantly or slowly increasing)'. This he believed 'would impose a quite different and probably much stabler pattern of behavior on the economy than any we have hitherto experienced'. Referring to Angell (1933a, 1933b), he continued: 'This proposal is nearly the same as some suggestions I made in an address at the end of 1932'.

Watkins (1938, 16–7), Graham (1936, 428, n. 2) and Reed (1942, 436–7) all noted that the 100% proposal had been 'first revived in recent years' by Soddy, the 1921 Nobel Laureate in Chemistry. Soddy (1943, 11) regarded Fisher's 100% money plan as 'practically identical' to his own and when banking reform was discussed in a broader context Soddy's proposal was regarded as having been 'popularized' by the advocates of the Chicago Plan (Watkins, 1938, 20).

An asymmetrical 'hysteresis' explanation underpinned part of Soddy's (1933a, 175) objection to the quantity theory which 'works beautifully *one way* [emphasis in original]'. Increasing the quantity of money would in the short run increase wealth but in the long run increase prices alone. Reducing the quantity of money would permanently reduce 'virtual wealth'. Thus Soddy (1934, 100) explained that 'It is not necessary to consider this old "quantity theory" of money farther than this, because enough has been said to show that it really is a fraud'.[22]

The hunt for precursors to Soddy began in the *AER* (Bromberg 1939, 553).[23] Knight (1927, 732) was critical of the 'cocky airs of the novice' that Soddy displayed. Simons (1935, 1421) described Soddy as a 'presumptuous charlatan' but failed to mention the connection between Soddy's 100% money proposal and the Chicago Plan. Alvin Hansen (1938, 111–3) – with whom Simons was feuding – sarcastically noted that it was 'strange' that the Chicago Plan had not explicitly been connected to Soddy's proposal. Hansen believed that the novelty of Simons' exposition of Soddy's proposal was its appropriation as part of the libertarian agenda. Simons (1939, 273, n. 1) took exception to being 'chided' by Hansen who was guilty of a worse crime by allowing his discussion of precursors to come to a 'stop with mention of Soddy!'. Simons was also outraged by Hansen's association of the 'Chicago group' with Angell's monetarism:

'He classes us, along with Angell, as proponents of the fixed-quantity scheme and, by way of documentation, cites an article of mine ... which is a complete disavowal of that scheme and an exposition of its crucial shortcomings. I cannot believe that Hansen has read this article with even ordinary care, for on other points as well his representation is distressingly unfaithful'. Hansen had 'grossly misrepresented the views of [himself] and the so-called Chicago group on monetary policy'.

The process by which the monetary Chicago Plan proceeded through the political market place casts further light on the uniqueness case. It also illustrates the lack of one-to-one correspondence between monetarism and ideology highlighted by Aschheim and Tavlas (pp. 115–34 [1981]). Watkins (1938, 30, n. 11) noted that 'Agitation for the plan has brought together 'strange bedfellows''. Indeed, the Chicago Plan may have acquired its name as a specific attempt to appeal to both Rexford Tugwell and Frederic A. Delano, President Roosevelt's uncle and the chairman of the New Deal National Planning Board (1933–43), which became a vehicle for Alvin Hansen's version of Keynesianism (Brinkley, 2000, 175).[24] In correspondence with Wesley Claire Mitchell, ex-President Hoover described the purpose of such a Board as the creation of 'a Socialist State – or at least a Regimented one' (cited by Karl, 1974, 244).

Delano had been interested in monetary reform since the 1896 US presidential election and after the panic of 1907, had founded a League to promote reform of the banking system. From the outset until 1918, he served on the Federal Reserve Board; between 1929–33 he was President of the Stable Money Association (Reagan, 1982, 47–8, 59). In the 1880s, he entered the railroad industry in Chicago during its period of maximum expansion.[25] He became closely involved in what was known as the 'Chicago Plan' of City Beautification and urban development.[26]

Chicago was infamous throughout the world for its housing problems. Berliners had hoped that their city would become 'Athens on the Spree', but with the decline in the quality of their housing stock their city became known as 'Chicago on the Spree'.[27] The *JPE* published Delano's (1913, 831) essay on 'The Chicago Plan, with Particular Reference to the Railway Terminal Problem' in which the Chicago Plan was presented as the coordinated 'blow' which would strike at the heart of Chicago's urban housing and congestion problems. The Chicago Plan became the prototype of other 'Progressive' Plans including the Regional Plan of New York, unveiled in 1929 (Reagan, 1982, 55).[28]

The original Chicago Plan envisaged a city larger than any other in the world ('an American Paris'), exerting primacy over a mid-continent domain larger than most European countries (Scott, 1969, 107). In 1933, at the start of Chicago Second World's Fair, the Chicago Plan Commission published *The Chicago Plan in 1933 – Twenty-Five Years of Accomplishments* (Wrigley, 1983, 70). In 1933 Roosevelt appointed Tugwell as Director of the Resettlement Administration. He was regarded as 'America's green-belt advocate' with strong intellectual affinities with the Garden City ideals' which 'included a belief in planning is a device to implement a broader social and economic restructuring of society' (Sies and Silver, 1996, 5; Schuman and Sclar, 1996, 437). In September 1932, Paul Douglas (one of the co-signatories of the Chicago Plan of Banking Reform) advocated planning as a vehicle to facilitate the provision of 'great areas of forests and parks on the outside of every one of our cities [and] more decent housing within our cities' (cited by Aschheim and Tavlas, pp. 115–34 [1979], 124–5).

On 16 March 1933, Knight sent what became known as the Chicago Plan of Banking Reform to Henry A. Wallace, Roosevelt's first Secretary of Agriculture.[29] In a follow-up memorandum to the President on 23 March 1933, Wallace described the 'memorandum from the Chicago economists' as 'really awfully good' and 'a complete break with our present banking history' (cited by Phillips, 1995, 198). The administrative debate over the Chicago Plan became centred on Wallace's Department of Agriculture, where it was strongly supported by Gardiner Means and Tugwell. By 1934, the Chicago Plan had virtually become the Wallace–Tugwell–Means Plan; propagated by 'numerous memos' from Means (Phillips, 1995, 69–75).

The Department of Agriculture and the Wallace family were at the centre of many interwar controversies over proposals for economic reform. Agriculture Secretary Henry C. Wallace Sr (Wallace's father) supported the 1924 McNary-Haugen bill which proposed to fix the price of eight basic agricultural commodities (Hicks, 1960, 198). In consequence, Hoover described Wallace Sr, his Cabinet colleague, as an 'unwitting Fascist' (Barber, 1985, 51, 208, n25). Hoover thus became known to the farming lobby as 'the arch enemy of a fair deal for agriculture' (Hicks, 1960, 201).

In 1922, Henry A. Wallace pushed President Harding to accept Thorstein Veblen, from the University of Chicago, as an advisor to his Conference on Agriculture.[30] Wallace hoped that business civilisation would be replaced by the rule of 'production engineers' and 'statistical economists'. He embraced John Dewey's call for a 'new individualism' based on farm cooperatives which could be expanded to include other sectors of the economy. Wallace was 'contemptuous' of Hoover whom he regarded as 'agriculture's worst enemy' in the 1920s. After Hoover won the Republican nomination of 1928 he sought to mobilise support for a farm-orientated third party. When that push failed, he backed Hoover's Democratic opponent (Markowitz, 1973, 14, 18–9).

As Stigler (1962, 17) noted, Henry A. Wallace approved of institutionalised price fixing as a remedy for the farm problem. The agricultural plan of the brains trust (to restrict agricultural production) was in effect, a Chicago Plan, formulated by Wallace, Tugwell, and M. L. Wilson at two University of Chicago conferences on agriculture and planning in August 1931 and April 1932, just prior to Roosevelt's nomination (Schapsmeier and Schapsmeier, 1968, 149–52; Schlesinger, 1957, 403; Kirkendall, 1966, 31, 45). It was part of a wider belief that 'a planned economy needed to be substituted for laissez faire in the light of the collapse of our business civilisation' (Elliot, 1977, 193). Friedman (1962, 198) referred to the agricultural aspects of the New Deal reforms as 'a national scandal that has wasted public funds'.

Hoover (1934, 100–1) described Roosevelt's monetary initiatives as 'the negation of whole philosophy of Liberty. Executive power over the coin is one of the oldest components of despotism'. Two decades after his electoral defeat, Hoover (1952, 408) was still denigrating the activities of the New Deal: 'Along with currency manipulation, the New Deal introduced to Americans the spectacle of Fascist dictation to business, labor and agriculture'. Simons (1948 [1941], 91) provided similar abuse: 'Any literate person may now identify Mr. [Henry A.] Wallace as our leading advocate of the totalitarian or pre-totalitarian economy of negotiation among tightly organised, monopolizing functional groups'. Wallace's proposal to create post war international agricultural syndicates would create an American farming sector whose 'power may be as inimical to peace as was that of Prussian landowners in the past' (Simons, 1943, 442).

Tugwell was frequently accused of wishing to Sovietise America. In April 1934, Roosevelt nominated him as Undersecretary of Agriculture which led to him being grilled by the Senate about whether he was a communist (Sternscher, 1964, 309, 9, 256). Among those employed in Henry A. Wallace's Department of Agriculture were Alger Hiss and Adlai Stevenson (Schapsmeier and Schapsmeier, 1968, 193, 203). James Paul Warburg noted in 1934 that of all the New Dealers, Tugwell and Wallace were the most sympathetic to the Soviet experiment (Markowitz, 1973, 164). In 1946, despite pressure from the University President, the Chicago

Economics Department 'refused to appoint [Tugwell] to their faculty' (Friedman, 1983, 188).[31]

Henry A. Wallace believed that the New Deal needed to be run by a small group of economists: an economic Supreme Court or Council on the General Welfare (Zinn 1968, 68–76). His faith in planning led the American Liberty League to target him as a prime threat to capitalism. In response, he vigorously attacked the 1936 Republican candidate, Alf Landon, as an agent of the Liberty League. After the demise of NRA, the Department of Agriculture became the focus of administrative attempts to institute economic planning and social reform (Markowitz, 1973, 25–7).

Roosevelt insisted that Wallace be his vice presidential partner in the 1940 election. Had Roosevelt died a few months earlier, Vice President Wallace (1941–5) would have become President of the United States. As it was, he was removed from the platform, Truman succeeded Roosevelt, and Wallace served as Truman's Secretary of Commerce. In September 1946, Wallace made a speech to a pro-Soviet audience which was interpreted by some Europeans as evidence that the Americans were preparing to abandon them to the Russians. As a consequence, Truman sacked him (Manchester, 1975, 319; Markowitz, 1973, 28).

Eight days later a Conference of Progressives met in Chicago. With assistance from Tugwell, Paul Sweezy and Richard Watt (a University of Chicago Law professor), the 1948 Progressive party platform was organised with Wallace as the presidential candidate (Markowitz, 1973, 201, 286, 173, 186–90). Wallace denounced the Marshall Plan as an anti-Soviet 'Martial Plan' (Saunders, 1966, 73). His party was perceived to be a communist front organisation: he planned to have Harry Dexter White as Treasury Secretary and the President of the United Electrical Workers Union as Secretary of Labor (Moley, 1949, 85: Carr, 1952, 337; Latham, 1966, 396; Rees 1973, 408). William Buckley (1951, 87, 48, 94–5, 231–2) complained that Wallace's supporters (armed with text books co-authored by Chicago trained economists) had captured Yale University for subversive purposes. In 1947–8, Buckley had been taught Economics 10 by Alexander Brooks who 'energetically promoted Wallaces's Communist-dominated Progressive Party in the spring of 1948'.[32] Albert Hart (1948, 471, n) complained that the 'anti-Keynesian "party line"' had mobilised a constituency which could successfully defeat any proposal linked to the names of Keynes or Henry Wallace.

In the mid-1930s, several Senators and Congressmen introduced Bills to facilitate the operation of the Chicago Plan (Watkins, 1938, 23–4). One of these supporters was Californian Democrat Congressman, Jerry Voorhis

(1938, 14), who combined it with the 'monetarist' suggestion that 'We need to instruct our monetary authority – the Federal Reserve Board – to anticipate the nation's need for an annual increase of circulating medium of about 4%'. For Voorhis (1947, chapter 13) this was 'My Big Campaign'. Voorhis had been a member of the Yale University Liberal Club with Aaron Director in the early 1920s (Coase, 1998). Voorhis (1947, 7–8, 15, 164) was a registered Socialist who voted for the Socialist Norman Thomas in 1928. When he discovered the works of Irving Fisher in the mid-1930s he wondered why he had not been exposed to these views whilst at Yale.

Voorhis was swept into Congress in the Democratic landslide of 1936 (Bullock, 1978). He immediately enlisted Fisher into his own private 'brain trust'. Voorhis sponsored a bill in Congress which Fisher interpreted as a method of implementing 'central control of the circulating medium' (Fisher, cited by Fisher, 1956, 316). But the author of this Chicago Plan monetarism was defeated in the 1946 congressional election by Richard Nixon who declared the choice to be between 'a supporter of free enterprise, individual initiative, and a sound progressive reform, or for my opponent who has supported by his votes the foreign ideologies of the New Deal Administration'. According to Paul Douglas (1972, 237–8) Voorhis was 'truly one of the saints of the earth'. According to Nixon, Voorhis was also associated in some way with 'Wallace's proposal that Russia be given a free hand' (Nixon, cited by Voorhis, 1973, 15).

Twenty-six years later (August 1972), this episode of history became a potent contemporary weapon for President Nixon in his determination to defeat George McGovern, his 1972 Democratic Party opponent. Douglas (1972, 237) recalled that in 1946, 'anonymous character assassins' phoned electors to tell them that 'Voorhis was a Communist ... Jerry was defeated and Nixon was launched on a career that has now taken him to the White House'. Within the White House in 1972, it was calculated that McGovern could be portrayed as a subversive for his support of Wallace in the 1948 election (Safire, 1975, 645). The following month the *JPE* published the exchange between Friedman and Patinkin (Vol. 1, pp. 123–43 and Vol. 1, pp. 147–66 [1972/1974]) illustrating that for economists, too, history can be a contemporary weapon.

In his essay on 'The Literature of Economics' Stigler (1978, 200–201) compared controversy in economics to 'a series of simultaneous and intersecting fox hunts'. Economists tend to hunt in packs – driven in part by the thrill of the chase and perhaps even the scent of blood. Laidler (pp. 217–29 [1998]; Laidler, 1999, 238, n. 30) titled his second response to Tavlas as 'a final comment' – but since he also accused Tavlas of using 'sarcasm' and being 'patronizing' and 'condescending' in presenting 'irrelevant, and occasionally inaccurate' arguments, this particular foxhunt seems likely to continue.

Notes

[1] The Chicago Plan may have prompted the First National Bank of Englewood, located near the Chicago campus, to become 100% liquid in early 1934 (Phillips 1994, 18, n. 17).

[2] Pigou continued: 'It was, perhaps, a fault in Marshall that he discovered more truth in the writings of others than was actually there, and unduly depreciated his own contributions. There is no fault of that kind in Mr. Keynes!'. Marshall's generosity to his predecessors, was according to Pigou, 'a great man's fault, not a little man's'.

[3] Also, A. W. H. Phillips did not correct the errors that circulated about his work (Leeson forthcoming).

[4] Don Patinkin Papers, Box 2.

[5] In his analysis of *Monetary Reform Movements*, Joseph Reeve (1943, 210, 219, xi–xii) identified a wide academic constituency in the 1930s in favour of monetary expansion through public works: 'With the possible exception of the proposals for more aggressive open-market purchases and credit expansion by the Federal Reserve System during 1931–33, probably no major type of monetary expansion attracted more widespread public support from professional economists than did deficit spending, especially spending for public works construction'. Reeve reported that Harry Hopkins, the Works Progress Administrator, explained that the WPA dollar was 'the fastest moving dollar in America'. Reeve's book began as a Chicago PhD on 'Monetary Proposals for Curing the Depression in the United States, 1929–1935' with Mints as committee chairman (Patinkin, Vol. 1, pp. 87–120 [1969/1981], 108–9). Of the eight economists who either contributed 'fundamental ideas' or who read and criticised Reeve's manuscript before it 'neared its final form', five were Chicago economists (Mints, Viner, Lange, Simons and Knight), two were Chicago economists at one remove (Charles Hardy and Homer Jones) and the eighth was at the Cowles Commission, which was on the Chicago campus (Dickson Leavens). A ninth, Paul Douglas, 'first encouraged' Reeve to 'study monetary proposals for curing unemployment'. Reeve made no reference to a unique Chicago monetary tradition.

[6] Tavlas (pp. 56–61 [1979], 57) denied that he had only partially read Davis' book: 'So much for Mr. Davis' empiricism'.

[7] Hans Neisser (1934, 441–3), writing in the *JPE*, also described underconsumptionism as a non-monetary theory of crises. Neisser contrasted the 'classical type of underconsumption theory [which] rejects from the outset all purely monetary considerations based on the quantity theory of money' with the 'more primitive' approach of Foster and Catching in which the quantity of money increases in response to profit making transactions. Laidler (1999, 169, n. 16) commented that for Foster and Catching, the monetary system played a role in 'generating underconsumptionism'.

[8] Tavlas (pp. 70–9 [1981], 70, n. 2) stated that 'Humphrey [1971, 1973] never refers to Foster and Catchings'. In fact, Humphrey (Vol. 1, pp. 343–6 [1973], 344) does, in passing, refer to Foster and Catching.

[9] Aschheim and Tavlas (1996, 416, 409–10) described Laidler's *Golden Age of the Quantity Theory* as 'indispensable for future scholars of monetary thought'. They also disputed 'Laidler's attribution of the origination of the wage-stickiness hypothesis to Marshall and Pigou', offering as examples Henry Thornton's (1802) *Paper Credit* and John Gray who 'articulated 'one of the first monetary growth rules found in the literature and one that directly influenced the Chicago money-supply growth rate rule of the 1930s (see Tavlas 1977, [chapter 30 [1977])'. However, in *Golden Age of the Quantity Theory*, Laidler (1991, 116, n. 30) stated that he did 'not mean to suggest that [W. S.] Jevons originated the idea of money wage stickiness. It can be found, for example, in Thornton's *Paper Credit* (1802) …'.

[10] Douglas and Aaron Director (1931) devote a little over ten per cent of *The Problem of Unemployment to monetary factors.*

[11] After he retired from the Treasury, Hawtrey was Henry Price Research Professor at the Royal Institute of International Affairs, 1947–52 (Davis, 1981, 204).

[12] For a similar conclusion, see Patinkin (1995, 361–2). See also Johnson (1975, 124) for critical perspective on the influence of ideology on Cambridge economics.

[13] The editors of the *JPE* formed a different judgement about Tavlas' work than one of their nominated referees (such differences are, of course, the lifeblood of scholarly disputes).

[14] The last sentence of Laidler's (pp. 247–8 [1999], 248) letter to the *Journal of Economic Perspectives* was edited without his knowledge or permission. The last sentence of his submitted letter reads: 'A perusal of published work by, among others, Karl Brunner (1968), Thomas Humphrey (1971), Roger Sandilands (1990) Frank Steindl (1996) and myself (Laidler, 1993, 1998), all of which Tavlas has overlooked on this occasion, will reveal this in much more detail than can be set out in a letter'. This change may have exacerbated Tavlas' suspicion that his work was being ignored.

[15] For a discussion, see Leeson (2000).

[16] Laidler had been criticised a quarter of a century earlier by Joan Robinson (1973, ix) in her self-appointed role as one of Keynes' 'Bulldogs' (Samuelson, 1994, 25). Laidler was a young award-winning economist; but as President of Section F of the British Association for the Advancement of Science (BAAS) and editor of *After Keynes*, Robinson (1973) marred the award ceremony by expressing contempt for Laidler, the 1972 Lister Lecturer, who she thought was a co-conspirator in the attempt to return economics to pre-Keynesian (i.e. quantity theory) perceptions (the Lister Lecturer was chosen by the BAAS committee, including Harry Johnson, not the President of Section F). According to Robinson (1972, 86–7) the quantity theory had been revived by 'modern Chicagoans led by Milton Friedman … There is an unearthly, mystical element in Friedman's thought'. Citing uncritically Patinkin (pp. 87–120 [1969/1981]) Robinson continued: 'In so far as [Friedman] offers an intelligible theory, it is made up of elements borrowed from Keynes'.

[17] Although the discovery of this memorandum pre-dates the Laidler–Tavlas exchange (see the brief references in Rees 1973, 37, and Sandilands 1990), its significance had not been adequately appreciated until Sandilands obtained a copy of the full manuscript from Princeton University's Manuscript Library in 2000.

[18] Watkins found an 'obiter dicta' from *The General Theory* to indicate Keynes' (1936, 205–6, 234) support for components of the proposal. In 1934, Paul Samuelson (1996, 148–9), a Chicago undergraduate, became converted to this proposal to eliminate factional reserve banking.

[19] Albert Hart had been a graduate student with Friedman at Chicago (Phillips, 1995, chapter 4; Friedman and Friedman, 1998, 39–40). Hart's essay was reprinted in *Readings in Monetary Theory* selected by a committee of the AEA, co-chaired by Lloyd Mints (Lutz and Mints, 1952) and published just as Friedman began planning the Workshop in Money and Banking. It is safe to assume that Friedman was aware of Hart's essay in the period that he was writing his 'Restatement' since in the early 1950s he prescribed the *Readings* to his students (Hammond, 1999, 462). Shortly afterwards – as 'a student of Henry Simons and Lloyd Mints' – Friedman (1960, 65–6) referenced the Hart essay and proposed to expand on the 'original "Chicago Plan of Banking Reform" in only one respect' by proposing that interest be paid on the 100% reserves.

[20] Moreover, the 'Chicago Plan' involved the objective of an increase in prices which does not immediately appear to be easily reconcilable with the orthodox quantity theory: 'That the administration announce and pursue a policy of bringing about, by fiscal and monetary measures, an increase of fifteen (15) per cent in Wholesale Prices'. At the same time, 'Adoption of the reserve guarantee arrangements, far from being inflationary, would actually involve, by comparison with conditions of the recent past, a marked reduction in the quantity of circulating media' (cited by Phillips 1995, 196–7).

[21] The Plan was described in a Chicago Public Policy Pamphlet as having been 'presented in a number of different forms, varying in detail' (Whittlesey, 1935, 21; Gideonse, 1935, iii).

[22] Soddy was unlikely to have created an anti-quantity theory oral tradition since his students, such as Kenneth Boulding, slept through his chemistry lectures (Daly, 1980, 483, n. 4; see also Gaitskell, 1933, 383).

[23] Soddy (1934, 173, 131–2, 201; 1943, 25) opposed the 'proposals of the Socialists' to nationalise banking on the grounds that it would not help to secure a stable price level. He outlined a four per cent money growth rule which he attributed to Gustav Cassels and which he believed would preserve the value of money. He was also an early advocate of freely floating exchange rates as a vehicle to facilitate free trade, a proposal that Friedman would later be associated with. Friedman (pp. 33–51 [1956], 46) objected to the 'reaction against the quantity theory in the 1930s ... The demand for money, it was asserted was a will-o'-the-wisp'. Referring to Fisher's *Purchasing Power of Money* Soddy (1933a, xix–xxi) concluded that the velocity of circulation was 'a will-of-the-wisp'.

[24] Charles W. Eliot II became executive officer of the Board, Wesley Mitchell was also recruited as was Charles E. Merriam from Chicago's Department of Politics who

described the purpose of the Board as the creation of 'a plan for national planning' (cited by Brinkley, 2000, 174).

[25] Shortly afterwards, Chicago surpassed Philadelphia as the nation's second largest city and won the right to host the World's Fair celebrating the 400th anniversary of Columbus' 'discovery' of America. The Fair attracted millions of visitors and stimulated great interest in urban planning: 'nowhere was this matter discussed more than in Chicago (Wrigley, 1983, 58). Frederick Law Olmsted was recruited to recommend a site for the Fair. Two other architects involved in the project, Daniel Burnham and John Root, were associated with 'the so-called Chicago School that paved the way to contemporary design' (Reps, 1965, 498; Peterson 1996, 48). Simultaneously, John D. Rockefeller began his endowment of the University of Chicago (Turner, 1984, 172). The 'Chicago School of Sociology' was formed 'in the two decades after the *Plan of Chicago*' (Fishman, 2000a, 70; Knight, 1924, 250; Ogburn, 1934; Smith, 1988). 'The Chicago School" of politics also acquired a 'stunning impact ... on the profession' (Simon, 1991, 62). At a 1955 conference on 'The State of the Social Sciences' reference was made to the Chicago contributions to the social sciences made by John Dewey, J. Laurence Laughlin and James Angell's father, the psychologist, James Roland Angell (Harris, 1956, 1).

[26] Such concerns were reflected in the *JPE*, and later republished in *Landmarks in Political Economy* (Hamilton, Rees, and Johnson, 1962). One Chicago economist writing in the *JPE* referred to plans 'for relieving the terminal difficulties at Chicago' which had been 'advocated more or less urgently for twenty years' (Hill, 1962 [1906], 64). Chicago was regarded as 'typically a city of rugged individualism' (Wrigley, 1983, 58). But nationalisation was the preferred solution: 'It is hardly conceivable that the delay in adopting so great an improvement over the present method could have been worse under government ownership' (Hill, 1962 [1906], 64).

[27] In 1910, Charles Elliot Sr, Olmsted's associate, published an essay on 'A Study of the New Plan of Chicago' (Reagan, 1982, 25, 39, 73, n. 27; Fishman, 2000b, 12).

[28] President Theodore Roosevelt sought to initiate a 'second national plan' to 'control the mighty commercial forces' which American civilisation had unleashed. This 'national plan' involved conservation, railways and city planning (Lacey, 2000, 117). The motto of the City of Chicago is *Urbs in Horto* ('City set in a Garden'). In 1907, President Roosevelt described the Chicago parks as 'one of the most notable civic achievements in any American City' (cited by Draper, 1996, 100). Chicago was a pioneer in the search for 'the science of city planning' (Draper, 1996, 104). The onset of the depression encouraged the parks to form an amalgamated Chicago Park district. This was achieved in 1934, which enabled the parks to qualify for significant WPA assistance.

[29] Wallace had been one of Fisher's monetary reformers as the first Vice President of the Stable Money League (Fisher, 1934a, 104; Schapsmeier and Schapsmeier, 1968, 90–1; Markowitz, 1973, 17–18). He was one of two disciples of Henry L. Moore (who retired from Columbia in 1929). The other disciple was Henry Schultz who persuaded Friedman to spend his second graduate year at Columbia (Friedman and Friedman, 1998, 38–9; Stigler, 1962, 17).

[30] Veblen had been recruited to Chicago by Laughlin (Friedman, 1987).

[31] In 1947, Tugwell was appointed chairman of Chicago's graduate curriculum in planning (Scott, 1969, 468).

[32] This required textbook was *Economic Analysis and Public Policy* by Jean Bowman and a Chicago graduate George Bach (who had referred to the Chicago 'oral tradition' in his doctoral dissertation). Buckley noted with alarm that this text was also prescribed at Chicago and 65 other universities. In a more advanced course, Buckley was obliged to read Simons' *Positive Program for Laissez Faire* which outlined 'a sure program for the destruction of the free economy'. By 1950–1, Simons' essay had become required reading in Economics 10.

Bibliography

Angell, J. W., 'Monetary Prerequisites for Employment Stabilisation' in Roos (ed.), *Stabilisation of Employment* (Bloomington, Indiana, Principia, 1933a).

——, 'Monetary Control and General Business Stabilisation' in *Economic Essays in Honour of Gustav Cassel* (London, Allen and Unwin, 1933b).

——, 'The 100 Per Cent Reserve Plan', *Quarterly Journal of Economics*, 50 (November 1935), pp. 1–35.

Aschheim, J. and G. Tavlas, 'Doctrinal Foundations of Monetary Economics', *Journal of Monetary Economics*, 28 (1991), pp. 501–10.

——, 'Monetary Economics in Doctrinal Perspective', *Journal of Money Credit and Banking*, 28:3 (August 1996), pp. 406–17.

Barber, W. J., *Designs Within Disorder: Franklin D. Roosevelt, the Economists, and the Shaping of American Economic Policy, 1933–1945* (Cambridge, Cambridge UP, 1996).

Bigg, R. J., 'Ralph George Hawtrey' in Eatwell *et al.* (eds), *The New Palgrave: A Dictionary of Economics* (London, Macmillan, 1987).

Blitch, C., *Allyn Young: The Peripatetic Economist* (London, Macmillan, 1995).

Bowman, J. and Bach, G., *Economic Analysis and Public Policy*, 2nd edn (New York, Prentice-Hall, 1949).

Brinkley, A., *The End of Reform: New Deal Liberalism in Recession and War* (New York, Alfred Knopf, 1995).

——, 'National Resources Planning Board and the Reconstruction of Planning' in Fishman (ed.), *The American Planning Tradition: Culture and Policy* (Washington DC, The Woodrow Wilson Centre Press, 2000).

Bromberg, B., 'Two Neglected Twentieth Century 100 Per Cent Reserve Economists', *American Economic Review*, 29 (1939), p. 553.

Buckley, W. F. Jr, *God and Man at Yale* (Chicago, Henry Regnery, 1951).

Bullock, P., *Jerry Voorhis: The Idealist as Politician* (New York, Vantage, 1978).

Carr, R., *The House Committee on Un-American Activities* (Ithaca, New York, Cornell UP, 1952).

Coase, R., 'Aaron Director' in Newman (ed.), *The New Palgrave Dictionary of Law and Economics* (London, Macmillan, 1998).

Colander, D. and Landreth, H. (eds), *The Coming of Keynesianism to America* (Cheltenham, England, Edward Elgar, 1996).

Cole, G. D. H. (ed.), *What Everybody Wants to Know About Money* (London, Victor Gollancz, 1933).

Currie, L., *Supply and Control of Money in the United States*, 1st edn (Cambridge, Mass., Harvard UP, 1934).

Daly, H., 'The Economic Thought of Frederick Soddy', *History of Political Economy*, 12 (1980), pp. 469–88.

Davis, E. G., 'R.G. Hawtrey, 1879–1975' in O'Brien and Presley (eds), *Pioneers of Modern Economics in Britain* (London, Macmillan, 1981).

Davis, J. R., *The New Economics and the Old Economists* (Ames, Iowa, Iowa UP, 1971).

Delano, F. A., 'The Chicago Plan, with Particular Reference to the Railway Terminal Problem', *Journal of Political Economy*, 21 (1913), pp. 819–31.

Douglas, P. H., *In the Fullness of Time* (New York, Harcourt Brace Jovanovich, 1972).

Douglas, P. H. and Director, A., *The Problem of Unemployment* (New York, Macmillan, 1931).

Draper, J. E., 'The Art and Science of Park Planning in the United States: Chicago's Small Parks, 1982 to 1905' in Sies and Silver (eds), *Planning the 20th Century American City* (Baltimore, Johns Hopkins UP, 1996).

Eatwell, J., Milgate, M. and Newman, P. (eds), *The New Palgrave A Dictionary of Economics* (London, Macmillan, 1987).

Elliott, E. A., *Hoover, Roosevelt and the Brains Trust: From Depression to New Deal* (New York, Columbia UP, 1977).

Fisher, I., 'Irving Fisher Tells Controllers of Monetary Cure for Depression', *The Controller*, (October 1934a), pp. 155–68.

——, *Stable Money: A History of the Movement* (New York, Adelphi, 1934b).

——, '100% Money and the Public Debt', *Economic Forum*, 3 (1934–5), pp. 406–20.

——, *100% Money* (New York, Adelphi, 1935).

Fisher, I. N., *My Father Irving Fisher* (New York, Comet, 1956).

Fishman, R., 'The Metropolitan Tradition in American Planning' in Fishman (ed.), *The American Planning Tradition Culture and Policy* (Washington DC, The Woodrow Wilson Centre Press, 2000a).

——, 'The American Planning Tradition: An Introduction and Interpretation' in Fishman (ed.) , *The American Planning Tradition Culture and Policy* (Washington DC, The Woodrow Wilson Centre Press, 2000b).

——, (ed.), *The American Planning Tradition Culture and Policy* (Washington DC, The Woodrow Wilson Centre Press, 2000).

Freidel, F., *Franklin D. Roosevelt: Launching the New Deal* (Boston, Little Brown, 1972).

Friedman, M., *Essays in Positive Economics* (Chicago, Chicago UP, 1953).

——, *A Program for Monetary Stability* (New York, Fordham UP, 1960).

——, *Capitalism and Freedom* (Chicago, Chicago UP, 1962).

——, In Kitch, *Journal of Law and Economics*, XXVI (April 1983), pp 163–234.

Friedman, M. and Friedman, R., *Two Lucky People: Memoirs* (Chicago, Chicago UP, 1998).

Gaitskell, H., 'Four Monetary Heretics' in Cole (ed.), *What Everybody Wants to Know About Money* (London, Victor Gollancz, 1933).

Gideonse, H. D., 'Introduction by the Editor' in Whittlesey (ed.), *Banking and the New Deal*, Public Policy Pamphlet No. 16 (Chicago, Chicago UP, 1935).

Goldenweiser, E. A., *American Monetary Policy* (New York, McGraw Hill, 1951).

Graham, F. D., 'Partial Reserve Money and the 100 Per Cent Reserve Proposal', *American Economic Review*, (September 1936), pp. 428–40.

Hamilton, E. J., Rees, A. and Johnson, H. G. (eds), *Landmarks in Political Economy* (Chicago, Chicago UP, 1962).

Hammond, J. D., 'Labels and Substance: Friedman's Restatement of the Quantity Theory', *History of Political Economy*, 31:3 (Fall 1999), pp. 449–71.

Hansen, A. H., *Full Recovery or Stagnation?* (London, Adam and Charles Black, 1938).

Harris, C. D., 'Address of Welcome' in White (ed.), *The State of the Social Sciences* (Chicago, Chicago IP, 1956).

Hart, A. G., 'The "Chicago Plan" of Banking Reform', *Review of Economic Studies*, 2 (1935), pp. 104–16.

——, *Money, Debt and Economic Activity* (Englewood Cliffs, NJ, Prentice Hall, 1948).

Hicks, J. D., *Republican Ascendancy 1921–1933* (New York, Harper and Row, 1960).

Hill, W., 'Recent Utterances of Mr Hill and Mr Harriman on Railway Problems' reprint of 1906 article, in Hamilton *et al.* (eds), *Landmarks in Political Economy* (Chicago, Chicago UP, 1962).

Hoover, H., *The Challenge to Liberty* (New York, Charles Scribner's Sons, 1934).

——, *The Memoirs of Herbert Hoover: The Great Depression 1929–41* (New York, Macmillan, 1952).

Johnson, H. G., *On Economics and Society* (Chicago, Chicago UP, 1975).

Karl, B. D., *Charles E. Merriam and the Study of Politics* (Chicago, Chicago UP, 1974).

Kennedy, S. E., *The Banking Crisis of 1933* (Lexington, Kentucky UP, 1973).

Keynes, J. M., *The General Theory of Employment Interest and Money* (London, Macmillan, 1936).

Kirkendall, R. S., *Social Scientists and Farm Politics in the Age of Roosevelt* (Columbia, Missouri, Missouri UP, 1966).

Kitch, E. W., 'The Fire of Truth: A Remembrance of Law and Economics at Chicago, 1932–1970', *Journal of Law and Economics*, XXVI (April 1983), pp. 163–234.

Knight, F. H., 'The Limitations of Scientific Method in Economics' in Tugwell (ed.), *The Trend of Economics* (London, Kennikat, 1924).

——, 'Money', *The Saturday Review of Literature*, 16 (April 1927), p. 732.

——, *The Ethics of Competition and Other Essays* (New York, Book for Libraries Press, 1935).

Krueckenberg, D. A. (ed.), *Introduction to Planning History in the Unites States* (New Brunswick, Centre for Urban Policy Research Studies, Rutgers University, 1983).

Lacey, M. J., 'Federalism and National Planning' in Fishman (ed.), *The American Planning Tradition Culture and Policy* (Washington DC, The Woodrow Wilson Centre Press, 2000).

Laidler, D. E. W., 'The Rate of Interest and the Demand for Money – Some Empirical Evidence', *Journal of Political Economy*, 74 (December 1966), pp. 545–55.

——, *The Demand for Money: Theories and Evidence*, 1st edn (New York, Dun-Donnelly, 1969).

——, *The Demand for Money: Theories, Evidence, and Problems*, 3rd edn (New York, Harper & Row, 1985).

——, *The Golden Age of the Quantity Theory: The Development of Neoclassical Monetary Economics 1870–1914* (New York, Harvester Wheatsheaf, 1991).

——, *Fabricating the Keynesian Revolution: Studies of the Inter-War Literature on Money, the Cycle, and Unemployment* (Cambridge, Cambridge UP, 1999).

Lathan, E., *The Communist Controversy in Washington From the New Deal to McCarthy* (Cambridge, Mass., Harvard UP, 1966).

Leeson, R., *The Eclipse of Keynesianism: The Political Economy of the Chicago Counter-Revolution* (New York, Palgrave, 2000).

——, *The Political Economy of the Inflation–Unemployment Trade-Off* (forthcoming).

Lester, R., 'Check-Book Inflation', *American Scholar*, (Winter 1935), pp. 30–40.

——, *Monetary Experiments: Early American and Recent Scandinavian* (Princeton, Princeton UP, 1939).

Lutz, F. and Mints, L. (eds), *Readings in Monetary Theory* (American Economic Association; London, George Allen and Unwin, 1952).

Manchester, W., *The Glory and the Dream* (London, Michael Joseph, 1973).

Markowitz, N. *The Rise and Fall of the People's Century: Henry A. Wallace and American Liberalism 1941–1948* (New York, Macmillan, 1973).

Moggridge, D., *John Maynard Keynes: An Economist's Biography* (London, Routledge, 1992).

Moley, R., *27 Masters of Politics in a Personal Perspective* (New York, Funk and Wagnalls, 1949).

Neisser, H., 'General Overproduction', *Journal of Political Economy*, 42:4 (August 1934), pp. 433–65.

Newman, P. (ed.), *The New Palgrave Dictionary of Law and Economics* (London, Macmillan, 1998).

O'Brien, D. P. and Presley, J. R. (eds), *Pioneers of Modern Economics in Britain* (London, Macmillan, 1981).

Ogburn, W. F. (ed.), *Social Change and the New Deal* (Chicago, Chicago UP, 1934).

Patinkin, D., 'The Training of an Economist', *Banca Nazionale del Lavoro Quarterly Review*, 195 (December 1995), pp. 359–95.

Peterson, J. A., 'Frederick Law Olmsted Sr and Frederick Law Olmsted Jr, the Visionary and the Professional' in Sies and Silver (eds), *Planning the 20th Century American City* (Baltimore, Johns Hopkins UP, 1996).

Phillips, J. R., 'Safe Banking During the Great Depression: John M. Nichols, the FDIC and 100% Reserves', *Consumer Finance Law Quarterly Review*, 48:1 (Winter, 1994), pp. 15–21.

——, *The Chicago Plan and New Deal Banking Reform* (London, M. E. Sharpe, 1995).

Pigou, A. C., 'Mr. Keynes and Money', *Nation and Athenaeum*, (24 January 1931).

——, *Economics in Practice: Six Lectures on Current Issues* (London, Macmillan, 1935).

——, 'Mr J. M. Keynes' General Theory of Employment, Interest and Money', *Economica*, 3 (May 1936), pp. 115–21.

——, *Lapses From Full Employment*, reprinted 1978 (London, Macmillan, 1945).

——, 'John Maynard Keynes, 1883–1946', *Cambridge Review,* (May 18 1946), pp. 380–38.

——, *Keynes's "General Theory": A Retrospective View* (London, Macmillan, 1950).

Reagan, P. D., *The Architects of Modern American National Planning* (PhD thesis, Ohio State University, 1982).

Reed, H. L., *Money, Currency and Banking* (New York, McGraw Hill, 1942).

Rees, D., *Harry Dexter White: A Study in Paradox* (London, Macmillan, 1973).

Reeve, J. E., *Monetary Reform Movements: A Survey of Recent Plans and Panaceas* (Washington, American Council on Public Affairs, 1943).

Reps, J., *The Making of Urban America: A History of City Planning in the United States* (Princeton, NJ, Princeton UP, 1965).

Robinson, J., *Economic Heresies* (London, Macmillan, 1972).

—— (ed.), *After Keynes* (Oxford, Basil Blackwell, 1973).

Roos, C. F. (ed.), *Stabilisation of Employment* (Bloomington, Indiana, Principia, 1933).

Safire, W., *Before the Fall: An Inside View of the Pre-Watergate White House* (New York, Belmont, 1975).

Samuelson, P. A., 'Richard Kahn: His Welfare Economics and Lifetime Achievement', *Cambridge Journal of Economics*, 18 (February 1994), pp. 55–72.

——, 'Paul Samuelson' in Colander and Landreth (eds), *The Coming of Keynesianism to America* (Cheltenham, England, Edward Elgar, 1996).

Sandilands, R., *The Life and Political Economy of Lauchlin Currie: New Dealer, Presidential Adviser and Development Economist* (Durham, Duke UP, 1990).

Saunders, C. B. Jr, *The Brookings Institution: A Fifty-Year History* (Washington, Brookings Institution, 1966).

Schapsmeier, E. L. and Schapsmeier, F. H., *Henry A. Wallace of Iowa: The Agrarian Years* (Ames, Iowa, Iowa State UP, 1968).

Schlesinger, A. M., *The Crisis of the Old Order* (Boston, Houghton Mifflin, 1957).

Schneider, M., 'Underconsumptionism' in Eatwell *et al.* (eds), *The New Palgrave: A Dictionary of Economics* (London, Macmillan, 1987).

Schuman, T. and Sclar, E., 'The Impact of Ideology on American Town Planning from the Garden City to Battery Park City' in Sies and Silver (eds), *Planning the 20th Century American City* (Baltimore, Johns Hopkins UP, 1996).

Scott, M., *American City Planning since 1890: A History Commemorating the 50th Anniversary of the American Institute of Planners* (Los Angeles, California UP, 1969).

Seligman, L. G. and Cornwell, E. F., *New Deal Mosaic: Roosevelt Confers with his National Emergency Council 1933–1936* (Eugene, Oregon: University of Oregon Books, 1965).

Sies, M. C. and Silver, C. (eds), *Planning the 20th Century American City* (Baltimore, Johns Hopkins UP, 1996).

Simon, H. A., *Models of my Life* (USA, Basic Books, 1991).

Simons, H. C., 'Depression Economics', *The Christian Century,* (November 6 1935), p. 1421.

——, 'Review of Hansen's *Full Recovery or Stagnation?*', *Journal of Political Economy,* (1939), pp. 272–6.

——, 'Postwar Economic Policy: Some Traditional Liberal Principles', *American Economic Review*, XXXIII:1 (March 1943), pp. 432–45.

——, *Economic Policy for a Free Society* (Chicago, Chicago UP, 1948).

——, 'Rules Versus Authorities in Monetary Policy', reprinted in F. Lutz and L. Mints (eds), *Readings in Monetary Theory* (American Economic Association; London, George Allen and Unwin, 1952).

Smith, D., *The Chicago School: A Liberal Critique of Capitalism* (New York, St. Martin's Press, 1988).

Soddy, F., *Wealth, Virtual Wealth and Debt*, 2nd edn (London: George Allen and Unwin, 1933a).

——, 'Wealth, Capital and Money: The Resume of My Theories', *Economic Forum*, (Summer 1933b), pp. 291–301.

——, *The Role of Money* (London, George Routledge, 1934).

——, *The Arch-Enemy of Economic Freedom* (Knapp, Enstone, Oxon, published by the author, 1943).

Sternscher, B., *Rexford Tugwell and the New Deal* (New Brunswick, Rutgers UP, 1964).

Stigler, G. J., 'Henry L. Moore and Statistical Economics', *Econometrica*, 30:1 (January 1962), pp. 1–21.

——, 'The Literature of Economics: The Case of the Kinked Oligopoly Demand Curve', *Economic Inquiry*, 16:2 (April 1978), pp. 185–204.

——, *Memoirs of an Unregulated Economist* (New York, Basic Books, 1988).

Tavlas, G. S., 'Some Initial Formulations of the Monetary Growth Rule', *History of Political Economy*, 9 (Winter 1977), pp. 535–47.

——, 'Notes on Garvy, Synder and the Doctrinal Foundations of Monetarism', *History of Political Economy*, 14:1 (1982), pp. 89–100.

Thornton, H., *An Enquiry into the Nature and Effects of the Paper Credit of Great Britain*, reprinted with an introduction by F. A. von Hayek (London, George Allen and Unwin, 1802).

Tugwell, R. G. (ed.), *The Trend of Economics* (London, Kennikat, 1924).

Turner, P. V., *Campus: An American Planning Tradition* (Cambridge, Mass., MIT Press, 1984).

Voorhis, G., 'The Power of the Money Monopoly', *Dynamic America*, (February 1938), pp. 11–38.

——, *Confessions of a Congressman* (New York, Doubleday, 1948).

——, *The Strange Case of Richard Milhouse Nixon* (New York, Popular, 1973).

Watkins, L. L., *Commercial Banking Reform in the United States With Especial Reference to the 100% Plan and the Regulation of Interest Rates on Bank Deposits* (New York, Arno Press, 1938).

White, D. (ed.), *The State of the Social Sciences* (Chicago, Chicago UP, 1956).

Whittlesey, C. R., *Banking and the New Deal*, Public Policy Pamphlet No. 16 (Chicago, Chicago UP, 1935).

Wrigley, R. L., 'The Plan of Chicago' in Krueckenberg (ed.), *Introduction to Planning History in the United States* (New Brunswick, Centre for Urban Policy Research Studies, Rutgers University, 1983).

Zinn, H., *New Deal Thought* (New York, Bobbs-Merrill, 1966).

'Monetary Economics of Chicagoans and Non-Chicagoans'

G. Tavlas, 'Some further observations on the monetary economics of Chicagoans and non-Chicagoans', *Southern Economic Journal* (April 1976), pp. 685–92

SOME FURTHER OBSERVATIONS ON THE MONETARY ECONOMICS OF CHICAGOANS AND NON-CHICAGOANS*

GEORGE S. TAVLAS

New York University

I. INTRODUCTION

The increased acceptance of monetarist thought among economists during the past decade has been accompanied by a concurrent interest in the doctrinal historical character of the quantity theory of money. The outcome of this rekindled interest has been an outpouring of evidence shedding considerable light on the analytic and pragmatic nature of the American quantity theory tradition, circa, 1920-1950. This paper is an extension and elaboration of some recent work by Thomas Humphrey, J. Ronnie Davis, and Don Patinkin.

Humphrey [15] rightly challenges Milton Friedman's rigid representation of the extra-Chicago quantity theory during the 1930's and 1940's. As evidence, Humphrey outlines the relation of the present-day monetarist doctrines to the Fisherine analytic constructs of such writers as Carl Snyder, Lionel Edie, Lauchlin Currie, and Clark Warburton. In a later note [16], he cites the contributions of Holbrook Working, Morris A. Copeland and James Harvey Rogers. His conclusion is that,

> Friedman's implication that the contemporary version of the quantity theory was born and nurtured in the University of Chicago in the 30's and 40's, while the old version of the theory withered and died outside seems not be an accurate evaluation In fact, much of the opposite seems to have happened. Non-Chicago economists continued in the 20's, 30's and 40's to make important improvements and extensions of the old theory—improvements and extensions which anticipated Friedman's modern version but which are not to be found in the published works of his mentors during that time [16, 17].

Overlooked, however, by Humphrey and all other latter-day commentators is the very significant work of William T. Foster and Waddill Catchings.[1] Using the framework of the Fisherine equation of exchange, Foster and Catchings, writing in the 1920's, expounded views remarkably similar to those that Friedman now teaches. Some neglected doctrines of Foster and Catchings are outlined in Section II.

Davis [1; 2] meticulously re-examines the policy proposals of American economists, including Chicagoans, of the late 1920's and early 1930's. His results run contrary to the generally held notion that pre-Keynesian classical economists advocated the use of wage cuts and balanced budgets as means of combatting depression Quite the contrary, these economists instead recommended the use of deficit budgets to finance public works Hence "the policy proposals of Keynes and the Chicago economists were remarkably similar during the early 1930's" [1,481]. Davis has made a very real contribution to the history of doctrine by showing that American economists during this period were less classical in their policy recommendations and more Keynesian than postwar interpretation has led us to believe. But Davis is simply wrong when he extends his argument to equate the "*analytical* specifications concerning Keynes and the Classics" [2, 153] which gave rise to the similar policy proposals. Keynes, and especially his followers, advocated deficits within a theoretical framework that featured the impotence of monetary policy during depressions Ameri-

* The author wishes to thank James Becker, Dermot Gately, and William Silber for their comments

[1] Patinkin [20] does make brief reference to them, but only with respect to their being among the first American quantity theorists to replace "transactions velocity" by "circuit velocity" in the equation of exchange

can economists—especially members of the Chicago school—advocated deficit budgets precisely because monetary policy *did* matter Section III is an elaboration of this assertion.

Finally, Section IV is a note to Professor Patinkin's well-known article [19] on the Chicago school. Patinkin shows that the oral and written "tradition" that flourished at Chicago during the 1930's and 1940's used the framework of Fisher's equation of exchange in contrast to Friedman's "elegant exposition of the modern portfolio approach to the demand for money which. . .can only be seen as a continuation of the Keynesian theory of liquidity, preference" [19, 93]. The point at issue with Patinkin is his fifth, and final, proposition [19, 97–98] concerning the monetary framework of the Chicago tradition, namely, that to achieve budget deficits, a "variation of tax receipts is definitely preferable" over a variation in expenditures. A review of the relevant literature does not lend support to this contention.

II. FOSTER AND CATCHINGS: ADDITIONAL NON-CHICAGO INNOVATIONS

In outlining the contributions of Snyder, Edie, Currie, and Warburton, Thomas Humphrey [15] bridges these earlier versions of the quantity theory to the contemporary Chicago version. But even more pertinent to Friedman's Chicago, are the contributions of William T. Foster and Waddill Catchings. Writing jointly [7,8,9] in the 1920's, these two economists produced an abundance of material containing propositions strikingly similar to monetarist doctrines of today.

Foster and Catchings [8, 223; 9, 129] assert that the validity of Say's Law, that supply creates its own demand, holds only under conditions of pure barter. However, the introduction of money, defined as "suspended purchasing power" [8, 214] and treated within the Fisherine framework of $MV + M'V' = \sum pq$ [8, 159], upsets the full-employment equilibrium of Say's world. Unlike many of their classical forerunners and contemporaries, Foster and Catchings argued that "there cannot be intrinsically a more significant thing in the present economy of society than money" [8, 351]. The equation of exchange is a helpful device for gaining a better understanding of reality, but to assume, as was common practice among economists, that there is a proportional relationship between money and prices, one must realize that the other factors in the equation are being held the same. In the real world, however, "other factors never do remain the same" [8, 156] and those who believe they do are attacked as "rigid quantity theorists" [8, 161]. "Consequently when we say that the price-level varies directly with the quantity of money in circulation, ***all other factors remaining the same,*** we confine ourselves to hypothetical situations" [8, 162–163].

In criticizing the applicability of Say's Law within a monetary economy, Foster and Catchings [8, 212–24; 9, 121–31] launched a lengthy attack upon classical economics much like Keynes was to do a decade or so later in the ***General Theory*** [17]. Their reasoning [7, 409; 9, 71], and the source of the problem, was that the level of monetary purchasing power failed to keep pace with the annual trend rise in production, which from all available estimates was about 4 per cent a year. Hence, there would arise a general glut of goods in the market place. At this point, the classical prescription would call for a decline in the general price level. What the classical analysis failed to realize, however, was that decreases in today's product prices, in conjunction with yesterday's relatively higher costs which had already been paid out, result in lower profit margins and therefore lower future production levels. Consequently, the proper policy to follow should be one of maintaining monetary purchasing power, which in turn would maintain the inherent stability of the economy [8, 364]. A policy of maintaining monetary purchasing power could in turn be attained by either attempting to stabilize the general price level through the necessary variations in the money supply, or by following a simple growth rule of increasing the money supply at a rate of 4 per cent annually. The ideal policy would be one of discretionary changes in the money supply to achieve price-level stabilization, but such a policy was hampered by imperfectly understood lags.

> All discussion of this question [of price stabilization] is necessarily speculative nothing but experience could show exactly how long the "lag" would be between the corrective action and the desired effect Some of the factors that affect this "lag" are not even considered in current discussions of the methods for stabilizing prices [8, 354]

Therefore, much in line with Friedman's view [12] at the present, price stabilization was relegated to a future world with more and better information [8, 365] For the short, or immediate, run, a money growth rule was advocated They stated that,

> extreme flucuations in general business activity are themselves due chiefly to fluctuations in the volume of currency and bank credit which have taken place without reference to changing trade needs We are justified, therefore, in concluding that an increase of about four per cent per annum in the total volume of currency and bank credit in circulation would come much nearer to satisfying the legitimate needs of business than increases . under our present banking system [8, 364-365].

In any event, whether the policy adopted was direct price stabilization or a money growth rule, sharp changes in the money supply should be avoided because of the resulting destabilizing lags, and because they lead to changing price levels and therefore to destabilizing changes in the demand for money [8, 168]. Friedman likewise incorporates the rate of change of the price level as one of the independent variables in his demand function of money [10].

Briefly, some of the other pertinent views held by Foster and Catchings were advocacy of deficit financed public works as a means of increasing monetary purchasing power [7, 340; 9, 94-95; 99, 104, 156-158], the use of empirical data to verify their results [9], and a simplistic, yet Fisherine, theory of interest [8, 126-136] They were clear to note that budget deficits were expansionary only if financed by monetary expansion [2] Tax-financed or bond-financed deficits were not considered expansionary as they had offsetting—what we today call "crowding-out"—effects [7, 337-338] Although not very explicit in their interest rate theory, Foster and Catchings argued that increasing the money supply was likey, through its effect on prices, to raise, rather than lower, the rate of interest. Their long-run view was one that emphasized the neutrality of money "It is true .that, in the long-run, the physical volume of trade is not greatly enlarged by increases in the volume of money in circulation" [8,169]. Moreover, in the long-run, "the only safe guide to changes in the volume of currency is the price level" [8, 365].

William Foster and Waddill Catchings completed their joint work in the 1920's. But in the 1932, Foster [6], appearing before the U S. Senate Committee on Banking and Currency, on a bill dealing with public works sponsored by Robert Wagner of New York, again reiterated his support for deficit budgets as means of increasing monetary purchasing power and combatting the depression He argued that the causes of the depression were "wholly monetary," and implied that blame for the depression should be placed with the Federal Reserve authority:

> They [consumers] lack the currency and credit [to buy goods] mainly because it has been driven out of circulation The driving campaign has been deliberately carried out, with the "liquidation" hounds all the while barking at the heels of frightened business. So far as the United States had any private banking policy in 1930 and in 1931, it was a policy of deflation So far as the United States had any official public policy, during those years, it was a policy of deflation. . . Those in command piously accepted defeat, convinced apparently that the suffering was good for us, and that, in any

[2] Friedman [13, 915[1] states that, "Whether deficits produce inflation depends on how they are financed. If, as so often happens, they are financed by creating money, they unquestionably do produce inflationary pressure." Tax or bond financed deficits are expansionary only if they "somehow affect monetary policy."

event, it was foreordained and nothing could be done about it. They fervently believed in the economics of original sin [6, 63]

Thomas Humphrey states that, "Currie was the *only* American monetary theorist in the early 1930's to hold the Federal Reserve authorities responsibile for precipitating the Great Depression" [15, 14]. Surely, some acknowledgement must also be given to William T. Foster.

It can be seen, then, that there is a great deal of similarity between the doctrines of Foster and Catchings, and those which Friedman currently teaches. But Friedman never refers to the contributions of Foster and Catchings which include: (1) that money is suspended purchasing power (to Friedman, it is a temporary abode of purchasing power); (2) the economy is inherently stable; (3) the reason for instability is perverse changes in the money stock; (4) money is not neutral in the short-run; (5) the long-run neutrality of money; (7) as a result, the proper policy is one of expanding the money supply at 4 per cent annually; (8) direct price-level stabilization is a more desirable policy, but because of lags, it must be delegated to the long-run; (9) deficits are expansionary only if financed by monetary expansion; (10) deficits financed by either selling bonds or raising taxes have completely offsetting effects; (11) monetary expansion raises the level of interest rates; (12) a factor affecting the demand for money is the expected change of the price level; (13) the use of empirical evidence to verify the equation of exchange; (14) the subsequent argument by Foster that the Great Depression was caused by perverse changes in the stock of money.

III. DEFICIT BUDGETS AND THE CHICAGO SCHOOL

In his aforementioned testiomony before the Committee on Banking and Currency, William Foster emphasized that the way out of the depression was through an expansion of bank credit. But how was bank credit to be put into circulation? Foster's answer was as follows:

One of the most obvious ways is through public works. As you see, the next question becomes, 'What kind of public works?' Personally, that to me is a less important question. The absolute and immediate necessity is the putting of money into circulation, where it will be spent for commodities, because that is the only way which you can stimulate private industry to proceed to do its part toward using credit . . . [6, 56].

Soon, thereafter, Foster argues that,

We shall get out of the depression, therefore, soley by monetary measures [6, 57].

There is an ostensible similarity between Foster's view of the proper policy measures to take to rid the chains of depression, and the views of the Chicago school of this period, as presented by J. Ronnie Davis. This similarity is very real. Indeed, the names of Foster and Catchings might well be added to Davis' comprehensive study [2] of the policy prescriptions of the U.S. economists during the late 1920's and early 1930's. The addition of these two names can only further substantiate the validity of Davis' historical study and his surprising conclusion that American economists of this period advocated the utilization of deficit budgets to finance public works. These *were* Keynesian ideas, and as result the American economists, and Chicagoans in particular, were much "less susceptible to the Keynesian virus than their contemporaries" [2, 8].

To go on from here, however, and draw analogies, as Davis does, between analytic frameworks can and does lead one into unseen pitfalls. To state further, as Davis does, "that a large majority of leading U.S. economists affirmed, as did Keynes, the usefulness of fiscal policy" [2, 6] can only blur the very sharp differences between the U.S. economists, especially the residents at Chicago, and Keynes; Behind the similar policy proposals lay two alternative hypotheses concerning the determinants of the level of income. Following Friedman and Meiselman [11], these can be represented in simple algebraic fashion as follows:

(1) $$Y = a + K'A$$

(2) $$Y = b + V'M.$$

The former equation expresses income as a linear function of autonomous expenditures, A, where K' is the marginal multiplier. The second equation expresses income as a linear function of the stock of money, M, where V' is marginal income velocity. These two equaitons will be helpful in discussing the theoretical differences between the earlier Chicago school and Keynes.

It will be instructive at this point to return to the previously quoted congressional testimony by Foster. His policy recommendation, it will be remembered, was the use of public works. Yet underlying this policy was the need of "putting money into circulation." Getting out of the depression could be accompanied "soley by monetary measures." Recall, further, from Section II, that Foster and Catchings jointly had pronounced that deficit budgets used to finance public works were expansionary only when accompanied by increases in the money supply. Tax or loan-financed deficits had offsetting effects. To Keynes, in contrast, the financing aspect of the deficit made little difference, and this view remained imbedded, until recently, within most post-Keynesian thought

This asymmetry should not surprise us For Keynes, it was necessary to offset changes in autonomous expenditures, which were at the mercy of the businessman's "animal spirits". The easiest way of accomplishing the task of stabilization was through offsetting changes in goverment expenditure. Hence the need for public works. This is an equation (1) view of the world. To Foster and Catchings, on the other hand, the heart of the problem was that productive capacity, growing at roughly 4 per cent a year, had to be accompanied by monetary expansion to generate the needed purchasing power. In a depression, however, traditional monetary measures—rediscounting and open market operations—might fail, due to a lack of borrowers. An alternate method had to be found to increase the money stock. One such method was through the financing of public works. This is an equation (2) view of the world. Missing are the "animal spritis".

Beneath the apparent similarities in policy, however, lie important differences. The early Keynesian view of the impotence of monetary policy ran somewhat as follows.[3] An increase in the *stock* of money could be effective only through a simple portfolio adjustment process where the cost of capital was lowered, via an increased demand for the stock of other financial assets. Due to the high interest elasticity of the demand for money in depressions, and the interest inelasticity of investment expenditure, monetary policy was likely to be inefffective. This is the familiar Keynesian story. But to Foster and Catchings, causation ran directly from the increased *stock* of money to the increased *flow* of spending There is no intervening portfolio adjustment process Public works, because they generated monetary flow, were useful during depression. Therefore public works were entirely consistent within the Fisherine analytic framework where money matters. Said Foster, during his testimony:

> May I say that this bill [the Wagner bill for public works] as proposed, and as drawn in detail is entirely supported by the full body of economic theory which I endorse. To my mind, there is behind it, all the way through, as absolutely sound, demonstrated economic theory [6, 58]

Entirely consistent with the Foster and Catchings analysis, that public works and deficit budgets be used as instruments for conducting monetary, rather than fiscal, policy, is the view of the Chicago school of the early 1930's. Thus Paul Douglas, as early as 1927 [3], and throughout the early 1930's [4, 5] was also an advocate of deficit spending for public works. The analysis from which he reaches this policy conclusion is very similar to that of Foster and Catchings. Indeed, his acknowledgment to their work [3, 38] leads

[3] See Patinkin [19, 107–108]

one to deduce the derivature nature of his analysis. Like them, he eschews traditional monetary measures during depressions because these do little to raise the demand for loans. The problem is one of "creating more monetary purchasing power" [4, 11]. Such purchasing power will drive prices up, and with costs lagging behind, will increase profit margins and lead to increased production. Looked at from the viewpoint of the equation of exchange, there is a "neccessity of increasing the money side of the price equation" [3, 41]. This end can be accomplished by deficit spending financed by either issuing money or by floating bonds, but because the latter have offsetting effects, a policy of monetary expansion is definitely preferable provided that inflation can be controlled.

Other members of this earlier Chicago school shared with Douglas the view that public works financed by deficit budgets are expansionary because of their monetary effects—causation running directly from changes in the stock of money to changes in the flow of monetary purchasing power. Viner's view [25, 20] is much like Douglas' Changes in the money supply, with costs adjusting stickily, will affect profits initially and then production. The use of deficit budgets as means of conducting monetary policy was stated explicitly by Mints[4].

> If and when the Federal debt was reduced to the desirable minimum, it would be necessary to find other means of meeting the requirement of a policy of annual additions to the stock of money Two means are available: (1) the purchase of other assets than government bonds and (2) the introduction of a permanent deficit in the regular budget [18, 195].

Mints [18] goes on to explain that the latter can be attained by public works spending. His primary policy goal is one of direct price stabilization. Here, too, one can get and inkling of the rationale behind his advocacy of deficit budgets:

> Under these curcumstances [that policy is directed towards price stabilization] the amount of deficit needed for monetary purposes would be the starting point in making up the budget It should then be recognized that any extention of public expenditures beyond this amount should invariably be covered dollar for dollar by tax receipts, and that every item of expenditure should stand on its own merits, without regard to the problem of monetary policy [18, 221]

Finally we come to Henry Simons whose work Patinkin [19] considers definitive in the fields of monetary and fiscal policy at Chicago throughout the 1930's and 1940's. Though never presenting in writing a complete analytic framework of his views, Simons left no doubt that federal expenditures should be used as a means of conducting monetary policy [21, 55, 321; 22, 321; 23, 175]. Thus in his discussion on implementation of monetary rules he states that

> The responsibility for carrying out the monetary rules should be lodged in a federal authority, endowed with large administrative powers but closely controlled in their exercise by a sharply defined policy The powers of the monetary authorities should have to do primarily or exclusively with fiscal arrangements—with the issue and retirement of paper money (open-market operations in government securities) and perhaps with the relation between government revenues and expenditures—in other words, the monetary rules should be implemented entirely by, and in turn should largely determine, fiscal policy [22, 182].

As for the stabilization of autonomous expenditures, Simons argues,

> the direction of investment [should be] left to the control of competition and kept as far as possible outside the influence of political agencies (or central banks) [22, 82].

These latter statements demonstrate that Simons accepted an equation (2) view of the world and eschewed the view hypothesized in equation (1). Combined with the evidence here presented by his Chicago colleagues, and the further work of Foster and Catchings, it can be seen that these economists recommended deficit budgets precisely be-

[4] See Also, Mints [18, 197, 206, 221].

cause monetary policy did matter.[6] Although sharing with Keynes the need for public works, their analytic paradigm was different in conception. Because of the similarities in policy recommendations, they *were* less susceptible to the Keynesian virus. Perhaps they were further immune, because they rejected the Keynesian theoretical structure and its implication of the weakness of monetary policy.

IV. CHICAGO AND THE FINANCING OF DEFICITS

Professor Patinkin [19] in his article on the Chicago tradition, lists five propositions concerning the monetary approach of this school, the last of which states that its members, in advocating deficit budgets argued that the latter should be generated through variation of tax receipts. Of the four members of the Chicago school listed in the present paper only one, Lloyd Mints [18, 196], ever argued explicitly for deficits produced through revenue variation.

As for the other members of the Chicago school dealt with here, there is no evidence that any of them ever showed a strong preference for varying receipts. Viner [25, 24; 26, 133] was usually indifferent as to whether deficits be generated by changing expenditures or tax receipts, but where he did show favor, it was on the side of varying expenditures. Douglas [4, 13; 5, 138] was definitely in favor of expenditure induced deficits financed by printing money, or, if inflation could not be checked, by selling bonds. Simons [22, 23, 24] never showed preference either way.

Patinkin states that his five propositions on the Chicago school are "primarily a summary of Simons' views" [19, 96]. The rationale given in support of the fifth proposition is that,

> a tax system which depends heavily on the income tax is desirable not only from the viewpoint of distributive justice, but also from the viewpoint of automatically providing proper cyclical variations in tax receipts [19, 98].

The problems of distributive justice and stabilization, according to the preceding statement, can be tied together. This, however, is not Simons, view at all. The two problems are distinct and should be kept so. Thus,

> the problem of efficiency and of inequality may usefully be separated for purposes of discussion—and properly, if one accepts the view that the appropriate measures for improving efficiency and for mitigating inequality are, within fairly wide limits, distinct and independent [21, 46–47].

Of his five propositions on the Chicago school, the fifth is the only one in which Patinkin does not support with documented evidence.

V. CONCLUDING REMARKS

This paper has dealt with some issues recently raised concerning the state of monetary economics in the U.S. during the 1920's and 1930's. The evidence presented on the work of Foster and Catchings furnishes additional support for Thomas Humphrey's contention that Milton Friedman's quantity theory has its roots in the earlier non-Chicagoan, Fisherine equation of exchange. In addition, the work of Foster and Catchings can also be added to J. Ronnie Davis documented evidence showing that U.S. economists in the late 1920's and early 1930's advocated the use of deficit budgets to finance public works. Davis is simply wrong to extend the valid analogy between the policy proposals of U.S. economists and those of Keynes, to the invalid analogy concerning analytic paradgims. Furthermore, to state that these U.S. economists were less susceptible to the Keynesian virus because they already held Keynesian notions, is to haze the issue. Keynes argued for public works and fiscal policy, and had little faith in the

---

[6] This was stated explicitly by another Chicagoan, Harry Gideonse: "Expenditures for public works. . are definitely a part of [an administration's] monetary policy " [14, 750].

effectiveness of monetary policy during depressions. As has been shown, to Foster and Catchings, and the Chicagoans, public works were a means of conducting monetary policy. Indeed, in this respect, Friedman's [10] exegesis of a Chicago tradition where "money matters" can only be strengthened. Further, much like Friedman, and unlike many Keynesians, until recently, Foster and Catchings, Douglas, Viner, Simons and Mints recognized that the method of financing a budgetary deficit is most important in its own right. Finally, there is little support for Patinkin's contention that members of the Chicago school in the 1930's advocated the variation of tax receipts, rather than expenditures, as the proper method for generating deficit budgets.

REFERENCES

1. Davis, J. Ronnie, "Chicago Economists, Deficit Budgets, and the early 1930's," *A.E.R.* 58 (June 1968), 476–82
2. ——— *The New Economics and the Old Economists* Iowa Iowa State Press, 1971.
3. Douglas, Paul H., "The Modern Technique of Mass Production and its Relation to Wages," *Proceedings of Academy of Political Science*. (April 1927), 17–42
4. ——— . *Collapse or Cycle* Chicago: American Library Association, 1933
5. ——— . *Controlling Depressions* New York. Norton and Company, 1935.
6. Foster, William T. *Unemployment Relief*. U.S , Senate Committee on Banking and Currency, 72nd Cong., 1st sess , 1932. 55–63.
7. ——— and Catchings, Waddill, *Profits*. Boston: The Riverside Press, 1925.
8. ——— . *Money* Boston; The Riverside Press, 1927.
9. ——— *The Road to Plenty*, Boston· The Riverside Press, 1928.
10. Friedman, Milton, "The Quantity Theory of Money—A Restatement," in *Studies in the Quantity Theory of Money*, edited by Milton Friedman Chicago. University of Chicago Press, 1956
11. ——— and Meiselman "The Relative Stability of Monetary Velocity and the Investment Multiplier in the United States, 1897–1958," in *Stabilization Policies* Englewood Cliffs, N. J : Prentice Hall, 1963.
12. ——— , "The Monetary Theory and Policy of Henry Simons," *Journal of Law and Economics* October 1967, 1–3.
13. ——— , "Comments on the Critics," *Journal of Political Economy*. September/October 1972, 906–950
14. Gideonse, Harry D., "Money and Finance," *The American Journal of Sociology*, May 1934 749–758.
15. Humphrey, Thomas M , "Role of Non-Chicago Economists in the Evolution of the Quantity Theory in American 1930-1950," *Southern Economic Journal*. July 1971, 12–18
16. ——— , "On the Monetary Economics of Chicagoans and Non-Chicagoans. Reply," *Southern Economic Journal* January 1973, 460–463
17. Keynes, J. M *The General Theory of Employment. Interest and Money* New York· Harcourt, Brace, 1936
18. Mints, Lloyd W *Monetary Policy for a Competitive Society* New York McGraw-Hill, 1950.
19. Patinkin, Don, "The Chicago Tradition, The Quantity Theory, and Friedman," in *Studies in Monetary Economics*. New York· Harper and Row, 1972, pp 92–117
20. ——— , "On the Monetary Economics of Chicagoans and Non-Chicagoans Comment," *Southern Economic Journal*. January 1973, 454–459
21. Simons, Henry C , "A Positive Program for Laissez-Faire," (1934), in *Economic Policy for a Free Society* Chicago: University of Chicago Press, 1948.
22. ——— , "Rules versus Authorities in Monetary Policy," (1936), in *Economic Policy for a Free Scoiety*
23. ——— , "Hansen on Fiscal Policy," (1942), in *Economic Policy for a Free Society*.
24. ——— . "On Debt Policy," (1944), in *Economic Policy for a Free Society*.
25. Viner, Jacob. *Balanced Deflation, Inflation or More Depression*. Minneapolis, Minn.· University of Minnesota Press, 1933.
26. ——— , "Inflation as a Remedy for Depression," in *Proceedings of the Institute of Public Affiars* Athens, Ga. University of Georgia, 1933.

'Chicago Economists'

J. R. Davis, 'Chicago economists, budget deficits, and the early 1930s', *American Economic Review* (June 1968), pp. 476–82.

Chicago Economists, Deficit Budgets, and the Early 1930s

"There is clearly great similarity between the views expressed by [Henry C.] Simons and by [John Maynard] Keynes—as to the causes of the Great Depression, the impotence of monetary policy, and the need to rely extensively on fiscal policy" [2, p. 7]. Coming from an authority no less than Professor Milton Friedman, this statement undoubtedly surprised economists who are unaccustomed to hearing Simons and Keynes mentioned in the same breath. The more familiar impression of the views of these two giants was struck five years before Friedman's remarks: in a much-celebrated controversy [9, 5, 1], Professor Lawrence Miller charged that a School of economics crystallized at the University of Chicago during the tenure of Professors Knight, Simons, and Viner and that this School was "consistently less enamored with Keynesian ideas and terminology than the rest of the profession" [5, p. 68]. This apparent conflict is heightened by Friedman's lengthy comparison of the Keynes and Simons interpretations of 1929-33: they both argued that it is collapse of confidence which sets off a demand for liquidity, that this demand cannot be met but the attempts to meet it force liquidation, and that this liquidation includes bank loans with a resultant decline in the quantity of money [2, p. 6]. In short, Friedman argues that both Simons and Keynes emphasized the state of business expectations and the desire for liquidity. Accordingly, Simons and Keynes each turned to fiscal policy—changes in government expenditures and taxes—as their primary tool for promoting economic stability [2, p. 9]. Friedman suggests that the views which Keynes and Simons held in common were also widely shared by Simons' contemporaries [2, p. 4], thereby making Chicago students "much less susceptible to the Keynesian virus than their contemporaries in London, England, and Cambridge, Massachusetts, who were taught that the Great Depression was a necessary and ultimately healthy purgative" [2, pp. 8-9].

Friedman's appraisal of his predecessors surprises many observers because they have become accustomed to associating Chicago economists with the advocacy of limited government and the distrust of discretionary authority in government [5, p. 65]. While these themes might indeed characterize much of their work, they should not be allowed to obscure the facts that Frank H. Knight, Henry C. Simons, Jacob Viner, and their Chicago colleagues argued throughout the early 1930s for the use of large and continuous deficit budgets to combat the mass unemployment and deflation of the times, that they played an important role in the development of the notion of compensatory public spending, and that they attempted to persuade the Hoover Administration to adopt large budgetary deficits. Strangely enough, these contributions have gone largely uncredited.

While Knight, Viner, and others are understandably amused, if not annoyed, at charges that a School of economics was founded during their tenure, they surely do not deny that there was a remarkable consensus in support of fiscal policy rather than either monetary or wage policy during the early years of the Great Depression.[1] Accordingly, this paper is devoted to a study of this group's professional activities during the pre-Keynesian years 1931-33.

Jacob Viner (1931)

By 1931, the simple truths of compensatory public finance, i.e., that governments should execute budgetary deficits in depression periods and budgetary surpluses in boom periods, had already caught root in the United States. During that year, Jacob Viner was invited to lecture on "Problems of International Commercial and Financial Policy" at the Institute of Politics at Williamstown, Massachusetts. At the seventh meeting of his Round Table, Viner discussed and criticized prevailing American Treasury policy. Viner explained that the Treasury was still practicing traditional policies based on so-called sound principles of finance: taxing heavily, spending lightly, and redeeming debts. Although such policies were sound during periods of prosperity, Viner argued, they were unwise and inappropriate depression policies. Viner advised a precisely opposite depression policy: taxing lightly, spending heavily, and borrowing [7, p. 182]. During depression periods, government may borrow to defray expenditures which give rise to the employment of otherwise idle capital and labor. And inasmuch as the capital and labor would otherwise remain idle, Viner pointed out that "the public works or other useful services so financed during a period of economic depression are from the national economic point of view almost costless" [7, p. 183].

Viner's discussion at Williamstown was one of the first important statements of the "simple truth" of a compensatory role for government spending in this country. Viner was not speaking in isolation, however. According to him, "the idea [that government should utilize deficits in depressions and surpluses in booms] was then [1931] commonplace in my academic surroundings of the time, and I cannot recall that any of my Chicago colleagues would have dissented" [13, p. 264]. This relative unanimity was much in evidence a few months later when the Chicago economists issued an important memoran-

[1] This should not be interpreted as a suggestion that Chicago economists represented a monolithic point of view. For example, it has been pointed out that Paul Douglas and Harry Millis diverged from the consensus on the role of wage policy in recovery and that Jacob Viner and Simeon Leland were more willing then Frank Knight and Henry Simons to abandon "rules versus authorities" for the practical benefits of rapid recovery from the Depression. While supporting the thesis that the Chicago economists failed to be highly monolithic, these differences were not serious in the face of the remarkable policy consensus which characterized the group. Notably, even Knight and Simons proved willing to "weasel" on "rules versus authorities" when they signed the January 1932 telegram to President Hoover.

dum to Congressman Samuel B. Pettengill (Indiana) on the advisability of either borrowing or printing money as a depression remedy.

1932 Chicago Memorandum

In their April 26, 1932 memorandum to Congressman Pettengill, the twelve Chicago economists[2]—including Knight, Simons, Viner—argued strongly in favor of "fiscal inflation" as the means of checking depression and initiating recovery [10, pp. 524-27]. These economists were quick to dismiss recovery by automatic adjustments. Reliance on the automatic process involved "tremendous losses, in wastage of productive capacity, and in acute suffering" [10, p. 524]. They further pointed out that wage and price rigidities were largely the ground on which governmental action was justified. Their advice, therefore, was that recovery could be brought about by injecting enough new purchasing power which, while amenable to abuse, required only courageous fiscal policy on the part of the federal government. To the Chicago economists, action was needed to raise prices, and this action "should take the form of generous Federal expenditures, financed without resort to taxes on commodities or transactions" [10, p. 525].

One of the fears expressed by the Chicago economists was that in the event that their advice was followed, the "fiscal inflation" would be of token proportions. They warned of the danger of emergency-spending schemes whose "inadequate, temporary stimulation might well leave conditions worse than it found them" [10, p. 525]. Convinced that too meager or too short-lived "fiscal inflation" would induce at best only temporary revival and then serious relapse, the Chicago economists' recommendation was that heavy doses of stimulant should be administered, that they should continue until recovery was firmly established, and that only then should these expenditures be discontinued.

The Chicago economists realized that their recommendation would be received with alarm by some. Accordingly, they appended two arguments. First, they agreed that it was probably best, under the circumstances,[3] for the government to sell new issues of bonds directly to the reserve banks or, in effect, to exchange them for bank deposits and Federal Reserve notes: "much may be said, indeed, for issuing the bonds with the circulation privilege, thus permitting the reserve banks to issue Federal reserve bank notes in exchange; for this procedure does not much invite suspicion, has supporting precedent, and would greatly reduce the legal requirements with respect to gold" [10, p. 526]. Also, they pointed out that "fiscal inflation" was the most promising means of eventually restoring an annually balanced budget and that in the meanwhile Congress should intend to balance the budget over periods of five years or so.

[2] Signers of the memorandum were Professors Garfield V. Cox, Aaron Director, Paul H. Douglas, Harry D. Gideonse, Frank H. Knight, Harry A. Millis, Lloyd W. Mints, Henry Schultz, Henry C. Simons, Jacob Viner, Chester W. Wright, and Theodore O. Yntema.

[3] Some feared that drastic inflation threatened gold. The Chicago economists argued that their policy must be carried through, whatever that policy meant for gold.

Frank H. Knight (1932)

On April 20, 1932, Senator Robert F. Wagner decided to sample professional opinion of deficit budgets and addressed letters of inquiry to the foremost economists in the United States. On May 8, 1932, Frank H. Knight replied to Senator Wagner in favor of such tactics: "As far as I know, economists are completely agreed that the Government should spend as much and tax as little as possible, at a time such as this—using the expenditure in the ways to do the most good in itself and also to point toward relieving the depression . . ." [11, p. 10323].

Simeon E. Leland (1932)

Part of the widespread outspokenness which the Chicago economists levied against official budgeting philosophy was Professor Simeon E. Leland's lectures on the subject. In October, 1932, Leland addressed the International City Managers' Association Convention on "How Governments Can Best Meet the Financial Crisis." Leland's opinion, commonly shared by his Chicago colleagues, was that public expenditures should be "synchronized with economic rhythms" and that "no hesitancy should be shown in borrowing to finance" capital outlays [4, pp. 109-10]. Leland charged that concern for the annually balanced budget had been responsible for the bulk of real and imaginary crises facing government: "It is erroneously conceived that this is the only proper policy year in and year out, regardless of economic conditions" [4, p. 108]. Leland pointed out that the budget should be geared to economic conditions and that "equilibrium between surplus and deficits should be struck over a period of years rather than annually" [4, p. 108].

Jacob Viner (1933)

As the depression deepened, Jacob Viner in particular continued to press for the execution of deficit budgets. In 1933, for example, he delivered a paper in the Day and Hour Series of the University of Minnesota [12]. Here, Viner carefully and somewhat bitterly criticized the "fear campaign" directed towards deficit budgets because it unnecessarily discounted the value of an otherwise sound policy. Viner's point was that countercyclical balancing of the budget calling for deficits during depression periods was part of a sound fiscal policy. Viner chided Hoover for offsetting with fear the beneficial effects of the unintentional deficits executed during the early 1930s: "The outstanding though unintentional achivement of the Hoover Administration in counteracting the depression has in fact been its deficits of the last two years, and it was only its own alleged fears as to the ill effects of these deficits, and the panic which the big business world professed to foresee in these deficits should recur, which have made this method of depression finance seriously risky" [12, pp. 18-19].

Only a few months later but still in 1933, Viner again spoke out on depression policy. Speaking at the Institute of Public Affairs of the University of Georgia, Viner recommended that the most promising method of combating the depression was "that of governmental expenditures financed by borrowing from the banking system, with the hope that what the banks lend is newly created credit or credit which otherwise would have remained idle" [14, p. 133]. Again, Viner made it clear that sound principles of depression finance justified deficits being met either by new bank credit or by resorting to the printing press. Impatient by now with his antagonists, Viner lashed out that it was a mouldy fallacy to insist on balancing the budget in each year regardless of circumstances: "Why not in each month or week or hour?" [14, p. 129].

Viner then advanced a notion which Chicago economists had made familiar by 1933: the logical period for balancing the budget was the business cycle. And he pointed out that mere balancing was unsound during boom periods when a surplus should be executed either by building up cash reserves or by liquidating debt. This subject, however, became the object of still another pronouncement by the Chicago economists, this time in the form of a public policy pamphlet.

Public Policy Pamphlet No. 1 (1933)

Still in 1933, some of the Chicago economists[4]—notably Simons and Viner —helped in the preparation of a policy statement regarding balancing the budget [3]. In the Public Policy Pamphlet No. 1, they began by warning of the retarding effects which annually balanced budgets have during depressions. They argued that it was not axiomatic that the federal government should annually collect revenues sufficient to defray even its ordinary operating expenses. Instead, many types of expenditures should be financed by short-term borrowing, long-term funding, or issuance of fiat money.

This Chicago group then repeated the argument which by 1933 had been advanced before every conceivable type of audience: "The balancing of budgets should be regarded as a series of long-term operations in which deficits will be incurred and debts increased during years of economic adversity while Treasury surpluses and the rapid retirement of the public debt will be planned for during years of prosperity" [3, p. 10]. When a series of annual budgets is put together, they continued, the result should be an equilibrium between revenue and expenditures intentionally struck over a period of years rather than annually.

Concluding Remarks

On at least one occasion, the Chicago economists directly attempted to make their professional advice heard in Washington. In January, 1932, Henry Schultz, Jacob Viner, Garfield V. Cox, Frank H. Knight, John H. Cover, Lloyd W. Mints, Chester W. Wright, Harry D. Gideonse, Theodore O. Yntema, Harry A. Millis, Aaron Director, and Henry C. Simons were among the twenty-four participants of the Harris Foundation who signed a telegram to President Hoover, urging him to act favorably on (1) what later became the Glass-Steagall Act, which broadened the assets eligible for rediscounts with the Federal Reserve and permitted the Federal Reserve to use govern-

[4] Signers of the statement were Frank Bane, Paul Betters, Carl Chatters, Paul H. Douglas, Simeon E. Leland, H. A. Millis, Clarence E. Ridley, H. C. Simons, Donald Slesinger, Jacob Viner and L. D. White.

ment bonds as well as commercial paper as collateral for its notes; (2) a systematic campaign of Federal Reserve open-market purchases; (3) R.F.C. aid to banks with ineligible assets; and (4) financing a public works program (of a magnitude not less than 1930-31) with deficits[5] [6, pp. 413-15]. Although unintentional deficits occurred during the Hoover Administration, Hoover was not dissuaded from his fetish of an annual balanced budget: the efforts of Knight, Simons, Viner, and the others to persuade Hoover to utilize large budgetary deficits were met with increasing determination to close the unintentional excess of expenditures over revenues.

In a significant way, the policy proposals of Keynes and the Chicago economists were remarkably similar during the early 1930s. Then why were many of this group unsympathetic to the *General Theory?* Friedman's answer—Keynes and the Chicago economists shared views regarding 1929-33, making the latter unsusceptible to the "Keynesian virus"—is only a partial answer. Much of the answer lies in an explanation offered by one of the key figures in the Chicago tradition: those who argued for large deficits from the early 1930s on, but who were critical of (if not hostile to) the *General Theory,* based most of their opposition on an interpretation of it as advocating deficits as a desirable, normal practice and as seeing in deficits a cure-all for everything which ailed the western world. In short, the group which had labored in behalf of the notion of *compensatory* public spending was unsympathetic towards the notion of *secular* public spending which they read into Keynes' *General Theory.*

J. Ronnie Davis*

* The author is assistant professor of economics, Iowa State University. This paper is part of a study (cf. J. Ronnie Davis, "Pre-Keynesian Economic Policy Proposals in the United States During the Great Depression," University of Virginia, unpublished doctoral dissertation, 1967) made possible by a grant from the Ford Foundation, which, needless to say, shares no responsibility for its contents. The author would like to thank Frank H. Knight, Jacob Viner, Simeon E. Leland, and Harry D. Gideonse for conversations and letters in which they gave their account of this period and helped with bibliographical difficulties. Also, the author thanks his colleagues Dudley G. Luckett and Charles W. Meyer for their suggestions which improved earlier drafts of this paper.

References

1. M. Bronfenbrenner, "Observations on the 'Chicago School(s)'" *Jour. Pol. Econ.* Feb. 1962, *70,* 72–75.
2. Milton Friedman, "The Monetary Theory and Policy of Henry Simons," The Henry Simons Lecture delivered at The Law School, University of Chicago, May 5, 1967, *Jour. Law & Econ.,* Oct. 1967, *10,* 1–13.
3. H. D. Gideonse, editor, *Balancing the Budget,* Public Policy Pamph. No. 1. Chicago 1933.
4. S. E. Leland, "How Governments Can Best Meet the Financial Crisis," address to The International City Managers' Association Convention, October 24, 1932, *City Manager Yearbook,* 1933, pp. 105–21.

[5] In the Special Session which adopted this telegram, Jacob Viner emphasized that this was a *minimum* program on which they could agree [8, p. 2].

5. H. L. Miller, Jr., "On the 'Chicago School of Economics,'" *Jour. Pol. Econ.*, Feb. 1962, *70*, 64–69.
6. Norman Wait Harris Memorial Foundation, *Reports of Round Tables: Gold and Monetary Stabilization.* Chicago 1932.
7. *Report of the Round Tables and General Conferences at the Eleventh Session,* The Institute of Politics. Williamstown, Mass. 1931.
8. *Special Session of Economists In Attendance at the Norman Wait Harris Institute, January 31, 1932* (mimeographed).
9. G. J. Stigler, "Comment," *Jour. Pol. Econ.*, Feb. 1962, *70*, 70–71.
10. U.S. Congress, House of Representatives, Committee on Ways and Means, *Hearings, Payment of Adjusted-Compensation Certificates,* 72d Cong., 1st Sess., 1932.
11. U.S. Congress, *Congressional Record,* 72d Cong., 1st Sess., 1932, *75*, Part 9.
12. Jacob Viner, *Balanced Deflation, Inflation, or More Depression,* The Day and Hour Series of the University of Minnesota, No. 3, Minneapolis 1933.
13. ———, "Comment on My 1936 Review of Keynes' General Theory," in Robert Lekachman, ed., *Keynes' General Theory: Reports of Three Decades,* New York 1964.
14. ———, "Inflation as a Remedy for Depression," *Proceedings of the Institute of Public Affairs, Seventh Annual Session,* The University of Georgia, Athens, Georgia, 1933.

'The Last Remake of the New Economics'

J. R. Davis, 'The last remake of the new economics and the old economists', *Southern Economic Journal* (January 1979), pp. 919–25.

AND

'Reply'

G. Tavlas, 'The last remake of the new economics and the old economists', *Southerm Economic Journal* (January 1979), pp. 926–31.

The Last Remake of the New Economics and the Old Economists: Comment

Mr. George S. Tavlas recently has undertaken to contribute to the doctrinal history of the quantity theory of money [24]. In the judgment of Mr. Tavlas, the work of William T. Foster and Waddill Catchings[1] [5; 6; 7] has been slighted and the theoretical frameworks of Keynes and the classics have been equated without warrant. The corrective that Mr. Tavlas tenders is itself adulterated, however. In this paper, I endeavor to lay to rest representations that I thought already decently buried. The character of controversy as it is, I doubt that I shall fully succeed. Nonetheless, I remain hopeful that this is, indeed, the last remake of *The New Economics and the Old Economists* [1].

I.

In my book, I pointed out that the sharp distinctions between pre- and post-1936 economics were drawn principally from analytical models rather than from historical descriptions. Typically, economists denoted a system of equations as "classical theory," and then "classical policy" was deduced from the model. Often, the policy deduced in this manner was represented as historically descriptive of proposals characteristic of economists prior to 1936. Thus, I had wished to examine the historical record to see whether the "old economists" actually proposed wage cuts and annually balanced budgets, the policies often deduced from classical models [1, 4–5]. When I concluded that, based on my study of 1930–35, "the analytical specifications concerning Keynes and the Classics do not square well with these historical observations," of course I meant that, historically, the old U.S. economists generally did not propose the policies so readily deduced from analytical models declared to

1 Catchings was a prominent investment banker (of Goldman, Sachs and Co.) as well as an iron and steel magnate. Foster was director of the Pollack Foundation for Economic Research, founded by Catchings. Both were close to the Hoover administration. Their ideas were underconsumptionist. They thought that the cause of overproduction was that consumers cannot buy the output at going prices. The evidence was the investment of too much savings rather than the failure to find investments for all the savings which people desire. Keynes would have disagreed with Foster and Catchings, arguing that, in periods of unemployment, a high level of investment would stimulate income and promote prosperity. The only sense in which Foster and Catchings were true to the Keynesian spirit was in opposing deflationary adjustment of falling prices. For brilliant criticisms of Foster and Catchings, see Hayek [9, 199–263] and Phillips, *et al.* [22, 59–64].

represent theory prior to the publication of Keynes' *General Theory* [10]. I do not know where Tavlas got the idea or even what he means when he says that I "equate the 'analytical specifications concerning Keynes and the Classics' which gave rise to the similar proposals [24, 685]."

In a preview of coming attractions, as it were, I said in my book that "this study tries to demonstrate that a large majority of leading U.S. economists affirmed, as did Keynes, the usefulness of fiscal policy and the uselessness of money wage reductions in fighting business depression [1, 6]." Mr. Tavlas believes that my attempted demonstration "can only blur the very sharp differences between the U.S. economists, especially the residents at Chicago, and Keynes [24, 688]." What I showed in my book was that, historically, sharp differences in policy are more imagined that real. At least, this was true of 1930–35, the period that I studied.

Consider the 1931 meetings that were attended by Keynes as well as most Chicago economists and many other prominent U.S. and European economists. Henry Schultz, a Chicago stalwart, presented part of a paper that concluded that wage cuts would not reduce unemployment in a depression because (1) wage cuts reduced incomes and, in turn, aggregate demand, especially for consumer goods; and (2) thus, no additional labor was likely to be hired at lower wages since employers would see no market for any more output [21, 190 ff.]. There was no disagreement. Keynes said that he thought that the analysis was "extraordinarily good and most helpful," that he had "never seen it put quite so before," and that he had "very little to add to the actual scope of this or to criticize [21, 212]." Harvard's Summer Slichter concluded a later discussion when he said, "I think [wage-cutting] is practically a dead issue in this depression [21, 545]."

When expansionary public works programs were discussed, Keynes emphasized that, in the United States, "getting back to a state of equilibrium should be concentrated on the rate of interest [21, 303]."[2] Keynes explained that, in Great Britain, he had supported public works only because its economy was "such a center of an international system that we cannot operate on the rate of interest, because if we tried to force the rate of interest down, there is too much lending, and we lose our gold [21, 303]." "In Great Britain, one had to lay great stress on public programs," Keynes said, "but in this country I should operate on the rate of interest [21, 303]."

Lloyd Mints, a thoroughgoing Chicagoan, tried to exhort Keynes to concede a case for expansionary fiscal policy.[3] "As I understand your argu-

2. Throughout discussion, Keynes assumed that there was only *one* equilibrium and that at full employment. There is not as much as a hint on his part of an unemployment equilibrium. The other economists, however, argued that there were *infinite* equilibria, only one of which would be at full employment. The only exception among those who spoke up was, interestingly, Alvin Hansen, who, by assuming perfect competition, agreed with Keynes that there was never more than one equilibrium.

3. Only six months later, leading economists again gathered in Chicago. Jacob Viner, sometimes credited or blamed as a founder of the so-called "Chicago School," and others again

ment," Mints pointed out, "you want to reduce the interest rate in order to bring about an equivalence between saving and investment [21, 493]." Mints then tried to wring agreement from Keynes that public works would bring about precisely the same results, not through decreasing the rate of interest, but increasing the rate of investment. In other words, Keynes was counting on the interest rate to equilibrate saving and investment, whereas, Mints, on income. Acquiescing in Mint's understanding, Keynes granted only that, "I should use the public works program to fill in the interregnum while I was getting the interest rate down," and that, "I should be afraid of [public works] as a sole remedy [21, 494]."

To recapitulate, I did not "equate the 'analytical specifications concerning Keynes and the Classics' [24, 685]." I did show that the policy proposals of U.S. economists generally (1) were not those deduced from analytical models of classical theory and (2) were similar to those that, after 1936, were hailed as Keynesian. When Mr. Tavlas says of my book, "Davis is simply wrong to extend the valid analogy between the policy proposals of U.S. economists and those of Keynes, to the invalid analogy concerning analytic paradigms [24, 691]," I believe this to be a groundless criticism based on a misreading of my book.[4] Also, in criticizing my book—which, after all, is a study of 1930–35—I believe that Mr. Tavlas commits a serious error laid bare by the comments made by Keynes and other economists attending the 1931 Harris Foundation meetings. I am referring to Mr. Tavlas' criticism that:

> Furthermore, to state that these U.S. economists were less susceptible to the Keynesian virus because they already held Keynesian notions, is to haze the issue. Keynes argued for public works and fiscal policy, and had little faith in the effectiveness of monetary policy during depression [24, 691–2].

I shall leave to the reader's judgment whether, as evidenced by his comments in mid-1931, Keynes argued for public works and had little faith in monetary policy. Also, Mr. Tavlas attributes to Keynes the point of view that "the easiest way of accomplishing the task of stabilization was through offsetting changes in government expenditure [24, 689]." While this attribu-

---

argued strongly for expansionary public works programs. Only Alvin Hansen, who was still at Minnesota, seemed unmoved by the consensus:

> I have a feeling that public works has [sic] been accepted . . . too easily tonight. . . . There are a good many arguments against public works. . . You can't put public works suddenly in motion without an enormous waste, and . . . they do react upon the private economy [20, 244–5].

Viner parried each of Hansen's thrusts against public works. Among his comments, Viner said that public works would have an altogether favorable reaction on business. Also, Viner emphasized that "so far as wasting is concerned, assume that there was thirty, forty, or fifty percent wastage, it would be thirty, forty, or fifty percent of the wastage involved now in the idle capital resources and the idle labor resources that are available and not being used [20, 245]."

4. I do not believe that I can be faulted for misleading Mr. Tavlas. The only pages to which he refers from my book are the last page and two pages from the introductory chapter. I think the language and meaning are clear in the places cited, but certainly the intent is clear in the intervening pages.

tion must be qualified to be descriptive of Keynes in, say mid-1931, it seems an apt description of the point of view expressed in 1930–35 by any number of U.S. economists, including "the residents of Chicago." Indeed, even the U.S. reviews of the *General Theory* did not question policy at all. They challenged theory only. Among Chicago economists, Frank Knight [11], Henry Simons [23], and Jacob Viner [25], each reviewed the *General Theory*. They all agreed with Keynes on policy.

Furthermore, Mr. Tavlas suggests that, in a depression, "traditional monetary measures" are rediscounting and open-market operations, as though, prior to the influence of Keynes, economists endorsed such measures with confidence in their effectiveness [24, 689]. It was "Keynes, and especially his followers," Mr. Tavlas tells us, who "advocated deficits within a theoretical framework that featured the impotence of monetary policy during depressions [24, 685]." In fact, during 1930–35, countless U.S. economists pointed out that such measures would, in Mr. Tavlas' words, "fail, due to a lack of borrowers [24, 689]."

For example, Chicago's Paul Douglas clearly showed that such measures would be ineffective for the very reason that Mr. Tavlas cites, *viz.*, they would not stimulate borrowing [3, 118]. Douglas advocated budgetary deficits in part because the rediscount rate and open-market operations were "weak reeds [3, 118]." In a study for the National Bureau of Economic Research, Arthur D. Gayer flatly denied that monetary policy could stimulate aggregate demand during recessions [8] Gayer's argument was that the availability of funds for investment would not induce new investment because of low, if not negative, rates of expected return. The rediscount rate and open-market operations were impotent because they would not create bank deposits, increase consumer buying, or producer borrowing.

Also, at the 1932 meetings of the Harris Memorial Foundation, Irving Fisher suggested consideration of a laundry list of monetary measures [20, 198 ff]. The other economists, including the many Chicago economists who attended, dismissed the twenty-four measures [17]. Harold Moulton, of the Brookings Institution, was particularly outspoken for borrowing from the Federal Reserve and spending the proceeds for public works and the relief of unemployment. The differences between expansionary monetary and fiscal policy, Moulton said, was that deficit financing was money "spent in the market [setting] up a chain of demand all the qay back through the economic system [20, 224–8]." Among others, Jacob Viner agreed wholeheartedly. "What you probably need," Viner said, "is a means whereby the banks can take up the increased government indebtedness . . . and the funds getting to the consumers through public expenditure [20, 228–9]."

This position was reaffirmed in the 1934 *Report on Economic Reconstruction* [4], which included Viner, Alvin Hansen, and J. M. Clark among its commission members. The general report included the argument that increasing the supply of money by means of a low rediscount rate supported by open-market operations could be effective only if measures were taken to increase the demand for credit as well as its supply. The report also pointed out there is a surplus of idle funds during depression. The problem was, according to the report, the unwillingness to borrow [4, 34–5].

Thus, based on "traditional theory," as Simons called it [23, 1017], economists were concerned about the possibility of a "bank reserves trap."[5] Monetary policy could increase bank reserves, but such monetary measures as the rediscount rate and open-market operations were not likely to stimulate borrowing. An increase in the money supply could be trapped in bank reserves. Expansionary fiscal policy, however, directly stimulated spending, and, if supported by expansionary monetary policy, the funds borrowed to finance the deficit would be there in excess of bank reserves, so that no "crowding out" of private borrowing was likely.

II.

Mr. Tavlas champions the contributions of Foster and Catchings. Mr. Tavlas says that they asserted that (1) "the validity of Say's Law . . holds only under conditions of pure barter," and that (2) "the introduction of money . . . upsets the full-employment equilibrium of Say's world" [24, 686]. Mr. Tavlas continues to say that, "in criticizing the applicability of Say's Law within a monetary economy, Foster and Catchings launched a lengthy attack upon classical economics much like Keynes was to do a decade or so later in the *General Theory* [24, 686]." The inexactitudes in these comments contribute to a misunderstanding of Keynes' attack and of Say's Law in classical economics.

First, in the *General Theory*, Keynes' reference to Say's Law [10, 18–19] is to J. S. Mill's *Principles* [16]. Keynes infers that Mill denies therein the possibility of general gluts of commodities. This is a peculiar allegation, inasmuch as Mill's "denial" is in a chapter, "Of Excess of Supply," which lucidly describes "commercial crises" involving "an excess of all commodities above the money demand . . . , what may be indiscriminately called a glut of commodities or a dearth of money [16, 574]." In the passage that Keynes quotes in the *General Theory*, Mill is discussing a barter economy, and a general oversupply or an excess of all commodities over the demand is denied by Mill. However, later in the same paragraph and in subsequent sections of the chapter, Mill considers a money economy. Mill clearly states that one of the complications of introducing money is that general gluts of commodities are possible. Mill then discusses "commercial crises" or excess supplies of commodities in some detail.

5. The "bank reserves trap" should not be confused with Keynes' "liquidity trap." However, sometimes the argument is stated as an "excess reserves trap" and, because of the similarity between the two, they are classified under the same "liquidity trap" heading.

Axel Leijonhufvud [13, 101] has said that, had Keynes finished reading the paragraph and the rest of the chapter, he could not have attributed Say's Law to Mill.[6] Leijonhufvud believes that Keynes was careless. Robert Mundell speculates whether Keynes was careless or perpetrating a historical error calculated to win over disciples to the belief that there was a fatal logical defect in the classical system [19, 108 ff.]. There is evidence [2] that Keynes was careless, apparently "quoting" Mill from a secdonary source! The evidence is that, at the time he was writing pages 18–19 of the *General Theory*, Keynes read the passage that he "quotes" from Mill in either Marshall [14, 19; 15, 154] or Hobson [18, 102]. By carelessly quoting Mill from a secondary source that did not extend to Mill's discussion of general gluts of commodities, Keynes misrepresented Mill and contributed to a historical error that persists and, to this day, beckons others to its propagation.

The observations that Say's Law holds only for a barter economy and that gluts of commodities as well as unemployment are possible in a money economy are clear in Mill. Thus, Foster and Catchings' criticism of the applicability of Say's Law within a monetary economy could hardly be regarded as launching a lengthy attack upon Mill. While their criticism is an attack "much like Keynes was to do . . . in the *General Theory* [22, 686]," this is not to say that it was any more informed or pertinent than that of Keynes. Foster and Catchings may have represented their criticism as pertinent and informed, but their criticism would have been directed more appropriately at bad applications of classical theory. This criticism, however, was common to many economists, especially "residents at Chicago."

J. Ronnie Davis
University of Florida

6. At least not in the sense later given it by Lange [12], Leijonhufvud [13] says.

References

1. Davis, J. Ronnie. *The New Economics and the Old Economists*. Ames: Iowa State University Press, 1971.

2. ——— and Francis J. Casey, Jr., "Keynes' Misquotation of Mill." *Economic Journal*, June 1977, 329–30.

3. Douglas, Paul H. *Controlling Depression*. New York: Norton, 1935.

4. *Economic Reconstruction: Report of the Columbia University Commission*. New York: Columbia University Press, 1934.

5. Foster, William T. and Waddill Catchings. *Money*. Boston: Riverside, 1927.

6. ——— and ———. *Profits*. Boston: Riverside, 1925.

7. ——— and ———. *The Road to Plenty*. Boston: Riverside, 1928.

8. Gayer, Arthur D. *Public Works in Prosperity and Depression*. New York: National Bureau of Economic Research, 1935.

9. Hayek, F. A., "The 'Paradox' of Savings." *Profit, Interest and Investment*. London: Routledge and Kegan Paul, 1939.

10 Keynes, J M *The General Theory of Employment, Interest and Money* New York Harcourt, Brace and World, 1936

11. Knight, F H, "Unemployment And Mr Keynes' Revolution in Economic Theory" *Canadian Journal of Economics and Political Science* February 1937, 100-123.

12 Lange, O , "Say's Law A Restatement and Criticism," *Studies in Mathematical Economics and Econometrics*, edited by O Lange, F McIntyre, and T O Yntema Chicago University of Chicago Press, 1942, 49-68

13 Leijonhufvud, Axel *On Keynesian Economics and the Economics of Keynes* New York, Oxford University Press, 1968

14 Marshall, A *The Pure Theory of Foreign Trade, The Pure Theory of Domestic Values* London The London School of Economics, 1930

15 Marshall, A and A P Marshall. *The Economics of Industry* 2nd Ed London Macmillan, 1881

16 Mill, J S *Principles of Political Economy, with Some of Their Applications to Social Philosophy* Toronto University of Toronto Press, 1965

17 Minutes, 31 January 1932, Special Session of Economists in Attendance at the Norman Wait Harris Institute

18. Mummery, A F and J A Hobson *The Physiology of Industry* New York Kelly and Millman, 1956

19. Mundell, R A *Man and Economics* New York McGraw-Hill, 1968

20. Norman Wait Harris Memorial Foundation *Reports of Round Tables Gold and Monetary Stabilization* Chicago 1932

21 ______ *Reports of Round Tables Unemployment as a World Problem*. Chicago 1931

22 Phillips, C A , T F McManus, and R W Nelson *Banking and the Business Cycle*. New York Macmillan, 1937

23. Simons, Henry C . "Keynes Comments on Money" *Christian Century* July 22, 1936, 1016-17

24 Tavlas, George S., "Some Further Observations on the Monetary Economics of Chicagoans and Non-Chicagoans" *Southern Economic Journal* April 1976, 685-92

25. Viner, Jacob, "Mr Keynes on the Causes of Unemployment" *Quarterly Journal of Economics* November 1936, 147-67.

The Last Remake of the New Economics and the Old Ecomomists: Reply

J. Ronnie Davis makes the following assertions in reference to my article: (1) that I incorrectly argued that, in his work [1; 2], Davis attempted to equate the analytical specifications concerning Keynes and the classics; (2) that I wrongly suggested that prior to Keynes's *General Theory* [15] economists endorsed the use of traditional monetary measures to combat depressions; and (3) that my comparison of the respective attacks on Say's Law by Foster and Catchings, and by Keynes, was inappropriate.

The purpose of my paper was to inquire into the possible relationship between certain earlier formulations of the quantity theory of money and the modern version of that theory as espoused by Milton Friedman.[1] Specifically, I sought to examine the claim enunciated by Friedman in his 1956 Restatement of the quantity theory [9] that contemporary monetarism has its roots in an earlier Chicago monetary tradition. Davis's work, on the other hand, was concerned with ascertaining the policy views of American economists, circa 1930–36. Though our research motivations differed, our respective investigations into the Chicago School of the 1930s constituted an intersecting set.

In my paper, I demonstrated how earlier quantity theorists—notably Foster and Catchings and the Chicagoans—used a short-run version of the Fisherine equation of exchange to generate a framework whereby deficit budgets became desired depression policy. I also contrasted the stock-flow monetary transmission mechanism articulated by these economists with the Keynesian portfolio adjustment channel. Budget deficits were considered important within the context of the Fisherine framework because they effected monetary expansion. Accordingly, I concluded that, "to Foster and Catchings, and the Chicagoans, public works were a means of conducting monetary policy" [19, 692]. Furthermore, these economists recognized that tax-financed and bond-financed deficits entailed "crowding-out" effects. In this manner, I linked-up Foster and Catchings, and the Chicagoans, to Friedman, who also views money-financed deficits as the implementation of monetary, as opposed to fiscal, policy [10, 915].

1. Additionally, papers by Humphrey [11; 12] and by Patinkin [16] have dealt with the possible relationship between Friedman's monetary doctrines and non-Chicagoan versions of the quantity theory during the 1920s and the 1930s.

My criticism of Davis was that he failed to identify the Chicagoans of the 1930s as quantity theorists. On the contrary, in terms of the current debate of monetarism versus fiscalism, Davis presumes that the former Chicagoans were *fiscalists*. This misrepresentation, in turn, leads him to conclude that the Chicago School rejected the Keynesian revolution because it "had labored in behalf of the notion of *compensatory* public spending [and] was unsympathetic towards the notion of *secular* public spending which they read into Keynes's *General Theory*" (original italics) [1, 481]. But this interpretation conflicts with the fact that Chicagoan Paul Douglas saw the need for chronic deficits as early as 1935 [6, 185], to be joined the following year in this view by Henry Simons [18, 333]. In light of this evidence, Davis's interpretation as to why Chicago rejected the Keynesian revolution is undermined. A much more plausible explanation can be found in the continued Chicagoan adherence to the quantity theory of money. This explanation, however, is obviated in the context of Davis's fiscalist interpretation of the 1930s Chicago School.

Davis denies that he equated the "analytical specifications concerning Keynes and the classics." Mr. Davis's denial to the contrary, he *did* incorrectly describe the theoretical views of certain economists, "especially the residents at Chicago," along Keynesian income-expenditure—as opposed to quantity theory—lines. Consider, for example, his lengthy discussion of Paul Douglas [2, 47–60]. Davis presents Douglas's theory of the contractionary phase of the business cycle as follows: "there is first a decrease in production, causing a decrease in employment, causing a decrease in purchases and in purchasing power" [2, 48]. Davis proceeds to argue, that, following the work of Keynes and Wicksell, "Douglas pointed to the saving-investment nexus as the major culprit in depression making. The sperm of a depression was an excess of saving over investment" [2, 48–49]. And, "Paul Douglas clearly pointed to changes in the *rate* of investment as the initiating cause of depression" (original italics) [2, 49]. A discussion follows describing Douglas's use of the multiplier and acceleration mechanisms, and his attack on Say's Law, that supply creates its own demand. Davis then concludes:

> In the case of Paul Douglas we have witnessed an American economist who built an *explanation of* and a remedy for depression largely along *Keynesian* lines. . . . Like Keynes, he did disavow an older tradition of aggregate economics, principally identified with J. B. Say, whose followers treated total effective demand as transferable, but incapable of creation or destruction (italics supplied) [2, 58–59].

There was no "misreading" of Davis's book on my part.[2] And contrary to the foregoing line of interpretation, Douglas did not build "an explanation

2. In note 4 to his "comment," Davis implies that the reason I concluded that he equated the analytics concerning Keynes and the classical economists was because I really did not read his book, except for the introductory chapter and the last several pages. The evidence presented above certainly discounts Davis's inference. I might also note that on a previous occasion I have explicitly referred to other sections of his book [21]. So much for Mr. Davis's empiricism.

of . . . depression largely along Keynesian lines." In accordance with the reasoning of his Chicago colleagues, Douglas fashioned his business-cycle diagnosis in terms of the Fisherine equation of exchange. Douglas, however, cautioned that "The various terms are not as some of the more naive quantity theorists have believed, independent of each other. On the contrary, they are inter-related in a somewhat organic fashion" [6, 26]. In numerous papers and speeches throughout the late 1920s and the 1930s, Douglas argued that depressions were caused by the failure of the money supply to increase proportionately with the annual trend rise in the production of goods.[3] He cited this failure "as an important reason I believe for the great depression which began in 1929" [5, 161]. Accordingly, depressions could be avoided "if the quantity of purchasing power were to be increased at the rate of 3 to 4 percent a year, or the long time gain in production" [6, 185]. This policy norm, which Douglas stated repeatedly, is a seminal formulation of the monetary growth-rate rule currently advocated by monetarists.[4]

As I have noted above, Davis's discussion of the other Chicagoans suffers from the same failure to perceive their quantity theory orientation. Instead, the Chicago economists are depicted as fiscalists. "Individually and collectively," according to Davis, "the Chicagoans stressed the need to rely extensively on fiscal policy" [2, 62]. And they "share an unusual position in the development of modern fiscal policy" [2, 145]. Furthermore, their theoretical framework is portrayed in terms suggestive of the Keynesian income-expenditure identity:

> Throughout the Chicagoans' contributions, there is the notion that total spending, private plus public, should be great enough to take off the markets an output associated with full employment and stable prices. The argument constituted a type of macroeconomic model out of which compensatory fiscal policy was easily extracted as the means of stabilization in general and recovery from depression in particular [2, 62–63].

Significantly, the only reference to quantity theorists as such in Davis's book appears under the heading "Tutelaries of Retrenchment" [2, 35]. Though this may be an accurate characterization of non-Chicago quantity theorists during the 1930s,[5] it disregards the former Chicago School's quantity theory

3. For a detailed account concerning the mechanics of Douglas's business-cycle analysis, and for additional references to Douglas's writing during the 1920s and 1930s, see Tavlas [21]. Incidentally, Douglas continued to champion the quantity theory even after he became a U.S. Senator in 1949. In this capacity, he became a moving force behind the Treasury-Federal Reserve "accord" of 1951. He viewed the Fed's failure to control the money supply prior to the "accord" as a "vindication of the quantity theory of money, supposedly known to every student of elementary economics" [7, 332].

4. Douglas's version of the monetary growth-rate rule traces back to the neglected monetary writings, during the 1830s and 1840s, of the British economist, John Gray. See Tavlas [22].

5. In an interesting article, Humphrey attributes "the crude version of the quantity theory prevalent in the 1930s" to the empirical studies of Holbrook Working and Carl Snyder [13, 300–301].

proclivity. Moreover, acknowledgement of this quantity theory orientation of the earlier Chicago tradition permits further investigation into the evolvement of that tradition, culminating in the appearance of Friedman's 1956 Restatement of the quantity theory. For example, I have shown elsewhere [20], that contributions to the quantity theory—including the elaboration of portfolio analysis and the development of a broad monetary transmission mechanism—by Chicago economists throughout the 1940s and early 1950s provide evidence that Friedman's Restatement is, indeed, an outgrowth of the 1930s Chicago tradition.

Davis is correct when he states that prior to the influence of the *General Theory* economists did not generally endorse traditional monetary measures. Nor did I ever state that this was the case. In my paper, I demonstrated that it was precisely their dissatisfaction with such measures which induced the Chicagoans to endorse budget deficits in order to attain monetary expansion. Incidentally, this view—that changes in the money supply should be pursued via changes in the federal budget due to the impotence of traditional monetary tools—also characterized Friedman's early work in monetary economics.[6]

Davis's final point is that my comparison of the respective attacks on Say's Law by Foster and Catchings, and by Keynes was inaccurate. The rationale offered in support of this view is that Keynes's criticism of Mill was impertinent because Keynes was quoting Mill from a secondary source—either from the Marshalls or from Hobson. As evidence, Davis cites a recent paper dealing with this premise, which he co-authored with F. J. Casey [3].

Several observations are in order. First, as I have demonstrated in this note, Davis draws a similar analogy between the attacks on Say's Law made by Keynes and by Paul Douglas. Moreover, in the pages which Davis cites from Douglas's *Controlling Depressions* [6, 67–77], Douglas clearly states that his criticism was directed at J. S. Mill's version of Say's Law. In a 1927 paper, Douglas acknowledged that his attack on Mill and Say's Law was based on the "brilliant and suggestive writings" of Foster and Catchings [4, 37]. Hence, any validity concerning Davis's criticism of my paper also pertains to his own analogy between the attacks on Say's Law by Douglas and by Keynes.

Second, in a recent comment on the Davis-Casey paper, Patinkin has argued that "the fact (if we accept it as such) that Keynes quoted Mill from the Marshalls can 'explain' Keynes's misrepresentation of Mill only if the Marshalls themselves were guilty of such misrepresentation—and this point is completely overlooked by Davis and Casey" [17, 341]. Patinkin provides evidence which leads him to conclude: "Clearly, however, the Marshalls were not guilty of such misrepresentation" [17, 341].

In a broader context, the monetary views of Foster and Catchings—including their attack on Say's Law—and of the Chicagoans are important be-

6. See, for example, Friedman [8].

cause they help identify the historical foundations of the monetarist counter-revolution, including the reasons underlying the Chicago School's resistance to the Keynesian "virus." As H. G. Johnson has stated, the validity of the monetarist counter-revolution requires the establishment of a "plausible linkage with pre-Keynesian orthodoxy" [14, 10].[7] It is precisely this linkage that my work has served to establish. As I stated in my paper: "Davis has made a very real contribution to the history of thought" [19, 685]. Fortunately—from the imperative perspective of "setting [the] record straight" [2, 7]—his research has not remained "The Last Remake of the New Economics and the Old Economists." In particular, my paper has extended and corrected Mr. Davis's significant but nonetheless incomplete work.

George S. Tavlas
United States Department of State

7. A fuller discussion of this matter is provided in Tavlas and Aschheim [23].

References

1. Davis, J. Ronnie, "Chicago Economists, Deficit Budgets, and the Early 1930s." *American Economic Review*, June 1968, 476–82.

2. ——. *The New Economics and the Old Economists*. Iowa. Iowa State Press, 1971.

3. Davis, J. Ronnie and Francis J. Casey, Jr., "Keynes's Misquotation of Mill" *Economic Journal*, June 1977, 329–30.

4. Douglas, Paul H., "The Modern Technique of Mass Production and its Relation to Wages." *Proceedings of the Academy of Political Science*, April 1927, 17–42.

5. ——, "Technological Aspects of Unemployment." *Proceedings of the Institute of Public Affairs*, August 1933, 150–61.

6. ——. *Controlling Depressions*. New York. Norton, 1935.

7. ——. *In the Fullness of Time*. New York: Harcourt Brace, 1972.

8. Friedman, Milton, "A Monetary and Fiscal Framework for Economic Stability" *American Economic Review*, June 1948, 245–64.

9 ——, "The Quantity Theory of Money—A Restatement," in *Studies in the Quantity Theory of Money*, edited by Milton Friedman. Chicago· Univ. of Chicago Press, 1956.

10 ——, "Comments on the Critics" *Journal of Political Economy*, September/October 1972, 906–50.

11 Humphrey, Thomas M., "Role of Non-Chicago Economists in the Evolution of the Quantity Theory in America: 1930–1950." *Southern Economic Journal*, July 1971, 12–18

12. ——, "On the Monetary Economics of Chicagoans and Non-Chicagoans. Reply" *Southern Economic Journal*, January 1973, 460–63

13. ——, "Empirical Tests of the Equation of Exchange: 1900–1930." *History of Political Economy*, Spring 1973, 285–316.

14. Johnson, H. C., "The Keynesian Revolution and the Monetarist Counter-Revolution" *American Economic Review*, May 1971, 1–14.

15 Keynes, J. M. *The General Theory of Employment, Interest and Money* New York Harcourt, Brace and World, 1936.

16. Patinkin, Don, "On the Monetary Economics of Chicagoans and Non-Chicagoans." *Southern Economic Journal*, January 1973, 454–59.

17. ——, "Keynes's Misquotation of Mill: Comment" *Economic Journal*, June 1978, 341 42

18. Simons, Henry C., "Rules versus Authorities in Monetary Policy." *Journal of Political Economy*, February 1936, 1–30. Reprinted in *Economic Policy for a Free Society*, by Henry Simons. Chicago: Univ. of Chicago Press, 1948.

19. Tavlas, George S., "Some Further Observations on the Monetary Economics of Chicagoans and Non-Chicagoans." *Southern Economic Journal*, April 1976, 685–92.

20. ———. "Chicago Schools Old and New on the Efficacy of Monetary Policy." *Banca Nazionale del Lavoro Quarterly Review*, March 1977, 52–73.

21. ———, "The Chicago Tradition Revisited: Some Neglected Monetary Contributions of Senator Paul Douglas." *Journal of Money, Credit, and Banking*, November 1977, 529–35.

22. ———, "Some Initial Formulations of the Monetary Growth-Rate Rule." *History of Political Economy*, Winter 1977, 535–47.

23. Tavlas, George S., and Joseph Aschheim, "On Monetarism and Ideology." Unpublished manuscript, 1978.

'Keynes on Monetary Theory and Policy'

T. Cate, 'Keynes on monetary theory and policy: comment', *Southern Economic Journal* (April 1981), pp. 1132–6.

AND

'Reply'

G. Tavlas, 'Keynes on monetary theory and policy: reply', *Southern Economic Journal* (April 1981), pp. 1137–42.

Keynes on Monetary Theory and Policy: Comment*

Professor Friedman suggests that from the 1920s through the 1950s the only advances which occur in monetary theory and policy take place within the walls of the University of Chicago. Humphrey [4, 5], with support from Patinkin [12], notes that the work of Foster and Catchings [1; 2, 3] provides evidence that progress in the area of monetary theory did occur outside the confines of the University of Chicago. Tavlas's [13] efforts provide an excellent follow-up to the work of Humphrey and Patinkin. In his presentation, however, Tavlas has a serious error in his argument. Tavlas argues that [13, 685–86]

> Keynes, and especially his followers, advocated deficits within a theoretical framework that featured the impotence of monetary policy during depressions. American economists especially members of the Chicago School— advocated deficit budgets precisely because monetary policy did matter

The time frame for Tavlas's quote is the Harris Foundation Lectures, 1931 The question the quote raises is at the time of these lectures, does Keynes advocate the use of deficit spending (a loan-financed, domestic investment program) within a theoretical framework that features the impotence of monetary policy during depressions *for the United States?* The answer to this question must be in the negative

In 1931, Keynes's *Treatise on Money* has been out for about one year and he is still three to four years from circulating the first draft of the *General Theory*. In the *Treatise* [8, 336], Keynes argues that the United States *could use* monetary policy as a means of resolving the problems of the slump of 1930. In the *General Theory*, however, Keynes, using a theoretical framework which differs from that found in the *Treatise*, advocates the use of a loan-financed, domestic investment program as the means whereby the level of unemployment within the British economy can be raised. I suggest, therefore, that Tavlas, in his haste to make a point, refers to the wrong text

To support my hypothesis, this paper will take the following form Section II will discuss the *Treatise* and the three views on monetary policy contained therein Section III will discuss the *General Theory* and how its policy conclusions differ from the *Treatise's* Section IV will point out the source of Tavlas' error

II. The Treatise

In a *Treatise on Money*, Keynes advocates three public policy recommendations which are designed to stabilize the general level of prices First, for a nation whose international sector

* I would like to thank E. Ray Canterbery, Irvin Sobel, Philip Sorenson, Vincent J Tarascio and an anonymouse referee for their insightful comments If any errors remain, I must bear the sole responsibility for them

constitutes a very small percentage of its total output, the goal of price stabilization could be achieved by having that nation's central bank bring the market rate of interest into equilibrium with the natural rate of interest (i.e., that rate of interest which equated the volume of current savings with the value of new investment) [7, 138–39, 10, 336]. With the market rate of interest in equilibrium with the natural rate of interest, the cost of new investment would be equal to the value of new investment and both equal to the volume of new savings [7, 137–38]. This policy proposal, Keynes argues, applies to the United States. Keynes had first broached the idea of using the bank rate to stabilize the general level of prices in an article entitled "The Depression of Trade" which appeared in the *Sunday Times* on September 4, 1921 [10, 259–265]. Keynes expanded this argument in *A Tract on Monetary Reform* and "The Economic Consequences of Mr Churchill."

Second, for a nation whose international economies constitutes a significant percentage of its total output, Keynes advocates that the nation's central bank adopt a trident of control namely, the bank rate, the forward-exchange rate, and the buying and selling points of gold [8, 292–93]. The trident of control would permit that nation's central bank to set different short-term rates of interest for domestic funds and foreign funds and that would permit the central bank to stabilize the general level of prices without having a balance of payments crisis short-circuit the stabilization policy of the bank. This policy recommendation, except for some institutional details adhering to the rules of the gold system *versus* having that nation's stock of gold completely separated from the note issue of its central bank--is identical to the trident of control recommendation advocated by Keynes in the *Tract* [10, 355–369]. Keynes notes that this policy proposed applies to Great Britain.

Third, for those occasions when, because of misadventure, a declining market rate of interest, rather than increasing domestic borrowing, provokes foreign lending and an outflow of gold on a scale larger than that nation could afford, Keynes advocates the adoption of a reserve weapon, a loan-financed, government-sponsored program of domestic investment, which is to be used to stabilize the general level of prices [8, 337–38]. Keynes suggests [8, 337].

> but if foreign borrowers are ready and eager, it will be impossible in a competitive open market to bring the rate down to the level appropriate to domestic investment. Thus the desired result can only be obtained through some method by which, in effect, the Government subsidises approved types of domestic investment or itself directs domestic schemes of capital development.

To Keynes, this reserve is but another way of achieving the equilibrium of the cost of new investment, the value of new investment and the volume of new savings, the result of which would be stable prices.

Thus, the policy recommendations which Keynes articulates in the *Treatise*, except for some differences in institutional structures, are identical to the policies which he advocates in his earlier writings. All of these recommendations are based upon the working out of the Ricardo-Marshall model of equilibrium at full employment. Although there are references to unemployment in these writings, in them Keynes takes the view that unemployment would be *periodic and temporary*. Finally, one of the policy recommendations is designed for use by the United States in order to resolve the problems of the slump of 1930. The other two are designed for use by Great Britain.

III. The General Theory

Keynes suggests that the *General Theory* [11] represents a continuation of work begun in the *Treatise* [7, xxvii, 9, 172, 243]

> I should add in conclusion, that after a year and a half of further reflection and after having had the advantage of much criticism and discussion of my theories, I naturally made many *addenda* and *corrigenda* in what follows It is not, however, my intention to revise the existing text of this *Treatise* in the near future I propose, rather, to publish a short book of a purely theoretical basis of my views as set forth in Books III and IV below

The *General Theory*, however, differs from the *Treatise* in one important way While the *Treatise* concerned itself with price stabilization policies assuming the level of output to be nearly constant, the *General Theory* is concerned with the ways by which the government is able to increase the level of effective demand in the economy, as a means of restoring the economy to a full employment level of output. That is to say, in the *Treatise*, unemployment is regarded as being a temporary phenomenon, a disequilibrium situation In the *General Theory*, however, that same unemployment problem is viewed in terms of an equilibrium situation

Keynes poses two questions in the *General Theory* First, what determines the volume of employment in the economy? Second, by what means may the economy be moved to a position of full employment? Keynes approaches the question of what determines the volume of employment in the following way Keynes argues that the economy is divisible into two, more or less, distinct groups: consumers and entrepreneurs The consumers, having received an increment of income, are able to do two things with that increment expend it for the purpose of acquiring consumption goods, or increase the volume of current savings Meanwhile, the entrepreneurs decide quite independently of consumers into what proportions the economy's output should be divided as between consumption goods and investment goods Keynes concludes that it is the interaction of these two groups and their independently conceived plans that determine the volume of employment

Three theories may be used to explain the forces that influence these independently conceived plans: the theory of investment, the theory of liquidity preference, and the theory of expectations R F Harrod, in a letter to Keynes dated 30 August 1935, explains how the volume of employment is determined in a slightly different manner The chart below summarizes Harrod's remarks [9, 553]

Volume of investment determined by	marginal efficiency of capital schedule rate of interest
Rate of interest determined by	liquidity preference schedule quantity of money
Volume of employment determined by	volume of investment multiplier
Value of multiplier determined by	propensity to save

The second question of how to achieve a full employment level of output is approached by Keynes in the following manner. Having examined the determinants of the volume of employment. Keynes concludes that there is no mechanism which forces the economy to always produce a full employment level of output Keynes notes the theoretical possibility of having the economy producing a level of output that is associated with a chronically depressed volume of employment and having that situation persisting over a number of years That is, Keynes argues that the British economy has settled into an equilibrium at less than full employment, an idea that is completely foreign to the economics of Ricardo and Marshall and to the economics of his own earlier writings

Thus, in the *General Theory*, Keynes argues that the depression of the 1920s, combined with the slump of the 1930s, has so demoralized the business class that the economy has settled down into an unemployment equilibrium Keynes, therefore, advocates the immediate adoption of the following policy recommendation a loan-financed, domestic investment program Such a program, if implemented, raises the volume of employment and with it the level of aggregate demand of the economy. That, however, is only the beginning, for Keynes, by modifying Kahn's multiplier [6], is able to show that the initial change in the volume of employment leads to a series of secondary changes in the volume of employment Keynes concludes that monetary policy, even monetary policy *a outrance*, is not capable of stimulating the economy, the volume of employment fails to increase because the business class is convinced that the yield on money is superior to the expected future yields from a capital-asset

In other words, this policy proposal, unlike those of the *Treatise*, is based upon a theoretical framework which emphasizes the notion that monetary policy is unable to resolve the problems of Great Britains's economy At that time and place, monetary policy is impotent and an alternative means of resolving Great Britain's economic woes must be developed

IV Tavlas's Error

Let us review again the main points covered in this paper First, the *Treatise* has three major policy recommendations, all of which are designed to stabilize the general level of prices or, if you prefer, the internal purchasing power of a nation's currency. The historical origins of two of these policies are the articles and memoranda which Keynes had published either in the *Sunday Times* or the *Manchester Guardian Commercial*'s Reconstruction Supplements, and later gathered together in the *Tract* and "Economic Consequences of Mr Churchill" The third policy recommendation has as its origins articles and memoranda written by Keynes while a member of the Treasury and the British Peace Delegation or as a member of the Cambridge faculty, and later gathered together in *Economic Consequences of the Peace* and the *Revision of the Treaty* The policy recommendation of the *General Theory* is designed to move the economy from an unemployment equilibrium to one of full employment The *General Theory*'s recommendation drew on Kahn's article on the multiplier and is first articulated in "The Means to Prosperity"

Thus, as I suggested earlier, the origins of the policy recommendations developed by Keynes in the *Treatise* are found in his earlier writings which he wrote between 1919-29. This is not the case, however, for the recommendation that one finds in the *General Theory* Keynes's earlier writings are based upon the economics of Ricardo and Marshall which recognize only one equilibrium a full employment equilibrium. In the *General Theory*, however, the problem of unemployment is no longer one of disequilibrium (periodic but temporary movements away from a full employment equilibrium) but one of equilibrium, an idea that is completely foreign to the economics of Ricardo and Marshall.

Tavlas's error should now be apparent: he inadvertently references the policy conclusion of the *General Theory*. During the Harris Foundation Lectures, however, it was Keynes of the *Treatise* who suggested the following [14, 303].

> I think the argument for public works in this country is much weaker than it is in Great Britain. In Great Britain I have for a long time past agitated very strongly for a public works program, and my argument has been that we are such a center of an international system that we cannot operate on the rate of interest, because if we tried to force the rate of interest down, there is too much lending, and we lose our gold The advantage of a government program in Great Britain is that the government can borrow at whatever the world rate of interest is, regardless of whether the investment yields that.
>
> In this country you haven't a problem of that kind. Here you can function as though you were a closed system, and I think all your arguments hitherto have been rather based on the closed system assumption. For such a system I would use as my first method operating on the long term rate of interest. If I could not do that, I should be afraid we would be open to the difficulty you suggested.

Thus, it is Tavlas's inaccurate reading of the *Treatise* and the *General Theory* and the subsequent mixing of their policy conclusions and recommendations which result in the error in Tavlas's presentation.

Tom Cate
Northern Kentucky University
Highland Heights, Kentucky

References

1 Foster, William T. and Waddill Catchings *Profits* Boston The Riverside Press, 1952

2 ——— *Money* Boston The Riverside Press, 1927

3 ——— *The Road to Plenty* Boston The Riverside Press, 1928

4 Humphrey, Thomas M, "Role of Non-Chicagoan Economists in the Evolution of the Quantity Theory in America 1930–50" *Southern Economic Journal*, July, 1971, 12–18.

5 ———, "On the Monetary Economics of Chicagoans and Non-Chicagoans Reply" *Southern Economic Journal*, January, 1973, 460–63

6. Kahn, R F, "The Relation of Home Investments to Unemployment" *Economic Journal*, June, 1931, 173 98

7. Keynes, John Maynard *A Treatise on Money* Vol I *The Pure Theory of Money*, The Collected Writings of John Maynard Keynes New York. Macmillan Press Ltd, 1971

8 ——— *A Treatise of Money*, Vol II. *The Applied Theory of Money*, The Collected Writings of John Maynard Keynes New York: Macmillan Press Ltd, 1971

9 ———. *The General Theory and After, Part I: Preparation*, The Collected Writings of John Maynard Keynes New York Macmillan Press Ltd, 1971

10 ——— *Activities 1919–1922 Treaty Revision and Reconstruction*, The Collected Writings of John Maynard Keynes New York Macmillan Press Ltd, 1977

11 ———. *The General Theory of Employment, Interest, and Money* London Macmillan, 1936, reprint ed New York Harcourt, Brace and World, A Harbinger Book, 1964

12. Patinkin, Don, "On the Monetary Economics of Chicagoans and Non-Chicagoans Comment" *Southern Economic Journal*, January, 1973, 454–59

13 Tavlas, George S, "Some Further Observations on the Monetary Economics of Chicagoans and Non-Chicagoans." *Southern Economic Journal*, April, 1976, 685–92.

14 Normal Wait Harris Memorial Foundation *Reports of Round Tables Unemployment as a World Problem* Chicago: The University of Chicago Press, 1931

Keynes on Monetary Theory and Policy: Reply

Tom Cate contends that my attempt to distinguish between the theoretical specifications concerning Keynes and the Chicagoans suffers in that I inadvertently attribute views to the *Treatise on Money* [9] which were really not part of Keynes' thinking until the appearance of the *General Theory* [10]. Cate proceeds to argue that the *Treatise* was essentially an elaboration of Keynes' earlier views as articulated during the early 1920s in *A Tract on Monetary Reform* [8] and that the real transformation in Keynes' monetary economics occurs during the interval between the appearance of the *Treatise* in 1930 and the publication of the *General Theory* in 1936. As evidence in support of his interpretation of Keynes' thinking during the early 1930s, Cate refers to Keynes' qualification regarding the efficacy of public works projects during depressions as enunciated at the 1931 Harris Foundation Lectures shortly after the publication of the *Treatise*.

The references in my article [23] to the Keynesian theoretical framework which rendered monetary policy impotent were directed at the standard Hicks-Hansen interpretation of Keynes. Thus, in neither the article to which Cate refers, nor in a subsequent exchange in this journal [26],[1] do I ever mention the *Treatise*. The only references to Keynes' work in my papers occur in the explicit context of the income-expenditure model as incorporated in the *General Theory* [2]. Nevertheless, in that my discussion of the Chicagoans centered on the period circa 1930-36, the frame of reference of the *Treatise* might be interpreted as having been implicit in my work. To that extent, Cate is justified in indicating the differences in Keynes' views with respect to the *Treatise* and the *General Theory*. At the same time, Cate's categorization of the *Treatise* as a continuation of views set forth earlier in the *Tract* obscures the transformation of Keynes' own thinking on monetary economics and obviates one of the reasons why, in its initial stages, the monetarist counter-revolution was centered in Chicago. In particular, in the *Tract* Keynes expounded views on monetary theory similar to those which were to later categorize the 1930s Chicago School. Keynes' rejection of these views in the *Treatise* explains, in part, the Chicago School's resistance to the Keynesian revolution.

Keynes of the *Tract* was a quantity theorist very much in the Cambridge tradition of Marshall and Pigou. Keynes stated: "This theory is fundamental. Its correspondence with fact is not open to question" [8, 61]. He formulated the quantity theory in terms of the demand for money, $n = p(k + rk')$, where n is the amount of cash in circulation, p is the price

1 The exchange was with Davis [2].

2 In a similar vein, Cate, in his opening paragraph refers to my work as being a follow-up of the work of Humphrey [5, 6] and Patinkin [18] on Foster and Catchings. But Humphrey never refers to Foster and Catchings, while Patinkin mentions them only in passing as having been among the first American quantity theorists to replace transactions velocity with income velocity in the equation of exchange.

level, k is the number of consumption units which the public decides to hold in cash, r is the banks' ratio for checking accounts, and k' is the number of consumption units which the public decides to hold in checking accounts. Pigou, in a 1917 article on *The Value on Money* [20, 74] had referred to the Fisherine transactions-velocity approach to the quantity theory as "something that seems at first sight accidental and arbitrary." Similarly, Keynes argued that his formulation of the quantity theory "seems less artificial than Professor Fisher's [version]" [8, 63].[3] Specifically, by approaching the quantity theory in terms of the demand function for money, Pigou and Keynes imparted a choice-theoretic content to that theory

In the *Tract* Keynes used his cash-balance version of the quantity equation to articulate a theory in which the business cycle was initiated by shifts in the demand for money Thus·

> Cyclical fluctuations are characterized, not primarily by changes in n or r, but by changes in k and k'. It follows that they can only be cured if we are ready deliberately to increase and decrease n and r, when symptoms of movement are showing in the values of k and k' [8, 69]

Moreover, once set in motion by changes in k or k', the cycle would be exacerbated by changing expectations with respect to the price level

> There is a further aggravation of the case, in that an expectation about the course of prices tends, if it is widely held, to be cumulative in its results up to a certain point If prices are expected to rise and the business world acts upon this expectation, that very fact causes them to rise for a time and, by verifying the expectation, reinforces it, and similarly if it expects them to fall [8, 34]

Accordingly, Keynes opted for a stabilization policy based on "deliberate decision" and aimed at "controlling the standard of value" by varying the money supply in such a manner so as to offset changes in the demand for money [8, 35 6]

As noted, a striking aspect of the foregoing views is their basic similarity with the macroeconomics of the Chicago School of the 1930s Thus, as I have shown elsewhere [24], the earlier Chicago economists argued that business cycles were caused by variations in the velocity of circulation or the demand for money (i.e. hoarding),[5] that the cycle was exacerbated by changing price expectations, and that, accordingly, the cure for the cycle consisted in offsetting changes in velocity by varying the money supply in order to achieve price-level stabilization. Said Chicagoan Frank Knight "An approximate constancy in general prices can in the nature of the case be achieved by deliberate action, based on constant attention, correcting or offsetting incipient tendencies to expansion or contraction" [13, 224] Moreover, compare Keynes' statement on the role of price expectations with the following remark by Chicagoan Paul Douglas

> during a depression, the velocity of circulation of both money and credit is appreciably reduced Consumers hold dollars in their pockets longer because they expect prices to fall still further and their money will consequently be worth more Such is the so-called 'hoard-

3 Other formulations of the quantity theory prior to the appearance of the *General Theory* included the income-expenditure approach developed chiefly by Wicksell, the mathematical approach stressing the classical dichotomy issue and homogeniety postulate identified with Cassel and discussed recently by Samuelson [21], and the American empirical approach of whom Snyder and Working were leading expositors For discussions of the latter version see Humphrey [7] and Tavlas [28] I might also note that the Cambridge formulation of the demand for money was itself to become increasingly "accidental and arbitrary" following the publication of the *General Theory* See Tavlas [27]

4 See, also, Patinkin [17]

5 The exception is Paul Douglas, who thought that depressions were caused by a failure of the money supply to increase in proportion to the secular advance in production For a discussion of Douglas's views, see Tavlas [25]

ing' at the present time The effect is to decrease the quantity of money offered for goods and hence again to cause prices to decrease [3, 79]

By the time of the publication of the *Treatise* and Keynes' participation in the Harris Lectures, his theoretical thinking had undergone a marked change The demand for money approach to the quantity theory had been replaced by the controversial and short-lived fundemental equations The cash-balance mechanics of the *Tract* where a change in the stock of money exerts its initial impact in the goods market had been replaced by the income-expenditure approach of the *Treatise*, in which a change in the money stock initially affects the short-term rate of interest via portfolio substitution in the bond market Keynes appended this transmission mechanism with a theory of the term structure of interest rates whereby the initial change in the short-term rate would lead to a change in the long-term rate and thereby influence profits and the level of investment.

In order to highlight the transformation in Keynes' thought, consider his discussion at the Harris Lectures The business cycle, he argued, "is a function of costs of production moving at a different rate from prices" [16, 73] So far this sounds like the diagnosis of business cycles developed in the *Tract*, as well as that formulated by the Chicago School of the 1930s But to Keynes of the *Tract*, as well as to the Chicagoans, changes in the level of output during the cycle were thought to be caused by the failure of costs to move as quickly as prices due to the rigid nature of the cost, or wage, structure At the time of the Harris Lectures, however, Keynes argued that the disparity between costs and prices is due to "a failure of the rate of interest to be as sensitive as it ought to be to changes in the minds of the business community" [16, 74] Accordingly, Keynes abandoned his earlier persuasion as to the desirability of price-level stabilization and opted instead for stabilization of the level of investment, to be achieved through manipulation of the interest rate He stated "What we ought to get rid of are the wastes of the credit [i e , business] cycle, and *that is not primarily a price problem, it is primarily a rate of interest problem*" (italics supplied) [16, 74]. One of those present at the Harris meetings was Alvin Hansen, then of the University of Minnesota, who pressed Keynes on the issue of the proper target of stabilization policy

Hansen What would be your criterion guiding your central banks in their rate of interest? Would it be the movement of the price level? [16, 93]

Keynes I think as much as anything the volume of impending construction [i e investment] is a symptom I should look at it more than I should look at the price index [16, 93 4]

Despite the changes which occurred in Keynes' monetary thought, there was one notable similarity between the *Tract* and the *Treatise* which is of fundamental importance in assessing the Chicago School's resistance to the Keynesian revolution. Thus, as Cate documents, Keynes in both the *Tract* and the *Treatise* argued that stabilization policy should be implemented through the banking system via the operation of traditional monetary measures—specifically, through manipulation of the bank rate In contrast, the Chicago quantity theorists had begun to evince a lack of faith in traditional monetary policy by the early 1930s. Such measures were considered (1) time-consuming, (2) subject to the offsetting influence of confidence which induced banks not to want to lend, nor business to borrow; (3) further subject to the unstable character of fractional-reserve banking which made expansion by a small number of banks self-defeating [6] Accordingly, the Chicagoans opted for bud-

6 For documentation, see Tavlas [24]

get deficits in order to attain the necessary variations in the money supply. But they were careful to note that such deficits were entirely consistent within their short-run version of the Fisherine framework. As I stated in the article to which Cate refers: "to the Chicagoans, public works were a means of conducting monetary policy" [23, 692].

Actually, by the time of the Harris Lectures, Keynes, too, had begun to display some reservations concerning the efficacy of traditional banking tools. For example, he noted that attempts to expand the money supply might well be thwarted if the banking system chose to hold additional reserves rather than lend them out to business [16, 449]. Nevertheless, he did not regard this as a sufficient qualification to reject the use of traditional monetary measures. Subsequently, he began to share the Chicago view that banking measures were insufficient in dealing with the 1930s depression. Moreover—and in accord with the Chicagoans—Keynes increasingly opted for budget deficits to combat the depression. Where he departs from the Chicagoans, however, is in his rejection regarding the compatibility of budget deficits within the framework of the quantity theory. Instead, Keynes elected to construct a new theoretical structure to support his practical recommendations of pulic works projects.

As evidence in support of the foregoing argument, consider a most revealing exchange which occurred between D H Robertson and Keynes in 1933. Robertson never did become a convert to the *General Theory*, and this exchange explains, in part, why he -as well as the Chicagoans-- refused to partake in the Keynesian offensive. The point at issue was how to best justify public works theoretically. Said Robertson in a letter dated April 1, 1933

> I know I shall never reconvert you to the old K and V [i e , quantity theory] method, but I can't refrain from suggesting how much stronger they make the *prima facie* case for public works For on your and [R.F] Kahn's short period method, all new money becomes completely inert in the end, and most of it pretty quickly Hence your arguments can do nothing to allay the objections of those who argue that the budgets *of future years* will be burdened by the interest charges on the loan But surely *prima facie* money once effectively introduced into circulation may be expected to stay there, and to circulate (thus affecting prices or employment as the case may be) with a velocity approximating to that of existing money, unless and until it is withdrawn by taxation, deflation, etc (original italics) [11, 17]

To which Keynes retorted in a May 3, 1933 letter

> I doubt that either version of the Cambridge equation is of any serious utility and I can't remember that I have ever come across a case of anyone ever using either of them for *practical purposes of interpretation* ... *All the versions of the quantity theory*, which make no distinction between swaps and intermediate transactions and genuine production-consumption transactions, *seem to me to tell one nothing* (italics supplied) [11, 18]

Robertson's point regarding the financing aspect of budget deficits was to become a distinguishing feature of the Chicago School For example, such Chicagoans as Mints [15], Simons [22], and more recently, Friedman [4], have argued that debt-financed deficits are contractionary because they fail to operate on the supply of money In contrast, to Keynesians the financing aspect of deficits was, until recently, of secondary importance

The important issue, however, concerns the development of Keynes' monetary views and their relation to those of the Chicago School of the 1930s Tom Cate is correct in noting the similarity in Keynes' policy recommendations with respect to the *Tract*, on the one hand, and the *Treatise* and Harris Foundation Lectures, on the other. Indeed, it was Keynes' continued espousal of traditional monetary measures which initially distinguished him from the Chicagoans. But there is an additional aspect to the story Specifically, Keynes' monetary theory in the *Tract* stressing direct stock-flow monetary mechanics and its associated emphasis on price expectations and price-level stabilization ran along similar lines to the monetary views characterizing the 1930s Chicago School. The transformation of Keynes' thought in the *Treatise*, accordingly, served to set him apart along *theoretical* lines from the Chicagoans—a transformation which became accentuated with the appearance of the *General Theory*.[7] But by that time it had become clear that the Chicagoans had accepted the compatibility of the quantity theory with a policy of deficit budgets, while Keynes, rejecting that notion, had chosen to set off in another direction.

George S. Tavlas
Organization for Economic Cooperation and Development
Paris, France
and
U S. Department of State
Washington, D. C.

7 Recent work by Leijonhufvud [14] and Davidson [1] attempts to rehabilitate Keynes' views on the importance of money as articulated in the *General Theory* by stressing the link of that volume with the *Treatise* Patinkin [19] has been critical of this work in Keynesian interpretation The evidence presented above lends support to Patinkin's view

References

1 Davidson, Paul *Money and the Real World* London Macmillan Press, 1978
2 Davis, J Ronnie, "The Last Remake of the New Economics and the Old Economists Comment" *Southern Economic Journal*, January 1979, 919 25
3 Douglas, Paul H , "Money, Credit and the Depression" *The World Tomorrow* March 1932, 78–80
4 Friedman, Milton, "Comments on the Critics" *Journal of Political Economy*, September/October 1972, 906–50
5 Humphrey, Thomas M , "Role of Non-Chicago Economists in the Evolution of the Quantity Theory in America 1930 1950" *Southern Economic Journal*, July 1971, 12 18
6 ———, "On the Monetary Economics of Chicagoans and Non-Chicagoans Reply" *Southern Economic Journal* January 1973, 460 63
7 ———, "Empirical Tests of the Equation of Exchange 1900 1930" *History of Political Economy*, Spring 1973, 285 316
8 Keynes, John M *A Tract on Monetary Reform*, 1923 As reprinted in Keynes' *Collected Writings*, Vol IV
9 ——— *A Treatise on Money*, Vols I and II As reprinted in Keynes' *Collected Writings*, Vols V and VI
10 ——— *The General Theory of Employment, Interest, and Money* As reprinted in Keynes' *Collected Writings* Vol VII
11 ——— *The General Theory and After A Supplement* Edited by Donald Moggridge Vol XXIX of Keynes' *Collected Writings*, 1979
12 ——— *Collected Writings* London Macmillan, for the Royal Economic Society, 1971 79
13 Knight, Frank H "The Business Cycle Interest, and Money A Methodological Approach" *Review of Economic Statistics* May 1941, 53 67 Reprinted in Knight, *On the History and Method of Economics* Chicago University of Chicago Press 1956
14 Leijonhufvud, Axel, *On Keynesian Economics and the Economics of Keynes* New York Oxford University Press, 1968
15 Mints, Lloyd W "Monetary Policy" *Review of Economic Statistics*, May 1946, 60 69
16 Norman Wait Harris Memorial Foundation, *Reports of Round Tables* Chicago 1931
17 Patinkin Don, "The Chicago Tradition, the Quantity Theory, and Friedman" *Journal of Money, Credit and Banking* February 1969 46 70
18 ———, "On the Monetary Economics of Chicagoans and Non-Chicagoans Comment" *Southern Economic Journal* January 1973, 454 59

19 ———, "Keynes' Monetary Thought A Study of its Development " *History of Political Economy*, Spring 1976, 1–150.

20 Pigou, A C , "The Value of Money " *Quarterly Journal of Economics*, November 1917, 38 65

21. Samuelson, Paul A , "What Classical and Neoclassical Monetary Theory Really Was " *Canadian Journal of Economics*, February 1968, 1–15

22 Simons, Henry C., "Hansen on Fiscal Policy." *Journal of Political Economy*, April 1942 161 96 Reprinted in Simons, *Economic Policy for a Free Society* Chicago University of Chicago Press, 1948

23. Tavlas, George S , "Some Further Observations on the Monetary Economics of Chicagoans and Non-Chicagoans " *Southern Economic Journal*, April 1976, 685–92

24. ———, "Chicago Schools Old and New on the Efficacy of Monetary Policy " *Banca Nazionale del Lavoro Quarterly Review*, March 1977, 52–73.

25 ———, "The Chicago Tradition Revisited Some Neglected Monetary Contributions of Senator Paul Douglas." *Journal of Money, Credit and Banking*, November 1977, 529–35

26 ———, "The Last Remake of the New Economics and the Old Economists Reply " *Southern Economic Journal*, January 1979, 926–31

27 ———, "Keynesian and Monetarist Theories of the Monetary Transmission Process Doctrinal Aspects " *Journal of Monetary Economics*, April 1981, forthcoming

28. ———, "Notes on Garvy, Snyder, and the Doctrinal Foundations of Monetarism " *History of Political Economy*, 1981, forthcoming.

'The Chicago Tradition Revisited'

G. S. Tavlas, 'The Chicago Tradition revisited: some neglected monetary contributions: Senator Paul Douglas (1892–1976)', *Journal of Money Credit and Banking*, 9 (November 1977), pp. 529–35.

GEORGE S. TAVLAS*

The Chicago Tradition Revisited: Some Neglected Monetary Contributions

Senator Paul Douglas (1892–1976)

INTRODUCTION

In his 1956 "Restatement" of the quantity theory, Milton Friedman presented his analytic and pragmatic framework as one that "conveys the flavor" of the Chicago quantity-theory tradition of Simons, Mints, Knight, and Viner [15, p. 4]. As a result of Friedman's attempt to bridge his contemporary quantity theory to that of his mentors, there has been an increased interest in the doctrinal historical character of the Chicago School of the 1930s. Important contributions have included (a) Patinkin's study [20] concerning the theoretical nature of the earlier Chicagoans and his conclusion that, contrary to modern quantity theorists, these economists placed primary reliance on sharp fluctuations in the velocity of circulation (with the money stock responding passively) in interpreting changes in the level of economic activity; and (b) Davis's survey [1] of the policy orientation of the members of the Chicago School during the early 1930s and his surprising finding that these Chicagoans advocated the use of public works and deficit budgets as means of combating depression.

The culmination of this doctrinal historical research has been the recent exchange between Friedman [15] and Patinkin [21]. Friedman now seems to accept the validity of Patinkin's criticisms concerning the difference in conceptual frameworks between earlier and contemporary quantity theorists and thus no longer claims theoretical lineage to the former Chicagoans. Yet following Davis, he notes, "so far

*I would like to thank Martin Bronfenbrenner, Milton Friedman, and William Silber for their helpful comments.

George S. Tavlas is economist, U.S. Department of State.

as policy was concerned, Keynes had nothing to offer those of us who had sat at the feet of Simons, Mints, Knight, and Viner" [15, p. 937]. Though the doctrines of the aforementioned Chicagoans are undoubtedly of importance in contributing to the monetary economics that Friedman now teaches, even more relevant to the theme of the anticipatory nature of the earlier Chicago School are the neglected contributions of Paul Howard Douglas.[1]

Douglas, who was born March 26, 1892, in Salem, Massachusetts, joined the faculty at the University of Chicago to teach economics in 1920 (the following year he was awarded his Ph.D. at Columbia University). Douglas taught at Chicago until 1942, when he enlisted in the Marines. He returned to Chicago in 1946 and remained there for two more years–until his election to the U.S. Senate. During his eighteen years as a senator, Douglas established a reputation as a champion of liberal causes. He died on September 24, 1976.

MONETARY CONTRIBUTIONS DURING THE 1920s AND 1930s

As a minimum statement, Douglas was the first Chicagoan to advocate the use of public works and deficit budgets to combat depression, doing so originally in a 1927 article [8]. This fact has been overlooked by latter-day commentators. Moreover, he continued to argue for budget deficits throughout the early 1930s [3, 9, 12] financed preferably by printing money, as tax-financed and bond-financed deficits had offsetting effects [8, p. 42; 9, p. 80; 4, pp. 136–38]. In accordance with the views of his Chicago colleagues (see [1]), Douglas had originally called for the balancing of the budget over the course of the cycle [3, p. 14; 12, p. 149]. But by the time of his *Controlling Depressions* in 1935, he recognized that chronic deficits would have to be expected [4, p. 185]. The following year, Simons joined Douglas in foreseeing the need for chronic deficits [22, p. 333]. Thus if credit is to be given to the other Chicagoans "for developing relevant policy prescriptions" [15, p. 3] some acknowledgment seems due to Paul Douglas.

Yet even more pertinent to contemporary Chicago are Douglas's theoretical views on money. Using as his analytic framework the Fisherine equation of exchange, $P = (MV + M'V')/T$, he was careful to note: "The various terms are not, however, as some of the more naive quantity theorists have believed, independent of each other. On the contrary, they are inter-related in a somewhat organic fashion" [11, p. 26].[2]

[1] Davis [2] does refer to Douglas's 1935 work [4]. Davis, however, is not concerned with Douglas's monetary economics, but rather with his advocacy of fiscal measures as cures for depression. He also describes how Douglas's views were influenced by Keynes and Wicksell and led to Douglas's adoption of a saving-investment analysis. But Davis is in error when he states that: "Douglas pointed to the saving-investment nexus as the major culprit in depression making. The sperm of a depression was an excess of saving over investment" [2, pp. 48–49]. As this paper will demonstrate, this was not how Douglas interpreted the initiating cause of depressions.

[2] That Douglas's monetary writings are representative of the Chicago tradition is evidenced by the fact that when Patinkin refers to a similar interpretation of the quantity equation, as described in Lloyd Mints's lecture notes, he observes: "[this] has always represented to me 'the flavor of the Chicago tradition'" [20, p. 55].

Unlike his Chicago colleagues, who interpreted depressions as due to independent movements in velocity,[3] Douglas argued that depressions were caused by the failure of the money supply to increase as rapidly as the annual trend rise in production [8, pp. 31–41; 11; 4, p. 77]. The annual rise in production was attributed to improvements in technical efficiency and increased savings. The failure of the money supply to keep pace with increases in production would result in an induced fall in the general price level in order to clear the market of the excess supply of goods. Because present product prices have embodied within them relatively higher costs that have been paid out previously, profit margins would shrink, and curtailed output would ensue. Much in line with Friedman's recent criticism of the London School of Economics tradition of the 1930s [15, pp. 936–41], Douglas observed: "The orthodox economists of the English classical tradition, whose reasoning tends to be permeated with the assumptions of a pre-capitalistic and barter economy, see few or no evil consequences in a fall in prices. But the results may be serious in the money and credit economy of today, where business enterprises produce for a profit. For production takes time, and raw material and labor purchased at one period of time will not be fully combined into finished products and sold until some time later" [10, pp. 112-13].

Douglas applied his analysis directly to the Great Depression. He cited the failure of the money supply to increase proportionately with the annual rise in production "as an important reason I believe for the great depression which began in 1929"[4] [11, p. 161]. This is precisely the conclusion reached by Friedman and Schwartz [17] in their reinterpretation of the 1929 depression. In addition, another distinctive feature of Douglas's work was the emphasis he placed on empirical verification of his theoretical framework [4, 8, 10]. This, too, serves to link him more directly to the methodology of contemporary Chicago than do the nonempirical approaches of Simons, Knight, or Viner.

To prevent depressions, Douglas argued that primary reliance should be placed on two key indicators; either a general price index could be kept relatively stable or the unemployment rate prevented from rising above a maximum level of 4 or 5 percent [8, p. 42; 4, p. 195]. Attainment of either of these two goals could in turn be achieved "if the quantity of purchasing power were to be increased at the rate of 3 to 4 percent a year, or the long-time rate of production" [4, p. 185]. This is re-

[3]The other Chicagoans did not really express strong interest in the factors that might initiate a depression. In this context, Knight stated that, "Too much attention has been given to this problem of the cause of the collapse" [18, p. 214]. A similar opinion is expressed by Mints in [19, p. 60].

[4]Douglas's monetary economics and his interpretation of depression as being due to a failure of the money supply to increase proportionately with production were greatly influenced by the joint writings of the American economists William Foster and Waddill Catchings. I have discussed the monetary doctrines of Foster and Catchings elsewhere [23]. The point to be emphasized is that Douglas did not ascribe the initiating cause of depression to the "saving-investment nexus" as claimed by Davis [2] and as referred to in note 1. Indeed, he argued throughout the late 1920s and early 1930s that an excess of saving relative to investment was a cumulative cause of depression. Thus, after crediting Wicksell and Keynes for their saving-investment analyses, Douglas notes: "They are [however] describing characteristics and accelerating causes of the up and down swings rather than the initiating causes themselves" [4, p. 42].

markably similar to the growth-rate rule that is the hallmark of contemporary quantity-theory policy. Douglas advocated the monetary growth-rate rule as early as 1927, when he stated: "The primary need is for stability in the price level of those goods manufactured under the present technique of mass production and this can be secured by a general and proportionate increase in the supply of monetary purchasing power" [8, p. 40]. Douglas stated the growth-rate rule on numerous occasions during the late 1920s and early 1930s[5] but was the only Chicagoan to do so. It is *not* to be found in the published writings of Simons, Mints, Knight, or Viner during the early 1930s.

Entirely consistent with the aforementioned doctrines are the views contained in a neglected 1931 work, *The Problem of Unemployment*, which Douglas coauthored with Aaron Director (then in his first year on the Chicago faculty). The analysis of depressions in this volume—as due to the failure of the supply of monetary purchasing power to increase as rapidly as production—follows closely the reasoning that Douglas had been expounding since 1927 [14, p. 181]. Douglas and Director argued that depressions could best be combated through the use of public works and deficit budgets, "particularly where fresh monetary purchasing power is created to finance the construction work" [14, pp. 210–11]. Moreover, curtailment of economic activity could be avoided "if the supply of money and credit were to increase commensurately with the increase in production" [14, p. 183].

POSTWAR VIEWS

During Douglas's first senatorial term, he was appointed chairman of the Subcommittee on Monetary, Credit, and Fiscal Policies. In this capacity he presided over a series of hearings having to do with the Federal Reserve-Treasury conflict of the late 1940s and early 1950s. Throughout these hearings, Douglas continued to express his adherence to the quantity theory of money and to recognize the importance of monetary policy in the Chicago tradition.

The conflict between the Fed and the Treasury was a consequence of the Treasury's desire to peg interest rates on government debt. This required that the Federal Reserve lose its control over the money supply. Douglas viewed the conflict as particularly acute during periods of inflation or threatening inflation, when the Fed favored higher interest rates and the Treasury continued in its adherence for low interest rates [26, p. 533]. A subsequently published report of the Subcommittee on Monetary, Credit, and Fiscal Policies dealt directly with this issue. The report recommended that the primary responsibility for regulating the supply, availability, and cost of credit should be lodged with the Fed and that "Treasury actions in the Federal debt shall be made consistent with the policies of the Federal Reserve"

[5]Elsewhere he stated: "Since the long-time advance in production tends to be somewhere between 3 and 4 percent a year . . . it follows that the monetary purchasing power in the hands of consumers must normally be increased in approximately that rate" [3, p. 19]. See also [13, p. 32; 6, p. 190; 11, pp. 160–61; 7, p. 332]. The development of the growth-rate rule traces back to the early nineteenth century English economic literature. See [24].

[27, p. 2]. In addition, the report rejected the notion that fiscal policy could be very effective if monetary policy were neutral and stated that "a conflicting monetary policy could lessen still further the effectiveness of fiscal policy." Douglas's Subcommittee also criticized the contractionary policies pursued by the Fed during the first few years of the 1930s depression and suggested that the severity of that depression might have been substantially lessened had more expansionary policies been followed [27, pp. 18-19].

On February 22, 1951, Douglas took the floor of the Senate and delivered a lecture on his interpretation of the key issues regarding the Fed-Treasury conflict. "No one desires a high interest rate in and of itself," he stated. "However, I do not think that this states accurately the real issue before us. The real issue is inflation" [25, p. 1470]. Douglas proceeded to give his senate colleagues a verbal description of the equation of exchange. He argued that the rise in the general price level that had taken place since June 1950 was a consequence of prior increases in the supply of money made possible by the expansion of reserves by the Fed. But the blame does not lie with the Federal Reserve, for "over the shoulder of the Federal Reserve System has stood the Treasury, making threatening passes and gestures and from time to time cracking its whip. . . . Under this pressure the Federal Reserve System has gone along. The real responsibility has been that of the Treasury. The Treasury has pulled the strings, and the Federal Reserve has danced to its music" [25, p. 1473].

Douglas noted that he did not believe high interest rates would have much effect in halting inflation. But that was not the issue. Inflation could best be controlled not by raising the price of credit but "by helping to shut off the supply" [25, p. 1478]. Accordingly, he proposed that the Fed give primary emphasis to controlling the supply of money while continuing its policy of maintaining orderly conditions in the money market. Having completed his speech, Douglas presented his senate colleagues with a signed document that he had received from seven University of Chicago economists—including Milton Friedman and Lloyd Mints[6]—on "The Failure of the Present Monetary Policy." He noted that the analysis of inflation contained in the document, as well as the proposed inflation remedies, were entirely in accord with his own. Shortly after Douglas's speech—and a direct consequence of his persistent efforts in that direction—the Treasury and the Fed issued a joint statement acknowledging that they had reached "a full accord" (on March 2, 1951).[7]

CONCLUDING REMARKS

Paul Douglas is notably remembered today for his pioneering studies on the relative effects of labor and capital upon production. Yet at one time he remarked that

[6]Other signers of the document were: Lloyd A. Metzler, Frederick H. Harbison, D. Gale Johnson, Theodore W Schultz, and H. G. Lewis. See [25, pp 1481-82]

[7]Some twenty years later, Douglas reflected upon the Fed's actions prior to the accord as "a vindication of the quantity theory of money, supposedly known to every student of elementary economics" [7, p. 332].

he considered his contributions to monetary economics at least as important as his work on production functions [5, p. 507]. This note has sketched some of these contributions that have been overlooked and that serve to link him directly with the contemporary quantity theory. Combined with the innovations of his Chicago colleagues during the 1930s, Douglas's monetary economics serves to reinforce Milton Friedman's exegesis of a Chicago tradition where "money matters" and where the quantity theory "became a flexible and sensitive tool for interpreting movements in aggregate economic activity and for developing relevant policy prescriptions" [15, p. 3].

LITERATURE CITED

1. Davis, J. Ronnie. "Chicago Economists, Deficit Budgets, and the Early 1930's." *American Economic Review,* 58 (June 1968), 476-82

2. ——. *The New Economics and the Old Economists.* Iowa City: Iowa State University Press, 1971.

3. Douglas, Paul H *Collapse or Cycle.* Chicago: American Library Association, 1933.

4. ——. *Controlling Depressions.* New York: W. W Norton and Company, 1935.

5. ——. "Economist of Tomorrow: The Story of Paul Douglas." *The World Tomorrow,* 12 (December 1929), 507-10

6. ——. "An Economist's Idea of Good Government." *Annals of the Academy of Political and Social Science* (April 1933), 184-92.

7. ——. *In the Fullness of Time* New York: Harcourt Brace, 1972.

8. ——. "The Modern Technique of Mass Production and Its Relation to Wages." *Proceedings of the Academy of Political Science,* 12 (July 1927), 17-42.

9. ——. "Money, Credit and the Depression." *The World Tomorrow,* 15 (March 1932), 78-80.

10. ——. "Purchasing Power of the Masses and Business Depressions." In *Economic Essays in Honor of Wesley Clair Mitchell* New York: Columbia University Press, 1935.

11. —— "Technological Aspects of Unemployment." *Proceedings of the Institute of Public Affairs,* 33 (August 1933), 150-61.

12. ——. "The World Problem of Unemployment." *Proceedings of the Institute of Public Affairs,* 33 (August 1933), 136-49.

13. ——. *The World Unemployment Problem.* London: League of Nations Union, 1931.

14. Douglas, Paul H., and Aaron Director. *The Problem of Unemployment* New York: MacMillan, 1931.

15. Friedman, Milton. "Comments on the Critics." *Journal of Political Economy,* 80 (September/October 1972), 906-50.

16. ——. "The Quantity Theory of Money–A Restatement." In *Studies in the Quantity Theory of Money,* edited by Milton Friedman. Chicago: University of Chicago Press, 1956.

17. Friedman, Milton, and Anna J. Schwartz. *A Monetary History of the United States, 1867-1960.* Princeton, N. J.: Princeton University Press (for the National Bureau of Economic Research), 1963.

18. Knight, Frank H. "The Business Cycle, Interest, and Money: A Methodological Approach." *Review of Economic Statistics,* 23 (May 1941). Reprinted in *On the History and Method of Economics,* edited by Frank H. Knight. Chicago: University of Chicago Press, 1956.

19. Mints, Lloyd. "Monetary Policy." *Review of Economic Statistics* 28, (May 1946), 60–69.

20. Patinkin, Don. "The Chicago Tradition, The Quantity Theory, and Friedman." *Journal of Money, Credit, and Banking,* 1 (February 1969), 46–70.

21. ———. "Friedman on the Quantity Theory and Keynesian Economics." *Journal of Political Economy,* 80 (September/October 1972), 883–905.

22. Simons, Henry C. "Rules versus Authorities in Monetary Policy." *Journal of Political Economy,* 44 (February 1936), 1–30. Reprinted in *Economic Policy for a Free Society,* by Henry Simons. Chicago: University of Chicago Press, 1948.

23. Tavlas, George S. "Some Further Observations on the Monetary Economics of Chicagoans and Non-Chicagoans." *Southern Economic Journal,* 42 (April 1976), 685–92

24. ———. "Some Initial Formulations of the Monetary Growth-Rate Rule." *History of Political Economy,* 9 (Winter 1977).

25. U.S. Congress. Senate. *Congressional Record.* 82nd Cong., 1st sess., 1951, 97, pt. 2: 1468–82.

26. U.S. Congress. Senate. Subcommittee on Monetary, Credit, and Fiscal Policies. *Hearings.* 79th Cong , 1st sess., 1949.

27. ———. *Report of the Subcommittee.* 81st Cong., 2d sess., S. Con. Res. 26, 1950.

'Chicago Schools Old and New'

G. Tavlas, 'Chicago schools old and new on the efficacy of monetary policy', *Banca Nazionale Del Lavoro Quarterly Review* (March 1977), pp. 51–73.

Chicago Schools Old and New on the Efficacy of Monetary Policy

The exegesis of a Chicago monetary heritage by Friedman (1956, reprinted in Friedman 1969) where "money mattered" and which forms a direct link to his modern version of the quantity theory has recently been challenged by several writers. In a series of articles, Don Patinkin (1969, 1972a, 1972b, 1972c) contrasts the variable-velocity approach to the Fisherine equation adopted by former Chicagoans with Friedman's stable portfolio-demand function for money. The conclusion drawn by Patinkin is that Friedman's monetary framework can more accurately be described as an extension of Keynesian liquidity preference theory rather than as a direct outgrowth of an earlier Chicago quantity-theory tradition. Subsequent papers by Johnson (1971) and by Moggridge and Howson (1974, p. 227), relying on Patinkin's work as their source, take a more extreme view denying the validity of a unique Chicago monetary heritage and categorizing the delineation of such a heritage by Friedman as a mythical invention. Despite these criticisms, however, Friedman continues to view his monetary contributions as primarily an extension of the pre-Keynesian quantity-theory tradition, particularly as formulated by his mentors at Chicago during the 1930's and 1940's (Friedman 1972, pp. 932-45).

The failure to reach agreement concerning the possible existence and relevance of an earlier Chicago School of monetary economics is due in part to shortcomings in previous doctrinal-historical studies. In particular previous studies have not dealt adequately with the relationship between the monetary-policy orientations of earlier and modern Chicagoans. The purpose of this paper is to trace the evolvement of monetary-policy proposals at Chicago from the early 1930's up until the appearance of Friedman's classic "Restatement" of the quantity theory in 1956. It is divided into three sections. The first section examines the pragmatic nature of Chicagoan monetary economics during the depression-dominated 1930's. Contrary to recent interpretation, these Chicagoans had little faith in the efficacy of traditional monetary measures — open market operations and variations in the discount rate — as means to combat the depression.[1] Nevertheless, their advocacy of fiscal prescriptions in light of the effects of deficit budgets upon the stock of money suggests a unique approach to the Fisherine equation not shared by other American quantity theorists during the 1930's.

The second section describes the emergence of the Chicagoan affirmation in the efficacy of traditional monetary policy. This process entails extensions to the quantity theory by Chicago economists during the 1940's and early 1950's, especially by Frank Knight, Lloyd Mints, and Friedman. Following Patinkin (1969, 1972c), Friedman's " Restatement " is considered a pivotal contribution to contemporary monetarist thought. But Patinkin's implication — which is carried over into the work by Johnson, and Moggridge and Howson — that neo-Chicagoan monetary economics is largely a derivative of Keynesian monetary theory as integrated in the " Restatement " and stands in isolation of earlier Chicago views is shown to be in error. This paper argues that rather than representing a transmogrification of the monetary views of his predecessors, Friedman's "Restatement" more accurately reflects a culmination of post-Keynesian Chicago contributions on money. In addition, a common link binding Chicagoans throughout the period under study, is shown to be their interpretation of deficit budgets financed by money creation as the implementation of monetary — as opposed to fiscal — policy.[2] Concluding remarks are provided in the third section of the paper.

I. The Message from Chicago: 1930-1936

Professor Patinkin (1969, 1972a) has accurately described the theoretical nature of the monetary economics of the 1930's Chicago School in terms of Fisher's MV=PT, where velocity was considered

1 The Federal Reserve's power to alter reserve requirements did not come into effect until 1935.

2 J. Ronnie Davis has stated that Chicago economists " argued throughout the early 1930's for the use of large and continuous deficit budgets to combat the mass unemployment and deflation of the times " (Davis 1968, p. 476). Davis, however, interprets the Chicagoans desire for deficit budgets as the advocacy of *fiscal* policy. This paper shows that Chicagoans argued for deficits as means to conduct monetary policy.

unstable and responsible for initiating movements in economic activity. Moreover, as Patinkin rightly notes, the elder Chicagoans thought that proper stabilization policy required that fluctuations in velocity be offset with opposite variations in the stock of money. Unfortunately, Patinkin's valid generalization concerning countercyclical policy has been extended to an invalid generalization concerning the views of former Chicagoans with respect to the effectiveness of traditional monetary measures. Thus — perhaps the consequence of the failure of prior studies to examine adequately the monetary-policy content emanating from Chicago during the 1930's — Joseph Aschheim states:

> While contemporary Monetarists under Friedman's leadership are generally regarded as exponents of the efficacy of monetary policy, earlier adherents of the quantity theory even of the Chicago School have been quite eclectic as to the preferable way in which an increase in the quantity of money was to be engendered (Aschheim 1975, p. 227).

A review of the relevant literature, however, does not lend support to Aschheim's contention. On the contrary, an investigation of the works of those Chicagoans who wrote in the fields of monetary economics and stabilization policy during the 1930's — notably Jacob Viner, Paul Douglas, Henry Simons, A. G. Hart and Harry Gideonse — suggests a Chicago group characterized by its lack of conviction in monetary tools which operated via the borrowing and lending activities of the commercial banking system.

Thus Viner, in a 1933 speech on " Inflation as a Remedy for Depression " delivered before the Institute of Public Affairs at Athens, Ga., explored possible alternative methods of expanding the money supply. The most efficient means to this end, he argued, was the implementation of budget deficits of the federal government. Next, he analyzed the possible use of open market purchases:

> This method is inferior to the preceding one [budget deficits] in this respect: the preceding one gives more *immediate* stimulus to business. What this does is to increase the cash reserves of the banking system, and therefore, it is hoped, to give the banks the desire to put their idle funds to work. But the bankers have learned in recent years not how to make money without lending, but that under certain circumstances the rate at which they lose

> money is less if they stop lending, so it is conceivable that the banking system would welcome the additional liquidity and would not increase its loans or investments [italics supplied] (Viner 1933, p. 131).

Viner, in addition, supplemented his observations concerning the time-consuming nature of policies aimed at expanding the supply of bank reserves and the tendency of the banking system to hold such reserves idle during depression, with a reflection on the demand for reserves. In times of low confidence, he thought, where the future was filled with uncertainty, there would be no reason for businesses to want to borrow even at a lower rate of interest. Accordingly, "if the business community gets scared, if it does not acquire confidence, it is powerful enough to more than counteract expansionist activities" (Viner 1933, p. 130).

Viner perceived depression in terms of a maladjustment between prices and costs. Once velocity moved sharply downward — for whatever reason — product prices would fall, and with costs adjusting rigidly, the result would be a decline in profits and production. Therefore, "there will not be recovery... unless there is expansion in the use of means of payment" (Viner 1933, p. 133). Implicit in this view is the assumption that costs are inflexible in an upward direction as well, so that monetary expansion would have its initial impact on prices and profits which would lead to higher levels of production. "Theoretically, that is not inevitable," argued Viner, "but practically an inflation has always worked out that way... The costs lag behind" (1933, p. 122). Because of his strong reservations with policies operating through the banking system — indeed, "central banking systems have frequently fed booms and depressions instead of counteracting them" (1933, p. 123) — Viner opted instead for currency expansion via deficit budgets. But he was careful to note that deficits were expansionary only when financed by creating money. Depression required money expansion to offset velocity contraction. He stated this explicitly in his 1933 speech, and remained firm in this view well after Keynes' *General Theory* (1936) had made its initial impact. Thus, in a 1942 paper, Viner argued: "It is government expenditure [of newly created money] and not government borrowing which is inflationary; and given the expenditures, the borrowing is anti-inflationary" (1942, p. 696).

Paul Douglas' monetary views during the 1930's were in accord with those of Viner. As with Viner, he saw the necessity of increasing product prices faster than costs through monetary expansion in order to escape depression. And he also shared Viner's disenchantment of achieving such expansion by way of traditional monetary measures. Douglas reasoned that " it is not enough to give the banks the power to create more credit. It is necessary that the loans should actually be made in large quantities " (1933b, p. 10). During depressions, however, open market purchases would likely result in failure as " business does not want to borrow to build more factories and install new machines when those they already own are so largely idle. Nor do they want to borrow on short-time in order to produce more current goods since it is more than doubtful whether those goods could be sold at a profit to a public whose monetary purchasing power has so dried up " (1934, p. 14). Nor are the banks anxious to lend during contractions. For the banks are " afraid that they will not be repaid for their loans ". Hence, stated Douglas, " the combined result has been a stalemate " (1933a, p. 129). The same, he argued, applies to manipulations of the discount rate during a depression:

> At such times the volume of credit... shrinks and the banks have large accumulations of idle reserves. The banks, therefore, do not need to resort to re-discounting in order to make loans and hence a reduction in the re-discount rate offers no further bait... It is, therefore, an idle gesture for the Reserve System at such times to lower the re-discount rate (Douglas 1935, p. 116).

Since depression required expansion of the supply of money, and because of " this failure to obtain credit [through banking measures]," Douglas declared that " the problem must be attacked directly " (1933a, p. 129). Like Viner, he advocated the use of deficit budgets. Furthermore, Douglas called for the financing of such deficits through money creation as he argued that bond-financed and tax-financed deficits would have offsetting effects (Douglas 1935, pp. 136-138).

Analogous interpretations of depression and required depression policy were shared by A. G. Hart and Harry G. Gideonse. Both Hart and Gideonse were on the Chicago faculty during the 1930's, but their monetary writings have been overlooked in recent studies of the Chicago tradition. Thus Hart, in a neglected 1936 paper significantly titled " The ' Chicago Plan ' of Banking Reform " argued against combating depression through expansion of bank reserves. " Expansion requires not only the basis of an increased *amount* of reserve funds but the *acquisition* by member banks of earning assets" (Hart 1936, p. 108). Hart, however, doubted whether such an acquisition would actually materialize "if — as has happened recently — the banks are unable to find a sufficient volume of satisfactory short-term assets and hesitate to acquire further long-term assets for fear of capital losses" (1936, p. 108). He shared the Chicagoan view that depression required offsetting downward movements in velocity through monetary expansion. But given his disenchantment with attempting such expansion through the banking system, he asked: "How are the funds to be put into circulation?" His answer was that, "ideally we might propose manipulation by tax remission or increase of government expenditures *financed by printing money*" [italics supplied] (1936, p. 108). Here again, we have the view, that during depressions, fiscal measures be used in order to expand the supply of money.

Gideonse's contribution to the 1930's Chicago monetary literature was his 1934 article on "Money and Finance". His views were entirely consistent with those of his Chicago colleagues. At the risk of some repetition therefore — but for the sake of historical documentation — it may be noted that Gideonse likewise eschewed the use of traditional monetary tools during depression. "The banks," he stated, "are already provided with ample 'idle' reserves and a factor explaining their idleness seems to be a general lack of confidence" (1934, p. 751). Furthermore,

> bankers are at present the victims of a group prejudice that leads to pronounced conservatism. Speculative lending in the past has contributed to the present impasse. While the stigma of bad losses of the past is still upon them, new questionable lending is urged... Under the circumstances expansion is difficult to develop (1934, p. 754).

In accord with the Chicagoan interpretation of the depression, Gideonse observed that "many of our difficulties are due to differential rigidities in prices" and require upward movement of product prices induced through money expansion (1934, p. 756). But Gideonse stated, perhaps more explicitly than other Chicagoans, a theme that has been emerging from the present study. "[Public] expenditures," he argued, "are an essential part of a monetary program... [They] *are definitely part of monetary policy*" [italics supplied] (1934, p. 750).

Finally we come to Henry Simons, whose views on fractional-reserve banking have been dealt with previously by Friedman (1967, reprinted in Friedman 1969). Briefly, according to Simons, the character of a fractional reserve system was marked by its instability and acted to further impede the effectiveness of monetary policy.[3] Under a fractional reserve system, the velocities of both currency and deposits — V and V′ — are influenced by the *volume* of near-money substitutes. Therefore, during periods of low levels of confidence when the public moved to increase their cash hoards, banks would find their depositors turning deposits into cash. As a result, the fraction of reserves held against the withdrawn deposits would provide a small cushion against further withdrawals. Hence the banks would be forced to sell their earning assets in order to maintain the statutory reserve proportions. But the conversion process is self-defeating, for while any individual bank can turn its assets into cash, the economy as a whole cannot. Said Simons:

> No real stability of production and employment is possible when short-term lenders are continuously in a position to demand conversion of their investments, amounting in the aggregate to a large multiple of the total available circulating media, into such media... Short-term obligations provide abundant money substitutes during booms, thus releasing money from cash reserves; and they precipitate hopeless efforts at liquidation during depressions (1936, reprinted in Simons 1948, p. 166).

The ineptitude of a fractional-reserve banking system as the basis for expansionary monetary policy was stated succinctly by Douglas. Successful implementation of the expansionary policy requires that new loans and investments actually be made. But, said Douglas,

> if only a few banks start such a policy and the others do not follow suit, then the checks drawn on the newly created accounts will mostly find their way into other banks. The expanding banks will therefore have large adverse balances to meet which will drain their resources and force them to call a sufficient quantity of loans to preserve their balances. The expansion of credit by a fraction of the banks during such periods of depression is therefore self-defeating (1932, p. 79).

[3] This view was shared by the other Chicagoans as well. See, for example, Douglas (1935, pp. 165-177), Gideonse (1933, p. 754), Hart (1936), and Viner (1936, p. 106).

Additional evidence concerning the attitude of 1930's Chicago economists towards policies aimed directly at expanding bank reserves is provided in a joint memorandum dealing with possible depression remedies which was sent to Congressman Samuel B. Pettengill of Indiana on April 26, 1932. The memorandum was signed by twelve University of Chicago economists — including Douglas, Gideonse, Knight, Mints, Simons and Viner.[4] A much discussed depression proposal during the early 1930's was the Glass-Steagall bill of 1932, which aimed at expanding bank reserves by permitting the banks to receive federal reserve notes in return for government bonds. The (Smoot, 1933, p. 1010).

> We agree entirely... as to the inadequacy of the Glass-Steagall bill *and similar expedients*. Little is to be gained merely by easing the circumstances of banks, in a situation where, by virtue of cost-price relations, everyone, including the banks, is anxious to get out of debt. Such measures may retard deflation and prepare the way for recovery; but they can not much mitigate the fundamental maladjustments between prices and costs [italics supplied] (Pettengil, 1932, p. 824).

A year later in 1933, another Chicago memorandum was prepared and sent to Senator Reed Smoot, the chairman of the Senate Finance Committee. Titled *Balancing the Budget*, signees included Douglas, Simons and Viner.[5] Here Chicagoans argued that combating depression required "fiscal policies [which] can and should be controlled with reference to the monetary and credit situation of the nation" (Bane, et al. 1933, p. 1010).

Thus the picture which emerges from all of this is of a group of Chicago economists closely united in their views of depression and necessary depression policy. Chicago economists were arguing during the 1930's that depressions were caused by downward movements in velocity and that proper depression policy required expansion of the money supply to correct the "fundamental maladjustments between prices and costs". They were not, however, "eclectic" as to the proper means by which to implement monetary policy. Open

---

[4] Other signers of the memorandum were Professors Garfield V. Cox, Aaron Director, Harry A. Millis, Henry Schultz, Chester W. Wright, and Theodore O. Yntema.

[5] Other signers were Frank Bane, Paul Betters, Carl Chatters, Simeon E. Leland, Clarence E. Ridley, Donal Slesigner, and L. D. White. The credit for the discovery of both this and the Pettengill memorandums belongs to J. Ronnie Davis (1968).

market operations and rediscounting were considered: (1) time-consuming; (2) subject to the offsetting influence of confidence which induced banks not to want to lend, nor business to borrow; (3) further subject to the unstable character of fractional-reserve banking which made expansion by a small number of banks " self-defeating ". Hence they opted for fiscal measures and delegated traditional monetary policy to an accommodating role. But they were careful to note that deficit budgets were a means of attaining the necessary variations in the money supply. Bond-financed and tax-financed deficits had offsetting effects — indeed, debt-financing of deficits might even be contractionary — and therefore, fiscal measures were a direct way of conducting *monetary policy*.[6]

The consistency with which Chicago economists clung to these views is evidenced with reference to Simons. In a 1934 book review, he called for the "recognition of the decisive importance of fiscal policy for monetary policy" (1934, p. 788). In his 1934 "A Positive Program for Laissez Faire " he diagnosed the depression as a " cost-price maladjustment " (1934, reprinted in Simons 1948, p. 74) and argued that " monetary policy must ultimately be implemented through fiscal arrangements" (1948, p. 321). In a 1942 review article on the fiscal proposals of Alvin Hansen, Simons observed: " There is never any excuse for borrowing save to *prevent* expansion... If we want expansion, the way to get it is by noninterest-bearing issues " (1942, reprinted in Simons 1948, p. 196). Moreover, in his review of Hansen, Simons advanced an observation most pertinent to the present study. Discussing Hansen's earlier conversion from a saving-investment cycle theorist to his later adoption of Keynesian economics, Simons reflected:

> [A] distinction conceals the conversion, namely the distinction between monetary and fiscal measures. Hansen, advocating the latter, thus disassociates himself nominally from monetary theorists by representing such people as advocates of mere central bank action. This provides a lonely category for Mr. Hawtrey, while denying classification to those for whom central bank action is a feeble, inadequate and anomalous implementation of monetary

---

[6] Though the Chicagoans were apparently advocating " Keynesian " notions, this pertains only with respect to money-financed deficits. Keynesians were also arguing during the 1930's for tax-financed and debt-financed deficits and were thus truly advocates of fiscal policy. For a fuller discussion, including an analysis of the differing paradigms of Chicagoans and Keynesians, see (TAVLAS, 1976).

> policy. [The] name at issue [must] be granted to those advocating schemes of monetary... stabilization which would employ all the borrowing, spending, taxing and issue powers of the central government (Simons, 1948, p. 190).

II. Post-Keynesian Chicago Innovations: Frank Knigth (1941)

The preceding discussion has explicated the Chicagoan distinction, during the 1930's depression, between the efficacy of expansionary monetary policy when implemented through fiscal measures and the impotence of such policy when instituted by way of the commercial banking system. A corollary manifestation of the former Chicago tradition was its approach to the quantity theory — a fluctuating velocity variant of the Fisherine equation. During the 1940's and early 1950's, however, a transformation took place in Chicago monetary economics. The transformation was marked by several pertinent contributions, the earliest being Frank Knight's article on " The Business Cycle, Interest, and Money: A Methodological Approach " (1941, reprinted in Knight, 1956).

Knight's article in some respects represents a direct continuation of earlier Chicago views. Thus, though the depression was now part of the past, Knight continued to argue that traditional monetary policy was ineffectual. As his colleagues had argued before him, Knight stated that such policy was hampered by the nature of fractional-reserve banking which could create and destroy money substitutes at will. Hence, " the consequences " of such a banking system for the implementation of monetary policy " are peculiarly serious " (Knight 1956, pp. 211-212). But Knight added a further twist to the earlier Chicagoan view. In order to be effective, open market purchases and discount rate variations required stimulation of investment spending, induced through reductions in the cost of borrowing. Since " the borrowing rate on money, including the rate of yield at which bonds can be sold and the bank rate, is relatively quite unimportant " in the overall cost computations facing a firm, in the real world successful implementation of tradition monetary measures might require extraordinary low — perhaps even negative — rates of interest (1956, p. 215). Knight considered attainment of such low or negative rates unrealistic. Therefore, " any action operating through interest rates can only be effective for moderate fluctuations...

or as a detail in connection with those of major proportion" (1956, pp. 215-216).

Additional lines of continuity bridging earlier Chicago thought with Knight's "Business Cycle" article included similar interpretations of the 1930's depression in terms of price-cost maladjustments, analagous stock-flow monetary transmission mechanisms, and identical Fisherine, MV=PT, macro models. Knight's continued use of Fisher's equation is particularly noteworthy, not only because five years had passed since the appearance of Keynes' *General Theory*, but because he continued to define velocity in transactions terms rather than the more easily measurable (and hence easily defined) income concept.

Despite the foregoing similarities between the views of Knight and the earlier views of his colleagues, there were also important differences. Thus, for the first time, the significance of lag effects was brought home to the Chicago School. Successive implementations of a given economic policy, argued Knight, should be expected to produce variations with respect to both "timing and magnitude" upon a proposed target variable. Hence, he stated that, "variations in an economic cause can never be expected to produce strictly simultaneous variations in effect" (1956, p. 203). More importantly — from the standpoint of the anticipatory nature of his lag analysis — Knight perceived that "this phenomenon of 'disturbance' [between cause and effect] is especially important in monetary theory" (1956, p. 204). Also for the first time, Knight brought to Chicago the Fisherine distinction between real and nominal interest rates. He compared two rates of return — the real rate of return on capital [i.e. the marginal efficiency of capital] and the loan rate of interest on contracts between borrowers and lenders. Calculation of the loan rate requires that "allowance must be made... for foreseen changes in the value of money" (1956, p. 215). "In long-term contracts involving any stipulated exchange ratio, this contractual price will of course be influenced, in a mathematically simple way, by the general market *anticipation* of future price changes" [italics supplied] (1956, p. 218). Recognition of the effect of anticipated price changes on the loan rate of interest enabled Knight to make a distinction which contemporary monetarists make between real and nominal rates of interest. For "the stipulated rate in loan contracts becomes a monetary phenomenon... to the extent [of] prospective changes in the value of the unit in which such contracts are drawn" (1956, p. 221).

" The Business Cycle " introduced another factor which was to attain prominence in subsequent Chicago economics. Capital, which is part of wealth, according to Knight, is analagous to " the present worth of a future income stream " (1956, p. 217). The relevant " future income stream ", however, is not merely " the rate of return on [physical] capital ", but should include the return on *human* capital as well:

> In all essentials, the training or retraining of a laborer... is a matter of investment or the transfer of investment; and the economically rational management of such activity involves the same kind of investment yield calculation as the production of any material instrument or the replacement of such instrument by another (1956, p. 217).

A well-known aspect of Professor Friedman's work is his all-inclusive concept of wealth.

Finally, we come to Knight's treatment of the demand for money. For though the formal cyclical analysis of " The Business Cycle " was couched in terms of Fisher's MV=PT, Knight made several pertinent observations on the factors affecting money demand. Unlike most of his Keynesian contemporaries who included income along with the interest rate as the proper variables in the demand function for money, Knight argued that the relevant constraint upon total money holdings is wealth. Thus,

> The economic process in a pecuniary economy involves the holding or owning, by somebody, of wealth — all the wealth of the economy — and also the entire stock of money. Hence every property owner has the alternative either of holding money up to the amount of his fortune or of choosing the concrete kind of wealth other than money that he will hold (1956, p. 210).

As to the relevant opportunity cost of holding cash balances, Knight was critical of Keynes' notion that the rate of interest on long-term bonds be used to represent this cost. Here he was essentially repeating an argument he had originally advanced in a 1937 review of the *General Theory*:

> The things equilibrated are the desirability of holding cash and the desirability of holding wealth in any other form, the relation between the two being dependent upon the relative quantities of

> cash and other forms of wealth and upon other factors, among which the money prices of other wealth items can hardly be ignored (1937, p. 112).

Hence,

> [Anyone] can consume or hold wealth, and if he holds wealth he can hold it in the form of money or real things — and the latter, of course, in innumerable forms (1937, p. 113).

These statements are suggestive of a portfolio analysis of the demand for money, the importance of which is heightened when coupled with the following remark from his "Business Cycle" article concerning the effects of an expanded money supply:

> Of course if created currency is used exclusively to buy bonds, or to construct new equipment, it can temporarily raise the relative price which the principal, or source, will yield. Such an occurrence is a temporary disturbance only. As a monetary change diffuses through the economy, it comes to affect all classes of prices in the same way... (1941, p. 223).

Apparently Knight visualized a monetary transmission mechanism affecting a broad spectrum of assets — "bonds or new equipment" — "in the same way". Such a perception of the monetary process follows directly from his 1937 suggestion of a portfolio demand for money encompassing assets in "innumerable forms".

It can be seen, then, that there is much in Knight's earlier work which was to anticipate later Chicagoan views. Knight's contributions include: (1) recognition of the importance of lags for monetary theory; (2) adjustment of the loan rate of interest for anticipated price changes, thereby distinguishing the monetary (or loan) rate from the real rate; (3) the division of capital into human as well as physical components; (4) the constraint on the demand for money is wealth; (5) a demand function for money which included a broad spectrum of assets; (6) a monetary transmission mechanism incorporating direct effects on both financial and real assets. In many respects, Knight's particular formulations of these aforementioned contributions were simplistic. Nor did he succesfully integrate them into a consistent analytic framework. But they remain significant nonetheless, for they convey a definite indication of the flavor of the ideas that must have filled the air at Chicago during the early 1940's.

Lloyd Mints (1946, 1950)

The Chicago version of the quantity theory underwent further evolvement as a result of the contributions of Mints. As with Knight, however, much of Mints' monetary economics is repetitive of earlier Chicago views. This is especially so with respect to Mints' evaluation of the ineffectiveness of open market operations and discounting as policy instruments. Thus in a 1946 paper on "Monetary Policy" and in a subsequent volume *Monetary Policy for a Competitive Society* (1950), Mints was arguing against stabilizing aggregate demand through traditional monetary measures.[7] "It takes time", he said, "for the central bank to make its rates policy effective in the market and in the short-run the demand for funds, particularly short-term funds, is inelastic" (1946, p. 63). Therefore, "it is unlikely that there would be much, if any, immediate effect on aggregate demand in consequence of open market operations [or discount rate manipulations]" (1950, p. 202). Nevertheless, stabilization, according to Mints, required offsetting changes in aggregate demand (MV) with countercyclical variations in the money stock. Such necessary variations in money could in turn be achieved through use of fiscal measures. As his colleagues were arguing during the 1930's, Mints was arguing a decade later that "fiscal operations of the national government have monetary consequences". They are a way by which to "carry through monetary policy" (1946, p. 63). And, "budget deficits and surpluses... and the borrowing and redemption operations of the Treasury, all have monetary significance" (1946, p. 63). In periods of contracting aggregate demand, deficits should be created for the purpose of expanding the monetary stock. However, deficits financed by selling government bonds were thought, by Mints, to be contractionary: "To finance federal expenditures... the need is for money, and that being the case, money, not bonds, should be issued; and when inflation is imminent, money should be withdrawn" (1946, p. 66). The preceding views are entirely consistent with those emanating from Chicago during the 1930's.

But there were also extensions of former Chicagoan thought in Mints' writings. Recall that while Knight had made some important insights into the demand for money, his formal cyclical analysis was

---

7 In addition to the reasons advanced in the text, Mints also eschewed traditional monetary tools due to the unstable character of fractional-reserve banking (MINTS 1950, p. 7).

couched in terms of velocity. Mints' formal analysis of depressions, however, involved a simultaneous juxtaposition of velocity with money demand — symbolic of the gradual Chicagoan replacement of the former concept with the latter. Said Mints: "Unemployment growing out of a rise in the propensity to hoard is a monetary phenomenon... in the sense that the proximate cause is a change in the velocity of circulation of money" (1950, p. 29). And while velocity (or the demand for money) was still considered an unstable function of the volume of near moneys and price expectations (i.e. confidence) it by no means was definite that depressions were due solely to downward shifts in velocity as had been previously argued by Chicagoans. For "though a depression [may be initiated] by an increase in liquidity preferences" it may also "be caused by a reduction in the quantity of money" (1946, p. 60). "It is quite possible that in some instances a decline in the stock of money has been the initiating factor in bringing on depressions" (1950, p. 37). Mints, therefore, was on the road to the modern Chicagoan view which adduces business fluctuations primarily to movements in the money stock.

In his *Monetary Policy for a Competitive Society* Mints discussed the demand for money in detail. Keynes, he argued, assumed that an increase in the demand for money would raise the level of interest rates. But said Mints, "we have three factors to be kept in equilibrium: the quantity of money [demanded], the rate of interest, and the general price level" (1950, p. 34). Keynes' view was that changes in the demand for money primarily affect the demand for long-term bonds. Mints, however, stated that "an increase... in the demand for cash may be at the expense of any one or more of several ways [an individual] might have disposed of income" (1950, p. 30). He listed the following possibilities:

(1) Purchase of consumers' goods.
(2) Purchase of producers' goods.
(3) Lend on short-term.
(4) Purchase of long-term bonds.
(5) Purchase of corporation shares (1950, p. 30).

Mints argued that an increase in the demand for money is primarily at the expense of consumers' and producers' goods though it probably also affects the demand for long-term bonds. Hence "the rate of interest [is] a matter of decidedly minor importance" in the "total demand of the community for cash" [8] (1950, p. 35). It can be seen then, that Mints stated in a more explicit manner than Knight a portfolio approach to the demand for money. Knight's portfolio analysis was heightened when presented in conjunction with a simplistic, but broad monetary transmission mechanism. The same applies to Mints who — though he had little faith in the efficacy of open market operations — observed:

> The effect of changes in cash balances on aggregate demand in consequence of open-market operations might conceivably come either indirectly, through changes in the rate of interest, or directly, through an immediate effect on the demand for consumers' or producers' goods (1950, p. 198).

In both his 1946 paper on "Monetary Policy" and in his 1950 volume on *Monetary Policy for a Competitive Society* Mints advanced another view which is currently associated with contemporary Chicago. This had to do with Federal Reserve behavior during the early stages of the 1930's depression. According to Mints, rather than being characterized by expansionary monetary policies, the period was instead characterized by a lack of "sufficiently vigorous action... taken by central banks, and particularly... by the Federal Reserve System" (1946, p. 62). Thus,

> Our mistakes are to be found... in our failure to follow an enlightened policy in the months and years immediately following the autumn of 1929. Neither the Reserve System nor the Federal government made any significant effort to prevent a drastic decline in the quantity of money, to say nothing of the much needed increase, from 1929 to 1932. This is where we blundered (1950, p. 129).

In his 1950 work, Mints supplied empirical data confirming the correlation between the decline in the money stock with the concurrent drops in wholesale prices and industrial production during the depres-

---

8 Friedman states: "I too tend to minimize changes in market interest rates as the primary channel through which changes in the quantity of money affect spending, output, and prices" (1972a, p. 945).

sion. Some years later Friedman and Schwartz (1963) validated Mints' insight concerning the Federal Reserve's behavior during the period, 1929-1933.[9]

To avoid depressions in the first place, Mints thought that the general (wholesale) price level should be kept stable. Because he viewed velocity as variable, he thought price stability might best be attained through the necessary variations in the supply of money. Nevertheless, in his 1946 article he considered the possibility of increasing "the quantity of money at some constant rate, roughly equivalent to the rate of increase in output" (1946, p. 61). Mints thought this growth-rate rule an "acceptable" alternative, but opted instead for discretionary price stabilization. A growth-rate rule was not suited to take account of fluctuations in velocity. He maintained his preference for direct price-level stability in his 1950 work, but with less conviction. There were, he recognized, "difficulties" which were associated with such a policy:

> The possible difficulties that might be encountered in price-level stabilization are two: (1) the lag in the effect of the monetary action, and (2) the discretionary power that would have to be given to some administrative official in regard to the amount of open-market operations (1950, pp. 171-172).

Friedman has advanced similar arguments against discretionary stabilization. Thus he states that "monetary changes take time to affect the economy, and the time delay is itself highly variable". Furthermore, he prefers a monetary rule because, for one thing, it "would insulate monetary policy... from the arbitrary power of a small group of men not subject to control by the electorate" (1972b, p. 66).

Moreover, from the standpoint of the overall philosophy of the role of monetary policy in economic life, there is striking similarity between Friedman's view and that of Mints. In his important 1967 Presidential address before the American Economics Association, Friedman's theme was partly "what monetary policy cannot do". As to what monetary policy can accomplish, Friedman states that it can "provide a monetary climate favorable to the effective operation of those basic forces of enterprise, ingenuity, invention, hard work and thrift that are the true springs of economic growth. That is

[9] During the 1930's Viner was critical of the Federal Reserves' behavior during the initial years of the depression. But Viner's view was not shared by other Chicagoans and therefore not part of Chicago's "mainstream" economics.

the most that we can ask from monetary policy at our present stage of knowledge " (1968, reprinted in Friedman 1969, p. 110). Similarly, Mints observed:

> The level of production and employment are not amendable to control by monetary measures, except in the sense that monetary stability will provide the conditions in which a high level of output and employment will be maintained (1950, p. 117).
> Monetary policy is no panacea for the ills of society; but it can be of powerful, even though indirect, aid in dealing with them (1950, p. 229).

Thus as in the case of Knight, the Chicago quantity theory continued to undergo improvement at the hands of Mints. The latter's contributions include: (1) incorporating the concept of the demand for money on an equal setting with velocity into his formal cyclical analysis; (2) recognition that reductions in the quantity of money — independently of velocity — could initiate a depression; (3) the development of a more clearly stated portfolio demand for money than had earlier been formed by Knight; (4) an associated broad monetary transmission mechanism resulting from open market operations; (5) criticism of the Fed's failure " to prevent a drastic decline in the quantity of money " during the early years of the depression; (6) empirical validation of the decline in the money stock from 1929-1932; (7) consideration of a monetary growth-rate rule as an " acceptable " policy guide; (8) recognition of lag effects and problems of discretionary power involved with direct price-level stabilization; (9) the view that monetary policy should be considered an indirect, yet powerful, instrument from which to pursue economic expansion.

Milton Friedman (1948, 1951, 1952)

Friedman's early monetary work is in many respects a continuation of the views of his Chicago mentors and colleagues. Thus in a 1948 paper, " A Monetary and Fiscal Framework for Economic Stability " (reprinted in Friedman 1953), he shares the Chicagoan disenchantment towards traditional monetary tools. Fractional reserve banking, he argues, allows the monetary authorities to have large discretionary powers over the creation and destruction of the money supply. Hence, Friedman calls for the adoption of Simons' plan of 100 per cent reserves. But Friedman goes further. Noting that the adoption of 100 per cent reserves would "reduce the discretionary powers of the reserve system by eliminating re-discounting and existing powers over reserve requirements", he also calls for "the elimination of... the existing powers to engage in open-market operations" (1953, p. 136). As a result, monetary policy should be conducted with reference to the government's fiscal operations:

> Deficits or surpluses in the government budget would be reflected dollar for dollar in changes in the quantity of money; and conversely, the quantity of money would change only as a consequence of deficits or surpluses. A deficit means an increase in the quantity of money, a surplus a decrease (1953, p. 140).

Moreover, Friedman recognized that financing deficits through money creation is more expansionary than either levying taxes or issuing interest-bearing securities (1953, p. 140).

Given that deficits should be financed by the issue of money, what particular monetary transmission mechanism did Friedman envisage? Purely one in which additions to the money stock represent additions to assets and thereby increase the average propensity to consume via wealth effects. "The resultant increase in the aggregate stock of money [a result of the deficit]", he says, "must further raise the real value of the community's stock of assets and hence the average propensity to consume" (1953, p. 152). It was not until his "Comments on Monetary Policy" in 1951 (reprinted in Friedman 1953) that Friedman began to envisage a broader transmission mechanism along the lines previously suggested by Knight and Mints. Discussing the effects of a rise in the rate of interest — brought about by open-market sales — on investment expenditure, Friedman stated,

> 'Investment' in this context includes not only expenditures on plant and equipment but also business expenditures on inventories and goods in process and consumer expenditures on durable goods and houses (1953, pp. 269-270).

In addition, "Comments on Monetary Policy" included a turnabout on Friedman's views concerning the implementation of monetary policy — though largely a result of his desire to halt inflation. Nevertheless, he stated: "At the present time and under existing conditions [of inflation], monetary policy... must take the form primarily of open-market operations in government securities" (1953,

p. 265). Once inflation was controlled, however, Friedman reiterated his belief that 100 per cent reserve banking be instituted and discretionary monetary policies be abolished. But such reform was now delegated to the " long-run " (1953, p. 265). Finally, " Comments on Monetary Policy " contained explicit reference to the " two alternative languages " through which the monetary process could be discussed — " that of the quantity theory or that of Keynesian analysis" (1953, p. 268). Friedman implied his preference for the former and then proceeded to present his broad view of investment spending.

Friedman's demarcation between the quantity theory approach and that of Keynesian income-expenditure analysis was carried over into his " Price, Income and Monetary Changes in Three Wartime Periods " (1952, reprinted in Friedman 1969). But Friedman here presented the two approaches — perhaps for the first time in the literature — as two alternative, empirically testable hypotheses. The empirical results of the article are important because they led Friedman to conclude that " the velocity of circulation of money is [an] empirical variable that behaves in a stable or consistent fashion " and that changes in the money stock are primarily responsible for changes in nominal income and prices (1969, pp. 166-170). Friedman continued to assert, however, — in the tradition of Chicago — that: " The level of expenditures and of taxation... [are important] because of their effects on the stock of money per unit of output, and they are only important insofar as they have such effects " (1969, p. 170).

Concluding Remarks

The 1930's Chicago School is especially notable for its unique variable-velocity approach to the quantity theory and the consensus of its members that depression should be combated by expanding the money supply. The consensus among the Chicagoans extended to the view concerning the inefficacy of traditional monetary policy in correcting price-cost maladjustments and to the efficacy of monetary policy when conducted through variations in government expenditures and receipts. These views continued to be representative of Chicagoan monetary economics during the 1940's and early 1950's. Moreover, contributions by Knight, Mints, and Friedman extended the quantity-theory foundations at Chicago throughout these latter years. The current Chicagoan view that deficits financed solely by money creation are a means of conducting monetary policy (Friedman 1972, p. 715) dates back to the Chicago tradition of the 1930's.

In light of the aforementioned contributions by Knight, Mints, and Friedman, the " Restatement " of the quantity theory by Friedman in 1956 is accordingly a culmination of the evolvement of the Chicago tradition. The " Restatement " should not, however, be viewed as a reflection of the then existing state of Chicago monetary economics. For as Friedman has rightly acknowledged: " After all, I am not unwilling to accept some credit for the theoretical analysis in that article " (1972a, p. 941). But Friedman's contributions in the " Restatement " *should* be viewed as a sequential extension of the Chicagoan approach rather than reflecting the adoption of Keynesian monetary economics by Friedman. If Friedman's portfolio demand for money is Keynesian, it is also Chicagoan due to the elaborations of portfolio analysis by Knight and Mints. Moreover, the development of a broad monetary transmission mechanism by Knight, Mints and Friedman, in conjunction with the latter's empirically-determined stable velocity function in 1953, led to the affirmation of traditional monetary policy at Chicago during the mid and late 1950's. At about the same time, the Keynesian monetary tradition bred Radcliffism elsewhere. For these reasons, and from the additional vantage of the hereditable nature of his entire monetary framework, Friedman's monetary economics forms a direct bridge to the quantity-theory views of his Chicago mentors.

New York

George S. Tavlas

REFERENCES

Aschheim, Joseph, " Monetarism Versus Fiscalism: Towards Reconciliation ", in this *Review*. 114, September 1975, pp. 223-31.

Davis, J. Ronnie. " Chicago Economists, Deficits Budgets, and the Early 1930's. " *A.E.R.* 38 (June 1968), pp. 476-82.

Douglas, Paul H. " Money, Credit and the Depression. " *The World Tomorrow*. 15 (March 1932), pp. 78-80.

Douglas, Paul H. " Should We Reflate? " *The World Tomorrow*. 16 (February 1933), pp. 129-30. (a).

Douglas, Paul H. *Collapse or Cycle?* Chicago: American Library Association, 1933. (b)

Douglas, Paul H. " Introduction " to *No More Unemployed* (by J.B. Cheadle, H.O. Eaton, and A.M. Ewing). Norman, Oklahoma: University of Oklahoma Press, 1934.

DOUGLAS, PAUL H. *Controlling Depressions*. New York: W. W. Norton and Company, 1935.

FRIEDMAN, MILTON. " A Monetary and Fiscal Framework for Economic Stability. " *A.E.R.* 38 (June 1948), pp. 245-64; reprinted in Friedman 1953.

FRIEDMAN, MILTON. " Comments on Monetary Policy ". *Review of Economics and Statistics. 33* (August 1951), pp. 179-200; reprinted in Friedman 1953.

FRIEDMAN, MILTON. " Price, Income, and Monetary Changes in Three Wartime Periods. " *A E.R.* 42 (May 1952); reprinted in Friedman 1969.

FRIEDMAN, MILTON. *Essays in Positive Economics*. Chicago: Univ. of Chicago Press, 1953.

FRIEDMAN, MILTON. " The Quantity Theory of Money - a Restatement ". In *Studies in the Quantity Theory of Money*, edited by M. Friedman. Chicago: Univ. of Chicago Press, 1956; reprinted in Friedman 1969.

FRIEDMAN, MILTON. " The Monetary Theory and Policy of Henry Simons. " *J. Law and Econ.* 10 (October 1967); reprinted in Friedman 1969.

FREDMAN, MILTON. " The Role of Monetary Policy. " *A.E.R.* 58 (March 1968); reprinted in Friedman 1969.

FRIEDMAN, MILTON. *The Optimum Quantity of Money and Other Essays*. Chicago: Aldine, 1969.

FRIEDMAN, MILTON. " Comments of the Critics. " *J.P.E.* 80 (September/October 1972), pp. 906-50. (a)

FRIEDMAN, MILTON " The Case for a Monetary Rule. " In *An Economist's Protest* by M. Friedman. New Jersey: Thomas Horton, 1972. (b).

FRIEDMAN, MILTON, and SCHWARTZ, ANNA J. *A Monetary History of the United States, 1867-1960*. Princeton, N.J.: Princeton Univ. Press, 1963.

GIDEONSE, HARRY D. " Money and Finance. " *The American Journal of Sociology*. 39 (May 1934), pp. 749-58.

HART, ALBERT G. " The ' Chicago Plan ', of Banking Reform. " *The Review of Economic Studies*. 2 (1934-35), pp. 104-116.

JOHNSON, HARRY G. " The Keynesian Revolution and the Monetarist Counter-Revolution. " Richard T. Ely lecture. *A.E.R.* 61 (May 1971), pp. 1-14.

KEYNES, JOHN MAYNARD. *The General Theory of Employment, Interest and Money*. New York: Harcourt Brace, 1936.

KNIGHT, FRANK H. " Unemployment: And Mr. Keynes's Revolution in Economic Theory. " *Canadian Journal of Economics and Political Science*. 3 (February 1937), pp. 100-23.

KNIGHT, FRANK H. " The Business Cycle Interest, and Money: A Methodological Approach. " *Review of Economic Statistics*. 23 (May 1941); reprinted in F. Knight 1956.

KNIGHT, FRANK H. *On the History and Method of Economics*. Chicago: Univ. of Chicago Press, 1956.

MINTS, LLOYD W. " Monetary Policy. " *Review of Economic Statistics*. 28 (May 1946), pp. 60-69.

MINTS, LLOYD W. *Monetary Policy for a Competitive Society*. New York: McGraw Hill, 1950.

MOGGRIDGE, D.E., and HOWSON, SUSAN. " Keynes on Monetary Policy 1910-1946. " Oxford Economic Papers. 26 (1974), pp. 226-47.

PATINKIN, DON. " The Chicago Tradition, the Quantity Theory, and Friedman. " *Journal of Money, Credit and Banking*. 1 (February 1969), pp. 46-70.

PATINKIN, DON. " On the Short-Run Non-Neutrality of Money in the Quantity Theory." In this *Review*. 100 (March 1972), pp. 3-22. (a)

PATINKIN, DON. " Keynesian Monetary Theory and the Cambridge School. " In this *Review*. 101 (June 1972), pp. 138-58. (b)

PATINKIN, DON. " Friedman on the Quantity Theory and Keynesian Economics. " *J.P.E.* (September/October 1972), pp. 883-905. (c)

PETTENGILL, SAMUEL B. " Memorandum: Payment of Adjusted-Compensation Certificates. " *U.S. Cong., House of Representatives*, Committee on Ways and Means, 72d Cong., 1st Session, 1932.

SIMONS, HENRY C. " Economic Reconstruction: The Columbia Report. " *J.P.E.* 42 (December 1934), pp. 795-99.

SIMONS, HENRY C. " A Positive Program for Laissez Faire " in *Economic Policy for a Free Society*. Chicago: Univ. of Chicago Press, 1948.

SIMONS, HENRY C. " Hansen on Fiscal Policy. " *J.P.E.* 50 (April 1942), pp. 161-96; reprinted in Simons, 1948.

SMOOT, REED. " Memorandum on Balancing the Budget. " *U.S. Cong.*, Senate Finance Committee. 72d Cong., 2d Session, 1933.

TAVLAS, GEORGE S. " Some Further Observations on the Monetary Economics of Chicagoans and Non-Chicagoans. " *Southern Economic Journal*. 42 (April 1976), pp. 685-92.

VINER, JACOB. " Inflation as a Remedy for Depression. " *Proceedings of the Institute of Public Affairs*. Athens, Ga.: Univ. of Georgia, 1933.

VINER, JACOB. "Inflation: Menace or Bogey?" *Yale Review*. 31 (June 1942), pp. 684-702.

'On Monetarism and Ideology'

J. Aschheim and G. S. Tavlas, 'On monetarism and ideology', *Banca Nazionale Del Lavoro Quarterly Review* (June 1979), pp. 167–86.

On Monetarism and Ideology*

I. Introduction

In the course of the current probing of monetarism versus fiscalism, a newly raised subject is the relationship, if any, between monetarism and ideology. Specifically, does monetarism imply or presuppose espousal of a laissez-faire political economy? In turn, have all notable monetarists been laissez-faire proponents? Correspondingly, does any rejection of monetarism imply or presuppose opposition to a laissez-faire political economy? In turn, have all notable nonmonetarists been laissez-faire opponents? In recent writings, such authors as Tobin (1974, pp. 62-3), Mayer (1975, pp. 307-08), and Stein (1976, p. 2) have suggested that the association of right-wing ideology with monetarism is not inherent in the content of monetarism.[1] Tobin, in particular, argues that the widespread attribution of right-wing ideology to the modern quantity theory of money is due to the institutional coincidence of the espousal of both the theory and the ideology in the University of Chicago. Beyond these passing references, however, little supporting evidence and little probing of the monetarism-ideology nexus are to be found in the literature.

The indication of a unique 1930s Chicago monetary tradition by Friedman (1956) provides a useful point of departure for consideration of the conceptual connection between monetarism and ideology.

---

* We have benefited from helpful comments by Thomas Mayer

[1] Mayer (1975) does, however, discuss the interrelations between various monetarist propositions and Keynesian economics. Mayer also distinguishes between the quantity theory of money and monetarism in terms of a set of criteria among which the quantity theory is included. Alternatively, monetarism may be viewed as having undergone an evolution in the early phases of which the quantity theory itself was coterminous with monetarism.

Acknowledging Nobay and Johnson's affirmation that "The historical perspective has been a relatively neglected dimension in much of the debate between monetarism and Keynesianism" (1977, p. 471), this essay examines the evolution of the quantity theory at Chicago during the formative 1930s in the context of the ideological articulations of the theory's principal exponents. In turn, the essay also probes into the linkage between opposition to monetarism and the left-right ideological cleavage.

Briefly to anticipate, the coexistence of two strands of monetarism can be identified in Chicago's 1930s monetary tradition. The distinctiveness of these two strands is marked by a variety of features: (a) the interpretation of the causal role of money in initiating cyclical fluctuations, (b) policy prescription for economic stabilization, and (c) the ideological bent of the expositors. It turns out that Friedman's advancement of the quantity theory reflects the dominance of a right-wing version of Chicago's 1930s monetarism over a coexisting left-wing version. Thus, the irony of this dominance, and of the consequent neglect of the left-wing version in the current literature, is that the left-wing version is in important respects more anticipatory of modern Chicago monetary economics than the dominant right-wing version. Hence, it is demonstrated that monetarism is not uniquely assignable to a single ideological bent. Correspondingly, it is also demonstrated that the negation of monetarism, despite the dominance of left-wing ideology among its expositors, does not necessarily presuppose or imply rejection of a laissez-faire political economy.

II. Money, the Business Cycle, and the Chicago Tradition

Though the exegesis of a distinctive Chicago monetary heritage where "money mattered" had been provided by Friedman in his 1956 "Restatement" of the quantity theory, more than a decade was to elapse before the polemics concerning the relevance of that heritage were kindled. Evidently, this was because consideration of the writings and teachings of an earlier generation of Chicago economists increased in importance only as monetarist interpretations began to dominate the macro-economic literature. The increased acceptance of monetarism in the late 1960s and early 1970s induced several of its foremost adherents — notably Friedman (1970 [a]) and Brunner

(1970) — to aver the existence of a monetarist counter-revolution. However, the validation of a counter-revolutionary movement requires the establishment of a "plausible linkage with pre-Keynesian orthodoxy" (Johnson, 1971, p. 10). Yet the claim to such a linkage had already been made in Friedman's "Restatement", and, as a result, the emergence of the neo-quantity theory of money stimulated research into the monetary doctrines of the 1930s Chicago School.

A definitive delineation of the contributions of Chicagoans who wrote on and/or taught monetary economics during the 1930s — in particular Henry Simons, Frank Knight, Lloyd Mints, and Jacob Viner — is due to Patinkin (1969; 1972 [a]; 1972 [b]). Patinkin contrasts the earlier Chicago tradition, characterized by its variable velocity adaptation of the Fisherine equation of exchange, with Friedman's stable portfolio approach to the demand for money. Thus, whereas contemporary monetarists attribute fluctuations in economic activity and the occurrence of inflation to prior movements in the money stock, Friedman's Chicago predecessors were arguing that business cycles were generated by a fluctuating velocity of circulation. The money supply was a passive element in the business-cycle diagnosis developed by the 1930s Chicago School, an element capable of exacerbating, but not of initiating, economic fluctuations.[2] Evidently, the volume of money was not considered most important.[3]

There is however, more to the earlier Chicago business-cycle diagnosis than has been conveyed in the recent literature. As noted in the preceding section, there did exist at Chicago a particularly anticipatory adaptation of Fisher's MV = PT, distinguishable both by the causal role it assigned to money in initiating economic fluctuations and by its policy orientation. This largely neglected strand of 1930s Chicago monetarism was contributed by Paul Douglas, as will be discussed below. Additionally, further consideration of the Simons-Knight approach reveals that though monetary factors were ascribed a subordinate role in the causal mechanism underlying the cycle, proper control of the money stock was deemed essential in preventing the cycle from occurring. Accordingly, money was ushered-in through the back door and ultimately held center stage.

---

[2] A description of this process is provided in FRIEDMAN (1967).

[3] Several writers, using Patinkin's work as their source, deny outright the existence of an earlier Chicago quantity-theory tradition. In this context, see JOHNSON (1971; 1972), TEIGEN (1971, p. 244) and MOGGRIDGE and HOWSON (1974, p. 227).

In addition to the primacy accorded to a variant velocity of circulation as the *modus operandi* of its analysis, a striking aspect of the Simons-Knight formulation of business-cycle causation is its unsystematic endeavor to inquire into the factors underlying the variations of velocity. For example, Simons, in an unpublished 1933 monograph, attributed depressions to "some fortuitous disturbance (perhaps a mere speculative scare) which happens to establish a sharp reversal of the trend in product prices" (1933, p. 5). The following year, Simons adduced a declining velocity as due to an overtaking of product prices by factor costs "for any reason" with adverse subsequent implications for business profits (1934, p. 55). Similarly, Knight attributed depressions to such factors as "the overtaking of prices by costs, a crop failure, any calamity in the business world, or mere 'psychology'" (1941, p. 214). Viner argued that a declining velocity was due to a general prevalence of "fear" within the community resulting in sudden reversals of confidence (1932, p. 18). Such attitudes of "fear", according to Viner, were sparked by specific events such as the occurrence of a stock-market crash (1931, pp. 174-75).[4] Still another Chicagoan, Harry Gideonse, in a neglected 1934 paper on "Money and Finance", argued in terms of "structural difficulties which exhaust the private stimulus to enterprise" (1934, p. 749).

The 1930s Chicagoans perceived a continually fluctuating unit of value as an inherent aspect of economic life. For whatever reasons the variation in the unit of value occurs, they regarded it as leading through rigid costs to corresponding changes in profits and production. Thus,

> A standard of value fluctuating erratically in its own value must be an important factor in initiating and in accentuating the recurrent cycles of expansion and depression from which the world has suffered: Jacob Viner (1932, p. 35).
>
> Surely nothing could be more unsettling to an economic system than the fundamental uncertainty of its measure of value: Harry Gideonse (1932, p. 5).
>
> The currency system [is one of] the roots of the immediate difficulty: Frank Knight (1933, p. 422).

---

[4] In 1964, VINER argued that the 1930s depression "resulted from epidemic fear, and one of the major fears was that prices would fall still further (given an initial decline)" (1964, p. 19).

Indeed, Friedman's Chicago predecessors were so firmly convinced that a fluctuating price level — in the face of a rigid cost structure — was the rationale of the business cycle, that further theoretical exploration was considered unnecessary. In this vein, Knight succinctly stated: "Too much attention has been given to this problem of the cause of the collapse" (1941, p. 214). Likewise, Simons observed: "I am strengthened in the conviction that the sooner we quit talking about business cycle theory as a major field of inquiry, the better" (1942, p. 186). And Mints argued that the study of the causal forces underlying upswings and downswings "is a matter of secondary importance" (1946, p. 60).

In contrast to the short shrift they gave the diagnosis of economic fluctuations, the aforementioned Chicago monetarists were preoccupied with the policy aspects of countering the cycle, and recent research supporting the relevance of that tradition appropriately stresses its policy orientation.[5] Given the volatility of the price level and the consequently fluctuating velocity of circulation of money, economic stabilization was deemed to require discretionary variations in the money supply to maintain price-level stability. In the words of Knight: "An approximate constancy in general prices, or in the relation between product prices and wages, can in the nature of the case be achieved by deliberate action, based on constant attention, correcting or off-setting incipient tendencies to expansion or contraction" (1941, p. 224). Accordingly, in view of the overriding importance attached to regulation of the money stock in the pursuit of economic stability, the message emanating from the earlier Chicago tradition clearly was that the behavior of money did matter.

In turn, money behavior was also important in the neglected and largely isolated version of 1930s Chicago monetarism developed by Paul Douglas.[6] Celebrated for his work on production functions, Douglas independently formulated a theory of the business cycle directly relevant to contemporaneous monetarist thought. Briefly summarized, Douglas, who in accord with his Chicago colleagues, used the Fisherine equation of exchange as his analytic framework, stressed the interdependence of the various terms within the equation. But unlike his colleagues who ascribed cycles to variations in

---

[5] See Davis (1968; 1971), Friedman (1972), and Tavlas (1976; 1977[a]; 1977 [b]).

[6] A systematic discussion of Douglas's monetary views is contained in his *Controlling Depressions* (1935). For additional references, see Tavlas (1977 [b]).

velocity, Douglas argued that business fluctuations were caused by the failure of the money supply to increase proportionately with the secular rise in the production of goods. Thus, if the money stock expanded at a slower pace than production, prices would have to fall in order to permit the glut of goods in the market to be cleared. But because current product prices would embody relatively higher costs that were previously paid out, profit margins would fall and output would decline, thus triggering a recession. A conversely expansionary sequence would ensue, were the money stock to grow in excess of the secular pace of expansion in the production of goods. Hence, according to Douglas, the root cause of the business cycle was entirely a monetary one.

In consequence, Douglas held that economic stability necessitated reliance on either of two key indicators. Either the unemployment rate could be maintained within a certain range, or the price level could be kept stable. Attainment of either of these two goals could be achieved "if the quantity of purchasing power were to be increased at the rate of 3 to 4 percent a year, or the long-time rate of production" (1935, p. 185). This policy norm is, of course, strikingly reminiscent of the monetary growth-rate rule advocated by contemporary monetarists. Douglas originally espoused this norm in a 1927 paper on "The Modern Technique of Mass Production and its Relation to Wages" (1927, p. 40), and continued to do so in a series of writings culminating in his 1935 volume *Controlling Depressions*.

No similar advocacy of the monetary growth-rate rule, however, is to be found in the writings of Douglas's Chicago colleagues during the 1930s who opted instead for discretionary changes in the money stock. Additionally, Douglas broadened the quantity theory framework to incorporate such innovations as a Wicksell-Keynes savings-investment analysis, an accompanying multiplier mechanism à la Keynes-Kahn, and an accelerator principle in the vein of J.M. Clark. Such broadening of the quantity theory is not paralleled in the writings of Douglas's Chicago colleagues Simons, Knight, Mints, and Viner.

In sum, we have delineated the coexistence of two disparate threads of monetarism at Chicago during the 1930s. The Simon-Knight formulation relates to the contemporary quantity theory primarily in terms of the essential role assigned to money regulation as a stabilization device — with the important contrasting proviso that money regulation is to be discretionary. On the other hand, Douglas is seen to anticipate more directly subsequent monetarist doctrine in terms of his monetary theory of the business cycle and in his seminal formulation of the monetary growth-rate rule.

The two diverse versions of the 1930s Chicago monetarism have in common several elements of fiscal and monetary policy. Indeed, as early as in 1927, Douglas has advocated the use of governmental budget deficits financed by money creation as a means to combat depressions. His argument was that traditional banking measures might fail during a depression because of the existence of low levels of confidence among both lenders and borrowers of funds. Since proper depression policy required an expansion of the supply of money so as to raise product prices and thereby profits, an alternative method of conducting monetary policy would be to create public-works projects financed by printing money. Douglas noted that bond-financed and tax-financed deficits were less desirable as they entail crowding-out effects.

The next Chicagoan to be associated with the advocacy of money-financed deficits as a depression tool was Aaron Director, who did so in 1931 (his first year on the Chicago faculty), in a volume which he coauthored with Douglas, titled *The Problem of Unemployment* (1931). In subsequent years two joint memoranda[7] from Chicago were coauthored, both advocating the use of public works projects and money-financed deficits as essential antidepression policy. The rationale of the memoranda was entirely in accord with Douglas's 1927 paper: money creation-financed deficits would be effective because they would raise product prices faster than factor costs. The signatures of Douglas, Simons, and Viner appeared on both memoranda, while those of Director, Gideonse, Knight, and Mints appeared on either of the two. Given the similarity between the reasoning of these documents and the views that Douglas had been advancing as early as 1927, it is reasonable to infer that Douglas was primarily responsible for the Chicagoan advocacy of budget deficits during the early 1930s. Douglas, in turn, had accepted Simons's argument during this period concerning the disruptive influence of near-monies on economic stability as well as Simons's accompanying policy proposal of 100 percent reserve requirements.

---

[7] See PETTENGILL (1932) and SMOOT (1933).

III. The Chicago Tradition and Ideology

The University of Chicago is widely regarded as a fulcrum for the espousal of the free-enterprise economy.[8] This pre-eminent fosterage of the virtues of laissez-faire is traceable to the writings of Knight, Simons, Viner, and Mints during the 1930s. Concurrent, however, with the extolling of private enterprise by these economists was the contrary ideological pronouncement in the writings of Paul Douglas.

According to Douglas, the doctrine of laissez-faire was not as detached from material interests as its philosophical proponents were prone to argue. "On the contrary, it acquired dominance because the owners of industrial, commercial, and financial capital correctly judged that it would most favor them" (1933, p. 185). Hence, capitalistic governments had an inherent propertied-class proclivity:

> Those who own the property in this country have an enormous advantage. They can withhold the use of their property but the worker cannot withhold very long the use of his labor (1932[b], p. 104).

Thus, challenging the norm of the neutral state enshrined in laissez-faire advocacy, Douglas contended that there was much truth in the Marxian claim that "we have in reality a class state which reflects the interests of the most powerful economic classes both in what it does and what it does not do in the fields of legislation, administration, and judicial opinion" (1933, p. 186). And though the working class could strike against the source of power, the existing political structure would assure the futility of such action. For:

> there were always the police and the army upon whom the strong could call, and who, in the existing legal and political set-up, would hasten to respond (1933, p. 185).
>
> The dominant classes might be advocates of laissez-faire in other matters, but they never proposed to disband the police or the army... The real question, therefore, is not whether government should participate in the social and economic life of our times, but for whom and how (1933, p. 185).

---

[8] Discussions of the political philosophy of the Chicago School are provided in MILLFR (1962), and MISHAN (1975). See also the comments on Miller's paper by BRONFENBRENNER (1962) and STIGLER (1962).

Douglas's ideological perception of capitalism in terms of what he viewed as its inherent class character was antithetical to the dominant Chicago view of the 1930s. Indeed, on at least one occasion Douglas averred that he was a socialist (1929, p. 508). Further consideration of several specific issues sheds added light on the underlying ideological schism that prevailed between Douglas and the other Chicago economists.

Issue A: The Labor Movement. According to the Simons-Knight business-cycle theory, changes in the general price level would be transformed into corresponding variations in profits and production because of the downward rigidity of the cost structure. Thus, Simons stated that "the existence of extreme inflexibility in large areas of the price structure is one of the primary factors in the phenomenon of severe depression" (1936, p. 54). Since the downward rigidity of costs was ascribed to the expanding labor movement, trade unions were constantly attacked by Chicagoans throughout the 1930s. So intense were these attacks, that it has recently been documented that Simons was subjected to delay in his promotion to full professor at the University of Chicago "due to the opposition of a dean who was incensed by Simons's attack on labor unions" (Stigler, 1974, p. 2). Moreover, the economic benefit of unions to the working class itself was denied by Chicagoans. For example, in 1932 Knight stated,

> I submit that there is no greater wrong to laborers or to humanitarian progress than to encourage the belief that general wages are determined by bargaining position, or can be substantially raised by organization, even if *it possesses monopoly power* (original italics) (1932, p. 823).

In contrast to the foregoing line of interpretation, Douglas (1935) maintained that the severity of the Great Depression was experienced because real wages had not risen enough during the 1920s, rather than the other way around. Specifically, in his statistical work on production functions, Douglas found that costs had been declining throughout the 1920s while prices had been reduced only slightly. As a result, profits increased at a higher pace than real wages. Since profits accrue to employers who in turn invest them in mass-production industries, the consequence of higher profits can be increased production of consumer goods. But profit recipients, he argued, spend only a small fraction of their profit incomes on mass-production goods, and a larger fraction on luxury goods and services. Hence, throughout the 1920s, commodity markets evinced a mounting glut of mass-production goods that could not be afforded by the working class because of the prevalence of low wages. In turn, had the general price level been allowed to decline gradually during the decade of the 1920s, the ensuing depression would not have been so severe. In this vein, Douglas linked-up his theory of the business cycle with his perception of the inferior position of wage-earners. He stated:

> The present depression has caused many economists to ascribe both the origin and the continuance of the depression to the stickiness of wage rates in the face of falling prices (1935, p. 55).
>
> (However) it is evident that at least in the United States high wage rates did not initiate the present depression, but that, on the contrary, the pegging of prices by management was largely responsible for both the initiation and the continuance of the depression... (1935, p. 64).

Accordingly, Douglas considered it imperative for laborers to organize. Labor unions, he thought, succeeded in imparting "to people who are individually weak a collectively greater strength so that in the wage market they stand in a position of better equality with employers" (1932 [b], p. 103). Union-organizing movements among wage earners would become more frequent, according to Douglas. "Instead of disparaging them, we should welcome them" (1932 [b], p. 98).

Issue B: Planning. A further object of scorn by Simons was what he designated the "mongrel system of 'national planning'". He deemed it "unlikely that any planners or controllers, with the peculiar talents requisite for obtaining dictatorial power, would be able to make decisions wise enough to keep an elaborate economic organization from falling apart" (1934, p. 52). Likewise, Knight criticized planning as an irresponsible overhauling and reconstruction of the social system (1933, pp. 421-22). Douglas, on the other hand, argued that "Society will have to take up sooner or later a planned economy" (1932 [b], p. 108). Planning, he thought, would allow society to enjoy "great areas of forests and parks on the outside of every one of our cities [and] more decent housing within our cities" (1932 [b], p. 107).

Issue C: The Reconstruction Finance Corporation. Both Simons and Douglas opposed the Reconstruction Finance Corporation established by the U.S. Government during the Great Depression to rescue faltering enterprises. But whereas Simons thought it "terrifying to reflect on the amount of arbitrary power delegated to the administrators of the R.F.C., and thus viewed it as a means of fostering monopolistic pricing (1934, p. 322), Douglas, in typical fashion, opposed it because of its "class character". The R.F.C., according to Douglas, was created "in order to buoy up the propertied classes" (1932, [a], p. 80).

IV. The Emergence of Chicago Monetarism

During the early 1930s an intense cleavage developed between Douglas, on the one hand, and Simons and Knight on the other. Thus, beginning in 1932 and for some time thereafter, Douglas strenuously opposed renewal of Simons's appointment on the Chicago faculty.[9] Simons's staunchest defender against Douglas was Knight. As the 1930s wore on, Douglas increasingly took refuge in local politics in the ranks of the Democratic Party. In the early 1940s he departed Chicago on academic leave and volunteered for wartime service in the U.S. Marine Corps. Upon his postwar return to the University, he found that ideological conservatives had attained an almost total dominance of this department. The doctrine of laissez-faire did not square well with the economist who in 1933 had argued that "society (should) move sooner or later into a system of public ownership rather than backward into unrestrained competition" (1933, p. 191). His thoughts on returning to Chicago are noteworthy:

> The university I had loved so much seemed to be a different place... Knight was now openly hostile, and his disciples seemed to be everywhere. If I had stayed, it would be in an unfriendly environment. I felt stifled and did not think I could live in that atmosphere. My emotions turned outward and not inward. (1972, p. 128).

[9] See Stigler (1974).

As a result, Douglas successfully campaigned as a candidate for the U.S. Senate in 1948. Significantly, he continued to champion the quantity theory of money as a senator, and became a moving force in the Congress behind the Treasury-Federal Reserve Accord of 1951.[10]

Thus, at the very least, Douglas's simultaneous adherence to the quantity theory and to left-wing ideology is a direct challenge to the facile presumption of conflict between the two. It is plainly undeniable that the quantity theory that found consensus in Chicago during the 1930s was underlain by an ideological battle of Douglas versus Knight and Simons. The latter two gained the upper hand with the consequence that Douglas filled a less and less active role in his department during the late 1930s and eventually took permanent leave of Chicago altogether. In turn, the theory of money that is identified with Chicago of the 1930s has come to be viewed in splendid isolation of the left-wing ideology of which Paul Douglas was a consistent adherent. Yet when brought to the fore, the case of Douglas versus Knight and Simons illustrates the compatibility of monetarism with varied segments of the ideological spectrum within Chicago and without.

V. Keynesian Anti-Monetarism: The Case of Kaldor

Since Keynes's *General Theory*, it has become axiomatic that fiscalism or Keynesianism, poses an ideological, and not only a logical, challenge to monetarism. Certainly Keynes's own espousal of the socialization of investment (1936, p. 378) as a suggested reform in economic policy-making was bound to be perceived as implying rejection of a laissez-faire political economy. But whether Keynesian monetary analysis as a rival to Chicago monetarism implies such rejection is an open question, albeit a tenet of conventional wisdom that Keynesianism is tantamount to welfare statism. It is, therefore, instructive to consider the case of Nicholas Kaldor, a leading fiscalist or Keynesian, whose anti-monetarist analysis has been noted and directly rebutted by Friedman (1970 [b]).

In terms of ideology, Kaldor is evidently an anti-laissez-faire, British left-wing adherent. That his political-economy orientation contrasts, if it does not clash, with the ideology of American liberta-

[10] Douglas's role in initiating the Treasury-Federal Reserve Accord is discussed in Tavlas (1977[b]).

rianism as well as of conservatism, is beyond question. Suffice it to note that while Keynes himself was officially a Liberal (Party) Lord, the Keynesian Kaldor is a Labour (Party) Lord. Yet consider Kaldor's anti-monetarist analysis in terms of the demand function for money, the nature of money, the velocity of circulation of money, and the variability of the money supply. Though on all these counts Kaldor differs with Friedman openly and directly, does Kaldor's monetary analysis as such presuppose or imply a leftist ideology?

In challenging Friedman's proposition of the existence of a stable demand function for money, Kaldor first probes the economic basis for the presence of seasonal variation of currency in circulation. Regarding the rise of currency at Christmas time, he asks: "Could the 'authorities' prevent the [Christmas] buying spree by refusing to supply additional notes and coins in the Christmas season?" (1970, p. 6). If the central bank deliberately attempted to do so, retorts Kaldor, it could instruct banks not to cash more than a specified amount at any one time for each customer and to keep down the number of cashiers at Christmas time so as to drastically lengthen the queues for cash at bank tellers' windows. But would such measures stop the Christmas buying spree? No, answers Kaldor: "There would be chaos for a few days, but all kinds of money substitutes would spring up: credit cards, promissory notes, etc., issued by firms and financial institutions which would circulate in the same way as bank notes. Any business with a high reputation — a well-known firm which is universally trusted — could issue such paper, and anyone who could individually be 'trusted' would get things on 'credit'" (1970, p. 6). Others, such as the mass of wage-earners who might have no credit, continues Kaldor, "would get paid in chits which would be issued in lieu of cash by, say, the top five hundred businesses in the country (who would also, for a consideration, provide such chits to other employers). And these five hundred firms would soon find it convenient to set up a clearing system of their own, by investing in a giant computer which would at regular intervals net out all mutual claims and liabilities" (1970, p. 7). The upshot of such spontaneous adaptation of the private sector to the central bank's attempt to suppress the upsurge in the volume of currency in circulation at Christmas time, according to Kaldor, is, therefore, the emergence of "a complete surrogate money system and payments system" that "would exist side by side with official money" (1970, p. 7).

Thus, what at any time is regarded as "money", maintains Kaldor, "are those forms of financial claims which are commonly used as means of clearing debts. But any shortage of commonly used types is bound to lead to the emergence of new types; indeed, this is how, historically, first bank notes and then checking accounts emerged" (1970, p. 7). Hence, Kaldor concludes that "When the central bank succeeds in controlling the quantity of 'conventional money', lending and borrowing is diverted to other sources, and the 'velocity of circulation', in terms of conventional money, is automatically speeded up" (1970, p. 8).

Addressing himself to Friedman's claim that the velocity of circulation of conventional money has been relatively stable empirically, Kaldor readily concurs. His reason, however, is that in the historical periods analyzed by Friedman, the supply of money was unstable. In Kaldor's words: "in one way or another an increased demand for money evoked an increase in supply. The money supply 'accomodated itself' to the needs of trade: rising in response to an expansion, and vice versa" (1970, p. 8).

In sum, Kaldor's retort to Friedman's stability of the demand function for money is that the money supply is endogenous, not exogenous.[11] In turn, the monetary base, according to Kaldor is itself automatically responsive to changes in the demand for money: "if variations in the money supply were closely related to changes in the 'monetary base', this is mainly because the latter has also been 'endogenous', as well as the former" (1970, p. 12).

It turns out that Kaldor's anti-monetarist monetary analysis is itself rooted in his attribution to the initiative, drive and spontaneity of the private sector, under the leadership of financial and nonfinancial private enterprises, the capacity to supply money in creative response to the private sector's demand for money. Kaldor's anti-monetarism or anti-Friedmanism in thus grounded in the conception of a profit-oriented private enterprise, nay, a laissez-faire analysis of the nature and behavior of a monetary economy. Manifestly, whatever his political ideology, Kaldor's anti-monetarist monetary analysis does not presuppose or imply socialism, communism or welfare statism. It is as readily reconcilable with a laissez-faire political economy as monetarism itself.

---

[11] KALDOR expresses a similar view concerning the endogeniety of the money supply in his article on the "The Radcliffe Report" (1960).

VI. Non-Monetarism and Laissez-Faire

Finally, we turn to the question of the relationship between professed laissez-faire adherence and monetarism. Having found that monetarists need not be laissez-faire adherents, and that anti-monetarists need not be laissez-faire opponents, we now query: do laissez-faire proponents need to be monetarists?

In the camp of contemporary laissez-faire proponents, the preeminence of the University of Chicago has been noted previously in this paper. The fact of this preeminence is widely perceived as suggesting that laissez-faire adherence connotes monetarism. Our task is to probe this laissez-faire-monetarism nexus.

As would be expected, the contemporary laissez-faire camp itself meets the test of laissez-faire in monetary analysis. In other words, despite the preeminence of the University of Chicago among both monetarists and laissez-faire adherents, the laissez-faire camp is not limited exclusively to monetarists. Two non-monetarist strands of monetary analysis coexist with monetarism in the camp of laissez-faire ideology. Though distinguishable from each other, the two non-monetarist strands of thought share a major analytical feature as a point of emphasis: the treatment of money as an international (i.e., open-economy) phenomenon. Monetarism itself is fully reconcilable with an open-economy analytical framework, as recent work by Johnson[12] effectively illustrates. Yet the conceptually seminal development of monetarism has not featured the open-economy framework as have the non-monetarist strands of thought to be considered.

A. Metallism. A time-honored non-monetarist conception of optimality in the supply of money propounded by some outstanding laissez-faire advocates is that of precious metallism: the classical specie-flow mechanism. The line of reasoning here involved, derives from the proposition that the preservation of voluntary exchange, and, therefore, of private property, is ultimately contingent upon the monetary stability that only a specie-based monetary system is deemed capable of imparting. This proposition finds its clearest expression in terms of the von Mises-Rothbard money-regression theorem: A medium of exchange "can arise only out of a commodity previously *used directly in*

[12] See, for example, Johnson (1977).

a barter situation, and therefore having had an array of prices in terms of other goods. *Money must develop out of a commodity with a previously existing purchasing power, such as gold and silver had.* It cannot be created out of thin air by any sudden 'social compact' or edict of government'' (original italics), (Rothbard, 1962, pp. 235-36).

Thus, fiat money, in this laissez-faire view, is inherently the product of an authoritarian or collectivist state. As such, fiat money is inconsistent with the role of the state as preserver of the viability of private property. Hence the policy norms that monetarism would provide for a fiat-money economy are themselves considered as contrary to the rules of the game required for restoration of the classical specie-flow mechanism. Such metallism advocates, therefore, regard monetarism as undermining the application of laissez-faire economics to the monetary system.

Yet remarkably enough, while proponents of restoration of the gold standard are typically laissez-faire advocates, there is no presumptive basis for barring laissez-faire opponents from gold-standard advocacy as well. Thus, presiding over French indicative planning as a convinced dirigiste, General Charles de Gaulle delivered a paean to gold so ardent that it has been aptly depicted as ''perhaps the most remarkable lecture in monetary economics ever mouthed by a head of state'' (Hirsch, 1969, pp. 258-59).

B. Functionalism. A contemporary non-monetarist conception of a monetary regime diverging from the von Mises-Rothbard metallist approach but likewise sharing the voluntary-exchange tenet of laissez-faire advocacy has been stimulated by the international monetary developments ensuing from the Smithsonian Agreement of 1971. Applying the theory of the second-best, this conception focuses upon the emergence of abstract international units of account (numeraires) introduced at will by private enterprises as well as by national governments and international organizations, units depicted by Aschheim and Park (1976) as ''artificial currency units''. The transformation of such units of account into media of exchange is here viewed as an experimental process in the emergence of functional currency areas whereby a variety of ACUs come into being and coexist, each tailormade for the range of international and national exchange transactions that its sponsor seeks to enhance.

The Aschheim-Park concept of the formation of functional currency areas implies a regime of laissez-faire or do-it-yourself monies within the private sector. Yet it also recognizes the capacity of national governments and international governmental organizations to participate in the ACU proliferation process for both economic and political reasons of their own.

Perhaps the foremost laissez-faire proponent in the world, Friedrich A. Hayek has recently espoused the notion of private-money proliferation as an integral part of his laissez-faire advocacy (1976; 1977). Specifically, Hayek proposes allowing private individuals to print money instead of the governments, and letting the public decide whose money is the most valuable. Hayek's propounding this proposal is vivid testimony to the pluralism of non-monetarism among laissez-faire advocates. Clearly, laissez-faire ideology is not the exclusive domain of monetarists any more than monetarism is the exclusive domain of laissez-faire ideologists.

VII. Concluding Remarks

This paper has examined: (a) the relationship between monetarism and ideology; and (b) the relationship between non-monetarism and ideology. The identification of two coexisting strands of 1930s Chicago monetarism, distinguished in terms of business-cycle theory and stabilization policy, provides the basis for the suggestion that monetarism is not the exclusive domain of conservatism. Furthermore, the delineation of the ideological battle during the 1930s and 1940s between Chicago monetarists Frank Knight and Henry Simons, on the one hand, and Paul Douglas, on the other, highlights the subsequent emergence of Chicago monetarism in association with right-wing ideology.

In turn, non-monetarism or even anti-monetarism is also found to encompass a diversity of approaches to monetary economics with no single ideological connotation as the overriding one. It is demonstrated that a Keynesian monetary analysis does not necessarily presuppose or imply opposition to a laissez-faire political economy. On the other hand, a non-Keynesian challenge to monetarism, whether of the precious-metallism or of the international-functionalism variety, is seen to be reconcilable with more than one ideological preference.

Washington J. ASCHHEIM - G.S. TAVLAS

REFERENCES

ASCHHEIM, JOSEPH and PARK, Y.S., *Artificial Currency Units: The Formation of Functional Currency Areas*, Princeton: Princeton University Press, 1976.

BRONFENBRENNER, M., "Observations on the Chicago School(s)", *Journal of Political Economy*, 70 (February 1962), pp. 72-75.

BRUNNER, KARL, "The 'Monetarist Revolution' in Monetary Theory", *Weltwirtschaftliches Archiv*, 105 (Number 1, 1970), pp. 1-30.

DAVIS, J. RONNIE, "Chicago Economists, Deficit Budgets, and the Early 1930s", *American Economic Review*, 58 (June 1968), pp. 476-82.

DAVIS, J. RONNIE, *The New Economics and the Old Economists*, Iowa: Iowa State Press, 1971.

DOUGLAS, PAUL H., The Modern Technique of Mass Production and its Relation to Wages." *Proceedings of the Academy of Political Science*, 12 (July 1927), pp. 17-42.

DOUGLAS, PAUL H., "Economist of Tomorrow: The Story of Paul Douglas", *The World Tomorrow*, 12 (December 1929), pp. 507-10.

DOUGLAS, PAUL H., "Money, Credit, and the Depression", *The World Tomorrow*, 15 (March 1932), pp. 78-80 [a].

DOUGLAS, PAUL H., "The Farmers, The Wage Earners, and Our Political System." *Proceedings of the Institute of Public Affairs*, 33 (September 1932), pp. 96-111 [b].

DOUGLAS, PAUL H., "An Economist's Idea of Good Government", *Annals of the Academy of Political and Social Science* (April 1933). pp. 184-92.

DOUGLAS, PAUL H., *Controlling Depressions*, New York: W.W. Norton and Company, 1935.

DOUGLAS, PAUL H., *In the Fullness of Time*, New York: Harcourt Brace, 1972.

DOUGLAS, PAUL H., and DIRECTOR, AARON. *The Problem of Unemployment*, New York: MacMillan Company, 1931.

FRIEDMAN, MILTON, "The Quantity Theory of Money - A Restatement." In Friedman, Milton, ed., *Studies in the Quantity Theory of Money*, Chicago: University of Chicago Press, 1956.

FRIEDMAN, MILTON, "The Monetary Theory and Policy of Henry Simons", *Journal of Law and Economics*, 10 (October 1967), pp. 1-14.

FRIEDMAN, MILTON, *The Counter-Revolution in Monetary Theory*, London: Institute of Economic Affairs, 1970 [a].

FRIEDMAN, MILTON, "Comment on the New Monetarism", *Lloyds Bank Review*, 98 (October 1970), pp. 52-53 [b].

FRIEDMAN, MILTON, "Comments on the Critics", *Journal of Political Economy*, 80 (September/October 1972), pp. 906-50.

GIDEONSE, HARRY D., "Silver, Gold, and Depressed Trade", *Proceedings of the Institute of Public Affairs*, 32 (February 1932), pp. 1-12.

GIDEONSE, HARRY D., "Money and Finance", *The American Journal of Sociology*, 39 (May 1934), pp. 749-58.

HAYEK, FRIEDRICH A., *Denationalisation of Money*, London: Institute of Economic Affairs, 1976.

HAYEK, FRIEDRICH A., "Toward a Free Market Money", *The Wall Street Journal*, (August 19, 1977).

HIRSCH, FRED, *Money International*. New York: Doubleday, 1969.

JOHNSON, HARRY G., "The Keynesian Revolution and the Monetarist Counter-Revolution", *American Economic Review*, 61 (May 1971), pp. 1-14.

JOHNSON, HARRY G., *Inflation and the Monetarist Controversy*, Amsterdam: North Holland, 1972.

JOHNSON, HARRY G., "The Monetary Approach to Balance of Payments Theory and Policy: Explanation and Policy Implications", *Economica*, 44 (August 1977), pp. 217-30.

KALDOR, NICHOLAS, "The Radcliffe Report", *Review of Economics and Statistics*, (February 1960). Reprinted in KALDOR, NICHOLAS, *Essays on Economic Policy*, New York: W.W. Norton and Company. 1965.

KALDOR, NICHOLAS, "The New Monetarism", *Lloyds Bank Review*, 97 (July 1970), pp. 1-18.

KEYNES, JOHN MAYNARD, *The General Theory of Employment, Interest and Money*, New York: Harcourt Brace, 1936.

KNIGHT, FRANK H., "Comment on Mr. Slichter's Comment", *Journal of Political Economy*, 40 (December 1932), pp. 820-25.

KNIGHT, FRANK H., "Review of A Planned Society", *Journal of Political Economy*, 41 (July 1933), pp. 421-23.

KNIGHT, FRANK H., "The Business Cycle, Interest, and Money: A Methodological Approach", *Review of Economic Statistics*, 23 (May 1941). Reprinted in KNIGHT, FRANK H., *On the History and Method of Economics*, Chicago: University of Chicago Press, 1956.

MAYER, THOMAS, "The Structure of Monetarism", *Kredit und Kapital*, 8 (Heft 2 and Heft 3, 1975).

MAYER, THOMAS, "Monetarism: Economic Analysis or Weltanschauung?", in this *Review*, 126 (September 1978), pp. 233-250.

MILLER, H. LAURENCE, "On the 'Chicago School of Economics'", *Journal of Political Economy*, 70 (February 1962), pp. 64-69.

MINTS, LLOYD, "Monetary Policy", *Review of Economic Statistics*, 28 (May 1946), pp. 46-70.

MISHAN, ERZA J., "The Folklore of the Market: An Inquiry into the Economic Doctrines of the Chicago School", *Journal of Economic Issues*, 9 (December 1975), pp. 681-752.

MOGGRIDGE, D.E. and HOWSON, SUSAN, "Keynes on Monetary Policy 1910-1946", *Oxford Economic Papers*, 26 (1974), pp. 226-47.

NOBAY, A. ROBERT and JOHNSON, H.G., "Monetarism: A Historic-Theoretic Perspective", *Journal of Economic Literature*, 15 (June 1977), pp. 470-85

PATINKIN, DON, "The Chicago Tradition, the Quantity Theory, and Friedman", *Journal of Money, Credit and Banking*, 1 (February 1969), pp. 46-70.

PATINKIN, DON, "On the Short-Run Non-Neutrality of Money in the Quantity Theory", in this *Review*, 100 (March 1970), pp. 3-22[a].

PATINKIN, DON, "Friedman on the Quantity Theory and Keynesian Economics", *Journal of Political Economy*, 80 (September/October 1972), pp. 893-905 [b].

PETTENGILL, SAMUEL B., "Memorandum: Payment of Adjusted-Compensation Certificates", *U.S. Congress, House of Representatives*, Committee on Ways and Means, 72nd Cong., 1st Session, 1932.

ROTHBARD, MURRAY N., *Man, Economy, and State; A Treatise on Economic Principles*, Princeton: Van Nostrand, 1962.

SIMONS, HENRY C., *Banking and Currency Reform*. Unpublished Manuscript.

SIMONS, HENRY C., "A Positive Program for Laissez Faire"; *Public Policy Pamphlet*, No. 15. Chicago: University of Chicago Press, 1935. Reprinted in SIMONS, HENRY C., *Economic Policy for a Free Society*, Chicago: University of Chicago Press, 1948.

SIMONS, HENRY C., "Rules versus Authorities in Monetary Policy", *Journal of Political Economy*, 44 (February 1936), pp. 1-30. Reprinted in SIMONS 1948.

SIMONS, HENRY C., "Hansen on Fiscal Policy", *Journal of Political Economy*, 50 (April 1942), pp 161-96 Reprinted in SIMONS 1948.

SMOOT, REED, "Memorandum on Balancing the Budget", *U.S. Congress*, Senate Finance Committee, 72nd Cong., 2nd Session, 1933.

STEIN, JEROME L., "The Monetarist Critique of the New Economics", in STEIN, JEROME L., ed., *Monetarism*, Amsterdam: North-Holland, 1976, pp. 1-16.

STIGLER, GEORGE J., "Comment", *Journal of Political Economy*, 70 (February 1962), pp. 70-71.

STIGLER, GEORGE J., "Henry Calvert Simons", *Journal of Law and Economics*, 17 (April 1974), pp. 1-6.

TAVLAS, GEORGE S., "Some Further Observations on the Monetary Economics of Chicagoans and Non-Chicagoans", *Southern Economic Journal*, 42 (April 1976), pp 685-92.

TAVLAS, GEORGE S., "Chicago Schools Old and New on the Efficacy of Monetary Policy", in this *Review*, 120 (March 1977), pp. 51-73 [a]

TAVLAS, GEORGE S., "The Chicago Tradition Revisited: Some Neglected Monetary Contributions of Senator Paul Douglas", *Journal of Money Credit and Banking*, 9 (November 1977) [b].

TEIGEN, RONALD L., "Some Observations on Monetarist Analysis", *Kredit und Kapital*, 4 (Heft 3, 1971), pp. 234-63.

TOBIN, JAMES, *The New Economics One Decade Older*, Princeton: Princeton Univ. Press, 1974.

VINER, JACOB, "Problems of International Commercial and Financial Policy", *Institute of Politics* (11th Session, 1931), pp. 165-93.

VINER, JACOB, "International Aspects of the Gold Standard", in Wright, Quincy, ed. *Gold and Monetary Stabilization*, Chicago: University of Chicago Press, 1932.

VINER, JACOB, "Inflation as a Remedy for Depression", *Proceedings of the Institute of Public Affairs*, Athens, Ga.: University of Georgia, 1933.

VINER, JACOB, *Problems of Monetary Control*, Princeton: Princeton University Press, 1964.

'Hawtrey, Harvard and the Origins of the Chicago Tradition'

D. Laidler, 'Hawtrey, Harvard and the origins of the Chicago Tradition' *Journal of Political Economy*, 101 (December 1993), pp. 1068–103.

Hawtrey, Harvard, and the Origins of the Chicago Tradition

David Laidler

University of Western Ontario

Milton Friedman has claimed that his monetary economics derives from a Chicago Tradition that, in the 1930s, offered a monetary explanation of cyclical fluctuations in general and the Great Depression in particular, an optimistic view of the power of monetary policy, and a case for governing it by rules rather than discretion. It is argued that all the elements of this tradition except the last are to be found in earlier writings of Ralph Hawtrey, Allyn Young, and Lauchlin Currie and that there is much evidence to point to a direct influence running from Hawtrey, through Harvard to Chicago.

I. Introduction

The existence of a "Chicago Tradition" in monetary economics was first brought to general attention by Milton Friedman's (1956) claim that his version of the quantity theory of money derived from a doctrine that had been under continuous development at the University of Chicago since the 1930s. While agreeing that an oral tradition in monetary economics existed at that institution in the 1930s and 1940s, Don Patinkin (1969) showed beyond any reasonable doubt that whatever its contents might have been, the notion that the quantity theory

This paper forms part of a larger study being carried out with the financial support of the Lynde and Harry Bradley Foundation. I am grateful to Lauchlin Currie for much helpful correspondence; to Milton Friedman for comments and for providing me with a copy of the unpublished Chicago manuscript on "Banking and Currency Reform" (Simons et al. 1933), to which extensive reference is made below; and to Mark Blaug, Charles Blitch, Bernard Corry, Sue Howson, Peter Howitt, Mary Morgan, Don Patinkin, Roger Sandilands, Anna Schwartz, Frank Steindl, and James Tobin for helpful comments on earlier drafts. Toni Gravelle has provided invaluable research and bibliographic assistance. The usual disclaimers apply.

[*Journal of Political Economy*, 1993, vol 101, no 6]

of money was primarily a theory of the demand for money was not among them. Friedman (1974) subsequently conceded that his model of the demand for money owed little to Lloyd Mints, Henry Simons, or Jacob Viner, but went on to describe in some detail a tradition at Chicago, not unlike that sketched by Patinkin ([1969] 1981, pp. 245–52), which had offered a monetary explanation of economic fluctuations, and in particular of the Great Depression of 1929–33, as well as an essentially optimistic assessment of the power of monetary policy to deal with the Depression. And Friedman (1967) had already drawn attention to Henry Simons's advocacy of governing monetary policy by legislated rules rather than the discretion of politicians and central bankers, though he noted that Simons had favored a price stability rather than a money growth rule.

Thomas Humphrey (1971) documented the appearance of ideas closely related to this Chicago tradition in the writings of such non-Chicagoans as Carl Snyder (e.g., 1924), Lauchlin Currie (e.g., 1934*b*), and, later, Clark Warburton (e.g., the papers reprinted in *Depression* [1966], which date from 1945 onward and hence are late enough to be outside the period with which this paper deals). His study, together with Patinkin's (1973) comment on it, left the overall impression that the Chicago tradition was less the product of a single department than it was a manifestation of a widely influential and essentially Fisherian approach to monetary economics.

This paper proposes a rather different account of the matter. Specifically, and without denying the existence of a pervasive Fisherian influence, it argues that two of the three distinctive characteristics that Friedman has attributed to 1930s Chicago monetary economics also distinguish the analysis of such Harvard economists as Allyn Young and Lauchlin Currie from the broader tradition of American monetary economics of the period. It argues further that those characteristics are to be found in the writings of the British economist Ralph Hawtrey, who, from 1913 onward, developed a monetary theory of the cycle that provided a far richer description of the phenomenon as a "dance of the dollar" than Irving Fisher ever produced.[1] Even though the work of Young and Currie was systematically empirical and was clearly influenced by the American Institutionalist tradi-

[1] Indeed, Fisher himself wrote of his work before 1932 in the following terms: "The vast field of 'business cycles' is one on which I had scarcely ever entered before, and I had never attempted to analyze it as a whole" (1932, p. vii). Before that date, Fisher's work on cycles (e.g., Fisher 1923) had mainly been devoted to showing how variations in the rate of inflation were associated with fluctuations in various measures of real activity, and he had been an active supporter of legislating price stability as a goal for the Federal Reserve System. Thus he supported the Strong Bills of 1926–27, not to mention the Goldsborough Bill of 1932. Nevertheless, the question "Why not Fisher, rather than Hawtrey?" inevitably recurs throughout this paper.

tion in which Young had been trained at Wisconsin, and to that extent differed from Hawtrey's, the theoretical vision that underlay it was, as we shall see, close indeed to his. And this paper not only demonstrates the presence of similar theoretical ideas in the writings of Hawtrey, these Harvard economists, and the originators of the Chicago tradition, but also provides evidence that the people concerned were aware of, and took particularly seriously, the work to which influence is attributed.

It will be shown in the following pages (*a*) that the monetary interpretation of the Great Depression, which we nowadays associate with Friedman, but which Currie (1931*a*, 1931*b*, 1934*a*, 1934*b*) undoubtedly pioneered, was the natural outcome of applying to that specific episode ideas that appeared first in Hawtrey's *Good and Bad Trade* (1913) and were then developed in *Currency and Credit* (1919), a book that played an important part in an oral tradition, recognized as such by contemporaries, developed at Harvard by Young; (*b*) that Hawtrey himself analyzed the Depression in similar terms, though by no means as systematically as Currie; (*c*) that optimism about the power of monetary policy also marked the work of Hawtrey, Young, and Currie but arrived rather late in the day in Chicago; and (*d*) that, with due recognition of the priority of Frederick Soddy (1926), proposals to establish a regime of what Fisher (1935) was to call 100 percent money (i.e., to subject checkable deposits to 100 percent reserve requirements of high-powered money) were developed independently by both Simons et al. (1933) and Currie (1934*b*) as responses to the phenomenon that Hawtrey had labeled the "inherent instability of credit."[2] At this last point, however, we encounter a fundamental difference between Harvard and Chicago. Whereas Currie's intention, even as early as 1934, was to render activist monetary policy a more useful component of a generally interventionist policy regime, Simons's aim was to make adherence to a monetary rule a more effective feature of a competitive economic order. Thus the distinguishing feature of Chicago analysis was normative, namely to forge a link between a monetary explanation of the cycle and a liberal political agenda.[3]

[2] It is generally acknowledged that Fisher's (1935) book was a development of the Chicago proposals and in no sense an original contribution. There is no sign of the 100 percent money proposal in his writings of 1932 or 1933, contrary to Tobin's (1987) suggestion that Fisher had been developing the proposal since the mid-1920s. Perhaps Tobin had in mind Fisher's commitment to price-level stability by way of a compensated dollar, which goes back, of course, to 1911 and was written into the Goldsborough Bill, though it was deleted from the version of that bill passed by the House of Representatives but defeated in the Senate in 1932.

[3] Much evidence to support the story just outlined is already scattered through the secondary literature. For example, there is no doubt that Hawtrey's work attracted

To interpret the positive theoretical content of the "Chicago Tradition" as being essentially the same as that of the work of Hawtrey and certain Harvard economists is also to suggest that it has the same origins as much of the macroeconomics of the New Deal, to which Currie in particular made a major contribution.[4] That is perhaps one reason why the "monetarism" that emanated from Chicago in the mid-1950s has turned out, on closer and more dispassionate inspection than it was originally accorded, to have, from an analytic point of view, a good deal more than a capital theoretic approach to modeling the demand for money in common with the American "Keynesian" orthodoxy to which it was opposed.

II. Hawtrey's Analysis

As I argued in Laidler (1991), among the leading pre–World War I exponents of the quantity theory of money, only Fisher offered a purely monetary explanation of the cycle. Hawtrey's prewar work on the topic, as it appeared in his *Good and Bad Trade* (1913), drew explicitly on the Fisherian tradition—Fisher (1911) was the only work cited there—but much of its detail was of recognizably Marshallian origin. Though Hawtrey should not be characterized as a quantity theorist

widespread attention during the 1920s and early 1930s. Gottfried von Haberler's (1937) authoritative survey of business cycle literature presents Hawtrey as the leading exponent of a purely monetary theory of the trade cycle, and, as Patrick Deutscher (1990) has told us, before the publication of John Maynard Keynes's *General Theory*, Hawtrey was cited with impressive frequency in the journal literature on macroeconomics, indeed with the same frequency as Fisher over the 1931–35 period. As to the visibility of his work in the United States, Deutscher has also documented the attention paid to it by Allyn Young, who was instrumental in arranging Hawtrey's only academic appointment, as a visitor at Harvard during 1928–29. Joseph Schumpeter would later note the frequent references made to Hawtrey's analysis by defenders of Federal Reserve policy as it was conducted before 1928 (see Schumpeter 1954, p. 1121). Moreover, Currie's anticipation of what would come to be called the "monetarist" interpretation of the Great Depression has already been discussed by Karl Brunner (1968), Humphrey (1971), Patinkin (1973), Roger Sandilands (1990), and Frank Steindl (1991).

[4] To take this position is to endorse Sandilands's (1990) view that Currie the New Dealer, a strong advocate of fiscal policy in the later 1930s, held at that time views that had developed naturally from, rather than in opposition to, those that earlier had led him to blame monetary policy for the onset of the Great Depression and to argue that a monetary cure, if applied quickly and vigorously enough, could have dealt with it. Currie believed that the economy itself had changed during the 1930s and required policies different from those that would have sufficed earlier. The prime evidence for this is that he never repudiated his interpretation (Currie 1934*a*, 1934*b*) of the events of 1928–32. This is not, of course, to argue that so creative a thinker as Currie remained wedded throughout the 1930s to each and every idea he had advanced in the early years of the decade. To attribute continuity to an economist's thought is not the same thing as saying that his thought never changes. For a detailed account of these matters, see Sandilands (1990, chaps. 2–3).

as the term would have been understood by his contemporaries, his work certainly falls within a monetary tradition of business cycle analysis that built on the quantity theory.[5] The distinctive variations on that tradition that Hawtrey developed in *Good and Bad Trade* were to remain central features of his postwar work and differentiate it rather sharply from Fisher's. In particular, where Fisher had written *The Purchasing Power of Money* (1911) primarily about the secular relationship between money and prices, and had discussed the cycle in only one chapter dealing with "Transition Periods," the whole of *Good and Bad Trade* was about the cycle, and Hawtrey's next work, *Currency and Credit* (1919), retained this emphasis. Young (1920) remarked explicitly on this characteristic in his review of its first edition: "Mr. Hawtrey is less interested in imagined states of monetary equilibrium than in what Professor Irving Fisher would call 'transition periods'" (pp. 522–23), as he did also in a subsequent review (Young 1924) of its second (1923) edition.[6]

Hawtrey's attitude toward the quantity theory, in the sense of a hypothesis about a long-run proportional relationship between money and the general price level, was expressed succinctly in the preface to *Currency and Credit:*

> Scientific treatment of the subject of currency is impossible without some form of the quantity theory. . . . But the quantity theory by itself is inadequate, and it leads up to the method of treatment based on what I have called the consumers' income and the consumers' outlay—that is to say, simply the aggregates of individual incomes and individual expenditures. [1919, p. v]

[5] Patinkin (1969) (and elsewhere) has rightly insisted that the phrase "quantity theory" at this time was almost universally understood to mean a proposition about a unidirectional and proportional effect running from the quantity of money to the general price level. The phrase, or derivatives such as "quantity theoretic," should not, therefore, be used to characterize a theory of the business cycle, particularly one in which chains of causation running from money income to money, as well as in the opposite direction, play a prominent role. At the same time, the qualifier "monetary" is too broad to describe the tradition to which I refer here, since it can encompass the very different Austrian cycle theory of Friedrich von Hayek (1931, 1933); "monetarist" is anachronistic and conjures up stable demand for money and natural unemployment rate hypotheses that are not to be found in the literature dealt with here. In what follows, I shall therefore try to avoid shorthand labels of this type altogether.

[6] Thus the pervasive Fisherian influence on Hawtrey's work was recognized by Young, but so was the fact that Hawtrey had carried many elements of Fisher's analysis a good deal further than its originator. On this matter, see also James Angell (1926, p. 182 ff.), where a discussion of Hawtrey's work based explicitly on Young's writing and teaching is to be found. The novelty of Hawtrey's work, not least in the way in which "the older machinery, of quantities of money and goods and transactions, is . . . put into the background" (1926, p. 183), is explicitly stressed by Angell. I am informed by Mark Blaug that Hawtrey's *Currency and Credit* still appeared on Angell's undergraduate reading lists in the early 1950s.

And this early version of an income-expenditure approach was by no means Hawtrey's only departure from a more conventional Fisherian viewpoint. In 1919, the word "money" usually referred to "currency," and that indeed is how Hawtrey then used it; but he regarded "credit," by which he meant, as Currie (1934*b*, p. 48) was later to stress, checkable demand deposits, as playing a far more important role in the financial system, so much so that he actually began *Currency and Credit* with an analysis of a simplified monetary system from which currency was totally absent.[7] This is exactly the opposite simplification to that adopted by Fisher at the beginning of the *Purchasing Power of Money*, where an economy using only currency is first considered, and its purpose was to enable Hawtrey to develop from the outset, and in a clear-cut fashion, a hypothesis that was always utterly central to his work, namely "the inherent instability of credit": the hypothesis that any shock to the system that disturbed bank lending, and therefore the volume of deposits, particularly in an upward direction, would tend to generate a perpetual and perhaps accelerating movement.

In the case of contraction, falling interest rates induced by "the self-interest of the bankers and the distress of the merchants combined to restore the creation of credits . . . . But in the case of the expansion of credits there is no such corrective influence at work" (Hawtrey 1919, p. 13). This cumulative process of credit expansion has about it a strong flavor of Knut Wicksell's (1898) "pure credit economy" (see Laidler 1991, chap. 5), though there is no evidence that, in 1919, Hawtrey was aware of this work. Two important elements in the mechanism driving it, however, have no parallel in Wicksell. The first involved the inventory holding decisions of wholesale merchants: in the face of expanding demand not immediately matched by an increase in short-term interest rates, they would seek to increase, or at least maintain, the levels of those inventories with the aid of loans from the banks. The second, closely related, involved the way in which the deposits created in this process would swell the economy's "unspent margins" (money holdings, in modern terminology) beyond the levels desired by agents and, hence, induce increased expenditure, which would, in turn, frustrate wholesalers' plans for

[7] There does arise a question about whether Hawtrey thought it was the injection of bank deposits into the system per se that was important, or the fact that the injection came in the form of loans to the business community. The fact that Hawtrey believed that public works expenditure per se would not affect aggregate demand, but that if financed by money creation it would, with the money creation being responsible for the expansionary effects of the policy, suggests that the former interpretation is the right one. Note that Angell (1926, p. 182) draws explicit attention to the novel feature of Hawtrey's analysis that it begins with a world without currency, and that John H. Williams (1932) also follows this example, albeit without a direct reference to Hawtrey. See the discussion in Sec. IV below.

inventory accumulation. In the absence of currency, this process could continue forever, but in fact currency's dual role as a reserve for the banks, and an alternative means of exchange to deposits for the public, placed a limit on it. In Hawtrey's words, "money [i.e., currency] . . . has to correct the instability of credit" (1919, p. 15). An expansion of money incomes and expenditures would lead to a drain of currency from the banks and induce them to increase the nominal interest rate sufficiently to bring to an end, and indeed to reverse, the upward cumulative process.

In Hawtrey's view, two factors in particular made a reversal, rather than the attainment of a new higher-equilibrium price level, virtually inevitable. First, during the boom, expenditures would rise, not in proportion to money creation, but in greater proportion because the rate of increase, as well as the level, of deposits would have a positive effect on consumers' expenditures (pp. 38–46); and second, the demand for currency relative to deposits in the makeup of the public's "unspent margins" would depend on the distribution of national income between wages and profits:[8] "It is only after a considerable interval that the prosperity of the manufacturer is reflected in an increase of *wages*. Consequently it is only very gradually that the bankers can become aware that the growth of credits is threatening their reserves of coin" (p. 23). And the stickiness of wages posited here, because it operated in a downward as well as an upward direction, had a further consequence: namely, fluctuations in employment as an inherent characteristic of the cycle:

> The alternation of expansions and contractions would be comparatively harmless but for the dislocation and distress which accompany the contraction. . . . The working classes have the greatest interest in the stable currency, and . . . the question of justice between debtor and creditor is less important than the effect of currency movements on employment and real wages. [P. 376]

Hawtrey conceded that what amounted to a competitive banking system did have it within its powers to stabilize the cycle:

> If the bankers keep large reserves and take early steps to safeguard them, not merely when the proportion of reserve to liabilities falls below their conventional limit, but as soon as trade begins to become suspiciously profitable, and if they have the courage to avoid panic measures even when their

[8] Dennis Robertson (1915) had noted the originality and importance of this element in Hawtrey's analysis. It has no parallel in Fisher's work, where the currency/deposit ratio is assumed to be stable except during and immediately after, rather than in advance of, the crisis phase of the cycle.

> reserves seem to be melting away to nothing, they are likely to keep control of the situation. But bankers are human. [P. 28]

Hence, as a practical matter, if the inherent instability of credit was to be counteracted, and the cycle mitigated, a central bank was required. Even the operation of an international gold standard with variations in the supply of currency linked rigidly to variations in gold reserves (as they were under the 1844 Bank Charter Act, which had regulated the Bank of England's behavior until 1914) did not change this in Hawtrey's view. In a monetary system dominated by deposit banking, "The note-issuing authority which regulates the supply of legal tender paper money is really dependent upon the control of credit for passing the notes into circulation" (p. 49). And "in fact, experience has shown that even with an automatically regulated paper currency, which does not need to be managed on banking principles, a central bank for the control of credit is almost indispensable. For a long time the United States was an example, or rather a warning, of the contrary system" (pp. 78–79).

Now Hawtrey's best-known contribution to specific matters of policy involved the Genoa Conference of 1922 and the resolutions (never acted on) that emanated from it concerning the desirability of cooperation among central banks to ensure that their efforts at restoring and maintaining stability in domestic monetary systems were compatible with the restoration and maintenance of an international gold standard in the wake of its disruption by the First World War. But more important in the context of this paper is his knowledge of U.S. experience, and the comment above on the workings of the national banking system is no mere isolated remark. Hawtrey was a well-informed observer of the U.S. monetary system. The analysis first set out in *Good and Bad Trade* had treated open-economy considerations as peripheral to cyclical mechanisms, and, even though from *Currency and Credit* onward Hawtrey paid more attention to international factors, this analysis remained at the heart of all his later work on the cycle. As he subsequently pointed out (in the foreword to the 1962 reprint), *Good and Bad Trade* was a response, not to any specifically British experience, but to the depression that followed the crisis of 1907 in the United States, which, among other effects, had helped provoke the establishment of the Federal Reserve System. It is no surprise, then, that Hawtrey's analysis proved readily applicable to, and provided the basis for, much commentary on the system's operations in the 1920s and early 1930s; and, indeed, a wide range of issues that were to become important in subsequent American discussion had been broached in his work by 1919.

For example, Hawtrey had already argued in the first edition of

Currency and Credit that, though stock market speculation was usually a feature of the boom phase of the cycle and that in "the more usual sequence of events . . . [a] serious fall in the prices of securities will precede the crisis itself" (1919, p. 141), it was important not to attach too much significance to this point: "Speculators in stocks are so especially exposed to the strain of a crisis, that particular crises are very commonly explained as due to 'over-speculation.' In point of fact, however, there are examples of periods of furious speculation which led to no crisis at all" (p. 147). This was later to be his position, and that of others, notably Currie (1934*a*, 1934*b*), with respect to the particular events of 1929.[9] *Currency and Credit* also contains an early and undogmatic discussion of another matter much debated in subsequent years, namely the relative desirability of aiming monetary policy at stabilizing prices or money wages. Hawtrey's treatment of this question was mainly concerned with the matter of fairness between debtors and creditors, and concluded that "either view seems to be perfectly tenable, and neither seems necessarily to represent the last word of justice" (1919, p. 375). For Hawtrey, this issue was "less important than the effects of currency *movements* on employment and real wages" (p. 376; italics added).

Hawtrey also told his readers in 1919 that commercial banking "comprises two distinct functions—temporary lending, and the provision of transferable credits as means of payment. Their union is a matter of convenience and not of necessity" (p. 378). He thus stated one basic premise of the case subsequently made for "100 percent money," though he did not go on to make that case. On the contrary, he argued that to separate these functions so that "the supply of purchasing power would lose its elasticity" (p. 378) would not put a stop to merchants' economizing on cash by obtaining credit by other means. For Hawtrey, indeed:

> Far from causing the cyclical fluctuations, a banking system diminishes their violence and facilitates their control. Nevertheless, though credit institutions are not themselves the cause of this phenomenon, yet where such institutions exist it is through them that the fluctuations take effect.
>
> It is these credit movements which determine the "rapidity of circulation" of money and of credit. There is no need to dwell on the futility of any theory of currency which accepts the "rapidity of circulation" or the "needs of trade" as something given, something determined from outside independently of the currency system itself. [P. 379]

[9] But it was not the position of Fisher, whose "debt-deflation" hypothesis led him to accord an altogether more important role to the stock market crash (see Fisher 1932, p. 85 ff.).

As we shall see, these issues raised by Hawtrey in 1919—the variability of the currency/deposit ratio as a crucial characteristic of the cycle; the debatable role of stock market speculation and its collapse in foreshadowing a cyclical downturn; the question of tying monetary policy to a rule and, if so, which; the possibility of divorcing the provision of means of payment from the granting of short-term credit; and the dangers of treating the "needs of trade" as independent of the behavior of the monetary system, the basis of what is now known as the "real-bills" doctrine—all played prominent roles in the subsequent monetary debates in the United States. As we shall also see, Hawtrey's undogmatic skepticism about the need for rules or radical reforms, something surely to be expected from one who regarded central banking as an "art," found more sympathy among Harvard economists than those at Chicago; but this does not alter the fact that, in both places, the agenda for discussion was dominated by questions that he had raised as early as 1919. Many of these issues were, of course, raised by others, at about the same time. It is not claimed that Hawtrey single-handedly invented the agenda for monetary debates in the 1920s and early 1930s.[10] But it is nevertheless the case that the comprehensiveness of *Currency and Credit* made it unique among English-language works of the early 1920s as a statement of that agenda. In his review of its second edition, Young called it "one of the most significant—possibly *the* most significant—of modern treatises on money" (1924, p. 349), and it occupied a prominent place on reading lists at Harvard, his and then Currie's, throughout the 1920s and early 1930s.[11]

III. Allyn Young, Lauchlin Currie, and the Harvard Tradition

Harvard's reputation in monetary economics in the years immediately preceding the arrival of Keynesian ideas is one of mediocrity; and even if one allows for the tendency to disparage anything thought, said, or written before 1936 that accompanied the Keynesian revolution, that reputation is not altogether undeserved.[12] Anyone who

[10] Though it is worth pointing out that the only item in the list above that figures prominently in Fisher's writing before 1919 is the matter of a monetary rule, in the form of his proposals for a "compensated dollar."

[11] In a letter to Charles Blitch, dated October 15, 1973, Overton H. Taylor refers to Young's using *Currency and Credit* as the textbook for his graduate course in Money and Banking in 1924–25. I am grateful to Charles Blitch for this information.

[12] This was acknowledged by Mason (1982) in his history of the Harvard department, a history in which, it is sad to note, the name of Lauchlin Currie appears but once, with no reference to his work. Sandilands (1990) complains, with some justice, that Friedman and Schwartz (1963, 1970) paid insufficient attention to Currie's work, and in a recent letter to me, Friedman acknowledges this criticism with an explicit "mea

doubts this is invited to peruse the 1934 commentaries on *The Economics of the Recovery Program* (Brown et al. 1934) prepared by members of the department, most of which verge on the incoherent and do no credit to their distinguished authors. Only Schumpeter's contribution to this volume is something of an exception. It is at least coherent in its presentation of the Austrian view of the Depression, namely that it was the result of overinvestment and that any attempt to use expansionary policy to mitigate it would only make matters worse. But, until as late as 1934, outstanding work in monetary economics was done at Harvard, the best of it at least as good as anything that would emanate from Chicago in the 1930s and, indeed, if careful empirical analysis is valued, far better.

Most of this work was due to Allyn Young and Lauchlin Currie, though John H. Williams made at least one noteworthy contribution as a transmitter of ideas, as we shall see below. The fact that this work is not well known nowadays is mainly due to a series of unfortunate events that cut short its progress. First, Young died in early 1929, at the age of 52, in the penultimate year of what he had intended to be a temporary appointment at the London School of Economics. Second, Currie was a graduate student and then an instructor at Harvard, but never a tenured member of the faculty; and having been selected by Jacob Viner to join the Roosevelt administration's "freshman brains trust," he was refused leave by Harvard to extend his stay in Washington beyond the summer of 1934, thus forcing his resignation. His subsequent career in Washington, as Sandilands (1990) shows, gives him a strong claim to be considered as a major intellectual force in the development of the macroeconomic policies of "the New Deal," but he also became distanced from the academic community.

To complicate matters further, more monetary analysis seems to have been discussed and taught at Harvard than found its way into

culpa." Currie's neglect by the profession began earlier, however, and was comprehensive enough to verge on the scandalous. For example, Mints gives but three grudging references to his work in *History of Banking* (1945) and none in *Monetary Policy* (1950), despite the fact that the latter book expounds a version of the monetary explanation of the Depression pioneered by Currie (1934*a*, 1934*b*). Currie's name does not appear at all in the 45-page bibliography of "Articles on Monetary Theory" prepared by Harlan Smith, with the "constant advice" of Lloyd Mints, and appended to the American Economic Association's (1952) *Readings in Monetary Theory,* a collection that was, for a good decade, the standard source of graduate student reading material in the area. Nor did Currie fare any better at the hands of Harvard economists. His name fails to appear in such products of that department as Hansen (1941, 1951) or Harris (1945). Karl Brunner's introduction to the 1968 reprint of Currie (1934*b*) is an honorable exception to all this, as was the inclusion by Harry G. Johnson and Albert Rees of Currie (1934*a*) in their selection of *Landmarks in Political Economy* (1962) from earlier issues of the *Journal of Political Economy.*

print. Currie tells readers of *Supply and Control of Money* that "most of the subject matter . . . has been taught in the first half of the money and banking courses at Harvard for some years" (1934*b*, p. ix), courses that Currie taught as an assistant to Williams, who also acted as his Ph.D. supervisor. There is also a book that did not get written. Young had projected a treatise on monetary economics that presumably would have provided a systematic written account of ideas, which, according to Oskar Morgenstern (1929, p. 488), had "become at Harvard a matter of oral tradition just as—according to Keynes—Marshall's theory of money in Cambridge" (also quoted by Deutscher [1990, p. 196]). He was working on it from 1927 onward, but whatever he had completed was lost, presumably destroyed, when his office at the London School of Economics was cleared out after his death.[13]

But though Young left no systematic exposition of monetary economics, he nevertheless published enough work on monetary issues for us to be able to get a flavor of his thought. He was, as we have seen, a great admirer of Hawtrey, but he was far too individual a thinker simply to adopt and repeat Hawtrey's views, or those of anyone else, for that matter. Thus the chapter on "Business Cycles" that he prepared for the 1923 edition of Richard Ely's widely used textbook *Outlines of Economics* refers its readers to *Good and Bad Trade* (which Young thought easier reading than *Currency and Credit* [Young 1920, p. 521]). But Robertson's *Industrial Fluctuations* (1915) is also recommended, and Young pays more attention to fixed investment than Hawtrey did. Hawtrey's emphasis on the role of traders was not, in fact, to be a feature of subsequent Harvard or Chicago work on the cycle, and we know from Nicholas Kaldor's notes on his 1927–29 LSE lectures that Young regarded this element as overemphasized in Hawtrey's analysis (see Sandilands 1990, pp. 82–83). All in all, Young is more eclectic than Hawtrey in his views on the sources of economic instability, mentioning "maladjustments, born in part of the redistribution of incomes" not to mention "crop failures, or crises in other countries" as factors in addition to "the exhaustion of bank reserves"

[13] I am indebted to Charles Blitch for this information, who also tells me that the only written contemporary record of the existence of this work is a complimentary reference to it in a 1927 letter from Wesley C. Mitchell to Young. Blitch speculates that Young's wide-ranging curiosity, combined with the generosity with which he gave time to the work of others, would have made it difficult for him to complete a systematic treatise on a single topic. In recent years, Young's work on the role of increasing returns to scale has attracted attention among exponents of modern growth theory, and two relatively recent accounts of his life and works—Blitch (1983) and Peter Newman (1987)—have appeared. Neither of these cites Young's empirical work on the U.S. monetary system discussed below, and my attention was first drawn to it by Deutscher (1990, pp. 195–99).

likely to bring a cyclical upswing to an end (see Young 1923, p. 335). And he also makes a case for public works expenditure as a countercyclical device, a position quite contrary to that taken by Hawtrey in the 1920s.

Nevertheless, there is strong circumstantial evidence of Hawtrey's influence in the 1923 edition of the *Outlines.* The role of the banking system in the cycle gets more emphasis there than in its 1916 predecessor, which does not contain a separate chapter on the cycle; and though the capacity of the newly established Federal Reserve System to use its rediscounting mechanism, and open-market operations, to render cyclical fluctuations "less frequent and less violent than in the past" was recognized in the third edition (1916, p. 312), discussion of the "proposal . . . that the control of the volume of bank credit be used as the means of controlling the fluctuations of the business cycle" is much more extensive in the fourth edition (1923, p. 337). This edition also notes that the Bank of England's use of discount policy in earlier years had been designed primarily to protect its gold reserves rather than to stabilize the cycle, a distinction to be found in Hawtrey's work, and one that leads to important insights about the essential novelty of attempting systematic countercyclical monetary policy.

At the beginning of the 1920s, to use Hawtrey's later words,

> the authorities in control of the Federal Reserve System deliberately departed from that mechanical subservience to [gold] reserve proportions which had previously been supposed essential to the art of central banking. Under the wise guidance of Governor Benjamin Strong of the New York Bank they pursued a policy of stabilisation, which prevented any serious fluctuations of the price level from 1922 to 1929. . . . It was a disaster for the world that Governor Strong died in the autumn of 1928, and the experiment came to an end. [1932, pp. 208–9]

During much of this 1922–28 period, Young was, as Blitch (1983) tells us, a consultant to the New York Bank, and he also carried out an extremely careful *Analysis of Bank Statistics for the United States,* published first in a series of four articles in the *Review of Economic Statistics* and then gathered together in a 1928 book of the same title. The statistics in question appertained to national banks only, and only the last of the four articles deals with post-1914 data—1915–26, to be precise. But they document the pronounced seasonal movements of currency out of New York in the autumn that, when combined with the propensity of New York banks to hold call loans to the financial markets as secondary reserves, did much to contribute to the fragility of the national banking system; and above all, they document New York's central place in what even before 1914 had become (perhaps with the exception of California) an integrated nationwide monetary system. The work is mainly descriptive, but Young did remark, with respect to the movements of funds into New York banks from the hinterland, and thence through financial markets and out to the hinterland again, and their associated fluctuations in reserve and currency/deposit ratios, that "I have little doubt but that relations such as we are now considering lie at the very heart of the problem of the instability of the modern mechanism of bank credit and of those business activities which depend upon credit. The discussion of that problem falls outside the limits set for the present study" (1928, p. 28). And to this aside he appended a footnote: "I know of no better analysis of the essential instability of the volume of bank credit than is to be found in R. G. Hawtrey's work, *Currency and Credit*" (p. 28, n. 1).[14]

One other work of Young's deserves our attention, an essay, evidently written for lay readers, that first appeared in two parts in a weekly called *The Annalist* and was reprinted as chapter 5 of his collection *Economic Problems New and Old* (1927), on "The Structure and Policies of the Federal Reserve System." Young begins by noting the following:

> The fundamental principle of central banking is very simple. It is merely that there should be a bank or group of banks set apart from ordinary commercial banks by the circumstance that their policies are shaped with an eye not merely to their own profits and their own solvency, but to the continued solvency of the banking system of the country, taken as a whole. [Pp. 77–78]

But he extends this essentially Bagehotian proposition by also pointing out that "since the war new importance has been attached to the effects which the operations of central banks have on the general conditions of business, and it is quite generally held that their policies should be determined with primary reference to the securing of the

[14] It should be noted that an important study dealing with, among other things, the role of New York banks in holding reserves for the national banking system, the unsuitability of call loans to Wall Street as secondary reserves for the system as a whole, and the desirability of creating a central bank to act as a lender of last resort had been carried out for the National Monetary Commission by another Harvard economist, Oliver Sprague (1910). Young also referred to this work in *Analysis of Bank Statistics*. The reader is reminded that the 1907 crisis, the last of those described by Sprague, helped provide the impetus for Hawtrey's first book, *Good and Bad Trade* (1913), and that a well-informed discussion of the national banking system appears in that book (p. 169 ff.).

maximum practicable degree of business stability" (p. 80). He also stresses the importance of "that practical wisdom which is born only of experience" in enabling the Federal Reserve Banks to fulfill their task, and is quite explicit that "a sound tradition would not be the kind of thing which could be formulated in a set of rules and maxims" (p. 82), thus echoing the position taken in the previous year by Governor Strong in opposing legislation that would have established the single-minded pursuit of price-level stability as a rule for Federal Reserve policy.[15]

This essay also states the policy implications of Young's abovementioned work on U.S. banking statistics. Its second half is devoted to the following argument:

> Those who planned the Federal Reserve System confidently expected that the system would operate so as to do away with the "artificial" concentration of banking power in New York. . . .
>
> These expectations were bound to be disappointed, for they were based upon a mistaken analysis of the situation that existed in the United States before the Federal Reserve System was installed, and upon a failure to take into account some very important aspects of the operations of central banks in other countries. [P. 84]

Two features of the U.S. system were particularly important here, namely the fact that "New York still retains its unique position as the center in which the surplus banking funds of the country are concentrated" (p. 86) and the fact that New York is "our only really important point of contact between the domestic and the international money markets" (p. 90). For Young, these facts inevitably meant that "the New York Bank has come to have a position of primacy in the Federal Reserve System merely because it has not tried to shun the responsibilities which are naturally assigned to it by the structure of the national money market" (p. 92); and they suggested to him the wisdom of "frankly conceding larger responsibilities and larger powers to the New York Bank . . . [rather] than to run the danger of 'unifying' the system into a cumbrous and slow-moving substitute for a single central bank, with divided authority and divided responsibilities" (p. 94).

The warning implicit here was prophetic: conflict between the New York Bank and the Federal Reserve Board about their respective

[15] The reference here is to the first (Congressman James) Strong Bill, on which hearings were held in 1926–27. Charles Hardy (1932, chap. 10) gives an excellent account, from a contemporary standpoint, of the intellectual background to these hearings.

powers and responsibilities was already evident in 1927 and would be a major contributor to the ineptitude with which monetary policy was conducted after what Hawtrey termed the "disaster" of Benjamin Strong's death. Young, too, died before his warnings materialized, but the analysis from which they derived continued to be developed, particularly by Lauchlin Currie.

Currie would have been Young's assistant, but for the latter's death, and he had served Hawtrey in a similar capacity during the latter's visit to Harvard in 1928–29.[16] His Ph.D. thesis, entitled "Bank Assets and Banking Theory," was submitted to Harvard in January 1931 (Currie 1931*a*), and in the next few years Currie wrote and published extensively on matters of monetary theory and policy, gathering the main results of his work in a monograph, *The Supply and Control of Money in the United States* (1934*b*). Though Currie's book was not a reworking of his thesis, it did contain some material taken from this earlier work, notably a thorough discussion of "The Meaning of Credit," which supplemented a vigorous critique of what Lloyd Mints (1945) would later call the "real-bills doctrine," but what Currie termed, following the usage of the period, the "Commercial Loan Theory of Banking." An intermediate version of this chapter was published in the *Journal of Political Economy* (1933*c*). Another article of Currie's, "The Failure of Monetary Policy to Prevent the Depression of 1929–32" (1934*a*), whose substantive message was also incorporated into his monograph, appeared in the same journal. And anyone concerned with assigning priorities among exponents of a monetary interpretation of the onset of the Great Depression should note that an outline of Currie's views was published as early as 1931, in a book review in the *American Economic Review* (1931*b*). The dangers of confusing money and credit and the role of that confusion in permitting a monetary contraction to begin in 1928, not to mention the possibility that the subsequent downturn of 1930 was due to that contraction, are all discussed there, as indeed they are in Currie's dissertation.

The influence of Young on Currie's work is pervasive, and *The Supply and Control of Money* is in fact dedicated to Young. By far the greater part of that book's quantitative content documents variations

[16] In a personal communication to me (July 8, 1992), Currie says that his work for Hawtrey involved attending his graduate lectures and grading papers. He acted in a similar capacity for Schumpeter, and he recalls getting little out of his lectures and disagreeing with his interpretation of the cycle as the result of waves of innovations. This letter also refers to the plan that Currie would become Young's assistant on the latter's return to Harvard from the London School of Economics in 1930. Currie's work has, as I have already noted, been the subject of commentaries by Brunner (1968), Humphrey (1972), Patinkin (1973), Sandilands (1990), and Steindl (1991), and the following discussion was, no doubt, influenced by all these sources.

in the public's currency/deposit ratio, not to mention the behavior of excess reserves within the banking system, all very much in the spirit and style of Young (1928). But just as Young was no mere exponent of other people's ideas, so Currie too made his own considerable contribution to the tradition in which he was working. Like Hawtrey, whose monetary theory of the cycle had formed the basis of a chapter on "Bank Assets and the Business Cycle" in Currie's dissertation, where it was accorded nine pages (pp. 211–19) of exposition and criticism, Currie was cautious about pushing the quantity theory of money too far.[17] Also like Hawtrey, he was aware of the dangers of ignoring its implications altogether:

> In the past an altogether disproportionate amount of importance was attached to variations in the supply of money. In consequence of the almost universal abandonment of the quantity theory of money, however, there is danger that the pendulum may swing too far in the opposite direction so that the effect of variations in the supply of money may be unduly minimized. [1934*b*, p. 3]

Hence Currie was particularly critical of Keynes (1930) for placing too much emphasis on interest rate variations in the *Treatise,* arguing that his "viewpoint tends . . . to obscure the really important rôle played by changes in the supply of money" (p. 5), and "money" in Currie's view was to be defined as "those instruments possessed by the public by delivery of which debt contracts and price contracts are discharged" (p. 11). In the United States, this meant currency in the hands of the public plus demand deposits, and this point is of some importance. A tightening of U.S. monetary policy in 1928 is much more evident in Currie's data for this aggregate than in the series constructed at the same time by another former student of Young's, James Angell (1933), which included time deposits; and that is surely one reason why Currie was far more definite in attributing the onset of the Depression to Federal Reserve policy than Angell, or indeed

[17] It is interesting to note that, in this chapter, Currie takes up the criticism of Hawtrey's work that it overemphasizes the role of short-term lending to traders for inventory finance and concludes that "Hawtrey's theory does not rest solely on the movement of commercial loans. He only uses the wholesaler's and merchant's demand for loans as a means of bringing about an expansion of credit [i.e., deposit money], which is the essential thing in his theory" (p. 217). It should also be pointed out that, like Young (1928), Currie pays attention to Sprague (1910), but also that he twice criticizes Sprague's later work for coming uncomfortably close to embracing what we would now call the "real-bills doctrine" in discussions of the Federal Reserve System (see Currie 1931*a*, pp. 15–16, 68–70).

Henry Simons, who in 1935 criticized Currie for his allegedly over-narrow definition of money.[18]

Currie, again like Hawtrey, to whose work he explicitly referred on this point (see Currie 1934*a*, p. 146, n. 2), believed that "the shrinkage of spending power and the Wall Street crisis [of October 1929] were both effects of a common cause, . . . credit contraction" (Hawtrey 1932, p. 80), and he attributed this "credit" (i.e., money supply) contraction to the Federal Reserve System's adherence to the "commercial loan" theory of banking, or as Charles O. Hardy (1932, pp. 124–25), whom Currie also cited with approval at this point, termed it, the "Washington" view of the matter (as opposed to the "New York" view, which Hardy associated in particular with Benjamin Strong).[19] Currie was, of course, a strong exponent of this "New York" view. He saw disagreement as stemming in some measure from semantic confusion: "the term [credit] was in the way of acquiring, among monetary writers, a fairly precise connotation: means of payment represented by demand deposits" (1934*b*, p. 48) (he cited both Hawtrey and Young, among other authorities, for this usage), but unfortunately, "particularly in America, [the term] has become increasingly identified with something else—loans of all kinds, and particularly bank loans and investments" (p. 48), with the result that "much of the monetary theory of the past, built up in connection with the control of money by the central bank, has been misapplied by the banking authorities to loans and investments" (p. 56).

[18] Angell (1936) subsequently published data that appeared to show that "outside currency and circulating [i.e., checkable] deposits alike tend to move with or after, but apparently never *before* . . . indices of production, trade, and the like," but he was careful to note that "the conclusion cannot fairly be drawn from this, however, that the quantity of money is a purely passive factor in business activity" (1936, p. 60). His series differed from Currie's as a result of his using a different statistical technique to allocate unclassified nonmember bank deposits between demand and time deposits, and Currie (1936) argued that his own method was more reliable. Moreover, Warburton ([1946] 1966, p. 82) was later to argue, with specific reference to the 1927–32 period, that this description of the timing of variations was "contrary to his [Angell's] data." Nevertheless, the fact remains that Angell, who was a Ph.D. student of Young and Frank Taussig, took a rather pessimistic position on the power of monetary policy—more akin to what Currie (1934*b*, p. 116) attributed to Taussig (and to Mitchell) than to Currie's own position. Note that Friedman (1967) does not attribute to Simons a monetary explanation of the onset of the Depression, and indeed it is hard to decide, from Simons's writings, just what he thought about this matter. Friedman (1974) was later to cite Viner (1932, 1933), not Simons, as the Chicago economist who had most nearly anticipated his own views on the Depression. See, however, the discussion in Sec. IV below.

[19] Hardy was at this time at the Brookings Institution, but he had been an instructor at Chicago between 1916 and 1922, and his students had included Mints and Simons. It is presumably this association that caused Friedman (1974, p. 164, n. 19) to refer to him as a Chicagoan "at one remove."

In 1928, in an effort to check stock market speculation, the authorities had tried to cut down bank lending for financial transactions, while maintaining its availability to commercial and industrial borrowers. The effort had been a partial success in its own terms but had led to the reduction in the money supply, which, in Currie's view, precipitated a downturn in economic activity. Thereafter, according to Currie, the transformation of a downturn into a depression was also largely the responsibility of the Federal Reserve System. Already in his dissertation he had expressed the opinion that "a much greater expansion of credit ought to have been brought about after the downturn in business in 1929 than did in fact take place" (1931*a*, p. 238), and by 1934 he was arguing that

> much of the current belief in the powerlessness of the reserve banks appears to arise from a complete misreading of the monetary history of 1929–32. It is generally held that the reserve administration strove energetically to bring about expansion throughout the depression but that contraction continued despite its efforts. Actually the reserve administration's policy was one of almost complete passivity and quiescence. [1934*b*, p. 147]

That the banking system had increased its holdings of excess reserves and stayed away from the discount window, and that the public had begun to hoard currency in increasing amounts during 1930–32 was as well known to Currie as anyone, but this meant to him not that the authorities were powerless, but merely that "the initiative must be taken by the reserve banks themselves, through increased purchases of bills and securities" (p. 103). Though he conceded that such open-market operations would have been more effective had they been undertaken promptly, he did not believe, as most of his contemporaries did, that the public's unwillingness to borrow from the banking system had presented an insuperable barrier to their effectiveness. Currie (1934*b*, p. 116) cites Taussig and Mitchell as holding this latter view, but on this point he could have included even Hardy, whose criticism of Federal Reserve policy during the Depression for being too cautious (1932, pp. 55–60) was nevertheless tempered by considerable skepticism about the effectiveness of monetary policy: "It would be unjustifiable to impute to the Reserve system primary responsibility either for the prosperity which the country enjoyed during the major portion of the period under review, or for the disasters with which the decade closed" (p. 239).

In a review essay on Keynes's *Treatise*, Williams (1931), who had become Currie's Ph.D. supervisor as a result of Young's death, had also been skeptical about both the central role of monetary factors in generating cyclical fluctuations, including the then rapidly developing downturn, and the power of monetary policy to deal with it, though by 1932 his position had, as we shall see, changed somewhat. But Hawtrey had expressed considerable faith in the power of monetary policy in general, and open-market operations in particular, to offset the Depression in his *Art of Central Banking* (1932), a work with which, as we have seen, Currie was both familiar and sympathetic:

> Obviously, however intense the depression, the unwillingness of borrowers can never be absolute and universal. That would only occur if all economic activity had been completely shut down. To some extent borrowers will be induced to come forward.
>
> . . . If . . . the bills offered and the suitable applications for advances are inadequate and do not increase fast enough, the banks have the alternative of buying long-term investments of a suitable marketable character. . . .
>
> . . . There must ultimately be a limit to the amount of money that the sellers will hold idle, and it follows that by this process the vicious circle of deflation can always be broken, however great the stagnation of business and the reluctance of borrowers may be. [Hawtrey 1932, pp. 173–74]

Though Currie agreed with Hawtrey about this, even in the light of the experience of 1929–32, which "should not be cited as evidence of the *inability* of a central bank to arrest contraction of money and bring about expansion" (1934*b*, p. 148), he nevertheless believed that a better system of monetary control "in which expansions and contractions of the supply of money could be brought about easily and quickly to any required extent" (p. 151) could be devised. Specifically, "It appears to the writer that the most perfect control could be achieved by direct government issue of all money, both notes and deposits subject to check" (p. 151). Thus Currie was an independent originator of one version of what came to be called "the Chicago Plan" for 100 percent money, whose "difference from the present system would lie in the substitution of certainty and precision of control for the existing uncertainty and lack of precision" (p. 156).[20]

[20] I refer here to "one version" of this plan, because a variety of plans were "in the air" as well as in print in the early 1930s. Albert G. Hart (1935) is an excellent source of information about the main alternatives discussed. Though Currie was to submit a detailed proposal for such a scheme to the then Secretary of the Treasury, Henry Morgenthau, in September 1934 (see Currie [1934*b*] 1968, p. 195 ff.), earlier in the year he had thought that "it [could] hardly be regarded as practicable at the present time" (1934*b*, p. 157). Hence the final three chapters of his book were devoted to proposals for modifying the then existing system. These proposals included replacing the extremely cumbersome decision-making process within the Federal Reserve System with a small board of "not more than three or four members," the introduction of

Now it is clear that in the writings of Hawtrey, Young, and Currie are to be found many elements of what Friedman (1974) has termed the "Chicago Tradition": a monetary approach to cycle theory that derived from but went far beyond the quantity theory of money as it was then understood as a proposition about the relationship between money and the price level; opposition to the "real-bills" doctrine; a belief that the Great Depression was largely the result of inept policies pursued by the Federal Reserve System under the influence of that doctrine; confidence in the effectiveness of properly conceived monetary policies to alleviate the Depression; and a version of the 100 percent money scheme; all are there.[21] As we have also seen, certain of these crucial elements were missing, or explicitly denied, in the works of other influential contemporary economists—Taussig, Mitchell, and indeed Hardy, to whom Friedman (1974) was later to refer as a Chicagoan "at one remove"—and Chicago itself in the 1920s was still, to some extent, under the influence of that arch-opponent of the quantity theory, J. Laurence Laughlin. But it is nevertheless the case that some Chicago discussion of these issues began to appear in 1932 and 1933, before much of Currie's work, where these ideas are most fully developed, saw print. The question must arise, therefore, whether the Chicago tradition was a simultaneous and independent development, responding to influences other than those described here, or whether it derived from them. And this question is made all the more interesting by the fact that one important element in the

uniform reserve requirements, along with the obligation of all banks emitting demand deposits to be members of the system, the abolition of the rediscounting privilege, and the introduction of nationwide branch banking. The effectiveness of these measures, Currie well understood, would depend on "a radical change . . . in the whole attitude toward banking at present held by the reserve administration" (p. 157). He specifically referred to the administration's commitment to the erroneous "commercial loan" theory of banking at this point, and noted that "it is . . . useless to increase the administration's control over money if what it is really trying to do is to control the quality of bank assets" (p. 157).

[21] It should be pointed out, as Steindl (1991) has shown, that even in *The Supply and Control of Money* there is a certain ambiguity in Currie's views about the extent to which the banking system's demand for free reserves had become a passive factor in the determination of the money supply and that his inclination to the latter view became stronger as the 1930s progressed and the volume of free reserves continued to grow. In 1936 Currie advocated increasing required reserve ratios to mop up reserves, and again as Steindl stresses, his explanation of the 1938 downturn did not therefore anticipate that of Friedman and Schwartz in attributing it to increases in required reserve ratios. Rather he blamed a tightening of fiscal policy. However, there is no evidence to support the view that Currie's beliefs about what the Federal Reserve System could have accomplished in 1930–32, had it acted soon and vigorously enough, changed as the 1930s progressed. He did not abandon his monetary explanation of the onset of the Great Depression, even though his skepticism about the power of monetary policy alone to combat it grew as the Depression persisted. I am grateful to Roger Sandilands and Frank Steindl for helpful correspondence about this point, but they are not necessarily implicated in the views I express on it.

Chicago tradition—namely a commitment to governing monetary policy by rules rather than discretion—is not merely missing from the writings of Hawtrey, Young, and Currie, but rather is considered and explicitly rejected by all three and by the fact that the systematic and careful empirical analysis of Young and Currie has no parallel in the work of the Chicago economists.[22]

IV. The Chicago School

It is easy to show that, in the early 1930s, Chicago economists were well aware of Currie's work. Two of his most important articles appeared in the *Journal of Political Economy* in 1933 and 1934; and by the early summer of 1934, Jacob Viner, an editor of that journal, who seems to have first met Currie in 1932, had evidently got to know him well enough, and come to think highly enough of his work, to invite him to Washington as a member of the "freshman brains trust."[23] There must also have been contact between Currie and his former undergraduate student Albert Hart, who had moved on to Chicago and in 1935 would provide the definitive account of the "Chicago Plan" for 100 percent money. The published record makes it clear that Hart drew Currie's attention to the now well-known, though never published, Chicago manuscript dealing with this issue

[22] Patinkin (1973) has noted the lack of interest in empirical work of Mints and Simons, which differentiates their contributions so strongly from Friedman's. It is beyond the scope of this paper to investigate the origins of Friedman's empiricism. As I have suggested above, Young's empiricism, and that of his students, among whom Angell should be explicitly included in this context, presumably comes from his training in the American Institutionalist tradition at the University of Wisconsin. But of course Fisher (1911) had made extensive studies of U.S. monetary data, and in the 1920s, so did Carl Snyder, who was much influenced by Fisher. Snyder was on the staff of the Federal Reserve Bank of New York, to which Young acted as a consultant. Given the absence of formal statistical analysis from Hawtrey's work, it is in this regard rather than any other that the case for a Fisherian influence on the Harvard economists might be easiest to make. Against this, it should be noted that, unlike Snyder, both Angell (1933) and Currie (1933*b*) adopted income (or circuit, in Angell's terminology) velocity as opposed to Fisher's transactions velocity as a foundation for their empirical work. Angell (1926, chaps. 7, 8) shows that he was completely familiar with the British as well as Austrian origins of this concept. Note also that the third (1928) edition of Hawtrey's *Currency and Credit* contains a sharp critique of the concept of transactions velocity.

[23] In a personal communication to me (July 8, 1992), Currie notes that his relation with Chicago occurred through Viner, who occasionally lectured at Harvard. The earliest exchange of letters between Currie and Viner in Viner's papers dates from November 1932 and refers to lectures delivered by Viner at Harvard a little earlier that autumn. Viner's letter to Patinkin of January 15, 1970 (reprinted in Patinkin [1981, pp. 267–68]), in which there occurs the phrase "When I went to the Treasury in 1934 I encountered Lauchlin Currie," ought not, therefore, to be interpreted as indicating that this was Viner's *first* encounter with Currie. However, apart from the above-mentioned pair of letters between the two in 1932, the correspondence between Currie and Viner that now survives all dates from 1935 and later.

(Simons et al. 1933) sometime between late 1933, when it was prepared, and the autumn of 1934, when Currie's book, containing a similar proposal, appeared (see Currie 1934*b*, p. 156, n. 1). Furthermore, Simons reviewed the book in question in the August 1935 issue of the *Journal of Political Economy* and referred to it as expounding "a set of views . . . firmly established in the 'oral tradition' of some schools" [note the plural] (1935, p. 555).

Chicago economists must have been aware of Young's work too. Not only had he been Frank H. Knight's thesis supervisor and remained his friend and correspondent thereafter, but, more to the point, the 1928 journey, shortly after which Young contracted his fatal influenza, was a trip between London and Chicago. It had been undertaken, as Blitch (1983) tells us, partly to attend the American Economic Association meetings in that city, but mainly to decline in person the offer of the chairmanship of the Department of Economics at the University of Chicago. Is it too much to presume that members of the Chicago department would have taken the trouble to make themselves aware of at least the outlines of the work Young then had in progress? And that work was, by all accounts, on money.

There is also the matter of the Harris Foundation conference on Gold and Monetary Stabilization, held at the University of Chicago early in 1932, out of which came a manifesto, sent by telegram to President Herbert Hoover, which, among other things, "recommend[ed] that the Federal Reserve banks systematically pursue open-market operations with the double aim of facilitating necessary government financing and increasing the liquidity of the banking structure" (Wright 1932, p. 162). The manifesto was, as Friedman (1974) points out, signed by 12 University of Chicago economists, and following J. Ronnie Davis (1968), he treats it as illustrative of the "intellectual climate at Chicago," though he is careful to observe that the views it expressed were not confined to that institution. As he notes, it was signed as well by 12 others, from nine institutions, "including Irving Fisher of Yale, Alvin Hansen of Minnesota, and John H. Williams of Harvard" (1974, p. 164). But though 12 Chicago economists, including Frank H. Knight, Henry Simons, and Jacob Viner, were among the signatories, Paul Douglas (perhaps not surprisingly) was not; and Douglas was later to remark, with explicit reference to the debates of early 1932 in general, and the proceedings of the Harris Foundation conference in particular, that "those who, like myself, expressed their disbelief that any real stimulation of business would follow [big open-market operations], were either laughed aside or regarded as rather loose-brained heretics" (1935, p. 117). It is of some interest that, in this context, Douglas mentions James H. Rogers, of Yale, rather than any of his colleagues, as being a particularly vigorous advocate of expansionary open-market operations at this 1932 conference.[24]

Nor should it be thought that, Douglas aside, the manifesto was a product of Chicago thinking, to which certain other conference participants were willing to put their signatures. As Davis (1971, p. 129) records, it was in fact drafted by a committee consisting of Irving Fisher, Alvin Hansen, Charles Hardy, Henry Schultz, Jacob Viner, and John H. Williams, and of this group, it was "Professor Williams, who . . . was asked to contribute [an] article . . . on the practical problems of relieving depression, with special attention to the subject matter of these recommendations" for inclusion in the conference proceedings (Wright 1932, p. x). Williams, it will be recalled, was not merely from Harvard, but had just finished supervising Currie's Ph.D. thesis and was involved with Currie in teaching monetary economics.[25]

A comparison of Williams's paper with the one presented at the same 1932 conference by Viner shows interesting similarities—but even more interesting differences. Viner and Williams were both critical of recent Federal Reserve policy, and both placed much of the blame on the Federal Reserve Board's belief in the "commercial loan" theory of banking. Viner's remarks on this matter (from which Friedman [1974] also quotes) were particularly pithy:

> While the New York Federal Reserve Bank has made more effort than any other central banking institution to develop a program and a technique of credit control with a view to

[24] Rogers gave no lecture at the conference but did take part in a roundtable. Douglas refers to the mimeographed proceedings of the conference rather than the published lectures, and though Rogers was not a signatory of the manifesto, the views it expresses are quite compatible with his own comments at the winter 1931 meetings of the Econometric Society: "Under present distressing conditions, *easy money* [by which he meant a low discount rate] is of little importance. *Plentiful money* would probably bring effective relief" (Rogers 1933, p. 70). Rogers was a former student of Fisher, and Sterling Professor at Yale. These facts, along with Fisher's membership on the committee that drafted the manifesto, provide the strongest evidence of which I am aware of a direct Fisherian influence on Chicago thinking. For an account of the monetary analysis developed by Yale economists during this period, notably Fisher, Rogers, and Harry Gunnison Brown, see Steindl (1992).

[25] In his personal communication to me of July 9, 1992, Currie remarks that the fact that he had been kept on at Harvard in anticipation of his acting as an assistant to Young on the latter's expected return affected his relationship with Williams. Though they were personally friendly, Williams never regarded himself as Currie's "patron," and Currie did not attend the lectures in the course in which he acted as assistant. Indeed Currie goes so far as to remark that "I probably had more influence on his thinking than he on mine." This judgment, similar to the judgment many Ph.D. students make about their interaction with supervisors, is nevertheless consistent with the published record.

> stabilization, it has at critical moments found itself at cross-purposes with, and inhibited from action by, a Federal Reserve Board with an attitude toward its functions resembling with almost miraculous closeness that of the Bank of England during its worst period. [1932, p. 28]

Viner and Williams were both unenthusiastic about the gold standard, not only as a general framework for organizing monetary systems, but also because, in 1932, adherence to it inhibited the U.S. authorities from undertaking otherwise desirable monetary stabilization policies, though neither was willing to advocate its outright abandonment.

But there was an important difference in emphasis between their views about what could be accomplished by monetary policy if it were not constrained by the gold standard. Viner, noting that "for over a century writers have pleaded for the abandonment of the gold standard and the substitution of a managed paper currency" (p. 35), expressed "an individual view, [that] we know too little as yet of the possibilities of stabilization to take immediately any major steps in that direction" (p. 37). The most he would concede was that

> We could soon learn a great deal more than is now known of the possibilities of comprehensive stabilization, if some country now off the gold standard were to attempt by credit control or otherwise to raise its price level somewhat above its present level, and then were to regulate the volume of bank credit so as to approximate a constant level in some significant index of prices. [P. 38]

Williams, on the other hand, was more confident:

> Granting . . . the dangers of expecting too much from credit management, and granting also the deficiencies of our understanding, it is safe to say that both our ability to control and our knowledge of why to control considerably outrun our performance. . . .
>
> . . . The immediate problem is to restore normal conditions. The greatest single help, internally, would be a vigorous open-market policy designed to reduce rediscounts of member banks and to increase the supply of purchasing power. . . . The logical end of the evolution of credit management, and the only real hope of solution of the conflict between external and internal stability, would be closer cooperation of central banks looking toward some form or degree of supernational management. [1932, pp. 156–58]

The differences between Viner and Williams revealed here do not concern matters of theory, but rather of empirical judgment. Viner is skeptical but nevertheless open-minded about what open-market operations might achieve; Williams is more confident, although that confidence is of relatively recent origin.[26] The views he had expressed in 1931 had, as we have noted, been more cautious.

Is it going too far to see the influence of Hawtrey, and Currie too, on Williams's paper? Certainly, and as we have already seen, optimism about the power of open-market operations is expressed in *The Art of Central Banking* (1932) and is the major factor distinguishing Hawtrey's attitude, one shared by Currie, from that of Charles Hardy (another author of the 1932 manifesto) as set out in his own book of the same year. Furthermore, the phrase "closer co-operation of central banks looking toward some form or degree of supernational management" provides an excellent summary of the aims of the 1922 Genoa resolutions, of which Hawtrey had been the principal architect. And the opening theoretical section of Williams's paper adopts Hawtrey's (1919) method of focusing on banking behavior in the absence of currency in order to demonstrate propositions, also closely associated with Hawtrey, namely, "that under central banking the control [of credit] can never be 'automatic' [and that this] would seem to follow from the nature of the credit mechanism" (Williams 1932, p. 135). The circumstantial evidence is strong, but the fact remains that Williams does not cite Hawtrey. This suggests that, if we are seeing Hawtrey's influence here, it was exercised indirectly, perhaps by way of Currie, or indeed by way of Keynes's *Treatise,* which Williams (1931) had only recently reviewed. As Deutscher (1990) has shown, Hawtrey's contributions had left a considerable mark on this latter work.

Even so, the only explicit mention of Hawtrey in the Harris Foundation volume is critical. It occurs in the course of Haberler's (1932) defense of Hayek's (1931) views, which, contrary to those of Hawtrey, were that expansionary, rather than contractionary, monetary policy had caused the Depression in the first place and that expansionary policy, if implemented in 1932, would serve only to prolong it. Haberler was a visitor at Harvard that year, but he was not, needless

[26] Friedman (1974) also refers to Viner's (1933) Minnesota lecture, and the views Viner there expresses are indeed somewhat more optimistic about the powers of monetary policy to alleviate the Depression than those he had set out in early 1932 (but this paper was written about a year after the Harris Foundation conference). Even then, as Friedman notes, Viner was still inhibited from recommending vigorous expansion in the United States by the difficulties he believed to be imposed by the maintenance of the gold standard, which was of course abandoned only a few months later.

to say, a signatory of the manifesto that emerged from the Harris Foundation conference; Viner and Hardy, despite their reservations about what might be achieved by expansionary policy, had participated in drafting it. We should not, therefore, make too much of institutional affiliations at this point, nor should we overstress the extent of the differences of opinion between Williams and colleagues. But the facts remain that, if we follow Friedman in looking to the 1932 Harris Foundation conference for evidence of that "hopefulness" that he tells us marked the Chicago tradition, we shall find more of it in the contribution of Williams than anywhere else; and if we look further afield, we shall also find it in the work of Hawtrey—by then published—and Lauchlin Currie—then in progress.[27]

Another important early record of Chicago analysis cited by Friedman, namely, the appendix on "Banking and Business Cycles" attached to Simons et al. (1933), concisely and vigorously elaborates the view that

> in any money economy there will be some tendency toward cumulative maladjustment over periods of a few years, largely because of two circumstances: (a) The relative inflexibility of those prices which largely govern operating costs of production; and (b) the sensitiveness or responsiveness of money "circulation" to changes of business earnings. [1933, app., p. 1]

That input costs, and particularly money wages, were relatively inflexible had been a key proposition in cycle theory, particularly British theory, since the work of Alfred Marshall and Mary Paley Marshall (1879), and it had been a standard feature of Hawtrey's analysis since 1913. And the "sensitiveness . . . of money 'circulation' to changes of business earnings" is precisely what Hawtrey meant when he referred to the "inherent instability of credit." This Chicago theoretical analysis is neither original nor unusual, although there is no way of knowing whether Hawtrey directly influenced the appendix in which it is set out, which lacks any references to the literature.[28] However, as Hayek suggested to Friedman in a 1967 letter dealing

[27] The reader is, nevertheless, reminded of Douglas's reference to Rogers's informal contribution to this conference and the written record of the latter's position as expressed in Rogers (1933). See also Steindl (1992).

[28] But we may be reasonably confident that Irving Fisher did not. The last sentence of this appendix states that "it follows as a corollary, incidentally, that the problem of unemployment is not, to an important extent, a problem of debt" (Simons et al. 1933, app., p. 6). To my eye, this reads like a direct repudiation of Fisher's "Debt-Deflation Theory of Great Depressions" as set out in Fisher (1932, 1933), and probably as discussed at the 1932 Harris Foundation conference, too.

with common intellectual influences on Keynes and Simons, and quoted in Friedman ([1967] 1969, p. 88, n. 7), "We all held similar ideas in the 1920's. They had been most fully elaborated by R. G. Hawtrey who was all the time talking about the 'inherent instability of credit' but he was by no means the only one." But if Hawtrey was "not the only one," he was beyond a doubt the leading exponent of the style of monetary cycle analysis deployed by Simons and his colleagues.[29]

Simons et al. (1933) advocated 100 percent money and the subjection of monetary policy to a legislated rule. They were somewhat more original in this normative analysis, but even here there are precedents in earlier literature. The 1921 Nobel laureate in chemistry, Frederick Soddy, wrote a number of unconventional works on economic matters during the 1920s and 1930s and advocated a 100 percent money scheme in *Wealth, Virtual Wealth and Debt* (1926, pp. 197–99); at least one Chicagoan was familiar with this work, namely Frank H. Knight, who, as Herman Daly (1980) noted, had reviewed it favorably in the *Saturday Review of Literature*. More generally, there had been widespread discussion in the United States of governing monetary policy by a legislated rule for nearly a decade: the Strong Bills of 1926 and 1927 had sought to do just that with a price stabilization rule and had been supported by such economists as Gustav Cassel, John Commons, and Irving Fisher; the Goldsborough Bill of 1932 had revived this idea. Constant money growth, which would later reappear in Friedman's work, had also been advocated as a suitable aim for monetary policy, with varying degrees of enthusiasm by Carl Snyder (1924) and Lionel Edie (1931), while the "neutral money principle" of stabilizing money expenditures (*MV* in Fisherian terms), developed by the Austrian School in the late 1920s, had by 1932 become well enough known in the United States to attract the

[29] But it was disingenuous of Hayek to try to associate himself with Hawtrey's analysis. In the 1920s and 1930s, he had been the outstanding exponent of the very different "Austrian" theory, and he had then also been highly critical of analysis based in any way on the quantity theory and on the idea of the "general price level." Austrian analysis focused on the effects of money on relative prices and led to an extremely pessimistic, indeed nihilistic, view of the scope for fighting the Depression with any sort of policy, either monetary or fiscal. Friedman refers explicitly to this style of theory as representing "the atrophied and rigid caricature [of the quantity theory] that is so frequently described by proponents of the new income-expenditure approach" (1974, p. 163; bracketed phrase in original). There are two difficulties with Friedman's comments on this matter. First, the Austrian approach was explicitly offered by its exponents as an alternative, theoretically superior, doctrine to anything associated with the quantity theory; and second, Friedman correctly identifies Ludwig von Mises and Lionel Robbins as among its exponents but fails to mention even the name of the leading figure in this group, namely Hayek (see Hayek 1931, 1933). On Hayek's analysis, see Laidler (1992).

cautious support of Charles Hardy among others (see Hardy 1932, p. 324).[30]

But for all that, Simons et al. did make a unique and important contribution. As Hart pointed out in his 1935 discussion of the "Chicago Plan," "The '100 per cent. system' . . . [was] an effective remedy for the weaknesses of the banking system which now unfit it *either for automatic functioning or for use as an instrument of monetary management*" ([1935] 1952, p. 444; italics added). Currie, to whose "masterly account" of the way in which "conversion of chequing deposits into cash or *vice versa* influences the total quantity of both in existence" (p. 442) Hart paid tribute, very clearly advocated it for the latter purpose. As Currie had remarked in 1933, "In such a delicate and difficult task as the determination of proper central banking policy it would appear to be a safe generalization that automatic rules render more difficult the task of central bankers, while discretionary powers facilitate it" (1933*a*, p. 356). Douglas also took such a view, listing among the advantages of 100 percent money that it would "provide complete social control over monetary matters" (1935, p. 187).

Not so Simons, for whom "managed currency without definite, stable, legislative rules is one of the most dangerous forms of 'planning'" (1935, p. 558). The importance that Simons attached to this point may be gauged from the fact that, though this quotation is drawn from his review of Currie (1934*b*), almost the same phrases are to be found in Simons et al. (1933, pp. 4–5), Simons (1934, p. 24), and Simons ([1936] 1952, p. 339).

Readers of Hart (1935) are given the impression that the "Chicago Plan" and "100 percent money" are one and the same thing, but the 1933 manuscript makes it quite clear that 100 percent money is but one component of a plan that *also encompasses a legislated rule for the conduct of policy*. Moreover, Hardy had remarked, with reference to the debate about legislated monetary rules in 1926–27, that "*the controversy over the stabilization issue hinges chiefly upon differences of economic theory*. It does not involve party traditions or conflicting sectional or class interests" (1932, p. 202). But Simons in 1934 presented a monetary rule as an integral part of *A Positive Program for Laissez Faire*.[31]

[30] The policy nihilism of the Austrians was not shared by Hardy, but he was skeptical about how much of the Depression should really be blamed on monetary policy and how much could be expected of it by way of a cure. Even so, as his participation in drafting the 1932 Harris Foundation manifesto attests, he still thought that the experiment of expansionary open-market operations was worth trying.

[31] And much of the rest of the program was concerned with eliminating the various monopolies that, in Simons's view, were responsible for the cost rigidities that had made the Depression so severe. It is worth noting that Simons was explicitly opposed to nationwide branch banking of the type favored by Currie, because of his general aversion to business concentration.

The originality of Simons's contribution to the discussion of monetary policy thus lay in linking his positive analysis to liberal political values. It was this, rather than any characteristic of that positive analysis, whether theoretical or empirical, that separated Chicago work from that of Hawtrey and those Harvard economists whom he influenced.[32]

Simons discussed a range of possible monetary policy rules: "At one extreme is the rule of fixing the quantity (*M*) or the total turnover (*MV*); at the other is the rule of stabilizing some index of commodity prices" (1934, pp. 24–25), and the change in his position between 1933 and 1936 about which was best is worth some discussion. His first preference, in 1933, had been for fixing the quantity of money. Among the disadvantages of price-level stabilization that he then found compelling was that "it is sadly lacking in definiteness as a rule of long run management. Thus it leaves too much room for administrative discretion and political manipulation. (This will be clear immediately to anyone familiar with the technical, statistical problems of price level measurement over long periods)" (Simons et al. 1933, p. sup. 7). A constant money supply rule was preferable because, among other things, it implied, under a 100 percent money regime, a balanced budget rule for fiscal policy too, and because it implied that input prices, and particularly wages, which Simons believed to be sticky in nominal terms, would not have to move.[33] It was even preferable to stabilizing *MV*—the neutral money principle—because of difficulties in establishing procedures for offsetting changes in *V* "without in effect granting to the monetary authority large freedom for discretionary action. Moreover, if we be not alarmed by the thought of some discretionary action, is there any feasible way of permitting discretionary measures in the short-run and still assuring realization of the long run objectives?" (p. sup. 4). And in any event, "some of us are inclined to feel that the disturbances occasioned merely by changes in velocity are unlikely to be of serious magnitude" (p. sup. 3).

Friedman (1967) conjectured that Simons's (1936) advocacy of a price-level rule was the result of ignorance of the monetary facts of the Great Depression, but Patinkin (1979) questioned this interpretation, arguing that by 1936, and as a reviewer of Currie's (1934*b*) book, Simons must have had a reasonable grasp of those facts, even if he

[32] To say this, of course, is also to say that Jacob Viner should not be categorized as a member of the Chicago School, a judgment with which, one suspects, he would not have been entirely unhappy. See Viner's letter to Patinkin of November 24, 1969 (reprinted in Patinkin [1981, pp. 265–66]).

[33] Though Simons did see the need for a period of transition, involving reflation, before the constant money supply rule was to be enforced.

himself was not deeply impressed by empirical work. The evidence above supports Patinkin's position, for it suggests that in 1933 Simons's empirical judgment was reasonably accurate. This is perhaps not surprising, because Currie's (1932) basic work documenting both the mild contraction of deposits of 1928–29 and what he called their "catastrophic decline" in 1931, the very facts which underlay his later (1934*a*, 1934*b*) critique of Federal Reserve policy, had already been published, and both Currie's (1933*b*) estimates of narrow money velocity and Angell's (1933) for broad money velocity appeared in November of that year.

What had come to concern Simons in 1936 was not short-run cyclical instability of velocity per se, based on a misreading of recent experience, but the potential for such instability to appear in the future as a consequence of the institutional change that the introduction of a rule might create. Readers will recognize what we nowadays call "the Lucas critique" or "Goodhart's law" as underlying Simons's position, though he himself dealt with only one special case of what we now think of as a pervasive problem: "The fixing of the quantity of circulating media might merely serve to increase the perverse variability in the amounts of 'near-moneys' and in the degree of their general acceptability, just as the restrictions on the issue of bank notes presumably served to hasten the development of deposit (checking-account) banking" ([1936] 1952, p. 341).

This matter had been discussed earlier by Hart, who noted that "a repetition of the fiasco of bank-note regulation—which drove monetary transactions into the less manageable form of chequing on bank balances—would be disastrous" ([1935] 1952, p. 451). Neither Hart nor Simons identified the specific historical evidence that he had in mind here, but I conjecture that both were referring to British experience with Sir Robert Peel's Bank Charter Act of 1844, which failed to achieve its purpose because, among other weaknesses, it imposed 100 percent marginal reserve requirements against only Bank of England notes, leaving deposit banking essentially unregulated. They could, though, have been referring to the development of deposit banking among state-chartered banks in the United States in response to the prohibitive taxation of their note issues instituted in 1863.[34]

[34] Hart (1952, p. 438, n. 3) explicitly discusses the similarities and differences between the Chicago Plan and Peel's act, but does not refer to American experience. Among the Chicago department, Viner would have been well enough aware of this episode to see its potential relevance and draw his colleagues' attention to it; we also know from Hart's paper that Viner commented on the "Chicago Plan," though the explicit reference to him does not concern this point (see Hart 1952, p. 454, n. 30). However, Viner's *Studies in the Theory of International Trade* (1937), with specific reference to the provisions of Peel's act, does draw attention to "changes in the ratio between bank notes and deposits and in their relative velocities . . . which the regulation of one type of means of payment might itself tend to bring about" (p. 253).

Whatever prompted Simons's shift from a money supply rule to a price-level rule, however, two things are clear: it did represent for him a shift to a second-best position that opened up uncomfortably large scope for the exercise of discretionary power; but, even more important, he did think it nevertheless feasible to enforce a price stabilization rule, so that its legislation remained a far superior alternative to leaving government authority in the monetary area unfettered: as he put it, "If price-level stabilization is a poor system, it is, still from a liberal viewpoint, infinitely better than no system at all" (1952, p. 358). The link between a monetary approach to business cycle analysis and a liberal political agenda, that is to say, which I have suggested was the major distinguishing feature of the early "Chicago" tradition, remained firmly in place in 1936, as it would in the later work of Mints (1950) and Friedman.

V. Concluding Comments

The year 1936 was of course crucial in the development of macroeconomics. Keynes's *General Theory* filled intellectual vacuums in a number of important places. Before then, the main rival to the analytic tradition deriving from the quantity theory, discussed in this paper, was Austrian business cycle theory, which taught that the only cure for the Depression was to leave well enough alone and allow it to come to a natural end. As Friedman has plausibly suggested, this negative policy message did much to predispose economists exposed to it to embrace Keynesian ideas.[35] Friedman is surely right also in claiming that, *after* 1936, Chicago was unique among major centers in preserving and developing further the analytic tradition discussed in this paper as the basis of an important body of ongoing work and in suggesting that the failure of the Keynesian revolution immediately to overwhelm this center had much to do with the dominance there of this tradition.[36]

[35] That is surely why, in Britain, not just Cambridge economists, but many at the London School of Economics, too, quickly took up the new doctrine. Austrian nihilism had made inroads at Harvard as well, where the combined effects of the death of Young, the departure of Currie, and, perhaps also, Williams's accession in 1937 to a senior administrative position ensured that the once vigorous tradition in more traditional monetary analysis on which this paper has focused had died out. There, too, the triumph of Keynesian thought after 1936 was quick and close to complete. In Currie's case, of course, the economics of the New Deal, which he did so much to create once in Washington, easily assimilated Keynes's (1936) analysis and came to be called simply, but unfairly to its American creators, Keynesian economics. On the American roots of the economics of New Deal fiscal policy, including those nurtured at Chicago, particularly by Schultz, Viner, and Douglas, see Davis (1971).

[36] Which is not to say that particular individuals in other places did not continue to work in the tradition discussed in this paper. Rogers's death in 1939 seems to have cut short further developments at Yale, but Angell at Columbia, Arthur Marget (1938, 1942) at Minnesota (who was also, incidentally, a student of Young's and a signatory

It is beyond the scope of this paper to describe the subsequent development of Chicago thought and to show how some of the theoretical innovations of the *General Theory* became incorporated into it. It will suffice here (1) to express agreement with Patinkin's (1969) judgment that Friedman's (1956) capital theoretic model of the demand for money betrays a deep and unmistakable Keynesian influence; (2) to draw attention, nevertheless, to the essential similarity between Friedman's interpretation of the causes of the Great Depression and his views on what appropriate monetary policy could have accomplished between 1929 and 1933, and the positions taken by Hawtrey, Williams, and Currie on the same questions; (3) to note that advocacy of monetary rules as a central component of a broader liberal policy agenda is what gave Chicago work of the 1930s its distinctive character; and (4) to conclude that it is only the latter feature that links what has come to be called "monetarism" to any tradition uniquely associated with the Chicago of the early 1930s.

References

Angell, James W. *The Theory of International Prices: History, Criticism and Restatement.* Cambridge, Mass.: Harvard Univ. Press, 1926.

———. "Money, Prices and Production: Some Fundamental Concepts." *Q.J.E.* 48 (November 1933): 39–76.

———. *The Behavior of Money: Exploratory Studies.* New York: McGraw-Hill, 1936. Reprint. New York: Kelley, 1969.

Blitch, Charles P. "Allyn A. Young: A Curious Case of Professional Neglect." *Hist. Polit. Econ.* 15 (Spring 1983): 1–24.

Brown, Douglas V., et al. *The Economics of the Recovery Program.* Cambridge, Mass.: Harvard Univ. Press, 1934.

Brunner, Karl. "Introduction." In *The Supply and Control of Money in the United States,* by Lauchlin Currie. New York: Russell & Russell, 1968.

Currie, Lauchlin. "Bank Assets and Banking Theory." Ph.D. dissertation, Harvard Univ., 1931. (*a*)

———. Review of *Federal Reserve Policy, 1921–1930,* by Harold L. Reed. *A.E.R.* 21 (March 1931): 162–64. (*b*)

———. "Member Bank Indebtedness and Net Demand Deposits in the Federal Reserve System." *Q.J.E.* 46 (May 1932): 509–25.

———. "Member Bank Reserves and Bank Debits." *Q.J.E.* 47 (February 1933): 349–56. (*a*)

———. "Money, Gold, and Income in the United States, 1921–32." *Q.J.E.* 48 (November 1933): 77–95. (*b*)

———. "Treatment of Credit in Contemporary Monetary Theory." *J.P.E.* 41 (February 1933): 58–79. (*c*)

———. "The Failure of Monetary Policy to Prevent the Depression of 1929–32." *J.P.E.* 42 (April 1934): 145–77. (*a*)

———. *The Supply and Control of Money in the United States.* Cambridge, Mass.: Harvard Univ. Press, 1934. (*b*) Reprint. New York: Russell & Russell, 1968.

of the 1932 Harris Foundation conference manifesto), and Warburton at the Federal Deposit Insurance Corporation all continued to work in the older tradition.

———. Review of *The Behavior of Money: Exploratory Studies*, by James W. Angell. *A.E.R.* 26 (December 1936): 789–91.

Daly, Herman E. "The Economic Thought of Frederick Soddy." *Hist. Polit. Econ.* 12 (Winter 1980): 469–88.

Davis, J. Ronnie. "Chicago Economists, Deficit Budgets, and the Early 1930's." *A.E.R.* 58 (June 1968): 476–82.

———. *The New Economics and the Old Economists.* Ames: Iowa State Univ. Press, 1971.

Deutscher, Patrick. *R. G. Hawtrey and the Development of Macroeconomics.* London: Macmillan, 1990.

Douglas, Paul H. *Controlling Depressions.* New York: Norton, 1935.

Edie, Lionel D. *The Banks and Prosperity.* New York: Harper and Bros., 1931.

Ely, Richard T. *Outlines of Economics.* 3d ed. New York: Macmillan, 1916; 4th ed. 1923.

Fisher, Irving. *The Purchasing Power of Money: Its Determination and Relation to Credit, Interest and Crises.* New York: Macmillan, 1911.

———. "The Business Cycle Largely a 'Dance of the Dollar.'" *J. American Statis. Assoc.* 18 (December 1923): 1024–28.

———. *Booms and Depressions: Some First Principles.* New York: Adelphi, 1932.

———. "The Debt-Deflation Theory of Great Depressions." *Econometrica* 1 (October 1933): 337–57.

———. *100% Money.* New York: Adelphi, 1935.

Friedman, Milton. "The Quantity Theory of Money: A Restatement." In *Studies in the Quantity Theory of Money.* Chicago: Univ. Chicago Press, 1956. Reprinted in *The Optimum Quantity of Money and Other Essays.* London: Macmillan, 1969.

———. "The Monetary Theory and Policy of Henry Simons." *J. Law and Econ.* 10 (October 1967): 1–13. Reprinted in *The Optimum Quantity of Money and Other Essays.* London: Macmillan, 1969.

———. "Comments on the Critics." In *Milton Friedman's Monetary Framework: A Debate with His Critics,* edited by Robert J. Gordon. Chicago: Univ. Chicago Press, 1974.

Friedman, Milton, and Schwartz, Anna J. *A Monetary History of the United States, 1867–1960.* Princeton, N.J.: Princeton Univ. Press (for NBER), 1963.

———. *Monetary Statistics of the United States: Estimates, Sources, Methods.* Princeton, N.J.: Princeton Univ. Press (for NBER), 1970.

Haberler, Gottfried von. "Money and the Business Cycle." In *Gold and Monetary Stabilization,* edited by Quincy Wright. Chicago: Univ. Chicago Press, 1932.

———. *Prosperity and Depression: A Theoretical Analysis of Cyclical Movements.* Geneva: League of Nations, 1937.

Hansen, Alvin H. *Fiscal Policy and Business Cycles.* New York: Norton, 1941.

———. *Business Cycles and National Income.* New York: Norton, 1951.

Hardy, Charles O. *Credit Policies of the Federal Reserve System.* Washington: Brookings Inst., 1932.

Harris, Seymour E., ed. *Economic Reconstruction.* New York: McGraw-Hill, 1945.

Hart, Albert G. "The 'Chicago Plan' of Banking Reform." *Rev. Econ. Studies* 2 (February 1935): 104–16. Reprinted in *Readings in Monetary Theory.* London: Allen and Unwin (for American Econ. Assoc.), 1952.

Hawtrey, Ralph G. *Good and Bad Trade: An Inquiry into the Causes of Trade Fluctuations.* London: Constable, 1913. Reprint. New York: Kelley, 1962.

———. *Currency and Credit.* London: Longmans, Green, 1919. 2d ed. 1923. 3d ed. 1928.

———. *The Art of Central Banking.* London: Longmans, Green, 1932.

Hayek, Friedrich A. von. *Prices and Production.* London: Routledge, 1931.

———. *Monetary Theory and the Trade Cycle.* London: Routledge and Kegan Paul, 1933.

Humphrey, Thomas M. "Role of Non-Chicago Economists in the Evolution of the Quantity Theory in America, 1930–1950." *Southern Econ. J.* 38 (July 1971): 12–18.

Johnson, Harry G., and Rees, Albert, eds. *Landmarks in Political Economy.* Chicago: Univ. Chicago Press, 1962.

Keynes, John Maynard. *A Treatise on Money.* 2 vols. London: Macmillan, 1930.

———. *The General Theory of Employment, Interest and Money.* London: Macmillan, 1936.

Laidler, David. *The Golden Age of the Quantity Theory.* Princeton, N.J.: Princeton Univ. Press, 1991.

———. "Hayek on Neutral Money and the Cycle." Manuscript. London, Ont.: Univ. Western Ontario, 1992.

Marget, Arthur W. *The Theory of Prices: A Re-Examination of the Central Problems of Monetary Theory.* 2 vols. New York: Prentice-Hall, 1938, 1942.

Marshall, Alfred, and Marshall, Mary Paley. *The Economics of Industry.* London: Macmillan, 1879.

Mason, Edward S. "The Harvard Department of Economics from the Beginning to World War II." *Q.J.E.* 97 (August 1982): 383–433.

Mints, Lloyd W. *A History of Banking Theory in Great Britain and the United States.* Chicago: Univ. Chicago Press, 1945.

———. *Monetary Policy for a Competitive Society.* New York: McGraw-Hill, 1950.

Morgenstern, Oskar. "Allyn Abbott Young" (in German). *Zeitschrift für Nationalökonomie* 1 (May 1929): 143–45. Reprinted in *Selected Economic Writings of Oskar Morgenstern,* edited by Andrew Schotter. New York: New York Univ. Press, 1976.

Newman, Peter. "Allyn A. Young." In *The New Palgrave: A Dictionary of Economics,* edited by John Eatwell, Murray Milgate, and Peter Newman. London: Macmillan, 1987.

Patinkin, Don. "The Chicago Tradition, the Quantity Theory, and Friedman." *J. Money, Credit and Banking* 1 (February 1969): 46–70. Reprinted in Patinkin (1981).

———. "On the Monetary Economics of Chicagoans and Non-Chicagoans: Comment." *Southern Econ. J.* 39 (January 1973): 454–59. Reprinted as "More on the Chicago Monetary Tradition" in Patinkin (1981).

———. "Keynes and Chicago." *J. Law and Econ.* 22 (October 1979): 213–32. Reprinted in Patinkin (1981).

———. *Essays on and in the Chicago Tradition.* Durham, N.C.: Duke Univ. Press, 1981.

Robertson, Dennis H. *A Study of Industrial Fluctuations: An Enquiry into the Character and Causes of the So-called Cyclical Movements of Trade.* London: King, 1915.

Rogers, James H. "The Absorption of Bank Credit." *Econometrica* 1 (January 1933): 63–70.

Sandilands, Roger J. *The Life and Political Economy of Lauchlin Currie: New Dealer, Presidential Adviser, and Development Economist.* Durham, N.C.: Duke Univ. Press, 1990. (*a*)

———, ed. *Nicholas Kaldor's Notes on Allyn Young's LSE Lectures, 1927–29. J. Econ. Studies* 17, nos. 3/4 (1990): 2–114. (*b*)

Schumpeter, Joseph A. *History of Economic-Analysis*. New York: Oxford Univ. Press, 1954.

Simons, Henry C. *A Positive Program for Laissez Faire: Some Proposals for a Liberal Economic Policy*. Public Policy Pamphlet no. 15. Chicago: Univ. Chicago Press, 1934.

———. Review of *The Supply and Control of Money in the United States*, by Lauchlin Currie. *J.P.E.* 43 (August 1935): 555–58.

———. "Rules versus Authorities in Monetary Policy." *J.P.E.* 44 (February 1936): 1–30. Reprinted in *Readings in Monetary Theory*. London: Allen and Unwin (for American Econ. Assoc.), 1952.

———, et al. "Banking and Currency Reform." Manuscript. Chicago: Univ. Chicago, 1933.

Snyder, Carl. "New Measures in the Equation of Exchange." *A.E.R.* 14 (December 1924): 699–713.

Soddy, Frederick. *Wealth, Virtual Wealth and Debt: The Solution of the Economic Paradox*. New York: Dutton, 1926.

Sprague, Oliver M. W. *History of Crises under the National Banking System*. Washington: Government Printing Office, 1910.

Steindl, Frank G. "The Monetary Economics of Lauchlin Currie." *J. Monetary Econ.* 27 (June 1991): 445–61.

———. "Yale and the Monetary Interpretation of the Great Depression." Manuscript. Stillwater: Oklahoma State Univ., 1992.

Tobin, James. "Irving Fisher." In *The New Palgrave: A Dictionary of Economics*, edited by John Eatwell, Murray Milgate, and Peter Newman. London: Macmillan, 1987.

Viner, Jacob. "International Aspects of the Gold Standard." In *Gold and Monetary Stabilization*, edited by Quincy Wright. Chicago: Univ. Chicago Press, 1932.

———. *Balanced Deflation, Inflation, or More Depression?* Minneapolis: Univ. Minnesota Press, 1933.

———. *Studies in the Theory of International Trade*. New York: Harper and Bros., 1937.

Warburton, Clark. *Depression, Inflation, and Monetary Policy: Selected Papers, 1945–1953*. Baltimore: Johns Hopkins Univ. Press, 1966.

Wicksell, Knut. *Interest and Prices* (in German). Jena: Fischer, 1898. Translated by R. F. Kahn. London: Macmillan (for Royal Econ. Soc.), 1936.

Williams, John H. "The Monetary Doctrines of J. M. Keynes." *Q.J.E.* 45 (August 1931): 547–87.

———. "Monetary Stability and the Gold Standard." In *Gold and Monetary Stabilization*, edited by Quincy Wright. Chicago: Univ. Chicago Press, 1932.

Wright, Quincy, ed. *Gold and Monetary Stabilization: Lectures on the Harris Foundation*. Chicago: Univ. Chicago Press, 1932.

Young, Allyn Abbott. Review of *Currency and Credit*, by Ralph G. Hawtrey, and *Stabilizing the Dollar*, by Irving Fisher. *Q.J.E.* 34 (May 1920): 520–32.

———. "Business Cycles." In *Outlines of Economics*, 4th ed., by Richard T. Ely. New York: Macmillan, 1923.

———. Review of *Currency and Credit* (2d ed.) and *Monetary Reconstruction*, by Ralph G. Hawtrey. *A.E.R.* 14 (June 1924): 349–51.

———. *Economic Problems New and Old*. Cambridge, Mass.: Riverside, 1927.

———. *An Analysis of Bank Statistics for the United States*. Cambridge, Mass.: Harvard Univ. Press, 1928.

'The Doctrinal Foundations of Monetary Economics'

G. S. Tavlas, 'Chicago, Harvard, and the doctrinal foundations of monetary economics', *Journal of Political Economy*, 105 (February 1997), pp. 153–77.

Chicago, Harvard, and the Doctrinal Foundations of Monetary Economics

George S. Tavlas

Bank of Greece and International Monetary Fund

The relationship between Milton Friedman's monetary economics and the views espoused by Chicago and non-Chicago quantity theorists during the years 1930–36 is examined. Contrary to recent interpretations, Chicago economists advanced the efficacy of monetary policy as the means of escaping from the Great Depression, provided that such a policy was implemented by the use of budget deficits to generate monetary expansion. The use of the quantity theory of money to provide a theoretical rationale for budget deficits distinguished the Chicago economists from other quantity theorists and left them less susceptible to the Keynesian revolution. The claim that Harvard was an important center for monetary research in the early 1930s is refuted.

I. Introduction

Milton Friedman's claim, in his restatement of the quantity theory of money (1956), that his monetary economics is a direct outgrowth of an earlier Chicago quantity theory tradition (as reflected in the writings of Henry Simons, Frank Knight, Jacob Viner, and Lloyd Mints) has provoked a long-running debate about the relationship

This paper was prepared while I was guest scholar at the Brookings Institution. For encouragement and guidance, I am grateful to Milton Friedman. I have benefited from helpful comments and discussions with Martin Bailey, Edward Bernstein, Benjamin Cohen, David Fand, Morris Marget Goldings, Peter Kenen, David Laidler, Robert E. Lucas, Jr., Walter Salant, Robert Solomon, W. Allen Wallis, and an anonymous referee. The views expressed are those of the author and do not necessarily reflect those of the Bank of Greece or the International Monetary Fund.

Journal of Political Economy, 1997, vol. 105, no. 1]

between Friedman's monetary framework and the views of the Chicago School of the 1930s and of other academic centers of that period. In a recent article in this *Journal,* David Laidler (1993) argues that during the 1920s and 1930s, Harvard economists Allyn Young, Lauchlin Currie, and John H. Williams, influenced by British economist Ralph Hawtrey, anticipated Friedman's views in several important respects. Specifically, these economists developed a monetary interpretation of cyclical fluctuations in general and of the Great Depression in particular and were optimistic about the power of monetary policy. In contrast to the views of the Harvard economists, Laidler argues that "optimism about the power of monetary policy . . . arrived rather late in the day in Chicago" (p. 1070) and that "*after* 1936, Chicago was unique among major centers in preserving and developing further the analytic tradition discussed in this paper as the basis . . . in suggesting that the failure of the Keynesian revolution immediately to overwhelm this center had much to do with the dominance there of this tradition" (p. 1099).

This paper argues otherwise. Evidence is presented, much of it for the first time in the literature, showing that while economists at Harvard and other academic institutions argued during the 1930–36 period that either the Great Depression should be allowed to run its course or traditional monetary measures were sufficient to deal with the Depression, Chicago economists became increasingly disenchanted with such measures. Unlike most of the profession, including Harvard, Chicagoans used the quantity theory framework to advocate public works projects and budget deficits during cyclical downturns as a means of putting money directly into circulation. The importance of this policy stance with respect to the influence of John Maynard Keynes's *General Theory* (1936) is evidenced in Don Patinkin's (1987, p. 24) argument that "the advocacy per se of public-works expenditure was not the purpose of the *General Theory;* rather it was to *provide a theory* which would, among other things, rationalize such a policy" (italics supplied). As will be shown below, the Chicagoans already had such a theory, were unique in applying the quantity theory in this manner, and for this reason were less susceptible than other academic centers, such as Harvard, to the Keynesian revolution.

The remainder of this paper is organized into four sections. Section II briefly summarizes the recent literature on the Chicago tradition and the views of earlier non-Chicago quantity theorists. Section III traces the process, beginning in the late 1920s, that led to a consensus Chicago view that budget deficits should be used as a means of conducting monetary policy. The key characteristics of the mid-1930s to the mid-1940s Chicago monetary tradition described by Patinkin (1969) in his influential article on that tradition are shown already to have been in place by 1933. Section IV deals with the relationship between the monetary economics at Chicago and the views held by non-Chicagoans during the 1930–36 period, including those at, or associated with, Harvard; the section also deals with Hawtrey's policy stance during the Great Depression and discusses reactions of Chicago economists to Hawtrey's work. Section V presents conclusions.

II. Back to the Past

A. *The Chicago Monetary Tradition*

The doctrinal-historical literature on the 1930s and 1940s Chicago tradition has dealt with the following aspects of that tradition: (1) the theory of economic cycles, (2) countercyclical policy, and (3) anticipations of Friedman's views in terms of his monetary interpretation of the Great Depression or advocacy of a money supply, growth rate rule or both. The analytic framework used by the earlier Chicagoans (primarily Simons, Viner, Mints, and Knight) has been described by Friedman (1967) and Patinkin (1969), and discussions of the Chicago tradition's countercyclical policies include work by Friedman (1967, 1972), Davis (1968, 1971), Patinkin (1969), and Tavlas (1976). The key characteristics of the Chicago monetary tradition, as presented in this literature, are the following: (i) with the $MV = PT$ framework, economic fluctuations are caused by autonomous variations in V; (ii) variations in V are cumulative in nature because of changes in price expectations and changes in the state of business confidence; (iii) the effects of cumulative changes in V are exacerbated by the perverse behavior of the banking system, which expands credit in booms and contracts it in depressions; (iv) antidepression policy requires a countercyclical expansion in M; (v) such an expansion in M can best be achieved by generating budget deficits, which are a mechanism for conducting monetary policy; and (vi) budget deficits produced during economic contractions should be counterbalanced through surpluses generated during expansions. Characteristics i–v correspond to Patinkin's (1969) five propositions describing the Chicago tradition. Characteristic vi is due to Davis (1968), who showed that the Chicagoans favored budget deficits *only* during depressions.

In terms of Friedman's empirical orientation, his monetary interpretation of the Great Depression, and his monetary growth rate rule, the earlier Chicago monetary tradition provided few forerunners. Two exceptions have been noted in the literature. First, Viner, both in a 1932 Harris Foundation lecture (Viner 1932) and in a lecture the following year delivered in Minneapolis (Viner 1933*b*), criticized the Federal Reserve Board for allowing the Depression to *worsen.* Second, in Tavlas (1977), I added an additional cross-sectional observation, in Paul Douglas, to the Chicago core monetary group of Simons, Knight, Viner, and Mints. Specifically, in the early 1930s, Douglas had argued that the failure of the money supply to grow in accordance with the long-term rate of advance of production (i.e., 3–4 percent per year) was an important cause of the Depression. Accordingly, he espoused a 3–4 percent monetary growth rate rule.

B. *Non-Chicago Anticipations of Friedman*

Non-Chicago economists who have been shown to have proposed a monetary growth rate rule similar to that of Friedman during the years encompassing the 1920s through the 1940s include the following: Carl Snyder (Humphrey 1971; Garvy 1978); Lionel Edie (Humphrey 1971; Patinkin 1973); James Harvey Rogers (Humphrey 1971); James W. Angell (Lee and Wellington 1984); Harold Reed (Humphrey 1971); Clark Warburton (Humphrey 1971; Bordo and Schwartz 1979; Cargill 1979); and, jointly, William T. Foster and Waddill Catchings (Tavlas 1976). With respect to the view that the Federal Reserve Board was responsible for precipitating the Great Depression, Humphrey (1971) provided evidence showing that Lauchlin Currie espoused this thesis in the early 1930s. The upshot of this general line of research has been summarized by Patinkin as follows: "the picture of monetary economics in the 1930s that emerges . . . is one of widespread ferment with respect to questions of both monetary theory and policy. Thus contrary to Friedman's implication, the Chicago School of that time cannot be represented as an isolated center of monetary studies and of belief in the importance of money" (Patinkin [1973] 1981, p. 281).[1]

Laidler argues that the monetary approach developed at Harvard during the 1920s and 1930s was more directly linked to Friedman's monetary economics than the earlier Chicago tradition was, thus reinforcing the view that Friedman's monetary economics is not a direct outgrowth of an earlier, unique Chicago tradition. In this connection, Laidler refers to the 1932 Harris Foundation conference on Gold and Monetary Stabilization, held at the University of Chicago, and contrasts the papers presented at that conference by Viner (1932) and Williams (1932*b*), with Williams considerably "more con-

[1] This research has led some writers to argue that Friedman's claim of a Chicago monetary tradition is an "invention" (see Johnson 1971, pp. 10–11; Moggridge and Howson 1974, p. 227).

fident," according to Laidler, "about what open-market operations might achieve" (1993, p. 1093). Laidler interprets these facts in the following terms:

> If we follow Friedman in looking to the 1932 Harris Foundation conference for evidence of that "hopefulness" that he tells us marked the Chicago tradition, we shall find more of it in the contribution of Williams than anywhere else; and if we look further afield, we shall also find it in the work of Hawtrey—by then published—and Lauchlin Currie—then in progress. [P. 1094]

Laidler's argument turns the distinguishing characteristic of the 1930s Chicago tradition upside down. The Chicago tradition *did* believe in the importance of monetary policy during depressions provided that it was conducted through changes in the government's budgetary stance. It was *this* position that set it apart from the work of most other quantity theorists during the 1930s. Contrary to Laidler's interpretation, Viner was not less hopeful about the effects of injections of the quantity of money than Williams, but about the usefulness of open-market operations for accomplishing this objective during the Depression. As shown below, by 1933 Viner was to become even less enthusiastic about the use of open-market operations than he had been one year earlier.

III. Messages from the Midway

A. *Who Said What and When Did They Say It?*

In order to document the preceding arguments regarding the main attributes of the Chicago monetary tradition, in what follows, key writings of the earlier Chicagoans during the period 1927–33 are presented in order to show (1) the convergence toward the consensus Chicago view by 1933 concerning the six propositions presented above and (2) the emergence of the Chicago view about the inefficacy of open-market operations. Several key differences between the following presentation and Patinkin's (1969) description of the Chicago monetary tradition should be noted. Patinkin stated that the Chicago tradition he described "is primarily a summary of Simons' views, which were largely accepted by Mints. . . . For Viner, I have been able to find clear evidence only on the first proposition [i.e., characteristic i above]" ([1969] 1981, p. 245, n. 8). Patinkin's data set begins in November 1933 and ends in the mid-1940s. The following discussion deals primarily with the period 1927 to mid-1933, although several papers dealing with the years 1934–36 are described, and includes the writings of Douglas, Aaron Director, Viner, and Simons. By focusing on the period prior to the publication of Keynes's *General Theory*, the discussion shows that Patinkin's rendition of the Chicago monetary tradition for the period from the end of 1933 to the mid-1940s had already been conceived and, as such, was in place and was ready to withstand the Keynesian revolution. For Viner, clear evidence will be presented for all six propositions as of 1933.

Douglas (1927–33)

During the years 1927–33, Douglas wrote a series of articles on monetary issues.[2] The substance of his monetary analysis and policy position is contained in the article "The Modern Technique of Mass Production and Its Relation to Wages" (1927). He ascribed depressions to the failure of the money supply to increase as rapidly as the annual trend rise in production, which he thought would result in a fall in the general price level in order to clear the market of the excess supply of goods. Because the present structure of prices has embedded within it relatively higher costs (mainly wages) that have been paid out previously, profit margins would shrink and output would therefore contract. To prevent depressions, Douglas argued that "the primary need is for stability in the price level . . . and this can be secured by a general and proportionate increase in the supply of monetary purchasing power [i.e., money]" (1927, p. 40). In order to generate the necessary purchasing power, Douglas advocated that the government undertake public works projects financed by money creation if "proper safeguards could be provided to prevent inflation" (p. 42).

After the Great Depression had begun, Douglas continued to write on monetary issues, using the Fisherine equation as his monetary framework. He argued that "the various terms are not, however, as some of the more naive quantity theorists have believed, independent of each other. On the contrary, they are inter-related in a somewhat organic fashion" (1935, p. 26). His monetary analysis included the view that the cycle contains the following forces (corresponding to Chicago characteristics ii and iii above) "which . . . act in a cumulative way to create an intensified depression" (1932*b*, p. 78): when prices are falling, "consumers hold dollars in their pockets longer because they expect prices to fall still further and their money will consequently be worth more" (p. 79) and because "banks find their deposits melting and in self-defense are compelled to call and re-

[2] See Tavlas (1995) for a more detailed account of Douglas's monetary writings during this period.

duce their loans" (p. 79). With regard to policy, Douglas thought that traditional monetary reasons were unlikely to be effective during depressions because in periods of high uncertainty, businesses would be reluctant to borrow and banks would not want to lend (p. 79). Accordingly, he argued "that a more direct method of attack should be made upon the problem of building up monetary purchasing power" of "having the federal government run a deficit during the depression period" (p. 80). Over the course of the cycle, however, the budget should be balanced: the "government should tax during prosperity and spend during depression" (Douglas 1932*a*, p. 612).

These statements made by Douglas in the early 1930s contain all five of Patinkin's summary characteristics describing the mid-1930s to mid-1940s Chicago tradition, with the exception that Douglas was eclectic about the cause of the cycle (see Tavlas 1995). He continued to espouse these views over the next several years in numerous articles and in several monographs, culminating in his *Controlling Depressions,* published in 1935.

Director (1930–32)

Aaron Director's work has been completely overlooked in the literature on the Chicago tradition. He began teaching at the University of Chicago in the fall of 1930, having been brought there by Douglas.[3] In August 1930, Director published an article on "Making Use of Public Works" in which he advocated the use of public works during depressions and set forth the Chicago view with regard to the use of compensatory public finance. Davis (1968, p. 477) has cited a 1931 lecture by Viner as "one of the first important statements of the 'simple truth' of a compensatory role for government spending in this country" and as the first instance of such a statement by a Chicagoan. However, in his 1930 paper, Director argued that "it seems clear that planned public works can, to an appreciable extent, increase the demand for labor in times of depression and decrease it in times of prosperity" (p. 428).

In 1932, Director published a monograph, *Unemployment,* in which he argued that it is the stickiness of costs that leads to changes in profits and production, thereby generating the cycle (pp. 25–28). Accordingly, during depressions, there is a need to increase the money supply in order to raise prices. Director thought that traditional monetary measures, while suitable for stabilization (i.e., avoiding the cycle) purposes, were not adequate as antidepression

[3] I am grateful to W. Allen Wallis for providing me with this information.

policy because of "the prevalence of a lack of confidence on the part of businessmen during a depression so that even if banks were willing to extend credit at low rates of interest businessmen are reluctant to demand credit. And we also noted that the banks themselves are cautious and reluctant to extend credit where there is the slightest risk involved" (p. 37). According to Director, "the possibilities are at least "*hopeful*. . . of alleviating the needs of the unemployed workers once a depression is upon us" (p. 34; italics supplied). Specifically, the "real possibilities . . . consist . . . in the planning of public construction over long periods of time, contracting the expenditures in times of prosperity when there is full employment in private industry and expanding the expenditures in times of depression when there is much unemployment" (p. 35).

Douglas and Director (1931)

During the course of 1930, Douglas and Director jointly worked on a book, *The Problem of Unemployment,* published in early 1931. This study is, in part, a wide-ranging survey of then-existing theories of the business cycle as well as a presentation of Douglas and Director's views. The neglect of this book is striking in light of its elucidation for the first time of several of the key attributes now associated with the earlier Chicago tradition.

Douglas and Director set forth a theory of cycles similar to that contained in Douglas's 1927 article: when output rises at a faster rate than the money supply, prices fall and, with sticky wages, profits and production decline. Accordingly, Douglas and Director proposed the following policy guide for preventing depressions: "If the supply of money and credit were to increase commensurately with the increase in production, the price level would be held constant and the goods produced would be sold at prices which would permit industry to go on with undiminished profits and without curtailment of activity" (1931, p. 183). They also assessed various methods of increasing the supply of money. Indirect methods—that is, open-market operations or a lowering of reserve ratios—were considered unlikely to be of much use during depressions because "it is not certain that the reduction in cost [i.e., lowering of interest rates] will be sufficient to induce business men to take full advantage of it in view of the increasing unprofitableness of business" (p. 245). Therefore, they opted for "more direct methods for seeing to it that the increased potential credit is actually put into circulation so that it can buoy up prices" (p. 245). Specifically, Douglas and Director advocated public works projects, preferably financed by "the issuance of added money by the government rather than by taxes" (p. 248).

Two other contributions of the Douglas and Director study are important to mention. First, the authors introduced into the Chicago literature the view that the cycle can be cumulative in nature. Specifically, once a downturn gets underway, "there is a progressive breakdown of business, which in its cumulative process is essentially similar to that of a forest fire" (p. 182). Second, they explicitly introduced the Chicago view that rules are preferred over discretion. In this regard, after assessing Irving Fisher's compensated dollar proposal, they criticized the proposal for being "tied up with the consequences of the future gold production of the world" (p. 235). Nevertheless, Douglas and Director argued that "Professor Fisher's proposal has the merit of being automatic and not depending on the discretion of government or banking officials" (p. 235).

Viner (1931–33)

In a 1931 lecture on "Problems of International Commercial and Financial Policy," Viner advocated "a policy of using the Federal Reserve system to stimulate recovery by an expansion of credit" (p. 188) and the use of expansionary open "market operations on a considerable scale" (1931, p. 189).[4] By 1932, Viner was somewhat less sanguine about the effectiveness of open-market operations. Laidler has pointed out that in Viner's 1932 Harris Foundation lecture, Viner was "skeptical but nevertheless open-minded about what open-market operations might achieve" (1993, p. 1093) but certainly less confident than Harvard's John H. Williams. In August 1933, Viner gave a lecture on "Inflation as a Possible Remedy for the Depression" (Viner 1933*b*) at the University of Georgia. That lecture is pivotal in elucidating the emergence of the Chicago monetary tradition because it shows that Viner was even more skeptical about the efficacy of open-market operations than he had been in 1932. Yet, contrary to Laidler's argument, Viner's increased skepticism is not evidence of a less "hopeful" Chicago monetary tradition concerning the importance of monetary policy compared with the views espoused by Williams. Rather, Viner's skepticism about open-market operations should be viewed in conjunction with the in-

[4] Viner set down the following analytic framework:

$$P = \frac{GV^1 + NV^2 + DV^3}{TV^4},$$

where "*P* is the level, *G* the monetary stock of gold, *N* the amount of paper money in circulation, *D* the bank deposits, *T* the physical volume of transactions, and *V* the velocity of circulation" (p. 186).

creased importance attached by him in 1933 to the use of budget deficits as a mechanism of putting money *directly* into circulation, a policy that Director explicitly called "hopeful."

Viner argued that the key characteristic of a depression is that "there exists a perverse excess of cost over product prices" (1933*b*, p. 120). The way to escape from a depression is "with the aid of monetary measures" (p. 124) that increase inflation. Viner noted that he preferred to define inflation "simply as a rise in prices resulting from a deliberate increase by or under the auspices of government, of means of payment" (p. 124). He argued that "this process of putting purchasing power into circulation will operate to increase the total volume of money income, prices will rise, but less than in proportion than business expenditures, and the result will be an increased physical output, which will mean an increased employment of productive factors" (p. 122). According to Viner, "Theoretically, that is not inevitable; but practically an inflation has always worked out that way, at least in its early stages. The costs lag behind" (p. 122).

Viner then assessed the "possible methods of inflation" (p. 126). One such "method of bringing inflation is to acquire an excess of government expenditures over revenues, that is an unbalanced budget, with the deficit met by new bank credit or by resort to the printing press" (p. 128). Next he turned to the use of open-market operations:

> This method is inferior to the preceding one in this respect: the preceding one gives more immediate stimulus to business. What this [i.e., open-market operations] does is to increase the cash reserves of the banking system, and therefore, it is *hoped,* to give the banks the desire to put their idle funds to work. But the bankers have learned in recent years, not how to make money without lending, but that under certain circumstances the rate at which they lose money is less if they stop lending, so it is conceivable that the banking system would welcome the additional liquidity and would not increase its loans or investments. [P. 131; italics supplied]

Accordingly, Viner concluded that

> the most promising method, I think, is that of government expenditures financed by borrowing from the banking system, with the hope that what the banks lend is newly created credit or credit which would otherwise have remained idle and not funds that would otherwise have been used by

> private business. There will not be recovery through the method of inflation unless there is an expansion in the *use of means of payment.* [P. 133; italics supplied]

These statements by Viner show that he set forth the following characteristics of the earlier Chicago monetary tradition: antidepression policy requires a countercyclical expansion in *M* (i.e., characteristic iv); such an expansion in *M* can best be achieved by generating budget deficits, which are a mechanism for conducting monetary policy (characteristic v). In his lecture, Viner also enumerated characteristics iii and vi. With regard to the former, he stated that "central banking systems have frequently fed booms and depressions instead of counteracting them" (p. 123). With respect to the latter, he argued that "it is obvious that in the long run the budget must balance. . . . During a period of depression, a government should allow deficits to pile up" (p. 129). In his lecture at the University of Georgia, Viner did not state Chicago characteristic ii dealing with the cumulative nature (apart from the banking system) of velocity changes during the cycle, though it is evident that he had this mechanism in mind in his discussion of the "general boom psychology" that is part of the inflationary phase of the cycle (p. 123). In any event, he had already stated this characteristic several months earlier, in April 1933, in his lecture on *Balanced Deflation, Inflation, or More Depression* delivered at the University of Minnesota: "The [cyclical] process, moreover, is cumulative or contagious. If one business man contracts his operations, . . . this compels other business men further to contract their expenditures and production, and so on indefinitely, in a vicious spiral" (1933*a*, p. 7).

The development of Viner's views from 1931 to 1933, in terms of both the efficacy of budget deficits as a means of putting money directly into circulation and the notion that during depressions open-market operations were less effective in this regard, is evidence of the distinctive character that marked the Chicago monetary tradition. As discussed below, Viner's explicit argument in favor of inflation (i.e., an increase in "the means of payment") stands in marked contrast to the views of much of the profession during the 1930s, as exemplified in the writings of those quantity theorists who have been singled out as the antecedents of Friedman.

Some Further Evidence (1932–36)

In the several years following Viner's 1933 lecture, the connection between the use of fiscal measures and the implementation of monetary policy was explicitly stated in Chicago writings. In this regard, in a 1934 review article, "Economic Reconstruction: The Columbia Report," Henry Simons referred to "the decisive importance of fiscal policy for monetary policy; an adequate monetary system could not possibly be made effective without the most careful ordering of fiscal practice in conformity with the dictates of that system" (1934, pp. 798–99). The connection between fiscal and monetary measures was perhaps best articulated by Simons two years later in his classic paper "Rules versus Authorities in Monetary Policy":

> The responsibility for carrying out the monetary rules should be lodged in a federal authority, endowed with large administrative powers but closely controlled in their exercise by a sharply defined policy. The powers of the monetary authority should have to do primarily or exclusively with fiscal arrangements—with the issue and retirement of paper money (open-market operations in government securities) and perhaps with the relation between government revenues and expenditures; in other words, the monetary rules should be implemented entirely by, and in turn should largely determine, fiscal policy. [(1936) 1948, p. 182]

A final set of evidence, in the form of two memoranda prepared by the Chicago faculty, also demonstrates the importance attached by Chicago economists to the use of public works projects as a means of increasing the money supply. The first memorandum (Cox et al. 1932) was addressed to Congressman Samuel B. Pettengill and dated April 26, 1932; it was signed by (among others) Director, Douglas, Knight, Mints, Simons, and Viner.[5] According to the memorandum,

> we have developed an economy in which the volume and velocity of credit is exceedingly flexible and sensitive, while wages and pegged prices are highly resistant to downward pressure. This is at once the explanation of our plight and the ground on which governmental action may be justified. Recovery can be brought about, either by reduction of costs to a level consistent with existing commodity prices, or by injecting enough new purchasing power so that much larger production will be profitable at existing costs. The first method is conveniently automatic but dreadfully slow; and it admits hardly at all of being facilitated by political measures. The second method, while readily amenable to abuse, only requires a courageous fiscal policy on the part of the central government. [P. 524]

[5] Other signers were Garfield V. Cox, Harry D. Gideonse, Harry A. Millis, Henry Schultz, Chester W. Wright, and Theodore O. Yntema.

The second memorandum (Bane et al. 1933) was sent to Senator Reed Smoot and dated January 16, 1933; it was signed by (among others) Douglas, Simons, and Viner.[6] This memorandum also espoused the use of fiscal measures as a way of putting money into circulation: "What is needed to-day is an increase in the circulation of money and credit" (p. 1018). In this connection, the memorandum stated that "the repercussions of the ordinary fiscal operations of the Federal Government on the Nation's currency system must not be ignored" (p. 1014). Both memoranda recommended the balancing of the budget over the course of the cycle (Cox et al. 1932, p. 527; Bane et al. 1933, p. 1021). Finally, it is interesting to note that the *only* reference to open-market operations in *either* document occurred in the 1932 memorandum:

> We agree . . . as to the inadequacy of the Glass-Steagall bill and similar expedients. Little is to be gained merely by easing the circumstances of banks, in a situation where, by virtue of cost-price relations, everyone, including the banks, is anxious to get out of debt. Such measures may retard deflation and prepare the way for recovery; but they can not much mitigate the fundamental maladjustments between prices and costs. [1932, p. 524]

B. *The Chicago Tradition and Friedman*

Can anyone who has read the preceding statements by the earlier Chicago economists, individually and collectively, subscribe to the view set forth by Laidler that optimism about the power of monetary policy arrived rather late in the day in Chicago? To do so is to confine monetary policy solely to measures operating through the banking system. In the next section, I show the critical manner in which Simons reacted to such a strict characterization of the conduct of monetary policy. Moreover, a distinguishing feature of Friedman's monetary economics compared with the views of Keynesian economists during the 1960s and early 1970s was Friedman's proposition that the impact of a budget deficit on the economy depends on how the deficit is financed. As Friedman stated, "the monetary effect [of deficit spending] is 'alchemy of a much deeper significance' than

[6] The memorandum, entitled *Balancing the Budget,* was a pamphlet edited by Harry D. Gideonse. Other signers were Frank Bane, Paul Betters, Carl Chatters, Simeon Leland, Harry A. Millis, Clarence E. Ridley, Donald Slesinger, and Leonard D. White. The congressional proceedings named the author of the introductory letter to Senator Smoot as H. A. Willis. W. Allen Wallis has told me that this is an error; the letter was written by Harry A. Millis, who was chairman of the Economics Department.

the fiscal effect" (1972, p. 916).[7] This connection between Friedman's view and the Chicago monetary tradition, prior to 1936, is obvious and direct. Finally, the Chicago tradition's transmission mechanism, running from changes in the money supply to changes in prices and, via sticky wages, to changes in profits and production, is very similar to the *short-run* Phillips curve process described by Friedman in his presidential address before the American Economic Association (Friedman 1968). I suggest that the Chicago tradition's preoccupation with the short run during the 1930s was well placed.

IV. Views from Outside the Midway

In order for one to appreciate the uniqueness of the Chicago tradition's policy stance, this section first summarizes the policies prescribed by those non-Chicago quantity theorists who have been singled out as the real precursors of Friedman in terms of their empirical orientation and espousal of a monetary growth rate rule. In this regard, Patinkin ([1973] 1981, p. 281) has argued that Friedman's monetary thought "is closer in spirit [to that of the non-Chicagoans] than to the original Chicago School." The section next considers Laidler's contention that Harvard was an important center for the study of monetary economics until 1934. The policy views of Hawtrey are then discussed. Finally, comments are made on issues related to the post-1936 years.

A. *The "Precursors" of Friedman*

In Tavlas (1995), I document the policy views during the Great Depression of those economists who have been claimed to be the precursors of Friedman: Lionel Edie (Investment Research Corp.), James W. Angell (Columbia), James Harvey Rogers (Yale), Harold Reed (Cornell), and Carl Snyder (New York Fed). Apart from advocating money supply growth rate rules, the policy views of these economists can be summarized as follows: (i) Angell, Reed, and Snyder argued that the Depression was an inevitable outcome of the previous expansion, and Angell and Snyder thought that the Depression should be allowed to cure itself. Friedman has referred to this view of the cycle as the "London School (really Austrian) view" (1972, p. 936).[8] (ii) Reed thought that expansionary open-market opera-

[7] This view has long characterized Friedman's work. See, e.g., Friedman ([1948] 1953, p. 140).

[8] Friedman's discussion of the London School view occurred in the context of his "Comments on the Critics," which was part of the *Journal of Political Economy's* symposium on "Friedman's Theoretical Framework." Friedman described his reply to Patinkin's comment, dealing with the Chicago monetary tradition, as "the reply that concerns me most" (1972, p. 907).

tions may be insufficient in dealing with severe depressions and it was, therefore, necessary to prevent the cycle from occurring. (iii) Edie and Rogers argued in favor of open-market operations but believed that such a policy stance had been tried (in 1932) and had been found wanting in light of the adverse effects on confidence stemming from the government's deficit budgets. (iv) In 1936, a year in which the U.S. unemployment rate hovered near 17 percent, the (consumer price index) inflation rate was 1.0 percent, and Keynes published his *General Theory*, Rogers advocated a policy of monetary and fiscal *tightening* to deal with what he thought was a potential for inflation. (v) A year earlier, Angell had also come out in favor of fiscal and monetary tightening. With the prevalence of such views, it is not surprising that students at such academic centers as Columbia, Cornell, and Yale were attracted to the policy message of the *General Theory*. This brings us to Harvard.

B. Harvard and the Great Depression

Laidler has claimed that "as late as 1934, outstanding work in monetary economics was done at Harvard, the best of it at least as good as anything that would emanate from Chicago in the 1930s and, indeed, if careful empirical analysis is valued, far better" (1993, p. 1078). He also argues that "most of this work was due to Allyn Young and Lauchlin Currie, though John H. Williams made at least one noteworthy contribution as a transmitter of ideas" (p. 1078). The picture that emerges from Laidler's account is of a small, but vibrant, group of economists at Harvard working on relevant monetary issues until 1934. The year 1934 is a critical cutoff point in assessing the work done at Harvard. For if, following the onset of the Depression in 1929, Harvard produced "outstanding" work in monetary economics as late as 1934, the issue arises as to why Harvard, unlike Chicago, became so susceptible to Keynesian ideas. It is therefore important to take another look at what Young, Williams, and Currie had to say, and *when* they said it.

As Laidler points out, 1934 marked the publication of *The Economics of the Recovery Program* (Brown et al. 1934),

> prepared by members of the [Harvard] department, most of which [commentaries] verge on the incoherent and do no credit to their distinguished authors. Only Schumpeter's contribution to this volume is something of an exception. It is at least coherent in the presentation of the Austrian view of the Depression, namely that it was the result of overinvestment and that any attempt to use expansionary

> policy to mitigate it would only make matters worse. [1993, p. 1078]

Laidler contrasts this publication with the work of Young, Currie, and Williams. Yet Young's contributions were made *before* the onset of the Great Depression in 1929. As Laidler states, Young *left* Harvard in 1927 for an appointment at the London School of Economics and died in early 1929. That leaves Williams and Currie as having shouldered the brunt of the monetary contributions at Harvard during the critical years 1929–34.

As noted above, Laidler singled out Williams's 1932 Harris Foundation lecture as showing that Williams was confident about the efficacy of expansionary open-market operations as a means of dealing with the Depression. Apart from expansionary open-market operations, the main policy message in Williams's writings during the 1930s was that world economic cooperation was the most hopeful method of emerging from the Depression. He argued the following:

> Granting that the chief emphasis already is, and must be, upon central bank management, it seems probable that the gold standard still provides the best general framework within which management can function effectively. The logical end of the evolution of credit management, and the only real *hope* of solving the problem of monetary instability, would seem to be closer coöperation of central banks looking toward some form or degree of super-national management. [Williams 1932*a*, p. 19; italics supplied; see also Williams 1933, p. 8]

Such views continued to characterize Williams's writings at least until 1936. Consider his paper "Monetary Stabilization and the International Flow of Capital" (1936). With respect to the relationship between capital flows and economic cycles, Williams noted that international investment is attracted to profits, and

> the inflow of capital drives prices higher, makes profits larger for the time being, and there will be another inflow of capital.
>
> So the thing goes on as in a spiral and . . . continues until there is a collapse, either in the capital-receiving country or by the drainage of funds from the lending countries. [P. 58]

Regarding the appropriate policy, Williams had the following to say:

> Now for our own country. What should be the policy? My time is getting short. Well, what are the alternatives? We,

> too, could go in for flexible exchanges. But if we do not do that, should we leave international capital movements wide open or should we subject them to some measure of control? I am very skeptical of governmental control. In England today it is not possible to bring out a new loan without approval of the Treasury. Indefinitely continued, such a policy might raise many questions. In the long run, political, economic and diplomatic questions are intertwined. With governmental control of loans in this country we might hear a good deal more about imperialism and dollar diplomacy. Are governments going to hold themselves responsible for the mistakes they make in foreign investment? Are they going to collect with troops the loans which they sanction? [P. 60]

Williams concluded that "you cannot have domestic monetary stability without some measure of international good health, and you cannot have international monetary stability unless you keep your house in order at home" (p. 60). There simply is nothing more specific in this paper regarding policy. If one likes this sort of thing, I recommend Williams's article, which has much more of the same. I suggest, however, that the differences between such views and the views that filled the air at Chicago are striking.

We now come to the work of Lauchlin Currie. As Laidler shows, Currie made important contributions in the monetary area during the early 1930s, culminating in his 1934 book, *The Supply and Control of Money in the United States.* Two key questions, however, need to be addressed: (1) Were Currie's monetary views representative of those at Harvard during the 1930s? (2) If not, in what respect did they differ? In fact, Currie differed from his Harvard colleagues precisely because he did *not* believe in the efficacy of open-market operations, but instead—like the Chicagoans—advocated the use of expansionary budgets. Answers to both questions have been supplied by Currie himself. Thus, in a 1978 paper, he reflected back on his years at Harvard:

> After the upturn in business in early 1930 proved abortive, I despaired of the efficacy of monetary measures in the conditions of the times and started both in my classes and in discussions advocating deficit spending. But this had to be done almost surreptitiously. Even so, the heresy became known and I fell from grace and was reprimanded by the Chairman of the Department. The prevailing Harvard attitude remained that expressed in the publication, as late as 1934, of *The Economics of the Recovery Program* written by

> the more senior members of the Economics Department. [P. 541]

Currie goes on to state that "by 1934, what was later called a Keynesian approach had not as yet made the slightest dent on a set of beliefs so firmly entrenched as to be articles of faith and as such not to be questioned" (pp. 541–42).

Two important points emerge from these remarks. First, in terms of policy, Currie was a lone wolf at Harvard at least from 1930. Second, the distinguishing characteristic of Currie's policy stance, that is, the inefficacy of open-market operations and the need for budget deficits, was precisely part of the policy stance (in addition to the balancing of the budget over the cycle) that distinguished the earlier Chicago economists from much of the profession. In light of the preceding factors, it is not surprising that Viner, who met Currie while delivering a lecture at Harvard in 1932 and who brought Currie to work for the U.S. Treasury in 1934, pronounced that Currie "was too good for Harvard" (as quoted in Mason [1982, p. 422]).[9]

Several other aspects regarding Harvard should be noted. First, Arthur Marget, one of the most prolific writers on monetary economics throughout the 1930s, taught at Harvard from 1923 to 1927 before moving on to the University of Minnesota. It is interesting that Marget was not given tenure in the same year that Young's departure created a void in the monetary area. It may well have been the case that Marget was not given tenure at Harvard because of anti-Semitism at that institution.[10] Second, Frank Taussig was the senior member of the Harvard faculty during the early 1930s, the editor of the *Quarterly Journal of Economics,* and a leading figure in the area of international trade. Taussig's views on the Depression have not previously been reported. This fact is not surprising since his views appear to have been confined to nonprofessional outlets. His views are not, however, without interest. In a National Broadcasting Company radio broadcast, reported in the *New York Times* on July 24, 1932, Taussig was quoted as saying that "the public's spending activi-

[9] Unlike the Chicagoans, however, Currie does not seem to have provided a quantity theory rationale for his position on budget deficits (see Tavlas 1995). As pointed out by the referee, Viner's admiration for Currie also stemmed from Viner's knowledge of two articles that Currie published in the *Journal of Political Economy* in the 1930s. For a discussion of these articles, see Laidler (1993).

[10] This information has been independently provided to me by two sources: Morris Marget Goldings, nephew of Arthur Marget and a leading U.S. First Amendment attorney as well as the trustee of his uncle's professional writings; and Edward Bernstein, who did his graduate work in economics at Harvard during 1927–31. It is of interest to point out that the one Jewish member of the Harvard Economics Department in the 1920s who received tenure (in the 1930s) was Seymour Harris, whose name before it was changed was Seymour Cohen.

ties should not be hurried. . . . A grand orgy of expenditure is a dangerous stimulant, likely to be followed by a relapse'' (1932*b*, p. 5). He also argued ''that a readjustment of supply and demand is a slow process'' (p. 5). The following month, Taussig published an article, ''Doctors, Economists, and the Depression,'' in *Harper's Magazine.* He described the use of public works during depressions as ''a matter of palliation—of dealing mercifully and carefully for the time being with a distressing condition'' (1932*a*, p. 360). Taussig's view of the Depression was that ''somehow or other the thing seems to cure itself. Minor crises and depressions are got over with comparative ease. Even the great and deep-reaching ones, such as we are now in the midst of, run their course, and health sets in again. . . . We do not know quite how it happens. . . . I take it this will happen with the present depression'' (p. 364).

Finally, it is worth noting that Alvin Hansen, who did not leave the University of Minnesota to go to Harvard until 1937, held similar views prior to 1936, perhaps explaining his attraction to the *General Theory*'s policy message (Tavlas 1995).

C. *Hawtrey, the Great Depression, and Chicago*

According to Laidler, issues raised by Hawtrey in the first edition of his *Currency and Credit,* published in 1919, directly influenced Harvard economists in particular and the monetary debates in the United States in the 1920s and 1930s more generally. A subject not discussed by Laidler is Hawtrey's policy position during the Great Depression. During the early stages of the Depression, Hawtrey advocated a position similar to Friedman's view regarding the effects of budget deficits. Over the course of the Depression, however, Hawtrey was to change his policy stance in such a manner that he became viewed by the Chicagoans as an extreme exponent of central bank measures.

In his 1931 book *Trade Depression and the Way Out,* Hawtrey proposed an antidepression policy consisting of expansionary central bank actions along with large wage cuts (see Tavlas 1995). In that book, Hawtrey also assessed the possible use of money-financed deficits. While he thought that such measures would be effective, he believed that they were ''quite unnecessary . . . if the central bank is willing to take the requisite steps'' (1931, p. 62).

While Hawtrey's perception that expansionary open-market operations and money-financed expenditures are equally effective during depressions served to set him apart from the early 1930s Chicago tradition, it also served to establish a connection between Hawtrey's view on this issue and that of Friedman. Specifically, unlike the earlier Chicago economists, Friedman (1972, pp. 916–17) has argued that money-financed expenditures and expansionary open-market operations are equivalent in their effectiveness.[11] Hawtrey's view on this issue, however, was to be modified after 1931. As the Depression continued, he became increasingly pessimistic about the efficacy of government expenditures and more and more an advocate of central bank measures (see Tavlas 1995).

As a result of the change in Hawtrey's policy position toward the use of strictly central bank measures for dealing with the Depression, during the course of the 1930s and early 1940s he became viewed as an extreme advocate of the use of such measures, as is evidenced by the reactions of the Chicago School. Indeed, although Laidler argues that Hawtrey's work must have influenced Chicago thinking via the writings of Young and Currie, it is not necessary to take the indirect route to investigate the Chicago School's reactions to Hawtrey's policy stance. For Douglas, Director, Mints, and Simons referred directly to Hawtrey.

As early as 1931, Douglas and Director alluded to Hawtrey's reputation as a distinctive supporter of central bank measures for dealing with the Depression. In this connection, in their discussion about the efficacy of government spending during depressions, Douglas and Director stated that "where the funds for government expenditures come directly or indirectly from an increase in the total supply of bank credits, *even Mr. Hawtrey* has admitted the possibility of increasing the demand for labor by the construction of public works" (1931, p. 210; italics supplied). In a similar vein, Mints, in his *History of Banking Theory* (1945), stated that Hawtrey "is today the stoutest believer in the ability of a central bank to stabilize business conditions, although *even he is willing to concede* that, if action is not prompt, a 'credit deadlock' may develop which will not yield to a low bank rate" (p. 278; italics supplied).

Finally, we come to Henry Simons. In his book *Economic Policy for a Free Society* (1948), there is but one reference to Hawtrey; with regard to a major argument made in this paper—that is, the view that fiscal measures can be used to conduct monetary policy—it is a cru-

[11] In a recent letter to me, Friedman states that "I agree with Hawtrey's perception. However, that statement conceals a very complicated issue. In the first place, much depends on whether government deficits emerge via additional expenditures or via reductions in taxes. If via reductions in tax, it may well be that creating money in that way is more effective thanks to supply-side effects. On the other hand, if via expenditures on public works, they might be less effective. In either case, that analysis does not apply to the situation as it was in 1932, 1933, 1934, given the extraordinary extent of unemployment at that time. The WPA and PWA could be amply justified in terms of bringing help to people who needed help desperately while the economy recovered even though on monetary grounds alone the money created would have no different effect than a similar amount of money created through open-market operations."

cial one. The reference occurs in Simons's essay "Hansen on Fiscal Policy," which was published in 1942. The specific context of the reference concerns Simons's discussion of Hansen's conversion to Keynesian economics. According to Simons, Hansen's earlier view of the cycle was "that its causes were to be found in exogenous happenings, immutable and beyond reach of policy" ([1942] 1948, p. 189). Simons argued that "Hansen now confidently proclaims the efficacy of monetary weapons" (p. 189). He then stated the following:

> But another distinction conceals the conversion, namely, distinction between monetary and fiscal measures. Hansen, advocating the latter, thus dissociates himself nominally from monetary theorists by representing such people as advocates of mere central-bank action. This provides a lonely category for Mr. Hawtrey, while denying classification to those for whom central-bank action is feeble, inadequate, and anomalous implementation of monetary policy. If the name at issue be granted to those advocating schemes of monetary compensation or stabilization which would employ all the borrowing, spending, taxing, and issue powers of the central government, then Hansen not only belongs among them but stands as an extremist in that company. [P. 190]

D. *The Post-1936 Years*

Laidler agrees that after 1936 Chicago was a unique center, working in the quantity theory tradition. He also states, however, that this "is not to say that particular individuals in other places did not continue to work in the [quantity theory] tradition . . . . Angell at Columbia, Arthur Marget (1938, 1942) at Minnesota . . . and Warburton at the Federal Deposit Insurance Corporation all continued to work in the older tradition" (1993, pp. 1099–1100, n. 36). The following points, however, need to be made. Although Angell taught at Columbia until 1966 and published a book, *Investment and Business Cycles*, in 1941 criticizing Keynes's theory of investment, as Milgate and Levy (1987, p. 94) observe, "most of his [Angell's] original work on monetary economics was undertaken in the decade between 1926 and 1936." Indeed, by the 1950s it appears that Angell had been converted to Keynesian ideas; in his classroom lectures he spent much of the time defending the analysis contained in *General Theory* against the neoclassical synthesis.[12] With regard to Marget, the two volumes of his

12 Two sources provided me with this information: Benjamin Cohen, a student of Angell's in the late 1950s, and Peter Kenen, a colleague of Angell's in the 1950s and 1960s.

scholarly *Theory of Prices* (1938, 1942) were critical assessments of Keynes's work. Marget, however, left academia in 1942, never to return, apparently a victim of hostility toward his quantity theory views.[13] He moved on to the Federal Reserve Board and stopped publishing original research. This leaves Clark Warburton. It is interesting that perhaps the lone individual outside of Chicago conducting important research in the older quantity theory tradition during the 1940s in the United States was situated outside of an academic institution. It is also interesting to note that Warburton's contributions were largely ignored until the publication in 1963 of Friedman and Schwartz's *Monetary History of the United States, 1867–1960,* which contains generous acknowledgments of, and citations to, Warburton's work and was followed by the publication of a selection of his writings under the title *Depression, Inflation, and Monetary Policy* (1966).

After 1936, Friedman's use of money demand analysis and empirical methodology combined to widen the Chicago approach so as to embrace the efficacy of open-market operations, as advocated by some earlier non-Chicago quantity theorists. As Robert Lucas (in Klamer [1984, p. 53]) has noted, however, the reception to Friedman's early work was not always cordial. An irony of history is that the monetary economics that emerged from Chicago encompassed the policy views of the earlier Chicagoans and non-Chicago quantity theorists alike. The link connecting these respective policy stances, forged at Chicago during the 1940s and 1950s, is the view that money creation—whether due to expansionary open-market operations or budget deficits—matters.

V. Conclusions

This paper has presented evidence of the pre-1936 monetary economics at Harvard and Chicago considerably different from Laidler's presentation. With regard to Laidler's claim that outstanding work was done at Harvard at least until 1934, the following considerations are relevant: (i) Young had already left Harvard (in 1927). (ii) Williams argued (on occasion) for expansionary open-market operations, a policy stance that the Chicagoans found to be inadequate in dealing with the Great Depression, and for world economic cooperation as the most hopeful method of restoring world monetary stability. (iii) Taussig, along with the Austrian members of the Harvard faculty, thought that the Depression would cure itself. (iv) True, Currie made outstanding contributions in terms of his statistical work. But in terms of his policy views, according to his own recol-

[13] I am grateful to Morris Marget Goldings for providing me with this information.

lections he was a lone wolf at Harvard. In terms of antidepression policy, Harvard during the 1930–36 period provided an easy prey for the Keynesian revolution, brought there by that former expositor of that old-time religion, Alvin Hansen.

With regard to Hawtrey, his policy stance increasingly emphasized central bank actions to the exclusion of other policy measures. The reactions of the Chicago economists to his work illustrate precisely the distinctiveness that marked the Chicago tradition's approach to the conduct of monetary policy: that such policy should be viewed as including the government's budgetary operations. The key issue, therefore, addressed in this paper is the following: Would Chicago have been as likely to emerge as the important academic center for the study of monetary economics after 1936 if the dominant approach prior to 1936 was not that of such economists as Viner and Simons, but that of the economists at Harvard or of the so-called precursors of Friedman? I suggest that it is not merely a coincidence of history that the monetarist counterrevolution originated in Chicago.

References

Angell, James W. *Investment and Business Cycles.* New York: McGraw-Hill, 1941.

Bane, Frank, et al. *Balancing the Budget: Federal Fiscal Policy during Depression.* Public Policy Pamphlets, no. 1. Chicago: Univ. Chicago Press, January 16, 1933. Reprinted in *Investigation of Economic Problems: Hearings before the Committee on Finance.* U.S. Senate, 72d Cong., 2d sess., February 1933.

Bordo, Michael D., and Schwartz, Anna J. "Clark Warburton: Pioneer Monetarist." *J. Monetary Econ.* 5 (January 1979): 43–66.

Brown, Douglas V., et al. *The Economics of the Recovery Program.* Cambridge, Mass.: Harvard Univ. Press, 1934.

Cargill, Thomas F. "Clark Warburton and the Development of Monetarism since the Great Depression." *Hist. Polit. Econ.* 11 (Fall 1979): 425–49.

Cox, Garfield V., et al. Memorandum to Congressman Samuel B. Pettengill. In *Payment of Adjusted-Compensation Certificates: Hearings before the Committee on Ways and Means.* U.S. House of Representatives, 72d Cong., 1st sess., April 1932.

Currie, Lauchlin. *The Supply and Control of Money in the United States.* Cambridge, Mass.: Harvard Univ. Press, 1934.

———. "Comments and Observations." *Hist. Polit. Econ.* 10 (Winter 1978): 541–48.

Davis, J. Ronnie. "Chicago Economists, Deficit Budgets, and the Early 1930's." *A.E.R.* 58 (June 1968): 476–82.

———. *The New Economics and the Old Economists.* Ames: Iowa State Univ. Press, 1971.

Director, Aaron. "Making Use of Public Works." *Survey* (August 15, 1930), pp. 427–28.

———. *Unemployment.* Chicago: American Library Assoc., 1932.

Douglas, Paul H. "The Modern Technique of Mass Production and Its Relation to Wages." *Proc. Acad. Polit. Sci.* 12 (July 1927): 17–42.
———. "Dividends Soar, Wages Drop." *World Tomorrow* 15 (December 28, 1932): 610–12. (*a*)
———. "Money, Credit and the Depression." *World Tomorrow* 15 (March 1932): 78–80. (*b*)
———. *Controlling Depressions.* New York: Norton, 1935.
Douglas, Paul H., and Director, Aaron. *The Problem of Unemployment.* New York: Macmillan, 1931.
Friedman, Milton. "A Monetary and Fiscal Framework for Economic Stability." *A.E.R.* 38 (June 1948): 245–64. Reprinted in *Essays on Positive Economics.* Chicago: Univ. Chicago Press, 1953.
———. "The Quantity Theory of Money: A Restatement." In *Studies in the Quantity Theory of Money.* Chicago: Univ. Chicago Press, 1956.
———. "The Monetary Theory and Policy of Henry Simons." *J. Law and Econ.* 10 (October 1967): 1–13.
———. "The Role of Monetary Policy." *A.E.R.* 58 (March 1968): 1–17.
———. "Comments on the Critics." *J.P.E.* 80 (September/October 1972): 906–50.
Friedman, Milton, and Schwartz, Anna J. *A Monetary History of the United States, 1867–1960.* Princeton, N.J.: Princeton Univ. Press (for NBER), 1963.
Garvy, George. "Carl Snyder, Pioneer Economic Statistician and Monetarist." *Hist. Polit. Econ.* 10 (Fall 1978): 454–90.
Hawtrey, Ralph G. *Currency and Credit.* London: Longmans, Green, 1919.
———. *Trade Depression and the Way Out.* London: Longmans, Green, 1931.
Humphrey, Thomas M. "Role of Non-Chicago Economists in the Evolution of the Quantity Theory in America, 1930–1950." *Southern Econ. J.* 38 (July 1971): 12–18.
Johnson, Harry G. "The Keynesian Revolution and the Monetarist Counter-revolution." *A.E.R. Papers and Proc.* 61 (May 1971): 1–14.
Keynes, John Maynard. *The General Theory of Employment, Interest and Money.* New York: Harcourt Brace, 1936.
Klamer, Arjo. "Conversations with New Classical Economists: Robert E. Lucas Jr." In *Conversations with Economists: New Classical Economists and Opponents Speak Out on the Current Controversy in Macroeconomics.* Totowa, N.J.: Rowman and Allanheld, 1984.
Laidler, David. "Hawtrey, Harvard, and the Origins of the Chicago Tradition." *J.P.E.* 101 (December 1993): 1068–1103.
Lee, Joong-Koon, and Wellington, Donald C. "Angell and the Stable Money Rule." *J.P.E.* 92 (October 1984): 972–78.
Marget, Arthur W. *The Theory of Prices: A Re-examination of the Central Problems of Monetary Theory.* 2 vols. New York: Prentice-Hall, 1938, 1942.
Mason, Edward S. "The Harvard Department of Economics from the Beginning to World War II." *Q.J.E.* 97 (August 1982): 383–433.
Milgate, Murray, and Levy, Alastair. "Angell, James Waterhouse." In *The New Palgrave: A Dictionary of Economics,* vol. 1, edited by John Eatwell, Murray Milgate, and Peter Newman. London: Macmillan, 1987.
Mints, Lloyd W. *A History of Banking Theory in Great Britain and the United States.* Chicago: Univ. Chicago Press, 1945.
Moggridge, Donald E., and Howson, Susan. "Keynes on Monetary Policy, 1910–1946." *Oxford Econ. Papers* 26 (July 1974): 226–47.
Patinkin, Don. "The Chicago Tradition, the Quantity Theory, and Friedman." *J. Money, Credit and Banking* 1 (February 1969): 46–70. Reprinted

in *Essays on and in the Chicago Tradition.* Durham, N.C.: Duke Univ. Press, 1981.

———. "On the Monetary Economics of the Chicagoans and the Non-Chicagoans: Comment." *Southern Econ. J.* 39 (January 1973): 454–59. Reprinted as "More on the Chicago Monetary Tradition" in *Essays on and in the Chicago Tradition.* Durham, N.C.: Duke Univ. Press, 1981.

———. "Keynes, John Maynard." In *The New Palgrave: A Dictionary of Economics,* vol. 3, edited by John Eatwell, Murray Milgate, and Peter Newman. London: Macmillan, 1987.

Simons, Henry C. "Economic Reconstruction: The Columbia Report." *J.P.E.* 42 (December 1934): 795–99.

———. "Rules versus Authorities in Monetary Policy." *J.P.E.* 44 (February 1936): 1–30. Reprinted in *Economic Policy for a Free Society.* Chicago: Univ. Chicago Press, 1948.

———. "Hansen on Fiscal Policy." *J.P.E.* 50 (April 1942): 161–96. Reprinted in *Economic Policy for a Free Society.* Chicago: Univ. Chicago Press, 1948.

———. *Economic Policy for a Free Society.* Chicago: Univ. Chicago Press, 1948.

Taussig, Frank W. "Doctors, Economists, and the Depression." *Harper's Mag.* 165 (August 1932): 355–65. (*a*)

———. "N.B.C. Radio Broadcast." *New York Times* (July 24, 1932). (*b*)

Tavlas, George S. "Some Further Observations on the Monetary Economics of Chicagoans and Non-Chicagoans." *Southern Econ. J.* 42 (April 1976): 685–92.

———. "The Chicago Tradition Revisited: Some Neglected Monetary Contributions: Senator Paul Douglas (1892–1976)." *J. Money, Credit and Banking* 9 (November 1977): 529–35.

———. "The Light in the Secret Shrine: Chicago, Harvard, and the Doctrinal Foundations of Monetary Economics." Manuscript. Washington: Internat. Monetary Fund, 1995.

Viner, Jacob. "Problems of International Commercial and Financial Policy." In *Report of the Round Tables and General Conferences at the Eleventh Session,* edited by Arthur Howland Buffington. Williamston, Mass.: Williams Coll., Inst. Politics, 1931.

———. "International Aspects of the Gold Standard." In *Gold and Monetary Stabilization,* edited by Quincy Wright. Chicago: Univ. Chicago Press, 1932.

———. *Balanced Deflation, Inflation, or More Depression.* Day and Hour Series, no. 3. Minneapolis: Univ. Minnesota Press, 1933. (*a*)

———. "Inflation as a Possible Remedy for Depression." In *Proceedings of the Institute of Public Affairs,* 7th annual session. Athens: Univ. Georgia, 1933. (*b*)

Warburton, Clark. *Depression, Inflation, and Monetary Policy: Selected Papers, 1945–1953.* Baltimore: Johns Hopkins Press, 1966.

Williams, John H. "The Effect of Currency Depreciation on International Trade." *Proc. Acad. Polit. Sci.* 15 (May 1932): 13–19. (*a*)

———. "Monetary Stability and the Gold Standard." In *Gold and Monetary Stabilization,* edited by Quincy Wright. Chicago: Univ. Chicago Press, 1932. (*b*)

———. "The United States Tariff and Our International Financial Positions." *Proc. Acad. Polit. Sci.* 15 (June 1933): 1–8.

———. "Monetary Stabilization and the International Flow of Capital." *Proc. Acad. Polit. Sci.* 17 (May 1936): 54–61.

‘Was the Monetarist Tradition Invented?’

G. S. Tavlas, ‘Was the Monetarist Tradition invented?’, *Journal of Economic Perspectives*, 12:4 (Fall 1998a), pp. 211–22.

Retrospectives
Was the Monetarist Tradition Invented?

George S. Tavlas

This feature addresses the history of economic words and ideas. The hope is to deepen the workaday dialogue of economists, while perhaps also casting new light on ongoing questions. If you have suggestions for future topics or authors, please write to Joseph Persky, c/o *Journal of Economic Perspectives,* Department of Economics (M/C 144), University of Illinois at Chicago, 601 South Morgan Street, Room 2103, Chicago, Illinois 60680.

Introduction

Milton Friedman's (1956) restatement of the quantity theory of money is widely regarded as having been the initial shot fired in the monetarist counterrevolution against the then-existing Keynesian orthodoxy. In his essay, Friedman claimed that his monetary framework was an outgrowth of a 1930s and 1940s oral quantity theory tradition at Chicago that differed sharply from other versions of the quantity theory during those years. The earlier Chicago economists, according to Friedman (p. 3), developed a "subtle and relevant version" of the quantity theory that "became a flexible and sensitive tool for interpreting movements in aggregate economic activity and for developing relevant policy prescriptions."

■ *George S. Tavlas is Special Adviser to the Governor of the Bank of Greece, Athens, Greece, and the Bank's Alternate Member to the Monetary Committee of the European Union. He is on leave from the International Monetary Fund, Washington, D.C., where he was Deputy Chief of the Financial Relations Division.*

Friedman's exegesis of an earlier Chicago quantity theory tradition went unchallenged for about 15 years. But in the late 1960s, it came under fire. Don Patinkin (1969) produced evidence showing that from about the mid-1930s through the mid-1940s, the Chicago economists used Irving Fisher's velocity-based equation of exchange MV = PT as their theoretical model—where M is the quantity of money, V is the velocity of circulation of money, P is the price level, and T is a measure of output. This implied that the "Chicago" tradition had neither been original nor unique. Patinkin also argued that this approach differed from Friedman's (1956) approach of presenting money demand as a portfolio decision with respect to alternative assets. Furthermore, he showed that the earlier Chicagoans thought that velocity was highly unstable, which he argued was in opposition to Friedman's view that the demand for money is stable. Patinkin concluded that Friedman's analytic framework was an extension of Keynesian liquidity preference theory, rather than an outgrowth of a distinctive Chicago tradition.

The year after Patinkin's article, Harry Johnson (1971 [1978]) used the occasion of his Richard T. Ely Lecture before the American Economic Association to engage in the controversy surrounding the origins of Friedman's monetarism.[1] Johnson's lecture dealt with the characteristics that underpinned successful revolutions and counterrevolutions in economic theory. One vital characteristic needed by a counterrevolution is to establish "some sort of continuity with the orthodoxy of the past" (p. 223). Johnson (p. 224) charged that the monetarist solution to this problem was found through "the invention of a Chicago oral tradition that was alleged to have preserved understanding of the fundamental truth among a small band of the initiated through the dark years of the Keynesian despotism." Drawing on Patinkin's work showing that the earlier Chicagoans regarded velocity as inherently unstable, Johnson agreed that Friedman's analytic framework owed much more to Keynes than to pre-Keynesian quantity theorists—including those at Chicago. Johnson proceeded to charge (p. 225) that Friedman had engaged in "scholarly chicanery used to promote a . . . counter-revolution in economic theory. . . . There was no lonely light constantly burning in a secret shrine on the Midway, encouraging the faithful to assemble in waiting for the day when the truth could safely be revealed to the masses: that candle was made, and not merely lit, only when its light had a chance of penetrating far and wide and attracting new converts to the old-time religion."

The notion that the Chicago oral quantity theory tradition was an invention spread rapidly and became widely accepted. Moggridge and Howson (1974, p. 227), for example, argue that the "famous oral tradition of Chicago [is] a mythical invention." Skidelsky (1992, p. 579), in his biography on Keynes, writes that the

[1] Johnson's (1971 [1978]) article continues to be the subject of discussion For example, see Snowdon and Vane (1996)

"recollections of Friedman [with respect to the Chicago tradition] should be taken with a pinch of salt." In his well-regarded survey of the history of economic thought, Blaug (1996, p. 640) states that "Patinkin . . . destroyed the notion of a Chicago 'oral tradition' about the quantity theory."

Was the Chicago oral tradition invented? The following account argues that there was indeed a unique Chicago oral tradition during the early 1930s, which enabled Chicago to withstand the Keynesian virus while other academic institutions succumbed. Furthermore, that tradition contained important links with Friedman's analysis, culminating in his restatement of the quantity theory.

The Chicago Monetary Tradition

During the years 1930–36, a group of Chicago economists developed a unique approach to the quantity theory that represented a near-consensus among Chicago economists, but was not used outside of Chicago. The group included Henry Simons, Jacob Viner, Frank Knight, Lloyd Mints, Paul Douglas (best remembered for his work on production functions and for his career as a U.S. Senator), Aaron Director, and Albert G. Hart. The context of their analysis was confined to the short-run—appropriate for an economy mired in Depression—and the group was aggressive in pursuing the policies implied by its views, using books, articles, conferences, public pamphlets, radio broadcasts, and letters and memoranda to congressmen and senators to get its message across (Tavlas, 1997).

The analytic framework used by the early Chicagoans did begin with the Fisherine equation of exchange, $MV = PT$. With this framework, the Chicagoans argued that a basic feature of economic life is the "danger of sharp changes on the velocity side," or in other words, "the danger of extreme alternations of hoarding and dishoarding" (Simons, 1936 [1948], p. 164). These sharp changes in velocity are cumulative in nature, because if individuals expect prices to fall and earnings to be poor, they will hoard—that is, decrease velocity. In this way, expectations will be self-justifying, for the act of hoarding will cause prices to fall even further. As Viner (1933b, p. 7) put it: "The [cyclical] process . . . is cumulative or contagious. If one business man contracts his operations, . . . this compels other business men further to contract their expenditures and production, and so on indefinitely, in a vicious spiral." Furthermore, the effects of cumulative changes in velocity are exacerbated by the perverse behavior of the banking system, which expands the money supply in booms with its greater willingness to lend and contracts the money supply in recessions (Tavlas, 1997).

To combat the 1930s depression, the Chicago economists thought it necessary to generate a countercyclical expansion in the stock of money. Such an increase in M would be used to buy goods and, thus, increase prices; with wages lagging, profits and production would rise. According to Viner (1933b, p. 122), "Theoretically, that is not inevitable; but practically an inflation has always worked out that way, at least in its early stages. The costs lag behind." The pro-cyclical behavior of velocity would then reinforce the recovery process. However, traditional monetary measures like open market operations were unlikely to be effective during depressions, because in periods of high uncertainty, businesses would be reluctant to borrow and banks would not want to lend (Douglas and Director, 1931, p. 245). Nevertheless, an expansion in the money supply could be achieved by generating budget deficits, which were viewed as a mechanism for conducting monetary policy. The use of fiscal measures to effectuate immediate changes in the money supply—as opposed to the indirect and time-consuming methods operating through the banking system—was put succinctly by Viner in a 1933 article. After presenting the case for money-financed government expenditures, Viner (1933b, p. 133) stated: "There will not be recovery . . . unless there is expansion in the use of means of payment."

The view that fiscal measures could be used to implement monetary policy was brought to Chicago by Paul Douglas in the late 1920s (Tavlas, 1997). A memorandum prepared by the Chicago faculty demonstrates the importance attached by Chicago economists to the use of fiscal measures as a means of increasing the money supply. The memorandum was addressed to Congressman Samuel B. Pettengill and dated April 26, 1932. It was signed by (among others) Director, Douglas, Knight, Mints, Simons, and Viner. According to the memorandum (Cox et al., 1932, p. 524):

> We have developed an economy in which the volume and velocity of credit is exceedingly flexible and sensitive, while wages and pegged prices are highly resistant to downward pressure. This is at once the explanation of our plight and the ground on which governmental action may be justified. Recovery can be brought about, either by reduction of costs to a level consistent with existing commodity prices, or by injecting enough new purchasing power so that much larger production will be profitable at existing costs. The first method is conveniently automatic but dreadfully slow; and it admits hardly at all of being facilitated by political measures. The second method, while readily amenable to abuse, only requires a courageous fiscal policy on the part of the central government.

A second memorandum, dated January 16, 1933, was sent to Senator Reed Smoot. It was signed by Douglas, Simons, Viner, and others. This memorandum also espoused the use of fiscal measures as a way of putting money into circulation: "What is needed to-day is an increase in the circulation of money and credit" (Bane et al., 1933, p. 1018). In this connection, "the repercussions of the ordinary fiscal operations of the Federal Government on the Nation's currency system must not be ignored" (p. 1014).[2]

[2] Similarly, Simons (1934, p 799) stressed "the decisive importance of fiscal policy for monetary policy."

In addition, the lack of confidence in traditional measures of monetary policy and concerns over how the banking system might exaggerate booms and busts with procyclical expansions and contractions of credit led Chicago economists to emphasize certain policy lessons. One example was support for 100 percent reserve requirements for banks, to prevent banks from exacerbating economic cycles, a proposal that was known as "The 'Chicago Plan' of Banking Reform" (Hart, 1934–35). Another example was the belief that monetary policy should be conducted by rules, rather than left to the discretion of the monetary authority. Simons (1936) preferred a rule where the money supply would be adjusted to stabilize the price level, both to stabilize price expectations and to limit the monetary authorities; in modern terminology, this is now called "inflation targeting." Douglas and Director (1931, p. 235) favored a rule where the money supply would be expanded at a rate according to the average annual increase of output.

At a minimum, the Chicago faculty seemed to believe that these elements added up to a cohesive and unique oral tradition. For example, Simons (1935, p. 555) referred in a 1935 review of Lauchlin Currie's *The Supply and Control of Money in the United States* (1934) to the "oral tradition" at Chicago and elsewhere, while noting that these views were "meagerly represented in the accessible literature."[3] In Leland Bach's 1940 Ph.D. thesis at Chicago, supervised by Mints, Simons and Viner, Bach includes a footnote following a description of the business cycle : "On this reduction to essentials I am indebted to Professor Mints, although it has been in the nature of an 'oral' tradition at Chicago for some time . . ."

Answering the Patinkin Critique

At this point, the reader may have noted that Patinkin's (1969) critique did not drop out of an empty sky. It is correct that the Chicago tradition was based on Fisher's MV = PT model. It is correct that the Chicago monetarist tradition of the 1930s focused on sharp and cumulative changes in velocity. It is true that Friedman's restatement cast the demand for money as part of a general theory of the choice of an optimum portfolio of assets. However, these points are not dispositive; they surely do not sum up to Johnson's (1971) argument that Friedman was guilty of "invention" and "chicanery." The Chicago tradition did follow the quantity theory, but in a unique way that Patinkin's critique does not appreciate. Moreover, the Chicago tradition was strikingly different from Keynesian views.

The Chicago tradition was distinctive both in how it used the Fisherine equation of exchange to describe the economic cycle and in its policy responses. No

[3] Steindl (1990, p. 431) points out that Simons left little doubt that he was referring to the Chicago quantity theory tradition

other U.S. quantity theorist during the 1930s formulated a theory of the cycle combining the particular elements used at Chicago: that is, the role of autonomous variations in velocity, the cumulative nature of velocity as a function of price expectations and the volume of near moneys, and a monetary transmission process involving flexible prices, sticky wages and changes in profits and production.[4] During the 1930s, many quantity theorists—including James W. Angell at Columbia, Alvin Hansen at Minnesota, Carl Snyder at the New York Fed, and Frank Taussig at Harvard—were in favor of allowing the Depression to run its course (Tavlas, 1982, 1997). Others favored expansionary open market operations, but believed that such operations had been tried and found wanting because expansionary fiscal measures had dampened business confidence. The Chicagoans thought that open market operations would probably be ineffective given the adverse business climate of the times and, even if ultimately effective, would take too much time to operate, and that during the severity of the Depression, a more immediate, direct method of increasing the money supply was needed. While some economists outside of Chicago advocated the use of expansionary fiscal measures, only the Chicagoans used the quantity theory to rationalize such a policy. Only the Chicagoans identified the use of fiscal measures as a direct mechanism to effectuate an increase in the money supply.

To bring home the uniqueness of the Chicago approach, consider how the Chicagoans differed in terms of theory and policy from Fisher and Keynes. Fisher's work during the 1930s stressed the effect of deflation on the real burden of nominal debt. The "big bad actors" in the cyclical process, as Fisher (1933, p. 341) called them, were "debt disturbances and price-level disturbances," which caused debtors to default on loans and led to runs on banks. The effect of deflation on debt was not, however, part of the Chicago cyclical mechanism. Turning to anti-depression policy, Fisher favored reflation but, like others, thought that the use of government expenditures to generate an expansion in the money supply would be counterproductive because it would undermine business confidence. He set forth his theoretical and policy frameworks while attending the 1932 Harris Foundation discussions at Chicago, prompting a rebuttal from Viner. During these discussions, Fisher circulated a list containing 24 ways he proposed to increase money and/or velocity. The use of government expenditures was not on the list. Viner took exception, arguing that such expenditures—if accompanied by currency expansion—would directly cause reflation and have a favorable effect on confidence (Harris Memorial Foundation, 1932, pp. 412–15).[5]

[4] While other economists used some of the individual elements in their cyclical analysis, the Chicago tradition was unique in combining them into a cohesive theory of the cycle The view that price changes generate changes in output via sticky wages dates back at least to Henry Thornton at the beginning of the 19th century See Aschheim and Tavlas (1996)

[5] Fisher wanted to send his list, signed by the other participants, to President Hoover The list that was

In the *General Theory*, Keynes presented a portfolio approach to the demand for money which allowed him to analyze the effects of changes in money on an individual's balance sheet. This approach emphasized that to persuade people to hold an increased stock of money, the rates of return on competing assets in their portfolios must fall. The approach differs from most velocity-based theories, which typically (but not always, as in the case of the Chicago approach) stress the mechanical aspects of the payments process in analyzing velocity behavior. Keynes used the rate of return on bonds as the relevant opportunity cost to holding money and thought that at low rates, the demand for money becomes highly elastic with respect to the interest rate, so that increases in the quantity of money will simply be absorbed in portfolios without any fall in interest rates. An increase in the money supply need not increase output.

There are clearly similarities between the earlier Chicagoans and Keynes in terms of policies. Both the Chicagoans and Keynes thought that traditional monetary measures were likely to be ineffective during depressions. Both favored increased government expenditures. But the Chicagoans—unlike Keynes—confined the range of ineffective monetary measures to those operating through the banking system. Expansionary monetary policy would be ineffective, not because it would fail to lower interest rates, as Keynes thought, but because banks might choose not to lend their increased reserves and businesses might decide not to borrow them. For Keynes, *any* increase in money would likely be ineffective. Increased government spending, however, would be effective because it produced an offsetting flow to the decline in autonomous private investment expenditure. For the Chicagoans, increased government spending was a way of raising the stock of money, offsetting the cyclical decline in velocity, and directly affecting the flow of spending without an intervening interest-rate effect. The Chicagoans and Keynes reached similar policy conclusions, but they traveled very different theoretical roads.

Patinkin's claim that Friedman's (1956) monetarist theory, with its idea of money demand in the context of a portfolio of assets, was not apparent in the Chicago tradition of the 1930s, and should instead be seen as a descendent of the Keynesian views on liquidity preference, has an element of truth; the Chicago tradition of the 1930s did not emphasize money demand in the portfolio context. But Patinkin (and Johnson) missed essential connections between Friedman and the earlier Chicago economists. First, work by Knight (1941) and Mints (1946, 1950), which were cut from the same cloth as the 1930s Chicago writings, explicitly developed models of money demand based on a portfolio view. Second, unlike Keynes, who viewed bonds as the only substitute for cash holdings, Friedman regarded all

agreed upon and sent to President Hoover was pared down to five recommendations, one of which was the use of public expenditures. See Harris Memorial Foundation (1932, pp 412–15) types of wealth as potential substitutes, including real goods. He therefore included the change of the price level of goods in his portfolio analysis and interpreted this new variable as the "expected rate of change in prices" (p. 14); as noted, price expectations were a key determinant of velocity behavior for the 1930s Chicagoans. Third, since Friedman viewed money as a substitute for real goods, as well as for bonds, changes in the quantity of money would spill over into the market for consumer and producer goods, thereby exerting a direct effect on spending and not just an indirect effect via the interest rate. Friedman's transmission mechanism was, therefore, part Keynes and part 1930s Chicago.

Finally, and most fundamentally, we come to the stability of Friedman's money demand. This is perhaps the crucial issue, for velocity and money demand can be viewed as merely alternate ways of analyzing business cycles. Indeed, Friedman and Schwartz's *Monetary History* (1963) contains ten references to money demand and over 50 references to velocity. If money demand was indeed stable in Friedman's cyclical analysis, then this would mark a clear departure from the Chicago tradition. However, the role of a stable money demand function in Friedman's work actually constitutes Patinkin's weakest argument.

As Friedman (1972, p. 933) has pointed out, Patinkin was a Walrasian, concerned with abstract completeness. Patinkin's own work (1965) used comparative static analysis within a general equilibrium setting. When Patinkin analyzed Friedman's money demand formulation, he did so after the dust had settled—after equilibrium had been achieved. Friedman's empirical work (1959) on money demand was, to be sure, pure long run; the empirical specification did not include a lagged endogenous variable to pick up adjustment costs, the time series used covered a long horizon (1869 to 1956!), and the data frequency treated each business cycle as constituting a single observation—in other words, the data *abstracted* from the cycle. This long-run context, and the empirical finding that money is neutral, might have appealed to Patinkin the theorist, whose comparative static analysis was concerned with demonstrating the conditions necessary for money neutrality.

The Chicago tradition, however, was preoccupied with the short run, and if Friedman's work is to be compared with that tradition, the comparison should take place *before* the dust has settled. Here the picture changes. In Friedman's work, money is nonneutral in the short run, with the lags between changes in money and changes in nominal income being long and variable. Accordingly, velocity behavior is not predictable with enough accuracy that it can be used as the basis of an activistic countercyclical policy. Velocity, in other words, is unstable. As Friedman (1958, pp. 199) stated, "The direction of influence between the money stock and income and prices is less clear-cut and more complex for the business cycle than for longer movements." Indeed, it is because of our ignorance about the exact timing and effects of given policies that Friedman has long favored a monetary growth-rate rule.

Writing in the midst of the Depression, the earlier Chicago economists stressed that the business cycle is cumulative due to changes in business confidence and the fractional-reserve banking system. In Friedman's own work, the chapter on "The Great Depression" in the *Monetary History*, Friedman and Schwartz (1963, p. 419) stated: "Yet it is also true that small events at times have large consequences, that there are such things as chain reactions and cumulative forces. It happens that a liquidity crisis in a unit fractional reserve banking system is precisely the kind of event that can trigger—and often has triggered—a chain reaction. And economic collapse often has the character of a cumulative process." Friedman and Schwartz (1963, p. 302) also showed that velocity varies pro-cyclically during the course of the cycle. This analysis of velocity not only grows from the earlier Chicago tradition, but is distinctly different from Keynesian analysis where one reason for the ineffectiveness of monetary policy was that velocity and money move in opposite directions. The cyclical behavior of velocity constitutes an important distinction between the earlier Chicago tradition and Friedman, on the one hand, and Keynesian economics, on the other.

In the light of the above similarities in business-cycle analyses, it is not surprising that Friedman's policy position is very much consistent with that of the Chicago tradition. Friedman also favors rules over discretion (a money-supply growth rate rule a la Douglas and Director) and 100 percent reserve requirements, and views fiscal policy accompanied by money creation as conducting monetary policy. Friedman, of course, extended the Chicago approach in a number of directions. For example, his empirical research demonstrated the importance of traditional monetary measures, the causal role of money in the business cycle, and, yes, the long-run neutrality of money.

Conclusion

There has been a long-running controversy in the literature over what constitutes the main contribution of Keynes's (1936) *General Theory*. Patinkin and Johnson, however, agreed on this issue. Patinkin (1987, p. 27, italics supplied) argued that "the advocacy of public-words expenditure was not the purpose of the *General Theory*; rather it was to *provide a theory* which would, among other things, rationalize such a policy." Similarly, Johnson (1971 [1978], p. 226) stated: "The *General Theory* was successful precisely because, by providing an alternate theory to the prevailing orthodoxy, it rationalized a sensible policy [public works] that had hitherto been resisted on purely dogmatic grounds." However, Patinkin and Johnson overlooked that lonely spot on the Midway that used the quantity theory to provide an alternate rationale for a policy of public works during the Depression. The Chicagoans called this monetary policy, since they viewed it as operating on the quantity of money. Patinkin and Johnson also did not acknowledge that Friedman's business cycle analysis was, in key respects, consistent with the Chicago tradition, including the notions that, during the cycle, velocity behavior varies pro-cyclically and is cumulative and unstable.

It's worth remembering that in the years following the publication of Keynes's *General Theory* (1936), while Chicago economists continued to work in the quantity theory tradition, quantity theorists at many other U.S. academic institutions either converted to Keynesian ideas or left academia altogether (Tavlas, 1997). In the United Kingdom, Keynes's disciples severely attacked the quantity theory as a framework of analysis, leading to a commonly-held view that money did not matter (Tavlas, 1981). However, Chicago economists were possessed of a version of the equation of exchange that could be used to advocate public works expenditure to raise the stock of money and combat depressions, and thus were not susceptible to Keynes's theoretical message.

Milton Friedman joined the Chicago faculty in 1946, in the midst of this turmoil. His 1956 essay, heralding the beginning of the monetarist counterrevolution, served as the introductory chapter to a volume consisting of four essays by his students, two of which were concerned with estimating velocity behavior. In his essay, Friedman adopted and extended elements of Keynes's liquidity preference theory while acknowledging that his perspective was heavily shaped by Chicago's distinctive monetarist tradition using the quantity theory. Accordingly, the restatement also heralded the culmination of an ongoing research tradition at Chicago extending back into the 1930s and expounding the old-time religion which insisted that money matters.

■ *I wish to thank Meyer Burstein, Robert Clower, Milton Friedman, and participants at the History of Economics Society conference at the University of South Carolina for helpful comments and suggestions on an earlier draft. Special thanks to the editors of this journal, Timothy Taylor and Brad De Long, for their extensive and insightful comments, and to Joseph Persky for his encouragement and guidance. The views expressed are the author's own and should not be interpreted as those of the Bank of Greece or the International Monetary Fund.*

References

Aschheim, Joseph, and George S. Tavlas, "Monetary Economics in Doctrinal Perspective," *Journal of Money, Credit and Banking,* August 1996, *28,* 406–17

Bach, George L., *Price Level Stabilization. Some Theoretical and Practical Considerations.* Unpublished Ph D. Dissertation, University of Chicago, 1940.

Bane, Frank, et al., "Balancing the Budget· Federal Fiscal Policy during Depression " In U.S Senate, 72d Cong , 2d sess., *Investigation of Economic Problems Hearings before the Committee on Finance,* February 1933.

Blaug, Mark, *Economic Theory in Retrospect* Cambridge, U K. Cambridge University Press (fifth edition), 1996.

Cox, Garfield V., et al., "Memorandum to Congressman Samuel B Pettengill " In U S House of Representatives, 72d Cong , 1st sess , *Payment of Adjusted-Compensation Certificates Hearings before the Committee on Ways and Means,* April 1932

Currie, Lauchlin, *The Supply and Control of Money in the United States* Cambridge, Mass· Harvard University Press, 1934

Douglas, Paul H., and Aaron Director, *The Problem of Unemployment* New York. Macmillan, 1931

Fisher, Irving, "The Debt-Deflation Theory of Great Depressions," *Econometrica,* October 1933, *1,* 337–57.

Friedman, Milton, "The Quantity Theory of Money A Restatement " In Friedman, Milton, ed , *Studies in the Quantity Theory of Money* Chicago University of Chicago Press, 1956, 3–21

Friedman, Milton, "The Supply of Money and Changes in Prices and Output," U.S Joint Economic Committee, 85th Congress, 2nd sess , *The Relationship of Prices to Economic Stability and Growth,* 1958 Reprinted in Friedman, 1969, 171–87

Friedman, Milton, "The Demand For Money: Some Theoretical and Empirical Results," *Journal of Political Economy,* August 1959, *67,* 327–51

Friedman, Milton, *The Optimum Quantity of Money and Other Essays* London: Macmillan, 1969

Friedman, Milton, "Comments on the Critics," *Journal of Political Economy,* September/October 1972, *80,* 906–50

Friedman, Milton, and Anna Schwartz, *A Monetary History of the United States, 1867–1960* Princeton. Princeton University Press, 1963

Harris Memorial Foundation, *Reports of Round Tables Gold and Monetary Stabilization* Chicago The University of Chicago, 1932

Hart, Albert G., "The 'Chicago Plan' of Banking Reform," *Review of Economic Studies,* 1934–35, *2,* 104–16

Johnson, Harry G., "The Keynesian Revolution and the Monetarist Counter-Revolution,"*American Economic Review,* May 1971, *61,* 1–14 Reprinted in Harry G Johnson, ed , *Selected Essays in Monetary Economics* London George Allen, 1978, 210–30

Keynes, John Maynard, *The General Theory of Employment, Interest and Money* London· Macmillan, 1936.

Knight, Frank H., "The Business Cycle, Interest and Money: A Methodological Approach," *Review of Economic Statistics,* May 1941, *23,* 53–67 Reprinted in Knight, 1956, 202–26

Knight, Frank H., *On the History and Method of Economics* Chicago University of Chicago Press, 1956

Mints, Lloyd W., "Monetary Policy," *Review of Economic Statistics,* May 1946, *28,* 60–69

Mints, Lloyd W., *Monetary Policy for a Competitive Society* New York McGraw Hill, 1950

Moggridge, Donald, and Susan Howson, "Keynes on Monetary Policy, 1910–46," *Oxford Economic Papers,* July 1974, *26,* 226–47

Patinkin, Don, *Money, Interest and Prices* New York Harper and Row, 1965

Patinkin, Don, "The Chicago Tradition, the Quantity Theory, and Friedman," *Journal of Money, Credit and Banking,* February 1969, *1,* 46–70

Patinkin, Don, "Keynes, John Maynard " In John Eatwell, Murray Milgate, and Peter Newman, eds., *The New Palgrave A Dictionary of Economics.* London Macmillan, 1987, 19–42

Simons, Henry C., "Economic Reconstruction The Columbia Report," *Journal of Political Economy,* December 1934, *42,* 795–99.

Simons, Henry C., "Review of 'The Supply and Control of Money in the United States,' by Lauchlin Currie," *Journal of Political Economy,* August 1935, *43,* 555–58.

Simons, Henry C., "Rules versus Authorities in Monetary Policy," *Journal of Political Economy,* February 1936, *44,* 1–30 Reprinted in Henry C. Simons, ed., *Economic Policy for a Free Society* Chicago University of Chicago Press, 1948

Skidelsky, Robert, *John Maynard Keynes The Economist as Savior, 1920–1937* London Macmillan, 1992

Snowdon, Brian, and Howard Vane, "The Development of Modern Macroeconomics Reflections in the Light of Johnson's Analysis after Twenty-five Years," *Journal of Macroeconomics,* Summer 1996, *18,* 381–401

Steindl, Frank G., "The 'Oral' Tradition at Chicago in the 1930s," *Journal of Political Economy,* April 1990, *98,* 430–32.

Tavlas, George S., "The Chicago Tradition Revisited Some Neglected Monetary Contributions of Senator Paul Douglas," *Journal of Money, Credit and Banking,* November 1977, *9,* 529–35

Tavlas, George S., "Keynesian and Monetarist Theories of the Monetary Transmission Process," *Journal of Monetary Economics*, May 1981, *7*, 317–37.

Tavlas, George S., "Notes on Garvy, Snyder, and the Doctrinal Foundations of Monetarism," *History of Political Economy*, Spring 1982, *14*, 89–100

Tavlas, George S., "Chicago, Harvard, and the Doctrinal Foundations of Monetary Economics," *Journal of Political Economy*, February 1997, *105*, 153–77

Viner, Jacob, *Balanced Deflation, Inflation, or More Depression* Minneapolis. University of Minnesota Press, 1933a.

Viner, Jacob, "Inflation as a Possible Remedy for Depression " In *Proceedings of the Institute of Public Affairs*, 7th annual session. Athens, Georgia. University of Georgia Press, 1933b

'More on Hawtrey, Harvard and Chicago'

D. Laidler, 'More on Hawtrey, Harvard and Chicago', *Journal of Economic Studies* 25:1 (1998a), pp. 4–16.

More on Hawtrey, Harvard and Chicago

David Laidler
University of Western Ontario, Canada

Introduction

In Laidler (1993) I drew attention to the fact that Milton Friedman's views on monetary factors in the business cycle are close to those espoused by Ralph Hawtrey in the 1920s and 1930s (as indeed are his opinions on the relative effectiveness of monetary and fiscal policy, though I did not discuss this issue in the paper in question). I further showed that Allyn Young, who taught monetary economics at Harvard until 1927, did much to bring Hawtrey's ideas into US discourse in the 1920s; that Lauchlin Currie, Young's student and Hawtrey's assistant during the latter's tenure of a visiting appointment at Harvard in 1928-1929, came closer to anticipating some of Friedman's major conclusions about the role of monetary factors in the "great contraction" of 1929-1933, than did any Chicago economist of the period; and that one of the prime contributions cited by Friedman (1974) in his discussion of the links between his own work and an earlier "Chicago tradition", namely the manifesto that emerged from the winter 1932 Harris Foundation conference, was drafted by a committee that included John H. Williams, also a Harvard professor, who contributed a paper to the conference volume (Wright, 1932) justifying that manifesto, and who, as a result of Young's death in 1929, had supervised the PhD thesis out of which most of Currie's significant publications on these matters developed. I concluded, on the basis of this evidence, that the "Chicago tradition" invoked by Friedman was not unique to that university in the early 1930s, but had strong links to Harvard and, by that route, indirect links to Hawtrey too.

This conclusion has recently been criticized by George Tavlas (1997), who takes me to task, among other things, for neglecting contributions of the Chicago economist, Paul Douglas, writing both alone and in collaboration with Aaron Director, to the Chicago tradition[1]. The significance of this aspect of Tavlas' critique stems from the fact that Douglas started writing on these matters in the later 1920s, and that his book with Director appeared in 1931. If

Without implicating them in the views I express, let me acknowledge helpful conversations and correspondence with Milton Friedman, Dan Hammond, Tom Humphrey, Perry Mehrling, Paul Samuelson, Roger Sandilands, Frank Steindl and George Tavlas. My correspondence with Don Patinkin on the issues dealt with here was brought to an end by his untimely death in 1995. Let this paper stand as a small personal tribute to a sometime colleague, great friend and magnificent scholar. The financial support of the Lynde and Harry Bradley foundation, and of the SSHRCC are gratefully acknowledged.

Douglas is a key contributor to Friedman's Chicago tradition, then, it has an earlier origin at that university than 1932 or thereabouts. In this paper, I shall answer many of Tavlas' criticisms, and in the course of doing so, present a little new evidence that bears on the major points of contention between us.

In the following pages, I shall discuss in turn: the views of Hawtrey (e.g. 1925) and Friedman (e.g. 1974) on the powers of monetary and fiscal policy, and contrast them with those of Douglas and Director (1931) to which Tavlas draws attention; the role of monetary factors in causing and exacerbating the great contraction of 1929-1933, and what monetary policy might have accomplished to mitigate it, as seen by Hawtrey (1932), Currie (1934a, 1934b), Friedman and Schwartz (1963) and Douglas (1933, 1935); and the relationship between Douglas' work and that of some of his Chicago colleagues. I shall conclude that the scepticism I expressed in (1993) about the uniqueness in the early 1930s of a Chicago tradition to which Friedman's work is related remains well justified.

Before proceeding to the substance of my case, however, let me explicitly set aside two matters. First, though I disagree with Tavlas on many issues, his treatment of Douglas in particular, there is nevertheless much to admire in his paper, not least his discussion of the hitherto unappreciated contribution of Aaron Director to the Chicago tradition, and his analysis of the evolution of Jacob Viner's work. Second, there are two important aspects of Friedman's work whose antecedents are not in contention, namely his advocacy of rule guided monetary policy and his careful and systematic empiricism. Neither Hawtrey nor Currie, nor Young for that matter, favoured governing monetary policy by rules. As Humphrey (1971) showed, some non-Chicago economists did advocate such measures in the 1920s and 1930s, but I have no doubt that Friedman's position on monetary rules, and his linking of it to a liberal (in the old-fashioned sense) political agenda, derived from the Chicago tradition in general and Henry Simons' contribution to it in particular. Nor, despite the fact that Young and Currie did carry out important and systematic empirical work, do I see any reason to doubt J. Daniel Hammond's (1996a, 1996b) contention that Friedman's own empiricism derives primarily from the NBER tradition of Wesley C. Mitchell and Arthur F. Burns.

Friedman, Hawtrey, and Douglas and Director on fiscal policy

Tavlas relates Friedman's views on fiscal and monetary policy to those of Douglas and Director (1931). They are most succinctly set out in Friedman's reply to James Tobin's criticisms of his position on these matters, contained in Gordon (Ed.) (1974, pp. 137-43). Friedman's argument may be paraphrased, in terms of the IS-LM schema, which he there uses to express them, as follows: government expenditure financed by borrowing from the public will shift the IS curve to the right, and mainly affect interest rates; only to the extent that the LM curve deviates from the vertical will the level of money income be increased. If, on the other hand, government expenditure is financed by money creation, then the LM curve will also shift to the right, inducing a much more significant increase in money income. This analysis provides the context of Friedman's remark, quoted by Tavlas (1997, pp. 165-6) that the deficit's "...monetary effect is 'alchemy of a much deeper significance' than the fiscal effect" (Friedman, 1974, p. 141). This comment does not derive, as Tavlas would have it, from any tradition developed at, and unique to, Chicago. Rather it is an expression of the so-called "treasury view" developed by Hawtrey (see Hawtrey, 1925 in particular). Friedman's IS-LM exposition of the matter deviates from John Hicks' (1937) original IS-LM characterization of the treasury view only in allowing the logical possibility that the LM curve might not be completely vertical; an effect whose empirical significance he clearly thought trivial[2].

It was Hawtrey's contention that bond financed public expenditure would normally do no more than displace private sector expenditure, because "...it is only in exceptional circumstances that government expenditure on public works will itself bring about an increase in velocity" (Hawtrey, 1929, p. 637), while money financed expenditure would be effective, but only because it increased the money supply. According to Hawtrey, if the money supply was increased by the same amount as was needed to finance a public works programme, but by other means, the effects on aggregate demand would usually be the same[3]. Hawtrey's conclusions here, so close to Friedman's, differ in emphasis, but crucially so, from those of Douglas and Director, to which Tavlas (1997) relates Friedman's position. Douglas and Dirctor argued that, although in the case of either tax or bond financed public works expenditure, it was necessary to allow for some offsetting reduction in private demand caused by these methods of finance, the overall effect would definitely be "a net addition to the demand for labour" (Douglas and Director, 1931 p. 210). Noting that "where the funds for government expenditures come directly or indirectly from an increase in the total supply of bank credits, even Hawtrey has admitted the possibility of increasing the demand for labour by the construction of public works" (p. 210) they also concluded that "...it is possible for government to increase the demand for labour without a corresponding contraction of private demand, and that this is particularly the case when fresh monetary purchasing power is created to finance the construction work" (pp. 171-2).

Tavlas (1997, pp. 171-2) suggests that, after 1931, Hawtrey became "increasingly pessimistic about the efficacy of government expenditures and more and more an advocate of central bank measures." (Tavlas, 1997 p. 172) All. I can say to this is that I do not read Hawtrey this way, nor, as far as I can see, does his intellectual biographer Patrick Deutscher (1990, see particularly pp. 65-6, 217-9). On my reading, from 1913 until after the publication of the *General Theory* (Keynes 1936), Hawtrey never deviated from the view that, except in certain extreme circumstances which he thought were of purely theoretical significance (see, e.g. 1925, pp. 44-5) government expenditures would be insufficient to combat unemployment, unless financed by money creation, and that anything they might accomplish if they were so funded could also be accomplished if the central bank put money into circulation by other means, specifically by open market operations, or by financing a deficit created by cutting taxes. He remained, that is to say, steadfast in his support of a position that Friedman would later hold, and which was not held at Chicago in the early 1930s, as Tavlas, in apparent contradiction of his own earlier arguments, at one point concedes (cf. Tavlas, 1997, pp. 165-6, 171-2).

Monetary factors in the great contraction

Friedman and Schwartz (1963, ch. 7) portrayed "the great contraction" of 1929-1933 as "a tragic testimonial to the importance of monetary forces" (p. 300) and argued that "the failure of the federal reserve system to prevent the collapse reflected not the impotence of monetary policy, but rather the particular policies followed by the monetary authorities and, in smaller degree, the particular monetary arrangements in existence" (p. 300). They contrasted these conclusions with the then prevailing opinion that the contraction had shown that orthodox "monetary policy is of extremely limited value in promoting stability" (p. 300)[4].

As I showed in 1993, the Chicago economists of the early 1930s were at best guarded about what could be expected of open market operations, noting for example that Viner (1932) was less confident in their powers than was John Williams (1932). Tavlas takes me to task for neglecting the Chicago economists' optimism about the expansionary potential of money financed deficits. He points out, correctly, that Douglas in particular was an advocate of such measures, and suggests that he influenced Aaron Director, Jacob Viner and Henry Simons on this issue. Tavlas is right that advocacy of this unorthodox means of increasing the money supply did become an integral part of Chicago teaching, including that of Lloyd Mints, as the 1930s wore on. Patinkin (1969) provides ample evidence of this, and Steindl (1995) has documented this advocacy on the part of Douglas in 1932, Viner in 1933, and Mints in later years (cf. Steindl, 1995, p. 84, 88, 94 *et. seq.*). The position in question is, however, conspicuous by its absence from the 1932 Harris Foundation conference manifesto, as reprinted in Wright (Ed.) (1932), which Douglas did not sign, and to which Friedman, nevertheless, drew attention as an important document embodying the thought of members of the Chicago department. Since it was my claim that the "hopefulness" which, in Friedman's view, characterized the Chicago tradition was more apparent in the contribution of Williams to that 1932 conference than that of any members of the Chicago department, and since I also noted that, for example, Viner did become a little more optimistic in 1933, I fail to see how Tavlas' arguments, correct as they may be, bear on this aspect of my case.

Douglas' advocacy of deficit finance as a means of increasing the money supply during, and even before (see Douglas, 1927), the great contraction, hardly makes him a forerunner of Friedman and Schwartz (1963) either. The latter argue that orthodox monetary measures, particularly open market operations, could have done much to counter the contraction, had they only been pursued with sufficient vigour. Douglas did not believe that, either during or after the event. Thus, Douglas and Director (1931, p. 243) expressed considerable and, for the time, rather conventional, scepticism about the expansionary powers of open market operations in any slump. After 1932, moreover, Douglas explicitly argued that open market operations had been proven impotent by the events of that year. In 1933, he wrote about the open market operations of 1932 in the following terms:

> The expectation was that the banks would be so choked with cash that they would have to increase their loans.
>
> The hoped for results did not occur. It is not enough to give banks the power to create more credit. It is necessary that the loans should actually be made in large quantities. That did not happen because in a period of depression businessmen are afraid to borrow and banks are afraid to lend (p. 10).

Contrast Douglas's position, which Steindl (1995, p. 93) characterizes as "real-bills oriented", with the general view expressed by Ralph Hawtrey (1932, ch. 4) about what could be accomplished in a period of depression. Should what he called "a deadlock" arise in credit markets, it "can best be broken by injecting money into the system. Now the central bank has the power of creating money" (p. 172). Hawtrey did indeed believe, as Mints (1945), quoted by Tavlas (p. 172), would much later note, that such a situation would "not yield to a low bank rate", but this is beside the point in contention between Tavlas and myself, because, as Tavlas fails to point out, it was also Hawtrey's position that, when

> ...the bills offered and the suitable applications for advances are inadequate and do not increase enough, the banks have the alternative of buying long term investments of a suitable marketable character...
>
> There must ultimately be a limit to the amount of money that the sellers will hold idle, and it follows that by this process the vicious circle of deflation can always be broken, however great the stagnation of business and the reluctance of borrowers may be (1932, pp. 173-4).

It is even more instructive to contrast Douglas's interpretation of the particular events of 1932, with that offered by Lauchlin Currie in (1934b).

> It has been held that security purchases by a central bank in the downswing of business will bring about an expansion of money. In 1932 the reserve banks bought an unprecedented amount of bonds and money did not expand. Therefore open market operations cannot bring about expansion in periods of depression. The answer to this line of argument is, of course, that the major premise as stated is incomplete. The assumption is that the purchases will result in an actual increase in member bank reserves. The open market policy of 1932 was offset by an outflow of gold and the liquidation of member bank indebtedness to the reserve banks so that only a comparatively small increase in reserves occurred (p. 147).

Currie's conclusions then followed:

> Much of the current belief in the powerlessness of the reserve banks appears to arise from a complete misreading of the monetary history of 1929-32. It is generally held that the reserve administration strove energetically to bring about expansion throughout the depression but that contraction continued despite its efforts. Actually the reserve administration's policy was one of almost complete passivity and quiescence (p. 147).

and

> The drastic contraction of money from 1929 to 1932 proceeded automatically with no real effort made to offset it. Hence the course of events during this period should not be cited as

evidence of the *inability* of a central bank to arrest contraction of money and bring about expansion (1934b, p. 148, italics in original).

If any doubts remain about Currie's views as of 1934 on the role of monetary policy in the great contraction, they can surely be settled by referring to the title of the article in which, in that year, he summarized them: namely, "the failure of monetary policy to prevent the depression of 1929-1932" (Currie, 1934a).

Currie's monetary analysis of the great contraction was not brand new in 1934. Chapter IX of his PhD thesis "Bank assets and banking theory", supervised by John H. Williams, and submitted at Harvard in January 1931, bore the title "Bank assets and the business cycle". In this chapter he pointed to a "normal relation" of "movements in demand deposits ...to the business cycle" with "a contraction preceding the downturn in business in 1920, 1923 and 1929" (Currie, 1931, p. 229), and he argued, with respect to federal reserve policy in 1929 and 1930, "...that a much greater expansion of credit might have been brought about after the downturn in business in 1929 than did in fact take place" (Currie, 1931, p. 237)[5]. Currie's discussion of US experience over the 1920-1930 period was, moreover, cast in terms of a monetary analysis of the cycle which, as he explicitly acknowledged, derived from Hawtrey, to whose theoretical views the first eleven pages (pp. 211-21) of this chapter are largely devoted.

The influence of Hawtrey on Currie has not been sufficiently appreciated, largely one suspects because he himself later downplayed it. Even in the version of his thesis submitted for the Wells Prize competition in October 1932, the first eleven pages of chapter IX (by then chapter XI) dealing with Hawtrey were deleted, and the subsequent discussion modified so that Keynes' *Treatise on Money* (1930), not published when this chapter was first drafted, as Currie explicitly pointed out in its first version, seemed to be the inspiration for its optimistic discussion of the powers of counter-cyclical monetary policy[6]. But downplayed later or not, Hawtrey's influence on Currie is demonstrable and important.

In the course of criticizing my 1993 paper, Tavlas, p. 169, quotes from a memoir of Currie's (1978) and concludes on its basis that, while still at Harvard, Currie believed in "the inefficacy of open market operations and the need for budget deficits". What Tavlas does not tell his readers is that this memoir was written as part of a symposium dealing with Currie's post-1934 contributions to the economics of deficit finance, and not as an account of his overall contributions to monetary economics in the 1930s. The fact is that Currie (1934a) was published just as Currie was leaving Harvard, and (1934b) after he had left; and the passages I have quoted above from the second of these quite evidently contradict Tavlas's attribution of a belief in the inefficacy of open market operations to Currie in 1934 and earlier, while the title of the first refers to the failure, not the inability, of monetary policy to prevent the depression. Furthermore, Currie makes no mention of unbalanced budgets as a tool of expansionary policy in either work, nor does he do so in any of his other publications up to that date, so far as I am aware. In the face of so evident a conflict between what Currie wrote while still at Harvard, and the view which Tavlas attributes to him on the basis of what he wrote more than 40 years later, it is surely appropriate to rely on the contemporary source in establishing Currie's views.

This is not to deny that Currie advocated unbalanced budgets as a means of fighting depression in his teaching at Harvard. He may well have done so, and in so doing he would have been taking up a position that his mentor Allyn Young had defended in the 1920s, as Mehrling (1996, p. 623, fn. 25) has noted. It is, moreover, quite uncontroversial that, as the 1930s wore on, and free reserves continued to build up in the banking system, Currie began to lose faith in the reliability of open market operations. From 1935 onwards, the period with which his 1978 memoir is concerned, he did indeed become a very vigorous advocate of fiscal policy. Furthermore, Sandilands (1990) and Steindl (1995) have discussed his views in the late 1930s, and have established that his explanation of the 1938 downturn in terms of fiscal policy is very different from Friedman and Schwartz's monetary explanation of this event[7]. But, and more to the point of my disagreement with Tavlas, none of this can alter the fact that what Currie wrote in (1934b) was far closer to the (1963) views of Friedman and Schwartz on the role of monetary factors in the great contraction of 1929-1933 than anything written by Douglas or any of his Chicago colleagues, with the possible exception of Simons who, in a 1935 review of Currie (1934b), expressed broad agreement with his conclusions, which, he said were "firmly established in the 'oral tradition' of some schools" (Simons, 1935, p. 555).

Douglas and the Chicago tradition

In (1993) I treated Paul Douglas only briefly, and as something of an outlier at Chicago, partly because of positions he took in his 1935 book, *Controlling Depressions*, but also because of his failure to sign the 1932 Harris Foundation conference manifesto. Tavlas, on the other hand, argues that he occupied an important place in the mainstream of that department's monetary thought[8]. As it happens, Eric Lundberg was a visiting student at Chicago in 1931-1932, the academic year immediately prior to Milton Friedman's arrival there, and his 1934 report to the Rockefeller Foundation on his two-year visit to the USA (September 1931-September 1933) has recently (1995) been published for the first time. It contains the following unflattering comment, which nevertheless identifies Douglas as a leading contributor to Chicago discussions of the cycle at that time:

> In the field of business cycle theory the University of Chicago had very little to offer. Professor Mints touched on some of the problems in his lectures on monetary theories, while Douglas offered a very simple overproduction and underconsumption theory (Lundberg, 1934, pub. 1995, p. 51).

One might question Lundberg's overall assessment of the state of cycle theory at Chicago, because visiting graduate students do not, after all, necessarily learn all there is to be learned about a department. His characterization of Douglas is, however, demonstrably accurate in the light of the written record.

Tavlas presents a 1927 paper by Douglas as an early exposition of the "Chicago" case for steady money growth. However, the case that Douglas makes in that paper is not based on any version of the quantity theory of money, but rather on the underconsumptionist theory of William T. Foster and Waddill Catchings, to whose "brilliant and suggestive writings" (Douglas, 1927, p. 37) he pays explicit tribute. It is easy to confuse these two very different strands in US economic thought, because both do indeed call for regular injections of new money into the economy as the best means of stabilizing it[9]. However, the under-consumptionist doctrine developed by Foster and Catchings insists that, if it is to be effective in curing a chronic tendency of consumer expenditure to fall short of the nominal value of consumption goods coming onto the market, the new money in question must be placed, in the first instance, in the hands of consumers. That is exactly what Douglas argued in 1927, and would argue again in 1932, 1933 and 1935.

Tavlas points out that, in 1927, "Douglas advocated that the government undertake public works projects financed by money creation if 'proper safeguards could be provided to prevent inflation' (p. 42)" (Tavlas, 1997, p. 158). This is correct as far as it goes, but Douglas also told his readers that public works expenditures would be effective because they

> ...would give purchasing power to the workers and stabilize the price level. Since the services of these public works would later largely be offered gratuitously to the public, they would not enter into the volumes of commodities offered for sale and hence would not cause a fall in the price level (Douglas, 1927, p. 41).

This is a quintessential underconsumptionist argument in the style of Foster and Catchings.

Underconsumptionism went into temporary eclipse in Douglas and Director (1931), a fact which I am unable to explain, but which would merit further investigation. Thus the cycle theory presented there is best summarized as an eclectic amalgam of Pigou (1927) and Mitchell (1927). Tavlas (1997, p. 161) argues that in their treatment of this topic, Douglas and Director "...introduced into the Chicago literature the view that the cycle can be cumulative in nature". Since, however, that view was central to the cycle theories of J.S. Mill, Alfred Marshall, Irving Fisher, and a host of others, including of course Hawtrey, Mitchell and Pigou, there could hardly be stronger testimony than this to the derivative nature of Chicago's analysis of the cycle in the early 1930s. The case for steady money growth in Douglas and Director (1931) is motivated with reference to the empirical work of Willard Thorp (1926), as discussed by Mitchell (1927, pp. 407 *et seq.*). This work appeared to show that secular deflation was associated with cycles whose depression phases were relatively long, and whose booms were relatively shortlived, and the theoretical arguments that Douglas and Director advance to explain why such results should be taken seriously have a greater affinity to the *Tract on Monetary*

Reform (see Keynes, 1923, pp. 33-5), a book which they do cite but not in this context, than to anything in the writings of Foster and Catchings.

Be that as it may, Douglas's (1933) pamphlet *Collapse or Cycle* and his longer (1935) monograph *Controlling Depressions* return to the underconsumptionist theme. Though Foster and Catchings are not cited, as they had been in 1927, Douglas's analysis is nevertheless clearly a variation on theirs, adapted to conditions prevailing in the USA in the early 1930s[10].

> The chain of revival runs primarily from the *increased purchasing power of the consumers and greater demand by consumers,* to increased borrowings and bank loans, rather than from increased bank loans to business, to greater purchasing power by consumers, to increased purchases (1933, pp. 10-11, italics added).

What is required to promote such revival, then, is "the liberal financing of relief, and extremely large expenditures on public works" (p. 11). Spending on relief is required to meet "...actual human needs"; but also, and crucially, it will satisfy "the *necessity for increased purchasing power by consumers* which will start the cumulative process of revival" (p. 11, italics added). Public works will also, following the argument of Keynes, as presented in *The Means to Prosperity* (1933), generate "...a multiplicative effect in stimulating business" (p. 12) Douglas expected such a programme to be effective whether financed by bond issue or money creation, but "It should be realized that bonds require the payment of interest by the government while money does not. So if the issuance of money can be controlled, this would seem to be by far the more economical way" (p. 13).

Whatever may have been the views of his Chicago colleagues on these matters, it should be clear that Douglas was not here advocating fiscal deficits as merely a reliable means of increasing the money supply in conditions of what Hawtrey called a "credit deadlock". Rather he was advocating: first, putting money in the hands of consumers in order to enable them to increase their expenditure and hence alleviate the chronic underconsumption which he believed to be an inherent characteristic of a market economy; and second, setting a Keynesian multiplier process in motion by public works expenditures. Methods of finance, though not irrelevant, were of secondary importance to Douglas' programme, whereas, in the Chicago tradition as described by Patinkin (1969), and Steindl (1995, ch. 5), they were all-important since the whole object of the exercise was to increase the quantity of money in circulation.

To be sure, in 1933, Douglas also advocated the goal of price stability once recovery had been achieved (see. p. 14ff); and he made a brief case for what later came to be called "100 per cent money" (see pp. 19-20)[11]. However, though it is not immediately apparent from this pamphlet, it is quite clear from a book written a year earlier, namely *The Coming of a New Party* (1932) (see ch. 4, and particularly pp. 102-6) that Douglas regarded these proposals as an integral part of a comprehensive socialist (albeit democratic) policy agenda that included a large role for planning, and would permanently and radically change US economic and social life. None of this looks to me like the economic thought, or even the monetary thought, of someone whose work lay at the centre of an intellectual tradition whose principal exponent in the 1930s was Henry Simons, but also included Lloyd Mints, Jacob Viner, not to mention Frank H. Knight, and would later produce Milton Friedman. Friedman himself (1974) refers to these four as exponents of the doctrines that influenced him while he was a student at Chicago, but he does not mention Paul Douglas.

Be that as it may, Friedman's views are, as he himself has argued, (cf Friedman, 1967, repr. 1969 and 1974) most akin to those of Henry Simons. Simon's views were first revealed in the 1933 unpublished manuscript in which the "Chicago plan" for 100 per cent money was first fully articulated (Simons *et al.*, 1933). The theory of the cycle there set out is a monetary one, very much in the spirit of Hawtrey. An increase in the price level brought about by monetary expansion is presented as the *sine qua non* of recovery, and an unbalanced budget is presented, not as expansionary in and of itself, but solely as the best way of engineering this result: "at the present time, increase of expenditures or reduction of taxes would be far more immediately effective toward raising prices than conversion of the federal debt into the non-interest-bearing form" (Simons *et al.*, 1933, p. 12).

Furthermore, Simons himself made it abundantly clear the following year that he regarded such measures as an integral part of an altogether broader *Positive Program for Laisser Faire* (see Simons, 1934). Though his programme was a radical one, embodying a vigorous use of anti-trust measures and a significant degree of redistribution too, and hence differed from the, in many ways, more traditional agenda that we nowadays associate with Friedman, it was nevertheless far closer to what we have come to think of as a "Chicago" position than anything that Douglas offered in the 1930s.

Concluding comment

Friedman's monetary economics is certainly related to ideas that were current at the University of Chicago in the 1930s; that is not in dispute. However, there were sharp divisions among the Chicago economists of that time. Friedman himself has particularly stressed his indebtedness to Simons, but I have been unable to find a single reference to Paul Douglas in his monetary writings. The contemporary record gives us good reason to trust his judgement here.

However, in a number of key respects, Friedman's monetary theory of the cycle in general, as well as his position on the relative efficacy of monetary and fiscal policy, place him closer to Hawtrey than to any of his Chicago predecessors, and Hawtrey's analysis of these matters was fully developed long before the "Chicago tradition" had come into being. Moreover, Friedman's specific views on the causes of the great contraction were more closely anticipated by Lauchlin Currie, a graduate student and instructor at Harvard, than by anyone else writing in the early 1930s, as Humphrey (1971) long ago pointed out; Hawtrey's most important US advocate was Allyn Young, a professor at Harvard until 1927; and the only academic appointment Hawtrey ever held was at Harvard in 1928-1929, where his assistant was Lauchlin Currie. Moreover, John H. Williams, the supervisor of Currie's doctoral dissertation had a major hand in drafting the 1932 Harris Foundation conference manifesto, which Friedman has cited as an important and early manifestation of 1930s Chicago thought. In light of all this, I am still inclined to suggest that there was a Hawtrey-Harvard connection to the origins of the 1930s Chicago tradition[12].

Notes

1. It should be pointed out that I am not the only one to raise most of the matters referred to in the proceeding paragraph. On the similarity between Hawtrey and Friedman, see, for example, John R. Presley (1986) (to which I failed to refer in 1993); on Hawtrey's influence in the USA, and Young's role in promoting it, see Patrick Deutscher (1990, pp. 195-9) and Perry Mehrling (1996); and on Currie's anticipation of Friedman, see, *inter alia*, Karl Brunner (1968), Thomas Humphrey (1971) and Roger Sandilands (1990). Tavlas' quarrel, therefore, is not with me but with an extensive secondary literature. The only one of the above contributions to which he refers is Humphrey (1971).
2. See Hicks (1937, repr. 1967, p. 133, fn.1).
3. This would also happen in the case of expenditure financed by borrowing abroad. "The desired end can be achieved by dropping out the expenditure on development works, and using the proceeds of the loan to extinguish government floating debt in the hands of the banks and the money market" (Hawtrey, 1932, ch. 8 p. 438). This chapter was originally prepared in 1930 as evidence to the Macmillan committee.
4. I add the qualifier "orthodox" here, because, as did I in 1993, Friedman and Schwartz employ the phrase "monetary policy" in the usual sense of discount policy and open-market operations, rather than in the broader sense favoured by Tavlas, which also encompasses the finance of government expenditure by money creation.
5. Note that Currie here discusses demand deposits rather than the money stock. Steindl (1995, ch. 4) draws attention to this difference between his analysis and that of Friedman and Schwartz (1963).
6. Currie's reasons for making this change are unknown. I am indebted to Roger Sandilands for helpful correspondence and for providing me with a copy of the relevant section of the 1932 version of Currie's thesis.
7. I discussed aspects of this matter in Laidler (1993, p. 1071, fn. 4 and p. 1088, fn. 21). Note that Currie's post-1935 advocacy of fiscal policy was based on an analysis which stressed the possibility that the issue of government bonds would provide instruments which banks could purchase, thereby mobilizing their excess reserves and increasing the money supply, rather than on a simple multiplier theory. This is essentially the case which Hawtrey (1925) treated as an exception, albeit a purely theoretical exception, to his general advocacy of the Treasury view. I am indebted to Roger Sandilands for helpful correspondence on this point.
8. Tavlas (1977) has earlier made the case for Douglas as an important contributor to the Chicago school. In preparing Laidler (1993) I simply overlooked this paper, as I did Presley (1986). I owe apologies to Tavlas, to Presley, and to my readers for these oversights. Had the first of them not occurred, I might well have included a brief explanation of why I disagreed with Tavlas about Douglas at the point at which the latter came into my story.
9. Tavlas (1997, p. 156) includes Foster and Catchings among the non-Chicago predecessors of Friedman, and has argued that case in more detail in (1976). A little later, writing with Joseph Aschheim (Tavlas and Aschheim, 1981) he refers to Foster and Catchings as "American quantity theorists" (p. 76). Thus, lying behind my disagreement with Tavlas about the place of Douglas in the Chicago tradition, is another about the place of Foster and Catchings in US monetary thought. For a discussion of Foster and Catchings as exponents of underconsumptionism, a completely conventional interpretation of their work see, for example, Lawrence Klein (1966, pp. 138-40).

10. Compare Douglas's views to Foster and Catchings (1925, p. 364): "The chief economic need, therefore, is a flow of money to consumers sufficient to provide for the necessary growth in their savings, and yet enable them to buy, and to continue to buy at an appropriately stable price level, all the goods that are *actually* ready for final consumption" (italics in original) See also Foster and Catchings (1925, pp. 338-9).
11. There is some inconsistency in Douglas's 1933 analysis, since he also advocates a secularly balanced, or even surplus, budget. Douglas did get this point straight two years later: see (1935, p. 185, fn. 8).
12. This is not to say that I accept Tavlas' (1997, p. 167) suggestion that in 1993 I painted a picture of "a small, but vibrant, group of economists at Harvard working on relevant monetary issues until 1934." This simply misrepresents my assessment of that department's contributions, which was a good deal more mixed than that, as Tavlas' own subsequent discussion of my arguments seems to concede (see Laidler, 1993, p. 1077 *et seq.* and Tavlas, 1997, pp. 167-8). Nevertheless, in spring and summer, 1933, Eric Lundberg seems to have found Harvard having more to offer by way of discussions of the business cycle than Chicago a little earlier. He singled out Professor (sic) Currie for special mention in this regard. See Lundberg (1934, 1995, p 62).

References

Brunner, K. (1968), "Introduction" in Currie, L. (Ed.), *Supply and Control of Money in the United States*, (reprinted), Russell & Russell, New York, NY.

Currie, L. (1931), "Bank assets and banking theory", unpublished PhD thesis, Harvard University (revised 1932).

Currie, L. (1934a), "The failure of monetary policy to prevent the depression of 1929-32", *JPE*, Vol. 42, April, pp. 145-77.

Currie, L. (1934b), *The Supply and Control of Money in the United States*, Harvard University Press, Cambridge, MA, reprint, Russell & Russell, New York, NY, 1968.

Currie, L. (1978), "Comments and observations", (on new deal fiscal policy and the publication of two of Currie's federal reserve board memoranda from the 1930s), *History of Political Economy*, Vol. 10 No. 4, Winter, pp. 507-48.

Deutscher, P. (1990), *R.G. Hawtrey and the Development of Macroeconomics*, Macmillan, London.

Douglas, P.H. (1927), "The modern technique of mass production and its relation to wages", in Moon, P.T. (Ed.), *Stabilizing Business, Proceedings of The Academy of Political Science in the City of New York*, Vol. 12 No. 3, July, pp. 17-42.

Douglas, P.H. (1932), *The Coming of a New Party*, Whittlesey House, New York, NY.

Douglas, P.H. (1933), *Collapse or Cycle*, American Library Association, Chicago, IL.

Douglas, P.H. (1935), *Controlling Depressions*, Norton, New York, NY.

Douglas, P.H. and Director, A. (1931), *The Problem of Unemployment*, Macmillan, New York, NY.

Foster W.T. and Catchings, W. (1925), *Profits*, Houghton Mifflin, Boston and New York.

Friedman, M. (1967), "The monetary theory and policy of Henry Simons", *J. Law and Econ*, Vol. 10, October, pp. 1-13, reprinted in *The Optimum Quantity of Money and Other Essays*, Macmillan, London, 1969.

Friedman M. (1974), "Comments on the critics", in Gordon, R J. (Ed.), *Milton Friedman's Monetary Framework: A Debate with His Critics*, University of Chicago Press, Chicago, IL.

Friedman M. and Schwartz, A.J. (1963), *A Monetary History of the United States, 1867-1960*, Princeton University Press (for NBER), Princeton NJ.

Hammond, J.D. (1996a), *Theory and Measurement – Causality Issues in Milton Friedman's Monetary Economics*, Cambridge University Press, New York, NY

Hammond, J.D. (1996b), "Labels and substance: Friedman's restatement of the quantity theory", mimeo, Wake Forest University, Whinston-Salem, NC, September.

Hawtrey, R.G. (1925), "Public expenditure and the demand for labour", *Economica*, Vol. 5, March, pp. 38-48.

Hawtrey, R.G. (1927), *Currency and Credit*, Longmans, Green, London.

Hawtrey, R.G. (1929), "The monetary theory of the trade cycle", *EJ*, Vol. 39, September, pp. 636-42.

Hawtrey, R.G. (1932), *The Art of Central Banking*, Longmans, Green, London.

Hicks, J.R. (1937), "Mr. Keynes and the classics: a suggested interpretation", *Econometrica*, Vol. 5, April, reprinted in *Critical Essays in Monetary Theory*, Oxford University Press, London, 1967.

Humphrey, T.M. (1971), "Role of non-Chicago economists in the evolution of the quantity theory in America 1930-1950", *Southern Economic Journal*, Vol. 38, July, pp. 12-18.

Keynes, J.M. (1933), *The Means to Prosperity*, Harcourt, Brace, New York, NY.

Keynes, J.M. (1936), *The General Theory of Employment, Interest and Money*, Macmillan, London.

Klein, L.R. (1966), *The Keynesian Revolution* (2nd ed.), Macmillan, London.

Laidler, D. (1993), "Hawtrey, Harvard, and the origins of the Chicago tradition", *JPE*, Vol. 101, December, pp. 1068-103.

Lundberg, E. (1934), "Report of my studies as a Rockefeller fellow of economics", *Studies in Economic Instability and Change*, SNS Foerlag, Stockholm, 1995.

Mehrling, P. (1996), "The monetary thought of Allyn Abbott Young", *History of Political Economy*, Vol. 28 No. 4, Winter, pp. 607-32.

Mints, L.W. (1945), *A History of Banking Theory in Great Britain and the United States*, University of Chicago Press, Chicago, IL.

Mitchell W.C. (1927), *Business Cycles: The Problem and its Setting*, NBER, New York, NY.

Patinkin, D. (1969), "The Chicago tradition, the quantity theory, and Friedman", *Journal of Money, Credit and Banking*, Vol. 1, February, pp. 46-70.

Pigou, A.C. (1927), *Industrial Fluctuations*, Macmillan, London.

Presley, J.R. (1986), "Modern monetarist ideas: a British connection", in Collison Black, R.D. (Ed.), *Ideas in Economics*, Macmillan, London.

Sandilands, R.J. (1990), *The Life and Political Economy of Lauchlin Currie: New Dealer, Presidential Adviser, and Development Economist*, Duke University Press, Durham, NC.

Simons, H.C. (1934), *A Positive Program for Laisser Faire: Some Proposals for a Liberal Economic Policy*, Public Policy Pamphlet No. 15, University of Chicago Press, Chicago, IL.

Simons, H.C. (1935), Review of *The Supply and Control of Money in the United States*, Currie, L. (Ed.), *JPE*, Vol. 43, August, pp. 555-8.

Simons, H.C. *et al.* (1933), "Banking and currency reform", manuscript, University of Chicago, Chicago, IL.

Steindl, F.G. (1995), *Monetary Interpretations of the Great Depression*, University of Michigan Press, Ann Arbor, MI.

Tavlas, G. (1976), "Some further observations on the monetary economics of Chicagoans and non-Chicagoans", *Southern Economic Journal*, Vol. 43, April, pp. 685-92.

Tavlas, G. (1977), "The Chicago tradition revisited: some neglected contributions: Senator Paul Douglas (1892-1976)", *Journal of Money, Credit and Banking*, Vol. 9, November, pp. 529-38.

Tavlas, G. (1997), "Chicago, Harvard and the doctrinal foundations of monetary economics", *Journal of Political Economy*, Vol. 105, February, pp. 153-77.

Tavlas, G. and Aschheim, J. (1981), "The Chicago monetary growth-rate rule: Friedman and Simons Reconsidered", *Banca Nazionale del Lavoro Quarterly Review*, Vol. 136, March, pp. 75-89.

Viner, J. (1932), "International aspects of the gold standard", in Wright, Q. (Ed.), *Gold and Monetary Stabilization*, University of Chicago Press, Chicago, IL.

Viner, J. (1933), *Balanced Deflation, Inflation or More Depression?*, University of Minnesota Press, Minneapolis, MN.

Williams, J.H. (1932), "Monetary stability and the gold standard", in Wright, Q. (Ed.), *Gold and Monetary Stabilization*, University of Chicago Press, Chicago, IL.

Wright, Q. (Ed.) (1932), *Gold and Monetary Stabilization*, University of Chicago Press, Chicago, IL.

'More on the Chicago Tradition'

G. Tavlas, 'More on the Chicago Tradition', *Journal of Economic Studies*, 25:1 (1998b), pp. 17–21.

More on the Chicago tradition

George S. Tavlas
Bank of Greece and International Monetary Fund

David Laidler's article (1998) in this journal is a continuation of the line of argumentation made in Laidler (1993) – namely, "there was a Hawtrey-Harvard connection to the origins of the 1930s Chicago tradition" (1998, p. 14), while expressing doubt about "the uniqueness in the early 1930s of a Chicago tradition to which Friedman's work is related" (1998, p. 4). Laidler will have the opportunity to provide a reply to my comment. In so doing, it would be helpful – for the sake of clarifying the issues that separate us – if he could address the following question: Why did Chicago remain an important centre for the development of the quantity theory of money in the late 1930s and the 1940s while Harvard (and other academic centres) succumbed to the Keynesian revolution?

In Tavlas (1997b), I provided an answer to this question. Specifically, I showed that during the early 1930s the Chicago economists developed a unique approach to the quantity theory of money. According to the earlier Chicagoans, anti-depression policy required an expansion in the money supply (M). Such an increase in M would be used to buy goods, and thus raise prices. With wages considered to be sticky in the short run, profits and production would rise. Traditional monetary measures (i.e. those operating through the banking system), however, were viewed as being too time consuming to be relied on during the Great Depression, and (even if they were not overly time consuming) not likely to be effective during the Depression because, in periods of high uncertainty, business would be reluctant to borrow and banks would not want to lend. Nevertheless, an expansion in M could be achieved by generating budget deficits, which were viewed as a mechanism for conducting monetary policy.

The consensus standing attained by this policy – i.e. that fiscal measures are a way of conducting monetary policy – among the Chicago economists during the early 1930s is remarkable. Consider a memorandum, prepared by the Chicago faculty and sent to Senator Reed Smoot on 16 January 1933. It was signed by (among others) Paul Douglas, Henry Simons, Jacob Viner, and Harry Gideonse: "What is needed to-day is an increase in the circulation of money and credit" (Bane *et al.*, 1933, p. 1018). In this connection, "the repercussions of the ordinary fiscal operations of the Federal Government on the nation's currency system must not be ignored" (Bane *et al.*, 1933, p. 1014). Similarly, Simons (1934,

I have benefited from helpful conversations with Roger Sandilands. The views expressed are those of the author and should not be interpreted as those of the International Monetary Fund or the Bank of Greece.

p. 789) stressed "the decisive importance of fiscal policy for monetary policy," and Gideonse (1934, p. 750) emphasized that "expenditures for public works...are definitely part of monetary policy."

The importance of this policy stance with respect to the influence of Keynes's *General Theory* (1936) is evidenced in Patinkin's (1987, p. 24) argument that "the advocacy *per se* of public works expenditure was not the purpose of the *General Theory*; rather it was to *provide a theory* which would, among other things, rationalize such a policy" (italics supplied). The Chicagoans already had such a theory – their particular formulation of the quantity theory of money. Moreover, the Chicagoans were unique in applying the quantity theory in such a manner that fiscal measures were considered a means of conducting monetary policy. I am not aware of a single US economist during the early 1930s outside of the University of Chicago who explicitly and consistently used the quantity-theory framework in such a manner. At Chicago, however, this policy posture continued into the 1940s. For example, in a 1946 article, Lloyd Mints argued: "Fiscal operations of the national government have monetary consequences – (they are way to) carry through monetary policy" (1946, p. 63). Similarly, in a 1948 paper, Milton Friedman (1948) argued that monetary policy should be conducted through fiscal measures.

Although the 1930s Chicagoans advocated what came to be called Keynesian policies to combat the Great Depression, the analytical underpinnings of the Chicago approach were much different from that of the *General Theory*. For Keynes, increased government spending produced an offsetting flow to the decline in autonomous private investment expenditure (also a flow) via the income-expenditure identity (i.e. $Y = C + I + G$); an increase in the stock of money could be effective only through a portfolio adjustment process that lowered the cost of borrowing via an increase in the demand for the stock of other financial assets. For the Chicagoans, increased government expenditure was a way of raising the stock of money, offsetting the autonomous decline in velocity via the equation of exchange ($MV = PT$), and directly affecting the flow of spending. An increase in the stock of money was viewed as raising the flow of spending on goods and services, thereby increasing prices, profits (due to sticky wages) and production. Moreover, with velocity assumed to be positively related to price anticipations and the state of business confidence (Tavlas, 1997b), an increase in the supply of money would lead to increases in velocity, reinforcing the expansionary thrust of the initial monetary stimulus. Thus, velocity was a propagation element in the cyclical process, moving in the same direction as the money supply. This formulation is in direct contrast to that of Keynes's *General Theory*, which viewed velocity behaviour as passive and moving in the opposite direction of changes in the money supply. The formulation is, however, remarkably similar to Friedman's cyclical analysis, in which velocity behaviour is unstable and varies procyclically (Tavlas, 1997c).

Laidler devotes considerable attention to Paul Douglas's writings and makes the following arguments:

(1) Douglas's analytic framework was underconsumptionist theory.

(2) Douglas wrote a book in 1932 advocating "a comprehensive socialist (albeit democratic) policy agenda that included a large role for planning, and would permanently and radically change US economic and social life" (Laidler, 1998, p. 12).

(3) Although Friedman mentions his indebtedness to Simons, Viner, Knight and Mints while he was a student at Chicago, "he does not mention Douglas" (Laidler, 1998, p. 13). Laidler goes on to state : "I have been unable to find a single reference to Paul Douglas in (Friedman's) monetary writings. The contemporary record gives us good reason to trust his judgment here" (Laidler, 1998, p. 13) I agree, let the contemporary record speak for itself.

Let me, therefore, briefly respond to each of these points.

(1) Douglas was an underconsumptionist all right, but he used the quantity theory to formulate his underconsumptionist views. Above all he was a quantity theorist. After he became a US Senator in 1948, he played a pivotal role in the famous "accord" reached between the Fed and the US Treasury. Prior to the accord, the Fed had been pegging interest rates, losing control over the quantity of money and inciting inflation. In his autobiography, published in 1972, Douglas called the Fed's actions prior to the accord as "a vindication of the quantity theory of money, supposedly known to every student of elementary economics" (1972, p. 332).

(2) Was Douglas at one time a socialist? Perhaps he was, but Douglas also was the first Chicagoan to state the view that fiscal measures can be used to implement monetary policy. If his role at Chicago after 1936 diminished, what he brought to Chicago prior to 1936 was a major reason why Chicago became immune from the Keynesian virus.

(3) On Friedman's not mentioning Douglas, this in no way diminishes what Douglas brought to Chicago – i.e. the use of the equation of exchange as a theoretical underpinning for expansionary fiscal measures during the Great Depression, a policy that was subsequently adopted by Simons, Mints, Knight, Viner, and other Chicagoans. In 1976, while a graduate student, I submitted a comment describing Douglas's role in the development of the Chicago tradition during the early 1930s to the *Journal of Money, Credit and Banking*. The paper was published in that journal in November of 1977 (see Tavlas, 1977a). The referee was such an enthusiastic supporter of my paper, that he had me double its length – so that it became a full article – by including a discussion of Douglas's role in the Fed-Treasury accord. The referee was Milton Friedman. The contemporary record has spoken.

In his influential article on the mid-1930s to mid-1940s Chicago tradition, Patinkin (1969) listed five key characteristics that characterized that tradition. In Tavlas (1997b), I presented evidence showing that Douglas advocated each of those characteristics prior to the mid-1930s. Therefore, Douglas's work was in the Chicago monetary tradition and served to bring that tradition forward in time – that is, the Chicago monetary tradition was in place in the early 1930s. Laidler's attempt to decouple Douglas's writings from the Chicago monetary tradition is a deflection. Suppose Douglas's work was not in the Chicago monetary tradition. As I showed in Tavlas (1997b), by 1933 Viner also had advocated each of the five key characteristics listed by Patinkin. Douglas aside, the Chicago tradition, in which money mattered, was in place *prior* to 1936 and ready to withstand the Keynesian revolution. Does Laidler disagree?

With regard to Laidler's claim that certain members of the Harvard faculty were important precursors of Friedman, I will let my 1997b paper stand on its own on the issue of Harvard except for one additional point. Laidler (1993) claims that Harvard economist Allyn Young anticipated Friedman's work in several important respects. Specifically, Laidler argues that Young developed a monetary interpretation of cyclical fluctuations and was optimistic about the power of monetary policy. In this connection, it is important to point out that Mehrling (1996), in his study of Young's monetary thought, argues that:

(1) on the international side, Young's view was that "overexpansion of money was the result of depreciation, not its cause" (Mehrling, 1996, p. 620); and

(2) on the domestic side, "fluctuation is not monetary in *origin*, but it is definitely monetary in character, since business expansion depends on the expansion of bank credit" (italics supplied, Mehrling, 1996, pp. 620-21).

Did Young believe that monetary changes *cause* business fluctuations or *respond* to such fluctuations? Will the real Allyn Young please come forward?

In summary, there was a unique Chicago quantity-theory tradition in the early 1930s that:

(1) embodied a policy framework which left it immune from the Keynesian revolution (Tavlas, 1997b); and

(2) contained important linkages with Friedman's views in its business-cycle analysis and policy positions (Tavlas, 1997c).

Chicago economists continued to write in the quantity-theory tradition in the 1940s and 1950s, which explains why Chicago – not Harvard – originated the monetarist counter-revolution.

References

Bane, F. *et al.* (1933), *Balancing the Budget: Federal Fiscal Policy during Depression*, Public Policy Pamphlets, No.1, 16 January, University of Chicago Press, Chicago, IL, reprinted in

Investigation of Economic Problems: Hearings before the Committee on Finance, US Senate, 72nd Congress, February 1933.

Douglas P.H. (1972), *In the Fullness of Time*, Harcourt Brace, New York, NY.

Friedman, M. (1948), "A monetary and fiscal framework for economic stability", *American Economic Review*, Vol. 38, June, pp. 245-64.

Gideonse, H.D. (1934), "Money and finance", *The American Journal of Sociology*, Vol. 39, May, pp. 749-58.

Keynes, J.M. (1936), *The General Theory of Employment, Interest and Money*, Harcourt Brace, New York, NY.

Laidler, D. (1993), "Hawtrey, Harvard and the origins of the Chicago tradition", *Journal of Political Economy*, Vol. 101, December, pp. 1068-103.

Laidler, D. (1998), "More on Hawtrey, Harvard and Chicago", *Journal of Economic Studies*, Vol. 25 No. 1, pp. 4-16.

Mehrling, P. (1996), "The monetary thought of Allyn Abbott Young", *History of Political Economy*, Vol. 4, Winter, pp. 607-32.

Mints, L.W. (1946), "Monetary policy", *Review of Economic Statistics*, Vol. 28, May, pp. 60-9.

Patinkin, D. (1969), "The Chicago tradition, the quantity theory, and Friedman", *Journal of Money, Credit and Banking*, Vol. 1, February, pp. 46-70.

Patinkin, D. (1987), "Keynes, John Maynard", in Eatwell, J., Milgate, M and Newman, P. (Eds), *The New Palgrave : A Dictionary of Economics*, Vol. 3, Macmillan, London.

Simons, H.C. (1934), "Economic reconstruction: the Columbia report", *Journal of Political Economy*, Vol. 42, December, pp. 795-9.

Tavlas, G.S. (1977a), "The Chicago tradition revisited: some neglected monetary contributions: Senator Paul Douglas (1892-1976)", *Journal of Money, Credit and Banking*, Vol. 9, November, pp. 529-38.

Tavlas, G.S. (1997b), "Chicago, Harvard, and the doctrinal foundations of monetary economics", *Journal of Political Economy*, Vol. 105, February, pp. 153- 77.

Tavlas, G.S. (1997c), "Was the monetarist tradition invented?", paper presented at the History of Economics Society Conference, Charleston, SC

'Hawtrey, Harvard and Chicago'

D. Laidler, 'Hawtrey, Harvard and Chicago: a final comment', *Journal of Economic Studies*, 25:1 (1998b), pp. 22–4.

Hawtrey, Harvard and Chicago: a final comment

David Laidler
University of Western Ontario, Canada

Introduction

George Tavlas (1997 and 1998 this issue) disagrees with the story I have told about the origins of the Chicago tradition, but he has not shown that the extensive body of evidence with which I supported it, drawn from both primary and secondary sources, will not bear its weight. Instead, he has, in the main, raised issues which are irrelevant, and occasionally inaccurate, some of which I now take up.

Tavlas on Harvard

Tavlas (1997, pp. 167-71) includes interesting discussions of the attitude of what we might term the "Harvard establishment" to the Great Depression, showing that their often confused analysis bore no resemblance to that emanating from Chicago; true enough, but this has no bearing on my case, which rested on the work of Ralph Hawtrey, a visiting professor at Harvard for one year (1928-1929), Allyn Young, who left Harvard in 1927 and died in 1929, and Lauchlin Currie who was a lowly instructor in that department until 1934.

I did refer to John H. Williams, who certainly was a member of the Harvard establishment, but only as someone who "made at least one noteworthy contribution as a transmitter of ideas" (Laidler 1993, p. 1078) from Harvard (where he had supervised Currie's PhD) to the Harris Foundation conference held at Chicago in 1932. Williams helped to draft the manifesto which emerged from that conference, a document which Friedman (1974) cites as an important early example of the "Chicago tradition", and he also contributed a paper to the proceedings of the conference (Wright (Ed.), 1932) explaining and justifying the manifesto in question. Thus, Tavlas' (1997) patronizing criticism of Williams' writings between 1932 and 1936, like the rest of his discussion of the Harvard establishment's work of that period, is irrelevant to my case.

Tavlas (1997, pp. 169-70) did discuss the nature of Currie's contribution, and in terms that could suggest to an unwary reader that I misrepresented it in Laidler (1993). I have nothing here to add to my earlier response to this discussion (cf. 1998, this issue, pp. 4-16). Now Tavlas (1998, this issue, pp. 17-21) turns to my treatment of Young. He says that "Laidler argues that Young developed a monetary interpretation of cyclical fluctuations and was optimistic about the power of monetary policy." He contrasts this with Perry Mehrling's (1996) view that, for Young "fluctuation is not monetary in *origin*, but it is definitely monetary in character, since business expansion depends on the

---

The financial support of the SSHRCC and the Lynde and Harry Bradley Foundation is gratefully acknowledged.

expansion of bank credit" (Mehrling, 1996, pp. 620-1, as quoted, with added italics, by Tavlas). Tavlas then asks "will the real Allyn Young please come forward?" Let me quote from my (1993, pp. 1079-83) discussion of Young:

> All in all, Young is more eclectic than Hawtrey in his views on the sources of economic instability, mentioning "maladjustments, born in part of the redistribution of incomes" not to mention "crop failure, or crises in other countries" as factors in addition to "the exhaustion of bank reserves" as likely to bring a cyclical upswing to an end... And he also makes a case for public works expenditure as a counter-cyclical device, a position quite contrary to that taken by Hawtrey in the 1920s (1993, pp. 1079-80).

I have a question of my own. Will Tavlas please read my paper (as opposed, perhaps, to its unintentionally ambiguous abstract) before subjecting it again to his sarcasm?

Tavlas on Douglas

Tavlas (1997) argued that in (1993) I paid insufficient attention to Paul Douglas, thus overlooking an important and, more to the point, since temporal priorities are at stake here, early contributor to the Chicago tradition. Here, as in (1977), Tavlas characterized Douglas as a quantity theorist. But, (apart from a brief venture into eclecticism in 1930-1931) Douglas was an underconsumptionist between 1927 and 1935 (see Laidler, 1998, this issue, pp. 4-16). Tavlas now concedes this point, but goes on to say that "...he used the quantity theory to formulate his underconsumptionist views. Above all he was a quantity theorist" (1998, this issue, pp. 19). A division between underconsumptionism and the quantity theory has been a key feature of economics since the days of Ricardo and Malthus, and it remained such in the 1920s and 1930s. Perhaps other historians of economic thought will agree with me that it is utterly unhelpful to gloss over this division, as Tavlas now seems intent on doing.

In the post-war years, as a US senator, Paul Douglas did indeed adopt positions that one might nowadays characterize as "monetarist"; and it is interesting to learn that Milton Friedman was an enthusiastically positive referee of Tavlas' (1977) paper on Douglas. What any of this has to do with the nature of Douglas' economic ideas in the 1920s and 1930s, the relationship of those ideas to those held by his Chicago colleagues at the time, or their influence on Friedman's own monetary thought, is, however, quite beyond me.

Let me repeat: in the 1930s, Douglas was an outlier in the Chicago department. From late 1933 and well into 1934, he and Frank Knight were barely on speaking terms, as George Stigler (1988, ch. 12) has recounted. Douglas believed that Knight regarded him "as something of a charlatan and a demagogue", and as "a publicity seeker craving to get his name in the newspapers" (letters from Douglas to Knight, as quoted in Stigler (1988, p. 184 and p. 188, respectively)). Furthermore, a major point of contention between these two was Douglas' belief that Henry Simons, even then a central figure in the development of the Chicago tradition, was unworthy of tenure at that institution.

An answer to Tavlas' question

Tavlas (1998, this issue, p. 17) asks me to address the question: "Why did Chicago remain an important centre for the development of the quantity theory of money in the late 1930s and the 1940s while Harvard (and other academic centres) succumbed to the Keynesian revolution?" This question is only peripherally related to my (1993) paper, which was concerned with the origins of the Chicago tradition in the early 1930s, and not with its influence after 1936; but let me hazard a reply, necessarily assertive, given considerations of space, and tentative as well: my answer is that the premise of the question is very likely false on two counts.

First, with such additions to the Chicago department as Oscar Lange in 1939 and Jacob Marshak in 1943, not to mention its close association with the Cowles Commission, whose staff included Lawrence Klein, it in fact became, for a few years, an important centre for the development of a Keynesian research agenda (see Patinkin, 1981, "introduction"). Second, though the "Chicago tradition" of the early 1930s persisted throughout the 1940s, and left a mark on the writings of some Chicago economists, notably Lloyd Mints, in the early post-war period, I am unable to recall any further "development of the quantity theory of money" that carried the tradition in question beyond the point to which Viner, Knight, and Simons had taken it by, say, 1936 or 1937.

Further advances had to await the arrival of Milton Friedman at Chicago in 1946, who thereafter "...proceeded to establish three lines of work, which together constituted his fundamental contributions to the formation of the Chicago school. First, he revived the study of monetary economics, which had become moribund" (Stigler, 1988, p. 150). I am inclined to accept Stigler's verdict on this matter for the moment, but further research on the matter might overturn it in future.

References

Currie L. (1931), "Bank assets and banking theory", unpublished PhD thesis, Harvard University, January.

Friedman, M. (1974), "Comments on the critics", in Gordon, R.J. (Ed.), *Milton Friedman's Monetary Framework*, University of Chicago Press, Chicago, IL.

Laidler, D. (1993), "Hawtrey, Harvard and the origins of the Chicago tradition", *Journal of Political Economy*, Vol. 101, December, pp. 1068-103.

Laidler, D. (1998) "More on Hawtrey, Harvard and Chicago", *Journal of Economic Studies*, Vol. 25 No. 1, pp. 4-16.

Mehrling, P. (1996), "The monetary thought of Allyn Abbott Young", *History of Political Economy*, Vol. 28, Winter, pp. 607-32.

Patinkin, D. (1981), *Essays on and in the Chicago Tradition*, Duke University Press, Durham, NC.

Stigler, G. (1988), *Memoirs of an Unregulated Economist*, Basic Books, New York, NY.

Tavlas, G. (1977), "The Chicago tradition revisited: some neglected monetary contributions: Senator Paul Douglas (1892-1976)", *Journal of Money, Credit and Banking*, Vol. 9, November, pp. 529-35.

Tavlas, G. (1997), "Chicago, Harvard, and the doctrinal foundations of monetary economics", *Journal of Political Economy*, Vol. 105, February, pp. 153-77.

Tavlas, G. (1998), "More on the Chicago tradition", *Journal of Economic Studies*, Vol. 25 No. 1, pp. 17-21.

Wright, Q. (Ed.) (1932), *Gold and Monetary Stabilization: Lectures on the Harris Foundation*, University of Chicago Press, Chicago, IL.

'The Chicago Monetarist Tradition'

D. Laidler, 'The Chicago Monetarist Tradition', *Journal of Economic Perspectives*, 13:3 (Summer 1999), pp. 240–1.

AND

G. Tavlas, 'Response from G. Tavlas', *Journal of Economic Persepctives*, 13:3 (Summer 1999), pp. 241–2.

The Chicago Monetarist Tradition

George Tavlas (Fall 1998, pp. 211–222) has presented arguments for the existence of close links between the work of Milton Friedman and an earlier "Chicago Tradition" that in turn was firmly rooted in the quantity theory of money. Though I agree with Tavlas that a Chicago Tradition existed, and that Friedman's work is, in some respects, related to it, these matters are a good deal more complicated than he suggests, as the following examples demonstrate.

Tavlas (p. 214) is right that Paul Douglas (1927) was responsible for introducing into the Chicago Tradition the idea that money creation undertaken to finance fiscal measures would be a particularly effective expansionary policy. Douglas, however, did not derive this idea from an application of the quantity theory, but rather from the at-that-time well-known underconsumptionist analysis of William Foster and Waddill Catchings (for example, 1923). Douglas's later (1933) advocacy of such policies was also based on an underconsumptionist approach, rather than the quantity theory, and by that time he was supplementing the case for public works spending with reference to their expansionary multiplier effects, as expounded by Keynes in *The Means to Prosperity* (1933).

Douglas was, of course, something of an outlier among Chicago monetary economists in the 1930s, but Tavlas is again right in stressing that many of the latter shared his lack of faith in the expansionary powers of orthodox monetary policy implemented through open market operations. He is also right (p. 219) that, on the matter of the powers of traditional monetary measures, Friedman's later analysis (as in Friedman and Schwartz, 1963) differs from that of the earlier Chicago Tradition. He might, however, have mentioned that Friedman and Schwartz's position, particularly as it appertained to the Great Contraction, was largely anticipated by Lauchlin Currie (1934), as Karl Brunner (1968) long ago pointed out. As Currie (1934, p. 147), at that time an instructor at Harvard, remarked, "Much of the current belief in the powerlessness of the reserve banks appears to arise from a complete misreading of the monetary history of 1929–32. It is generally held that the reserve administration strove energetically to bring about expansion throughout the depression but that contraction continued despite its efforts. Actually the reserve administration's policy was one of almost complete passivity and quiescence."

In the light of the strong similarity between Currie's views on this matter and those of Friedman and Schwartz, it is interesting to note that, as can be documented from Currie's own writings, he arrived at them under the influence of Allyn Young, Ralph Hawtrey, and Keynes of the (1930) *Treatise on Money*. Currie's analysis of the contraction owed essentially nothing to a Fisherian version of the quantity theory.

Evidently, the relationships among Friedman's monetarist analysis, the Chicago Tradition of the 1930s, and the quantity theory of money, are a good deal more complicated and hard to pin down than Tavlas suggests. As a starting point, a perusal of published work by Karl Brunner (1968), Thomas Humphrey (1971), Roger Sandilands (1990), Frank Steindl (1996) and myself (Laidler 1993, 1998), will reveal this in much more detail.

David Laidler
University of Western Ontario
London, Ontario, Canada

References

Brunner, K. 1968. "On Lauchlin Currie's contribution to Monetary Theory," in *The Supply and Control of Money in the United States*. Currie, L., ed. 1934 [1968]. Cambridge MA: Harvard University Press. Reprinted by Russell and Russell, New York.

Currie, L. 1934 [1968]. *The Supply and Control of Money in the United States*. Cambridge MA: Harvard University Press. Reprinted by Russell and Russell, New York.

Douglas, P. H. 1927. "The Modern Technique of Mass Production and its Relation to Wages." *Proceedings of the Academy of Political Science*. July, 12:3, pp. 17–42.

Douglas, P. H. 1933. *Collapse or Cycle?* Chicago: American Library Association.

Foster, W. T. and W. Catchings. 1923. *Money*. Boston: Houghton Mifflin.

Friedman, M. and A. J. Schwartz. 1963. *A Monetary History of the United States 1867–1960*. Princeton NJ: Princeton University Press.

Humphrey, T. M. 1971. "The Role of Non-Chicago Economists in the Evolution of the Quantity Theory in America." *Southern Economic Journal*. July, 38, pp. 238–53.

Keynes, J. M. 1930. *A Treatise on Money*. London: Macmillan.

Keynes, J. M. 1933. *The Means to Prosperity*. New York: Harcourt Brace and Co.

Laidler, D. 1993. "Hawtrey, Harvard and the Origins of the Chicago Tradition." *Journal of Political Economy*. December, 101, pp. 1068–1103.

Laidler, D. 1998. "More on Hawtrey, Harvard and Chicago." *Journal of Economic Studies*. 25, pp. 4–16.

Sandilands, R. 1990. *The Life and Political Economy of Lauchlin Currie: New Dealer, Presidential Advisor and Development Economist*. Durham NC: Duke University Press.

Steindl, F. G. 1996. *Monetary Interpretations of the Great Depression*. Ann Arbor MI: Univ. of Michigan Press.

Response from George S. Tavlas

My *JEP* paper demonstrated the relationship between Milton Friedman's monetary views and the contributions of the early 1930s Chicago tradition. The paper corrected the misleading characterization created by, among others, the writing of Laidler (1993, p. 1070) that "optimism about the power of monetary policy . . . arrived rather late in the day in Chicago." It is reassuring to have Laidler write: "I agree with Tavlas that a Chicago Tradition existed, and that Friedman's work is, in some respects, related to it . . ." Obviously, matters are more complicated than he once argued.

In another paper I dealt with the views of Currie, who was at Harvard in the early 1930s, Young, who left Harvard in 1927 and died in early 1929, and Hawtrey (Tavlas, 1997). That paper refuted Laidler's (1993, p. 1078) claim that a small group of Harvard economists produced "outstanding work in monetary economics" as late as 1934. Currie certainly made important contributions in the monetary area during the early 1930s, but he was a lone wolf at Harvard. As I documented, he began advocating deficit spending during this period. Reflecting back on his years at Harvard, Currie (1978, p. 541) noted that his advocacy of deficit spending "had to be done surreptitiously. Even so, the heresy became known and I fell from grace and was reprimanded by the Chairman of the Department." Unlike the Chicagoans, Currie did not provide a quantity theory rationale for his advocacy of budget deficits.

Laidler puts a lot of weight on the underconsumptionist views of Douglas. But Douglas was, above all, a quantity theorist. After he became a U.S. Senator in 1948, he played a pivotal role in the famous "accord" reached between the Federal Reserve and the Treasury. Prior to the accord, the Fed had been pegging interest rates and losing control over the quantity of money and inflation. In his autobiography *In the Fullness of Time*, Douglas (1972, p. 380) called the Fed's actions "a vindication of the quantity theory of money, supposedly known to every student of elementary economics."

I agree with Laidler that the issue of the development of monetary economics during the early 1930s is a complicated one. A reader who wants a good idea of the broad range of issues involved would benefit from examining the many fine studies that Laidler cites. But if the reader wants to learn about the interconnections between Harvard and Chicago of the early 1930s and Friedman's monetary thought—the focus of the debate between Laidler (1993) and me, both in my *JEP* article and in Tavlas (1997)—the reader might focus on these sources and judge accordingly. Indeed, it is interesting that Laidler does not focus on that debate—he does not even refer to my 1997 paper—but deflects attention away from it by diverting the reader to references that are not aimed at addressing the particular issues.

George S. Tavlas
Bank of Greece, Athens, Greece
International Monetary Fund, Washington, D.C.

References

Currie, L. 1978. "Comments and Observations," *History of Political Economy*, Winter, 10, 541–48.

Douglas, P. 1972. *In the Fullness of Time.* New York: Harcourt Brace.

Laidler, D. 1993. "Hawtrey, Harvard and the Origins of the Chicago Tradition," *Journal of Political Economy*, December, 101, 1068–1103.

Tavlas, G. S. 1997. "Chicago, Harvard, and the Doctrinal Foundations of Monetary Economics," *Journal of Political Economy*, February, 105, 153–77.

'Anti-Depression Policies'

D. Laidler and R. Sandilands, 'An early Harvard memorandum on anti-depression policies. An introductory note', *History of Political Economy* (Fall 2002), pp. 515–32.

AND

L. B. Currie, P. T. Ellsworth and H. D. White, 'Memorandum', *History of Political Economy* (Fall 2002), pp. 533–52.

An Early Harvard Memorandum on Anti-Depression Policies: An Introductory Note

David Laidler and Roger Sandilands

The memorandum that this note introduces was completed by three young members of the Harvard economics department sometime in January 1932. Two of them, Lauchlin Currie and Harry Dexter White, were soon to play key roles on the American, indeed the worldwide, policy scene. Both of them would go to Washington in 1934 as founding members of Jacob Viner's "Freshman Brains Trust." In due course, first at the Federal Reserve Board and later at the Treasury and the White House, Currie would become a highly visible and leading advocate of expansionary fiscal policy, while White, at the Treasury, was to be a coarchitect, with Keynes, of the Bretton Woods system. Both would fall victim to anti-Communist witch-hunts in the late 1940s, in White's case perhaps at the cost of his life, since he died of a heart attack in 1948 three days after a strenuous hearing before the House Committee on Un-American Activities (HUAC). The third author, Paul Theodore Ellsworth, later a professor of economics at the University of Wisconsin, is perhaps best

Correspondence may be addressed to David Laidler, Department of Economics, University of Western Ontario, London, Ontario N6A 5C2; e-mail: laidler@uwo.ca. The typescript whose text is reproduced below is from box 12, folder 29, Harry Dexter White Papers, Seeley G. Mudd Manuscript Library, Princeton University Library. Published with permission of Princeton University Library. Its title, authorship, and date are written at the top of its first page, in handwriting identified by Bruce Craig and Roger Sandilands as that of White. In preparing the text for publication, we have corrected obvious typographical errors. We are grateful to Daniele Besomi, Milton Friedman, Perry Mehrling, and an anonymous referee for comments on an earlier draft of this introduction.

History of Political Economy 34:3 © 2002 by Duke University Press.

remembered nowadays as the author of a leading textbook on international economics (Ellsworth 1937), although it is worth noting that he was also a very early (December 1936) but hitherto unrecognized discoverer of what came to be called the IS-LM model as a means of elucidating issues raised by Keynes's (1936) *General Theory*.[1]

It is not known how widely this memorandum was circulated, but the fact that it is a piece of policy advocacy, combined with its relatively polished style, makes it inconceivable that it was meant for the eyes and files of its authors alone. As readers will see, it sketches out an explanation of the then rapidly developing Great Contraction, as well as a comprehensive and radical policy program for dealing with it. In keeping with its authors' explanation of the contraction as a consequence of a collapsing money supply, the main domestic components of that program were to be vigorously expansionary open-market operations and substantial deficit spending that, particularly in its early stages, was to be financed by money creation; its international dimension involved a return to free trade and serious efforts to resolve the problems of international indebtedness that had originated in the Great War and in the Treaty of Versailles that had brought it to an uneasy end in 1919.

The Memorandum's Significance

The existence of this memorandum has recently been noted in one or two publications, but apart from a brief discussion in Sandilands 2001, its significance has not been adequately appreciated. First, it is self-evidently a coherent work of high intellectual quality and provides documentary evidence about an original and provocative element in the macroeconomic thought of an important intellectual center, namely Harvard, in the early years of the depression, before the New Deal and before the importation of the theoretical ideas of Keynes's *General Theory* (1936). Second, it provides considerable insight into the early intellectual

1. The standard source of information on Currie's life is Sandilands 1990; on White, see Rees 1973 and Boughton 2001. We are unaware of any biography of Ellsworth, but the editors tell us that some information about him is in Lampman 1993, although no single section of that book is devoted to him. Ellsworth's (1936) exposition of a version of the IS-LM model, published when he held an appointment at the University of Cincinnati, seems to be the second to have appeared (after that of W. B. Reddaway in 1936) and antedates J. R. Hicks's (1937) exposition of the system. Warren Young (1987) does not refer to it in his now standard history of the "IS-LM-ization" of Keynesian economics.

development of Currie and White, both of whom had great influence on the course of U.S. domestic and international economic policy in the years of the Roosevelt administration. The importance of a document in which these two had a hand, and which deals extensively with domestic macroeconomic policy and international economic relations, is surely obvious. It merits the attention of any historian of interwar economic thought for this reason alone.

The memorandum is also interesting for a third reason. There are strong similarities between the program it sets out and the one embodied in the recommendations sent to President Herbert Hoover over the signatures of twenty-four economists who participated in the conference on gold and monetary stabilization held under the auspices of the Norman Wait Harris Foundation at the University of Chicago on 27–31 January 1932, and published in its proceedings (Wright 1932, 161–63). This conference took place at the end of the very month in which this memorandum was completed. Given its venue, and the fact that no fewer than twelve of the signatories of its recommendations occupied posts at the University of Chicago, the letter containing the recommendations has long been cited as one of the seminal documents of what has sometimes been claimed to be a unique "Chicago tradition" in monetary analysis.[2] But as one of us (Laidler 1993) has earlier noted, one of the non-Chicago economists involved in drafting the recommendations was John H. Williams of Harvard. As we shall see, the record of his oral contributions to the Harris Foundation conference suggests that he was probably familiar with the Harvard memorandum, and certainly well acquainted with some of the ideas emphasized in it.[3] These considerations constitute strong circumstantial evidence of a Harvard influence on one of the Chicago tradition's earliest documents. But even if this conjecture

2. The first mention of this Chicago tradition seems to have been by Milton Friedman (1956), and its nature and claim to uniqueness were subsequently discussed by, among others, Don Patinkin (1969, 1973), Thomas Humphrey (1971), and Friedman (1974). The links, or absence thereof, of this tradition to ideas current at Harvard are debated by Laidler (1993, 1998a, 1998b) and George Tavlas (1997, 1998a). Tavlas (1998b) later restates the view that the Chicago tradition was unique. Friedman (1974) makes much of the 1932 Harris Foundation conference as an example of the Chicago tradition, and in so doing he draws on the work of J. Ronnie Davis (1968), who also discussed it extensively. See also Davis 1971.

3. A complete transcript of the conference's deliberations (Norman Wait Harris Foundation 1932) is to be found in the Regenstein Library at the University of Chicago.

is discounted, it is clear from the following memorandum that there was nothing unique about the Chicago tradition as it stood in early 1932.[4]

We shall now elaborate on these matters in turn.

Harvard Economists and the Depression

The best-known product of the Harvard economics department dealing with economic policy in the early 1930s is a collection of essays titled *The Economics of the Recovery Program* (D. V. Brown et al. 1934), which the department's historian Edward Mason (1982) has tactfully characterized as "not very distinguished." We prefer to stand by the verdict of Laidler (1993, 1078), that most of the essays "verge on the incoherent and do no credit to their distinguished authors." The only intellectually coherent contribution to this collection, which offered a comprehensively negative assessment of President Roosevelt's policy plans, was that of Joseph Schumpeter. He advanced an essentially "Austrian" interpretation of the depression, locating its causes in a bout of overinvestment that had collapsed in 1929, and arguing forcefully that attempts at a cure by monetary or fiscal expansion would serve only to prolong the slump. This was also the view of another member of the Harvard department, albeit a visitor from Vienna at this time, Gottfried von Haberler, who gave it a thorough airing in a paper (Haberler 1932) presented to the very Harris Foundation conference that produced the recommendations referred to earlier, which, by the way, he did not sign.

There is, then, no question that Harvard's reputation for mediocrity and policy pessimism in the early 1930s is founded in fact, but this has never been the whole story. Its economics department had until quite recently been an important center for the development of balance of payments theory under the leadership of Frank Taussig, and monetary economics, largely under the leadership of Allyn A. Young. Among Taussig's supervisees in earlier years had been Jacob Viner, Frank Graham, and John H. Williams, and among Young's, at Harvard, had been James

4. In a letter to Laidler, dated 22 January 2001, Milton Friedman remarks that the memorandum "is a truly remarkable and impressive document, and it certainly supports your position that Chicago had no monopoly on the quantity theory approach to the Great Depression and to measures required to recover from it. I have no doubt, as you suggest in your introductory comments, that more than coincidence explains the similarity of the views expressed by the Harvard trio and the recommendations coming out of the Harris conference." We are grateful to Professor Friedman for permission to quote from this letter.

Angell, Arthur Marget, and E. H. Chamberlin, while Currie had expected to become another.[5]

Taussig was still on the Harvard faculty in the early 1930s, and still editor of the *Quarterly Journal of Economics*. He also remained involved with graduate students' work, supervising the thesis of Harry White, one of the authors of the memorandum; Currie was also closely enough associated with him to contribute to a collection of essays in his honor in 1936.[6] However, Taussig was by then in his seventies and, as George Tavlas (1997, 170–71) has noted, such public comments of his on the depression that survive were few and noncommittal. Young, moreover, had left Harvard in 1927 to take up a temporary appointment at the London School of Economics, from which he had expected to return in 1930, but he died of influenza in March 1929 at the early age of fifty-two.

As Perry Mehrling (1997) has argued, Young's work in monetary economics had sought a middle ground between the quantity theory of Irving Fisher and the real-bills approach of James Laurence Laughlin and Henry Parker Willis that dominated thinking at the Federal Reserve Board in the 1920s and early 1930s; and it had informed his efforts as an adviser to Benjamin Strong at the Federal Reserve Bank of New York.[7] Young was also a great admirer of, and was in turn admired by, Ralph Hawtrey, an official of the United Kingdom Treasury, whose only academic appointment, as a visitor to Harvard in 1928–29, Young was instrumental in arranging.[8] In common with Hawtrey, Young was a supporter of the gold standard and an advocate of discretionary monetary policy aimed at ironing out the cycle, but unlike Hawtrey, he was also an advocate of public works expenditure as a tool of stabilization policy in its own right. Young's death left a vacuum in the field of what we would now call macroeconomics among the senior ranks at Harvard that Joseph Schumpeter was soon to fill.

5. Earlier, at Cornell, Young had supervised Frank H. Knight and Harold Reed.

6. See Sandilands 1990, 54. Also, in a letter to Taussig, written in October 1934, Viner remarks, "I have had a few Harvard men working for me here [in Washington], Currie, [Alan] Sweezy, and White, and have been very favorably impressed indeed with them, especially the two former." We are grateful to Bruce Craig for this information.

7. In addition to Mehrling's study of Young, the reader's attention is also drawn to Mehrling and Sandilands's preface to their 1999 collection of work by Young, much of it hitherto unknown, as well as to Charles Blitch's 1995 biography.

8. For Young on Hawtrey, see for example his 1924 review of *Currency and Credit*, and for Hawtrey on Young, his 1927 review of *Economic Problems New and Old*.

Currie, one of the three authors of the memorandum that is the focus of this note, had been Young's student and Hawtrey's assistant during his year at Harvard. He had expected to write his Ph.D. thesis (Currie 1931) under Young's supervision, but it was, in fact, completed under the guidance of Williams and submitted in January 1931. This thesis is a clear antecedent of the memorandum.[9] It blended Hawtrey's monetary cycle theory with Young's empirical approach to the analysis of the U.S. monetary system, and offered (among other things) a quantity-theory-based explanation of the downturn that began in 1929, a critique of the Federal Reserve System's passive response to it, and the suggestion that a more vigorously expansionary monetary policy would have been appropriate during 1929–30. It is worth noting that the quantity theory he deployed was an income velocity version of the doctrine, such as Hawtrey and Young customarily used, rather than the Fisherian transactions velocity variant.[10] And Currie's slightly later *Supply and Control of Money in the United States* (1934), dedicated to Young's memory, further developed these themes, and was (indeed still is) particularly notable for expounding the thesis that, far from having engaged in expansionary policy as it claimed at the time, the Federal Reserve System had remained largely passive as the depression gathered momentum into 1932–33. He can, then, reasonably be regarded as having largely anticipated the monetary explanation of the Great Contraction that was later developed by Milton Friedman and Anna J. Schwartz (1963). Only in his sometimes ambiguous discussions of the buildup of excess reserves in the banking system during 1932–33 does his analysis differ from theirs.[11]

9. Currie would later suggest that Williams's role in shaping his thesis was rather minor. He remarked in a 1992 letter to Laidler that "I probably had more influence on his [Williams's] thinking than he did on mine." For further discussion of this point, which corroborates the suggestion we make below that the memorandum influenced Williams's contributions to the 1932 Harris Foundation conference, see Laidler 1993, 1091 n. 25.

10. Currie's thesis in its original 1931 version contains an extensive discussion of Hawtrey's work, but this material was deleted from the draft later submitted for the Wells Prize competition at Harvard. See Laidler 1999, 234 n. 25. We speculate, without any direct evidence, that he may have done this because Haberler, one of the judges for the competition that year, was known to be hostile to Hawtrey, having, for example, explicitly and sharply criticized him in his 1932 Harris Foundation paper (Haberler 1932, 193). Whatever the reason, however, the modification was to no avail. The prize that year was awarded to White. See Sandilands 1990, 23.

11. Karl Brunner (1968) and Humphrey (1971) were the first to note Currie's contribution here. Frank Steindl (1995, chap. 4) defends the uniqueness of Friedman and Schwartz's interpretation, largely on the basis of his reading of Currie's discussions of the role of excess reserves. See note 16 below for further comment.

Particularly important given the joint authorship of the following memorandum, there already exists evidence that Currie did not develop these ideas in isolation. It is well known that he and White were already close friends and worked together when at Harvard (see Sandilands 1990, 23). Furthermore, when Erik Lundberg spent time at Harvard in 1933 he found the department a center of lively debate, and he described its environment in the following terms:

> Schumpeter had gathered around him a group of young economists, all working with modern monetary theories. During most of the summer I had discussions with some of them, especially on monetary questions concerning the business cycle. In Washington, and also to a large extent in New York, I had repeatedly heard of the tremendous inflation during the years leading up to 1929. At Harvard, reputed for its conservatism, I now learned that there had been no inflation, but rather the contrary. Professor [*sic*] Currie was the most eager advocate of this theory . . .; *Currie was not alone in holding this opinion. He, as well as the others who held this belief at Harvard* were good economists, as were the people with the opposite view in New York and Washington. (Lundberg [1934] 1995, 62; emphasis added)[12]

Evidently Currie was no lone wolf at Harvard in the early 1930s, as Tavlas (1997) characterized him, but nor was he a professor as Lundberg had it; he was an untenured instructor.

It would be a mistake to think that divisions of opinion about macroeconomic questions at Harvard lay solely along lines demarcated by age and rank, with mediocrity and pessimism being concentrated among the department's "establishment." Although they would in due course become members of that establishment, some contributors to the *Economics of the Recovery Program* were, after all, young and untenured in 1934 (e.g., Wassily Leontief, Edward Chamberlin, Seymour Harris), while, as we shall see, at least one member of that establishment, John H. Williams, was quite sympathetic to proposals like those of Currie and

12. In this passage, the word *inflation* should be read, in accordance with the common usage of the time, as referring to the expansion of money and credit, rather than to a rise in the price level. The view that the depression was the inevitable consequence of a previous overexpansion of credit in the 1920s was held in common by Austrian analysts such as Haberler and by advocates of the real-bills doctrine such as Henry Parker Willis. On this, see Laidler 1999, 214–17. Currie and his coauthors of the following memorandum clearly blamed it on the contraction of the money supply, which began in a mild way in 1928 but quickly gathered momentum after October 1929, an interpretation already developed by Currie (1931).

his associates. Even so, as the 1930s progressed, those younger members of the department whose macroeconomic views were hostile to the New Deal won promotion and stayed, while those who, like the authors of the memorandum, took the more radical and intellectually coherent position it epitomizes, either left or were eased out. By 1936, therefore, when "Keynes came to America" with a new crop of graduate students who had studied with him at Cambridge and then migrated to Harvard, the department was perhaps a less interesting and lively place than it had been only a few years earlier.[13]

The Harvard memorandum may be read, then, as giving some indication of the character and quality of an alternative intellectual tradition that might have developed at Harvard in the 1930s, had the department's promotion and tenure policies been different. And in the background here perhaps there stands the shade of Young, who had advocated activist monetary and fiscal stabilization policies during the 1920s, and had also, incidentally, written extensively on the monetary problems created by the international indebtedness left over from World War I and the Versailles Peace Conference, which he had attended as a senior adviser to the American delegation.[14]

Currie's Economics

Currie was among those eased out of Harvard. As we have already noted, he was, along with White, a founding member of Jacob Viner's Freshman Brains Trust in Washington. This appointment, which began in June 1934, was supposed to be for a matter of months, and when he was invited to extend it into the autumn of that year, Harvard refused to grant him further leave, in effect forcing his resignation (see Sandilands 1990, 56–57).

By his own account, Currie (1978) had been in difficulty with some of his senior colleagues for advocating unbalanced budgets as a means of fighting the depression long before 1934. Though no one, to the best of our knowledge, has ever questioned this particular claim, it does at first

13. Colander and Landreth 1996 contains a series of conversations with some of the economists involved in this later episode.

14. We nevertheless hesitate to enroll Young as a posthumous supporter of Currie and his colleagues in every aspect of their recommendations. During his life, Young attached great importance to the gold standard, and may well have hesitated to support wholeheartedly measures that might have put U.S. adherence to it at risk. But that his work profoundly influenced Currie is beyond question.

sight sit oddly with the so-far available published record of his work at Harvard, which deals solely with monetary policy.[15] At the very least, it leaves open the question of how his analysis of fiscal policy at that time might have fitted in with his work on monetary questions. One commentator, Tavlas (1997, 170), has gone so far as to suggest, largely on the basis of Currie's (1978) own retrospective account, that his policy stance rested on a belief in "the inefficacy of open market operations and the need for budget deficits." The following memorandum clarifies all of this. It first of all confirms the evidence of his other writings of the time that, contrary to Tavlas, Currie did indeed strongly and systematically advocate open-market operations as an important policy measure in their own right. Even more striking, although written before the events of 1932, it also discusses in some detail the likelihood that the commercial banks' first response to open-market operations would be to reduce their indebtedness to the Fed. Thus the stress that Currie laid on this same point in 1934, in his after-the-event discussion of the inefficacy of the open-market operations that were actually executed in 1932, was in no way an ex post rationalization.

Nevertheless, Currie and his associates were unduly optimistic on two matters. They underestimated the chances that open-market operations would provoke a gold outflow, and they did not foresee the buildup of excess reserves in the banking system, which would do so much to inhibit the effectiveness of these operations, although they did appear to believe that neither of these problems would arise if their recommendations were implemented in full.[16] Most striking of all, however, this

15. Indeed, an unpublished December 1934 memorandum to Marriner Eccles titled "Confidence" is the earliest substantive item dealing with expansionary fiscal policy to appear in Sandilands's 1990 bibliography of Currie's work. In his January 1931 Ph.D. dissertation, however, Currie did explore the links between monetary policy and the incentive to expand public works. Furthermore: "In so far as the policy of expanding public works in times of depression is adopted, and banks purchase bonds of public authorities, the additional bank credit will be spent directly and will not involve any decrease in the spending ability of private individuals" (Currie 1931, 236).

16. Although Currie largely anticipated Friedman and Schwartz's (1963) explanation of the Great Contraction itself, his interpretation of the later years of the depression differs markedly from theirs, particularly over the matter of the buildup of excess reserves after 1934. Currie came to regard this buildup as a sign that, whatever it might have accomplished up until the end of 1932, orthodox monetary policy alone was not likely to be effective in bringing about expansion unaided as the depression continued (see Laidler 1999, 243–44, for further discussion). Friedman and Schwartz on the other hand treat this same phenomenon as a result of an increase in the liquidity preferences of a badly shocked banking system. Currie was among those who recommended the increase of reserve requirements in 1936–37, which, in Friedman

memorandum shows that, as early as January 1932, Currie and his associates had concluded that the economic situation was sufficiently serious that open-market operations alone might not be enough to deal with it: hence their advocacy of fiscal expansion. They were well aware of the potential for what we would now call "crowding out" effects to mute the influence of fiscal expansion, however, and argued the necessity of financing budget imbalances with money creation, particularly in the early stages of any such program.

Here it is worth drawing attention to a certain similarity between their views and those of Hawtrey, whose assistant Currie had recently been. Hawtrey is rightly regarded as the originator of the "Treasury view" that fiscal policy not financed by money creation would usually be fully crowded out, and that, when deficits were financed by money creation, it was this money creation, and not any direct expenditure associated with fiscal policy, that would do the work. The memorandum comes close to this position in raising the possibility of fiscal policy's effects being crowded out if it is financed by bond issues. It should also be recalled, however, that Hawtrey (1925, 41–42) discussed possible exceptions to his basic position. In particular, he allowed that an increase of confidence among the general public in an initially depressed economy could create a rise in velocity and prevent the government expenditures from having any crowding out effect on output; and he also argued that this would only be possible if such expenditures were initially accompanied by money creation so as to permit a confidence-building expansion to get under way in the first place.[17] It is, furthermore, worth recalling that

---

and Schwartz's (1963, 520–34) view, provoked a subsequent downturn in the money supply and recession in 1937–38. Currie attributed this recession to an inadvertent tightening of fiscal policy in that year. See Sandilands 1990, 87–92. Note finally that the claim here is not that Currie was in any general way a precursor or early exponent of Friedman's so-called monetarism. It is only that in one important respect, namely the analysis of the Great Contraction of 1929, Currie's work anticipated Friedman's later findings, as Friedman has himself acknowledged. See Laidler 1993, 1077–78 n. 12.

17. See Laidler 1999, 125–28, for further discussion of Hawtrey's treatment of this and related matters. It is interesting to note that, on the second page of the memorandum, there is a reference to "recommendations recently made by Dr. [Warren] Persons." Although we have not been able to track this reference down to a precise source, Robert S. Herren (1997, 523) remarks that "as the depression deepened, Persons became actively involved in attempts to promote economic recovery. His proposals included monetary expansion, increased taxes, eliminating price-fixing policies, and retaining the gold standard. Although over fifty prominent economists and statisticians endorsed his program in 1932, Persons' ideas did not alter U.S. economic policy."

Currie's later expositions of the case for expansionary fiscal policy invariably paid more attention to the interaction of such measures with the quantity and velocity of money than did more explicitly Keynesian treatments of the topic.[18] Evidently, these later expositions rested on principles that he and his colleagues had begun to develop while at Harvard in the early 1930s, and owed nothing to any later influence emanating from Keynes's *General Theory*; but they may have owed something to Hawtrey's analysis of exceptions to his own central position.[19]

The Harris Foundation Recommendations

Finally we turn to the extremely strong similarities between the Harvard memorandum and the recommendations to President Hoover that emerged from the Harris Foundation conference of January 1932. These recommendations (along with Jacob Viner's contribution to the conference that produced them) are the earliest of the sources cited by Milton Friedman (1974, 162–68) as epitomizing the economics of the Chicago tradition of the 1930s, from which, he claimed, his own work ultimately drew its inspiration. Quoting J. Ronnie Davis (1968, 476), Friedman (1974, 163) called attention to Chicago economists' advocacy of (in Davis's words) "large and continuous budget deficits to combat the mass unemployment and deflation of the times," and he went on to remark, now quoting from one of the recommendations (Wright 1932, 162), that

> they recommended also "that the Federal Reserve banks systematically pursue open-market operations with the double aim of facilitating necessary government financing and increasing the liquidity of the banking structure." (163)

Friedman contrasted the "hopeful and 'relevant' view" epitomized by these passages with the

> London School (really Austrian) view that I referred to in my "Restatement" [1956] when I spoke of "the atrophied and rigid caricature

18. On this matter, see Currie 1978 and Sandilands 1990, 68–78.

19. And to Keynes's own earlier writings. He is quoted explicitly in the memorandum in a passage about "the bogy of inflation" that Daniele Besomi has identified as coming from *Can Lloyd George Do It?* (Keynes and Henderson 1929, 118).

[of the quantity theory] that is so frequently described by the proponents of the new income-expenditure approach." (163)

Now Friedman was careful to note that the recommendations bore the signatures of twelve non-Chicago economists in addition to twelve from that university, and he did not therefore claim that "this more hopeful and 'relevant' view" of what could be done about the depression "was restricted to Chicago" (1974, 163–64).[20] But a comparison of the Harris Foundation recommendations with the following memorandum, completed, it should be recalled, earlier in the same month, forces us to conclude that, at this early stage in the development of the Chicago tradition, there was nothing at all unique about them.[21]

The recommendations urged President Hoover to support vigorous open-market operations and public works programs (paras. 2–4); so did the Currie, Ellsworth, and White memorandum, although the latter was more enthusiastic about the second of these measures. The recommendations urged that the Federal Reserve System be empowered to issue notes against government securities, thus effectively increasing the amount of "free gold" available to the system (para. 1); so did the memorandum. Finally, they urged that attention be given to reducing or canceling intergovernmental debts, and to beginning international negotiations with

20. The signatories, and their affiliations, were James W. Angell (Columbia), John H. Cover (Chicago), Garfield V. Cox (Chicago), Aaron Director (Chicago), Irving Fisher (Yale), Harry D. Gideonse (Chicago), Max Handman (Michigan), Alvin H. Hansen (Minnesota), Charles O. Hardy (Brookings), Frank H. Knight (Chicago), Arthur W. Marget (Minnesota), Harry A. Millis (Chicago), Lloyd W. Mints (Chicago), Harold G. Moulton (Brookings), Ernest M. Patterson (Pennsylvania), Chester A. Phillips (Iowa), Henry Schultz (Chicago), Henry C. Simons (Chicago), Charles S. Tippets (Buffalo), Jacob Viner (Chicago), John H. Williams (Harvard), Chester W. Wright (Chicago), Ivan Wright (Illinois), and Theodore O. Yntema (Chicago). Among those who were at the conference, but did not sign the letter listing the recommendations, were Gottfried von Haberler (Vienna, visiting Harvard), Henry Parker Willis (Columbia), and Paul H. Douglas (Chicago).

21. If, however, we follow Don Patinkin (1969) and George Tavlas (1997, 1998a, 1998b), and focus on advocacy of public works policies as a means of injecting money into circulation as a key characteristic of Chicago thinking, then it should be noted that a brief reference to this position occurs in Jacob Viner's contribution to the informal discussions that took place at the Harris Foundation conference, during the session of 29 January titled "What Should Be Done in the Present Emergency." He argued that earlier experience with public works expenditures was irrelevant to the current situation because, among other things, "none [were] connected with a program of expansion of currency or banking funds" (Norman Wait Harris Memorial Foundation 1932, 245). Steindl (1995, 84–85) also quotes this passage, but cites Viner 1933 as the principal source for his advocacy of this typical Chicago position. Laidler (1999, 237–39) also dates its emergence from 1933, and now notes that an explicit reference to Viner 1933 was inadvertently omitted from or edited out of this passage.

a view to securing a substantial reduction in tariffs and other trade barriers (paras. 5–6); so, once again, did the memorandum. The similarities between the two documents are so great that we find it hard to believe that they are coincidental.[22] Moreover, there is a direct connection between these two documents, in the person of John H. Williams. He was beyond doubt familiar with Currie's earlier work, having supervised his thesis, and he not only signed the Harris recommendations, but also had a hand in drafting them sufficiently important to have been chosen by his colleagues to prepare an essay for the Harris conference volume putting them in context (Williams 1932).

That essay, it must be said, makes no explicit reference to Currie, Ellsworth, and White, nor did Williams refer directly to them or their memorandum in his extensive contributions to the oral deliberations of the conference. Moreover, his essay has nothing to say about fiscal policy, despite the fact that one of the recommendations it was justifying was that "the federal government maintain its program of public works and public services at a level not lower than that of 1931–32." However, Williams's (1932, 157) conclusions—that "the greatest single help, internally, would be a vigorous open-market policy designed to reduce rediscounts of member banks and to increase the supply of purchasing power" and that "the greatest help of international character would be the substantial reduction, or cancellation, of war debts, and the scaling down of tariff barriers"—echo not only the other recommendations emanating from the conference, but also, as we have already seen, proposals set out in great detail in the memorandum. Furthermore, the transcript of the oral deliberations of the Harris Foundation conference shows that

22. It must be recalled that, contrary to later myths surrounding the so-called Keynesian revolution, support for vigorous open-market operations was no novelty at this time—e.g., Keynes (1931), Hawtrey (1932)—nor was advocacy of expansionary fiscal policy—e.g., Pigou (1927), Robertson (1928), Douglas and Director (1931). However, all of the last four just-mentioned advocates of expansionary fiscal policy based their support on a belief that monetary policy measures, including open-market operations, were too weak to engender recovery. Thus, the main claim to originality of the Currie, Ellsworth, and White memorandum and the Harris conference recommendations is that they both, and particularly the first, canvassed the joint and consciously coordinated use of monetary and fiscal measures at a very early stage of the depression. In this connection it might be noted that Tavlas (1977, 1997, 1998a, 1998b) has long taken the view that Douglas is a key figure in the Chicago tradition, and that his 1931 book, written with his then research assistant Aaron Director, is one of its important documents. In our view, this book's pessimism about the effectiveness of expansionary monetary policy puts it outside that tradition as it is usually understood. Douglas's earlier and later espousal of underconsumptionism also seems to separate him from an intellectual tradition based on the quantity theory. See Laidler 1999, 206–11, 222–28, and Steindl 1995, 93–94, for further discussions.

Williams stressed the importance of existing commercial bank indebtedness to the Federal Reserve System as a factor affecting the likely efficacy of open-market operations, just as the memorandum does, and he also gave a quantitative assessment of the scale of open-market operations needed to influence the economy that ran exactly parallel to a similar discussion in the memorandum. Where Currie, Ellsworth, and White wrote

> At the moment of writing the indebtedness [of commercial banks to the Fed] amounts to over $800,000,000. We strongly recommend, therefore, that the reserve banks purchase upwards of a billion dollars of bills and securities. This action would satisfy member banks' desire for liquidity and in addition give them large surplus reserves,

Williams remarked

> If we examine our situation today we would find that it would take something like double the present security holdings of the Federal Reserve banks merely to get the banking system out of debt. Apparently the first desire of the banking system would be to clear itself from debt, so that I can express my point . . . quantitatively by saying that it would take, for example, $1,600,000,000 of Federal Reserve assets merely to get ready to get started to pump money into circulation. (294)

If he had not actually read the memorandum, then, Williams demonstrably held essentially identical views to those of its authors about the scale of open-market operations needed at the beginning of 1932.[23] An

23. The reader's attention is drawn to the fact that Williams here estimates the total *amount* of Federal Reserve assets needed to *establish conditions* for the further pursuit of expansionary policy, while Currie, Ellsworth, and White estimate the *amount by which such assets need to be increased* if monetary policy is to exercise an expansionary effect. According to Friedman and Schwartz (1963, 347–48), the open-market purchase program of 1932, which lasted from April till July of that year, resulted in the system's acquiring roughly one billion dollars worth of government securities. About half a billion of this increase was offset by an outflow of gold, but a reversal of gold movements thereafter saw gold holdings increase slightly over the year as a whole. However, discounts and bills bought (mainly the former) fell by half a billion between July 1932 and January 1933. Overall, the operation was sufficiently strong to keep the stock of high-powered money expanding slowly during 1932 and to stabilize the growth rate of the money supply in the second half of the year. Note that Currie, Ellsworth, and White, who were optimistic that member banks "out of debt and in possession of surplus reserves could be . . . relied upon to bring about an expansion of deposits," did not foresee the growth in the ratio of reserves to deposits that would continue throughout 1932. But this was partly because

opinion on a critical question of monetary policy, with roots in discussions then going on at Harvard, was thus clearly represented at the Harris Foundation conference by one of the principal authors of its recommendations. It is hard to believe, as we have already remarked, that these two documents are totally independent of one another.

Conclusions

To summarize then: the following memorandum is interesting from a number of points of view. It provides concrete evidence that, whatever it may have been like later in the decade, in 1931–32 the Harvard economics department was the scene of vigorous and constructive discussion of the depression and how to deal with it, with an optimistic activist viewpoint well represented. Lauchlin Currie's role here has long been recognized, and this memorandum throws important new light on it, showing clearly that he was not a lone wolf at Harvard. More important, it provides a unique source of evidence on just how far his views on the use of fiscal policy had developed while he was still at Harvard, and how they fitted together with his, by now well known, monetary interpretation of the causes of the depression. Finally, the similarities between this memorandum's contents and those of the famous Harris Foundation recommendations of 31 January 1932 provide conclusive evidence that many of the ideas that characterize the pre–*General Theory* "Chicago tradition" in monetary economics, of which so much has been written in the last twenty-five years, were also current at Harvard at the time when that tradition was developing. For all these reasons, then, the following memorandum is an important document.

References

Blitch, C. P. 1995. *Allyn Young: The Peripatetic Economist.* Houndmills, U.K.: Macmillan.

Boughton, J. M. 2001. The Case against Harry Dexter White: Still Not Proven. *HOPE* 33.2:219–39.

Brown, D. V., et al. 1934. *The Economics of the Recovery Program.* Cambridge: Harvard University Press.

---

they had linked their advocacy of open-market purchases with a call for the government to increase its borrowings from banks, just as Currie (1931, 236) had done.

Brunner, K. 1968. On Lauchlin Currie's Contribution to Monetary Theory. Introductory material to *The Supply and Control of Money in the United States*, by L. Currie (1934), ix–xxxv. New York: Russell & Russell.

Colander, D., and H. Landreth, eds. 1996. *The Coming of Keynesianism to America: Conversations with the Founders of Keynesian Economics*. Cheltenham, U.K.: Edward Elgar.

Currie, L. 1931. Bank Assets and Banking Theory. Ph.D. diss., Harvard University.

———. 1934. *The Supply and Control of Money in the United States*. Cambridge: Harvard University Press.

———. 1978. Comments and Observations. *HOPE* 10.4:541–48.

Davis, J. Ronnie. 1968. Chicago Economists, Deficit Budgets, and the Early 1930s. *American Economic Review* 58 (June): 476–82.

———. 1971. *The New Economics and the Old Economists*. Ames: Iowa State University Press.

Douglas, P. H., and A. Director. 1931. *The Problem of Unemployment*. New York: Macmillan.

Ellsworth, P. T. 1936. Mr. Keynes on the Rate of Interest and the Marginal Efficiency of Capital. *Journal of Political Economy* 44 (December): 767–90.

———. 1937. *International Economics*. New York: Macmillan.

Friedman, M. 1956. The Quantity Theory of Money—A Restatement. In *Studies in the Quantity Theory of Money*. Chicago: University of Chicago Press.

———. 1974. Comments on the Critics. In *Milton Friedman's Monetary Framework*, edited by R. J. Gordon, 132–77. Chicago: University of Chicago Press.

Friedman, M., and A. J. Schwartz. 1963. *A Monetary History of the United States 1867–1960*. Princeton, N.J.: Princeton University Press.

Haberler, G. von. 1932. Money and the Business Cycle. In *Gold and Monetary Stabilization: Lectures on the Harris Foundation*, edited by Q. Wright. Chicago: University of Chicago Press.

Hawtrey, R. G. 1925. Public Expenditure and the Demand for Labour. *Economica* 5 (March): 38–48.

———. 1927. Review of *Economic Problems New and Old* by Professor Allyn A. Young. *Economic Journal* 37 (December): 605–6.

———. 1932. *The Art of Central Banking*. London: Longmans.

Herren, R. S. 1997. Warren Milton Persons (1878–1937). In *Business Cycles and Depressions: An Encyclopedia*, edited by D. Glasner. New York: Garland Publishing.

Hicks, J. R. 1937. Mr. Keynes and the Classics—A Suggested Interpretation. *Econometrica* 5 (April): 147–59.

Humphrey, T. M. 1971. Role of Non-Chicago Economists in the Evolution of the Quantity Theory in America 1930–1950. *Southern Economic Journal* 38 (July): 12–18.

Keynes, J. M. 1931. An Economic Analysis of Unemployment. In *Unemployment as a World Problem: Lectures on the Harris Foundation*, edited by Q. Wright. Chicago: University of Chicago Press.

———. 1936. *The General Theory of Employment, Interest, and Money*. London: Macmillan.

Keynes, J. M., and H. Henderson. 1929. *Can Lloyd George Do It? An Examination of the Liberal Pledge*. London: *The Nation and Athenaeum*.

Laidler, D. 1993. Hawtrey, Harvard, and the Origins of the Chicago Tradition. *Journal of Political Economy* 101 (December): 1068–1103.

———. 1998a. Hawtrey, Harvard, and Chicago: A Final Comment. *Journal of Economic Studies* 25:22–24.

———. 1998b. More on Hawtrey, Harvard, and Chicago. *Journal of Economic Studies* 25:4–16.

———. 1999. *Fabricating the Keynesian Revolution: Studies of the Inter-war Literature on Money, the Cycle, and Unemployment*. Cambridge: Cambridge University Press.

Lampman, R. J. 1993. *Economists at Wisconsin: 1892–1992*. Madison: The Board of Regents of the University of Wisconsin System.

Lundberg, E. [1934] 1995. Report of My Studies as a Rockefeller Fellow of Economics. In *Erik Lundberg: Studies in Economic Instability and Change*, edited by R. G. H. Henricksson. Stockholm: SNS Förlag.

Mason, E. S. 1982. The Harvard Department of Economics from the Beginning to World War II. *Quarterly Journal of Economics* 97 (August): 383–433.

Mehrling, P. G. 1997. *The Money Interest and the Public Interest: American Monetary Thought 1920–1970*. Cambridge: Harvard University Press.

Mehrling, P. G., and R. J. Sandilands. 1999. Editors' Preface. In *Money and Growth: Selected Papers of Allyn Abbott Young*. London: Routledge.

Norman Wait Harris Memorial Foundation. 1932. *9th Institute—Gold and Monetary Stabilization Reports of Round Tables*. 27–30 January. Typescript, Regenstein Library, University of Chicago.

Patinkin, D. 1969. The Chicago Tradition, the Quantity Theory, and Friedman. *Journal of Money, Credit, and Banking* 1 (February): 46–70.

———. 1973. More on the Chicago Monetary Tradition. *Southern Economic Journal* 39 (January): 454–59.

Pigou, A. C. 1927. *Industrial Fluctuations*. London: Macmillan.

Reddaway, W. B. 1936. The General Theory of Employment, Interest, and Money. *Economic Record* 12 (June): 28–36.

Rees, D. 1973. *Harry Dexter White: A Study in Paradox*. New York: Coward McCann and Geoghegan.

Robertson, D. H. 1928. *Money*. 3d ed. London: Nisbet.

Sandilands, R. J. 1990. *The Life and Political Economy of Lauchlin Currie: New Dealer, Presidential Adviser, and Development Economist*. Durham, N.C.: Duke University Press.

———. 2001. The New Deal and "Domesticated Keynesianism" in America. In *Economist with a Public Purpose: Essays in Honour of John Kenneth Galbraith*, edited by M. Keaney. London: Routledge.

Steindl, F. 1995. *Monetary Interpretations of the Great Depression*. Ann Arbor: University of Michigan Press.

Tavlas, G. 1977. The Chicago Tradition Revisited: Some Neglected Contributions: Senator Paul Douglas. *Journal of Money, Credit, and Banking* 9 (November): 685–92.

———. 1997. Chicago, Harvard, and the Doctrinal Foundations of Monetary Economics. *Journal of Political Economy* 105 (February): 153–77.

———. 1998a. More on the Chicago Tradition. *Journal of Economic Studies* 25:17–21.

———. 1998b. Retrospectives: Was the Monetarist Tradition Invented? *Journal of Economic Perspectives* 12 (fall): 211–22.

Viner, J. 1932. International Aspects of the Gold Standard. In *Gold and Monetary Stabilization: Lectures on the Harris Foundation*, edited by Q. Wright. Chicago: University of Chicago Press.

———. 1933. *Balanced Deflation, Inflation, or More Depression?* Minneapolis: University of Minnesota Press.

Williams, J. H. 1932. Monetary Stability and the Gold Standard. In *Gold and Monetary Stabilization: Lectures on the Harris Foundation*, edited by Q. Wright. Chicago: University of Chicago Press.

Wright, Q., ed. 1932. *Gold and Monetary Stabilization: Lectures on the Harris Foundation*. Chicago: University of Chicago Press.

Young, A. A. 1924. Review of R. G. Hawtrey's *Currency and Credit* (2nd ed.) and *Monetary Reconstruction*. *American Economic Review* 14 (June): 349–51.

Young, W. 1987. *Interpreting Mr. Keynes: The IS-LM Enigma*. Cambridge, U.K.: Polity Press.

Memorandum Prepared by L. B. Currie, P. T. Ellsworth, and H. D. White (Cambridge, Mass., January 1932)

Edited by David Laidler and Roger Sandilands

The depression has been in progress more than two years. During this period the index of business activity has declined over a third; unemployment has assumed very grave proportions; partial employment has seriously reduced the weekly earnings of a large proportion of those listed as gainfully employed. In terms of real income the depression has already cost the American people more than the Great War.[1] Nor can the loss be measured in terms of real income alone. The widespread and long drawn out period of unemployment and greatly reduced incomes has been accompanied by increasing physical suffering and anxiety. It has, further, engendered a loss of confidence in American leadership and American institutions which is becoming more marked as the depression lengthens.

The end is not yet in sight, nor can any precedent be used as a forecast of duration; the significant factors of the present crisis have no parallel in modern economic history. The situation has passed the bounds of a business depression and has assumed the aspect of an international calamity.

1. In 1930 the national income, according to the National Industrial Conference Board, showed a decline from the peak year 1929 of 14 billion dollars, or 10 billion dollars from the average of 1927–28–29. For 1931 the decline has been considerably greater. During the three years 1917–18–19 the *total* federal government expenditures—converted into 1931 dollars—were only about 17 billions, and of that sum a portion was expended for normal government purposes and a larger portion consisted of loans to the Allies. In the 24 months from January 1, 1930 to January 1, 1932 the loss has amounted to double the money expenditure caused by the war, and if the situation continues, it will double again before the year is over.

History of Political Economy 34:3

With the reparations problem involved, economic distress throughout Europe on the increase, with the progressive maldistribution of gold reserves, the growing loss of confidence in banks, the mounting trade barriers, disorders in Spain, India, and China, the outlook for recovery in the near future is not encouraging.

In view of the manifest uncertainty as to the duration of the depression, the likelihood of its continuance for another year or longer and the failure on the part of the government to adopt other than palliative measures, there devolves upon the economist the responsibility of recommending a course of action which will hasten the approach of recovery. There are some economists who believe that the course of the depression cannot be checked, that political and economic changes are beyond human control, that to attempt to influence their direction is an attempt to interfere with the "natural" operation of economic principles; there are others who believe that the factors involved are so complex that economists can safely recommend no way out, and that the only policy to follow is one of patient submission to the as yet little understood operations of economic maladjustments; there are even a few who believe that the depression should be permitted to run its course because they regard it as a vehicle for the wholesome purging of inefficiency from our industrial system. A great number of economists, however, are not in sympathy with such views; they believe with Dr. Persons that "the depression will not cure itself and requires prompt, intelligent, and vigorous action"; they believe that recovery can and should be hastened thru the adoption of proper measures.

The recommendations recently made by Dr. Persons and signed by a number of eminent economists are a first step towards a vigorous grappling with the situation. We feel, however, that the proposals are stated in terms too vague, and the program offered is not sufficiently comprehensive to insure the desired goal of business recovery. We therefore venture to submit the following specific program together with a brief discussion of the economic principles involved.

Banking Policy

Production and prices have been and are falling, not because of a decline in the need for goods, but because of a decrease in monetary demand. This decrease, in turn, is due both to decreased monetary incomes and to the decreased spending of those incomes. Monetary incomes, broadly speaking, are determined by the volume and the rate of spending of the community's means of payment, which consist of money and demand deposits. The banking system can influence the rate of spending only indirectly. It can, however, thru its control of demand deposits, control within wide limits the volume of the means of payment, and it can offset, to a large degree, changing rates of spending by changing the volume of the means of payment.

Our banking policy has not exerted any effective influence to check the decline in the means of payment. Instead of offsetting the decline in the demand for goods caused by the decreased rate of spending, our policy has intensified it by permitting a contraction of the volume of the means of payment. The contraction has resulted chiefly from the extremely high level of indebtedness of member banks to the reserve banks. This indebtedness arose from the necessity placed upon the member banks of meeting customers' demands for notes and gold, and it has been maintained at that high level by the action of the reserve banks, which, from October to the end of January, decreased their holdings of acceptances by some $600,000,000. A decrease in the holdings of acceptances reduces correspondingly the reserve accounts of member banks and so forces them to increase their borrowings from the Federal Reserve Banks. To reduce this indebtedness, the member banks resort to a policy of credit contraction.

Why, it may be asked should banks wish to reduce their indebtedness to the reserve banks? There are various reasons. In the first place, there is the understanding—virtually an unwritten law—that recourse to the reserve banks should be for temporary and emergency purposes only. Continuous indebtedness to the reserve banks has, in the past, been frowned upon by the authorities. In addition there is the urgent desire of conservative bankers to be in a liquid condition, and it is considered that borrowings impair liquidity. For these and other reasons, member banks have been selling bonds in unprecedented amounts and have not been renewing old loans nor making new ones. As a consequence we have been experiencing an enormous contraction of demand deposits.

The results of this contraction have been uniformly unfortunate. It has unquestionably contributed to the demoralization of the bond market, and so to bank failures and the postponement of bond issues for construction purposes. In addition it has deepened the depression in less obvious ways. When an individual having a deposit buys a bond from or pays off a loan to the banking system and the system cancels the deposit, precisely the same effect is brought about as if the government were to issue bonds for banknotes and then destroy the banknotes. Individuals acquire means of payment from current production; they save, that is refrain from exercising a demand for the goods they have contributed in producing, and with their savings pay off a loan or buy a bond. If the bond is issued by a borrower who uses the proceeds to finance construction, no net decrease in spending or demand for goods has taken place. If, on the other hand, it is bought from a bank, as has recently been the case, the deposit is wiped out and a net decrease in the demand for goods is the result. In other words, a deposit which is not spent by the original owner on goods cannot, since it has been wiped out, be spent by anybody.

Obviously, continued liquidation of this nature will hinder any plan to overcome the depression. It is of the utmost importance, therefore, that liquidation be terminated as soon as possible. We do not believe that it will be terminated as long as member banks are so heavily in debt, and we believe, therefore, that it is absolutely essential for the indebtedness to be reduced. How can this be done?

Broadly speaking, indebtedness to the reserve banks can be reduced in four ways: (1) by an inflow of gold; (2) by an inflow of money from circulation; (3) by purchases of bills and securities by reserve banks; (4) by a contraction of member bank loans and investments and hence of deposits. A contraction of deposits sets free a proportion of the member banks' reserves which can be used to pay off rediscounts with the reserve banks. It is, however, important to note that a reduction of a billion dollars in deposits reduces reserve requirements, and hence rediscounts with the reserve banks, by only one hundred millions (assuming a 10 per cent reserve ratio). In default of the first three ways member banks have been forced to have recourse to this last method of reducing rediscounts. After four months of contraction, however, they found themselves more heavily indebted than ever, owing to the diminution in the holdings of acceptances by the reserve banks.

Since we dare not wait for an inflow of gold or of cash, and it is obviously undesirable that banks should continue to reduce indebtedness by contracting deposits, the only alternative is for the reserve banks to enter upon a vigorous open market purchasing policy. At the moment of writing the indebtedness amounts to over $800,000,000. We strongly recommend, therefore, that the reserve banks purchase upwards of a billion dollars of bills and securities. This action would satisfy member banks' desire for liquidity and in addition give them large surplus reserves. Member banks, out of debt and in possession of surplus reserves, could be relied upon to increase their holdings of short term government bonds and in this way bring about an expansion of deposits in place of the present contraction.

The reserve and member banks' purchases of bonds would aid in the recovery of the bond market and this, in turn, would enhance the solvency of bond holding institutions and would enable borrowers to secure loans at better rates. Further, this policy would unquestionably result in an increase in consumers' incomes, demand for goods, and production. What is needed at the present time is a net increase in the effective demand for goods. If the government borrows from the reserve banks and other banks, it receives deposits which have been *newly created* and which have not been taken from individuals. In this way a net increase in spending can be achieved. If, however, as is pointed out elsewhere in this plan, the government attempts to finance its deficit solely by taxation, or even by bonds sold to individuals, there is a probability that most of the increased government spending will be offset by the decreased spending of taxpayers and bond buyers.

An objection to our proposal that the reserve banks buy bonds, which probably carries some weight with the reserve administration, is that it would decrease the "free gold" of the system. There is a provision in the Federal Reserve Act that federal reserve notes must be backed 40 per cent by gold plus 60 per cent by eligible paper or gold. Member bank rediscounts secured by government securities bought in the open market are not. If, therefore, a policy were adopted which would result in the displacement of bills discounted by government bonds in the reserve banks' earning assets, the amount of gold that would have to be held against notes would be increased. We believe that this provision in the act has no valid justification and recommend, therefore, that government bonds be declared eligible as collateral against federal reserve notes. The reserve banks need not, however, wait for a change in the law. Their reserves are ample, and in any case they could purchase at least $600,000,000 of acceptances if they raised their buying price sufficiently. Acceptances are eligible paper.

Some people feel that an increase in means of payment would have no perceptible effect since, they say, there is plenty of money now; the real difficulty is in getting it spent. We can dispose of this objection very briefly by pointing out that we have provided for the spending of the increased means of payment by linking the plan for deposit expansion to one providing for public works with no immediate rise in taxes. If there is one point on which everyone is agreed, it is that any money borrowed by public bodies will be spent.

A criticism of an entirely different character is that our proposal is "inflationary." It should be noted that the people who make this criticism concede fully the efficacy of a policy of expansion on the part of the central bank. Their fear is, apparently, than an upturn started in this way would get out of control and eventually involve us in a situation similar to that of war time. We do not believe that there is the slightest justification for this fear. We concede and, indeed, think it desirable that some recovery in prices should take place. In this connection, it is important to distinguish between an increase in monetary incomes when the factors of production are fully utilized and when they are only partially utilized. In the former case the output of goods can rise but slowly. In the latter, which corresponds to the present situation, an increase in monetary demand for goods could very shortly be met by increased output. It is only after much of the present enormous slack in our economic system has been taken up that the danger of inflation becomes real. Before that point is reached, the production of goods and services will have greatly increased. This additional production in answer to an increased demand is just what is wanted; it is the very goal of our economic system. As Keynes has so aptly said, "To bring up the bogy of Inflation as an objection to capital expenditures at the present is like warning a patient who is wasting away from emaciation of the dangers of excessive corpulation." It is true that an approach to prosperity—i.e., the upswing in the movement of business activity—brings with it danger of inflation; the very nature of expanding business activity contains the impetus to expanding bank deposits and rising prices. But the danger can be avoided, as it has been in the past. The reserve banks will be in an excellent position to apply brakes on the upswing by virtue of their very large holdings of bills and securities which they can sell and so place member banks heavily in debt. We find it difficult to understand why the spending of newly created means of payment should be any more inflationary than an increased rate of spending of the existing means of payment, which is universally advocated today.

It may be objected that a banking policy designed to check deflation would result in such an outflow of gold as to endanger the maintenance of the gold standard here. Our present gold stock is, however, approximately four and a half billions. French balances in this country were variously estimated in January to amount to between $400,000,000 and $450,000,000 and were being steadily reduced. Other foreign balances are much smaller. We could, therefore, well stand, if need be, the loss in gold of all foreign balances. It has been intimated that foreigners would also sell their holdings of our securities for gold. This is, of course, a matter of opinion and is, by its nature, incapable of definite refutation. We can only state it as our belief that such a reaction is unlikely. It seems more probable that a continued fall in our stock and bond prices would cause more foreign selling than would arise in those brought about by the anticipation of business recovery.

It must be remembered that only a few countries remain on the gold standard, and that they have received enormous quantities of gold in the past two years. It appears doubtful that they could absorb the upwards of two billions that we could spare, without any effect on their internal price structures. As long as the United States continues, by its policy, to raise the value of gold, central banks in countries off the gold standard feel constrained to adopt restrictive measures in order to prevent continued depreciation of their exchanges. Should we succeed in starting a business recovery independently, it is probable that foreign exchanges would move initially against us. This would enable central banks in countries off the gold standard to relax their present drastic restrictive policies and pave the way for a world upturn. It need hardly be pointed out that a policy which leads to an increase in our aggregate money income to be spent on both home and foreign goods would do much to lighten the pressure on Germany and other debtor countries without causing any diminution in demand for home goods.

In conclusion, we believe that the most serious danger to the maintenance of the gold standard would be an internal drain of money into "circulation," which would result from a policy of continued liquidation. Such a policy, involving a steady decline in all values, would result in increased bank failures, which, in turn, would lead to increased hoarding. Suspensions of specie payments in the past have occurred as a consequence of internal rather than external runs on our banking system.

Public Expenditures

While it is true both that an easing of credit conditions will tend to encourage private investment, and that any increase in credit, resulting in greater expenditure, will create additional employment, it is doubtful—in the present situation—whether the desired increase in private borrowing will take place. With confidence as badly shaken as it is at present, and with prices continuing to fall, there is little in the current outlook to make it attractive to business men to borrow in amounts sufficient to stimulate recovery. And while presumably the fall in prices will some day stop and confidence revive, the policy of waiting for this day to come involves us in a continuation of the present unemployment and business losses for an indeterminate period. Such measures as the National Credit Corporation and the Reconstruction Finance Corporation are in the main designed to prevent the liquidation from becoming more serious, not to give business an impetus which would start it on the upward path.

Since the initiation of a voluntary program of expansion by independent, scattered producers must wait upon the appearance of the prospect of profits, and since the Federal Government is the sole agency in a central position and strong enough to undertake drastic remedial action, it is strongly recommended that the Government immediately commence a program of public construction on a nationwide scale. Such a program would stimulate directly the building and construction industry and those industries engaged in the production of raw materials and tools, and indirectly a large number of other lines of enterprise, thru the expenditure of the earnings of the re-employed. The revival of these industries would involve a further, secondary increase in employment, which in turn would stimulate recovery in other lines in ever widening circles. As employment in industry at large increased, a gradual reduction in government expenditure on construction would be called for, and would permit the return of men engaged on such work to their ordinary occupations.

This program should be financed, not by taxation, which serves principally merely to divert expenditure from one channel to another, but by an issue of bonds, under conditions specified below. It is recommended that United States bonds be issued in amounts sufficient to the purpose. The bonds should be sold, not in one block, but after an initial issue of $500,000,000, at such a rate as the progress of construction makes necessary. It is expected that it will not be necessary to issue more than one to two billions to achieve the desired results. These bonds should be made eligible for rediscount at the Federal Reserve Banks, and also as collateral for the issue of Federal Reserve notes. Partial retirement should be provided out of a surtax on incomes, the remainder out of generally higher taxation to be imposed as soon as recovery has been attained, the retirement to take place as rapidly as is consistent with the state of business activity, preferably at a rate of 15 per cent a year. Public utterance of prominent individuals to the contrary notwithstanding, it is deemed obvious that a period of national poverty is the worst time to increase federal taxes, and a period of prosperity the worst time to reduce them.

Increased taxes result normally in a transfer of purchasing power from the individual to the government; it is only when taxes come from hoarded or idle funds that an increase rather than a transfer of purchasing power results. If the government employs this purchasing power (i.e., collected taxes) instead of borrowing "created" or idle funds, the result is a drop in the effective demand for bonds at a time when the government should be doing everything in its power to build up the effective demand. When at the same time the government adopts a policy of retrenchment, of ruthless cutting of expenditures, the effect is doubly bad. In times of intense depression a paring down of productive expenditures that can be financed thru the borrowing of "created" or idle funds is inexcusable. A course of action which may be proper for a private corporation, for a municipality, for a state, or for some other country is no criterion of the proper policy for the United States Government. The City of New York may find it expedient to reduce its deficit, notwithstanding the resulting intensification of the depression, because it may not be able to borrow unless it reduces its budgetary deficit. If the important bankers refuse to support a municipal loan, New York has no alternative; it must reduce its deficit by increased taxes and decreased expenditures. But the United States Government is never in such a predicament; it always has a choice: it can make possible such credit conditions as will facilitate the flotation of its bonds, and can, if necessary, even supply the funds with which its own bonds may be purchased.

It cannot be emphasized too strongly that financing public works through domestic bond flotations by the federal government *does not* saddle future generations with a burden. Even the 25 billion dollar loan raised to finance the war did not pass on to later years any portion of the burden of conducting the war. It doubtless caused in later years some redistribution of the national income (to what extent and in what direction involves an analysis of the incidence of the taxes raised to liquidate the loan and of the factors connected with the rapidity of liquidation, changed rates of interest, effect of loan and redemptions on prices, etc.—matters extremely complex for the economist and wholly beyond the layman—but it did not decrease the aggregate real income. The economic burden of the war on future generations consisted of the loss of benefits that would have been derived from the use of such capital, actual and potential, as was destroyed. The loss of future generations would have been neither more nor less had the war been financed wholly out of current taxes. Those who reiterate that domestic borrowing by the Federal Government saddles future generations with a burden should familiarize themselves with the A B C of economics. It is the *failure* of the Federal Government to increase its outstanding indebtedness during a period of depression that in a sense saddles the future with a burden; the capital goods that could be and are not produced deprive the future of the continuous stream of utilities that would have been derived from those capital goods. Every month's delay in setting idle equipment and idle men to work not only denies to us currently an enormous amount of consumer's goods and service, but also deprives future generations of the utility to be derived from the additional factories, schools, parks, roads, machinery, and so forth that could be produced if the Government now embarked on the program here outlined.

It is claimed that any large issue of bonds would destroy confidence in the United States Government and cause the value of its outstanding bonds to decline seriously. Such objection is wholly unwarranted. From 1921 to 1929 the Government reduced its indebtedness from 26 to 16 billions. Had the Government deemed it expedient, it could without difficulty have maintained the higher tax rates and by 1929 wiped off another ten billions of the debt. But it chose rather to lower taxes and to reduce the debt less rapidly. In 1930 the debt was 16.8 billion dollars, or about $134 per capita, a sum less than one-third the per capita indebtedness of France and less than one-fifth that of Great Britain. The tax burden in the United States, on the other hand, is considerably less than in either of these two countries. The United States, in short, has (in per capita terms) a much greater income, a smaller debt, and considerably lower taxes than any of the great nations. In the light of these facts there are those who continue to affirm that if in this emergency—an emergency certainly as great as the war if privation and national loss be the measure—the outstanding domestic debt is to be increased by a few billion dollars, confidence in the United States Government will be destroyed. Those who make the claim point to the decline in the price of United States Government bonds during the fall of 1931 as evidence of a loss of confidence, but there is no sound basis for such a view. A loss of confidence in the financial stability of a government is quite different from a loss of confidence in the financial stability of a corporation or municipality. In the case of the federal government it does not and cannot mean that the government is in any danger of suspending payment on its domestic debt. It can mean only that the government may cease to pay its debt in money redeemable in gold; in other words, that the government is in danger of being forced off the gold standard. If such fears were entertained in the fall of 1931, the first sign would have been a hoarding of gold, and we know that this did not occur. Hoarding took place, but it was the hoarding of paper money, not gold, and indicated a loss of confidence in the banks, not in the Government. The decline in government bond values was caused definitely not by loss of confidence, but by the suddenly increased supply of bonds coming from those banks which were liquidating their investments in order to reduce their indebtedness to the reserve banks.

It is to be expected that a great increase in the demand for funds would probably depress the bond market unless the Federal Reserve Banks or member banks come to its support, as they did during the war, by purchasing a large portion of the government issues. Indeed, such action by the Federal Reserve Banks will be essential to the success of the plan herein outlined; otherwise a large bond flotation will heighten the long term borrowing rate and discourage new undertakings on the part of private corporations and municipalities. A result to be sedulously avoided. The Federal Reserve Banks need support the market with large purchases only at the start of the program. Once the upturn in business activity begins, there will be a return of business optimism, confidence in the banks will be revived, and the 1.3 billions of hoarded funds, which the Government is trying to "coax" and "reason" back, will flow of its own accord (either by direct deposits or by the purchase of securities) into the banks. The demand for securities brought about by the inflow of hoarded funds will alone prevent the interest on long term borrowing from rising.

It has also been claimed that such a large government loan would merely have the effect of causing an equal decline in private investment. In view of the fact that new corporate issues of securities during the last six months of 1931 averaged well under $100,000,000 per month, the lowest figure since 1918, this is hardly a serious objection at the present. The proposed rate of issue of new government securities would far offset even a complete abandonment of private investment. Furthermore, as the effects of the increased expenditure on employment, prices, and profits began to be felt, the prices of industrial securities could scarcely fail to rise, and as business revived, new industrial issues would be needed and would appear. Better security prices would be the inevitable result of rising monetary incomes of corporations. Again, more profitable business would mean both higher taxable capacity and higher tax returns, and this, together with the diminished burden of unemployment, would raise the value of the securities of states and municipalities, many of which have recently been forced to abandon their own public works programs because of low revenue and high cost of borrowing.

The program should begin with the letting of contracts to private contractors to an initial sum of $1,000,000,000, the work to be pushed as rapidly as possible; where feasible, by the employment of two or three separate shifts a day. In the awarding of the first group of contracts, preference should be given to those works that can be completed within the shortest possible time. It is essential that enough contracts be completed each month to make possible a decrease in total expenditures as business conditions improve. The emergency nature of the expenditure should be kept uppermost in planning the details. A high rate of expenditure at the outset should be aimed at, and bonds sold as rapidly as need be to meet the payments coming due. In view of the large number of public projects that have been postponed thruout the country by states and municipalities, it should be possible in a short time to achieve a rate of expenditure of $300,000,000 per month. As the stimulus of this expenditure spreads to other lines of activity, the rate of expenditure should be reduced. The value of contracts let after the first billion is spent should be scaled down as the index of production of the Federal Reserve Board rises. When the index reaches 90 (in 1928–29 it averaged 114), only those projects as yet incomplete should be finished and no new contracts should be let in.

The expenditure of the emergency funds should be governed by the following considerations: (1) facility with which projects may be initiated at the earliest possible date and completed within a short time; (2) amount of labor that will be employed, directly or indirectly; (3) number and diversity of the industries which will be affected, directly or indirectly, by the projects; (4) value of the projects to the economic and social welfare of the country; (5) economical administration of the work. While waste and duplication should be avoided so far as is humanly possible, the object of the expenditure is to put men to work at useful tasks immediately instead of waiting until we are forced to relieve them in idleness—hence the emphasis on speed and on the numbers employed.

As to the objects upon which the funds should be spent it is clear that there is a wide variety of useful public works which need to be undertaken, and which, if done, will leave the country definitely ahead in a tangible way. Specifically, it is recommended that the proceeds of the loan be used in the construction of roads, the elimination of grade crossings, the erection of bridges and public buildings for which there is a clear need and for which plans are ready, the elimination of unsightly areas in municipalities, and in carrying out a program of flood prevention and reforestation, both directly by the Federal Government and thru loans to states and thru them to municipalities. In order to ensure a coordinated policy in the execution of the program of construction, it is recommended that there be created an Administration of Public Works, along the lines laid down in the bill (S. 2419), presented to the Senate by Senator La Follette.

It will doubtless be argued that such public work will be costly, that some things will be done which do not seriously need doing, and, in general, that such vast expenditure by the Government is unwise. Admittedly the work done will probably involve a larger outlay than ordinary public works, but it is the object of the program to meet a specific emergency—men are to be given employment because they are unemployed. The alternative is direct unemployment relief, which, to be adequate, would require a large outlay, would leave nothing behind to show for the expenditure, and would prove demoralizing to the recipients.

Innumerable difficulties lie in the path of a rapid and successful execution of so large a program. Yet those difficulties are not insurmountable. In 1917 the United States demonstrated its ability to execute a far more difficult program. The seriousness of the present emergency warrants the straining of every effort to achieve quickly an adequate rate of public expenditure which will do so much to bring about business recovery.

Tariff Policy

One of the factors that has in no small way contributed to the present world wide depression and is an additional obstacle in the way of recovery is the determination on the part of the nations to keep out goods of other countries. Since 1925 the tariff schedule of every important country has been revised upward at least once. Not content with mere increases in duty, many countries have set up import quotas, licensing restrictions, and embargoes. Germany in a desperate attempt to prevent an outflow of gold has instituted a system of licensed imports and control over foreign exchanges, designed effectively to cut her imports to the bone. Austria, Czechoslovakia, Turkey, Greece, Jugoslavia, and Roumania exercise close control over exchange, and Spain, incensed by the restrictions imposed on her exports, has recently retaliated with import quotas. Even France, whose gold reserves are in no way threatened, is adding import quotas to her already high tariff schedule. This concerted rush to place more and more obstacles in the path of international trade has operated to increase not only the real costs of production of innumerable international commodities, but also the maladjustments which are now playing economic havoc. The relationship between the world supply and demand of many important world commodities has been seriously disturbed: the present ruinous prices of wheat, sugar, textiles, and a host of other manufactured articles are in part traceable to the policy of expanding home industries and domestic crops by means of subsidies provided by protective duties, regardless of the fact that in the exporting countries crop areas and plant capacities are not reduced until long after prices have become ruinous.

Heightened tariff barriers, by rendering more difficult the adjustments of international accounts, have magnified the problem of debt settlements, both private and public, and have contributed materially to the maldistribution of gold reserves. The higher the import duties in the creditor countries, the harder the task of developing export surpluses in the debtor countries. Forced to adopt extreme measures to develop the export surplus necessary to meet payments abroad, the debtor countries have cut imports to a minimum, and have maintained high discount rates. The difficulty of developing a sufficient export surplus has in some cases led to virtual abandonment of the gold standard. The concentration of gold in the United States and France, where it is not needed, at the expense of gold reserves in countries where its loss proved disastrous, has been encouraged by their high tariff policies. In an attempt to stem the outward flow of gold or encourage an inflow, tariff barriers in other countries have been increased, and have in turn incited retaliatory increases. And so the mad march toward declining trade, increasing costs, and economic maladjustment goes on.

The United States has been in the forefront in the building up of tariff walls; it is only fitting that she take the lead in the downward revision so necessary to a return to economic sanity. A step by her in that direction may well initiate a general reduction in the tariff schedules of all important countries, but whether or not other countries follow America's lead, the reduction of import duties in the United States would be an important step towards economic recovery and a means of increasing the real aggregate national income. We therefore recommend a reduction in all duties protective in design or in effect. We indorse also that portion of the tariff bill (now before Congress) calling for the creation of a commission to confer with European governments with the express intent of securing the scaling down of tariff schedules. International conferences, however, are certain to be long drawn out, and the present situation calls for immediate action. Let the United States by a reduction in her import duties demonstrate to the world that she no longer will contribute to the dangerous spirit of unenlightened nationalism and international bitterness which high protective policies foster.

It is important to recognize, however, that a sharp reduction of duties would involve injustice to vested interests in the protected industries, and would result in additional short-time maladjustments. The diversion of capital and of workers from protected industries to others should be so gradual as to cause minimum losses to the owners of protected industries and a minimum of additional temporary unemployment. It is therefore recommended that all import duties in excess of twenty per cent *ad valorem* be reduced by one fifth of the existing duty. Such a reduction would avoid serious maladjustments and losses: many of the duties in the present schedule, being much in excess of the differences in the domestic and the foreign costs of production, would continue to keep out the foreign commodities; others, being completely ineffective, would merely continue so; while commodities taxed twenty per cent *ad valorem* or less (the *ad valorem* equivalent of specific duties to be based on the average import price of 1930) would not be touched by the revision. The employment of a flat rate of reduction applying to all commodities (except those taxed twenty per cent or under) would have a double advantage: it would obviate the delay and the uncertainty of lengthy consideration of the separate items, and it would immediately make clear to the world that an important downward revision of the tariff schedule had been made. The proposed reduction would have, we believe, a beneficial economic effect out of all proportion to the actual changes involved.

Reparations and Interallied Debts

We feel confident that the adoption of the foregoing recommendations in regard to banking policies, public works, and the tariff will bring about business recovery in the United States; but we cannot overlook the fact that extreme distress in Europe must tend to retard our progress. Europe consumes normally one-fourth of our exports, and the sharp decline in her demand for our products will continue to be a depressing factor in many of the export industries, particularly in agriculture. Americans have invested, moreover, five billion dollars in European countries, and the income from these investments has been curtailed by the depression abroad. We believe, therefore, that business recovery in the United States will be more easily attained, and will reach a higher level, if accompanied by recovery in Europe.

Reparations are the chief obstacle to European prosperity. They hang like a storm cloud over Europe, presaging possible chaos, shutting out the influences essential to a resumption of normal international relations, and inducing a state of mind wholly inimical to business recovery. In Germany—the crucial country, whose situation so largely affects conditions in the rest of Europe—the very high interest rates, the budgetary difficulties, the interference with the normal course of trade, the precarious banking situation, are all in a large measure a consequence of the reparations tangle. Unemployment is now approaching six millions, and political strife is assuming more and more a threatening aspect, while the growing determination among all parties in Germany that reparations be cancelled, or at least greatly reduced, is keeping France in a state of great uneasiness that is reflected in increased hoarding, a cautious banking policy, and a growing pessimism.

The Young Plan has not provided a solution to the reparations problem; payments are not being made, and there is little likelihood that they ever will be made on the scale fixed by the plan. Germany balks at the prospect of saddling the next two generations with burdens she holds them to have in no way merited, and is becoming less and less inclined to submit to terms she believes to be unreasonable. Any attempt to force from Germany larger payments than she is willing to make can result, as France discovered in 1923, only in disaster to all concerned. It is evident, therefore, that German reparations must be revised, and in a manner that will receive the co-operation of the German people.

Interallied debts are, as every economist recognizes, inextricably bound up with reparations. It may be political wisdom for United States government officials to continue to deny that such is the case, but the fact remains that France will not make her annual payments to the United States and England if she does not receive annuities from Germany, and that England will not pay the United States if Germany and France default in their payments to her. An extension of the moratorium will not be a settlement of the tangle; it will serve merely to perpetuate the uncertainty. If, on the other hand, a definite and *permanent* arrangement be made on a basis satisfactory to the principal nations concerned, Europe will be rid of the great impediment that bars the road toward her economic recovery. With intergovernmental debts permanently out of the way, the next decade may well see a great stride towards a higher standard of living and better international relations.

We believe that the quickest, most equitable, and most effective way to settle the problem of reparations is thru a *complete cancellation* of interallied debts and reparations. The principal justification for cancellation rests upon other than economic grounds, but our economic interests alone, we believe, warrant the step. The greatest monetary loss of such a settlement would fall upon the United States, yet if by a cancellation of all intergovernmental debts we can achieve a ten per cent higher level of business activity, even for a single year, the United States will have lost nothing, while Europe will have gained much. Those who oppose cancellation on the ground that the American people would lose $300,000,000 a year, base their attitude on the questionable assumptions that the Allies are going to meet their obligations, and that intergovernmental debts in no way retard economic recovery or prevent a higher level of prosperity. As we have pointed out, whether or not the United States receives $300,000,000 a year depends upon whether or not Germany pays her reparations in accordance with the Young Plan. Germany, we repeat, will not make those payments, and cancellation, therefore, does not mean a loss of $300,000,000, for in no case would the United States receive this sum. Cancellation would mean an end to the bickerings, moratoriums, uncertainties, political and economic disturbances, and international frictions which are contributing so much to the downward movement of business activity in Europe, and which cannot but affect the situation in the United States. But public sentiment, however unjustified, remains strongly opposed to cancellation. We recommend, therefore, as an alternative the following plan, which while gaining the support of those who resent cancellation, will achieve a measure of its benefits.

The United States loaned the Allied Governments about ten billion dollars. This sum, compounded at 4¼ per cent annually would amount to 15 billions. Of this sum 2.5 billions have already been paid, leaving the current indebtedness, on the foregoing basis, at 12.5 billions. (For purposes of brevity only approximate figures are used.) At the time these funds were loaned the purchasing power of the dollar was about one-half what it is today. Since it is palpably unfair to expect our allies to pay back double the amount of goods and services they borrowed for the conduct of a joint war, the sum owing to the United States ought to be adjusted to its present purchasing power. In terms of 1932 dollars the debt to the United States would be only 6.25 billions. This sum of 6.25 billions, it must be emphasized, represents no real reduction from the amount borrowed by the Allies plus the interest which would have accrued from the date the loan was made until the present time. However, in its arrangements with the various debtor countries, the United States has already demonstrated its willingness to scale down the real burden of the debt. In its agreement with Italy the effective reduction, in view of the low interest rate and dates of payment, amounted to 74 per cent; with Belgium, 46 per cent; with France, 50 per cent; with England, 18 per cent. If these reductions were applied to the deflated value of the loan (namely, 6.25 billions), the remainder due the United States would be 3.75 billions. The reduction of 2.5 billions, or 40 per cent of the debt, would then be the contribution of the United States toward a permanent settlement of the debt problem, the reduction being contingent upon a similar treatment of German reparations. The annual loss of revenue to the United States from the 2.5 billion dollar reduction would be a negligible portion of our annual income, and would be much more than offset by the good results of a permanent solution of the inter-allied debts and reparations problem.

We recommend that this 3.75 billion dollar debt be paid in the following manner:

Each country will give to the United States, in place of bonds already given, its bonds, bearing an interest rate of 7 per cent per annum, payable in gold, to an amount equal to the sum due the United States after correction is made for the changes in the purchasing power of gold, and after the reductions listed above for each country are made. The bonds will be equally divided into three classes—A, B, and C,—the only difference in the classes being the date and the callable price. Class A bonds will be dated August 1, 1932, and will be callable (by lot) for the first two years at 103, and thereafter at par; Class B bonds will be dated August 1, 1933, and will be callable for the first three years at 110, during the second three years at 105, and thereafter at par; Class C bonds will be dated August 1, 1934, and will be callable during the first three years at 115, during the next three years at 110, during the following three years at 105, and thereafter at par. All bonds will be payable in 20 years, with redemption required at the rate of 2 per cent, beginning in the seventh year and increasing at the rate of 2 per cent every second year. This splitting of the bonds into different classes would delay maximum interest payment until 1935.

The United States Government will offer these bonds to the public at not less than par. Because of the attractive rate of interest, the bonds will be rapidly absorbed by individuals and banks in the United States. The sale of these bonds will not depress the bond market, because the proceeds will be used to liquidate its own bonds; in fact, it might be easily arranged to permit the holders of United States government bonds to exchange them for the 7 per cent foreign government bonds. The debts to the United States Government would thus be liquidated and removed from the field of governmental consideration. To prevent exchange difficulties arising in the issuing countries from a possible extensive purchase of these bonds by the residents of the issuing countries, a tax could, if necessary, be imposed by those countries on their purchase or interest payment.

Improvement in the credit of the debtor governments is certain to follow a satisfactory solution of the reparations problem and the return of prosperity. The issuing governments could then refund one-third of the loans at a lower rate of interest, followed by another third three years later, and so forth. Before ten years had passed, the interest payments would in all probability have been reduced one-fourth by virtue of the lower rates, made possible by improved credit conditions. A portion of these bonds would doubtless replace some of the foreign securities now held in the issuing countries, and the transfer problem would thereby be further reduced.

A settlement of the debts in this manner is conditional, of course, upon a similar settlement to be made by the Allied Governments with regard to reparations. The Young Plan fixed the remainder of reparations due from Germany at 9 billions. Since the payments already made under this plan have amounted to no more than the interest on that amount, the reparations due remain at 9 billions. In terms of 1932 dollars this sum would equal about 6 billions. From this sum is to be deducted an amount equal to the reduction made by the United States to the Allies—namely, 40 per cent. This will leave about 3.6 billions due from Germany to the Allies. In settlement of this debt Germany will give to each of the Allies, in such proportion as shall be agreed upon among themselves, German Government 7 per cent bonds, payable in gold. The service on those bonds shall have priority over any other government loan except the $300,000,000 loan of 1925. The bonds, like those given to the United States by the Allies, are to be divided into three classes with the same provisions. The first payment to be made by Germany would be $84,000,000 in 1934, followed by $168,000,000 in 1935, and by $252,000,000 in 1936. Under the Young Plan the annuities were to [be] $450,000,000 in 1934, $465,000,000 in 1935 and $475,000,000 in 1936. The new plan thus considerably reduces the transfer problem. As soon as Germany's credit improves, she can refund the 7 per cent bonds for others bearing a lower rate of interest, and, if advisable, reduce the rate of redemption. The transfer problem may thus be reduced still further.

Under the favorable conditions following the virtual elimination of the transfer problem and the reduction of Germany's debt, the 7 per cent bonds will pass into the hands of private holders. Once this occurs, the reparations problem will lose all political importance and will cease to be a disturbing factor in international affairs. Long before this final absorption of the bonds takes place, however, Europe will have been relieved of the demoralizing burden of uncertainty and fear, and will have taken forward steps toward prosperity.

Part Four

Towards a Resolution of the Dispute

Towards a Resolution of the Dispute

> … it would be interesting to know whether there was a line of influence running from Keynes (1923) to Chicago (1934).
>
> Robert Skidelsky (1992, 579, n.) *John Maynard Keynes: The Economist as Saviour 1920–1937*

Overview

Prior to Don Patinkin's assault on Milton Friedman, the major dispute over macroeconomic lineage (and bastardry) related to John Maynard Keynes, not to Henry Simons and Lloyd Mints. Patinkin was a major participant in both disputes. Joan Robinson (1962a, 690–1) first used the term 'Bastard Keynesianism' in print in 1962. Simultaneously, Patinkin sought to establish the legitimate tradition of both Keynes and the Chicago Fathers.

Patinkin asserted that Keynes supported the Walrasian general equilibrium (IS-LM) interpretation of the *General Theory.* In contrast, Axel Leijonhufvud (1969 [1968], 302) accused Patinkin and his fellow general equilibrium theorists of providing 'a seriously misleading framework for the interpretation of Keynes' theory'. Robert Clower (1969 [1965], 270, 295–6, 283) argued that Patinkin was carrying forward this 'Keynesian counter-revolution … with such vigour'. But in Clower's view this vigour was not accompanied by rigour: 'much of what now passes for useful theory is not only worthless economics (and mathematics), but also a positive hindrance to fruitful theoretical and empirical work'. Patinkin was guilty of '*ad hoc* theorizing – inventing a solution to a problem which has actually been evaded rather than resolved'.[1]

Patinkin objected to what he regarded as 'history-mining' to add respectability to contemporary policy recommendations. Thus Patinkin (1980, 25, 23) advised economists to 'cut the umbilical cord to Keynes'. According to Patinkin (1989, 235–6, 211) in the 1960s attempts were made to 'identify Keynes' theory with that of the 'Modern Cambridge School' [and] to invoke Keynes' authority for the more radical policy views of this School'. This involved driving 'a wedge' between 'the economics of Keynes' and those who were denigrated as 'bastard Keynesians'. Friedman (1974 [1972], 133–4; 1974, 18) approved of this wedge. For him,

'Keynes was a true Marshallian in method'. Friedman (1970, 7–8) also asserted that 'if Keynes were alive today he would no doubt be at the forefront of the [monetarist] counter-revolution. You must never judge a master by his disciples'.

Volume 2, part 2 falls into four sections. The first three chapters represent Patinkin's ongoing scholarly interest in explaining the evolution of Keynes' economics and his relationship to the Chicago economists. In his Sir Dennis Robertson lecture, Patinkin (pp. 317–44 [1974], 318, 326, 341) explained that he was using the term 'Keynesian monetary theory' in contrast to 'the quantity theory' to describe 'the *General Theory* and the literature to which it gave rise – though I should note that the aspect of the theory that is my primary concern here (namely, the treatment of money from the viewpoint of the choice of an optimum portfolio) is in some respects more precisely developed in Keynes' *Treatise on Money* ... There is no doubt that Keynes of the *General Theory* is at one with Keynes of the *Tract* (1923, pp. 78–9) in taking as his point of departure the individual's demand for money holdings'.

Patinkin explained that his general approach to doctrinal history was that 'isolated passages do not a theory make'. Therefore the crucial distinction between the Cambridge School and the Keynesian School was that the latter – but not the former – recognised the 'implications of the optimal-portfolio approach'. Patinkin cited Robertson's (1928, 37) reference to the choice-theoretic marginal calculation underpinning an individual's demand for money but concluded that 'the Cambridge economists did not recognise the full implications of the optimum-portfolio approach to monetary theory; they did not really integrate it into their thinking'. Patinkin (pp. 317–44 [1974], 324) also argued that 'the novelty of Keynesian monetary theory' related to the distinction between stocks and flows. However, Robertson (1928, 29) explained that 'we can fix our attention either on the *stock* of money in existence at a given *point* in time, or on the *flow* of money being used during a given *period* of time. Each of these procedures has its own advantages, and it will be well to be familiar with both of them before we are done' [Robertson's emphases]. Patinkin interspersed his lecture with 'various facetious remarks' – mostly aimed at Milton Friedman.

Pages 347–69 is a review of *The Collected Writings of John Maynard Keynes: From the Tract to the General Theory.* According to Patinkin (pp. 347–69 [1975], 352–3, 355–6, 367) 'monetary theory' in the *Treatise* means, first and foremost, a theory that explains the determination of the price level'. Patinkin interpreted Keynes as a co-author of the Keynesian Neoclassical

Synthesis: 'the General Theory is not a static theory of unemployment equilibrium but a dynamic theory of *dis*equilibrium' [emphasis in original]. Patinkin also appropriated Keynes as a keen econometrician: a pioneer in estimation of reduced form models (see also Patinkin, 1976).

Patinkin (1979, 156) thought that it was 'essential' to realise that 'Keynes did not live in the world of academe. He was not a professor'. Patinkin (pp. 347–69 [1975], 352, 365, 367) noted that the *Treatise* was 'designed to firmly establish his academic reputation'. Patinkin sought to encourage the reading of the *General Theory* but to discourage the reading of the *Treatise*: 'least enjoyable as a reading experience is the *Treatise* ... I can (from the viewpoint of macroeconomic theory) see little profit (and certainly no pleasure) from reading it today ... one cannot help the feeling that it represents a Keynes out of character: a Keynes attempting to act the role of a Professor, and a Germanic one at that'.[2] In contrast, in the General Theory 'we once again find the true Keynes ... the stirring voice of a prophet who has seen a new truth, and who is convinced that it – and only it – can save a world deep in the throes of crisis. It is a sharp polemical voice directed at converting economists all over the world to the new dispensation – and combating the false prophets among them who perversely continue with the erroneous teachings of the earlier gods whom Keynes had already abandoned'.

Keynes visited the University of Chicago in June–July 1931 to attend the Harris Foundation lectures and seminars on 'Unemployment as a World Problem' (Wright, 1931a). In his Henry Simons Lecture on 'Keynes and Chicago', Patinkin (pp. 373–92 [1979/1981], 373–4, 383) ridiculed the simplicity of the 'obscure' and 'strange' notation of Keynes 'fundamental equation!' In his discussion of the Chicago reviews of the *General Theory*, Patinkin noted that Frank Knight framed his criticism of Keynes' theory of liquidity preference in the context of an optimal portfolio analysis. This style of analysis 'does not appear in earlier Chicago writings on money, and so can itself be regarded as reflecting the influence of Keynes' theory of liquidity preference – an influence that was to manifest itself in' Friedman's writings.

The next four sections capture the response of Jacob Viner, Henry Simons and Knight to Keynes' and his *General Theory* (p. 395 [1932]; pp. 399–401 [1936/1964]; pp. 443–4 [1936]; pp. 447–70 [1937]). The following three chapters are part of a post-war symposium on monetary policy between Mints and Alvin Hansen, with a commentary by Howard Ellis (pp. 473–90 [1946]). Pages 493–525 consist of a previously unpublished essay which attempts to resolve aspects of the dispute by examining

Friedman's lecture notes and readings from Mints' Economics 330 in 1932–3.

The Evolving Chicago Response to Keynes and the Keynesians

While Keynes' *Treatise on Money* (1930) was apparently welcomed in Chicago, his *General Theory* (1936) was not. This appears to be true even for Paul Douglas, who was regarded as being on the left-wing component of the Chicago spectrum. Douglas (1931, 9; 1933a, 80) described the *Treatise* as 'brilliant' and 'the most stimulating single work on money'.[3] But he was 'not convinced' by 'the school of thought ... based on Keynes's *General Theory of Employment, Interest and Money*'. Instead, Douglas (1972, 455) preferred a *Treatise*-style explanation: 'the rate of interest was higher than the marginal productivity of capital'.

The period following Keynes' visit to Chicago was highly productive both for him (culminating in the *General Theory* and the Keynesian revolution) and for Simons (it corresponded with the effective beginning of his publishing career). After the publication of the *General Theory*, Keynes became a widely 'hated' figure in some American circles (Harrod, 1951, 448–9). Since Friedman learnt monetary economics at Chicago before this period it is important to precisely delineate the chronology and the components of this North American animosity towards Keynes and his disciples.

Before the *General Theory* Keynes and the Chicago economists had begun to proceed down divergent evolutionary paths as a section of the Cambridge school evolved into the Keynesian school. Keynes' journey reflected, in part, the influences of two young disciples, Richard Kahn and Joan Robinson. They (together with Austin Robinson, Pierro Sraffa and James Meade) were 'among the irritants' that propelled Keynes from the *Treatise* to the *General Theory* (Austin Robinson, 1992, 211). They were also among the irritants in the oyster that created the anti-Keynesian reaction.

The February 1946 Employment Act was perceived as having 'in effect, enacted Keynesian policies into law' (Friedman and Friedman, 1980, 122). In September 1946 Friedman returned to Chicago after a gap of eleven years. In between these two dates both Keynes and Henry Simons died: Keynes on 21 April 1946 aged 62, and Simons on 19 June 1946 aged 46, apparently by suicide (Coase, 1993, 244; Friedman and Friedman, 1998, 155). The post-war configuration was, in part, a dispute between the heirs of Keynes and the heirs of Simons.

There were at least five overlapping aspects to the anti-Keynesian reactions. First, there were some personal elements. Secondly, there was the political dimension of Keynesianism. Thirdly, there was an irritation at the manner in which Keynes and the Keynesians ridiculed their 'classical' predecessors. Fourthly, there was some resistance to the replacement of the quantity theory by the income–expenditure–multiplier. Finally, there was the contribution that Keynes made to policies such as tariffs and protection.

With respect to personal characteristics, economists sometimes see themselves as exerting an influence in the evolution of world history; but few would portray themselves individually as playing an heroic but tragic role in such a cosmic drama. Keynes (JMK, IX [1931], xvii), however, published a volume almost entitled *Essays in Prophesy and Persuasion*. Dropping the 'Prophesy' from the title he nevertheless claimed to have been a tortured Cassandra since the publication of the *Economic Consequences of the Peace*, 'painfully conscious that a cloud of witnesses would rise up against me and very few in my support'.

Keynes' attack on President Wilson in *Economic Consequences of the Peace* caused 'particular resentment'. Herbert Hoover regarded Keynes as 'one of the most conceited men he had ever met' (Stein, 1969, 134, 142). Keynes retorted that 'Attempts to humour or placate the Americans or anyone else seems quite futile' (Skidelsky, 1983, 342, xxii). Keynes had established himself as 'a person to listen to'. But the *New York Times* suggested that Keynes' attitude towards foreigners equated to Samuel Johnson's remark that 'So far as I can see, foreigners are mostly fools' ([1926] cited by Stein, 1969, 134, 484, n. 33).

With respect to his opponents, Keynes often saw stubborn reactionaries, not highly endowed with intelligence. In March 1933, he wrote to Kahn (who was then in the US) that 'it seems hardly an exaggeration that there are no longer any serious obstacles to a reasonable policy, except Neville Chamberlain, Hilton Young and, perhaps, the Governor [of the Bank of England]'. When Chamberlain, the Chancellor of the Exchequer, invited Keynes to discuss some of his recent articles, Keynes wrote to Kahn: 'Could it be that the Walls of Jericho are flickering?' (cited by Moggridge, 1992, 573).

During a visit to the US in 1917, Keynes did not like what he found and made 'a terrible impression for his rudeness' (JMK, XVI [1918], 264). He was not averse to ridiculing his disciples. In 1934, during a third visit, Keynes received a visit at his hotel from Calvin Hoover (1965, 173, 125). Using Keynes' bathroom, Hoover's careful use of only one towel was ridiculed by Keynes, who swept a bunch of clean towels to the floor so as to demonstrate how to stimulate the American economy. According to his disciple and first biographer, Keynes was 'not predisposed to admire the American way of life'; his preferred style of 'cultured' civilisation required 'ample domestic service' (Harrod, 1951, 4–5).[4]

Some of his more radical disciples displayed a similar propensity. In 1936, Roy Harrod and Hubert Henderson complained that '2 people in Cambridge together with a few undergraduates' were propagating the belief that those who did not accept the *General Theory* were 'intellectually inferior beings' (cited by Clarke, 1988, 308). Joan Robinson with her 'bleak Cambridge rudeness' generated a mixture of intense admiration and irritation, with the latter perhaps the dominant reaction (Turner, 1989; Skidelsky, 1992, 538; Tobin, 1972, 105; Tobin, 1978, 452).[5] In 1934, Kahn advised Robert Bryce (1996, 43) that when he took up his scholarship at Harvard he should boycott the lectures and seminars.

Two years previously, Kahn travelled to America on a boat appropriately called 'Majestic' (Marcuzzo, 2001, 22). From the US, Kahn wrote to Joan Robinson and Keynes of his contemptuousness of Americans: 'the people are so desperately dim, and far too frequently grubby into the bargain ... in respect of society, I had to lower my standards considerably, in respect of both age, eminence, intelligence and quality ... after watching the struggle of these wretched people I shall for the first time realise my good fortune in being a member of the King's High Table, and take more pleasure in its society than I had in the past'. Kahn was especially contemptuous of American academics: 'I believe that Americans being what they are, it is only the unfitted who were relegated to academic life ... I feel that if I wanted to do academic work in the States the thing to do would be to get a job at one of their banks'. At the University of Chicago, Kahn was disgusted by 'the grubbiness of their style of living' and the 'revolting food that is served up in all their halls and clubs' (15 February 1933, 8 January 1933, 27 February 1933, cited by Marcuzzo, 2001, 54–7).[6]

Kahn (15 January 1933) also reported to Joan Robinson that Viner tried to be 'extremely contemptuous of Cambridge ... Viner gave me proudly to understand that he never devotes more than an hour to the [Economic] Journal' and was 'very proud of not having read more than a few passages from the Treatise'.[7] Yet Viner (p. 395 [1932]) was (or had very recently been) full of praise for the diagnoses and remedies contained in *Essays in Persuasion*, which he described as being widely accepted as 'substantially and brilliantly right'. Moreover, Keynes stood 'head and shoulders' above other economists as a 'propagandist' whose work was 'undiluted by academic scruples to disclose all the qualifications and the uncertainties of his logical argument'. Keynes also displayed 'fearlessness in assigning to his opponents their appropriately low intelligence quotas ... Perhaps what the world has needed and most urgently needs today, is a few more Keynes'. Viner had a reputation for being a ruthless teacher who sought to maintain the strictest standards by humiliating students (Domar, 1992, 121; Minsky, 1985, 218; Samuelson, 1972, 5–6; Friedman and Friedman, 1998, 35; Stigler, 1988, 19–20; Becker, 1991, 145). In 1932–3, Friedman attended Viner's Economics 301 simultaneously with Mints' 330; such praise of Keynes could only have added to the impression that the *Treatise* was of great significance.

Viner (pp. 399–430 [1936/1964], 420, 427, 430) later highlighted the distinction between the 'heroic' Keynes of the 1940s and his American disciples. He continued to express strong reservations about the *General Theory.* Viner was not sympathetic to Keynes' 'after us the deluge' approach. He objected to the mythology (expressed by Seymour Harris) that the Keynesian 'truths' about the need for expansionary fiscal policy in times of depression needed to be 'repeated hundreds of times before they made the required impression'. Viner noted that he had made exactly that point in August 1931 and that his Chicago colleagues did not need 'to learn it from Keynes'.

With respect to the political dimension of Keynesianism, Schumpeter (1951, 287–8) saw sociological analogies between the Keynesian school and the Marxist school: 'a group that professes allegiance to One Master and One Doctrine'. Keynesianism became an especially suspect ideology during the post-war McCarthyite period. During the Great Inflation of the 1970s, *The New Economics* (Harris, 1947) became associated with *The New Inflation* (Jones, 1973). In consequence, anti-Keynesianism became as virulent as anti-Communism. Paul Sweezy (1996, 84, 78) reflected that the early 1930s was a time of uninhibited discussion; later this freedom of association 'came back to haunt people who weren't very careful during the 1930s. They were accused of being Communists and subversives'. Sweezy was uncertain at which point prior to 1936 the term 'Keynesian' became used as a 'general nomenclature', but it was clear that an economist could be 'a kind of left wing socialist Keynesian or a conservative business Keynesian'.

This aspect of the early Keynesian movement was apparent to Alvin Hansen by April 1933. Hansen's view was that 'it is wholly fallacious to assume that a government can, in a private capitalist economy, spend its way out of depression'. Hansen added that there were similarities between

Keynes' *Treatise* and Marx's *Das Kapital*: 'Both the truth and the error have been used by ardent propagandists in the political arena to support practical policies in which they believe' (Hansen and Tout, 1933, 342, 143).

The radical nature of some Keynesians was apparent to Paul Sweezy (1996, 76, 78) who returned to Harvard in 1932 after a year at the London School of Economics (LSE). Sweezy regarded himself at that time as 'a Marxist and as a radical' but noted that Joan Robinson was 'far to the left of many of the Marxists, in terms of her instincts and sympathies'. Sweezy (1934, 805, 807) reviewing Pigou's *Theory of Unemployment* in the *JPE*, noted that members of the 'Cambridge' school had some 'unpublished' arguments which purported to show that a reduction in nominal wages would not necessarily reduce real wages. The neoclassical view would 'receive the ascent of most economists'; the Cambridge school was interpreted as launching an assault on this paradigm.[8]

With respect to tariffs, on June 13 1930, the Senate passed the Hawley-Smoot tariff, which the President signed four days later. The previous month virtually every respectable American economist (including 1,038 AEA members) had signed a petition urging Congress to reject the bill (Hicks, 1960, 220–2). This led to what Paul Douglas (1972, 477) described as 'a deadly international trade war'. Albert Hart (1948, 370) described it as a 'notable event' in the 1930s '"economic warfare". This struggle was not merely one of the Nazis against the democratic powers, but a struggle in which "every man's hand was against every other"'. In their January 1932 *Memorandum* on Anti Depression Policy, Lauchlin Currie, Paul Theodore Ellsworth and Harry Dexter White (pp. 271–90 [1932]) noted that since 1925 all major countries had revised upwards their tariff schedules which had caused 'maladjustments which are now playing economic havoc ... The United States has been in the forefront of the building up of tariff walls; it is only fitting that she take the lead in the downward revision so necessary to economic sanity'.

In contrast, in July 1930, Keynes (JMK, XX 378, 488, 494–5) advised the British Prime Minister that he had 'become reluctantly convinced that some protectionist measures should be introduced'. As his first biographer noted, this was a 'momentous proposal'. When Keynes arrived to give a talk at Oxford, Harrod's (1951, 424–7) 'face fell' upon hearing that he planned to speak in favour of a revenue tariff. Harrod was so inconsolable that Keynes was obliged to talk about the much safer *Treatise* instead. According to Skidelsky (1983, xxii), Harrod 'believed that a bright future depended upon "selling" Keynes to the United States. This required downplaying all those aspects of Keynes' character and thought likely to give offence across the Atlantic'. Referring to Keynes' advocacy of protection, Harrod (1951, 428) asked: was Keynes 'a little too ready to be an iconoclast?'.

Prior to his visit to Chicago in 1931, Keynes (JMK, XX [1931], 501, 505, 519, 523) was obliged to defend his position. Perceiving the choice to be between tariffs and exchange rate flexibility Keynes explained that 'if I look into the bottom of my own heart, the feeling which I find there is … that a tariff is a crude departure from *laissez-faire*, which we have to adopt because we have at present no better weapon in our hands, but that it will be superseded in time, not by a return to *laissez-faire*, but by some more comprehensive scheme of national planning'. Keynes complained that 'new paths of thought have no appeal to the fundamentalists of free trade … I appeal for a reconsideration of the whole matter with a fresh head, and a clear one'.

Keynes' 1930–1 advocacy of tariffs caused 'a sensation' in Britain (JMK, XX, 489). It also led to a rejoinder – *Tariffs: the case examined* – by a group of LSE economists under the chairmanship of Sir William Beveridge (1932).[9] Joan Robinson (1962b, 84, 64) referred to this 'great outcry against Keynes' treachery towards Free Trade' and noted that Viner was the authority cited by the LSE economists. Viner (p. 395 [1932]) argued that Keynes was 'seriously wrong' in advocating that Britain join the 'crowded ranks of tariff sinners', had 'contributed greatly to a further weakening of the already waning faith of the English public in the virtues of free trade'. For Simons (1948 [1944], 1213; 1943, 443–4), tariffs were part of the government-sponsored 'racketeering' which his 'rules' were designed to thwart. Simons sought to defend 'Traditional Liberal Principles'; his 'faith and hope' for the post-war world rested on the construction of a 'free-trade front'.

Viner's (pp. 399–430 [1963], 430) admiration for Keynes was qualified both by the *General Theory* and 'the journalistic and polemical Keynes of the 1920's and early 1930's'. But judging by the reviews, this animosity appeared not to cloud the reception to the *Treatise*. Indeed, the only genuinely critical review of the *Treatise* came from Cambridge and from A. C. Pigou. Pigou (1931, 544) complained that 'There is too much carping at "current economic theory" – whatever precisely that may be; too much adverse comment upon classes of persons, "the bankers", "the financial press", and so on, names not specified; too many naively patronising remarks. It was, perhaps, a fault in Marshall that he discovered more truth in the writings of others than was actually there, and unduly depreciated his own contributions. There is no fault of that kind in Mr. Keynes!'

Dimand (1988, 56) noted that this was an 'extreme outlier among the reviewers'.

In May 1931, Pigou (JMK, XIII [1931], 214–8) wrote to Keynes indicating that he had suspected that the *Treatise* was purporting to offer a formula which 'revealed price changes which could not be revealed by the "Cambridge equation"'. Pigou was temporarily appeased. But as word spread about the developments that would lead to *The General Theory*, 'spies ... members of the fifth column' from London came to listen to Keynes' lectures (Austin Robinson, 1947, 40).

In 1934, Pigou gave a series of lectures at LSE, entitled *Economics in Practice*. In his first lecture, Pigou (1935, 22–4) made several cryptic comments about developments in Keynes' career since Marshall's death: 'Not long ago one of my most distinguished colleagues urged his fellow economists to "eschew the Treatise, pluck the day, fling pamphlets to the wind" [a reference to JMK, X [1924], 199]. A few years later he himself offered, and we gratefully received, a work with the title Treatise'. Keynes was apparently compared, unfavourably, to Marshall, whose generosity to his predecessors, according to Pigou, was 'a great man's fault, not a little man's ... Controversy for its own sake is a prodigious waste of time ... Are we, in our secret hearts, wholly satisfied with the manner, or manners, in which some of our controversies are carried on? A year or more ago, after the publication of an important book, there appeared an elaborate and careful critique of a number of particular passages in it. The author's answer was, not to rebut the criticisms, but to attack with violence another book, which the critic had himself written several years before! Body line bowling! The method of the duello! That kind of thing is surely a mistake. It is a mistake, not merely in general and in the abstract, but also for solid reasons of State. Economists in this country lack influence which – in their own opinion – they ought to have, largely because the public believe that on all topics they are hopelessly divided. Controversies conducted in the manner of Kilkenny cats do not help to dissipate this opinion'.

Pigou (1949, 21) acknowledged that both the *Treatise* and the *General Theory* 'broke that dogmatic slumber' which had descended upon interwar economics: 'The period of tranquillity was ended ... For this the credit is almost wholly due to Keynes'. Pigou (1953, 26–7) was also curious about 'the explanation of the tone of Keynes's criticisms ... the red flags for bulls'. Since autumn 1930, Keynes had been referring to Kahn as 'the little priest' (Moggridge, 1992, 532). In his LSE lectures, Pigou (1935, 2) referred to the 'priests' and 'priestesses', who regarded anyone in trade as 'being essentially inferior to oneself'. This – combined with an analogous generational conflict – was also a component of the American animosity to the Keynesians which increasingly revealed itself in the early 1930s.

In April 1931, Keynes made some remarks to an American radio audience which, according to Stein (1969, 145), were 'typical of many that alienated businessmen and endeared him to young economists'. The *New York Times* reported that Keynes had ridiculed the experts who 'talk much greater rubbish than an ordinary man can ever be capable of'. At Harvard there was a generational conflict in which the juniors regarded many of the seniors as '"retreads" who had outlived their usefulness'. Frank Taussig was 'the grand old man' of Harvard economics who liked to humiliate students with all the venom of a 'prosecuting attorney' (Mason, 1982, 394, 427; Douglas, 1972, 33). Taussig (1932, 356, 359–61) adopted a similar attitude towards what he regarded as 'quack' economic remedies: 'The doctors are sure that most of the proposed and advertised remedies for cancer are worthless, or worse than worthless – not only do no good, but may do harm. The economists have the same conclusion about sundry popular measures for depressions'. In his classification scheme, 'public and private charity ... this business of providing for all the claimants by indiscriminate relief has its dangers as well as limitations ... they may stand in the way of return to health'. Taussig was very uncertain about the benefits of public works: 'The very fact that public works are searched for in advance – that they are so to speak cooked up – indicates that they are not keenly wanted'. He also stated that he was 'unable to see that unemployment insurance or unemployment reserves can operate as a preventive'; they should be classed 'among the palliatives'.

A few months after this article was published, Kahn (3 March 1933) wrote to Keynes from Harvard, explaining that Taussig objected to Kahn's 'arrogance' and his 'impertinent' approach: he 'very much resented my abusive attitude towards the businessman ... He was appalled that a young man should imagine that he could venture to advise the experienced business man. This cocksure attitude of mind was typical of the Keynesian school, but was particularly deplorable in the young. Things were far more complicated than was allowed for in my philosophy'.[10]

Joan Robinson (1977, 8) located the immediate origins of the Keynesian revolution to 1929 'with a debate about the case for government loan expenditure on public works as a means of reducing unemployment ... a great storm of controversy broke out in Cambridge' when the *Treatise* was published. Advocacy of public works was acquiring some revolutionary implications. Joan Robinson told Keynes (JMK, XIV [1937], 149–9) her primary motive for writing a 'told-to-the-children' *Introduction to the Theory of Employment* was to provide ammunition for the Workers' Education Association. In her attempt to popularise the Keynesian message, Joan Robinson (1937, 126–7) noted that the debate over public works gave rise to 'violent conflicts of interest ... the adherents of laissez faire ... fear that, if it once became clear to the public that state intervention can reduce unemployment, the public might begin to think that state intervention could do much else besides'. Friedman (Vol. 1, pp. 33–51 [1956], 33) asserted that the 'subtle' inter-war Chicago quantity theory 'became a flexible and sensitive tool for interpreting movements in aggregate economic activity and for developing relevant policy prescriptions'. In contrast, Joan Robinson (1937, chapter 10, appendix) contemptuously explained that 'For detailed discussion of changes in trade activity the Quantity Equation is a weak and treacherous instrument ... in inexpert hands the Quantity Equation can lead to great confusion'. She later referred to the 'pitiful state of confusion' epitomised in the 1930s by the work of Friedrich Hayek and Henry Simons: 'Prices were conceived to be something to do with money'. In the post-war period the quantity theory continued to be 'so implausible' (Robinson 1972, 2, 5).

Kahn's first multiplier paper appeared in June 1931. Kahn (1933) presented his American multiplier essay on 'Public Works and Inflation' at the 1932 joint AEA-American Statistical Association meeting in Cincinnati. After the meeting Kahn (10 February 1933) wrote to Joan Robinson about the 'filthy kind of bilge' which passed for monetary thought amongst those in America who had not been influenced by Keynes (cited by Marcuzzo, 2001, 59). Kahn (30 January 1933) informed Keynes that the 1932 AEA meeting 'provided a most shocking spectacle. These people are still living in the Dark Ages. It was all about the helplessness of trying to expand the economy ... I am thinking that the only way to save humanity is to lead a campaign against the Quantity Theory. I tried it on the [Chicago] Graduate Club here and they didn't very much like it, but didn't quite know what to say. These people can see nothing absurd in the president elect being "opposed to currency inflation but in favour of credit inflation". I am enjoying the spectacle'.[11]

Kahn's Chicago audience may not have enjoyed his sarcastic and supercilious assault on orthodox economics. According to his handwritten notes, Kahn set out the 'Quantity Equation for hairpins' which Joan Robinson (1933, 22, 23, 26) wrote up in October 1933 for the first issue of *Review of Economic Studies*. Orthodox economists were portrayed as ridiculous figures, analogous to the Pope seeking to outlaw bobbed hair on moral grounds. The 'violent revolution' which had taken place in Cambridge after the publication of the *Treatise* had left 'many academic economists ... bewildered'. The 'Analysis of Output' had dethroned the 'Theory of Money ... once Mr Keynes had shown us how to crack the egg, it appears the most natural thing in the world to attack the interesting part of the problem directly, instead of through the devious route of the Quantity Theory of Money'. Keynes himself had failed 'to realize the nature of the revolution that he was carrying through'. However, 'once it becomes clear what has happened the confusion disappears'.

Kahn's (1984, 170–1) 'antipathy to the Quantity Theory of Money dated from boyhood'. His animosity made an impression on his audience: 'The long and short of Mr Kahn's method of discussion is that, as soon as he notices the faintest trace of 'quantity theory' he no longer bothers about the specific problem or the specific argument in question, but tackles the adversary by trying to give him a lesson about the true meaning of that ill-fated doctrine' (Neisser, 1936, 148).

Keynes' (JMK, XXI, 171–8) essay on the multiplier was published on April Fools Day, 1933. On Independence Day, 1933, Keynes wrote that: 'What I call the Multiplier ... may in the United States today be very large indeed' (cited by Skidelsky, 1992, 491). Kahn (1933, 168, 173) argued that for recovery it was necessary to turn 'to the state ... it is only in this kind of way that the wheels of private investment and spending can be set revolving so that the system could be left to carry on once again under its own momentum ... This secondary employment, which, if I am right, is of an extraordinary magnitude, is usually completely ignored in discussions on the adequacy and the cost of various measures for dealing with unemployment'. On 15 April 1933, Alexander Sachs, having just received a visit from Kahn, wrote enthusiastically to the prominent New Dealer, Raymond Moley, about the much larger value of the American multiplier relative to the British (Freidel, 1972, 430). Joan Robinson (1937, Chapter III) reiterated this message.

On 31 December 1933, Keynes (JMK, XXI [1933], 294) published an 'Open Letter to the President' in the *New York Times* in which he referred to 'a crude economic doctrine commonly known as the quantity theory of money'. To Americans, Keynes' letter sounded 'like a letter from a school teacher to the very rich father of a very dull pupil' (Stein, 1969, 150). In May 1934, Keynes met both Rex Tugwell and President Franklin D. Roosevelt with whom he may have taken the opportunity to discuss the multiplier; this was certainly the subject of his conversation with the Secretary of Labor (Perkins, 1946, 226; Barber, 1996, 83). Some economists, however, believed that the secondary employment components of the multiplier were 'largely imaginary' (Kazakevich, 1935, 351). In August 1934, possibly in response to this type of scepticism, Roosevelt, at a meeting of the National Emergency Council, asked for a precise calculation of the multiplier associated with the public works construction projects. He was told that it would 'double to triple the numbers directly employed' (Seligman and Cornwell, 1965, 131, 276).

Douglas (1933b, 52–4) supported countercyclical budgetary policy operating through unemployment insurance to 'lesson the violence of business fluctuations and hence provide a net stabilising effect'. Douglas explained that the world behaved differently from the way 'most of us were taught and in turn taught others ... this naïve view has been well exposed by Wicksell and Keynes'. Douglas then proceeded to make a precise multiplier calculation of 2.8 (1933c, 12; 1935, 125). Even some Keynesians, such as Samuelson (1939, 75), complained that the Keynes–Kahn multiplier was becoming an 'extremely simplified mechanism ... in danger of hardening into a dogma'.

Shortly after Roosevelt's inauguration, Keynes' name became closely connected to the New Deal. In June 1933, Calvin Hoover (1965, 149–50) returned to the US 'obsessed' by the potential parallels between what he had observed in Nazi Germany and the consequences of maintaining the 'orthodox economics' that had, he thought, hitherto dominated Washington: 'I was no longer an orthodox economist. I had become a "Keynesian" as early as had Keynes himself'. In the *Theory of Unemployment*, Pigou (1933, 155–6) argued that 'all gratuitous payments to poor people and all social services' would reduce the labour demand schedule. Seymour Harris (1934, 314, 324; 1935, 21, 43) regarded this as 'an offset to the excessive influence of inflation and purchasing power theories'. Pigou was interpreted as having taken 'an anti-Keynes and anti-Roosevelt Administration position' and being hostile to the 'Keynes-Kahn wing of the Cambridge school'.

Thus Keynes became known as the 'father of the "new" or "non-Hoover" economics ... "New Deal" and "Keynesianism" later became synonymous profanities to some people' (Stein, 1969, 36, 147). This aroused the suspicions that he was 'an evil spirit' (Harrod, 1951, 448–9). Keynes reinforced this association. In spring 1934, during a further visit to the United States, the 'first thing' Keynes asked Calvin Hoover (1965, 172) was 'What is this "Brain Trust" I read about?'. In June 1934, Keynes presented an early version of parts of the *General Theory* to the American Political Economy Club. Keynes ridiculed 'flat earth' microeconomic solutions to real world problems which required 'central controls' and 'sufficient effective demand'. Keynes learnt first hand of the depth of business animosity towards the New Deal. Yet he 'commended Washington's efforts to New York. The New Deal, he said, had aroused his 'deepest sympathy'' (Skidelsky, 1992, 504–7; Moggridge, 1992, 582; JMK, XIII, 456–68; Winch, 1969, 234).

Ex-President Herbert Hoover also reinforced a supposed connection between the New Deal, Marx, Keynes and inflation. In October 1936, during the US Presidential election campaign, Hoover stated that the 'New Deal attack upon free institutions has emerged as the transcendent issue in America'. During his Presidency he had 'refused national plans to put the government into business in competition with its citizens. That was born of Karl Marx. I vetoed the idea of recovery through stupendous spending to prime the pump. That was born of a British professor ... I stopped attempts at currency inflation ... That was born of the early Brains Trusters' (cited by Leuchtenburg, 1968, 203–4).

The same amalgam of suspects reappeared during the post-war anti-communist hysteria. In *God and Man at Yale*, William F. Buckley Jr made what was regarded (in the Preface) as a 'devastating' case against the Yale Economics Department. Students were exposed to textbooks which contained material 'brewed out of Keynes, the Fabians, and Karl Marx himself' without the countervailing arguments of Ludwig von Mises, Friedrich Hayek and Knight (Chamberlin, 1951, ix).

There were other tensions at Chicago in the 1930s. Kahn (30 January 1933) referred to Douglas as one of Chicago's 'minor men' who he 'mildly' liked.[12] But Samuelson (1996, 149–50, 154–5) recalled that Douglas was 'a reflationist, and not on very good terms with Simons and Knight; they regarded him as a power-hungry do-gooder'. Kahn (15 January 1933) reported to Joan Robinson that Douglas' 'work has been almost completely ignored over here, where he is regarded as a somewhat silly sort of communist politician' (see also Douglas, 1976, 905).[13] Shortly afterwards, the Chicago Economics Department erupted into a full-scale internal Civil War. This was 'Academic Life on the Battlefront' with Douglas pitted against Knight and his disciples, in particular Simons (Stigler, 1988, chapter 12; Neff, 1973, 109; Patinkin, 1980, 5, n8). Friedman recalled that Douglas and Knight were at 'very serious odds with one another. There was a feud' (cited by Blumenthal, 1986, 96–7).

Shortly after this feud, Simons (1962 [1936]) created what Richard Selden (1962, 323) described as the 'Rules Party' with his 'Rules Versus Authorities in Monetary Policy'. In the same month (February 1936) Keynes (1936, 164, 220–1, 378) explained that he had become 'somewhat sceptical of the success of a merely monetary policy directed towards influencing the rate of interest. I expect to see the State, which is in a position to calculate the marginal efficiency of capital-goods on long views and on the basis of the general social advantage, taking an even greater responsibility for directly organising investment ... I conceive, therefore, that a somewhat comprehensive socialisation of investment will prove the only means of securing an approximation to full employment'.

Samuelson (1996, 148) recalled that 'from 1932 to 1936 I was besotted on Frank Knight'. Samuelson (1992, 239) had been taught at Chicago 'that business freedom and personal freedoms have to be strongly linked'. But the Keynesians argued that business freedom had to be curtailed in the interests of macroeconomic stability. In his review of the *General Theory*, Knight (pp. 437–60 [1937], 456) complained that Keynes was using the 'the language of the soap box reformer' with 'phrases like socialisation of investment'. According to his disciples, Keynes 'trusted to human intelligence. He hated enslavement by rules. He wanted governments to have discretion and he wanted economists to come to their assistance in the exercise of that discretion' (Cairncross, 1978, 47–8). In Aaron Director's (1948, v) judgement, Keynes' work provided the foundations for 'collectivism' while Simons' work provided the foundations for 'freedom and equality'.

Simons (pp. 433–4 [1936]) believed that the *General Theory* could easily become 'the economic bible of a fascist movement'. Keynes' *Treatise*, like the *General Theory* was 'full of brilliant insights and occasionally devastating criticisms of other writers'; but the *General Theory* was 'a revision (if not a repudiation)' of the first volume of the *Treatise*. Keynes had 'now' embarked on a mission which Simons found repellent: an authentic genius 'becoming the academic idol of our worst cranks and charlatans'.

Between 1936 and 1951 the Keynesian and Chicagoan paths became even more distinctly divergent. Some of the American Keynesians were 'more royalist than the King' (Stein, 1969, 162). The anti-Keynesian economists who briefed Herbert Corey (1944, 39) drew analogies between Alvin Hansen's proposals and the concentration of power in Stalin's Russia: 'They ask what is it if it is not State Socialism in high gear'. Herbert Stein (1995, 11, 220) was a student at Chicago when the *General Theory* was published: 'As a contemporary of mine at Chicago, Albert Hart, has said, one could be pro-Keynesian or anti-Keynesian, but one could no longer be pre-Keynesian'.[14]

Hansen was regarded as the American Keynes. Simons (1939, 275) complained that if Hansen' proposals would generate 'a continuing contest between the monetary authority seeking to raise employment and trade-unions seeking to raise wage rates'. Simons also bemoaned that 'the gods are surely on his side. What he proposes is exactly what many of us, in our most realistic and despairing moods, foresee ahead as the outcome of recent trends'. If Hansen succeeded in establishing a monetary system 'dictated by the *ad hoc* recommendations of economists like himself ... the outlook is dark indeed'.

Notes

[1] Patinkin (1952; 1956; pp. 347–69 [1975], 355) interpreted the *General Theory* as a dynamic theory of disequilibrium rather than a static theory of unemployment equilibrium. Referring to 'the mechanics of disequilibrium states' Clower (1969 [1965], 280) argued that the 'Keynesian consumption function and other market relations involving income as an independent variable cannot be derived explicitly from any existing theory of general equilibrium', adding that 'This was apparently overlooked by Patinkin [1956] when he formulated his 'general theory' of macroeconomics'. In his editorial commentary in *Monetary Theory Selected Readings*, Clower (1969, 121) suggested that 'Patinkin's conceptual universe now appears to be just a more precise and elaborate portrait of the barter world of Mill, Walras and Marshall, its only novel feature being that "money" appears among the set of commodities bartered. The significance of Patinkin's work thus lies not so much in what he says about monetary theory as in what he unintentionally reveals about the analytical and empirical weaknesses of established price theory'.

[2] Patinkin (1979, 157) thought that Keynes' 1931 performance in Chicago was an immodest 'song of praise to the *Treatise* ... Keynes apparently knew the Bible – and on various occasions (e.g. the "widow's cruse") even alluded to it – but the verse "Let another man praise thee, and not thine own mouth" (Proverbs 27:2) does not seem to have been one of his favourites'. But Keynes' fiscal policy prescriptions preceded advances in his theory. As he directing his theoretical vision towards the *General Theory* it was 'like the Children of Israel at the foot of Mount Sinai proclaiming, "we shall do – and we shall listen"'.

[3] Laidler (1999, 223) noted that the quantity theory tradition to be found in Douglas and Director (1931) was 'the Cambridge version, as developed by Keynes (1923)'.

[4] Keynes, however, explained to his mother that he could live in Canada (Moggridge, 1992, 767).

[5] Even to her admirers she could be highly offensive (Harcourt, 1993; 1995a; 1995b). When John Kenneth Galbraith (1981, 63) visited her in Cambridge in the early fifties, he asked who the promising young Cambridge economists were. Robinson 'looked at me sternly, which in her case could be very stern indeed, and said, "My dear Ken, we were the last good generation"'.

[6] I am grateful to Don Moggridge for pointing out to me that Kahn's diet was strictly kosher at this time.

[7] Richard Kahn Papers, RFK/13/90/1/44–51.

[8] The multiplier that Sweezy believed undermined the Cambridge view was driven by an expansion of purchases from non-wage earners' income caused by the cut in money wages.

[9] After Britain left the gold standard, Keynes abandoned his advocacy of a tariff. On 28 September 1931 he wrote to *The Times* that 'the immediate question for attention is not a tariff but the currency question' (JMK, IX, 243; Moggridge, 1992, 529).

[10] Keynes Papers, L/K/43–4.

[11] Keynes Papers, L/K/35–8. Kahn's judgment is supported by Willis and Chapman (1935, 56) who report that in 1933–4 amongst public officials and their economic advisers there was an 'uncritical acceptance of the view that changes in the money unit would be immediately reflected in similar changes of commodity prices'.

[12] Keynes Papers, L/K/35–8.

[13] Richard Kahn Papers, RFK/13/90/1/44–51.

[14] See Hart 1948, vii. Stein continued: 'the Chicagoans took a middle-of-the-road, "none of the above" point of view' towards the *General Theory*.

Bibliography

Arestis, P. and Sawyer, M., *A Biographical Dictionary of Dissenting Economists* (Cheltenham, England, Edward Elgar, 1992).

Barber, W. J., *Designs Within Disorder: Franklin D. Roosevelt, the Economists, and the Shaping of American Economic Policy, 1933–1945* (Cambridge, Cambridge UP, 1996).

Becker, G., 'Milton Friedman' in Shils (ed), *Remembering the University of Chicago …* (Chicago, Chicago UP, 1991).

Beveridge, W. *et al.*, *Tariffs: the Case Examined*, by a committee of economists under the chairmanship of Sir William Beveridge (London, Longmans, Green, 1932).

Blumenthal. S., *The Rise of the Counter-Establishment from Conservative Ideology to Political Power* (New York, The *Times*, 1986).

Bryce, R., 'Robert Bryce' in Colander and Landreth (eds), *The Coming of Keynesianism to America* (Cheltenham, England, Edward Elgar, 1996).

Buckley, W. F. Jn, *God and Man at Yale* (Chicago, Henry Regnery, 1951).

Cairncross, A., 'Keynes and the Planned Economy' in Thirwall (ed.), *Keynes and Laissez-Faire* (London, Macmillan, 1978).

Chamberlain, J., 'Introduction' in Buckley, *God and Man at Yale* (Chicago, Henry Regenery, 1951).

Clower, R., 'The Keynesian Counter Revolution: A Theoretical Appraisal' in Clower (ed.), *Monetary Theory. Selected Readings* (Harmondsworth, England, Penguin, 1969).

Coase, R., 'Aaron Director', in P. Newman (ed.), *The New Palgrave Dictionary of Law and Economics* (London, Macmillan, 1998).

Colander, D. and Landreth, H. (eds), *The Coming of Keynesianism to America* (Cheltenham, England, Edward Elgar, 1996).

Corey, H., 'Oh, Debt, Where is Thy Sting!', *Nation's Business*, (June 1994), pp. 34–9.

Dimand, R., *The Origins of the Keynesian Revolution: The Development of Keynes' Theory of Employment and Output* (Cheltenham, England, Edward Elgar, 1988).

Director, A., 'Prefatory Notice' in Simons (ed.), *Economic Policy for a Free Society* (Chicago, Chicago UP, 1948).

Domar, E., 'How I Tried to Become an Economist' in Szenberg (ed.), *Eminent Economists: Their Life Philosophies* (Cambridge, Cambridge UP, 1992)

Douglas, P. H., *World Unemployment and its Reduction through International Co-operation* (London, League of Nations Union, 1931).

——, *Know America: Its Ills and Cures* (Chicago, Buti-Lami Press, 1933a).

——, 'Economics of Unemployment Relief – Discussion', *American Economic Review*, XXIII:1 (March supplement 1933b), pp. 51–4.

——, *Collapse or Cycle?* (Chicago, American Library Association, 1933c).

——, *Controlling Depressions* (London, George Allen and Unwin, 1935).

——, *In the Fullness of Time* (New York, Harcourt Brace Jovanovich, 1972).

——, 'The Cobb-Douglas Production Function Once Again: Its History, Its Testing, and Some New Empirical Values', *Journal of Political Economy*, 84:5 (1976), pp. 903–15.

Fels, R. (ed.), *The Second Crisis of Economic Theory* (Morristown, NJ, General Learning Press, 1972).

Freidel, F., *Franklin D. Roosevelt Launching the New Deal* (Boston, Little Brown, 1972).

Friedman, M., *The Counter-Revolution in Monetary Theory* (London, Institute of Economic Affairs, 1970).

——, 'A Theoretical Framework for Monetary Analysis' in R. J. Gordon (ed.), *Milton Friedman's Monetary Framework: A Debate with his Critics* (Chicago, Chicago UP, 1974), pp. 1–62.

——, 'Comments on the Critics' (1972) in R. J. Gordon (ed.), *Milton Friedman's Monetary Framework: A Debate with his Critics* (Chicago, Chicago UP, 1974), pp. 132–4.

Friedman, M. and Friedman, R., *Free to Choose: A Personal Statement* (New York, Harcourt Brace Jovanovich, 1980).

——, *Two Lucky People: Memoirs* (Chicago, Chicago UP, 1998).

Galbraith, J. K., *A Life in Our Times: Memoirs* (Boston, Houghton Mifflin, 1981).

Greenfield, H. I., Levenson, A. M. Hamovitch, W. and Rotwein, E. (eds), *Theory for Economic Efficiency: Essays in Honour of Abba P. Lerner* (London, MIT Press, 1979).

Hansen, A. H. and Tout H., 'Annual Survey of Business Cycle Theory: Investment and Saving in Business Cycle Theory', *Econometrica* (April 1933), pp. 119–47.

Harcourt, G. C., 'Joan Robinson' in Arestis and Sawyer (eds), *A Biographical Dictionary of Dissenting Economists* (Cheltenham, England, Edward Elgar, 1992).

——, 'Talking About Joan Robinson', *Review of Social Economy*, LIII:1 (Spring 1995a), pp. 31–64.

——, 'Joan Robinson 1903–1983', *Economic Journal* (September 1995b), pp. 1128–243.

Harrod, R., *The Life of John Maynard Keynes* (London, Macmillan, 1951).

Harris, S. E., 'Professor Pigou's Theory of Unemployment', *Quarterly Journal of Economics*, 49 (1934), pp. 286–324.

—— (ed.), *The New Economics: Keynes' Influence on Theory and Policy* (New York, Dennis Dobson, 1947).

Hart, A. G., *Money, Debt and Economic Activity* (Englewood Cliffs, NJ, Prentice Hall, 1948).

Hicks, J. D., *Republican Ascendancy 1921–1933* (New York, Harper and Row, 1960).

Hoover, C., *Memoirs of Capitalism, Communism, and Nazism* (Durham, Duke UP, 1965).

Jones, A., *The New Inflation: The Politics of Prices and Incomes* (London, Penguin, 1973).

Kahn, R. F., 'The Relation of Home Investment to Unemployment', *Economic Journal*, (June 1931), pp. 173–98.

——, 'Public Works and Inflation', *Journal of the American Statistical Association*, Supplement (1933), pp. 168–73.

——, *The Making of Keynes' General Theory* (Cambridge, Cambridge UP, 1984).

Kazakevich, V. D., 'Inflation and public works', in Willis and Chapman (eds), *The Economics of Inflation: the Basis of Contemporary American Monetary Policy* (New York, Columbia UP, 1935).

Keynes, J. M., *A Treatise on Money: The Applied Theory of Money* (London, Macmillan, 1930).

——, *The General Theory of Employment Interest and Money* (London, Macmillan, 1936).

——, *Collected Writings of John Maynard Keynes* (London, Macmillan, 1972–89).

Leijonhufvud, A., 'Keynes and the Keynesians: A Suggested Interpretation', in Clower (ed.), *Monetary Theory. Selected Readings* (Harmondsworth, England, Penguin, 1969).

Leuchtenburg, W. E. (ed.), *The New Deal: A Documentary History* (New York, Harper and Row, 1968).

Lutz, F. and Mints, L. (eds), *Readings in Monetary Theory* (American Economic Association; London, George Allen and Unwin, 1952).

Marcuzzo, C. (ed.), *Economists in Cambridge: The Letters Between Kahn, Keynes, Harrod, J. Robinson, Sraffa, Kaldor and Hayek, 1921–1946* (Dipartmento di Scienze Economiche, discussion papers, 2001).

Mason, E. S., 'The Harvard Department of Economics from the Beginning to World War II', *Quarterly Journal of Economics*, XCVII:3 (August 1982), pp. 383–433.

Minsky, H., 'Beginnings', *Banca Nazionale Del Lavoro Quarterly Review* (1985), pp. 211–21.

Moggridge, D., *Maynard Keynes: An Economist's Biography* (London, Routledge, 1992).

Neff, J. U., *Search for Meaning: The Autobiography of a Nonconformist* (Washington, Public Affairs Press, 1973).

Neisser, H., 'A Rejoinder', *Review of Economics and Statistics* (August 1936), pp. 147–8.

Newman, P. (ed.), *The New Palgrave Dictionary of Law and Economics* (London, Macmillan, 1998).

Patinkin, D., 'Keynes and Econometrics: On the Interaction Between Macroeconometric Theory Measurement in the Interwar Period', *Econometrica*, 44:6 (November 1976), pp. 1091–123.

——, 'The Development of Keynes's Policy Thinking' in Greenfield *et al.* (eds), *Theory for Economic Efficiency: Essays in Honour of Abba P. Lerner* (London, MIT Press, 1979).

——, 'New Material on the Development of Keynes' Monetary Thought', *History of Political Economy*, 12:1 (1980), pp. 1–28.

——, 'On Differing Interpretations of the General Theory', *Proceedings of the British Academy*, LXXV (1989), pp. 201–42.

Perkins, F., *The Roosevelt I Knew* (New York, Harper, 1946).

Pigou, A. C., 'Mr. Keynes and Money', *Nation and Athenaeum* (24 January 1931).

——, *Economics in Practice: Six Lectures on Current Issues* (London, Macmillan, 1935).

——, 'The Economist' in *John Maynard Keynes, 1883–1946, Fellow and Bursar* (memoir prepared by the Direction of the Council of King's College, Cambridge, 1949).

——, *Alfred Marshall and Current Economic Thought* (London, Macmillan, 1953).

Robinson, E. A. G., 'John Maynard Keynes, 1883–1946', *Economic Journal* (March 1947), pp. 1–68.

——, 'My Apprenticeship as an Economist' in Szenberg (ed.), *Eminent Economists: Their Life Philosophies* (Cambridge, Cambridge UP, 1992).

Robinson, J., 'The Theory of Money and the Analysis of Output', *Review of Economic Studies*, 1:1 (October 1933), pp. 22–6.

——, *Introduction to the Theory of Employment* (New York, Macmillan, 1937).

——, 'Review of H.G. Johnson's *Money, Trade and Economic Growth*', *Economic Journal*, LXXII:287 (September 1962a), pp. 690–2.

——, *Economic Philosophy* (London, Penguin, 1962b).

——, 'The Second Crisis of Economic Theory' in R. Fels (ed.), *The Second Crisis of Economic Theory* (Morristown, NJ, General Learning Press, 1972).

——, 'Michael Kalecki on the Economics of Capitalism', *Oxford Bulletin of Economics and Statistics*, Special Issue (February 1977), pp. 7–18.

Samuelson, P. A., 'Interactions Between the Multiplier Analysis and the Principle of Acceleration', *Review of Economic Statistics*, 21 (May 1939), pp. 75–8.

——, 'Jacob Viner', *Journal of Political Economy* (January–February 1972), pp. 5–11.

——, 'My Life Philosophy: Policy Credos and Working ways' in Szenberg (ed.), *Eminent Economists: Their Life Philosophies* (Cambridge, Cambridge UP, 1992).

——, 'Paul Anthony Samuelson (b. 1915)' in Colander and Landreth (eds), *The Coming of Keynesianism to America* (Cheltenham, England, Edaward Elgar, 1996).

Schumpeter, J., *Ten Great Economists: From Marx to Keynes* (New York, Oxford UP, 1951).

Selden, R. T., 'Stable Monetary Growth' in Yeager (ed.), *In Search of a Monetary Constitution* (Cambridge, Mass., Harvard UP, 1962).

Seligman, L. G. and Cornwell, E. F., *New Deal Mosaic: Roosevelt Confers with his National Emergency Council 1933–1936* (Eugene, Oregon, University of Oregon Books, 1965).

Shils, E. (ed.), *Remembering the University of Chicago: Teachers, Scientists and Scholars* (Chicago, Chicago UP, 1991).

Simons, H. C., 'Review of Hansen's *Full Recovery or Stagnation?*', *Journal of Political Economy* (1939), pp. 272–6.

——, 'Postwar Economic Policy: Some Traditional Liberal Principles' *American Economic Review*, XXXIII:1 (March 1943), pp. 432–45.

——, *Economic Policy for a Free Society* (Chicago, Chicago UP, 1948).

——, 'Rules Versus Authorities in Monetary Policy' reprinted in E. J. Hamilton, A. Rees and H. G. Johnson (eds), *Landmarks in Political Economy* (Chicago, Chicago UP, 1962).

Skidelsky, R., *John Maynard Keynes: Hopes Betrayed 1883–1920* (London, Macmillan, 1983).

——, *John Maynard Keynes: The Economist as Saviour 1920–1937* (London, Macmillan, 1992).

Stein, H., *The Fiscal Revolution in America* (Chicago, Chicago UP, 1969).

——, *On the Other Hand ... Essays on Economics, Economists, and Politics* (Washington, DC, AEI Press, 1995).

Stigler, G. J., *Memoirs of an Unregulated Economist* (New York, Basic Books, 1988).

Sweezy, P., 'Professor Pigou's Theory of Unemployment', *Journal of Political Economy*, 42 (1934), pp. 800–11.

——, 'Paul Sweezy' in Colander and Landreth (eds), *The Coming of Keynesianism to America* (Cheltenham, England, Edward Elgar, 1996).

Szenberg, M. (ed.), *Eminent Economists: Their Life Philosophies* (Cambridge, Cambridge UP, 1992).

Taussig, F. W., 'Doctors, Economists and the Depression', *Harper's Monthly Magazine*, 165 (1932), pp. 355–65.

Thirlwall, A. P. (ed.), *Keynes and Laissez-Faire* (London, Macmillan, 1978).

Tobin, J. 'Cambridge (U.K.) versus Cambridge (Mass)', *The Public Interest* (1972), pp. 102–9.

——, 'Harry Gordon Johnson', *Proceedings of the British Academy* (1978), pp. 442–58.

Turner, M. S., *Joan Robinson and the Americans* (Armonk, NY, M. E. Sharpe, 1989).

Willis, H. P. and Chapman, J. M., *The Economics of Inflation: The Basis of Contemporary American Monetary Policy* (New York, Columbia UP, 1935).

Winch, D., *Economics and Policy: A Historical Study* (London, Hodder and Stoughton, 1969).

Yeager, L. B. (ed.), *In Search of a Monetary Constitution* (Cambridge, Mass., Harvard UP, 1962).

'Keynesian Monetary Theory and the Cambridge School'

D. Patinkin, 'Keynesian monetary theory and the Cambridge School' in H. G. Johnson and A. R. Nobay (eds), *Issues in Monetary Economics* (London, Oxford UP, 1974), pp. 3–30.

KEYNESIAN MONETARY THEORY AND THE CAMBRIDGE SCHOOL*

DON PATINKIN
(*Hebrew University of Jerusalem*)

I AM indeed honoured to be invited here this evening in order to present the Sir Dennis Robertson lecture. I still remember with pleasure my first—and, unfortunately for me, only—meeting with Robertson some twenty years ago, as well as the discussions we continued to carry on by correspondence in subsequent years. And I find it particularly appropriate that my subject for this lecture deals with the very school of which Robertson himself was such an illustrious member.

Let me, then, turn to my subject. The monetarist revival of the last decade and more has been accompanied—especially in recent years—by a renewed interest in the nature of the quantity theory before Keynes. In this connection it seems to me that present-day adherents of this theory have claimed too much for it—and correspondingly too little for the Keynesian theory.[1]

The exaggerated claims for the quantity theory have expressed themselves in the attempt (especially by Milton Friedman) to present Keynes's monetary theory not as a new theory, but as a variation on the Cambridge cash-balance theory. It is this contention that I shall here examine—and, on the basis of this examination,

* I am very grateful to Stanley Fischer for helpful comments on an earlier draft. I am also indebted to Lord Robbins for illuminating discussions of various points dealt with here.

I wish to thank Allan Drazen and Akiva Offenbacher for their assistance. I am also indebted to the Central Research Fund of the Hebrew University of Jerusalem, and to the Israel Academy of Sciences and Humanities for research grants to cover the costs of technical assistance.

The reader is asked to keep in mind that this paper was delivered as the opening address of a conference—and to excuse accordingly various facetious remarks. A version of the paper has been previously published in the journal of the Banco Nationale De Lavoro.

[1] In what follows, I shall make free use of Patinkin (1969, 1972a, and 1972b).

reject. And lest I be misunderstood (though there is really no reason that I should), I should like to emphasize at the outset that this examination should not be interpreted as a criticism of the Cambridge school. For I would certainly consider it unjustified to criticize these economists for not having fully understood and integrated into their thinking what we have succeeded in learning only in the course of the subsequent development of Keynesian monetary theory. My criticism is only of those who make exaggerated claims for the Cambridge economists.

Before embarking on this examination, I would like to say a few words about my general approach to doctrinal history—which is certainly not an unusual one. This approach can be succinctly summarized by the statement that isolated passages do not a theory make. Instead, one of our major concerns in the study of the history of theory is the determination of the extent to which ideas expressed at various points in a work are integrated into—and hence really part of—its main theoretical framework. And this accordingly will be my major concern this evening.

Another point that I should clarify at the outset is my use of the terms 'quantity theory' and 'Keynesian theory'. By the first of these I mean—quite pragmatically—the monetary theory expounded at the end of the nineteenth century and through the late 1920s by Irving Fisher in the U.S. and by the Cambridge school (Marshall, Pigou, Robertson, Lavington—and the younger Keynes) in this country.

By 'Keynesian monetary theory' I mean the one developed in the *General Theory* and the literature to which it gave rise—though I should note that the aspect of the theory that is my primary concern here (namely, the treatment of money from the viewpoint of the choice of an optimum portfolio) is in some respects more precisely developed in Keynes's *Treatise on Money* and Hicks's 'Suggestion for Simplifying the Theory of Money'.[2] In so far as the later development is concerned, I have in mind in particular the work of James Tobin and his colleagues. And in a small voice I add: and Milton Friedman too. A small voice—because I do not want right at the beginning of this Conference to run the risk of setting off a violent argument. Nor do I want to offend the man who is really responsible for my being here this evening; for surely you

[2] Keynes (1930, i, pp. 36, 140–6, 248–57); Hicks (1935). Shackle (1967, pp. 222–7), however, claims that there are important differences between these two treatments.

would not have brought me all the way from Israel to speak on this antiquarian subject in a conference devoted to such currently pressing matters as European monetary integration, commercial bank behaviour, and U.K. monetary policy in the 1970s, were it not for the reawakened interest in the doctrinal history of the quantity theory that has been sparked in recent years by Friedman's repeated and provocative assertions about its alleged nature.

By the foregoing definition of the quantity theory, I obviously do not mean to imply that Fisher and the Cambridge school are coterminous with the quantity theory. Indeed, at the same time that they were doing their work, Léon Walras in Switzerland was developing his version of the quantity theory in terms of the *encaisse désirée*. And Knut Wicksell in Sweden (whom I continue to regard—by virtue of his own repeated declarations—as a quantity theorist) was making his invaluable contribution to our understanding of the way the quantity theory manifests itself through the interest-rate mechanism in an economy with a banking system.

But since neither Walras nor Wicksell had the sense to write in English, the sad fact—that at the time prompted the gentle chiding of Myrdal (1939 (1933), p. 8) about 'the attractive Anglo-Saxon kind of unnecessary originality'—the sad fact is that Wicksell's work, for instance, did not become known in this country until the mid-1920s. Furthermore—if I make the proper inference from Keynes's *Treatise* (i, pp. 186–8, 196–9, and especially p. 199, footnote 2)—the development of Keynes's thinking even then was not influenced by Wicksell. For this reason the work of Walras and Wicksell has no bearing on the question that concerns us, namely the relationship of Keynesian monetary theory as here defined to the quantity theory that Keynes knew and, indeed, at one time helped to develop.

I would like to emphasize one further point: what interests me now is monetary theory, not monetary policy. These represent two different spheres of discourse. And whatever the relationship between the two, it is clearly not a one-to-one correspondence: different policy recommendations can emanate from the same conceptual theoretical framework; and different frameworks can lead to the same policy recommendation.

Some of the clearest examples of this can be taken from the monetary field itself. Thus those of us who studied at Chicago under Henry Simons did not need the conceptual framework of the *General Theory* to advocate vigorously government deficits to combat depressions; for quite independently of Keynes—and, indeed, before the *General Theory*—Simons taught this to his students on the basis of the conceptual framework embodied in Fisher's $MV = PT$. Indeed, Simons taught us not to suffer patiently those conventional souls who continued to preach the righteous orthodoxy of a balanced budget even in the face of mass unemployment.

I might digress for a moment to note that Simons was far from being a voice in the wilderness at that time in the U.S.—and that there were then also similar voices here in England. Thus in a most remarkable passage in a work systematically based on the quantity theory, Pigou (1933, p. 213) made the distinction that only Keynesians are supposed to make between the efficacy of monetary policy in countering expansionary forces in the economy by raising the bank rate sufficiently and the limitations to which monetary policy is subject in countering 'a contraction in aggregate money income'. For though it is 'always possible for the Central Bank, by open market operations, to force out money into balances held by the public . . . there may be *no* positive rate of money interest that will avail to get this money used'. (A 'liquidity trap' at zero interest!) In such circumstances, Pigou continued, a purely monetary policy is 'bound to fail. If, however, at the same time that the banking system keeps money cheap, the government adopts a policy of public works, the risk of failure is greatly reduced.'[3]

Thus both quantity theorists and Keynesians—each from their own conceptual framework—advocated policies of combating unemployment by public-works expenditures and/or deficit financing. Conversely—and once again I must speak in a small voice—the common conceptual framework of most monetary theorists today—Friedman as well as Tobin—is (as I shall argue this evening) the Keynesian one; but this has clearly not precluded the emergence from this framework of quite different policy recommendations, based both on different political philosophies and on different interpretations of the empirical findings.

(As an aside, I might quite frankly note that what generates in me a great deal of scepticism about the state of our discipline is the

[3] Italics in original.

Actually, this passage is not as Keynesian as it sounds; for Pigou presents his argument in the Wicksellian terms of the effect of such public-works expenditure on the difference between the actual bank rate and the 'proper' one. At the same time, he does recognize that a decrease in public-works expenditures 'directly contracts to [the?] real demand for labour' (Pigou, 1933, pp. 213–14, especially footnote 1).

high positive correlation between the policy views of a researcher (or, what is worse, of his thesis director) and his empirical findings. I will begin to believe in economics as a science when out of Yale there comes an empirical Ph.D. thesis demonstrating the supremacy of monetary policy in some historical episode—and out of Chicago, one demonstrating the supremacy of fiscal policy.)

In any event, the examples of Simons, Pigou, and others have led me to suspect that the real Keynesian Revolution took place not in the sphere of economic policy (where changes were already occurring in the early 1930s), but in that of economic theory. I suspect that the real change wrought by Keynes's *General Theory* was in the conceptual framework from which we viewed the problems of employment, interest, and money. But that is a question that I shall defer for discussion on another occasion.[4]

I. On the meaning of a new theory

Let me return to our main question. Consider the familiar representation of the Keynesian model in terms of a simultaneous analysis of the markets for commodities and money. I think that everyone would agree that the conceptual framework of effective demand that Keynes developed to analyse equilibrium in the commodity market was indeed a new one (leaving aside the case of Kalecki and perhaps one or two other possible precursors). The question is whether the same can be said for the conceptual framework of liquidity preference that Keynes developed to analyse equilibrium in the money market. In order to answer that question, we must first clarify what we mean by a 'new theory'.

Those of us who live in Jerusalem need not be reminded of the words of a wise man of our city—many, many centuries ago—that there is nothing new under the sun. Clearly, every theory advanced at one point in time has some antecedents in earlier theories. Nevertheless, there are stages in the development of a science where, by consensus, a 'new' theory is said to develop. And one of the major questions discussed by philosophers and historians of science are the characteristics which justify calling a theory 'new'.[5] Some

[4] I might, however, note that I find support for the foregoing view in Winch's study (1969) of English economic thought and policy in the 1920s and early 1930s, and in Davis's corresponding study (1971) for the U.S.A. See also Hutchison (1953, ch. 24, 1968 Appendix).

[5] Cf. Kuhn (1970); see also Joseph Agassi (1968) and Stigler (1955).

related questions that I have already alluded to are the difference between 'the asides' referring to an idea in the antecedent theories, as compared with its 'systematic development' in the 'new theory'; and the difference between 'mentioning an idea in passing' or 'as an aside', as compared with 'integrating it into one's thinking'.

By their very nature, questions of this type are not susceptible of hard-and-fast answers. The general type of answer that has on occasion been given—and that I would like to give here—is that a theory is 'new' if it deals in a different manner with one of the central concepts of the science. Similarly, it is 'new' if it stimulates concentrated research along hitherto neglected directions.

Now, that does not take us very far, for it has merely replaced the mystery of 'new' by that of 'central' and 'neglected'. Still I think it can help us on the question now at issue.

Before turning to this issue, I would like to illustrate these distinctions in terms of another recent episode in the history of economic theory—the development of Friedman's permanent-income hypothesis. As we all know, the essence of this theory is that the individual's current consumption depends not on his current (or 'measured') income, but on his wealth or its surrogate, permanent income.

Now, in a sense this theory can be said to be incorporated already in Fisher's 1907 analysis, in his *Rate of Interest*,[6] of the individual maximizing his utility over two periods subject to the present value of his income stream. And, indeed, by his generous references to Fisher, Friedman (1957, p. 7) even encourages us to think in this way.

Even more to the point is Hicks's detailed and systematic 1939 discussion in his *Value and Capital* of the meaning of income—to which Friedman also refers (1957, p. 10, footnote 4); for in this discussion Hicks addressed himself directly to the question of the proper measure of an individual's income during a given period of time—and explains why, in a non-stationary economy, 'we should not regard the whole of his current receipts as income' (1939, p. 172). Instead, Hicks went on to explain, 'the calculation of income consists in finding some sort of *standard* stream of values whose present capitalized value equals the present value of the stream of receipts which is actually in prospect' (ibid., p. 184, italics in original).

But despite these discussions, the earlier Keynesian literature—

[6] This analysis is essentially repeated in Fisher's later *Theory of Interest* (1930).

and the related econometric studies in particular—all analysed consumption as a function of current income—with no one (not even—to the best of my knowledge—Hicks) criticizing this procedure. And even after the post-war failure to predict consumption correctly[7] led to the introduction of additional variables into these functions—including lagged income, and even lagged consumption—there was no full understanding of what this meant. Thus, for example, Klein and Goldberger (1955, p. 8) explained their introduction of lagged consumption into the function in terms of their contention that 'consumer behavior tends to be repetitive to some extent'.

Now 'all' that Friedman did was to infer from Fisher's analysis that the proper measure of income for use in the consumption function is an estimate of permanent income provided by an average of income over several periods of time. (Friedman's rationalization of this procedure is far more sophisticated—as is also the average he uses—but for our present purposes we can look at it in this over-simplified way.) But this 'simple suggestion'—as well as some related ones—sufficed to bring about a revolution in the way economists viewed the process of consumption, and to stimulate accordingly concentrated empirical research along hitherto neglected directions. Consumption has never been the same since.

This episode illustrates, better than any other that I can think of, one of the fundamental facts of the history of ideas: namely, that in general the full implications of a set of ideas are not immediately seen. Indeed, as frequently noted, if they were, then all mathematics would be a tautology; for its theorems are implicit in the assumptions made.

I think that all of us must be aware of these aspects of *la condition humaine*. I am sure all of us will empathize with my colleague Nissan Liviatan, who in one of our recent departmental seminars quietly answered the criticism that something he said was a tautology with the words 'Whether or not something is a tautology depends on how fast you think.'

Similarly, I am sure that all of us have had the experience of saying in the course of our work on a certain problem: 'Now why didn't I see that before?' If we are fortunate, we say this at some

[7] The role of these failures in generating the new theories of consumption can well be interpreted in terms of Kuhn's emphasis on the general feeling of dissatisfaction ('crisis in the scientific community') that leads to the development of a new theory (Kuhn, 1970, chs. 7–8).

later stage of the work when we indeed achieve that 'moment of truth' that enables us to see the deeper meaning of what we have done. And if we are less fortunate, we say it only after someone else has pointed it out.

II. The novelty of Keynesian monetary theory: stocks and flows

This is the viewpoint from which I approach the question of the novelty of Keynesian monetary theory.

To begin with, I think that we are all agreed that one of the central distinctions of economic theory is that between stocks and flows. Correspondingly, what I would consider to be one of the hallmarks of Keynesian monetary theory is the sharp distinction it draws between the two sets of decisions an individual has to make: the decision as to the forms in which to hold his stock of wealth at a given instant of time, and particularly the amount to be held in money; and the decision as to the rate at which to add to this wealth over time—i.e. the decision as to the flows of savings and investment.

The Keynesian approach has led to the development of the theory of the demand for money as part of a general theory of the choice of an optimum portfolio of assets. Correspondingly, the emphasis of this theory is on the optimal relationship between the stock of money and the stocks of other assets, as influenced primarily by the alternative rates of return available on these assets. Other determinants of this demand are the total wealth of the individual (which defines the wealth restraint that must be satisfied by the portfolio of assets) and the flow of income (which is the major determinant of the transactions demand for money).[8]

All agree that this conceptual framework is quite different from that of Fisher. The question is whether it is also different from that of the Cambridge school. (I might incidentally note that the sharp contrast that is traditionally drawn between the 'mechanical' Fisher and the 'behaviouristic' Cambridge economists is, in my opinion, largely a Cantabridgian tale; but the discussion of that question too must be deferred to another occasion.) Let me, then,

[8] This approach has received its most formal development at the hands of James Tobin (1955, 1963, 1969) and, more recently, Duncan Foley and Miguel Sidrauski (1971). The individual in this development is conceived as making his optimizing decisions while being subject to a wealth (stock) restraint as well as an income (flow) restraint.

See also Gurley and Shaw (1960).

contrast the foregoing conceptual framework with that of the Cambridge school—and with that of Keynes of the *Tract on Monetary Reform* in particular.

There is no doubt that Keynes of the *General Theory* is at one with Keynes of the *Tract* (1923, pp. 78–9) in taking as his point of departure the individual's demand for money holdings. Thus in his exposition of the *Tract* (which he explicitly bases on Marshall (1923) and Pigou (1917–18)) Keynes wrote that the demand for real 'purchasing power' in the form of money holdings depends

> partly on the wealth of the community, partly on its habits. Its habits are fixed by its estimation of the extra convenience of having more cash in hand as compared with the advantages to be got from spending the cash or investing it. The point of equilibrium is reached where the estimated advantages of keeping more cash in hand compared with those of spending or investing it about balance. The matter cannot be summed up better than in the words of Dr. Marshall [1923, p. 78].

And here Keynes quotes at length from Marshall's well-known discussion in his *Money, Credit and Commerce* (1923, pp. 44–5)—which goes back to much earlier statements—about 'the fraction of their income which people find it worth while to keep in the form of currency', as well as Marshall's example of an economy whose inhabitants 'find it just worth their while to keep by them on the average ready-purchasing power to the extent of a tenth part of their annual income, together with a fiftieth part of their property'.[9] Keynes also notes, when referring to Marshall's discussion of the antecedents of this approach in the writings of Petty and others, that 'in modern conditions the normal proportion of the circulation [of money] to this national income seems to be somewhere between a tenth and a fifteenth' (Keynes, 1923, p. 79, footnote 1).

Actually, the clearest statement of the Cambridge approach—though one that Keynes does not cite, possibly because he was restricting himself to the writings of his teachers, as distinct from his contemporaries—is that of Lavington,[10] who also based himself on Marshall. After discussing 'the general principle on which an

[9] These passages are cited at length and further discussed in the Appendix below.

[10] Frederick Lavington (1881–1927) began his university studies (at Cambridge) relatively late (in 1908) after eleven years' service in a bank. He began his academic career at Cambridge in 1918, after a further period in administrative work. This late start—as well as his illness and early death—undoubtedly helps explain why his role in the development of Cambridge monetary thought was less than it otherwise would have been. But I suspect that an at least

individual distributes his resources among their various uses', Lavington wrote:

Resources devoted to consumption supply an income of immediate satisfaction; those held as a stock of currency yield a return of convenience and security; those devoted to investment in the narrower sense of the term yield a return in the form of interest. In so far therefore as his judgement gives effect to his self-interest, the quantity of resources which he holds in the form of money will be such that the unit of resources which is just and only just worth while holding in this form yields him a return of convenience and security equal to the yield of satisfaction derived from the marginal unit spent on consumables, and equal also to the net rate of interest (1921, p. 30; the reference to Marshall is on p. 27).

I might note that no such passage appears in the first (1922) edition of Dennis Robertson's celebrated little volume on *Money* in the Cambridge Economic Handbooks series—though there is one in the third (1928) and later editions.

At first sight, these passages seem to indicate that the conceptual approach of the Cambridge school did not differ much from that of the later Keynesian monetary theory. What I shall, however, now show is that this is not the case: First of all, there are some substantive differences in the description of the optimum portfolio—though less so with respect to Lavington than the others. Secondly—and more important—the Cambridge economists did not recognize the full implications of the optimum-portfolio approach to monetary theory; they did not really integrate it into their thinking. In particular, as I shall show in the next section, they failed to take account of the implications of this approach at the appropriate points in their discussions.

By my first point I mean that Cambridge monetary theory did not draw the sharp and basic distinction Keynesian theory draws between stocks and flows—and sometimes it even indiscriminately interchanged 'wealth' and 'income'. Thus, it is not clear from the foregoing passages whether the Cambridge economists conceived of the individual as holding a quantity of money that is optimum

---

equally important factor was Lavington's self-effacing outlook on his own work as reflected in his favourite saying that 'It's all in Marshall, if you'll only take the trouble to dig it out.'

Cf. the obituaries of Lavington by H[arold] W[right] and C. R. F[ay] in *Economic Journal*, xxxvii (1927), 503–5. (I am indebted to Lord Robbins for the identification of Harold Wright, and for the information that Wright was the author of the Cambridge Economic Handbook, *Population* (1923).)

with reference to his stocks of other assets, or optimum with reference to his income, or optimum with reference to some combination of the two.

In order to prevent any misunderstanding, I must emphasize that in actual fact the individual's holdings of money should be optimum with respect to both his wealth and his income. This, after all, is the view implicit in Keynes's liquidity-preference function $L_1(Y) + L_2(r)$—and explicit in the presentation of the demand for money by Tobin (1955, p. 208; 1969) and Foley and Sidrauski (1971, pp. 30–1). My point is, however, that some Cambridge economists (Pigou, Robertson, and possibly Lavington) expressed the demand for money as a function of income—without referring at all to wealth; and that even those who did refer to both wealth and income (Marshall and Keynes of the *Tract*) did so in a way that does not reveal awareness of the basically different roles these magnitudes play in determining the demand for money: namely, that tangible wealth is the variable that constitutes the total budget restraint on the holding of assets, including money—so that an increase in wealth generally results in increased holdings of all assets; whereas income is one of the relevant variables explaining the (transactions) demand for money in a portfolio of a given size—so that an increase in income increases the demand for money, at the expense of other assets.

In order to make this criticism more concrete, consider the basic passages from Marshall's *Money, Credit and Commerce* that Keynes cites in the *Tract* as an expression of his position too (above, p. 11). At one and the same time these consecutive passages present a theory of people's demand for money as a 'fraction of their income' and as 'a tenth part of their annual income, together with a fiftieth part of their property.' It is inconceivable to me that Marshall and Keynes of that time could have understood the full implications of the distinction between stocks and flows (and of the corresponding distinction between wealth and income), and yet that Marshall could have juxtaposed two such different descriptions of the demand for money—and that, even more so, Keynes could have cited them without comment.[11]

As further evidence on this point, consider Marshall's statement

[11] For further discussion of this point, see the Appendix below.

This failure of neoclassical economists to distinguish sharply between wealth and income may be related to the corresponding absence of a sharp distinction in the writings of the classical economists (and of Smith and Ricardo in particular), for whom capital (i.e. wealth) was last year's crop carried over to the current year.

that the 'relation between the volume of this currency and the general level of prices may be changed permanently by changes in . . . population and wealth, which change the aggregate income' (1923, p. 45). Marshall is clearly assuming here that an increase in wealth increases the demand for money only by first increasing the subsequent flow of income, and hence the transaction needs for money; there is no awareness here of the possibility that an increase in wealth may directly increase the demand for money as one of the assets in which form this wealth is held. In brief, if in modern monetary theory we sometimes use income as a proxy for wealth, here Marshall is using wealth as a proxy for income.

Significantly enough, my criticism on this point would seem to be related to one that Keynes of the *Treatise* makes of the Cambridge school, including explicitly Keynes of the *Tract*: namely, that the Cambridge equation $P = kR/M$—in which R represents 'the current income of the community'—can explain the demand for income (or demand) deposits, which are held for transactions needs; however, contends Keynes, it does not explain the demand for savings (or time) deposits. This demand, too, can be said to depend on the 'resources' of the individuals; 'but resources in this connection ought not be interpreted, as it is interpreted by Professor Pigou, as being identical with current *income*' (1930, i, pp. 231–2, italics in original).

I wish I could go on to say that Keynes explicitly states here that 'resources' in this connection should be interpreted as wealth. Unfortunately for me, he does not; but that this is what he meant is, I think, quite clear from Keynes's analysis earlier in the *Treatise* of the holding of saving deposits, in which he explicitly relates these holdings to the individual's total wealth, and not to the 'current increment' to this wealth (1930, i, pp. 140–1).

I must admit that Keynes's criticism here does not apply to Lavington, who explicitly stated that that part of the demand for money that is held as a contingency reserve changes 'in some measure independently of the volume of payments' (1921, p. 33). On the other hand, Lavington—unlike Keynes of the *Treatise*—does not relate this contingency reserve to the individual's wealth; nor does he relate its magnitude to the price of the securities that can be held as an alternative (Keynes, 1930, i, pp. 141–3). Instead, Lavington speaks only in general terms of the magnitude of this reserve being 'regulated largely by the general level of confidence' (1921, p. 33). It is also significant that Lavington himself considers his description of the demand for money as a contingency reserve to be 'rather different from (though not inconsistent with) that laid down by the Quantity theory' (1921, p. 32). Finally, it is significant that though Robertson ((1933) 1940, pp. 92–3)) defends the Cambridge equation against Keynes's criticisms here, he (Robertson), too, makes no mention of Lavington in this context.[12]

III. The novelty of Keynesian monetary theory: the recognition of the implications of the optimum-portfolio approach

The preceding discussion has explicated the distinction between Keynes and the Cambridge school that is reflected in their respective treatments of stocks and flows. A related distinction manifests itself in the already-noted fact that despite its description of an optimum portfolio, the Cambridge school did not realize the full implications of the portfolio approach to monetary theory. Conversely, it is the systematic application of this approach that is the hallmark of Keynesian monetary theory.

This distinction reflects itself, first of all, in the way these two approaches analyse the effects of a monetary increase on the economy. Keynesian theory analyses the initial impact of this increase on the balance sheet of the individual: it emphasizes that in order to persuade the public to hold a portfolio with such an increased stock of money, the rates of return on the other assets in this portfolio must fall. That is, stock equilibrium can be achieved now only at lower rates of return on these other assets. This decline in interest and other rates of return then increases the demand for the flow of consumption and (primarily) investment goods, thus disturbing the equilibrium in the commodity-flow markets, and thus causing an increase in output and/or prices (depending on the state of unemployment).

In brief, Keynesian theory analyses the impact of a monetary increase in terms of the substitution effects that it generates. I am sure that it will come as no surprise to anyone if I say that Keynesian economics is to be criticized for this concentration on the substitution effects, to the exclusion of the possible wealth—or real-balance—effect. For though there are indeed cases in which monetary changes do not generate a wealth effect (namely, some open-market operations),[13] there are other cases (namely, monetary changes generated by deficit financing) in which it does.

[12] For further details, see Appendix below.

[13] Cf. Patinkin (1965), ch. XII:4, especially p. 294, footnote 23.

On the other hand, I cannot think of a case in which a monetary change generates only a wealth effect, and not a substitution effect. And it is the fact that the Cambridge school nevertheless frequently analysed a monetary change precisely in this way that distinguishes it so sharply from the later Keynesian economics.

Ironically enough, this distinction is clearest from a passage by Keynes himself in the *Tract* that reads as follows: 'When people find themselves with more cash than they require . . ., they get rid of the surplus by buying goods or investments, or by leaving it for a bank to employ, or, possibly, by increasing their hoarded reserves' (1923, pp. 75–6; see also 1911). Thus Keynes here conceives of the individual as directly using his 'cash surplus' to increase his 'hoarded reserves', and makes no mention whatsoever of the variation in interest required to induce him to do so.[14] In this way Keynes fails to realize the full implications of his own description (cited above) of 'equilibrium [as being] reached where the estimated advantages of keeping more cash in hand compared with those of spending or investing it about balance' (1923, p. 78). He does not recognize the fact (that he was later to emphasize so systematically in the *General Theory*) that the monetary increase will disturb the foregoing balance at the margin—and that the individual's holdings of money and other assets can accordingly be in equilibrium once again only at a lower rate of interest.

The lack of appropriate references in the Cambridge literature to the dependence of the demand for money on interest is of great significance in the present discussion, not because such a dependence is necessarily of empirical importance, but because the recognition of such a dependence seems to me to constitute a critical and unambiguous indicator of whether the Cambridge economists really understood the analytical apparatus they described. Let me then provide some additional instances in which their writings fail to indicate such a recognition.

Thus, despite what I have said above, Cambridge economists did indeed assign an important role to changes in the rate of interest in their analysis of the effects of a monetary increase. But the

[14] I am indebted to Dr. Luigi Ceriani, editor of the Banco Nazionale del Lavoro: *Quarterly Review*, for pointing out an error in my original discussion of this passage. In that discussion I interpreted 'investments' as 'investment goods'—whereas it should have been clear from Keynes's use of 'investments' in other parts of the *Tract* (1923, pp. 5–7, 13 *et passim*) that what he meant by the term is *financial* investment—that is, the purchase of securities of various kinds.

way in which they discussed this role is itself evidence of how different their conceptual framework really was from that of the Keynesians. In particular, Marshall, Pigou, the younger Keynes, and other quantity theorists all analysed the effects of a monetary increase that reflected itself in the first instance in an increase in bank reserves. Indeed, this was the major case they considered. They argued that the resulting excess reserves would lead to an increased desire on the part of banks to make loans, hence to a decrease in the rate of interest[15] (Wicksell's 'money rate' or 'bank rate', though the Cambridge economists did not describe it in these terms), hence to increased borrowings, hence to increased demand for goods by the borrowers, and hence to a rise in prices.

Now, the interesting aspect of this description of the adjustment process is that none of these Cambridge economists even alluded to the fact—implicit in their analyses of the demand for money cited above—that the changes in the rate of interest would affect not only the amount of the public's borrowing, but also the quantity of money it chooses to hold.

A similar picture emerges when we consider the instances—unfortunately, few—in which Cambridge economists supplemented their theoretical monetary analysis with empirical observations.

Thus Pigou (1929, pp. 163–72) tried to apply to British data for the period 1878–1914 the same techniques used by Carl Snyder (1924) in his study of the equation of exchange for the U.S. Pigou concludes from the data that the higher price level of 1914 as compared with 1878 was the result of a higher velocity of circulation at that time (1914). Now, what is interesting about Pigou's discussion is that he does refer to the possibility that velocity is increased by an increasing price level (by Pigou's data (ibid., p. 592)—though he does not explicitly refer to them—prices had been *falling* before 1878, and had remained *constant* in the period 1912–14, which could have explained part of the higher velocity in the latter period). On the other hand, Pigou does not refer to the possible effect of changes in the rate of interest on velocity (though it must be conceded that the yield on consols in 1914 (3·3 per cent) was only slightly higher than in 1878 (3·2 per cent)) (*British Historical Statistics*, p. 455). Thus the evidence here is ambiguous.

[15] This can be interpreted as reflecting the optimum-portfolio adjustment of the banks; but the Cambridge economists did not present such an interpretation—nor should they be expected to have done so. Once again, however, Lavington (1921, pp. 30–1) is something of an exception; see Appendix below.

The situation with reference to Keynes is clearer. In his *Tract* (pp. 83–4) Keynes compares the data for prices and money supply in October 1920 with those for October 1922—and concludes that his k (which, of course, equals the Cambridge KT in the equation $M = KPT$) had increased significantly during this period. Now, Keynes does mention (though as the effect of the increase in k, and not as its cause) the sharp (33 per cent) decline in the price level during this period. On the other hand, he does not cite as a possible explanatory factor the fact that the yield on consols fell from 5·3 per cent in 1920 to 4·4 per cent in 1922—or that the maximum rate on three-month bills fell from 6·5 per cent in 1920 to 2·7 per cent in 1922. Of course, one might say that in accordance with Fisher's distinction between nominal and real rate of interest, this decline in nominal interest reflected in part the fact—which Keynes did mention—that the price level was declining. But it would be carrying things too far to try to explain away in this way Keynes's failure even to mention the rate of interest in this context.

Furthermore, in his immediately following discussion about the ways to stabilize k' (i.e. the real value of the demand for current deposits), Keynes states that 'a tendency of k' to increase may be somewhat counteracted by lowering the bank-rate, because easy lending diminishes the advantage of keeping a margin for contingencies in cash' (*ibid.*, p. 85). Now this sentence can be interpreted as reflecting the effect on the demand for money of the more ready availability of money substitutes like easy credit facilities. But however it is interpreted it will not yield a reaffirmation of the contention that, *ceteris paribus*, lowering the rate of interest causes an increase in k—and hence in the real amount of money demanded.

I might note that Pigou and Keynes are representative of what seems to have been a systematic tendency of quantity theorists to explain observed variations in the velocity of circulation in terms, not of the rate of interest, but of variations in the rate of change of prices (Patinkin, 1972a). Keynes's procedure on this score is particularly enigmatic; for in his description of the post-World War I inflations in his *Tract on Monetary Reform* (pp. 45 ff.), he provides a precise analysis of the influence of a high rate of increase of prices in causing the public to develop 'economizing habits' with reference to its demand for money; yet in his systematic presentation of the Cambridge demand for money (ibid., pp. 78 ff.) he does not mention this factor at all, but does analyse the influence of the rate of interest. In this discrepancy, too, I see additional evidence of the failure of the Cambridge economists to integrate the different elements of their monetary theory into their thinking.

A similar difference characterizes Pigou's analysis of the trade cycle (1929). Changes in the velocity of circulation play an important rôle in this analysis—but they are never related to the concurrent changes taking place (according to Pigou) in the rate of interest. Instead, the changes in velocity are attributed solely to the anticipation of price changes—and to changes in 'confidence'. A similar statement holds for Lavington's analysis (1922). As an aside, I might also note that the emphasis that both these writers placed on 'confidence' makes it clear that—in contrast with the 'modern quantity theory'—they did not think of velocity—and hence the demand for money—as a stable function of stipulated economic variables.

I would like to conclude this examination of the Cambridge literature with another indication of its failure to realize the full implication of its conceptual framework. It seems to me that if an economist has a full understanding of the portfolio approach to monetary theory, then one of the natural questions he will be led to ask is about the effects on the rates of returns of the various assets of a shift in tastes with reference to the forms in which individuals wish to hold their assets (of which Keynes's shift in liquidity preference is the archetype). It should be emphasized that such a shift will affect the rate of interest (and rates of return in general) even under conditions of full employment and perfectly flexible prices.[16] Correspondingly, the complete absence from the Cambridge literature of an analysis of such a shift in taste—in contrast with the attention paid to the effects of a shift in tastes with respect to the desired level of K—is to me clear evidence that the Cambridge quantity theorists did not really approach monetary problems from the viewpoint of an optimally composed portfolio of assets.

IV. Concluding remarks

My conclusion from the evidence presented here is that the conceptual framework of the Cambridge school was not really the Keynesian one described in the opening section of this paper: namely, a framework that conceives of the individual as deciding on the amount of his money holdings as a component of a portfolio of assets that is optimally composed with reference to the alternative rates of return available on these assets. A framework

[16] See Patinkin (1965), ch. X:4.

that (in contrast with the Cambridge school) distinguishes between the initial *stock* (or balance-sheet) adjustments generated by a monetary change, and the subsequent effect on the demand for *flows* of commodities of the changes in rates in interest generated by these adjustments.

One indication of this fact is the failure of the Cambridge school to analyse the effects on the equilibrium rate of interest of a shift in the tastes of the individual with reference to the desired asset-composition of his portfolio. Another indication is that despite the fact that the Cambridge school referred to the influence of the rate of interest on the demand for money, it did not really integrate this influence into its thinking: it did not call it into use in explaining observed variations of the velocity of circulation; nor did it cite it as a factor in its theoretical explanations of variations of the velocity of circulation over the trade cycle.

It is because of these differences from the Cambridge school that the Keynesian theory of liquidity preference can properly be considered only as a 'new theory'—one that makes it impossible for us today to approach monetary problems without taking account of these factors.[17]

I would like to end with some personal reminiscences that I hope will support this interpretation of the Cambridge school—though I am sure that for some it will merely be an indication of my prejudices.

There is some effrontery in claiming that though scholars described a certain analytical apparatus, they did not really understand its full implications. I dare nevertheless to advance this contention not only because of what I feel to be the convincing evidence presented here, but also on the basis of my own recollections of how I, too, failed at one time to see these implications. For though my studies of economics at Chicago began some years after the appearance of the *General Theory,* I was educated in the analytical spirit of the quantity theory that prevailed there. Hence, even though we also studied the *General Theory,* I know that I did not think then in terms of the sharp Keynesian distinction between stock and flow equilibrium. I know that my instinctive way of thinking of monetary influences at that time was directly from the increase in the stock of money to the increase in the demand for the flow of commodities—without the aid of any intervening portfolio-adjustment substitution

[17] It is for these reasons that I cannot accept the contrary conclusions of Eshag (1963), pp. 62–8.

effects. I know that I thought of a change in the velocity of circulation solely in terms of a change in tastes as to the desired proportion between the stock of money and the flow of expenditure on current commodities; not in terms of the consequence of a change in tastes as to the desired proportion between the stock of money and the stocks of other assets in a portfolio of a given size.

Knowing these things about the workings of my own mind, I hope that I will not be considered presumptuous if I interpret the detailed evidence from the writings of the Cambridge economists that I have here presented as evidence that they too were subject to a similar failure to see what is so clear to us today—as a result of the changes wrought by Keynesian monetary theory.

Appendix

The passages from Marshall's *Money, Credit and Commerce* (1923, pp. 44–5) referred to in the text are reproduced here, together with the relevant footnote:

> To give definiteness to this notion, let us suppose that the inhabitants of a country, taken one with another (and including therefore all varieties of character and of occupation) find it just worth their while to keep by them on the average ready purchasing power to the extent of a tenth part of their annual income, together with a fiftieth part of their property; then the aggregate value of the currency of the country will tend to be equal to the sum of these amounts. . . .
>
> Thus the position is this. In every state of society there is some fraction of their income which people find it worth while to keep in the form of currency; it may be a fifth, or a tenth, or a twentieth. A large command of resources in the form of currency renders their business easy and smooth, and puts them at an advantage in bargaining; but, on the other hand, it locks up in a barren form resources that might yield an income of gratification if invested, say, in extra furniture; or a money income if invested in extra machinery or cattle. . . . But, whatever the state of society, there is a certain volume of their resources which people of different classes, taken one with another, care to keep in the form of currency; and, if everything else remains the same, then there is this direct relation between the volume of currency and the level of prices, that, if one is increased by ten per cent., the other also will be increased by ten per cent. Of course, the less the proportion of their resources which people care to keep in the form of currency, the lower will be the aggregate value of the currency, that is, the higher will prices be with a given volume of currency.

This relation between the volume of the currency and the general level of prices may be changed permanently by changes in, first, population and wealth, which change the aggregate income; secondly, by the growth of credit agencies, which substitute other means of payment for currency; thirdly, by changes in the methods of transport, production, and business generally, which affect the number of hands through which commodities pass in the processes of making and dealing, and it may be temporarily modified by fluctuations of general commercial confidence and activity.*

* The above statement is reproduced from my answers to Questions 11,759–11,761 put by the Indian Currency Committee in 1899. In fact a considerable part of the present discussion of the problems of money and credit may be found in my answers to Questions 11,757–11,850 put by that Committee: and my answers to Questions 9623–10,014 and 10,121–10,126 put by the Gold and Silver Commission in 1887–8.

In his memoir on Marshall, Keynes (1924, pp. 27–8) states:

We must regret still more Marshall's postponement of the publication of his *Theory of Money* until extreme old age, when time had deprived his ideas of freshness and his exposition of sting and strength.

. . . his theories were not expounded in a systematic form until the appearance of *Money, Credit and Commerce* in 1923. By this date nearly all his main ideas had found expression in the works of others. He had passed his eightieth year; his strength was no longer equal to much more than piecing together earlier fragments; and its jejune treatment, carefully avoiding difficulties and complications, yields the mere shadow of what he had had it in him to bring forth twenty or (better) thirty years earlier.

It does not take any expertise in textual criticism to see how the passage cited here from *Money, Credit and Commerce* reflects such 'piecing together'. In particular, the first paragraph of this passage—in which the demand for money is expressed as 'a tenth part of their annual income, together with a fiftieth part of their property'—clearly presents a different theory of the demand for money than does the second paragraph—which refers only to the 'fraction of their income which people find it worth while to keep in the form of currency'. This difference is a reflection of the fact that the second and third[1] paragraphs in the passage cited essentially reproduce Marshall's 1899 testimony before the Indian

[1] The reader is reminded of the discussion in the text above emphasizing that the allusion in this paragraph to the influences of changes in wealth on the demand for money visualizes this effect not as a direct one, but as an indirect one exerted through the influence on this demand of the increase in income generated by the increase in wealth.

Currency Committee (1926, pp. 267–9) to which he refers in the first sentence of the footnote he attached to this passage. And this testimony essentially goes back to an unpublished manuscript that Marshall wrote around 1871.[2]

On the other hand, the first paragraph in this passage does not appear in any of Marshall's various testimonies as reprinted in *Official Papers*; nor, to the best of my knowledge, does it appear in any of his published works; nor, finally, does it appear in the unpublished manuscript for 1871 just mentioned. Thus it may have been written at the time Marshall was preparing his *Money, Credit and Commerce.*

In view of the circumstances under which Marshall wrote his *Money, Credit and Commerce* (as described by Keynes), it may be that one should not attach too much importance to the fact that Marshall described the demand for money in two different ways. But this cannot explain why Keynes in his *Tract* (1923, pp. 78–9) cites the foregoing passages from *Money, Credit and Commerce* at length—and makes no comment that would indicate his realization of the fact that from the stock-flow viewpoint there are indeed two different descriptions here.

In addition to the foregoing passages that he cites from Marshall, Keynes also describes this demand repeatedly (1923, pp. 76, 78 *et passim*) by the statement that the demand of individuals for money 'depends partly on their wealth, partly on their habits.' As the reader can verify, this statement does not appear in the above-cited passages from *Money, Credit and Commerce.* It does, however, appear in one of the memoranda that Marshall submitted in 1887 to the Gold and Silver Commission in which he states that 'the volume of the business in each country which requires the use of coin [is] determined by each country's wealth and habits' (1926, p. 177).

In this material we also find another example of the failure of Marshall to distinguish sharply between wealth and income in this context:

Assuming the habits of business to remain unchanged, the amount of coin which a person finds it convenient to carry about, taking one with another, depends upon his general *wealth.* A shopkeeper with an *in-*

[2] See pp. 13–14 of this manuscript, which is to be found in the Marshall Library of Economics in Cambridge (see Bibliography below). I am indebted to the Senior Assistant Librarian of the Library and to Professor Robin Matthews for providing me with a Xerox of the manuscript.

This manuscript is referred to by Keynes in his memorial essay on Marshall (1924, p. 28).

come of £1,000 a year would be likely to use a great deal more gold than an architect with the same *income*, but if prices rose generally so that the money income of each increased 10 per cent, and the expenditure of each in every direction increased also 10 per cent, then (their habits of business remaining unchanged) each of them would, I believe, keep 10 per cent more money in his purse. (1926, p. 43, italics added.)

The passages cited in the text above from Pigou's 'Value of Money' (1917–18, pp. 164–7) are the following—where once again the relevant footnote has been reproduced:

There is thus constituted at any given moment a definite demand schedule for titles to legal-tender money. Let R be the total resources, expressed in terms of wheat, that are enjoyed by the community (other than its bankers) whose position is being investigated; k the proportion of these resources that it chooses to keep in the form of titles to legal tender; M the number of units of legal tender, and P the value, or price, per unit of these titles in terms of wheat. Then the demand schedule just described is represented by the equation $P = kR/M$. When k and R are taken as constant, this is, of course, the equation of a rectangular hyperbola.

. . . consider the variable k. When the aggregate wheat value of the community's resources is given, the quantity of wheat value kept in the form of titles to legal tender is determined by the *proportion* of his resources that the average man chooses to keep in that form. This proportion depends upon the convenience obtained and the risk avoided through the possession of such titles, by the loss of real income involved through the diversion to this use of resources that might have been devoted to the production of future commodities, and by the satisfaction that might be obtained by consuming resources immediately and not investing them at all. These three uses, the production of convenience and security, the production of commodities, and direct consumption, are rival to one another. For our present purpose, the use of immediate consumption need not be particularly considered. Its presence mitigates, but never does more than mitigate, the effect of the principal causes with which we have to deal. Practically, the critical question for a business man—and the same class of question has to be asked by everybody—is, as Professor Carver well observes: 'will it pay better to have one more dollar in his cash drawer and one less on his shelves, or will it pay better to have one less dollar in his cash drawer and one more on his shelves.'*

* *American Economic Association Papers* (1905), 131.

Incidentally, I think that this was the first appearance in print of the Cambridge equation.

In view of Lavington's distinctive contributions to the Cambridge school, I should like to cite at length from Chapter 6 of his *English Capital Market* (1921):

> In a modern community each person with resources at his disposal needs some means by which he can employ these resources in order to obtain goods from other parties, to pay his dues to the State and to meet more uncertain demands to which he may be exposed. . . . Each therefore will find it convenient to hold a part of his resources in the form of a stock of something which, being generally acceptable and easily transferable, serves as general purchasing power and may be readily passed from hand to hand as a means of making payments.
>
> He will of course have to forego interest upon the resources which he invests in this particular form of a stock of money, but he will obtain instead facilities for making payments, which may be expressed as a return of convenience and security. His stock yields him an income of convenience, for it reduces the cost and trouble of effecting his current payments; and it yields him an income of security, for it reduces his risks of not being able readily to make payments arising from contingencies which he cannot fully foresee. The investment of resources in the form of a stock of money which facilitates the making of payments is then in no way peculiar; it corresponds to the investment by a merchant in the office furniture which facilitates the dispatch of business, to the investment of the farmer in agricultural implements which facilitate the cultivation of his land, and indeed to investment generally.
>
> Such being the *nature* of an individual's demand for money, we have now to consider the causes governing its *amount*. In order to do so, let us first state the general principle on which an individual distributes his resources among their various uses, and then pass on to consider the causes determining the amount which he invests in this particular use—money.
>
> This general principle is familiar enough. As a person extends the application of resources in any particular use, the yield from each successive unit of resources so applied satisfies a less and less urgent need. Accordingly he presses their employment in each use up to that point where in his judgment the marginal yield is equal all round; for if this yield differed as between any two uses it would pay him to transfer resources from one to the other. Resources devoted to consumption supply an income of immediate satisfaction; those held as a stock of currency yield a return of convenience and security; those devoted to investment in the narrower sense of the term yield a return in the form of interest. In so far therefore as his judgment gives effect to his self-interest, the quantity of resources which he holds in the form of money will be such that the unit of resources which is just and only just worth while holding in this form yields him a return of convenience and

security equal to the yield of satisfaction derived from the marginal unit spent on consumables, and equal also to the net rate of interest.

This distinction between the yield of convenience and security brings out the consideration that the stock of money held by a business man serves not only to effect his current payments but also as a first line of defence against the uncertain events of the future. . . .

If we arrange a business man's investments in order of their marketability, we may regard his resources as distributed among a series of uses ranging from his stock of the supremely acceptable thing, money, up to his investments in the permanent plant from which he draws his main money income. This arrangement conveniently illustrates the essential similarity between the distribution of resources by a business man and the distribution effected by a bank, where the two main considerations, the need to meet current and contingent demands and the need to earn a profit, are shown in clearer contrast. . . .

Even in normal circumstances, therefore, the size of the stock of money held by a business man depends partly on the volume of his current transactions, partly on his individual business outlook. . . .

These considerations lead to a definition of the demand for money rather different from (though not inconsistent with) that laid down by the Quantity theory. In that theory the demand for money during the year is taken to be the aggregate of goods (and services) exchanged against money during that period. . . . Can this total, the volume of payments to be effected, be properly regarded as forming the demand for money? This question must be answered in the light of the considerations which have just been noticed. . . .

. . . In order to carry through his payments quickly and conveniently each person holds a part of his resources in the form of a stock of money. The size of that part of this stock which he holds to carry through current transactions depends directly upon the volume of his payments; . . . But the size of that part of this stock which he holds as a first line of defence against emergencies depends less directly upon the volume of his payments; it depends upon his *estimate* of contingent payments, and consequently varies with his state of mind, or, more concretely, with the business outlook. . . . It seems reasonable, therefore, to regard this latter part of the aggregate money stock as a reserve whose size is regulated largely by the general level of confidence—a reservoir from which money flows into active circulation when times are good, and into which money flows from active circulation when times are bad. . . . Accordingly it seems that theory is brought into closer relation with the facts when we recognize that part of the demand for money arises from the need to make provision against contingent payments, and that this part of the demand fluctuates in response to changes in the general condition of confidence in some measure independently of the volume of payments. (1921, pp. 29–33, italics in original.)

In its clear distinction between the two incentives for holding money—and in its explicit statement that that part held as a contingency reserve changes 'in some measure independently of the volume of payment'—this striking passage is, to the best of my knowledge, unique in the Cambridge literature. I find it accordingly significant that Lavington himself considers this description of the demand for money to be 'rather different from (though not inconsistent with) that laid down by the Quantity theory'.

As noted in the text, there is no discussion of the relative advantages of holding different assets in the first (1922) edition of Robertson's book on Money. In the third (1928) and later editions, however, Robertson wrote that

> . . . taking the country as a whole at any given time, we can express its demand for money—that is, the real value of its money supply—as a proportion of its real national income . . .
>
> On what then does the magnitude of this proportion depend? It depends on the one hand, as has been said, on the convenience and sense of security derived from the possession of a pool of money, and on the other, on the strength of the alternative attractions of increased consumption, or lucrative investment in trade capital or in Government or industrial stocks, against which these advantages have to be weighed up. Thus the magnitude of the demand for money, like that of the demand for bread, turns out to be the result of a process of individual weighing-up of competing advantages *at the margin* . . . (1928, pp. 38–9, italics in original; the same passage appears on pp. 36–7 of the 1948 edition.)

Keynes's criticism in the *Treatise* of Pigou's presentation of the Cambridge equation, $P = k\,R/M$ (cited above), is as follows:

> the introduction of the factor R, the current income of the community, suggests that variation in this is one of the two or three most important direct influences on the demand for cash resources. In the case of the income-deposits this seems to me to be true. But the significance of R is much diminished when we are dealing, not with the income-deposits in isolation, but with the total deposits. Indeed the chief inconvenience of the 'Cambridge' Quantity Equation really lies in its applying to the total deposits considerations which are primarily relevant only to the income-deposits, and in its tackling the problem as though the same sort of considerations which govern the income-deposits also govern the total deposits [i.e. income-deposits *plus* savings deposits—or in U.S. terminology, demand deposits *plus* time deposits] . . .
>
> The prominence given to k, namely the proportion of the bank-deposits to the community's *income*, is misleading when it is extended beyond the income-deposits. The emphasis which this method lays

on the point that the amount of real balances held is determined by the comparative advantages of holding resources in cash and in alternative forms, so that a change in k will be attributable to a change in these comparative advantages, is useful and instructive. But 'resources' in this connection ought not to be interpreted, as it is interpreted by Prof. Pigou, as being identical with current *income*. (1930, i, pp. 231–2, italics in original.)

I might note that even though Robertson defends the Cambridge equation against Keynes's criticisms here, he does not question Keynes's interpretation of Pigou's term 'resources' as 'income'. Robertson's not very convincing answer to Keynes is as follows:

> It is of course true (as is recognized in Marshall's own illustration of the 'Cambridge' theory) that many people will have other quantities than their income in mind (for instance, their capital or their business turnover) in deciding upon their monetary requirements. But from the fact that their money stock is not exclusively *determined* as a proportion of their income, it does not follow that it cannot usefully be *expressed* as such a proportion; still less that the real value of the whole community's total money stock cannot usefully be expressed (as in the equation $M/P = KR$) in terms of the constituents of real income or output. For the whole of M is *potentially* expendable against output, and if in any period of time more or less of it were to be so expended than was previously the case, P would alter. It is of the utmost importance that under certain conditions money which has been imprisoned in what Mr. Keynes calls the 'savings deposits' and 'business deposits' may seep out, raise the aggregate of incomes and 'income deposits,' and drive up P. Such a change is represented in the 'Cambridge' approach by a diminution of K: it would not be represented by any change in a symbol which stood for the proportion borne to R by the real value of 'income deposits' alone. ((1933) 1940, pp. 92–3, italics in original.)

I presume that what Robertson had in mind in his reference to 'Marshall's own illustration of the "Cambridge" theory' is Marshall's discussion in the first paragraph of the citation from *Money, Credit and Commerce* (1923, p. 44) that is cited at the beginning of this Appendix. In any event, as already noted in the text, it is puzzling that Robertson does not refer here to the far more substantive discussion in Lavington (1921, pp. 32–3) cited above in this Appendix (last three paragraphs of the passage cited).

REFERENCES

Agassi, Joseph (1968). 'The Novelty of Popper's Philosophy of Science', *International Philosophical Quarterly* (Sept.), pp. 442–63.

DAVIS, J. Ronnie (1971). *The New Economics and the Old Economists* (Ames, Iowa: Iowa State University Press).
ESHAG, Eprime (1963). *From Marshall to Keynes* (Oxford: Blackwell).
F[AY], C. R. (1927). '[Obituary of] Frederick Lavington', *Economic Journal*, pp. 503–5.
FISHER, Irving (1907). *The Rate of Interest* (New York: Macmillan).
—— (1930). *The Theory of Interest* (New York: Macmillan).
FRIEDMAN, Milton (1957). *A Theory of the Consumption Function* (N.B.E.R.: Gen. Ser. No. 63) (Princeton, N.J.: Princeton University Press).
FOLEY, D. K., and SIDRAUSKI, M. (1971). *Monetary and Fiscal Policy in a Growing Economy* (New York: Macmillan).
GURLEY, John G., and SHAW, Edward S. (1960). *Money in a Theory of Finance* (Washington, D.C.: The Brookings Institution).
HICKS, J. R. (1935). 'A Suggestion for Simplifying the Theory of Money', *Economica*, pp. 1–19; reprinted in Lutz, F. A., and Mints, L. W. (eds.), *Readings in Monetary Theory* (London: Allen and Unwin, 1952), pp. 13–32.
—— (1939). *Value and Capital* (Oxford: Clarendon Press).
HUTCHISON, T. W. (1953). *A Review of Economic Doctrines 1870–1929* (Oxford: Clarendon).
—— (1968). *Economics and Economic Policy in Britain 1946–66* (London: Allen and Unwin).
KEYNES, J. M. (1911). 'Review of I. Fisher's "The Purchasing Power of Money"', *Economic Journal*, pp. 393–8.
—— (1923). *Tract on Monetary Reform* (London: Macmillan).
—— (1924). 'Alfred Marshall, 1842–1924', *Economic Journal* as reprinted in Pigou, A. C. (ed.), *Memorials of Alfred Marshall* (New York: Kelley and Millman, 1956), pp. 1–65.
—— (1930). *A Treatise on Money* (London: Macmillan).
—— (1936). *The General Theory of Employment, Interest and Money* (New York: Harcourt, Brace).
KLEIN, L. R., and GOLDBERGER, A. S. (1955). *An Econometric Model of the United States 1929–1952* (Amsterdam: North-Holland).
KUHN, Thomas S. (1970). *The Structure of Scientific Revolutions* (2nd edn.) (International Encyclopedia of Unified Science, vol. 2, No. 2), (Chicago: University of Chicago Press).
LAVINGTON, F. (1921). *The English Capital Market* (London: Methuen).
—— (1922). *The Trade Cycle* (London: King).
MARSHALL, Alfred (*c.* 1871). Unpublished Manuscript; Marshall Red Box 2 (Money and Banking, Exchanges), Item 6, in the Marshall Library of Economics, Cambridge.
—— (1923). *Money, Credit and Commerce* (London: Macmillan).
—— (1926). *Official Papers* (London: Macmillan).

MITCHELL, B. R., and DEANE, P. (1962). *Abstract of British Historical Statistics* (Cambridge: Cambridge University Press).

MYRDAL, Gunnar (1939). *Monetary Equilibrium* (Glasgow: William Hodge (trans. from the German work of 1933)).

PATINKIN, Don (1965). *Money, Interest, and Prices* (2nd edn., New York: Harper and Row).

—— (1969). 'The Chicago Tradition, the Quantity Theory, and Friedman', *Journal of Money, Credit and Banking* (Feb.), pp. 46–70.

—— (1972a). 'On the Short-Run Non-Neutrality of Money in the Quantity Theory', Banca Nazionale del Lavoro, *Quarterly Review* (Mar.), pp. 3–22.

—— (1972b). 'Friedman on the Quantity Theory and Keynesian Economics', *J.P.E.* (Sept./Oct.), pp. 883–905.

PIGOU, A. C. (1917–18). 'The Value of Money', *Q.J.E.*, as reprinted in Lutz, F. A. and Mints, L. W. (eds.), *Readings in Monetary Theory* (London: Allen and Unwin, 1952).

—— (1929). *Industrial Fluctuations* (2nd edn., London: Macmillan).

—— (1933). *The Theory of Unemployment* (London: Macmillan).

ROBERTSON, D. H. (1922). *Money* (New York: Harcourt, Brace; 3rd edn., London: Nisbet, and Cambridge: Cambridge University Press, 1928; 4th edn., London: Pitman, 1948).

—— (1940). 'A Note on the Theory of Money', in *Essays in Monetary Theory* (London: Staples Press), reprinted from *Economica* (1933).

SHACKLE, G. L. S. (1967). *The Years of High Theory* (Cambridge: C.U.P.).

SNYDER, Carl (1924). 'New Measures in the Equation of Exchange', *American Economic Review* (Dec.), pp. 699–713.

STIGLER, George J. (1955). 'The Nature and Role of Originality in Scientific Progress', *Economica* (Nov.), as reprinted in *Essays in the History of Economics* (Chicago and London: University of Chicago Press, 1965), pp. 1–15.

TOBIN, James (1955). 'A Dynamic Aggregative Model', *J.P.E.* (Apr.).

—— (1963). 'An Essay on Principles of Debt Management', in *Fiscal and Debt Management Policies* (Commission on Money and Credit) (Englewood Cliffs, N.J.: Prentice-Hall), pp. 143–218.

—— (1969). 'A General Equilibrium Approach to Monetary Theory', *Journal of Money, Credit and Banking* (Feb.), pp. 15–29.

WINCH, Donald (1969). *Economics and Policy* (London: Hodder and Stoughton).

WRIGHT, Harold (1923). *Population* (New York: Harcourt, Brace).

W[RIGHT], H[arold] (1927). '[Obituary of] Frederick Lavington', *Economic Journal*, pp. 503–5.

'Keynes' Collected Writings'

D. Patinkin, 'The collected writings of John Maynard Keynes: from the tract to the General Theory', *Economic Journal*, 85:338 (June 1975), pp. 249–71.

THE ECONOMIC JOURNAL

JUNE 1975

THE COLLECTED WRITINGS OF JOHN MAYNARD KEYNES: FROM THE *TRACT* TO THE *GENERAL THEORY*[1,2]

THE *Tract*, the *Treatise*, and the *General Theory*: this is the inter-war trilogy that marks the development of John Maynard Keynes's monetary thought from the quantity-theory tradition that he had inherited from his teachers at Cambridge; to his subsequent systematic attempt to dynamise and elaborate upon this theory and its applications; and, finally, to the revolutionary work with which he changed the face of monetary theory and defined its developmental framework for years to come.

These classic volumes have now been reprinted by the Royal Economic Society in the magnificent edition of Keynes's *Collected Writings* which it is publishing as its most appropriate memorial to Keynes. General responsibility for this edition rests with Richard Kahn, Roy Harrod, and Austin Robinson. The Society has also provided an invaluable service to scholarship by issuing two additional volumes—ably edited by Donald Moggridge from the papers that Keynes left behind him—containing the published and unpublished materials and correspondence that relate to the writing of the aforementioned trilogy. Most interesting of all here is the surviving written evidence of the by now legendary process of fruitful discussion and criticism that accompanied the development of the *General Theory*.

Truly to review these volumes would mean to survey the development of monetary theory as a whole during the inter-war period—and this is obviously not the task that can or should be undertaken here. What I shall,

[1] I would like to express my sincerest appreciation to my research assistant, Leonardo Leiderman, for his invaluable help. My thanks, too, to Mrs. Vera Jacobs for carefully and efficiently typing this article through its various drafts. The work on this article has in part been supported by research grants from the Ford Foundation (received through the Israel Foundation Trustees), the Central Research Fund of the Hebrew University, the Israel Commission for Basic Research, and the Israel National Academy of Sciences and Humanities—to all of which I am most indebted. Because of space limitation, I have not been able to provide detailed documentation for many of the statements that appear in this article. Such documentation is, however, provided in my forthcoming study *On the Development of Keynes' Monetary Thought* (1975*a*).

[2] A review article of the following volumes of the *Collected Writings of John Maynard Keynes* (London: Macmillan, for the Royal Economic Society): IV, *A Tract on Monetary Reform* ((1923) 1971, pp. xxii+172, £8.00); V, *A Treatise on Money*, 1: *The Pure Theory of Money*: ((1930) 1971, pp. xxvii+336, £8.00); VI, *A Treatise on Money*, 2: *The Applied Theory of Money*: ((1930) 1971, pp. vi+350, £8.00); VII, *The General Theory of Employment Interest and Money*: ((1936) 1973, pp. xxxv+428, £8.00, also available in a student edition at £1.95); XIII, *The General Theory and After*. Part I: *Preparation* (ed. Donald Moggridge, 1973, pp. xiv+653, £8.00); XIV, *The General Theory and After*. Part II: *Defence and Development* (ed. Donald Moggridge, 1973, pp. 584, £8.00). For convenience, I shall refer to these volumes by the following short-titles, respectively: *Tract*; *Treatise* I or *T.M.* I; *Treatise* II or *T.M.* II; *General Theory* or *G.T.*; JMK XIII; JMK XIV. Needless to say, all page references will be to the edition under review. I shall also use JMK I, JMK II, and so forth, to refer to the other volumes in this edition of *Collected Writings*.

instead, try to do is to take advantage of the opportunity now afforded of re-reading Keynes's three classic works in the light of the new and fascinating supplementary materials reproduced in JMK XIII and XIV in order to offer some general reflections on the development of Keynes's monetary thought during the period covered by these volumes.

I

This is a review not only of certain writings of Keynes, but of a new edition of those writings. It is therefore appropriate to begin with some comments—intended primarily for the specialist in the history of monetary thought who will use these volumes in his research—on the technical aspects of the edition itself.

In this context one is naturally led to make comparisons with another magnificent publication of the Royal Economic Society—Piero Sraffa's edition a quarter of a century ago of *The Works and Correspondence of David Ricardo* (1951–55). From the viewpoint of book-design, it seems to me that the present edition certainly matches the aesthetic achievements of the earlier one. On the other hand, as will be seen below, it has not fully met the standards set by the superb editorial apparatus that Sraffa appended to his texts.

At the same time, I must emphasise that as the consequence of a fundamental difference in conception as to the end-product to be presented to the reader, the scope of the editorial task in Volumes XIII–XIV of Keynes's *Collected Writings* is significantly broader than that of the corresponding volumes of Ricardo's *Works and Correspondence*. In particular, the latter was conceived as a reference work in the strict format of a scholarly edition. Accordingly, after the material had been classified by type (namely, "Pamphlets and Papers", "Speeches and Evidence", and "Letters"), it was (within each type) reproduced in chronological order, with few if any connective editorial comments—and with those that did appear relegated to special editorial introductions or footnotes, clearly separated from the texts themselves. In contrast, Volumes XIII–XIV of Keynes's *Collected Writings* have in effect been conceived not only as a reference work, but also as a "documented history" of the development of Keynes's monetary thought. For though the major emphasis of these volumes is unmistakably on the documents themselves, these documents have been interspersed with a running editorial commentary which integrates them into the outlines of a historical narrative (see pp. 251–2 below). Indeed, the needs of this narrative have frequently led the editor to depart from a strict chronological presentation of the material.

Though the conception of the Ricardo edition is the more usual one for scholarly editions, each of the foregoing conceptions is valid—and each has its advantages and disadvantages. Thus, almost by definition, the conception of the Keynes edition produces more coherent and readable volumes—and hence ones which will be of interest not only to the researcher in the field, but also to the general economist. On the other hand—and again, almost by definition—this conception imposes on the reader, to a greater extent than does that of the Ricardo edition, the judgment of the editor as to the relevance and significance of the documents in question (cf., e.g., pp. 253, 254 (fn. 3), and 269 below). This is the unavoidable tradeoff.

Let me turn now to some comments on the edition itself. In general, the editors of Keynes's *Collected Writings* have given much thought—and taken great care—to make this new edition of the "trilogy" as useful as possible to the reader. Thus the *General Theory*—around which an immense literature of detailed criticism and analysis has grown up—has deliberately been reprinted with an unchanged pagination (*G.T.* p. xix). And though the *Treatise* has been reset, it has been supplemented with an appendix providing the comparative pagination with the original edition. Unfortunately, however, though the *Tract* too has been reset, it has not been so supplemented. This is particularly regrettable in view of the fact that such an appendix could also have provided the comparative paginations with the already differently paged original British (1923) and American (1924) editions of this book.[1]

The editors have also provided each of the volumes of the "trilogy" with a brief unsigned introduction which most usefully describes the place of the volume in the general intellectual development of Keynes. Especially illuminating here is the "Editorial Introduction" to the *General Theory*. Another extremely useful addition are the special prefaces that Keynes wrote for the respective foreign editions of these books. These throw interesting light on the way Keynes himself viewed them subsequent to their publication. Needless to say, the editors have also taken advantage of this reprinting of the "trilogy" to correct the typographical errors that have been noted over the years (including some noted by Keynes himself) in the respective original editions of these books. Inevitably, however, a few—though I think very few indeed—new errors have crept in.[2]

The outstanding editorial achievement of the volumes under review is, of course, Donald Moggridge's editing of the published and unpublished materials that have been reproduced in JMK XIII and XIV, and which trace (with the aid of his invaluable running commentary) the development

[1] As indicated below (p. 254), one of the advantages of the new edition of the *Tract* is that it shows precisely how this book is largely based on the articles that Keynes had published earlier in the *Manchester Guardian Commercial*—a relation that the editors have further (and entertainingly!) highlighted by also reproducing the contemporary cartoons which Keynes chose to accompany his original articles (*Tract*, p. xiii). I must, however, confess that this advantage has unfortunately been achieved by using a multiplicity of footnotes (containing the variorum readings from the original articles) in a way which greatly interferes with the smooth reading of this enjoyable book—and which sometimes (e.g., p. 20) even leaves uncertainty as to how the original footnotes read. Both of these problems could have been largely averted—without impairing the objective of showing the relationship of the book to the original articles—by referring in the text of the present edition of the *Tract* to the footnotes containing the variorum readings by means of letter superscripts (instead of numbers), and by then printing such footnotes below a line at the bottom of the page. As it is, the problem has been further complicated by the unusual editorial practice of sometimes (but not always) placing Keynes's original footnotes in square brackets—a practice that on occasion has also been adopted in JMK XIII–XIV.

[2] There is, however, a larger number of typographical errors and slips in JMK XIII and XIV—the great complexity of whose material made proof reading a far more difficult task.

of Keynes's monetary thought from the *Tract* to the *Treatise* to the *General Theory*—and after. I think it is difficult for me or any other "outside" reader fully to appreciate the magnitude of the task that Moggridge and his staff have so ably carried out here: the careful sifting of the voluminous Keynes Papers in order to find, elucidate, and organise the great variety of materials (including unpublished lectures and reports, correspondence, incomplete drafts, scribbled notes, corrected galley proofs, and, of course, published articles) that were relevant to these volumes; the persevering attempts to complete the gaps in the correspondence found in these Papers by turning to those with whom Keynes had corresponded; and the extremely helpful supplementing at selected points of the material from these more standard sources with summaries based on interviews with contemporaries of Keynes and on lecture notes of his former students (see pp. 256 and 263 below). Only a hint of these prodigious and well-designed efforts can be discerned in the brief and modest "Editorial Foreword" to JMK XIII.

What I have found most valuable in these volumes is the reproduction of the surviving drafts of the *General Theory*—beginning with the fragments of the first drafts from 1931-32[1] (JMK XIII, pp. 381–405) and ending with the successive galley proofs of the book that began to flow in early 1935 (reproduced in the Appendix to JMK XIV, pp. 351–512). The value of the latter to the researcher has been immeasurably increased by the detailed editorial notes that enable him to trace the precise changes that Keynes made in these proofs.

The more dramatic aspect of the development of Keynes's thought is, however, revealed in his correspondence. Moggridge is always there to provide vital information about the context of the correspondence in question. In addition, he helpfully identifies the articles and books which may be implicitly or explicitly referred to in the correspondence, and usually also provides a few words of explanation about the writers of the respective letters.

On both of these scores, however, I feel that more could and should have been done. Thus the aforementioned articles and books are identified only by title and date of publication, and not by their full bibliographical details—and this sometimes makes it difficult to locate the reference in question.[2, 3]

[1] Unfortunately, the basis for dating these fragments is not indicated. Thus Moggridge states that the fragment reproduced on pages 381–96 of JMK XIII is the earlier one, and that the fragment reproduced on pages 397–405 is "from slightly later work, although still before the end of 1932" (JMK XIII, p. 380). To me, however, the correct order seems to be the reverse: for the fragment reproduced on pages 397–405 seems to be less finished than the one on pages 381–96; furthermore, the fragment on pages 397–405 seems to be more closely related to the *Treatise*—with its emphasis on the determination of the respective prices of consumption and investment goods.

[2] As a case in point, the source of the excerpt from Keynes's discussion in one of the seminars that took place in connection with the famous 1931 Harris Foundation Lectures is given (on page 367 of JMK XIII) as "*Unemployment as a World Problem: Reports of Round Tables* (1931)"—with no indication that this is an unpublished report of which only a limited number of mimeographed copies were issued. Again, the source of Keynes's published lecture on this occasion (reproduced in JMK XIII, pp. 343 ff.) is given as "*Unemployment as a World Problem* (1931)"—without listing the editor of this book (viz. Quincy Wright), under whose name the book is generally catalogued.

[3] In this context I might also note that advantage has not been taken of the new edition of the "trilogy" in order to fill out the original bibliographical references which appear there.

Similarly, it would have been helpful if these two volumes had been preceded by a list of biographical notes on the principal *dramatis personae* who appear in them—with particular emphasis on the respective relationships of these individuals to Keynes at the time that the action takes place.[1]

I should also note that the record of Keynes's correspondence as provided by JMK XIII–XIV is actually not as complete as it at first sight seems to be. There are omissions—resulting either from editorial decisions or from the chance oversights that are inevitable in a work of this scope and magnitude. The two that I have noticed are the omission of two or three minor notes that Keynes and John Hicks exchanged during the years 1933–35, and which Hicks (1973, pp. 7–8) has recently reproduced; and the omission of Keynes's correspondence with Simon Kuznets to which Keynes referred in the note that he published correcting the use that he had first made in the *General Theory* of Kuznets's estimates of net investment in the United States (*G.T.*, Appendix 2, p. 386; see also p. 258 below).[2]

Let me finally express a special word of appreciation for the excellent fifty-page classified index to these volumes (prepared by Barbara Lowe), which quickly and efficiently enables the reader to find his way through the 450-odd documents in the more than 1,150 pages of these volumes to the specific materials that are relevant to his purpose.

The editing of the six volumes under review—and especially of JMK XIII–XIV—is indeed a monumental task. It is accordingly only natural that there should be some criticisms and differences of opinion of the kind indicated above. But this in no way affects the basic debt that the profession as a whole owes to the Royal Economic Society for having conceived and carried through the noble idea of publishing these volumes—and to the editors and their staff for having so ably and commendably carried out their difficult and complex task. The volumes with which they have thus provided us are truly a "widow's cruse" from which students of the development of Keynes's monetary thought will gratefully continue to draw materials for years to come—without any diminution in the profits to scholarship.

II

Though I have referred to Keynes's three books on monetary theory as a "trilogy", they differ from each other greatly not only in substance (a difference that has, of course, been a major theme of all studies of the development of Keynes's thought), but also in form and purpose. Thus the *Tract* is not really a book, but a short and somewhat unsystematic revision and elaboration of the series of articles on post-war economic policy that Keynes first published in 1922 in the "Reconstruction Supplements" of the

[1] As was indeed done in the reprinting of Keynes's *Indian Currency and Finance* (JMK I).

[2] I first became aware that there had been such a correspondence from a chance conversation with Simon Kuznets. I have been informed by Moggridge that this correspondence (of which he has most kindly supplied me copies) may be published in a future volume of the *Collected Writings*.

Manchester Guardian Commercial. And one of the advantages of the present edition of the *Tract* is that it makes this relationship unmistakably clear by means of the variorum readings from these articles that it appends to the text.

In the *Tract*—as in these articles—Keynes dealt with the pressing problems of inflation, deflation, and exchange rate disequilibrium that then beset Europe. On the other hand, the brief, formal presentation of monetary theory that appears in the *Tract* (pp. 61–70)—and which, as Keynes tells us (*Tract*, p. 63, footnote 1) "follows the general lines of Professor Pigou...and of Dr Marshall"—is part of the material that Keynes added to these articles in making up the book. And just as this theoretical material was (by Keynes's "revealed preference") not necessary for an understanding of the original articles, so is it not really necessary for the book: its deletion would interfere very little with an understanding of the argument of the *Tract* at other points.[1] Conversely—and this is one of the clearest manifestations of the failure of the *Tract* to be an integrated whole—this added theoretical material on pages 61–70 barely reflects the penetrating and elegant analysis of inflation as a tax on real money balances[2] that Keynes reproduces from the aforementioned articles on pages 37–53 of the *Tract*.

Nor does the *Tract* incorporate the dynamic analysis of the way in which an influx of gold operates through the banking system—and thence on prices—that Keynes (basing himself on Marshall) had summarised in his 1911 review in this Journal of Irving Fisher's *Purchasing Power of Money*.[3] Thus the *Tract*—as a theoretical work—is not only not integrated within itself, but it even fails to reflect some major aspects of Keynes's thinking about monetary problems at the time it was published.

On both of these scores the *Treatise* is the exact opposite. It is as specifically designed for a professional audience with a major concern with the latest development in monetary theory as the *Tract* was designed for a general audience primarily concerned with current policy. Indeed, from the view-point of traditional scholarship, the *Treatise* is Keynes's most ambitious and weighty work: the two-volume work—on "The Pure Theory of Money" and "The Applied Theory of Money"—is designed to establish firmly his academic reputation. At its core (in Books III–IV of Volume 1) is a formal, rigorous presentation of a theory of money that deals in detail with both the static and dynamic aspects of the problem. And in the slow, methodical, dignified, and comprehensive manner in which an academic treatise customarily proceeds—but in which Keynes of the inter-war period so rarely proceeded[4] —it leads up to this core, first, by defining the nature of money and describing its historical origins (Book I); and then (in Book II) describing at length the

[1] Correspondingly, the theoretical pages of the *Tract* received little if any attention in most of the reviews of the book at the time.

[2] Including the notion of an optimum rate of inflation from the view-point of maximising tax receipts! (*Tract*, pp. 43–5).

[3] I would consider this long review essentially to be Keynes's first published writing on monetary theory—and hence feel that it should have been included in the Prologue to JMK XIII.

[4] See below, p. 267.

various index numbers that can be used to measure the value of money, which (to use one of Keynes's favourite terms) is the *quaesitum* of monetary theory. And afterwards comes Volume 2, which begins with a lengthy description of the respective empirical magnitudes of the critical theoretical variables described in the preceding volume—as well as of the institutional features of the financial sectors which bear upon these variables (Books V–VI). Only when all this is completed does Keynes finally proceed (in Book VII) to a systematic presentation of the monetary policy—both domestic and international—that he derives from his theory.

The *General Theory*, too, is—in Keynes's words of his preface—"chiefly addressed to...fellow economists" (*G.T.* p. xxi). It differs from the *Treatise* in being almost exclusively concerned with theory. Indeed, this is the whole purpose of the book as indicated by its very title. Thus the *General Theory* contains practically no description of institutional details. And for a work that is credited with having initiated a revolution in fiscal policy (see, however, p. 260 below), it contains surprisingly few explicit discussions of the policy implications of its analysis. Indeed, the major new policy conclusion of the *General Theory* as compared with the *Treatise*—namely, that monetary policy in the form of variations in the interest rate might not be enough, and that an effective full-employment policy may well require direct government spending—is never developed systematically and in detail. Instead, it is only referred to on one or two occasions in passing (e.g. *G.T.* p. 164)—and in brief "Concluding Notes" of a general nature (*G.T.* pp. 372–84). Similarly, the problem of the international monetary system—which was one of Keynes's major concerns in both the *Tract* and the *Treatise* (as it was once again to be at Bretton Woods after World War II)—is barely mentioned in the *General Theory*.[1] I shall return to this point below (pp. 259–60).

I should, however, emphasise that if from these viewpoints the *General Theory of Employment Interest and Money* was more narrowly conceived than the *Treatise on Money*, from another viewpoint it is—as its title indicates—much broader. For as I have already hinted above, "monetary theory" in the *Treatise* means, first and foremost, a theory that explains the determination of the price level. Accordingly, if the argument of the *Treatise* revolves about Keynes's "fundamental equations", these are (as the title of its chapter 10 makes clear) "The Fundamental Equations *for the Value of Money*" (*T.M.* I, p. 120, italics added). Again, Keynes explains the absence of a full analysis of the role of wage changes in these equations on the grounds that "this is a treatise on money, and not on the wages system" (*T.M.* I, p. 151). Similarly, he prefaces Book VI of the *Treatise* on "The Rate of Investment and Its Fluctuations" with the statement that it is "in the nature of a digression, which is doubtfully in place in a treatise on money" (*T.M.* II, p. 85).

[1] Aside from the references to the balance of payments in the "Notes on Mercantilism" in Chapter 23 of the *General Theory*—a chapter which is, after all, only an appendage to the main body of the book—the only references to an open economy that I have been able to find are the passing ones on pp. 121–2 and 270.

In conformity with this view—and in sharp contrast with the systematic attempt of the *General Theory* to base its analysis on the concepts of value theory—the term "marginal productivity" (of labour or of capital) does not appear in the *Treatise*. Correspondingly (as Moggridge points out) one of the first signposts on the road that leads from the *Treatise* to the *General Theory* is Keynes's change of the title of his autumn 1932 lectures from "The Pure Theory of Money" (which was the title he had used since 1929–30) to "The Monetary Theory of Production" (JMK XIII, pp. 343, 411–12).

Not that the *Treatise* was not concerned with changes in production. On the contrary, its main purpose was to explain the cyclical fluctuations of production and hence employment that then beset the economies of Europe and the United States. But the theory developed in the *Treatise* analysed these fluctuations not directly, but as the consequence of prior changes in prices. More specifically, the analysis proceeded as follows: Profits are the motive force of the economy (*T.M.* I, pp. 126, 163). The existence of profits causes firms to expand their respective outputs and hence their demands for the inputs of productive services—and conversely for losses. Now (in the Marshallian terms that Keynes used), profits are the difference between the "demand price" (i.e. market price) of a unit of output and its "supply price" (i.e. cost of production). Hence the study of cyclical movements of output reduces to a study of the causes of the differential movements of prices and costs—which study was the purpose of the fundamental equations of the *Treatise*.

At the same time—and in accordance with his view of the role of monetary theory as just described—Keynes insisted (in, for example, a letter to Ralph Hawtrey written immediately after the publication of the *Treatise* in October 1930) that "the question *how much* reduction of output is caused, whether by a realised fall of price or an anticipated fall of price, is important, but not strictly a monetary problem" (JMK XIII, p. 145, italics in original). And as Keynes was later to explain in the Preface to the book, it was with respect to this view of the role of monetary theory that the *General Theory* differed so fundamentally from the *Treatise*, by virtue of its being "primarily a study of the forces which determine changes in the scale of output and employment as a whole" (*G.T.* p. xxii).

What distinguishes the *General Theory* from the *Treatise* is not simply its more direct and precise concern with changes in output, but the crucial role that it assigns to such changes as an *equilibrating force* with respect to aggregate demand and supply—or, equivalently, with respect to saving and investment. Indeed, this is what Keynes's theory of effective demand is all about. And this is also what lends crucial significance to Keynes's "fundamental psychological law" of a marginal propensity to consume which is less than unity: for (as Keynes repeatedly emphasises) if it were unity, changes in output would have exactly the same effect on both aggregate demand and supply—and so could not act as an equilibrating force.

In this context let me emphasise that Keynes's notion of the less-than-full-employment equilibrium position to which (he contended) the foregoing mechanism might well bring the economy was, strictly speaking, one of *short-run* equilibrium only. In particular, Keynes's analysis of this position was carried out on the *temporary* assumption of constant money-wages. In Keynes's words (*G.T.* p. 27): "...this simplification, with which we shall dispense later, is introduced solely to facilitate the exposition" of Book I of the *General Theory*, in which the theory of effective demand was first outlined. And indeed after Keynes had (in Books II–IV) completed his detailed development of the basic building-blocks of his theory (namely, the consumption, marginal-efficiency-of-capital, and liquidity-preference functions, respectively), he abandoned this simplification and proceeded in Book V to apply the theory that he had thus developed to an analysis of the effects on the level of employment of a decline in money-wages—an analysis that (as Keynes explained) "could not be set forth clearly until the reader was acquainted with my [i.e. Keynes's] own method" (*G.T.* p. 257).

It is, accordingly, this Book V—and its opening chapter 19 in particular, a chapter explicitly entitled "Changes in Money-Wages"—that forms the apex of the *General Theory*. For it is here that Keynes finally achieves the *quaesitum* of the *General Theory*: namely, the rigorous theoretical demonstration that—contrary to the "classical theory" as Keynes understood it (*G.T.* p. 257)—lowering of money-wages was not an efficacious means of reducing unemployment. "The economic system cannot be made self-adjusting along these lines" (*G.T.* p. 267).[1]

Thus the *General Theory* is not a static theory of unemployment equilibrium, but a dynamic theory of unemployment *dis*equilibrium. What really concerns Keynes is not an economy in which the level of unemployment necessarily remains unchanged over time, but one in which (as a result of a declining money-wage) the level might be continuously declining, but much too slowly to solve the problem of unemployment within a reasonable period of time. Hence (concluded Keynes) an adequate full-employment policy could not rest on such automatic market forces—or even on central-bank interest-rate policy—but must instead impose upon the state "an ever greater responsibility for directly organising investment" at that level necessary for full employment (*G.T.* p. 164; see also page 378).[2]

[1] That this was a basic and recurrent theme of Keynes's thinking at this time is clear not only from the *General Theory*, but also from other materials reproduced in JMK XIII. See especially Keynes's November 1934 B.B.C. talk entitled "Is the Economic System Self-Adjusting?" (reproduced in JMK XIII, pp. 485–92). See also the passage in the mid-1932 draft of the *General Theory* reproduced on page 395 (*ibid.*), as well as Keynes's "Historical Retrospect" ("probably written in 1932") reproduced on pp. 406–7 (*ibid.*).

[2] I have developed this interpretation of the *General Theory* at greater length in my "Price Flexibility and Full Employment" (1951), Section 14, and *Money, Interest, and Prices* (first ed., 1956; second ed., 1965), Chapter XIV: 1. It is also elaborated upon—with further documentation—in my *Development of Keynes' Monetary Thought* (1975*a*), Chapters 9–10 (forthcoming).

III

Despite the foregoing differences between Keynes's three books on monetary economics, there are also important similarities. Thus a common element of these books is their concern with practical policy problems—and their related concern with the empirical aspects of these problems. At the same time I must emphasise that Keynes (like most of his contemporaries) largely used empirical data for illustrative purposes—or at most as a basis for rather impressionistic observations about the relations between the variables described by the data. Though there are partial exceptions (see the second paragraph below), Keynes practically never carried out a systematic statistical analysis of empirical data as a basis for conclusions.

Thus, for example, Keynes's excellent presentation of the purchasing-power-parity theory in the *Tract* is supported by charts and diagrams showing the generally corresponding movements of the actual exchange rates of England, France, and Italy with those respectively predicted by the theory (*Tract*, pp. 81–6). Similarly, Keynes's aforementioned analysis of inflation as a tax on real cash balances—and his explanation that this tax will decrease the volume of these balances that individuals will be willing to hold—is illustrated by data from the post-war hyperinflations of Germany, Austria, and Russia (*Tract*, pp. 45–6). Similarly, in the second, "applied" volume of his *Treatise*, Keynes presents empirical estimates of the variables that play a key role in the theory he developed in the first volume: namely, the quantity of money, the velocity of circulation, the volume of working capital—and he even adds a long chapter (30) providing historical illustrations of his theory.

Though there is less emphasis on empirical data in the *General Theory*, it is noteworthy that Keynes was quick to make use in it of Simon Kuznets's preliminary estimates of net investment in the United States in order to illustrate his (Keynes's) basic contention about the critical role of wide fluctuations in this variable in generating business cycles (*G.T.* pp. 102–5). What is even more noteworthy is Keynes's use of these data in order to make an empirical estimate (crude as it was) of the magnitude of the multiplier in the United States—and thence of the marginal propensity to consume of that country (*G.T.* pp. 127–8). Thus Keynes not only made the marginal propensity to consume a central component of macroeconomic analysis, but (to the best of my knowledge[1]) also provided the first estimate of its magnitude that was based on an examination of statistical time series![2,3]

[1] Unfortunately, the statistical basis of Richard Kahn's original estimate of this propensity in his celebrated article on the multiplier (1931, pp. 13–14) is not specified—except to say that it was supplied by Colin Clark.

[2] Thus Keynes's later (1944–45) serving as President of the Econometric Society was not simply honorific! Students of the history of econometric methods will also find it interesting to note that by deriving his estimate of the marginal propensity to consume from that of the multiplier, Keynes essentially estimated the former by means of the reduced-form method—and thus was (though obviously unknowingly) also the first to use this method of estimation!

[3] The significance of the "statistical revolution" that accompanied and interacted with the "Keynesian revolution" to their great mutual benefit is well attested by the fact that such estimates

Though all three of Keynes's books are concerned with policy issues, they nevertheless differ in the extent and sense of immediacy with which their policy discussions are presented. In view of the origin of the *Tract* in articles in the *Manchester Guardian*, it is not surprising that discussions on current policy issues are paramount in it. Indeed, having only a short time before dealt so successfully with prime ministers in his *Economic Consequences of the Peace* (1919, JMK II) and in his *Revision of the Treaty* (1922, JMK III), Keynes had no hesitations in sending out directly from the pages of the *Tract* advice on current matters to the finance ministers (or their equivalent), not only of England and the United States but also of Czechoslovakia (p. 120), Germany (pp. 50–2), and France (pp. xxi–xxii[1]).

In contrast—as befits a comprehensive, scientific work—Keynes's policy recommendations of the *Treatise* are for the most part of a more general nature, though here too there are references to specific, immediate issues (e.g. *T.M.* II, pp. 270 ff., 348 ff.). Least specific in its policy proposals (for reasons explained on p. 255 above) is the *General Theory*—though it clearly reflects the threatening air of immediate crisis generated by the mass unemployment of the period.

What were the specific policy problems that concerned Keynes? Naturally enough, they varied with the contemporary situation. Thus I have already mentioned Keynes's brilliant analysis in the *Tract* of post-war hyperinflation. But even countries (like England) that had not suffered disastrous extremes of hyperinflation in the post-war period, had nevertheless experienced years of rapid inflation that were followed by equally sharp deflations (*Tract*, p. 3). And against this background there emerged the problem of re-establishing an appropriate system of exchange rates among them.

This was one of the major problems that Keynes discussed in the *Tract*. In the course of this discussion he provided a lucid analysis (*Tract*, pp. 125–40) of the basic dilemma between the "alternative aims" of stability of the internal price level and stability of the exchange rate—and strongly argued the view that he was to re-affirm in the *Treatise* in favour of giving precedence to the aim of internal price stability.

The problem of the relation between internal price levels and exchange rates—and indeed (as noted on p. 255 above) the whole problem of the international monetary system, and of the impact of domestic policies on international reserves in particular—are not discussed in the *General Theory*.

---

of the overall volume of investment were not available only a few years before at the time when Keynes wrote his *Treatise* and had to suffice instead with "partial indicators" (*T.M.* II, p. 87). For further discussion of this question, see my forthcoming paper on "Keynes and Econometrics: On the Interaction Between Macroeconomic Theory and Measurement in the Interwar Period" (1975*b*).

[1] These pages are from the preface to the French edition of the *Tract*, which appeared in 1924.

The explanation for this fact too probably lies in the situation that prevailed in the Western world during the period that the *General Theory* was being written. In particular, this was the new world ushered in by England's abandonment of the gold standard in September 1931: a world of flexible exchange rates and/or severe restrictions on the flow of international trade, in which the aforementioned problems had accordingly largely lost their relevance.[1]

On the other hand, a problem that runs like a common thread throughout Keynes's "trilogy" is that of unemployment. Keynes's changing views on the appropriate policies for dealing with this problem reflected both the changing situation (viz. the duration and depth of the unemployment, as well as the just-described change in the framework of international economic relations) and his not entirely unrelated changing views on the validity of the quantity theory. Indeed, there are many who see Keynes's "trilogy" as The Saga of Man's Struggle for Freedom from the Quantity Theory—and I think there can be little doubt that Keynes himself so saw it.[2] Thus in the *Tract* Keynes embraced the Cambridge cash-balance form of this theory that he had received from his teachers. In the *Treatise* he continued to maintain the quantity theory in a macroeconomic (though not microeconomic) context—but criticised it as being restricted in its validity to comparative-statics analysis; accordingly, Keynes considered its supplementation by an appropriate dynamic analysis to be one of his major objectives in the book (*T.M.* I, pp. 120, 131–3, 137–8; II, pp. 4–5).[3] Finally, in the *General Theory* Keynes abandoned the quantity theory entirely, and in its place put the new theory that he had just developed (*G.T.* pp. 208-9).

There is, however, one point that I would like to make about the relationship between theory and policy in the *Treatise* and in the *General Theory*. It seems to me that in both cases the major contribution of the book is with respect to theory—and the purpose of the theory is to provide a rigorous underpinning for a policy position which already had many adherents. As Keynes himself indicated in Chapter 13 of the *Treatise*, this was certainly true for the bank-rate policy he advocated in that work. And as has been recently emphasised,[4] it is also true of the public-works-expenditure policy advocated by Keynes in the *General Theory*. Indeed, Keynes himself had already advocated such a policy in his famous 1929 election pamphlet (written together

[1] On the details of this world, see the classic study by Nurkse (1944). In this context it is also worth noting that Winch's study of *Economics and Policy* in England records many discussions of balance-of-payment problems during the decade that preceded the 1931 devaluation, but none in the years that immediately followed. See also Winch's reference to Harry D. White's report after a visit to Britain in 1935 that there was then "a complete lack of interest in British business circles in exchange problems" (Winch 1969, p. 201, footnote 4).

[2] As witness Keynes's statement in this preface to the French edition of the *General Theory* that "the following analysis [of money and prices] registers my final escape from the confusions of the Quantity Theory, which once entangled me" (*G.T.* p. xxxiv).

[3] For further details, see Patinkin (1975*a*, ch. 4).

[4] Cf. Winch (1969, chs. 6–8), Stein (1969, chs. 2, 7), Hutchison (1953, ch. 24; 1968 appendix), and Davis (1971). See also Patinkin (1969, pp. 96–8; 1974, pp. 5–7).

with Hubert Henderson) on "Can Lloyd George Do It?" (JMK IX, pp. 86–125). Accordingly, I feel that the major revolution affected by the *General Theory* was in the field of theory, and not of policy. And if (unlike the *General Theory*) the *Treatise* did deal at length with policy, it was not because it made any basic, new contribution to this issue, but because it was—as its name indicated—a comprehensive treatise, designed, *inter alia*, to describe the existing state of the science with respect to both theory and practice.

Just as Keynes's "trilogy" is bound together by a common concern with the problem of unemployment, so is it bound by a common lack of concern with the problem of economic growth. With respect to the *Treatise* and *General Theory*, this omission can well be understood as a "normal" characteristic of the economic literature of the depression years. For at a time when a dismaying percentage of the existing productive potential was idle, it would have taken an "unrealistic" soul indeed to have concerned himself with the problem of assuring the further growth of this potential. But I think that this lack of concern reflected an additional element in Keynes's thought—and probably in that of many of his contemporaries as well.

In particular, I think that Keynes viewed economic growth as a process that would emerge "normally"—and at a satisfactory pace—from a free-market system in which households saved, and then used these savings to purchase the securities[1] which firms issued in order to finance their expansion. "For a hundred years [before World War I] the system worked, throughout Europe, with an extraordinary success and facilitated the growth of wealth on an unprecedented scale" (*Tract*, p. 6)—and Keynes, like his contemporaries, was not much concerned with things outside Europe, in the broad sense of Western civilisation.[2] Now, what had seriously interfered with the growth process of Europe after the World War were the disastrous inflations which had wiped out the real value of past savings—and had accordingly discouraged further savings. Correspondingly, a necessary—and sufficient!—condition to re-activate the growth process at a satisfactory pace was to re-establish the confidence of the public in the future real value of its savings (*Tract*, pp. 16–17).

The *General Theory* introduced another factor that interferes with steady growth: unemployment. And parallel to his view in the *Tract*, Keynes felt that once this disturbing factor was eliminated, growth would again proceed at a satisfactory pace. Indeed, if full employment could be maintained, "a properly run community equipped with modern technical resources, of which the population is not increasing rapidly, ought to be able to bring

[1] Which is what Keynes means by the term "invest" throughout the *Tract* (cf., e.g., pp. 4–5, 7, 16 *et passim*).

[2] Keynes's *Indian Currency and Finance* (JMK I) is not a contrary indication: for, as the title of this book indicates, its concern is with the monetary aspects of India; it contains nothing on the "real" side. Indeed, one might almost say that Keynes was not interested in India *per se*, but in India as a convenient and outstanding example of the workings of a gold-exchange standard.

down the marginal efficiency of capital in equilibrium approximately to zero within a single generation" (*G.T.* p. 220).[1] The "zero" of the classical stationary state.

In brief, I would conjecture that in Keynes's view at this time there was no need for any special analysis of the process of economic growth. All that one had to do was to ensure the prevalence of two necessary preconditions: a stable value of money and full employment. And growth—to the extent that the economy was still interested in it—would take care of itself.

IV

The materials of JMK XIII afford us some behind-the-scenes views of the actual process of writing the *Treatise* and *General Theory*—and I would like to make a few observations about what is revealed. Here, too, there are similarities and differences. Among the basic similarities is the fact that the highly novel theoretical developments which mark both works were first presented to the profession at large as finished products: i.e. in the form of published books. In neither case was there any attempt by Keynes to exploit the relatively long period of preparation that was involved (roughly, five years) in order to publish articles in the leading scientific journals on the salient features of his new theories—and thus benefit from the exposure of these theories to the criticism of the profession at large before formulating them in final book form. It is true that such a "research strategy" was much less customary at the time Keynes wrote than it became later. But I would conjecture that Keynes's failure to follow such a "strategy" also reflected his belief that the quintessence of economic knowledge was concentrated in Cambridge—which geographical point need at most be extended to a triangle that would include London and Oxford.[2] So why bother publishing articles in order to benefit from criticism, if the most fruitful criticisms could be reaped more conveniently and efficiently simply by circulating draft-manuscripts and galley proofs among his colleagues in this fertile triangle?

And as the materials in JMK XIII show us, this is indeed the procedure that Keynes employed in the writing of the *General Theory*. On the other hand—and contrary to the accepted view of the matter—there is little if any evidence that the *Treatise* was subjected to much effective pre-publication criticism even within this triangle. And this is particularly true for what Keynes considered to be its major theoretical innovation—the fundamental equations. Correspondingly, there are many serious deficiencies in the *Treatise* which were pointed out immediately after its publication—and which (I conjecture) would have been avoided if only it

[1] Cf. also page 377 of the *General Theory* where Keynes speaks of accomplishing this aim "within one or two generations".

[2] Cf. Harrod (1951), pp. 322–3.

had been subjected to such criticism. And I would also conjecture that it was precisely this unfortunate experience with the *Treatise* that made Keynes so eager to seek out criticism as every stage of the writing of the *General Theory*.

Here again, however, the picture revealed by JMK XIII of the actual process of criticism and development is somewhat different from the commonly accepted one. More specifically, I think we can roughly distinguish here between three main stages: a first stage of (to borrow Moggridge's term) "arguing out the *Treatise*", which lasted until (say) the end of 1931; a second stage—the formative stage of writing the *General Theory*—which in part overlapped with the first stage, and which ended (at the latest) with the mid-1934 draft of the book; and a third stage which took up most of 1935 and which was devoted to obtaining detailed criticisms of the successive galley-proofs of the book. These stages differed not only with respect to their major emphasis, but to a certain extent also with respect to the individuals involved.

Prominent and fruitful roles in the "arguing out of the *Treatise*"—by means of correspondence, as well as published critiques—were played by Ralph Hawtrey (JMK XIII, pp. 130–73), Dennis Robertson (JMK XIII, pp. 201–2, 211–14, 219–38, 271–321), and (somewhat abrasively) Friedrich Hayek (JMK XIII, pp. 243–66). To this first stage also belong the discussions of the legendary "Cambridge Circus". This was the name given to the group of young economists at Cambridge (most of them then between 25 and 30) who—immediately after the publication of the *Treatise*—undertook a detailed critical examination of the book. The leading participants of the "Circus" were Richard Kahn, James Meade, Piero Sraffa, Joan and Austin Robinson—with Kahn serving as the channel of communication between Keynes and the group. And one of Donald Moggridge's most valuable contributions as editor of JMK XIII is his reconstruction—on the basis of the "pooled memories" of the aforementioned participants—of the major discussions of the "Circus" during the first half of 1931 (JMK XIII, pp. 337–43).[1]

As a result of all this criticism, Keynes—within a remarkably short time after the appearance of the *Treatise*, and certainly by the spring of 1932[2]—was already engaged in the basic re-examination of its analysis that was to lead ultimately to the *General Theory*. And the most important aspect of this re-examination was Keynes's recognition of the crucial necessity of

[1] At the same time I feel that James Meade's "cautious confidence" (as reported by Moggridge) that these discussions contained "most of the essential ingredients of the subsequent system of the *General Theory*" (JMK XIII, p. 342) claims too much. Thus, for example, the most essential ingredient of all—the theory of effective demand—does not appear even in the mid-1932 draft of the *General Theory* (on which see below).

[2] On this chronology, see the "Editorial Introduction" to the *General Theory* (p. xvi), as well as Moggridge's comments on page 337 of JMK XIII. See also Moggridge's illuminating article "From the *Treatise* to the *General Theory*: An Exercise in Chronology" (1973), as well as Lambert's "Evolution of Keynes's Thought from the Treatise on Money to the General Theory" (1969).

developing the theory of short-run output that—as Hawtrey and the various members of the "Cambridge Circus" had emphasised—was missing from the *Treatise*.

Unfortunately, relatively little material relating to this crucial, formative stage of writing the *General Theory* has survived. That which has (and for which we can only be most grateful) consists almost entirely of drafts of various chapters of the *General Theory* written in 1932 (JMK XIII, pp. 381–405) and 1934 (*ibid.* pp. 423–56, 471–84)—the latter of which already contained the basic conceptual framework of the *General Theory*. In addition, there are some odd notes and comments on these drafts that Keynes exchanged with Richard Kahn and Joan Robinson. It is, however, clear that there must have been many additional oral discussions of which no record has survived (cf. Keynes's references to such discussions with Kahn in JMK XIII, pp. 422, 484). Thus if we are to judge from the material that has survived to be reproduced in JMK XIII, the criticisms which influenced Keynes's work during the formative stage of writing the *General Theory* emanated almost entirely from his junior colleagues at Cambridge, and from Richard Kahn and Joan Robinson in particular.

Only after galley proofs of the *General Theory* started to flow in the beginning of 1935 did Keynes expose his work to the criticisms of economists outside the intimate world of his junior colleagues at Cambridge. For this purpose he renewed his correspondence with Dennis Robertson in January 1935 (JMK XIII, p. 493), and two months later with Ralph Hawtrey (*ibid.* p. 565). And a little later again—in June 1935—Keynes also began to send proofs to Roy Harrod at Oxford (*ibid.* p. 525). Needless to say, these proofs were also circulated to Richard Kahn and Joan Robinson. And almost all of the correspondence reproduced in the chapter of JMK XIII entitled "Towards the General Theory" is with these five individuals.

I have already expressed the opinion that the formative stage of the *General Theory* came to an end with the mid-1934 draft. Let me conclude this discussion by expressing the corollary opinion that even though the detailed criticisms of the proofs that stemmed from the aforementioned correspondence were undoubtedly of great value in leading Keynes to clarify the exposition and tighten the argument at various points, for the most part they did not affect the basic conceptual framework of the book.[1]

V

I turn now to some observations on Keynes's style—both analytical and literary. In so far as the analytical style is concerned, let me start by noting Keynes's failure to make use in his writings of graphical techniques—and this despite the fruitful precedent on this score set by his teacher Marshall,[2]

[1] For detailed documentation of the statements in this section, see my *Development of Keynes' Monetary Thought* (1975*a*), Chapters 6–7 (forthcoming).

[2] I might, however, note that Marshall relegated the analytical diagrams of his *Principles* to the footnotes: he never accorded them equal status with his text.

and despite the many passages (especially in the *General Theory*[1]) that almost cry out for the application of such techniques! Here and there in the "trilogy" there are diagrams of a statistical or schematic nature (*Tract*, pp. 83, 87; *T.M.* I, pp. 290–1; II, p. 317). But in all of these books there is only one diagram of an analytical nature. And even this one exception—which occurs in the course of his discussion of the classical theory of interest—is (as Keynes acknowledges) a diagram that Roy Harrod suggested to him (*G.T.* p. 180, footnote; see the fascinating correspondence on this diagram in JMK XIII, pp. 544–61).[2]

In connection with Keynes's analytical style, I should also note his oft-cited criticism in the *General Theory* of "symbolic pseudo-mathematical methods of formalising a system of economic analysis. . .which allow the author to lose sight of the complexities and interdepencencies of the real world in a maze of pretentious and unhelpful symbols" (*G.T.* pp. 297–8). We should not, however, uncritically accept this statement as if it were an expression of Keynes's unchanging and unequivocal view on the usefulness of mathematical methods. First of all, Keynes's own analysis in the *Treatise* was in fact largely based on fairly mechanical applications of the pseudo-mathematical "fundamental equations". Furthermore, the *Treatise* devoted an entire chapter (20) to "An Exercise in the Pure Theory of the Credit Cycle", in which Keynes explored in a very formalistic manner—and under a variety of alternative assumptions—the mathematical properties of his model of the cycle.

Indeed, it may have been Keynes's lack of success with such formal model building in the *Treatise* that led him to the more critical attitude expressed in the passage from the *General Theory* just cited. In any event, it is significant that in the *General Theory*—in contrast with the *Treatise*—Keynes did not attempt to provide a formal mathematical statement of the theory of employment that constitutes the major theme of the book. Instead, to the extent that Keynes made use of mathematical analysis in the *General Theory*, he did so with respect to such secondary themes as the relationship between the own-rates of interest of different goods (Chapter 17, Section II) and the theory of prices (Chapter 21, Section VI). And even in these instances, the mathematical formulation adds little to Keynes's literary exposition—and so could be deleted without much loss of continuity.

Actually, I think it fair to say that the *General Theory* reveals an ambivalent

[1] What I particularly have in mind is Keynes's diagram-less discussion in Chapter 3 of the determination of the equilibrium volume of employment "at the level given by the intersection of the aggregate demand function with the aggregate supply function" (*G.T.* p. 30; see also the similar statement on page 25).

[2] Keynes's failure to use graphical techniques in the *General Theory* is even more puzzling in the light of the fact that his chief disciples and critics during the formative period of writing the book—namely, Richard Kahn and Joan Robinson—played a leading role in the breakthrough that was then taking place in the use of such techniques! I am, of course, referring to Joan Robinson's *Economics of Imperfect Competition* (1933), in the writing of which she acknowledged the "constant assistance of Mr. R. F. Kahn" (*ibid.* p. v).

attitude toward the role of mathematical analysis in economics: for with all his reservations about the usefulness of such analysis, Keynes could not resist the temptation to employ it! Thus the quotation from the *General Theory* so critical of mathematical analysis with which I began this discussion, actually occurs in Section III of the same Chapter 21 that I have just cited as providing an instance of the use of such analysis—and indeed this quotation appears as part of Keynes's apologia for nevertheless going ahead and resorting to it in Section VI of that chapter! Thus when all is said and done, I strongly suspect that a comparison of the *General Theory* (and *a fortiori* the *Treatise*) with other works on economic theory that were written during this period would actually show Keynes's works to be among the more mathematical of them.

On the other hand, judging from the critical literature that subsequently grew up around Chapters 17 and 21, I think it fair to say that the mathematical analysis that appears in these chapters is not only not essential to the argument, but is also problematic. And this fact—together with the ineffectualness of the "fundamental equations" of the *Treatise*—makes it clear that whatever may have been Keynes's attitude toward the proper role of mathematical methods in economic analysis, his strength did not lie in the use of such methods.

Nor in general did Keynes's analytical strength lie in rigour and precision. Thus in both the *Treatise* and the *General Theory* Keynes frequently failed to specify the exact nature of the assumptions that underlay his argument. And the best evidence of the existence of such obscurities is the fact that forty years later disagreements continue to go on in the literature about the role played in the *General Theory* by such crucial assumptions as wage rigidities, the "liquidity trap", unemployment equilibrium and the like—not to speak of the protracted exegetical debate about the meaning of Keynes's aggregate supply function.

Instead, Keynes's analytical strength lay in his creative insights about fundamental problems that led him to make major "breakthroughs"—leaving for those that followed him to formalise and complete his initial achievements. In the *Treatise*, Keynes thought (erroneously, as it turned out) that his "fundamental equations" constituted such a breakthrough. In the *General Theory*, he saw his breakthrough as lying in his theory of effective demand—and this time he was undeniably right.

In view of this basic aspect of Keynes's analytical style, I should in all fairness also emphasise that the aforementioned lack of rigour and completeness in part reflects the "natural" deficiency of many a path-breaking work. As Keynes wrote to Joan Robinson:

> My own general reaction to criticisms always is that of course my treatment is obscure and sometimes inaccurate, and always incomplete, since I was tackling completely unfamiliar ground, and had not got my own mind by any means clear on all sorts of points [JMK XIII, p. 270].

Keynes made this comment in 1932 with reference to the *Treatise*; it is even more relevant for the *General Theory*.

These obscurities in the *Treatise* and *General Theory* frequently impede the flow of the reading. But despite these difficulties, there are constant reminders throughout the "trilogy" that we are in the presence of a master of English style. The language is generally rich and incisive, enhanced occasionally by well-turned phrases and apt literary allusions. For Keynes's objective is to appeal not only to the intellect, but also to the aesthetic senses.

This is particularly true of the *Tract*—and for two related reasons: first, because it is the least technical of the three books; second, because of its already noted origin (above, pp. 253–4) in Keynes's essays in the *Manchester Guardian*, where Keynes could give full expression to his brilliant publicist style.

Least enjoyable as a reading experience is the *Treatise*, whose generally heavy and constrained style reflects the stately scientific objective that Keynes set for himself in it (above, p. 254). Indeed, when one reads the *Treatise* against the background of Keynes's other writings, one cannot escape the feeling that it represents a Keynes out of character: a Keynes attempting to act the role of a Professor, and a Germanic one at that.[1]

In the *General Theory* we once again find the true Keynes. Here (as in so many of Keynes's writings) is the stirring voice of a prophet who has seen a new truth, and who is convinced that it—and only it—can save a world deep in the throes of crisis. It is a sharp, polemical voice directed at converting economists all over the world to the new dispensation—and combating the false prophets among them who perversely continue with the erroneous teachings of the earlier gods whom Keynes had already abandoned.

And so it is that these writings of Keynes are famous not only for their basic scientific contributions, but also for having become part of the literary heritage of every economist. For who does not know that "in the long run we are all dead" (*Tract*, p. 65); or that "the ideas of economists and political philosophers, both when they are right and when they are wrong, are more powerful than is commonly understood. Indeed the world is ruled by little else. Practical men, who believe themselves to be quite exempt from any intellectual influences, are usually the slaves of some defunct economist. Madmen in authority, who hear voices in the air, are distilling their frenzy from some academic scribbler of a few years back...The power of vested

[1] Among Keynes's economic writings, the only other one which is similar to the *Treatise* in its relatively dry academic style is his *Indian Currency and Finance* (1913, JMK I), which can best be characterised as corresponding to a Scandinavian Ph.D. thesis—or a German *habilitation*. If one goes outside Keynes's economic writings, then one must also mention in this context his *Treatise on Probability* (1921, JMK VIII), which originated in the fellowship dissertation that Keynes wrote during the period 1906–1909. In general, it would be worth while studying the intellectual interrelationships between this book and Keynes's economic writings, with particular emphasis on (*a*) Keynes's theory of the formulation of expectations under uncertainty, (*b*) his use of mathematical techniques, and (*c*) his views on the applicability of correlation analysis to economic data. In connection with (*c*), note Keynes's implicit reference to *The Treatise on Probability* (so I interpret it) in his 1939 critique of Tinbergen's work (JMK XIV, p. 315, last paragraph).

interests is vastly exaggerated compared with the gradual encroachment of ideas" (*G.T.* p. 383)?

VI

The *General Theory* was finally published in February 1936—and was immediately honoured with review articles by the leading economists of both the older and younger generations. And the major part of the text of JMK XIV is taken up with Keynes's published and unpublished reactions to practically all of these articles. These reactions varied from brief discussions carried out only by means of correspondence (as in the case of Harrod and Reddaway) to published replies that were in many cases preceded and/or followed by protracted correspondence (as in the case of Hawtrey, Hicks, Robertson, and Ohlin).

In general we can say that—in sharp contrast with the *Treatise*—having been formed and reformed in the fires of the detailed criticisms that Keynes solicited at every stage of its development, the *General Theory* stood up most successfully under the criticisms that followed its appearance. There were indeed some less integral parts of the book—for example, the attempt at formal rigour in Chapter 17 on "The Essential Properties of Interest and Money"—which proved to be deficient. But the basic structure of the *General Theory* not only remained intact, but also defined the framework of both theoretical and empirical research in macroeconomics for decades to come. Truly a scientific achievement of the first order.

The material of JMK XIV shows us Keynes not only defending the existing, but also continuously open to new ideas and developments. Thus, for example, we find him in the fall of 1936 and spring of 1937 discussing with Joan Robinson and Roy Harrod their respective extensions of his theory to international trade and the trade cycle (JMK XIV, pp. 134–79). And what is most revealing about the nature of the ever-active mind of the man, we find him already in August 1936 writing to Hawtrey about tentative plans to produce a book of "Footnotes to 'The General Theory'", "dealing with various criticisms and particular points which want carrying further"—and even preparing a table of contents for it (JMK XIV, pp. 47, 133–4). But the serious heart attack that he suffered shortly afterwards apparently put a halt to these plans (Harrod 1951, pp. 479–81; Austin Robinson 1947, p. 47). In any event, there are no further references in JMK XIV—which ends with material from December 1938—to the aforementioned book.

The *Treatise* began as a systematisation of the *Tract*; and the *General Theory* as a "short book" to develop the theory of the *Treatise* (*T.M.* I, p. xxvii). Who can know what form the "Footnotes to 'The General Theory'" would ultimately have taken?

VII

Let me conclude this review article with two further observations. First, the general reflections that I have presented on the development of Keynes's monetary thought have naturally been based on the materials in the six volumes of his *Collected Writings* under review. These are indeed the volumes that bear directly on this development. Yet it is quite possible that some further light on this question may be cast by forthcoming volumes in this edition of Keynes's *Writings*. What I particularly have in mind—in view of the vital interrelationship between Keynes's thinking on theory and policy that has been described above (pp. 258–9)—are forthcoming Volumes XIX–XXI on "Activities", that will contain Keynes's more policy-oriented writings during the period in question. And to a lesser extent I also have in mind forthcoming Volumes XI–XII on "Economic Articles and Correspondence (various)": for the integration of monetary and value theory carried out by Keynes in his *General Theory* means that in principle his correspondence on any aspect of economic theory may be of some (albeit tangential) relevance.

My second observation relates to the general question of the justification for reading the volumes of Keynes's "trilogy" today. From the substantive viewpoint, all of these volumes are now in the domain of the history of monetary doctrine: their basic scientific contributions have long since been incorporated in the current macroeconomic literature, so that, by definition, the volumes themselves are of importance only to students of this history.

From a broader viewpoint, however, there are sharp differences between these volumes. Thus in these times of world-wide inflation, I think that one can still read—with both pleasure and profit—Keynes's brilliant discussion of this problem in the *Tract*. On the other hand, the recent revival of interest in the *Treatise* notwithstanding, I can (from the viewpoint of macroeconomic theory) see little profit (and certainly no pleasure) in reading it today. Indeed, my re-reading of it now has only convinced me that the hitherto generally accepted view that it is not a good book is fully justified. Furthermore, though the *Treatise* does indeed help us achieve a deeper understanding of certain details of the *General Theory*, it does not provide such help with respect to the basic conceptual framework of this book (viz., the theory of effective demand), which differs so fundamentally from that of the *Treatise*.

In so far as the *General Theory* is concerned—this is the book that made the revolution which has continued to mould our basic ways of thinking about macroeconomic problems. And so the reading of it—at least in part—is an intellectual experience that no aspiring economist even today can afford to forego.

Don Patinkin

The Hebrew University of Jerusalem.

Date of receipt of final typescript: December 1974.

Bibliography

Davis, J. Ronnie (1971). *The New Economics and the Old Economists*, Iowa State University Press, Ames, Iowa.

Fisher, Irving (1911). *The Purchasing Power of Money*, Macmillan, New York.

Harrod, R. F. (1969). *The Life of John Maynard Keynes*, Macmillan, London, 1951, reprinted Augustus M. Kelley, New York.

Hicks, John R. (1973). "Recollections and Documents," *Economica*, Vol. XL (February), pp. 2–11.

Hutchison, T. W. (1953). *A Review of Economic Doctrines 1870–1929*, Clarendon Press, Oxford.

—— (1968). *Economics and Economic Policy in Britain 1946–1966: Some Aspects of their Inter-relations*, George Allen and Unwin, London.

Kahn, Richard F. (1931). "The Relation of Home Investment to Unemployment," Economic Journal, Vol. XLI (June), pp. 173–98. As reprinted in Richard Kahn (1972), *Selected Essays on Employment and Growth*, Cambridge University Press, pp. 1–27.

Keynes, John M. (1911). "Review of *The Purchasing Power of Money: Its Determination and Relation to Credit, Interest, and Crisis*, by Irving Fisher," Economic Journal, Vol. XXI (September), pp. 393–9.

—— (1913). *Indian Currency and Finance*, as reprinted in Keynes's *Collected Writings*, Vol. I.

—— (1919). *The Economic Consequences of the Peace*, as reprinted in Keynes's *Collected Writings*, Vol. II.

—— (1921). *A Treatise on Probability*, as reprinted in Keynes's *Collected Writings*, Vol. VIII.

—— (1922). *A Revision of the Treaty*, as reprinted in Keynes's *Collected Writings*, Vol. III.

—— (1923). *A Tract on Monetary Reform*, as reprinted in Keynes's *Collected Writings*, Vol. IV.

—— (1924). *Monetary Reform*, Harcourt, Brace and Company, New York. (U.S. edition of preceding, with different pagination.)

—— (1930). *A Treatise on Money*, Vol. 1: *The Pure Theory of Money*, as reprinted in Keynes's *Collected Writings*, Vol. V.

—— (1930). *A Treatise on Money*, Vol. 2: *The Applied Theory of Money*, as reprinted in Keynes's *Collected Writings*, Vol. VI.

—— (1936). *The General Theory of Employment Interest and Money*, as reprinted in Keynes's *Collected Writings*, Vol. VII.

—— (1973). *The General Theory and After*, Part I: *Preparation*, edited by Donald Moggridge, in Keynes's *Collected Writings*, Vol. XIII.

—— (1973). *The General Theory and After*, Part II: *Defence and Development*, edited by Donald Moggridge, in Keynes's *Collected Writings*, Vol. XIV.

—— (1971–3). *Collected Writings*, Macmillan, London, for the Royal Economic Society.

—— and Henderson, Hubert (1929). "Can Lloyd George Do It?", as reprinted in Keynes's *Collected Writings*, Vol. IX, pp. 86–125.

Lambert, Paul (1969). "The Evolution of Keynes's Thought from the *Treatise on Money* to the *General Theory*," *Annals of Public and Co-operative Economy*, Vol. XL (July–Sept.), pp. 243–63.

Marshall, Alfred (1920). *Principles of Economics*, 8th ed., Macmillan, London.

Moggridge, Donald E. (1973). "From the *Treatise* to *The General Theory*: An Exercise in Chronology," *History of Political Economy*, Vol. V (Spring), pp. 72–88.

[Nurkse, Ragnar] (1944). *International Currency Experience: Lessons of the Inter-War Period*, League of Nations, 1944.

Patinkin, Don (1948). "Price Flexibility and Full Employment," *A.E.R.*, Vol. XXXVIII (September), pp. 543–64, reprinted with revisions in *Readings in Monetary Theory*, edited by F. A. Lutz and L. W. Mints, Blakiston, Philadelphia, 1951.

—— (1956). *Money, Interest, and Prices*, Row, Peterson and Co., Evanston, Ill., 2nd ed., Harper and Row, New York, 1965.

—— (1969). "The Chicago Tradition, the Quantity Theory, and Friedman," *Journal of Money, Credit and Banking*, Vol. I (February), pp. 46–70, as reprinted in Don Patinkin, *Studies in Monetary Economics*, 1972, Harper and Row, New York, pp. 92–117.

—— (1974). "Keynesian Monetary Theory and the Cambridge School," in *Issues in Monetary Economics*, edited by H. G. Johnson and A. R. Nobay, Oxford University Press, pp. 3–30.

—— (1975*a*). "On the Development of Keynes' Monetary Thought," *History of Political Economy*, Vol. VII (Winter), forthcoming; to be reissued in book form by Duke University Press, Durham, North Carolina.

—— (1975*b*). "Keynes and Econometrics: On the Interaction Between Macroeconomic Theory and Measurement in the Interwar Period." *Econometrica*, Vol. XLIII, forthcoming.

Ricardo, David (1951–1955). *Works and Correspondence*. Edited by Piero Sraffa, with the collaboration of M. H. Dobb. Vol. I–IX. Cambridge: Cambridge University Press for the Royal Economic Society.

Robinson, E. A. G. (1947). "John Maynard Keynes 1883–1946," ECONOMIC JOURNAL, Vol. LVII (March), pp. 1–68.
Robinson, Joan (1933). *The Economics of Imperfect Competition*, Macmillan, London.
Stein, Herbert (1969). *The Fiscal Revolution in America*, University of Chicago Press, Chicago.
Winch, Donald (1969). *Economics and Policy: A Historical Study*, Hodder and Stoughton, London.
Wright, Quincy (ed.) (1931). *Unemployment as a World-Problem*. Chicago, University of Chicago Press, Chicago.
—— (1931). *Unemployment as a World-Problem. Reports of Round Tables*, 2 volumes, Norman Wait Harris Memorial Foundation, University of Chicago, mimeographed, unpublished.

'Keynes and Chicago'

D. Patinkin, 'Keynes and Chicago' (1979), reprinted in Patinkin (ed.) *Essays On and In the Chicago Tradition* (Durham, North Carolina, Duke UP, 1981), pp. 289–308.

12. Keynes and Chicago*

I am both honored and gratified to present this lecture in memory of Henry C. Simons—one of my first teachers at this University when I entered it as an undergraduate student in economics over thirty-five years ago, and a teacher who left an indelible impression upon me.[1]

I shall yet be returning to Simons this evening, but let me first emphasize that the subject of my lecture is not Keynesianism and Chicago, on which volumes could be written, but the far more restricted one of Keynes and Chicago. Specifically, there were two notable occasions on which Keynes had direct contact with Chicago: in 1931, when he came to The University of Chicago to participate in the Harris Foundation Lectures of that year; and in 1936, when his newly published *General Theory* was greeted by review articles by (among other leading economists) the two senior members of the Chicago School, Jacob Viner and Frank Knight, as well as by a brief review by that member in whose memory we have met here this evening, Henry Simons. And it is about these two occasions that I wish primarily to talk.

The subject of the 1931 Harris Lectures was the painfully current one of "Unemployment as a World Problem," and Keynes gave the keynote lecture (or rather, series of lectures) on "An Economic Analysis of Unemployment." In order to obtain a proper perspective on this lecture, we must remember that Keynes gave it less than a year after the publication of his *Treatise on Money* (1930), the work which at the time Keynes considered as his *magnum opus* and which he undoubtedly believed would be recognized for years to come as the definitive work on the pure and applied theory of money.

The Eighth Henry Simons Lecture, delivered at The Law School, The University of Chicago, May 2, 1979. Reprinted by permission from the *Journal of Law and Economics* 22 (Oct. 1979), pp. 213–32, with the addition of material on pp. 300–301 and on p. 304, fn 30, below.

*This paper was written while serving as Ford Foundation Visiting Research Professor at the Department of Economics and Graduate School of Business of The University of Chicago. I am greatly indebted to Shlomo Maital for providing me with materials from the Jacob Viner Papers at Princeton University. I would also like to express my sincerest appreciation to Marc Levin for his invaluable research assistance and to Mrs. Marie Marchese for so efficiently typing this paper through its various drafts The work on this paper was in part financed by NSF Grant SOC79–08281.

Because of its concern with historical questions, this paper refers to reprinted works by the date of original publication; for convenience, however, the page references themselves follow the pagination of the reprinted form as indicated in the bibliography. In particular, references to the writings of Keynes are to the new edition of his *Collected Writings*. For simplicity, I shall refer to the two volumes of his *Treatise on Money* as *Treatise* 1(2), respectively. The *General Theory* will sometimes be further abbreviated to *GT* Specific volumes of Keynes' *Collected Writings* will be referred to as *JMK* plus the volume number (for example, *JMK* 13)

1. See "Reminiscences," pp 4–5 above.

In retrospect, the approach of the *Treatise* was a fairly simple one. It claimed that business cycles, or (to use the term of Keynes and his contemporaries) credit cycles, are caused by the alternation of profits and losses. Now, profits are caused by the excess of the price of a product over its cost of production, and losses by a shortfall. And so Keynes' analysis of the business cycle evolved into an analysis of what determines the price per unit of output relative to the cost per unit. This is the subject and the purpose of the so-called fundamental equations—and Keynes' very choice of that term is ample indication of the significance he attached to them. I will not bother you with the obscure notation, so strange to us today, with which Keynes presented these equations. But when you finish examining these equations carefully, when you get down to their essence, what they say is the following:

$$\text{index of price} = \text{index of cost of production} + \text{index of profits}$$

—all per unit of output. And that is the fundamental equation!

Keynes recognizes that this is an identity, and indeed says so. But he also says that it is an identity which is useful for classifying causal relationships. However, if we read the *Treatise* carefully, we find that Keynes frequently shifts across the very thin and indefinite line that lies between repeating an identity and trying to endow it with more meaning than it really has. Thus by making use of a special definition of income (namely, defining it to exclude excess profits) Keynes showed that the excess of investment over saving was equal to excess profits—and then claimed that such an excess *caused* an increase in price relative to costs.

Similarly, Keynes supplemented his fundamental equations with a dynamic theory which stated that a decline in the rate of interest (more specifically, of the "market rate" relative to the "natural rate") generated an excess of investment over saving, hence raised prices relative to costs, hence generated excess profits, and hence led firms to expand their output; conversely, a rise in the interest rate would generate losses and hence a contraction of output. Correspondingly, the way to stabilize prices, hence avoid excess profits or losses, and hence cycles, is for the central bank to adopt a policy of varying the market rate of interest so as to keep it equal to the natural rate. And in particular, the cure for depressions and their unemployment is a central-bank policy designed to lower the rate of interest, hence stimulate investment, hence raise the price level relative to costs, hence generate business profits, and hence stimulate output and employment. In brief, by making use of the interest rate, the central bank could stabilize the price level, which policy was also the means of assuring the equality between saving and investment, and hence full employment.[2]

That is the policy position that we generally associate with the *Treatise*. But in recent years we have been reminded [3] that almost hidden away at the end of this book Keynes adds a crucial reservation about the applicability of this policy: namely, what he described as "the insuperable limitation on the power of skilled monetary management to avoid booms and depressions" that has its source in "international complica-

2. The preceding three paragraphs are reproduced in part from Patinkin (1977), pp. 4–5. For further details, see my *Keynes' Monetary Thought* (1976), chaps. 5, 6, and 12

3. In the excellent article by Moggridge and Howson (1974).

tions." More specifically, in a gold-standard world (and that was the world in which Keynes was then writing), a central bank acting in isolation cannot reduce the interest rate below that of other central banks, for this will lead to the outflow of gold and hence to a dangerous loss of international reserves (*Treatise* 2, p. 335). In such a situation Keynes advocates public works as the alternative "reserve weapon" by which the country in question can nevertheless combat unemployment. And Keynes makes it clear that this has indeed been the situation of Britain during 1929–30, for which (he notes) he has accordingly repeatedly advocated public works as a means of dealing with its problem (*Treatise* 2, pp. 337–38)—undoubtedly an allusion (*inter alia*) to his advocacy of such works in his famous 1929 pamphlet (together with Hubert Henderson) on *Can Lloyd George Do It?: An Examination of the Liberal Pledge*. On the other hand, says Keynes, the basic interest-rate policy of the *Treatise* is more appropriate for a country like the United States, which is much less dependent than Britain on "international trade and international lending" (*Treatise* 2, p. 336, especially fn. 1).

That was the background of Keynes' 1931 Harris Lecture. Indeed, this lecture was essentially a song of praise to his *Treatise*. Thus Keynes began his analysis of the slump in this lecture with a verbal rendition of the fundamental equations and with the accompanying proclamation, "That is my secret, the clue to the scientific explanation of booms and slumps (and of much else as I should claim) which I offer you" (*JMK* 13, p. 354). Which brings me to observe that though Keynes alluded to the Bible on more than one occasion in his writings (e.g., the famous "widow's cruse" of chapter 10 of the *Treatise*), the verse in the Book of Proverbs (27:2), "Let another man praise thee, and not thine own mouth" was apparently not one of his favorites.

In any event, Keynes summarized the "main theme" of his Harris Lecture in the following terms:

> The cure of unemployment involves improving business profits. The improvement of business profits can come about only by an improvement in new investment relative to saving. An increase of investment relative to saving must also, as an inevitable by-product, bring about a rise of prices, thus ameliorating the burdens arising out of monetary indebtedness. The problem resolves itself, therefore, into the question as to what means we can adopt to increase the volume of investment . . . . [*JMK* 13, p. 362]

Keynes then proceeds to describe three "lines of approach" for achieving this objective: first, restoring confidence, about which not much can be done deliberately; second, carrying out a program of public investment, which has the practical drawback that "it is not easy to devise at short notice schemes which are wisely and efficiently conceived and which can be put rapidly into operation on a really large scale" (*JMK* 13, p. 364); and, finally, lowering the long-run rate of interest by a vigorous central-bank policy of open-market purchases. And it seems to me quite clear that Keynes' preference is for the third method—a preference that, in the light of what I have said above, should be interpreted as a reflection of the fact that the world was still on the gold standard (though that situation was to change radically in the fall of that year, with Britain itself taking the lead in abandoning this standard), combined with the fact that Keynes was giving this lecture in the United States and not in Britain.

Not at all surprisingly, the conceptual framework of the *Treatise* (though it is not mentioned by name) also manifested itself in much of what Keynes had to say in the Round Table discussions that accompanied the Harris Lectures.[4] This is particularly true of his contributions (cf., e.g., *Reports*, pp. 73–74, 78–84, 92–92) to the Round Table which Alvin Hansen opened with a paper on "Business Cycles, Price Levels and Unemployment," and in which he actually referred a few times to Keynes' "book" (*Reports*, p. 49; see also pp. 62 and 66).[5,6] In this discussion Keynes also reaffirmed the policy-preferences of the *Treatise*:

> I should like to try the central bank method first, uncertain how far in practice it would lead us. If that proved to be incapable of keeping things reasonably steady, then I should go in for a very great degree of state control of the rate of investment [*Reports*, p. 93].

And in a later discussion of a paper by Otto Nathan on "Public Works Construction and Unemployment," Keynes made the *Treatise*'s differential (as between Britain and the United States) advocacy of public works most explicit:[7]

> I think the argument for public works in this country is much weaker than it is in Great Britain. In Great Britain I have for a long time past agitated very strongly for a public works program, and my argument has been that we are such a center of an international system that we cannot operate on the rate of interest, because if we tried to force the rate of interest down, there is too much lending,[8] and we lose our goal [gold?]. The advantage of a government program in Great Britain is that the government can borrow at whatever the world rate of interest is, regardless of whether the investment yields that.

4. A two-volume record of this discussion (designated on the title-page as "Confidential—Not for Publication") exists in mimeographed form under the title Norman Wait Harris Memorial Foundation, *Reports of Round Tables: Unemployment as a World Problem* (1931), referred to henceforth as *Reports*. In a prefatory note to these *Reports* (p. ii), Quincy Wright (who was Chairman of the meetings) states that the "reports have been in nearly every instance corrected by the speakers."

The contents of these 1931 *Reports* were surveyed (with extensive quotations) some years ago by J. Ronnie Davis (1971, pp. 107–24), though without placing them in the context of Keynes' writings in the immediately preceding period.

5. Hansen (1932) was shortly afterwards to write a brief note on a technical point in the *Treatise*.

6. Keynes again made use of the theory of the *Treatise* in his contribution to the discussion of the two papers by Henry Schultz and Carter Goodrich on "Is Wage Cutting the Way Out?" In particular, Keynes analyzed a wage cut primarily in terms of its effects on the relation between savings and investment, and concluded (as did most of the other participants in the Round Table) that he would not recommend such cuts as a means of dealing with employment (*Reports*, pp. 212–17, 222).

7. This point has already been made by Moggridge and Howson (1974, p. 236), who cite the passage as reproduced by Davis (1971, p. 120).

8 By which Keynes means lending abroad, which would generate an outflow of gold; compare this passage with that in *Treatise* 2, pp. 337–38 (pp. 376–77 of the original edition). Correspondingly, I believe the last word in this sentence should have read as indicated in the brackets. This is also the way that Davis (1971, p 120) has rendered it, though without indicating that it differs from the original text.

> In this country you haven't a problem of that kind. Here you can function as though you were a closed system, and I think all your argument hitherto has been rather based on the closed system assumption. For such a system I would use as my first method operating on the long term rate of interest.
>
> I think in this country deliberate public works should be regarded much more as a tonic to change the state of business conditions, but the means of getting back to a state of equilibrium should be concentrated on the rate of interest. That condition not being so in Great Britain, one had to lay great stress on public programs, but in this country I should operate on the rate of interest [*Reports*, p. 303].

At the same time, Keynes indicated that where a public-works policy was called for, he would recommend doing so vigorously. Again in his words:

> I am sure Dr. Nathan is right, that if we just depend on traditional methods, and keep to the traditional sphere, there never will be enough government work to be more than a small factor in curing a depression of the magnitude of the present one, but I should not be so sure that it is impractical to go beyond the traditional field [*Reports*, p. 294; see also p. 300].

When pressed to explain his preference for using interest-rate policy in the United States, as against public works, Keynes did so on the grounds that the former was more in accord with the philosophy of "individualism." In Keynes' words, "I use that [namely, interest-rate policy] because I am speaking in the country which is the last home of individualism" (*Reports*, p. 84; cf. also *ibid.*, p. 92). However, on the basis of my understanding of Keynes' personality, I would like to suggest that his preference for applying interest-rate policy in the United States was motivated by an additional consideration: namely, his already-noted belief in his fundamental equations as magic formulas that could solve the world's economic ills; his willingness (as he expressed himself the year before in a letter to the Governor of the Bank of England) "to have [his] head chopped off" if these equations should be false.[9] As against this absolute conviction, however, was his recognition of the frustrating fact that the major policy implication of these equations was not applicable to his own country, Britain. But it was applicable to the United States—and so under no circumstances would Keynes give up that unique opportunity to put his magic formula to the test.

Though the Harris Lectures brought Keynes to Chicago, they apparently did not bring him into contact with the Chicago School.[10] Viner was then spending the year at the Graduate Institute of International Studies in Geneva, which in that pre-jet age meant that he did not participate in the meetings at all. And though Knight's name

9. Letter cited by Howson and Winch (1977), p. 48. For other manifestations of Keynes' "magic-formula" view of his fundamental equations, see Patinkin (1976), chap 6

10. I am not including under this heading Henry Schultz, who, as already indicated, played an active role in the Round Table discussions. Nor am I including Paul Douglas, who in any event did not for some reason participate in these meetings (perhaps he was away from the University then). It might be noted that Douglas and, especially, Viner participated actively in the meetings of the following year

does appear among the members of the "Round Table Group," he participated in only one of the fourteen Round Tables which took place, and even then did not contribute more than one inconsequential remark (*Reports*, p. 481). Henry Simons (who was then an assistant professor) did participate in several of the Round Tables, but he too did so actively only once and inconsequentially (*Reports*, p. 88).[11] Only Lloyd Mints (then also an assistant professor) played a more active role. On one occasion he asked Keynes why "public works won't bring about precisely the same results" as a reduction in interest, and received the kind of answer that has already been described. Said Keynes:

> Certainly; therefore I am in favor of an admixture of public works, but my feeling is that unless you socialize the country to a degree that is unlikely, you will get to the end of the public works program, if not in one year, in two years, and therefore if you are not prepared to reduce the rate of interest and bring back private enterprise, when you get to the end of the public works program you have shot your bolt, and you are no better off. I should use the public works program to fill in the interregnum while I was getting the interest down. The public works program would in itself increase business profits, and therefore relieve people from that exceptional unwillingness to borrow.
>
> I should be afraid of that as a sole remedy. I should be afraid it would work itself out, come to an end, and then we should be back where we were unless we decided on a very definite further action [*Reports*, pp. 493–94].

On another occasion Mints asked Keynes what he thought of the possibility of reducing the rate of interest not only by "indirect means" (by which I think Mints meant open-market purchases of government securities), but also by purchasing "industrial and public utility bonds" [12]—to which Keynes replied that he would not favor such purchases "in order that the minds of those responsible for the central system should not have loaded on them the duty of judging the relative value of different classes of bonds" (*Reports*, pp. 479–80). I do not however know whether Mints was asking these questions out of conviction or out of intellectual curiosity.

Let me now jump roughly five years to the appearance of Keynes' *General Theory*. In the meantime, much has happened: Britain left the gold standard in September

11. Apparently, however, these Round Tables formed the basis for further contacts between Simons and Keynes Thus the Simons Papers contain a handwritten note from Keynes dated 31 March 1933—though without any designation of its addressee—which reads: "Much interested by the memorandum which you kindly send [*sic*] me." This may well be a reference to the memorandum on *Balancing the Budget: Federal Fiscal Policy During Depression* which was published in January 1933 as a University of Chicago *Public Policy Pamphlet*, and whose signers included Simons, Viner, and Douglas. The main message of the memorandum was that government budget should be balanced over the business cycle, rather than annually For details see Davis (1971), pp. 46–47

I am indebted to Donald Moggridge for advice on the reading of Keynes' note. Moggridge has also kindly informed me that there is no further correspondence on this point in the Keynes Papers in Cambridge; nor do these Papers, or the Marshall Library collection which came from Keynes' books, contain the aforementioned pamphlet.

12 The complete passage here refers to "purchasing industrial and utility bonds by the member banks themselves"; but from Keynes' reply and the discussion which follows (which describes Mints' proposal as one which would get the government "into the bond business") I think this passage should read " by the central banks themselves."

1931, which immediately led Keynes to advocate interest-rate reduction for it too. But after a short time, during which serious unemployment continued to prevail, it became clear to Keynes that such a policy was not adequate to the task. Accordingly he began to advocate public-works expenditures not as a second-best policy, but as a "first-best" one (Patinkin 1979b, pp. 162–64). And in the *General Theory* he developed the revolutionary macroeconomic theory which provided the underpinning for such a policy. According to this theory, the great degree of uncertainty which surrounds investment plans generates instability with respect to the volume of investment and also makes it unlikely that reductions in the rate of interest brought about by open-market purchases can stimulate investment (and hence employment) significantly. This effective interest-inelasticity of investment in turn implies that the additional money injected into the economy by the open-market purchase will largely be added to cash balances—that is, the demand for such balances under such uncertain circumstances is effectively highly interest-elastic. Correspondingly, government deficit-favored expenditures must be relied upon as a way of achieving full employment.

During this same period—as all good Chicagoans know, and as both Milton Friedman (on the occasion of the Henry Simons Lecture twelve years ago) and myself (on a somewhat later occasion) have spelled out in detail[13]—the Chicago School was independently developing the traditional $MV = PT$ quantity-theory approach in a way that led it to seemingly similar conclusions. In its analysis, the major cause of the cycle was the instability, not of investment, but of the velocity of circulation V, which set off cummulative movements of expansion or contraction in the economy. And the corresponding policy prescription of the Chicago School of the 1930s (more specifically, of Simons and Mints) was for the government to make appropriate changes in M that would offset these changes in V and thus maintain a constant level of what Simons called "total turnover MV" (1934, p. 64). Under the assumption of some downward flexibility in prices, it also advocated for this purpose the operational rule of varying M so as to stabilize the price level, P: increasing M when P tended to fall, and decreasing M when it tended to rise. The necessary variations in M were to be generated either by open-market operations or by budgetary deficits, which deficits in turn were to be generated by varying either government expenditures and/or tax receipts.[14]

Having mentioned Friedman's Simons lecture, let me digress briefly to dispute one of its major contentions. When in his "Rules versus Authorities in Monetary Policy" (1936) Simons chose the foregoing policy rule of keeping the price level constant, he

13 Though with some differences; see chap. 10 above, p 248, fn. 22, and p. 257, fn 3 A more significant difference—of another nature—will be discussed in the next two paragraphs.

The views of the Chicago School have also been described in J Ronnie Davis' *New Economics and the Old Economists* (1971), chap. 3.

14. For documentation and further details, see chap. 10 above, pp. 245–52, which also refers to the views of Knight and Viner. I have not been able to find any place where Viner explicitly supported this policy prescription; on the other hand, he was already in the early 1930s advocating deficit spending, as well as the more general policy of balancing the budget only over the cycle; see Davis (1971), pp. 39–46 Cf also Viner's letter to me of February 23, 1970, reproduced on pp. 270–71 above

did so after considering—and rejecting—an alternative rule of keeping the quantity of money constant. And he explained this choice in the following words:

> With all its merits, however, this rule [of holding the quantity of money constant] cannot now be recommended as a basis for monetary reform. The obvious weakness of fixed quantity, as a sole rule of monetary policy, lies in the danger of sharp changes on the velocity side, for no monetary system can function effectively or survive politically in the face of extreme alternations of hoarding and dishoarding. It is easy to argue that something would be gained in any event if perverse changes were prevented merely as to quantity, but the argument is unconvincing. The fixing of the quantity of circulation media might merely serve to increase the perverse variability in the amounts of "near moneys" and in the degree of their general acceptability, just as the restrictions on the issue of bank notes presumably served to hasten the development of deposit (checking-account) banking [1936, p. 164].

Now, Friedman quite reasonably says that Simon's belief in the instability of velocity was based on his interpretation of the Great Depression; but Friedman goes on to contend that had Simons then known the "facts which we now know and he did not" (1967, p. 84), he would not have interpreted the Great Depression in terms of such an instability of V, and would accordingly have chosen instead a policy rule stated in terms of the quantity of money.

I must confess that I have always found it difficult to understand the operational meaning of such statements: to understand how they can be subjected to empirical test. And what compounds my difficulty in this case is that Friedman does not specify which of the facts of the Great Depression—facts that he goes on to cite from his monumental study with Anna Jacobson Schwartz of *A Monetary History of the United States* (1962)—were not available to Simons. Surely it cannot be the facts about the decline in Federal Reserve credit outstanding to which Friedman refers (1967, p. 90); for current monthly data on the volume of this credit were being published in the *Federal Reserve Bulletin*. Nor can it be the broad facts about the changes in the money supply which Friedman cites: for monthly data on currency in circulation had long since been available, and ever since 1927 quarterly data on net deposits (including time deposits) of all banks were being published in the *Bulletin* as well as the *Annual Reports* of the Federal Reserve; and the addition of these two series yields an estimate of the money supply[15] whose changes during the Great Depression are broadly similar to those described by Friedman in his lecture.[16] Even more relevant to the question at issue (for reasons that will become clear in a moment) is the fact that in November

15. Which after subtracting deposits of mutual savings banks (for which the Federal Reserve provided separate estimates), conceptually approximates Friedman's M_2; needless to say, however, this procedure leads to double-counting of vault cash, a minor item.

16. Thus in terms of annual rates of change in M_2, Friedman (1967, pp. 89–90) describes (a) a decline at the rate of 2.3 percent from August 1929 to October 1930; (b) a decline at the rate of 13 percent from March 1931 to August 1931; and (c) a decline at the rate of 31 percent from August 1931 to January 1932. The corresponding estimates from the Federal Reserve data (for the quarters closest to these respective periods, and again in terms of annual rates of change) are (a) −5.7 percent; (b) −5 percent; and (c) −27 percent (Federal Reserve Board, *Twentieth Annual Report* (1934), pp. 141, 163).

1933 Lauchlin Currie published an article in the *Quarterly Journal of Economics* in which he provided annual estimates of the money supply for 1921–32 whose year-to-year percentage changes during the Great Depression are also similar to those described by Friedman and Schwartz.[17] And in April 1934 Currie used this series as the basis of an article which he published in the *Journal of Political Economy* on "The Failure of Monetary Policy to Prevent the Depression of 1929–32." Indeed, the major conclusion of this article was that "The [Federal Reserve] policy followed throughout 1929, so far from tending to prevent the depression, actually operated, in the view of this paper, to bring it on" (Currie 1934a, p. 176). Later in that year, Currie published a book on *The Supply and Control of Money in the United States* (1934b) in which he reproduced the monetary data of his 1933 article (pp. 31–33, 70) as well as the major conclusions of his 1934 one (pp. 144–48). And since—as the last link in this chain of events—Simons reviewed this book the following year for the *Journal of Political Economy* we can safely say that when he chose his price-stabilization rule, Simons had available to him not only monetary data that revealed roughly the same changes that Friedman has described in his lecture, but even an alternative interpretation of these data which in its broad lines agreed with the one that Friedman was later to give.[18,19]

Let me return now to our main subject. The *General Theory* appeared in February 1936 and in November of that year the *Quarterly Journal of Economics* published what was to become a celebrated symposium on the book in which Jacob Viner wrote the lead article (entitled "Mr. Keynes on the Causes of Unemployment"), followed by articles by Dennis Robertson, Wassily Leontief, and F. W. Taussig, who also acted as editor of the symposium. In a comment on this review written some twenty-five years later, Viner explained that he had been asked by Taussig to concentrate on Keynes' theory of changes in the volume of employment, which Viner interpreted as a short-run theory. As such (wrote Viner in this comment) he found the *General Theory* "a veritable landmark, in both its positive and negative or critical aspects, in the history of our discipline" (Viner, 1964, p. 255).[20] At the same time (said Viner in this comment) he remained "skeptical . . . with some propensity to be hostile" with respect to Keynes' denial "that (in a truly competitive economy) there

17. Thus the following are the percentage year-to-year changes in M_1 as respectively estimated by Currie and Friedman-Schwartz (the estimates of the latter appear in parentheses): 1928–29. 0.1 (1.7); 1929–30: −3.7 (−3.4); 1930–31: −6.4 (−5.6); 1931–32. −13 7 (−14.4) (Currie, 1933, p. 84; Friedman-Schwartz, 1963, pp. 710–14). A similar comparison holds with respect to the monthly estimates which James W. Angell presented in his *Behavior of Money* (1936, p. 175).

As noted above (p. 278, fn 1), the work of Currie and Angell is not referred to in Friedman and Schwartz' *Monetary History of the U.S.* (1963); the estimates themselves are however described in their subsequent volume on *Monetary Statistics of the U S* (1970). For more on Currie's contribution to monetary economics, see Brunner (1968), Humphrey (1971), and Jones (1978); cf. also the preceding chapter.

18 In 1935 Currie published a second edition of his book with slightly different estimates of M_1; these differences, however, have almost no effect on the percentage changes described in the preceding footnote.

19 For another aspect of Simons' review of Currie's book, see p. 283 above.

20. On the other hand, Viner (1951, p. 13) felt that "neither in his *General Theory* or after did Keynes himself make any important application of his new doctrines and concepts to theoretical issues in the international field " (I am indebted to Jacob Frenkel for bringing this passage to my attention.)

exist powerful automatic forces which in the long run, if not counteracted by perverse governmental intervention, will restore equilibrium'' (Viner, 1964, p. 255). Viner also explained that in his review he had not discussed ''Keynes' ventures in the *General Theory* into *Dogmengeschichte*,'' and added that ''as a historian of thought in areas in which he was emotionally involved as a protagonist and prophet, Keynes seemed to me to be seriously lacking in the unexciting but essential qualities for the intellectual historian of objectivity and of judiciousness'' (Viner, 1964, p. 254). Amen.

As can be gathered from this, Viner's review itself was a favorable one. Unlike such review articles as those by Hicks (1937) and Meade (1937), however, it did not attempt to summarize the basic conceptual framework of the *General Theory* and instead restricted itself to presenting a balanced criticism of various individual points in it. Thus Viner identifies one of the major differences between Keynes' position and the orthodox one as lying in Keynes' denial that reduction of money wages is a remedy for unemployment. Viner contends that Keynes had failed to take account of the possibility that the decline in prices might lag behind that of wages, thus giving a temporary boost to profits, which in turn would stimulate investment and thus output (Viner 1936, pp. 247–49). On another point, and in an adumbration of discussions twenty years later, Viner also argues that consumption should be assumed to be a function not only of current income, but also of wealth and of ''anticipations as to the prospective trend of income''—and that the influence of wealth acts as a stabilizing factor over the cycle (*ibid*., p. 239, fn. 3; pp. 250–52).

Viner's major criticism, however, is of Keynes' contention that the rate of interest is determined by liquidity preference in the sense of the propensity to hoard. As against this, Viner supports Robertson's point in his contribution to the symposium that the transactions demand—and the forces of consumption and investment which lie behind it—are equally important determinants of this rate. Viner also contends that in any event such hoards are quantitatively small, since most money holdings are for transaction purposes. And in what I interpret as an allusion to the teaching prevalent at Chicago (and elsewhere), Viner also claims that ''in modern monetary theory it [i.e., hoarding] is generally dealt with, with results which in kind are substantially identical with Keynes', as a factor operating to reduce the 'velocity' of money'' (Viner, 1936, p. 240).

In his reply to Viner (whose contribution Keynes described as ''the most important of the four'') Keynes contended that ''the monetary theorists who try to deal with it in this way are altogether on the wrong track'' (Keynes, 1936, p. 211). But at the later point at which Keynes seems to be expanding on this contention (*ibid*., p. 216), he fails to take account of the fact that an increased propensity to hoard means a decreased velocity of circulation. Nor does he concede to Viner or to Robertson—or for that matter to anyone else at any other time—that the rate of interest is determined by savings and investment, as well as liquidity preference (Patinkin, 1976, pp. 62–63, 99).

About a year later, Frank Knight published his review article of the *General Theory* in the *Canadian Journal of Economics and Political Science* under the title ''Unemployment: And Mr. Keynes' Revolution in Economic Theory'' (1937). In his opening footnote Knight states that the article will be ''primarily critical in nature,'' and he more than fulfills his promise. It is Knight at his irascible and sarcastic best—or worst. I have had the opportunity of examining Knight's copy of the *General Theory*, the one which he presumably read in preparation for writing his review, and it is filled with pencilled marginal notes of vehement dissent.[21] Thus on Keynes' statement in the Preface that ''It is astonishing what foolish things one can temporarily believe if one thinks too long alone, particularly in economics'' (*GT*, p. vii), Knight commented ''best statement in the book''—and we know of whom he was thinking. The expletive ''Nonsense!''—replaced on occasion by even stronger terms—makes a frequent appearance in these margins. There are, however, passages which Knight obviously enjoyed, such as like Keynes' scintillating description of the nature of speculative activity on the stock market, and on Wall Street in particular (*GT*, pp. 153–60—''Best thing in the Book?'').

In any event, Knight's published review is a fairly systematized—if expurgated—rendition of these marginal notes. And this is a pity: for lost in this sea of captious criticisms are some valid points. Thus Knight (1937, p. 103), alone of all reviewers, rightly criticizes Keynes' puzzling statement that profits are maximized at the intersection point of aggregate demand and supply (*GT*, p. 25).[22] Like Viner, Knight also shows that Keynes' statements about hoarding can be translated into more familiar statements about changes in velocity. In Knight's words, ''saving may be hoarded and by reducing monetary circulation lead to sales reductions or price declines with all the consequences of these in train; but familiar terms and modes of expression seem to be shunned on principle in this book'' (Knight, 1937, p. 108; see also p. 110). And like Viner and Robertson, Knight also rejects Keynes' purely monetary theory of interest. In particular, he criticizes Keynes' theory of liquidity-preference on the grounds that

> . . . it is self-evident that at any time (and at the margin) the rate of interest equates *both* the desirability of holding cash with the desirability of holding non-monetary wealth *and* the desirability of consuming with that of lending and so with both the other two desirabilities. For, to any person who has either money or wealth in any form, or to anyone who holds salable service-capacity, all three of these alternatives are continuously open (Knight, 1937, p. 113, italics in original).

Let me, however, note that this description of the desire for holding money as an alternative to holding other forms of wealth does not appear in earlier Chicago writings on money, and so can itself be regarded as reflecting the influence of Keynes' theory of liquidity preference—an influence that was to manifest itself in subsequent writings of other Chicagoans as well (see above, chapter 10, pp. 247–49, 253–56).

To the best of my knowledge, Knight's review is also the only one which points out

21. I am indebted to George Stigler for making this book available to me, and to Mrs. Frank Knight for permitting me to quote from its marginal notes

22. Cf. Patinkin (1979a), pp. 171–73.

that though Keynes contends that he has presented a theory of unemployment equilibrium, his language at various points in the book indicates that he is really talking about a short-period situation. In Knight's words:

> The next general comment which must be made on Mr. Keynes's book as a whole is that it is inordinately difficult to tell what the author means. This is true in particular because on general issues it appears certain that he does not mean what he says. The theory is ostensibly one of equilibrium with extensive involuntary unemployment . . . and in the bulk of the exposition there is no explicit reference to cycles or oscillations and little hint that such phenomena exist. Now I for one simply cannot take this new and revolutionary equilibrium theory seriously, and doubt whether Mr. Keynes himself really does so. Scattered through the work are innumerable references to the short period, several which indicate that reactions are more or less reversible (*e.g.*, pp. 248, 251), and a few which run frankly in terms of comparative stability or stickiness rather than fixity (pp. 236, 237); in particular, there is a reference (p. 249) to the capacity of the economic system for remaining in a "chronic" condition of sub-normal activity for a "considerable period". This is a far cry from the "stable equilibrium" of page 30 and the tone of most of the book (Knight, 1937, p. 121).

And for this general tone, a typical Knightian explanation is provided: in modern times "the demand for heresy is always in excess of the supply and its production always a prosperous business" (Knight, 1937, p. 122, fn. 22). Knight also repeatedly emphasizes that there can be a long-period position of unemployment equilibrium only if there is absolute rigidity of the money wage rate.[23]

The editor of the *Canadian Journal* wrote Keynes asking if he would care "to write a counter-blast" to Knight's review. But Keynes declined, saying that "with Professor Knight's two main conclusions, namely, that my book had caused him intense irritation, and that he had had great difficulty in understanding it, I am in agreement. So perhaps you will excuse me if I leave the article alone" (*JMK* 29, p. 217).

This difference between Knight's and Viner's views of the *General Theory* gave rise a few years later to an incident which to begin with was probably never known to more than a few people, which slipped into oblivion afterwards, and of which I have only now learned. In 1940 The University of Chicago was making plans for the celebration of its fiftieth anniversary the following year. Among these plans was the customary one of marking the occasion by awarding honorary doctorates to outstanding scholars of the world. In this connection Jacob Viner—and this was before their wartime contacts which so deeply impressed him (see fn. 30 below)—apparently proposed awarding such a degree to Keynes. I say "apparently" because the only evidence I have of this is a lengthy letter in the Viner Papers from Knight to Viner,

23. There is one major exception to the generally negative tone of Knight's review, namely (as might be guessed from the above description of Knight's marginal notes), his description of Keynes' discussion of "the speculative element involved in any decision to invest" (Knight, 1937, p. 11). Knight, however, questions the novelty of this discussion, and cites Keynes' own reference to Irving Fisher's marginal rate of return over cost (*GT*, p. 140). I do not, however, see the relevance of Fisher to this discussion, whereas I do very much see the relevance of Knight's own *Risk, Uncertainty and Profit* (1921)—to which Knight, quite characteristically, does not refer.

dated August 6, 1940, which begins by expressing Knight's "shock" at having heard that Viner had made such a proposal—and which then goes on to denounce it vigorously. The main substantive basis of Knight's objection was expressed in the following words:

> I regard Mr. Keynes' neo-mercantilistic position in economics in general, and with respect to money and monetary theory in particular,[24] as essentially taking the side of the man-in-the-street, against the effort of the economic thinker and analyst to get beyond and to dispel the short-sighted views and prejudices of the former. . . . His work and influence seem to me supremely "anti-intellectual," in the only meaning of intellectual life which is worthy of approval or support.

Whether because of Knight's objections, or for other reasons, the honorary degree was never awarded.[25]

Let me turn now to Henry Simon's brief review of the *General Theory*. This appeared in the *Christian Century* for July 2, 1936 and was almost as critical as Knight's. In accordance with the nonprofessional nature of this magazine,[26] the review is practically devoid of technical analytical details and instead dwells largely on what Simons saw as the policy implications of Keynes' book. Thus Simons began by explaining that:

> Mr. Keynes' main point is that our economic system has been excessively exposed and subjected to deflationary pressures—that individual savings are likely to get dammed up in hoards, instead of flowing on to finance the production of investment-assets. With this judgment, the reviewer is inclined definitely to agree. Indeed, if the whole book could be interpreted simply as a critical appraisal of the traditional gold standard, implemented through central-bank operations, one's judgment of its main ideas might be extremely favorable.

24. What I think Knight primarily had in mind here was Keynes' purely monetary theory of interest; cf pp. 33 and 299 above.

25. The foregoing excerpt from Knight's letter is reproduced here with the permission of the Princeton University Library. I have been informed by Shlomo Maital that there is no other material relating to this letter in the Viner Papers there. Nor is this letter or any related material to be found in the Frank Knight Papers at Chicago or in the files of the Department of Economics there

Of the members of the Department at that time who are still with us, Gregg Lewis and Lloyd Mints have informed me that they never knew of this incident; and John Nef wrote me as follows (cited with permission from a letter dated July 18, 1979):

> I was a member of the committee for recommending the awarding of honorary degrees to the president at the time you mention and I was also a member of the special committee which recommended degrees in connection with the social sciences at the time of the fiftieth anniversary celebration of the founding of the University. I cannot remember Lord Keynes' name being brought before either of these committees. So I assume that Viner did not force the issue with Knight

Among the individuals who did receive honorary degrees at the Fiftieth-Anniversary Convocation in September 1941 were R. H. Tawney and J. M. Clark. (From 1915–26, Clark had been a Professor of Political Economy at Chicago and a member of the teaching staff of both the Department of Political Economy and the School of Business. At the Convocation he was presented by the dean of the School of Business.)

26. I do not know why Simons chose it as a vehicle for his review, he had once before published a group of reviews there. See the bibliography in Simons (1948), p 314.

He then goes on to criticize Keynes for advocating that, in order to solve these problems, "the state should use taxation to curtail private saving; it should supplement private consumption and investment with its own spending and it should force down and keep down the rate of interest to promote new enterprise," vehemently declaring that by suggesting these and similar measures, Keynes "may only succeed in becoming the academic idol of our worst cranks and charlatans—not to mention the possibilities of the book as the economic bible of a fascist movement." And in an obvious allusion to his own policy Simons writes:

> Mr. Keynes nowhere suggests the need for economy in the kinds of governmental interference; and he seems to disregard, or grossly to underestimate, the possibilities of controlling all the variables which his analysis emphasizes merely by controlling the quantity of money—i.e., by ordering fiscal practice (spending, taxing, borrowing and currency issue) in terms of deliberate monetary policy. He overlooks the need (clearly suggested by his own analysis) for the minimizing of monetary uncertainties and the achievement of a monetary system based on definite and stable rules. Thus, while expressing decided preference for an economic system of free enterprise, he does not seriously consider what monetary arrangements or what implementations of monetary policy are most and least compatible with that system.

At first sight this strong opposition to the policy implications of the *General Theory* seems puzzling: for, as emphasized above, the Chicago School of the 1930s also advocated government deficit spending as a means of dealing with unemployment. But whereas it visualized this as a short-run necessity, which in the course of the cycle would be balanced by a budget surplus, Keynes saw it as a necessary long-run feature of a full-employment capitalist economy. This difference reflected in turn their different views as to the long-run marginal productivity of capital, which Keynes saw as highly inelastic and thus possibly declining to zero within a generation or two (*GT*, pp. 220, 375–77), and which Knight and Simons saw as highly, if not infinitely, elastic.[27] In this connection we should also note Viner's statement in his later comment on his review that

> Aside from details, however, I would have accepted the policy implications of the *General Theory* in the monetary and fiscal field were they presented as relating to short-run or cyclical fluctuations in employment but were not extended without further analysis to long-sustained or chronic unemployment [Viner, 1964, p. 263].

But I think that there was an important policy difference even within the short-term context. For Keynes, the purpose of a deficit was to increase aggregate demand directly, which meant to increase government expenditures G in $C + I + G = Y$. For the Chicago School, however, the purpose of a government deficit was to increase

27. Thus in his review of the *General Theory*, Knight (p. 117, fn. 18) termed Keynes' idea of a zero marginal efficiency of capital as "fantastic." For a general discussion of Knight's views on this matter, see above, chap. 1, pp. 32–33. On Simons, see his "Hansen on Fiscal Policy" (1942), pp. 186, 192–93.

M in $MV = PT$, and this could be done either by increasing expenditures or decreasing tax revenues. In his "Positive Program for Laissez Faire" (1934) and "Rules versus Authorities" (1936), Simons was neutral with respect to these two alternatives. But in his later writings, as the need arose to define his views relative to Keynesian ones, Simons (1942, p. 210; 1944, p. 265)—and after him Mints (1950, pp. 196, 205–12)—began to express a definite preference for generating deficits by means of reducing taxes: both because it was a more flexible procedure which could subsequently be reversed, and because it involved less government activity than did increasing expenditures. Indeed, there is one passage in Simons' writings (1942, p. 205, second paragraph) which, though obscure, seems to imply that the ideal method of changing the money supply is through open-market operations. Be that as it may, Mints (1946, pp. 62–63; 1950, pp. 200–203) did not have confidence in the efficacy of such operations. Nor did Viner, many years before that.[28,29]

Let me conclude with two brief comments. First, I have already stressed the common view of Keynes and the Chicago School on the short-run instability of the economy. Another common feature was the fact that each chose what we would today call a discretionary policy to deal with this instability: the Chicago School, a policy which took the price level as its target variable, and Keynes, one which took the level of employment. Yet another common feature, and what distinguishes both Keynes and Chicago, on the one hand, from both the monetarists and fiscalists of today, on the other—in brief, what distinguishes the 1930s from the 1970s—was the absolute confidence of the economists of this earlier period in the efficacy of their respective policies: their failure to realize (as both theory and sad experience have forced us to realize since then) that uncertainty about the actual state of the world at any given moment of time compounded by the possibly destabilizing effects of lags could seriously interfere with the success of their policies. Simons did not mention this problem, Keynes gave it at best passing attention, and in 1950 Mints (p. 138) even rejected Milton Friedman's "early warnings" of this danger—warnings that Friedman (1948, 1953, and 1961) was in the process of developing into one of his most important contributions to the analysis of macroeconomic policy (cf. p. 283 above).

28. Namely, in his 1933 article on "Inflation as a Possible Remedy for Depression," in which Viner said:

> Now, the government can also try another method [to overcome the depression] Instead of increasing its expenditures, it may buy its own bonds in the market with either new money printed by the printing presses or with funds which it has borrowed from the banking system for the purpose. This method is inferior to the preceding one in this respect: the preceding one gives more immediate stimulus to business. What this does is to increase the cash reserves of the banking system, and therefore, it is hoped, to give the banks the desire to put their idle funds to work But the bankers have learned in recent years, not how to make money without lending, but that under certain circumstances the rate at which they lose money is less if they stop lending, so it is conceivable that the banking system would welcome the additional liquidity and would not increase its loans or investments But it can be argued in support of this method that it does not weaken the budgetary situation of the government, but merely substitutes obligations of no definite maturity for long term obligations. If used at a time of growing business confidence, when business men were willing to borrow, it would make it easier and safer for bankers to lend [Viner 1933, p. 131; cited by Tavlas 1977, pp 53–54]

29 Cf above, chap. 10, p. 246, Proposition 5, for which this paragraph provides belated documentation (cf p. 257, fn. 2 above)

My second point is that I have restricted myself in this lecture to the relations between Keynes and Chicago in connection with the macroeconomic theory and policy of what is effectively a closed economy. There is yet another subject which I hope someone will some day study: namely, their relations in connection with international economics. Let me for the moment only say that with respect to one of Keynes' major activities in this field, his role in the Bretton Woods agreement, he earned the approval of both Viner and Simons. In view of Viner's general belief in the desirability of fixed exchange rates, this is not surprising. And though Simons saw flexible exchange rates as "perhaps closer to the ideal scheme of things" (1944, p. 265), he did not advocate this for the postwar world, for which "a strong case can be made for nominal return to the gold standard" (1943, p. 245). And so it was not only Viner who, in reaction to Keynes' plan, wrote him in July 1943 that "we are not really far apart on any important issues," [30] but also Simons, who a month before that wrote saying: [31]

> Please accept my enthusiastic praise and endorsement of your paper on *International Clearing Union*.[32] . . . I have just finished reading the document itself and am pleased beyond even my high expectations. It strikes me not only as sound in its proposals, but as eminently judicious and statesmanlike in its whole argument.
>
> These are the considered opinions of an American economist who, by slight reputation, has been bitterly anti-Hansen and, if not wholly anti-Keynesian, utterly opposed to your extreme American disciples. (I sometimes suspect that

30. Viner had sent Keynes an advance copy of his (Viner's) *Yale Review* article (1943) on the respective merits of the Keynes and White plans and this led to some correspondence between them. This correspondence is reproduced in *JMK* 25, pp. 320–35; the statement just cited appears on p. 326.

I might note here that there was an earlier wartime context in which Viner and Keynes met, apparently for the first time: namely, during Keynes' 1941 visit to the United States on behalf of the British government for the purpose of clarifying the terms of the Lend-Lease agreement. In particular, the Henry Morgenthau Diaries contain the minutes of several meetings in the United States Treasury during June and July 1941 (usually chaired by Morgenthau himself) in which both Keynes and Viner participated. From these minutes it would, however, appear that Viner's role in these meetings (in which there were always more than a dozen participants) was a minor one.

I am indebted to Donald Moggridge for informing me of these meetings and directing me to the Morgenthau Diaries. For a general description of Keynes' Lend-Lease negotiations (though without reference to Viner), see Harrod (1951), pp. 505–14.

It was apparently the impression of these wartime contacts, as well as of Keynes' posthumously published "Balance of Payments of the U.S." (1946), which brought Viner in later years to speak of Keynes in the following way:

> The [1946] article . . . survives as one among many other testimonies of the supreme level of statesmanship, of balanced vision, of dedication, and of endeavor to reconcile differences in conclusions when there was no difference as to basic objectives and values, on which he ended his brilliant career. The Keynes of that period was to me then, and continues to be, a heroic figure, and my admiration of him as he was then, of his personality and his intellect, was unalloyed by the qualifications which I felt, and still feel, about the Keynes of the *General Theory*, and even more, about the journalistic and polemical Keynes of the 1920's and early 1930's [1964, p. 266].

31. Typewritten letter of June 10, 1943, in Simons Papers, The Law School, The University of Chicago; reproduced with permission. Unfortunately, this letter is not reproduced in *JMK* 25.

32. The reference is presumably to the version which the British government issued as a Command Paper in April 1973.

you may not be much more tolerant than I am toward that weird amalgam of your doctrines and Schumpeter's preposterous *Entwicklungstheorie* [33] which constitutes the extreme "American Keynesism [*sic*].") As a vigorous but inconspicuous participant in recent monetary-fiscal controversies, I think I can testify to the statesmanlike quality of the document and to its success, among reasonable people, in adjourning a bitter academic controversy in favor of common pursuit of international monetary cooperation. . . .

I think I may say that my colleagues in the Department, if invited to do so, would join me in congratulating you on your great and timely service to the cause of winning the peace.

Keynes replied with a brief letter of thanks for Simons' "handsome letter"; but unfortunately for us, he did not rise to the bait of Simons' remark about Hansen. And so we lost this opportunity of learning something about Keynes' views of his "American disciples."

Bibliography*

J. W. Angell. *The Behavior of Money*. New York, 1936.

K. Brunner. "On Lauchlin Currie's Contribution to Monetary Theory." Introduction to reprint of L. Currie, *The Supply and Control of Money in the United States*. New York, 1968.

L. Currie. "Money, Gold, and Income in the United States, 1921–32" *Quarterly Journal of Economics*, Nov. 1933, *48*, 77–95.

______. "The Failure of Monetary Policy to Prevent the Depression of 1929–32." *Journal of Political Economy*, Apr. 1934, *42*, 145–77 (a)

______. *The Supply and Control of Money in the United States*. Cambridge, Mass., 1934 (b)

______. *The Supply and Control of Money in the United States*, 2nd ed., rev Cambridge, Mass., 1935.

J. R. Davis. *The New Economics and the Old Economists*. Ames, Iowa, 1971.

M. Friedman. "A Monetary and Fiscal Framework for Economic Stability." *American Economic Review*, June 1948, *38*, 245–64. As reprinted in *Essays in Positive Economics*. Chicago, 1953. Pp. 133–56.

______. "The Effects of a Full-Employment Policy on Economic Stability: A Formal Analysis. "In *Essays in Positive Economics*. Chicago, 1953. Pp. 117–32.

______. "The Lag in Effect of Monetary Policy." *Journal of Political Economy*, Oct. 1961, *69*, 447–66. As reprinted in *The Optimum Quantity of Money and Other Essays*. Chicago, 1969. Pp. 237–60.

______. "The Monetary Theory and Policy of Henry Simons." *Journal of Law and Economics*, Oct. 1967, *10*, 1–13. As reprinted in *The Optimum Quantity of Money and Other Essays*. Chicago, 1969. Pp. 81–93.

33. I do not know to what aspects of Schumpeter's theory of development Simons is referring And what increases my puzzlement here is that in his "Hansen on Fiscal Policy" (1942)—a reprint of which Simons enclosed with his letter to Keynes—there is a fairly favorable reference (on p. 187, fn. 2) to pp. 1032–50 of Schumpeter's *Business Cycles* (1939).

*References in text to works listed here as reprinted are to the date of original publication; the page references, however, follow the pagination of the reprinted form.

——— and A. J. Schwartz. *A Monetary History of the United States 1867–1960*. Princeton, N.J., 1963.

———. *Monetary Statistics of the United States*. New York, 1970.

A. H. Hansen. "A Fundamental Error in Keynes' 'Treatise on Money.' " *American Economic Review*, Sept. 1932, *22*, 462. As reprinted in *The Collected Writings of John Maynard Keynes*. Vol. 5, pp. 329–30.

——— *Fiscal Policy and Business Cycles*. New York, 1941.

Harris Memorial Foundation. *Unemployment As a World Problem*, ed. Q. Wright. Chicago, 1931.

———. *Reports of Round Tables: Unemployment As a World Problem*, 2 vols. Chicago, 1931 (mimeographed).

R. F. Harrod. *The Life of John Maynard Keynes*. London, 1951. Reprinted New York, 1969.

J. R. Hicks. "Mr. Keynes and the 'Classics': A Suggested Interpretation." *Econometrica*, Apr. 1937, *5*, 147–59.

S. Howson and D. Winch. *The Economic Advisory Council 1930–1939*. Cambridge, 1977.

T. M. Humphrey. "Role of Non-Chicago Economists in the Evolution of the Quantity Theory in America 1930–1950." *Southern Economic Journal*, July 1971, *38*, 12–18.

B. L. Jones. "Lauchlin Currie, Pump Priming, and New Deal Fiscal Policy, 1934–1936." *History of Political Economy*. Winter 1978, *10*, 509–24.

J. M. Keynes. *A Treatise on Money, Vol. 1: The Pure Theory of Money*. London, 1930. As reprinted in Keynes' *Collected Writings*, vol. 5.

———. *A Treatise on Money, Vol. 2: The Applied Theory of Money*, London, 1930. As reprinted in Keynes' *Collected Writings*, vol. 6.

———. "An Economic Analysis of Unemployment." In Harris Memorial Foundation, *Unemployment As a World Problem*. Chicago, 1931. As reprinted in Keynes' *Collected Writings*, vol. 13, pp. 343–67.

———. *The General Theory of Employment, Interest, and Money*. London, 1936. As reprinted in Keynes' *Collected Writings*, vol. 7 (same pagination as original).

———. "The General Theory of Employment." *Quarterly Journal of Economics*, Feb. 1937, *51*, 209–23. As reprinted in Keynes' *Collected Writings*, vol. 14, pp. 109–33.

———. "Proposals for an International Clearing Union" Cmd. 6437, London: HMSO April 1943. As reprinted in *The International Monetary Fund 1945–1965*, ed. J. K. Horsefield, vol. 3. Washington, D.C., 1969. Pp. 19–36. (Various drafts of these "Proposals" appear in Keynes' *Collected Writings*, vol. 25).

———. "The Balance of Payments of the United States." *Economic Journal*, June 1946, *56*, 172–87.

———. *The General Theory and After, Part I: Preparation*. Edited by D. E. Moggridge. Vol. 13 of Keynes' *Collected Writings*. 1973.

———. *The General Theory and After, Part II: Defense and Development*. Ed. D. E. Moggridge. Vol. 14 of Keynes' *Collected Writings*. 1973.

———. *Activities 1940–44: Shaping the Post-War World: The Clearing Union*. Ed. D. E. Moggridge. Vol. 25 of Keynes' *Collected Writings*. 1979.

———. *The General Theory and After: A Supplement*. Ed. D. E. Moggridge. Vol. 29 of Keynes' *Collected Writings*. 1979.

———. *Collected Writings*. London, 1971–79.

——— and H. D. Henderson. *Can Lloyd George Do It?: An Examination of the Liberal Pledge*. London, 1929. As reprinted in Keynes' *Collected Writings*. vol. 9, pp. 86–125.

F. H. Knight. *Risk, Uncertainty, and Profit*. Boston, 1921.

———. "Unemployment: And Mr. Keynes' Revolution in Economic Theory." *Canadian Journal of Economics and Political Science*, Feb. 1937, *3*, 100–123.

J. E. Meade. "A Simplified Model of Mr. Keynes' System." *Review of Economic Studies*, Feb. 1937, *4*, 98–107.

L. W. Mints. "Monetary Policy." *Review of Economic Statistics*, May 1946, *28*, 60–69.

———. *Monetary Policy for a Competitive Society*. New York, 1950.

D. E. Moggridge and S. Howson. "Keynes on Monetary Policy, 1910–1946." *Oxford Economic Papers*, July 1974, *26*, 226–47.

Norman Wait Harris Memorial Foundation. See Harris Memorial Foundation.

D. Patinkin. "The Chicago Tradition, The Quantity Theory, and Friedman." *Journal of Money, Credit and Banking*, Feb. 1969, *1*, 46–70. [Reproduced as chap. 10 above.]

———. "On the Monetary Economics of Chicagoans and Non-Chicagoans: Comment." *Southern Economic Journal*, Jan. 1973, 39, 454–59. (a) [Reproduced as chap. 11 above.]

———. "Frank Knight as Teacher." *American Economic Review*, Dec. 1973, *53*, 787–810. (b) [Reproduced as chap. 1 above.]

———. *Keynes Monetary Thought*. Durham, N.C., 1976.

———. "The Process of Writing the *General Theory*: A Critical Survey." In *Keynes, Cambridge, and the General Theory*, ed. D. Patinkin and J. C. Leith. London, 1977. Pp. 3–24.

———. "A Study of Keynes' Theory of Effective Demand." *Economic Inquiry*, Apr. 1979, *17*, 155–176. (a)

———. "The Development of Keynes' Policy Thinking." In *Economic Theory for Economic Efficiency: Essays in Honor of Abba Lerner*, ed. H. I. Greenfield et al. Cambridge, Mass., 1979. Pp. 151–66. (b)

D. H. Robertson. "Some Notes on Mr. Keynes' General Theory of Employment." *Quarterly Journal of Economics*, Nov. 1936, *51*, 168–91.

J. A. Schumpeter. *Business Cycles*. New York, 1939.

[H. C. Simons]. *Economics 201: The Divisional Course in Economics* Chicago, n d. (mimeographed).

———. *A Positive Program for Laissez Faire*. Chicago, 1934. As reprinted in Simons (1948), pp. 40–77.

———. Review of *The Supply and Control of Money in the United States* by L. Currie *Journal of Political Economy*, Aug. 1935, *43*, 555–58.

———. "Rules versus Authorities in Monetary Policy " *Journal of Political Economy*, Feb. 1936, *44*, 1–30. As reprinted in Simons (1948). Pp. 160–83.

———. "Keynes Comments on Money" [Review of the *General Theory*] *The Christian Century*, July 2, 1936, 1016–17.

———. "Hansen on Fiscal Policy." *Journal of Political Economy*, Apr. 1942, *50*, 161–96. As reprinted in Simons (1948). Pp. 184–219

———. "The U.S. Holds the Cards." *Fortune*, Sept. 1944, 156–59, 196–200. Reprinted with substantial revisions as "Money, Tariffs, and the Peace." As reprinted in Simons (1948) Pp. 260–76.

———. *Economic Policy for a Free Society* Chicago, 1948.

G. S. Tavlas. "Chicago Schools Old and New on the Efficacy of Monetary Policy *Banco Nazionale del Lavoro Quarterly Review*, Mar. 1977, *120*, 51–73.

University of Chicago Round Table. *Balancing the Budget· Federal Fiscal Policy During Depression Public Policy Pamphlets*, no. 1, ed Harry D Gideonse Chicago, Jan. 1933.

J. Viner. "Inflation as a Possible Remedy for the Depression." *Proceedings of the Institute of Public Affairs. Seventh Annual Session.* The University of Georgia, Athens, Ga. 1933, 120–35.

______ "Mr. Keynes on the Causes of Unemployment." *Quarterly Journal of Economics*, Nov. 1936, *51*, 147–67. As reprinted in *Keynes' General Theory. Reports of Three Decades*, ed. R. Lekachman. New York, 1964. Pp. 235–53.

______. "Two Plans for International Monetary Stabilization." *The Yale Review*, Autumn 1943, *33*, 77–107. As reprinted in Viner (1951). Pp. 192–215.

______. *International Economics*. Glencoe, Ill., 1951.

______. "Comment on My 1936 Review of Keynes' *General Theory*." In *Keynes' General Theory, Reports of Three Decades*, ed. R. Lekachman. New York, 1964. Pp. 253–66.

Q. Wright. See Harris Memorial Foundation.

Government Publications

U. S. Board of Governors of the Federal Reserve System, *Federal Reserve Bulletin*, vol. 20. Washington D.C., 1934.

______. *Twentieth Annual Report of the Federal Reserve Board*. Washington, D.C., 1934.

Unpublished Materials

Frank H. Knight Papers. Joseph Regenstein Library, The University of Chicago.
Henry Morgenthau Diaries. The Franklin D. Roosevelt Library, Hyde Park, N.Y.
Henry C. Simons Papers. The Law School, The University of Chicago.
Jacob Viner Papers. Princeton University Library, Princeton, N.J.

'Pessimism Vindicated'

J. Viner, 'Pessimism vindicated', *The Saturday Review of Literature* (6 February 1932), p. 504.

Pessimism Vindicated

ESSAYS IN PERSUASION. By John Maynard Keynes. New York: Harcourt, Brace & Co. 1932.

Reviewed by Jacob Viner
University of Chicago

BEHOLD an economist who in this year of little grace for economic prophets presents a dated collection of his economic prophecies since 1919, not in the role of a sinner driven by an inner compulsion to repent in public, but with pride in his record and regret only that the world should have been under the governance of statesmen, bankers, business men, and labor leaders too stupid to follow his advice. The pride is in large part justified, even if a little veiling would have made it more becoming. Keynes has been since 1919 predicting serious economic difficulties for the world at large and England in particular if the proper steps were not taken to regulate the currency; reduce the burden of reparations and inter-allied debts to manageable proportions; remove some of the barriers to international trade; and, in general, by raising world prices to the level of English costs, make the world safer for the pound sterling and English trade. He won more attention from statesmen and bankers than has ever before in recent years been given to any economist. He failed, however, to secure their active acceptance and promotion of his policies And now the world is enduring the woes he had predicted while pursuing more vigorously than ever the practices which he has condemned.

This record for a prophet would appear an excellent one. It may be objected, however, that between 1922 and 1929 a large portion of the world was getting along very well, better, in fact, than ever before, while following policies diametrically opposed to those which Keynes advocated. There was after all a new economic era, judged in terms of past experience, and for those countries which enjoyed it its only serious drawback was its brevity. That currency mismanagement, tariff orgies, perverse policies of government finance, and excessive reparations and inter-allied debt claims were undermining this prosperity and were limiting its geographical incidence even while it was under way, and that these factors were responsible in large part for the intensity and duration of the collapse which followed, no economist outside of France has to my knowledge denied. But any economist—and there were many such—who in the period 1922 to 1929 predicted an impending economic crisis, but who maintained a cautious reticence as to the date when that crisis would make its appearance, would have established for himself a basis for satisfactory claims for his prophetic capacity. In fact, this would have been true at any time during the last two centuries. In any case, all that was necessary in the post-war period to establish a successful record as a prophet was a pessimistic temperament, an absence of confidence in the wisdom of our political and financial rulers, patience, and indefiniteness as to the date at which the impending doom would fall. All of these qualities Keynes displayed in high degree.

I am nevertheless convinced, and I find that most of the economists, English, Continental, and American, with whom I have discussed these matters, are convinced, that in his diagnosis of the world's situation and in the remedies which he proposed for its already existent and impending ills, Keynes was substantially and brilliantly right. On only one major item in his record, an item not exhibited in this book, do I believe that he was seriously wrong, namely, his vigorous campaign to persuade England to adopt a protective tariff, and thus seek relief by eating a hair of one of the dogs that were biting it. While at the time he failed in this as in other phases of his propaganda, he undoubtedly contributed greatly to a further weakening of the already waning faith of the English public in the virtues of free trade, and thus indirectly contributed his bit to the subsequent entrance of England into the crowded ranks of tariff sinners.

But where Keynes stands head and shoulders above other economists is as a propagandist. This book demonstrates his capacity for vigorous and sustained polemic, undiluted by academic scruples to disclose all the qualifications and the uncertainties of his logical argument, his command of a forceful, flexible, and imaginative prose style, his fearlessness in assigning to his opponents their appropriately low intelligence quotas, his ability to disturb the unearned complacency of statesmen and bankers In spite of these qualities, however, he has completely failed in his task. Alas for the world, these "Essays in Persuasion" have so far been unsuccessful essays in persuasion. But economists have rarely, if ever, succeeded in persuading the world that theirs were the right paths to economic salvation Perhaps what the world has needed, and most urgently needs today, is a few more Keynes.

Jacob Viner, who is a professor in the University of Chicago, is an expert on international financial problems such as the inter-allied debts, the distribution of the world's gold supply, etc.

'Keynes on the Causes of Unemployment'

J. Viner, 'Mr Keynes on the causes of unemployment and comment on my 1936 review' in R. Lekachman (ed.), *Keynes' General Theory: Report of Three Decades* (London, Macmillan, 1964), pp. 235–66.

JACOB VINER

Mr. Keynes on the Causes of Unemployment

[1936]

THE INDEBTEDNESS OF ECONOMISTS to Mr. Keynes has been greatly increased by this latest addition to his series of brilliant, original, and provocative books, whose contribution to our enlightenment will prove, I am sure, to have been even greater in the long than in the short run. This book deals with almost everything, but the causes of and the future prospects of unemployment, cyclical and secular, are its central theme. It brings much new light, but its display of dialectical skill is so overwhelming that it will have probably more persuasive power than it deserves, and a concentration on the points where I think I can detect defects in the argument, though it would be unfair if presented as an appraisal of the merits of the book as a whole, may be more useful than would a catalogue—which would have to be long to be complete—of its points of outstanding intellectual achievement.

Written though it is by a stylist of the first order, the book is not easy to read, to master, or to appraise. An extremely wide range of problems, none of them simple ones, are dealt with in an unnecessarily small number of pages. Had the book been made longer, the time required for reading it with a fair degree of understanding would have been shorter, for the argument often proceeds at breakneck speed and repeated rereadings are necessary before it can be grasped. The book, moreover, breaks with traditional modes of approach to its problems at a number of points—at the greatest possible number of points, one suspects—and no old term for an old concept is used when a new one can be coined, and if old terms are used new meanings are generally assigned to them. The definitions provided, moreover, are sometimes of unbelievable complexity. The old-fashioned economist must, therefore, struggle not only with new ideas and new methods of manipulating them, but also with a new language. There is ample reward, however, for the expenditure of time and attention necessary for even partial mastery of the argument.

"INVOLUNTARY" UNEMPLOYMENT

Mr. Keynes claims that the "classical"[1] economists recognized the possibility only of "frictional" and of "voluntary" unemployment, and that a vitally important chapter of economic theory remains to be written about a third class of unemployment, for which there was no place in the "classical" scheme of things, namely, "involuntary" unemployment. The concept of "frictional" unemployment relates to the inevitable loss of time between jobs, and presents no difficulties. "Voluntary" unemployment is defined as the unemployment "due to the refusal or inability of a unit of labor . . . to accept a reward corresponding to the value of the product attributable to its marginal productivity," but is used in such manner as to require the addition to this definition of the proviso that the money wage offered must not be below what the laborer regards as a proper minimum rate of *money* wages. If laborers refuse available employment at a money rate below this minimum, or if employed laborers refuse to permit a prevailing money rate to be lowered and unemployment results for themselves or for others from this refusal, Keynes would apparently regard it as "involuntary" unemployment, but deny its possibility or probability. He defines "involuntary" unemployment as follows: "Men are involuntarily unemployed if, in the event of a small rise in the price of wage-goods relatively to the money wage, both the aggregate supply of labor willing to work for the current money-wage and the aggregate demand for it at that wage would be greater than the existing volume of employment." (p. 15). What he seems to mean by this is that any unemployment which would disappear if real wages were to be reduced by a rise in the prices of wage goods, money wages remaining the same or rising in less proportion, ***but not falling,*** would be involuntary. It is with "involuntary" unemployment so understood, its causes and its remedies, that Keynes' analysis of unemployment is primarily—and almost solely—concerned.

[1] Used by him to mean the later economists, such as J. S. Mill, Marshall, Edgeworth, Pigou, who in the main were adherents of the Ricardian tradition; a usage which I shall follow here.

In Keynes' classification of unemployment by its causes, unemployment due to downward rigidity of money wages, which for the "classical" economists was the chief type of cyclical unemployment and the only important type of secular or persistent unemployment, therefore finds no place. As will be seen later, it is excluded on the ground that resistance to reductions in money wage rates generally does not involve a reduction in the volume of employment and is, if anything, favorable to employment rather than the reverse. The omission charged against the "classical" economists is their failure to note the lesser resistance of labor to reductions in real wages if unassociated with reductions in money wages *per se*, and their failure to recognize the existence of a large volume of unemployment for which the former is an available and practicable remedy, but not the latter. Keynes' reasoning points obviously to the superiority of inflationary remedies for unemployment over money wage reductions. In a world organized in accordance with Keynes' specifications there would be a constant race between the printing press and the business agents of the trade unions, with the problem of unemployment largely solved if the printing press could maintain a constant lead and if only volume of employment, irrespective of quality, is considered important.

The only clash here between Keynes' position and the orthodox one is in his denial that reduction of money wage rates is a remedy for unemployment. Keynes even follows the classical doctrine too closely when he concedes that "with a given organization, equipment and technique, real wages and the volume of output (and hence of employment) are uniquely correlated, so that, in general, an increase in employment can only occur to the accompaniment of a decline in the rate of real wages" (p. 17). This conclusion results from too unqualified an application of law-of-diminishing-returns analysis, and needs to be modified for cyclical unemployment, as well as for the possibility that the prices of wage goods and of other goods may have divergent movements. If a plant geared to work at say 80 per cent of rated capacity is being operated at say only 30 per cent, both the per capita and the marginal output of labor may well be lower at the low rate of operations than at the higher rate, the law of diminishing returns notwithstanding. There is the further empirical consideration that if employers operate in their wage policy in accordance with marginal cost analysis, it is done only imperfectly and unconsciously, and the level of wages they can be persuaded to establish is strongly influenced by the profitability of their operations as a whole, and not solely—if at all—by calculations of the marginal contributions of labor to output.

Keynes uses the term "full employment" to signify the absence of any involuntary unemployment (p. 16). He describes it also as the condition which would prevail "when output has risen to a level at which the marginal return from a representative unit of the factors of production has fallen to the minimum figure at which a quantity of the factors sufficient to produce this output is available" (p. 303). There are implied here several questionable propositions. The concept of diminishing marginal productivity is generally used in economics in a partial differential sense to indicate the diminishing increments of output which would result when some particular factor or group of factors was being increased, the remainder of the working combination being held constant. If all the factors are being increased simultaneously and in uniform proportions, it requires some such assumption as that of the general prevalence of external technical diseconomies from increased production if it is to be accepted that output and return per compound unit of the factors must be negatively correlated. There is also implied here the assumption that any increase in real wages (money wages remaining constant, or rising) will result in an increase in the amount of labor available. If, as widely held opinion since the seventeenth century has maintained, and as Professor Paul Douglas' recent investigations for urban labor in the United States appear to confirm, the supply schedule of labor with respect to real wages is, for part of its range at least, negatively inclined, the volume of employment could conceivably be much greater when there was "involuntary" unemployment than when there was "full" employment, and Keynes' conditions of "full" employment might be met at an indefinite number of levels of employment.

"Full" employment rarely occurs, according to Keynes, and the main immediate responsibility for the persistence of "involuntary" unemployment lies with the persistence of interest rates at levels too high to induce employers to bid for all the labor available at the prevailing money rates of wages. An elaborate and strikingly novel analysis of the causes determining the level of interest rates leads to the conclusion that high "liquidity preferences" of savers, an excessive disposition to save, and a low marginal productivity of investment are responsible for the absence of such a relation between the rates at which savers are willing to lend and the rates at which entrepreneurs are willing to borrow for investment as would result in an approximation to "full" employment.

Mr. Keynes claims further: (1) that there can be "full" employment only when entrepreneurs make investments sufficient to absorb any excess of income paid out by entrepreneurs over expenditures on consumption by income recipients; (2) that the amount of investment entrepreneurs are prepared to make, or their "investment demand for capital," is governed by the relation of their anticipations as to the yield of additional investment, or what Keynes calls the "marginal efficiency of capital"[2] to the interest rates at which funds can be borrowed; (3) that the amount which income recipients are willing to spend of their current income, or their "propensity to consume," a function primarily of the amount of their incomes,[3] determines the quantity of saving; and (4) the rate of interest is determined by (*a*) "liquidity preferences" and (*b*) the quantity of cash available to satisfy such preferences. The quantity of cash is generally assumed to be a constant. I accept most of this as valid in its general outlines, but I am unable to to accept some of Keynes' account of how these "propensities" operate in practice or his appraisal of their relative strength.

THE PROPENSITY TO HOARD

Keynes maintains that for centuries back the propensity to save has been so much stronger than the inducement to invest as to create a substantial barrier to "full" investment. He finds fault with the "classical" economists for their alleged neglect of the gulf between the desire to save and the desire to invest, i.e., for their neglect of "liquidity preferences." It was a shortcoming of the Ricardian wing

[2] "*Anticipated* marginal efficiency of capital" would seem to me a more accurately descriptive label for the concept.

[3] It is, in my opinion, probably dependent appreciably also on anticipations as to the prospective trend of income, and is surely affected significantly by amount of accumulated wealth at current valuations as well as by current income. See *infra*, "Propensity to Consume," for further comments on this point.

of the classical school that in the face of strong criticism they steadfastly adhered to their position that hoarding was so abnormal a phenomenon as not to constitute a significant contributing factor to unemployment even during a period of severe deflation. In static equilibrium analysis, in which perfect price flexibility is assumed and monetary changes are abstracted from, there is no occasion for consideration of hoarding. In modern monetary theory it is generally dealt with, with results which in kind are substantially identical with Keynes', as a factor operating to reduce the "velocity" of money. There has been, I believe, common agreement among economists that when price rigidities are important hoarding could present a serious and continuing problem, and that it is always a significant factor in the downward phase of a short business cycle. Keynes, however, attaches great importance to it as a barrier to "full" employment at almost all times, and apparently irrespective of the degree of flexibility of prices.

There are several reasons why "liquidity preferences" loom so large to Keynes as a source of trouble in the economic process. He takes it for granted that they are ordinarily so strong for the average person in control of liquid resources that a substantial interest rate is required to overcome them; and apparently that they cannot be overcome by *any* rate of interest if a still higher rate of interest is anticipated in the near future. He assigns to them the role of sole determinant (given the amount of cash available, which he treats ordinarily as a constant) of the rate of interest. He believes that the marginal productivity function of capital and therefore the investment demand for capital have little elasticity. Finally he assumes in general that nothing can satisfy liquidity preferences except that "cash" whose quantity is one of the determinants of the interest rate.

We have almost no reliable information about the strength of liquidity preferences under varying circumstances, and in the absence of statistical information of a genuinely relevant character discussion must be based largely on conjecture. Nevertheless, I venture to present a series of considerations which, in the aggregate, seem to warrant the conclusion that Keynes has grossly exaggerated the extent to which liquidity preferences have operated in the past and are likely to operate in the future as a barrier to "full" employment.

(*a*) Keynes stresses the pressure which is exercised by the expectation of a rise in the interest rate on potential purchasers of securities, leading them to postpone their purchases in order to escape a capital loss. There are, however, in every country large numbers of investors who have been taught to buy gilt-edge securities on the basis of their yield to maturity and to disregard the fluctuations in their day-to-day market values. Even investors of a speculative type are ordinarily as anxious not to miss a "low" as not to buy too high. There are many opportunities for investment which are—or seem at the time to be—of the "now-or-never" type. There is a widely prevalent aversion to the waste of "dead" cash.

(*b*) Keynes seems to exaggerate the actuarial valuation of postponement of investment during a period of anticipated rise in interest rates. Rising interest rates are frequently associated with periods of greater confidence in the security of the investment, as far as payment of principal and interest according to schedule are concerned; or in the case of equity securities, with periods of more favorable anticipations of long-run yields. Hence periods of rising interest rates are often associated with periods of rising rather than falling prices of securities, especially for equity securities. Keynes seems to be in error also when he asserts that, abstracting from the risk of default on principal or interest, it will be equally profitable to hoard as to invest at par in a long-term security paying 4 per cent if the market interest rate is rising by 0.16 per cent per annum. In the first place, hoarding and investment in a long-term security are not the only alternatives. Let it be provisionally granted that hoarding and the purchase at par of a 4 per cent long-term bond would prove equally profitable at the end of the first year if the interest rate during that year had risen by 0.16 per cent. The purchase at the beginning of the year of a one-year maturity security paying anything over 0.16 per cent would then have been more profitable even if it had to be exchanged for cash within six months, and even if the short-term interest rate were also gradually rising by as much as 0.16 per cent per annum. Secondly, even a purchaser of the long-term 4 per cent security would have been richer at the end of the first year than if he had hoarded his cash, unless the security were a *perpetual* bond.

(*c*) Even if it be granted that liquidity preferences are as strong ordinarily as Keynes indicates, their operation as a barrier to investment would necessarily be important only if it be assumed (1) that liquidity preferences can be satisfied solely by the holding of non-investment assets, and (2) that the quantity of such assets does not automatically respond to the demand for them. Keynes takes care of this second qualification by his assumption that the quantity of money—in the assumed absence of a positive central monetary control—is constant. Here, indeed, he concedes more than is necessary, for if liquidity preferences are assumed to be stronger during depressions than during periods of business expansion, then the quantity of money, under such monetary systems as have existed in the past, varies inversely with the strength of liquidity preferences. But he does not give adequate consideration to the first qualification.

The satisfaction of liquidity preference on the one hand and of investment on the other are opposite phenomena only if the range of assets which can satisfy investment demand corresponds with the range of assets which can satisfy liquidity preferences, so that it shall be impossible to satisfy both by the same transaction. If liquidity preferences can be satisfied by the holding of resources which are not identical with the "money" whose surrender satisfies investment demand, the satisfaction of the former does not necessarily entail failure to satisfy the latter. Keynes explains liquidity preference as a wish to retain one's resources in the form of money. There is no systematic examination of what is to be included as "money" for this purpose, but incidentally to his analysis of one particular form of surrender of liquidity, namely, exchange of money for a debt, he states:

> . . . we can draw the line between "money" and "debts" at whatever point is most convenient for handling a particular problem. For example, we can treat as *money* any command over general purchasing power which the owner has not parted with for a period in excess of three months, and as *debt* what cannot be recovered for a longer period than this; or we can substitute for "three months" one month or three days or three hours or any other period; or we can exclude from *money* whatever is not legal tender on the spot. It is often convenient in practice to include in *money* time-deposits with banks and, occasionally, even such instruments as (e.g.) treasury bills. As a rule, I shall . . . assume that money is co-extensive with bank deposits (p. 167, note).

If everything which satisfies liquidity preference is to be included as money, then money must be broadly defined so as to include not only demand deposits and time deposits, but also short-term securities, any other assets which are readily marketable without serious risk of loss through depreciation of value, and even the command over credit from banks or others. But the conversion of newly acquired cash into any other form of asset either involves investment directly or transfers the decision as between hoarding and investment to a banker or other intermediary between the original saver and the ultimate borrower for investment. If the banker permits his investments to remain constant while his cash reserves are increasing, or if he maintains the same cash reserves for idle as for active demand deposits, or for time deposits as for demand deposits, or for deposits as for banknotes in circulation, then the propensity to hoard which manifests itself in the maintenance of idle bank deposits does operate to check investment, but only with the connivance and support of the banking mechanism.

It may be objected that even if liquidity-preferences operate only, or in the main, to check purchases of long-term securities, they still operate as a check to investment; because the latter is and must be largely in durable goods, or in assets far removed from the stage of the consumers' goods. But the relation between the period of investment intended by the saver and that intended, or in fact resulting, by the borrowing entrepreneur is not a simple one of necessary equality. It is highly flexible and approaches to free variability at the discretion of the borrower. Every money market has an elaborate machinery for transmuting short-term loans into long-term investments and long-term loans into short-term investments, to suit the convenience of original lenders and ultimate borrowers. The typical entrepreneur will shift from long-term to short-term borrowing, or vice versa, even though the time period involved in the particular operation is unchanged, or (as often) unknowable in advance. He may also be able to shift from long-term to short-term investment if the interest rate at which the latter can be financed is much lower than that at which he can conduct admittedly long-term borrowing. If savers have a 5 per cent per annum preference for cash over investment in 10-year bonds but only a ¼ per cent preference for cash over time deposits or short-term securities, and if entrepreneurs want funds for 10 years and are unwilling to incur the sacrifice of their own liquidity which would be involved in the attempt to finance 10-

year operations with, say, 3-month borrowings, middlemen will step in who are prepared to lend on long-term funds which they have borrowed on short-term. The modern money market is fortunately equipped to some extent with procedures for satisfying liquidity preferences without providing genuine liquidity.

(*d*) The propensity to hoard exercises its influence as a restraint on investment through its tendency to raise interest rates. But in what seems to me the most vulnerable part of his analysis, his explanation of the determination of the rate of interest, Keynes assigns to the desire for cash for hoarding purposes a grossly exaggerated importance.

Keynes denies the validity of the "classical" doctrine that interest is the reward for saving and is directly determined by the supply schedule of savings with respect to the interest rate and the investment demand schedule for capital, and his exposition leaves the impression that the interest rate is not dependent to any important extent on these two factors. He denies that interest is the "reward" for saving on the ground that, if a man hoards his savings in cash, he earns no interest, though he saves just as much as before (p. 167), and claims that, on the contrary, it is the reward for surrender of liquidity. By analogous reasoning he could deny that wages are the reward for labor, or that profit is the reward for risk-taking, because labor is sometimes done without anticipation or realization of a return, and men who assume financial risks have been known to incur losses as a result instead of profits. Without saving there can be no liquidity to surrender. The saver who has no concern about liquidity gets the same reward as the person who saved with liquidity as his initial objective but is persuaded by the interest rate to lend; and the return is granted for loans irrespective whether it is reluctance to postpone consumption or reluctance to surrender liquidity which keeps the supply of funds for investment down to the level at which borrowers are willing to pay the prevailing rate of interest for it. The rate of interest is the return for saving without liquidity.

Keynes explains the rate of interest as determined by the schedule of liquidity preferences and the available quantity of money, the prevailing rate of interest being simply that price for the sacrifice of liquidity at which the desire to hold cash is equated with the quantity of available cash (p. 167). The rate of interest determines the amount of investment, given the investment demand for capital; but a change in the investment demand for capital will not affect the interest rate "if nothing has happened to the state of liquidity preference and the quantity of money." (See especially the figure on p. 180, and the text on p. 181).

There have been previous attempts to discover a basis on which the interest rate could be held to be determined independently of the demand for capital, the level of wages, and other important elements in the economy, but the growing recognition of the basic interdependence of all the important economic variables has led to widespread scepticism that any such attempt could succeed. In Keynes' present attempt the fatal flaw is, to repeat, the exaggerated importance attributed to hoarding. In his discussion of liquidity preferences Keynes distinguishes between the desire for cash for use in the current transaction of personal and business exchanges, and the desire for cash as a security against loss from unsuccessful investment. As I have already argued, the latter consideration should not operate as a barrier to short-term investment, and while it may induce a high long-term interest rate, it will be compensated for in part by a shift of borrowing to the short-term market. The pattern of behavior of the desire for transaction liquidity is probably very largely the inverse of that of security liquidity, or hoarding proper. As D. H. Robertson points out in his contribution to this symposium, the transactions desire for cash is for cash to be used and not for cash to be held unused. It must therefore vary positively with the volume of investment, of income, and of expenditures for consumption. In so far as it consists of demand for cash from entrepreneurs for business uses, it is but a reflection of their investment demand for capital. In so far as it is a demand for cash from consumers who are living beyond their current income, it is the demand for consumption loans of older theory. Whatever its origin, demand for cash for transaction purposes is, dollar for dollar, of equal influence on the rate of interest as demand for cash for hoarding purposes. The demand for capital and the propensity to save (which is the reciprocal of the propensity to consume) are thus restored—though, I admit, in somewhat modified and improved fashion—to their traditional roles as determinants of the rate of interest.

While (to repeat again) relevant statistical information is scarce, what we do know about the holders of cash balances in the United States points strongly to the importance of the transactions motive for liquidity and to the relative insignificance in ordinary times of hoarding. It is the corporations, institutions, and governments that hold at all times the bulk of the cash balances, especially if savings deposits are excluded as constituting investments rather than cash. Moreover I suspect (I know of no data on the question) that at least in prosperous times the savers—those who add each year to their estates—who are supposed by Keynes to be a source of so much trouble because of their hoarding propensities, typically hold in cash a smaller percentage of their incomes, let alone of their total resources, than do the spenders. The former have investment habits, and abhor idle cash as nature abhors a vacuum. The latter hold cash until the bills come in for settlement. It would at least be interesting to know whether these are facts or fancies.

The importance of the transactions demand for cash makes it easy to explain a whole series of historical phenomena which do not fit into Keynes' theory. Because the demand for cash for business use varies positively with the investment demand for capital, and the demand for cash for personal use varies positively with the level of income and of expenditures for consumption, there is no need for treating as a perplexing puzzle the facts that business is active when interest rates are high and slack when interest rates are low, and that the quantity of money and the interest rate are historically correlated positively rather than negatively. There is an important stabilizing influence, moreover, in these circumstances. During a depression entrepreneurs and spenders release some of the cash to supply the demand of hoarders for security, and during an expansion of business the absorption of cash by business and by spenders, serving as it does to raise the interest rate, keeps the expansion from going beyond bounds; or, Keynes would say, from even approaching reasonable bounds.

MONEY WAGE FLEXIBILITY AND VOLUME OF EMPLOYMENT

Keynes expresses sweeping dissent with the "classical" doctrine that money wage rigidity is a major cause both of cyclical and of secular unemployment, although he freely grants that in general increased employment must mean lower real wages. He maintains that labor strongly resists money wage reductions but takes reductions in real wages much more calmly, and therefore that even if money wage reductions were logically a remedy for unemployment they would not be a practicable one. His view is that a lowering of money wage rates, unless it proceeded simultaneously and uniformly all along the line, would chiefly alter the relative rates of wages of different labor groups. It would not be likely to increase the aggregate volume of employment of labor, and on the balance of probabilities would be more likely to reduce it. He does not discuss the effects on employment which would result from pressure from labor for *increases* in money wages, or from increases of money wages made voluntarily on the part of employers, whether for humanitarian reasons or because of belief that high wages mean prosperity or in response to public opinion.

Keynes presents his own position mainly in terms of a criticism of a theory which he imputes to the "classical" economists, according to which a reduction of money wages *and a simultaneous corresponding reduction in prices* would increase employment because the same volume of monetary expenditures would purchase a greater physical output of commodities. He easily demolishes this by pointing out that, if money wages paid out were to fall in amount and investment by entrepreneurs (measured in wage units) did not increase, the amount of money income available for expenditures would fall to an equivalent extent. His discussion of the effects of the wage reduction on the volume of investment is mainly in terms of its influence on the expectations of entrepreneurs as to the future trend of wages, and he concedes that if entrepreneurs are led to expect further changes to be in an upward direction its effect will be favorable. He urges, however, that "it would be much better that wages should be rigidly fixed and deemed incapable of material changes than that depressions should be accompanied by a gradual downward tendency of money-wages" (p. 265).

This does not meet the argument for wage reduction—or rather money cost reduction[4]—during a depression which I had understood

[4] From the point of view of effect on *output*, the reduction of any part of variable costs is dollar for dollar of the same importance as the reduction of any other part of such costs, and it is only as against re-

to be the prevalent one in recent years. In this other doctrine, factor prices are to be reduced, but not, or not in the same degree, the prices of consumers' goods. In Keynes' analysis perfect and active competition is assumed, and prices are supposed to fall immediately and in full proportion to the fall in marginal variable[5] costs. If this occurred, and output remained the same, prices per unit would fall in greater absolute amount than would average variable costs,[6] and even more, if current labor cost were a negligible element in the fixed costs, than would average aggregate costs. The profit status of entrepreneurs would then be less favorable than before. What I understand to be the current doctrine is different. It looks to wage reductions during a depression to restore profit margins, thus to restore the investment morale of entrepreneurs and to give them again a credit status which will enable them to finance any investment they may wish to make. It relies upon the occurrence of a lag between the reduction in wage rates and a response in reduced volume of sales at the previous prices, during which interval entrepreneurs find prices to be higher than marginal costs and extensions of output therefore profitable, provided buyers can be found for the increased output. Increase in expenditures to restore depleted inventories and to replace inefficient equipment is relied upon to increase pay rolls sufficiently to provide the incomes with which the increased output can be bought, and the gain in employment—and in security of employment for those previously employed—is

---

duction of outstanding fixed costs, to the extent that they also do not consist of labor costs, that there is anything to be said for reduction of labor costs in preference to other costs. But from the point of view of the effect on the employment of *labor*, the reduction of labor cost is more favorable than the reduction to an equivalent amount of any other cost, because it will tend to lead to a substitution of labor for other factors, though it will not be as favorable as the reduction of both or *a fortiori* of all costs simultaneously and in the same proportions.

[5] Keynes distinguishes between "factor costs" and "user costs," the two combined comprising "prime" costs. By user costs he means the amounts paid out to other entrepreneurs for purchases from them and sacrifices incurred (extra wear and tear presumably) in employing equipment instead of leaving it idle. He claims that economists have generally equated supply price with marginal factor cost, ignoring user cost, whereas it should be equated with prime cost. I see no point in the distinction between purchases from entrepreneurs and direct

expected to release for expenditure the emergency reserves of the wage earning class. On the assumption that a large part of an entrepreneur's expenditures are ordinarily of the postponable class in the sense that they can be deferred without forcing a reduction of the scheduled rate of current output, even though not without increasing the current cost of production, and on the further assumption that operations at a loss are conducive to the postponement of every expenditure not essential for current operation, the supporters of this doctrine maintain that recovery of a profit margin can lead for a time to an increase in entrepreneurs' expenditures many times the increase in their net income, or, alternatively, the reduction in their net loss. They do not contend that this is certain to occur, but on the ground that the chief factor in governing the action of entrepreneurs with respect to postponable expenditures is the current profit status of their operations as compared to their immediately preceding experience, they say that it is a reasonable probability. Where external pressure on prices in the face of rigid costs has been an important factor in the depression, they also expect a favorable influence on the volume of employment from the effect of a wage reduction on profits and therefore on the volume of postponable expenditures, rather than from its effect on prices. While Keynes' analysis provides materials for strengthening this doctrine at a number of points, I cannot find in it any refutation of its general validity.

PROPENSITY TO CONSUME

Mr. Keynes himself tells us that the functional relationships of the various economic variables are more complex in fact than is formally recognized in his analysis. Simplification of this sort is inevitable, if analysis is to proceed at all. In the case, however, of Keynes' "propensity to consume" function, it seems to me that the

purchases of the services of the factors. What is the point in distinguishing between the cost of coal to a steel mill according as it is bought from an outside mine or produced in its own collieries? Where is the line to be drawn between entrepreneurs and "factors"? I am sceptical as to whether any economists have, explicitly or by implication, excluded cost of purchased materials or depreciation of equipment through use from the costs supposed to determine supply price.

[6] Because marginal costs would fall in the same proportion as average variable costs but would be greater in amount per unit than average variable costs.

simplification has been carried further than is necessary to prevent the analysis from becoming entangled in its own complexities, and further than is permissible if the concept is to be used fruitfully in the analysis of the short cycle.

Keynes explains the propensity to consume as a functional relationship between the amount of consumption measured in money wage units and the amount of income similarly measured. On the assumption that income in terms of money wage units corresponds substantially in its variations with the variations in level of employment, it is concluded that income, consumption, and level of employment are related to each other in a simple pattern. Writing C_w for amount of consumption in wage units and Y_w for income in wage units, and accepting as a close approximation that Y_w is a unique function of the level of employment, he states the propensity to consume function as: $C_w = \chi(Y_w)$ (p. 90).

Keynes lists a number of factors, (p. 96) "subjective" and "objective," which might affect the value of χ, Y_w remaining constant, but he assumes in general that the "subjective" factors remain constant, at least over short periods, and that, given Y_w, χ depends only on changes in the "objective" factors, which in the aggregate he takes to be of minor importance as compared to changes in Y_w. Several "objective" factors which he does not appear to have taken into account seem important enough in the short cycle to be deserving at least of mention.

Keynes believes that, apart from the effect of a change in the wage unit on the distribution of income between entrepreneurs and rentiers, who might have different propensities to consume, he has made adequate allowance in his formula for changes in expenditure resulting from changes in the wage unit by measuring both consumption and income in wage units. This disregards the possibility that, for short periods at least, the distinction which Keynes' makes in his supply function of labor between the response of labor (1) to changes in real wages accompanied by corresponding changes in money wages, and (2) to changes in real wages resulting from the changes in the prices of wage goods, money wages remaining the same, may have a parallel in the propensity to consume function. The response of consumption to a reduction in real income may be, for a time, substantially different if the reduction takes the form of a decrease in money income, prices remaining the same, from what it would be if money income remained the same but prices increased.

Mr. Keynes claims that in general rich countries are worse off than poor countries with respect to avoidance of "involuntary" unemployment because of the lesser propensities to consume in the former than in the latter, and thus the greater potential importance of hoarding. Since I would contend that over long periods, given a flexible price system, the propensity to consume will affect the rate of capital accumulation rather than the volume of employment, I will confine myself to a consideration of the comparative situation of the rich and poor countries with respect to the short cycle. The possession of large accumulated resources should operate to level out the rate of consumption in the face of fluctuations in income, and therefore to check both the downward and the upward phases of the cycle. Corresponding to the charges against the entrepreneur's budget which are fixed in aggregate monetary amount regardless of current output, there are in the ordinary consumer's budget items of monetary expenditure which are fixed for a time, very much regardless of changes in his money income as far as reductions therein are concerned, and which tend to be increased only as the result of careful deliberation in response to anticipation of a change of some duration in the individual's economic status. Aside from the probability that such fixed charges are ordinarily a greater proportion of the expenditures of the rich than of the poor, the poor in times of severe depression have a partial means of escape from them, in the form of defaults, to which those with resources subject to levy cannot resort. What this amounts to is that C_w should be treated as a function not only of Y_w, but also of the amount of accumulated resources measured in wage units held by the individual. In so far as the possession of resources operates in the manner suggested here, wealth becomes a stabilizing rather than a disturbing factor. The explanation of the apparently indisputable fact that the cyclical disturbances are more severe in rich than in poor countries would then have to be sought elsewhere than in the differences between rich and poor in propensities to consume. My own guess is that it is to be sought largely in the differences between the cyclical behavior of rich and poor with respect to the disposition of the income which they do not spend. The rich hoard only during depressions and dishoard for investment during prosperity, whereas the poor hoard some of their emergency reserves during prosperity and dishoard during depression.

Mr. Keynes says that a fundamental psychological law, upon which we have a right to depend both on a priori grounds and on the basis of experience is that $\frac{dC_w}{dY_w}$ is positive and less than unity; i.e., that in terms of wage units consumption varies in the same direction as income, but in smaller absolute amount than income (p. 96). This seems altogether reasonable. It leaves unanswered, however, a question of some interest: does C_w ever, except perhaps under war conditions, exceed Y_w? Since the community excess of Y_w over C_w constitutes new investment, if C_w never exceeded Y_w there would be continuous, though fluctuating, accumulation of capital resources, even through the depths of depression. Mr. Keynes apparently must believe that for the world as a whole the C_w's must often and substantially exceed the Y_w's, for he holds that in spite of "several millenia of steady individual saving" the world is poor in accumulated capital assets.[7] But what evidence there is seems to indicate that, if any acceptable mode of measuring physical amount of capital could be found and applied, it would show that the western world has been getting wealthier fairly steadily during say the past century and a half, not only in terms of aggregate resources but per capita, in spite of a three- or four-fold increase of population.

In connection with the propensity to consume concept, as with most of Keynes' concepts, the question arises in my mind how these concepts would have to be restated in order to provide specifications for the construction of statistical series by which his conclusions as to the nature and mode of behavior through time of the various functions could be inductively tested, and I regret that no suggestions of this sort are provided in this book. I am disposed to support Mr. Robertson in his claim that concepts expressed in more "monetary" terms, and expressions for the relationships between variables

[7] "That the world after several millennia of steady individual saving, is so poor as it is in accumulated capital-assets, is to be explained, in my opinion, neither by the improvident propensities of mankind, nor even by the destruction of war, but by the high liquidity-premiums formerly attaching to the ownership of land and now attaching to money" (p. 242).

which make specific allowance for time lags instead of assigning uniform time units to all the variables, have for purposes of a priori analysis some points of superiority over Keynes' "propensity" concepts expressed in terms of a single time unit. For purposes of inductive verification, assuming that the statistical data available will ever be in a form relevant to the answer of important questions, it seems obvious to me that the analysis would have to be extensively restated in terms of directions and degrees of time lags.

Comment on My 1936 Review of Keynes' *General Theory*

[1963]

MY 1936 REVIEW OF KEYNES' *General Theory*, here revived from the dead, no doubt had limitations of which I was then unaware and continue to be unaware. It also had, however, some deliberate limitations which were imposed on it by the circumstances of its publication. It was written as part of a symposium under the editorship of Professor Taussig. He encouraged me to include in my contribution a paragraph or two appraising the importance and quality of the book as a whole, but asked me aside from this to concentrate on a discussion of Keynes' theory of the causes of changes in the volume of employment. I interpreted Keynes' theory as in fact, whatever its intent, a theory only of the *short-run* determinants in changes in employment, and kept my comments within that limited framework. I consequently refrained from any attempt to assess the contribution of the *General Theory* to policy formulation, or to long-run analysis, or its serviceability as a foundation for long-run forecasting. I would not have denied that it contained, or probably contained, materials which could be profitably embodied, perhaps after appropriate adaptation, in long-run theorizing, but I would have conceded that I had only hazy notions of how that task could be performed and that its performance would require new insights and the invention of new analytical tools. I refrained also from discussing the various considerations which keep a theory of employment from being automatically a satisfactory theory of output.

Another deliberate limitation of my review was its abstention from any discussion of Keynes' ventures in the *General Theory* into *Dogmengeschichte,* although it was this phase of his book which I felt myself best qualified to appraise and regarded as most vulnerable. As a historian of thought in areas in which he was emotionally involved as a protagonist and prophet, Keynes seemed to me to be seriously lacking in the unexciting but essential qualities for the intellectual historian of objectivity and of judiciousness. Even when he was engaged in selecting those upon whom to bestow laurels for having in some degree anticipated his discoveries, his selection seemed to me then, and still seems to me now that I have acquired more knowledge of the older literature, often to have been random when not eccentric. I would nevertheless have agreed with him on what I take to be his major complaint against the main line of "orthodox" English economics from Ricardo to Marshall and Pigou that it failed miserably as an explanation of the causes of (nonsecular) fluctuations in output and employment, although I would have seen their failure more in their not making any serious attempt at such explanation than in the erroneous character of their product. I had myself been trained in that tradition, but by 1930 or 1931 I had realized that to an appreciable extent it gave no light, or misleading light, on the nature and origins of major economic fluctuations. I took it for granted, however, that the unsuitability of its standard analytical procedures for analysis of "depression" and "boom" was the result not of general stupidity or perverse bias on their part but of lack of professional interest in and of dedication to short-run analysis, a lack even more conspicuous in two other great schools of economic theory, the Austrian School and the Lausanne School. Keynes, however, was writing in a white heat of revolt from the English classical tradition, and treated its neglect of or deliberate abstraction from short-run phenomena as deliberate and stupid denial of their existence, while himself abstaining from acknowledging or exploring the possibility that in the short-run phenomena there were inherent forces which tended to produce quite different long-run than short-run consequences.

Almost the only references to my review that I know of were by Keynes himself and by two avowed Keynesians. All of them, of course, took issue with me on some major points, but none of them, I am glad to say, seemed to regard my review as hostile on the whole, in fact or intent. As best I can remember, I found the *General Theory* dazzling in its brilliance, and, if interpreted as primarily and admittedly a contribution to short-run theorizing, a veritable landmark, in both its positive and negative or critical aspects, in the history of our discipline. If I failed to make this clear, it was the consequence of inadequacy of exposition, not of intent. My appreciation of the quality and originality of its analysis as *short-run* analysis has grown since rather than shrunk, as I have struggled with its difficulties and as my understanding of it has improved thanks to the efforts of its many dedicated exegetes and perhaps also to my own later efforts, with the assistance of my students, to master its intricacies of thought and peculiarities of vocabulary. Within the boundaries of short-run analysis, and especially of short-run depression analysis, I regard the claim made for its having achieved a "Keynesian revolution" in economics as a permissible manifestation of an enthusiasm for which there is substantial justification, subject, however, to possible rival claims on the part of the "Swedish School" which I am not qualified to assess. On its adequacy as long-run analysis, and especially on its denial that (in a truly competitive economy) there exist powerful automatic forces which in the long run, if not counteracted by perverse governmental intervention, will restore "equilibrium," I still remain sceptical at least, with some propensity to be hostile. It may be that these long-run equilibrating forces operate with painful slowness. Real historical time, moreover, does not exclude those short-period disturbances which traditional theory tended to overlook or to segregate in a pound of abstraction whose characteristics it did not closely or penetratingly scrutinize. A year or two of the Great Depression sufficed to convince me, "orthodox" theorist though I was by training and temperament, that a substantial shift of emphasis in economic theory to short-period analysis was called for, and that the greater the degree of crisis the greater was the relative importance of the forces whose impact was predominantly short-run in character. Probably also by 1936, and certainly later, there was no reluctance on my part to concede that even analysis on strictly long-run assumptions had much to gain from inclusion of considerations such as Keynes was emphasizing. Nevertheless, without denying that "in the long-run we will all be dead," I still find "after us the deluge" an unsatisfactory guiding maxim for mankind in general or for economic theory in particular. What we should concede, with acknowledgments to Keynes, is that in counting our putative long-run blessings we should not disregard as trivial the short-run woes that they may have involved merely because they were, or may have been, present for a period substantially short of infinity, a procedure which is tolerable, if anywhere, only in theological discourse.

Within the field of short-run theory, Keynes—and his Cambridge associates—has great claims to originality. Many of the elements in his system were by no means new, or even of recent origin, as others have demonstrated, and as Keynes was even over-ready to concede provided it was not the "classical school" on whose behalf the anticipation was claimed. I will shortly cite a few instances of such anticipation, but will confine myself to out-of-the-way texts that have perhaps escaped notice hitherto.

From the seventeenth century on, there was an almost continuous stream of expositions of the view that unemployment and sluggish trade were the consequences of the failure of purchasing power to keep step with the expansion of productive power. Keynes found to his delight that the literature of mercantilism was saturated with this idea; it persisted into the nineteenth century and did not need the prodding of Keynes to continue to flourish in the twentieth century outside the realm of orthodox economic theory. One of the many curious items in this literature was a treatise of twelve hundred pages on this single theme which paused for breath only for paragraphing and thus constituted what was probably the longest chapter by far on record.[1]

---

[1] David Laurie, *New System of Finance*, Glasgow, 1815.

Among the ideas of narrower scope on which Keynes had anticipators, in some instances a host of them, were: the explanation of interest as the reward for surrendering (cash) liquidity;[2] the dependence of employment and output on the sum of consumption expenditure and investment expenditure; a loan-fund theory of the determination of the interest rate; the absence of inflationary pressure as long as there are involuntarily-unemployed resources;[3] and even the necessary equivalence of (realized or effective) investment with (realized or effective) saving, so that the outcome of increased effort to save may be less rather than more saving.[4]

Even, however, if few of the bricks Keynes used to build his theoretical structure were completely novel, he refined and remoulded them to more precise and rigorous specifications. More important, Keynes was strikingly original in the skill and comprehensiveness with which he combined these separate ideas or theorems into a complex and coherent system.

Keynes gave to his integrated system the label "*General* Theory" because he thought its claims to originality lay largely in its demonstration of the possibility of "equilibrium" at *any* level of employment, with equilibrium at "full employment" only a special and not very probable case. This is a legitimate use of the term "general," but it should not be confused with its meaning as used in Walrasian theorizing, which is "general" in the sense that the Walrasian purports to account for all the significant interrelations between variables or functions. Even in this latter sense, however, Keynes' system,

[2] "Since the Statute against usurie [13 Eliz. c. 8 (1571)] did tolerate ten upon the hundred everie man hath found such a sweetness in that usurial gaine that smalle store of money is hoorded up." (From a 1594 manuscript quoted by H. M. Robertson, *Aspects of the Rise of Economic Individualism,* Cambridge, Eng., 1933, p. 198).

[3] E.g., Hugo Bilgram, *Involuntary Idleness,* Philadelphia, 1889.

[4] After a discussion of "the propensity of man to lay up in store or to consume:" "Savings do not become capital, unless they are employed reproductively; and it is the difficulty of finding modes of so applying them, not the strong inclination of man to spend all that he can obtain, that opposes a bar to the rapid accumulation of capital. Any plan, therefore, of increasing the capital of a country by an artificial diminution of the consumption, proceeds upon a supposition of very dubious truth. You may, by such means, diminish the amount of the unproductive consumption of the country, but you will not necessarily increase its productive consumption. The more probable result

as a short-run system, was in some, though not all, respects, a more "general" system than any other earlier short-run system. I find it a good working rule to test the degree of generality, in the Walrasian sense, of an economic system by counting the ratio of variables to constants in the system. On this, as on other grounds as well, neither Walras's system as a long-run system nor Keynes' system as a short-run one is as "general" as it could ideally be made to be. In my review of the *General Theory,* most of my criticisms related to this issue, although I did not make this point explicit. The *General Theory* relies too heavily for its conclusions on the treatment of variables as constants, that is, on rigidities, and on the treatment of structures, or complex matrices, such as the wage structure, the price structure, the rate of interest structure, each marked by complicated internal as well as external interrelations, as if they were simple, single-layer, concepts. It disturbs me, therefore, when I think I see "Keynesians," and especially Keynesian econometricians and geometricians, endeavor to develop and improve upon the contribution of the *General Theory* by stripping it of some of the Walrasian-type of generality it does possess, instead of making it more Walrasian in its analytic character. I think I have grounds for believing that I am here closer to Keynes' beliefs, at least as they were in 1946, than are some of his avowed disciples, although in the conversations I had with him in that year neither of us made any use of this specific way of formulating the analytical issue.

One manifestation of Keynes' reliance on too restricted a set of variables in the *General Theory* was his treatment of *the* rate of interest as the product of the relationship of the demand for "money" to the stock of "money," with "money" defined or identified, in the *General Theory,* and in later writings, as "cash," as "hoards," as "idle balances," or expressly left to be defined by the reader to his taste. I found fault with this in my review as gross oversimplification, but I should have given my criticism a wider

will be, either that the amount of annual production will be lessened, or that a proportion of the unproductive consumption will be shifted from one class of commodities to another [presumably because one man's saving will be offset by another man's dissaving]." An anonymous review of James Mill's *Elements of Political Economy, The British Review, and London Critical Journal,* xix (1822), 158.

scope, more range, although perhaps no more weight or intensity, than I did. The flow of funds to borrowers is restrained not only by the interest charged but also by "rationing" or limiting availability. In England the grant of a line of credit, in the United States a commitment to lend, is from the point of view of "liquidity" a close equivalent to an actual loan, but neither gets into statistics of the stock of "money," or into the diagrams. In the United States the "compensatory balances" which banks often require borrowers to maintain are spurious parts of the statistical "money" stock when they exceed the maximum working balances which borrowers would maintain if they were free to choose. Probably everywhere in some degree banks control their volume of lending by rationing and changes in "availability" of loans as well as by changes in discount rates, and in England before the 1850's and in Canada before World War I the maintenance of discount rates by law or custom at substantially constant levels was an additional factor, which receives no attention in the *General Theory*, weakening the connection between variations in the stock of money and variations in the interest-rate structure.

In his reply to the *Quarterly Journal of Economics* symposium on the *General Theory*, Keynes dealt with me gently and generously, and took sharp issue with me on only two closely related points: my complaint that he had grossly overemphasized "hoarding" as a major element in "liquidity preference" and thus as an influence on the rate of interest, and my claim that "in modern monetary theory the propensity to hoard is generally dealt with, with results which in kind are substantially identical with Keynes', as a factor operating to reduce the 'velocity' of money."[5]

To take first the question of the role of "liquidity preference" as a force operating to create, or sustain, or raise the level of, the interest-rate structure, Keynes in his reply to me wrote:

> Again, when Professor Viner points out that most people invest their savings at the best rate of interest they can get and asks for statistics to justify the importance I attach to liquidity-preference, he is overlooking the point that it is the *marginal*

---

[5] J. M. Keynes, "The General Theory of Employment," *The Quarterly Journal of Economics*, LI (1937), 209-225. The direct references to me are on pp. 210-212 and p. 219, note.

> potential hoarder who has to be satisfied by the rate of interest, so as to bring the desire for actual hoards within the narrow limits of the cash available for hoarding [p. 211].
>
> When Professor Viner charges me with assigning to liquidity-preference "a grossly exaggerated importance," he must mean that I exaggerate its instability and its elasticity. But if he is right, a small decline in money-income would lead, as stated above, to a large fall in the rate of interest. I claim that experience indicates the contrary. [p. 219, note].

"Liquidity preference" was Keynes' term, and when I charged him with exaggerating its importance, I had reference to the meaning he gave it in many passages in the *General Theory*, which is also the meaning he gives it in the two passages from his reply to me which I quote above, namely, a preference for "hoards," for money deliberately to be kept idle, as the consequence of the "propensity to hoard." Keynes was surely also using "liquidity preference" in this narrow sense when he said: "The rate of interest obviously measures . . . the premium which has to be offered to induce people to hold their wealth in some form other than hoarded money. . . . The rate of interest is the factor which adjusts at the margin the demand for hoards to the supply of hoards" (p. 216). I did not then deny, and I would not deny now, that "liquidity preference" broadly conceived, so that it included preference for "hoards" only as one element, and probably a very minor one, in the liquidity complex, was an important determinant or "regulator" of the interest-rate structure. Keynes in his reply did state "nor is my argument affected by the admitted fact that different types of assets satisfy the desire for liquidity in different degrees," but he must have meant, if he was being relevant, that his argument as to the importance of the propensity to hoard did not need qualification because of this capacity of other assets than money to satisfy "liquidity preference."

The passages I have quoted from Keynes' reply have continued to puzzle me, but as I was preparing this paper I at last saw what I now think Keynes meant by them, why he thought them an adequate reply to me, and how he had originally reached his theory of the importance of the propensity to hoard as the causal factor regulating, with the stock of money, the rate of interest. It all rests, I fear, on a basic misunderstanding or misapplication of marginal analysis of the Marshallian kind, in a pattern of error which has occasionally been perpetrated in the textbooks and with which I have been familiar for more years than I can remember.

In a statement of the processes of equilibration in a competitive market, the conditions of (or at) equilibrium are not to be confused with the causal forces producing that equilibrium. It is not the marginal contribution to supply, or to demand, of an individual, or of a minor sector of the supplying agents or the demanding agents, or even of all the supplying or demanding agents in the aggregate, which determines what the equilibrium level of price shall be, but the whole supply functions and demand functions. If a distinguishable sector of demand (or of supply) is quantitatively a minor fraction, under any likely circumstances, of the aggregate demand (or supply), it cannot be a major or an important determinant of the equilibrium level of price. The whole equilibrium complex, once established, will determine for that sector what quantity it will take, or provide, on the basis of equality between the equilibrium price and that sector's marginal demand (or supply) price. It will, however, be the equilibrium price determined by the market as a whole which will (predominantly) regulate where the margin is located for the sector in question, and not the other way around. For a homogeneous commodity in a well-ordered competitive market, it will not make sense, even theoretically, to talk of equilibrium between the demand of a particular sector of aggregate demand (e.g., the demand for money *to hoard*) and the supply of a particular sector of aggregate supply (e.g., the supply of money *for hoarding purposes*). In almost every respect possible, Keynes' theory of the role of "the propensity to hoard" as regulator of the interest rate contradicts these propositions. In especially sharp contradiction is Keynes' emphasis, in his reply to me, on the importance of the degree of elasticity and stability of the demand for money to hoard, *if* such demand is, at almost any conceivable range of interest rates, small in relation to the total demand for money. This is where the need for "statistics" that I referred to and that Keynes rejected enters into the picture.

In the only comment on this interchange between Keynes and myself that I can recall seeing in print, Lawrence R. Klein reports me as not agreeing "with the theory of liquidity-preference because he [that is, I] thought that the transaction motive has as much influence on the rate of interest as the speculative motive." What I said went further than this: the hoarding motive was a minor force as compared to all the other motives taken together which influenced the demand for money. Klein thought that this question had been answered "by the events of recent years." The answer, I presume, was supplied by the statistical record of what went on in those years, and Klein found it unnecessary to state so obvious a fact as that that answer confirmed Keynes' position.[6] I am unfamiliar with that record and cannot therefore contest any inferences drawn from it, but I at least welcome the implied agreement with me that a "propensity to hoard" theory of the determination of the level of the interest-rate structure needs supporting quantitative data.

With respect to the existence of liquid assets other than money, of "near-money," of "half-hoards,"[7] possessing in some degree "liquidity preference" satisfying-power, aside from the question of their role in the determination of interest rates I would continue to press the point that the accumulation of such assets constitutes simultaneously both a satisfaction of liquidity preference *and* investment, so that the two are not, as they are in the case of "hoards," functional opposites. I would now add that there is no fixed or stable scale of liquidity for different classes of assets, and that depending on circumstances, as, for example, the existence of fear of extreme inflation or of exchange depreciation, or the loss of confidence in the solvency of banks, the "propensity to hoard" may become a propensity to hoard anything except domestic money or claims to such money.

Keynes' disapproval of my attachment to the "velocity" concept as a tool of analysis, with which Klein heartily expressed agreement, is certainly supported by the record since the publication of the *General Theory;* velocity analysis seems to have been totally abandoned by all except one minority group of monetary theorists. I am impressed, however, by the quality of the products of this group. I note also that in his one endeavor to define the "money" which plays so

[6] Lawrence R. Klein, *The Keynesian Revolution,* New York, 1950, pp. 101-102.

[7] Thomas Gisborne, "Accumulations of Capital," *Quarterly Review,* LXXII (1847), 206-231, an article which contains much of interest for the history of liquidity preference theorizing, makes pertinent use of this term.

fundamental a role in his "propensity to hoard" theory of interest, Keynes was not able to dispense with "velocity" as a criterion of what was and what was not "money" for the purposes of this theory. It is conceivable to me that if he had ever tried to locate precisely the line between money and not-money, "velocity" would have turned out to be almost the sole criterion.

The *General Theory* had policy objectives very much in mind, but in the main concentrated on providing theoretical foundations for the formulation of policy and the selection of policy instruments with respect to the problem of unemployment. To keep within my assignment, and also because my entanglement with the U.S. Treasury at the time, a time of some internal controversy within the Administration with reference to fiscal and monetary policy, inhibited me from public discussion of related policy issues, I also refrained from discussing policy except for a warning that there was an inflationary bias in Keynes' thinking. Aside from details, however, I would have accepted the policy implications of the *General Theory* in the monetary and fiscal field were they presented as relating to short-run or cyclical fluctuations in employment but were not extended without further analysis to long-sustained or chronic unemployment. Seymour Harris has said of Keynes, with reference, I believe, to the early thirties:

> He preached what has become a commonplace since he wrote: 'Government should spend more and tax less in depression; and spend less and tax more in boom.' These simple truths were discoveries of Keynes's which had to be repeated and repeated hundreds of times before they made the required impression.[8]

This formula may have been a discovery of Keynes, but I used it at least as early as the summer of 1931, and I don't think I derived it from Keynes, with whose journalistic writings I then had little acquaintance. The idea was then a commonplace in my academic surroundings of the time, and I cannot recall that any of my Chicago colleagues would have dissented, or that they needed to learn it from Keynes, or from me. In any case, a talk I gave at the Institute of

[8] Seymour Harris, *John Maynard Keynes, Economist and Policy Maker*, New York, 1955, p. 149. I do not know whether this formula is a close paraphrase of something Keynes wrote.

Politics at Williamstown on August 14, 1931, was reported in the next day's *New York Times* as follows:

> Tax heavily, spend lightly, redeem debts, are sound Treasury principles during a period of dangerously rapid business expansion: tax lightly, spend heavily, borrow, are equally sound Treasury principles during a period of acute depression. . . .
>
> Really sound Treasury policy in a world in which business depression is a recurrent phenomenon should be a function of the state of business conditions and should be conducted so as to contribute to the smoothing out of business fluctuations rather than so as either to accentuate them or to insulate itself from them regardless of the repercussions on business in general.

Two conservative journals which commented on this passage (*The Journal of Commerce*, August 17, 1931; *The Financial World*, September 9, 1931) agreed with it on principle, but warned that in practice governments would happily conform to the rule during depression but would disregard it during boom, so that its long-run outcome would be inflation. There is much in the historical record since then to justify this warning, but I would then and later have been willing to take the risk, provided the rule was not extended to chronic unemployment, as I believe Keynes would have extended it. There is nowhere in the *General Theory* any warning about the evil or the danger of inflation, and Keynes there defines "true" inflation in such a manner that the historical circumstances which would justify taking anti-inflationary action could exist only in the rarest of circumstances; not even, say, in the Brazil of 1962 when the price level rose by over 50 per cent. "When a further increase in the quantity of effective demand produces no further increase in output and entirely spends itself on an increase in the cost-unit fully proportionate to the increase in effective demand, we have reached a condition which might be appropriately designated as one of true inflation" (p. 303). The advocacy this year (1963) by the Administration at Washington of a deliberate increase in the budgetary deficit at a time of increasing output and employment, with the implied promise that it will not result in inflation, is hard for me to understand unless the Administration has this Keynesian definition of "true inflation" up its sleeve, ready to be produced if it should be charged with inflationary tendencies.

The prophet and the politician, in their professional roles, generally find it necessary to abandon a rhetoric which is disciplined and solid but liable to be painfully unpersuasive and to adopt one which, if it has elements of wildness in it, at least promises to be effective as persuasion. The issue of sincerity is, with respect to them, not worth raising, since what men hear themselves repeating they soon come to believe. Keynes, I am sure, often interpreted his role as that of the prophet and the politician, and it was in such a period, I presume, that he once wrote: "Words ought to be a little wild, for they are the assault of thoughts on the unthinking." I do not challenge this for prophets and politicians, for they have special occupational license to promote their objectives free from stodgy inhibitions on the exercise of all their rhetorical resources for persuasion. I believe in the virtues of professional division of labor, however, and I am troubled, therefore, when economists adopt the role and the tactics of the prophet or the politician, especially when there is any ground for suspicion that what is involved is false prophecy.

In the early 1940's, "Keynesians" were forecasting that the cessation of hostilities would be followed by a disastrous degree of depression and of unemployment unless governments deliberately engaged in massive deficit financing. In a series of conversations I had with Keynes in March 1946, shortly before his death, I tried to tease him about this, but found him invulnerable. He told me that he had just met with a group of younger economists in Washington who regarded themselves as his followers, and who claimed that they had on hand econometric demonstrations based on Keynesian logic that disastrous deflation was imminent. Keynes himself, however, was optimistic and disowned any responsibility for their gloomy prognostications; he especially objected to their reliance on restricted and mechanical manipulations of a few statistical series, rather than making a broad survey of the significant factors and using judgment in assaying their importance and the nature of their impacts. His last publication, which was in galley for the *Economic Journal* when he died, startled his disciples by its optimistic tone, and there was serious consideration of the desirability of suppressing it, on the ground, I gathered, that it manifested some weakening, in his last days, of his analytical powers, and that to publish it posthumously would be to participate in perpetrating an unwarranted blemish on his record.

The article was not suppressed, and it survives as one among many other testimonies of the supreme level of statesmanship, of balanced vision, of dedication, and of endeavor to reconcile differences in conclusions when there was no difference as to basic objectives and values, on which he ended his brilliant career. The Keynes of that period was to me then, and continues to be, a heroic figure, and my admiration of him as he was then, of his personality and his intellect, was unalloyed by the qualifications which I felt, and still feel, about the Keynes of the *General Theory*, and even more, about the journalistic and polemical Keynes of the 1920's and early 1930's.

'Keynes Comments on Money'

H. C. Simons, 'Keynes comments on money', *The Christian Century* (22 July 1936), pp. 1016–17.

Keynes Comments on Money

THE GENERAL THEORY OF UNEMPLOYMENT, INTEREST AND MONEY. *By John Maynard Keynes. Harcourt, Brace & Company, $2.00.*

THE PUBLICATION of a general treatise on money by the most famous economist of our time is, of course, an important event. Mr. G. D. H. Cole has announced—as promptly and as injudiciously as did Sir Josiah Stamp in reviewing Mr. Keynes' earlier "Treatise on Money"—that it marks a new era in the progress of economic thought; and the book has received serious and respectful attention in circles where its contents must be about as palatable as the communist manifesto. Mr. Keynes is popularly accepted as one of the authentic geniuses of his generation; and, in spite of his warning that he is writing for specialists, the book will enjoy a wide circulation outside, as well as within, academic circles. It is thus a choice item for laymen who cultivate reputations for serious reading and brilliant conversation.

The book is largely in the nature of a revision (if not a repudiation) of the first volume of the "Treatise on Money" and, like that work, is full of brilliant insights and occasionally devastating criticism of other writers. As a general treatise on money, however, it lacks form and structure and represents simply a collection of interesting propositions, expounded awkwardly and presented with little or no indication of the special assumptions and postulates within which they might be valid or meaningful. Strange and novel terms of the analysis are seldom explicitly defined; and those necessary assumptions which the author does recognize (e.g., the assumption of fixity of wage-rates) are insinuated obscurely. Nowhere, moreover, can one discover, even from insinuation, the nature of the monetary system which the argument presupposes. Thus the author gives us a theory of unemployment, interest and money which attains generality by being about nothing at all.

Mr. Keynes' main point is that our economic system has been excessively exposed and subjected to deflationary pressures—that individual savings are likely to get dammed up in hoards, instead of flowing on to finance the production of investment-assets. With this judgment, the reviewer is inclined definitely to agree. Indeed, if the whole book could be interpreted simply as a critical appraisal of the traditional gold standard, implemented through central-bank operations, one's judgment of its main ideas might be extremely favorable. The author, however, does not invite such interpretation. Moreover, if the book is good as criticism of monetary arrangements of the past, it certainly is not to be commended for its suggestions and implications regarding the desirable arrangements for the future.

Announcing a general theory, Mr. Keynes delivers merely a collection of generalizations and practical judgments which have substantial validity with reference to the particular conditions of post-war England, and of other countries since 1930. The nominal eschewing of practical proposals serves only to keep them in an obscure and ambiguous form. Clearly, however, his notions of solution run now in terms of a great and curious variety of expedients—in terms of a highly diffuse kind of political interference. The analytical passages indicate, often illuminatingly, how monetary disturbances are manifested in different aspects of economic behavior and in different phases of the economic process; and they seem intended to demonstrate that wise governmental policy must deal directly with many particular relationships. Thus, the state should use taxation to curtail private saving; it should supplement private consumption and investment with its own spending; and it should force down and keep down the rate of interest to promote new enterprise. At times the author seems to suggest outright fixing of the volume of investment and of the rate of interest by the government.

Mr. Keynes nowhere suggests the need for economy in the kinds of governmental interference; and he seems to disregard, or grossly to underestimate, the possibilities of controlling all the variables which his analysis emphasizes merely by controlling the quantity of money—i.e., by ordering fiscal practice (spending, taxing, borrowing and currency issue) in terms of deliberate monetary policy. He overlooks the need (clearly suggested by his own analysis) for the minimizing of monetary uncertainties and the achievement of a monetary system based on definite and stable rules. Thus, while expressing decided preference for an economic system of free enterprise, he does not seriously consider what monetary arrangements or what implementations of monetary policy are most and least compatible with that system.

Mr. Keynes submits his treatise as a frontal attack upon traditional economic theory. Orthodox economists are rather defenselessly exposed to the charge of making bad applications of their relative-price analysis—of applying carelessly an analysis which abstracts from monetary disturbances in the discussion of practical questions for which monetary problems are crucially important. (The usual academic lecture or textbook chapter on foreign trade and tariff policy is the striking case in point.) But the author attacks, not the bad applications of traditional theory, but the theory itself—with results which will impress only the incompetent.

If the attack upon orthodoxy is misdirected, it is also indiscreet. Not content to point out the shortcomings of traditional views, Mr. Keynes proceeds to espouse the cause of an army of cranks and heretics simply on the grounds that their schemes or ideas would incidentally have involved or suggested mitigation of the deflationary tendencies in the economy. The fondness for a labor theory of value may be pardoned as mere intellectual dilettantism; but the author might adequately have criticized economists for their neglect of monetary problems without endorsing mercantilism, *autarchie*, social credit, stamped money, fantastic governmental spending, the single tax, underconsumption theories and usury laws. The reviewer is not inclined to be more generous toward monetary orthodoxy than is Mr. Keynes. But the sophistical academic leg-pulling which he perpetrates in this volume, however delightful and entertaining in its proper place, should not be done publicly in times like these, least of all by persons of Mr. Keynes' repute.

Readers should be warned against the presumption that the author has eschewed advocacy of practical expedients in favor of objective analytical inquiry, and cautioned against hasty or credulous acceptance of analysis, arguments and critical judgments which are always highly sophisticated and often merely sophistical. Critical readers will find grounds for suspicion either that Mr. Keynes has become overly susceptible to his own clever persuadings or that, having few more laurels to win as an economist, he now aspires to be remembered also as a great wit. Attempting mischievous and salutary irritation of his peers, however, he may only succeed in becoming the academic idol of our worst cranks and charlatans—not to mention the possibilities of the book as the economic bible of a fascist movement.

Many economists, including the reviewer, will welcome opportunity to defend Mr. Keynes against all advocates of reactionary monetary policies, and against those who think they can talk sense about our urgent economic problems while abstracting them from monetary disturbances. But only a kind fate can spare him the approbation which he has invited from fools.

HENRY C. SIMONS.

'Unemployment and Keynes' Revolution'

F. Knight, 'Unemployment and Mr. Keynes's revolution in economic theory', *Canadian Journal of Economics and Political Science*, 3 (February 1937), pp. 100–23.

REVIEW ARTICLE

UNEMPLOYMENT: AND MR. KEYNES'S REVOLUTION IN ECONOMIC THEORY[1]

I. *The Revolutionary Approach to the Problem*

WHAT Mr. Keynes ostensibly does in his already widely discussed volume published over a year ago is to effect a revolution in general economic theory. His work does not purport to be an extension of theory in the way of removing abstract generalizations and bringing it into closer touch with reality under particular conditions; rather its fundamental assumptions are rejected outright and others are substituted. These are still more general, and the accepted notions are treated as "special case" propositions not justified by the facts. The general character of the argument is indicated by the title, which is not "The Theory of Unemployment", but in contrast, "The Theory of Employment". In particular, the book is not ostensibly or directly a treatise on the business or trade cycle, to be incorporated into, and by qualifying to supplement, a general theory of stable equilibrium. It claims to be itself a theory of stable equilibrium, like the conventional systems in being free from cycles, but different in that instead of full employment a large amount of unemployment, involuntary and not due to friction, is characteristic of the equilibrium position.

I may as well state at the outset that the direct contention of the work seems to me quite unsubstantiated. Its value is, I think, to be sought in the opposite direction from that of its pretensions, as just indicated; *i.e.*, the treatment suggests modifications of conventional equilibrium analysis to account for temporary, possibly more or less chronic, disequilibrium conditions or, in other words, makes indirect contributions to the theory of business fluctuations. The argument, therefore, requires extensive re-interpretation and integration with a general theory running in terms of equilibrium with full employment, before it can be accepted as sound or useful.

[1]*The General Theory of Employment, Interest, and Money*. By JOHN MAYNARD KEYNES. London: Macmillan and Co. [Toronto: The Macmillan Company of Canada.] 1936. Pp. xii, 403. ($1.50) In view of the late date of this review, and particularly of the number of extensive reviews already published, some familiarity with the content of the book may be assumed, and this article will be made primarily critical in character.

Mr. Keynes himself sets his position in contrast with that of "the classical economics" at every opportunity. He begins with an introductory chapter of a single short paragraph which, repeating statements in his Preface, condemns the classical economics for dealing with a "special case", the characteristics of which "happen not to be those of the economic society in which we actually live", and follows with a full-length chapter entitled "The Postulates of the Classical Economics". In this chapter and throughout the book, his references under this phrase are, in general, the sort of caricatures which are typically set up as straw men for purposes of attack in controversial writing. I mean, of course, that that is the way in which they impress me. In the great majority of cases the doctrines so labelled seem to be quite at variance with, and often contradictory to, anything I was ever taught as classical doctrine in any modern sense—and I went through the academic "mill"; and they are certainly alien to anything I have ever taught as such, and I have been rated, and have supposed myself, an adherent of the general type of position referred to by the term. On the other hand, many of Mr. Keynes's own doctrines are, as he would proudly admit, among the notorious fallacies to combat which has been considered a main function of the teaching of economics. The general issue—in so far as there is an issue, and not merely the sort of amiable misrepresentation customarily assumed to be necessary to make an interesting fight—has to do with procedure in analysis. The accepted view among theorists has been that theory must begin with drastically simplified situations, described in abstract and over-general terms, and must proceed by stages toward the complexity of real life. In particular, it has been assumed that the theorist must consider a society free from the complications of speculation and of monetary changes, and hence from cyclical unemployment, before taking up these phenomena.[2] In the interest of clarity as to the underlying meaning, the reader of Mr. Keynes's book would do well to keep in mind that references to "the classical economics" are to be interpreted as relating to economic analysis *at the stage* at which uncertainty and monetary disturbances are assumed absent. It may also be helpful to suggest that Mr. Keynes's own procedure is typically that of replacing conventional assumptions which do not tell the whole story, and were never represented as doing so, with some antithetical proposition, or familiar qualification, which is then treated as quite general, though the context of the book itself makes it clear enough that the argument cannot be taken as meaning what it says.

[2]On page 292 the author finally mentions satirically the fact that traditional economics may get around to monetary phenomena, "in Vol. II, or more often in a separate treatise".

In chapter 2, Mr. Keynes states two "postulates", both having to do with labour and wages. The first is that "the wage is equal to the marginal product of labour"; the second, that "the utility of the wage when a given volume of labour is employed is equal to the marginal disutility of that amount of employment". The first is accepted, "subject only to the same qualifications as in the classical theory" (p. 17), the second rejected. The argument on this point need not be considered in detail; the main conclusion is that money wages are not revised downward in case of involuntary unemployment, because "fortunately", the workers are "instinctively more reasonable economists than the classical school" (p. 14).[3] In more general terms, the contention is that in the labour market the prevalence of a price which leaves a large quantity of the commodity in question unsalable but with the owners willing and anxious to sell, produces no effective tendency to reduce the price to a level which will "clear the market". It is almost, if not quite expressly, stated that workers bargain through an organization as a unit, *i.e.*, a monopoly, yet the situation conspicuously is not brought under the principles of monopoly price, and, of course, nothing is said of any arrangement for distributing the burden of loss of sale (*i.e.*, of unemployment). Mr. Keynes states repeatedly that the normal presence of a large amount of involuntary and non-frictional unemployment is a fact of common observation (pp. 7, 10, 16, 32, *etc.*). There is no reference to depression conditions. As neither the relation to friction nor even the involuntariness of unemployment is open to direct observation, the conclusion must be that his belief is based on deduction from the principles of his "system",—just the crime of which he accuses the classical writers (p. 16) in connection with the contrary conviction.

II. *The General Statement of the Theory*

It is imperative to keep the fundamental position above stated clearly in mind in interpreting the book as a whole, for little more is said about it, yet it is assumed throughout. It represents the first main step in the author's argument. Viewed as a theory of unemployment, the drift of this argument may be sketched as follows (as far as I am able to figure it out). To explain unemployment, Mr. Keynes first *assumes* (*a*) unemployment, and (*b*) such a price situation, and (*c*) such a mode of operation of the price mechanism, that growth in employment is blocked. This blocking is the fundamental mystery. It does not seem to be a matter primarily of wages being too high in relation to product prices, plus wage

[3]Chapter 19, entitled "Changes in Money-Wages", deals with the *effects* of wage *increases*.

and price "stickiness", but rather a matter of rigidity in the total monetary circulation, plus rigidity as regards decline in both prices and wages. The first step in the argument is intended to dispose of the popular heresy (derived from "classical" reasoning) that employment might be increased through a downward adjustment of wages. It has been argued (in chapter 2) (*a*) that the pressure of unemployment does not tend effectively to lower wages, and (*b*) that if it did, or if effective pressure in this sense were somehow brought to bear, wage reduction would not tend to increase employment, and hence "ought" not to happen. The bulk of the book, then, assuming initially more or less "correct" relative levels of wages and product prices, attempts to explain the failure of employment to increase spontaneously, and to suggest the type of social policy to be pursued in connection with the problem. The explanation runs in terms of the workings of the monetary system, especially in relation to the investment market.

In chapter 3, "The Principle of Effective Demand", the main argument of the book is sketched out in the form of a relation between aggregate demand and supply functions, *i.e.*, functions expressing supply-price and demand-price of amounts of employment (labour) as functions of the amount. The demand-price for labour (D in Mr. Keynes's notation) is the "proceeds" to be expected by entrepreneurs from employing a given amount. The supply-price is represented by Z and the quantity of employment by N. We read (p. 25):

> Now if for a given value of N the expected proceeds are greater than the aggregate supply price, *i.e.* if D is greater than Z, there will be an incentive to entrepreneurs to increase employment beyond N and, if necessary, to raise costs by competing with one another for the factors of production, up to the value of N for which Z has become equal to D. Thus the volume of employment is given by the point of intersection between the aggregate demand function and the aggregate supply function; for it is at this point that the entrepreneurs' expectation of profits will be maximized. The value of D at the point of the aggregate demand function, where it is intersected by the aggregate supply function, will be called *the effective demand*. . . . This is the substance of the General Theory of Employment, . . .

For "factors of production", we clearly should read "labour", and for "costs", "wages". In view of the fixity (against downward change) of the wage-level, this ought to say that there is a tendency to increase N until D is lowered, in consequence of diminishing returns, to equality with Z. What is meant by maximizing profits, I cannot see (the same statement is repeated on page 89), as the author surely does not assume that all entrepreneurs are organized as a monopoly, and if they were, the marginal productivity of labour would not be made equal to wages—the first "assumption of the classical economics", which he has said he accepts.

The page following the paragraph quoted again emphasizes the contrast with "the classical doctrine". The contrast is exceedingly strained and almost seems designed to distract attention from the essential assumption of the (downwardly) fixed supply-price for labour. The "special assumption as to the relation between these two functions" which classical economists are accused of making (p. 24 at bottom), which Mr. Keynes forcibly identifies with "Say's Law", actually means precisely the assumption that there is no such fixity of price preventing an adjustment which will clear the market.[4]

In the following section (of the same chapter, ch. 3) is given a "brief summary of the theory of unemployment to be worked out in the course of the following chapters". We read (pp. 27-8):

> The outline of our theory can be expressed as follows. When employment increases, aggregate real income is increased. The psychology of the community is such that when aggregate real income is increased aggregate consumption is increased, but not by so much as income. Hence employers would make a loss if the whole of the increased employment were to be devoted to satisfying the increased demand for immediate consumption. Thus, to justify any given amount of employment there must be an amount of current investment sufficient to absorb the excess of total output over what the community chooses to consume when employment is at the given level. For unless there is this amount of investment, the receipts of the entrepreneurs will be less than is required to induce them to offer the given amount of employment. It follows, therefore, that, given what we shall call the community's propensity to consume, the equilibrium level of employment, . . . will depend on the amount of current investment. The amount of current investment will depend, in turn, on what we shall call the inducement to invest; and [this] will . . . depend on the relation between the schedule of the marginal efficiency of capital and the complex of rates of interest. . . .[5]

[4]Mr. Keynes quotes Mill on Say's Law, but does not mention either Mill's explicit exception for crisis conditions which occurs a few pages previously in his *Principles*, or, of course, Mill's doctrine that the demand for products is not a demand for labour, which (however absurd) was one of his chief bids for fame.

[5]The first difficulty in following up and interpreting this statement is the confusion between what is dependent upon the actual magnitude of a variable and what is dependent on changes in that variable. It is no exaggeration to say that the book is "packed" with examples of this confusion. If we interpret the statement in accord with what it actually says, the questions raised have to do with speed of change and differences in speed of change between independent and dependent variables, *i.e.*, with "lags" in response, and the length of time required to establish a new equilibrium of the same sort which must be assumed as the starting point of the initial change, to make sense of the statement. But this view is contradictory to the conception of equilibrium in terms of which the theory as a whole is couched. The main assumption as to the psychology is repeatedly referred to in the book as a "law". The statements alternate more or less at random between the form of a relation between changes (almost always increases) in income and changes (increases) in "non-consumption" (as to saving, see below) and the form of a relation between income itself and non-consumption. For the latter, see page following quotation (p. 28 at bottom) and the apparently crucial definition on

III. *The Monetary Demand for Labour*

So far we have been dealing with what is essentially introductory material; the title above (of this present section of our study) is practically the subject of Mr. Keynes's book. (On page 89, he remarks that the aggregate supply function involves few considerations which are not already familiar, that it is the part played by the aggregate demand function which has been overlooked.) The thesis of the work is, first, that unemployment is due to the failure of effective demand, that neither actually nor properly, naturally nor artificially, is unemployment to be remedied otherwise than by an increase in the effective (monetary) demand for labour.[6] The reader's task could have been made indefinitely lighter if key sentences in the early part of the book had been so worded as to make it clear that, theoretically in the course of nature, and practically as a matter of policy, supply-price is fixed and the adjustment is all on the demand side, instead of being worded so as to give the impression that the supply-price function is a real function in the sense ordinarily understood.[7]

After dividing the monetary demand for labour into the two parts, demand for consumption purposes and demand for investment, the logical order of procedure might seem to be that of examining the forces which

---

page 90, which calls the propensity to consume the functional relation between income and expenditure on consumption out of that income. But on page 96 "the fundamental psychological law" is again a relation between increases, and on page 97 the two formulations are apparently identified. (*Cf.* also pp. 115, 121, 251, 247.)

It is to be noted as a separate source of confusion that a relation between changes in one direction does not necessarily hold for changes in the other. A sufficiently industrious and painstaking reader will finally discover that in this case the reverse change, decrease in monetary flow, is supposed not to occur. (*Cf.* p. 307, at middle, and discussion below in this review.)

[6]Secondly, as we shall presently see, the thesis is specifically that the failure occurs in the demand for labour for use in connection with investment, not in connection with consumption.

[7]Immediately following the last long quotation above (*General Theory*, p. 28), the author reiterates his special-case accusation (without using the words "classical economics"), asserting that the equilibrium level of employment cannot correspond to more than full employment, since wages cannot exceed marginal productivity, but that there is no reason for expecting employment to be as much as full, that this will be the case only "when the propensity to consume and the inducement to invest stand in a particular relationship to one another". He means when they stand in a particular relationship to wages, the interest-rate, and general prices, which is obvious. What is mysterious and difficult to state clearly is the manner in which Mr. Keynes sets up an economic system on the basis of assumptions which imply that these variables or variable-complexes are either fixed or are determined by other forces than the mutual adjustment of supply and demand, *i.e.*, by "bargains" or public authority, or "psychology", or some other *deus ex machina*.

control the division of money income between the two fields and then following through the course taken by the "money" in the two channels until it either results in a demand for employment or for some explained reason fails to do so. But before taking the suggested next step, Mr. Keynes finds it necessary to insert a group of four general chapters under the caption, "Definitions and Ideas" (book II, chs. 4-7). These are chiefly devoted to explaining the meaning of investment.

The main task of chapter 4, on "The Choice of Units", is to assume out of existence the complicating circumstance that the demand for labour is a two-stage affair of prices, a price offered by entrepreneurs to secure the labour for use in making products which either are to be sold at prices or have an estimated money value to the entrepreneurs themselves. It might well have been made clear that the discussion of the chapter deals only with the demand for consumers' goods, since in Mr. Keynes's set-up only these are assumed to be sold by entrepreneurs in the market. Capital goods are held by them for use. The nominal capitalized value of such goods is, however, the crucial factor in the workings of the author's theoretical system. The argument advanced for treating the demand-function for labour as a single function is that the notion of a general price level is unnecessary and lacks "perfect precision —such as our analysis requires". The subject of prices is henceforth almost entirely avoided, sometimes apparently with effort, until the last chapter in the body of the work. The assumption is that prices, like wages, are fixed in one direction; they may go up, but never go down. This is virtually stated in so many words in chapter 21 (p. 307). And again, the sellers who according to the theory never cut prices, are, like the workers who refuse to accept lower wages, held to be pursuing the right policy (though in this case their superiority in wisdom to classical economists is not explicitly asserted).[8]

[8]As already remarked, the question of the reversibility of functional relations predicated for change in one direction is a confusing feature of Mr. Keynes's argument as a whole. The most general and pervasive example is the fact that the whole work explains unemployment by showing why increase in employment is brought to a stop, or blocked before it can get started. Except in chapter 22, "Notes on the Trade Cycle", which is really an appendix with a different point of view, little or no intimation is ever given that unemployment might result from a decrease in employment. In historical fact, as far as I know, unemployment on the scale of a serious social problem is not a typical state of affairs, and in every known case such a situation has followed at no long remove a period of relatively full employment—and has followed upon a sequence of change fairly uniform and familiar in its more general features and, similarly, periods of serious unemployment have in due course come to an end. But the question of how unemployment comes to pass is excluded from this work by the predetermination to make it a "normal" phenomenon, characteristic of an enterprise economy in stable equilibrium. It always follows upon equal or greater unemployment, never upon more

The consumption demand for employment (for labour) need not detain us much longer, as it is the failure of demand in the investment field which is the crux of the theory. It may be observed that labour applied to given equipment is assumed to be subject to diminishing returns (pp. 17, 40, *etc.*) and that this fact is made to imply rising prices with increasing employment (p. 249, *etc.*). The reasoning is doubtfully sound under the actual conditions in which serious unemployment occurs, *i.e.*, when the equipment has been built for use with a much larger complement of labour; but it would hold under ideal and instantly effective competition, and in any case the point plays no important role in the general argument. We pass for the present over chapter 5, on "Expectations", which contains important matter but it is properly relative to the theory of investment, and is badly stated, out of order, and not effectively integrated with the main argument. Chapter 6, on "The Definition of Income, Saving and Investment", begins with a discussion of production in terms of revenue and cost. This seems intended to illuminate the relation of costs, especially capital depreciation (a special formulation of which is here called user cost), to the producer's decisions affecting volume of production. But the argument is confused and unrealistic, and is hardly used in the later discussion, where marginal wage cost seems to be treated as controlling.[9]

The outstanding point made in book II is that saving and investment are so defined as to be necessarily and continuously equal. What this amounts to in the first place is simply that saving money is treated as "investing" in money, which is logically correct from the point of view of the saver. But in Mr. Keynes's first definition of investment, "current" investment is defined as "the current addition to the value of the capital equipment which has resulted from the productive activity of the period" (p. 62). This is correct only if the "productive activity" is interpreted

employment. In this connection the interpretation of Mr. Keynes by Professor Alvin H. Hansen (*Journal of Political Economy*, Oct., 1936) is interesting in that the position of equilibrium is established on the way down and not on the way up, as in the book itself.

[9]It is difficult to tell what is Mr. Keynes's conception of the relation between short-run and long-run conceptions and of their role in managers' decisions. The weakness of chapter 5 is again in point. It should be recognized that in the shortest short-run all, or virtually all, production of goods is for stock (in possession of some one) and all sales are sales from stock, hence that both are a matter either of speculative conversion of investment between goods and money, or of choice between consumption and investment. On the other hand, in the ultimate long-run there are no fixed costs, and for a system in equilibrium, stationary, or with growth (*i.e.*, unless the system as a whole is decadent), there is no capital charge except interest. In the "theoretical" long-run, moreover, there is no speculative factor; but in reality the farther ahead plans must look the greater this factor becomes.

to include everything that has happened during the period in question which affects values in any way, especially any shrinkage in general values due to money saving *not* resulting in investment as ordinarily understood and as implied in the phrase "productive activity"; and it must include any change in values in either direction consequent upon any monetary changes. Mr. Keynes's exposition seems calculated to conceal these facts, though in them lies the core of the explanation of depression and unemployment in accord with his own theory, if the latter is interpreted so as to make it defensible or intelligible. In this connection we may quote what seem to be the two most important sentences in the book (pp. 83-4): "The error [in the "old-fashioned view that saving always involves investment"] lies in proceeding to the plausible inference that, when an individual saves, he will increase aggregate investment by an equal amount. [This] conclusion . . . fails to allow for the possibility that an act of individual saving may react on someone else's savings and hence on someone else's wealth." In familiar language this, of course, means simply that the saving may be hoarded and by reducing monetary circulation lead to sales reductions or price declines with all the consequences of these in train; but familiar terms and modes of expression seem to be shunned on principle in this book.

In book III ("The Propensity to Consume", chs. 8-10), we finally arrive at the author's development of his view as to the forces determining the division of individual money income between consumption and saving. In substance, little is added to the "psychological law" first stated in the summary of the theory in chapter 3 (already cited) and several times repeated in the meantime. Objecting (characteristically) to any designation already in use, the author has in the meantime regularly referred to the determining psychological principle or attitude by the name which is used as a title to book III. (See especially, at end of chapter 6, p. 65.) As already indicated above, the point emphasized is that the amount saved out of income increases when the income increases, *i.e.*, a part of the increase will be saved. The amount saved is supposed to be dependent only on the size of the income (or change in its size), or at least substantially independent of other influences, notably the interest rate. There is nothing novel in this last view; it is familiar in "classical" writings, where it is commonly emphasized that saving is an "institutional" matter, dependent upon social psychology rather than economic comparisons in terms of price. More interesting is the fact that in an elaborate analysis filling three chapters, the prices of consumption goods (or their price changes) are not mentioned. Perhaps they are assumed to be tied to the wage level, for it is specified that income is measured in wage units.[10]

It would have helped the reader to avoid confusion if the author had stated explicitly that by "amount" saved he meant the absolute amount, and not the proportional amount or fraction of the income. (At least this reader puzzled some time over the question as to just why the author so emphasized the increase of saving with increased income, making the natural assumption that an increase meant an increased proportion.) The importance of the "psychological law" is, in fact, that while money spent on consumption may supposedly be counted upon to result in demand for employment, that which is "saved" may fail to do so.[11] What is essential is that social money income shall increase with increased employment. This presumably must happen if wages are fixed as to decline, as the entire increase in total wages would hardly come out of profit or other outlay cost. Again, it would have been an aid in following the argument if Mr. Keynes had been clearer as to the nature of his organization set-up, particularly as to what decisions are made by whom. It seems to be assumed for the most part that wages represent the only outlay cost, or certainly the only variable outlay cost (apart, in chapter 6, from differential depreciation), and the express statement that interest paid is considered a part of profit (p. 290) indicates that wages and profit are the only forms of income. It would be particularly interesting to know whether anyone except the labourer is supposed to save (money).

As Mr. Keynes states the theory, the fact that some fraction of an increment of income "would be" saved "if" it were disbursed prevents its being disbursed in the first place, unless some "special conditions" insure that investment will keep pace with monetary saving. (The unconscious assumption that such conditions always obtain is the most important flaw found in classical theory.) In this form the theory seems to depend on the assumption that all entrepreneurs are organized and act as a unit, or at least that the consumption-goods and investment-goods industries are carried on in combination by the same firms. Under competition, the

[10]As already noted, it is expressly stated (p. 249) that prices rise, in terms of wage-units, with increasing employment—which seems to be the same as increasing income—in consequence of increasing cost (diminishing returns) in the short period.

[11]On page 83 (quoted above) it "may" fail. When we come to Mr. Keynes's theory of interest, we shall see that there is no indication of any way in which monetary saving, though it "is" an equal investment, can lead to any investment in the sense of technical production. The questions whether money savings are made by entrepreneurs as well as "owners of productive factors" (and *rentiers?*) and whether "owners of factors" means simply labourers, become important in connection with the effort to form any inclusive picture of the motives of saving and the way in which they operate; but I have not been able to find answers to them.

fact that employing an additional labourer in one enterprise would cause disemployment in another would not prevent the first increase in employment, and to establish equilibrium this process would have to be followed through to a defensible general adjustment, in which no single employer and unemployed worker would find it advantageous to make an employment agreement.[12]

This brings us to the theory of the "Multiplier", to which chapter 10 is largely devoted. It represents a drastic simplification of an argument developed by Mr. R. F. Kahn[13] to afford some basis for estimating the additional employment consequent upon "repercussions", beyond what would be directly provided by an expenditure on public works or the like. Mr. Keynes assumes (as he has done throughout the argument just summarized) that an increment of investment is made and paid for with new money from "somewhere", that the expenditure is divided by its recipients (owners of unemployed productive factors, *i.e.*, labourers) between consumption and "savings" (meaning hoarding) in the proportions corresponding to the prevalent "propensity to consume", and that the fraction devoted to consumption is divided in the same way by its recipients, and so on *ad infinitum*. The result, easily calculated, is that if the propensity to consume is represented by $\frac{r-1}{r}$, the total employment due to repercussions will be r times the direct expenditure (if the public spends three-fourths of its income and hoards one-fourth, the multiplier is 4). As usual, Mr. Keynes's arithmetic is correct, but the result is somewhat strange. It is undoubtedly true that "the logical theory of the multiplier . . . holds good continuously, without time lag, at all moments of time. . . " (p.122). This is rigorously correct because all money which exists at all must exist in some "hoard" at any moment of time. But it would surely be more realistic to assume that an addition to the monetary circulation simply continues to circulate at the prevalent velocity (or some other, to be explained), which would yield entirely different results.

Leaving the underlying usable meaning of the entire scheme for later consideration, we turn now to the theory of the investment demand for employment. This is necessarily the crux of any theory of unemployment and cycles, since it is a well-known empirical fact that it is in the capital-goods industries that boom and depression—and unemployment as a phase of the latter—are largely concentrated.

[12]As already suggested, Mr. Keynes's whole argument in connection with labour apparently assumes that it bargains as a unit, and that the complete unemployment of particular individuals (leaving them with no income? or none except "relief"?), will affect the supply price of labour in the same way as a fractional reduction in the employment and wages of a given group of employed men.

[13]*Economic Journal*, June, 1931.

IV. *The Investment Demand for Labour*

This topic is the pivotal one for Mr. Keynes's new theoretical system as well as for any realistic treatment of the problem of unemployment. It is discussed especially in book IV, "The Inducement to Invest", which occupies eight chapters (11-18) and well over a third of the volume, apart from two chapters which are really appendices. It is certainly in connection with this subject that we meet the most important ideas in the work, and also the most confused thinking and exposition. To begin with, the title of book IV is hardly in strict accord with the author's new-fangled definitions of investment and saving, as the intention clearly is not that of discussing the inducement to invest in the sense in which the latter is automatically and identically equal to saving. The reference is to investment in the ordinary acceptation, the use of money to hire productive services to create capital goods, which is done by entrepreneurs. In chapters 11 and 12 is discussed a "reformulation" of the doctrine of the marginal productivity of capital, renamed "marginal efficiency" for the purpose of emphasizing appreciation as an element in yield. (It is said to have been left out of account in "classical" theory.) The next two chapters (13, 14) deal with the rate of interest, contrasting Mr. Keynes's own theory with classical theory (Mr. Keynes's version). The significance of the rate of interest, for Mr. Keynes as in part for "classical" economists, is that it is the negative inducement, the impediment, to investment in the real sense. Chapter 15 ("The Psychological and Business Incentives to Liquidity") discusses the grounds of choice between holding money and holding wealth, apparently from the standpoint of entrepreneurs considering (real) investment. This argument must then be seen in relation to that of book III, where grounds of choice between "saving" (hoarding) and spending for consumption are treated from the standpoint of the income-receiver (in this system, the labourer, and possibly also the *rentier*). The next two chapters (16, 17) contain various observations on capital, money, and interest, and chapter 18 is a general restatement of the theory as a whole.

The crucial assumptions in this crucial part of Mr. Keynes's system, viewed as a theory of unemployment, relate to the decision to save money and the decision to invest money in the creation of real capital. The two decisions are absolutely separated, as suggested above; they are made by two different sets of persons, with apparently no possibility of contact between their spheres of action in this connection. The rate of interest, it is to be observed, has nothing to do with the first decision, but is decisive in connection with the second; men do not save to get interest and never invest (in real production) except at the cost of interest. Saving, which appears to be done exclusively by owners of factors (labourers), neither influences the rate of interest nor is affected by it. (The novelty is in the first of these two positions.) Mr. Keynes's theory of interest is even more original than his theory of wages, but runs along somewhat the same lines. It is curious that no mention was made of it in his opening chapter dealing with the postulates of the classical economics, for it is much more important in the system and more of a departure from orthodox doctrine. In the capital market, saving has no influence on the interest rate, while on the other side demand is similarly without effect on price, even, apparently, in an upward direction. Men get control of capital through borrowing money, but there is never any connection between saving money and the offer of funds in the loan market. It almost seems as if the money which is saved is completely distinct from the money which is lent and borrowed, and that the former, if it ever reaches a bank, or any lending agency, is still kept entirely separate. The theory of interest is the most difficult part of the whole construction to take seriously.[14]

According to Mr. Keynes, interest is a purely monetary phenomenon. He is repeatedly explicit and emphatic that "the rate of interest at any time, being the reward for parting with liquidity, is a measure of the unwillingness of those who possess money to part with their liquid control over it. The rate of interest is *not* the 'price' which brings into equilibrium the demand for resources to invest with the readiness to abstain from present consumption. It *is the 'price' which equilibrates the desire to hold wealth in the form of cash with the available quantity of cash. . .*" (my italics; *cf.* also pp. 174, 236, 246, ch. 14 *passim, etc.*). The positive part of the statement, asserting that the rate of interest does, at any time, equilibrate the desirability of holding cash with the quantity of cash, is not only badly worded (a desirability is not comparable with a quantity of cash), but is definitely beside the point. The things equilibrated are the desirability of holding cash and the desirability of holding wealth in any other form, the relation between the two being dependent upon the relative quantities of cash and of other forms of wealth—and upon other factors, among which the money prices of other wealth items can hardly be ignored!

The negative part of the statement is entirely indefensible; it is self-

[14]In the first of the chapters on "The Propensity to Consume" (ch. 8, p. 93), the rate of interest is referred to as being nearly the same thing as the ratio of exchange between present and future goods. But in the text no move is made to integrate this notion with the theory of interest. There is no indication of any causal relation either way between the interest rate and the exchange ratio or between either and the general price level. (*Cf. General Theory*, 140-1, reference to Fisher.)

evident that at any time (and at the margin) the rate of interest equates *both* the desirability of holding cash with the desirability of holding non-monetary wealth *and* the desirability of consuming with that of lending and so with both the other two desirabilities. For, to any person who has either money or wealth in any form, or to anyone who holds salable service-capacity, all three of these alternatives are continuously open. He can consume or hold wealth, and if he holds wealth he can hold it in the form of money or real things—and the latter, of course, in innumerable forms, and with various sorts of claims to money as intermediaries, other wealth being always the security back of such claims. The statement also involves all the abstractions which are involved in assuming that the rate of interest is merely a price ratio between present and future income, *i.e.*, that there always is a single known interest rate in terms of which either capital value or yield is known when the other is known.[15]

In the first two chapters of book IV, which bear directly on the incentive to invest, the main point emphasized is the speculative element involved in any decision to produce durable wealth. It is, I think, a point which has needed more emphasis than it has received and a matter on which the book should render service. (But as to its novelty, *cf.* again Mr. Keynes's reference to Fisher, p. 140.) My criticism of Mr. Keynes's treatment of anticipation, apart from the exasperating difficulty of following his exposition, would be that he does not follow through in accord with the importance and universality of the speculative aspect of capital production (and, in a lesser degree, capital-maintenance) in real life. In a pecuniary enterprise economy, production only very exceptionally takes place on direct order for the final consumer; consequently, as already noted, every act of production is a speculation in the relative value of money and the good produced. (This, of course, applies only to the production of goods, not of services from given agencies; *i.e.*, it applies to capital production.) The speculative element varies directly with the length of time the good may be expected to remain in the possession of the producer, and affects every purchaser of anything for resale, as well as technical producers; it varies inversely with the development of a market for the article in question. Above all, in practical import, such speculation affects producers or purchasers of durable goods for actual use, whether in consumption or in production. It does not seem to me an im-

[15]It will be noticed that Mr. Keynes's discussion of the interest rate (the terms of investment) comes in between the treatments respectively of the two alternatives compared by the entrepreneur who makes a real investment, namely, the incentive to invest and the incentive to hold cash, the latter called "the incentive to liquidity". But in fact neither of these alternatives has any reality apart from the other, or from the necessity of comparing them and making a choice.

provement in terminology to insist on lumping value changes into the concept of the productivity of capital, without discrimination. This is particularly dubious because, in the cases which are crucial for the problem of the cycle and of unemployment, the value change is due to something that has happened outside the field of real supply and demand for the particular good, namely in the field of money. It seems to me imperative rather to keep the different factors entering into demand and supply sharply separate, but, of course, that does not excuse neglecting any of them, as has perhaps happened until recently with respect to speculative anticipation.

The point which I think Mr. Keynes is really trying to get at is that the decision to produce is a speculation on the general price level, thought of as controllable from the money side. Again, his use of the term "liquidity" to designate everything that makes it desirable to hold money, apart from its purely relative character, already noted, does not seem to be an advance or justifiable. Of the four specified and numbered motives for holding money, the first two, income motive and business motive, might be lumped together as the convenience motive. The real issue for cycle and unemployment theory arises in connection with the third and fourth—the precautionary motive and the speculative motive—which are different cases of the speculative motive. Convenience and speculation or provision against contingencies are factors in any decision and are only conceptually separable, but it is the second of these which is suggested by the word liquidity, the general "feeling" that money is for the time being the safest form of property to hold. The feeling may, of course, be present when in fact the value of money is an especially dubious risk. The convenience motive is the familiar non-coincidence of barter of "classical" phraseology. There is finally no distinction between the two functions. For, as we approach the ideal of the perfectly stationary state with all economic activity reduced to an unvarying routine, uncertainty, and with it the need for money, tends to disappear. The essential function of money is that of meeting contingencies, and in the ultimate limit velocity becomes infinity, cash holdings, or "M", zero; physical money is replaced by some conventional unit of account or *numéraire*. In any case, why not call the general psychological attitude simply the "relative money preference", and keep the elements in, or grounds for, it a matter for separate discussion?

And in any case, it is the speculative motive for holding money which varies widely in connection with the cycle and immediately causes the trouble. (What causes this variation is the central problem of cycle theory.) Of course this is not necessarily true of the individual "holder". A man with an obligation to meet in a specified number of money units on a specified day will try harder to accumulate cash, apart from his own speculative feelings, when loans are costly and especially when they are precarious; for at such times it is quite erroneous to assume a perfect market for the use of cash.[16] This applies to anyone in business when there comes to be a general demand for, and premium on, cash. Practically speaking—apart from the short period of crisis when there is danger of actual inability to secure cash for contractual or otherwise fixed needs—the speculative consideration which causes the trouble is opinion or fear as to prospective unfavourable change in the price-level or such a change in the relation between product prices and cost prices as results directly from changes in the general level. In the ordinary course of events, changes in relative prices are a risk of the individual business and are related only as effect, not as cause, to cycles, depression, or general unemployment.

Conversely,—as Mr. Keynes, like most writers on capital, fails to see or to make clear—in every case where either risk or futurity in any form is in question, the activity is necessarily one of investment, or disinvestment. Any act or outlay by way of production which does not yield its fruit instantly and finally in the form of a service enjoyed, yields it in the form of an addition to the value of some specifiable thing, hence a quantity of capital. If it does not instantly yield either service or capital value, it is not productive, and if intended to be, represents failure and waste. The opening sentences of chapter 5, for example, are ambiguous and will undoubtedly be generally read in a sense which commits the author to the widely accepted but fallacious doctrine that present production typically results in a future value. The discussion in chapter 16 (pp. 213 *ff.*) endorsing the old classical (as well as pre-classical) view that everything is produced by labour, still further commits him to this untenable position. (What *can* anyone think he means by a physical unit of labour? Yet from beginning to end Mr. Keynes treats labour as a homogeneous fluid with a uniform price per unit.) Moreover, in a world in which capital goods were actually produced by labour, or any "primary factors", and worn out in use in a fairly short period, the Austrian view that "capital formation occurs when there is a lengthening of the period of production" would be sound, and Mr. Keynes has expressly repudiated it (p. 76). In contrast with his general position in this connection, which is muddy if not unequivocally wrong, we find on page 105

[16]It would surely have been in accord with Mr. Keynes's line of attack to emphasize the fact that at a time of deep depression there is little relation between the prices of capital goods or even securities (relative to yield) and any market rate of interest. Interest rates and capital values are both abnormally low. See above, p. 113, and below, p. 116.

the correct statement that wants are satisfied by objects produced previously only in connection with disinvestment. However, we still lack anything definitive, since real disinvestment means disinvestment at one point in a capital system without reinvestment somewhere else in the system, and everything depends on what are considered to be the boundaries of the "system".

What this all finally amounts to for a theory of employment or unemployment, we have another chance to attempt to find out in the last three chapters of book IV, especially the last (18), which is a formal restatement. I cannot see that we are really carried beyond the argument developed in the earlier summary chapters already summarized, including especially the statement quoted from *General Theory*, pp. 83-4 (see above, p. 108), but with the predicate regarding possible effects of monetary saving changed from a contingency to a positive assertion. We must take as the starting point, as given and unexplained, an economic system in which there is (*a*) extensive unemployment, (*b*) such an adjustment and pegging of prices and of quantity and distribution of exchange medium, and (*c*) such attitudes, especially such a relative desire to own "money" in comparison with other forms of wealth (at existing prices?) that the only possibility for absorbing unemployment is an interference by some "god" outside the economic system leading to increased real investment. Any new light on the question why this is so must be obtained from such statements as the following, which surely deserves quotation as a sample of lucid exposition (p. 236).

> Our conclusion can be stated in the most general form (taking the propensity to consume as given) as follows. No further increase in the rate of investment is possible when the greatest amongst the own-rates of own-interest of all available assets is equal to the greatest amongst the marginal efficiencies of all assets, measured in terms of the asset whose own-rate of own-interest is greatest.
>
> In a position of full employment this condition is necessarily satisfied. But it may also be satisfied before full employment is reached, if there exists some asset, having zero (or relatively small) elasticities of production and substitution, whose rate of interest declines more slowly, as output increases, than the marginal efficiencies of capital-assets measured in terms of it.

This, if I understand it at all, is, taken with the context, Mr. Keynes's way of saying that if new capital wealth is to be produced, its anticipated yield, including appreciation, must exceed interest on the money expended in its production. Possibly this is a revelation in economic insight. There is no reference to any possible difference between interest actually paid and interest which might have been received, and apparently the author assumes a perfect market, in which there would be no difference; there is also no reference to any speculative element in either the holding or the lending of money.[17] In reality, of course, every choice between forms in which wealth is to be held, including money, reflects a speculative comparison, a comparison between speculative prospects.

Discussion of this section may be brought to a conclusion by noticing one or two statements of the implications of the system as regards policy, which serve as a basis for the positions taken in the final chapter of the book, to which we must now turn. In the final section of chapter 16, we read (p. 220) of "steps to be taken" to "ensure that the rate of interest is consistent with the rate of investment which corresponds to full employment". This means, of course, that the rate is to be artificially kept down to such a point. Immediately following we are asked to assume that "state action enters in" to regulate "the growth of capital equipment". This is followed with a statement of conviction that it would be "comparatively easy to make capital-goods so abundant that the marginal efficiency of capital is zero" (p. 221).[18] The rest of the section briefly argues for the desirability of this result.

V. *Social-Philosophical Implications of the New Theoretical System*

In his final chapter (24, following two chapters which are really digressions), Mr. Keynes sets down a number of "inferences" from his general theory which have to do with the problem of social-economic reform, reconstruction, or revolution, as the case may be. This section is of especial interest to the present writer—as one inclined to take economics as a "serious subject" rather than an intellectual puzzle for the diversion or even the improvement of the mind.

The first inference drawn is that the new economic theory removes "one of the chief social justifications of great inequality of wealth". For "in contemporary conditions the growth of wealth, so far from being dependent on the abstinence of the rich, as is commonly supposed, is more likely to be impeded by it" (p. 373).[19] This inference is held to affect

[17]This is probably more or less in accord with the general thinking of the business community, which fact, and its relation to the realities of the situation, might have been worth noting. Mr. Keynes makes no reference to the patent fact of the business cycle that men rarely borrow money to hold money, but do so to hold other forms of wealth (or to pay off some other debt) and that the rate of interest is highest when exchange medium is most abundant and its velocity of circulation most rapid (with the exception of the brief period of acute crisis, when the demand for cash rests primarily on actual, prospective, or feared needs to meet contractual or other obligations fixed in monetary terms.)

[18]I think this idea fantastic, but the issue cannot be argued here.

[19]This indeed is qualified to apply "up to the point where full employment prevails" (p. 372), but the text of this chapter, as well as the book as a whole, makes it clear that the qualification is essentially "theoretical".

particularly our attitude toward death duties; but even within any given generation, "much lower stakes will serve the purpose equally well, as soon as the players are accustomed to them", in stimulating those "valuable human activities which require the motive of money-making and the environment of private wealth-ownership for their full fruition" (p. 374). From the standpoint of moral idealism, this is an agreeable conclusion to draw, and is not implausible, with sufficient emphasis on the qualification, "as soon as they are used to it", with what it may be taken to imply regarding caution and gradualness in taking measures.

It is not so clear what the conclusion has to do with Mr. Keynes's particular theories, or, still less, what "measures" would be implied. The indirect and subtle social-psychological accompaniments of wealth ownership are (in my opinion) far more important than its direct consequences, and the same applies even more to any political substitute for the economic machinery of private property; and some political substitute is the only conceivable possibility, unless one plans for such a moral-religious conversion of human nature as would make a completely anarchistic utopia feasible. Such facts make the issues much less simple to me than they evidently seem to Mr. Keynes. When he goes on, for example, to say that institutional saving is now "more than adequate" (p. 373), very large questions regarding ideals of policy, as well as regarding facts, are raised in my mind. The difficulties, and dangers, in any ambitious programme of deliberate social reorganization make too large a topic to go into here.[20] In my own opinion, the distribution of actual consumption not only is rather a side issue in importance (the statistical facts set narrow limits to the possible gains from mere redistribution), but in addition, the distribution could not be much less unequal under any conceivable system of socialism, and the concentration of power, which is a more important issue, would certainly be much greater.

In any event, the mere mechanical problem of securing a supply of capital presents no serious difficulty, if productive efficiency is maintained. Any government in effective control of the economic life of a nation can certainly set aside any fraction of the social product it may

[20]One difficulty which may be mentioned is that if modern technology, with specialization and large scale organization of production, is not to be simply scrapped, great concentration of authority in the hands of individual human beings, or committees or "boards", is unavoidable, and the issue is one of methods of selecting, motivating, and remunerating such functionaries, and of maintaining "responsibility" in the face of social objectives which must also be formulated through the workings of the social system itself. Reformers seem characteristically to pass somewhat lightly over the fact that these are human problems, essentially political problems, that there is no way which men will generally agree upon as valid to call in God and the angels to make the decisions and carry out the policies.

decide upon, and can also invest it in any way it pleases. It is pertinent to note that Mr. Keynes has explicitly provided for all that, in advocating "a somewhat comprehensive socialization of investment" in addition to "the influence of banking policy on the rate of interest" as "the only means of securing an approximation to full employment" (p. 378). I can only comment that phrases like socialization of investment, with no indication of what procedure is in mind, sound (to me) more like the language of the soap-box reformer than that of an economist writing a theoretical tome for economists. Even the "influence of banking policy" cannot, in fact, be carried far without the banking authority passing upon the soundness of, and taking responsibility for, real investment for long periods, which would necessitate a large measure of actual management. That is, this in itself involves socialization of investment, which again certainly cannot be carried far without largely "socializing" economic life in general, and this means taking it out of business and putting it into politics. More specifically, it is hard for me to believe that Mr. Keynes has tried very hard to picture in his mind the effects on the competitive economy of having a political banking authority dedicated to the permanent policy of maintaining an artificially low rate of interest. He calls such suggestions "moderately conservative" (p. 377)! (I wish to state explicitly that—as I think Mr. Keynes might also have recognized—any statement as to what would, or would probably, happen in consequence of any considerable politico-legal-administrative measure is a political rather than an economic prediction.)

The second inference drawn by Mr. Keynes, and labelled "much more fundamental", repeats a statement already quoted, along the same general line. It is that since "the extent of effective saving is necessarily determined by the scale of investment and [since] the scale of investment is promoted by a *low* rate of interest" (up to full employment), "it is to our best advantage to reduce the rate of interest to that point relatively to the schedule of the marginal efficiency of capital at which there is full employment" (pp. 374-5). Passing over the fact that there is no way of knowing at all accurately when there is full employment, meaning no "involuntary" or "frictional" unemployment, there are two notable omissions. Again, nothing is said either as to the consequences, monetary and other, of having a central bank unremittingly pumping money into the system by an arbitrarily low interest rate, or as to the political status of the official or board by whom it would be done. It surely requires an optimist to believe that it would or could be done without resulting in an unbalanced capital structure in industry, and more of an optimist to believe that the resulting situation could be cured—as Mr. Keynes must imply—by a further overdose of the same medicine which would have brought it about.

Mr. Keynes ends his chapter and volume with a short and very optimistic section on the favourable effects for world peace which would result from abandoning the international gold standard, and a final short section on the great power and influence of economists' ideas. Whether this faith is also optimistic or not depends on one's opinion of the quality of economists' ideas, and whether the faith itself is justifiable is another question.

VI. *Concluding Summary and Comment*

From the standpoint of economic theory, the important fact is that all these conclusions are supposed to depend on the principles of Mr. Keynes's system. These are formally summarized at the beginning of chapter 18 (pp. 245 *ff.*): "We take as given the existing skill and quantity of available labour, the existing quality and quantity of available equipment, the existing technique, the degree of competition, the tastes and habits of the consumer, the disutility of different intensities of labour . . . the social structure." "Our independent variables are, in the first instance, the propensity to consume, the schedule of the marginal efficiency of capital and the rate of interest."

> The schedule of the marginal efficiency of capital depends, however, partly on the given factors and partly on the prospective yield of capital-assets of different kinds; whilst the rate of interest depends partly on the state of liquidity-preference (*i.e.*, on the liquidity function) and partly on the quantity of money measured in terms of wage-units. Thus we can sometimes regard our ultimate independent variables as consisting of (1) the three fundamental psychological factors, namely, the psychological propensity to consume, the psychological attitude to liquidity and the psychological expectation of future yield from capital-assets, (2) the wage-unit as determined by the bargains reached between employers and employed, and (3) the quantity of money as determined by the action of the central bank.

"Our dependent variables are the volume of employment and the national income . . . measured in wage units."[21] It would surely appear that if

[21]As to the import of the "sometimes" I have no inkling. Why the national income is measured in wage units is also obscure to me; presumably there is some connection with the dictum in the next section of the chapter, where it is explained that an increase in employment will increase the demand for money because of increased quantity and value of output, the latter in turn being due to rising wages and diminishing returns from labour "in the short period". Why either money or real wage rates should rise before unemployment is absorbed is not explained and the increase in labour cost under conditions of unemployment is dubious; and granting both, the rise in prices rests on the dogma that they "must" equal or correspond to wage cost, which is the kind of reasoning we have been told earlier (p. 12) would have been expected of the classical school. More interesting is the fact that in the formal classification itself, prices were not mentioned, either as given, as independent variable, or as dependent variable.

one is willing to make assumptions of this sort—along with those already pointed out, namely, that there *is* unemployment, that wages and prices cannot fall (but are free to rise), that wages are uninfluenced by the supply-offering of labour, that the price of capital-service is dependent only on the speculative attitude of the public toward money (*i.e.*, toward general prices) and the quantity of money fixed by the arbitrary fiat of a central banking authority entirely uninfluenced either by saving or by the demand for capital—one should indeed find little difficulty in revolutionizing economic theory in any manner or degree or in rationalizing any policy which one might find appealing.

The next general comment which must be made on Mr. Keynes's book as a whole is that it is inordinately difficult to tell what the author means. This is true in particular because on general issues it appears certain that he does not mean what he says. The theory is ostensibly one of equilibrium with extensive involuntary unemployment, and with the things taken as given, or independently variable, which have been set out in our preceding paragraph. Moreover, as already emphasized, it is an equilibrium reached "on the way up", and in the bulk of the exposition there is no explicit reference to cycles or oscillations and little hint that such phenomena exist. Now I for one simply cannot take this new and revolutionary equilibrium theory seriously, and doubt whether Mr. Keynes himself really does so. Scattered through the work are innumerable references to the short period, several which indicate that reactions are more or less reversible (*e.g.*, pp. 248, 251), and a few which run frankly in terms of comparative stability or stickiness rather than fixity (pp. 236, 237); in particular, there is a reference (p. 249) to the capacity of the economic system for remaining in a "chronic" condition of sub-normal activity for a "considerable period". This is a far cry from the "stable equilibrium" of page 30 and the tone of most of the book. Then, of course, there is chapter 22, "Notes on the Trade Cycle", which hardly seems to be a part of the book, but, along with a few other allusions to cycles, cannot be left entirely out of the picture.

As suggested at the beginning of this article, it is my own conviction that we must simply "forget" the revolution in economic theory and read the book as a contribution to the theory of business oscillations. This, of course, involves laborious interpretation, amounting to rewriting the book as one reads—or re-reads for the *r*th time. Even from this point of view, I cannot see that it gets very far or says anything very original, but perhaps its wild overstatement may serve to emphasize some factors which have been relatively neglected. In my own case, which is that of one who has happened to work primarily in economic theory at the more general levels, and who pretends to no expert knowledge of monetary and cycle theory, the book has been useful in emphasizing the need of more effective integration of monetary theory and general equilibrium economics.[22] Perhaps I may also be allowed to add that as a theorist, I have always made a special point of emphasizing (along with rigour in theorizing) not only the dangers of drawing conclusions from the propositions of a theoretical construction without carefully making allowance for all the factors ignored in building it, but also the dangers of taking any step in the theoretical construction itself without full awareness of all the abstractions involved. Among these abstractions (or "disturbing factors"—speaking from the standpoint of practical implications), "monetary repercussions" constitute an item or a group of items the importance of which can hardly be over-estimated.

Whether this point has been neglected, or especially needed urging against the "classical" economics is a matter of opinion. Personally I had not been aware of any striking dearth of publication in the field indicated, in the period in which I have been a student and teacher of economics, and am inclined to guess that the issue is one of kind and quality rather than quantity; but that may be a prejudice. Speaking from the same point of view, I am disposed to echo and to underline the doubt expressed by Mr. Robertson whether the "multiplier"—and I should add

[22]This, of course, is a line on which a number of thinkers have been working and writing in recent years. I am thinking especially of the work of Mr. Hawtrey, the Swedish school, and Mr. Robertson; but only an authority on subject-matter can be an authority on the literature.

In the very first paragraph of his Preface, Mr. Keynes says: "Those, who are strongly wedded to what I shall call 'the classical theory', will fluctuate, I expect, between a belief that I am quite wrong and a belief that I am saying nothing new. It is for others to determine if either of these or the third alternative is right." The prediction has been largely correct in my own case, though I should say that my difficulty (and no little annoyance) has been that of choosing between interpretations, one apparently nonsensical and the other more or less commonplace. "It is for others to determine" whether such a result proves that the one who arrives at it is "wedded" to some antique mode of thought. This, of course, is one of two "arguments" regularly hurled by revolutionary thinkers at those who do not immediately join up, the other being that the refusal is based on a vested interest. This the revolutionary is sometimes "polite" enough to imply is done unconsciously (*i.e.*, blindly instead of intelligently); Mr. Keynes may be thanked for omitting the second. Since it has become quite the fashion to account for differences in intellectual position by psycho-analysing, or somehow "explaining", one's opponent (and the example of following the fashion having in this case been set by Mr. Keynes), it may be permissible to note that our civilization of to-day, being essentially romantic, loves and extols heretics quite as much as its direct antecedent a few centuries back hated and feared them. The demand for heresy is always in excess of the supply and its production always a prosperous business. Where once it was necessary in writing to pose as merely restating and interpreting doctrine handed down from the Fathers, the surest way to public interest and acclaim now lies through pulling down and overturning everything established or accepted.

the other novel conceptions of Mr. Keynes, in so far as they are novel—constitute much advance over more crudely "monetary" weapons of thought;[23] and I would also insert the adjective "classical" before the word "monetary". It seems to me that the value of the book is in emphasizing the need of a sound monetary theory, rather than in contributing to the construction of such a theory. At least, after much labour spent in trying, I have extremely little conception of Mr. Keynes's monetary theory, if he has one. It seems to me reasonable to interpret the entire work as a new system of political economy, built around, and built to support, Mr. Keynes's conception of inflation as the cure for depression and unemployment—with especial reference to a situation in which this condition has become more or less "stabilized", such as Mr. Keynes's own country in and since the later 1920's. With this general position, I happen to be in sympathy—for whatever that statement may be worth. But I had hopes of learning more about the problems involved, especially whether society should wait until such a situation is existent before taking action or should rather take steps to prevent its arising; and also what concrete measures are likely to be effective without aggravating the situation, or preparing for a recurrence, possibly worse, or introducing other evils more than offsetting the gain. In this regard, I must confess that the labour I have spent on *The General Theory of Employment, Interest, and Money* leaves me with a feeling of keen disappointment. The chief value of the book has seemed to lie in the hard labour involved in reading it, which enforces intensive grappling with the problems.[24]

F. H. KNIGHT

The University of Chicago.

[23]See *Quarterly Journal of Economics*, Nov., 1936, p. 175.

[24]Perhaps a constructive suggestion from a "mere theorist" may not be entirely out of order. It has long been in my mind that in the welter of cycle theories (most of which have merit in pointing to real factors in the problem) one point is still neglected which must be of some importance. It has been recognized for at least a century that within some limits speculative psychology tends to give rise to a kind of momentum or cumulative tendency in price changes. The equilibrium point being uncertain, the tendency of speculation for a rise to create a rise in the price of any commodity within limits outweighs the "force" tending toward equilibrium—and conversely. Reasoning which cannot be developed here would show that this tendency should be especially strong in the case of money, the essential function of which is to be held speculatively. I should not be surprised if this is the most important factor in the general tendency to oscillation in an economic system—in contrast with specific "cycles" affecting particular commodities, which according to the laws of chance should be distributed in periodicity and phase and so cancel out for the system as a whole.

'Monetary Policy'

L. W. Mints, 'Monetary Policy', *Review of Economic Statistics* (1946), pp. 60–9.

'Notes on Mints' Paper'

A. Hansen, 'Notes on Mints' paper on monetary policy', *Review of Economic Statistics* (1946), pp. 69–74.

'Comments'

H. S. Ellis, 'Comments on the Mints and Hansen papers', *Review of Economic Statistics* (1946), pp. 74–7.

A SYMPOSIUM ON FISCAL AND MONETARY POLICY

MESSRS. MINTS, HANSEN, ELLIS, LERNER, AND KALECKI

MONETARY POLICY

Lloyd W. Mints
The University of Chicago

My contention will be that general economic equilibrium and a high level of employment can be maintained by means of monetary-fiscal policy, and without highly variable expenditures by the federal government. However, if this end is to be attained we shall have to give more heed than heretofore to the need for protecting the freedom of the market from encroachments by both business men and laborers. A simple governmental policy of laissez-faire is indefensible in an enterprise economy, since if the government is purely passive private groups will then not fail to take advantage of the opportunity to impose monopolistic restrictions of various kinds on the community. Such restraints will mean not only outright reduction of output, but also a rigid price structure. Unless we have a fairly flexible price system a dynamic economy will be subject to an inordinately high level of frictional unemployment, and unless we also have monetary stability it will be subject to intolerable fluctuations in employment.

In what follows I shall include only incidental reminders of the need for free markets and price flexibility, but I should like to emphasize the fact that these factors are of equal importance with monetary stability if we are to have a stable economy and a high level of employment.

MONETARY STABILITY

A depression is initiated by a decline in aggregate demand. Whether this decline is caused by a reduction in the quantity of money, or by an increase in liquidity preferences is a matter of secondary importance, although if it were always the former, the problem of maintaining demand manifestly would be simplified. It also does not matter greatly whether the initial decrease in demand comes from a lessened demand for consumers' or for capital goods. In fact, it is probable that it usually and predominantly originates in the market for producers' goods, although it is quite likely that there should be a concomitant decrease in the demand for durable consumers' goods. In any event, however, the important thing is the decline in aggregate demand, and the consequent reduction of employment and income. The initial disturbance and decline in income promptly produce an adverse effect on expectations, which further reduces aggregate demand. The worsening conditions of business result in a decrease in bank assets, and thus the quantity of money is reduced. These forces continue to interact upon each other, with the effect of progressively deepening the depression.

If we had a definite, announced monetary policy, based upon legislation and firmly accepted, and if Congress provided ample means of implementation, there would be no reason why aggregate demand should continue to decline after an initial disturbance. On the contrary, aggregate demand could be quickly restored by monetary-fiscal measures, if not by mere expectations of such measures, and thus nothing more than a minor recession in business activity need ever arise.

Any one of a number of possible guides to monetary action would be about equally acceptable. We might either increase the quantity of money at some constant rate, roughly equivalent to the rate of increase in output, stabilize an index of the price level, stabilize per capita money incomes, or follow some similar rule. In any case aggregate demand could be maintained. Stabilization of a price level index is most familiar; it is simple; it is definite; and it would require that changes in velocity be offset. Everything considered, it is probably preferable to any of the alternatives. In what follows, therefore, I shall assume that a price index is to be the guide to monetary action.

Granted a reasonable degree of flexibility of prices (absence of monopoly), a decline in aggregate demand will be reflected promptly in a fall in the price level. It follows that if we stabilize the price level, under competitive conditions, aggregate demand will be sustained, and thus unemployment will be kept to tolerable levels. If a given increase in the stock of money does not raise aggregate demand to the desired level, there is nevertheless some larger increase that will, and there is no serious obstacle to as great additions to the stock of money as may be required — or to subsequent subtractions, if the need for large additions proves temporary.

Unemployment can be kept to tolerable levels by monetary measures under even the most extreme conditions of high liquidity preferences and low investment opportunities. If the marginal efficiency of capital were zero, and if the propensity to save and liquidity preference were extremely high, it would still be feasible continuously to maintain aggregate demand, and thus a high level of employment, without any public investment whatever. As a portion of the public saved and hoarded, which would be the same thing as a constantly rising demand for money, new money would be injected into the system. Thus the demand for additional money would be met. The desired effect would be achieved whether the new money went exclusively to savers or to non-savers, although in practice it would go to both.

If it went to the savers a somewhat larger injection of money would be required than would be the case if it went to the non-savers, since the savers, being those with higher incomes, would have a more rigid propensity to consume. Nevertheless, it is inconceivable that the marginal propensity to consume would be zero even for the savers, if we consider them as a group, although it might be for some individuals. If the savers who received the additions to their cash balances spent, on either consumers' or producers' goods, any small portion of an increment to their cash, the problem could be solved. To be sure, if the marginal propensity to consume were very low, and if none of the additional cash were spent on producers' goods, the necessary additions to the quantity of money would be large, but these circumstances would constitute no bar to success. It is hardly likely, however, that the savers would permit their cash balances to rise indefinitely without turning to investment in some measure so long as the prospective rate of return was in excess of zero.

If the new money went to the non-savers, which is to say, to the lowest income groups, it is preposterous to suppose that consumption would not increase markedly. To the extent that it did go to this group, the program here outlined would bring about a redistribution of real income in favor of the lower income groups. This fact has perhaps been overlooked because a period of inflation has unfortunate effects on the distribution of income. Thus, even though the economy were in an extreme position of "maturity," aggregate demand could be maintained by using all resources for the production of consumers' goods. This situation could continue indefinitely, and without any rise in the level of prices.

Actually, it is hardly conceivable that a technique for increasing the stock of money could be found that would make it possible to increase the cash balances of only the lower income groups. It is also highly improbable that any western industrial nation has reached the degree of "maturity" wherein employment could be maintained only by devoting all resources to the production of consumers' goods; but these are matters of secondary importance if the preceding analysis is correct.

To me it seems evident that, given monetary stability and an absence of restrictive practices on the part of industry and labor, opportunities for investment will be plentiful at rates of return which will not lead to liquidity preferences greatly in excess of those prevailing before 1929. If this is true it means that no large continuous increase in the stock of money would be necessary, although a relatively small secular increase would probably be required so long as the volume of output continues to grow. Minor variations in the rate of injection of money might be required to offset variations in the propensity to hoard, although it is at least conceivable that such fluctuations would be virtually non-existent in the absence of disturbances originating in the quantity of money. It is more likely, however, that changes of such magnitude in the propensity to hoard will occur as to require some variation in the rate of addition to the stock of money; and occasional withdrawals might become necessary. In any case, I am convinced that the problem is not of greater magnitude than these statements suggest. However, even though secular stagnation is neither present nor imminent, a program of price level stabilization would actually avoid more than frictional unemployment if such conditions should develop.

While the numerous current attempts to estimate postwar income, savings, and private investment under conditions of full employment are of some interest, they have little necessary relevance to the problem of public policy. The estimates may be made by able men, as many of them are; they may represent a close approximation to the truth; and they may superficially appear to be very alarming; but nevertheless they should not in fact disturb us. Whatever the magnitude of the difficulty shown by these estimates, it can be managed by an appropriate monetary-fiscal policy; or, rather, there is in fact no serious problem if only we will adopt a reasonable monetary policy and vigorously oppose the development of monopolistic restrictions. The really serious problem is that of restraining the growth of monopoly; and a successful attack on this problem is as much necessary to the success of a program of maintaining employment by means of federal expenditures as to the policy which I am defending.

Free markets and monetary stability are not so much remedies for unemployment as they are essential conditions for the functioning of an economy of private enterprise. Given these conditions, autonomous responses to disturbances will ceaselessly operate to maintain a close approach to general equilibrium. A high level of employment will be the incidental but certain result. Unless we provide these conditions, there is no point in attempting to encourage private investment by means of a suitable tax structure, by devices for increasing the volume of foreign investment, or by other remedial measures currently urged upon us. I am wholly in sympathy with such measures as these, but they are minor (though important) refinements in the constitution of a competitive system, whereas free markets and monetary stability are part of the essential framework.

IMPLEMENTATION

Opinion is not unanimous concerning the best means of purposively adding to, or subtracting from, the quantity of money in circulation. During the nineteenth century and approximately the first third of the twentieth, the theory was developed that this could be done by means of changes in the rate of interest, induced by a central bank. This theory runs to the effect that changes in the central bank discount rate and open market operations will affect the market rate of interest, but particularly the rate charged by the member banks. If a lower rate is made effective, business men will increase their borrowings from the banks, and thus the quantity of money, in the form of bank deposits, will be increased.

There is some tendency to believe that the events of the thirties have proved that central bank policy is ineffective. This contention is entirely unwarranted. Not sufficiently vigorous action was taken by central banks, and particularly not by the Federal Reserve System, during the early thirties to warrant any simple inferences from the actual course of affairs of those years. The Reserve Banks did, indeed, reduce their rediscount rates promptly after the panic of the autumn of 1929; but the reduction thereafter was only gradual, a rate of 1½ per cent at the New York Bank not being reached until May 1931. Moreover, and this is of more importance, open market operations were not employed on a scale sufficient to increase the reserves of the member banks, despite the fact that the volume of circulating medium (deposits and hand-to-hand currency) was actually declining. Meanwhile, the wholesale price index declined from 96 (1926 = 100) in September 1929 to 73 in May 1931. Although the Reserve Banks purchased large volumes of government bonds in 1932 and again in 1933, the reserves of the member banks had increased by October 1933 by only an inconsequential amount. The price index declined to its low point of 63 in May 1933, and the volume of money dropped to a low level in the summer of 1933 which was 25 per cent below that in 1929. In the light of these facts one cannot say that the Federal Reserve System made any serious attempt to maintain the quantity of money in the early thirties. We therefore are not justified in asserting that the course of events during those years has proved the inadequacy of conventional central-bank measures.

Nevertheless, I believe the critics of central banking are right, even though the reasons for their conclusions are not acceptable. It takes time for a central bank to make its rate policy effective in the market, and in the short run the demand for funds, particularly short-term funds, is inelastic. Under these circumstances, the cumulative forces of a depression are likely to operate so much faster than a reduction of bank rate that a situation will be reached in which pessimistic expectations will overwhelm the effect of the lowest rate of interest which it is feasible to obtain.

Open market operations by a central bank may have an influence in the desired direction, both because they will induce changes in the rate of discount and because they will directly affect the size of the cash balances of the public. The latter effect will be the more immediate of the two, and it is likely that it would be sufficient to maintain substantial stability of the price level when disturbances were minor in character. Nevertheless, open market operations immediately affect the cash balances of only a small proportion of individuals and corporations, and consequently they are unlikely to be sufficiently effective, in the presence of severe disturbances, to serve as a sole reliance for the implementation of monetary policy.

The doctrine of central bank control fell into disrepute during the thirties, although some few men continue to have faith in it — notably R. G. Hawtrey. In place of it there has arisen the belief that only by means of fiscal policy can adequate control of the quantity of money be had. I subscribe to this later point of view.

The case for implementation of monetary policy by way of the fiscal operations of the national government does not rest exclusively upon skepticism concerning the effectiveness of the operations of a central bank. The final monetary authority is and must be the legislature, and it is therefore impossible to provide a politically independent agency for the management of the monetary system. If Congress is convinced that the policies followed by some supposedly independent agency are undesirable, it will and should intervene.

One of the traditional fears of the American public is that of "political" or "arbitrary" interference with the currency. This attitude ignores the fact that the fiscal operations of the national government unavoidably have monetary consequences. Such an attitude leads to failure on the part of the government to adopt and carry through a rational monetary policy. The major difficulty in governmental control of the monetary system lies in the fact of limited knowledge of monetary matters on the part of the public and of governmental officials. The tradition against political interference serves to absolve the officials of responsibility for their actions which in fact have monetary significance, and to prevent the development of the requisite knowledge upon which a rational monetary policy can be based.

The Secretary of the Treasury is in effect the agent of Congress in carrying out the directions of the latter in fiscal matters, and the federal finances may, and at times do in practice, become the major factor in determining the quantity of money in circulation. Budget deficits and surpluses, the shifting of the working balances of the Treasury between the member and the Federal Reserve Banks, and the borrowing and redemption operations of the Treasury, all have monetary significance. Since these matters must be managed by a financial department of the government, it follows that it is impossible to create a monetary agency that either is independent of Congress or, without an intimate association with the Treasury, has exclusive control of the quantity of money. This means that if there is a central bank it must be a second monetary agency, and monetary policy must therefore be implemented by two agencies, each independent of the other, but both deriving their authority from Congress.

Monetary policy consists of regulating the quantity of circulating medium in accordance with some criterion. To have two agencies with power to change the volume of money will in all probability lead, at times, to conflict, indecision, irresponsibility, and failure to follow any rational policy. The only reasonable conclusion seems to be, therefore, that the powers of the Board of Governors of the Federal Reserve System and certain powers of the Secretary of the Treasury should be lodged in some one agency. In this way, responsibility to the extent of the powers delegated by Congress would be centralized; and this agency could not escape responsibility on the grounds that it had less than full authority within the limits of the powers so delegated.

While there is now agreement among a large proportion of economists to the effect that monetary stability can be obtained only through directing fiscal policy to this end, there is much disagreement concerning the kind of policy that should be pursued. (1) There are those who would rely upon either a high or variable volume of federal expenditures for achieving full employment. (2) There is a second group who would also rely on fiscal policy, but who would both minimize and substantially stabilize the volume of federal expenditures. They would vary tax collections in such manner as to produce deficits and surpluses and thus to change the quantity of money in accordance with some predetermined criterion of policy, such as an index of the price level. It is this policy which I am defending.

Manifestly, deficits and surpluses can be produced by stable revenues and variable expenditures, by variable revenues and stable expenditures, or by a combination of these two methods. The second of these methods is distinctly preferable to the first, and also to the third — with minor and improbable exceptions. Either variations in tax liabilities and collections, or the promise of such variations, can be obtained within a short period of time. If the monetary agency were given authority, within prescribed limits, to vary exemption levels under the income tax, the volume of tax collections could be greatly changed within a short time. This is particularly true since we now have "current" collection, largely at source. This method is simpler than variation of expenditures, and it could be brought into operation more quickly.

Implementation of monetary policy by means of variable federal expenditures would require the central government to undertake construction work or other projects which would largely redound to the benefit of local communities. One need consider only the log-rolling incidental to legislation for the improvement of rivers and harbors to deter one from urging an expansion of the activities of the federal government in comparable directions.

An expansion of the volume on public expenditures merely for the purposes of monetary policy would mean that the aggregate of such expenditures would be larger than otherwise would be the case. This fact would increase the area within which the public authorities would determine the allocation of resources, in other words, the ends of economic activity. We defend political democracy in part because it permits the will of the majority to prevail, but in this one respect a competitive economic system has more to commend it. In a system of free markets the desires of even very small minority groups are duly registered, and the appropriate amount of resources is devoted to their satisfaction. I do not mean to imply that the technique of the market can be applied to political affairs, or that this criterion alone can serve as the final basis for an appraisal of democracy or of private enterprise; but it does suggest that we should not resort to political control in areas where the mechanism of the market will function, unless there are overwhelmingly strong reasons for so doing. Since simpler means are available, implementation of monetary policy is not one of those reasons.

I am by no means opposed to public investment that is clearly required to promote the general welfare. I would merely urge that projects for the expenditure of public funds should be decided upon in view of their merits, independently of the requirements of monetary policy, and that, having been so decided upon, their volume should be substantially stabilized.

The administration of monetary policy requires that all monetary powers delegated by Congress be centralized in a single agency. For this purpose a Monetary Agency should be established. The powers of the Board of Governors of the Federal Reserve System, as well as certain powers of the Treasury Department, should be given to this agency. The agency should acquire all the outstanding stock of the

Federal Reserve Banks; it should be given the power of varying the exemption levels under the income tax law within prescribed limits; it should be given such powers as are delegated by Congress to determine the maturity of, and rates of interest on, government bonds; it should be given the power to determine the division of Treasury balances between the member and Reserve banks; and it should be given large powers to buy and sell government bonds in the open market. Finally, it should be explicitly charged by Congress with responsibility for maintaining stability of a wholesale price index, the technical problem of constructing the index to be left to the agency.

Since this agency would have little discretionary power, it would have little need for deliberation or determination of policy. It could and should, therefore, be small. Under the circumstances a board of three men would seem to be appropriate. Preferably the Secretary of the Treasury should be ex officio a member and chairman of the board. If he were not, then the chairman should be a member of the cabinet, in order that he might represent the administration in fiscal matters before Congress. All members of the board should be appointed by the President.

This board or agency would operate in somewhat the following manner. Let us assume that the index is to be stabilized at 100. It would hardly be likely that any action to change the quantity of money would be required if it rose to 101 or fell to 99. There might be some doubt if it rose to 102 or fell to 98, but without much doubt action should be taken if it rose to 103 or fell to 97. Just where these limits of tolerance should be placed might have to wait upon experience. If, for example, the index fell to 97, the Monetary Agency would immediately enter the open market and purchase government bonds. The volume of purchases could not be prescribed in advance, although experience in time should furnish some guide. In this matter, therefore, some discretionary authority would have to be granted to the agency. In any case, however, purchases would continue until the index rose to 100. Contrariwise, the agency would sell if the index rose to 103, although it might be wise to discontinue sales at 101. There would be need for a secular increase in the quantity of money; consequently, a continued change in the quantity until the index reached 100 would probably be less desirable in the downward direction than the upward. These are matters upon which no very definite statements can be made; we would have to rely upon an accumulation of experience for satisfactory guides to action.

How effective open-market operations would be we cannot say, since no central bank or governmental agency has ever given them an adequate test. (Our experience in 1923–24 and 1927 is at best inconclusive.) It would be my hope, however, that they would be sufficient to bring the index back to "normal" after a minor disturbance, or if the decline in the index were due to technological improvements or a secular increase in the volume of transactions. In any event, if the decline were not halted in a very short time, exemption levels under the income tax would be raised. The deficit thus created would afford opportunity to inject additional money into circulation. If the decline still were not halted — but I am convinced that it would be — it would become necessary for Congress to pass legislation providing for a further raising of the exemption level beyond that which the agency had been authorized to make. In an extreme case, it is conceivable that the tax rates themselves would have to be reduced.

Maintenance of price level stability would be powerfully aided by the spontaneous action of the public under conditions wherein it was generally understood that the government would take energetic steps to maintain substantial stability of a price index at some announced level. The program might have some rough going for a few years following its inauguration if there chanced to be serious disturbances, but as the public gained familiarity with, and confidence in, the policy it would to an increasing extent become self-maintaining. It is probable that after the first few experimental years had passed success would be achieved more easily than at first one might suppose.

The federal budget is not likely to be less than 15 billion–20 billion dollars per annum for many years to come. This amount of money could therefore be added to the system each year by the device of reducing tax collections to zero. It may be doubted, however, that a complete elimination of taxes on the wealthy would be desirable, or indeed, that any reduction in the tax collections from the higher income brackets should be made. However, a deficit of 10 billion dollars could easily be achieved, and I am convinced that far less than this amount would be ample to maintain a price index if action were taken promptly when the index had declined sufficiently to indicate the need for an addition to the stock of money. Furthermore, with the huge public debt now outstanding, vast additional sums could be put into circulation merely by purchasing government bonds in the open market. In fact, the public debt could be entirely eliminated in less than fifty years, merely by retirement of new money to the extent of the (probable) secular need for increase in the quantity of money. However, to achieve this result, interest on the debt would have to be paid in large part out of tax revenues, and the banks could not be permitted to make further additions to the stock of money.

This program would permit resort to borrowing by the national government only as a means of withdrawing money to be impounded when inflation threatened. Contrariwise the government would buy securities in the open market only as a means of adding to the stock of money, and thus combatting deflation So long, therefore, as the secular advance in transactions continued, this policy would operate to decrease the amount of the federal debt. Such a debt policy would be precisely the opposite of the recommendations of those who would borrow to finance federal expenditures. The latter policy would lead to a continuous rise in the debt in an expanding economy. When deflation threatens, the need is for more money, and that being the case money, not bonds, should be issued; and when inflation is imminent, money should be withdrawn. All bond issues should be consols, since they would fluctuate more in price than short-term government issues and hence would be less acceptable than the latter as a substitute for cash in "cash" balances. If we borrow on short term, we give the lender a security that is almost as liquid as cash itself, and the result must be to increase velocity in some measure. Likewise, if short-term governments were bought in the open market, the security withdrawn would be only slightly less liquid than the cash received for it, and consequently the antideflationary effect would be less than would be the case if consols were bought.

Briefly, consols should be bought and tax collections reduced in the face of deflation, and consols should be sold and tax collections increased when inflation threatens.

While the federal budget and debt clearly will be adequately large for the purpose of adding to the stock of money for many years to come, we should not ignore the possibility that at some more distant date the debt may (should) be eliminated and the budget reduced to a figure below 15 billion dollars. I believe that, even with a budget as low as 5 billion, we could prevent deflation by a reduction of tax collections. This, however, is by no means certain, and we should therefore consider what other means might be used under these circumstances.

If there were no debt to be monetized, and if tax reductions were insufficient to meet the need for additional money, it would become necessary in some way to increase the outlay of the federal government. This, of course, could be done by means of an expansion of public works, and while some expansion of this kind should not be a cause for great concern under conditions wherein it would be neither permanent nor large in amount, it nevertheless is desirable, for the reasons already given, to avoid resort to this device if possible.

On grounds of monetary effectiveness, the most attractive device, by a wide margin, is a manufacturers' or retail sales subsidy. Whereas a sales tax is regressive, the relative benefits of a sales subsidy would be inversely related to the income of the purchaser. Such a subsidy would at the same time reduce the purchase price of commodities to buyers and add to the stock of money. Since it would apply to all consumers and since the subsidy could be made large if necessary, an enormous addition to the stock of money could be made within a short period of time. A large proportion of the additional money would go directly to those with the lower incomes; and inasmuch as their marginal propensity to consume is high, it could be confidently expected that most of the new money would promptly be offered for goods and services. While success in maintaining aggregate demand would not depend upon a high marginal propensity to consume, such conditions would require a smaller addition to the stock of money than would be needed with a low marginal propensity to consume. This fact leads to the conclusion that a sales subsidy would have to be neither high nor long continued in effect.

The drawback to a sales subsidy lies in the fact that it would be difficult to administer. This is true of a sales tax, and would undoubtedly be true in substantially the same measure of the subsidy. However, I am doubtful that in this respect it would be significantly worse than a program of public works; and since it could be instituted and withdrawn more promptly, it would offer some advantage over the latter program.

A publicly announced program such as I have outlined would in a significant degree be self-enforcing, once the public became convinced that it was to be rigorously followed. Under the conditions of the past, it was reasonable to assume that if the price level declined to some extent this fact would lead to unemployment, a decline in bank loans and consequently in the quantity of money, and a further decline in prices. The wise thing to do, therefore, was to stay off the market, either in the hope that still better bargains could be had in the future, or in the fear that adverse developments would give rise to a need for cash. If it were generally known that vigorous action would be taken to combat a decline in the price level, and if it were believed that this effort would be successful, it would then be reasonable to re-enter the market. Such a development would bring about the desired result of restoring aggregate demand before any addition to the quantity of money had actually taken place.

I can see no avoidance of the conclusion that, granted an absence of an undue upward pressure on monopolistically controlled prices, including wage rates, stabilization of the price level would maintain fairly continuously a high level of employment. To deny this is to assert that additional money in unlimited amounts would be hoarded in its entirety. Some hoarding of the new money there might be; but, so long as any portion of it was spent, the program could attain a high degree of success. Much hoarding would simply require a larger addition to the stock of money.

That there would be a complete elimination of unemployment or of fluctuations in employment is out of the question. If some important industry was confronted with a drastic decline in the demand for its output, it would not be practically possible to bring about the necessary adjustments in the economy so quickly as to prevent some increase in unemployment. Nevertheless, by means of an addition to the cash balances of the public, if it should become necessary, the maintenance of aggregate demand could be assured, and thus there would be other industries which would find the demand for their products rising. In this way, the reallocation of resources would be facilitated, even though it could not be made instantaneous. Under these circumstances no widespread depression would occur. In a changing economy readjustments are constantly necessary, and frictional unemployment of some minimum amount is therefore unavoidable. This is a problem, however, which cannot be solved by monetary means. It requires flexibility of prices, information available to the public, particularly to workers, concerning the regions and industries in which additional workers are in demand, and geographic and occupational mobility.

It is as much a governmental function to provide the means to a minimization of these obstacles to mobility as to maintain conditions of monetary stability. To say, therefore, that some fluctuating minimum of frictional unemployment is unavoidable as a practical matter, is not to say that governmental policies should not be adopted which are irected toward reducing this minimum to a low level. Monetary stability would aid in reducing frictional unemployment only in that it would, through the maintenance of aggregate demand, insure that when the demand for labor declined in one region or industry it would correspondingly rise in others.

As nearly as I can discover, the essential differences between those who propose a policy of price level stabilization by means of variations in tax revenues and those who favor federal expenditures — either in fluctuating amounts to prevent variations in employment, or in continuously large amounts to avoid the effects of what is believed to be a condition of economic "maturity" — are (1) a difference as to the size of the federal budget which is deemed necessary, (2) a decided difference concerning stabilization of the price level, and (3) a difference concerning either the desirability or possibility of maintaining an essentially competitive organization.

The defenders of public expenditures in effect desire a relatively large federal budget. Explicitly they assert that this is necessary to maintain employment, but there seems frequently to be implicit in their discussions a feeling to the effect that the central government should do more than it now does by way of direct investment to promote the general welfare. The proponents of price level stabilization, on the other hand, are opposed to federal centralization if not to reduction of the area within which the market decides the allocation of resources, and to handing these decisions over to authorities. Nevertheless, they of course concede that there is some amount of public expenditure which is highly desirable, and which should be undertaken quite independently of the requirements of monetary policy.

It is my impression that those who would implement monetary policy by means of a variable volume of federal expenditures would subscribe to the view that stability in the price level is desirable. They look upon this matter, however, as a secondary consideration. They would presumably call it a desirable end, but not a sufficient means of achieving the more important goal of a reasonably high level of employment. In any case, they for the most part ignore the question, and they enormously underemphasize the importance of monetary stability. They do not, therefore, provide any definite means for maintaining this stability, or indeed, of surely avoiding a very marked degree of inflation. Those who would stabilize the price level assert that a stable price level is the evidence that aggregate demand is maintained, and that therefore nothing more than frictional unemployment will appear.

Those who would rely upon variable federal expenditures for maintaining employment have little to say concerning the need for free markets. Their position therefore is problematical. The truth is, however, that avoidance of rigidity in the presence of downward pressure on prices and of undue upward pressure, but particularly the latter, is as necessary to the success of their program as to that of a policy of price level stabilization. An attempt to maintain employment by means of public expenditures can lead only to endless inflation if product and labor monopolists are given a free hand. They will constantly raise their prices above the equilibrium level, and, if the monopolies themselves are to be undisturbed, the only possible means of meeting, or rather, of attempting to meet, the difficulty will be to raise the level of expenditures and increase the quantity of money. This action will lead to further price increases by the monopolists, and thus inflation will proceed. To be sure, for a short time immediately following the inauguration of the public expenditures program, constantly increasing tax collections or borrowing from the nonbanking public might prevent rising prices, but taxes and borrowing would soon reach levels beyond which they could not be increased.

The above program pertains to the long-run. It does not have particular reference to the immediate postwar monetary conditions. During the reconversion period it is somewhat problematical what the nature of the monetary problem will be. There are those who believe that deflation is likely, while there are others, including myself, who believe that for some time inflation will remain the greater danger. If deflation develops it can be opposed in the manner I have suggested above. If, on the contrary, inflation threatens, somewhat different weapons may be required to combat it.

The existing large cash balances of the public and the enormous amount of near moneys in the form of government bonds may well lead to a level of spending so high as to bring about a serious inflation, provided nothing is done to prevent such a development. The means of preventing a postwar inflation, however, are readily available, if only we will use them. Taxation at a level that will yield a surplus, and the destruction of money to the extent of this surplus, is, of course, the logical device. Nevertheless it is not our sole resource.

It would be a simple matter to enforce a reduction of bank assets and consequently of deposits. This could be done either by refunding the short-term government debt now held by the Reserve Banks at rates of interest which would induce the public to buy the refunding issues, which should be long-term (preferably consols), or by raising the required reserve ratio for the member banks. This latter measure should be used, however, only for the purpose of raising the ratio permanently to a level higher than now prevails; that is to say, raising and lowering the reserve requirement should not become a permanent instrument for the implementation of monetary policy.

The institution of a policy of price level stabilization at any other time than one of general equilibrium and a fairly high level of employment would present some difficulties. The program could not be started at a time of a large amount of unemployment, since such conditions require, as a practical matter, both an increase in the quantity of money and some rise in the price level as a means of restoring employment. If an act were passed providing for stabilization of the price level while these conditions prevailed, it would be necessary to give some discretionary power to the Monetary Agency during the period of re-employment.

NOTES ON MINTS' PAPER ON MONETARY POLICY

Alvin H. Hansen
Harvard University

I welcome Mints' paper. The more I study it, the more clearly stand out the essential issues on which we differ.[1]

I fully agree that both anti-monopoly policy and monetary policy are important. Adequate liquidity, after the turning point in 1929, could have achieved a good deal in preventing the continued liquidation of assets by banks, the calling in of loans, and the consequent acceleration of the deflation.

On the other hand, it seems to me that Mints underestimates the structural financial defects of the twenties. The banking structure was seriously deficient, and an institution such as the Federal Deposit Insurance Corporation was lacking. In another area, if the Federal Housing Administration (with the reforms it has instituted in the house mortgage field) had been in the picture, the housing boom and collapse would certainly have been less violent. The same can be said about the Securities and Exchange Commission and the securities market. Had these institutions been in exsitence throughout the twenties, many unsound elements in the boom would have been absent or present in less degree. The wrong structure of exchange rates with no machinery for correction and adjustment was also important. The *structural* defects in the economy after World War I seem to me very serious, and I see little or no recognition of them in Mints' analysis, though it is possible that he would wholly agree with what I have said.

With respect to fiscal and monetary policy, granting that a decline in income and employment is under way (however caused), or that there is inadequate demand to provide full employment (whatever the reason), what can we do about it?

Mints admits that buying bonds in exchange for money in depression periods and selling bonds in exchange for money in boom years (W. I. King's solution) is not likely to be adequate. He suggests, therefore, tax reduction, first in the form of raising the income tax exemptions and finally by lowering the rates, as a means of increasing private spending in the depression phase. He would hold government expenditures constant and increase private spending by tax reduction. He does not approve fluctuating public expenditures and he wants to hold the federal budget to a low minimum figure.

For myself I should want both to vary public outlays contracyclically and also to vary taxes with the cycle. I would use both expenditures and taxes in a stablization program.

I think we should miss certain very positive

[1] Also see Henry C Simons, "On Debt Policy," *Journal of Political Economy*, LII (1944), pp 356–61.

benefits from holding public outlays rigorously constant as Mints suggests. Take for instance the matter of the construction industry. If we merely held *public* outlays on construction constant, the construction industry as a whole might fluctuate pretty violently. To stabilize the whole construction industry, public and private, it would be necessary to use the public sector as a balance wheel — to offset fluctuations in private construction by varying the rate of public construction. Public construction is, however, done usually under private contract. If public construction were used as a balance wheel, private contractors would, in depression periods, shift from private projects to public projects, but the industry as a whole would be fairly stabilized. This would be a very great gain. Without such variation the construction workers would have to be shifted out of construction into other lines. Obviously when I favor a stabilization of construction in general, I do not favor the stabilization of any particular *part* of the construction industry. It is an enormously varied industry covering hundreds and thousands of different kinds of projects and scattered all over the country. I do not intend to stabilize any one of these kinds of construction or to stabilize it in any one small area. The stabilization of the construction industry in no way involves the regimentation of a sector of the economy. The stabilization of the industry, by varying public outlays to offset private construction, would operate exclusively through the market and would not represent regimentation of the industry by means of production quotas or direct controls. Stabilization of the construction industry as a whole over the cycle cannot be achieved without varying public capital outlays.

Another reason why I think there is a definite advantage in using both methods — variation in outlays and variation in taxes — is that under this program the deficit would be materially smaller. Complete reliance on tax reduction is a pretty drastic procedure. Even moderate tax variation (such as I propose) is politically difficult. For this reason, some writers on fiscal policy, while perhaps favorable to my suggestion, nevertheless deem it wise to advocate a *stable* tax structure (Beardsley Ruml, for example) under which tax revenues would rise and fall with the national income not because rates or exemptions were changed but because of the progressivity of the tax structure. This would provide at least some measure of cyclical compensation. While it is possible that tax reduction alone if carried to the limit might do the job, it is certainly not clear that it is the best method.

Apart from cyclical fluctuations there is (or there may be) the problem of inadequate demand from the long-run standpoint. This also could, presumably, be solved by tax reduction to the point of zero if necessary. Mints believes that his program involves a better use of resources, that the requirements of a high standard of living can best be served by minimizing to the utmost public expenditures and maximizing to the utmost private expenditures. I cannot help wondering if he has really made any study of the most serious deficiencies in the present-day American society. Consider the wholly inadequate educational facilities in the southern and other backward states which include about 40 per cent of American children, and the grave deficiency in public health facilities as revealed by the military draft. Consider the housing situation in this country. While very much can be done to stimulate more private housing, no one has yet been able to show how we can get rid of the seven or eight million slum and substandard houses unless we undertake a systematic program of demolition and a substantial program of public housing. In the two decades between the World Wars we demolished houses in this country only at the rate of forty thousand per annum. It is just because the substandard houses remain occupied that high vacancies repeatedly develop after a few years of high construction volume. There is nothing in a hundred years of experience in this or any modern country to indicate that the price system, even though there were full employment, can get rid of slum housing. Similarly, the development of our resources (TVA and MVA) requires public capital outlays. So also with urban redevelopment. These outlays in turn would open up new private investment.

For myself I am convinced that a study of the serious deficiencies in this country will indicate that large public outlays are necessary. They are necessary in areas where private enterprise cannot enter. It is just because a rational use of our resources — one that would satisfy the most urgent needs — requires large public outlays (much larger than we have had in the past) that we cannot be satisfied with a bare minimum of public spending even though tax reduction toward zero might achieve full employment.

Now whatever the relative merits of tax reduction versus loan expenditures for achieving adequate aggregate demand, the question still remains: how should the deficit be financed? [2] It could be financed in one of three ways or a combination of two or three methods. They are (a) sale of government securities to the public, (b) sale of securities to commercial banks, and (c) issue of currency.

The last two methods are alike in that both increase the money supply. In both cases demand deposits would rise. In one case the banks would hold against their deposit liabilities government securities; in the other they would hold currency. I assume that whichever method were used, the volume of currency which the *public* will wish to hold would be the same, since for the most part the public will wish to hold money in the form of demand deposits.

Both of these methods would increase liquidity and drive down the rate of interest. While from a long-run standpoint I should favor a low rate of interest, I should think that a sudden drastic fall in the rate of interest such as would follow a vast and rapid increase in liquidity (incident to a vigorous monetary policy in a deep depression) would have pretty disturbing effects in various directions.[3] At any rate, the multiplication of money as an anti-depression policy would, I should think, necessarily be conditioned by one's philosophy with respect to what the interest rate should be. I find no analysis of this very fundamental question in Mints' paper. There seems to be no limit to his multiplication of money other than the limit imposed by stabilization of the price level. What rate of interest that would give us depends upon several factors that he has not considered.

In so far as the multiplication of money is desirable to provide adequate liquidity both in terms of (a) the transaction's demand for money and (b) the demand for money as a liquid asset, I cannot see that the issue of currency is to be preferred to the sale of securities to banks. If the currency issue method is used (essentially the 100 per cent reserve proposal), the banks will have to cover expenses by heavy service charges. If the securities method is used, bank expenses will be covered by interest payments on the securities held, financed from general taxation. In my view, the service charge is essentially a regressive form of taxation that weighs heavily on the small depositor. The checking service is an important factor in a well functioning exchange economy. We do not charge a toll for the use of our free highways. Neither should we charge a toll on our money transactions. There are better ways of financing this service. I very much prefer (in so far as bank expenses cannot adequately be covered by interest on commercial loans, private mortgages, and private securities) to support them by interest earned on government bonds. The interest banks earn on the public debt can always be adjusted so as to prevent excessive bank earnings, or, alternatively (which I think is to be preferred), excessive earnings may be whittled down by special taxation. The matter of managing debt held by the banking system presents no serious difficulty, and such debt is burdenless on the community as a whole in the sense that the cost of bank services must be covered somehow or other. Hence, why so much worry about an established practice? Why upset the apple-cart by proposals that are novel and revolutionary unless indeed there are some very great advantages? I am unable to see what they might be.

There remains the first of the three methods enumerated above, namely, the financing of the deficit by the sale of bonds to the public.

The assumption that the issue of bonds is deflationary while the issue of currency is inflationary is surely a vast oversimplification. It

[2] It should be noted that full employment could also be achieved by tax-financed expenditures, but this route to adequate aggregate demand, for purposes of this analysis, need not be considered here

[3] " . I reiterate the practical possibility as well as the advisability of low interest rates after the war, although I believe it is wise to move gradually and to avoid sensational changes in a factor so interwoven as is the rate of interest with our social as well as our economic fabric" Sir John Anderson in the House of Commons, April 24, 1945

all depends upon what the public and what the government do with the money. If bonds are issued to individuals who had previously been holding money as an idle asset, the issue of bonds is not deflationary even though the government should hoard the money. If the government spent the money, the effect would be expansionist. If currency is issued to individuals who decide to hold the new money idle, the issue of currency (or alternatively borrowing from banks) is not inflationary. In the usual case, both the issue of bonds (assuming that the government does not hoard the cash received from the sale of bonds) and the issue of currency will probably have an expansionary effect; the issue of bonds less so to the extent that the funds raised by borrowing from the public would probably more or less restrict private outlays whether on consumption or on investment. Thus in practice there is no such sharp dichotomy between "currency" and "consols" as Mints and Simons suggest.

How much should be financed by borrowing from the public and how much from an increase in the money supply (however effected) depends, I think, fundamentally upon one's view with respect to the desirable level of the rate of interest. The rate of interest — not the price level — will be determined by the relative use made of (a) the multiplication of money or (b) borrowing from the public. Having decided upon an appropriate level of interest rates, however, various combinations of (a) public spending, (b) tax revenues, (c) borrowing from the public, and (d) multiplication of money can be applied to produce full employment at substantially stable prices. A stable price level by itself alone is no adequate criterion on the basis of which it can be decided how much of a deficit shall be financed from borrowing from the public and how much by multiplication of the money supply.

Full employment at a substantially stable price level could, of course, be achieved quite well without financing by securities sold to the public. It could be achieved by varying (a) expenditures, (b) taxes, and (c) the multiplication of money. This alone, however, in no way answers the question whether (a) borrowing from the public, (b) no borrowing, or (c) retirement of debt held by the public, is desirable policy. Many other matters must be taken into account.

In my view a widespread ownership of property claims (assets) is a positive social benefit. Property claims may be broadly classified into the following categories:

1. Equities
2. Private debt (other than demand deposits)
3. Public debt
4. Money (demand deposits and currency)

In all advanced countries the amount of assets which the public desires to hold far exceeds the property claims represented by equities and private debt. Equities and private debt, while mostly representing specific things, like houses, factories, etc. (tangible wealth), derive their value from expected future income. Capitalization of goodwill, however, represents no tangible asset, but is based exclusively on expectations of income. So also with respect to money and public debt. Not being based on any *specific* goods, they represent claims of more general applicability. As property claims they depend exclusively upon confidence that the economy will continue to function effectively to produce a large flow of goods and service. What is important is the expectation of a high and rising real national income. The value of these assets is based upon expectations with respect to the value of money and confidence in the credit of the government. These in turn depend upon the capacity of the economy to turn out goods and services.

The total volume of highly liquid assets (money and public debt) may rise to greater or smaller magnitudes, without producing inflation, varying with (a) the intensity of the desire of the public to hold assets (to save or to hoard) and (b) the burden of taxes. The stronger the desire to hold assets, the greater the volume of highly liquid assets (money and public debt) which can be issued without producing inflation. Similarly, very large assets in these forms may be held without producing inflation if current income is heavily taxed, since under this situation the tendency to spend (stimulated by the large assets held) is restrained by the deterrent effect of high taxes on spending.

On the one side, a society enjoys obvious advantages if it holds large claims; on the other side, there is a limit to which claims can be held without creating inflation — this limit depending in part upon the tax rate. Since taxes have in various ways deleterious effects on the economy, it is reasonable to suppose that there is an optimum volume of property claims for any given society. Thus, while some level of public debt may be desirable, there are nevertheless limits beyond which the disadvantages become serious. The same holds true for the money supply. There are limits beyond which liquid claims (money and bonds) will be inflationary. It is a question of balancing advantages and disadvantages. And with respect to debt, public or private, I do not see at all why Mints and Simons assume (so far as I can see without argument) that there is some peculiar virtue in limiting the property claims of a society wholly to equities and money. So far as private debt is concerned, there are both advantages and disadvantages. But the disadvantages would become negligible under a high and stable level of income and employment.

It may now be useful to contrast the Mints-Simons program with that urged by Lerner. Lerner, if I understand him correctly, would raise the propensity to consume to a level adequate to ensure full employment by thoroughly saturating the desire on the part of the public to save. He would do so by tax reduction, by an increase in public spending, or both. He would finance the deficit by sale of bonds to the public or by expanding the money supply.[4] He is not concerned with how large the interest-bearing debt may become, since even the interest on the debt may be financed, in his view, by further borrowing or by increasing the money supply Eventually, however, an equilibrium would be reached, and the public debt or the money supply would cease to rise. This equilibrium would be reached because the assets held by the public would eventually become so vast that there would be a tendency to spend all of the current income in excess of that invested in private capital formation. At this point full employment could be maintained without public loan expenditures. All public expenditures would indeed have to be financed by taxes in order to prevent property claims from rising to a point at which the inducement to spend would become inflationary.

According to Lerner, the propensity to consume might be raised either by ever larger bond holdings or by the multiplication of the money supply. The propensity to consume could be raised by saturating the desire to hold assets, whether money or securities. The two methods, however, would have very different effects upon the rate of interest. Alternatively, the desire to hold money and the desire to hold securities might both be satisfied simultaneously in proportions that would tend to hold the rate of interest stable or to cause it to move in any desired trend.

The degree to which the desire to hold assets can be satisfied without creating inflation depends on the level of taxes which is deemed appropriate after balancing all the advantages of holding property claims against the disadvantages of paying taxes. With Lerner — assuming that the desirable level of public expenditures has been determined and that account has been taken of (a) the best use of resources and (b) the total level of expenditures, public and private, necessary to produce full employment — the tax rate should be as low as possible consistent with the prevention of inflation and an appropriate distribution of wealth and income.

For myself, I think that much can be said, on practical grounds, for the proposal to cover (over the cycle) operating government expenses by means of taxes, while financing developmental and improvement projects from borrowing. I would, however, by no means be dogmatically tied to this rule. (The ultimate criteria that ought in the final analysis to control are (1) full employment, (2) the best use of resources — social priorities, (3) prevention of both inflation and deflation, and (4) the most favorable distribution of income, socially and economically.) Even the rough rule referred to would involve deficit financing of operating or current expenses in depression years. With respect to borrowing for developmental and improvement projects, the financing should, I think, involve borrowing from banks to the de-

[4] Lerner calls this "printing money," which I regard as obsolete language since the modern method of increasing the money supply is through an increase in bank credit — either commercial bank credit or central bank credit, or both.

gree necessary to achieve liquidity adequate to ensure a low rate of interest. The rest should be borrowed from the public.

Thus from the secular standpoint I should favor a combination of three methods of financing — taxes, borrowing from the public, borrowing from banks. And from the cyclical standpoint I should favor varying both expenditures and tax revenue, financing the deficit partly by borrowing from banks and partly by borrowing from the public, the proportion between the two being determined by the requirements of liquidity and interest rate policy.

This program would satisfy reasonably well, I should think, a number of relevant criteria for fiscal policy:

(1) The preservation of the value of money or a substantial stability in the cost of living price index.

(2) The preservation of government credit through the continued demonstration of adequate fiscal capacity and taxing power.

(3) A reasonably satisfactory distribution of wealth controlled in part by the relative use made of taxation and of borrowing and by the progressivity of the tax structure.

(4) Full employment and optimum use of resources, and rising national income as rapidly as productivity permits.

COMMENTS ON THE MINTS AND HANSEN PAPERS

Howard S. Ellis

University of California

Professor Mints believes that the achieving of full employment "is in fact no serious problem *if only* [italics mine] we will adopt a reasonable monetary policy and vigorously oppose the development of monopolistic restrictions." I heartily agree that the two most promising procedures against under-utilization of resources are first monetary-fiscal measures of some such general character as Mints envisages, and second, a concerted attack against monopoly, wherever it is reasonably clear that monopoly results in a lesser volume of output than competition. Agreement with Professor Mints is for me easier and safer than disagreement, for I agree with most of the explicit contentions of his paper, whereas my misgivings attach only to some uncomfortable inferences.

It will not be overlooked that Professors Mints and Hansen agree completely upon the desirability of federal deficits to meet depressions. Professor Hansen advocates increasing government expenditures as well as reducing taxes, whereas Professor Mints would rely almost exclusively on the latter. I do not think we can definitely promise not to resort to large government outlays if other devices fail to stem recession. But the revenue-variation method has very definitely in its favor that the division of economic activity as between private and government could be settled upon the merits of each case, if this division were not subject to the violent alternations involved in contra-cyclical variations in public works. There is bound always to be a political wing favoring a very large amount of government activity, and another wing which, mistrustful of the concentrated power which the bureaucracy would possess under these circumstances, would reduce it to a minimum. In a parliamentary and democratic government, a compromise will be worked out between extreme positions, as for example, between Hansen with his visions of vast "developmental" projects, and Mints with his general mistrust of public works. But Mints is right that, if government activity could be allowed to settle down to a coherent and stable basis, it would be much easier for everyone to form a seasoned judgment of the issue of public vs. private in specific cases. With a federal budget of 20 billion–30 billion dollars there would seem to be a fair prospect that the drastic reduction of income-tax withholding could stop a shrinkage of private outlay. The experiment would be worth trying; and it does not seem chimerical to look for a limited delegation of tax authority — limited as to duration without Congressional review —

for anything so generally popular as *reducing* taxes.

More than passing notice should be given also to Professor Mints' radical proposal of a sales subsidy for the stubborn case of shrinking markets and employment even with drastically reduced or zero tax revenues. With so powerful a fiscal device it is conceivable that the volume of purely compensatory public works would not need to be large. A sales subsidy would presumably stimulate demand with a minimum of delay and loss; it would avoid diverting resources from channels of consumer preference; and it would not extend public undertakings at the expense of the private enterprise sector. But there are undoubtedly severe political problems involved in any subsidy system; and the application of subsidies even to as broad a category as consumers would not automatically avoid these difficulties. In the light of this fact, it seems scarcely warrantable completely to reject compensatory public works upon the grounds simply that they involve "politics."

Generally speaking, Professor Mints links together monetary-fiscal policy with the idea of an anti-monopoly program; and this combination is emphasized in a passage in which he describes "free markets and monetary stability" as essential conditions of sustained high-level employment, while other policies such as reform of the tax structure, increasing foreign investment, etc., are "minor (though important) refinements." But he offers nothing toward formulating the policies necessary to realize those "free markets"; and he does not apparently think of a multitude of structural and institutional reforms as necessary to the realization of full employment in a free society.

Indeed, despite the repetition at several points of the necessity for competitive markets, Professor Mints creates the general impression of being ready to cure unemployment by large dosages of money. Professor Hansen apparently has such an impression for he begins his criticism by casting doubt upon the sufficiency of monetary-fiscal measures in the late twenties without some underlying institutional reforms. For Professor Hansen this would have signified some additional federal lending agencies and financial regulatory bodies. I find very significant, however, the institutional changes envisaged by the six Oxford writers of *The Economics of Full Employment*,[1] who rely primarily upon the liquidity method of reaching full employment. To prevent sporadic outbursts of inflationary spending in a society assured of jobs for all, price control and rationing would have to be available for immediate use; furthermore, as the Oxford economists hold, inflationary pressure could be avoided only by vigorous measures to increase labor mobility, by what is virtually government veto over wage advances, by authoritarian allocation of capital for new ventures, etc. Perhaps Professor Mints would be the first to reject this course; but if so, I believe he would create a correct impression of his economics, not by presenting an outline of "Monetary Policy" in isolation, but by a well-rounded program for securing "free markets" while the recommended monetary-fiscal measures are being put into force.

"Free markets" in the sense of workably competitive markets are not to be built in a day. Here are problems of great complexity, involving the institutional structure of our entire economy. In some markets it may eventually be found that monopoly is technically more or less inevitable; and government regulation or ownership, despite Professor Mints' distaste for public works, may be the only solution. In others, as in slum clearance and other "welfare" undertakings, the drawback of free markets may not be monopoly but rather a complete lack of action. Finally, in those cases where monopoly restriction does yield to skillful public policy and can be supplanted by workable competition under private enterprise, the goal may be reached slowly and tortuously.

One who ardently desires the political and economic benefits of free markets should not maintain that "unemployment can be kept to tolerable levels by monetary measures under even the most extreme conditions of high liquidity preference and low investment opportunities." Saturating the public with money will induce full employment but at the cost of quasi-collectivist controls. By contrast, the maintenance of a liberal capitalist regime requires an attack upon unemployment along a very broad front.

[1] Oxford, England, 1944. Six studies in Applied Economics prepared at The Oxford University Institute of Statistics

Fiscal and monetary measures must indeed, as Professor Mints insists, be complemented by coping with monopoly restriction. But this is no simple "if only" proposition. It involves some defensible national wage policy, and a solution of the still more difficult question as to how a national policy can be implemented without authoritarian determination of wage rates. It involves some substitute for the artificial demand-limitation of our agricultural price parities. It involves working solutions of the international cartel problem, of our unsatisfactory patent situation, of allowable margins for selling costs, etc. Outside this nexus there are other impressive problems: the encouragement of new firms and new lines of production, the reform of the tax structure favorable to venture capital, the facilitating of foreign capital investment, the furtherance of low-price large-volume corporate policies, etc. Indeed, precisely because the elements in the economic scene are amazingly complex, there is a corresponding multiplicity of ways to further high and stable employment. Aggregate fiscal and monetary measures are among the most potent weapons; but they are not the whole story, especially in anything resembling a private enterprise economy.

Somewhat similar reflections are pertinent to price-level stability as a goal of monetary policy. Even in a reasonably competitive society we cannot be at all certain that stability of prices necessarily gives us full employment. In saying this I do not imply my adherence to Professor Hansen's belief that there are underlying conditions making for what he designates as "secular stagnation," at least none which cannot be obviated by compassable reforms of our capitalistic institutions without resort to continued high levels of spending or investment by government. My reason for differing with Mints is that I do not believe there is any inherent stability in even a reasonably competitive economy. Equilibrium can easily be upset by a number of exogenous and indigenous factors which have long been stressed by the cycle theorists. Once thrust away from equilibrium the economy can move progressively toward lower and lower outputs — or if the thrust is in the opposite direction, to more and more intense activity — until it meets with certain limits either at the lower or upper turning point. Professor Mints would probably respond that if prices did not undergo marked movements we would not have these great oscillations. I agree with him to the degree that greater price stabilization would contribute substantially toward economic stabilization. But there is no identity between the two. I do not believe that the rather gradual drift of commodity prices during the late twenties can in any way account for the events of 1928 and 1929 (during which years, indeed, commodity prices actually declined). Nor do I believe that the gradual rise of prices from 1933 to 1937 can at all explain the degree of economic activity during that period. Indeed, both these periods can be characterized as periods of relatively small changes in the level of commodity prices. During the earlier period we had a reasonably adequate level of employment and during the latter we had a distressingly large amount of unemployment. Price level stability, while it constitutes one of several legitimate aims of monetary and fiscal policy, does not constitute the only or even the most important aim and it is certainly not synonymous with maintaining full employment. During the twenties there was probably a tendency amongst monetary theorists to over-emphasize the benefits flowing from price-level stability, and during the thirties a somewhat excessive repudiation of these ideas. Professor Mints probably contributes to redressing the balance in current discussions.

Even though I should welcome a fair trial of the revenue variation method of compensating for cycles in private economic activity, Professor Hansen seems to me to be justified in refusing to be bound by an absolute rule against utilizing public works, particularly in housing and construction, if need be. Much can be said in favor of Hansen's rules of public finance — balancing operating expenses over the cycle and borrowing for developments and improvements — in preference either to Lerner's "functional finance" or to Mints' price-level guide of money creation. I would agree further with Hansen that as long as the capital market seems to require a variety of maturities, there is no especial merit in requiring the Treasury to issue either money or consols.

Professor Hansen is unwarrantably dogmatic

in declaring that "the rate of interest — not the price level — will be determined by the relative use made of (a) the multiplication of money or (b) borrowing from the public." The discussion since the publication of Keynes' *General Theory* has certainly demonstrated that the quantity of money bears on both prices and interest rates. There may be something banal — but nevertheless true — in adding the observation that *institutions* determine whether interest rates or prices are the more sensitive to variations in the quantity of money. In the present and near future, when government dominates capital markets much more than commodity markets, and when it does so by the direct method of simply selecting the rates it wishes to prevail, commodity prices would be expected to respond more to monetary variations.

'From Keynes to Friedman via Mints'

R. Leeson, 'From Keynes to Friedman via Mints: a resolution of the dispute', unpublished.

From Keynes to Friedman via Mints: a Resolution of the Dispute

1. The Keynes Before Keynes

Milton Friedman (Vol. 1, pp. 33–51 [1956], 33–4) asserted that 'Chicago was one of the few academic centres at which the quantity theory continued to be a central and vigorous part of the oral tradition throughout the 1930's and 1940's'. Friedman sought to 'nurture' the revival of the quantity theory by linking it to this Chicago 'oral tradition'. According to Friedman the 'flavor' of this oral tradition was captured in a model in which the quantity theory was 'in the first instance a theory of the demand for money'. Friedman added that to 'the best of my knowledge no systematic statement of this theory as developed at Chicago exists, though much of it can be read between the lines of [Henry] Simons' and [Lloyd] Mints's writings'. He also enlisted the names of Frank Knight and Jacob Viner in support of his assertion.

It is inherently difficult to resolve a dispute over an oral tradition that may or may not have existed decades before. Friedman began his Chicago graduate studies in the autumn of 1932, and his primary exposure to Chicago monetary economics was through Mints' Graduate Study of Money and Banking course (Economics 330).[1] Don Patinkin carefully marshalled evidence from his own Chicago lecture notes (taken from Mints' Economics 330 in the summer of 1944) and from contemporary Chicago writings and thesis titles. Patinkin (Vol. 1, pp. 123–43 [1972/1974], 127–8; Vol. 1, pp. 87–120 [1969/1981], 92–3) concluded that Friedman's use of the quantity theory differed significantly from interwar Chicago usage: 'the basic assumption of the Chicago School analysis was that the velocity of circulation is unstable'. Simons' writings (beginning in 1933) 'represent the Chicago tradition in its pristine – and pre-Keynesian – form'. With respect to the demand function for money, Patinkin (Vol. 1, pp. 123–43 [1972/1974], 127) asserted that Simons 'never even mentioned this concept!'[2] However, Simons (1948 [1946], 340, n. 4) stated that: 'Empirical evidence as to secular increases in the demand for money or liquidity is, however, a precarious basis for long term policy'.

Patinkin (Vol. 1, pp. 87–120 [1969/1981], 95) concluded that 'by the 1940s the Chicago School had – quite understandably – been influenced by Keynesian monetary theory'. The relevant doctoral theses of the period 'generally took [John Maynard] Keynes as their point of departure'. Mints (1950) analysed the asset demand for money – but this analysis, Patinkin explained, was followed by 'a special appendix on Keynes' theory of liquidity preference'. On two occasions, Patinkin (Vol. 1, pp. 87–120 [1969/1981], 102; Vol. 1, pp. 361–6 [1986], 365) used Friedman's (Vol. 1, pp. 71–84 [1968], 77) reference to the modern reformulated quantity theory as having been 'strongly affected by the Keynesian analysis of liquidity preference' as evidence that Friedman had been obliged to retreat from his original position. Thus Michael Parkin (Vol. 1, pp. 349–61 [1986]) was represented as 'more Friedmanian than Friedman' for not accepting this as a 'fact'.

However, as Herbert Stein (1969, 133) put it, there was a 'Keynes Before Keynes'. Lauchlin Currie (1972, 139, 141) considered himself 'a Keynesian from way back ... my theoretical approach had been influenced by Keynes since my London School of Economics days in 1922–25'. Currie (13 June 1979) informed Patinkin that in the early 1930s he was 'using the Treatise in classes at Harvard'.[3] Erik Lundberg (1994 [1934], 48, 51–2, 62) recalled that in Chicago in 1931–2, 'Our speeches and discussions centred around the monetary formulations of the business cycles given by Hayek, Mises and Keynes ... I dare say the Keynesian side mostly won the battles'. 1933 cannot be characterised as 'pre-Keynesian' in so far as the demand for money is concerned because that framework was already present in the *Treatise on Money* published in 1930. Patinkin (pp. 000–000 [1981/1973], 282) 'strongly suspected' that the Chicago 'classroom teaching' of the 1940s 'differed' from 'that of a decade before' in some respects – but he apparently made no attempt to inspect Friedman's 1932 Economics 330 lecture notes.

These 1932 lecture notes indicate that Friedman was exposed to a version of the quantity theory which stressed the importance of the demand for money. Moreover, this version of the quantity theory was stated to be part of a (Cambridge) oral tradition. In 1932, Mints' placed great stress on Keynes' *Treatise on Money* (1930) and to a lesser extent on Keynes' *Tract on Monetary Reform* in which this Marshallian oral tradition was discussed. In response to Patinkin, Friedman (Vol. 1, pp. 147–66 [1972/1974], 157; see also 1967, 8–9) maintained that 'Keynes's discussion of the demand curve for money in the *General Theory* is for the most part a continuation of earlier quantity theory approaches, improved and refined but not basically modified. As evidence, I shall cite Keynes's own writings in the *Tract on Monetary*

Reform (1923) – long before he became a Keynesian in the present sense'. But like Patinkin, Friedman did not refer to his 1932 lecture notes.

This chapter uses these lecture notes to resolve this long-standing dispute about the nature of inter-war Chicago monetary economics. To avoid ambiguity, section 2 of this chapter provides a precise description of the aspects of the debate that can be regarded as resolved. Section 3 examines the existing literature (including Patinkin's work) which emphasised that the demand for money framework was already to a large extent present in the *Treatise*. Sections 4, 5 and 6 describe the transmission process of the quantity theory money demand approach from Keynes to Friedman via Mints. Section 4 examines the interactions between Keynes and the participants of the Harris Foundation lectures and seminars at the University of Chicago in 1931. Section 5 specifically examines the interaction between Keynes and Mints in Chicago in 1931. Section 6 examines Friedman's 1932 Economics 330 lecture notes and readings: 6.1 the course outline, 6.2 Friedman's readings and lecture notes and 6.3 the reviews of the *Treatise*. Section 7 outlines Friedman's defence against Patinkin. Concluding comments are provided in section 8.

2. Issues Resolved and Issues Not Resolved

Since this essay purports to resolve this dispute it may be helpful to summarise the six issues that, it is claimed, can be regarded as being resolved (2.1–2.6). No *conclusive* evidence, however, is offered with respect to Viner, Knight, Simons or Douglas (2.7).

2.1 First, the documentary evidence clearly indicates that in 1932–3 Mints organised Economics 330 around Keynes' *Treatise*. The first words that Friedman wrote were 'Econ 330 Keynes'. Friedman then wrote that Mints concluded that 'General Framework of Keynes likely to endure much longer than details'.

2.2 Secondly, within a few years the framework of the *Treatise on Money* had been replaced by the framework of what Arthur F. Burns (1946, 12) described as Keynes' 'treatise on unemployment equilibrium'. When Burns wrote that in the 'last decade the world has moved swiftly in a Keynesian direction' he was, of course, referring to the *General Theory* as the 'Keynesian' framework that endured. As Kenneth Boulding (1956, 141) put it the 1936 Keynesian Revolution was 'the Great Change in economics'.

In the process, the *Treatise* came to be viewed as a stepping-stone in the 'natural evolution' of Keynes' (1936, vi) thought. After 1936, much of the theoretical apparatus of the *Treatise* was 'discarded' (Boulding 1956, 133). Alvin Hansen (1936, 668, 686) in his *Journal of Political Economy* (*JPE*) review of the *General Theory*, noted that Keynes had now 'wholly abandoned ... the imposing edifice erected in a *Treatise on Money*'. Hansen described economics as standing 'in danger of a sterile orthodoxy'; but the *General Theory* would 'stimulate thinking on fresh lines in the field of economic dynamics'.

Roger Weiss (1 July 1987) wrote to Mints (on the occasion of his 100th birthday) to remind him that for post-1936 students 'you worked your way patiently through the *General Theory*'.[4] By the time Patinkin attended Mints' Economics 330 – in 1944 – the *General Theory* not the *Treatise* dominated monetary theory. Mints apparently devoted one lecture (17 July 1944) to deriving the fundamental equations of the *Treatise*, and a part of a lecture (19 July 1944) to Keynes' discussion of the market and natural rates of interest. Mints concluded his discussion with 'By now concept of "natural rate" pretty well evaporated'.[5]

Keynes (1936, v) apologised in advance if his 'controversy is itself too keen'. The controversy over the Keynesian framework of the *General Theory* became more intense after the publication of *Studies in the Quantity Theory of Money*, until this alternative Chicago framework evolved into the 'natural' rate counter-revolution and displaced its Keynesian competitor (Friedman, 1968). Even before this counter-revolution, Roy Harrod (1951, 404) noted that the publication of *General Theory* 'greatly militated against the reading of the *Treatise*'. One of Keynes' American popularisers described the *Treatise* as being 'confined to a pretentious monetary theory of the trade cycle' (Dillard, 1948, 310).

2.3 Thirdly, one of the novel features of Keynes' work in the *Treatise* was an increased emphasis on money demand in a revised quantity theory framework. Like his followers (including Patinkin), Keynes (1936, 343–4) sought 'a genuine synthesis' – but Keynes' emphasis in this context was the synthesis between the 'twin quantity theories' one of which sought to determine the price level (or 'value in exchange') and the other which sought to determine the rate of interest (or the 'value in use'). This specific synthesis was, as Friedman put it, 'a continuation of earlier quantity theory approaches, improved and refined but not basically modified'. Patinkin (16 November 1959) complained to Friedman that 'to me it seems that with perhaps one exception (Karl Schlesinger) an exposition with the contents and spirit of yours could not have been written (and was not written) before Keynes. I find it particularly difficult to accept your implication that your essay represents the kind of thing that was taught at Chicago by Knight, Viner, Simons and Mints. My own recollections are different'.[6] Friedman's 1956 essay could not have been written (and was not written) before Keynes of the *Treatise* – but the publication of that book preceded Friedman's training at Chicago.

2.4 Fourthly, there was an important generational aspect to this dispute. As Stein (1969, 162) noted, both Paul Samuelson and Boulding responded to Keynes with 'Wordsworthian or Keatian emotions'. Both described their feelings using the words 'Bliss was it in that dawn to be alive, but to be young was very heaven'. Samuelson (1915–) was describing his reaction to the *General Theory*; Boulding (1910–95) to the *Treatise*. Both were twenty-one when they encountered these respective books. Friedman (1912–) was twenty when he attended Mints' 330 course; Patinkin (1922–95) was twenty-two.

Boulding (1956, 133) recalled that he would 'never forget the excitement, as an undergraduate [at Oxford] of reading Keynes' *Treatise on Money* in 1931'. He recounted to his biographer that the *Treatise* provoked 'a spiritual experience as well an intellectual one ... *now* the world made sense; history made sense for the first time' [emphasis in original]. One of the unpleasant shocks he received upon taking up his first teaching position in Edinburgh, in autumn 1934, was that 'Keynes had scarcely been heard of' there (Kerman, 1974, 104–5, 242).

Boulding spent the intervening period (1932–4) as a graduate student at Chicago.[7] He was not impressed with much of the formal teaching but wrote to a friend, 'There are a large number of Bright Young Men in the graduate school. We meet every week in a seminar to rend Mr Keynes' (cited by Kerman, 1974, 236–7). George Stigler (1988, 25) recalls that students and junior faculty "of whom Albert G. Hart was the most prominent, organised a seminar and invited a stream of visiting scholars (Oskar Lange and Fritz Machlup, among others) to give talks that led to remarkable stimulating discussions". Economics Chairman Harry Millis was prepared to transform this seminar into a departmental course; but given the state of "extraordinary intellectual ferment" that existed among the students, they declined for fear that their autonomy might be undermined.

Friedman, Stigler and Allen Wallis (1993) avidly discussed the idea they were exposed to. Indeed, Milton and Rose Friedmans' (1998, 35, 39–40) 'most vivid memory' of their fellow graduate students was Boulding and Hart vigorously debating: 'Both believed it was wasteful for only one person to talk at a time'. Friedman (correspondence to the author, 15 February

2002) has reiterated that Boulding was a dominant influence among graduate students at Chicago; a status that may have been reinforced by his having already published in Keynes' *Economic Journal* (Boulding 1932).

Albert Hart (1948, vii) located in Hicks' (1935) article on 'A suggestion for simplifying the theory of money' the 'most direct intellectual influence' on his *Money, Debt and Economic Activity.* Hicks (1935, 3) emphasised the marginal portfolio analysis in the *Treatise*, as 'the most important part of [Keynes'] theoretical contribution'. Hart (1948, vii, 167) also described Keynes as 'the most fertile monetary thinker of the interwar years'. The revolution in monetary thinking occurred during Hart's time at Chicago: 'Down to the Great Depression of the 1930's, the stability of velocity made this mechanistic [quantity-velocity] approach reasonable'. However, with the breakdown of the stability of velocity, it was necessary to analyse 'people's motives and plans; and this is more conviently carried out in the framework of the payments approach and cash-balance approach'. In the chapter on 'The Cash-Balances Approach', Hart (1948, 191–2) stated that 'This chapter is about motives to hold cash ... [this] approach has a long history and has been widely used – particularly in England ... Among British economists of the twentieth century, Alfred Marshall, A. C. Pigou, D. H. Robertson and J. M. Keynes (in the earlier stages of his monetary thinking) took this approach'. Hart (1948, viii) also stressed the influence of Mints and Simons on his book.

It therefore seems likely that Friedman took the ideas he was exposed to in Economics 330 and used them as an organising framework with which to understand the 'macroeconomic' dislocation of the 1930s. If intense student discussion is admissible as an 'oral tradition' then Friedman's assertion has some validity. A version of the quantity theory which was 'in the first instance a theory of the demand for money' was apparently 'a central and vigorous part of the oral tradition' at Chicago at least among graduate students in 1932–3 (and possibly until the *General Theory* made Keynes a suspect figure).

2.5 Fifthly, Friedman's initial assertion about Chicago uniqueness in this context must now appear unreliable. The *Treatise* made a profound impression on a variety of economists in a variety of universities. John Kenneth Galbraith (1971, 280) spent 1931–4 at Berkeley where 'Leo Rogin discussed Keynes with a sense of urgency that made his seminars seem to graduate students the most important things then happening in the world'. Boulding (1956, 133) had a similar sense of excitement at Oxford in 1931. In summer 1930, A. F. Plumptre left Cambridge with a hundred proof copies of the *Treatise*, from which he taught his University of Toronto students, including Lorie Tarshis (1977, 49).[8] When in 1932–3, Richard Kahn visited the United States (including a four week visit to Chicago) he reported to Keynes that 'The *Treatise* plays an enormously prominent role wherever I go' (16 February 1933; cited by Marcuzzo, 2001, 22).

John Williams taught money and banking at Harvard (Mason, 1982, 419). In his forty-one page lead article review of the *Treatise*, Williams (1931, 549, 552–3, 559, 580) noted in the *Quarterly Journal of Economics* that Keynes was 'turning away from old versions of the quantity theory'. In Williams' view, Keynes' primary innovation related to the composition of money demand: 'a shift of deposits from demand to time deposits'. Thus 'the concept of the idle savings deposit, and the consequent distinction between saving and investment, underlie Keynes' whole treatment and constitute a valid claim to his having broken new and significant ground in monetary theory'. This was 'an important advance. Fisher's equation, for example, deals exclusively with demand deposits. So far as I know all theories previous to Keynes' have failed to make use of the statistical division of deposits into demand and time ... in monetary terms, the crux of the matter is that, while banks control the physical quantity of deposits, depositors control the spending of them, and changes in quantity may be offset by changes in velocity or in direction'.

Joseph Schumpeter described the *Treatise* to Keynes (JMK, XIII [1930], 201) as 'a Ricardian *tour de force*' and as a result tore up his own uncompleted work on monetary theory (Moggridge, 1992, 593). Erik Lundberg (1994 [1934], 48, 51–2, 62) found that at Harvard in 1933, Schumpeter had 'gathered around him a group of young economists all working with modern monetary theories. During the summer I had discussions with some of them, especially on monetary questions concerning the business cycle'. This contrasted favourably with what Lundberg found in Chicago in 1931–2. With respect to business cycle theory, Lundberg thought that Chicago had 'very little to offer. Professor Mints touched on some aspects of the problem in his lectures on monetary theories'.

It is therefore improbable that the *Treatise* – with its emphasis on money demand – informed 'macroeconomic' discussions in Chicago only. Indeed, Friedman in the preface to these volumes has retreated from his initial assertion about Chicago uniqueness. The texts in Volume 2, Part 1 also tend to undermine the uniqueness assertion.

2.6 There has been much speculation about Friedman's motives. He was clearly highly stimulated by the Chicago environment of the 1930s. His teachers 'left a unique imprint' on their students. In this Chicago tradition 'what mattered in intellectual discourse was only the cogency of the argument'. After his return to Chicago in 1946, he self-consciously modelled his teaching style on Viner's. Friedman's (Vol. 1, pp. 33–51 [1956]) essay introduced a collection of dissertations written by students from his Chicago Workshop in Money and Banking. The purpose was 'to supplement what I did with related work by students and colleagues. This combination gave birth to what became known as the Chicago School of Monetary Economics' (Friedman and Friedman, 1998, 35, 156–7; Friedman, 1983, 211; Stigler, 1988, 156–7).

Friedman sought to provide an enthusiastic 'teamwork approach' for his Workshop (Hammond, 1996, 47).[9] His pedagogical mission was 'to fuel intensive discussion' (Friedman and Friedman, 1998, 35, 41, 49, 202). But one energising ingredient, present for Friedman's generation, was missing for students of the 1950s: extreme macroeconomic dislocation. The oral tradition linked the students of the second-generation Chicago School to their predecessors, thus assisting the cultivation of an institutional affiliation.

Friedman (1962a, viii) thought that his role was to act as an intellectual 'matchmaker'. Some of his students found his 'magic' comparable in excitement to 'a date with a beautiful woman' (Becker, 1998).[10] If his 'Restatement' exaggerated the degree of continuity with respect to earlier Chicago versions of the quantity theory this may have been a rhetorical flourish designed to provide an additional motivational stimulus to his students. Friedman (Vol. 1, pp. 33–51 [1956], 34, 51) emphasised 'the part which students have played in keeping that tradition alive and vigorous'. That tradition 'nurtured' his students' essays.

It was a highly successful pedagogical device. Not only did Friedman produce a cohort of students committed to analysing macroeconomics through the quantity theory,[11] some such as Robert Lucas (1976, 41) and Thomas Sargent and Neil Wallace (1976, 169) constructed a third generation Chicago School 'rules party'. So potent was this teaching style that many others 'picked up the Chicago business by osmosis' (Bork 1983, 196). Stigler (1962, 71) claimed that Friedman was the intellectual leader, not merely of the Chicago School, but of a much broader church: the 'Berkeley–Cambridge axis'.

2.7 This chapter does not purport to offer decisive evidence with respect to Knight, Simons, Viner or Douglas. Prior to 1936, these Chicago economists may have used Keynes' framework to analyse the Great Depression, orally, despite the paucity of published references. Friedman's cohort had extensive social and intellectual interactions with their teachers (Stigler, 1983, 168; 1988, 19; Friedman, 1983, 179; Wallis, 1983, 179; Director,

1983, 179; Minsky, 1985, 220). Paul Douglas (1931, 9; 1933, 80) described the *Treatise* as 'brilliant' and 'The most stimulating single work on money'. Viner (p. 397 [1932]) concluded that the diagnoses and remedies contained in Keynes' *Essays in Persuasion* were widely accepted as 'substantially and brilliantly right'. Moreover, Keynes stood 'head and shoulders' above other economists as a 'propagandist' whose work was 'undiluted by academic scruples to disclose all the qualifications and the uncertainties of his logical argument'. Keynes also displayed 'fearlessness in assigning to his opponents their appropriately low intelligence quotas... Perhaps what the world has needed and most urgently needs today, is a few more Keynes'. However, during a visit to Chicago, Kahn (15 January 1933) reported to Joan Robinson that Viner was 'very proud of not having read more than a few passages from the Treatise'.[12]

With respect to post-war published work, Viner, as Mints (1950, 116–7) pointed out, was a 'proponent of discretionary authority'. Viner (1947, 210–1) proposed that 'until better techniques are discovered, the problem of inflation and of deflation needs to be dealt with by improvisation, by ad hoc and prompt reactions to changes in circumstances as they occur rather than by fixed policies set long in advance in accordance with long-run forecasts'.[13] Viner's (1958 [1954], 365) use of the quantity theory was different from that asserted by Friedman: he defended the quantity theory against Schumpeter's attacks, on the basis that the theory 'is understood as holding only: (1) that an authority powerful enough to make the quantity of money what it pleases can so regulate that quantity as to make the price level approximate to what it pleases, and (2) that the possibility of existence of such a power is not inconceivable a priori'.

Friedman (1962) and Viner (1962) both contributed essays to *In Search of a Monetary Constitution*. Viner's contribution to the rules versus discretion debate was entitled 'The Necessity and the Desirable Range of Discretion to be Allowed to a Monetary Authority'. Viner concluded that it was impractical to conduct monetary management 'in conformity with a "rule"', in part, because in the US 'the degree of decentralisation of direct and indirect control over the quantity and velocity of money, as well as of official powers to influence the supply of near-moneys and their velocities, is nothing short of fantastic' (1962, 262, 273; see also 1961, 232–3). Viner (1962, 252, 256–8, 261) followed Simons in preferring the 'flexible rule' and 'judgment' associated with a price-level goal, brought about by variations in the money supply. Indeed, the bulk of Viner's paper was a highly critical commentary of Friedman's x% money growth rule. Viner could not 'exorcise' from his mind Friedman's 'faith' and 'claims'. In

Friedman's analysis 'an improbable constancy is being projected into the future ... Staking our future on present prophesizing seems a high price to pay for escaping from the bondage of a discretionary authority'.[14]

Knight (1964 [1948], xlv, xliii) also objected to the 'whole project of making monetary theory the centre and starting point of systematic economics' in part because the 'supply and demand curves for 'liquidity' have no solid foundation and are not a solid basis for action but are 'theoretical' in the bad and misleading sense'.[15] According to Knight (1941, 65) 'that a monetary theory of interest should be defended by economists of repute is especially mysterious in view of the facts, which are directly contrary to what the theory calls for'. Knight explained that 'The monetary system can never be made automatic. An approximate constancy in general prices, or in the relation between product prices and wages, can in the nature of the case be achieved only by deliberate action, based on constant attention, correcting or offsetting incipient tendencies to expansion or contraction'. In the rules versus discretion debate over monetary policy, Knight (1960, 105) lent 'rather strongly towards the side of administrative discretion and judgement, being sceptical about how far rules can be made in advance or especially how far they would be made wisely by the agencies that would in fact make them'.

However, since this essay highlights the perils of the regression line approach to the history of thought, no definitive judgement is offered with respect to Douglas, Knight, Simons, Viner. Likewise no definitive judgement is offered with respect to Mints' written work. Friedman's primary exposure to monetary economics at Chicago was through Mints' 330: the evidence presented here is sufficient to absolve him of the charges laid by Patinkin and Johnson. However, constraints of space and time prohibit a systematic examination of these other aspects of the issue, which would, of course, be a valuable contribution to the literature. However, it is not undertaken here.

3. The Demand for Money prior to the General Theory

To Friedman's students he displayed 'the missionary's zeal in the worship of truth' (Becker 1991, 145). Patinkin (to Hicks, 19 August 1957) also shared an 'open-minded search for the truth'.[16] Patinkin (Vol. 1, pp. 87–120 [1969/1981], 88) sought to use the 'true nature of the Chicago monetary tradition' as a powerful weapon to attack Friedman. But in a letter to Phillip Cagan commenting on his forthcoming contribution to *Studies in the Quantity Theory of Money* (Cagan, 1956), Patinkin (16 May 1955) modestly acknowledged what he regarded as an intellectual weakness: 'seeing how my own thinking frequently gets compartmentalized – and fails to recognize in one context what it recognizes in another'.[17]

What Patinkin apparently failed to adequately realise – in the compartment of his dispute with Friedman – is that the *General Theory* created a structural break in Chicagoan reactions to Keynes and that the concept of liquidity preference was largely contained in the *Treatise*. The history of monetary economics – like the Keynesian Neoclassical Synthesis – develops through 'irony' and 'error' (Patinkin, 1952, 269–70).[18]

Patinkin (1981, 3, 16–7, 247, n. 17) was at Chicago between 1941–7, the last two years as a doctoral student and research associate at the Cowles Commission. He used his recollections of these years to further undermine Friedman's assertion: 'In so far as the empirical estimation of the demand function for money was undertaken at Chicago, it was done so under the auspices of the Keynesian model builders of the Cowles Commission, which was then located at the University of Chicago. See in particular Lawrence Klein [1947, 1950a]'. At Cowles 'Truth in the form of maximum-likelihood estimates identified and enthroned' battled 'Error in the form of simultaneous equation error ... Armed with this truth Lawrence Klein developed his econometric models of the United States economy (1947, 1950[a])'.

In 1944, as Patinkin attended Mints' Economics 330, Klein, supervised by Samuelson, wrote his MIT doctoral dissertation on the *Keynesian Revolution*. Patinkin (1981 [1947], 155, n.) read and commented on what he described as Klein's 'excellent' thesis in manuscript form. In his discussion of the *General Theory*, Klein (1950b, ix, 8, 16, 97) emphasised that 'the interest theory of this system is the solution to the entire set of equations *which is based on the liquidity-preference building block* [emphasis in original]'. But Klein also emphasised that 'the major theoretical innovation of the *Treatise* was an analysis of the functions of money and the motives which lead people to hold cash balances ... the foundations of Keynes' later liquidity preference theory of interest'.

Klein's (1950b, 96, 101) thesis also reflected some of the polemics of the emerging modern configuration. Referring to the reviewers of the *General Theory* Klein described Knight as one of 'the mob in the stoning of the revolutionary dissenter' and Viner as someone who 'did not agree with the theory of liquidity preference ... He was not able to give up the quantity equation'.

In '1923, as a faithful pupil of the classical school', Keynes (1936, 334–5) argued that 'the claim to cure Unemployment involves the Protectionist fallacy in its grossest and crudest form'. But in the *General Theory*, Keynes

(1936, 339, 341–4, 351) sought to unravel and undermine the 'domination of the classical school' and to locate antecedents to his emphasis on money demand. With fixed exchange rates, the interest rate could not be used to facilitate 'full employment' and had been sacrificed 'to the operation of blind forces'. In contrast, mercantilists opposed high interest rates: 'they were even aware that the rate of interest depended on liquidity-preference and the quantity of money'. Between these two positions stood economists with varying degrees of confusion. David Hume had 'a foot and a half in the classical world', while the 'great' John Locke had managed to have 'one foot in the mercantilist world and ... one foot in the classical world'. One of the defining characteristics of those who had (partially) escaped the 'classical' nonsense was an understanding of liquidity preference. Not only had Locke failed to proceed to 'a genuine synthesis' but he was also 'confused' and 'overlooked altogether the possibility of *fluctuations* in liquidity preference' [emphasis in original]. As usual Keynes added some provocative spice to his analysis: 'One recurs to the analogy between the sway of the classical school of economic theory and that of certain religions'.

In the *General Theory*, Keynes (1936, 174, 194–5) explained that 'the concept of *Hoarding* may be regarded as a first approximation to the concept of *Liquidity-preference*'. Liquidity preference was 'substantially the same as that which has been sometimes discussed under the heading of the Demand for Money ... In my *Treatise on Money* I studied the total demand for money under the headings of income-deposits, business-deposits, and savings-deposits, and I need not repeat here the analysis which I gave in Chapter 3 of that book'. Keynes (1936, 176, n3, 179) specifically associated Knight with a theory of interest which was 'precisely in the traditional, classical mould'. In Keynes' judgement, Knight and the other 'classical' theorists were guilty of propagating a 'nonsense' and had failed to 'furnish material for a theory of interest'. When 'we introduce the state of liquidity-preference and the quantity of money ... then the whole position becomes determinate'.

Knight scribbled 'Nonsense' and sometimes even stronger comments throughout his copy of the *General Theory* (Patinkin, 1981, 289). In his milder published review, Knight (pp. 437–60 [1937], 459, n. 22) objected to the tone of the *General Theory*: 'it has become quite the fashion to account for differences in intellectual positions by psycho-analysing, or somehow "explaining" one's opponent (and the example of following the fashion having in this case been set by Mr Keynes)'.[19] In 1940, Knight opposed the award of an honorary degree to Keynes on the grounds that

'His work and influence seem to me supremely 'anti-intellectual'' in that he had sought to pander to the 'prejudices' of 'the man-in-the-street' (cited by Patinkin, 1981, 301).

As Harrod (1951, 409) pointed out, 'the greater part of the doctrine of the *General Theory* on liquidity preference is to be found quite clearly set out in the *Treatise*'. In the *Treatise* Keynes (1930, 249) discussed the motives for 'the main variation in the total demand for money'. In the *Econometrica* article which launched the IS-LM formalisation of the *General Theory* John Hicks (1937, 147) declared that that it was 'the liquidity preference doctrine which is vital' in distinguishing the 'classical' from the Keynesian equations: 'Liquidity Preference transports us from the "Treasury View" to the "General Theory of Employment"'. Both Knight and Viner took exception to Keynes' analysis of money demand: 'His use of the term "liquidity" to designate everything that makes it desirable to hold money ... does not seem to be an advance or justifiable'. Keynes' assertion 'that the rate of interest does, at any time, equilibrate the desirability of holding cash with the quantity of cash, is not only badly worded ... but is definitely besides the point' (Knight pp. 437–60 [1937], 449). Viner (pp. 399–430 [1936/1964], 245–6, 422–7) complained about Keynes' 'gross oversimplification' of the issue. However, the focus of Chicagoan opposition remained the *General Theory* not the *Treatise*.

In 'Some Notes on Liquidity Preference', Kahn (1954, 245, 250) explained that Keynes never really escaped from the idea of a 'stable' money demand relationship. Kahn was seeking to undermine Dennis Robertson's attempt to put liquidity preference theory on stronger grounds by replacing the speculative motive for holding money. He was responding to Robertson's (1946, 25) assertion that 'the older Cambridge theory is kinder to "liquidity preference" than is Mr Keynes' of the *General Theory*. Kahn concluded that: 'Sufficient has been said to demonstrate the unsuitability of thinking of a schedule of liquidity preference as though it could be represented by a well-defined curve or by a functional relationship expressed in mathematical terms or subject to econometric processes. Keynes himself often gave way to the temptation to picture the state of liquidity preference as a fairly stable relationship, despite his intuitional horror of undue formalism, but his treatment at least can be justified by the need at the time for a forceful and clear-cut exposition if it was to carry any weight at all'.

Kahn (1984, 51, 53, 59, 137, 171) heard Keynes lecturing from early drafts of *Treatise* and 'found his lectures extremely puzzling, based, as they were, on the Quantity Theory. (The great change occurred in the Summer

Term of 1932)'. Kahn complained that the *Tract* was 'far more strictly monetarist than Marshall and Pigou'. But Keynes then 'spent a considerable part of the next twelve years of his life in a struggle to escape from the stranglehold of the Quantity Theory'. When the *General Theory* was published, 'that was the end of the Quantity Theory until its recent resuscitation. Keynes in his long fight for release had conquered'. In this battle for mental liberation the *Treatise* represented 'an intermediate phase'. Kahn reflected that 'the origins of the liquidity preference theory of the rate of interest go back to Marshall ... In a primitive, but extremely interesting form, the theory is to be found in a section of the *Treatise*'.[20]

Patinkin (chapter 45 [1975], 260; 1976, 7, 45, 81, 136) also described the *Tract*, the *Treatise* and the *General Theory* as Keynes' interwar 'trilogy ... The Saga of Man's Struggle for Freedom from the Quantity Theory'. Keynes had inherited this quantity-theory tradition 'from his teachers at Cambridge'. Patinkin cited the preface to the French edition of the *General Theory* in which Keynes stated that 'the following analysis [of money and prices] registers my final escape from the confusions of the Quantity Theory, which once entangled me'. Patinkin provided what he regarded as 'conclusive evidence that a significant shift took place in Keynes' views on the efficacy of monetary policy between the *Treatise* and the *General Theory*'. In the *Treatise* there was 'the unmistakable ring of the quantity theory' plus 'the essence of the theory of liquidity preference'.

In autumn 1932, Keynes delivered lectures at Cambridge on 'the Monetary Theory of Production' (Patinkin, 1976, 72).[21] In those lectures, Keynes (JMK, XIII [1932], 397–8) referred to 'the state of liquidity-preference ... which tells us what ... the rate of interest exclusive of risk-allowance, will be, given to [the ?] quantity of money'. Keynes also discussed a fall in output 'in accordance with the argument in my *Treatise on Money.* Consequently the demand for money in the active circulation will fall, which in turn will affect the state of liquidity preference so that there will be a lowering cet. par. of the rate of interest corresponding to the given quantity of money' (Keynes, cited by Patinkin, 1980, 18). Patinkin (1976, 72) commented that 'The voice is that of the *General Theory*: but the analytical framework is still largely that of the *Treatise*'.

Patinkin (1976, 33) explained that 'One of the standard tasks with which every student of Keynes' writings is confronted if that of tracing the intellectual relationship between the *General Theory* and the *Treatise*'. Patinkin also noted that 'economists who did their graduate training after the appearance of the *General Theory* – that is, the vast majority of professional economists today – are unlikely ever to have studied the *Treatise* systematically'. As an historian, Patinkin qualified for this minority status. As someone who did his graduate training between the *Treatise* and the *General Theory*, so too did Friedman.

4. 1931: Keynes and the Chicago School

Keynes spent a fortnight in Chicago (22 June–2 July 1931) attending the Harris Foundation lectures and seminars on 'Unemployment as a World Problem' against the background of two parallel banking crises, in both Europe and in Chicago. The 1931 European financial crisis had started with the failure of the Credit Anstalt bank in Vienna on 11 May. This financial contagion began to spread to Austria's neighbours, including Germany. From late May, the Reichbank began to suffer heavy losses of reserves. On 20 June 1931, President Hoover proposed a two-year moratorium on war debts and reparation payments. On 24 June 1931, the Reichbank obtained a central-bank credit of $100 million which temporarily calmed the markets. This 'unexpected' development forced Karl Pribram (1931, 112, 118) from the University of Frankfurt, to rewrite part of his Harris Foundation lecture. With respect to unemployment, 'the situation has nowhere reached such a critical state as in Germany. And this reflection brings us back to the hopes of recovery attached to the execution of Mr Hoover's relief action'.[22]

Between December 1929 and the end of 1932, two thirds of banks in Chicago failed, a higher proportion than any other major US city (Phillips, 1994, 17). When Roosevelt received the Democratic nomination in Chicago in June 1932, the city was in the midst of a banking crisis: 'great crowds gathered at the banks' (Hoover, 1952, 170; Kennedy, 1973, 40–2). Keynes (JMK, XX, 555–7, 571) was shocked by the banking crisis that he found upon his arrival in Chicago. On the same day that he gave his first Harris Foundation lecture he wrote to Hubert Henderson: 'Quite apart from the immediate situations, German or other, the effect on the situation here which I had most underestimated before I came was the position of many banks in the country … Owing to the number of banks which have actually failed there is great unrest among depositors. There is a possibility at any moment of bank runs breaking out in different parts of the country, similar to what was lately experienced at Chicago. The consequence is that depositors not infrequently take their money out in cash and keep it in a safe deposit box. This has been particularly marked in recent weeks in the Chicago district, where safe deposit boxes are no longer obtainable. Everyone agrees that there must be at least $400,000,00 to $500,000,000 being actually hoarded by the public in the shape of currency in boxes. The same movement which has been occurring in Chicago might break out at any time in the Middle West if suspicions as to the position of the banks were to increase'. On his return to Britain, Keynes reflected that 'The Chicago situation is largely a reflection of a quite appalling real estate collapse from which it may take years to recover'.

Keynes (1931a, 3, 4, 16–17, 27, 35, 40) began his Harris lecture in apocalyptic fashion: 'We are today in the middle of the greatest economic catastrophe – the greatest catastrophe due almost entirely to economic causes – of the modern world. I am told that the view held in Moscow is that this is the last, the culminating crisis of capitalism and that our existing order of society will not survive it'. Keynes dissented from this pessimism: 'I believe that our destiny is in our own hands and that we can emerge from it if only we choose – or rather if those choose who are in authority in the world'. He explained that a 'secure basis for a return to an equilibrium of prosperity' could only be achieved by increasing volume of investment and allowing a revival of the price level. He suggested that interest rates needed to be reduced via an increase in 'the quantity of liquid assets' through open market operations which 'involves technical questions of some difficulty with which I must not burden this lecture'.

The United States (and presumably Chicago) in 1931 had a profound impact on Keynes (JMK, XX [1931], 586): 'Before I went to the United States I was disposed to hold with some confidence that the first impetus to recovery in the rest of the world would have to come from America. I held as you say firmly that it was sometime before I even questioned it. But eventually it was put to me point blank in discussion that perhaps the opposite was true. And in the end I came to wonder whether this might not be the more probable opinion. We may have to drag along what seems an endless period until something happens to stir the dry bones elsewhere then in North America'.[23]

Keynes' Harris lecture certainly made an impression on J. Laurence Laughlin, the founding chairman of the Chicago economics department and the founding editor of the *JPE* (1892–5). In *The Federal Reserve Act its Origin and Problems*, Laughlin (1933, 222, 229, 231–2) abused the quantity theory, Fisher and his 'unquestionable error ... the American inflationist school of Irving Fisher has called in for reinforcement ... John Maynard Keynes'. Keynes' 'remarks on the abandonment of the British gold standard and the sacerdotal nature assigned to the influence of the quantity of money on prices are scarcely credible'. Presumably referring to the Harris lectures, Laughlin continued: 'Coming to this country [Keynes] was, of course, given a hearing in magazines and as a speaker, but his method of going off into difficult ground, where it was hard for the untrained mass to follow kept him from making much of an impression. On the gold standard and its substitution by sterling, he could not easily be followed ... Such exposition sounds most like the theorising taken from Alice's Adventures in Wonderland. It would seem as if Keynes in this process has stepped off the firmer earth into the violent instability of dreams. It is too fantastic to be taken seriously'.

But Patinkin (pp. 373–92 [1979/1981], 377–8) asserted that the Harris lectures 'apparently did not bring [Keynes] into contact with the Chicago School ... Henry Simons (who was then an assistant professor) did participate in several of the round tables, but he too did so actively only once and inconsequentially (*Reports*, p. 88). Only Lloyd Mints (then also an assistant professor) played a more active role'. Given the pivotal importance of Mints' Economics 330 in the dispute over Chicago oral tradition this seems a surprising assertion. Virtually all of the Chicago economists were listed as members of the 1931 roundtable group, including Garfield Cox, Aaron Director, Harry Gideonse, Frank Knight, Harry Millis, Samuel Nerlove, Henry Schultz, Chester Wright, Quincy Wright and Theodore Yntema (Davis, 1971, appendix B). The evidence suggests that the Harris lectures unambiguously brought the Chicago School into contact with Keynes, oral traditions and the quantity theory–money demand nexus.

Simons contributed to the session led by Hansen (24 June) on 'Business Cycles, Price Levels and Unemployment'. Hansen (1931, 59–60) argued that 'one of the things that tends to prolong the depression at the present time as against earlier periods is the fact that it takes a longer time to reach a readjustment in the internal price structure, because our price and wage systems are becoming increasingly rigid. That means there is a longer lag, a longer time before you reach a new equilibrium in the internal price structure, which I think is a fundamental condition for an increase in the rate of investment'. Hansen (1931, 62) dissented from the analysis provided by the *Treatise*: 'It seems to me that the maladjustment between the rate investment and the rate of savings, which Mr Keynes discusses so clearly in his book, is fundamentally to be found not on the saving side, but on the investment side'. The proposal to increase wages, Hansen (1931, 64–5) argued 'invert[ed] cause and effect ... this thesis entirely overlooks all the fundamental principles which I am not willing to abandon, that we have had worked out through a long development of economic theory of the relation of money and prices, a theory, in other words, of the value of money. You cannot control the price level by raising the price of one agent of production. That, in a nutshell, is the point'. Keynes (1931a, 73–4) responded: 'I find it very difficult to discuss this question without making a distinction between the level of prices and the level of costs ... The quantity theory, I think, is essentially an equilibrium theory. When the two are in adjustment, when costs and prices are adapted to one another, the level of the two of them depends on the quantity of money'.

Keynes (JMK, XX [1931], 580) later reflected that at the Chicago conference the majority opinion favoured the view that the wage-price nexus operated in reverse: 'I heard the question of the advisability of wage reductions discussed in a large gathering of academic economists. The voice of the "equilibriumists" ... was heard, but I think it would be true to say that the balance of opinion was decidedly in favour of the view that the immediate advantages to employment from wage reductions would not be large and were outweighed by other considerations (social and the effect on the price level in relation to monetary indebtedness)'.

Lewis Lorwin (1931, 84) asked Keynes about his preference for an 'indirect' solution to unemployment by manipulating the interest rate as opposed to more 'direct' methods. Keynes (1931a, 84) replied: 'I use that because I am speaking in the country which is the last home of individualism'. Wright, Director, Cox, Simons and Mints all took part in the subsequent discussion. Keynes (1931a, 92) thought that this discussion 'brings us back to the question asked about individualism, whether private capitalism is capable of solving the problem completely. I do not feel at all certain.' Referring to the idea that 'the conditions which lead to prosperity have within them the seeds of depression ... so long as you have as a guiding force the desire for profit', Wright (1931b, 93) asked Keynes 'whether at least that degree of inevitability is inherent?' Keynes (1931a, 93) responded: 'I should agree that the capitalistic society as we now run it is essentially unstable. The question in my mind is whether one could preserve the stability by the injection of a moderate degree of management; whether in practice it is beyond our power to do this, and that we will have to have some further plan of control. I should like to try the central bank method first, uncertain how far in practice it would lead us. If that proved to be incapable of keeping things reasonably steady, but I should go in for a very great degree of state control of the rate of investment'.

As a result of this questioning, Keynes (1931a, 94) outlined two aspects of the philosophy to which Simons and the 'rules party' objected. Keynes advocated discretionary macroeconomic management to 'keep the price index and the employment index steady'. Hansen (1931, 94) asked whether it was not the case that 'in our present state of knowledge we have no guide at all dependable, and consequently the system you propose is a purely Utopia one?'

Keynes (1931a, 94) defended himself by explaining that 'statistics are becoming more adequate … I think we economists have given the practical business men very little real help in the past. If they were aided by more complete statistical data, then I think we should find central banks doing their best duty'. When asked by Hansen (1931, 94) about the reliability of the 'judgment' of the central bankers, Keynes (1931a, 94) replied: 'I think we already know enough to give them general suggestions … Painful experience works wonders. It is really the economists who are primarily at fault. We have never given any sort of scientific conclusions, such as you would expect. So long as the supposedly experts fail to agree among themselves, it seems to me reasonable for the practical business men to pay only moderate attention to them'. Magnusson (1931, 96) asked him: 'Must we not be very careful in our use of the word 'scientists'? Are we justified in really flirting with the word?' In reply, Keynes (1931a, 96) explained that 'Ours is a very complex science. It possesses the subject matter of science'.

5. 1931: Keynes and Mints

In the June 23 seminar on 'Public Works Construction and Unemployment', Keynes (1931a, 303) stated that he thought 'the argument for public works in this country is much weaker than it is in Great Britain. In Great Britain I have for a long time past agitated very strongly for a public works program, and my argument has been that we are such a centre of an international system that we cannot operate on the rate of interest … In this country you haven't a problem of that kind. Here you can function as though you were a closed system … For such a system I would use as my first method operating on the long term rate of interest … I think in this country deliberate public works should be regarded much more as a tonic to change the state of business conditions, but the means of getting back to the state of equilibrium should be concentrated on the rate of interest'.

Mints had an extensive exchange with Keynes during the Harris Foundation seminars. Keynes led the discussion on 'Is it possible for Governments and Central Banks to do Anything on Purpose to Remedy Unemployment?' Chairman Quincy Wright (1931b, 461) invited the audience 'to take up the cudgels with Mr Keynes'. Mints (1931, 479) asked Keynes: 'Your means of reducing a long-term rate of interest has been an indirect means. I wonder what you would say to a more direct means, namely purchasing industrial and public utility bonds by the member banks themselves'.

Mints did not receive a satisfactory reply. Later, Keynes (1931a, 493) stated that 'the forces of supply are the savings of the community: the forces of demand are the amount of construction that will take place at different rates of interest, and I want to fix the rate of interest at the point where the supply and demand meet'. Mints (1931, 493–4) pressed Keynes again: 'I should like to revert for a moment to the question of the relative importance of lowering the interest rate and public works. As I understand your argument, you want to reduce the interest rate in order to bring about an equivalent between saving and investment. As a matter of fact, won't public works bring about precisely the same results, not through decreasing the rate of interest, but increasing the rate of return for business firms, thereby increasing the rate of investment, even at current rates of interest?'

Keynes (1931a, 494) replied: 'Certainly; therefore I am in favour of an admixture of public works, but my feeling is that unless you socialise the country to a degree that is unlikely, you will get to the end of the public works programme, if not in one year, in two years, and therefore if you're not prepared to reduce the rate of interest and bring back private enterprise, when you get to the end of the public works programme you have shot your bolt, and you are no better off. I should use the public works programme to fill in the interregnum while I was getting the interest down. The public works program would in itself increase business profits, and therefore relieve people from that exceptional unwillingness to borrow. I should be afraid of that as a sole remedy. I should be afraid it would work itself out, come to an end, and then we should be back where we were unless we decided on a very definite further action'.

According to Kahn (1974, 368–9), Keynes had previously been 'curiously conventional for a genius'. Influenced by Kahn's (1931, 1933) multiplier articles, Keynes gradually began to embrace a position much closer to that espoused in 1931 by Mints. By 1951, it appears that Mints' pre-*General Theory* advocacy of public works had undergone a transformation. Dennis Robertson (1951, 466–7), in a review of Mints' (1950) *Monetary Policy for a Competitive Society* suggested that Mints' opposition to public works looked as if it was 'tinged with fanaticism'.

Samuelson (1996, 149–50, 154–5) may have witnessed part of this transformation during his undergraduate years at Chicago (1932–5). He was taught undergraduate monetary economics by Mints using Robertson's *Money* and another text from which he 'was taught MV=PQ'. When, in 1935, he was considering whether to go to Harvard graduate school he was 'warned by Lloyd Mints that Seymour Harris in macroeconomics was an inflationist ... Mints must have had some keen sense of smell, because after Harris did get tenure he became a flaming Keynesian'.[24]

But in Chicago, Keynes (1931a, 16–17, 27, 35, 40) explained that a 'secure basis for a return to an equilibrium of prosperity' could only be achieved by increasing volume of investment and allowing a revival of the price level. Keynes suggested that interest rates needed to be reduced via an increase in 'the quantity of liquid assets' through open market operations which 'involves technical questions of some difficulty with which I must not burden this lecture'. Keynes explained that he was limited by 'the medium of oral exposition' adding that 'Those who may wish to pursue the matter further I must refer to my *Treatise on Money*'. There is common agreement that in June 1931, Keynes essentially repeated the analysis contained in the *Treatise* (Patinkin, 1976, 68; Moggridge, 1992, 518; Skidelsky, 1992, 391; Dimand, 1988, 143–4; Klein, 1950b, 35).

Lorie Tarshis (1996, 55) recalled that on 10 October 1932, Keynes arrived for the first lecture of a course that had been scheduled as 'The Theory of Money and Prices'; but announced that the lecture series had a new title: 'The Monetary Theory of Production', a change that Keynes declared was 'significant'. Tarshis reflected that this was 'the opening bugle of the Keynesian revolution'. In October 1932, before the modern configuration had fully emerged, Friedman scribbled on his 330 bibliography: 'Look up Keynes' lectures for Harris Foundation on reserve at E11 under Q. Wright's name'. Friedman, like other attentive 330 graduate students, presumably wrote these words in at Mints' suggestion.

6. 1932–3: Mints and Friedman

6.1 Economics 330 Course Outline

There are in effect two relevant Economics 330 bibliographies in the Friedman archives.[25] The first is the version that Mints presumably circulated in the first class of the course and the second is the version that Mints actually used for the course (which consists of the first version plus Friedman's handwritten additions).

The only two items in the first bibliography that are added to in the second relate to Irving Fisher's *Purchasing Power of Money* and Keynes' *Treatise*. With respect to the first, Friedman (to Patinkin, 19 July 1972) recalled 'that Mints paid a great deal of attention to Irving Fisher's work and in particular to the book on the *Purchasing Power of Money* in the monetary course that I remember taking from him. Certainly I recall when I left Chicago after being a graduate student there in the period from 1932 to 1935, I left with a definite opinion that Fisher was one of the great men of the time and one of the great contributors to monetary analysis. Perhaps I got that somewhere else, but I think I got it in large measure from Mints' course'.[26] Since Mints informed Patinkin (1981, 285) that 'I have always had the greatest respect for Irving Fisher' Friedman's recollection appears to be justified.

Amongst the nineteen items on the second section of the first bibliography were 'Fisher, Purchasing Power of Money, chs. 2–5' which Friedman corrected by hand to read '2–5 + 8'. Chapters 2 to 5 largely outlined the equation of exchange. The purpose of chapter 8 ('Influence of quantity of money and other factors on purchasing power and on each other') was 'to set forth the causes determining the purchasing power of money ... It is proposed in this chapter to inquire how far these propositions are really *causal* propositions' [Fisher's emphasis]. The chapter concluded that 'we find nothing to interfere with the truth of the quantity theory that variations in money (M) produce normally proportional changes in prices' (Fisher, 1922 [1911], 149, 151, 183).[27]

Patinkin (Vol. 1, pp. 87–120 [1969/1981], 91, 96) concluded that the Chicago quantity theory was 'first and foremost, not a theory of the demand for money, but a theory which relates the quantity of money (M) to the aggregate demand for goods and services (MV), and thence to the price level (P) and/or level of output (T); all this in accordance with Fisher's MV=PT'. According to Patinkin's notes from Mints' 1944 lectures: 'Mints prefers following statement of quantity theory: P is the dependent variable (in the long-run) of the equation MV=PT. But in the short run all variables tend to move together'.

At one level, the structure of the 1932 version of 330 appears to support Patinkin's account. According to the course outline there were three sections. The first section was devoted to 'The functions of money and banking (a) the origins of money; (b) the functions of money (c) the functions of banking'; the second to 'Statement of theories concerning the relation of money and banking to the price level'; and the third to 'Appraisal of these theories by means of (a) logical analysis; (b) examination of the process of changes in the price level'.

At a deeper level, the evidence supports Friedman's memory. In the first bibliography there are two entries for 'Keynes, Monetary Reform': the first under section II, 'Statement of theories concerning the relation of money and banking to the price level' ('pages 81–95') and the second under 'Some general references on the theory of international prices' ('pp. 95–116'). Both entries come from chapter 3 ('The theory of money and of the foreign exchanges').

Keynes had been teaching the material contained in chapter 3 of the *Tract on Monetary Reform* at Cambridge since 1911 (Skidelsky, 1992, 153; 1983, 214–21; Moggridge, 1992, 197–200). In that year, Keynes (JMK, 1983, 11 [1911], 375–6) in his review of Fisher's *Purchasing Power of Money* stated that 'the theory of money, as it has ordinarily been understood and taught by academic economists in England for some time past, is considerably in advance of any published account of it. It is hardly an exaggeration to say that monetary theory, in its most accurate form, has become in England a matter of oral tradition. These preliminary remarks are necessary in order to explain that it is from the standpoint of this oral tradition, rather than from that of any printed book, that an English economist must approach Professor Fisher's very important contribution to the subject'.

Chapter 3 of *Monetary Reform* began with the statement that 'The quantity theory of money ... is fundamental. Its correspondence with fact is not open to question'. Keynes (1923, 74, 84–6, 95–116) explained that the supply of money was 'under the direct control (or ought to be) of the central banking authorities' but that the public's holding of cash and deposits was 'not directly controllable, and depends on the mood of the public and the business world'. Keynes then argued that 'Cyclical fluctuations' were characterised primarily by changes in the latter and not the former. Stabilising the price level, Keynes argued, required the authorities to vary the money supply so as to 'counterbalance' the movements of money demand.

6.2 Friedman's Readings, 330 Lecture Notes and Examination Paper

At the end of the course, Mints required his students to answer four examination questions from a total of five. The first two were invitations to critically examine statements made by Friedrich Hayek and Ralph Hawtrey (the second relating to Irving Fisher's equation of exchange). The third was an invitation to examine the *ceteris paribus* assumption of the quantity theory. Question 4a was: 'Discuss the relation between the k of Keynes' earlier equation and the velocity of circulation'. 4b was 'Discuss the statement that changes in the velocity of circulation of goods cannot bring about changes in the price level because of the fact that they necessarily bring about compensating changes in the velocity of circulation of money'. Question 5 was 'According to Keynes' analysis what would it be necessary to do in order to eliminate the business cycle? State and support your opinion of Keynes' conclusion'.

Milton and Rose Friedman both took this examination, which was scheduled immediately following Viner's examination. Rose Friedman recalled that Viner was 'an extreme disciplinarian in the classroom. Some students found the course forbidding and lived in fear of the man and of his subject. I found the course stimulating but the man forbidding, in part because of the tales I had heard as an undergraduate about how tough he was. The gossip was that he failed at least a third of the class every year'. Because her brother, Aaron Director, was on the faculty she 'was nervous about embarrassing him by not making the grade ... I was so nervous at the end of Viner's exam that I could not read the questions in Mints's exam'. When Mints saw her paralysed in his examination room 'he came over and asked what was wrong. I explained my problem. In a very fatherly way, he said, "Just relax for a few minutes and you'll be fine". But that didn't happen. When Mints came around a second time when I was in no better mental condition, his answer was, "You can write a paper on Keynes's *Treatise on Money* instead"' (Friedman and Friedman, 1998, 35, 38). This could only be interpreted as an act of kindness if the *Treatise* was such a prominent component of the course as to be easily accessible even to a student suffering from Viner-paralysis.

Not only were the last required words of the course about Keynes, but also the first words that Friedman wrote in his notes were 'Econ 330 Keynes'. Mints concluded that: 'General Framework of Keynes likely to endure much longer than details. 1. Equality of Investment + Savings. Is this idea something entirely new? Mints says no'. The evidence suggests that in autumn 1932 Mints allocated more attention to the *Treatise* than he had intended to. The *Treatise* appeared as item 18 in the original bibliography under section II with the required readings listed as 'Vol I, chs. 9–12 and 14'. Friedman underlined the whole of item 18 and crossed out the original chapters and replaced the entry with 'chs. 9–19'. Under section IIIa. Friedman added 'Keynes Treatise vol I Pages 53–120 (part. 53–88), also 221–239'. Friedman initially took thirty pages of notes from Chapters 9–19 of the *Treatise*, and then took an additional fifty-one pages of detailed notes from Volume one and six pages of notes from Volume two.

Chapter 19 of the *Treatise* began with the observation that 'The experience of the postwar period led many of us to advocate stability of the price level as the best possible objective of practical policy. Amongst other things, this would mean an attempt on the part of the banking authorities to eliminate the credit cycle at all costs'. Chapter 10 ('The Fundamental

Equations for the Value of Money') began with the observation that 'The Fundamental Problem of Monetary Theory is ... to treat the problem dynamically, analysing the different elements involved, in such a manner as to exhibit the causal process by which the price level is determined, and a method of transition from one period of equilibrium to another. The forms of the Quantity Theory, however, on which we have all been brought up – I shall give an account of them in detail in Chapter 14 – are but ill adapted for this purpose' (Keynes, 1930, 133, 293).

Chapter 14 was devoted to 'Alternative Forms of the Fundamental Equation'. Section 1, outlining 'The 'Real Balances' Quantity Equation', almost perfectly captured Friedman's (Vol. 1, pp. 33–51 [1956], 33–4) description of the Chicago oral tradition in which it was vitally important to explain 'why people are willing to hold the particular nominal quantity of money in existence ... The quantity theory is in the first instance a theory of the demand for money'. In section 2 of Chapter 14 ('The "Cambridge" Quantity Equation'), Keynes (1930, 229) explained that he was doing little more than capturing a Cambridge oral tradition: 'The "Real-balances" Equation discussed above is descended from a method of approach long familiar to those who have heard Professors Marshall and Pigou in the lecture-rooms of Cambridge'.[28] It appears that Chapter 14 made a special impression on Friedman. Under his notes entitled '1. "Real-Balances" Quantity Equation' Friedman provided what appears to be the only cross-reference in these fifty-seven pages: '[see notes on Monetary Reform]'.

Keynes (1924, 336) explained that Alfred Marshall's 'main ideas became known to pupils in a general way, with the result that there grew up at Cambridge an oral tradition, first from Marshall's own lectures and since his retirement from those of Professor Pigou, different from, and (I think it may be claimed) superior to, anything that could be found in printed books until recently'. Keynes then added a footnote: 'Professor Irving Fisher being the first, in several instances, to publish in book-form ideas analogous to those which had been worked out by Marshall at much earlier dates'.

Keynes (1924, 338) summarised the Marshallian approach to money as reflected in *Money Credit and Commerce*: 'Marshall also expounded long ago the way in which distrust of a currency raises prices by diminishing the willingness of the public to hold stocks of it – a phenomenon to which recent events have now called everyone's attention; and he was aware that the fluctuation in the price level, which is an accompaniment of the trade cycle, corresponds to a fluctuation in the volume of "ready command" which the public desire to hold'. After 'ready command' Keynes added a footnote: 'This is Marshall's phrase for what I have called "real balances"'.

In 1932, Mints required his 330 students to read Marshall's *Money Credit and Commerce* and Friedman took two pages of notes from Chapter IV, 'Total Value of the Currency Needed by a Country'. Friedman wrote: 'Function of Currency. A. Money demand not for own sake but its possession gives ready command of general purchasing power in a convenient form ... Total value of a country's currency, multiplied into the average no. of times of its changing hands for business purposes each year, is of course = to the total amount of business transacted in that country by direct payment of currency in that year. But this identity statement does not indicate the causes that govern the rapidity of circulation of currency: to discover that we must look to amount of purchasing power which the people of that country elect to keep in form of currency'.

In his 330 bibliography, Friedman wrote 'read' underlined four times alongside 'Hansen Business Cycle Theory, chs. 1 and 6' and took thirty pages of notes from the book. Hansen (1927, iv, 3, 7) explained that his purpose was to enable the student 'to cut a path through the tangled mass of apparently contradictory explanations of the business cycle'. In Chapter 1 ('A Classification of Business Cycle Theories') Hansen identified 'three broad type of business cycle theories'. The first two types believed that the business cycle was a 'function of the capitalist economy'; the first seeking remedies through redistributing income in a more egalitarian fashion; the second focusing attention on the inherent nature of technology. The third type of explanation saw the business cycle as 'a function of the money economy'.

In Chapter 6 ('The Money Economy as a Cause of the Business Cycle'), Hansen (1927, 139, 143–4) explained that Ralph Hawtrey's 'theory of the business cycle may be said to be the culmination of the line of analysis which we have been tracing'. The central element of this type of theory was that 'It is the *flow* [Hansen's emphasis] of purchasing power that is important, not the outstanding aggregate of money units. The "unspent margin" in terms of money units, is made up of the money in circulation and the bank credit outstanding ... Hawtrey's "command over wealth which the people hold in reserve" appears to be similar to J. M. Keynes's 'volume of real balances ... [which] may fluctuate violently even though there is little change in the volume of cash or in the reserve policy of the banks'. Hansen (1927, 144) proposed that this Hawtrey–Keynes type of theory be called 'deflations and inflations of real balances'.

In 1932, Mints also prescribed 'Pigou, The Value of Money, in the Quarterly Journal of Economics for 1917–18, pp. 38–65'. Two decades later Mints co-edited an AEA volume of *Readings in Monetary Theory* in which Pigou's essay was reprinted (Lutz and Mints, 1952). In the 1950s Friedman presumably had an opportunity to reread Pigou's article since he recommended the Lutz–Mints volume to his students (Hammond, 1999). Pigou (1952 [1917–8], 163, 173–4, 183) explained that he was 'not in any sense an "opponent" of the quantity theory or a hostile critic of Professor Fisher's lucid analysis'. But to 'tackle' the problems associated with the value of money 'without tools is like going into a modern battle unhelmeted and unarmed. The "quantity theory" furnishes a tool which in the skilled hands of Professor Irving Fisher has accomplished great things. But less experienced craftsmen need, I think, a better – a more completely fool-proof tool. It is this that, in the preceding pages, I have endeavoured to provide'.

The bulk of Pigou's article was devoted to the demand for money, its supply and the interaction between the two. Having derived 'the demand schedule for money ... the dry bones of my equation of demand' Pigou explained that 'it remains to explain the relation in which that equation stands to the "equation of exchange" made familiar in the "quantity theory" – an equation, by the way, which would itself be more properly described as an equation of demand'. Pigou claimed that the money demand formulation of the quantity theory was 'a somewhat more effective engine of analysis ... I offer this specification of it in order that those interested in monetary theory may test its powers in actual work upon concrete problems'.

In 1932, Mints also prescribed 'Robertson, Money, revised edition, chs. 2, 3 and 4'. Two-thirds of a century later it remained, in Friedman's judgement, 'one of the most lucid and profound presentations of the central principles of monetary theory' (Friedman and Friedman, 1998, 247). In contrast, Samuelson (1996, 148–9) used Robertson's *Money* to support Patinkin's assault on Friedman.[29] However, in Chapter 2 on 'The Value of Money' Robertson (1928, 30, 37, 39) explained that he was describing 'the underlying psychological forces determining the value of money ... *given the conditions of demand for money*, its value depends on the quantity of it available'. The 'truth' of the matter was that 'in estimating the demand for money we must take into account not only the volume of goods to be disposed of within a given time, but also the frequency with which each of them changes hands ... the magnitude of the demand for money, like that of the demand for bread, turns out to be the result of a process of individual weighing-up of competing advantages *at the margin*' [Robertson's emphases].[30]

Patinkin's (Vol. 1, pp. 87–120 [1969/1981], 101) 'main point' was that Friedman (Vol. 1, pp. 33–51 [1956]) presented 'an elegant and sophisticated statement of modern Keynesian theory ... whose analytical structure as it now exists stems from the publication during the 1930s of Keynes' *Treatise on Money* (vol 1, pp. 140–46)' plus John Hicks (1935, 13–32) and Keynes (1936, 166–72, 22–9). But years before the *General Theory*, Keynes (1924, 337) stressed that this marginal portfolio analysis of an individual's demand for money was part of the Marshallian heritage. Hicks (1935, 3) also emphasised that in the *Treatise*, Keynes had 'put substance' into the analysis of 'choice at the margin ... by his doctrine that the relative preference depends upon the "bearishness" or "bullishness" of the public, upon their relative desire for liquidity or profit'. This was 'the most important part of his theoretical contribution'.

Thus Patinkin (Vol. 1, pp. 87–120 [1969/1981], 88, 101) argued that Friedman's (Vol. 1, pp. 33–51 [1956]) supposed 'reformulation' of the quantity theory was 'a misleading designation' because 'what Friedman has actually presented is an elegant exposition of the modern portfolio approach to the demand for money which, though it has some well-known (albeit largely undeveloped) antecedents in the traditional theory, can only be seen as a continuation of the Keynesian theory of liquidity preference'. Friedman (Vol. 1, pp. 33–51 [1956]) was 'in direct continuation of this intellectual line of descent'. Yet Patinkin included the *Treatise* in this lineage.

6.3 Reviews of the Treatise

On the back of his 330 bibliography Friedman wrote a list of reviews of the *Treatise* which included the Keynes–Robertson and Keynes–Hayek exchanges, plus reviews from Pigou, Hawtrey, Williams, Josiah Stamp and Charles Hardy. Mints recalled that in the 1930s, he, Simons, Knight and probably Director met weekly at Hardy's home. Samuel Nerlove observed that Hardy exerted an 'exceedingly significant' influence on both Mints and Simons, having taught the latter (cited by Patinkin, 1981, 284–5). Homer Jones (9 October 1962) wrote to Margaret Porter that during his time at Chicago in 1933–4 'Hardy's book on the Federal Reserve System was regarded as the best critique of the policies and actions of that central bank'. Hardy was also an early critic of the New Deal, which he described as an attempt to 'substitute centralised authority of one sort or another for what is left of free competitive enterprise' (cited by Saunders, 1966, 54). These libertarian credentials were later reflected in Hardy's appointment as the founding treasurer of the Mont Pelerin Society (Hartwell 1995, 45). Friedman (Vol. 1, pp. 147–66 [1972/1974], 153, n. 19) appears to be justified in describing Hardy as a Chicagoan 'at one remove'.

In the first part of his review, Hardy (1931a, 150–2) predicted that Keynes' work would be the most influential book published since the war and would 'profoundly' modify the 'serious work of the next generation on business cycles, central banking, and international finance'. In the second part, Hardy (1931b, 394) argued that Keynes' analysis should be 'supplemented by Professor Fisher's well-known theory as to the relation between the rate of interest and the anticipated depreciation or appreciation in the value of money ... Keynes' rejection of Fisher's doctrine on this point (II, 202) reflects such a complete and obvious misunderstanding of the whole point that they can hardly be other than a *lapsus calami*'.

Robertson's (1931, 409–10) review was highly critical of several aspects of the *Treatise*. But he also concluded that 'I have no doubt that Mr Keynes is right in laying stress on hoarding as a dominant feature of trade depression. In this respect I feel sure his work is of high significance ... Where I suspect there is still work to be done is in clearing up the nature of the forces which lead the spirit of hoarding down'. Keynes (1930, 138) had previously explained that his fundamental equations 'resemble all other versions of the Quantity Theory'. In his reply to Robertson, Keynes (1931b, 419) made it clear that he was moving still further in the direction of focusing on the demand for money within this quantity theory framework: 'I should like to repeat that the amount of the hoards of the public is as much outside their control as is the quantity of money, and for the same reasons ... This is why it is so important to distinguish the forces determining the quantity of hoards (which is the affair of the banker) from the forces determining the propensity to hoard (which is the affair of the public). The old quantity equations did not reveal this to me ...'.

The first part of Hayek's review provoked Keynes (JMK, XIII [1931], 243–66) both privately and publicly. As Patinkin (1976, 58) pointed out 'as a result of these foregoing criticisms' Keynes was jolted further down the path to the *General Theory*. But Hayek (1932, 34–5) made clear in the second part of his review that Keynes' discussion of hoarding was 'the most interesting aspect of his theoretical analysis ... there is no doubt that he is here breaking new ground and that he is opening up new vistas ... the practical importance of this phenomenon is much greater than most economists used to suppose'.

Friedman found at Chicago a 'vibrant intellectual atmosphere of a kind that I had never dreamed existed' (Friedman and Friedman, 1998, 35).

The excitement associated with his monetary education must have been intensified both by spatial proximity to the Great Depression and by temporal proximity to these debates: the second part of Hayek's review was published February 1932, eight months before the start of Economics 330.[31]

7. 1968–74: Friedman's Defence

Patinkin and Stanley Fischer worked on 'The Chicago Tradition, the Quantity Theory, and Friedman' in the year following Friedman's AEA presidential address. Upon receiving a draft from Patinkin, Friedman (5 December 1968) replied that: 'I continue to regard what I wrote as a reformulation of the quantity theory of money, just as I continue to regard Keynes' Monetary Reform, and large parts of his Treatise, and some parts of his Gen. Theory, as the writings of a quantity theorist ... I would argue that much of K's analysis of liquidity preference is a carry-over from his earlier quantity theory orientation and only the absolute liquidity preference element as truly Keynesian'.[32]

Friedman offered the same defence at a social gathering on 16 March 1971, attended by Homer Jones, Gary Becker, David Meiselman, Robert Gordon and Fischer. That night Fischer wrote to Patinkin describing what had transpired: 'The major points which Milton made is that there is nothing particularly Keynesian about the liquidity preference function, and that the demand for money sections of the *General Theory* are simply a slightly inferior version of Keynes' views in the *Tract*. In response to arguments that the interest rate and rate of inflation were to be found as arguments in the velocity function only in Lavington and Pigou (or most explicitly in those two authors) he pulled the *Tract* off the shelves and with the aid of Gary Becker found some parts under the chapter on "Inflation as a Tax" which were quite suggestive. Anyway, Milton argues that there is nothing inconsistent in having a demand-for-money function similar to that of the *General Theory* and being a quantity theorist, quoting as evidence Keynes of the *Tract* who claimed that there was no disputing the quantity theory'.[33]

Friedman (Vol. 1, pp. 147–66 [1972/1974], 160) subsequently cited the chapter on 'Inflation as a Method of Taxation' in his response to Patinkin. In correspondence, Friedman (5 December 1968) told Patinkin that 'I find your description of the oral tradition entirely acceptable and much better and more comprehensive than mine. In extenuation, I can only say that the 1956 essay did not set out to be an essay in history of thought but an introduction to a collection of studies. Unquestionably, however, had I had your paper before me when I wrote that paper, I would have written the first part of it differently'.[34] Fischer (16 March 1971) reported to Patinkin that Friedman 'said that there was only one thing to which he seriously objected – and that was the implication that he had made up the "Chicago tradition (oral)" out of whole cloth'.[35] Fischer continued: 'When pressed on the point of the instability of velocity emphasised in Simons and Mints, Milton agreed to Simons, but was more hesitant about Mints. Both Becker and Meiselman said that Mints of the early 50's did not believe that velocity was unstable, and Homer Jones said that Mints of the late 20's also emphasises the stability of velocity ... Milton was fairly careful: he seemed to argue that the only statements about the oral tradition which are to be taken seriously are those at the beginning of the article, before he begins to number points. Thus he would say that the oral tradition essentially was the approach that money matters, and little more'.[36]

Friedman (1912–) was only a decade older than Patinkin (1922–95); but when the 1972 *JPE* symposium appeared (Gordon 1974), four decades had elapsed since he attended Mints' Economics 330. In contrast, Patinkin was in his mid-forties when he became so agitated by what he perceived to be the conflict between his own memory and Friedman's introductory essay. He was in his mid-thirties when he first noted and commented (in correspondence and in conversation) on the discrepancy. As a younger man in his prime, Patinkin had great confidence in the accuracy of his own recollections and stated that Friedman's account 'strikes no response chord in my memory' (Patinkin, Vol. 1, pp. 87–120 [1969/1981], 88). Friedman (to Patinkin, 5 December 1968) was left wondering whether 'I can trust my retrospective memory'.[37]

Perhaps Friedman was taken aback by the vehemence of the attack by someone he regarded as a friend. In addition, Patinkin was an historian of economic thought; Friedman was not. Indeed, Friedman (12 July 1951) described himself to Lionel Robbins as 'a tyro in the history of thought'.[38] Besides, the *JPE symposium was A Debate with His Critics* (plural). Fischer (16 March 1971) reported to Patinkin that Friedman indulged in 'some minor grumbling about not having the time to be involved in polemics'.[39] This may explain why he did not examine his 330 lecture notes or course outline. More importantly, in the early 1970s Friedman was entering his period of peak influence: 'The Transition from Fixed Exchange Rates to Money Supply Targets' (Parkin, 1977).

8. Concluding Remarks

Memory, as Friedman has acknowledged, is not an entirely reliable source of historical information (Friedman and Friedman, 1998, 112, 115, 123). Patinkin (1976, 64) was also justified in concluding that 'an author is not necessarily the best authority on the history of the development of his own work; and by definition he certainly is not an *objective* authority' [Patinkin's emphasis]. However, the archival material clearly indicates that Friedman's account of the oral tradition contains a large kernel of truth with respect to Mints in 1932, even though he *may* have exaggerated the extent of this tradition by invoking the names of Knight, Simons and Viner.

Patinkin (1977, 125) regarded the history of economic thought as an 'empirical science' and suggested that a 'regression line' approach was warranted. But when Martin Bronfenbrenner disagreed with his evaluation of Simons' influence, Patinkin (Vol. 1, pp. 87–120 [1969/1981], 92) noted that 'Bronfenbrenner's recollections refer to the period 1934–36 whereas mine are for 1941–46' adding 'I am not sure it is relevant'. It was a reasonable first approximation for Patinkin to extrapolate backwards from 1944, although the presence of a structural break in 1936 rendered his extrapolation unreliable. It was, in any case, an inadequate substitute for an examination of the 1932 archival material.

Friedman (correspondence to the author, 29 October 1999) regards 'the fuss over the Chicago oral tradition' as 'much ado about very little' which has produced a lot of 'wasted paper'. But as Stigler (1988, 153–4) pointed out (in a brief reference to the dispute over the oral tradition) Friedman was 'quite talented in outraging his intellectual opponents'. Moreover, Friedman used the quantity theory 'as a powerful weapon to attack the Keynesian theory'. Viner (pp. 399–430 [1936/1964], 403–4) noted that Keynes had identified liquidity preference as a 'source of trouble' for the economy; Friedman identified (apparently) stable money demand functions as a major source of trouble for Keynesians.

Keynes (1922, vi) edited a series of books written by those who perceived themselves to be 'orthodox members of the Cambridge School of Economics'. Robertson (1922, viii), the author of the handbook on *Money*, defended Keynes' (JMK, 11 [1911], 375–6) assertion about the 'oral tradition' as 'an almost pardonable exaggeration'. Patinkin was not inclined to be so tolerant towards Friedman.[40] To Patinkin it was as if Moses had presented a 'Restatement' that perverted the wisdom transmitted to him on Mount Sinai. The intensity of the resulting controversy can only be adequately explained by reference to the passions engendered by the modern configuration of economics.

Both sides of the Keynesian–monetarist debate claimed that the evidence supported their conclusions in 'a strikingly one-sided way' (Friedman, 1963, 8; Desai, 1981, 203). However, Patinkin performed a great service by undertaking such a one-sided historical examination. Had he been more dispassionate, and not played the role of 'economist-as-matador' the dispute may never taken place and we would presumably know a lot less about the evolution of monetary thought than we do today. Hence the dispute over the oral tradition illustrates the pervasiveness of the principle of unintended consequences. Patinkin, like Friedman, was 'led by an invisible hand to promote an end that was no part of his intention'.

Notes

[1] Friedman's lecture notes are currently in his possession and have not been processed into his archives at the Hoover Institution.

[2] Stanley Fischer, his research assistant, wrote a memorandum for Patinkin in spring 1968 stating that 'I've found no explicit mention of the demand for money' in Simons' writings. Don Patinkin Papers, Box 2.

[3] Don Patinkin Papers, Box 41.

[4] Don Patinkin Papers, Box 2.

[5] Don Patinkin Papers, Box 3.

[6] Don Patinkin Papers, Box 32.

[7] Kahn (15 January 1933) wrote to Joan Robinson from Chicago: 'The two Commonwealth students are a terrific godsend to me. Boulding of Oxford is a nice, unkempt kind of youth, and is regarded as good, particularly by Knight'. Richard Kahn Papers, RFK/13/90/1/44–51.

[8] From the 1930s to at least the 1950s, Dennis Robertson examined Cambridge undergraduates with questions about the relationship between the *Treatise* and the quantity theory (Johnson, 1975, 114).

[9] Gary Becker (1991, 144) recalled that as an Assistant Professor, he spent half his time assisting Friedman in running the workshop; which involved he and Friedman searching second hand stores for used Marchant and Monroe calculating machines for graduate students to use.

[10] 'Being a student of Milton's was magic indeed. People would always ask me, Why are you so excited? Are you going out on a date with a beautiful woman? I said, no, I'm going to a class in economics' (Becker, 1998).

[11] One of the contributors to *Studies in the Quantity Theory of Money* criticised Gardiner Ackley's analysis of inflation and the theory of administered pricing. At the 'heart' of Selden's (1959b, 455–6) criticism was that Ackley had failed to embed his discussion within 'the framework of generally accepted macro-tautologies'. Selden, one of the self-confessed 'reactionaries', corrected Ackley's supposed error by analysing the issue through the quantity theory. This revealed that the traditional theory of inflation was 'alive and kicking'.

[12] Richard Kahn Papers, RFK/13/90/1/44–51.

[13] Viner also advised the CEA about post war counter cyclical fiscal stabilisation (Strayer, 1950, 837, n. 14).

[14] One Mt Pelerin supporter, citing Viner, described the 'Anachronism of the Liquidity Preference Concept' (Hahn, 1947, 204, n. 3).

[15] In 'Theory of the Firm and of Investment' Hurwicz (1946, 131–2) stated that Knight's *Risk Uncertainty and Profit* had 'served to give a more realistic theory of the demand for cash, inventories and the like'.

[16] Don Patinkin's Papers: http://scriptorium.lib.duke.edu/economists/patinkin.

[17] Cagan (13 April 1955) had highlighted an elementary error in Patinkin's reasoning about the relationship between prices and money during hyperinflation. Patinkin (16 May 1955) informed Cagan that he 'felt hopelessly stupid … All this makes me now feel that I am missing the main point of your study. Maybe I'll just have to wait to read it in its entirety when it is published'. Don Patinkin Papers, Box 25.

[18] In his discussion of real balances, Patinkin (1952, 269–70) raised 'the interesting question of how this set of forces, [emphasised by Haberler and Pigou] could have been overlooked by Keynesian economists, in general, and Keynes himself, in particular. Questions of this type can rarely be answered satisfactorily – and perhaps should not even be asked. Nevertheless, I think it is both possible and instructive to trace through the exact chain of errors in Keynes's reasoning which caused him to overlook these factors'. Keynes' 'fundamental error' related to the relationship between real cash balances and consumption. Keynes erred by concentrating 'exclusively' on the tendency of real cash balances 'to lower interest rates' through the liquidity function. Patinkin then added a footnote: 'the following passage [from the *General Theory*] is especially interesting: 'It is, therefore, on the effect of a falling wage- and price-level on the *demand for money* [Patinkin's emphasis] that those who believe in self-adjusting quality of the economic system must rest the weight of their argument; though I am not aware that they had done so''. Patinkin concluded that 'looking back on the nature of these errors, we cannot but be struck by the irony that they should have emanated from the man who did most to demonstrate the fundamental inseparability of the real and monetary sectors of our economy'.

[19] On 19 April 1937, he wrote to Roy Harrod explaining that his review had stopped a long way short of expressing his real anger (Besomi forthcoming).

[20] Eprime Eshag in his thesis on *From Marshall to Keynes an Essay on the Monetary Theory of the Cambridge School* noted that 'Keynes' propositions on incentives to liquidity were largely obtained from Marshall's analysis of the demand for money' (1963, 65; see also Bigg, 1990, 99; Bridel, 1987, 28, 130). Patinkin (pp. 317–44 [1974], 334, n. 17) disagreed with Eshag's conclusions. Joan Robinson (1933, 77) complained that the 'simple minded reader [of the *Treatise*] finds that the Quantity Theory has led him to concentrate too much on Demand'. George Shackle (1967, 215, 209) concluded that the *Treatise* provided 'a better account of liquidity preference, because more impregnated with the feel of markets and their constant tip-toe alertness to every breath of suggestion, than is to be found in the *General Theory*'. In Shackle's judgement, the Treatise was 'in large part, an analysis of the economy's total need for a stock of money into various sources of demand'.

[21] On 14 November 1932, Keynes delivered a section of a lecture headed 'Parameters of the Money Economy'. In notes taken from these lectures, Robert Bryce recorded: 'Quantity [Theory] of Money [has] these [three] 3 fundamental factors – of market and psychology and attitude to[wards] future liquidity preference, expectation of quasi-rent – and state of time preference'. From Keynes' lecture on 4 December 1933, Lorie Tarshis recorded: '"liquidity preference" – really the demand for money – the way of summing up the eagerness of people to hold their wealth in money rather than other forms ... Motives for holding money, as in Treatise ... We now have the essential determinants of the rate of interest – A (L [iquidity] Pref[erence]) – W (State of News) – M (Quantity of Money) ... This is Keynes 'quantity equation' ... Keynes thinks it best to relate M to [the rate of interest]' (Rymes, 1985, A39, J33, J36).

[22] Pribram (1931, 62) also referred to Fisher's (1926) 'very interesting' 'Philips curve'.

[23] Keynes may also have been stimulated by the assertion that 'there is and can be no economic Einstein' and by the statement that the 'the pure doctrine of laissez-faire had gone and we could no longer think in the abstract terms of Ricardo' (Phelan, 1931, 155, 191). As he was pondering how to maximise the influence of the work that would, from late 1933, be called *The General Theory* (second draft table of contents), he met Albert Einstein, the author of another theory with a similar name and a similar claim: 'The old theory is a special limiting case of the new one' (Einstein, cited by Clark, 1984, 257). Keynes had used the Einstein analogy before (JMK, IX [1929], 91), and was aware of the rhetorical possibilities of presenting his revolution as the social science equivalent of the revolution that had conquered the physical sciences in the inter-war period: 'The classical economists resemble Euclidean geometers in a non-Euclidean world ... the postulates of classical theory are applicable to a special case only and not to the general case, the situation which it assumes being a limiting point of the possible positions of equilibrium ... We are thus led to a more general theory which includes the classical theory with which we are familiar, as a special case' (1936, vii, 3, 16).

[24] Currie (5 August 1971) explained to Alan Sweezy that his career had been blocked at Harvard by Harold Burbank, Gottfried Haberler and Harris who 'didn't get on the [Keynesian] bandwagon until it was perfectly safe to do so and he had his position secured at Harvard'. Lauchlin Currie Papers, Correspondence, Alan Sweezy file. Tavlas (pp. 175–99 [1997], 192, n. 10) recounts that Harris (whose surname was Cohen before he changed it) was the only Jewish member of the Harvard Economics department of the 1920s who received tenure.

[25] There is a third 330 bibliography which obviously relates to a later version of the course. Milton Friedman Papers, Box 5.

[26] Don Patinkin Papers, Box 32.

[27] In the third bibliography the entry reads 'Fisher, Purchasing Power of Money, chapters 1–6 and 8'. Thus it seems likely that Fisher figured slightly more prominently in the course from autumn 1932 onwards. Milton Friedman Papers, Box 5.

[28] The remaining sections of Chapter 14 discussed the Fisher quantity equation and its relationship with the Cambridge quantity equation.

[29] Samuelson (1996, 148–9) stated: 'it's not true, I'll say categorically, what Milton Friedman at one time tried to sell: that there was a very subtle Chicago oral tradition on the demand for money and monetary theory. Read Robertson's handbook on *Money*, and you will have plumbed the depths of Chicago's monetary sophistication'.

[30] Robertson (1928, 17) prefaced this chapter with the same words from Humpty Dumpty that Patinkin (Vol. 1, pp. 123–43 [1972/1974], 123) later used as the preface to his assault on Friedman (When *I* use a word ... it means just what I choose it to mean').

[31] On Roosevelt's inauguration day, 4 March 1933, thirty-eight states had closed their banks and, for the first time since 1848, the Chicago Board of Trade shut its doors (Leuchtenberg, 1963, 39). Re-establishing confidence in the money supply and the banking system was Roosevelt's first priority. Friedman recalled that the collapse of the monetary system and the associated calamities 'did not pass unnoticed in the Economics Department' (Friedman and Friedman, 1998, 40). In April 1933, Knight (1933, 244) wrote in the *JPE* that 'the devil in person could not have invented a device more obviously "intended" than is commercial banking to increase the amplitude of any incipient swing by an indefinite multiple'.

[32] Don Patinkin Papers, Box 2.

[33] Don Patinkin Papers, Box 32.

[34] Don Patinkin Papers, Box 32.

[35] Don Patinkin Papers, Box 2.

[36] Don Patinkin Papers, Box 2.

[37] Don Patinkin Papers, Box 32.

[38] Friedman Papers, Correspondence, Robbins file.

[39] Don Patinkin Papers, Box 2. Perhaps Friedman was growing weary of his opponents. On 30 December 1970, the *New York Times* reported that Johnson's Ely Lecture was an indication that Friedman's influence over policy was waning (Silk 1970). In March 1971, Friedman had apparently just heard that Johnson's Lecture (Vol. 1, pp. 169–82 [1971]) was to be published in both *Encounter* and the *American Economic Association Papers and Proceedings*. The previous month, Murray Rothbard (1971, 3, 4) described Friedman as the 'Establishment's Court Libertarian ... In many ways we have Milton Friedman to thank for the present monster Leviathan State in America'.

[40] There are some similarities between Robertson's relationship with Keynes before and after the writing of the *General Theory*, and Patinkin's relationship with Friedman before and after 1956 (although Patinkin had never been Friedman's student or long term colleague). Patinkin (1980, 10) referred to the Keynes–Robertson 'vendetta' as 'an originally close relationship steadily deteriorating over the years into repeated disagreements, inability to communicate, and mutual distrust – all exacerbated by deep emotional forces whose nature it is not for economists as such to analyse' (see also Blaug, 1986, 205; Danes, 1987, 210). Earlier, Patinkin (1958, 316–17) in his rather contemptuous account of the revival of the liquidity preference-loanable funds dispute had referred to the 'psychology of intellectual processes'. In his History of Thought course at the University of Western Ontario, Patinkin complained, or at least noted, that 'economists seem to have some deep need to use terms like "classical", "neoclassi-

cal", "Marxian", "Keynesian"'. He also stated that 'tracing development of thought – how the mind works – history of ideas' was a 'Useless subject – you've been warned'. Don Patinkin Papers, Box 20 (see also Backhouse, 2002).

BIBLIOGRAPHY

Backhouse, R., 'Don Patinkin – Interpreter of the Keynesian Revolution', *European Journal of the History of Economic Thought*, 9:2 (Summer 2002), pp. 186–202.

Becker, G., 'Milton Friedman' in Shils (ed.), *Remembering the University of Chicago: Teachers, Scientists and Scholars* (Chicago, Chicago UP, 1991).

Besomi, D. (ed.), *Roy H. Harrod, Interwar Papers and Correspondence* (Ann Arbor, Michigan UP, forthcoming).

Bigg, R., *Cambridge and the Monetary Theory of Production. The Collapse of Marshallian Macroeconomics* (London, Macmillan, 1990).

Blumenthal. S., *The Rise of the Counter-establishment from Conservative Ideology to Political Power* (New York, Times, 1986).

Bork, R., in Kitch, *Journal of Law and Economics*, XXVI (April 1983), pp. 163–234.

Boulding, K. 'The Place of the "Displacement Cost" Concept in Economic Theory', *Economic Journal*, 165:42 (March 1932), pp. 137–41.

——, 'Economics – the Taming of Mammon' in White (ed.), *Frontiers of Knowledge in the Study of Man* (New York, Harper and Brothers, 1956).

Bridel, P., *Cambridge Monetary Thought: the Development of Savings-Investment Analysis from Marshall to Keynes* (London, Macmillan, 1987).

Brunner, K. and Meltzer, A. (eds), *The Phillips Curves and Labor Markets*, Carnegie-Rochester Conference Series on Public Policy 1 (Amsterdam, North Holland, 1976).

Bryce, R., 'Robert Bryce' in Colander and Landreth (eds), *The Coming of Keynesianism to America* (Cheltenham, England, Edward Elgar, 1996).

Burns, A. F., 'Economic Research and the Keynesian Thinking of our Time', *Twenty-sixth Annual Report of the NBER* (New York, NBER, 1946).

Cagan, P., 'The Monetary Dynamics of Hyper-Inflation' in Friedman (ed.), *Studies in the Quantity Theory of Money* (Chicago, Chicago UP, 1956).

Coase, R., 'Aaron Director' in Newman (ed.), *The New Palgrave Dictionary of Law and Economics* (London, Macmillan, 1998).

Colander, D. and Landreth, H. (eds), *The Coming of Keynesianism to America* (Cheltenham, England, Edward Elgar, 1996).

Currie, L., 'Keynesian Revolution – Discussion' in Fells (ed.), *The Second Crisis in Economic Theory* (Morristown, NJ, General Learning Press, 1972).

Davis, J. R., *The New Economics and the Old Economics* (Ames, Iowa, Iowa State UP, 1971).

Desai, M., *Testing Monetarism* (London, Frances Pinter, 1981).

Dillard, D., *The Economics of John Maynard Keynes: The Theory of a Monetary Economy* (London, Crosby Lockwood and Sons, 1948).

Dimand, R., *The Origins of the Keynesian Revolution: The Development of Keynes' Theory of Employment and Output* (Cheltenham, England, Edward Elgar, 1988).

Director, A., in Kitch, *Journal of Law and Economics*, XXVI (April 1983), pp. 163–234.

Domar, E., 'How I tried to become an Economist' in Szenberg (ed.), *Eminent Economists: Their Life Philosophies* (Cambridge, Cambridge UP, 1992).

Douglas, P. H., *World Unemployment and its Reduction Through International Co-operation* (London, League of Nations Union, 1931).

——, *Know America: Its Ills and Cures* (Chicago, Buti-Lami Press, 1933).

Douglas, P. H. and Director, A., *The Problem of Unemployment* (New York, Macmillan, 1931).

Eshag, E., *From Marshall to Keynes: An Essay on the Monetary Theory of the Cambridge School* (Oxford, Basil Blackwell, 1963).

Fells, R. (ed.), *The Second Crisis in Economic Theory* (Morristown, NJ, General Learning Press, 1972).

Fisher, I., *The Purchasing Power of Money*, 2nd edn, 1st edn 1911 (New York, Macmillan, 1922).

——, 'A Statistical Relationship Between Unemployment and Price Changes', *International Labour Review*, 13:6 (June 1926), pp. 785–92.

Friedman, M., 'Should there be an Independent Monetary Authority?' in Yeager (ed.), *In Search of a Monetary Constitution* (Cambridge, Mass., Harvard UP, 1962).

——, 'The Present State of Monetary Theory', *Economic Studies Quarterly*, XIV:1 (September 1963), pp. 1–15.

——, 'The Role of Monetary Policy', *American Economic Review*, LVIII:1 (March 1968), pp. 1–17.

——, in Kitch, *Journal of Law and Economics*, XXVI (April 1983), pp. 163–234.

——, (ed.), *Studies in The Quantity Theory of Money* (Chicago, Chicago UP, 1998).

Friedman, M. and Friedman, R., *Two Lucky People: Memoirs* (Chicago, Chicago UP, 1998).

Friedman, M. and Schwartz, A., *A Monetary History of the United States* (Princeton, Princeton UP, 1963).

Galbraith, J. K., *Economics, Peace and Laughter* (Middlesex, Penguin, 1971).

Gordon, R. J. (ed.), *Milton Friedman's Monetary Framework: A Debate with his Critics* (Chicago, Chicago UP, 1974).

Hahn, L. A., 'Anachronism of the Liquidity Preference Concept', *Kyklos* (1947), pp. 203–20.

Hamilton, E. J. Rees, A. and Johnson, H. G. (eds), *Landmarks in Political Economy* (Chicago, Chicago, 1962).

Hammond, J. D., *Theory and Measurement: Causality Issues in Milton Friedman's Monetary Economics* (Cambridge, Cambridge UP, 1996).

——, 'Labels and Substance: Friedman's Restatement of the Quantity Theory', *History of Political Economy*, 31:3 (Fall 1999), pp. 449–71.

Hansen, A. H., *Business Cycle Theory: Its Development and Present Status* (Boston, Hyperion, 1927).

——, 'Discussion' in Wright (ed.), *Unemployment as a World Problem* (Chicago, Chicago UP, 1931).

——, 'Mr Keynes on Underemployment Equilibrium', *Journal of Political Economy*, (October 1936), pp. 667–86.

Hardy, C. O., 'Review of "A Treatise on Money"', *American Economic Review*, (March 1931a), pp. 150–55.

——, 'Savings, Investment, and the Control of Business Cycles', *Journal of Political Economy* (June 1931b), pp. 390–400.

Harrod, R., *The Life of John Maynard Keynes* (London, Macmillan, 1951).

Hart, A. G., *Money, Debt and Economic Activity* (Englewood Cliffs, NJ, Prentice Hall, 1948).

Hartwell, R. M., *A History of the Mont Pelerin Society* (Indianapolis, Liberty Fund, 1995).

Hayek, F. A., 'Reflections on the Pure Theory of Money of Mr. J. M. Keynes (continued)', *Economica* (February 1932), pp. 22–44.

Hicks, J. R., 'A Suggestion for Simplifying the Theory of Money', *Economica* (February 1935), pp. 1–35.

——, 'Mr Keynes and the "Classics": A Suggested Interpretation', *Econometrica*, 5 (April 1937), pp. 147–59.

Hoover, H., *The Memoirs of Herbert Hoover: The Great Depression 1929–41* (New York, Macmillan, 1952).

Hurwicz, L., 'Theory of the Firm and of Investment', *Econometrica* (1946), pp. 109–36.

Johnson, H. G., *On Economics and Society* (Chicago, Chicago UP, 1975).

Johnson, H. G. and Nobay, A. R. (eds), *Issues in Monetary Economics* (London, Oxford UP, 1974).

Kahn, R. F. 'The Relation of Home Investment to Unemployment', *Economic Journal* (June 1931), pp. 173–98.

——, 'Public Works and Inflation', *Journal of the American Statistical Association*, Supplement (1933), pp. 168–73.

——, 'Some Notes on Liquidity Preference', *The Manchester School of Economic and Social Studies* (September 1954), pp. 229–57.

——, 'On Re-Reading Keynes', *Proceedings of the British Academy* (1974), pp. 361–91.

——, *The Making of Keynes' General Theory* (Cambridge, Cambridge UP, 1984).

Kennedy, S. E., *The Banking Crisis of 1933* (Lexington, Kentucky UP, 1973).

Kerman, C. E., *Creative Tension. The Life and Thought of Kenneth Boulding* (Ann Arbor, Michigan UP, 1974).

Keynes, J. M., 'Introduction to the Series' in Robertson (ed.), *Money* (Cambridge, Cambridge UP, 1922).

——, *A Tract on Monetary Reform* (London, Macmillan, 1923).

——, 'Alfred Marshall, 1842–1924', *Economic Journal*, 34:132 (September 1924), pp. 311–72.

——, *A Treatise on Money: The Applied Theory of Money* (London, Macmillan, 1930).

——, 'Discussion' in Harris Memorial Foundation Reports of Round Tables: Unemployment as a World Problem, 2 vols (Chicago, mimeo, 1931a).

——, 'A Rejoinder', *Economic Journal*, XLI:163 (September 1931b), pp. 412–23.

——, *The General Theory of Employment Interest and Money* (London, Macmillan, 1936).

——, *Collected Writings of John Maynard Keynes* (London, Macmillan, 1972–89).

Kitch, E. W., 'The Fire of Truth A Remembrance of Law and Economics at Chicago, 1932–1970', *Journal of Law and Economics*, XXVI (April 1983), pp. 163–234.

Klein, L., 'The Use of Econometric Models as a Guide to Economic Policy', *Econometrica* (15 April 1947), pp. 111–15.

——, *Economic Fluctuations in the United States 1921–41*, Cowles Commission Monograph No. 11 (New York, Cowles, 1950a).

——, *The Keynesian Revolution* (London, Macmillan, 1950b).

Knight, F. H., 'Review of Hansen's *Economic Stabilisation in an Unbalanced World*', *Journal of Political Economy* (April 1933), pp. 242–5.

——, *The Ethics of Competition and Other Essays* (New York, Book for Libraries Press, 1935).

——, 'The Business Cycle, Interest and Money: A Methodological Approach', *Review of Economic Statistics*, XXIII:2 (May 1941), pp. 53–67.

——, 'The Role of Principles in Economics and Politics. *American Economic Review*, XLI:1 (March 1951), pp. 1–29.

——, *Intelligence and Democratic Action* (Cambridge, Mass., Harvard UP, 1960).

——, *Risk Uncertainty and Profit*, reprints of Economic Classics (New York, Kelly, 1964).

Laidler, D., *Fabricating the Keynesian Revolution: Studies of the Inter-War Literature on Money, the Cycle, and Unemployment* (Cambridge, Cambridge UP, 1999).

Laughlin, J. L., *The Federal Reserve Act: Its Origin and Problems* (New York, Macmillan, 1933).

Leuchtenburg, W. E., *Franklin D. Roosevelt and the New Deal* (New York, Harper and Row, 1963).

Lorwin, L., 'Discussion' in Wright (ed.), *Unemployment as a World Problem* (Chicago, Chicago UP, 1931).

Lucas, R. E., 'Econometric Policy Evaluation: A Critique' in Brunner and Meltzer (eds), *The Philips Curves and Labor Markets* (Amsterdam, North Holland, 1976).

Lundberg, E., *Studies in Economic Instability and Change*, ed. R. Henriksson (Stockholm, SNS Forlag, 1994).

Lutz, F. and Mints, L. (eds), *Readings in Monetary Theory* (American Economic Association; London, George Allen and Unwin, 1952).

Magnusson, L., 'Discussion' in Wright (ed.), *Unemployment as a World Problem* (Chicago, Chicago UP, 1931).

Marcuzzo, C. (ed.), *Economists in Cambridge: The Letters Between Kahn, Keynes, Harrod, J. Robinson, Sraffa, Kaldor and Hayek, 1921–1946*, Dipartmento di Scienze Economiche: discussion papers (2001).

Mason, E. S., 'The Harvard Department of Economics from the Beginning to World War II', *Quarterly Journal of Economics*, XCVII:3 (August 1982), pp. 383–433.

Minsky, H., 'Beginnings', *Banca Nazionale Del Lavoro Quarterly Review* (1985), pp. 211–21.

Mints, L., 'Discussion' in Harris Memorial Foundation Reports of Round Tables: Unemployment as a World Problem, 2 vols (Chicago, mimeo, 1931).

——, *Monetary Policy for a Competitive Society* (New York, McGraw Hill, 1950).

Moggridge, D., *John Maynard Keynes: An Economist's Biography* (London, Routledge, 1992).

Newman, P. (ed.), *The New Palgrave Dictionary of Law and Economics* (London, Macmillan, 1998).

Parkin, M., 'The Transition from Fixed Exchange Rates to Money Supply Targets', *Journal of Money Credit and Banking*, IX:1 (February 1977), pp. 228–42.

Patinkin, D., 'Price Flexibility and Full Employment' in Lutz and Mints (eds), *Readings in Monetary Theory* (American Economic Association; London, George Allen and Unwin, 1952).

——, 'Liquidity Preference and Loanable Funds: Stock Flow Analysis', *Economica*, 38:4 (November 1958), pp. 300–18.

——, *Keynes' Monetary Thought: A Study of its Development* (Durham, North Carolina, Duke UP, 1976).

——, 'Discussion' in Patinkin and Leith (eds), *Keynes, Cambridge and The General Theory* (London, Macmillan, 1977).

——, 'New Material on the Development of Keynes' Monetary Thought', *History of Political Economy*, 12:1 (1980), pp. 1–28.

——, *Essays On and In The Chicago Tradition* (Durham, North Carolina, Duke UP, 1981).

——, 'On Differing Interpretations of the General Theory', *Proceedings of the British Academy*, LXXV (1989), pp. 201–42.

Patinkin, D. and Leith, J.C. (eds), *Keynes, Cambridge and The General Theory* (London, Macmillan, 1977).

Phelan, E. J., 'International co-operation and unemployment', in Wright (ed.), *Unemployment as a World Problem* (Chicago, Chicago UP, 1931).

Phillips, J. R., 'Safe Banking During the Great Depression: John M. Nichols, the FDIC and 100% Reserves', *Consumer Finance Law Quarterly Review*, 48:1 (Winter 1994), pp. 15–21.

Pigou, A. C., 'The Value of Money' in Lutz and Mints (eds), *Readings in Monetary Theory* (American Economic Association; London, George Allen and Unwin, 1952).

Pribram, K., 'World unemployment and its problems' in Wright (ed.), *Unemployment as a World Problem* (Chicago, Chicago UP, 1931).

Robertson, D. H. (ed.), *Money*, 1st edn (Cambridge, Cambridge UP, 1922).

——, *Money*, 3rd edn (Cambridge, Cambridge UP, 1928).

——, 'Mr Keynes' Theory of Money', *Economic Journal*, XLI:163 (September 1931), pp. 395–411.

——, *Essays in Monetary Theory* (London, Staples Press, 1946).

——, 'Review of Mints' *Monetary Policy for a Competitive Society*', *American Economic Review*, XLI:3 (June 1951), pp. 465–9.

Robinson, J., 'A Parable of Savings and Investment', *Econometrica* (February 1933), pp. 75–84.

Rosen, S., 'George J. Stigler and the Industrial Organisation of Economic Thought', *Journal of Political Economy*, 101:5 (October 1993), pp. 809–17.

Rothbard, M. N., 'Milton Friedman Unravelled', *The Individualist* (February 1971), pp. 3–7.

Rymes, T. (ed.), *Keynes's Lectures, 1932–35: Notes of Students* (Carleton Economic Papers, Carleton University, Ottawa, 1985).

Samuelson, P. A., 'Interactions Between the Multiplier Analysis and the Principle of Acceleration', *Review of Economic Statistics*, 21 (May 1939), pp. 75–8.

——, 'Jacob Viner', *Journal of Political Economy* (January–February 1972), pp. 5–11.

——, 'My Life Philosophy: Policy Credos and Working Ways' in Szenberg (ed.), *Eminent Economists: Their Life Philosophies* (Cambridge, Cambridge UP, 1992).

——, 'Paul Anthony Samuelson (b. 1915)', in Colander and Landreth (eds), *The Coming of Keynesianism to America* (Cheltenham, England, Edward Elgar, 1996).

Sargent, T. and Wallace, N., 'Rational Expectations and the Theory of Economic Policy', *Journal of Monetary Economics*, 2 1976), pp. 169–83.

Saunders, C. B. Jr, *The Brookings Institution A Fifty-Year History* (Washington DC, Brookings Institution, 1966).

Schumpeter, J., *Ten Great Economists: From Marx to Keynes* (New York, Oxford UP, 1951).

Scitovsky, T., 'My search for welfare' in Szenberg (ed.), *Eminent Economists: Their Life Philosophies* (Cambridge, Cambridge UP, 1992).

——, 'Tibor Scitovsky' in Colander and Landreth (eds), *The Coming of Keynesianism to America* (Cheltenham, England, Edward Elgar, 1996).

Seligman, L. G. and Cornwell, E. F., *New Deal Mosaic: Roosevelt Confers with his National Emergency Council 1933–1936* (Eugene, Oregon, University of Oregon Books, 1965).

Shackle, G. L. S., *The Years of High Theory Invention and Tradition in Economic Thought 1926–1939* (Cambridge, Cambridge UP, 1967).

Shils, E. (ed.), *Remembering the University of Chicago: Teachers, Scientists and Scholars* (Chicago, Chicago UP, 1991).

Silk, L., 'Battle of the Theorists. Attack by Young Turk on Monetarism May Presage Shift in Economic Policy', *New York Times* (30 December 1970).

Simons, H. C., 'Postwar Economic Policy: Some Traditional Liberal Principles', *American Economic Review*, XXXIII:1 (March 1943), pp. 432–45.

——, *Economic Policy for a Free Society* (Chicago, Chicago UP, 1948).

——, 'Rules Versus Authorities in Monetary Policy' reprinted in Hamilton *et al.* (eds), *Landmarks in Political Economy* (Chicago, Chicago UP, 1962).

Skidelsky, R., *John Maynard Keynes: Hopes Betrayed 1883–1920* (London, Macmillan, 1983).

——, *John Maynard Keynes: The Economist as Saviour 1920–1937* (London, Macmillan, 1992).

Stein, H., *The Fiscal Revolution in America* (Chicago, Chicago UP, 1969).

Stigler, G. J., in Kitch, *Journal of Law and Economics*, XXVI (April 1983), pp. 163–234.

——, *Memoirs of an Unregulated Economist* (New York, Basic Books, 1988).

Strayer, P. J., 'Stabilisation of Personal Incomes A Limited Fiscal Policy', *American Economic Review* (1950), pp. 827–44.

Szenberg, M. (ed.), *Eminent Economists: Their Life Philosophies* (Cambridge, Cambridge UP, 1992).

Tarshis, L., 'Keynes as seen by his students' in Patinkin and Leith (eds), *Keynes, Cambridge and The General Theory* (London, Macmillan, 1977).

——, 'Lorie Tarshis' in Colander and Landreth (eds), *The Coming of Keynesianism to America* (Cheltenham, England, Edward Elgar, 1996).

Thirlwall, A. P. (ed.), *Keynes and Laissez-Faire* (London, Macmillan, 1978).

Viner, J., 'Can We Check Inflation?', *The Yale Review,* XXXVII:2 (December 1947), pp. 193–211.

——, *The Long View and the Short: Studies in Economic Theory and Policy* (Glencoe, Illinois, Free Press, 1958).

——, 'Hayek on Freedom and Coercion', *Southern Economic Journal* (1961), pp. 230–6.

——, 'The Necessity and the Desirable Range of Discretion to be Allowed to a Monetary Authority' in Yeager (ed.), *In Search of a Monetary Constitution* (Cambridge, Mass., Harvard UP, 1962).

Wallis, W. A., in Kitch, *Journal of Law and Economics*, XXVI (April 1983), pp. 163–234.

White, L. T. (ed.), *Frontiers of Knowledge in the Study of Man* (New York, Harper and Brothers, 1956)

Williams, J. H., 'The monetary doctrines of J. M. Keynes', *Quarterly Journal of Economics* (August 1931), pp. 547–87.

Wright, Q. (ed.), *Unemployment as a World Problem* (Chicago, Chicago UP, 1931a).

——, 'Discussion' in Harris Memorial Foundation Reports of Round Tables: Unemployment as a World Problem, 2 vols (Chicago, mimeo, 1931b).

Yeager, L. B. (ed.), *In Search of a Monetary Constitution* (Cambridge, Mass., Harvard UP, 1962).

INDEX